HOUGHTON
★ **MIFFLIN** ★
ECONOMICS
PROGRAM

★ ★ ★

The

Houghton Mifflin Company · Boston

Atlanta · Dallas · Geneva, Ill. · Hopewell, N.J. · Palo Alto

American Economy

Analysis

Issues

Principles

ROY J. SAMPSON

WILLIAM P. MORTENSON

IRA MARIENHOFF

with the editorial assistance of
HOWARD R. ANDERSON

About the authors and editor

Roy J. Sampson, professor of economics in the College of Business Administration at the University of Oregon, formerly taught at Texas Technological College, Pacific University, and the University of Utah. Professor Sampson has served in consultant and research capacities for private and public organizations and as an economist with the Office of Price Stabilization. He is co-author of *American Economic Development, Domestic Transportation,* and *Economics: Concepts, Applications, Analysis,* and has written many monographs and articles on economic topics.

William P. Mortenson, professor emeritus of economics at the University of Wisconsin, has also taught at the University of Wyoming and Kansas State University. He is the author of numerous articles in professional and technical journals. Professor Mortenson served as an economist with the War Food Administration during World War II and has been an economic consultant with the United States Bureau of the Census.

Ira Marienhoff, chairman of the social studies department at Hunter College High School, formerly was a teacher of economics at the High School of Music and Art in New York City. Mr. Marienhoff is a member of the board of directors of the New York State Council for Economic Education.

Howard R. Anderson, consulting editor, has served as provost of the University of Rochester, New York. A past president of the National Council for the Social Studies, he was formerly professor of education at Cornell University and director of social studies in the Ithaca, New York, public schools.

Contents

part one

The science of economics

What economics is all about

1. How does economics concern the individual?
2. In what sense is economics a "science"?
3. How should economic information be evaluated?

If we begin with certainties, we shall end in doubts, but if we begin with doubts, and are patient in them, we shall end in certainties.
FRANCIS BACON, De Augmentis

"The Big Rock Candy Mountain" was the name of a folk song popular in the early 1900's. This song described a place where food and clothing were free, and there were lemonade springs and many other good things. Since everything was free, money was unnecessary, and no one had to work!

This fabulous place was a product of the songwriter's imagination. In the real world most people must work to obtain the necessities, comforts, and luxuries of life. The economy in which people live affects the kind of work they do, how much they earn, what they can buy with their earnings, and how much they can save. To make the most of one's opportunities, therefore, it is necessary to have a knowledge of the economy.

Economics deals with everyday life. It is not a subject that only specialists can understand. Most persons already have enough knowledge of economics to use as a basis for further learning. It is important to approach the study of economics with an open mind. Economic judgments should be based on verified evidence and an analysis of the facts, or they are likely to be incorrect.

1

How does economics concern the individual?

Everyone makes economic choices. Every person must decide how to spend his own money. Such a decision may involve a choice of what clothes to buy, or a choice between spending for clothes or for amusements. To have more money to spend, for example, a student may decide to get a summer job. He may want to save some money toward a college education or toward the purchase of a car. On the other hand, when he thinks about what he could do with his time, the student may prefer not to work, even though this means having less money to spend. All of these instances involve economic choices and decisions.

Every family must make economic decisions.
In this country a family must decide how to use its available funds to best advantage, regardless of its wealth or poverty. Families, like individuals, must make economic decisions.

In the typical American family, monthly and weekly bills and day-to-day expenditures for necessary items and comforts take most of the family income. The family must choose carefully to get the most satisfaction from its expenditures. The wife may want a new refrigerator, whereas the husband may feel that a new family car should have higher priority. The children may want a color television set or an extension telephone. At the same time, the house needs repairs or a rug may be wearing out. Almost certainly some members of the family need new clothes. And probably everyone would like to have more money to spend for recreation.

A wealthy family may have to choose between a summer abroad or sending the children to private instead of public schools. A poor family may have to make much more difficult choices—such as whether to spend more on food and clothing, or what cuts to make in spending for food and clothing in order to pay the rent.

Regardless of income, all families are likely to have one thing in common. They *want* more things than they can *afford*. All of their wants cannot be completely satisfied. Some purchases must be postponed until times are better or until enough money has been saved, or at least until there is money to make a down payment. Wants always are much greater than one's limited means of satisfying them.

Individuals and families must decide between spending now and saving for the future.
Nearly everyone saves at least a small part of his income. A high school girl may save the money earned by babysitting to buy a new dress for a dance. Her family may put aside part of its income each month for years in order to buy a house, or to help the children go to college. People save because they think that future satisfactions made possible by saving will be greater than would be the satisfactions from spending money as fast as it is earned. The family breadwinner may feel it necessary to save to insure that the family would not be destitute should he die.

The choice of an occupation involves many economic factors. In addition to deciding how to spend one's money, most persons have to decide, at some point in their lives, how to earn a living. Acquiring the necessary education and skills for one's work involves a series of decisions. Throughout one's life, a great many choices and decisions have to be made. These decisions determine where, how, and how well one will live. Most of these decisions directly or indirectly involve economic considerations. Indeed, almost everything a person does is influenced in some way by economics.

Economic choices and decisions are affected by local, national, and international economic conditions. The economic system is made up of many interrelated parts that work together as a whole. The activities of business firms, farmers, banking and financial institutions, labor unions, government agencies and foreign governments all significantly influence people's everyday lives.

Obscure items in newspapers or newscasts about the actions of unfamiliar groups in remote places may fail to make a deep impression on the reader's mind at the time of

---

ORIGIN OF THE TERM *ECONOMICS*
The English word "economics" goes back to an ancient Greek source. Actually, two Greek words were combined into one: *oikos*, house, and *nemein*, to manage. In his work entitled *Politics*, Aristotle made certain observations about the economy of the Greek city-state, basing them on good management of the household. The word he used was *oikonomikê*—"household management." A nation, like a household, prospers when there is skillful management of the resources nature has provided.

their announcement. But these same little-noticed events may directly influence the availability and kind of jobs and also determine the prices of things people buy. To make the most of one's talents and to get the greatest satisfaction from public and private resources, it is necessary to understand the overall economic process.

Even small economic transactions may involve many persons and industries. Viewed singly, one's particular day-to-day acts of getting and spending may seem insignificant. But such commonplace transactions assume importance in the total economy. A buyer of a malted milk shake, for example, becomes a *consumer* of a milk product to which many people and agencies have contributed.

A typical malted milk contains (1) ice cream and fluid milk, (2) dried malted milk, and (3) a sweet syrup with flavoring, perhaps chocolate. Each of these ingredients originated in a different place and went through various processes.

The far-flung origins of a simple consumer product—a chocolate malt

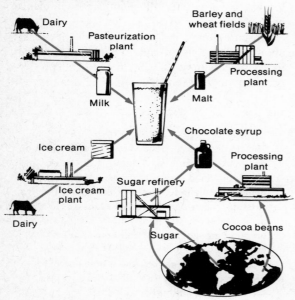

1. Both the milk used in the ice cream and the fluid milk came from dairy farms and were pasteurized under sanitary conditions.
2. Another important item in this drink is a specially prepared dried malted milk. The malt was made from cereals by a process that requires specialized equipment and involves several workers.
3. The sugar and the chocolate are imported and then refined separately before being combined into a syrup.

Among the factors that made possible the malted milk are transportation, national and international trade, several manufacturing plants, and many different employees and employers. Various economic considerations have influenced the pricing of the ingredients. Perhaps bank loans have helped to finance the dairy farmers or the manufacturers and processors of products used in preparing the malted milk. Tariff duties probably were paid on the imported cocoa, and government regulations insured sanitary conditions on the dairy farms, in the various processing plants, and in stores selling the drink.

Millions of such business transactions, taking place every day in all parts of the country, generate income and employment. The study of economics helps one to understand problems related to such transactions and how these transactions affect persons' lives.

A simple job may be part of a complex economic process. Many people work at various stages of an assembly line, each person doing the same thing again and again. For example, an employee in an airplane factory may drill a few holes in the frame of the aircraft. But the total task of bringing together the materials needed to build the airplane, of planning the assembly line, of operating the plants, of test-flying finished planes, and of pricing and selling the finished product, is a complex affair. It requires the skills of a great number of workers, engineers, and business managers. Each person makes a vital contribution to the successful completion of the whole undertaking.

Government plays an important role in economic affairs. A few generations ago, economics actually was called "political economy." This term reflected the close connection between political and economic activity. The political environment at any given time may help or hinder business in general, or a specific industry, or the economic well-being of all citizens. National goals help to determine government spending, levels and kinds of taxes levied, and wage and price levels. Indeed, national goals and policies determine the kind of economy that exists—free enterprise, government ownership, or mixed.

Every society must answer certain general economic questions. The answers to certain basic questions to a large extent determine both the kind of economy a country will have and the economic life of its people. These questions are: (1) What is to be produced? (2) How much is to be produced? (3) By what method and by whom will this production be accomplished? and (4) How shall what is produced be divided among the groups and individuals of society?

There probably would be general agreement that for a people to be economically prosperous two conditions must be met. First, *there must be an ample production of goods and services.* Second, *these goods and services must be distributed among the population in an equitable manner.* Considerable disagreement, however, may exist over the precise meaning of such terms as "ample" and "equitable." Violent controversies often grow out of government efforts to influence production and distribution.

The American political system encourages free enterprise. The government of the United States reflects the will of the people insofar as that will is expressed through voting. If people generally do not approve the policies of their elected officials, the voters can put the other party into office. Most Americans believe in the principle of *free* (or *private*) *enterprise.* This term means that private individuals or

How the American economy answers basic economic questions

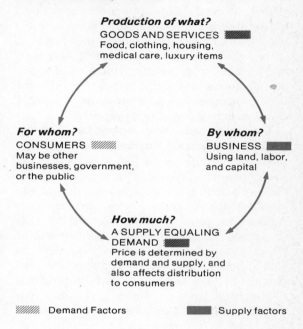

Production of what?
GOODS AND SERVICES
Food, clothing, housing, medical care, luxury items

For whom?
CONSUMERS
May be other businesses, government, or the public

By whom?
BUSINESS
Using land, labor, and capital

How much?
A SUPPLY EQUALING DEMAND
Price is determined by demand and supply, and also affects distribution to consumers

Demand Factors   Supply factors

companies control the land, factories, machines, and money used to produce goods and services. Government interference in the workings of the economic system is kept within relatively narrow limits. *Capital* is the term often used to designate the factories, machinery, and other physical elements (which may include money) invested in the production of goods and services. *Capitalism* refers to the economic system in which capital is privately owned and these owners have the right to earn profits from it. The terms capitalism and free, or private, enterprise, are often used interchangeably.

"Free enterprise" does not imply total lack of restraint. Most Americans doubtless favor certain kinds of restrictions on economic activity. Laws designed to prevent fraudulent advertising or the sale of adulterated food do in a sense interfere with "free enterprise." But such interference insures the greatest good for the greatest number by protecting the many from the unscrupulous few. Most Americans eligible for Social Security upon retirement or for unemployment compensation when they are out of work do not reject such payments on the ground that they are examples of "government interference" in economic matters. And many manufacturers not only accept but demand tariff protection, just as many farmers demand and accept agricultural price supports.

The American "free enterprise" system actually is a "mixed" economy. To protect the economic welfare of the general public, the government is empowered to *regulate* certain kinds of activities and to *encourage* or *promote* other activities or goals. For example, the government regulates the rates charged by railroads, and has encouraged the development of jet air transportation in various ways. And, as will be brought out in later chapters, the government at times and in various ways promotes such general goals as economic stability, economic security, and economic growth. Because both private enterprise and government play an important role in shaping this country's economy, the system is often termed a *mixed economy*.

Government taxation, borrowing, and spending significantly affect the economy. The federal government alone spends some 200 billion dollars per year. This large sum comes from taxing and from borrowing. Add to this huge sum the taxing, borrowing, and spending of 50 state governments, and of a host of county, city, and other local governments. The total is impressive.

Government policies not only affect employment and production, but also influence what is produced. Money used to pay taxes cannot be used to buy food and clothing. Men serving in the armed forces cannot be employed simultaneously in industry.

Men, management, and materials can be used for only one thing at a time. Society has to make economic choices, just as individuals do. Sometimes the choices are difficult to make.

• **America is a fortunate country.** The success of this country's economic system stems in part from the abundance of its natural resources. America's temperate climate, fertile fields, vast forests, rich mines and oil deposits, and her relatively small population have combined to make possible a high standard of living. Private initiative has exploited these resources and has been encouraged by a government that by and large imposes only those restrictions on economic activity that seem necessary to "promote the general welfare." Even though the supply of some important resources is limited, scarce items can be obtained from abroad if part of this country's production is exported in order to earn the foreign money needed to buy imports.

CHECK UP

1. How does a family in its economic planning face up to the fact that resources are limited and needs unlimited?

2. What are some factors a person needs to take into account in making a wise economic choice or decision? Relate the answer to a specific situation.

3. What four general economic questions must each society answer? What two conditions must obtain for a people to be prosperous in an economic sense?

4. Define *free enterprise* and *mixed economy*. Give examples of "government interference" in the economy. Are these desirable? Why or why not?

5. What factors have contributed to the success of this country's economic system?

2

In what sense is economics a "science"?

Economics has been called "the science of the production of wealth." Others have referred to it as "a science of choices" and "a maximizing science." Actually, all of these terms are pertinent. Economics is concerned with production, as well as with distribution and consumption. It does deal with making choices, and its aim is to obtain maximum benefit or satisfaction from the use of resources.

From a personal viewpoint, economics can be considered as *the field of study which deals with the ways people make their living.* From the broader viewpoint of society, economics is the field of study that deals with *the various possible ways for society to manage its resources in order to achieve the greatest amount of satisfaction.*

All the sciences employ a scientific method of analysis. That is, they use logical reasoning, measurement, observation, and sometimes experimentation to answer questions, solve problems, and reach conclusions. Every event is caused by some preceding event or events, and in turn affects future events. Scientists are interested in what causes things to happen. They search for orderly patterns among events where order is not readily visible or apparent. Stated differently, sciences explore the relationships between causes and effects. By these broad standards, economics may be considered a science.

Scientists deal with facts, hypotheses, theories, and laws (or principles). Persons who are not scientists often fail to understand what such terms as "fact," "hypothesis," "theory," and "law" mean to scientists. For example, some who assert that they are "practical" persons may be heard to say that they are interested in "facts" and not in "theories." Such persons are using scientific terms without knowing what they mean. It is important to establish the meaning of these terms and the relationships between them.

"Facts" grow out of experience. A fact is something which is generally accepted as true. It is a fact, for example, that a person gets burned when he touches a hot piece of metal with his bare hands. But a very young child might not know this, and magicians give the appearance of handling fire without being

harmed. Long ago, the existence of dragons, unicorns, and witches was accepted as fact. What is factual to one person or generation, therefore, may not be to another, and what people accept as facts may vary from time to time and from place to place.

Yet in any field of learning at a particular time there exists a basic body of facts which provide the foundations upon which the field rests. Knowing these facts, and how to use them, is the starting point in solving any problem.

Hypotheses are the first step in relating one set of facts to another. Once certain facts have been gathered about an occurrence, some idea may be formed about its causes and consequences. A tentative explanation may be drawn up which tries to relate causes and effects, and this first step is called the hypothesis. A hypothesis, however, is unproved. It may or may not be correct, but it provides a framework and a point of departure for further investigation. Its correctness can only be demonstrated by testing, that is, by logical reasoning, observation, and (if possible) experimentation.

Less than 300 years ago, very little was known about lightning, although man has been observing lightning for thousands of years. Then some people began to study electricity. Eventually some of them came to believe that lightning actually is a form of electricity. But this was merely an hypothesis, based upon a study of such facts as were then available. It could not be established through the use of reason alone. Observation was difficult and dangerous, and no significant experiments had yet been conducted. Few "practical" persons were willing to accept such unusual ideas about the nature of lightning.

Then in 1752 Benjamin Franklin decided to perform an experiment. He reasoned that if electric sparks could somehow be drawn from lightning, this would prove that lightning is a form of electricity. Most people are familiar with the story of Franklin's famous kite experiment. During a thunderstorm, he managed to fly a kite attached to a long cord at the end of which he had fastened metal keys. When lightning flashed, Franklin observed that electric sparks were given off by these keys. He had successfully used reason, observation, and experimentation to test his hypothesis.

Theories are hypotheses which have been confirmed by testing. A theory is more than an hypothesis. It is a statement about cause and effect relationships which has held up under whatever tests have been made. Franklin's hypothesis about lightning, after its successful testing, might properly have been called a theory. But a given theory may not be universally accepted, because sometimes more than one theory will give equally satisfactory explanations of relationships between causes and effects. Of course, old theories are constantly being replaced by more useful or more accurate theories.

Scientific laws are widely accepted theories. When a theory has stood up for a long period of time, and has become widely accepted by leading experts on the subject, it may be called a scientific law. Occasionally references are made to the "law of gravity" or to the "law of supply and demand." Wide acceptance of such laws, of course, does not mean that the people who refer to them really understand how they work. Laws, just as theories, may in time be replaced by more accurate ones. For this reason, to avoid an appearance of permanence, some scientists substitute the word "principle" for "law."

Scientific laws eventually may become facts. After most people have accepted a scientific law (or principle) for a long period of time, it usually comes to be regarded as a fact. Thus, the so-called "practical" man of today who rejects theory in favor of facts actually may be relying on facts that once were in the realm of theory. In defense of the practical man, however, let it be said that much of what he dismisses as theory is not even theory. Laymen tend to confuse untested hypotheses with tested theories. They make this mistake because laymen generally are less careful than scientists in the use of terms. Practical persons, therefore, may be justified in rejecting much of what they label theory if they actually are rejecting mere hypotheses.

Scientific method encourages constant reexamination of existing theories. The scientific approach starts with generally accepted facts. Study of these facts leads to hypotheses—that is, possible explanations or solutions. Testing of hypotheses by observation, experimentation, and logical reasoning leads to theories, or workable solutions or explanations. Theories, in turn, may become so widely accepted that they are called scientific laws or principles. Finally, these laws or principles may become so generally accepted that they are incorporated into our body of factual knowledge. Eventually, these "new" facts may be used as a basis for developing still more hypotheses, theories, laws, and facts.

Scientists often express their findings in the form of "models." A scientific model is simply a brief way of stating key relationships between the facts being studied. Such a model is commonly written as a mathematical equa-

The use of scientific method in solving problems and developing new knowledge

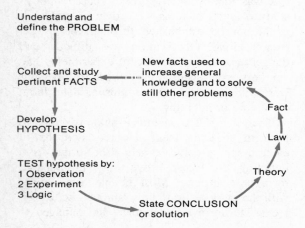

Understand and define the PROBLEM

Collect and study pertinent FACTS

Develop HYPOTHESIS

TEST hypothesis by:
1 Observation
2 Experiment
3 Logic

State CONCLUSION or solution

New facts used to increase general knowledge and to solve still other problems

Fact

Law

Theory

Philosopher of Facts
Aristotle

(384–322 B.C.)

Since Aristotle first wrote about economics more than 23 centuries ago, the subject has been developing into a science. As in other fields of learning, new ideas are constantly being added to the existing body of knowledge. Especially during recent years, economics has become a subject of interest to the "man on the street" as well as to the scholar. Under the heading PIONEERS IN ECONOMIC THOUGHT, thumbnail sketches are provided of a representative group of men who have helped to develop ideas basic to the evolving science of economics. These short biographical essays appear in chapters developing subjects to which the given economist made a significant contribution.

The great thinker Aristotle, the "philosopher of facts," was perhaps the first to recognize that economics should be considered a separate science or area of study. In fact, Aristotle analyzed and classified a number of different branches of learning, including economics.

Throughout history scholars have had a high regard for the simple but productive life of the farmer. Aristotle was one who expressed great respect for those who farmed, hunted, fished, or raised livestock. He believed that these people were producing natural goods for all, and were acquiring property in a most legitimate fashion. What constitutes "proper acquisition" has always concerned economists. Aristotle praised those who worked for the necessities of life, for he considered these to be wealth. He disapproved of anything not of use or in excess of one's needs. Thus he criticized those who profited from carrying on trade or commerce. "Buying cheap and selling dear," he condemned as immoral. He considered the payment of interest on loans deplorable, and called money "sterile" because it produces nothing.

Manual laborers did not deserve the privileges of citizenship, in Aristotle's view. Their bodies were ruined by lack of exercise and fresh air, and their labors did not leave them sufficient time to think about and take part in the civic life of Athens.

Aristotle rejected the idea that property should be held in common. He felt that such a practice clashed with man's natural disposition and wounded the pride which an individual has in himself and his possessions. However, Aristotle favored a strong government in which a wise ruler would use his power to prevent extremes of wealth or poverty. He favored a policy of sending surplus population to colonies if the home territory became overcrowded.

Aristotle's writings have influenced thinking in economics and related sciences for more than 2000 years. Many of his ideas on these subjects later became a part of Christian thought.

tion. This allows convenient mathematical manipulation by scientists, and permits numbers to be inserted in place of symbols as necessary.

One of the most famous and most important scientific models of this century was developed by Albert Einstein in his formula $E = mc^2$. Very simply, this means that energy (E) equals mass (m) times the velocity of light squared (c^2). Einstein's model, among other things, describes the behavior under certain conditions of light radiation and radioactivity and expresses a relationship between energy and matter.

Einstein had worked on the development of his model for many years before he published it. Starting with an hypothesis, he evolved a theory which has, in effect, become a scientific law. When it was first announced, this model was understood by only a handful of leading scientists. Eventually, however, it led to the development of the atomic and, later, the hydrogen bomb. Subsequently, nuclear-powered submarines and nuclear-powered generators of electricity grew out of this research. And other new practical applications of this concept are being sought and found constantly.

In the field of economics, a simple model of this type would be: $Y = C + I$. This is a shorthand way of stating that the total income (Y) of all the people in an economy equals the total expenditures made for consumption purposes (C) plus the total expenditures made for investment purposes (I) in the economy.

Or another economic model might say: $MV = PT$. This means that the total amount of money in an economy (M) times the speed at which this money changes hands (V) equals the price level (P) times the total number of transactions (T) occurring in the economy.

Actual numerical values may be substituted for the letter symbols in any of these or similar models. Then if one number in the equation is changed, it follows necessarily that some other number or numbers also must change. For example, in the $MV = PT$ model, if M is increased without any changes in V or T, the model will show an increase in the price level (P).

Scientific models and scientific methods often are very complex in practice. This discussion of models has been simplified, since it is unlikely that many readers of this book will become specialists in economics. Even so, some knowledge of scientific terminology and the scientific approach is important for a proper understanding of economics. For economics is often quantitative and analytical and not merely descriptive.

Economics is a social science. All human knowledge is classified by subject matter or content. Broadly speaking, there are (1) natural sciences, and (2) social sciences. The first of these includes the physical sciences, such as physics and chemistry, which deal primarily with inanimate matter, and the astronomical sciences, which deal with planets, stars, and galaxies. It also comprises the biological sciences, which deal with living organisms. These branches of natural science are sometimes referred to as the "exact" sciences, although in many respects they are far from being mathematically exact.

The social sciences, on the other hand, deal primarily with *relationships between people and people* (*that is, with society*), *or between people and their environments*. In addition to economics, the social sciences include history, sociology, psychology, political science (government), geography, and anthropology.

Because they are all concerned with human beings and human activity, branches of the social sciences are to some extent interrelated. Therefore, a knowledge of one social science contributes to understanding of the others. Also, an understanding of a physical science can be quite helpful in understanding the social sciences. All science—indeed all knowledge— is interrelated. Each of the sciences has its own specialized body of knowledge and its own techniques of analysis, however.

The task of the social scientist is difficult. The subject matter of social science is man himself, the most complex form of life. Persons differ greatly from one another, and react differently in groups than they do as individuals. The social scientist himself is a part of the mankind he is studying. Thus he may not be able to approach his study in as detached a manner as another scientist would approach the study of a lump of coal or the movements of the stars. Nor can the social scientist employ the techniques of experimentation, observation, and measurement to the same degree as does the physical scientist. For this reason, the social sciences are considered less "exact" than other sciences.

Economics probably is the most "exact" of the social sciences. Doubtless economics is more exact than the other social sciences. That is because many of the things dealt with in economics can readily be measured (numbers of people, automobiles, or houses, dollars, bushels of wheat, tons of coal, and the like). Such quantifiable items can be subjected to rigorous logical and mathematical analysis. To sum up, economics possesses a large body of facts, proven scientific methods of measurement and analysis, and a widely accepted toolkit of theories and principles. For this reason, people have a right to expect a higher degree of reliability from economics than from most of the other social sciences.

The American economy is based on two premises. The American economic system operates on two important assumptions. One is that *human wants are never completely satisfied*. No one ever has all of everything he wants. The second premise on which the economy is based is that *the things (resources) available to satisfy human wants are limited in amount*. There are not enough goods and services to permit all consumers to have everything they would like to have. If everyone could have anything he wanted and could get it instantly and without effort, as in the mythical "Big Rock Candy Mountain," there would be no need for a study of economics.

The realities of existence compel people to decide (a) *what they want most* and (b) *how best to go about getting it*. As someone has put it, "We do the best we can with what we've got." People make these choices as individuals, as families, as owners or managers of businesses, and as nations.

Economics is not concerned with telling people what they want; that is a matter of personal taste or circumstance. But economic analysis can be used as an aid in making a choice among alternative possibilities. And once the choice has been made, economics can provide assistance in making the most efficient use of avail-

BRANCHES OF ECONOMICS
Perhaps a better idea of what economics is about can be obtained from looking at the divisions of the subject made by professional economists themselves. The American Economic Association lists 14 specialized areas of economics, as follows:

1. Price theory, income theory, history of economic thought
2. Economic history, economic development, national economics
3. Economic statistics
4. Economic systems, planning and reform, cooperation
5. Business fluctuations
6. Money, credit, and banking
7. Public finance, fiscal policy
8. International economics
9. Business finance, investment and security markets
10. Business administration, marketing and accounting
11. Industrial organization, government and business, industry studies
12. Agricultural economics, economic geography, housing
13. Labor economics
14. Population, welfare programs, standards of living

And these 14 major subject-matter classifications are further broken down into 44 subgroups.

able resources in pursuit of an objective.

In the broad sense, the science of economics is concerned with the efficient use of *land, labor, capital,* and *entrepreneurship* (or management). It makes use of a variety of basic concepts such as *marginal utility, marginal cost,* the principles of *supply and demand, opportunity costs, increasing returns* and *decreasing returns,* the *circular flow of income, comparative advantage,* and others. (These terms will be explained as they are encountered later in this book.)

Social scientists specializing in economics are called economists. There are some 20,000 persons in the United States today who can be called professional economists. A recent survey by the American Economic Association found that about 45 per cent of the professional economists listed in the *National Register of Scientific and Technical Personnel* were engaged in teaching, mainly in colleges and universities. Almost one-third were employed in business and industry, and more than 12 per cent were working for the federal government. The remainder were employed by state and local governments, nonprofit organizations, and miscellaneous other employers, or were self-employed. Many economists are employed in research or policy-advisory positions. Some of them do part-time research or advisory work, and others write extensively in their special field. Economists change from one type of position to another from time to time, as from teaching to government to business, and back to teaching. Anyone who wishes to come to grips with some of the nation's major problems will find a rewarding career in the field of economics.

Non-economists often are puzzled by disagreements among economists. Two equally qualified economists may analyze the same problem in very different ways, and recommend wholly different solutions. This does not necessarily mean that one is wholly wrong and the other entirely correct. "Experts" in all fields frequently disagree with each other. For example, it is not unusual for two physicians to disagree in the diagnosis of a person's illness, and to prescribe different treatment based on their differing evaluations. Similarly, two engineers may recommend different ways of building a given bridge. In economics, as in other fields, many problems do not have a single "right" solution. There may be more than one solution to the same problem.

Recommended economic solutions to national problems usually are based on broad policy goals or objectives. Economics as a science may be neutral, but economists as individuals—like other scientists—have different personal values. Recommendations in any field are likely to reflect the personal values or beliefs of those making them.

For example, one economist may prefer a high rate of inflation to a high rate of unemployment, while another may prefer the opposite. If so, their recommendations on the joint problem of inflation and employment would be different. In the same way, during the early 1950's many prominent physicists opposed building a hydrogen bomb while many others favored it. In the late 1960's, many scientists opposed the deployment of an anti-ballistic missile (ABM) system but others favored it. These disagreements were not scientific disagreements as such, but rather were disagreements about how scientific knowledge should be used.

Disagreements can arise not only from differing points of view about goals, but also from incomplete technical knowledge. In late 1967, it was shown that the designers of the TFX fighter bomber had grossly underestimated its cost and grossly overestimated its performance. In the same way, economists can be mistaken in their predictions of the costs and benefits to be expected from new economic programs or policies. Therfore economists will easily disagree about the relative merits of alternative programs for attaining an agreed upon goal.

Agreement usually is not newsworthy; disagreement is. The public hears much more about a small number of disagreements among scientists than about the more frequent instances when they agree. In economics, as in other sciences, there is a broad area of general agreement among economists with respect to factual information, use of the scientific method, and the content of various theories. There is much more disagreement about what *ought* to be done than about what *can* be done. The question of what ought to be done, however, is more a matter of value judgment than it is an economic problem.

CHECK UP

1. Why is the term "economics" defined in so many different ways?

2. Explain and illustrate the meaning of these terms: facts, hypotheses, theories, laws (or principles), scientific method.

3. Why is the task of the social scientist more difficult than that of the physical scientist?

4. Explain the meaning of these terms: value judgment, social goal. How do differences in values and goals help to explain why social scientists disagree on the best solution to a problem?

3

How should economic information be evaluated?

The public is exposed constantly to a barrage of economic facts, opinions, recommendations, and conclusions. Newspapers, magazines, and newscasts contain a great deal of this kind of material. One frequently hears people talking about economic problems. But how is one to make up his mind about these matters intelligently?

First, it is necessary to understand the language of economics. Like every field of human activity, economics has its own terminology. Also, like every science, it has a specialized "jargon." Often the economists' specialized scientific terminology differs from that of non-economists. To understand any speaker or writer, one must understand the meanings of the terms he uses.

Statistical information must be considered. Economic information generally is summarized and presented in the form of tables, graphs, charts, and index numbers. Failure to understand such presentations will lead to wrong conclusions. Even when graphs and charts are based on accurate facts and are correctly drawn, they can be misleading to those who do not understand how they were constructed.

Then, too, information may be factually correct, well presented, and easily understood, but have little bearing on the question at hand. One should therefore check to see whether a set of stated facts are related to the problem, and whether they are the most pertinent facts available.

The source, reliability, and adequacy of the information must be determined. What are the sources of the facts? How have they been collected? Have they been correctly compiled and tabulated? These are some of the questions that might well be asked in verifying information. An equally important consideration is whether or not the information is adequate to support conclusions based on it. Even when there is no question about accuracy and relevance, there may not be *sufficient* reliable data to justify a conclusion. Decisions based on *insufficient* information may be as unsatisfactory as those based on *erroneous* information.

Does the information come from biased sources? A careful evaluation of the source of one's information should be made. If it comes from an individual, one should consider whether the person is qualified by education and experience to provide acceptable data. Is he recognized as an authority by the general public or by those in the same field? What has he stood for and what has he accomplished in the past? Is he attempting to "sell" the program of some special interest group, or is he "neutral" in his presentation? Has he made a careful study of the question? What are his personal value judgments, and how may these values have influenced his position?

The conclusions drawn should be one's own. After considering the best information available, each person must make up his own mind. Various alternative "solutions" to problems should be weighed in the light of how they might affect the individual, his or her family, community, and country, and even mankind as a whole. A person's final decision should be influenced by his own personal scale of values concerning what is "right" and "wrong," what is "good" and "bad." Science itself is not primarily concerned with values, but values do provide the limits within which the findings of science are applied.

The nature of the connection between scientific expertise and values in the choice of a public policy is illustrated blow:

Alternative proposed policies

$$P_1 \quad P_2 \quad P_3$$
$$\downarrow \quad \downarrow \quad \downarrow$$
$$R_1 \quad R_2 \quad R_3$$

The hypothesized chain of cause and effect underlying the expert's prediction of the results of each policy.

Predicted result of each policy

P_1, P_2, and P_3 stand for competing policy proposals submitted to the citizens as alternative courses of action for meeting a particular problem. The arrow below each proposed policy represents some expert's prediction of the effects of the policy—what kinds of effects and how big they may be. R_1 stands for the predicted end results of Policy 1, R_2 for the predicted results of Policy 2, etc. The responsibility of the citizen is to decide which package

of results, R, he thinks is best. His values, his moral or ethical beliefs, influence this choice.

The role of the scientist is to provide the citizen with as careful a prediction as he can make of the kind of results, R, to be anticipated from a given policy, P.

Because a scientist is also a citizen, with his own values, he will tend to favor one set of results over another. But his preference should carry no special weight, because his expertise in prediction does not make his values more legitimate than the values of the layman. His expertise only means that his prediction of the results of a particular policy may be more reliable than the layman's.

The real headache for the citizen arises when the experts disagree about their predictions; when one expert predicts that Policy 1 will lead to one package of results and another expert predicts that Policy 1 will lead to a different set of results. Then the citizen has no alternative but to trespass in the expert's territory and decide which prediction seems more reliable.

CHECK UP

1. In thinking about an economic problem, why is it necessary to understand the meaning of the terms used? To be able to interpret statistical material? To probe the reliability of data? To check information for bias?

2. Why must each person reach his own decision about the best among alternate solutions suggested for a given problem? What should be the basis for this decision?

Clinching the main ideas

In a broad sense, economics explains the activities of people earning their living. In doing this, it considers the affairs of individuals, families, businesses, and nations. It deals with the problems of these groups in a scientific manner, seeking to derive principles which will provide workable solutions to their economic problems.

Much of the study of economics centers around the key assumptions that people's wants are without limit, and that resources available to satisfy these wants are limited in quantity. Very few people have enough money to buy all the goods and services they would like to have.

From the viewpoint of an individual's immediate interest, the important economic questions are those concerned with his present and future wants. He asks how he can best prepare himself to satisfy his wants for food, shelter, clothing, comforts, and conveniences, now and in the future. The study of economics helps the individual to answer these important questions.

From society's viewpoint, individuals have the responsibility of choosing between various programs of action or policies designed to further the general welfare. (Of course, there is considerable dispute concerning what is "the general welfare" and what is meant by "furthering" it.) Taxes, poverty, the national debt, worker-employer disagreements, foreign trade, and aid to farmers are among the many general economic problems that citizens are faced with every day. These problems must be faced intelligently, and satisfactory choices or decisions must be made, if the national economy is to prosper and adequate standards of living are to be maintained or improved.

Experts on government maintain that *informed* voters generally choose the best political leaders from among rival candidates. Likewise, economically informed citizens should be able to make the most satisfactory choices from among the economic courses of action confronting them as individuals and as a nation. The following chapters will assist the reader in making more informed economic decisions now and in the years ahead.

Chapter 1 review

Terms to understand

1. economics
2. economy
3. free enterprise
4. mixed economy
5. hypothesis
6. theory
7. principle (law)
8. model
9. value
10. social goal
11. social sciences
12. analysis

What do you think?

1. Has this country's system of free enterprise become less free during the past century? Why? Give examples.

2. Why is it necessary to re-examine economic theories and laws (principles) and to modify them, and even to formulate new ones? Give examples.

3. How is it possible for competent economists to disagree on the best solution to a given economic problem? Give examples.

4. Why is the task of meeting the economic needs of present-day American society a more complicated process than it was 300 years ago?

5. What would be the effect on the American economy if the wages of all workers were doubled? Why?

Extending your knowledge of economics

1. The pollution of the environment is one of the nation's major problems. Read articles dealing with this problem and listen to pertinent programs on radio and television. Prepare a report in which the following questions are discussed: What are major causes of pollution? What can be done in each case? What progress is being made? What obstacles stand in the way of greater progress? How can these be overcome? What values and social goals are reflected in the positions taken by persons and agencies responsible for pollution? How are they working to lessen pollution? Are they seemingly unconcerned about the problem?

2. The paragraph headed, "America is a fortunate country," page 6, explains in general terms why the United States enjoys a high standard of living. So do Switzerland and Japan, though perhaps to a somewhat lesser degree. Do these two countries enjoy any or all of the advantages listed for this country? How do you account for the comparatively high standard of living enjoyed by the Swiss and the Japanese? You will need to use *Reader's Guide* to find articles in current magazines about Switzerland and Japan.

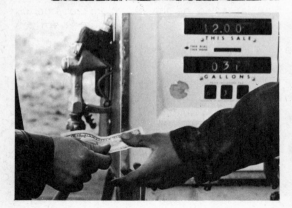

Figures can lie: interpreting statistics and graphs

General background

This textbook stresses the importance of thinking about and analyzing economic issues: identifying various points of view, seeking to understand why those who favor a given viewpoint believe as they do, weighing evidence for and against various positions, and then trying to make up one's own mind on the question. To provide special practice in analysis, a number of cases are included in the book. The next one starts on page 58.

The soundness of the conclusions one reaches in thinking about an issue depends in part on the reliability of the available information. In economics, many of the problems discussed involve statistics and comparisons based on statistics. Much of this statistical material is presented in tables, charts, and diagrams. Indeed, the reader would have difficulty understanding many topics in economics if data were not grouped or presented in graphic form. Although charts and graphs have eye appeal, and often are much easier to grasp than a long verbal explanation, they may also give a wrong impression.

The issues: the use and abuse of statistical information

1. DRAWING CONCLUSIONS FROM STATISTICS

Statistics, once gathered, must be interpreted. Much of the disagreement over a set of statistics is really disagreement over the approaches used in analyzing them. This may be illustrated by considering preliminary figures on changes in the economic status of black Americans during the decade 1960 to 1970. The statistics were discussed in *The New York Times*:

Negro median family income was, by 1968, 60 per cent of the white level, a 6 per cent increase . . .

since 1960. . . . In 1968, one-third of all nonwhite families had incomes of $8000 or more, as compared with only 15 per cent in 1960; the proportions for whites were 58 per cent in 1968 and 39 per cent in 1960, indicating a slightly higher relative gain for whites. On the other hand, 29 per cent of Negro families had incomes below the poverty line ($3553 for a nonfarm family of four in 1968) as opposed to only 8 per cent of white families; in 1959 the proportions were 48 per cent for Negroes and 15 per cent for whites. The decline in poverty was somewhat greater for whites.

The unemployment rate in 1969 for nonwhites was the lowest since the Korean war, but was still double the white rate. Between 1960 and 1969 the percentage of workers in highly skilled occupations increased more rapidly for Negroes and other races than for whites, and nonwhites also experienced a greater decrease in persons employed as laborers, domestic servants and in farm occupations. In spite of large relative gains, nonwhites were still represented in the two most skilled and best paying occupational groups (professionals and managers) by less than half their proportion of the total population. . . . The percentage of Negro males aged 25 to 29 who had completed four or more years of high school rose from 36 in 1960 to 60 in 1969; the comparable figures for whites were 63 and 78.

Few of the advances made are remarkable, and the "glass of water" parable clearly applies to them: optimists may declare the glass "half full" while pessimists are at liberty to describe it as "half empty." Both, of course, are right. One may also select from the statistics to stress for polemical purposes either absolute differences between blacks and whites, relative differences or unequal rates of change in a wide variety of areas. All demographic data lend themselves to such manipulation. From the standpoint of proclaimed aspirations, rhetorical commitments and time and energy—if not money—invested at all levels of government as well as by private organizations in efforts to right the historical injustice of the Negro's position in American society, one may readily conclude that a mountain labored throughout the sixties to bring forth a mouse. Moreover, some gains registered by blacks may owe less to policies adopted than to unplanned consequences or other, possibly transitory, circumstances such as a temporarily favorable age distribution among Negroes or the effects on the economy and on employment of the Vietnam war.[1]

1 From "Portrait of a Decade" by D. H. Wrong, printed in *The New York Times Magazine* (August 2, 1970), p. 30. © 1970 by The New York Times Company. Reprinted by permission.

Table 1. Population of the 25 largest cities, by rank

city	1970 census	1960 census	—change 1960 to 1970— number	per cent	—rank— 1970	1960
New York	7,894,862	7,781,984	112,878	1.5	1	1
Chicago	3,366,957	3,550,404	−183,447	−5.2	2	2
Los Angeles	2,816,061	2,479,015	337,046	13.6	3	3
Philadelphia	1,948,609	2,002,512	−53,903	−2.7	4	4
Detroit	1,511,482	1,670,144	−158,622	−9.5	5	5
Houston	1,232,802	938,219	294,583	31.4	6	7
Baltimore	905,759	939,024	−33,265	−3.5	7	6
Dallas	844,401	679,684	164,717	24.2	8	14
Washington	756,510	763,956	−7,446	−1.0	9	9
Cleveland	750,903	876,050	−125,147	−14.3	10	8
Indianapolis	744,624	476,258	268,366	56.3	11	26
Milwaukee	717,099	741,324	−24,225	−3.3	12	11
San Francisco	715,674	740,316	−24,642	−3.3	13	12
San Diego	696,769	573,224	123,545	21.6	14	18
San Antonio	654,153	587,718	66,435	11.3	15	17
Boston	641,071	697,197	−56,126	−8.1	16	13
Memphis	623,530	497,524	126,006	25.3	17	22
St. Louis	622,236	750,026	−127,790	−17.0	18	10
New Orleans	593,471	627,525	−34,054	−5.4	19	15
Phoenix	581,562	439,170	142,392	32.4	20	29
Columbus, O.	539,677	471,316	68,361	14.5	21	28
Seattle	530,831	557,087	−26,256	−4.7	22	19
Jacksonville	528,865	201,030	327,835	163.1	23	61
Pittsburgh	520,117	604,332	−84,215	−13.9	24	16
Denver	514,678	493,887	20,791	4.2	25	23

Source: Bureau of the Census

2. LOOKING BEYOND THE OBVIOUS

To gain an understanding of a problem or phenomenon, it is necessary not only to gather accurate data, but to gather enough data. An incomplete statistical picture can be as misleading as an inaccurate one. For example, in describing population changes affecting cities, one must consider whether all the relevant data are included. The 1970 census reported a general decline in the population of cities. But the Census Bureau cautions that such a conclusion does not tell the whole story of urban growth. *The New York Times* of September 3, 1970, explained the census figures on cities as follows:

WASHINGTON, Sept. 2—The population of New York City is:

  (A) 7,894,862

  (B) 11,571,899
  (C) 15,396,515
  (D) All three

The correct answer, it is apparent from new census data for American urban areas obtained today, is (D). It all depends on one's definition of a city.

The new figures for metropolitan areas, and not just central cities, show 11,571,899 for New York, an increase of 8.2 per cent over the 10,694,633 metropolitan population in 1960....

[For the city proper, the population figure of 7,894,862 marks an increase of about 112,000 since 1960.]

The 11,571,899 figure keeps the New York metropolitan area far out in front of other American urban areas, but even that larger number may not be large enough to define the urbanized area that is dependent on the city....

Table 2. Population of the 25 largest metropolitan areas, by rank

metropolitan area	1970 census	1960 census	—change 1960 to 1970— number	per cent	—rank— 1970	1960
New York City	11,571,899	10,694,633	877,266	8.2	1	1
Los Angeles-Long Beach, Cal.	7,032,075	6,038,771	993,304	16.4	2	3
Chicago	6,978,947	6,220,913	758,034	12.2	3	2
Philadelphia	4,817,914	4,342,897	475,017	10.9	4	4
Detroit	4,199,931	3,762,360	437,571	11.6	5	5
San Francisco	3,109,519	2,648,762	460,757	17.4	6	6
Washington	2,861,123	2,076,610	784,513	37.8	7	10
Boston	2,753,700	2,595,481	158,219	6.1	8	7
Pittsburgh	2,401,245	2,405,435	−4,190	−0.2	9	8
St. Louis	2,363,017	2,104,669	258,348	12.3	10	9
Baltimore	2,070,670	1,803,745	266,925	14.8	11	12
Cleveland	2,064,194	1,909,483	154,711	8.1	12	11
Houston	1,985,031	1,418,323	566,708	40.0	13	15
Newark	1,856,556	1,689,420	167,736	9.9	14	13
Minneapolis-St. Paul	1,813,647	1,482,030	331,617	22.4	15	14
Dallas	1,555,950	1,119,410	436,540	39.0	16	20
Seattle	1,421,869	1,107,213	314,656	28.4	17	21
Anaheim-Santa Ana-Garden Grove, Cal.	1,420,386	703,925	717,461	101.8	18	39
Milwaukee	1,403,688	1,278,850	124,838	9.8	19	17
Atlanta	1,390,164	1,017,188	372,976	8.8	20	24
Cincinnati	1,384,851	1,268,479	116,372	9.2	21	18
Paterson-Clifton-Passaic, N.J.	1,358,794	1,186,873	171,921	14.5	22	19
San Diego	1,357,854	1,033,011	324,843	31.4	23	23
Buffalo	1,349,211	1,306,957	32,254	3.2	24	16
Miami	1,267,792	935,047	332,755	35.6	25	26

Source: Bureau of the Census

Cluster of 4 Areas

The Census Bureau also provided new figures for the New York consolidated area, covering the metropolitan areas of New York, Jersey City and Newark and the Paterson-Clifton-Passaic, N.J., cluster.

This total, 15,396,515, may very likely uphold the city's claim to be the largest in the world. Prof. Kingsley Davis of the University of California, using consistent definitions, has ranked the New York urban area well ahead of Tokyo and London. . . .

Over all, the new census data illustrated how unreliable city population figures have become as a guide to metropolitan population.

Although they do not even appear on the list of metropolitan areas, eight cities are included on the list of the 25 largest cities. In large part this is because they are still able to annex surrounding territory as it develops, or because of city-county consolidations. . . .

Indianapolis, which now encompasses most of its metropolitan area under a new "unigov" system, rose from 26th to 11th on the city population list, ahead of areas whose city population is smaller but whose metropolitan total is much larger.

Houston and Dallas have annexed territory that would remain independent in other cities. Hence they rank much higher on the city population list (sixth and eighth) than on the metropolitan list (13th and 16th).

Similarly, Boston, long rimmed with suburbs, is 16th on the city list but eighth on the metropolitan roster. San Francisco, 13th among cities, is sixth among metropolitan areas. Pittsburgh, the 24th city, is the ninth metropolitan area.[2]

[2] Adapted from *The New York Times,* September 3, 1970, p. 1. © 1970 by The New York Times Company. Used by permission. (The preliminary figures in the original article have been changed to show final figures.)

Graph 1. U.S. population 1790 -1970

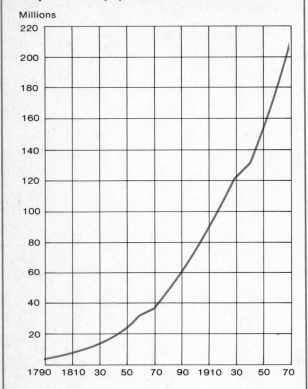

Millions

Graph 2. U.S. population 1790 - 1970

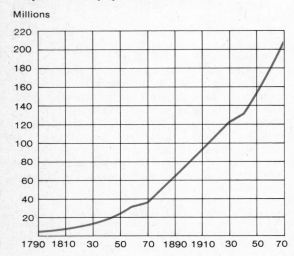

Millions

For a complete picture of urban growth, compare Tables 1 and 2 on pp. 18–19, showing the population of cities and metropolitan areas of the United States.

3. GRAPHS AND DIAGRAMS MAY BE MISLEADING

Many readers find tables of statistics comparatively uninteresting and much prefer to have data presented in graphic form. But as was stated earlier, a graph or diagram may create a wrong impression. The problem is not whether the basic data are accurate. It has to do with the way in which the data are pictured. Fundamentally, the issue is the proper use of *scale*.

The importance of scale can be illustrated by comparing the impressions created by a series of graphs which are based on the growth of population in the United States. (The figures used in the table and graphs have been rounded to the nearest whole number or decimal thereof.)

4. STRETCHING THE VERTICAL SCALE CREATES A STEEP RISE

Example: Population of the United States 1790–1970. Both graphs on this page were constructed to show the growth of population. But notice the difference between them.

Graphs 1 and 2 present exactly the same data, yet they create an entirely different impression. Because in Graph 2 the intervals are smaller on the vertical axis than on the horizontal, the growth of population seems much less impressive than it does in Graph 1. Graph 1, on the other hand, uses smaller intervals on the horizontal axis than on the vertical. It is easy to understand the effect created by these graphs when one compares them directly. However, if only one graph were used, the reader might get an impression of more dynamic growth or less dynamic growth, depending on the scale used.

Table 3 on page 21 shows the population increase by decades, both in numbers (millions) and relatively (in terms of per cent). Note, for example, that an increase of 1.4 million between 1790 and 1800 is an increase of 36 per cent; an increase of 19 million between 1940 and 1950 is an increase of only 14 per cent. It is possible to show the rate of growth (per cent) and net growth (millions) on the same graph. See Graph 3.

5. RELATIVENESS CAN BE PICTURED BY USING A RATIO (SEMILOGARITHMIC) SCALE

Table 3 on United States population growth shows the population increase not only in numbers but also in per cent of change for each decade. Should one wish to plot the population increase of the United States in such a way as to show relativeness accurately, it would be necessary to use what is termed a ratio (or semilogarithmic) scale. With ratio scaling an equal vertical distance at any level of the graph shows the same relative change. (Remember that a ratio, such as 1:2, can be expressed also as a percentage, 50%.) Turning to the data shown in the table below, one might wish to show that 3.9 is to 5.3 as 5.3 is to 7.2, or as 17.1 is to 23.2. Were a semilogarithmic scale used, the population curves on page 20 would

Table 3. Population of the United States, 1790–1970

year	population (millions)	increase in past decade (millions)	increase in past decade (per cent)
1790	3.9		
1800	5.3	1.4	36
1810	7.2	1.9	36
1820	9.6	2.4	33
1830	12.9	3.3	34
1840	17.1	4.2	33
1850	23.2	6.1	36
1860	31.4	8.2	35
1870	38.6	7.2	23
1880	50.2	11.6	30
1890	62.9	12.7	25
1900	76.0	13.1	21
1910	92.0	16.0	21
1920	105.7	13.7	15
1930	122.8	17.1	16
1940	131.7	8.9	7
1950	150.7	19.0	14
1960	179.3	28.6	19
1970	208.0	24.7	13

Graph 3. U.S. population increase 1800-1970

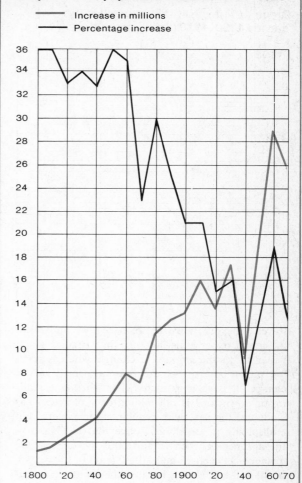

Increase in millions
Percentage increase

show the same relative change (as measured by vertical distance) for the nation's population growth between 1790 and 1800, 1800 and 1810, 1840 and 1850. Graph 4 is a graphic representation of population growth constructed on a ratio scale.

Graph 4, and others like it in this book (see, for example, pages 51 and 53) are constructed on special graph paper known as "semi-log" or "ratio" paper, obtainable at draftsmen's supply

Graph 4. Growth of U.S. population by decade 1790-1970 (semilogarithmic scale)

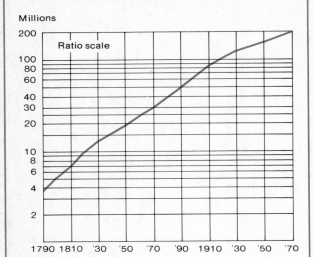

stores. The difference between regular and semi-log graph paper boils down to this: regular graph paper shows the *amount* of change, whereas semi-log paper best shows the *rate* or percentage of change. It is so constructed that when one reads up or down, one is not adding or subtracting (as would be the case with regular graph paper), but multiplying or dividing. Notice that in Graph 4, the distance between 10 and 20 is the same as the distance between 15 and 30, 20 and 40, 25 and 50, or 40 and 80. That is because these particular distances indicate a doubling. A given percentage increase measures the same distance anywhere on the chart. The distance from 10 to 11 is the same as from 20 to 22 or from 50 to 55 since all these distances represent an increase of 10 per cent. Semilogarithmic graphs facilitate the plotting (and predicting) of growth rates, such as interest on money (see Graphs 5, 6, and 7). Graphs 5 and 6 both show the growth of $100 in fixed amounts and in percentages. In Graph 5, the *straight line* shows what happens to $100 increased by $10 a year; the *curve* shows what happens to $100 when it is increased 10 per cent a year. In Graph 6 the reverse is true, because the graph employs a ratio

or semilogarithmic scale. Graph 7 shows how one may use semi-log graph paper to determine the future value of $100 deposited in a savings account yielding 5 per cent interest compounded annually. First locate 100 on the left edge of a semi-log sheet, then pinpoint 105 at the end of the first year. A straight line drawn from the first point through the second and extended across the graph will show how much the deposited sum will be worth at any time in the future. For example, it will be worth $163 in ten years, and $265 in 20 years.

6. THE SAME GRAPH MAY SHOW MORE THAN ONE SET OF DATA

Graph 3 uses data from the table on United States Population Growth (page 21). For each decade it compares percentage change with the numerical increase, but it does not show the total population for each decade. For 1870, for example, the graph shows an increase of 23 per cent and a numerical increase of 7.2 million. It does not show the total population for 1870, nor, for that matter, for any other year. Graph 4, however, does represent the total population for each decade, and also the numerical change in population from one decade to the next.

7. SUPPRESSING THE ZERO PROVIDES AN OPPORTUNITY TO STRETCH THE VERTICAL SCALE

At times data are represented in such a way that it becomes virtually impossible for the reader to draw a correct inference from the diagram. This difficulty may be the result of deliberate intent to deceive, or it may reflect lack of insight on the part of the author. Graph 8, for example, purports to show the net public debt for the years 1953–1961. Except for two plateaus, the graph pictures a steady and sharp increase in the national debt. An unfair and partisan author might suggest that this graph shows what happened to the public debt during a Republican administration. Two points should be remembered. First, the net public debt includes state and local debt as well as federal debt. More important, the graph does not show how the debt climbed to the total of about 257

Graph 5. Growth of $100 by $10 a year and by 10 per cent annually (regular scale)

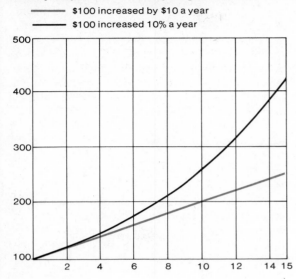

Graph 6. Growth of $100 by $10 a year and by 10 per cent annually (semilogarithmic scale)

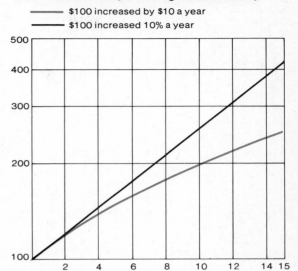

Graph 7. Growth of $100 at 5 per cent interest, compounded annually (semilogarithmic scale)

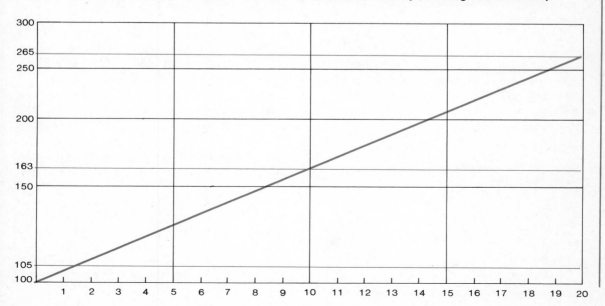

Graph 8.   Net public debt 1953-1961

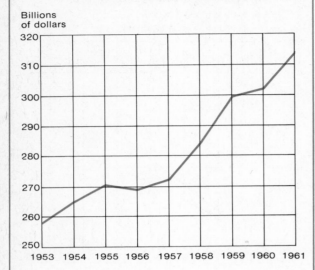

Billions
of dollars

320	
310	
300	
290	
280	
270	
260	
250	

1953 1954 1955 1956 1957 1958 1959 1960 1961

billion dollars, the figure for 1953. This second point is an example of what is known as "suppressing the zero."

8. PICTOGRAMS DRAWN TO SCALE IN ONE DIMENSION MAY MISREPRESENT RELATIONSHIPS

In an effort to make graphics more interesting, many authors are using pictorial symbols. To illustrate, one might wish to compare the population of this country in 1880 (50.2 million) and in 1950 (150.7 million). This might be done in either of two ways.

Pictograms showing U.S. population growth, 1880 -1950

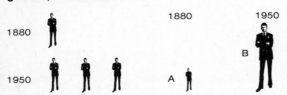

1880

1950   1880   1950

                                             B

                                      A

Each figure equals 50 million   Figure A equals 50 million

In the pictograms below, the symbol at left represents 50 million people, the population in 1880. Since the population in 1950 was about three times as great, the three symbols suggest the correct relationship. But in providing more "body" for the 1950 symbol, the artist created a burly giant who certainly looks much more than three times the size of the 1880 symbol. Almost certainly the reader would not draw the correct inference from this pictogram.

Toward better understanding

QUESTIONS TO CONSIDER IN ANALYZING THIS MATERIAL

1. Using the quoted selection on the economic status of black Americans, 1960–1970, what data would you use if you wished to give the impression that blacks had made great gains during this period? That they still were seriously disadvantaged compared to whites? Why is it that these data can be used to serve quite different ends? What do you consider the valid conclusions that can be derived from these data?

2. Why does the Census Bureau provide four sets of figures "to tell the whole story of urban growth"? What is the special value of each? Why may a city rank much higher on the city population list than on the metropolitan area list, or vice versa? Which of the following cities have the best chance of making great gains on the city population list between 1970 and 1980: Indianapolis, Dallas, San Francisco, Pittsburgh? Why?

3. How can differences in the scale used in line graphs create different "impressions" of the data represented? What can be done to make readers aware of this fact?

4. What possibilities of misrepresentation are present when "the zero is suppressed" in a graph? Explain.

5. Why is scale a problem in the case of certain types of pictograms and not in the case of others? Explain and give examples.

6. In graphic representation of growth statistics, why is it important to present rate of growth and thus bring out the factor of "relativeness"? How can this be done?

7. What is the advantage of using two sets of data to show population increase? (See Graph 3.)

THINKING ABOUT THE PLACE OF STATISTICS IN ECONOMICS

1. Why is "quantitative thinking" and therefore statistics important in economics?

2. What have the authors said about economics as a science and about the importance of a scientific approach to the study of economic problems?

3. Are statistics necessarily reliable? Why might incorrect statistics be "manufactured"? Why might persons be tempted to cite statistics in a "tricky" manner? Can you give examples?

4. Should the producers of statistics also provide an estimate of their probable accuracy? Why?

5. Why would it be difficult to provide reliable estimates of this country's population on a given date? Or the size of the national debt? Or how much the federal budget will be "in the red" at the end of the fiscal year?

6. Do the graphs and diagrams included in Part I of this book meet the standards just suggested? Explain why you think they do or fail to do so.

How wants lead to production

1. **How do economic wants become demands?**
2. **How do producers meet demands?**
3. **How is production adjusted to demands?**
4. **What provision is made for future demand?**

Industry is the soul of business and the keystone to prosperity.

CHARLES DICKENS,
Barnaby Rudge

In Chapter 1, it was shown that everyone has many wants, and that in general many of these go unsatisfied. To satisfy a want, one's desire must be so strong that he is willing to *give up something else* (usually money) in order to get it. When this happens, there is a *demand* for the thing in question.

Demands are satisfied by goods and services *produced* by others who desire the things offered in exchange. In other words, *wants backed by willingness and ability to pay constitute demands* which are met by *production*.

This chapter shows (1) how people transform some of their strongest wants into demands and (2) how these demands get translated into production.

The process by which consumers play such a large part in determining what is produced is basic to a free market economy, and the same principles that apply to individual consumers apply to business consumers as well.

1

How do economic wants become demands?

People have so many wants that choices are difficult. Everyone requires at least a minimum of food, clothing, and housing. Wants for such physical needs are basic. Nourishment and protection from the elements are essential for man's survival.

But who is satisfied with just the bare essentials of food, clothing, and shelter? Although food sufficient for survival could be produced for a few cents a day, most people prefer variety and flavor in their food. Likewise, a person could probably survive in a cheap tent and could protect his body against the weather with just one outfit of clothing. But most persons would rather live in more permanent dwellings, such as houses or apartments, and own a larger and more varied wardrobe. Most people in this country can afford some choice and variety in their shelter and clothing.

Wants include services as well as material goods. Some kinds of services are almost as essential as the food, clothing, and shelter which are indispensable for human survival. Medical services are required by most people from time to time. Transportation by private car or by public transport is necessary for getting to work, shopping, and many other purposes. Most persons now regard electric power —used in lighting and in communications systems—as essential in any modern society. And there are many other services that it would be a hardship to do without.

Most people want education for themselves and their children. In this country people are required by law to attend school until a certain age. A half-century ago, high school education was obtained by only a minority of citizens, now schooling through high school and beyond is practically a necessity. A college degree has become a prerequisite for an increasing number of jobs. Employers recognize that it is advantageous to hire the best-educated persons they can get. Government also encourages education, because it too requires the services of intelligent and well-trained people.

Most parents want their children to have as good an education as possible. The expense of keeping children in high school and college is a major item in many family budgets. Many parents make great sacrifices in order to help finance their children's education. Clearly the desire for education ranks high on the American people's list of priorities.

The need for recreation is universal. Everyone wants and needs a certain amount of recreation and relaxation. Some people can satisfy this need through participation in athletics. Others play musical instruments. Motion pictures, television and the theater provide escape for millions. Often a coffee house or a skating rink serve as social centers. Then there are those who like to "get away from it all" by going fishing. Everyone has his own favorite pastime. The desire for some form of diversion and relief from one's daily routine has come to be recognized as a natural and normal human need.

Expenditures for needed items for family of 4

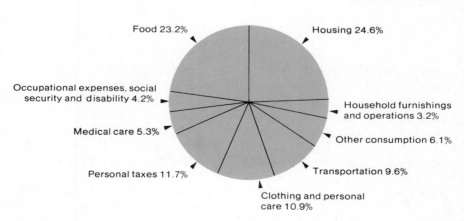

Total income = $11,232

Food 23.2%

Housing 24.6%

Occupational expenses, social security and disability 4.2%

Household furnishings and operations 3.2%

Medical care 5.3%

Other consumption 6.1%

Personal taxes 11.7%

Transportation 9.6%

Clothing and personal care 10.9%

Based on intermediate budget for family living in a metropolitan area (1971)

Source: Statistical Abstract

Want leads to demand

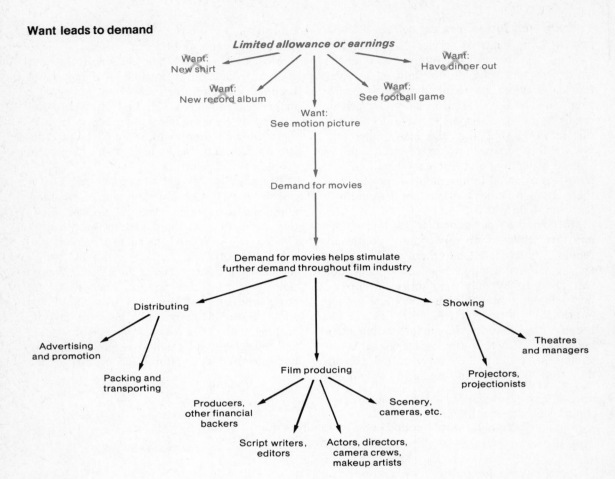

Limited allowance or earnings

Want: New shirt

Want: New record album

Want: See motion picture

Want: See football game

Want: Have dinner out

Demand for movies

Demand for movies helps stimulate further demand throughout film industry

Distributing

Showing

Advertising and promotion

Packing and transporting

Film producing

Theatres and managers

Projectors, projectionists

Producers, other financial backers

Scenery, cameras, etc.

Script writers, editors

Actors, directors, camera crews, makeup artists

Human beings have social needs. The wish to be associated with other people in various activities is one of the deep-rooted instincts of human nature. Whereas the basic want for food is based on physical needs, the desire to have meals with members of one's family, or with friends, is a social want. The desire of a young person for a car often is based on social reasons, as is the desire to acquire new clothing in the latest style.

Some families have an urge to "keep up with the Joneses," or even to surpass the Joneses in material possessions. Some families take pride in owning the biggest house in the neighborhood. An individual may go to great lengths to wear the most expensive wristwatch or necklace, or drive the most luxurious car. Spending often reflects a desire to impress others. The satisfaction of wants motivated by a desire for prestige is a legitimate concern of economics, since such wants lead to demand and to production, just as do other wants. People have different tastes and wants, and different ways of satisfying those wants.

There is a difference between wants and demands. Demands grow out of wants, but not all wants become demands in the economic sense. *Desire* for a product, backed by *money* and a *willingness to part with that money* for the product, makes *demand*. In the economic sense, there is no demand for a product unless people have money which they are willing to spend for the product. *Demand is desire plus ability and willingness to pay for something.*

The real cost of a thing is the value placed on what a person must give up to obtain it. Because one's resources are limited, choices always involve "trade-offs" of one thing for another. Leisure time must be sacrificed if one wishes to earn money. Then the money earned is given in exchange for whatever goods or services one values more highly than the money paid. Economic life is a constant process of exchanges that reflect views about relative values. The value of whatever is given up to acquire something else is sometimes called an "opportunity cost."

Economic *goods* (such as a house or a pair of shoes) are *material things* that are *scarce,* have *value,* and are wanted by people. An economic *service* has the same characteristics as an economic good except that it is not a material commodity. Services include any beneficial acts performed for people, such as those received from a doctor, a teacher, or an appliance repairman.

Goods or services that are not scarce have no economic value. If one gives up nothing to obtain a given item, it is in economic terms a "free good." The air one breathes is necessary for life, but nothing is paid for it. The air is therefore a free good.

In certain kinds of manufacturing, costs are involved in keeping the air unpolluted. In such a case, if the community demands clean air, the manufacturer may be required to install expensive antipollution devices. This expenditure uses up resources that could be used for other purposes. Manufacturing costs, and perhaps the prices of manufactured goods, are thereby increased. Society as a whole, as well as individuals, has wants and demands, and pays in various ways for the satisfaction it receives.

A thing that is not wanted has no value. Regardless of how much it costs to produce a thing, it cannot be sold unless someone wants it. An Eskimo probably would not want a bikini, or a South Sea Islander a heavy fur coat. Wants are influenced not only by tastes and preferences, but also by particular circumstances.

Demand is subject to the law of diminishing utility. In economics, the amount of satisfaction one gets from a good or service is called *utility*. But utility or usefulness changes with circumstances. Generally, the more of a particular thing one has, the less valuable become additional quantities of it. That is, the first item has most value, while succeeding items have less and less value. At some point one would not give anything in exchange for more of this particular good or service.

The general law of diminishing utility can be stated in these words: *Each succeeding unit of any good satisfies a less intense desire than the previous one,* until eventually some successive unit has no utility whatever, and one would

The law of diminishing utility

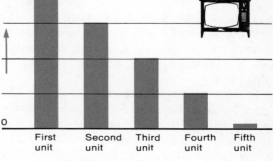

The utility of one television may be high, but the utility of additional televisions decreases.

pay nothing for it. This law applies not only to a good, but also to entertainment or other services for which one spends money. For example, at a musical recital one might enjoy the first hour, begin to tire during the second hour, and perhaps become bored during a third hour.

Everyone tries to get the greatest total utility for his money. In thinking about the law of diminishing utility, one usually has in mind the acquiring of successive units of one good. But in real life one buys many kinds of goods during the period of a week. For that reason, choices must be made to achieve the most satisfaction from spending a limited amount of money.

The greatest amount of satisfaction obviously is obtained when, under the prevailing circumstances, one buys that thing which gives the most satisfaction. But circumstances change in at least two ways when this thing is bought. The buyer now has less money, and the utility of another item of the same kind probably would be less than for the item just brought.

Successive dollars devoted to buying more of any one product yield less and less extra utility. This is true for all of the goods one may be planning to buy. If one has decided tentatively how much of each good he should purchase, and then decides that he could "do better" by switching a dollar, for example, from records to paperbacks, how was this decision reached? Subconsciously the shopper calculated that another dollar spent for records would provide less utility than if spent for paperbacks. The best allocation of a given sum of money among several goods is one where the last dollar spent on each different good seems to promise an equal utility.

Income influences demands. Money, like other items, is subject to the principle of diminishing utility. The more money a person has, the less utility a given amount of it (a marginal amount) has for him. Or the less one has, the higher one prizes a given sum, no matter how small.

A person who has ten dollars in his pocket may decide to take a cab on a rainy day. If he has only one dollar, he may choose to walk or wait for a bus. In the first case, the utility of the cab ride is greater than the marginal utility of the money required to pay the cab fare. In the second case, the person places a higher value on his dollar than on the services of the cab driver. Wants are not limited because of limited resources, but demands are.

Family expenditure patterns, like individual expenditures, vary with income levels. The size of a family's income largely determines the per cent of income spent for various kinds of goods and services. Families with very low incomes typically spend at least one-third of total income for food and another one-third for housing. They are not able to save much from their incomes. High-income families, on the other hand, may spend only 3 or 4 per cent of their income for food, 10 per cent for housing and clothing, and save perhaps 25 per cent or more.

High-income families are buying better and more varied food, housing, and clothing than low-income families can afford. Yet a much smaller per cent of their total incomes are required to provide these basic necessities. And because the marginal utilities of given amounts of money are lower for them, high-income families buy many more kinds of goods and services, both necessities and luxuries, and in much larger quantities, than do low-income families.

Total demand in a nation's economy is made up of demands from consumers, businesses, and government. In addition to the expenditures of individual and family consumers, all kinds of businesses, as well as farmers, and various nonprofit organizations, buy goods and services to be used in producing things for ultimate sale to consumers. During a typical year, these producer groups spend almost one-fourth as much for production facilities as all individuals and families spend for consumption. This does not include the amount spent by producers for the raw materials made into consumer goods.

Family budgets for three incomes compared (family size: 4)

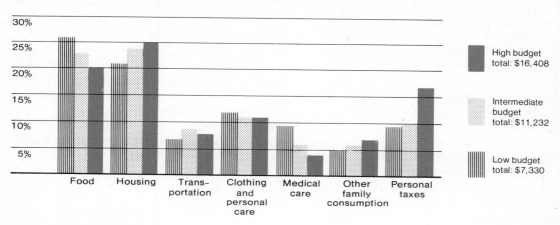

Source: Bureau of Labor Statistics

Government—federal, state, and local—also buys large amounts of goods and services. During a recent year, government purchases in this country amounted to more than one-third as much as the total amount of individual and family consumption expenditures. Government purchases are used to supply goods and services such as highways, dams, airports, schools, fire and police protection, national defense, and the like.

Total demand, in other words, is made up of the sum of demands for direct consumption plus demands for goods and services to be used in further production (for later consumption) by private producers and by government. Direct consumption demand currently is only a little more than three-fifths of this total.

The demands of private producers and governments differ from personal consumption demands. Governments hope that whatever they produce will be beneficial and pleasing to citizens. A business establishment buys goods and services for use in producing other goods and services, and not for immediate consumption. It is hoped that whatever is produced will be desired by individual and family consumers, and that the product can be sold at a profit.

CHECK UP

1. What are some major wants of an American family? Why are there differences between one family and another? How does demand differ from want?

2. How does one get the greatest total utility for his money?

3. Why do family expenditure patterns vary with income levels? Give examples.

4. What types of expenditures are included in a nation's total demand? How do the demands of governments and private producers differ from personal consumption demands?

2

How do producers meet demands?

Production is the creation of utility. A producer takes something of little value and makes it more valuable. Any process that makes goods more useful in satisfying wants is production. It is often said that production creates *place utility, form utility,* and *time utility.* This refers to the fact that wants can be satisfied only when something is available where it is wanted, in the condition that it is wanted and when it is wanted. Those who transport a product to where it is wanted, merchants who sell it to the public, and moneylenders who provide financing for production activities or for installment purchases, are producers just as are farmers, miners, or manufacturers.

Coal hundreds of feet underground in West Virginia cannot satisfy any wants. But miners dig this coal and bring it to the surface. A railroad transports it to an electrical power generating station. The power company uses the coal to generate electricity. The electricity is transported by wires into homes. The demand for light has thus been met by an involved production process which began when underground coal was mined hundreds of miles away from where the light was turned on in the home of the user.

Many steps are involved in production to satisfy consumer demands. The example just given illustrates some of the complexities of production. But actually much more is involved. Someone had to anticipate the demand for electric lighting. Plans had to be drawn up, money raised, materials bought, and labor hired to build and operate the facilities of the electric power company. The same is true for the coal mine and the railroad and for all of the many separate companies which produced equipment, materials and supplies used by these organizations. Finally, the owners or managers of the power company, the mine, and the railroad had to reach agreements on prices, payment terms, time schedules, and a variety of other matters.

The labor of many thousands of persons employed in various occupations in many parts of the country over a period of many years makes it possible to have light in the home by simply pushing a button. The same kind of complexity is back of most of the everyday goods and services that people take for granted.

Production is not limited to tangible goods. Persons who work with their minds or provide services are also producers: scientists, technicians, business managers, artists, television performers, teachers, authors, policemen, soldiers, elected public officials, and those engaged in many other creative and useful professions. All of these persons are engaged in satisfying the wants of individuals or of society as a whole. In this country, about two-thirds as much is spent annually for services of this kind as for tangible goods.

Production turns out "producer goods." *Consumer goods* are items to satisfy personal consumption wants; *producer goods* are used in making consumer goods available. The latter include such things as buildings, machines, tools, supplies, and materials used in production. As already mentioned, the spending of American private producers for production facilities of this type amounts to almost one-fourth of the total spending for personal consumption. During a recent year, about 130 billion dollars was spent for producer facilities in this country.

Most consumer goods are produced by "roundabout" production methods. At the time of the Revolutionary War nine out of every ten persons lived on farms. They produced most of their own food, made much of their own clothing, and built their own houses and barns.

Today, only about one American in twenty lives on a farm. Most people live in large or small cities or suburban areas, and cannot produce for themselves most of the things they want. Instead, they buy and sell to obtain most goods and services. Generally people "sell" their labor services and skills to employers, mainly businesses or government, and with the income earned buy what is needed for everyday life. Even modern farmers produce only a small part of the things they consume. Today most farmers sell most of their products and use the money received to buy the major portion of their consumer and producer goods.

"Roundabout" production is essential in a modern economy. Without complicated, efficient, and expensive manufacturing, agricultural, and transportation machinery and equipment, it would be impossible to maintain even present living standards. Roundabout production, involving the production and use of producer goods to mass produce consumer goods greatly reduces the cost of goods bought. For example, a man could build an automobile if he had the necessary knowledge, manual skills, tools, and materials, but it would take much longer and cost him many times more than it does to produce a car in an automobile plant.

The acquiring and bringing together of the producer goods used in roundabout production requires a complicated system of financing as well as a great deal of management talent and planning. Highly specialized workers are also needed at all stages of the operation.

The typical worker has only a small part in the manufacturing of a finished product. Instead of one man making an entire product, today each man is likely to make but one small part. He may spend his time making as many like parts as possible. This division of labor gives each worker only a limited part in the manufacture of an entire product. When all the parts produced in quantity through the division of labor are assembled into the final product, "mass production" has been accomplished.

Many businesses have programs of research and development. Large businesses, if they are to excel, must continually develop new products and cheaper methods of producing them. To this end engineers, research workers, and other specialists carry on a program of research and development. A large company can afford to employ specialists in research and development because the cost of their services is small in relation to the increased volume of production and the larger profits that result, ultimately, from their activities.

Machine power has largely replaced manpower. In an industrialized economy, work

"Get busy—it's the boss!"

© *Punch*—Ben Roth Agency

done by machines usually costs less than work done by human muscles. Consequently, machines are used wherever possible. Mechanized operation makes it possible to produce goods at relatively low costs even though wage rates are high. A machine may achieve in one operation what formerly involved separate operations by several men. Furthermore, the machine usually does the job in much less time, thus reducing another production cost. Machines that make machines (producer's goods) are increasing, and are speeding up the process of production even more.

Modern machinery is most efficient in large-scale operations. The large-scale manufacturer hires specially trained people to do the various specialized tasks involved in the process of manufacturing. He employs designers to develop styles that will appeal to the majority of customers. A large clothing manufacturer, for example, uses a power cutter to cut many identical pieces of cloth for men's suits at the same time. This reduces cost and waste. Since each suit is mass produced, the expense of each of the different operations amounts to very little per suit. And the total cost of producing the suit is far lower than that of a hand-tailored suit. This low cost makes possible low prices, and low prices enable people to buy more suits.

Rate of production may affect unit cost. The owner of a shop making only a few suits especially designed for wealthy customers may have a high *overhead* per unit of output. Overhead can be defined as *expenses which do not change significantly with the number of units of output produced.* These expenses include rent, property taxes, light and fuel bills, managers' salaries, and the like. Such expenses sometimes are called *fixed costs.* Expenses which change significantly with changes in the number of units produced are called *direct* or *variable costs.* Piece-work wages paid to a suit-cutter are an example of variable cost. Because the suit-cutter gets paid for each piece, the more he cuts the more wages he receives.

Total production costs include both variable and fixed costs. Variable costs increase as output increases, although they may remain about the same for each unit of output. But as fixed costs remain constant, the higher the production the lower the fixed costs per unit.

The future may be an age of automation. The most revolutionary development in the use of machines is called *automation.* In simple mechanization men use machines to facilitate and speed up their work. An automated (literally, "self-operating") system extends the principle of mechanization to the point where machines are used to operate other machines. Indeed automation devices not only run the machines, they also detect errors in production, and stop the process when something goes wrong. They may even correct or adjust operating mistakes. Wherever it has been introduced, automation has drastically reduced the number of workers needed. It has, therefore, once again raised the specter of *technological unemployment*—large-scale layoffs caused by labor-displacing machinery. Economists, taking a long view of the situation, tend to believe that such unemployment would be temporary. That, however, would be scant consolation for those affected.

Producers try to control their costs. If a producer's costs are too high, he may be unable to sell his product at prices high enough to cover his costs. Sales go to those who sell at the lowest prices. In a competitive economy, the efficient producer survives and the inefficient goes out of business. Consequently, producers are constantly searching for ways to reduce costs, to improve products without increasing costs, and to develop new products.

The "social overhead capital" contributes much to efficient production. Transportation systems, communications systems, electrical power systems, and educational systems sometimes are called *social overhead capital.* Without these, production would be limited and few present-day wants could be satisfied. Much of the economic aid provided developing countries by the United States since World War II has been used to develop these types of facilities.

The transportation system is a vital part of the nation's economy. Goods and people are transported by railroad, by vehicles using highways, and in airplanes and ships. Pipelines bring gas and petroleum to many parts of the country. Ships and airlines form a network serving the entire world.

Transportation enters into almost every step of production (including the distribution) of goods. The economics of mass production could not be achieved without a transportation system to move goods efficiently and cheaply from sources of supply to processing centers and then to consumer markets. The transportation system creates *place utility.*

Railroads form a unified transportation system. Railroad lines provide a network to move goods from one place to another almost anywhere in the country. Even though there are several hundred different railroad companies all the railroads operate as a unified system. Trains run on tracks with rails the same distance apart, so that the cars of any company can travel on the tracks of other companies. By switching cars from one railroad line to another, it is possible to move goods from any

The shifting transportation pattern

In freight traffic

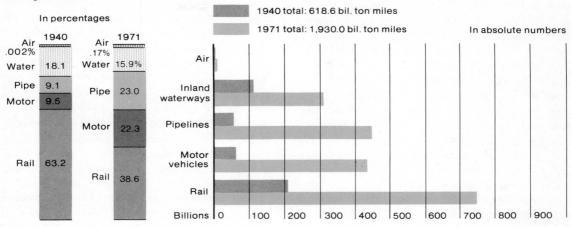

In passenger traffic (public transport only)

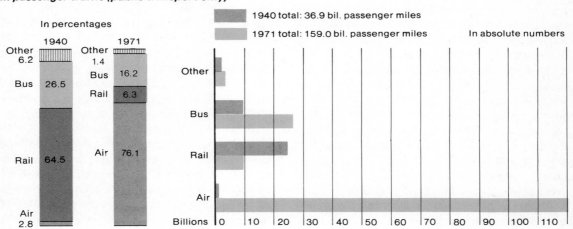

Railroad traffic has been marked by a decline in passenger travel but a sharp rise in freight transport. Note also the greatly increased use of air travel and of shipment by motor vehicles and pipelines.

Source: Statistical Abstract

part of the country to any other part without unloading and reloading goods. This flexibility greatly increases transportation efficiency.

Highways and trucks provide essential services in the economy. Most goods are brought at least a part of the way to consumer markets by truck. Agricultural products and livestock are hauled from farms and ranches to processing centers by truck. The lumber and plywood used in building homes and furniture, and the paper used in books and newspapers, started their journey from a forest on a log truck.

Much of the fluid milk consumed in the great cities is carried by tank trucks, sometimes for hundreds of miles.

For some purposes, trucks have advantages over railroads. On short hauls trucks usually provide faster and less expensive service. Unlike railroad cars, a truck in most cases can move the goods transported from the loading platform to the final unloading point. Speedy movement from the point of origin to the final destination is especially important for perishable products. For small shipments trucks provide faster and more economical service than do railroads. Trucks also serve areas where there are no railroads.

Waterways connect this country with almost every major producing region of the world. Surrounding oceans place the United States "next door" to all parts of the world. The great bulk of water transportation is ocean transportation between the various nations. Millions of tons of goods are constantly being moved from one country to another by cargo ships.

A large amount of freight moves coast-wise by ship and barge between ocean ports in the United States. On the Great Lakes ships carry such cargoes as iron ore, grain, coal, lumber, cement, and oil. Ships operate through the Panama Canal between the Pacific Coast and the Atlantic and Gulf Coasts. Barges move bulky materials on the rivers, especially in the great Mississippi Valley, and on canals.

Airplanes have become increasingly important to the economy. Today, air service reaches all large and most medium-sized cities. Planes also operate between the United States and virtually every other country in the world. Airlines provide a fast, dependable, and efficient passenger transportation at reasonable cost. Air-passenger miles (one passenger for one mile) exceed railroad- or bus-passenger miles in the United States.

Most of the mail and a growing amount of goods are moved by air. Many things are moved by air which otherwise could not be transported. For example, Californians can enjoy

Maine lobsters, and the people of New York can obtain orchids from Hawaii by air transport.

Pipeline systems transport fuels. Pipelines are an economical and efficient means of moving large amounts of petroleum and natural gas from oil wells to refineries and thence to consumers. Pipelines are sometimes owned and operated by oil and gas companies and are used only by the owners. Other pipelines carry oil and gas for all the co-operating companies within a single state or between different states. The pipeline system generally transports these specialized products at a lower cost than can railroads and trucks.

Communication networks span the nation. Modern communication includes telephone and telegraph, radio and television, postal service and photographs sent by wire. By tuning in his radio or television set a cattleman in Texas learns the market price of steers in Omaha and Kansas City. If he wants to sell some of his cattle in a hurry, he can telephone or telegraph the railroad or trucking company to be ready to ship the cattle to whatever market he chooses. A North Dakota wheat farmer or the operator of a grain elevator can use communication facilities in a similar manner.

If a grocer or the proprietor of a clothing store runs short of merchandise, he can call his supplier. In a short time the shipment will be on its way. If a farm-equipment company wants to feature a new machine or to push sales of one of its regular machines, it can notify its many dealers by telephone or telegraph within the hour.

Many buyers and sellers conduct much of their business by telephone, telegraph, or by mail. The communications system keeps not only these men but the public informed on business matters. They have access to up-to-the-minute reliable information which enables them to buy and sell almost any commodity advantageously.

Transportation and communications go hand-in-hand. Were it not for communications, the transportation system could not run smoothly. Even the railroads and airplanes could not operate safely and efficiently without information about weather conditions, schedules, and cargoes.

Likewise, communications could not function effectively without transportation. Radio and television notices of changes in the market could not be acted on by buyers and sellers. Telephone requests to reserve railroad cars or trucks could not be met. Passengers would be left stranded.

Americans are seldom without transportation or communication. The first men on the job after floods, hurricanes, and other disasters are usually telephone, highway, and railroad repairmen.

Transportation and communications systems are largely privately owned and operated. In many countries, transportation and communications facilities are "nationalized" (owned by the government). The United States, however, relies largely on private ownership because most persons believe this to be more efficient and less costly.

Highways, streets, and waterways in this country are publicly owned, as are most airport and many seaport facilities. But the cars, trucks, ships, barges, and planes are privately owned. Railroads and pipelines, with only a few minor exceptions, are privately owned. Telephone and telegraph services are provided by private companies, as are radio and television networks and stations. Mail service, a major form of communication for most people, is provided by a government corporation, but mail is actually moved (except for pickups and deliveries) by privately owned transportation.

Electrical services are valuable both to consumers and producers. As consumers, Americans know how important electricity is to this country. Try to imagine what would happen if homes in a community were without electrical services for a week. Most people would be without lights, many would find it difficult to prepare food, refrigerated foods would spoil,

and there would be no television programs.

A sizable portion of business and industry, and much of transportation and communication is dependent upon electrical power. Without electrical energy, factories would close, many workers would be without employment, and the prices of many goods would be much higher. Electrical service is so important that private businesses supplying it are closely regulated by government, and much of the power is actually supplied by government-owned facilities.

A high level of education is essential in a complex economy. A century ago, most people had little formal education. A typical wage earner could read well enough to read his Bible, write well enough to sign his name, and knew how to tell the time, count money, and do simple arithmetic. Although more education may have been desirable, it was not necessary for the work he did. Only professional people, such as physicians, lawyers, clergymen, and a few others among the wealthy, received an extensive education.

Today's worker may perform complex tasks, using expensive precision machinery and equipment. Mental as opposed to purely physical work involves a rapidly growing per cent of the total work force. Indeed the entire economic system depends on skills and abilities developed through education.

CHECK UP

1. What is the purpose of production? Who are producers? What are producer goods? What is "roundabout" production? Why does machinery tend to displace manpower? Why is there a trend toward large-scale operations? Automation?

2. Explain these terms: fixed costs, variable costs, automation, technological unemployment, "social overhead capital."

3. Why are the following of vital importance to the nation's economy: transportation systems, communications systems, electrical power, education?

3

How is production adjusted to meet demand?

Producers try to anticipate demands. Private producers want to make a profit in their businesses. If too much of a particular good is produced, all of it cannot be sold, or some of it must be sold at a price below the cost of production. In either case, producers' profits are reduced or losses may be incurred. On the other hand, if too little is produced, profits are smaller than if more of a given product were available for sale.

In some countries the government determines "what" and "how much" will be produced. (Such an economy is often termed a "command economy.") In the free enterprise system most of these decisions are made by private producers. Most Americans believe that the judgments of thousands of independent businessmen, all striving to make a profit, are

to be preferred to those of economic planners in government offices. Individual businessmen make mistakes, of course. Some of them may anticipate that demand will be greater than proves to be the case, and others may underestimate demand. Thus to some extent high and low anticipations may cancel each other out.

Demand for a particular product seldom remains constant for any considerable length of time. Consumer tastes and preferences change, and new products take the place of older ones. Demands for many kinds of products also vary from season to season. One of the most crucial and most difficult tasks of business owners and managers, therefore, is that of correctly estimating what the demand will be a few weeks, months, or years in the future.

Many large businesses spend thousands and even millions of dollars each year in *marketing research* designed to provide information about future demand. In that way, they hope to be able to adjust operations so as to provide consumers with what they want in quantities that will be profitable. Although small businesses obviously cannot spend as much on marketing research as larger businesses, their need to make the proper adjustment to changing demands is equally important. Those that do so successfully survive and prosper; those that fail to do so end up in bankruptcy.

Agricultural producers usually have more difficulty in adjusting to changes in demand than do manufacturers. Once a crop has been planted, a farmer cannot reduce production unless he foregoes harvesting. Furthermore, some agricultural products cannot be stored for long periods of time without spoilage. Finally, the output of any one farmer is so small a part of the total agricultural output for the given crop, that what he does has little influence on the total amount produced.

Manufacturers, on the other hand, often can adjust rather quickly to changing demands. More workers can be hired and more overtime

Demand leads to production

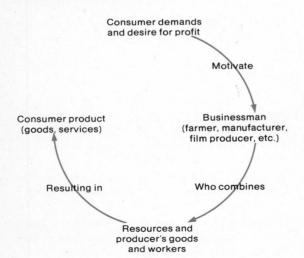

Consumer demands and desire for profit

Motivate

Businessman (farmer, manufacturer, film producer, etc.)

Who combines

Resources and producer's goods and workers

Resulting in

Consumer product (goods, services)

The cost of advertising in the United States

Percentage expenditures by advertising medium are shown for four years.

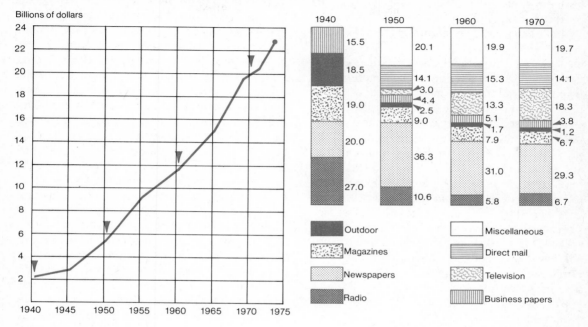

Source: Statistical Abstract

work introduced if demand increases. Conversely, workers can be laid off or the manufacture of other products stressed if demand declines for a particular good. In some industries a few large businesses provide most of a given product. In such cases, any change in output by one producer will affect total production substantially.

Regardless of the number of producers in an industry, all producers are eager to find profitable markets for their goods. They want to sell more. To do this, they must sell at prices as low or even lower than competitors. This *price competition* tends to hold the prices charged consumers to the lowest levels that production costs permit. This is perhaps the chief reason why consumers favor competition among those selling them goods.

Producers, including sellers, often try to influence demand by advertising. About 20 billion dollars a year is spent for advertising in this country. Some 150 large businesses spend more than a million dollars, and a few more than 100 million dollars, on various kinds of advertising.

People viewing television in the United States often protest that commercials distract from their enjoyment of programs. The total costs of commercial television are met by advertisers who believe that people watching TV will buy their products. Without advertising, viewers would have to pay a fee to the television companies, or pay higher taxes so that the government could operate television.

Television, of course, is only one of many methods of advertising. Advertisers also use radio, newspapers, magazines, outdoor billboards, street car posters, and the like. Some businesses also depend on direct mailing to potential customers.

Advertising enables one to make selections among various kinds of products. Sellers want consumers to know about new products. Many new products are developed each month. But if purchasers are not made aware of these products, they obviously cannot buy them.

Advertisers also want consumers to remember and continue to use already established products and services. If parents and children are constantly exposed to advertisements for a particular breakfast food, they are more likely to buy it than brands that are less well known.

Advertising can be informative. Grocery stores want housewives to know about weekend specials. If they shop for specials, they probably will buy other products in the same store. Purchasers also may want technical information about certain kinds of products, such as appliances, cars, or furniture. And people are always interested in low prices.

Advertisers try to "differentiate" their products. Much advertising is devoted to pointing out the special characteristics of a given product that are not found in competing products. Each seller would like buyers to believe that what he is selling is different from (but better than) what others are selling for the same price. Or, that his product is as good as products sold by others at higher prices.

Even when there are no noticeable differences in the physical characteristics or the prices of competing products, advertisers try to create a difference in the public mind. Often this is done by appealing to one's emotions or to the natural human desire for prestige or popularity. That is the basis for the advertising of many brands of toothpaste, cosmetics, and automobiles, for example.

Advertising is often criticized. Many critics of advertising assert that it is designed to increase the incomes of advertisers rather than

to help consumers. At times it may omit or distort pertinent information. It uses appeals to the emotions rather than to the intellect in an effort to persuade consumers to buy products which they do not really need or cannot afford. Large advertisers may influence the kinds of programs presented on television and radio, or the policies of newspapers, by threatening to withhold their advertisements. Obviously large companies, with millions of dollars to spend on advertising, have an advantage over small business. And in the end, it is the consumer who is forced to pay for advertising in the form of higher prices. All of these criticisms, and others of a similar nature, are true in part. But there is another side that also deserves consideration.

Advertising helps to raise living standards. The nation's high standard of living would not be possible without efficient production in agriculture and industry. But efficient production also is not enough. There must be consumers to purchase and use the goods produced.

Advertising is a powerful factor in building up sales and markets. National advertising and modern production methods combine to make more and better goods available at lower prices. When automobiles, radios, and television sets were first introduced they were so expensive that only families with high incomes could afford to buy them. As greater sales were developed and more units were produced, part of the savings resulting from more production were passed on to consumers. Because advertising helps to create and to maintain markets, it encourages businessmen to invest in new machinery and new products. In general, this trend has provided more job opportunities and increased the purchasing power of workers.

Without large-scale advertising mass marketing and mass production would be impossible. The fact that some advertisers resort to undesirable practices does not make all advertising undesirable. But it may suggest a need for stricter controls to eliminate such practices.

1. Under free enterprise, how are "what to produce" and "how much" determined? Contrast this with a command economy.

2. Why does agriculture have more difficulty in adjusting to changes in demand than industry?

3. What is the role of advertising from the point of view of producers? Consumers? What criticisms have been directed at advertising?

4

What provision is made for future demand?

This chapter so far has discussed mainly the various processes of production to meet the current demand. Some attention will now be given to this country's natural resources, to discover what is being done to conserve them. It would be short-sighted not to look beyond the present and attempt to provide for expected future demand. Careful planning is a "must."

More than 150 years ago several economists called attention to the possibility that food supplies might someday become scarce and other natural resources might be exhausted. At that time there was more concern about the food supply than about other natural resources.

Malthus warned that in future years the increasing population might outstrip the food supply. In 1798 Thomas R. Malthus, an English clergyman and economist, in a widely-quoted book, argued that population, if left unchecked, would increase at a "geometric ratio." That is, for every two people in the present generation, in the next generation—say 25 years—there would be twice two, or four, people. In the following generation there would be eight people, and so on. Thus population, through natural increase, would double itself every 25 years.

But Malthus said, food supplies from generation to generation increase in an "arithmetic ratio" only. In other words, the present supply of food can double itself in the next generation. But in the following generation, instead of

Two kinds of progressions

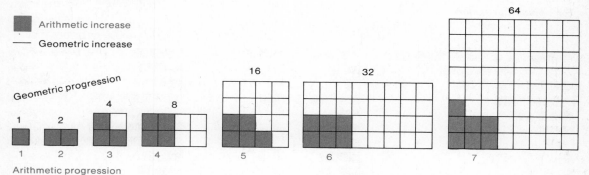

Here is one way of showing Malthus' theory graphically. Let the shaded *area within each figure stand for the food supply, the* total *area for the world population. Population increases at a faster rate than the food supply, hence the white squares would stand for people* without *food.*

The population explosion...

Projected world population increase

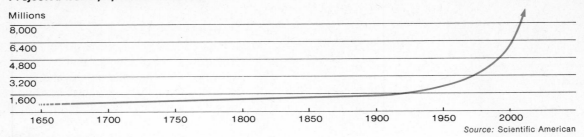

Millions

8,000
6,400
4,800
3,200
1,600

1650   1700   1750   1800   1850   1900   1950   2000

Source: Scientific American

World population density

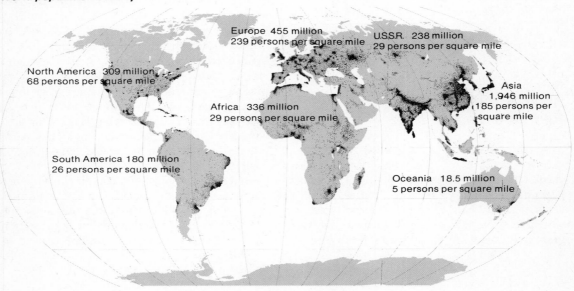

Europe 455 million
239 persons per square mile

U.S.S.R. 238 million
29 persons per square mile

North America 309 million
68 persons per square mile

Africa 336 million
29 persons per square mile

Asia
1,946 million
185 persons per
square mile

South America 180 million
26 persons per square mile

Oceania 18.5 million
5 persons per square mile

Ten population leaders

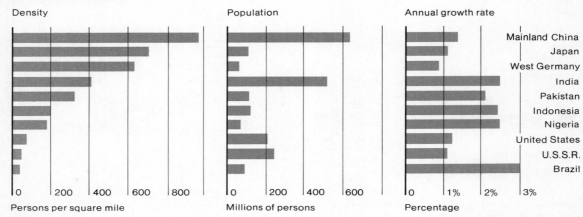

Density

Population

Annual growth rate

Mainland China
Japan
West Germany
India
Pakistan
Indonesia
Nigeria
United States
U.S.S.R.
Brazil

0   200   400   600   800
Persons per square mile

0   200   400   600
Millions of persons

0   1%   2%   3%
Percentage

Source: Pocket Data Book

42

Can the earth sustain the increase?

Acres per head of world population

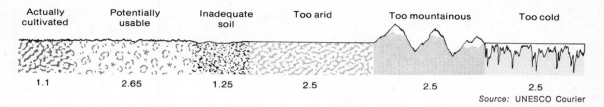

Actually cultivated	Potentially usable	Inadequate soil	Too arid	Too mountainous	Too cold
1.1	2.65	1.25	2.5	2.5	2.5

Source: UNESCO Courier

Habitable land

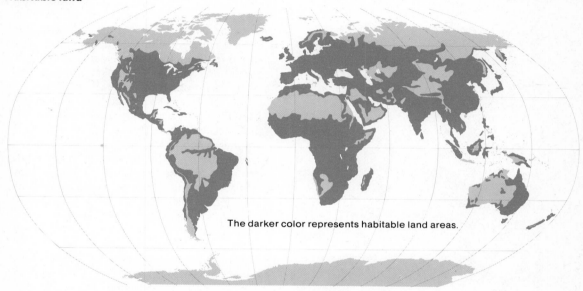

The darker color represents habitable land areas.

World food production

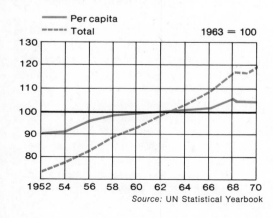

Per capita

Total

1963 = 100

130
120
110
100
90
80

1952 54 56 58 60 62 64 66 68 70

Source: UN Statistical Yearbook

World food consumption

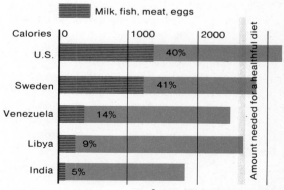

Milk, fish, meat, eggs

Calories	0	1000	2000	
U.S.		40%		
Sweden		41%		
Venezuela	14%			
Libya	9%			
India	5%			

Amount needed for a healthful diet

Source: UN Statistical Yearboo

43

Pessimistic Parson
Thomas Malthus
(1766–1834)

Picture smokestacks belching smoke and casting a shadow over the surrounding area. Then enter one of the factories and observe the workers—haggard men, women, and children, whose wizened faces reveal their misery. Observe also how these miserable people live out their lives crowded together in squalid tenement houses. Then you will understand why some men in eighteenth-century England dreamed of a better future. They foresaw an era when the machine might serve man, instead of vice-versa, and would free people from the burdens of routine labor for more creative and artistic tasks. Other persons, however, saw the future in a gloomier light,

and predicted that, far from emancipating mankind, industry would eventually reduce people to the level of automatons.

Thomas Malthus belonged to this second group. His views of economic and social trends were pessimistic and even alarming. A graduate of Cambridge University and an ordained minister, he had studied population statistics and agricultural production. Comparing his two sets of figures, he concluded that unless the birth rate were drastically reduced, the food supply would be inadequate to sustain the growing population. Mankind seemed doomed to pestilence, famine, and death. Malthus set forth these views in his now-famous *Essay on the Principle of Population As It Affects the Future Improvement of Society* (published in 1798). The world's food supply was increasing, said Malthus, but at a far slower rate than the expanding population. And now that science and industry were eliminating some of the age-old causes of early death, the prospect of an overpopulated planet loomed ahead. Starvation, he said, would be the lot of more and more people.

Malthus' essay was intended as an attack on the English Poor Laws. Direct relief to the poor would only make matters worse, according to Malthus. Gifts of food and clothing, especially to large families, would tend to encourage laziness and still larger families.

Parts of the world in this century have indeed suffered from overpopulation and food shortages. But in the United States and western Europe, at least, the Malthusian theory of overpopulation has not become a reality. Why? First, because in these areas improved farming techniques and soil conservation have greatly increased agricultural output. Second, in spite of longer life expectancies, the population of these areas has not grown at the enormous rate predicted by Malthus.

As a pioneer in the study of population growth, Malthus has influenced the thinking of economists and other social scientists to this day.

again doubling itself as can unchecked population, the food supply can be only three times as great as it was originally. Thus, without population checks, the food supply would be incapable of supporting the greater increase in population. Finally the world would be faced with actual famine. Malthus felt that only the evils of war, disease, and vice kept population in bounds. Without these evils starvation would necessarily have to keep population in balance with available food supplies.

Malthus' theory made a great impression when it was first introduced to the public. Although the accuracy of his ratios was questioned, many thought that his theory implied that most people would forever be faced with the constant threat of starvation or of other disasters. During the late nineteenth century, however, the Malthusian theory was gradually discredited. Only recently, since people have become aware of the soaring increases in population and the rapid depletion of some natural resources in many parts of the world, has it been revived.

Although food supplies are plentiful in America, other nations often lack food. Americans have seldom experienced actual food shortages; instead, they have often produced more food than could be disposed of profitably. The productivity of the land, combined with a widespread use of fertilizers and efficient farm machinery and farming techniques, has led to high crop yields. Science has advanced rapidly to increase efficiency in producing both crops and livestock. Even so, some demographers (specialists in the study of populations) speculate that the time may come when there will actually be a shortage of food supplies.

Not infrequently one reads of conditions in China, India, and other economically "underdeveloped" nations where serious food shortages occur. In those countries the rate of population growth has been extremely high. Consequently many millions of people go to bed hungry every night. In years when crop yields are below average, vast numbers of people in these countries die from malnutrition.

In many parts of the world efforts are now being made to conserve the soil, including aid to supervise soil conservation. The United States government, through its technical assistance programs, sponsors many of these projects; so does the Food and Agricultural Organization (FAO) of the United Nations. Their aims are: (1) to enrich the existing soil, (2) to prevent it from being washed away or worn out by overuse, (3) to build fertile soil from exhausted or arid land to meet the needs of their people, and (4) to assist the people in attaining maximum possible crop yields without exhausting the soil. Such programs can be of great value in nations where food supplies are inadequate. In America, where present food supplies are ample, soil conservation is important for future generations.

Equally important is the conservation of other natural resources. Unless natural resources are conserved, they may someday become exhausted. Conservation was not an issue during the early growth of America. Natural resources seemed more than ample, and efforts were concentrated on obtaining the bare necessities of life. However, after Americans learned to harness steam, unlock the power in coal, and release the energy in oil and natural gas, their standards of living began to rise, and they began to use their resources at a faster rate. Today some of the resources which the pioneers considered ample are not sufficient to meet the needs of an expanding population.

There is no assurance that this country's various resources will continue to be available for use and enjoyment in the indefinite future. Will there always be enough iron and coal? Will existing oil and natural gas reserves continue to meet the nation's needs? Will other resources continue to be plentiful? Even now formerly abundant resources are being depleted at an alarming rate.

The environmental crisis: natural resources

New concern about the environment and ecology has emerged recently to supplement the efforts of conservationists. Ecology is the study of living things and their environment—"the balance of nature." Ecologists have pointed out not only the importance of replanting forests and conserving soil, but also the dangers of the air and water pollution which accompany mining and industrial production. There are many economic considerations involved; principally revolving around two questions: (1) Who will pay for cleaning up the environment? (2) Who will "pay" if it is not cleaned up?

*Forest fires have long been of concern to conservationists. The one shown here, **a,** has destroyed all the foliage in this gulch. Soil erosion is sure to follow. Below, **b,** erosion began in this Idaho landscape after a storm in early August. The U.S. Soil Conservation Service estimates that 200 tons of earth were lost per acre.*

a

b

A beautiful, healthy forest is shown at right, **c.** The trees are redwoods in the Del Norte State Park, California. New trees are grown on farms, **d,** where genetic research is also carried out. These seedlings are the result of grafting a cutting from a superior forest tree to ordinary root stock. Grown trees must be protected too, from insects and plant diseases. In **e,** a helicopter sprays against hemlock looper. Defoliated trees near the helicopter have already been damaged by insects.

c

d

e

f

Water pollution has ruined many rivers and lakes near large cities. Fish (alewives) dead from pollution surface in Lake Michigan, **f.** Skyline shown is Chicago. Below, **g,** is an aerial view of a chemical complex in Charleston, West Virginia. Industrial waste pours into the Kanawha River at nine different locations.

g

The recovery of minerals and oil is often accompanied by danger to the environment. Oil has been discovered on the North Slope of Alaska, **h,** and ecologists are concerned about the effects of using pipelines to transport it. The above-ground pipelines must be heated and many fear that their warmth will melt the frozen soil, called tundra, causing it to sink. Depletion of copper resources is causing the U.S. to rely increasingly on imported copper. The photo of a Utah copper mine, **i,** illustrates the disruption of land which occurs in mining copper. Strip-mining of coal in Appalachia has aroused much opposition. The steepness of hills has rendered most reclamation efforts unsuccessful, **j.** Some stripping is done with bulldozers and steam shovels; below, **k,** large drills called augers are used. The holes shown are 6½ feet across.

h

i

j

k

It is clear that, to insure a supply of resources for generations to come, a definite program of conservation and control must be followed. More careful mining of mineral resources will give higher yields of raw materials. New and better methods of production can lead to a recovery of many so-called "waste products". Replanting forests and constructing dams will help to conserve trees and soil for future generations.

An expanding economy depends on fuel resources. Among the more important natural resources are fuels—coal, oil, and natural gas. (Wood as a fuel has been almost completely replaced by the other fuel resources.) Without these fuels, homes would be unheated; the engines of automobiles and of industry would not move. It will be useful to examine the outlook for some of these fuel resources.

1. *Oil and gas.* Oil and natural gas are both vital to the American economy. Together they supply more power than all other fuels combined. The increasing use of machines, the greater use of oil and natural gas in the home, and the development of more and more petroleum by-products contribute to the widespread, growing demand for oil.

However, the known available supplies of oil and natural gas are small when viewed in comparison to the nation's annual consumption. No one knows where new supplies may be found or how large those supplies will be. Shortages of oil and natural gas began to appear in 1973. Less fuel became available for transportation companies, electrical utilities, industry, home heating, and automobiles. Prices of fuels, and of goods requiring large amounts of fuels in their production, increased sharply. Government priorities and quotas for fuel and electricity were established. Highway speed limits were reduced to conserve gasoline and diesel oil, lights were turned off to save electricity produced by oil or gas, thermostats were turned down, and many other fuel-saving practices were adopted. Despite these efforts, many people were inconvenienced

and some manufacturing plants were forced to lay off workers. Gasoline rationing loomed.

Fuel shortages were caused by a combination of events. Growing populations, greater industrialization, and prosperity in the United States and abroad, led to increased demands for energy sources. Larger automobiles, equipped with pollution-control devices, burned more gasoline. Oil and natural gas were substituted for coal to reduce air pollution. Finally, Arab oil production, a principal source of the world supply, was reduced (and its export to the United States stopped) as a means of pressuring countries to withhold support for Israel in the Middle East war.

These shortages led to increased efforts to develop the rich Alaskan oil fields and to construct a pipeline. More attention was paid to methods of extracting oil from coal, from shale rock (found in abundance in the Rocky Mountains), and from rich oil-bearing tar sands (found in Canada). Nevertheless, it appears that fuel shortages and higher fuel prices may be with us for several years, or until acceptable energy substitutes are developed (see pages 51–52).

2. *Coal.* Today coal is valuable not only as a fuel but also for its many by-products which have hundreds of uses.

Almost the entire growth of the use of coal in industry in this country has taken place during the past 150 years. In 1824 only about 81,000 tons of coal were used in the United States. The country now consumes more than 5000 times that amount each year. Despite this tremendous coal consumption, the United States has a sufficient supply for many years to come. It is estimated that the United States has over 31 per cent of the world's coal reserves.

However, already many high-grade coal fields have been exhausted, leaving only poorer or more heavily polluting grades for future generations. Steps are now being taken, therefore, to conserve the remaining supply and to cut down on waste in coal consumption.

Changing energy requirements in the United States, by source (projected to the year 2000)

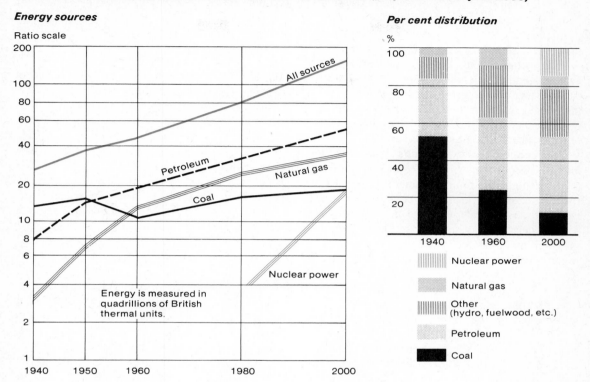

Energy sources

Per cent distribution

Best estimates indicate that coal will remain an important, if gradually declining, source of power through the year 2000. Nuclear energy will assume a much bigger role. (See pages 21–23 for an explanation of ratio scale).

Source: Resources in America's Future, *Resources for the Future, Inc., by the Johns Hopkins Press*

Present fuels may be supplemented or replaced by other forms of power. In some areas, electricity is used extensively as a substitute for coal, oil, or gas. If this electricity is produced by steam generators run by these other fuels, coal, oil, and gas may not be conserved. If it is produced by hydroelectric generators, however, other fuels are not needed. But only in a few parts of our country, such as the Pacific Northwest, upper New York State, and the Tennessee Valley, is large-scale use presently being made of hydroelectric power to generate electricity.

During recent years, much public and private experimentation in atomic-generated electricity has been conducted. This method is based upon the use of uranium to power steam generators. Large deposits of uranium exist in the United States and in several other countries.

It has been estimated that a pound of uranium is capable of producing as much energy as three million pounds of coal. In the years to come, better ánd less expensive atomic techniques are sure to be developed. Then, as other power supplies become more costly, atomic energy no doubt will be more widely used. Indeed, in some fuel scarce parts of the world, it is less expensive to generate electricity from uranium than from coal or oil even today.

Also, studies and experiments designed to harness geothermal power (underground steam or hot water) in the production of electricity are underway. And considerable research on the use of ordinary sunlight, through solar batteries or other devices, is being conducted.

The economy also depends upon nonfuel mineral resources. Among the more important of the exhaustible nonfuel mineral resources of the United States are iron, copper, zinc, and lead. These minerals are used in pure or alloy form in nearly every industry and home. Alloys, in which two or more metals are mixed in varying proportions, have qualities that are different from those of the "parent" metals.

A brief study of existing supplies and uses of a few of these mineral resources will afford some idea of the importance of conserving them.

1. *Iron*. About 85 per cent of the iron ore used in the United States during the past 30 years has come from the Lake Superior area. Mining operations have been concentrated there because of the immense supply of high-grade ore. Since this supply of high-quality ore is becoming exhausted, producers have sought new fields of like quality elsewhere. The United States now imports ore from the world's largest high-grade deposits in South America and from the extensive fields of the Labrador-Quebec region.

Fortunately, reserves of low-grade iron ore are practically inexhaustible. Mining engineers say that the supply of this quality of ore is so great that all iron mining for generations can come from this source without exhausting the supply. If to this reserve is added the extensive supplies of high-grade ore obtainable from friendly neighboring countries, one can be reasonably sure of an ample supply of iron ore for years to come. These supplies, together

with the immense reserves of coal within the United States, give assurance that there will be enough coal and iron ore to maintain and even surpass the present rate of industrial production.

2. *Copper*. Copper, the metal first used extensively by man, has within the past 100 years become tremendously important as a transmitter of electric current. It is difficult to estimate the amount of available copper within this country.

Although about one-fourth of the copper used each year is recovered and reused in later years, the United States now imports from 20 per cent to 30 per cent of its copper supplies. Unless new deposits are discovered, or better and less costly substitutes are developed, the percentage of imported copper will increase as the American economy expands and the demand for this metal grows.

3. *Zinc*. Zinc was little used until the nineteenth century, when the Industrial Revolution brought its great changes. Now zinc and zinc alloys are used in many products such as radiator grills, typewriters, and kitchen equipment.

Until recently, the sources of zinc in the United States were sufficient to meet the industrial demands. But since the beginning of World War II, the United States has had to import nearly all of the zinc it needs in making some of its most important alloys. It has been estimated that existing reserves of zinc ore may be seriously depleted within the next quarter-century unless new deposits are found.

4. *Lead*. Lead is widely used in the United States—for instance, to make cables, insecticides, and printing type. Sizable deposits of lead are well distributed over the country. But since 1936 the United States has had to import lead to meet yearly needs, and by 1949 it was importing more than one fourth of all the lead used. Other countries now supply large quantities of the lead demanded by American industries.

5. *Scarce metals*. There are many metals which are found only in minor quantities in the

United States. For still other scarce metals this country will have to depend entirely upon other countries. Though these metals—such as nickel, tungsten, chromium, cobalt, and manganese—are used in relatively small quantities, they are as necessary as coal and iron. Without them, it would be impossible to make the various alloy steels. Some alloys are harder than steel, others are more elastic or tougher. Still other alloys are brilliantly colored, rust proof, or can take a high, permanent surface polish.

Forest resources have served man since the beginning of civilization. Man has always needed a supply of timber for fuel, shelter, and weapons.

This country's extensive forests led early settlers to believe that there were trees enough for an indefinite period of time. Gradually the realization came that the nation's forests were being used up too rapidly. In 1871 a federal

Consumption of principal metals in the United States

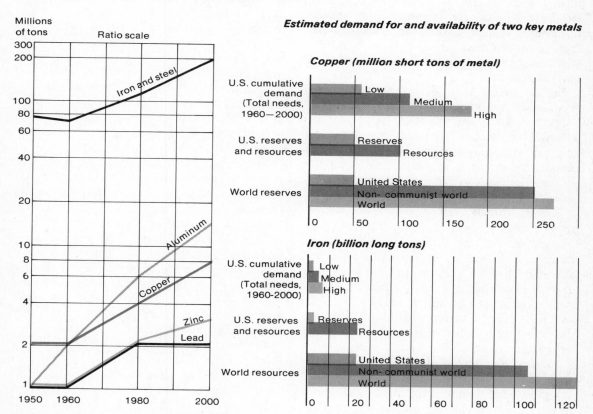

Requirements for nearly all principal metals are expected to increase through the year 2000. For copper—to take just one example—note that if high estimates prove true, the United States will have to lean heavily on imports. ("Reserves" are estimated deposits which can be mined profitably at current prices, with current technology).

Source: Resources in America's Future, *Resources for the Future, Inc.,* by the Johns Hopkins Press

committee was appointed to make a survey of the nation's forest supply. This committee estimated that in less than two centuries nearly one half of the originally forested land had been cleared.

Only about 25 per cent as much standing timber remains as when Europeans first settled here. Until recently standing timber was being used at a much faster rate than it was being grown. It has only been in the last several years that large-scale attempts have been made to replace cut timber with new forest growth.

Wood, in the form of lumber, plywood, boards, and shingles, is a basic building material. It is used for furniture and interior furnishings. Although substitute materials have frequently been used in recent years, these substitutes are more costly and less satisfactory to many consumers.

Forests supply most of the nation's paper needs, and contribute to many other important industries. They are extremely important in watershed protection (reducing the losses of flood and erosion, and maintaining stable water supplies for industry, irrigation, and domestic consumption). Also, forests provide opportunity for many forms of outdoor recreation.

Though forests are replaceable, timber grows slowly. Growth of timber depends upon the type of tree, the climate, and the soil of the area. Some species of softwoods (such as white pines) which were planted 100 years ago are now large enough to cut for lumber. Other kinds of trees such as walnut, maple, elm, and gum will grow to maturity within 120 years. Still other types of trees, such as Douglas fir and western pines, which form the greatest bulk of existing saw-timber, take even longer to reach their full growth.

An increasing number of states and communities are now planting trees in nurseries to help to maintain a future timber supply. The federal government and some states have set aside many forested areas as reserves and parks to prevent growing timber from being carelessly destroyed. Campaigns are constantly being waged against carelessness which may cause disastrous forest fires. The Forest Service posters of Smoky the Bear are nationally recognized.

It is widely accepted today that timber is a crop, even though a slow-growing one. This being so, from the long-term viewpoint, the nation can be assured only of as much timber as it is willing to pay for. Efficient conservation and methods of use are necessary, however, to keep the costs of timber production low and to insure protection of forest reserves.

Water is an essential resource. An accessible water supply is an indispensable requirement for human life. People must have water to drink. Without water to irrigate the soil and grow plants, man and animals would soon starve. Rivers, lakes, and oceans are great transportation highways. Natural waterfalls and dams are sources of power for homes and industry. Many processing and manufacturing firms require vast quantities of water. Wars have been waged for water rights; famines have occurred because of water shortages.

For thousands of years man has built irrigation systems to make arid land fertile. Today the United States is carrying on an extensive program of reclaiming arid or unproductive land by vast power-irrigation systems. By controlling the flow of water with dams, man is providing irrigation and is harnessing water power for generating electricity. But it is only during very recent years that many communities in this country have realized that their growth and living standards may be seriously hampered by insufficient water reserves.

Water is scarce in many areas. Although three fourths of the earth's surface is covered by water, serious students of water problems have pointed out that large areas of the United States may be faced with actual water shortages within the next few years. Water itself is plentiful, but enough may not be available where and when it is needed. Research is now being conducted to find low-cost ways of transforming sea water into fresh water.

Water pollution has reached critical proportions. A few decades ago, the major problem of water pollution was the bacteria that caused typhoid fever. But filtration and chlorination techniques were developed which ended typhoid epidemics and made municipal water supplies safe. In recent years, however, there has been a tremendous volume of municipal and industrial waste, including many chemical contaminents which were practically nonexistent a decade ago. As population grows and industry continues to expand, distances between points for waste discharge are becoming shorter, so that streams have less chance to recover. Sediment from soil erosion and pollutants from farms (seepage from strong fertilizers, insecticides, and herbicides) and from mines are also causing serious deterioration of water resources in this country.

The United States Public Health Service classifies pollutants entering the water supply into eight broad categories: (1) domestic sewage and other oxygen-demanding wastes; (2) infectious agents; (3) plant nutrients; (4) organic chemicals, such as insecticides, pesticides, and detergents; (5) other minerals and chemicals, including chemical residues, salts, acids, silts, and sludges; (6) sediment from land erosion; (7) radioactive substances; and (8) heat from power and industrial plants. Only the first of these categories will be considered here.

Organic wastes are those that originate with plants and animals. As these wastes decompose they use up oxygen that is naturally present in water or supplied artificially in sewage treatment processes. Many communities, however, still dump untreated garbage into the ocean or other bodies of water. Domestic sewage is the most widespread of these wastes, but about an equal amount comes from industries—with food, pulp, and paper industries generating the greatest amount of waste. If an excessive amount of oxygen is used in decomposing these wastes, fish and other aquatic life are killed, pollution sets in and the water gives off offensive odors and becomes unsightly.

Strong measures are needed to control pollution. Control of water pollution will require (1) the development of a suitable technology to process waste, and (2) modification of industrial and agricultural practices. Products now used will have to be changed if they result in pollution. There must be better management of available water supplies, including management of river basins to insure maximum usage. A promising solution in some areas is the reuse of the existing supply. But this will have to be accompanied by new methods of renewing the supply for agricultural, industrial, recreational, and even municipal use. Impetus for such developments and the needed regulations will doubtless have to come from the federal government. (See Case Analysis 2 on pages 58–61 for a discussion of federal actions already taken in the vital area of air pollution.)

CHECK UP

1. What prediction was made by Malthus? Has it come true? Why? What is the situation in developing countries?

2. Why is conservation of major importance in this country with respect to fuel resources? Metals? Forest resources? Water?

3. What are the sources of pollution? What are the basic approaches to controlling the pollution of water?

Clinching the main ideas

Most persons have numerous wants and limited incomes. Wants become demands only when they are backed by the willingness and the ability to pay for a good or service. In choosing how to distribute available income among many wants, one is influenced by the *utility* (want-satisfying capability) of a given expenditure. Utility, in turn, is influenced both by the *law of diminishing utility* and by the size of one's income.

In addition to personal consumer demands, the demands of private producers and government must be included in total demand. Such organizations compete with consumers for the available but limited resources. These organizations purchase goods and services for use in further production, however, rather than for immediate personal consumption.

Producers create *place, form,* and *time utility* to meet demands. Unlike some countries, the United States depends mainly upon private producers for goods and services. These producers, seeking to make profits, are constantly attempting to anticipate future demands and to reduce their production costs. They also use advertising to influence demand. The nation's complex production system is greatly aided by its well-developed facilities of *social overhead capital.*

In a competitive economy, those producers who best succeed in anticipating demands and reducing costs and prices prosper. Those who do not give consumers what they want at prices they are willing to pay usually fail. It is often said that "The consumer is king."

Whether or not the American economy will be able to meet future demand will depend in large measure on how prudently its natural resources are used. A rapidly growing population is making increased demands on available forest, mineral, land, and water resources. Efforts to protect the environment also limit the ways in which resources may be used. New, safe, and economical sources of energy will need to be developed.

Chapter 2 review

Terms to understand

1. social want
2. opportunity cost
3. marketing research
4. place utility
5. total demand
6. law of diminishing utility
7. overhead
8. pipeline system
9. product "differentiation"
10. mass marketing
11. geometric ratio
12. arithmetic ratio

What do you think?

1. "Economic life is a constant process of exchanges that reflect views about relative values." What does this statement mean?

2. If "production is the creation of utility," does that not limit the use of the term to the production of tangible goods? Explain.

3. "Without large-scale advertising, mass production and mass marketing would be impossible." Is this true? Why or why not?

4. Today the consumer gets much more protection than he did a century ago. Why?

5. Although transportation is vital to the nation's economy, most railroads are in serious economic difficulty. Why? What should be done?

Extending your knowledge of economics

1. Draw a cartoon to illustrate the law of diminishing utility.

2. Study advertising in newspapers and newsmagazines to find examples of advertising that render service to the nation's economy. Explain why, in each case.

3. Try to find out what is being done about conservation of resources or coping with pollution in the community or state where you live. What more needs to be done? What can your school do to help?

The population explosion: analyzing the charts and graphs on pages 42–43.

1. What was the world's population in 1960?

2. In a map of the world which showed areas drawn according to population rather than square miles of territory, how many times larger would Asia appear than (a) Europe; (b) Africa; (c) Australia? What would be the ratio in size of Europe to North America? Of Africa to the Soviet Union?

3. From the information on the bar graphs, could

one expect India to surpass China in population by 1980? Why?

4. What would happen to the per capita line (see bottom of page 43) if the population of Communist China were not included? Why?

5. In what respect is the diet of the average person in Venezuela superior to that of his counterpart in Libya?

6. For what reasons may the areas on the map on page 43 be classified as nonproductive?

7. According to the information presented on page 43, how many acres of nonproductive land are there for each person in the world? How much land is actually cultivated?

8. Would it be possible to double the amount of usable land? Why or why not?

Automobiles and air pollution: private benefits versus social costs

General background

In thinking about many of the nation's most important problems one must consider both economic and noneconomic factors. Air pollution, much of it caused by automobiles, is an example of such a problem. In addition to its purely economic aspects, it has implications for public health and the natural environment. Those interested in its "solution" must draw on the knowledge of experts in the fields of medicine, biology, physics, chemistry, mechanical engineering, politics, and law.

The total situation which gives rise to such a problem as air pollution may involve both benefits and costs which cannot easily be measured in dollars and cents. For example, what is the "value" to society of 100 million automobiles, as compared to the "value" of 25 million fewer or more cars? Or no cars at all? Or what is the value of "pure" (pollution-free) air as compared to air which is 90 per cent pure or 50 per cent pure?

The issues

There are about 100 million automobiles in the United States, almost all powered by internal combustion engines. The development of this type of engine during the late nineteenth century made the modern automobile possible. And it led to the rise of several of the nation's major industries.

About 80 per cent of all households in the United States own an automobile, and about 30 per cent of American households own two or more cars. In 1969, retail sales of new and used motor vehicles in this country amounted to 62 billion dollars, gasoline sales to 25 billion dollars, and sales of tires, batteries, and accessories to almost five billion dollars. Altogether, the automotive and closely related industries provide employment for six million or more workers. Clearly, anything affecting these industries will also significantly affect the American economy and way of life.

It has truly been said that "America is a nation on wheels," and that "Americans are in love with their automobiles." It would be extremely difficult to list all the social benefits brought by the automobile. But, according to the old adage, "There are no gains without pains." The "benefits" received from car ownership are offset by "costs." Increased air pollution is one cost associated with the use of the present generation of motor vehicles.

The gasoline-burning internal combustion engine produces at least four major types of pollutants: carbon monoxide, gaseous hydrocarbons and benzene compounds, nitrogen oxide compounds, and nongaseous heavy particles, the most important of which is lead. These pollutants combine in chemical reactions with sunlight and atmospheric dust particles to produce much of the "smog" or "smaze" which is becoming increasingly common in and around heavily populated centers and heavily traveled routes.

In addition to discomfort caused by this pollution and the reduced visibility which may be a contributing factor in accidents, the medical profession has warned that continual breathing of polluted air creates a serious human health hazard. For instance, they point out that the rate of lung cancer and emphysema among nonsmoking city dwellers is several times that of rural residents who breathe cleaner air. Biologists have warned that we are on the verge of poisoning our entire atmospheric environment, with probable disastrous chain-reaction consequences to many species of plant and animal life as well as to human life.

A 1970 report of the National Air Pollution Control Administration, a federal agency, described a community in which air pollution had caused grass to turn blue and cows to lose both their teeth and their appetites. It has been reported that trees in a national forest more than 100 miles away from Los Angeles are dying because of air pollution stemming from that city. Do we wish to continue to live in such an environment? Can we do so?

For decades, some people have been interested in working for cleaner air. Factory smokestacks, the most visible source of air pollution, have long been under attack. But it was not until the so-called "environmental revolution," which began in the late 1960's, that the automobile began to be identified as a major source of air pollution.

It was not easy for Americans to "see" pollution that was not readily visible to the naked eye, and to which most people contributed. But a 1970 scientific report stated that the amount of air pollution caused by automobiles in this country as a whole amounts to *three times* the weight of pollution from all industrial sources. In some areas, as much as 90 per cent of the air pollution is caused by automobiles. Obviously there can be no significant improvement in the quality of the air until this major source of pollution is controlled.

Automobiles continue to increase in number. More and better freeways and roads are being built and a larger number of motorists drive more miles each year. All recognize the direct benefits derived from the automobile. Furthermore, no individual driver contributes very much to the pollution problem, nor can any one person be billed in dollars and cents for the pollution which he causes. As a result, few Americans are willing to reduce their contributions to pollution by giving up the benefits they enjoy from using their automobiles. In a very real sense, each individual's benefits are his own, whereas most of the "costs" of air pollution are borne by others. That is, the latter are "social costs," not individual costs. Everyone's problem, or society's problem, is no one's problem! And if it is not solved by the voluntary action of individuals, it must be solved by society as a whole. But how?

Proposed alternatives

ACTIONS BY PRIVATE ENTERPRISE

One possibility in thinking about what to do in the case of a given problem is to do nothing. It appears that the American public is not willing to accept this approach to the problem of polluted air. Various positive approaches to coping with air pollution have been suggested. Some of these are briefly described below.

1. Americans could drive fewer automobiles and drive them fewer miles. Americans have not been willing to do this in the past, and there is no reason to expect that such a policy will be adopted in the future unless some other conditions change. It is not likely that the demand for travel and mobility will decrease. Indeed the opposite seems likely. But public mass transportation could be made more available in some communities (at a considerable cost), and individuals could be forced to use public transportation by making it more expensive to own and operate automobiles (higher automobile and fuel taxes, higher parking fees, etc.) and by banning cars from some areas. Most car owners, which means most of the nation's households, probably would consider this an unacceptable alternative, however.

2. Automobiles which do not use internal combustion engines could be developed. There has been considerable experimentation in recent years with automobiles powered by steam, electric batteries, and gas-turbine engines. The introduction of such vehicles would decrease air pollution. But engineering technology has not yet developed a vehicle powered by any of these methods that is comparable in performance to the present automobile. At the present stage of technological development, widespread adoption of one of these "new" types of vehicles would be a trading of one cost (air pollution) for another cost (poor performance). The automobile-owning public would be reluctant to do this. Also, such conversion might cause serious temporary disruptions in the automobile industry and in related industries.

3. New types of fuel may be developed for the internal combustion engine. It is possible, for example, to reduce the lead component of air pollution by using lead-free gasoline. The compression ratio of most modern automobiles, however, is designed for leaded gasoline. It would be difficult and expensive to modify the engines of most of the nation's 100 million autos, but without such modifications performance would be lower and maintenance costs higher with the use of unleaded gasoline. Also, some experts have stated that the use of lead-free gasoline would lead to an increase in benzene and other gaseous forms of pollution. No one can be certain that this approach provides a satisfactory solution even to a part of the total problem.

4. Pollution control devices can be added to present types of automobiles. These devices are designed to capture and recycle a portion of an automobile's exhaust pipe, crankcase, and fuel system emissions. Some automobiles have had anti-pollution accessories since the early 1960's, and certain types of such devices were required by law on all new cars sold in California beginning in 1970, and on all new cars sold in the United States beginning in 1971. These devices are not completely effective even under the best of conditions. Indeed they actually may increase pollution unless they are carefully and expertly maintained and serviced. Also, they are expensive to install and difficult to keep operational on old cars.

GOVERNMENT ACTIONS

Although the state of California led the way in attempting to control automobile air pollution as early as 1965, most people agree that this is a national problem rather than a state or local problem. Neither automobiles nor air pollution are limited to any one area. As stated in a 1970 speech by A. W. Clausen, President of the Bank of America: "This planet's ecology is unimpressed by political boundaries and subdivisions. Polluted air can and does cross rivers and mountains and oceans."

The National Air Pollution Control Administration has established standards and issued orders requiring that 1980 models emit no more than 10 per cent of the air pollution of 1970 model cars. The automotive industry, at considerable cost (which will be reflected in car prices), is working on this project by planning and testing better emission control devices and modified (lower compression) internal combustion engines. This approach, however, does not seem fast or sweeping enough for some lawmakers.

Late in 1970, Senator Edmund Muskie introduced a "clean air" bill which would require that the 1980 pollution control standards be met by 1975. And Senator Gaylord Nelson sponsored a bill which would ban the sale of automobiles powered by internal combusion engines by that year. Understandably, this proposed legislation upset persons in the automotive industry. The President of American Motors, Mr. William Luneberg, was quoted as saying, "They're asking me to cope with something that I'm genuinely striving to do and I can't get there. I don't know anybody that knows how to get there."

Late in 1970, the Nixon Administration proposed a tax on lead additives used in gasoline. This proposal was opposed by spokesmen for the petroleum industry, who argued that the tax would be inflationary and that it was unnecessary because many oil companies were already marketing non-leaded or low-lead gasoline. The United States Chamber of Commerce objected that the proposed tax would penalize lower-income motorists who drive older cars which cannot use nonleaded gasoline. Andrew J. Biemiller, legislative director for the AFL-CIO, was even more blunt. In testimony before the House Ways and Means Committee, he called the proposed tax "a license to pollute if you can pay the price."

Toward better understanding

QUESTIONS TO CONSIDER IN ANALYZING THIS CASE

1. What have been the economic implications of the development of the internal combustion engine? What benefits (other than economic) have stemmed from its development? What are some problems that directly or indirectly can be traced to increased dependence on the internal combustion engine?

2. In discussing automobiles and air pollution, the authors recall the adage, "There are no gains without pain." In other words, the advantages of automobile transportation are offset by social costs. Give examples of both. Would the elimination of the automobile be too high a social cost to pay for pure air? Why? Would it insure pure air? What are some alternative solutions to the problem of insuring purer air and also providing essential transportation? Evaluate each of these.

3. What are the hazards of polluted air to health? To plant and animal life? Explain the meaning of the statement that "most of the 'costs' of air pollution are borne by others." How does this make a solution of the problem more difficult?

4. Do you agree with the authors' evaluation of possible solutions to the problem through "actions by private enterprise"? Explain in each case.

5. What do you see as the implications of the enactment by Congress of legislation that in a given number of years air pollution by automobiles must be reduced 90 per cent? What are the implications of imposing a tax on lead additives used in gasoline? Should Congress enact legislation banning the sale of automobiles powered by internal combustion engines? Explain.

THINKING ABOUT THE BASIC ECONOMIC ISSUES

1. Would dealing with the problem of air pollution by automobiles be easier or more difficult in the Soviet Union than in the United States? Take into account differences in both government and economy. (Consult Chapter 17 of the text if you need facts about the Soviet economy to answer this question.)

2. What would be your reaction to the basic problem posed in this case if you were a major stockholder in one of the great corporations manufacturing automobiles? An urban resident who owned no car and used public transportation? A taxicab driver? Explain why in each case.

3. Should most of the costs of solving problems of air pollution be borne by all the people? By automobile manufacturers? By car owners?

4. Should the government launch an all-out attack on all forms of pollution—water, noise, pesticides, littering, industrial waste, etc.—rather than focusing on the contribution of automobiles to air pollution? Why or why not?

 **Prices in a free market economy**

1. **How do demand and supply influence prices?**
2. **How do production costs affect prices?**
3. **How does the total amount of money affect the general level of prices?**
4. **How are price changes measured?**

Things of greatest profit are set forth with least price.

JOHN LYLY, Euphues.

Probably no subject except the weather gives rise to more discussion and complaints than do the prices of things people buy. Usually the merchant is blamed if the prices seem too high. An understanding of how prices actually are determined in the economy may change such a conclusion. Usually the seller's control over prices is very limited.

In some countries, most prices are set by the government. But in the United States, prices are determined by the market. In a truly competitive market, no one seller can exert any great influence on prices.

This chapter will bring out how most prices are influenced by the principle of *supply and demand*. It also explains the influence of production costs and of the use of money, and considers how prices change with the passage of time. Finally, it will show the ways in which price changes are measured by the government through the use of various price indexes.

1

How do demand and supply influence prices?

Someone has said that a parrot taught to answer "supply and demand" to every question concerning economics would be an economist. This statement suggests the great importance of supply and demand in the economy. No one can really understand economics without knowledge of how supply and demand work.

The law of demand and the law of supply are basic in determining prices. The law of demand is that *the higher the price of a product, the less of that product people will be willing to buy; the lower the price, the more people will be willing to buy.* Or, stated from the seller's viewpoint, the larger the number of units offered to buyers, the lower will be the price at which each successive unit can be sold.

The principle of buyers' paying less and less for each successive unit holds true anywhere that buyers and sellers meet to carry on trans-actions. It applies whether the buyer is the consumer or is merely buying for purposes of ultimate resale.

The law of demand operates in this manner because of the law of diminishing utility. For any consumer, each successive unit of a good satisfies a less and less intense desire than the one before. This is why consumers will buy successive units of a good, beyond a certain number, only if each unit can be bought at a lower price than the previous one. The influence of the consumer is carried back through the marketing system and finally to the producer of the good.

An equally important economic law is the *law of supply,* which can be stated in these words: *An increase in the price of any product will generally call forth a larger amount as soon as it can be made available. Likewise, a decrease in price will reduce the rate of supply.* Not only is the immediate supply of the product reduced, but also the amount which will be produced in the days and months ahead. To express the law of supply in another way, the lower the price, the smaller the amount supplied, and vice versa.

The price of every product is established in a "market." In economics, the word "market" does not refer to any one specific place. Rather, it means any area within which potential buyers and potential sellers are in communication with each other. It may be two schoolboys dickering over the price of a used wristwatch which one wants to sell and the other wants to buy. It may be the corner grocery store where house-wives shop for staple food items. Or it may be nationwide or even worldwide in the case of many kinds of basic commodities or raw materials. The point is that *a market is an area within which prices are established by negotiations between buyers and sellers.*

Some markets operate very simply, while others are quite complex. At the corner grocery store, for example, a housewife sees a price tag for a pound of hamburger meat. This is the storekeeper's *offer* to sell at the indicated price. The housewife either *accepts* this offer and buys, or she *rejects* it. If there are enough rejections, the storekeeper either lowers his price or stops selling hamburger meat altogether. On the other hand, if the demand for hamburger at the posted price is so great that it threatens to exhaust the supply, the storekeeper may raise the price.

Large and complex markets basically operate in the same way as do small markets. The major differences are that many more people, both potential sellers and potential buyers, may be involved, and that they may make their offers and counter-offers by mail, telegraph, or telephone. In all cases, however, buyers want to buy at the lowest possible price, and sellers want to sell at the highest possible price.

The demand of buyers and the supply of sellers act upon each other to determine actual market prices. When buyers and sellers dicker in a market, the price at which transactions occur is determined both by the available supply and by the intensity of buyer's demands. The determination of the price of wheat provides a good illustration of this interaction between supply and demand in a large and well organized market. The following illustration, like all models in economics or other sciences, is somewhat simplified, but it brings out clearly the key relationships between supply and demand.

Buyers and sellers bargain for an advantage. Generally, when a number of buyers and sellers meet, some buyers will make purchases. But some will wait, believing that if they wait a day, a week, or a month, prices will go down. These are potential buyers. For example, some of the wheat buyers may be buying for flour mills. The price they are willing to pay is determined in part by whether a supply of wheat is needed to keep the flour mill busy and also by what they think they can get for the flour when it is sold. On a particular marketing day, some sellers will sell part or all of their stock; others will hold out because they think that prices will go up a little later.

A "demand schedule" shows the extent and intensity of demand. To illustrate the demand side of the market, a hypothetical *demand schedule* has been prepared to show how much will be bought at any particular price, and at all possible prices.

In the accompanying table, demand is represented by seven buyers. Each is willing to pay the price shown in column 2.

Buyer 1, the most eager buyer, would be willing to pay $2.40 per bushel for 80 units (10,000 bushels per unit) if necessary. But he knows that many sellers have supplies of wheat

Demand schedule for wheat, showing relationship between price and amount of wheat demanded

	price per bushel	amount demanded by each buyer	total amount demanded
Buyer 1	$2.40	80	80
Buyer 2	2.38	20	100
Buyer 3	2.36	20	120
Buyer 4	2.34	20	140
Buyer 5	2.32	20	160
Buyer 6	2.30	20	180
Buyer 7	2.28	20	200

(in units of 10,000 bushels each)

Demand and price are related

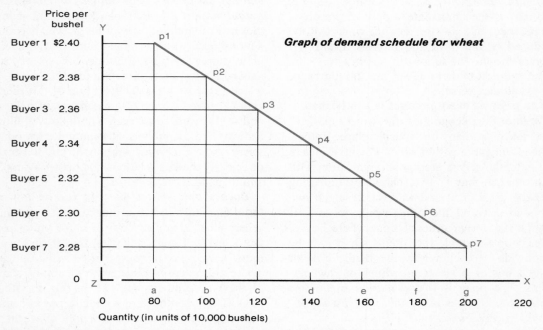

Graph of demand schedule for wheat

The relationship between the price of a good (such as wheat) and the quantity demanded is shown here by the line connecting p1 with p7. As the price goes down, the quantity demanded may be expected to increase.

on the market and will perhaps sell them at lower prices. So instead of offering the $2.40, he waits. He does not want to pay more than he has to.

Buyer 2, less eager than Buyer 1, is willing to pay $2.38 per bushel for 20 units rather than go without. But he, too, knows that it may not be necessary to pay as much as that, so he waits to see what the supply situation will be. He keeps an eye on the market so that he can jump in and buy when he thinks the price is as low as it will be that day.

Buyer 3 stands ready to buy 20 units at $2.36. Buyer 4 would buy 20 units at $2.34; Buyer 5 would take them at $2.32; and Buyer 6 would pay $2.30 per bushel. Buyer 7 is the least eager of all the buyers. He would take 20 units but would pay no more than $2.28 per bushel. This means that a total of 200 units of 10,000 bushels each would be bought if the price went as low as $2.28 a bushel.

It will be easier to follow this demand schedule if it is set forth in the form of a graph. On this graph the prices are shown along the perpendicular line ZY, and the amount of wheat along the horizontal line ZX.

Note that this graph illustrates the same principle as the table. Notice that Buyer 1 would be willing to pay a price of $2.40 per bushel for 80 units of wheat. (This is shown by lines *ap1* and *aZ*.) Buyer 2 would pay $2.38 for 20 units. (This is shown on the graph by lines *bp2* and *ba*.) The rest of the purchases may be determined by following the graph.

If the points *p1* to *p7* are connected with a line, the result is commonly known as a *demand curve* (or line). Note again that it corresponds to the demand schedule shown in the table.

The supply schedule shows present and potential supply. The *supply schedule* shows the sellers' side of the market; that is, the amount which would be offered for sale at any given price and at all possible prices. As already pointed out, a high price will bring forth more wheat than will a low price. As prices go up, new sellers will be tempted to part with some of their supplies. This is true of any product. The supply schedule is similar to the demand schedule, except that it applies to sellers (suppliers) rather than to buyers. The table illustrates a supply schedule for wheat in the market just discussed.

According to this schedule, at a price of $2.40 per bushel, 220 units would be supplied. However, at a price of $2.38 per bushel only 200 units would be made available. If the price dropped down to $2.28 per bushel suppliers would sell only 100 units. Thus the higher the price, the more wheat will be put on the market.

Supply schedule, showing relationship between price and amount of wheat supplied

	price per bushel	number of units each would sell	total number of units suppliers will sell
Seller 7	$2.40	20	220
Seller 6	2.38	20	200
Seller 5	2.36	20	180
Seller 4	2.34	20	160
Seller 3	2.32	20	140
Seller 2	2.30	20	120
Seller 1	2.28	100	100

(In units of 10,000 bushels each)

Supply and price are related

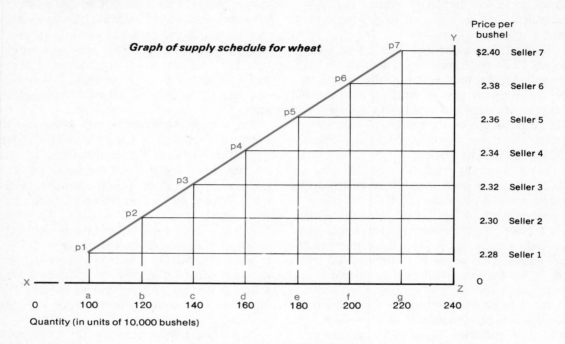

Graph of supply schedule for wheat

Price per bushel

$2.40 Seller 7

2.38 Seller 6

2.36 Seller 5

2.34 Seller 4

2.32 Seller 3

2.30 Seller 2

2.28 Seller 1

Quantity (in units of 10,000 bushels)

In the supply curve (above), it can be seen that a seller of wheat will supply 100 units (= 1,000,000 bushels) at a price of $2.28 per bushel. At a higher price farmers will be willing to devote more acreage to wheat, and thus increase the supply. When the amount supplied equals the amount demanded—shown (page 67) by the intersection of the supply and demand curves at P—an "equilibrium price" results. Here it is $2.33 per bushel for 150 units.

VALUE VERSUS PRICE
The great nineteenth-century British wit, Oscar Wilde, once defined a cynic as one "who knows the price of everything and the value of nothing." The economist has long recognized that there are many things whose value to human life cannot be measured in terms of dollars and cents. Social value is not always equal to economic value (price), in this sense. Such commodities as opium and marijuana, for example, may have a high price tag, but their value to society may be low if it is agreed that they are injurious to health. Also, whenever one refers to authorities other than economists—such as the clergyman, the politician, the philosopher—for value judgments, one is, in effect, recognizing the existence of values other than those of the price system. The student should remind himself that determining value can be a complicated and difficult problem.

How demand and supply may determine price

The "equilibrium price" in a wheat transaction

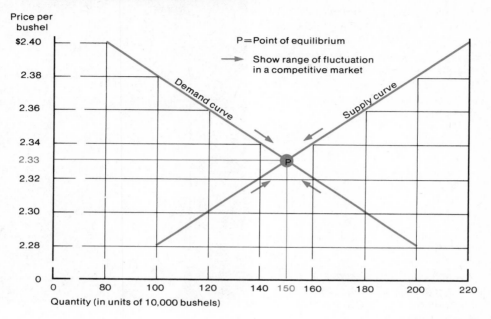

Seller 1 would sell 100 units at $2.28 a bushel. However, he wants to get the best price he can. Before he lets go of his wheat, he waits to see what the buyers will do. Seller 2 would sell 20 units at $2.30 per bushel. But like Seller 1 he waits, hoping to get a higher price. Seller 3 would sell 20 units at $2.32.

The table at the bottom of page 65 shows how much each seller wants for his wheat. Those who are keeping their prices high may not be able to sell at the prices they have in mind. In fact, some of them may not sell their wheat on that day. These are potential sellers. Other sellers, more anxious to get rid of their supply, may have all the supply that is demanded and be willing to sell it at prices that buyers consider favorable.

The supply schedule may now be expressed in the form of a graph which is the common way of showing a *supply curve* (or line). It should be noticed that the supply curve slopes to the right and upward, whereas the demand curve slopes to the right and downward.

A price is established. Prices are established at the point where the amount demanded at a certain price equals the amount offered at the same price. The following illustration will show how the demand schedule and the supply schedule affect each other.

After much bargaining, buyers and sellers arrive at a point where the amount demanded and the amount supplied equal each other. In the above graph, that amount is 150 units (each of 10,000 bushels of wheat) and the price arrived at between buyers and sellers in the day's sales averaged $2.33. Some units were

Setting a price: markets

The term "market" comes from the Latin word mercatus which meant "having traded." In the original sense of the word, there was a "market" whenever two people agreed to trade with each other. By trading they also set a price which depended, for instance, on how many melons one was willing to give for a hoe and how many the hoe maker would accept for his handiwork. Markets have grown into organized institutions, but they still operate in much the same way.

*The price of shares in America's biggest corporations is determined in the marketplace of the New York Stock Exchange, **a** and **b**. Here brokers representing would-be sellers and buyers meet each other face to face in thousands of separate transactions every day. Price tabulators must be alert since the value of a stock can change from minute to minute as bids are raised and lowered "to find a market"—the price level at which a transaction can take place.*

Since the development of villages and towns, people who wanted to trade found it convenient to meet in one spot. Open-air markets have flourished ever since. At right, **c,** is an open-air market in the lower east side of New York during the early 1900's. Markets became specialized early, too. The Fulton Fish Market in New York, **d,** has flourished since the 1800's, **e.** The tobacco auction, **f,** is another old American marketplace where tobacco farmers sell their crop every year.

sold at prices slightly below this $2.33 and some slightly above this amount. The price was established by the *interaction of demand and supply at the point where they are equal to each other* (shown on the graph at the point where the supply line and demand line cross). This is sometimes called an *equilibrium price*. It is the price which just "clears the market" by balancing the quantity buyers are willing to take with the quantity sellers are willing to let go. In a well-organized competitive market, prices tend to move up and down, within a narrow range, around such an equilibrium price.

The total supply available for sale during this trading day was 220 units. Seventy units were left unsold. The price went no lower than what the *last buyer* was willing to pay. By the last buyer we mean the least eager buyer who actually made a purchase. There are always, however, the *potential buyers* who would buy if the price dropped a little lower. And there are also *potential sellers* who would sell if the price went a little higher.

This illustration of buying and selling wheat shows how a rise in price will reduce the amount of sales and a drop in price will increase the amount sold. This basic economic principle tends to hold true for all products exchanged in a free marketing situation; that is, in a competitive market which is free of both monopoly control and government regulation. One can best observe the workings of the laws of supply and demand in a market that is highly organized, such as in the grain market just described. But it functions even under conditions where such well organized trading is absent.

As already indicated, some markets are small and some are large. Also, there are times when buyers greatly outnumber sellers, and other times when the two groups may be more equally balanced. Often buyers are not so well informed about market conditions and prospects as are sellers, while sometimes buyers are much better informed. All these and similar complicating factors influence prices.

What has been said means simply that prices are likely to fluctuate more or to move farther from the equilibrium price than would be true under more nearly perfect conditions.

Government sometimes intervenes in the pricing process. The prices of transportation services and of utility services (telephone, telegraph, electricity, gas, water) often are set by federal, state, or local governmental agencies. During World War II, the Korean War, and again in 1971 and following years, maximum prices for goods and services were set by the federal government. Furthermore, the federal government, for many years, has attempted to limit the supply of certain kinds of agricultural products and to "guarantee" minimum prices to the farmers growing these products.

Critics of such government activities often suggest that government is attempting to "repeal the laws of supply and demand." Is this really true? Or is government attempting to "regulate" the principles of supply and demand in order to further certain social goals? A student can reach his conclusion by using the above example of the determination of wheat prices. One should refer to the chart showing the equilibrium price of wheat at $2.33 per bushel.

First, assuming that nothing changes, except that the government allows only 120 units of wheat to be sold, what effect would this have on the price per bushel? Or, if the government should decide to set the maximum price of wheat at $2.30 per bushel, what effect would such action have on the supply of wheat?

Note that when supply is "artificially" limited, prices increase; that when prices are "artificially" lowered, supply decreases. In both cases, however, consumption is decreased. In the first case some people refuse to buy at the higher price. In the second case, some sellers refuse to sell (or producers to produce) at the lower price.

In the latter case, if the price set is far enough below the equilibrium price, and is maintained for a long period of time, some form of rationing of the product may be required to insure that all consumers get their "fair share" of the product. Rationing was used extensively during World War II. Prices higher than the equilibrium price, however, in effect themselves perform the "rationing" function. In one way or another, supply, demand, and prices inevitably are adjusted to each other.

In short, governmental or other "intervention" cannot abrogate the principles of supply and demand. But unless those manipulating supply and demand fully understand the economic effects of their manipulations, the end results may be different from those expected.

CHECK UP

1. What is the law of demand? Of supply? How are market prices determined?

2. Interpret the demand and supply schedules on pages 64 and 65.

3. How has the government intervened at times to regulate prices? Explain why in each case.

2

How do production costs affect prices?

The statement is often made that rising production costs cause higher prices. That is true in some circumstances. But this statement does not contradict our previous conclusions concerning the influence of supply and demand upon prices. Why not?

Supply is affected by production costs. Producers or sellers naturally do not like to sell at prices below their own costs. To do so would mean losses to them. If a producer thinks that he will not be able to sell his product for as much as it costs him to produce it, he will not produce. Therefore, supply is decreased.

Different kinds of costs have different effects upon supply and prices. Chapter 2 brought out that some production costs are *fixed* and that others are *variable*. That is to say, some costs *during a given period of time* will not change with changes in the amount produced, whereas others will. Whether or not costs are fixed or variable, and whether or not they affect supply and prices, depends upon the time period involved. To illustrate, consider the case of a farmer growing melons.

At planting time the price of melons was high enough so that it seemed possible for a melon grower to make a good profit. Later in the season, when the melons were half grown, it became clear that the crop of melons in the area would be unusually large. It seemed likely that the large supply would force down prices so low that production costs, starting at seeding time, could not be covered. How, then, would production costs influence the prices that a grower could obtain for his melons in the fall? Even though a grower finds out, after his crop is half grown, that prices will be too low to cover his entire costs, should he still continue the process of production until the melons are ready to be harvested?

Some of the grower's costs, such as those of preparing the land for seeding and the cost of the seed, are *sunk costs* or *fixed costs*. That is, they are fixed for the season whether the farmer continues his operations of growing, harvesting, and selling the melons, or abandons the crop —leaving the melons to rot in the field. Whatever happens to the crop, these expenditures already have been incurred and there is nothing the farmer can do to escape them.

Variable costs influence supply. But in addition to these fixed costs, there are such *variable costs* as irrigation, harvesting, and delivering the crop to the market. The latter costs would be incurred only if the farmer decided to harvest and sell the crop.

At this particular stage of production, these variable costs are the only ones the farmer

Factors that determine the price of a commodity: a summary

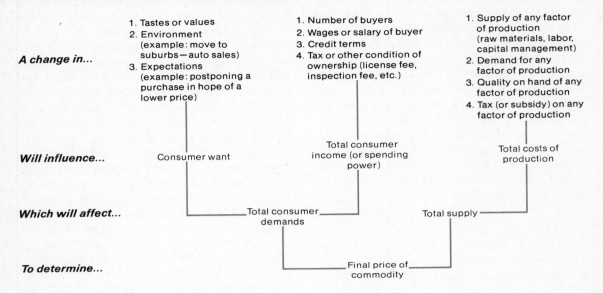

A change in...

1. Tastes or values
2. Environment (example: move to suburbs—auto sales)
3. Expectations (example: postponing a purchase in hope of a lower price)

1. Number of buyers
2. Wages or salary of buyer
3. Credit terms
4. Tax or other condition of ownership (license fee, inspection fee, etc.)

1. Supply of any factor of production (raw materials, labor, capital management)
2. Demand for any factor of production
3. Quality on hand of any factor of production
4. Tax (or subsidy) on any factor of production

Will influence...   Consumer want   Total consumer income (or spending power)   Total costs of production

Which will affect...   Total consumer demands   Total supply

To determine...   Final price of commodity

would take into account in deciding whether or not to harvest and sell his melons. The fixed (sunk) costs would not influence his decision; they have already been incurred and there is no way to eliminate them. It is *only the variable costs* that will influence the price of the crop. The melon farmer will continue his project if he thinks that he can cover his variable costs. Otherwise, he will not.

The example just given illustrates two important economic principles concerning production costs:

(1) Once production has been fully accomplished—that is, all costs have been incurred—prices are determined purely by market forces. The producer then has to accept the best price he can get, regardless of how high his production costs may have been. (Economists refer to this as a "market-pricing situation," or a "market-time period.")

(2) If production is to be continued, producers must get a price that will at least cover their variable costs. (Economists sometimes call prices based on the need to cover one's variable costs "short-run prices.")

Variable costs are affected by time. To return to the melon farmer, what costs would he consider were he starting a new crop the following spring? In making a decision whether or not to plant another melon crop, he would try to determine whether the price would be high enough to cover all costs of growing the crop. In other words, in what economists sometimes call the "long-run period" *all costs become variable costs.*

Note that the farmer has more variable costs when he calculates costs before planting than if he calculates them after the crop is well underway. At mid-season, the costs of the seed and the planting have become *fixed costs,* while at seedtime they were *variable costs.* Hence *the longer the period of time covered, the greater will be the influence of total costs on prices.* Producers expect to cover all costs in the long-run. Otherwise, they would not go into business.

Since many producers are growing or manufacturing the same product, should prices drop below costs *over a long period of time,* the least efficient producers who have the highest costs will suffer the greatest losses. They are likely to be forced out of business. Other producers may cut back production until the supply is reduced and prices again increase. Under free competitive conditions, it is also true that if prices rise considerably above long-run costs, production will be increased. This additional production will come both from new producers and from the increased outputs of old producers. Eventually the added supply will tend to force prices down to the point where they are again reasonably close to production costs.

Some production costs are difficult to determine. Consider the costs of a retail grocery store. The grocer has such costs as rent, heat and light, labor, and many others. He can determine his total cost without much difficulty. But it is extremely difficult for him to compute the cost of handling any one item.

The average retail store handles hundreds of different items, some of which are sold the day they come in. Because of the rapid turnover, the storekeeper does not have his money tied up for long in fast-selling items. But items with a slow turnover may remain on his shelves for a week, a month, or longer. His money is tied up in these slow-moving items for a long time. Some items require more handling than others. How can he make the correct charge for any one of them? How much of his total costs should the grocer charge for handling a loaf of bread, a pound of butter, or a pound of sugar?

The retailer "marks up" from wholesale prices. When the retailer puts a price on his bread, sugar, or meat, he must first consider what he paid the wholesaler (or other seller) for them. To this cost price he adds a certain *margin* or *markup* to cover his other expenses and to give him a small profit on the products he handles. The size of the markup and the amount of profit (or loss) depend on the extent to which he can raise his own prices and still compete with other retailers. Retail food stores,

clothing stores, and hardware stores all follow this general practice. But unfortunately, there is no assurance that the goods can be sold in large quantity at the prices listed. The retailer may find that he has to reduce some prices.

Wholesalers also add a margin or markup to the prices they pay for manufactured goods. The wholesaler who buys articles from manufacturers establishes his selling prices in much the same manner as does the retailer. He, too, must sell his goods for more than he paid for them, or he will be forced out of business. Much the same holds true of the manufacturer. It is often said that all middlemen and manufacturers receive for their goods what those goods cost them plus a reasonable margin of profit for handling. That is not the whole story, however.

Competition affects costs and prices. A manufacturer of men's suits will serve as an illustration. After he designed certain types of suits, he found that they would cost $86 each to manufacture. He then made a survey to learn what prices were being charged for similar suits by competing manufacturers. He discovered that some manufacturers were selling such suits at $65, others at $70, some at $75, and a few at $80. He also learned that relatively few suits were being sold at $90 or higher.

Clearly his cost of $86 per suit was out of line with the costs of his competitors. In fact they were selling suits for less than it cost him to manufacture them. He soon recognized that competition made it necessary to market his suits at $80 or less, and not at prices higher than $86, his estimated cost.

This clothing manufacturer, therefore, must adjust his operations and reduce his costs in order to meet price competition. He may be able to reduce costs (1) by more careful buying of cloth, (2) by more efficient use of his manufacturing plant, and (3) by keeping managers' salaries and the wages of workers within reasonable limits. He might also install more machines to reduce the amount of hand labor needed. In other words, he must try to reduce costs by slashing operating expenses. This manufacturer knows that a lower price will probably mean more sales, and that increased sales will reduce overhead cost per suit. Many business firms, in a highly competitive situation, follow such procedures to reduce costs.

The volume of sales affects costs and prices. Suppose that this suit manufacturer pays $1000 per month rent for his factory building. If he sells 100 suits per month, the amount of rent (a fixed cost) that must be charged to each suit is $10. But if he sells 500 suits per month, the rent cost per suit is only $2. Thus, by increasing volume, the manufacturer can lower his costs of production per suit. His other fixed costs will behave in the same fashion, and even his variable costs may decline with increased volume. In other words, within certain ranges of output, the manufacturer may be able to operate under conditions of *decreasing costs.*

Businesses with decreasing costs usually are very interested in increasing their volume of production and sales. To that end, they often lower prices to increase sales. As long as their price decreases are less than their corresponding production cost decreases, it will pay them to do this. With a large volume of sales, a small profit on each unit sold may result in greater total profits.

There is no simple formula for relating per unit costs to prices. Production costs are important in determining prices, but this is true only in a very general and long-run sense. It is not necessarily true for any particular product at any given time.

At best, producers and sellers typically can make only "informed guesses" at actual production costs and the appropriate prices for given articles. In addition to their own estimated costs, they have to consider general consumer demand for their products as well as the prices charged for similar products by competitors. If the price is set too high, consumers will either not buy the product or will buy from a competitor who sells at lower prices. Or if the price is set so low that costs are not recovered, sellers will lose money and eventually will have to go out of business.

In short, in order to be successful and remain in business, a seller must be able to price his product at a price high enough to cover his costs but low enough so that purchasers will buy his product. Sometimes this is not easy.

How volume of sales affects profit

Given: elastic demand, selling price of $1 per unit

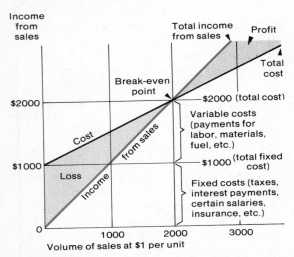

In this situation the "break-even" point is reached by selling 2000 units at $1 each.

CHECK UP

1. Explain the terms *fixed costs* and *variable costs.* Why did the melon farmer consider the latter in deciding whether or not to abandon the crop? Next spring, what costs will he consider in deciding whether or not to plant another melon crop? Why?

2. Why is it difficult to determine some production costs? The costs of handling goods at the retail level?

3. How do retailers and wholesalers establish prices?

4. How does competition affect costs? Prices? How does volume of sales affect costs? Prices?

3

How does the total amount of money affect the general level of prices?

Prices of the things one buys and sells, including one's own labor services, generally are expressed in dollars and cents, that is, in monetary terms. In a modern economy, very few goods and services are directly exchanged for each other. It is important, therefore, to understand the general nature of money, and the relationship between money and prices.

Money serves several useful purposes. It is often said that money has three functions, namely: (1) It serves as a "medium of exchange," (2) it serves as a "standard of values," and (3) it serves as a "store of value." What do these terms mean?

First, money provides a standard against which the exchange values of other things are measured. For example, a wheat farmer may want to buy a new tractor. He knows that a local farm implement dealer has a tractor for sale for 6000 dollars. The farmer has wheat for sale, and he knows that the current price of wheat is $1.50 per bushel. Thus, he can calculate that in order to obtain enough money to buy the tractor he will have to sell 4000 bushels of wheat. It is much more convenient to think of the price of a tractor as being 6000 dollars and the price of wheat $1.50 a bushel than it is

to think of the price of a tractor as being 4000 bushels of wheat (or 200 beef cattle, or 12,000 dozens of eggs, or 3000 hours of labor).

Money is a standard for future payments, as well as for immediate cash transactions. Most people do not pay cash for all their purchases, especially such more expensive items as homes, cars, furniture, and the like. People generally buy such products on charge accounts, or on installment contracts, paid off over a period of months or years. These obligations are expressed in terms of dollars and cents.

Third, money is a method by which one can store or save the values of present goods for future use. The wheat farmer, for example, would find it inconvenient to store the entire wheat crop on his farm, selling a few bushels from time to time to obtain money for living and farming expenses. Wheat storage is costly, wheat may deteriorate with age, and wheat prices change. It is far more convenient for the farmer to sell the wheat at harvest time and "store" the money received for it in a bank. In this manner, he can meet his current expenses by withdrawing funds from the bank or by writing a check.

Many things have been used for money. In olden times and far-away places, many things have been used as money. Among others, people have used cattle, animal skins, grain, sea shells, certain kinds of rocks, glass beads, precious jewels, arrowheads, fishhooks, salt, beer, cigarettes, and a host of other goods, have been used as a medium of exchange. Money can be anything that is readily acceptable in exchange.

Types of commodity money

commodity	people	area	period
shells	Indians	all over U.S.	precolonial
tobacco	pioneers	Virginia	colonial
nails	Puritans	New England	colonial
beaver skins	Indians	Northwest	colonial
whiskey	Railroad builders	West	nineteenth century
cigarettes	soldiers	Europe and Asia	World War II

Gold and silver came into common use as money in many parts of the world. Certain characteristics of gold and silver led to their widespread use. They are scarce. They wear well, especially if small amounts of other metals are mixed with them. They are easily recognized, and easily transported. The exchange value systems generally adopted were such that relatively high values could be represented by relatively small volumes of these precious metals.

Various kinds of "token money," made of less valuable metals (copper, lead, or zinc, for example) have been commonly used alongside gold and silver money for small transactions. For example, when gold and silver money was used in this country, 100 copper pennies were worth one silver dollar, or 500 pennies were the equivalent in value to a five dollar gold piece. Although the copper in 500 pennies may not have been as valuable as the gold in a five dollar gold piece, people accepted the pennies because others also accepted them, and because they could be exchanged for gold. When people lose faith that their money is worth its face value, economic chaos usually results.

Metals and other goods which have been used for money often have value apart from their monetary use. Money made of things having a value of their own is called *commodity money*. This kind of money is not much used today in our country or in most other major countries.

Today most money is "representative money" or "credit money." The paper used in a dollar bill is worth only a fraction of a cent. But this country's paper money is readily accepted by everyone. The United States government requires that it be accepted in payment of all public and private debts—that is, it is *legal tender*. People throughout the world are eager to get dollars because they represent purchasing power which can be used to acquire goods and services. The dollar is accepted readily in many countries because it is considered a highly stable currency. The price of gold is usually expressed in dollars. Formerly the British pound occupied the position now held by the dollar.

"Credit money" is rapidly replacing paper money, just as paper money has replaced commodity money. Actually, the great bulk of present-day transactions are handled by checks rather than paper money or coins. Most wages and salaries, and most payments for large purchases, are made by checks. The person receiving the checks deposits them in his checking account at the bank. Then, when large purchases are made or payments on bills fall due

---

WHAT BACKS UP THE DOLLAR?

For several years, the United States has not maintained gold backing for Federal Reserve Notes (popularly known as dollars). Although Americans have not been able to turn in their paper money for gold bullion since 1933—when the country went off the domestic gold standard—the government did maintain a gold backing of 25 per cent until March, 1968.

Heavy demands abroad for U.S. gold has reduced the nation's gold supply from $24.2 billion to $10.1 billion in the 20 year period ending in 1970. In 1968, only about one billion dollars' worth of gold was available for exchange. An international monetary crisis was threatened because so many foreign countries were demanding gold bullion in exchange for dollars. The crisis passed when the gold previously backing the dollar at home was freed for international monetary payments.

While gold remains an important factor in international finance, many economists claim that the strength of the dollar or any other currency should not be judged by the gold behind it. They say that the real backing behind the dollar is the total wealth of the United States, not just its wealth measured in gold—which is, after all, an arbitrary standard.

By total wealth, economists mean the dollar value of all the goods and services produced in the United States in a given year.

real purchasing power. Some groups, such as well-organized union workers or those whose incomes are primarily from business profits, may be able to maintain their purchasing power, or even to increase it, despite inflation. But this certainly is not true for most people.

In general, then, either inflation or deflation will help some and harm others. It is likely that rapid and drastic inflation harms more people than it benefits. This kind of inflation is likely to be more harmful than either mild deflation or a stable price level.

The chief victims of inflation are the old, the poor, salaried workers, and wage earners who are not union members or who are represented by weak unions. These groups usually are in no position to increase their incomes to keep pace with rapid and high price increase.

CHECK UP

1. How does money serve these purposes: medium of exchange, standard of value, store of value?

2. What is commodity money? Token money? What is representative money? Credit money? Why has representative money tended to replace commodity money? Credit money to replace representative money? Why may credit cards increasingly replace checks?

3. Explain the terms *inflation* and *deflation*. What are the basic causes of each? How does each affect the standard of living of a couple living on a fixed income? Of a union worker? Why does an increase in monetary income not necessarily increase real income?

4

How are price changes measured?

The foregoing discussion has brought out that prices of goods and services are always on the move. There is a strong tendency for the prices of all commodities and services to move up and

Changes in wholesale prices of farm products and all commodities

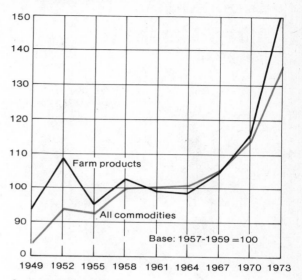

Source: Statistical Abstract

down together. Thus there is a general price level which may be either high or low—"high" and "low," of course, in comparison to some earlier period.

Sometimes it is quite important to know just how much prices have changed over a given period. Wage "cost of living" contracts often are negotiated by unions for their members. If prices increase by a specified amount, wages, too, are increased by a specified amount. Government officials may want to know about price changes so that policies to combat severe inflation can be adopted. Some payments to farmers are keyed to changes in prices, as are welfare and social security payments.

A base period is used to measure changes in general price level. To get a reliable measure of changes in the general price level, the prices of a large number of different products as a group are compared at different periods of time. Since prices of most commodities tend to move up and down together, they are treated as a group in order to get an overall measure. Com-

Mathematical Economist
Alfred Marshall
(1842–1924)

Alfred Marshall spent almost 40 years teaching and doing research at Cambridge University in England. He was an "economists' economist" in the sense that Marshall is not as well known as Adam Smith, Karl Marx, or John Maynard Keynes. During his long career of research, writing, and lecturing, however, Marshall exerted more influence on economists, and through them on "popular" economic ideas, than perhaps any other man who lived during the years between Karl Marx and John M. Keynes. Interestingly enough, Marshall began his university teaching the year after the publication of Volume I of Marx's *Das Kapital.* Marshall's most important book, *Principles of Economics,* first published in 1890,

appeared in eight editions during his lifetime, and has been reprinted many times since. It was a restatement of the whole body of economic thought and was a standard university textbook for more than 40 years. It is still required reading in most advanced economics courses.

Marshall's primary contributions were: (1) the gathering together and the updating of the best of classical economics, and (2) his attempt, then new, to apply mathematical analysis to economic problems. Much of Marshall's formal education had been in mathematics and ethics. He believed that economics, as a "pure science," deals with things that can be measured in terms of money, and that this science should be used for the betterment of society.

Private enterprise and *laissez-faire* economics were under bitter attack when Marshall became active. Although a staunch defender of private enterprise, he recognized weaknesses in the system and favored correcting them. As a humanitarian, he was interested in relieving poverty without overturning the existing economic order. He favored trade unions and collective bargaining to achieve a "standard of comfort" above mere subsistence.

With Marshall, classical economic theory attained a new exactness. Much of what students have learned about how supply and demand interact to determine prices in competitive markets was first clearly explained by Marshall. The same holds true for the differing effects that production costs have on prices over varying periods of time. Even today, many economic studies are simply elaborations of matters briefly discussed by Marshall. Just as Adam Smith has been called the "Father of Economics," Marshall may be called the "Father of Neoclassical Economics." (*Neo-* means "new" or "recent.")

The extensive use of mathematics as an analytical tool in economics has made that subject the most precise of the social sciences. It is Marshall's influence that is largely responsible for this trend.

parisons are made to show the relationship of the price of goods in two or more different months or years, or in two different periods of several years each. One of the periods is taken as a base period, and the other periods are measured in relation to it.

The base period chosen is usually one during which prices were neither especially high nor especially low, but any desired period may be used. In order to make it easy to compare different periods with the base period, the money value of the goods during the base period is generally regarded as 100 per cent. Changes from this base period to the other periods are shown in the percentages above or below the 100 per cent. Suppose 1950 is taken as a base period and prices in 1960 and 1970 compared with those of 1950. In all comparisons, the 1950 prices are given a value of 100 per cent.

A simple problem will illustrate how price changes are calculated. The prices of the eleven different food products are listed below. To find out how prices have changed, one first lists the prices of the various products for the three different years—1950, 1960, and 1970. Second, it is assumed that the prices in 1950 have a value of 100 per cent. The price figures for 1960 and 1970 are then divided by the actual 1950 prices in dollars and cents.

Milk, for example, was 19.3 cents per quart in 1950, 21.9 in 1960 and 26.6 cents in 1970. If 19.3 cents is taken as 100 per cent and divided into 21.9, the result is 113.5 per cent. This means that in 1960 the price of milk was 113.5 per cent of what it was in 1950. It had risen in price 13.5 per cent. By 1970 the price had risen to 26.6 cents per quart. The change in percentage from the 1950 base period to 1970 is obtained by dividing 26.6 (the price in 1970) by 19.3 (the price in 1950), getting the answer 1.378. This indicates that the price of milk in 1970 was 137.8 per cent of the price of milk in 1950.

Similar steps are taken to determine the price changes for each of the other products included in the table.

For this illustration, food products com-

Retail prices of eleven selected food products (1950 = 100)

products	price (in cents)		index number	price 1970[1]	index number
	1950	1960			
Milk, per quart	19.3	21.9	113.5	26.6	137.8
Eggs, per dozen	60.4	57.3	94.9	57.3	94.9
Butter, per pound	72.9	74.9	102.7	86.0	118.0
Bread, per pound	14.3	20.3	142.0	23.9	167.1
Hamburg, per pound	56.6	52.4	92.6	66.3	117.1
Bacon, per pound	63.7	65.5	102.8	97.6	153.2
Coffee, per pound	79.4	75.3	94.8	88.7	111.7
Apples, per pound	12.0	16.2	135.0	20.7	172.5
Sugar, per pound	9.7	11.6	119.6	12.8	132.0
Potatoes, per pound	4.6	7.2	156.5	9.0	195.7
Chicken, per pound	59.5	42.7	71.8	40.9	68.7
Overall index for eleven products:			111.5		133.5

[1] April 1970

Source: Statistical Abstract

monly used in the average household have been selected. They show the prices for each of those two years in relation to what they were in 1950, the base period. Prices of seven of these products were higher in 1960 than in 1950. However, in 1970, nine of the eleven were higher than they were in 1950. This shows that there was a general inflationary period from 1950 to 1970.

An "index number" is a useful measure of price changes. The average of all eleven price changes from 1950 to 1960 and 1970 may now be calculated. The resulting averages (one for 1950 and the other for 1970) are overall index numbers.

The purpose of an index number is to measure overall changes of the price level of similar products and services from one period of time to another. The overall index of prices of the eleven selected food products in 1960 was 111.5 per cent as compared with 100 per cent in 1950. This means, of course, that as an average the prices were 11.5 per cent higher in 1960 than in 1950, only ten years earlier.

In 1970 the price picture was quite different. All but two of the eleven food products were higher in price than they were in either 1950 or 1960. As an average the 1970 price of the eleven products was 133.5 per cent as compared with 100 per cent in 1950. This gives a rough idea of how useful index numbers are in telling how much, on the average, prices have gone up or down from one period of time to another.

Of course, an index number measuring the general price level is more complex than the sample index just illustrated. The index number commonly used is prepared by the United States Bureau of Labor Statistics. It is composed of several hundred commodities representing several different groups of products.

Weighted index numbers are used to calculate the cost of living. In the table on page 81, it was assumed that each product accounts for the same amount of expenditure in the family

food budget as every other product. That, of course, is not the case. The average family spends many times as much for milk as for apples. Even though the price of apples in 1970 was 172.5 per cent of the 1950 level, that in itself does not signify a dramatic overall increase in the family food expenditures. The average family, of course, spends only a relatively small amount for apples in a single month. Much the same thing is true of sugar. These two items do not add much to the family food bill whether the price is high or low.

But that is not the case with food products such as milk, eggs, bread, butter, and meat. The monthly expenditure for any one of these adds up to a considerable part of the total monthly food bill. For that reason a change in these prices is much more important to a household than a price change in sugar or apples.

It is clear that if the relative importance of price changes of several food products is to be measured, each product should be weighted *in accordance with its importance in the total expenditure for food.* That is, a 10 per cent

Calculating the weighted index for selected foods

product	weight	×	index	=	result
Milk	16.15	×	137.8	=	2273.7
Eggs	14.06	×	94.9	=	1334.3
Butter	4.75	×	118.0	=	560.5
Bread	10.83	×	167.1	=	1809.7
Hamburg	11.78	×	117.1	=	1379.4
Bacon	6.46	×	153.2	=	989.7
Coffee	7.22	×	111.7	=	806.5
Apples	3.61	×	172.5	=	622.7
Sugar	10.83	×	132.0	=	1429.6
Potatoes	4.56	×	195.7	=	892.4
Chicken	8.93	×	68.7	=	613.5
Total	100.00 (adjusted)				12,712.0

Weighted index for eleven food products: 12,712.0 ÷ 100 = 127.1

price change in milk or eggs is more important than a 10 per cent price change in apples or sugar. An index number can reflect the comparative amount spent for each of the several items included in the index only if a system of *weighting* is employed. That is, each item (bread, milk, sugar, etc.) is assigned weight in proportion to its importance in the family food expenditures.

For example, one may wish to calculate a price index for the four major dairy products— fresh milk, cream, butter, and cheese. Let us assume, for example, that milk prices have increased by 5 per cent, cream and butter by 15 per cent, and cheese by 20 per cent since a given base period. Studies indicate that the typical family in the area for which the index number is being prepared makes 60 per cent of its total dairy products expenditures for milk, 20 per cent for butter, and 10 per cent each for cream and cheese. By assigning proportionate weights to each of these products (that is, by multiplying each percentage increase by the percentage that product represents in total expenditures, adding the results, and dividing by 100) one can determine the percentage increase for dairy products. In this case, the increase is 8 per cent. The index number, in other words, has increased to 108 from the base year index of 100.0.

The same procedure has been followed with the eleven food products discussed on page 81. Weights compiled by the U.S. Bureau of Labor Statistics are applied to the unweighted index numbers for those commodities, yielding the weighted index numbers shown on page 82.

These simple examples are much less complicated and involve fewer details than is true of actual index number calculations, but they illustrate the basic principles and methods used.

Many price indexes are used by government and private industry. There are a number of different price indexes in common use. One of the most important is the *cost of living index,* which is usually another term for the "Con-

sumer Price Index" calculated by the Bureau of Labor Statistics of the United States Department of Labor. This is a general weight index, covering all the commodities normally bought by consumers in all parts of the country. It is also further broken down by various major commodity groups and by different localities.

Other indexes often used include the "Wholesale Price Index," the "Index of Comparative Living Costs in Specified Areas," the "Index of Retail Prices of Food in Selected Areas," and the "Index of Industrial Production." Someone, for some purpose, calculates price indexes for almost everything that is bought and sold. These indexes may be presented in figures such as used in this chapter, or they may be shown in tables or charts or graphs prepared from the figures. Some of these presentations are found on the financial pages of almost any newspaper.

CHECK UP

1. What is the purpose of a price index? How is it computed?

2. What are weighted index numbers? Why are they usually used in representing price changes?

Clinching the main ideas

Chapter Two brought out how wants plus ability and willingness to buy create demand, and how demand leads to production. This chapter pointed out that the market prices of the things one buys are determined basically by supply and demand.

The *law of demand* states that people will buy more of a product if its price is low and less if its price is high. The *demand schedule* shows the quantities that would be bought at all possible prices. The *law of supply* states that sellers will offer to sell more of a product if its price is high and less if its price is low. The *supply schedule* shows the quantities that would be offered for sale at all possible prices. Interactions between demand and supply establishes an *equilibrium price,* around which actual *market prices* tend to fluctuate.

Supply is influenced by production costs, which are both *fixed* (do not change during the time period under consideration) and *variable* (change with changes in output, although not necessarily in direct proportion). *All* production costs are variable in the long-run, but most pricing decisions are made on a short-run (or variable cost) basis. If all costs are not covered in the long-run, the seller eventually will be forced out of business.

Prices are expressed in terms of money. Today, Americans mainly use *representative money* and *credit money* rather than *commodity money.* The total amount of all forms of money in circulation, operating through the demand side of demand-supply forces, affects prices and price levels. More money without more production tends to lead to *inflation,* or generally rising price levels. These tend to decrease in the *real incomes* of those persons whose *monetary incomes* have not kept pace with the price increases. Likewise, general decreases in monetary incomes without corresponding production decreases lead to *deflation,* or a generally falling level of prices. Both inflation and deflation usually benefit some groups or individuals at the "expense" of others.

The general price level and individual prices are constantly changing. It is important for many reasons to know when these changes occur and how large they are. Consequently, *index numbers* are widely used to measure price changes in percentage terms over specified time periods. Many such indexes, some of them very complicated, are calculated by various agencies.

Chapter 3 review

Terms to understand

1. demand schedule
2. supply schedule
3. equilibrium price
4. charge account
5. markup
6. credit card
7. checking account
8. monetary income
9. real income
10. "fixed" income
11. base period
12. weighting

What do you think?

1. Explain this statement: "Costs affect prices; prices affect costs."

2. Explain this statement: "Prices are determined at markets, not by markets."

3. Below freezing temperatures ruin more than one third of the Florida citrus crop. Is it likely that this disaster will lead to higher prices for Florida citrus already harvested? For Florida citrus that escaped the freeze? For citrus from other states where temperatures were normal? Explain.

4. If prices drop below costs over a long period of time, what type of producer is most likely to be forced out of business? Why?

5. Most big banks issue "individualized and coded" books of checks to checking account customers. Why are these used? What are the advantages to banks and customers? Are there any disadvantages?

Extending your knowledge of economics

1. Prepare a supply schedule showing how many hours per week you would be willing to work at various hourly rates of pay. Use some part-time job you actually perform: baby-sitting, caring for lawns, snow removal.

2. Prepare a report on how the economy of Spain and Western Europe was affected by the treasure Spain brought from the New World during the 1500's. Or on how this country's economy was affected by the gold found in California during the decade following 1849. Be sure also to explain why.

3. Present a report on "How to Manage a Checking Account." Perhaps the local bank will provide the forms used by its customers.

Economic equality for women: an old issue receives new attention

During the late 1960's and early 1970's concern about the unequal status of women in the economy increased. At the behest of Eleanor Roosevelt, President Kennedy appointed a Commission on the Status of Women, which in 1963 made several recommendations. One of these resulted in the Equal Pay Act of that year. In the latter half of the 1960's, a new feminist movement received widespread support in its efforts to improve the status of women. Economic equality became a prime goal of this movement. By the early 1970's, women's liberation had become a factor of political significance.

Historical background

For centuries in Western Europe, and in America, women had few if any legal or political rights. Women, and any property or income that they might have, were almost completely under the control of their fathers or guardians until they married—usually at an early age, and often to someone whom they had not chosen. Once they were married, they came under the control of their husbands. Women were thought (at least by most men) to be physically and mentally inferior to men, emotionally unstable, and not capable of voting, managing their own properties, benefiting from higher education, or participating significantly in their religion. These views generally were supported by law, custom, religious teachings, and "folk wisdom."

An active women's rights movement in this country got started in 1848 under the leadership of Elizabeth Cady Stanton, Lucretia Mott, and a few other determined women. During that year, in a convention at Seneca Falls, New York, a Declaration was adopted asking that women be given (1) the right to vote, (2) legal equality, (3) educational equality, and (4) equal employment opportunities.

Seventy-two years later, in 1920, the Nineteenth Amendment to the United States Constitution gave women the right to vote. (Several states had granted this right earlier.) Despite the views expressed by those supporting and opposing this Amendment, no significant changes, for better or worse, were noted in the country's political affairs. Fifty years later, only one woman was serving in the Senate and only ten in the House of Representatives. Less than 4 per cent of all judges were women, and most of these served in the lowest courts. No woman had become a major contender for President of the United States, and none had served on the Supreme Court. Only two women had served in the President's Cabinet. Although women outnumber men in this country, the right to vote certainly has not brought them proportionate representation in major government positions.

Over the years, women gradually have been accepted in most colleges and universities (at least in most fields of study), and most (not all) of the discriminatory property laws have been changed. But discrimination against women still exists in employment and in the economic rewards for the work done. Support for this contention is provided in the Report of the President's Commission on the Status of Women, which found that the capacities of many women "are clearly not being developed to their full potential" and that women's earnings are "still far lower than men's."

The issue: economic inequality in the '70's

EVIDENCE OF ECONOMIC INEQUALITY

Females account for 51 per cent of this country's population and for 38 per cent of its work force. About 42 per cent of all women over 16 years of age (and 50 per cent of those between 18 and 64) work outside their homes. Three out of five of these working women are married, one fifth are single, and one sixth are widowed or divorced. One half of all women workers are more than 39 years old. The "typical" woman employee has some educational training beyond the high school level.

These figures suggest that women make up a substantial part of the country's permanent work force. They make clear that female employment is not confined to young women who work until they marry, or for a short time thereafter, or to other "temporary" or "part-time" work. Consequently, if employment and wage discrimination against women exists, clearly such inequality has important economic implications. What evidence is there of discrimination?

Government statistics show that the average wages or salaries received by women employees are only 58 per cent of those received by male employees. (This is a decline from 64 per cent in 1955.) Are there justifiable economic reasons for this great difference?

In the past, the following views seemed to be widely accepted: (1) women are only temporary employees, (2) absenteeism from the job and employment turnover rates were higher than for men, (3) their working life was likely to be shorter than that of males, and (4) "by nature" they are best suited for particular kinds of work (such as clerical or secretarial, retail sales, teaching, nursing, or social work). Recent experience and research suggests that the first three of these traditional assumptions are not valid. The fourth assumption needs to be examined more closely.

It is true that almost half of all employed women hold jobs in the fields just listed. Another 30 per cent of women workers are unskilled or semiskilled operatives or provide personal or institutional services. All of these are relatively low-paying occupations—in part because of the large number of women competing for these jobs. It is also true that unions have not yet organized women workers in many of these types of employment.

Very few women have entered the ranks of the higher paid in the professions and in management. Very few women, for example, have reached top positions in business. Only 1 per cent of American engineers, 3 per cent of the lawyers, and only 7 per cent of doctors of medicine are women. Less than 3 per cent of working women earn more than 10,000 dollars per year. Clearly, there can be no substantial improvements in the average earnings of women until more of them enter the higher-paid fields.

Women's rights advocates claim that the number of women entering professional fields has been limited by the admissions policies of university professional schools. They express the view that a woman must be better qualified than most male candidates to be admitted to a program of professional education or to receive consideration for a top technical, scientific, or management position. Even those universities which grant Ph.D.'s to women do not hire the same proportion of women to serve on their faculties.

Statistics show that in most occupations college

Table 1. Expected salaries for June college graduates, by sex and selected field (1970)

field	average monthly salary	
	women	men
Accounting	$746	$832
Chemistry	765	806
Economics, finance	700	718
Engineering	844	872
Liberal arts	631	688
Mathematics, statistics	746	773

Source: Frank S. Endicott, *Trends in Employment of College and University Graduates in Business and Industry* (Northwestern University, 1970). Figures based on jobs and salaries offered by 206 companies during campus recruitment.

educated and professionally trained women receive lower average starting salaries than do men with equivalent training.

Table 1 shows that expected salaries of June college graduates in 1970 were considerably lower for women than for men. Furthermore, women generally never catch up with men through promotions and salary increases.[1]

Table 2 shows that women workers in factories are often paid lower wages than are paid to men holding comparable jobs.

THE EFFECTS OF ECONOMIC INEQUALITY

What are the overall economic effects of discrimination against women workers?

If workers are not employed at their highest levels of ability, thus insuring optimum utilization of their talents, total production of goods and services (GNP) is lower than it could be. The nation as a whole is poorer, to say nothing of the underutilized individuals themselves. If there is a shortage of doctors, it is a waste of economic resources not to recruit for the profession women who might become competent physicians.

A substantial shift of women from the lower-paid labor-abundant occupations to the higher-

1 See *Handbook on Women Workers* published annually by the U.S. Department of Labor.

paid labor-short occupations would bring about changes in overall wage and price structures. With fewer women competing for jobs in a limited number of occupations, wage rates (and prices of goods and services) in these limited fields probably would increase. On the other hand, more worker competition should lead to lower wages (and prices) in occupations now effectively barred to women. But society as a whole, and most (but not all) individuals, probably would gain as a result.

Furthermore, the relegation of any large segment of the population to low-paying jobs pulls down the wage level for all workers. If wages for the lowest-paid jobs are increased, those holding better-paid jobs will also benefit. As long as women can be employed at lower wages than men, the possibility of employing "cheap labor" poses a threat to the income of male workers.

Historically, many jobs once filled entirely by men have become less prestigious and well paid when filled by women. This is especially true of clerical jobs. During a recession, it often is easier for women to find work than for men, simply because they will work for lower wages. If men and women received the same pay for identical work, there would be no economic reason for discrimination in hiring and promotion. But for too many employers, traditional hiring and wage practices seem more profitable despite the loss of talent which often occurs.

Table 2. Median wage or salary income of full-time year-round workers, by sex and selected major occupational group

major occupational group	median wage or salary income		women's median wage or salary income as a percentage of men's
	women	men	
Professional and technical workers	$6691	$10,151	65.9
Nonfarm managers, officials, and proprietors	5635	10,340	54.5
Clerical workers	4789	7351	65.1
Sales workers	3461	8549	40.5
Operatives	3991	6738	59.2

Source: U.S. Department of Commerce, Bureau of Census, *Current Population Reports.*

WHAT IS BEING DONE ABOUT SEX
DISCRIMINATION?

The two federal laws which deal with sex discrimination are: (1) the Equal Pay Act of 1963, and (2) Title VII of the 1964 Civil Rights Act. The Equal Pay Act provides that employers engaged in interstate commerce must pay men and women equally for equal work. The law is administered by the Wage and Hour Division of the Department of Labor, which makes routine investigations of sex discrimination in conjunction with its enforcement of minimum wage legislation.

Title VII of the 1964 Civil Rights Act provides that employers engaged in interstate commerce must hire and promote men and women equally unless a bona fide occupational qualification restricts a job to one sex. Very few occupations have such bona fide qualifications; actor and actress are two examples.

States often prohibit discrimination in hiring and promotion because of sex, but many states also have on their books laws originally enacted to protect women. These laws, for example, prohibit women from working more than a specified number of hours per week, from working at certain times of night, and from lifting objects that weigh more than a given amount—usually 30 or 40 pounds.

Many women have brought suit to gain rights guaranteed under antidiscrimination laws, and some have sued to erase the restrictions imposed by protective legislation. In the latter case, women complain that the protective legislation often denies them an opportunity to earn more money. They point out that women in their household work often lift weights greater than those prohibited on the job. They also point out that since cleaning women, waitresses, nurses, and others are not prohibited from working nights, there seems to be no good reason for retaining protective legislation that restricts other kinds of night work.

Those who support protective legislation argue that without it women would be forced to lift weights or work hours that would endanger health or cause hardship. Both supporters and opponents of protective legislation, however, agree that women are in a relatively weak position as members of the labor force, and need legal protection to make a better living.

The Equal Employment Opportunity Commission. The federal Equal Employment Opportunity Commission (EEOC) has the responsibility of enforcing Title VII of the 1964 Civil Rights Act. Its rulings can in turn be appealed to federal courts.

An example of EEOC activity can be cited in the case of the airline industry. Airlines were accused by EEOC of 1) hiring only women for the job of stewardess on domestic flights, 2) compelling stewardesses to retire at age 32, and 3) forcing stewardesses to retire when they got married.

The airlines argued (1) that only women could be stewardesses because women are feminine, gracious, charming, and interested in personal service. . . . The airlines justified the lack of male flight attendants on the basic ground that the clientele preferred to be served by stewardesses, that the frequent fliers chose airlines on the basis of the quality of stewardesses. . . . (2) The reasons given for terminating women who reached the ancient age of 32 was that the position requires enthusiasm, motivation, and physical endurance lost with age. . . . The airlines . . . argued that women's endurance and enthusiasm deteriorates proportionately faster than do men's. . . . (3) As for terminating married stewardesses, the airlines reasoned that since married women are unwilling to work around the clock, are unwilling to be absent frequently from home, they should therefore be terminated.[2]

The stewardesses countered that 1) male stewards were hired for international flights and performed well, and that if all airlines complied with the law, no one airline could be justified in discriminating against men.

2) Retirement from flight duty at age 32 was not imposed on male airline pilots, stewards, copilots or engineers. These jobs also included hard work and considerable tension. Stewardesses pointed out that in fact, women live longer than men, and might be expected to have more endurance rather than less.

3) The airlines assumed that the frequent absence of women from the home tended to harm

2 David A. Garcia, "Sex Discrimination," *University of San Francisco Law Review* (April, 1970), pp. 335–336.

marriage more than did the frequent absence of men from the home. The stewardesses rejected this conclusion, and held that in any case it was not the concern of the airlines. In fact, many stewardesses married to flight personnel might see their husbands more frequently if they were able to keep their jobs.

In essence, the EEOC agreed with the stewardesses. It concluded that the restrictions imposed upon stewardesses were not bona fide occupational qualifications, and that the airlines must hire men and women for the job of steward and stewardess and treat them equally.

Court cases under Title VII of the 1964 Civil Rights Act. Cases which have been taken to court under Title VII have increased markedly in the past few years. One typical case is that of *Cheatwood v. South Central Bell Telephone*. In this case, the employer refused to consider women for the position of commercial representative. The employer maintained that the job, which included rural canvassing, bill collecting, and occasional lifting, was better performed by men.

The court held that the average performances of men are not proof that men perform the job better than women. The employer must in each case consider the qualifications of each applicant, regardless of sex. In addition, the employer cannot refuse employment to a woman on the grounds that she might suffer harassment—a reference to the common response "this is no job for a lady!"

Another case dealt with the conflicts between state protection laws and Title VII. In *Richards v. Griffith Rubber Mills,* a woman was denied promotion to the job of press operator. The job was awarded to a man with less seniority. The company maintained that the job required occasional lifting in excess of 30 pounds, the limit set by the state for female workers.

The court held that the state law was invalid. Title VII was federal law, which overrides state law. The court opinion stated, "Individuals must be judged as individuals and not on the basis of characteristics generally attributed to . . . sexual groups."

Court cases under the Equal Pay Act. Suits have also been filed under the Equal Pay Act by the Secretary of Labor. One such suit was *Wirtz v.*

Basic Industries, Inc. The company employed three laboratory analysts—two female and one male. The male analyst received higher pay than the females, and received an additional bonus because he worked a late shift every two weeks. He did not begin working a late shift until several months after the Equal Pay Act went into effect.

The company defended its unequal pay policy by stating that the male was in a special job category—"swing analyst," referring to the fact that he worked the late, or "swing" shift every two weeks. It said that the male analyst, therefore, was employed under different working conditions and deserved higher pay.

The court held, however, that the male and females did identical work.

We think these facts compel the conclusion that the job classification "Swing Analyst" is a paper classification unrelated to the true working conditions, and the five cent pay differential bonus for swing shift work is intended to compensate for the different working conditions.[3]

The two women were awarded back pay to the date the Equal Pay Act went into effect, as provided by law. It should be noted that in such a situation the employer is forbidden to lower the pay of the male in order to achieve equality.

Unresolved problems

All the above cases resulted in women's gaining better working conditions and wages. But not all cases have turned out that way. The issues are complicated in some instances by whether or not a bona fide occupational qualification is sex-related. A recent case which involves this issue, *Phillips v. Martin Marietta,* has reached the Supreme Court.

The company, Martin Marietta, maintained a policy to exclude women with preschool-age children from a certain job. Many other women, however, were hired, as were men regardless of whether or not they had preschool-age children. The company claimed it did not discriminate against women, but only against women with small children.

3 *Wirtz vs. Basic Industries,* 256 Federal Supplement 786.

Lawyers for Ida Phillips, who was denied a job by the company, maintained that since the qualification of no small children applied only to women, the company *did* discriminate on the basis of sex. They further agreed that whether or not a female job applicant had preschool children was not a bona fide occupational qualification.

The lower courts decided in favor of the company in this case. They said that since a mother had a special relationship with her small children —a relationship the father did not have—she might be absent from work more often.

In appealing to the Supreme Court, the lawyers representing Mrs. Phillips argued that her relationship with her children was her own affair. The Civil Rights Act, in their view, required that she be considered as an individual and not stereotyped as the member of a group. They also noted that the mother of preschool children might need a given job just as much as any other person.

In 1970, federal guidelines were issued requiring employers with federal contracts to present plans of "affirmative action" to eliminate sex discrimination. This means that another arm of government—the Office of Federal Contract Compliance in the Department of Labor—will be brought into the fight to eliminate sex discrimination in addition to the Equal Employment Opportunity Commission, the various state commissions, and the Wage and Hour Division.

Toward better understanding

QUESTIONS TO CONSIDER IN ANALYZING
THIS CASE

1. What kinds of inequality between the sexes had legal sanction in this country during the early 1800's? What types of equality were demanded by the women at the Seneca Falls Convention? How do you explain the fact that comparatively few women have been appointed or elected to important positions in government 50 years after the Nineteenth Amendment was ratified?

2. What assumptions about women workers have been widely held in the past? Which of these were not supported by data gathered by the President's Commission on the Status of Women?

3. What conclusions do you draw from data in Tables 1 and 2? (Compare wages in each field.)

4. Evaluate each of the statements made about "the overall economic effects of discrimination against women workers."

5. What protection against discrimination is provided by (a) the Equal Pay Act of 1963 and (b) Title VII of the 1964 Civil Rights Act?

6. Evaluate the reasons given by the airlines for their policy in the case of stewardesses. Note the rejoinder of the stewardesses. Why did EEOC agree with the stewardesses?

7. What was the basis for the ruling in *Cheatwood v. South Central Bell Telephone?* In *Richards v. Griffith Rubber Mills?* In *Wirtz v. Basic Industries, Inc.?*

8. Evaluate the arguments on both sides in *Phillips v. Martin Marietta.*

9. Study advertisements in the "Help Wanted" columns of a daily newspaper for evidences of discrimination in hiring on the basis of sex and also on other grounds. Present this evidence to the class and discuss its implications for the economy.

THINKING ABOUT THE BASIC ECONOMIC ISSUES

1. Are women an important part of this country's labor force? Do women more nearly enjoy equality of opportunity in other lands, such as Sweden or the Soviet Union? Did women enjoy more nearly equal economic opportunities in this country during World War II? Explain.

2. Why are the average wages and salaries received by women substantially less than those received by male employees? Why would the differences between the two increase between 1955 and 1970?

3. Why is the percentage of women holding top positions in business, industry, and the professions smaller than that at lower levels?

4. Would you expect more discrimination or less in periods of full employment? Why?

5. If the principle of "equal pay for equal work" were enforced universally, what might be the effect on the economy? How might the employment situation change—in terms of wages and job availability—if women were admitted in large numbers and on an equal basis with men to fields where males predominate, such as construction and police work?

chapter four

Uses and rewards of the factors of production

1. **What do economists mean by "land" and "rent"?**
2. **What are the economic characteristics of labor and wages?**
3. **What is the role of capital and interest?**
4. **What is the role of entrepreneurship and profits?**
5. **Why and how are the factors of production often interchanged?**
6. **How do the factors of production share the "rewards" of production?**

We have not the power to produce more than there is a potential to consume.
LOUIS D. BRANDEIS

The level of productivity of any society depends mainly upon the uses made of its natural and human resources.

Economists frequently speak of the "four factors of production." These are *land* (natural resources, in the broadest sense of this term), *labor* (human productive resources), *capital* (man-made resources, used in further production), and *entrepreneurs* (a French word, referring to those who organize and direct the three factors of production, and assume some of the risks involved—often called "enterprisers"). Combinations of these four factors produce all economic goods and services.

This chapter examines the economic characteristics of these factors of production and the "rewards" each receives for its contribution to production. The payments to these four factors are, from one point of view, the *costs of production*. From another viewpoint they are the *incomes earned* in the economy. To some extent these factors can be substituted for one another, and the amount used (as well

as the prices paid) for each, is influenced by supply and demand. This chapter also considers what "economic efficiency" in resource use means, how this is related to the prices (or "rewards") of each of the four factors of production, and the role of entrepreneurs in promoting efficiency.

1

What do economists mean by "land" and "rent"?

Land is a basic resource. As used in economics, land refers to all natural resources. It includes all the earth's soils and waters, and everything found underneath and within them.

Land provides the space man needs to live and carry on his activities. Fertility of the soil and favorable climatic conditions permit plants to grow, thus providing man with food, fiber, and other materials. Minerals, such as oil and iron ore, are essential to everyday life. Animals, dependent upon land and water plants for their

Factors in production

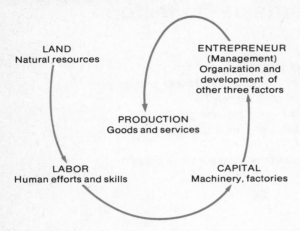

own food, provide man with food and many other necessities. Pure water and clean air are essential to all living things. All the goods that man uses and consumes originally came from what economists have called "land."

Traditionally, economists have maintained that land differs from the other three factors of production in that its quantity is virtually fixed for all time. Man cannot create more soil, water, or minerals, and the rate at which natural resources were being used up seemed so slow that it could be ignored. Recently, however, it has become apparent that current rates of depletion of critical natural resources can soon bring disaster. If man continues to poison the air, water, soil, plants and animals at the current rate, he will be poisoning mankind on a massive scale within a few decades. Consequently, it has become necessary to treat many natural resources with the same care as that bestowed upon most man-made instruments of production—machines, factories, homes. As natural resources wear out or diminish, they must be repaired or replaced to insure that their quality and quantity are maintained or even increased.

The owner of a paper mill, if he wishes to continue to produce paper, maintains his ma-chinery in good repair during its normal life, and then replaces it with as good or better machinery. In the same way, the water taken from the river and used in the paper-making process (and polluted in that process), should be purified by the paper mill owner and returned to the river at approximately its original level of purity.

Going one step further, if the amount or quality of a natural resource can be *decreased,* they can also be *increased.* If effective antipollution devices are soon installed in automobiles, the quality of the air in Los Angeles, Chicago, and New York will improve. Heroic measures might even reverse the process which has converted Lake Erie into a vast sewer, and which has converted sections of the Cuyahoga River flowing through Cleveland into a fire hazard. More soil can be brought under cultivation by irrigation or drainage, and new sources of minerals can be "discovered" by geologists.

Nevertheless, in the short run and for some purposes, it may be realistic to think of some natural resource as relatively fixed in quantity. The amount of land of any given quality which is specially suited for growing corn in the United States is relatively fixed. There is just so much land available for office buildings, stores, restaurants, and the like, in downtown New York, St. Louis, or San Francisco. And there are just so many lake-shore lots available in Minnesota.

"Rent" is the price paid for the use of land (or the "reward" received for its contribution to production). One normally thinks of rent as an agreed-upon payment made by a *tenant* to a *landlord* for the use of a piece of land or a building. This is sometimes called "contractual rent." The economist thinks of rent in still different terms, however.

"Economic rent" is a payment made for the use of any resource which is fixed in supply. Assuming that one wishes to use a resource the supply of which is limited, the amount of economic rent which such a resource can command

Proponent of Economic Rent

David Ricardo

(1772–1823)

Ricardo was a successful London stock-broker who lived soon after Adam Smith and was a contemporary of Thomas Malthus. The writings of both these men influenced Ricardo. Like them, he is considered a classical economist who advocated *laissez-faire* rather than a government-controlled economy.

Ricardo is remembered for his writings on (1) the distribution of wealth among capital, labor, and land; (2) comparative advantage; and (3) rent. In discussing the theory of rent he noted that if there were an unlimited supply of equally good land, there would be no rent. That is, land would be a "free good" like air or sunshine. He believed that this once had been the situation and that the first farmers had taken the best land, forcing those who came later either to farm poorer land or to pay rent for good land.

Ricardo explained that if crops were grown on two kinds of land, Class A (which was highly productive), and Class B (which was less productive), Class A land would yield a rent; Class B would not. The amount of the rent per acre on Class A land would be equal to the difference between the crop yields on the two kinds of land. Were there even less productive land (Class C), then Class A would yield a higher rent than Class B, and Class C would yield no rent at all. Thus rent is considered a reward for the high productivity of land. This productivity may stem from the natural fertility of the soil or from improvements made by the person farming it. As cultivation is extended to poorer lands, rents for use of the best lands increase. The chief exception to the rule is land which has a particular advantage, such as location near a good market or in the heart of a large city.

Ricardo maintained that when rents are raised the employer is exploited, since he must pay higher wages to keep his workers alive. Yet he cannot raise his prices if he expects to compete successfully.

At the time Ricardo was writing, English farming methods were inefficient and much of the soil was exhausted. Prices of grain and rents on farmland were high because the Corn Laws (protective tariffs) raised the price on foreign grain. These were also the early years of the factory system when large amounts of capital were needed for machinery and buildings. Workers were the victims of what Ricardo called the "iron law of wages," in that they received pay barely sufficient to keep them alive at a time when prices were high. Ricardo's solution was to repeal the Corn Laws, import needed farm products, and concentrate on business and foreign trade. This was the policy that England adopted in the 1840's.

is based upon its *productivity in comparison to the productivity of similar resources*. The productivity of a resource is determined either by its inherent characteristics, such as soil fertility, or location.

Suppose that the price of wheat is two dollars per bushel. Farmer A owns land upon which wheat can be grown at a cost, excluding rent, of one dollar per bushel. Farmer B owns a less fertile farm upon which wheat can be grown for $1.50, and the land of Farmer C will grow wheat only at a cost of two dollars per bushel.

Under these circumstances, if all this land is used in growing wheat, the land of Farmer C would be *marginal land*. The term *marginal* refers to land in which the cost of *producing* income from it is equal to that income.[1] That is, if wheat prices were any lower (or production costs any higher) this land would not be used to grow wheat because it could not command any economic rent. The land owned by Farmer B, however, can command economic rent equivalent to 50 cents per bushel and that of Farmer A the equivalent of $1 per bushel.

Next consider two pieces of wheat-growing land of equal fertility and productivity. Assume that production costs are one dollar per bushel on each farm, and that the price of wheat is two dollars. But one of these farms is located so far from the market that it costs an additional one dollar per bushel to transport the wheat to market. The other farm is so near the market that the cost of transportation is only 50 cents per bushel. In this case the more distant piece of land would be marginal, while the nearer land could command an economic rent of 50 cents per bushel. Differential rents based on location often are as important, or even more important, in determining economic rent

than are differentials based on fertility characteristics of the land.

The same principles determine the economic rent of any other kinds of resources, including urban land. Economic rents based on location are particularly important in urban areas, where land is used for business or housing. Retail stores, for example, will have more customers, and yield higher returns to their owners, if they are located in districts where large numbers of people customarily come to shop. Gasoline service stations do best at intersections passed by large numbers of automobiles. Manufacturing plants and office buildings in which large numbers of people are employed must be located with convenient access to mass transportation. The economic rent of such installations is not much affected by soil quality.

There is a close relationship between economic rent and contractual rent. An owner, or landlord, can exact the full amount of economic rent as his contractual rent *if* he knows what level of economic rent his property can command. At anything less than the full economic rent, a tenant would still be better off paying the rent asked than by using marginal property. On the other hand, a tenant cannot afford to pay *more* than the full economic rent. If the landlord asks him to pay more than this, the tenant would do better to move to another property—down to a marginal property.

This means that under ideal conditions, such as keen competition and complete knowledge of the actual levels of economic rent, contractual rent and economic rent would be the same. As neither competition nor knowledge is likely to be perfect, contractual rent and economic rent may differ. That is, either the tenant or the landlord may not be driving the best bargain.

Economic rent is closely related to the market values of property. The "capitalization" of economic rent is a measure of market value. For example, if the economic rent of a property is 2000 dollars and the interest rate at which money can be borrowed to purchase the property is 10 per cent per year, buyers would be

[1] The terms *submarginal* and *supramarginal* are applied to land in which the costs of producing income from it are, respectively, greater and less than that income. It should be emphasized that these are not necessarily permanent conditions. Land once submarginal may become supramarginal if new, income-producing uses for that land can be developed.

willing to pay up to 20,000 dollars for the property. This is because if they were to lend the 20,000 dollars, they would only earn 2000 dollars a year in interest, and if they used the 20,000 dollars to buy the property, they would save 2000 dollars a year in rental payments.

A buyer, of course, might be willing to pay more, or a seller to take less, because they estimate the amount of economic rent differently, or because they expect that economic rent or the interest rate will change in the future. But the worth of a property to anyone is determined basically by what he thinks it will yield in comparison to the yields of alternate properties.

Does economic rent serve a useful economic purpose? Economic rent is the factor which motivates the user of each piece of land to use it for its most productive purpose under the prevailing conditions. To do otherwise would be costly. In this sense, the "reward" or payment of rent contributes to economic efficiency and thereby increases production. It is not economically efficient to use resources for a low-yield purpose when they can be used for high-yield production. If resources are not used at their highest levels of productivity, there will be less goods and services to satisfy human wants.

Some persons have suggested that landlords should be heavily taxed so that most of the economic rent based on differences in production or location is drained away. If tax income from this source mounted, other taxpayers could pay less, for taxpayers could receive more services from government. It is argued that landowners themselves often are not responsible for the economic rents which their properties can command. Soil fertility is a "gift of nature," and locational advantages usually are a result of population increases and the general economic growth in the community where the property exists. Since it would be to the landlord's interest to continue to rent the land to tenants, even if he could retain only a fraction of the economic rent, the land would continue

in use. Thus the taxation of the landlord would not adversely affect the supply of goods and services available to society.

Each tenant would continue to pay exactly the same contractual rent as he would had there been no taxation of that rent after its receipt by the landlord. The tenant of an acre of land in the center of New York City would pay a much higher rent than would the tenant of an acre on the plains of Kansas. But the net income of the landlord after tax payment might not be very different. The New York City land could not so well be used for growing wheat as for building skyscrapers because the landlord's tax liability would reflect the very high potential rent that could be obtained from a tenant who used the land to build a skyscraper. The landlord would be ruined unless he rented the land to the tenant who would put the land to its financially most productive use.

The argument against such taxation of economic rents is that often these are not "windfall" gains to landlords representing no contribution of productive effort. The landlord may have established a new shopping center which has attracted a large volume of homebuilding nearby. The latter, in turn, has increased the profitability and the economic rent yielded by the shopping center. In this case, the landlord's initiative may have given impetus to a development which is advantageous to all the people affected. The prospect of very heavy taxation on rents from the shopping center might have discouraged the entire enterprise.

CHECK UP

1. Explain these terms: land, economic rent, contractual rent. What determines the economic rent that a resource commands?

2. What is the relationship between economic rent and contractual rent? Between economic rent and the market value of a property?

3. What useful economic purpose is served by economic rent? How does the economic rent provide a measure of market value?

2

What are the economic characteristics of labor and wages?

Labor also is an essential factor of production.
No matter how abundant natural resources are, people cannot live without working. Australian bushmen gather plant seeds, search for bird's eggs, and hunt small animals in eking out a living. Those engaging in such activities are laboring, just as are American factory workers, store clerks, farmers, or engineers.

In economic terminology, "labor" as a factor of production is a human resource. It refers to those whose efforts contribute to production by adding value to economic goods or services through the creation of place, form, and time utility. The efforts of labor may be physical or mental.

Unlike land, labor is a *renewable resource.* The population from which labor comes reproduces itself, increasing from generation to generation. Additionally, its qualities (that is, its productive skills) may be improved by education, training, and experience.

Labor receives wages for its contribution to production. Like other prices, the prices paid for labor—or the *wages* received by labor—are influenced by supply and demand in the *labor market.* But as with other prices, the process of wage determination is extremely complicated.

Differences of skill and location distinguish the many labor markets. Different wages are paid in each of the various labor markets. In general, workers in one labor market do not compete for jobs with workers in other markets. Individual workers differ in natural abilities, education, and training. There are many kinds of occupational groups which do not compete with each other.

Workers often are classified as unskilled, semiskilled, skilled, and professional. But each of these classifications contains numerous subcategories of specialized occupations. Workers in a particular occupation in a given city or section of the country normally are not easily available in the labor market for that occupation in another city or section of the country.

The term "labor market," therefore, usually means the market for a particular kind of labor in a given location at a specific time. Certainly people do change their occupations. An unskilled worker may become highly skilled in some trade with training and experience. But these changes are gradual, and are more likely to occur from generation to generation than within a short period of time. Workers also move from labor-surplus low-wage areas to labor-scarce high-wage areas. American workers probably are more mobile than any other workers in the world. These movements, however, usually do not occur overnight.

The supply of labor resources differs from the supply of natural resources. A worker who offers his labor services to an employer necessarily must offer himself. The work usually is done on his employer's property or under his direct control. Labor is relatively immobile, both occupationally and geographically, and labor services are highly perishable. Labor not used is lost forever.

At any given time and place, the total labor market supply is based on the number of available workers and the number of hours they are willing to work. But this supply is also affected by how hard workers are willing to work and by their levels of skills and abilities. All the factors mentioned tend to change over the years. The population, from which labor is drawn, may increase or decrease. Laws or customs bearing on legal or customary working age or the types of position appropriate for men and for women may vary. New skills can be acquired, or old ones lost. Custom, laws, or union rules may affect how long and how hard people work.

Both the demand for labor and the wages

paid are based upon labor's productivity. Labor is desired because it can produce things to satisfy human wants. Thus, the demand for labor may be called a *derived demand;* that is, it stems from demands for goods and services.

An employer in the business of supplying goods and services finds it profitable to hire additional labor as long as the wages paid workers do not exceed the value of the products they produce. Thus, if labor productivity is high and there is a market for the goods produced, an employer can afford to hire more labor and pay higher wages.

The productivity of labor, with a fixed combination of other factors of production, is subject to the principle of diminishing returns. As more workers are hired for a given job, the productivity or output of additional workers declines. To illustrate, a small corner retail food store must have at least one clerk to serve customers and check their purchases at the cash register. Since the store could not operate without the one clerk, his productivity, therefore, is high. A second clerk might be almost as productive as the first, depending upon the store's volume of business. But at some point, it would not pay to hire an additional clerk. One more might add nothing to productivity.

It is sometimes said, therefore, that the wage level for any group of workers is determined by the productivity of the *marginal* worker; that is, by the last worker that it pays the employer to hire. All workers doing the same kind of job are *interchangeable* and usually are paid about the same wage. There is no reason for the employer to pay one more than another. Because the workers all are interchangeable, no worker gets a higher wage than the value of the output produced by the marginal worker. Economists call this the "marginal productivity theory" of labor.

The "marginal productivity theory," like other models, must be qualified by "real world" conditions. In the long run, wages and the amount of employment generally are sig-

nificantly influenced by productivity, but other factors influence particular short-run situations. There is a minimum level below which wages cannot fall if an employer expects to hire any workers.

Minimum wages are established by law. These apply to most employers and workers, but are relevant only to the lowest-paid occupations. Most skilled or experienced workers receive higher wages than these legal minimums. Unemployment insurance and welfare payments, in effect, help to establish floors for wages. Few persons would be willing to work for less money than they can receive for not working.

Many persons have ideas about what a particular job "should" pay, and are not willing to work for less. Also, opportunities for employment in other kinds of work may influence the wage one is willing to accept on a given job. Additionally, labor unions, by bargaining and by controlling the supply of certain kinds of labor in given labor markets, may significantly influence wage rates.

Neither employees nor employers are likely to know exactly what is the productivity of a given worker. At any given time, therefore, wages may be somewhat above or somewhat below actual marginal productivity. Perhaps it is most useful to think of marginal productivity as providing a central point (much as the "equilibrium price" discussed in connection with supply and demand) about which actual wages tend to fluctuate.

The marginal productivity model is useful nonetheless. In the long run, workers cannot expect to receive more, nor employers to pay less, than the value added to goods and services by the productivity of labor. If wages exceed productivity, employers eventually must either cut wages or lay off the least efficient workers. If productivity exceeds wages, employers can increase their profits by hiring more labor, up to the marginal point where wages and productivity become equal.

CHECK UP

1. Define *labor* as that term is used in economics.

2. What factors influence the "prices paid for labor" (wages)?

3. How does the supply of labor resources differ from the supply of natural resources? How does productivity influence demand for and wages paid to labor?

4. Why must the marginal productivity theory of labor be modified in the light of real life conditions?

3

What is the role of capital and interest?

The word "capital" may be used in ordinary conversation to refer to the amount of money one has, or to the amount of money that is invested in a business. In the economist's more precise terminology, capital has only one meaning.

Capital is a factor of production created by man from natural resources. Most of the things which people use or consume are produced by an indirect or roundabout productive process. *Capital consists of the "tools" used in indirect production.* Capital, therefore, is "real" rather than "monetary" in nature, although it is measured in monetary terms and money (or credit) usually is used to acquire it.

Capital tools may be anything produced by man to be used in further production. Fishhooks and screwdrivers are capital, as are airplanes, the buildings and machinery of automobile manufacturers, and the plows of farmers. Very little is produced anywhere without some use of capital.

The Australian bushman uses a boomerang or throwing stick to kill small animals for food. An Eskimo seal hunter may use a spear. These simple instruments are capital—they have been made for use in the "production" of food. In this sense, both the Russians and the mainland Chinese employ capital in their system of production, but they would indignantly deny that they are "capitalists."

Capitalism is based on private ownership of the means of production. In this country, the capital used is largely privately owned. Under capitalism, labor is performed for wages, and the workers usually do not own any substantial amount of the capital they work with. Labor is specialized; that is, the typical individual worker concentrates on doing one or a few tasks rather than a wide variety of tasks. There is widespread use of money and credit. Finally, capitalistic production is organized and managed by private *entrepreneurs* who seek to make a profit.

The use of capital requires prior savings. If people immediately consume everything produced they cannot accumulate capital. In order to build capital goods—tools, factories, machinery—one must have a *surplus*. That is, one must have more economic goods than are required for immediate consumption. There must also be the will to defer consumption of this surplus for a time.

Persons who save defer consumption with the expectation that they will be able to enjoy even more goods and services in the future. To illustrate, assume that an Australian bushman, through hard work or good fortune, was able to accumulate enough food to last his family for several days. Instead of feasting and remaining idle until the surplus food was consumed, he used his time and labor (with available natural resources) to make a boomerang. With this piece of capital equipment, he was able to kill more small animals than before. His productivity was increased greatly.

Other bushmen saw his success. They agreed to provide his family with food if he would devote his entire time to making boomerangs for them. Thus, out of savings from surplus product and *specialization of labor,* the use of a form of capital was introduced into the tribe. Labor productivity and total output increased,

Defender of Capitalism

Eugen von Böhm-Bawerk

(1851–1914)

Great economic thinkers play two roles: (1) they make original contributions in the field of economic theory, and (2) they evaluate theories put forward by other economists.

Böhm-Bawerk (pronounced bu(r)m-*bah′* vayrk) was an Austrian economist who excelled both as a critic and as an original thinker. He was especially critical of·the theory that labor was the standard by which the value of all commodities was to be judged. This view had been suggested by Adam Smith. During the 1800's Karl Marx restated the labor theory of value in his monumental work *Das Kapital.*

Böhm-Bawerk took issue with both Marx and Smith in one of his books, *The Positive Theory of Capital.* He claimed that Smith had never really decided what constituted value. Was it the amount of labor which went into manufacturing a produot? Or was it this, plus the cost of materials, the land on which the factory stood, the profit which must be given to those who put up the money for the corporation, and so on? Böhm-Bawerk and other economists said that "utility (usefulness) alone is the cause of value." They explained that no matter how much labor, capital, and machinery have gone into producing a good, it has no value unless people want it and are willing to pay money for it. They buttressed their arguments with a great deal of difficult mathematical calculation.

Böhm-Bawerk's development of this theory of marginal utility was not his only contribution to economics. His ideas on the function of capital and on the theory of interest on capital were also of major importance. Unlike many other economists, he did not try to justify interest rates or to explain them by saying they were a tax on the money borrowed. Instead, Böhm-Bawerk looked upon interest as a *time* payment. Interest represents the difference between the value of something now and its value in the future when we have saved the money for it. One hundred dollars is more valuable to us today than a year from now. Therefore, to make these amounts equal, interest must be paid for the privilege of having the money today rather than waiting a year for it.

Böhm-Bawerk also pointed out the advantages of what was then called the "round-about" process of production. Under this system one first manufactured producers' goods, such as tools and machines. These were then used in making consumers' goods. This "round-about" system made possible a great saving compared to earlier and slower methods of producing consumers' goods by hand. The "round-about" process of production is the basis for modern mass production.

and everyone had more food than before. This incident illustrates the basic motivations and principles of capital formation and use. The details of capital formation would be much more complex in an industrial economy.

The owners of capital receive interest **for its use.** From the viewpoint of a user of capital (a producer), interest is a price charged or a payment made for a facility which will enable him to produce more. It is a cost of production, just as are rents and wages. From the viewpoint of the owner of the capital, interest is a reward for saving, an inducement to defer some portion of his present consumption in favor of future consumption. Most persons prefer present goods to the same amount of future goods. For that reason, "time preferences" must be overcome by the promise of receiving still more in the future.

"Contractual interest" is the amount actually paid for the use of capital. In most cases, contractual interest is a payment made for money borrowed to acquire "real" capital. If one borrows 1000 dollars for one year at an annual interest rate of 7 per cent, one has incurred an obligation to repay 1070 dollars— the 1000 dollars *principal* plus 70 dollars interest—at the end of the year. By using the capital acquired with the 1000 dollars, a producer hopes to earn more than 1070 dollars during the year, so that he can repay his total debt (the principal plus interest), and have left over a net gain for himself.

Consumers who buy on installment plans pay contractual interest on these debts. Consumer loans, however, usually carry higher interest charges, and often are for shorter periods of time, than is typical of capital goods loans. (Consumer borrowing is discussed in the next part of this book.)

Contractual interest, whether for consumer or producer goods, is made up of three elements: a *pure interest rate,* a *risk premium,* and a *service charge.* The pure interest rate is that portion of contractual interest which is necessary to induce a lender to give up present consumption for greater future consumption. It is the necessary reward to get persons to save. The risk premium is the amount necessary to offset a lender's fear that a loan may not be repaid. Some loans, of course, are much more risky than others. A wildcat oil well drilling business, for example, doubtless would be considered more risky than a long-established and stable retail store or manufacturing company. The service charge covers the expense involved in administering and supervising a loan. This might involve the work of checking on the borrower's credit standing, the clerical work of filling out and signing forms, and mailing and collection expenses.

These three elements are not separately stated in a contractual interest agreement, but they are included as parts of all interest charges. The risk premium is likely to vary most from one loan to another. This factor accounts for most of the differences between interest charges in a given "loan market" at a particular time.

Interest rates, like other prices, are affected by supply and demand. If the supply of capital (or the loanable funds necessary to acquire capital) is low and the demand is high, interest rates will be high. Plentiful supply and low demand, on the other hand, will result in lower interest rates. The supply of real capital at any given time is determined by the population's ability and willingness to defer immediate consumption. The supply of loanable funds, money and credit, however, is much more flexible. As is shown in later chapters, monetary supply is greatly influenced by the policies of government and the banking system.

The demand for capital is based upon capital's productivity. Capital, as is the case with the other factors of production, is subject to the principle of diminishing returns. As additional units of capital are used in conjunction with fixed amounts of other resources its marginal productivity eventually decreases. When a borrower or capital user believes that the additional product obtainable from another unit of capital is lower than the interest charge he would have to pay for it, he will not acquire this additional capital. On the other hand, as long as he believes that capital's marginal productivity is higher than the interest rate, he will use additional capital.

Interest rates distribute capital to its most productive uses. If each person could acquire all the capital he wants without any interest charges, there would not be enough to go around. The fact that interest must be paid rations the use of capital. It will be used only for those purposes which its users feel will be productive enough for them to pay the required interest charges. It also means that producers will first use capital for those purposes which are the most productive.

To illustrate, assume that a producer must pay interest at the rate of 8 per cent per year for money to acquire capital. He could use his borrowed capital to operate a restaurant which he thinks will bring him a return of 20 per cent, thus leaving him 12 per cent over and above his 8 per cent interest payment. Or he could operate a clothing store for a return of 15 per cent, a jewelry store for a return of 10 per cent, or a bookstore for a return of 7 per cent.

Clearly, it would be to this producer's advantage to go into the restaurant business. If his community would not support more than one restaurant, and he wished to operate other kinds of businesses, he would next expand into clothing, and then into jewelry. He would not operate a bookstore since the interest rate would have channeled his available capital into its most productive use. His additional capital would thereafter go, in descending order of productivity, into other uses until the point is reached where productivity is so low that the interest rate prevents further expansion.

CHECK UP

1. Explain the meaning of these terms: capital, capitalism, entrepreneur, surplus product, specialization of labor, interest.

2. How does a user of capital regard interest? How does the owner of capital regard interest?

3. Explain why three elements are included in contractual interest: pure interest rate, risk premium, service charge.

4. How are contractual interest rates determined? What determines demand for capital?

4

What is the role of entrepreneurship and profits?

Someone must organize and supervise the use of land, labor, and capital. For production to take place, someone must decide what purchasers are likely to buy, and at what prices. Estimates must be made concerning the probable costs of production. It must be decided whether or not these costs will make possible the production of goods for sale at prices acceptable to purchasers. If the answer is affirmative, the various necessary factors of production must be acquired and put to work. This work must be supervised to make sure it is performed as efficiently as possible. Finally, the product must be sold. All of these responsibilities are functions of the entrepreneur, or enterpriser.

Entrepreneurs may operate one-man businesses or firms, or they may be responsible for the largest corporations. (Privately-owned— that is, non-governmental—production operations of all kinds commonly are referred to as *firms.*) Entrepreneurs may use their own land, labor and capital, or they may use the resources of others. Whatever the size, type of operation, or source of the resources used, however, the entrepreneur ultimately is responsible for what goes on in the organization. He makes the major decisions. He reaps the rewards of suc-

From grain to bread: production

Bread on the dining table is taken for granted by most Americans. Yet the first steps in its production may take place a thousand miles away in grainfields which supply the chief raw material of bread. Grain, harvested by a combine and pouring into trucks, *a,* already has involved a number of production factors—the farmer's land, his farm machinery, and his labor. Before the grain gains the additional utility which makes it bread, it must pass through many more stages of production.

b

a

c

The grain is brought to centrally located flour mills from the scattered farms and grain elevators. At the mill, grain is ground into one of the many kinds of flour which are used in making bread. It is then shipped by enamel-lined railroad cars to a bakery and unloaded by modern methods, flowing from the bottom of the freight car into the bakery's storage bins, **b.** At the bakery it is sifted and released from large bins into mixing machines where it is added to the other ingredients which make bread, **c.**

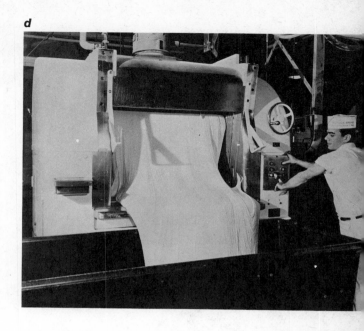

d

The dough pours out into big containers called troughs **d,** and then wheeled into a heated room, **e,** where the dough is left to rise, puffing up from tiny gas bubbles formed by the action of the yeast.

e

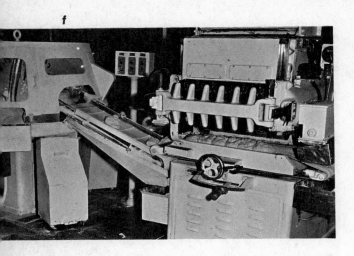

f

As soon as the dough has risen, it is fed into a series of processing machines, **f,** which cut the dough into loaf-sized lumps and shape it. The dough is then deposited in loaf pans, **g,** where it rises some more. A semi-automatic oven-loader, **h,** carries it slowly through an oven for baking. It emerges from the oven as bread, **i,** and is removed from the loaf pans. A checker inspects it, **j,** before it is moved through the slicing machine, **k.** The sliced loaves are then automatically wrapped and loaded on racks, **l,** ready for shipping to the supermarket. Transportation has played an important role in making bread; the grain, the flour, and the finished product, **m,** have all been transported by train or truck adding both utility and cost.

g

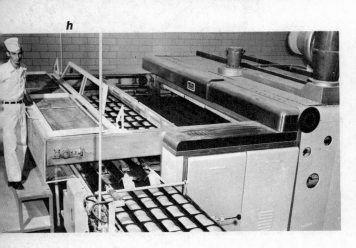

h

i

j

k

l

m

cess and assumes the risks of business failure.

In his book *The New Industrial State,* Harvard economist John Kenneth Galbraith points out how the concept of entrepreneurship has broadened with the rise of the large modern corporation. He suggests that while individuals may still be entrepreneurs in smaller firms or in family firms, large corporations are run by what is, in effect, collective entrepreneurship:

In the past, leadership in business organization was identified with the entrepreneur—the individual who united ownership or control of capital with the capacity for organizing the other factors of production and, in most contexts, with a further capacity for innovation. With the rise of the modern corporation, the emergence of the organization required by modern technology and planning and the divorce of the owner of the capital from control of the enterprise, the entrepreneur no longer exists as an individual person in the mature industrial enterprise. . . . It replaces the entrepreneur, as the directing force of the enterprise, with management. This is a collective and imperfectly defined entity; in the large corporation it embraces chairman, president, those vice presidents with important staff or departmental responsibility, occupants of other major staff positions and, perhaps, division or department heads not included above. It includes, however, only a small proportion of those who, as participants, contribute information to group decisions. This latter group is very large; it extends from the most senior officials of the corporation to where it meets . . . the white and blue collar workers whose function is to conform more or less mechanically to instruction or routine. It embraces all who bring specialized knowledge, talent or experience to group decision-making. This, not the management, is the guiding intelligence—the brain—of the enterprise. There is no name for all who participate in group decision-making or the organization which they form. I propose to call this organization the Technostructure.[2]

[2] John Kenneth Galbraith, *The New Industrial State* (Boston: Houghton Mifflin Company, 1967), pp. 70–71. Used by permission.

Entrepreneurs receive profits for their services and risks, and bear the losses if their businesses fail. Profits are the amount left over from a firm's income from sales of its product after all payments have been made to all the other factors of production for their services. This residual amount goes to entrepreneurs as a reward or payment for their contribution of services to the production process and for their assumption of the risks of failure and consequent losses. Losses occur if the firm's income is not enough to pay all the costs (that is, rent, wages, and interest) of production.

Profits are sometimes labeled as "accounting profits" or as "economic profits." Accounting profits are those monetary profits shown on a firm's *profit and loss statement* (an annual listing of all income and all expenses). This is what is commonly meant by "profits" in everyday conversation. Accounting profits, however, ignore the "costs" of factors of production owned by the entrepreneur. These costs are just as real, in an economic sense, as are the costs of these factors when they are not owned by entrepreneurs.

Consider the example of an entrepreneur who operates Firm A—a dry-cleaning establishment. He owns his building and the land upon which it is built. His dry-cleaning equipment and delivery truck are leased with monthly payments. He works full time in the establishment, and hires three assistants. At the end of the year, his profit-and-loss statement shows that this income from the business exceeds his payments for wages, leased equipment, and other operating expenses by 14,000 dollars. Is it correct, therefore, to say that the business made 14,000 dollars in profits during the year?

It is true that the firm's *accounting* profits stood at 14,000 dollars. Federal and state income tax payments would be based on this amount. But this figure does not include payments for the entrepreneur's own services, nor any payments for the rent of his land and building. By failing to "impute" these payments into his costs, he had ignored his "opportunity costs." That is, he did not consider the possible alternative earnings opportunities for the use of his own property and his own labor services.

Actually, this businessman could have earned wages of 8000 dollars per year by working for another dry-cleaning firm, and he could have rented his land and building to someone else for 4800 dollars per year. His opportunity costs, thus, amounted to 12,800 dollars. If this amount is deducted from his 14,000 dollars accounting profits, his economic profits—the actual amount attributable to his services as an entrepreneur—were only 1200 dollars.

Economic profits can be subdivided further into "normal profits" and "pure profits." In economic terminology, normal profits are those profits necessary to provide payments to entrepreneurs sufficiently large to induce them to keep their business in operation. The necessary size of these entrepreneurial rewards will vary from firm to firm and from time to time.

Pure profits, on the other hand, are the portion of economic profits which exceeds normal profits, and are over and above earnings necessary to keep entrepreneurs performing their services and operating their firms. Pure profits usually arise out of unexpected and unforeseen circumstances (often called "windfall gains") or because a particular firm has few or no competitors in the market for its product, and therefore can charge unusually high prices.

Assume that only one other dry-cleaning firm is in operation in Firm A's community. If this other firm should lose its building and equipment in a fire, it might not be able to rebuild and go back into business for several months. During this period, the owner of Firm A might find that his volume of business would increase considerably. He might even raise his prices. His profits might increase substantially because of lack of competition. These excess profits, which had not been anticipated by Firm A, and which are greater than are necessary for it to remain in business, would be pure profits.

Normal economic profits obviously serve a useful purpose. Without the hope of making such profits entrepreneurs would not organize and operate businesses. To avoid losses, firms must refrain from using resources to produce goods and services that people do not want to buy, or from producing at costs higher than the prices people will pay. If profits are abnormally high in some lines of production and abnormally low in others, the number and size of firms will gradually expand in the former and shrink in the latter. Profit differentials, therefore, tend to move production toward more useful activities in the same way that interest rates move capital into more useful activities.

Pure profits, therefore, usually do not continue in any given line of production for long periods of time. When other entrepreneurs realize that unusually high profits are being made in some particular type of endeavor, they are likely to start new businesses to share in the expected profits. Then competition will force prices down or force production costs up until only normal profits are being received. However, if barriers exist which prevent more competition where pure profits are being made, they do not serve to increase production, and purchasers can say justifiably that they are paying too much for the product concerned.

Profits vary considerably over a period of time as well as between different types of industries and different firms. At any given time some firms will be making large profits, others only normal profits, and still others will be suffering losses. But entrepreneurs, under a private enterprise system, must be willing to take such risks.

CHECK UP

1. What are the responsibilities of the entrepreneur? How has the entrepreneurship changed in large modern corporations? Why?

2. What compensation does the entrepreneur receive in the case of a small firm?

3. What is the difference between *accounting profits* and *economic profits*? *Normal profits* and *pure profits*?

5

Why and how are the factors of production often interchanged?

Entrepreneurs are interested in making the highest possible profits from the operations of their firms. Because prices usually are determined mainly by market forces of supply and demand, it is chiefly through control over production costs that the producer can increase profits.

Producers seek a "least-cost combination" of factors and methods of production. It may be possible to produce a given quantity of a particular product by using various combinations of land, labor, and capital. Within limits, factors of production can be substituted for one another.

More labor and less land may be used to produce a given number of bushels of wheat, or more capital and less labor may be used to manufacture a given number of automobiles. But usually there is only one combination of land, labor, and capital which insures the lowest production cost (measured in monetary terms) for a given volume of output. This is the least-cost combination which is constantly sought by businessmen and farmers. The lower their production costs are, the higher their profits.

To illustrate, a large high school used a duplicating machine to reproduce copies of examinations, assignments, and other instructional materials. One person was employed full time to operate this machine. Eventually the work load become so great that it was no longer possible to reproduce all the required materials on this machine during an eight-hour working day. After investigation, the principal found that by employing an office assistant part-time to operate the duplicating machine for four hours daily after school, the required work could be done. This would involve an additional expenditure of eight dollars per day in wages.

Another solution would be to trade in the old duplicating machine for a new model, which could turn out the necessary work in an eight-hour day. The principal decided to buy the new machine. By doing this, he saved eight dollars per day in wage costs by spending six dollars per day for capital equipment.

REARRANGING WORLD PRODUCTION

Jan Tinbergen, a Dutch economist who won the Nobel Prize, has arrived at what he considers a rational division of labor for the whole world. His division is based on the availability of capital and labor in different countries and the need for capital and labor in different industries. He assigned industries requiring the most labor to underdeveloped countries, and industries requiring the most capital to highly developed countries.

According to Professor Tinbergen, the countries of the world should produce the following, among other things:

United States—planes, chemicals, drugs, tele-communications equipment;

Western Europe—textile machinery, automobiles, turbines, animal and vegetable oils;

Japan—ships;

Soviet Union—computers;

The developing countries—textiles, shoes, glass.

The method of assigning industries involved listing the countries in eleven groups according to capital resources, and then listing 88 different industries according to capital requirements. However rational it may sound to economists, it is not likely to be embraced by world leaders. The political barriers to rearranging world production are simply too great.

In this case, the decision was a fairly easy one. Had the principal been able to hire a second assistant to do the additional work for four dollars per day, the decision also would have been easy. In that case, the least-cost combination would have led to a substitution of labor for capital.

Any change in the price (or the productivity) of a factor is likely to cause production cost changes leading to a different least-cost combination. If wage rates increase (or if labor productivity decreases) more capital equipment may be used as a substitute for labor. Likewise, if interest rates decline, thus reducing the cost of acquiring capital equipment, relatively more capital may be used. Or if land costs increase, more capital or labor, or both, may be used with a given quantity of land.

As long as it is possible for a producer to lower the costs of producing a given volume of goods or services by using other methods of production—that is, by varying the quantities or combinations of factors of production—it will pay him to keep seeking a least-cost combination. But no solution is likely to be a permanent one. The prices and the productive qualities of all factors of production are changing almost constantly. Thus, the producer's efforts to lower production costs—to increase the economic efficiency of his operation—never end. This is a major characteristic of a competitive private-enterprise economy.

Producers' efforts to increase their profits by lowering their production costs benefit the economy. Because all economic resources are limited in amount, it is desirable that *all* resources and *each particular kind* of resource be used as efficiently as possible under the prevailing circumstances. This is what occurs under least-cost production conditions.

In other words, producers' attempts to increase efficiency (or lower their costs) contribute to an economically wise use of resources. More goods and services are made available at lower costs than if profits-seeking producers were not striving to find less costly ways of production.

1. What is meant by a "least-cost combination" of factors and methods of production?

2. What factors may lead to a different least-cost combination? Why is no solution likely to be permanent?

6

How do the factors of production share the "rewards" of production?

It is not possible to calculate precisely how much is paid for the services of each of the four factors of production. The available statistical information almost always reports the "profits" and incomes of firms and individuals on an "accounting" basis. Such figures include the elements of wages, rents, interest, and entrepreneurial profits.

But by using data reported annually by the United States government, one can obtain a reasonably satisfactory picture of the per cent of the total costs of production paid to each factor for its services. These percentages usually change very little from year to year. It is important to recognize that the following statements apply to this country. The situation is quite different in many other countries.

Labor costs are the greatest factor in production costs. Government figures for the most recent year show that "wages and salaries" costs amounted to about 72 per cent of all production costs in the country as a whole. Even this figure, however, understates the situation.

During the same year, the profits (in the accounting sense) of businesses of all kinds, including farms, and the incomes of professional people, amounted to a little more than 21 per cent of all production costs. All of this 21 per cent, however, cannot be considered to be entrepreneurial payments. Certainly substantial portions of it were labor services performed by the owners of firms, and also the contributions made by land and capital equipment owned by them.

Interest costs based on reported dollar figures during the same year were a little less than 4 per cent of production costs, and rents were a little less than 3 per cent. Both of these figures, of course, are understated, as portions of the 21 per cent "profits" figure already mentioned actually were payments for interest and rent in the economic sense.

Payments made to factors of production are also income to those providing productive services. All incomes come from production. If no goods or services were produced there would be no incomes. All production costs something. These costs are no more and no less than payments made to the various factors for services used.

A payment made to anyone is income to the one who receives it. Thus every expenditure is also income to someone else. Total expenditures for the services of factors of production, therefore, must be the same as total incomes of these factors. Total expenditures, or production costs, and total incomes in an economy are merely the opposite sides of the same coin. This is what is meant by the "circular flow" of income or money. Individuals receive payments for their labor or for the services of other factors of production which they own. This is income. These individuals, in turn, use their incomes to buy the goods and services produced. With the payments (income) received from purchasers, producers buy more factor services to produce more, and so the flow continues.

For this reason, it has been said that "Supply creates its own demand." This statement is not true if it is understood to mean that all the monetary incomes generated in production will be used to buy the goods and services produced. Some persons may choose to save some portions of their incomes rather than spending all they receive. But if the statement is understood

to mean that all the goods and services produced *could be* bought by the incomes generated in their production, it is correct. Of course, there is a vast difference between "will be" and "could be." The importance of this difference will be brought out in Part Four of this book.

CHECK UP

1. About what per cent of the total costs of production is paid to each of the four factors?

2. Why is every payment to one of the factors of production also income to those providing productive services?

Clinching the main ideas

Everything that people consume or use is produced by some combination of the services of land, labor, capital, and entrepreneurs. These four factors of production receive, respectively, payments of rent, wages, interest, and profits for their contributions to production. (The precise economic meaning of these terms differs from their meaning in everyday usage.) Without these payments or "rewards," factor services would not be made available.

The various factors of production can be substituted for one another, at least within limits, in any particular kind of production operation. The quantities of land, labor, or capital which will be used, therefore, depends largely upon the respective costs (or prices) of these factors. Competitive entrepreneurs, seeking to lower production costs and thereby increase profits, constantly seek less costly ways of doing particular jobs. This search for a least-cost combination leads to more efficient resource use.

The expenditures made for the services of factors of production are the same as the incomes received in the economy. The payments made to others by "all of us" necessarily equal the incomes of "all of us." With presently available statistics, one cannot compute exactly what per cent of total production costs goes to each of the four factors of production for its services. But it is quite clear that by far the largest portion of payment (or income) in this country goes to labor involved in the production of both goods and services.

The four chapters in Part One have introduced much of the specialized terminology and many of the basic principles of the science of economics. A grasp of this material will help the student to understand better many of the economic issues and problems of today. Such understanding will also prove useful in dealing with economic problems that confront individuals and family groups.

Chapter 4 review

Terms to understand

1. land
2. labor
3. capital
4. entrepreneur
5. labor market
6. economic profits
7. least-cost combination
8. opportunity costs
9. economic rent
10. marginal productivity theory
11. contractual interest
12. profit and loss statement

What do you think?

1. Should landlords be taxed so heavily that most of the economic rent is drained away?

2. How can each of the following affect the productivity of labor: customs, laws, union rules? Give examples.

3. What useful purpose is served by interest?

4. Why has Professor Galbraith felt it necessary to coin the new term "Technostructure"?

5. How does the economy benefit from the efforts of producers to increase their profits by lowering production costs?

6. In what sense is it true that "supply creates its own demand"?

Extending your knowledge of economics

1. Prepare a chart or graph for a 50-year period to show the amount used of a given natural resource in this country. What has been the trend? How do you explain changes in the amount used? (See *Historical Statistics of the United States* published by the Census Bureau.)

2. Study the annual report of a large corporation. Note the various divisions, the products produced by each, and which operated at a profit. Relate what you have learned to Galbraith's comments about "Technostructure."

part two Family economics

chapter five

The family as a consuming unit

1. **What are the characteristics of family incomes in this country?**
2. **What are the characteristics of family consumption?**
3. **What safeguards have been provided for consumers?**

The individual serves the industrial system not by supplying it with savings and the resulting capital; he serves it by consuming its products. On no other matter, religious, political, or moral, is he so elaborately and skillfully and expensively instructed.

JOHN KENNETH GALBRAITH,
The New Industrial State

Chapter 2 brought out that direct consumption demand, or consumption spending, accounts for a little more than three-fifths of the total demand for goods and services in this country. This consumption spending amounts to about 600 billion dollars per year. This is the equivalent of nearly 3000 dollars annually for every man, woman, and child in the United States.

The family is the basic consuming unit. A family usually is defined as two or more related persons living at the same place. In this book, however, a single individual who maintains separate living quarters is also considered a "family." In other words, a "family," as this term is here used, may be made up of one or of several persons.

The heads of families—those who receive and spend most of the family income—con-

tinually face the problem of how much of the available income should be spent for what kinds of goods and services, and how much, if any, should be saved for the future. Most family heads want members of their families to have each day as many necessities, comforts, and luxuries of life as possible. But they are also concerned about the family's future economic security—retirement income for old age, meeting the expenses of serious illnesses, the possibility of the death, disability, or unemployment of the breadwinner, money with which to send children to college, and the like.

Very few families have sufficiently large incomes to live as well as they would like today and also to provide for tomorrow's eventualities. Choices must be made among present alternatives, and also between the present and the future. Economics, for good reason, has been called "a science of choices."

This chapter treats diverse patterns of family incomes, spending habits, and consumption problems in this country. The next chapter discusses family financial management in greater detail. The last two chapters in Part Two deal with saving and investing to further family security and with the use of insurance to protect the family from financial disasters.

1

What are the characteristics of family incomes in this country?

There are about 62 million families in the United States, of which more than four-fifths are made up of two or more persons. The remainder are single-member families. The median family income is more than 8000 dollars per year. (A "median" is the central or middle number in a distribution of numbers in descending order. A median family income, therefore, means that one-half of the country's families have higher incomes and one-half have lower incomes.)

There are wide differences in family incomes. The United States has the highest average incomes and the highest overall living standards of any country in the world. Even "the poor" in this country live better than many considered relatively "well off" in the developing countries. Furthermore, present-day "poor" have much more than did the nation's "poor" in earlier generations. But there is a vast gulf between the incomes of the very rich and of "middle-income" families, and a sizable difference between the middle income level and the poverty level.

Ten per cent of the lowest-income families in the United States receive only 1 per cent of the total income. At the opposite extreme, 10 per cent of the highest-income families receive 30 per cent of the total income. One-half of the country's families receives 22 per cent of the total income, whereas the other half receives 78 per cent. But these figures alone cannot bring out the wide spread in family incomes.

Income tax statistics give an indication of the range of incomes. Federal income tax returns are not always a measure of family income, because in some families more than one person may file returns. Nevertheless these individual tax returns may be used to bring out the wide differences in income.

During a recent year, more than 100 persons reported an income of more than 1 million dollars and about 2600 others reported incomes between 500 thousand and a million dollars. (It may be difficult to grasp the meaning of a million dollars. If a person should spend 100 dollars every day in the year, it would take him more than 27 years to spend a million dollars.) About 78,000 other persons had in-

---

THE DISTRIBUTION OF INCOME

The distribution of income among each 10 per cent of the population has hardly changed since World War II. While incomes in general have risen, each tenth of the population has remained in relatively the same position. The lowest tenth still garners only 1 per cent of the national income; the fifth tenth has received about 8 per cent, and the highest tenth receives about 30 per cent.

This inverted pyramid has been called by some a weakness in American society. The government has periodically moved to equalize the distribution of income through tax reform bills and anti-poverty measures. Nevertheless, the basic structure has not changed significantly in 25 years. Poorer Americans have voiced frustration at their inability to garner a larger share of the nation's income. During periods of economic stagnation, the middle class complains of its inability to "get ahead." At the same time, some economists advocate adoption of an "incomes policy" to combat inflation. This means a wage-price freeze, which would introduce more rigidity into the distribution of incomes. Clearly the situation is not an easy one to change.

Distribution of income among each tenth of the population

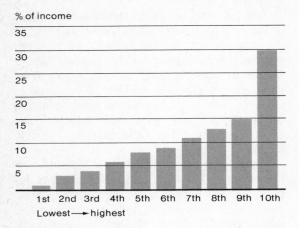

% of income

Source: Statistical Abstract

ferent ways. But whatever the definition, the amount of income needed to maintain an adequate livelihood depends also upon such factors as family size, the ages of family members, and where the family lives. To provide some usable income standards for determining the extent of poverty in this country, the federal government has defined "poverty income" levels for urban and rural areas, and for families of different size.

According to recent federal guidelines, a nonfarm family of four persons must have an income of more than 3600 dollars per year to be above the poverty line. A nonfarm family of six must receive 4800 dollars per year. The poverty line for farm families is lower. A farm family of four is in poverty if it receives less

comes of between 100,000 and 500,000 dollars per year, and an additional 300,000 had incomes of between 50,000 and 100,000 dollars annually. Altogether, the average income of all those receiving more than 50,000 dollars per year was about 96,000 dollars.

During that same year, more than 21 million persons reported incomes of less than 3000 dollars. The average income for this group was about 1412 dollars. Many of these persons, of course, were not family breadwinners. Some were students or housewives, while others worked only part-time or during only part of the year. Many, however, were full-time workers, or persons who would have worked full time had they been able to do so.

The "middle income" group—those with incomes ranging from 7000 to 15,000 dollars—had an average income of about 12,000 dollars per year. This group, which included 34.5 per cent of all the income-receivers, reported 46.3 per cent of the total income.

Many families live in poverty. A family is "poor," or living in "poverty," if it does not receive sufficient income to buy adequate food, clothing, shelter, and health services. Of course, different people may define "adequate" in dif-

Distribution of family income among income brackets

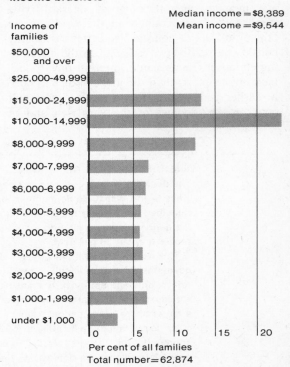

Median income = $8,389
Mean income = $9,544

Per cent of all families
Total number = 62,874

Source: Statistical Abstract

Number of top wealth-holders (thousands)

total	4,130
under $100,000	2,330
$100,000–199,000	1,130
$200,000–499,000	490
$500,000–999,999	120
$1,000,000 or more	50

Source: Statistical Abstract

than 3000 dollars, and a family of six if less than 4000 dollars. There are a number of other similar classifications.

Recent findings estimate that more than 25 million persons, or about 12.8 per cent of the country's population, are members of poverty-level families. The number and percentage of poor people in the nation's population, however, has decreased substantially in recent years, but this fact provides small comfort to those who still are below minimum desirable standards of living.

Poverty is not limited to any one race or place. In recent years a great deal has been written about the poverty of nonwhite people in the inner city. Such areas certainly have the greatest concentration of poverty, and this fact makes for explosive situations. But poverty exists in all parts of the country—in rural areas and small towns, as well as in the big cities.

About three-fourths of the poor in this country are white. On a percentage basis, however, poverty is more than twice as common among nonwhite families. Although most of the nonwhite poor are Negroes, the percentage of poor is greatest among reservation Indians and Eskimos. There also are large numbers of poor among Mexican-Americans in several southwestern states, and of Puerto Ricans in large cities in the East, especially in New York City.

About two-fifths of the country's poor live in rural communities. Figured as a percentage of the rural and urban populations, respectively, rural poverty is greater than urban poverty. It is less "visible" than urban poverty because the latter is far more concentrated. Since the range in income levels generally is smaller in rural areas, the contrast between the poor and the prosperous is less than in the big cities.

Many poor families are headed by women. About 1.5 million families living at the poverty level have a woman below 65 years of age as their head. About one-sixth of these families live in rural areas, the remainder in cities or in small towns. Almost one-half of them are nonwhite.

Many of these families depend on public assistance under the Aid to Families with Dependent Children (AFDC) program. The level of support is determined by the individual states, but each state program is supported by federal as well as state funds. Many women heading AFDC families cannot work outside the home because they must care for their small children. Moreover, if the earnings of a family receiving AFDC assistance exceeds a given small amount, its assistance is reduced. This restriction in effect discourages recipients from seeking outside work.

Many of the poor are old, ill, or disabled. About 5.5 million persons over the age of 65 are living at poverty levels. Because most of them are unable to obtain employment, they usually live on relatively fixed incomes. These come from Social Security, private retirement pensions, and various forms of public assistance. Rising prices for food, shelter, clothing, and other essentials create hardships for the aged poor. Increasing medical costs constitute a particularly serious problem, since illness is much more common among the old than among people of working age.

Among the poor of working age, a considerable number are unable to work because of illness or disability. The financial problems confronting these persons are similar to those of the aged poor.

Households in poverty, classified by head

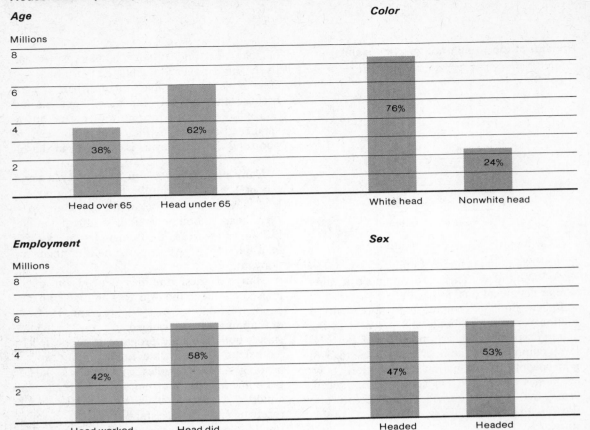

Age

Color

Employment

Sex

It is clear above that the incidence of poverty is disproportionately high among households headed by the aged, the unemployed, the nonwhite, and females.

Source: Statistical Abstract

Many poor families include an able-bodied person of working age. At least one-third of the country's poverty level families include persons able to work. Some of these persons work full-time and others part-time. They are poor because they cannot find regular employment at sufficiently high wages to bring them above the poverty income level. The great majority of the poor certainly do not prefer living in poverty to working.

It is a matter of grave concern to all citizens that in a country where living standards are high and rising, some able-bodied and willing workers cannot earn enough to support their families above poverty levels.

Many reasons are given in explanation of inadequate earnings. Doubtless discrimination against nonwhite minority groups has contributed to low income levels among these groups. Labor union policies, in some cases, have excluded qualified nonwhite workers from employment. Some employers in their hiring, training, and lay-off policies have favored whites for the higher-paying jobs. On the other hand, inferior education in segregated schools has handicapped members of minority groups in their efforts to qualify for well-paying occupations. Recent antidiscrimination laws and a growing sense of social responsibility on the part of union leaders and businessmen, and pressure from the minority groups themselves, are breaking down some of these barriers.

Although racial discrimination cannot be ignored as a cause of poverty, the elimination of discrimination would not eliminate poverty. The problem is more basic than this.

Low earnings may be related to low worker productivity. In discussing the relationship between productivity and wages (see Chapter 4), it was pointed out that an employer who must make normal profits to remain in business will try to hire the most productive workers.

Suppose that the going wage for a particular job is three dollars per hour, and the employer needs one additional worker. Two persons apply for the job. The employer estimates the productivity of one applicant to be five dollars per hour, and that of the other only four dollars per hour. Which would he be likely to hire? Should the employer find the productivity of neither worker to be as much as three dollars per hour, then what would he do?

Determining productivity, however, can be an elusive task. If an employer needs an accountant, he will have to pay one according to the prevailing salary scales for accountants. Productivity will have very little to do with it. The supply-and-demand market for workers with special skills will determine the wages an employer will have to pay such persons, quite apart from the degree they can "produce."

Since the 1930's, two other major factors have influenced the labor market. One is the Fair Labor Standards Act, which sets a "floor" under wages of $1.60 per hour for the millions of workers covered by the Act. The other is the labor movement, which has organized more

Federal support for work and training programs, 1973

Manpower Development and Training Acts	$ 425
Neighborhood Youth Corps	517
Concentrated Employment Program	155
JOBS (federally financed)	118
Work Incentive Program	155
Job Corps	202
Public Employment Program	962
Other	143
Total (in millions)	2,697

Source: Statistical Abstract

than 20 million workers into unions and has influenced the wages of millions more who are not yet unionized.

A rise in wages for low-income workers seems most likely to come about through a combination of job training and job placement services, the unionization of workers who are still unorganized, and the enforcement of state and federal antidiscrimination laws.

Government programs attempt to soften the blows of poverty. For the many families that have no member who can work, public (government) assistance seems likely to continue to be the only solution. The federal and state governments operate various programs to improve living standards for the poor. One of these, the AFDC program, has already been mentioned. Additionally, there are programs for the blind and the totally disabled. Food programs include "food stamps" which enable low-income families to buy food at low prices, "hot lunch" programs for schools, and some direct distribution of food packages. Public housing and rent supplements provide better shelter for a small number of poor families. Various kinds of public health service programs help the aged, the disabled, dependent children, and families on welfare.

Altogether, at the beginning of the 1970's, the federal government was spending approximately 15 billion dollars annually on various programs of direct relief to the poor. This is a very large sum. Yet, in terms of the national income, it amounts to only about 2 per cent. The important question to be raised about this spending is whether these programs provide the best approach to (1) making poor families self-supporting, and (2) earning incomes above estimated poverty levels.

Public assistance programs effect a "redistribution" of income. Governments obtain most of their funds from taxes levied on the incomes of persons and businesses. When funds are allocated to public assistance programs, there is a *redistribution of income.* Those paying the taxes have less money for consumption and savings; those receiving benefits have more.

Considerable redistribution of income is necessary for the survival of some of the very poor. Few Americans would oppose this policy. But there are definite limits to what can be accomplished by any reasonable redistribution plan.

It is sometimes said, for example, that no one person "should" have an income above some specified level—a million dollars, 100,000, or even 50,000 dollars per year. Such a statement implies that any incomes above the specified level "should" be drained away by taxation and then redistributed. The adoption of such a plan, however, could not completely resolve the problem of poverty.

Suppose that all income above 1 million dollars for persons receiving more than a million dollars per year is added to the total income of all persons receiving less than 3000 dollars per year. Were this sum divided among all members of the low-income group, the average income of each of them would be increased by about six dollars per month.

Or suppose that all persons with incomes above 100,000 dollars per year were required to put aside that portion of their incomes in excess of 100,000 dollars. Suppose again that all of this set-aside money were divided among

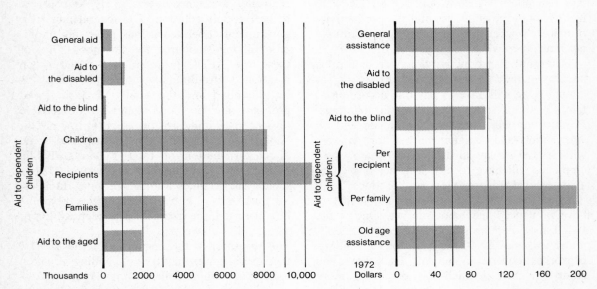

Number of welfare recipients by category

Average monthly payment by category

Source: Statistical Abstract (all four graphs)

low-income persons. The result would be that each individual in the low-income group would receive about 35 dollars of additional income per month. Only a very drastic redistribution of income, therefore, would completely eliminate poverty. One should ask what other means, if any, could be used to achieve the abolition of poverty from the United States.

If the productivity and income-earning ability of all persons receiving incomes of less than 7000 dollars per year could be brought up to the 7000-dollar level (which the Department of Labor considers the minimum income on which a family of four can be supported adequately), the total amount of consumer goods and services available in the country each year could be increased by more than one-third.

Income redistribution must continue to provide for those unable to work. But the best approach to helping low-income workers able to work, and the best solution for the country as a whole, is to provide programs that will increase productivity and thus increase their income and social mobility.

CHECK UP

1. What is the range in income of middle-income families? How was the poverty level defined in a recent federal guideline?

2. What general conclusions can be drawn about the poor? Why is urban poverty more "visible" than rural poverty?

3. What reasons are given to explain the inadequate earnings of many workers? What are some approaches to bringing about higher wages for low-income workers?

4. Describe programs provided by state and national governments to help the poor.

5. What are limitations to the redistribution of income as a solution to the problem of poverty?

Total public welfare expenditures by source

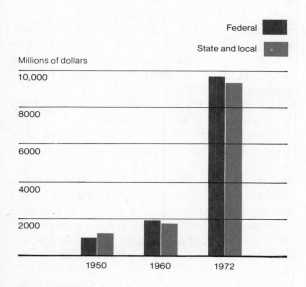

Total government expenditures for public welfare by program

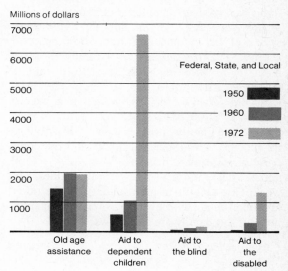

2

What are the characteristics of family consumption?

The size of a family's income limits and influences its consumption expenditures. Poor and low-income families must watch their spending very carefully. Only by buying cheap foods and inexpensive clothing and living in low-priced housing, can they make ends meet. These families usually must skimp on medical and dental services, spend very little for recreation, and save little, if any.

Families with higher incomes buy more and better food and clothing, live in better houses or apartments, and can afford more adequate medical services. Despite this higher level of spending, the percentage of income allotted to basic necessities by high-income families is much smaller than that of low-income groups. Families with higher income also spend more on recreation, travel, and other items that would be considered luxuries by low-income families. Usually they also are able to save some part of their incomes each month.

The "average" family spends about two-thirds of its income for food, clothing, and shelter. The Rosselinis are a family of four, living in a "working class" or "lower-middle income" district of a medium-sized city. Mr. Rosselini, in his mid-30's, works in a bakery and earns 8400 dollars per year. This is near the median family income. After withholdings for income taxes, Social Security, and the company pension plan, his "take-home pay" is 560 dollars per month. Mrs. Rosselini does not work. One child is in high school and the other in junior high. The average monthly expenditures of this family are as follows:

Food	$140.
Clothing	60.
Mortgage payments (house)	85.
Payments on furniture and household operations (utilities, minor repairs, etc.)	75.
Transportation	70.
Medical and dental care	25.
Recreation	35.
Education expenses for children	8.
Life insurance for Mr. Rosselini	12.
Miscellaneous expenses, and savings	50.
	$560.

The consumption pattern of the Rosselini family is fairly typical for urban families of similar income and size. They can afford basic necessities, but little money is left for luxuries and savings. They can make ends meet as long as the breadwinner holds his job. After the children have left home, perhaps their expenses will decrease.

In about another 30 years, Mr. Rosselini can retire. Their home will be paid for, and their annual income from Social Security and the company's retirement plan will amount to about one-half of the amount of Mr. Rosselini's average earnings during the last five years of his employment. This should be adequate for their old age unless there is considerable inflation.

Inflation causes hardships for retired middle-income families. Mr. Rosselini's Uncle Albert sold his small business and retired ten years ago. With the money from the sale of his business Uncle Albert purchased an "annuity" which pays him 420 dollars each month. He and his wife have no other income.

Uncle Albert had thought that the two of them would live comfortably on this fixed monthly income in their old age. But soon after retirement he noticed that prices were rising. Ten years later, the purchasing power of his annuity has been reduced by nearly one-fourth.

Uncle Albert and his wife have had to move into a smaller apartment in a less desirable neighborhood. They shop carefully for "bargains" such as "day-old" bread and "very ripe" vegetables and fruits. They study newspaper advertisements of special sales. Uncle Albert has not bought a new suit of clothes in three years. Because of the sharp increase in bus fares, he seldom goes back to the old neighborhood to visit friends.

Inflation has upset Uncle Albert's retirement plans, and he is too old to seek employment. Although his living standards are lower, he still is well above the "poverty line." Hence he is not eligible for public welfare assistance. Uncle Albert can only watch his purchasing power decline, and hope that things will get better. But compared to many families, Uncle Albert and his wife are well off.

The very poor have few choices in spending their income. Mrs. Cleveland lives in the inner city. In her early 30's, Mrs. Cleveland is the mother of six children ranging from three to thirteen years of age. She cannot work because of her small children. The total family income of 236 dollars per month comes from public welfare assistance. This family's consumption pattern differs significantly from that of the Rosselini family.

The Clevelands pay a rent of 70 dollars per month for three small rooms on the fourth floor of a "walk-up" apartment building. They share a bathroom with three other families. In winter their rooms are cold; in summer they are hot.

Mrs. Cleveland feeds her family for 96 dollars per month (about 46 cents per day per person). She uses surplus food from the federal food program, and the four oldest children get free lunches at school. The family consumes very little milk and fresh fruits. The children seldom are hungry, but their diet is far from well-balanced. This fact may explain why they tire easily and suffer from many colds and other minor illnesses.

Monthly payments on their few pieces of furniture (bought second-hand some years ago) and other household expenditures amount to 35 dollars a month. By using "hand-me-downs," patronizing the lowest priced clothing stores, and accepting clothes from charitable organizations, monthly clothing expenditures are held to an average of 24 dollars, or $3.43 per person. Some free medical service is available through the federal and state assistance programs.

The listed expenditures for necessities leave the Clevelands only 11 dollars per month, plus whatever small sums the older children can earn from odd jobs, for all other purposes.

Even high-income families often feel that they are financially hard pressed. Mr. Aldo, the principal owner of the bakery where Mr. Rosselini works, last year had an income after taxes of more than 40,000 dollars. He lives in the suburbs, owns a weekend cabin on a lake 200 miles north of the city, trades for a new car each year, and takes a month's annual vacation in Europe or the Caribbean. The Aldo children attend private schools. This is luxurious living compared to that of the Rosselinis, Uncle Albert, or the Clevelands. But Mr. Aldo often complains to his wife about the size of their bills.

After paying the living expenses "required" of a family in their situation, the Aldos last year saved about 3000 dollars. Mr. Aldo usually works at least 60 hours each week except during vacation. He is worried about the high cost of materials and labor, increasing taxes, and the competition from larger bakeries.

Although the Aldo standard of living is much higher than average, Mr. Aldo is troubled by economic problems similar to those that bother less well-off breadwinners. He wishes that he could make more money so that he could invest more to insure security in old age.

Very few people can afford to buy without regard to prices. No one has an unlimited supply of money. But a few families have sufficient incomes to buy whatever consumer goods and services they want without regard to prices and without concern for future financial security. Some members of this small group inherited large fortunes accumulated during the nineteenth and early twentieth centuries. Others have made their own fortunes. Some of them do no work and live lavishly. Others work long hours and live modestly—from choice, not from necessity.

Most people in this country live comfortably. Only a fraction of all American families are very poor, and far fewer are very rich. Each year many of the poor move into the lower-middle income class. The average present-day working class or professional family is well fed, well clothed, and well housed compared to earlier periods in this country's history. Most Americans take for granted a standard of living that would have seemed extravagant to their grandparents.

CHECK UP

1. The monthly budget of a lower-middle income family is given on page 122. Compute the per cent of monthly income spent for each item. Try to make estimates for Uncle Albert, Mrs. Cleveland and the Aldo family. What conclusions may be reached?

2. Why is inflation a problem for each family? How does the present standard of living for families at various income levels compare with that of their grandparents?

3

What safeguards have been provided for consumers?

Every family in the United States may be considered a unit of consumption. It may appear at first that families are relatively unimportant in the economy, but taken together, the routine purchases of all families amount to some 400 billion dollars per year. Nevertheless, most families do operate on a restricted budget. Chapter 2 brought out that satisfactions are maximized by balancing the utilities of various goods and services against the amount of money available for spending. Because families have limited budgets, the needs of each member must be weighed against the needs of the others. That is to say, the principle of marginal utility is applicable to the family as a whole, and not merely to one individual.

Besides utility, most consumers choose products for family consumption on the basis of advertising. Companies spend large amounts of money on advertising through radio, television, magazines, newspapers and billboards in order to attract and influence buyers. Products that are essentially the same, such as aspirin, detergents, or breakfast cereals, tend to have the largest advertising budgets.

The appeals of advertising often make intelligent choice difficult, because they present such a barrage of confusing and conflicting information. Packaging is another source of bewilderment for consumers. The significance of labels such as "family size," "jumbo," and "giant economy package" is lost in many cases.

The expression "Let the buyer beware" makes the point that ultimately the buyer must make a decision and bear the consequences of his action. Fortunately, various government and private agencies protect consumers against outright fraud and flagrantly harmful products. Available also are various kinds of information to help consumers in choosing between competing products.

Consumer protection is provided by federal, state, and local laws and agencies. When some flagrant abuse arouses the ire of consumers, they are likely to demand that the government do something about it. Sometimes a few crusading individuals are able to get people aroused. About the turn of this century, a novel by Upton Sinclair, which exposed unsanitary conditions in the meat-packing industry, brought about corrective changes in that industry and strict inspection of meat by the United States Department of Agriculture. A 1910 report on medical education by Dr. Abraham Flexner led to great improvements in the professional education of doctors and in the quality of medical services. More recently,

For the consumer: protection

Both private and governmental agencies are active in the effort to protect the consumer against goods which may be harmful or falsely advertised. Quality control by the manufacturer, inspection and consumer protection agencies of both the state and federal governments, and private testing services are all engaged in preventing the sale of sub-standard goods.

Before the Food and Drug Act was passed in 1906, a wide variety of "patent medicines" were advertised guaranteeing instant cures, **a.** The Food and Drug Administration now affixes its grading labels on many products, **b,** along with those of private testing laboratories and the manufacturers themselves. Below, **c,** a federal meat inspector looks at beef.

a

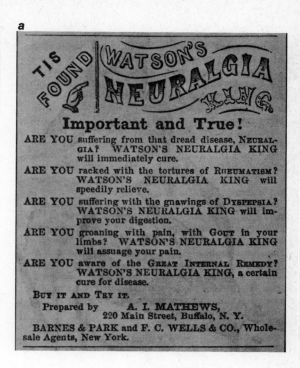

'TIS FOUND WATSON'S NEURALGIA KING.

Important and True!

ARE YOU suffering from that dread disease, NEURALGIA? WATSON'S NEURALGIA KING will immediately cure.

ARE YOU racked with the tortures of RHEUMATISM? WATSON'S NEURALGIA KING will speedily relieve.

ARE YOU suffering with the gnawings of DYSPEPSIA? WATSON'S NEURALGIA KING will improve your digestion.

ARE YOU groaning with pain, with GOUT in your limbs? WATSON'S NEURALGIA KING will assuage your pain.

ARE YOU aware of the GREAT INTERNAL REMEDY? WATSON'S NEURALGIA KING, a certain cure for disease.

BUY IT AND TRY IT.

Prepared by   A. I. MATHEWS, 220 Main Street, Buffalo, N. Y.

BARNES & PARK and F. C. WELLS & CO., Wholesale Agents, New York.

b

USDA CHOICE

U. S. GRADE B

38 U.S. INSP'D & P'S'D

INGREDIENTS

Oat flour, wheat starch, sugar, salt, calcium carbonate, sodium phosphate, artificial colors, iron, niacin, and thiamine. BHT added to packaging material.

USDA A GRADE

LISTED UNDER REEXAMINATION SERVICE OF UNDERWRITERS' LABORATORIES, INC.

UL

c

d

Another federal inspector, in a routine check, passes on shrimp being cleaned in a seafood plant, **d.** Automobile inspection is carried out by the manufacturer as the cars come off the assembly line, **e.**

e

QUALITY CONTROL EVALUATION AREA

Drags are inspected by the manufacturer as well as by the federal government, *f.* Here radioactive carbon is used to check the characteristics of a new drug before it goes on the market. Prepackaged foods are made with the aid of many automatic devices. In *g,* the quality and quantity of dehydrated soup ingredients are controlled by electronic equipment. The recipe for each variety of soup is contained in an electronic "plug board" which is inserted into the unit.

f

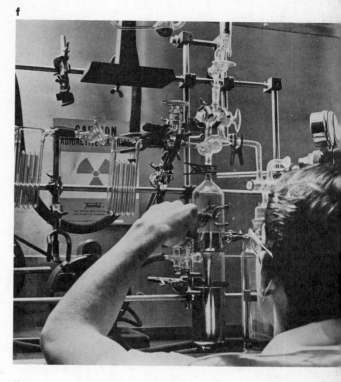

g

h

Private groups have become more important recently in pointing out new areas for government action. In **h,** consumer protection advocate Ralph Nader makes a point at a congressional hearing. His activities also have spurred government action in the field of consumer education. The informational leaflet in **i,** is one of many published by the consumer protection division of a state attorney general's office. Below, **j,** electric mixers made by different manufacturers are tested and compared in the laboratories of Consumers Union, a private group which publishes its findings. Consumers Union is one of the most highly respected organizations active in the consumer testing field.

i

j

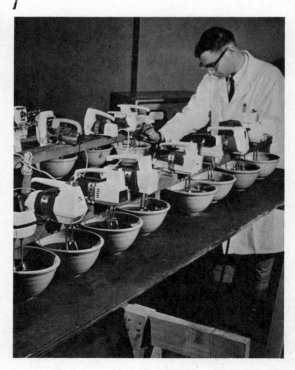

Silent Spring, a book by Rachel Carson, pointed out the dangers inherent in widespread use of harmful pesticides. Poisons that kill bugs may also kill birds and infect fish, with consequent ill effects on human beings. In the past few years a young attorney, Ralph Nader, gained prominence because of his "crusade" against motor vehicles which he alleged were "unsafe at any speed."

States have laws regulating weights and measures. Inspectors frequently check merchants' scales and gasoline pumps. By watching the scales carefully, one can be reasonably certain that he is not receiving short weights. The weights and volumes listed on the labels of packaged goods are generally accurate; however, because it is so easy to deceive consumers into thinking that they are getting more for their money, a number of states have passed "truth-in-packaging" laws which prescribe even stricter packaging and labeling standards.

Most state and local governments also have strict regulations to insure the quality of perishable goods. Milk, for example, is carefully checked at all stages of processing for compliance with approved hygienic standards. Restaurants must be licensed and must pass periodic inspection by health department officials. Food handlers who fail to meet specifications can be fined or their businesses closed if they are found guilty of persistent violations of sanitary codes.

The *United States Food and Drug Administration* (FDA) can order harmful food and drugs off the market and take legal action against their sellers. This agency's inspectors, scientists, and physicians do their utmost to guard the public from being harmed or deceived. Medicines must conform to the strength, purity, and quality claimed on the label, and must be safe if taken as directed.

The FDA is responsible for studying new pharmaceutical products. A few years ago, a new drug called thalidomide was widely prescribed as a sedative in Germany and certain other European countries. A skeptical FDA staff physician stopped this product from being approved for use in the United States. After a time, it was found that many expectant mothers who had taken this drug gave birth to seriously deformed children. Thousands of German babies were born without arms or legs. The FDA had prevented a similar major tragedy from occurring in this country. In a similar action in 1970 the FDA banned the use of cyclamates as "artificial" sweeteners in diet foods and low-calorie soft drinks because of evidence that when very large doses of cyclamates were administered to rats they developed cancer.

The *Federal Trade Commission* (FTC) prevents many kinds of unfair business practices. In particular, it seeks to end false and misleading advertising and practices which may lead

---

FEDERAL CONSUMER AGENCY PROPOSED

A federal consumer agency has been proposed by consumer protection advocates. They think that consumer representation at the agency level in Washington is necessary to deal with problems state and city agencies cannot handle.

Such an agency was outlined in a bill introduced in Congress in 1970. The bill provided that the new agency would represent consumers before federal regulatory bodies, other federal agencies, and federal courts. In addition, the agency would publish data on product performance by brand name, handle consumer complaints, and conduct research, investigations, and economic surveys useful to consumers.

Passage of a law setting up such an agency is probable in the near future.

Milestones in food and drug regulation

1897	The Tea Importation Act was passed, providing for inspection of all tea entering U.S. ports.
1906	The original Food and Drugs Act passed Congress and was signed by President Theodore Roosevelt.
1912	The Sherley Amendment prohibited labeling medicines with false and fraudulent therapeutic claims.
1923	The Filled Milk Act prohibited interstate traffic in milk or cream containing any fat other than milk fat.
1927	A separate law enforcement agency was formed, first known as The Food, Drug, and Insecticide Administration.
1938	The Federal Food, Drug, and Cosmetic Act was enacted.
1945	The FDC Act was amended to require certification of the safety and efficacy of penicillin.
1951	The Supreme Court ruled that a standardized food which does not meet its standard of identity cannot be sold legally unless it is marked "imitation."
1954	The Miller Pesticides Amendment streamlined procedures for setting safety limits for pesticidal residues on raw agricultural commodities and greatly strengthened consumer protection.
1960	The Federal Hazardous Substances Labeling Act was passed to require prominent warning labeling on hazardous household chemicals.
1965	Drug Abuse Control Amendments were enacted to deal with problems caused by abuse of three groups of dangerous drugs.
1966	The Fair Packaging and Labeling Act was enacted to require that consumer products in interstate commerce be honestly and informatively labeled.
1967	The St. Louis District converted into a national center for drug analysis to study intensively the Nation's drug supply.
1969	Reports on oral contraceptives denote current vital statistics on the efficacy of the drugs.

Source: Food and Drug Administration

to deceiving the public. Among other things, it sees that clothing, carpets, and rugs are properly labeled as to the content of cotton, wool, or other fabrics. The commission has recently cracked down on "promotional games" operated by food store chains and gasoline service stations.

The *United States Department of Agriculture* (USDA) is responsible for seeing that meat, fruits, vegetables, and various other foodstuffs sold in interstate commerce are not contaminated and that they are properly graded and labeled. The stamp of this agency, certifying the grade of a product, is highly reliable.

A *Consumer Advisory Council* was established by the President in 1962 to be "the voice of the consumer in the federal government." The activities and influence of this agency have been expanded by the Presidential appointment of a *Special Assistant for Consumer Affairs* and a twelve-member Committee on Consumer Interests. These have contributed to consumer welfare by pressing for the enactment of laws concerning packaging, labeling, and credit terms.

The *Truth-in-Packaging Act* of 1966 is intended to make it easier for consumers to compare prices. It encourages industry to limit and standardize package sizes of many common consumer items. This is only one of several consumer protection laws enacted by the national government in recent years.

Many private organizations also aid and protect consumers. The great majority of businessmen and professional people want to be fair and honest. But a few, including some of the biggest corporations, have resorted to illegal or unethical practices. Several influential private organizations or associations have been formed to apply pressure to those who violate generally accepted standards of conduct, and to aid consumers by making available pertinent information.

Better Business Bureaus are non-profit associations sponsored by reputable businessmen in many cities. They attempt to eliminate dishonest advertising and selling practices. One of their major targets has been door-to-door salesmen who descend upon a community to sell products and services which often are misrepresented or overpriced.

Older people, especially, have been victimized by high-pressure sales groups selling such services as "termite extermination" and "furnace repairs." Other groups may sell magazine subscriptions or encyclopedias which never are delivered, or undertake roofing, or siding, or spray-painting jobs at outrageously high prices. Uninformed consumers, many of them low-income families, provide fertile fields for such shady operators.

Better Business Bureaus also combat questionable practices in newspapers and on radio or television. If anyone has a question about some business organization, a phone call to the nearest office of the Better Business Bureau is likely to provide the information needed in deciding whether or not to buy. Of course all door-to-door salesmen are not crooks. And in a large community, a "local" business, even though it operates within the strict letter of the law, may be engaging in shady practices.

The *Consumers Union,* through its annual *Buying Guide* and monthly reports, keeps its members informed about "best buys" in many kinds of products. This organization purchases competing consumer goods on the regular market and tests them in its own laboratories. "Best buys" are recommended on the basis of the relationship of price to quality or performance. Some consumer co-operative associations perform similar services for their members.

The membership of the *American Medical Association* (AMA) and its state and local counterpart associations is made up of thousands of physicians throughout the country. Among other things, these organizations have as their goal high medical standards. They are interested in the training, qualifications, and professional conduct of medical doctors. They investigate and oppose medical practices that are a threat to the public's health. In particular, they fight "quack" cures, such as "miracle" cancer treatments by unlicensed doctors, and worthless or harmful "patent" medicines.

The AMA often is criticized for its alleged "conservative" viewpoints, lobbying practices, and "monopoly" control of the practice of medicine. It has opposed legislative efforts to bring medical care within the reach of the needy. It also has favored restricted enrollment in medical schools. The reason given was to insure the best possible preparation for the students admitted. But a result of this policy has been to create a serious shortage of physicians in many communities and to deny the admission of many qualified students to the profession.

Members of the *American Bar Association* and its affiliated state and local groups are concerned with the practice of law and the administration of justice. These groups recommend changes in laws and often recommend qualified attorneys for appointment as judges. Lawyers guilty of dishonest or unethical conduct may be reprimanded or even "disbarred" (expelled from their association). One who is disbarred usually cannot continue to practice his profession.

Many other private trade or professional groups, as well as hundreds of government agencies, attempt to curb sharp practices or to bring reliable information to consumers. But such organizations cannot be expected to protect all consumers in all situations.

The best form of consumer protection is provided by the informed consumer himself. An average person can make reasonably intelligent purchases most of the time, provided that he seeks pertinent information and follows some common-sense suggestions.

Only reputable sellers should be patronized. If there are any doubts about a seller's honesty or ethics, one is well advised to consult a Better Business Bureau office or one's friends and neighbors who have done business with the seller in question. One should avoid sellers who have a reputation for shoddy merchandise, poor workmanship, overcharging, and making unkept promises. Any document requiring a person's signature should be read with care—including the "fine print." On matters requiring an explanation, it may be desirable to consult a lawyer and pay his fee for services rendered.

Consumers should beware of strangers or recent acquaintances offering a "big bargain." Most "get-rich-quick" or "something-for-nothing" schemes benefit only the seller. Wise buyers realize that "there is no such thing as a free lunch." Intelligent shoppers, of course, do find bargains and save themselves money. But real bargains usually are not offered only to selected individuals. They are equally available to all potential buyers.

CHECK UP

1. What types of consumer protection are provided by local government? State government? National government? Private agencies?

2. What can the individual consumer do to protect his own interests?

FOR THE CONSUMER'S INFORMATION
The pamphlets listed below are published by various executive departments of the federal government for the benefit of consumers.

Buying Your Home Sewing Machine
Consumer's Quick Credit Guide
Borrowing for College, A Guide for Students and Parents
Money-Saving Main Dishes
Choosing a Hearing Aid
Pennywise Teenagers

These are only a few of scores of informative publications listed in *Consumer Information* (Price List 86) which may be obtained from the Superintendent of Documents, Washington, D.C., 20402. *Consumer Information* costs 10 cents; many of the publications are free, and others are available for a nominal charge.

Clinching the main ideas

This country has the world's highest overall family incomes and living standards. But all families must spend money wisely to obtain the most satisfaction possible, and to provide for possible future emergencies.

Incomes are not equally distributed. There is a small number of very high-income families and a considerably larger number of low-income or poor people. Poverty is not confined to any one racial group or geographic region. The largest number of poor are whites, and more poor live in rural areas and in small towns than in big cities. But in terms of a percentage, poverty is most common among nonwhites, and the greatest concentrations of poor are in big city ghettos.

This country's poor are a smaller percentage of the total population than is true in most other countries, and their numbers are decreasing. But the lot of the American poor may be more difficult than that of the poor in countries which provide socialized medicine, old-age care, and other similar services, as in Sweden or Britain.

Some low-income people are unable to work, while others have low productivity and therefore low earning power. Various government programs assist the poor. The best kinds of assistance programs, for those able to work, are programs designed to increase the productivity of workers.

Family consumption spending is determined largely by income levels. The principal buyer in the average family, usually the housewife, must make many decisions affecting the family's welfare. Most housewives, with a little experience, become shrewd shoppers.

A large number of government agencies and private organizations aid consumers by combating the "Let the buyer beware" philosophies of the relatively small number of unethical business operators. Although these agencies and organizations provide many helpful regulatory and informational services, they cannot protect consumers completely from their own follies. The best form of consumer protection is intelligent, informed, and alert buying.

Chapter 5 review

Terms to understand

1. median
2. single-member family
3. inner city
4. Social Security
5. AFDC program
6. FDA
7. FTC
8. AMA
9. Better Business Bureau
10. Consumers Union
11. American Bar Association
12. truth-in-packaging laws

What do you think?

1. What factors must be taken into account in deciding whether an income is adequate for a given family to maintain an adequate livelihood?

2. What are some of the shortcomings in current programs to help the poor?

3. If low wage rates are related to low worker productivity, what would be the effect of doubling the minimum wage?

4. To cope with the problem of inflation, some unions have obtained wage boosts and fringe benefits, and cost-of-living clauses to compensate for future price increases. What are the advantages and limitations of such contracts?

5. Since the purpose of advertising is to sell the goods advertised, does advertising help the manufacturer? The retailer? The consumer? All three? Explain.

6. Which person, publication, or organization do you feel is doing a good job of protecting the interests of consumers? Describe what is being done.

Extending your knowledge of economics

1. Turn to the "Help Wanted" page of the local newspaper and note: (1) jobs which seem to require no special skill and experience, and (2) jobs which call for specified skills, experience, and/or level of education, union membership, and the like. What conclusions can you draw about local job opportunities for skilled labor? For unskilled labor?

2. Study current federal income tax regulations to learn the size of exemptions and the amount of tax at various levels of income. Obtain the latest federal income tax form from the Office of Internal Revenue nearest you.

The welfare system— time for drastic change?

PROFILE OF THE POOR

Poverty in the United States is more prevalent among elderly persons than among any other age group. In 1968, the elderly poor (sixty-five years of age and over) numbered 4.6 million, or 18 per cent of the total poor, and they constituted about 25 per cent of all aged persons. . . .

The largest group of poor persons consists of children under eighteen. About 10.7 million children are poor, and they constitute 15 per cent of all children under eighteen. About 60 per cent of all poor live in families headed by a male, the remainder in families headed by a female. . . .

Poor children in . . . nonwhite families headed by women rose by more than a half-million (or 35 per cent) between 1959 and 1968, despite an overall decline (about 38 per cent) in the number of poor children in this period. . . . Poverty among children is also highly correlated with the size of families . . . about 44 per cent of all poor children are in families with five or more children. . . .

Of all population groups, households with dependent children that are headed by women increased by about 700,000 (or 24 per cent) between 1959 and 1968, despite an overall decline in the number of poor persons. The number of poor white persons in such families, on the other hand, declined by about 16 per cent, leaving the total number of persons about the same in 1968 as in 1959. The most obvious cause of poverty among families headed by women is the need of mothers to stay at home. . . .

Of the 39.5 million people who were classified as "poor" in 1959, some 7 million, or about 17 per cent, were receiving some form of cash allowances under public assistance. In 1968, of the 25.4 million poor people, some 10 million, or about 40 per cent, received such assistance. . . . Over the period from 1960 to 1969, the total amount of cash living allowances under public assistance almost doubled. . . .

Most southern states have had a reduced welfare population, while the northern industrial states have experienced a sharp increase in their rolls. To what degree public assistance payments, which are lower in the South than the North, account for this migratory pull is not known. Many authorities feel that the possibility of jobs at good pay has been a greater factor than welfare assistance in inducing migration.

. . . [An] unpleasant and unpalatable fact about the present welfare system in the United States is that those who must avail themselves of it in order to exist are consigned to a very low level of subsistence —even in states with the highest maximum benefits. . . . About half the states provided an allowance for a family of four of $2,400 or more, while below that the allowance ranged down to $600 a year. . . .

These figures speak eloquently of the real failure of the welfare "system," namely, its reflection of the larger national failure to have a proper regard and concern for the welfare of its less fortunate minority.[1]

Why have welfare?

An often-heard criticism of the American economic system is that poverty exists amid plenty. This charge cannot be refuted simply by pointing out that poverty has always existed, and still exists, under various other kinds of economic systems. There are in the United States several hundred persons with incomes of more than one million dollars per year and thousands receiving more than 100 thousand dollars. The median annual family income is 8000 dollars. Thus, many critics contend, the country is wealthy enough to improve the standard of living for millions of other people living in poverty.

Apart from the economic possibility that the United States is affluent enough to eliminate severe poverty, there are other considerations which make poverty more than an economic decision. Politically and socially, poverty poses a danger to society. People who think themselves unjustly consigned to live on the edge of existence are likely to rebel in one way or another. They may simply vote against the party in power, or protest policies to which they are opposed. Or some may feel driven to disrupt a society in which they have no place.

Once it has been decided to alleviate poverty, economic resources become the means to achieve that goal. Because economic resources are limited, optimum progress toward reducing or eliminating poverty can be made only if the most efficient use is made of the allotted resources. Some policies will achieve better results than others, even when

1 Committee for Economic Development, *Improving the Public Welfare System,* April, 1970.

expenses and number of persons involved are equal.

Public welfare assistance to the needy is one of several methods that can be used in fighting poverty. Private charity, and various forms of public assistance for some of the poor, have always existed in the United States. It was not until 1935, during the Great Depression, however, that the present form of public welfare assistance was organized. Most persons would agree that the present form of public welfare assistance does a better job than earlier forms. The important question is, however, whether an alternative form might not do a still better job. This is the question posed for analysis.

Background: the status of welfare in 1970

Public welfare assistance presently helps mainly families with dependent children (AFDC), and the needy blind, ill, or disabled. These needy persons include families and individuals of all racial backgrounds, living both in urban and rural areas in all parts of the country.

Actually, there are more rural and small-town poor than big-city poor, but the largest concentrations of poverty are located in large urban centers.

Aside from humanitarian considerations and the human and economic waste that results from poverty, dense concentrations of poverty in the big cities contribute to various social problems—crime, delinquency, broken homes, poor educational environment, drug abuse. These problems involve economic costs and wastes. While money spent on welfare and related programs is usually calculated at 1 per cent of the gross national product,[2] the real cost may be much higher. Mr. Joseph C. Wilson, chairman of the Xerox Corporation has put it this way:

Suppose that the true cost of poverty, discrimination, and deprivation in the country is not 1 per cent of the GNP, but more nearly 7 or 8 per cent. Not $10 billion, but closer to $70 or $80 billion a year. . . .

There is evidence that such is, indeed, the case. A sampling of a slum population in Sacramento, California, recently conducted by the U.S. Department of Health, Education and Welfare, showed that 20 per cent of the total population accounted for 60 per cent

of the use of the community's health services; 76 per cent of its tuberculosis; 41 per cent of its police protection; 36 per cent of its juvenile delinquency; 42 per cent of adult crimes; 26 per cent of the fires; and yet paid only 12 per cent of the city taxes. In a second city, for every dollar spent on police, fire, and health services in a good area, the costs in a blighted area were $1.87 for police, $1.67 for fire services, $2.25 for health services.[3]

The public welfare program adopted in 1935 (and continuing into the 1970's) gave major administrative control to the individual states. In general, each state had a fairly free hand in determining the maximum assistance to be given its citizens, and in setting the standards and conditions under which this assistance would be granted. This policy was adopted in recognition of differing needs, conditions, costs of living, and abilities to pay among the several states. It was also a concession to "grass roots" control of the program.

The accompanying graph shows the maximum monthly benefits received by a family of four under AFDC.

By the beginning of the 1970's, more than 9 million persons were drawing some form of public welfare assistance. Total expenditures for the program at all levels of government amounted to more than 5.5 billion dollars annually. Overall, a little more than one-half of these funds came from the federal government, about 12 per cent from local governments, and the remainder from state governments.

During the late 1960's many state and local governments had begun to complain that the burden of public welfare assistance was becoming too heavy for them to bear. They wanted the entire expenditure, or at least a larger amount of it, to be borne by the federal government. This was especially true in poorer sections of the country, and in the large cities where a large percentage of the population was receiving welfare assistance.

At the same time, however, many middle-income workers and taxpayers were complaining about "freeloaders" on public welfare. Many of them apparently believed that large numbers of able-bodied adults were receiving such large wel-

---

2 See Chapter 13 for an explanation of gross national product.

3 Joseph C. Wilson, "Welfare and Pragmatism," *Saturday Review* (May 23, 1970), p. 32.

The answer to the problem we have posed requires nothing less than a fundamentally reoriented approach to the problem of stability, so that full employment *without* inflation can be realized. Inevitably, as we shall see, there must be provision for public employment, as part of such a plan, as well as training and basic education for those who cannot get immediate jobs in private industry. But above all, the problem of instability must be frankly and boldly confronted.[7]

Toward better understanding

QUESTIONS TO CONSIDER IN ANALYZING THIS CASE

1. What trends are suggested by the data included under the heading "Profile of the Poor"?
2. Why does Joseph C. Wilson think that the true cost of poverty is not 1 per cent of the GNP but more nearly 7–8 per cent? Do you agree? Why or why not?
3. When the public welfare program was adopted in 1935, why was major administrative control given to the states? Currently, what are the sources of the money spent for welfare? On what grounds has the program of public welfare assistance been criticized? Which criticisms seem valid to you?
4. How does the "negative income tax" work? What criticisms of the plan are made by Faltermayer? What are your conclusions?
5. How does the "children's allowance" plan work? What criticisms of it are made by Faltermayer? What are your conclusions?
6. How does the "family assistance plan" proposed by President Nixon work? What are advantages to this approach? What doubts about the

plan are implied by Ulmer? What are your conclusions?

THINKING ABOUT THE BASIC ECONOMIC ISSUES

1. The Soviet Union boasts that under communism there is no unemployment. Why might unemployment be less of a problem in the Soviet Union than in the United States? What price would workers pay for such "security"?
2. Ulmer states, "The failure to provide jobs, of [all] . . . simple guaranteed income plans, is fatal to the avowed objective of fighting poverty." Yet more than half of the poor are 65 or older or children under 18. Would "full employment" necessarily solve the problem of poverty?
3. Ulmer states that "the American economy has teetered back and forth between excessive unemployment and rampant inflation, never pulling wholly free of either one. . . ." What does he mean? Do you agree? He also states that the nation's goal should be to provide "full employment *without* inflation," and that this goal cannot be achieved without "provision for public employment." What does this mean? Do you agree? Why or why not?
4. Clearly there are many jobs that need to be done in this country to insure a more beautiful and healthful environment. Litter in parks and streams, in streets and vacant lots is one example. Would public employment to "make America beautiful" be a wise expenditure of public funds? Would the unemployed wish to do such work?
5. "Training without job opportunities is like a larder without food. . . ." Apart from "the stop-go economy common to . . . welfare states," why is it difficult to predict what job skills will be in great demand five, ten, or 20 years hence?

[7] Melville J. Ulmer, *The Welfare State* (Boston: Houghton Mifflin Company, 1969), pp. 93–94.

chapter six

Managing the family's finances

1. How can expenditures be made to fit incomes?
2. How can families use credit wisely?
3. Where may families obtain credit?
4. What is the role of savings in family financial management?

If you would know the value of money, go and try to borrow some.

BENJAMIN FRANKLIN,
Poor Richard

The word "economics" comes from two ancient Greek words that mean "household management." Modern economics, of course, is concerned with much more than the economic problems of families. But for most people, day-to-day economic decisions usually are directly or indirectly related to the household. Wise management of its financial resources is of utmost importance to the family's welfare.

The family is similar to a small business firm in that it is concerned with obtaining the greatest amount of output (satisfactions) from the use of its limited resources (income). To do this, the family must choose between short-time and long-time objectives and among alternative courses of action. Much as a business, the family must plan and control its expenditures to obtain the "best" economic results.

Unlike most business managers, however, many family "managers" have little education or experience specifically designed to improve their efficiency as managers. They must learn through experience, and some are slow learners. That is one reason why some families with good incomes run out of funds long before payday. Generally, such families have not planned expenditures in line with their incomes.

This chapter discusses some of the major problems with which families must cope in spending their incomes, and suggests some useful methods for achieving family consumption and security goals.

1

How can expenditures be made to fit incomes?

Impulsive and unplanned buying often leads to financial difficulties. Many persons, when they have money in their pockets and see something they want, simply buy it. Next week they may see something that they want even more, but their money has already been spent. "Impulse buying" is a constant problem for many individuals and families. The very poor may have little choice about how their incomes are spent. But most families have sufficiently large incomes to permit some discretionary buying.

Families can avoid many financial difficulties by planning their expenditures. In order to plan, the family must know what it wants to achieve. Obviously no family can long permit its monthly expenditures to be larger than its monthly income. But in planning major expenditures, such as buying a home, a car, or a television set, it is necessary to look more than a month ahead. There is a need, too, to save something for a rainy day. Whatever spending the family has in mind, planning is valuable and may be essential.

A family budget is a useful device. A budget is a list of planned expenditures that takes expected income into account. The family usually knows approximately the income to be received next week, next month, or perhaps even next year. Members of the family can soon list about how much must be spent for "unavoidable items" such as rent or mortgage payments, utility services (gas, electricity, water, telephone, and the like), and for "time payments" on debts already incurred.

By deducting the amount of these relatively "fixed" expenses from expected income, the family determines how much more money it actually controls. This amount can be used to acquire the items most needed or wanted. Ideally, of course, a budget should make provision for saving some part of the income to build up a fund for emergencies or future needs. Unfortunately this may prove very difficult or even impossible for low-income groups.

It is important, of course, to follow a budget as closely as possible. But sometimes emergencies arise which throw the budget out of balance. This is one reason why it is desirable to budget some amount for savings. Should the family consistently spend more for certain items than was planned, either the budget is unrealistic or family members are not properly controlling expenditures and "balancing the budget."

Budgets may be useful aside from their value in helping to keep spending within income. Often the very preparation of a budget suggests the need to reduce certain expenditures in order to spend more wisely.

A budget cannot tell a family what it should buy. Patterns of spending, within the limits of one's income, are determined to some extent by the comparative intensity of various demands. Even within the same income group and in the same neighborhood, the budgets of two families may differ greatly. But regardless of priorities, a well-thought-out spending plan is likely to increase the satisfactions a family gets from its income.

Some families keep a balance sheet as a record of their financial condition. A balance sheet is a list of *assets* (what one owns and what others owe him) and *liabilities* (what one owes others). The difference between a family's assets and liabilities is its *net worth*.

Comparison of this year's net worth with the net worth in previous years reveals whether the family is holding its own, is moving ahead, or is falling behind financially. If the family is falling behind, or is not getting ahead as fast as seems desirable, a careful examination of the family budget should be undertaken to make whatever adjustments seem necessary and to control expenditures more carefully. Most families want to have their net worth increase from one year to the next.

In summary, to obtain the greatest amount of current and future satisfactions from family income, it is necessary to: (1) know where the family now stands financially; (2) know where the family wants to be financially in the future —perhaps next month, next year, five or ten years hence, or even at the age for retirement; (3) have a definite plan for achieving such financial goals; and (4) follow this plan insofar as possible. These procedures are essential for good financial management, whether for a family, a business, or even the nation.

What a typical urban family might include in a budget for one year

Fixed expenditures for year	**Savings**	335
	Emergencies not covered by insurance	165
	Seasonal outlays	2248
	Taxes	1400
	income and social security	1199
	property	120
	sales and excise	50
	gas and automobile license	31
	Insurance	608
	life	160
	personal property	75
	health and accident	111
	hospitalization	108
	fire and theft	78
	automobile	76
	Education expenses	55
	Debt reduction	185
		Total $2748

Regular monthly or periodic obligations	*Rent or mortgage payment*	1255
	Utilities	335
	telephone	65
	gas, electricity, and heat	270
	Installment payments	929
	furniture or equipment	179
	car	750
	Other	253
	club dues	30
	contributions to churches and charities	223
		Total $2772

Day to day needs	*Food*	2143
	Household expenses	216
	Clothing	684
	Transportation	534
	Medical and dental expenses not covered by insurance	373
	Recreation and travel	306
	Incidentals	724
	personal allowances	438
	haircuts and cosmetics	214
	laundry, dry cleaning, and clothing repairs	72
		Total $4980

Source: Studies by U.S. Department of Labor. Figures are estimates for a family of four with a yearly income of $10,500.

1. What are logical steps to take in preparing a family budget? What are the advantages of a budget?

2. What are the advantages of keeping a balance sheet?

2

How can families use credit wisely?

A family is using credit when it borrows money or buys goods or services without paying for them immediately. Credit is important to the consumer, to business, and to the nation. Perhaps as much as 90 per cent of the business transacted in this country uses credit in one form or another. This chapter, however, is concerned with the use of credit by consumers rather than by producers.

The use of consumer credit (debt) has expanded rapidly in recent years. Years ago, most consumers were reluctant to go into debt. They felt that being in debt was evidence of lack of thrift or of a sense of responsibility. Most families used credit only in an emergency. Today most families find the use of credit convenient and useful. Credit is widely used in buying homes, cars, furniture, clothing, food, gasoline, and a host of other goods and services. Many people even take vacations on a "go now and pay later." basis.

Today consumer debt is more than eight times greater than in the late 1940's. Recent figures show that family debt for housing (not including farm housing) is more than 300 billion dollars, and that other consumer credit is about 120 billion dollars. This means an average consumer debt of about 2100 dollars for every man, woman, and child in this country, or about 60 per cent of average personal income.

During most years, considerably more consumer debt is incurred than is repaid. This re-

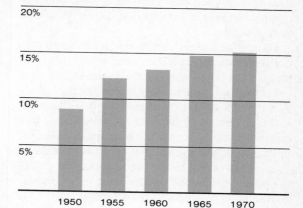

Total installment payments as a per cent of personal income after taxes

Source: *based on* Statistical Abstract

sults in part from a growing population and a rising level of average income, year to year. But it is also true that Americans are becoming more credit-minded. Twenty years ago, average consumer debt as a percentage of average consumer income was less than half what it is today.

Aside from housing, the largest items of consumer debt, in order, are for automobiles, other consumer goods bought on installment plans (that is, regular payments, usually monthly), personal loans, charge accounts, and home repair and modernization loans. Most families today, whatever their levels of income, make use of some form of credit.

Young families often use credit when their needs are greatest. When a young couple is starting out in life and bringing up children, family income often is low. The breadwinner, however, may reasonably expect to earn more later in life. Because current family expenses are high, the young married family may go into debt for a house, furniture, a car, and various other things. They expect to pay these debts later. Perhaps the house may not be fully paid for until the children have grown up, family expenses have decreased, and family income has risen. By going into debt, the family's wants have been met while the wants are greatest. This is a method of balancing income and expenditures over a long period rather than one year at a time.

A careful use of credit enables a family to consume while it earns or even before it earns, rather than postponing for years the satisfaction of its wants. Unfortunately, some families go so deeply into debt that they find it difficult to make payments when these are due. Credit can be useful, but it can also be misused. And it must also be recognized that credit is expensive.

Whether or not to use credit should be determined by the family in the light of its needs, wants, and resources. Before buying on credit, it is well to ponder these questions: (1) Is this purchase necessary, or merely a luxury or convenience that one can do without? (2) Can the family meet this obligation from future earnings without sacrificing other more important items? (3) Does the family understand the conditions and obligations it accepts under this credit contract? (4) Is this the best credit available?

Credit is often used for convenience. Even families that can afford to pay cash often use credit. Few would be willing to get up at the crack of dawn each morning to pay the milkman or the newsboy. Such payments usually are made once a week or once a month.

In the same way, many families use *charge accounts* at stores, or *credit cards* issued by large financial organizations for various kinds of purchases. The user is billed for these expenditures in one lump sum, usually once each month. Even though a small "service charge" may be added to such a monthly bill, many people find this procedure more to their liking than paying cash at all times or writing many small checks.

Emergencies may make borrowing necessary. Sometimes families are forced to seek credit to meet an unexpected financial crisis. Loss of or damage to property, sudden serious illness, or a long period of unemployment may place a heavy financial burden upon a family.

Under such circumstances, few families have saved enough to pay the bills. At such times credit is not a matter of choice but a necessity. Lending organizations refer to credit extended for such purposes as *remedial*. It is a remedy to help the family increase its income to meet extraordinary expenses.

In such a situation, money is borrowed directly from lending agencies. Money may also be borrowed for making a cash purchase of goods when a family determines that the amount of interest paid on the loan will be less than the expense of buying goods on the installment plan.

Large transactions such as buying a home are made easier by borrowing. Few families have saved enough money to pay cash in buying a home. Rather than wait until enough money has been saved, the family makes the purchase on credit while its earning power is still good. Members of the family are also agreed that they prefer home ownership to paying rent. After their debt is paid off, the house is theirs. When one buys a house on credit, the credit installment is known as a mortgage.

Under certain conditions a house will sell more easily with a mortgage than without one. Most families have to place a mortgage on the house they buy. Naturally they wish to obtain the loan at the lowest possible rate of interest. Interest rates vary but are usually high in a period of inflation. If a house offered for sale is carrying a mortgage at a lower rate of interest than could be obtained on a new mortgage, prospective buyers are attracted. They could save money by purchasing the mortgaged house and taking over the existing mortgage.

Installment buying may be wise or unwise. It is generally less expensive to pay cash for purchases. But if the cash is not available, an installment purchase may be made. The purchaser makes a small cash "down payment" and agrees to pay a certain amount each month until the debt is repaid. The monthly payment normally also includes the interest.

The "buying" of credit, like the buying of any good or service, should be done with care. The buyer should remember that he is not asking for a favor. Actually, he is buying a service (credit) from a business organization which engages in selling goods for profit. Just as a consumer should shop around to get the best buy for his money, so he should shop around for the best credit terms. Installment buying can become very expensive.

Consider the following example. A young secretary on her first job wanted to buy a wristwatch. She found just the watch she wanted, priced at $99.95, but she did not have that much money. The store clerk explained that she could buy the watch by making a "down payment" of nine dollars plus twelve monthly payments of the same amount. Although the secretary was strongly tempted to buy the watch on this basis, she decided to think it over for a day or so. She calculated that the total cost of the watch would be 117 dollars instead of

$99.95. This would mean that she paid $17.05 in interest on a debt which never could be greater than $90.95. Thus, she would be paying the equivalent of an annual interest rate of more than 40 per cent.

Another secretary suggested that she might borrow the money needed from the credit union operated for the benefit of the employees of the company. This was done and a loan of 90 dollars was arranged. With this money and $9.95 of her own money, she bought the watch. She had agreed to repay the loan at the rate of 15 dollars per month plus the credit charge of 1 per cent per month on the "unpaid balance" of the debt. She also paid a single "service charge" of two dollars. At the end of six months the secretary's debt to the credit union had been repaid. Altogether, the watch had cost her $105.10 rather than $117. Her interest charge, including the two dollars service charge, had been $5.15 rather than the $17.05 asked by the jewelry store.

WATCH YOUR CREDIT BUYING!

With an *installment loan*, interest rates may be twice as high as advertising seems to suggest. Under traditional ways of lending money the borrower repays a loan after having had the money for a specified length of time. For instance, a person borrowing $1200 at 6 per cent for one year has the use of the money for the full year and repays $1272 at the end of the year.

Interest on installment loans is not so easy to determine, however. Here the loan is repaid in time installments and the borrower does not have the full use of the principal for the full period of the loan. Yet he pays interest as if he did! For example, a consumer who borrows $1200 on installment credit has to pay back one twelfth of the principal each month. As the year goes by, therefore, he retains the use of less and less of the borrowed money; in fact, his average amount for the entire year is $650. Yet he has paid interest on $1200. We know that 6 per cent interest on $1200 is $72. But paying $72 interest on a loan that averages $650 amounts to paying interest at the rate of 11 per cent!

Not only must consumers be wary of types of loans, but they must also be careful in choosing their sources of credit. The table below shows the amount of interest which different credit institutions would charge for a one-year loan of $300 to purchase a refrigerator:

Credit Unions	$18–$ 36
Banks	$24–$ 52
Small Loan Companies	$54–$126
Installment Purchase Credit	$30–$ 72

Those who lend money or advance credit want reasonable assurance that the debt will be paid. Business concerns that lend money or extend credit are interested in the "credit rating" of prospective customers. They need to know whether the customer will be able and willing to repay his debt.

When asking for credit, one may expect to be asked such questions as: Have you borrowed or bought on credit before? If so, when and from whom? Did you make all payments when due? Is your present and expected income large enough to make the required payments after meeting other necessary expenses? Should some emergency arise, such as illness or loss of employment, can you still meet your payments?

Many businesses use the services of a *credit bureau* to obtain information about the credit ratings of prospective borrowers or credit customers. The expense of maintaining this agency is shared by most of the lenders and merchants in a community. The bureau maintains files showing the repayment performance of most local people who borrow, buy on installment plans or charge accounts, or use credit cards.

When a person fails to meet a payment that is due, this information may be noted in his file in some credit bureau. Then, when that person again asks for credit, it may be refused him because he is listed as a poor credit risk. It may thus be difficult to obtain credit if one's past record of repayment has not been satisfactory. If a person has never borrowed money and has always paid cash for his purchases, he will not have a file in a credit bureau. And, ironically, if a credit bureau has no file on an individual who is applying for credit, the applicant may have to answer many questions to establish a good credit rating. To obtain credit easily, it

Credit extended by retail outlets

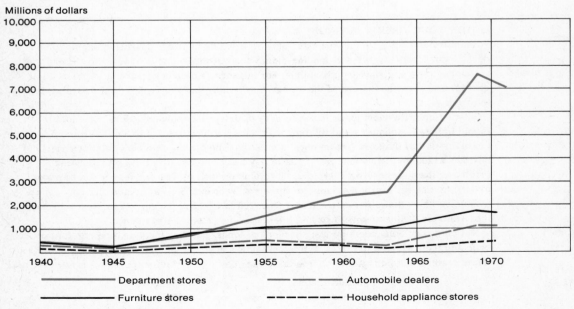

Millions of dollars

Source: Department of Commerce

helps to be a frequent borrower or credit user who makes payments on time. Many of those in the credit business are skeptical about persons asking for credit unless they have used credit before!

"Security" may be demanded by those extending credit or making loans. If a television set is bought on an installment plan or "conditional sales contract," the set may be "repossessed" by the seller if payments are not made when they are due. Homes, cars, furniture, and many kinds of major appliances customarily are sold on this basis. One should always read sales agreements carefully and make sure that he understands his rights and obligations.

Personal property (that is, property other than land or buildings) often is acquired by a *chattel mortgage*. This means that the possessor of the property can use it, and is entitled to any income received from its use. But he cannot sell or transfer the property to anyone else until the debt against it has been paid.

Banks and other lending agencies sometimes ask prospective borrowers to furnish *collateral* for a loan. This means that the borrower pledges some kind of property, often corporate stocks or bonds, as assurance that the loan will be repaid. Pawnbrokers make loans on this basis, although more tangible kinds of property —such as watches or jewelry—are usually involved. Loans supported by adequate collateral usually can be obtained more easily and at lower interest rates than is customary for unsecured loans. There is less risk and costs to the lender are usually lower.

Personal loans are often made without collateral. If one's credit rating is good, one may be able to borrow small amounts without pledging any specific security. But if a borrower does not pay his debt, the creditor may be able to *garnishee* the former's wages. To do that, the creditor must obtain a court order requiring the debtor's employer to pay him (the creditor) a certain amount of the debtor's wages each payday until the debt is repaid. A creditor may

also obtain a court order *attaching* a debtor's property to satisfy an unpaid debt. If the debt is not paid, the attached property may be sold.

Debtors, however, are protected by law against unjust or harsh garnishment or attachment. A creditor must follow established legal procedures, and the debtor is entitled to retain a certain minimum amount of his wages and property. But attachment or garnishment is expensive and ruins one's credit rating.

Cosigners may take the place of other security. In some instances credit sources are willing to accept the signature of a *cosigner* as sole security. Some lending organizations insist on a cosigner regardless of whatever other form of protection they receive. The person who cosigns a loan contract indicates his willingness to accept responsibility for paying the debt should the borrower fail to meet his obligation. Anyone who asks an acquaintance to cosign a loan contract is really asking a favor almost as great as if he were requesting a loan of the money itself. A cosigner must be prepared to pay the full value of a loan if the debtor fails to meet payments when they are due.

Credit involves an expense. A charge account at a store may increase the cost of the goods purchased. It entails an added operating cost for the businessman. The latter must keep records and send bills. Should he be unable to collect the amount owed, he must go to court to get his money. To meet these costs, he must charge more for his product. This added charge is usually borne in part by those who pay cash as well as by those who buy on credit. This situation leads some people to open charge accounts because they feel that they are paying for the convenience anyway. However, some businesses have a *carrying charge* for charge accounts so that they will not have to increase prices to cash customers.

Lenders are entitled to payment of interest. Those who lend money on installment contracts or extend credit over a long period of time usually add an interest payment to the amount of the account. By extending credit on large purchases they are taking a greater risk than businessmen who offer small charge accounts. Also, their own money is tied up longer in the goods sold on credit. They are, in effect, exchanging present cash for future cash. Chapter 4, in discussing capital goods used in production, stated that a person (or a business firm) normally must be paid something additional in the form of contractual interest to offset time preferences for present goods over future goods.

Money usually is borrowed by means of a promissory note. A promissory note is a contract under which a borrower agrees to repay the money borrowed, plus a certain percentage of interest, by a specific date. Sometimes such notes are repayable at the demand of the lender.

Usually, promissory notes are *negotiable*. That is, like most checks, they can be properly endorsed and transferred from one person to another. If the lender wants his money before the date required by the contract, he simply sells the note to someone else. (Installment and conditional sales contracts often are sold in the same way. Notes and contracts of this kind are a part of what is called the *commercial paper market.*)

In some cases, the interest on a promissory note is paid when the principal is repaid. On other notes, especially those used by banks, the interest may be paid in advance; this is called *discounting*.

For example, if one borrows a hundred dollars for a year at an interest rate of 8 per cent, with interest and principal payable at the end of the contract, he will have to repay 108 dollars. But if the 8 per cent interest is discounted at the time of the loan, he will receive only 92 dollars and repay 100 dollars at the end of the year.

In the latter case, since the borrower actually had use of only 92 dollars for the year, in reality he paid interest at the rate of almost 8.7 per cent rather than at the rate of 8 per cent.

Although the nominal rate of interest is 8 per cent, the true rate is 8.7 per cent.

CHECK UP

1. What is the trend in consumer debt? What are the largest items in this debt? What questions should a family ponder before buying on credit?

2. Why do most families buy a house on credit? Why may a mortgage make it easier to sell a house?

3. What procedures do business concerns follow before agreeing to lend money or extend credit? How can a creditor recover money owed on an unsecured loan?

4. What is a cosigner? Carrying charge? Promissory note? Discounting?

3

Where may families obtain credit?

This chapter already has shown that a great deal of credit is granted by sellers in the form of mortgages, charge accounts, installment or conditional sales contracts, and similar devices. It was also brought out that banks and other agencies, not themselves engaged in selling goods, make loans for use in consumer buying. This section concerns certain of these "non-merchandising" lending agencies. (Lending carried on by life insurance companies, however, will be treated in Chapter 8.)

Commercial banks are major lenders. Banks perform the useful functions of accepting demand deposits for safekeeping and honoring checks drawn on these deposits. Banks also accept *savings deposits* or *time deposits*. The bank pays the depositor interest on these accounts. The depositor, however, cannot write checks against his savings account and may be required to give the bank advance notification before making withdrawals. The major function of banks, however, is to lend people money.

Early banks were used mainly as places for the safekeeping of valuables. Banks had their beginnings hundreds of years ago when rich moneylenders had strong vaults and tough guards. Gradually, their neighbors and acquaintances began to leave their money, jewels, and other valuables with these moneylenders for safekeeping. The moneylender probably charged depositors a small fee for this early kind of banking service.

The "fractional reserve" system was developed. Money left for safekeeping with one of these early moneylenders might be called for in a few days, or it might be left for months, or even years. As the number of customers and the amounts deposited increased, the moneylenders found it was unlikely that all of their customers would ask for their deposits at the same time. Only a fraction of the deposits, therefore, had to be kept on reserve to meet day-to-day demands for withdrawals. For that reason moneylenders could, if they wished, lend some of their customers' money at interest —a safe practice as long as sufficient funds were kept on hand to meet the customers' daily demands. Thus began commercial banking, based upon the *fractional reserve system*. This is the principle upon which modern commercial banks operate.

Through the years some banks have failed. From the earliest times banks have attempted to provide sufficient reserves to protect themselves against "runs," that is, sudden withdrawals by a great many people. They have also attempted to operate on a sound financial basis. In spite of these precautions, however, there have been many bank failures down through the years.

In the United States, during the Great Depression of the early 1930's, there was an epidemic of bank failures. Many depositors lost all their savings or eventually recovered only a few cents of each dollar deposited. To deal with this problem, President Franklin D. Roosevelt,

Total consumer credit and credit extended by financial institutions

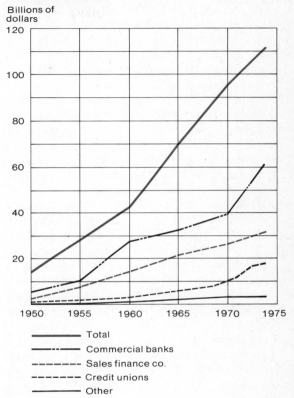

Billions of dollars

Source: Statistical Abstract

by an executive order, closed all of the nation's banks for a few days in 1933 until measures could be taken for the protection of their depositors. This became known as a "bank holiday," and led directly to the formation of the Federal Deposit Insurance Corporation (FDIC). All banks except a small number of state-chartered banks, are now members of this agency.

The FDIC initially insured the *first* 5000 dollars of each depositor's account. Later the amount insured was increased to 20,000 dollars. Since an individual may have accounts in as many different banks as he pleases, anyone of average means can now deposit his savings with complete assurance that they will be available when needed. If a bank fails, the depositors are insured against losses up to 20,000 dollars each. Bank failures in this country have been rare since the establishment of FDIC and the adoption of bank regulation and supervision.

Banks obtain most of their income by making loans. Banks incur costs but earn no income from funds which are left in their vaults. In order to cover their costs they must lend their funds to borrowers and obtain payment in the form of interest on the loans.

If a man wishes to borrow 3000 dollars to remodel his house, he may go to the local bank to borrow the funds. If his credit is good the bank will approve the loan and turn over the 3000 dollars. In order to be assured of payment when it is due, the bank may require a mortgage on the house. When the bank carries such a mortgage the loan is called a *mortgage loan*. Payments on such loans are often made as monthly installments over a period of, say, five years. Banks also make smaller loans which are not covered by mortgages. Generally these are for shorter periods of time, perhaps three to six months.

Banks lend money to responsible borrowers. Commercial banks lend money both to businesses and to individuals. Large loans to business and agricultural enterprises account for a sizable proportion of the total number of dollars loaned by most banks. In recent years, however, the personal-loan departments of banks have become increasingly important. Small loans are made to individuals who, in many cases, are the bank's own depositors. Such loans not only add materially to a bank's total volume of loans made, but also attract more customers.

Regular depositors in a bank require little or no investigation by the bank, hence little expense, before being given a loan. A bank is actually lending to some of its depositors money left in the bank by other depositors. Since depositors obtain no interest on demand deposits, and only a low rate on savings accounts, the bank gets its loanable funds at low cost.

Savings-and-loan associations are major suppliers of mortgage credit. A savings-and-loan association accepts savings deposits and pays depositors interest on them, just as do the savings departments of commercial banks. (Technically, the "interest" paid by these associations may be referred to as "dividends.") They do not accept demand deposits and may require from 30 to 90 days' advance notice for withdrawals. Their interest rates paid to depositors are usually a little higher than those paid on savings accounts by commercial banks.

Savings-and-loan associations specialize in making mortgage loans on *real* property, that is, on land and buildings, especially homes. These institutions presently hold about one-third of all the mortgage debt in the country. This is approximately twice as much as the total volume of mortgages held by either of the next most important mortgage lenders, life insurance companies and banks.

Mutual savings banks are important in some parts of the country. There are over 500 mutual savings banks in approximately 20 states. Most of them are in New England and the Middle Atlantic states, but there are some in the Midwest and the Northwest.

The first mutual savings banks were organized about 150 years ago, to enable persons of modest means to save small sums. In fact, the names of a number of banks include such terms as "Dime" or "Five Cents." Chartered by the states, they invest the bulk of their deposits in real estate mortgages.

One important characteristic of mutual savings banks is that after paying expenses and taxes and setting aside reserve funds, all earnings are distributed to the depositors as interest. Deposits are insured by the FDIC or by guaranty funds.

Mortgage debt outstanding by type of holder

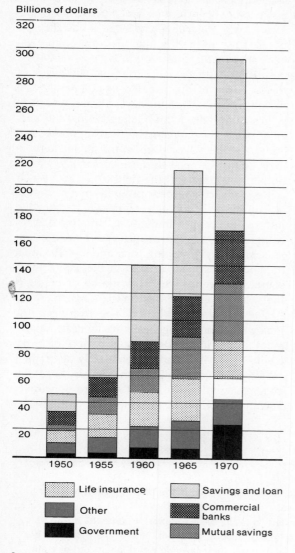

Billions of dollars

Life insurance | Savings and loan
Other | Commercial banks
Government | Mutual savings

Source: Statistical Abstract

Credit unions provide credit for groups with similar interests. A credit union is a co-operative association of people, usually having some common interest such as membership in a labor union, in a particular kind of business, or in a social group such as a church congregation. Members buy shares in the credit union for perhaps five dollars per share. A member may deposit his savings in the credit union, or he may borrow money from it. Ordinarily a fixed rate of interest is not paid on deposits as is done by banks, but dividends up to 6 per cent per year may be paid on the shares. These dividends represent the shared profits of the group's credit activities.

Shareholders elect the board of directors, who manage the investment of the deposits and capital of the group and determine the amount of credit which is to be extended. The maximum amount is determined by the size and economic condition of the group. The charge for credit is generally one per cent a month on the unpaid balance. Like other financial organizations, a credit union is regulated by state and federal laws.

Credit unions are able to give low-cost credit on small short-term loans because of their low costs of operation. They use regular banks for safeguarding their money. Their directors generally serve without pay. In most instances, because they know the persons to whom they are giving credit, they do not have to make costly investigations. Credit unions do little or no advertising, and the undistributed profit is kept low by state and federal regulations.

There are various types of licensed personal-loan agencies. Some licensed or legally recognized lending agencies specialize in "financing" installment purchases of cars, furniture, and appliances. In dealing with them, customers should always determine the true rate of interest charged. The fact that such goods can be repossessed makes it unnecessary for an installment buyer to seek a cosigner. But the very ease of such transactions should make one especially careful not to buy beyond his means. Should that happen, he may have to borrow cash, and without financial resources that is not easy!

Industrial banks (or the Morris Plan System) grant personal loans of money to persons of sound character who have little or no capital. These agencies generally require cosigners. Other organizations stress their willingness to save their customers the embarrassment of asking their friends and employers whether or not they are good financial risks. But a borrower must usually have such personal property as jewelry, furniture, or an automobile, or at least a good, steady job if he hopes to escape having to appeal to a relative or friend to guarantee his loan as cosigner.

Pawnbrokers make loans secured by pledged property. A pawnbroker makes loans, usually small, that are secured by such personal possessions of the borrowers as clothing, watches, or optical goods. This source of credit developed early in the history of credit because many families accumulated their wealth in personal property such as jewelry or art objects. By *pledging* or *pawning* these properties with a pawnbroker, people could borrow money on them when the need arose. As modern credit institutions have extended their services to include small loans, the pawnbroker has tended to pass from the scene.

Today, pawnbrokers must be licensed. They are regulated in their operation by state and municipal governments as well as by their own associations. A person wishing a loan takes his personal property—his "pledge"—to the broker, who determines its value for credit purposes. This amount is much less than the market value of the property. The customer, if he is satisfied with the appraisal and the terms of the loan, leaves his property as collateral for a period of from 30 to 90 days. Should he fail to return and redeem his pledge within the specified time by payment of the sum borrowed and the interest agreed upon, the pledge may, in most states, become the property of the pawnbroker, who then has the right to sell it.

Unlicensed sources provide much credit. A considerable amount of credit is extended informally between individuals. In almost every community there are people who extend credit as a means of investing their money. Personal judgment must be exercised in the use of these sources of credit. The best source of credit is that which is the cheapest in the long run.

Beware of loan sharks! The overwhelming majority of credit agencies are honest. To remain in business for a long period of time, credit agencies have to deal fairly with their customers. Nevertheless, the buyer of either goods or credit must accept some responsibility in choosing whom to patronize.

A LOOPHOLE IN LENDING LAWS

One loophole which remains in the field of loan protection is the nonregulation of loans made through the mail across state lines.

One company offering such loans mailed "a ready cash voucher" to persons not in its home state, offering them an unsecured loan of $600 at an annual interest rate of 34¾ per cent. Although most states outlaw such high rates, their laws do not apply to out-of-state firms.

One state attorney general contacted about this case said he would investigate whether the company was engaging in "unfair and deceptive advertising." The company's literature stated that it would not take wage assignments from loan applicants, implying that it would not garnishee wages. In fact, the company does use garnishment and lawsuits to recover its money.

The assistant attorney general of North Carolina said, "There's not one thing we can do for the poor suckers of this state who take the bait."

Low-income earners, unable to supply collateral to regular credit sources, sometimes find it necessary to obtain credit at unreasonable terms. They find themselves ready prey for *loan sharks,* unscrupulous operators who charge as much as they think they can get their victims to pay. Interest rates as high as 20 per cent a month (240 per cent a year) are not uncommon.

The notorious "six for five" plan is a favorite of big-city loan sharks. The borrower receives five dollars on Monday and must repay six dollars on Saturday. This is the equivalent of an annual interest rate of 1460 per cent! And woe to the victim who fails to pay on time. At best, the promised interest will be added to the principal debt, and it will be considered that a new loan for the total·amount is negotiated at the beginning of each five-day period. At the end of 30 days, the borrower will owe $14.92 for his original five-dollar loan. Even worse, if he does not pay promptly, he or some member of his family may suffer serious bodily harm. In some cities, loan sharking is a highly profitable operation for the most vicious elements in organized crime.

Loan sharks victimize the poor. Despite government efforts to curb abuses in moneylending, loan sharks do business in most large cities. They abound in the ghettos, where they victimize members of minority groups—Puerto Rican, Mexican, and especially Negro Americans. Since many members of these groups are in a desperate financial plight, they feel that they cannot bargain over interest rates. The legitimate credit channels are largely closed to them. Often they are unaware of laws that protect them against the illegal practices of loan sharks. Thus the condition of the urban poor is made yet more desperate. Here is a situation which cries out for change!

There are many state and federal laws for the protection of borrowers. To prevent excessive charges and undesirable and misleading credit practices, federal, state and local authorities constantly check the practices of lending organizations and those who sell on credit. The federal Truth-in-Lending Act, which became effective in 1969, for example, requires that persons using credit be informed of the true rate of interest that they are being charged and the total amount of the payments that they will have to make. Various state "small-loan laws" also impose restrictions on interest rates and credit practices.

This legal protection, and increased competition among those who supply credit, have improved the situation. Unfortunately, those most in need of protection are least informed about their rights, and therefore least able to protect their own interests. Government cannot completely shield citizens from those who would take advantage of them, and laws certainly cannot keep people from making foolish mistakes. As in many other matters affecting the welfare of consumers, the best protection is informed common sense.

CHECK UP

1. What is the primary purpose of banks? How does the fractional reserve system facilitate this function?

2. Describe how each of these carries on its business: savings-and-loan association; mutual savings bank; credit union; personal loan company.

3. What is the purpose of the Truth-in-Lending Law? Of small-loan laws?

4

What is the role of savings in family financial management?

Most families try to save a portion of their income. A plan for saving is just as much a part of good family financial management as is a plan for sensible buying or use of credit. Most married couples with young children recognize the need to provide for their future well-being.

Saving does not necessarily mean that a portion of one's income is deposited in a bank. Saving simply means that one does not spend all his income for immediate consumption purposes. The next chapter will discuss various forms that savings may take.

Savings are influenced by income levels. During a typical reasonably prosperous year, some 6 to 7 per cent of all "personal disposable income" (that is, income after taxes) in this country goes into savings. During the World War II years of 1943 and 1944, when consumer goods were scarce and employment high, savings amounted to about one-fourth of personal disposable income. Not since the severe depression year of 1933 have total personal expenditures exceeded total personal incomes. In that year, and in 1932, consumers as a group spent more than they received in income.

During recent years, the average amount saved in this country has been about 400 dollars per person. But averages of this kind may be misleading. During any year, many families, especially in the low-income group, save nothing. Some even draw upon past savings or go into debt. Most of the total saving is accomplished by the middle-income and higher-income groups.

Every family must meet such ordinary living expenses as those for food, clothing, shelter, and medical care. Higher-income families spend more for these necessities, but a smaller fraction of their total incomes, than do low income families. The higher the family income, the lower the percentage of income required for ordinary living expenses. This means that, in general, *the more money a family makes, the more it can save.* Most poverty-level families are not able to save anything.

Unforeseen factors influence individual family savings. Some families experience less illness and fewer accidents than others. Long illnesses or hospitalization, or unemployment of the principal family earner, not only reduces the ability to save, but may require the spending of past savings. Two families of the same size and with the same incomes, and living in the same neighborhood, may save very different amounts of money each year.

Even if family circumstances are not greatly different, savings patterns may differ. One fam-

Examples of savings growth through interest rates

At the end of—	*Amount of fund if $15 is deposited each month, with interest compounded semiannually at the annual rate of—*					
	2%	2½%	3%	3½%	4%	5%
	dollars	dollars	dollars	dollars	dollars	dollars
1 year	181	181	181	182	182	182
2 years	365	367	368	370	371	374
3 years	554	557	561	564	568	575
4 years	746	752	759	766	772	786
5 years	942	952	963	974	985	1,008
10 years	1,982	2,031	2,081	2,133	2,187	2,299
15 years	3,131	3,252	3,378	3,512	3,651	3,951
20 years	4,400	4,634	4,884	5,151	5,436	6,066
25 years	5,802	6,199	6,631	7,101	7,612	8,774

Source: U.S. Department of Agriculture, Consumer Research Division

ily may have a strong desire to spend and a weak desire to save; another family may have a much stronger desire to save and a correspondingly weaker desire to spend. The latter may save 15 per cent of its income; the former only 5 per cent. In the jargon of economists, the desire to spend is called "propensity to consume"; the desire to save, "propensity to save."

Generally, as people approach middle age, their propensity to save increases. They realize that eventually they will no longer be able to work. When they retire, they will have to live on their past savings and their retirement income.

Many private employers, as well as government, have programs for "enforced savings." The federal government requires employees in most occupations to pay a portion of their earnings into *Social Security* (discussed in Chapter 8). When a worker who has contributed to Social Security retires, he has a small but assured income for life.

Many private companies and governmental agencies have their own pension or retirement plans. Most of these plans are intended to supplement Social Security benefits. Typically, private or public employee pension plans plus Social Security benefits are designed to provide retired workers with an income of from one-third to one-half of their former annual earnings. Unfortunately, many retirement plans provide a fixed number of dollars monthly. Therefore they do not protect against inflation.

Planning and budgeting aid family saving. A family saves what it does not spend. In one sense, then, voluntary savings are "leftovers" from family incomes. The amounts of these "leftovers," however, are likely to be larger if family spending has been planned with specific goals in mind.

Many families find that they save more if a certain amount for savings is included as a regular item in their budgets. Some find it helpful to have a definite purpose in mind for their savings. A few persons seem to be instinctive savers, but most people in the middle and lower income groups have to work at saving.

How interest rates increase savings

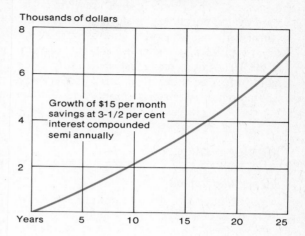

Thousands of dollars

Growth of $15 per month savings at 3-1/2 per cent interest compounded semi annually

CHECK UP

1. Why may two families of the same size and with the same income differ widely in the amount of income saved?

2. What are examples of "enforced savings"? Are these plans desirable? Why or why not?

Clinching the main ideas

Family financial management is like business financial management in many ways. Both businesses and families attempt to make the best uses of their limited resources. This involves numerous choices concerning how much to spend and how much to save, what should be bought, how much should be purchased for cash, how much on credit.

Families, like businesses, do best if they plan their financial affairs as carefully as possible. Many families use budgets as aids in their planning. Various other kinds of financial records also are essential for good financial management.

Credit is widely used by consumers (as by businesses). The proper use of credit may increase overall consumer satisfactions. But credit is furnished only at a price, and users must be wary of pitfalls. To get the greatest benefits for the least costs, one must shop around for credit, just as he shops around for the best buy in an automobile or refrigerator.

Most families save some part of their incomes, but some are unable to do so. Saving is dependent upon income levels and upon various other factors which one may be unable to control. Some saving is imposed upon most wage earners by government or private pension plans. Voluntary family saving is best accomplished through well-planned budgeting.

Chapter 6 review

Terms to understand

1. impulse buying
2. "fixed" expenses
3. net worth
4. liabilities
5. assets
6. collateral
7. chattel mortgage
8. credit bureau
9. pawnbroker
10. mortgage loan
11. conditional sales contract
12. commercial paper market
13. real property
14. loan shark
15. "six for five" plan

What do you think?

1. Why do not all families of the same size and at the same income level save about the same percentage of their income?

2. Why do many families prefer to use charge accounts and credit cards to paying cash for purchases?

3. The per capita consumer debt in this country is about 2100 dollars and is growing larger. Comment on the possible consequences of this trend.

4. Why has FDIC all but ended "runs" on banks?

5. During 1932 and 1933 consumers spent more than their total income; during 1943 and 1944 savings amounted to about one-fourth of personal disposable income; during a normal year 7 to 8 per cent of personal disposable income goes into savings. How might one account for such wide fluctuation?

Extending your knowledge of economics

1. Ask a local bank and other lending agencies for literature describing their services and the terms on which they extend various kinds of loans. Ask also for samples of the various types of notes a borrower signs in order to obtain a loan. Write a report summarizing your findings about loans.

2. The Social Security Administration is listed under "United States Government" in most big city telephone directories. From that office, obtain literature describing various Social Security programs, and prepare a summary. Ascertain how many students already have Social Security numbers and discuss the implications of having such a number on file in government records.

chapter seven

Investing for family security

1. Why is investing important?
2. What are common types of family investment?
3. How does one invest in corporate securities (stocks and bonds)?
4. What is a "good" investment?
5. What is meant by "real" investment?

Put not your trust in money, but put your money in trust.

OLIVER WENDELL HOLMES,
Autocrat of the Breakfast Table

Most people who save want their savings to earn additional income. That is, they want to *invest,* and thus to participate in the productivity and growth of the nation's economy. A given sum of money earning 6 per cent *compound interest* annually (that is, the interest is added to the principal each year, and in turn draws interest) will double itself in 12 years. Wise investment enables one to increase his savings substantially over a period of years.

Investment also is necessary for the growth of the country's economy. Chapter 4 points out that capital is necessary for production, and that capital is accumulated from savings. Unless savings are put to work, though, they contribute nothing to productivity. Most savers do not themselves use their savings to acquire real capital for production. What actually happens is that the relatively small savings of large numbers of people are channelled into the hands of firms or governmental agencies through various kinds of financial organizations, including banks.

Chapter 7 looks at the overall importance of investment, from the viewpoint of the individual and of the nation's economy. Consideration is given the common types of family investment, investment in corporate *securities* (stocks and bonds), and the characteristics of a "good" investment. Most people, especially those in the middle and low income brackets are not nearly as well informed about the matters as they should be.

1

Why is investing important?

Individual investment furthers family security and its income goals. Most family heads are concerned about the family's welfare both in the present and in the future. Through saving, the family can take care of possible future needs. But a given savings per month or per year will take care of many more needs if the money is earning interest in a bank or savings institution.

Should a family save 600 dollars per year—an average of 50 dollars each month—and their savings not earn anything, the family will have 12,000 dollars at the end of 20 years, or 18,000 dollars at the end of 30 years. But if these savings were earning compound interest at an annual rate of 4 per cent, the family would have more than 17,800 dollars after 20 years and more than 35,600 dollars after 30 years. If the earnings were compounded at an annual rate of 8 per cent, the amount would be more than 27,400 dollars after 20 years and more than 67,900 dollars after 30 years.

Investors are interested in safety and liquidity as well as in income. Since few families can afford to lose large sums by poor investment, the safety of an investment is of prime concern to small investors. Furthermore, since one reason for saving is to be able to meet unforeseen emergencies, most investors want at least a portion of their investments to be *liquid,* that is, invested in something that can be turned into cash readily.

Unfortunately, these three goals of safety, liquidity, and income are difficult to achieve at the same time. The safest investments usually do not yield the highest incomes and are not the most liquid. A wise investment program, for most families, first takes care of a minimum amount of safety and liquidity. After these conditions are met, additional investment can go into sources where earnings promise to be greater, but at some loss of safety and liquidity. Each investor must strike a balance that takes into account his circumstances and needs.

CHECK UP

1. Why should a family save some of its income? What are three major goals in saving?

2. Which of these goals are especially important for most families? Why?

2

What are common types of family investment?

Most families with savings maintain checking accounts, or demand deposits, in commercial banks. These accounts provide both safety and liquidity. They are insured in most banks (up to 20,000 dollars for each depositor in each bank) by the Federal Deposit Insurance Corporation (FDIC), and they are available upon

Interest-bearing deposits by type of holder

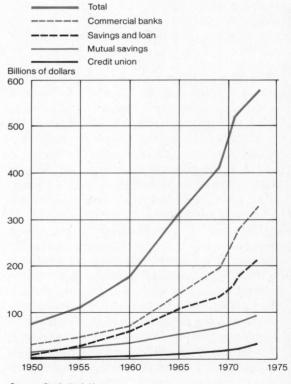

Source: Statistical Abstract

demand. But for the depositor, a checking account cannot be considered an investment. It earns nothing. Indeed a small "service charge" often is levied against checking accounts.

Savings accounts (time deposits) provide security and income. After a checking account reaches a level adequate for the family's routine transactions, a savings account often is started. Banks and savings-and-loan associations pay interest on time deposits in order to obtain funds for lending. Such accounts as are insured by the FDIC are safe. They are less liquid than checking accounts, however, since the depositor may have to give advance notice before withdrawal. Time deposits earn interest for the depositor, but the return is less than may be earned by less safe and less liquid investments.

Some form of life insurance is a common type of investment. Life insurance is a major form of investment for the average American family. This is often the only way in which a young family head, or one of small means, can provide funds for his family's security in the event of his untimely death.

One may receive an annual compound interest rate of about 4 per cent on a savings account. At this rate, it would take savings of 240 dollars per year for a period of about 25 years for one to accumulate 10,000 dollars. But a young man in good health can buy a 10,000 dollar life insurance policy for considerably less than 240 dollars per year. This means that in case of his death, 10,000 dollars would be paid to his beneficiary immediately. Life insurance is a quick way of providing essential financial protection for one's family. Additional information about life insurance is found in Chapter 8.

Buying a home may be a worthwhile investment. Owning rather than renting one's home has many economic advantages as well as some disadvantages. Some advantages are:

(1) The homeowner pays the actual costs of occupancy in his mortgage payments, taxes, insurance, upkeep, and *depreciation* (ordinary

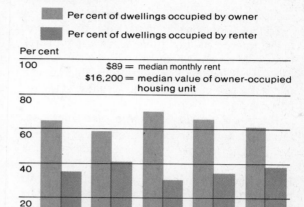

Ownership and rental of dwelling units by geographic area

Per cent of dwellings occupied by owner

Per cent of dwellings occupied by renter

$89 = median monthly rent
$16,200 = median value of owner-occupied housing unit

Source: Statistical Abstract

"wear and tear" stemming from use and the passing of time). Were he renting a house, his rent would include all these costs plus a profit to the property owner.

(2) After all the mortgage payments have been made (which may take 20 or 25 years), the homeowner has a debt-free house. In the future he is liable only for property tax, insurance, upkeep, and depreciation costs. The renter who has incurred comparably large expenses owns nothing and his expenses are not comparably reduced.

(3) The cost of rent tends to fluctuate considerably with changing economic conditions, while the costs of ownership tend to be more stable.

(4) Should the homeowner wish to sell his home, and the house is well built and in a good location, the value of his property will have remained relatively stable. During periods of inflation, the monetary value of a home tends to increase. It is equally true that during pe-

riods of deflation, property values tend to decrease. These economic forces are, of course, separate from aging and wear which gradually reduce the value of a house.

(5) A homeowner may save on income taxes. Interest paid on home loans and property taxes paid on one's home may be deducted from one's gross income in reporting taxable income for purposes of federal and usually state income taxes.

Home ownership has some disadvantages. Owning a home also raises problems:

(1) The average person selecting a house may fail to make a "good buy." Building materials and the quality of construction are so difficult to appraise that a purchase may be based on eye appeal rather than sturdiness, weather-resistance, and ease of upkeep.

(2) Many communities have tax problems. Young families with children desire schools, parks, recreational facilities, and police and fire protection. The cost of such services sometimes raises taxes to very high levels.

(3) The person who finds that he has bought a home in a deteriorating neighborhood may have difficulty selling the house for as much as he paid for it.

(4) If one buys a house in the outlying areas of a city, a portion of the savings effected by owning rather than renting will be offset by costs of transportation to places of work, schools, recreation areas, and shopping centers.

(5) Home ownership tends to limit freedom of movement. In a period when real estate prices are low, a better job in another community must be weighed against the disadvantage of having to sell one's home at the current market price.

(6) Some people would rather pay a higher monthly rent in order to be free of such chores as maintaining the yard and such unpredictable expenses as a leaking roof that has to be re-shingled.

Government bonds are safe and pay interest. A *bond* is a certificate of indebtedness. When a bond is issued by the local, state, or

U.S. savings bonds held by public

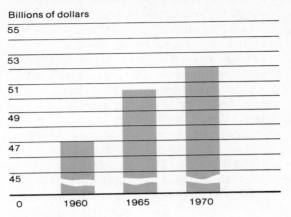

Source: Statistical Abstract

federal government, it is backed by that government's promise to pay. This is a *debenture* bond. The purchaser of the bond has loaned the government a fixed amount of money and will receive a fixed rate of return until the principal is paid back. Usually the agreement provides for an annual or semiannual interest payment for the life of the bond.

United States government bonds can be purchased through banks or through payroll-deduction plans. Most bonds of cities and states can be bought and sold through brokers, and in most cases the interest earned is not subject to federal income taxes.

City and state governments have been known to *default* (be unable to meet) their obligation to redeem their bonds on maturity. The bonds of the federal government, however, are as sound as the government itself. United States Savings Bonds are available in small denominations, but they pay a lower rate of interest than that earned on an equally safe savings account guaranteed by the FDIC.

Few small investors buy city and state bonds which usually are sold in amounts too large for small buyers. Many middle income families, however, buy some types of United States government bonds.

Some people invest in small local businesses. Many people with courage and initiative, who have acquired the necessary funds, use them to establish a commercial, farming, or manufacturing enterprise of their own. Some large present-day corporations began in this way. But a large proportion of small business ventures are short-lived, thus demonstrating the risk that is always involved when an investor puts all his eggs in one basket.

There are few opportunities to invest in a business that has already been established by an individual owner. Most of these businesses are financed by their owner-operators. If one does invest in such a business, the investment is usually a private loan, either with or without a mortgage as security.

CHECK UP

1. State the advantages and limitations of each of these forms of investment: savings account, life insurance, federal government bond, state or local government bond.

2. What are the advantages and limitations of home ownership as an investment? Of investing in a small local business?

3

How does one invest in corporate securities (stocks and bonds)?

Many families, after obtaining adequate life insurance, a nest egg of savings, and perhaps some equity in a home, turn to the stock market to invest additional savings. Corporation stocks and bonds, called *securities,* are bought for their expected earnings.

A corporate stock is a share of ownership in a corporation. A share of stock entitles its owner to receive *dividends* (that is, to share in the distribution of the corporation's earnings).

Stocks are bought both for dividend income and for anticipated growth in value as the corporation becomes more prosperous.

Sometimes the value of a stock increases rapidly; on the other hand, its value may also decrease. The possible return on an investment in stocks is greater than the usual return on savings accounts or government bonds, but the risks of loss also are greater. A person should not enter the stock market unless he knows what he is doing and unless he can afford to take the risk of possible losses.

Stock purchases are influenced by one's expectations for the future. Various factors may influence one in deciding which stock to buy. But the decision to buy stock, rather than to make some other kind of investment, usually reflects optimism about future economic conditions. An individual's expectations about future economic prospects, in turn, are influenced by the immediate past, as well as by his understanding of what has occurred over a longer period of time.

People vary greatly in their outlook on the future. Some are optimistic; others, pessimistic. Among investors as a group, optimism and pessimism seem to run in waves. This is reflected in the behavior of prices on the stock market. The nonprofessional investor is influenced by what others seem to be doing. For example, if stock prices have been declining, there may be a sudden rush to "sell at any price." Or if prices have been moving upward, small investors may rush to buy. These "ups and downs" in attitudes, through the working of supply and demand, often cause sharp fluctuations in the prices of stocks.

But for every sale there must be a buyer, and vice versa. Professional investors (both individuals and institutions), who deal with investments on a large scale, are well aware of the dictum "Sell when others buy, and buy when others sell." These professionals often exert a stabilizing influence on the market.

A pre-World War II stock market rule-of-thumb was that a stock is a "good buy" when its *price-earnings ratio* is about 10—that is, when the stock is selling at a price not more than ten times its annual earnings. This "rule" grew out of experience during the 1920's and 1930's.

Since that time investors have become accustomed to and accept stock price-earnings ratios considerably higher (and consequently yields considerably lower) than were acceptable during the pre-World War II era. Various reasons have been advanced for this change in the attitude of investors:

(1) They believe that a continued high level of economic growth in time will cause their investments to increase in value even though present dividends are low in comparison to the prices paid.

(2) They have faith in continued economic stability, which will prevent serious declines in stock prices from major depressions.

(3) They expect some degree of continued inflation. The ownership of common stock provides more protection against inflation than does investment in bonds or other securities yielding a fixed income.

Stock yields

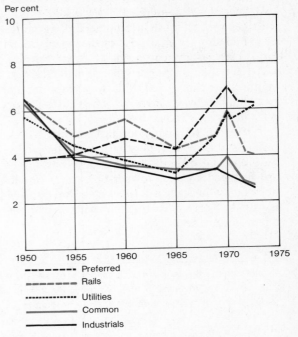

Source: Standard and Poor

STOCKHOLDERS' WINDFALL

In the early 1950's, few investors appreciated the importance of improvements being made in photocopying equipment. And fewer still could anticipate the sharp rise in demand for such equipment that would soon follow. But the "fortunate few" who bought shares in Haloid-Xerox (now Xerox) Corporation, leading manufacturer of copying machines, realized exceptional profits. First, Xerox's expansion led to several stock splits—each split giving two or more shares for each one held. Second, Xerox stock value rose steadily, going from $45 to $300 per share in about ten years. Thus an original investment of $450 for ten shares yielded the purchaser—through successive stock splits—some 640 shares, each share worth upwards of $300, for a total value of more than $192,000!

Unquestionably, there is some upper limit beyond which price-earnings ratios cannot climb (or conversely, some lower limit below which yields cannot fall) if investors are to continue buying stocks. Some authorities think we already are approaching this limit; others are not so sure. It is this difference of opinion, rather than actual changes in business conditions, that helps to keep the stock market active.

A corporate bond is a document acknowledging debt. In effect, when a corporation issues (sells) a bond, it borrows money from the buyer of the bond. A bond is an agreement by the corporation to pay the bondholder a specified rate of interest at specified times throughout the life of the debt, and to pay off the debt when it is due.

The income received by a bondholder is

Bond yields

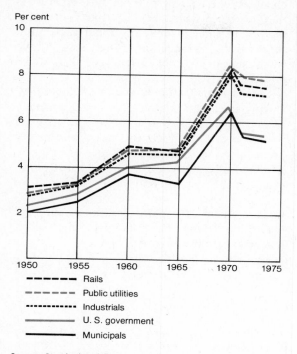

Per cent

Source: Standard and Poor

---

sell their securities through *investment bankers*. An investment banking firm, often called an *underwriter,* specializes in selling original issues of corporate securities to large investors. Thereafter, these securities may be traded (bought and sold) in large or small quantities through *stock exchanges* (or *security exchanges*) located in large cities. The New York Stock Exchange and the American Stock Exchange (also in New York) are the leading national exchanges. Several regional exchanges, such as those in Chicago, San Francisco, Boston, and Philadelphia, deal in stocks of local and smaller companies.

Buying stocks and bonds

1 Customer studies stock prices at local broker's office and places order for purchase with broker. He may tell broker to buy the stock at the best prices he can get, or at a specified price (*limit order*).

2 Broker transmits customer's order to the firm's New York office via telephone or teletype. The New York office phones in the order to the floor of the Stock Exchange.

3 The brokerage firm's telephone clerk on the floor receives the order. He goes to a spot on the floor where that particular stock is being traded.

4 The firm's Floor Member bargains with other representatives who are buying and selling the stock. When a price is agreed upon between buyer and seller, the order has been executed.

5 A record of the transaction (purchase or sale of a particular stock) is printed on ticker tape. This is flashed on screens in brokerage houses throughout the country.

---

fixed, according to the terms of the agreement. It does not fluctuate with the corporation's earnings. Bondholders usually have first claim against a corporation's income, and first claim against its assets should the firm fail. A bond, therefore, usually is not as risky as a stock. But if the corporation's earnings are high, the bondholder normally will receive less income from his investment than will a stockholder. On the other hand, if corporate earnings are low, bondholders may be better off, from the viewpoints of income and safety, than are stockholders.

Bonds usually are sold in large units, typically for 1000 dollars or more each. Consequently, they are bought less frequently than stocks by small investors.

It is easy to buy stocks and bonds of most large corporations. Large corporations usually

Securities are bought and sold on exchanges through brokers. A broker is a middleman, representing both buyers and sellers, who charges a commission or fee for his services. In order to trade on a stock exchange, a brokerage firm must own a *seat* on the exchange. These seats (memberships) are limited in number, and often sell for several hundred thousands of dollars. Ownership of a seat gives the broker the right to buy and sell for other people, its clients, or on its own account as a trader.

Large brokerage firms have offices in major cities throughout the country. These offices have direct telegraph, teletype, and telephone services with the home office at the stock exchange. This enables them to buy or sell any stock traded on an exchange within minutes.

In addition to buying and selling for their clients, brokers also give investment advice. As they are specialists, they are likely to know more than amateur investors about good buys. But there is no guarantee that their advice will result in a profit. Even specialists make mistakes.

Stocks are sometimes bought "on margin." Buying stock "on margin" is a practice usually limited to persons who want to speculate on fluctuations in the prices of stocks. It is a risky procedure for a small investor. Buying on margin really means buying stock listed on an exchange but paying only a percentage of its cost. For instance, an investor buys 10,000 dollars' worth of a particular stock, but pays only 5000 dollars. The remaining 5000 dollars he borrows from his broker.

Reading a stock market report

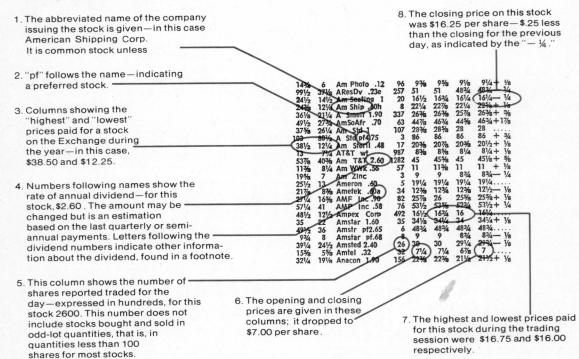

1. The abbreviated name of the company issuing the stock is given—in this case American Shipping Corp. It is common stock unless

2. "pf" follows the name—indicating a preferred stock.

3. Columns showing the "highest" and "lowest" prices paid for a stock on the Exchange during the year—in this case, $38.50 and $12.25.

4. Numbers following names show the rate of annual dividend—for this stock, $2.60. The amount may be changed but is an estimation based on the last quarterly or semi-annual payments. Letters following the dividend numbers indicate other information about the dividend, found in a footnote.

5. This column shows the number of shares reported traded for the day—expressed in hundreds, for this stock 2600. This number does not include stocks bought and sold in odd-lot quantities, that is, in quantities less than 100 shares for most stocks.

6. The opening and closing prices are given in these columns; it dropped to $7.00 per share.

7. The highest and lowest prices paid for this stock during the trading session were $16.75 and $16.00 respectively.

8. The closing price on this stock was $16.25 per share—$.25 less than the closing for the previous day, as indicated by the "— ¼."

If the price of the stock goes up, the man will sell his shares, pay the 5000 dollars plus interest and commission to his broker and enjoy his profits. But if the price of the stock goes down, he may have to sell his shares at a loss to get the money owed his broker. Should the price drop drastically the investor will probably receive a *margin call* from his broker asking him to put up more cash as a safeguard. If the investor cannot do this, the broker has the right to sell the stock.

In the given example, the investor paid 50 per cent of the total price of the stock and borrowed the rest. This 50 per cent put up by the investor is the *margin requirement* specified by the Board of Governors of the Federal Reserve System. Since 1934, the requirement has varied between 40 and 100 per cent.

Stock exchanges help investors and corporations needing funds. Large exchanges like the New York Stock Exchange are especially useful to corporations that may need additional capital. The large exchange through its widespread connections facilitates the sale of stock. People generally prefer to buy stock that is listed with a large stock exchange, since that offers the best prospects for a quick sale if they should wish to sell it.

In order to list stock on an exchange, a corporation must submit to the Securities and Exchange Commission (SEC) a statement of its financial condition and prospects. After it has been admitted to the exchange, the corporation must make periodic financial reports. In this and in many other ways the SEC supervises the operations of stock exchanges to protect large and small investors. The SEC, however, does not "guarantee" any stock.

Some stocks are sold in "over-the-counter" markets. Although the big city stock exchanges handle a large volume of stocks, their business is mainly confined to securities of the largest and best known corporations. Altogether, the securities of only about 3000 firms are traded on the New York and American Stock Exchanges. The securities of about 40,000 other

firms are bought and sold through brokers in the "over-the-counter" market. This simply means that these securities are not listed on an exchange, and that transactions usually are handled directly between brokers.

Many over-the-counter corporations are small or new; others are well established. Most United States Government securities, municipal bonds, bank and insurance company stocks, corporate bonds, Canadian and foreign securities, as well as the securities of many utilities and industrial companies, are traded over-the-counter.

Many millions of Americans own stocks or bonds. It has been estimated that about 25 million persons in this country own some type of corporate security. Most of these persons, of course, are in the middle or upper income groups. The poor and the low-income groups own practically no stocks or bonds. Even the average middle-income family which owns corporate securities has holdings worth only a few

Daily average of shares traded

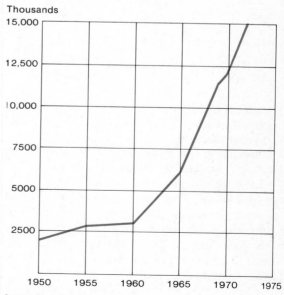

Thousands

Source: New York Times

Experienced investors utilize market indicators

Economists and stockbrokers study carefully all available figures relating to type and volume of stocks being traded. One familiar indicator is that published daily in the Wall Street Journal, the Dow-Jones industrial averages. These are shown both graphically and in tabular form.

MARKET DIARY

	Mon	Fri	Thur	Wed	Tues	Mon
Issues traded	1,667	1,613	1,612	1,580	1,597	1,617
Advances	899	831	578	342	638	496
Declines	488	444	703	939	617	801
Unchanged	280	338	331	299	342	320
New highs, 1970	17	11	4	6	12	2
New lows, 1970	12	25	28	22	15	22

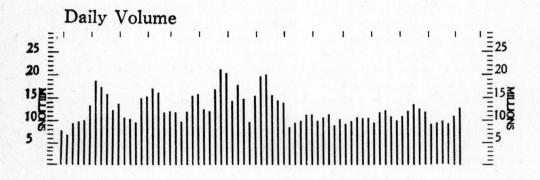

Daily Volume

DOW JONES CLOSING AVERAGES

	1970	—Changes—		1969
	-----MONDAY-----			
Industrials	767.52	+ 5.95	+0.78%	812.90
Transportation	148.00	+ 1.26	+0.85%	188.41
Utilities	112.22	+ 1.47	+1.32%	111.36
Composite	246.18	+ 2.19	+0.89%	271.08

OTHER MARKET INDICATORS

		1970	Change	1969
N.Y.S.E.	Composite	45.73	+ 0.26	52.12
	Industrial	48.38	+ 0.26	55.02
	Utility	36.85	+ 0.28	40.24
	Transportation	31.09	+ 0.26	40.76
	Financial	57.23	+ 0.29	68.51
Standard & Poor's Industrial ...		92.44	+ 0.53	102.72
American Exchange Price Index ..		21.47	+ 0.03	27.04
N.Q.B. Over-Counter Industrial		335.32	+ 1.57	432.00

Reprinted with permission of the Wall Street Journal.

hundreds of dollars. Two per cent or less of the population owns more than 80 per cent of all corporate securities.

Inexperienced investors may buy securities through investment clubs or companies. A person with limited means may feel that his capital is not large enough to enable him to open an individual account with an investment counseling firm, yet he may still wish to enter the stock market. Two ways open to him are through (1) an investment club, and (2) the investment company.

(1) *Investment clubs.* The formation of in-

vestment clubs is a recent trend in stock buying. Small groups of people with moderate savings pool their funds, time, and knowledge to purchase stocks that they otherwise could not afford. Because stocks in some corporations are expensive and are sold most economically in units of 100 shares each, this is one way in which small investors can enter the market.

(2) *Investment companies.* Another way for the person of limited resources to invest is by an arrangement variously known as the investment company, investment trust, or investment fund. The more familiar term is "mutual fund"

—although a mutual fund is only one kind of investment company. But regardless of the designation used, the same service is performed. The investor's money, instead of being put into a single corporation, goes into a general fund which buys stock in dozens of companies. His funds are *diversified,* or spread out through many corporations in different fields of business, as well as into bonds issued by municipal, state, and federal governments. The managers of the fund constantly "weed out" stocks they think may be declining in value, and substitute stocks which show promise. Since mutual funds employ trained investment specialists, the small investor reaps the benefit of their expertise. Profits are passed on to the stockholders in the fund through the payment of dividends.

More than one investment plan is available. There are many investment companies on the market, and finding the right one may be a problem. One might begin by considering their capital structure. There are two types—the *closed-end fund,* and the *open-end or "mutual" fund.* A closed-end fund is one which has a constant number of shares outstanding. It has already sold a block of shares to the public, but makes no continuous offering of additional shares. Shares of a closed-end fund are traded on the New York Stock Exchange or over-the-counter (see below) just as are the shares of any corporation. By contrast, an open-end or mutual fund is one which constantly sells new

---

THE OVER-THE-COUNTER MARKET

Brokers use many obscure terms. However, few are more misleading than "over-the-counter market," especially since there is neither a counter nor a market! Yet the securities of more than 50,000 companies are traded by this method. This is a sizable number, considering that the New York and American Stock Exchanges combined trade the stock of less than 3000 companies. The over-the-counter market has no particular location.

Many over-the-counter corporations are small or new, but others are well-established. Most United States Government bonds, municipal bonds, bank and insurance company stocks, corporate bonds, Canadian and foreign securities, as well as the securities of many utilities and industrial companies, are traded over-the-counter.

In an over-the-counter transaction a firm may act either as broker or as a dealer. As a dealer, the firm buys and sells stocks and bonds. As broker, it purchases the stock desired by a customer, and receives a commission.

Up until January 15, 1971, most business was done by telephone. On that date, a new computerized system of prices asked and prices bid began operation. The system gives 30,000 registered representatives and roughly 1000 wholesale and retail dealers up-to-the-minute information on 2500 leading stocks through a television hookup. At the end of each day, the information is transmitted to newspapers and wire services.

The new system provides buyers and sellers with information comparable to that carried by a stock exchange ticker tape. However, while the ticker tape records actual transactions, the new system records only offers to buy and sell. Nevertheless, the computerized system is expected to revolutionize the over-the-counter market. For the first time, buyers should be fairly certain of getting the price flashed on the screen (in the stock market, prices often change after the last transaction recorded on the ticker tape). Second, real competition is more likely, with prices for the same stock offered by different dealers jostling for the best level. Previously, the buyer could not determine the lowest price except by calling every dealer on the telephone. The new system is called NASDAQ, for "National Association of Securities Dealers' Automated Quotations System."

How a mutual fund operates

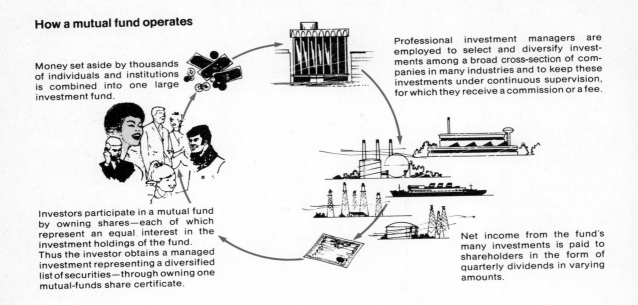

Money set aside by thousands of individuals and institutions is combined into one large investment fund.

Professional investment managers are employed to select and diversify investments among a broad cross-section of companies in many industries and to keep these investments under continuous supervision, for which they receive a commission or a fee.

Investors participate in a mutual fund by owning shares—each of which represent an equal interest in the investment holdings of the fund.
Thus the investor obtains a managed investment representing a diversified list of securities—through owning one mutual-funds share certificate.

Net income from the fund's many investments is paid to shareholders in the form of quarterly dividends in varying amounts.

shares and is willing to redeem old ones. Thus the number of outstanding shares of a mutual (or open-end) fund is always changing. Unlike closed-end shares, the shares of an open-end fund are not traded on the stock market, although buying and selling usually is done through a broker. When one wishes to buy open-end shares, one pays their dollar value (called the *net asset value*) plus a commission of about 9 per cent.

The commission one pays the person who sells open-end shares is another important factor to be considered by the prospective buyer. This commission is called "the load." Some mutual funds are sold by a contract which provides that a major portion of these charges for salesmen's commissions be paid in the first year of a normal ten-year plan of investment. This plan, with its *"front-end load,"* usually takes 50 per cent of ten years' commissions out of the investor's first year's payments into the mutual fund. The Securities and Exchange Commission has severely criticized this plan, and has proposed that legislation be enacted

to abolish or to place limits on this type of commission. Meanwhile, however, the investor has at his disposal a sizable number of no-load, open-end funds.

Commodity exchanges are central markets for dealing in raw materials or partly processed products. A commodity exchange operates somewhat as does a stock exchange, except that its traders deal in staple agricultural or industrial products instead of securities. These markets are located only in a few large cities. The Chicago Board of Trade is perhaps the best known commodity exchange. Some of the leading products dealt in—usually in very large quantities—are: wheat, corn, soy beans, cotton, sow bellies (for bacon), food oils, and certain kinds of metals.

Because fortunes can be made or lost very quickly in commodity exchange trading, professionals rather than small traders are usually involved. Commodity exchanges serve a useful purpose in stabilizing prices of the products concerned, by pitting one specialist's price judgment against another's.

4

What is a "good" investment?

How does one distinguish between "investment" and "speculation"? It frequently is difficult to distinguish between an investment and a speculation. It is sometimes said that an investment is made when a person merely wishes to get a set rate of return, and that a speculator buys with the hope of selling at a higher rate. These definitions, however, emphasize only differences in motives for buying. A more important difference between investment and speculation stems from the difference in risk. Purchase of a risky stock in the hope of getting a moderate return may be more speculative than a purchase of a sound stock in the hope that its price will go up.

A better statement of the difference, then, may be to say that as the risk becomes greater, the purchase becomes more speculative. To the extent that any investment involves some risk of losing part of the money invested, one may call the buying of any stock a speculation.

Only a very few professional speculators are able to make substantial gains through speculative ventures. These few are well informed and lucky enough to guess right most of the time. The person who has to work at a full-time job to earn his living is almost certain to lose in speculative ventures. He lacks the necessary information to guess right often enough to come out ahead. He will do better by making conservative investments and accepting a smaller but dependable return on his money.

The small investor should ask himself certain questions before making an investment. Any inexperienced trader who wishes to invest part or all of his savings should be careful! He is an amateur playing against professionals. The following are six important points to consider:

(1) *How safe is the investment?* A man may take an hour deciding what suit to buy. A woman may spend half a day shopping for a hat. Yet the cost of these items is small compared to making a lifetime investment that may amount to many thousand dollars. Nevertheless, some people reach a decision on this kind of investment merely by asking the opinion of a friend or neighbor!

Friends and neighbors may offer suggestions on investments, but their well-intended suggestions are not always dependable. Reliable investment brokers can usually give more dependable information. It is always a good plan to *investigate before you invest.* Also, it is generally safer to invest in a well-established company than in a new one. Some new companies may pay excellent returns when their business is good. But if general business conditions worsen, a new company may not be in as strong a position as one which has been in existence much longer.

Above all, one should be sure that his investment is not pure speculation. Businesses which offer unusually high dividend rates are often of the "fly-by-night" variety. They may go bankrupt before the investor receives any of the promised earnings. Worse yet, he may lose all or a part of the savings invested.

It is well to know the person with whom one is dealing before making an investment. In general, banks and licensed stockbrokers can be depended on for sound advice about investments. But there are many people who represent investments that are worthless or very unstable. Sometimes land is offered for sale at very attractive prices, but this land may be worth little or nothing, especially if it is advertised as located in a "boom" development which the prospective buyer cannot inspect beforehand.

(2) *How large is the return?* The return varies with each security and depends on a number of factors which cannot be predicted with complete accuracy. If one wishes to realize an assured income, he should probably consider bonds. While substantial dividends from stocks are possible, it is not standard practice to judge a stock's value by its dividend rate alone. Stocks are more susceptible to overall market changes than are other types of securities. On the other hand, if there is steady continued inflation, stock prices in general are likely to rise at about the same rate as the general level of prices. In sharp contrast, when bonds are finally redeemed, the lender receives a fixed amount in dollars which represents less purchasing power than the money invested when the bonds were purchased.

(3) *Is the value stable?* If one invests in something that has a high value at one time and a much lower one at another, one will be handicapped in the event he must sell at a time when the value is low. Generally it is better to invest in a security that has had a reasonably stable value from month to month and year to year. Stocks with a past record of frequent changes in price spell present and future danger.

(4) *How large are the units that one must buy?* It usually is easier for a family with a modest income to invest a certain amount each month. For that reason, it may not be feasible to invest in real estate where the purchase of a single unit may require an investment of several thousand dollars.

Government bonds are available in small denominations. Reliable brokerage and investment companies as well as banks usually are able to make arrangements for a person to invest a given amount in dependable commercial securities each month. These organizations usually furnish advice at no cost to the investor.

(5) *Can an investor get his money back if he needs it?* Anyone may need money to meet an emergency. For that reason, it is well to have a type of investment that can be disposed of at any time if necessary. It is usually possible to borrow money from a bank by using investments of recognized value as security. Many people raise needed cash in this way. Consequently an investment should be negotiable—easily sold or pledged

(6) *Should an investor put all his eggs in one basket?* If one buys stocks, it is wise not to put all one's savings into a single business, no matter how sound an investment it may appear to be. Should that business go bankrupt, the investor might lose everything put into it. If one invests in several stable companies, there is less of a risk. This practice is known as diversifying one's investments. Should a business fail, one would still be getting dividends from other investments. If one is investing chiefly in United States bonds, there is no need to worry about diversification. But the interest rate is very low on small-denomination bonds.

Investment opportunities meet varying needs. Some investors are primarily interested in current returns (yields). Others are more interested in long-range growth prospects. That is, they are willing to have lower returns for a time in the hope of receiving larger returns later. Thus, some stocks are referred to as *growth* stocks and others as *yield* stocks.

Stocks bought for current yield are expected to pay a steady dividend, quarter after quarter. Some companies have done this for decades, despite fluctuations in earnings. Such corporations retain enough earnings during prosperous years to continue paying regular dividends when earnings are less high.

"Growth" companies, on the other hand, typically retain a larger percentage of their income for reinvestment in the business. Consequently, they pay smaller current dividends. This is particularly true of new firms in newly developing industries. Reinvestment of earnings in the business is expected to increase the firm's future earning capacity. Such a policy would be expected to cause its stocks to increase in value and to make possible larger future earnings (and dividends).

All investments are risky. There is no such thing as a "riskless" investment. Risk is a part of every business just as it is a part of all other aspects of life. There is always the possibility that a business will fail or a local government default. Some types of investment, however, are less risky than others.

Inflation and depression are major sources of risk. During periods of prosperity (which usually are accompanied by some inflation) businesses tend to have higher earnings than during less prosperous times. There are exceptions, of course. This means that more money is available for dividends (or for reinvestment in the business). During recessions, however, bondholders are assured of fixed interest payments unless the organization issuing the bonds goes into bankruptcy. During a period of deflation, the purchasing power of a dollar is higher. But the nation has experienced no major decline in the general price level since the early 1930's.

It follows, therefore, that one usually is better off if he holds stocks during periods of prosperity and bonds during periods of recession. These ups and downs in the economy cannot be accurately predicted, however.

Most investment advisors, therefore, suggest that the head of a household first adequately protect his family by life insurance and home ownership. Then he should plan a *balanced* investment program. That is, some portion of his investments should be of the type expected to yield a steady though modest return. The remainder might be of a type which will yield a higher income in case of inflation.

CHECK UP

1. What questions should a small investor ponder before making an investment? Why should speculation be left to professionals?

2. What is the difference between growth stocks and yield stocks? How are stocks and bonds affected by inflation? Deflation?

3. What order of goals would an investment adviser be likely to suggest to the head of a household? Why?

5

What is meant by "real" investment?

The term "investment" has both a commonplace and a specialized meaning in economics. In the early chapters, the commonplace meaning of the term investment has been developed from the viewpoint of the individual with funds to invest. This is sometimes called "financial" investment. In the specialized language of the economist, however, the word "investment" is often used in referring to *real* (that is, tangible) property rather than to stocks and bonds. In this specialized sense, *real investment* refers only to expenditures which bring into being tangible assets which did not exist before.

For example, if one buys a corporate stock on the stock exchange, this would not be real investment. The corporate assets represented by this stock already are in existence. But if a person buys a share of stock when it is originally issued by the corporation, he will be providing funds to acquire productive assets for the corporation's use. This is real investment. Likewise, if one buys a house already in existence, he is making a financial investment.

But if one hires a contractor to build a new house, he has made an investment in the real or economic sense.

Businesses and governments are large investors in the real sense. Buildings, equipment, and machinery wear out. And older facilities often have to be modernized to keep abreast of new techniques in production. Businesses frequently buy or build additional facilities and invest surplus funds by building up inventories of raw materials, or of semi-finished products. These various forms of business investments account for a large part of the country's total real investment activity.

Governments (federal, state, and local) also invest in various types of facilities. These include highways, school buildings and city halls, subways and buses, power dams, recreational facilities, and a wide variety of other projects. Although these are not intended to earn profits, as are business investments, government investment expenditures are as "real" as those of business.

Real investment falls into two categories. Real investment sometimes is further classified into *net* investment and *gross* investment. Net investment is spending for *additional* facilities. Gross investment includes net investment expenditures plus expenditures for *replacing* existing facilities. For example, if an electric utility company's generator wears out and has to be replaced, no net investment has occurred. If the company installs an additional generator to expand its output of electricity, however, net investment has taken place.

During periods of prosperity, businessmen are optimistic. Businesses then are likely to increase their net real investments very rapidly at such times. During recessions, however, when businessmen are less optimistic, net investment may decline. In fact, *disinvestment* (failure fully to replace) occurs when inventories are reduced or allowed to dwindle or when producers do not renew worn-out facilities.

Businesses have several sources of investment funds. Individual proprietorships and partnerships may obtain investment funds from the personal resources of their owners. Corporations sell stocks. All types of businesses may also borrow. For example, when corporations sell bonds, this is one method of borrowing. All types of business organizations may also borrow from banks and other lending agencies, and they may buy on credit.

Businesses also may reinvest part of their profits rather than paying out all profits as dividends or distributed earnings. Replacement of facilities usually is made from "depreciation allowances" (portions of a firm's gross income regularly set aside to finance replacements). These depreciation funds are considered to be business expenses, not profits.

Business expenditures for new plant and equipment

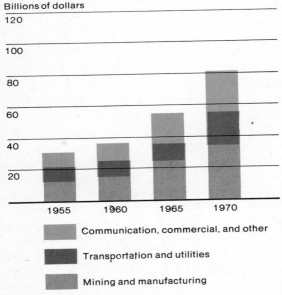

Billions of dollars

Source: Statistical Abstract

Governments have several sources of revenue. The principal source of government funds is taxation. Governments also borrow from various sources. The purchase of a government savings bond is one example of a loan to the United States government. In addition, many local, state, and federal government agencies receive income in the form of payments for goods and services which these agencies provide.

Real investment is of great importance to the nation's economy. It is hard to overestimate the importance of real investment. Its ups and downs affect the pocketbooks of all Americans. It replaces worn out or outmoded production facilities. It is necessary for the creation of new business, new industry, new consumer products, and new services. Equally important, real investment provides employment for a large portion of the working population. In many ways, it is a measure of how well the economy is doing.

When real investment declines, or when it grows too slowly, many people are thrown out of work. Their incomes cease or decline, and they buy fewer of the goods produced by other businesses. This decline in buying creates still more unemployment and generates pessimism in the business community. This in turn further discourages investment.

During the past generation, the government has become very conscious of how real investments by businesses affect the economy as a whole. Part Four of this book will examine policies employed by the government to promote economic growth, price stabilization, and greater prosperity.

CHECK UP

1. What is the difference between *financial investment* and *real investment*? Give examples of the latter in the case of business and government. Explain *net* and *gross* investment.

2. What are the sources of funds used by business for real investment? By government?

3. How does the rate of real investment affect the nation's economy? Why?

Clinching the main ideas

Bank accounts, home ownership, and life insurance are favorite forms of investment for small investors. In addition, some persons invest in their own small businesses, and others invest in corporate securities and government bonds.

Securities of large corporations sometimes are bought through investment clubs or mutual funds. Most, however, are bought through brokers operating on organized stock exchanges. Advice and assistance are available to inexperienced investors, and securities can be found to fit every investor's need. Some investors are interested primarily in current yields, others in long-term growth, and still others compromise by purchasing both types of securities.

All investments are risky, but some are much less risky than others. Generally, those promising the highest potential yields are the most risky. Future business conditions—depression or inflation—are important risks that should be taken into account. Wise investors should also consider such factors as safety, return, stability, negotiability, diversification, and terms of sale.

"Real" investment expenditures bring new productive facilities into being. Both business firms and governments engage in large scale net and gross real investment. These investments are extremely important in keeping the economy operating at a high and efficient level and in stimulating necessary growth.

During recent years, government policies frequently have been directed toward combating depressions by encouraging real investment. The reverse of these policies has been used to combat excessive inflation.

Chapter 7 review

Terms to understand

1. compound interest
2. depreciation
3. dividends
4. disinvestment
5. price-earnings ratio
6. over-the-counter market
7. growth stock
8. yield stock
9. commodity exchange
10. default
11. mutual fund
12. real investment

What do you think?

1. Which of the forms of investment discussed seems best from the point of view of safety? liquidity? income?

2. During a recession, would business or government be likely to make larger real investment? Why?

3. How do you explain the boom in the building of high-rise apartments in and near large cities?

4. Banks compound interest on savings accounts semi-annually, quarterly, monthly, and in some cases daily. What difference does this make to the investor?

5. In 1928 Mr. Jones had 20,000 dollars to invest. The Great Depression began the next year and was at its worst in 1933. Show how this depression would have affected each of the following investments Mr. Jones might have made: buying a home in a big city, buying a farm, buying government bonds, buying common stocks, putting the money in a bank which did not fail.

Extending your knowledge of economics

1. Invite a representative from a stock brokerage firm to discuss the buying and selling of stocks and bonds. Agree in advance on the questions to be put to him.

2. Let each member of the class choose three stocks, recording the "purchase price" for each. During a three-week period, the daily closing market price should be noted for each stock. The student may decide to sell one or more of the original stocks and to buy other stocks. If he does, he should keep track of both original and acquired holdings to discover whether he lost or made money by trading.

Insurance against family hardships

1. What is the basis of insurance?
2. What are the common forms of property insurance?
3. What kinds of life insurance are available?
4. How do private insurance companies operate?
5. What forms of insurance are provided by government?

Insurance, unlike the product of most other enterprises, is made available in reverse proportion to demand.

PETER HELLMAN

A family can work and save for years, only to see its property and financial accumulations wiped out by a disastrous fire, flood, or windstorm. Untimely death of a breadwinner, or a lengthy illness, can reduce a family to poverty. An automobile accident can tie up a substantial part of one's earnings for many years. It is impossible for the average family, even a well-off family, to meet a severe loss of the kinds mentioned from its own funds without great hardship.

During a recent and typical year, for example, fires occurred on the average in some American home every 47 seconds. Total losses from such fires (buildings and their contents) amounted to more than 1.7 billion dollars. During the same year, more than 53,000 persons died in car accidents; losses due to car thefts amounted to 666 million dollars; medical and hospital claims paid by private and public insurance organizations were more than 9.6 billion dollars.

Insurance does not prevent losses from occurring. It is a method for reimbursing those who have suffered losses of property or income for at least part of their financial loss. Almost, every family or adult is involved with insurance in some way. Within the next few years, the students reading this book doubtless will be paying for several kinds of insurance protection. An understanding of insurance, therefore, is necessary to help one obtain at the lowest costs the kinds of insurance that meets one's needs.

This chapter briefly explains the basic nature of insurance, the forms of property and income-protection insurance most commonly bought by families and individuals, and how private insurance companies operate. It also discusses several important types of government insurance. The discussion is focused on family and individual insurance rather than on the kinds of insurance purchased by businesses. However, some of the forms of insurance considered here also are used by business firms.

1

What is the basis of insurance?

Insurance differs from gambling. An uninformed homeowner might say, "I am betting the insurance company 100 dollars that my house will burn this year against its bet of 15,000 dollars that it will not." Such a remark reflects ignorance about the nature of insurance. When a person gambles, he deliberately creates a risk of loss which did not exist before. Insurance is a method of dealing with a risk which already exists.

Risks, including the risks of economic losses, are ever-present. Some kinds of risks and losses must be borne by the individual or family. Other kinds are partly transferred to others by a process of sharing. Insurance is an organized way of sharing certain kinds of economic losses.

Insurance "spreads the risk" of financial losses. Insurance protection basically is a method whereby a number of people facing similar risks spread the costs of these risks among themselves. Each person who is insured makes a small periodic payment—monthly, quarterly, or yearly—into a fund which is used to reimburse any member of the insured group who suffers a loss.

A HIGHLY PROTECTED PEOPLE
Nearly 1.7 trillion dollars' worth of life insurance protection is owned by American families. This is more than the nation's gross national product, and nearly four times the amount of the national debt! Since 1960, the amount of life insurance owned by Americans has trebled. Today the average family has about 23,000 dollars' worth of protection. During the year 1972, life insurance companies paid almost 30 billion dollars in benefits to policyholders.

The small regular payment made by each individual "covered" by a certain kind of insurance is his contribution to the losses suffered by the insured group as a whole. In effect, he is voluntarily accepting a small, regular, and certain loss (his insurance payments) to escape the risks of much greater but less certain losses.

A family can include regular and known payments for insurance in its financial planning and budgeting. A major loss not covered by insurance, however, can completely ruin the careful planning of a lifetime. Even though there are long odds against a major loss striking any given family, most people do not like to take such chances.

The costs of providing insurance protection can be calculated with reasonable accuracy. Statisticians called *actuaries* are employed by insurance companies and government insurance organizations. These actuaries collect vast amounts of information about the frequency and trends of fires, storms, car accidents, thefts, illnesses, deaths, and other hazards that people insure against. Through statistical analysis of this information, they can tell insurance companies approximately what charges must be made to cover the total losses for each type of risk.

A particular loss or death cannot be predicted, of course. But the total number of losses of any given type, or the total number of deaths within a given age group, can be predicted with surprising accuracy on a national or regional scale. No insurance company can predict whether or not a given driver will wreck the family car within the next year. But an automobile insurance company can closely estimate how many persons of a given age, and living in a given type of neighborhood, will be involved in car wrecks in this country during the coming year. No actuary can tell a given person how long he will live, but any life insurance company knows approximately how long the average person of this man's age will live. Charges made for insurance, therefore, are based largely on averages.

Losses through accidents and crime

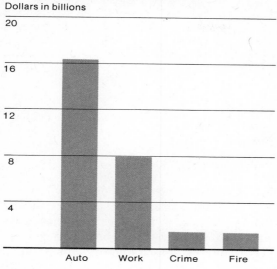

Dollars in billions

Source: Insurance Facts

How much insurance one should carry depends upon his income and needs. A sound and adequate insurance program is essential to family financial planning and management. But buying insurance is like buying other things, it involves choices. One must balance one's needs for insurance against other needs in order to keep within the family income.

As a minimum, a family owning its own home and furnishings should carry insurance sufficient to replace these items if they are lost through fire or some other disaster. Likewise, car owners should at least protect themselves against claims for injury or damage to the property of others in an accident. Failure to

Private insurance companies sell insurance policies. An insurance policy is a formal contract, usually written in legal and technical language. Under the terms of this contract, the *policyholder* or *insured,* the one buying the insurance, agrees to pay a stated amount, called the *premium,* to the insurance company. In return, the insurance company, the *insurer,* agrees to pay the insured up to the maximum *face value* stated on the policy should a loss insured against actually occur.

Anyone buying insurance should read the policy carefully, to make sure that he understands just what he is buying (as well as what he is *not* buying). An insurance company is legally obligated to live up to the terms of the insurance contract. It is not obligated to reimburse one for any loss not insured against, or to pay more than is called for in the contract. Most of the disputes between policyholders and insurance companies stem from the fact that the policyholder has not read or has not really understood his policy.

Net premiums collected by type of insurance excluding life and health

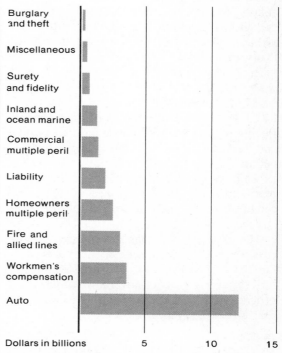

Dollars in billions

Source: Insurance Facts

have such protection may result in court judgments against one's property or future income in the amount of thousands of dollars, should one be found responsible for an accident.

The principal breadwinner of a family should carry sufficient life insurance to protect his family against undue hardship resulting from the loss of his earnings. Ideally, there should be enough insurance to pay off any mortgage on the family home and other major outstanding debts, and to provide a reasonable income until the family can become self-supporting. The principal breadwinner should also consider whether the family could stand the financial strain of a long illness or hospitalization, or the possible loss of his income.

No insurance program can provide complete protection against all risks. Almost any eventuality can be insured against if one is able and willing to pay for the insurance. Anyone sufficiently wealthy to insure against all eventualities, however, probably is wealthy enough to "self-insure" himself—that is, he does not need to buy insurance. Very few people, if any, are that wealthy!

In practice, demands for insurance, and purchases of it, are governed by the same principles of marginal utility (discussed in Chapter 2) as are demands for other goods and services. In choosing between insurance and other goods and services, one buys that thing which he believes will provide the most utility for a given expenditure. Then, if the choice is insurance, one buys that kind of insurance which is most valuable under one's own particular circumstances.

The next two sections of this chapter discuss the most important kinds of insurance for families and individuals. The final section describes several types of governmental insurance programs which supplement (or are substitutes for) private insurance.

CHECK UP

1. What is the purpose of insurance? How are the costs of insurance protection determined? Why should a policyholder read the terms of his policy carefully?

2. What types of protection should be included in a family's insurance program? How does the principle of marginal utility affect the demand for insurance?

2

What are the common forms of property insurance?

The most widely used types of family property insurance are homeowners' insurance against fire and associated risks, and automobile insurance. If one is buying a home, major items of furniture or home furnishings, or an automobile on credit, the creditor will insist that the property be insured for enough to pay off the debt in case the property is lost. The cost of this insurance is included in most monthly mortgage or installment payments. But when such property is fully paid for, most owners still want it to be insured.

Homeowners may insure against several types of property losses. Owners of homes (as well as property used by businesses) usually protect their investments against a variety of property risks. The most important among these risks are fire and associated water damage, and (in some areas) wind damage.

The property owner determines the value of his buildings or other property and the amount for which he wishes to insure them. If a building costs 20,000 dollars, or if that would be the cost of replacing it, he may insure it for that amount. Should he insure it for only 15,000 dollars, his premiums would be somewhat lower; but in case of complete loss by fire he would collect only 15,000 dollars, the face value, on a building worth 20,000 dollars. The insurance policy may also have a *coinsurance clause*. This means that on a partial loss, one collects only the amount determined by the ratio of the insured amount to the actual value of the property. Thus if a building worth 20,-000 dollars is insured for 15,000 dollars and a 10,000 dollar loss occurs, only 7500 dollars (three fourths) can be collected if the insurance policy has a coinsurance clause.

Property values are subject to changing economic conditions. Property owners need to review their insurance from time to time to make sure that it is adequate to cover the value of their property. A home built for 15,000 dollars may cost several thousand more to replace five years later. In case of loss, the insurance company pays the cost of replacement (up to the face value of the policy) less the amount of depreciation, if any. This depreciation deduction represents the gradual loss of value, because of age and use, that has occurred since the property was new. The insurance company under most contracts is only required to meet the amount of the "appraised value" of the property should it be destroyed. Even if the owner of the property carried an equal amount of insurance with two companies, he could only receive half of the appraised value from each insurance company. In brief, an insured property owner is not entitled to a "profit" from his insurance—he is, at best, entitled only to recover the amount of his actual loss.

Safety conditions are considered in fire insurance costs. Conditions of fire safety may change within a community over a period of time, and insurance costs are increased or decreased accordingly. It is general practice for a fire-insurance policy to be written to cover a period of one, three, or five years. The premium charge for an insurance policy is based upon the rate in effect at the time the policy is written or renewed. It is not affected by rate changes during the period of the contract. The premium for a three-year policy is generally two and one-half times the one-year amount, and that for a five-year policy is four times the one-year amount.

Several factors determine the size of insurance premiums. Premium rates are established partly on the basis of accumulated information on losses in the past. In the case of fire insurance, factors which help to determine the cost of protection include: (1) the use made of the building; (2) the type of construction (brick or frame); (3) the type of roof (wood shingles or fire-resistant materials); (4) the quality of fire protection provided in the city or town; and (5) the danger of catching fire if adjoining buildings should burn. In thinly populated areas rates depend also upon the distance from a fire station or fire hydrant, and upon the availability of a telephone to report fires.

Some fire insurance contracts can be expanded to include other risks. *Extended coverage* is an important type of fire-insurance protection included in many policies for an additional premium. This enlarges the scope of the policy to include damage from a variety of causes. Among these are windstorm, hail, explosion, smoke, falling aircraft, and motor vehicles out of control. Premium rates for insurance against damage to property from wind, water, smoke, and other causes are determined by a study of past experience, just as are those for fire losses.

PROTECTION FOR INVESTORS
A new form of federal insurance was passed by Congress in 1970. It would insure investors against a limited amount in losses of cash and securities which they leave with a broker should the brokerage firm go bankrupt. The insurance would be handled through a new federal insurance corporation made up of brokerage firms. The corporation would set standards for membership and firms which failed to meet the standards would be put on an "unsafe and unsound" list. They would be required by the corporation or by new legislation to correct unsound practices. The insurance plan resembles the Federal Deposit Insurance Corporation, which reimburses bank depositors up to a specified amount should a member bank fail.

Comprehensive insurance policies offer wide protection. During recent years a broad group of risks have been covered by a single insurance policy which has become known as a *package policy*. In addition to the fire and extended coverages just discussed, the risks insured by a package policy include water damage, freezing of plumbing or heating systems, glass breakage, collapse of roof, theft, and vandalism. Liability insurance (discussed below) is also included in the "package." Such a policy pays the full replacement cost of damage to buildings without deducting any money for depreciation, provided insurance is carried for 80 per cent of the full replacement cost of the damage, or provided the loss is small. The premium charge is considerably lower than it would be if these different risks were insured against in separate policies.

Liability insurance protects property owners. Many property owners, especially those operating income-producing property, carry *public-liability* insurance. Property owners are responsible for the security and safety of others who are in some way in contact with or using their property. For example, should a customer fall and injure himself while in a store, he may sue the store owner for the costs of injuries suffered. He may collect damages if he can prove that neglect on the part of the store owner contributed to the accident.

Liability insurance protects property owners against claims for damages up to a specified amount, in addition to the costs of defending lawsuits. For homeowners, there is a specific comprehensive personal-liability policy which protects the insured and his family against claims for personal injury or property damage up to a specified amount. Should a child leave his bicycle on the sidewalk in front of his home, his father, in some states, might be responsible for damages to a person injured by falling over it. Accidents caused by family pets, flying golf balls, or other hazards are also covered.

A special and very important kind of liability insurance is that part of automobile insurance which insures owners of automobiles and trucks against damage claims in the case of accidents.

Automobile insurance is essential in a motor age. Because of the increasing number of automobiles, the growing traffic congestion and the resulting hazards, every motorist runs the risk of being involved at some time in an accident. The large number of serious and costly automobile accidents in recent years has greatly increased the cost of liability protection. Despite seemingly high insurance rates, one cannot afford to operate an automobile without being adequately insured.

Many individuals have had to pay thousands of dollars in damages because they did not have adequate car-insurance coverage. The person responsible for an automobile accident is usually required to pay compensation to persons who because of the accident have suffered bodily injury or property damage. For that reason, automobile insurance is a "must." Otherwise, a court-awarded judgment may ruin a person financially.

Some states have "financial responsibility" laws. These laws require automobile owners to carry at least the required minimum amount of liability insurance to provide compensation for injuries or property losses caused to others. Other states require that such insurance be obtained, or a sizable bond posted, if a driver is involved in an accident. Laws requiring that liability insurance be obtained after an accident seem to be based on the principle that "Every dog is entitled to one bite."

The number of court judgments against the owners of automobiles involved in accidents have increased greatly in recent years, and so have the amounts awarded in compensation. Automobile insurance rates, consequently, have increased, and insurance companies have become selective in selling their policies. This has become a serious problem both for "poor insurance risks" and the victims of their driving.

Recently, some have been advocating a basic change in the form of automobile liability insurance. Under proposed plans, automobile injuries would be handled somewhat as are injuries received on the job under "workmen's compensation" insurance. All car owners would be required to make payments into a state fund or to private insurance companies closely supervised by the state. This fund would be used to pay a stated amount of compensation to anyone injured in a car accident, regardless of fault. The amount of the payment would depend on the seriousness of the injury.

Such a plan, if adopted, would eliminate most of the long and expensive lawsuits stemming from automobile injuries which now bog down the courts. Everyone receiving an injury would be assured of at least a minimum amount of compensation. Anyone not satisfied with this award still would have the option of starting a lawsuit.

Many persons and insurance companies oppose these proposed compensation plans. They say that such plans would be costly and difficult to administer. They also argue that these plans, by reducing personal legal responsibility for accidents, would encourage reckless drivers to be even more irresponsible. Careful drivers, therefore, might be penalized by having to pay even higher rates than they now do.

Despite such criticisms, however, it seems likely that some such plan will be adopted within the next few years. A growing number of people are very dissatisfied with the constantly rising costs of current automobile liability insurance programs and the unsatisfactory situation under present laws.

Automobile owners also insure for other losses. An automobile, especially a new one, is an expensive piece of equipment. If it is damaged in an accident, destroyed by fire, or stolen, its owner may be put to considerable expense. Consequently, insurance can be purchased to protect the owner from almost anything that might happen to his car. One may obtain insurance against collision (typically with a "deductible" of the first 50 or 100 dollars of loss to be borne by the insured), fire, theft, windstorm, flood, glass breakage, falling objects, and vandalism. Coverage usually includes the costs of emergency road service and towing. Premium payments are based on the value of the car and what it is insured against.

Automobile insurance premiums vary greatly. Premium rates on an automobile-insurance policy depend on a combination of several factors, including:

1. State laws which have a bearing on the comparative difficulty of collecting on a

---

"NO-FAULT" AUTO INSURANCE

In 1970, Massachusetts passed a "no-fault" insurance plan in response to complaints that auto insurance rates were too high. The new plan meant that inurance companies had to pay the policyholder in cases of personal injury regardless of who was at fault. It was expected that many costly court battles to determine fault would thus be avoided, and the expected savings in court costs were reflected in a 15 per cent reduction in premiums for compulsory personal injury liability. Property damage liability and fire, theft, and collision policies remained under the old system.

The results of this approach to car insurance will not be apparent for some time. Its benefits did not seem great to the average motorist, whose overall bill for full insurance coverage did not drop—due to a 38 per cent average increase in noncompulsory insurance. Nevertheless, the no-fault plan is being watched closely by other states to see whether it offers a solution to the problem of excessively high auto insurance rates.

claim for injury or damage to one's property;

2. The density of population—rates being highest on cars operated in large cities and lowest in rural areas;

3. The use of the car—highest rates on commercial vehicles of large size, lower on motor vehicles used for both business and pleasure, still lower on pleasure-type cars not used in business, and lowest on passenger vehicles operated by farmers;

4. The loss record of a particular community —higher rates in areas where claims have been high;

5. The age of the principal operator—premiums higher where the principal driver is either over the age of 65 or under a minimum designated age (usually 25 if single or 23 if married);

6. The driving record of the principal operator —that is, number and nature of arrests for operating (not parking) violations;

7. Driver education courses completed by younger drivers, if any.

CHECK UP

1. Against what types of loss might the owner of a house wish to be insured? The owner of business property? Why should the insured frequently review his insurance coverage?

2. What factors determine premium rates for fire insurance?

3. Explain these terms: extended coverage, a package policy, public liability insurance, personal liability insurance.

4. What new approach has been proposed to compensate persons injured in automobile accidents "regardless of fault"? Why? What criticisms have been directed at this policy?

5. In addition to liability insurance, what other types of insurance are needed by car owners? What factors determine the premiums they must pay?

6. "Insurance is made available in reverse proportion to demand." Explain why this applies to an inner city resident trying to obtain a package policy.

3

What kinds of life insurance are available?

Life insurance, available in many forms, is by far the most common type of income protection insurance. Various kinds of health, hospitalization, accident, and disability insurance also are widely used.

Life insurance protects against "untimely" death. Life insurance makes it possible to share with others the danger that *the insured person will die earlier than the average person of his age group.* If he does, he may have accumulated less property or savings by the time of his death than is usual for persons in his income bracket. Through life insurance, persons who live a long time help to pay death benefits to the survivors of those who lived a shorter time.

Life insurance benefits are paid to a beneficiary. When a person "takes out" insurance on his own life, the insurance company agrees to pay, on the death of the insured, the sum of money specified in the policy (face value). The person to whom this money is paid is known as the *beneficiary.* The policyholder's original choice of beneficiary is not necessarily final— in most cases the beneficiary can be changed if the policyholder so desires. Although anyone may be named, the beneficiary usually is the policyholder's wife or children.

Life insurance may be a form of investment. Life insurance policies, except for *term-insurance* (discussed below), usually have a "cash-in" value. They permit the policyholder to discontinue his premium payments and to surrender his policy at any time. The insurance company will then return a portion of the premiums already paid. At first this cash or *cash-surrender* value is only a small fraction of the face value. But as more premiums are paid, the cash value becomes a substantial part of the face value. This increase reflects the fact that

The cost of life insurance increases with age

Term insurance

Cost per $1,000

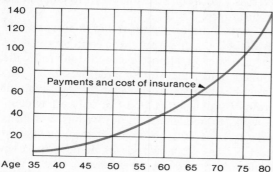

Straight life

Cost per $1,000

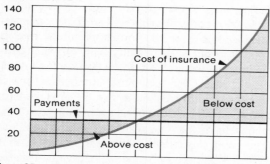

Payments on term insurance are related to actual insurance costs, whereas payments on straight life policies remain constant, and so do not cover total costs to the insurance firm of insuring older persons.

Source: Adapted from Paul Samuelson, Economics. Copyright 1961 by McGraw-Hill Book Company. Used by permission.

the time is approaching when the insurance company would be required to pay the face value of the policy.

The cash value of an insurance policy is a form of investment. A policyholder may properly include the cash value of his insurance policies among his assets. In fact, this cash value may be used by the policyholder as col-lateral in obtaining a loan from the insurance company. Usually insurance companies obligate themselves to lend a policyholder up to 95 per cent of his policy's accumulated cash value. The cost of such borrowing is generally comparable to the cost of other sources of credit.

Insurance contract terms are based on average life expectancy. When an insurance company enters into a life-insurance contract, it expects that the insured will live (and pay premiums) at least as long as the average person of his age. For this reason, the insured is usually required to take a physical examination when he applies for insurance. If, as a result of accident or illness, the insured dies soon after taking out the policy, the face value of the policy which will be paid to the beneficiary greatly exceeds the amount paid in premiums. On this particular policy, therefore, the insurance company loses money. If, on the contrary, the insured keeps paying premiums until an advanced age, his policy is profitable to the insurance company.

Insurance companies also sell contracts in which they assume that the given person will

Insurance mortality table

age	life expectancy	age	life expectancy
17	55.41	28	45.06
18	54.46	29	44.12
19	53.52	30	43.18
20	52.58	31	42.24
21	51.64	32	41.30
22	50.70	33	40.37
23	49.76	34	39.44
24	48.83	35	38.51
25	47.89	36	37.58
26	46.95	37	36.66
27	46.00	38	35.74

Source: Life Insurance Fact Book

not live longer than the average person of his age. This is known as an *annuity* contract. An annuity contract obligates the insurance company to pay the holder of the contract a stated sum at regular (usually monthly) intervals as long as he lives. Usually these annuity payments begin late in life. Suppose, for example, that a person bought an annuity contract which would start paying him a regular monthly income at age 60. In the United States, a person who is 60 years old lives on the average about 18 more years. If this person died at age 77

or earlier, the insurance company would have paid him less than it had expected; if he lived to be 79 or older, the company would pay him more than it had expected. An annuity, therefore, is a form of investment as well as a form of insurance.

Several major types of life insurance are available. A life-insurance contract can be tailor-made for almost every customer. In the United States there are more than 1100 life-insurance companies. Policies range in amount from 100 dollars, at a cost of only a few cents a week, to policies taken out by business firms on the lives of their executives at an annual cost of tens of thousands of dollars. In some contracts the goal of the insured is to buy protection for his dependents; in others, to buy protection for his own old age. Among the major types of life insurance are:

1. *Term life insurance.* The form of insurance with by far the lowest premium rate is *term insurance.* If a family with growing children wants the greatest protection for the lowest expenditure over a limited number of years, this is the form to choose. For 60 to 90 dollars a year a man of 30 can buy a fifteen-year term policy having a face value of 10,000 dollars. The great shortcoming of a term policy is that it builds up no cash value or loan value reserve for the policyholder. Once he stops paying premiums, his insurance under this policy comes to an end and he gets no premium refunds. Nor can he borrow on such a policy. Before his term insurance expires, however, he may convert it to a more permanent form of insurance at a higher premium rate.

2. *Straight-life insurance.* The straight life or "ordinary" life-insurance policy provides for payment of the face value to the beneficiary upon the death of the insured. Straight-life insurance is the most popular type of policy because it provides permanent life insurance at the lowest possible annual outlay. The premium paid each year depends upon the face value of the policy and upon the age of the insured at the time the policy was written. As an example,

Life insurance in force

Dollars
in billions

Source: Life Insurance Fact Book

a young man of 23 can buy a 10,000 dollar straight-life policy for 125 to 170 dollars a year. The premium remains the same as long as he lives. (See graph on page 185.)

The straight-life policy is a means of saving. If the policyholder just mentioned wants to stop premiums at 65, his 10,000 dollar policy has a cash value of more than 6000 dollars. He can either draw out this sum, or accept a paid-up policy with a face value less than that of the policy he surrendered.

Because a straight-life policy has a cash value, the policyholder can use it as a security in borrowing money from the insurance company. This loan value is useful in emergencies, because it enables a policyholder to obtain credit without a cosigner or other collateral. Many policyowners find this loan value helpful in making a down payment on a home. The loan can be repaid at any time. If the insured dies before the loan has been fully repaid, any unpaid balance is deducted from the amount paid to the beneficiary.

3. *Limited-payment life insurance.* If a man wants to limit payments on his life insurance to his best earning years, he should choose a *limited-payment* policy. His yearly premiums, compared to a straight-life policy, will be higher because the payments are made within a shorter period of years. If a man of 23 takes out a 20-year limited-payment policy, his annual premium would be between 250 and 320 dollars. However, at age 43 his 10,000 dollar policy would be paid. Thereafter the cash value would still increase, though more slowly than when payments were being made.

4. *Endowment life insurance.* When a person wants both life insurance protection while his children are growing up and a source of income after retirement, his best choice may be an *endowment* policy. This matures (becomes payable) to the policyholder when he reaches a given age. If one buys a 10,000 dollar policy, he will have life insurance protection for that amount. In addition, when the policy matures, he can either receive the face amount of the policy in a lump sum, or accept a regular income (annuity) for the rest of his life. In the case of a 10,000 dollar policy, this annuity amounts to about 740 dollars a year at age 65. While such an arrangement appeals to some, the yearly premium is considerably higher than for ordinary life insurance. This is necessary in order to build the cash value of the policy more rapidly.

The chief difference between regular or straight-life insurance and endowment insurance is the comparative speed with which cash value builds up. Since each builds up a cash value, each is an investment. In the case of regular life insurance, however, cash value does not equal the face value until an age which few persons reach. In the case of endowment insurance, the cash value "catches up with" the face value well within the expected lifetime of the insured. In the first case, the insured has to surrender his policy or use it as security in borrowing money if he is to use its cash value. In the second case, when the endowment matures the contract provides that the payment shall be made to the insured without a special request. If he chooses instead to accept an annuity, he is saved the trouble of "shopping around" among insurance companies to purchase an annuity. The annuity is one of the *options* allowed him in the policy.

Group life insurance is often available to employees. Group insurance is written to cover all the members of a given group regardless of race, sex, age, health, or special occupation. Normally this is a form of term insurance for which all employees of one firm, or all members of a labor organization are eligible. Insurance companies estimate how long the average member of a given group may be expected to live. Guided by this estimate, they offer a flat rate to all members of the group. Usually there is a requirement that 75 per cent or more of the eligible group must be insured if a group policy is to be written. The premium is withheld from the worker's pay check by his employer, thus reducing the cost of collection.

Most group insurance covers a worker only as long as he is employed by a given company. If an individual leaves the company, he usually has the right within 30 days to continue his policy under a new contract without taking a physical examination to establish that he is a good health risk. His new premium rate would depend upon his age at the time.

In recent years, many business organizations have provided employees with paid-up group insurance as an extra or "fringe" benefit. The amount of group insurance is frequently a subject of bargaining between employers and labor unions. Other fringe benefits of importance are hospitalization and surgical insurance, major medical insurance, loss-of-time benefits, and group pension benefits.

Many special types and combinations of life insurance are available. Except in term-insurance policies, several special provisions may be "written into" an insurance contract (policy) if the policyholder so desires. Any competent insurance company agent will explain to a prospective policyholder the special arrangements which might be advantageous to him. These will differ, depending on the income and obligations of the insured. Among such special provisions are some that (1) involve greater payments if death occurs as a result of an accident, and (2) relieve the insured of the obligation to continue paying premiums if he becomes totally disabled. Additional protection of this kind ordinarily involves additional premium cost.

Many combinations of different types of life insurance, or of life and other types of insurance, are available. Which combination best fits the need of the insured is usually decided in conference with the insurance agent whom the policyholder-to-be has chosen as his adviser.

One may purchase various types of annuities. Annuities are a sound investment for people who already have enough life insurance but wish to increase their retirement income. If a man aged 30 wants an income of 100 dollars a month for life beginning at age 65, he can get it by purchasing an annuity. Such a policy would require payments to the insurance company of about 350 dollars a year until age 65.

At age 65 he could either accept payments of 100 dollars a month for the rest of his life, or take the cash value, ranging from 16,000 to 17,000 dollars. Were he to die at 65, before starting to draw this income, the given amount would be paid to his beneficiary.

Generally it is unwise to take out a "straight" annuity on a single life, because if the policyholder dies soon after annuity payments begin, these payments cease. One might have paid thousands of dollars for a straight annuity and, because of premature death, have received only a few hundred dollars in annuity benefits. To avoid this risk, there are available, at additional cost (or for smaller annuity payments, which amounts to the same thing), annuity contracts which require the insurance company to continue payments to a designated beneficiary after the death of the annuitant (the person originally entitled to receive the annuity payments). Amounts to be paid and the length of the period during which they must be paid differ with the nature of the annuity contract. Also, a person may choose to receive larger annuity payments which cease at death, or smaller payments so that his beneficiary will receive the balance either in monthly installments or in a lump sum.

Health (medical) insurance is available to cover the costs of sickness, hospitalization, and accidents. Various nonprofit medical, hospital, and surgical plans, such as "Blue Shield" and "Blue Cross," provide for a substantial part of the costs of illness and accident for many families. These plans usually apply to groups such as workers for some company or organization, and part of the cost may be met by employers. Private insurance companies also sell similar policies to individuals. About half of the people in this country are covered by some form of health insurance.

Most health insurance policies do not provide

for extremely long illnesses or very high medical costs. They are designed only for average situations. During recent years, however, various types of "major medical" insurance policies have become more common and take over where ordinary health insurance leaves off.

For example, an "ordinary" expense, perhaps the first 300 to 500 dollars, will not be covered by a "major medical" policy because it is included in the more usual form of insurance. Beyond this excluded amount, however, the "major medical" policy will pay all, or some specified per cent, of one's medical expenses up to several thousands of dollars. In this way, for a reasonable premium, a family can be protected against the financial disaster of a long and serious illness.

Disability income protection is sold by some insurance companies. The usual type of health insurance policy pays only for medical and hospital costs. But if the chief wage earner is unable to work because of illness or injury, the family may have little or no income. Various kinds of disability insurance are available to provide protection against this eventuality. A disabled wage earner is paid a certain amount weekly or monthly, for a specified period of time, or perhaps even for life. This kind of insurance is not bought by many persons of moderate incomes, both because of its relatively high premiums and because other types of protection, such as Social Security, are available. It is becoming increasingly popular, however, among persons of better-than-average means.

CHECK UP

1. What two purposes are served by life insurance? What factors determine the premium?

2. What is term life insurance? Straight life? Limited-payment life? Group insurance? What are the advantages and disadvantages of each?

3. What type of protection is provided by annuities? Disability insurance? Blue Cross? Blue Shield? Major medical?

4

How do private insurance companies operate?

There are two main types of insurance companies. Insurance is sold by both mutual and stock companies. *Mutual companies* sell standard insurance contracts under the laws of the states in which they operate. Premiums are fixed in insurance contracts (policies), and reserve funds are maintained to save the policyholders from having to help meet unexpected expenses. Each policyholder is a part owner of the mutual company. He has a right to vote at its annual meeting, and shares in the company's profits through the distribution of annual dividends. These may be paid to him directly, or credited toward the premium currently due, or added to the cash value of his life insurance policy.

The *stock company,* on the other hand, is organized as a regular corporation. A person who takes out a policy with a stock company is simply a buyer of insurance. Unless he is also a stockholder in this insurance company, he cannot participate in making the company's business decisions or share in its profits. The profits are divided among the insurance company's shareholders.

Mutual companies are not necessarily preferable to stock companies. Few holders of mutual policies actually take a part in the business of the company, and the cost of insurance sold by mutual companies is frequently about the same as that of comparable policies sold by a stock company.

Insurance companies are chartered under state laws. Insurance companies are organized under the laws of the state in which each has its home office. State insurance commissions oversee insurance company operations and stand ready to serve policyholders who need help. During the depression of the 1930's, many small insurance companies failed. Since that time, state regulations have greatly reduced unsound insurance practices.

Insurance companies need large reserves. Usually the premiums charged are sufficient to meet policyholders' claims, but there may be exceptions. A great fire or a tornado might sweep over a great city, inflicting property damage amounting to hundreds of millions of dollars. Or a "flu" epidemic such as that of 1918 could make it difficult for a life insurance company to pay its claims. Insurance companies maintain large reserves to meet unexpected increases in the total volume of the claims which their contracts would obligate them to pay. Some insurance companies "reinsure" their pol-

icies with other companies, thus further "spreading the risk."

Insurance companies make extensive investments. The chief sources of profit to an insurance company are returns on investments made possible by the excess of premiums received over claims paid. But first insurance companies must set aside sufficient funds to pay operating expenses. Then such other funds must be deposited as premium reserves as may be required by state laws. After these amounts have been set aside, insurance companies invest money just as banks do. Their investments must satisfy four requirements: (1) the *principal,* or original amount invested, must be as safe as possible; (2) the return must be reasonably

Distribution of life insurance company assets

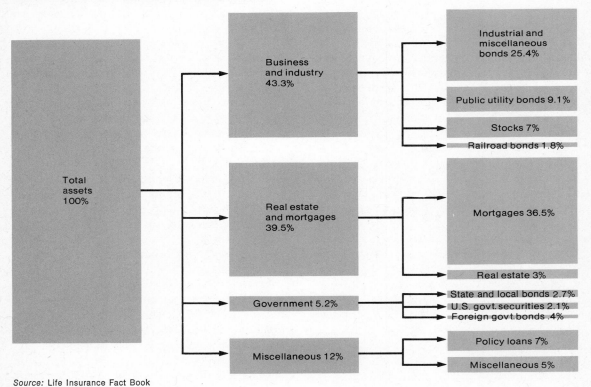

Source: Life Insurance Fact Book

dependable; (3) not too much money may be invested in bonds that mature, or become payable to the bondholder, in any one year; and (4) investments must vary in nature and be spread over different parts of the country.

Life insurance companies make loans. Many life insurance companies make loans for which homes, farms, and small business are pledged as security. The interest rates charged as well as their methods of doing business, are controlled by state agencies just as in the case of commercial banks. Life insurance companies are second only to savings-and-loan associations as a source of mortgage loans.

Policyholders also may obtain loans secured by the accumulated cash value of their life-insurance policies. In effect, the policyholder is borrowing back his own money from the insurance company. In the case of loans secured by an insurance policy, many banks compete with insurance companies, often charging lower interest rates. Whatever the lending agency, such a loan is attractive to the borrower because: (1) it is readily granted; (2) no cosigner is required; (3) interest charges are moderate; and (4) it can be continued for a long or indefinite term. Disadvantages of such a loan are: (1) Borrowing reduces one's insurance coverage by the amount of the loan; (2) the absence of a maturity date on the loan encourages the borrower to postpone repayment—which is to the insurance company's advantage; (3) the tendency to let the loan ride offsets the lower interest rate by prolonging the number of interest payments.

Insurance companies provide still other services. Insurance companies often provide valuable services to society through their educational advertising. Often this is designed to reduce the number of accidents, especially those involving motor vehicles. Fire insurance companies similarly promote measures for fire prevention. By stimulating interest in safety, life insurance companies have played leading roles in bringing about this kind of legislation.

1. What is a mutual insurance company? A stock company? How are insurance companies chartered? How is the size of reserves determined?

2. How has longer life expectancy affected life insurance companies? Why? How do these companies invest their funds? Describe various services they perform.

5

What forms of insurance are provided by government?

Privately owned and operated insurance companies have made it less necessary for the federal or state governments to provide life insurance for family protection. Besides the private insurance programs described in the preceding sections there is also social insurance—insurance in which the government participates or secures the participation of the employer and the wage earner in providing: (1) welfare payments to help the needy of all ages; (2) workmen's compensation in case of industrial accidents; (3) unemployment insurance; and (4) insurance plans to make possible retirement in old age.

In this country social insurance was first introduced by some of the states. Modern social legislation in the United States began in the early 1900's when laws were passed to help widows who had young children. The first mothers' pension law was passed in Illinois in 1911 to enable widowed mothers to keep children in the family rather than commit them to an orphans' home. Within ten years, about 40 states had passed similar laws under which communities gave assistance from local tax funds. Sometimes, also, the state paid part of the expense.

How the social security system functions

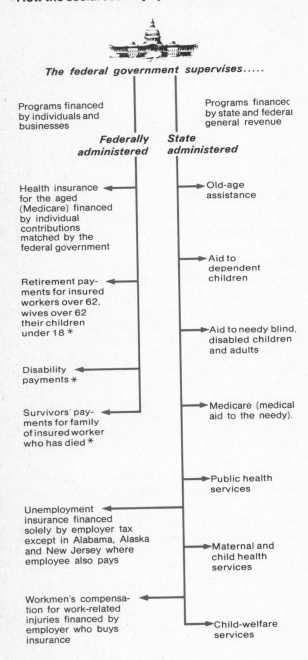

The federal government supervises.....

Programs financed
by individuals and
businesses

Programs financed
by state and federal
general revenue

**Federally
administered**

**State
administered**

Health insurance
for the aged
(Medicare) financed
by individual
contributions
matched by the
federal government

Old-age
assistance

Retirement pay-
ments for insured
workers over 62,
wives over 62
their children
under 18 *

Aid to
dependent
children

Disability
payments *

Aid to needy blind,
disabled children
and adults

Survivors' pay-
ments for family
of insured worker
who has died *

Medicare (medical
aid to the needy).

Public health
services

Unemployment
insurance financed
solely by employer tax
except in Alabama, Alaska
and New Jersey where
employee also pays

Maternal and
child health
services

Workmen's compensa-
tion for work-related
injuries financed by
employer who buys
insurance

Child-welfare
services

*Financed by "Social Security", i.e. compulsory employer
and employee contributions.*

In 1911, ten states passed laws providing for workmen's compensation. These laws required employers, when workmen were injured on the job, to provide weekly cash benefits to cover wage losses and medical care. To protect themselves, employers took out insurance with private companies or, in some instances, through state insurance programs.

The 1920's witnessed a slow growth of social insurance for other groups. During that decade, ten states passed old-age pension laws providing assistance to needy old persons. Funds for this assistance came from the general tax resources of the states.

Unemployment insurance is an important "cushion" against want. Insurance against loss of income from unemployment is relatively recent. In 1932 the state of Wisconsin established the first unemployment insurance program. Today all 50 states provide protection against the risk of involuntary unemployment to persons in certain occupations.

The cost of unemployment insurance is met partly by employers and partly by the federal government (through taxes on employers). The worker himself makes no contribution except in a few states. When a worker is unemployed, the amount he receives is based upon his previous wages. Minimum and maximum payments differ from state to state. As a rule, payments are made for a period of not more than 26 weeks, beginning two weeks after the person becomes unemployed.

Most states have state employment agencies which provide centralized services to help those drawing unemployment compensation find jobs. A person who refuses to work when jobs are available is likely to lose his compensation. To receive payments, one must be out of work through no fault of his own. He must also have been regularly employed, generally for at least ten weeks prior to becoming unemployed. Part-time workers are not eligible for insurance under this program.

Federal "Social Security" provides for old age and retirement. The most significant advance in social insurance was made possible by the federal Social Security Act (1935). One of this law's major aims was to provide a program of old-age and survivors' insurance to help the growing number of older people finance their retirement. A payroll deduction from the employee's wages is turned over to the federal Internal Revenue Service by the employer. It is credited to the worker's account in the wage record by the Old Age and Survivors Insurance Trust Fund. A matching amount, collected from the worker's employer, is also deposited. Self-employed persons pay their Social Security tax in submitting their income tax return. They pay an amount greater than that paid by other workers but less than the combined total paid by a worker and his employer.

A worker and his employer contribute to this fund until the worker reaches the age of 65 and is eligible for retirement benefits. Most wage earners, including farm workers and domestic help, have been covered by recent extensions of the act. Doctors and many teachers are not covered, and therefore neither pay Social Security taxes nor receive Social Security benefits. Workers, if they choose, may draw benefits at reduced rates as early as age 62. Fully covered workers who become totally and permanently disabled may draw benefits regardless of age.

The amount received in monthly retirement benefits depends on earnings subject to the Social Security tax. Persons who work after they reach age 65, and who earn more than a stated amount annually, must continue paying the social insurance tax even though they receive no benefits. All workers become eligible to receive benefits at age 72, regardless of what they may be earning. But such workers continue to pay the Social Security tax as long as they are employed.

Federal Social Security also provides financial help to certain specified dependents. Certain dependents of retired workers receive benefits while the latter are still living. Provision is also made in the Social Security program for aid to a deceased or disabled worker's dependents,

and for dependent children, the blind, and some others who are unable to support themselves and did not work in Social-Security-covered jobs.

Social Security is now a part of American life. When the national Social Security program was first proposed, many argued that it was "unsuited to our democratic way of life." They feared that it would lessen the incentive of workers to save and to provide for themselves. Some were opposed to the compulsory nature of the program. Others feared that Social Security would compete with the profits and growth of private insurance companies.

Some of this opposition continues, but most Americans have come to accept the idea of Social Security. This program has been extended under both Democratic and Republican administrations. American families, with the help of their insurance agents, are working out programs of private life insurance to supplement their Social Security protection.

"Medicare" is the newest form of social insurance. In July, 1966, a broad program of federal health insurance, popularly known as "medicare," went into effect for persons over 65. The program provides two kinds of health insurance: (1) *hospital insurance,* which covers a substantial amount of hospital and post-hospital expenses, including payments for nursing care and out-patient diagnostic services; and (2) voluntary *medical insurance* at low cost ($6.30 a month) covering 80 per cent of the cost of physicians' and surgeons' services, whether at home, in the doctor's office, or in the hospital, as well as home health visits and other medical services.[1]

Because of the costs of added retirement and other benefits, employees' contributions to Social Security (matched by employers) were raised by 1974 to 5.85 per cent of the first 12,600 dollars earned each year. Future increases were also scheduled.

---

[1] "Medicaid" pays for medical services to persons with very low or no income.

The government makes life insurance available for persons in military service. It has long been the policy of the United States to provide compensation or pensions to veterans of wartime military service or to their surviving dependents. During World War II those in active service were also given the privilege of taking out life insurance up to 10,000 dollars at a low premium rate, and to continue this insurance after their discharge.

In 1965 a new law provided for Servicemen's Group Life Insurance, with insurance benefits similar to those offered to World War II servicemen. The new law called for policies to be issued by private insurance companies under the supervision of the Veterans' Administration, rather than being issued directly by the government. The added risk costs resulting from combat service are paid out of government funds. At present, some six million servicemen and former servicemen hold various kinds of servicemen's life insurance. The total face value of their policies amounts to more than 40 billion dollars.

CHECK UP

1. What types of social insurance are provided by government? How is each financed?

2. How does Social Security provide for the retirement of workers? How does it help the dependents of workers? To what extent are Social Security and other forms of social insurance accepted as part of the American way of life?

3. What insurance protection has the government provided men and women in the armed forces? Why?

Clinching the main ideas

Insurance protection against the most likely and potentially most disastrous risks of loss of assets and income is as important for families as it is for businesses. No family financial plan can be considered complete without such protection. Minimum insurance protection is priced low enough to be included as a regular item in most family budgets.

Buying insurance is *not* the same as gambling with the insurance company. Whereas gambling deliberately *creates* a risk of loss, insurance provides protection in situations where risk *already exists*. It does this by spreading what would be a large loss for an individual among many persons. The "loss" of each insured person (that is, the premium he pays), is certain but small. Most people prefer a certain small loss of this type to a possible disastrous loss.

Insurance company actuaries, by studying the statistics of past experiences, can predict the number of future losses with reasonable accuracy. Thus, insurance companies can set premium rates which, combined with returns from investments, enable them to meet the obligations spelled out in policies. Insurance firms are either *stock companies* (regular profit-making corporations) or mutual companies (owned by policyholders). Both types of company are regulated by state governments.

The most common types of property insurance are fire and automobile coverages. Automobile insurance also usually includes liability insurance covering property damage or personal injury to others. A variety of additional types of property and liability insurance, as well as several forms of health and disability insurance, is commonly available.

The basic forms of life insurance are: (1) term; (2) straight life; (3) limited-payment life; and (4) endowment. All of these except term insurance combine investment features with protection. Policies can be tailored to fit almost any need.

Many people are covered by "group" insurance, usually under "term" contracts. Life insurance companies also sell annuities, which emphasize investment features more heavily than do regular life insurance policies.

Social insurance includes old-age and survivors' insurance (commonly known as Social Security), workmen's compensation for injured employees, and unemployment insurance. The last two are administered by states (although workmen's compensation in many states is placed with private companies), the first by the federal government. In 1966 a federal health insurance program ("Medicare") was established for persons over 65. It provides both hospital and medical insurance at low cost. Life insurance also is provided by the federal government for members of the armed forces and for some veterans. Other government social benefits are available to certain categories of the aged or needy, although not on an insurance basis.

Insurance buying is both important and complicated. Most persons buying insurance need the advice of professional representatives of reputable insurance firms.

Chapter 8 review

Terms to understand

1. coinsurance clause
2. appraisal value
3. term insurance
4. cash value
5. actuaries
6. face value
7. beneficiary
8. annuity
9. social insurance
10. public liability
11. personal liability
12. "no-fault" automobile liability insurance

What do you think?

1. How is it possible accurately to predict the total number of deaths or the dollar cost of losses by fire for a given year?

2. What factors determine how much a policyholder collects on a fire insurance policy when his house is destroyed by fire?

3. Why do some states require all drivers to carry personal injury and property damage liability insurance? Why do many owners of cars carry a greater amount of insurance than is required? Other types of automobile insurance than those required?

4. What is the best form of life insurance? Give reasons for your answer.

5. Has Social Security made life insurance less necessary? Has it caused a drop in the amount of life insurance sold? Explain.

6. Should the "no-fault" principle be adopted in the case of automobile liability insurance? Why or why not?

Extending your knowledge of economics

1. Discuss the merits and limitations of national health insurance. Members of the class may wish to find out how such a plan works in Great Britain or in other European countries.

2. Insurance brokers will be able to provide pamphlets and insurance forms that provide more detailed information about various kinds of insurance.

part three

Economic organization for production

chapter nine

How business is organized for production

1. **What are the chief characteristics of the nation's business system?**
2. **What is the nature of an individual proprietorship?**
3. **What is the nature of a partnership?**
4. **What is the nature of a corporation?**
5. **What is a co-operative?**
6. **What are the advantages and disadvantages of "bigness" in business?**

The business of America is business.
CALVIN COOLIDGE

Chapter 4 pointed out that production is accomplished by the use of land, labor, capital, and management (or entrepreneurship)—the four factors of production. The chapters in Part Three deal more specifically with how management organizes and supervises the use of the other three factors in producing a major portion of the nation's goods and services.

Chapters 9 and 10 consider the nature, role, and problems of nonagricultural business firms, as well as the relationships between private businesses and government. Chapter 11 deals with agriculture, which can be considered a form of business. The role of unionized labor, its relationships with government and the general public, and its influence on nonunion labor are discussed in Chapter 12.

Probably no social institutions except the family, government, and religion affect day-to-day living as much as does business. Most incomes, and most things consumed, stem from business activities. Regardless of where one lives or what one does, Americans are members of a business society from birth to death.

During recent years, much criticism has been directed at the so-called "military-industrial complex" or "business establishment." Some of this criticism no doubt is justified. Much of it, however, is merely uninformed.

1

What are the chief characteristics of the nation's business system?

Business enterprises, or firms, operate with the expectation of making profits; that is, that "income" will exceed "outgo." In a free enterprise economy, no business can survive unless it makes a profit. And a firm cannot make profits unless it gives consumers what they want at prices they are willing to pay. Furthermore, this must be done so efficiently that production costs will be less than the total payments received from consumers. A firm's overall income must be greater than its expenditures.

There are about twelve million business firms in the United States, excluding farmers. This country has some twelve million nonagricultural firms. These firms vary greatly in size, whether measured by total sales, investment in the business, or total number of employees. Some firms have only one employee (the owner), almost no physical assets, and annual sales of only a few thousand dollars. Eighty per cent of all businesses employ fewer than 20 persons.

At the opposite extreme, several thousand large firms each employ several hundred or several thousand workers. General Motors alone employs more than 750,000 persons, and American Telephone and Telegraph employs nearly 700,000. General Motors has total assets of more than 14 billion dollars, while American Telephone has assets of more than 40 billion dollars. During a recent year, General Motors' sales amounted to more than 22 billion dollars, and American Telephone's sales were more than 14 billion dollars.

Large businesses account for most of the production of goods and services. Large firms dominate manufacturing. A little more than 1 per cent of all manufacturing firms produce almost two-thirds of the manufactured goods as measured by sales values. A similar situation is characteristic of some other kinds of economic activities.

Big businesses tend to dominate those kinds of production in which capital can easily be substituted for labor; that is, where large and expensive machinery can be operated by a relatively small number of persons engaged mainly in routine and repetitive tasks. As was pointed out in Chapter 2, "roundabout" mass production, using specialized labor (division of labor) with modern machinery and equipment, tends to lower production costs. Low production costs enable large firms to undersell small and high-cost manufacturers. Since consumers like to buy at the lowest possible prices, there is little place for a small business in the manufacturing of goods that can be mass-produced readily.

Types of business organizations

By per cent of national receipts

By number of businesses

Source: Statistical Abstract

The average worker in this country is backed by substantial capital investment. It has been estimated that the average capital investment per manufacturing employee is about 23,000 dollars. This average is increasing yearly (it is up from about 5000 dollars a generation ago). In many kinds of production, the average capital per worker is much higher—in petroleum refining, for example, it amounts to about 75,000 dollars per worker. This explains why small businesses do not thrive in certain kinds of manufacturing. It also explains why manufacturing output per man-hour is high in this country compared to most other nations.

Small businesses are more common in the fields of personal services and retail distribution. There are fewer advantages of bigness in business activities which involve specialized or personalized services. Although there are large chains such as supermarkets in some of these fields, much of the retailing, repair work, and the like, is performed by small businesses. Small retail food stores, drug stores, restaurants, gasoline stations, laundry and dry-clean-

ing establishments, beauty parlors, barbershops, and appliance and automobile repair shops, are found in every community.

Many new businesses are started each year. About 20,000 or more new firms go into business each year. Some of them serve real consumer needs, and prosper under good management. Many, however, have little to keep them going except the optimism of their founders. One half of these new firms are no longer in business within two years. Some fail because of inadequate financing or poor management. Others sell out to larger establishments, or cease operations for various other causes. Of those that prosper, a few eventually grow into large businesses. Contrary to what is sometimes said, there still are many opportunities in this country for young persons with sound ideas, ability, and the willingness to work hard, to start and develop their own businesses.

Small business failures usually are a result of inadequate financing or poor mangement. Organizing and operating a business involves

Rate of business failure per 10,000 businesses

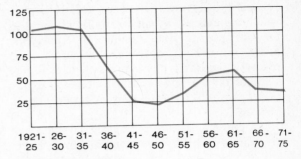

Source: Statistical Abstract

hard work, and most businessmen work much longer hours than do their employees. But this is not enough, because to succeed, a business, large or small, must be efficient. In addition, to produce something that people are willing to buy, the business must do this at least as well and as inexpensively as its competitors. Work must be planned carefully, and time-saving and labor-saving devices must be adopted wherever possible.

Large firms usually have sufficient funds to hire superior managers and to acquire whatever up-to-date equipment is needed. Consequently, the failure rate of large businesses is not nearly as high as that of small businesses. Most experts agree that small businesses fail when (1) they lack highly qualified managers or (2) do not have the financial resources to acquire modern capital equipment or to survive a temporary misfortune or a slump in business.

Minority groups are not represented proportionately in business ownership. Less than 1 per cent of all manufacturing businesses and less than 2 per cent of construction businesses are owned by blacks or members of other nonwhite minority groups. Most of the businesses owned by these groups are small. Even in the

Business failures in the United States

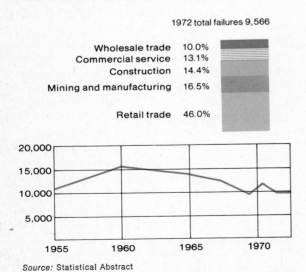

1972 total failures 9,566

Wholesale trade	10.0%
Commercial service	13.1%
Construction	14.4%
Mining and manufacturing	16.5%
Retail trade	46.0%

Source: Statistical Abstract

black and minority group neighborhoods, about four-fifths of the total dollar volume of business is controlled by white owners—most of whom do not live within the "ghetto" communities.

Since the late 1960's, there has been much talk about "black capitalism." This expression is used to suggest Negro or minority group ownership or management of business. From a social viewpoint it certainly is desirable that more members of minority groups be helped and encouraged to participate in the ownership and control of businesses. It seems unlikely, however, that this approach would solve the general problems of ghetto and minority group poverty, as some persons appear to believe. Control of most of the country's businesses by members of the white majority certainly has not eliminated poverty among white people.

Legally, business firms are organized and operated in three different forms: individual *proprietorships, partnerships, and* corporations. Although most businesses are individual proprietorships, virtually all large businesses are corporations. Legally co-operatives are corporations, but they differ in several ways from other corporations.

Each form of business enterprise has certain advantages and certain disadvantages. Under given specific conditions, one form is likely to be more appropriate than another. But no one form is "best" for all situations any more than any given size of business can be said to be "best."

CHECK UP

1. What characteristics of the nation's business system are discussed in Section 1?

2. What conclusions may be drawn in each case from the information provided?

The four principal ways of doing business under private enterprise

Type of Organization	Formation	Ownership	Control and Management	Net Profits; Losses	Termination
Sole Proprietorship	Individual decision of businessman, who starts it himself, or buys from another	Individual	By owner or persons delegated by him	Profits to owner; losses borne by him	By owner's decision to dissolve; death, disability, or retirement of owner
Partnership	By agreement between associates (partners)	Jointly by two or more individuals; or by terms of partnership agreement.	By partners or persons they delegate	Shared according to partnership agreement	By mutual decision to dissolve, resignation or death of any member, or bankruptcy of the firm
Corporation	Organized by associates and legalized through state charter	Stockholders, according to number of shares	Through Board of Directors, elected by the stockholders (usually 1 vote per share of stock held)	Dividends to stockholders according to number of shares	Bankruptcy or by legal dissolution, as when charter is violated
Co-operative	By agreement among interested persons. Usually incorporated under special laws that apply to co-operatives	Member-patrons	Through Board of Directors elected by the members (usually only 1 vote per member)	Profits distributed to members in proportion to amount originally bought	Bankruptcy or by legal dissolution of the co-op

Source: Statistical Abstract

2

What is the nature of an individual proprietorship?

An individual proprietorship is a business owned by one person. About four-fifths of all businesses in this country, more than nine million altogether, are of this form. This is the easiest kind of business to start. No legal formalities (except licenses for certain kinds of businesses) are required.

An individual owner can run his business to suit himself; he makes his own decisions. And should the business make a profit, it goes to the owner alone. It is not surprising that the individual proprietorship is the most popular type of business for small undertakings which do not require large investments of capital.

Number of sole proprietorships in nine major categories

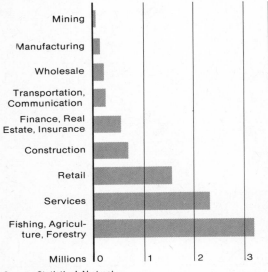

Source: Statistical Abstract

There is another side to this story, however. Should an individually owned and operated business suffer a loss or fail, the owner has no one to blame but himself. *Unlimited liability* makes the owner fully responsible for all losses and debts of the business. Any property or income of the owner, not just that property used in the business (with a few minor exceptions), may be legally seized and sold by the firm's creditors to pay the firm's debts. Thousands of small individual businesses fail each year, for a wide variety of reasons.

An individual owner does not have complete freedom of operation. On first thought it may seem that the person who operates his own business has complete freedom to run it as he pleases. This is not the case. For example, if a merchant rents a building to carry on his business, the landlord can exercise a degree of control when the lease expires. Comparatively few operators of small business concerns own the buildings they occupy. They usually rent their business space on a five- or ten-year basis. Should the operator of a men's clothing store seek to renew his five-year lease, the landlord may demand higher rent. If the clothier finds that this rent is too high, he will have to seek new quarters. If these cannot be found, he will be forced to close.

Like all other citizens, the businessman must operate within an established social, legal, and economic pattern. He is subject to laws and government regulations. He also has to consider the requirements of people he may employ. No employer has absolute control over hours of work, minimum-wage rates, or working conditions. A retail merchant, for example, may not be able to keep his store open as early or late in the day as he would like. Public opinion, laws and government regulations, and the policy of labor unions are among the factors which compel businessmen to conform to accepted standards. In a very real sense, it is the customer who ultimately is every businessman's "boss."

1. What are the advantages and limitations of the individual proprietorship?

2. What kinds of restrictions limit the owner's freedom of operation?

3

What is the nature of a partnership?

A *partnership* is an agreement between two or more persons to share the responsibilities and the profits (or losses) of a business. Legally, partnerships are easy to form. All that is necessary is an agreement between the partners. To avoid disputes, it is desirable to have the agreement in writing and witnessed. About 9 per cent of this country's businesses—a little less than one million altogether—are partnerships.

Individual proprietorships may become partnerships. A person who operates a business by himself may wish to expand it but lacks the necessary funds. For this and other reasons, he may decide that a partnership will be a suitable business arrangement.

A clothier, for example, may wish to enlarge his business. He needs about 50,000 dollars to buy his enlarged stock of goods and to pay higher rent for a new store. He can raise only 25,000 dollars, but one of his friends, who is interested in the business, can supply an equal amount. The two men therefore agree to become partners. The enlarged enterprise is expected to yield each partner a larger income than he could make by himself in a smaller store.

A partnership has both advantages and disadvantages. The usual arrangement between persons engaged in a partnership, whether written or not, is that each: (1) takes over a specific part of the management or work, (2)

Number of active partnerships in nine major categories

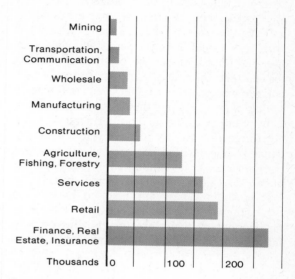

Source: Statistical Abstract

furnishes a stated amount of money, and (3) takes a certain percentage of the profits. This sharing of responsibility is one advantage that a partnership has over individual ownership.

There also are other advantages. The partners can divide responsibility for the store so that no partner has to work unduly long hours. If one partner wants to take a vacation, there will still be a responsible person in charge of the business. Each partner contributes his own special skills and experience to the business.

Partners of course sometimes disagree about how a business should be operated. If their disagreements cannot be resolved, the partnership may have to be dissolved. Whenever one partner leaves a business, or a new person becomes a partner, a completely new partnership must be arranged.

There is one serious disadvantage in the operation of a partnership. Each partner is legally responsible for all financial obligations of the business. That is, each partner has *unlimited liability*. If the mistakes made by one partner should cause the business to fail, or if one partner should embezzle the firm's funds and flee the country, the remaining partner (or partners) would become personally liable for the total obligations of the partnership. Should the partner who fled have no property, the partner who remained might even be forced to sell his property to pay the obligation in full.

In addition to the general partnership, there are forms of partnership, rarely found in this country, in which some member or members are not subject to unlimited liability. These members, called "silent partners," merely invest in the business but take no part in its management. Their losses, then, are limited to the amount of their investments. But even in this type of partnership, some member or members of the firm must have unlimited liability.

Number of active corporations in nine major categories

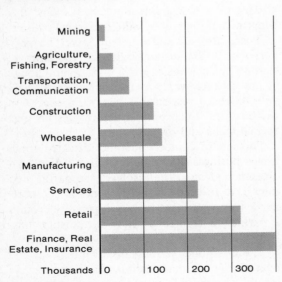

Source: Statistical Abstract

4

What is the nature of a corporation?

A corporation may be large or small, and may have only a few or several thousand owners. Regardless of the number of owners, the corporation is operated as a single firm, legally distinct from its owners. In the eyes of the law, a corporation is a separate legal "person."

Business is transacted in the name of the corporation. A corporation can sue and be sued in the courts under its own name, rather than under the names of its owners. The corporate form of enterprise is the easiest and quickest way to raise large sums of money for capital investment. This, in large part, explains why almost all big businesses are corporations.

Most of the manufacturing, mining, transportation, and communications, and much of the wholesaling and retailing, is carried on by corporations. Although about 12 per cent of American businesses are corporations, they account for about 80 per cent of all production (measured by the value of sales).

Corporations may grow from individual proprietorships or partnerships. Many large business firms started as small, individually operated concerns, and then perhaps expanded into partnerships and later into corporations. The clothier and his partner may again be used to illustrate this. They have operated their clothing store for ten years and built up a successful business. Their firm has become well known in the city, and the partners have decided that they want to expand still further. Even though they have been making a good profit each year, they have not accumulated sufficient money to carry out their plans for expansion. The landlord of the store on which their five-year lease is about to expire has just notified them that he must increase the rent because his taxes are going up. The partners must make a decision.

The clothier has been checking on shopping centers being developed on the outskirts of the city. These have ample parking space, and one of them would be an ideal location for a clothing store. To obtain the necessary funds he and his partner consider taking on more partners, but they are unwilling to yield part of the management of the business to someone else. After some study, they decide that the best way to expand is to change the form of business organization to that of a corporation. This would enable them to obtain the necessary additional funds without surrendering effective control of their business.

A corporation is owned by those who hold its common stock. For these two partners to control the new corporation, they must own at least 51 per cent of its *common* or voting *stock*. The owner of each share of common stock is entitled to vote in the corporation's business—one vote per share. He will also receive *dividends*—payments from a firm's profits whenever it is decided to distribute a part of the profits. Dividends are paid at a determined amount per share of stock. (The general nature of corporate securities—stocks and bonds—was discussed in Chapter 7.)

Before establishing the corporation, the clothier and his partner must determine the amount of common stock they can buy. They do not have much cash, but they do have (1) a large stock of goods, (2) fixtures and equipment that can be used in the new store, (3) what is known in business as *good will* (the

earning power of a going concern, its reputation, and its customer relations), (4) exclusive rights to purchase certain brands of clothing, and (5) "know-how." Suppose the estimated value of these items, plus the amount of cash they can raise, is 80,000 dollars. This amount must account for at least 51 per cent of the common stock if the two partners are to retain control. Neither one would have exclusive control, since each would own only a little more than 25 per cent of the stock. The partners decide to issue common stock to the amount of 156,000 dollars, of which they will retain 80,000 (about 51.3 per cent) to insure their control. The remaining 76,000 dollars in common stock will be sold in 50-dollar shares to anyone interested.

A corporation is created by law. Usually five or more incorporators file an application, known as the *articles of incorporation,* with the appropriate state official. The application states the purpose of the proposed corporation, the amount of its capital stock, and the names of the incorporators.

If the application is in order, a corporate charter is granted by the state. This charter allows the corporation to exist and to do business, subject to the laws of the state and the terms of the charter. Once the corporation has been legally authorized, the sale of the stock is arranged.

Large issues of stock sold by a corporation to the public must have the approval of a government agency, the Securities and Exchange Commission (SEC). This approval certifies that the sellers of the stock are not concealing information about the business from potential stock buyers. It is *not* an endorsement from the SEC that the stock is a "good buy." Severe penalties are imposed for giving incomplete or misleading information about stocks.

Small corporations usually sell their stocks to the organizers or their friends. Larger issues of stock are sold by *investment bankers* (often known as underwriters) for a fee.

Setting up a corporation

	legal steps involved	practical matters involved
1	Interested parties meet to decide basic questions.	a. Amount of existing assets (if any) of group desiring incorporation. b. Amount of money that must be raised. c. Division of ownership among interested parties.
2	Draw up *articles of incorporation*. (For a small fee, lawyer will draw up necessary papers.)	a. Name and purpose of proposed corporation. b. Address of main office. c. Duration (in perpetuity, or for limited period). d. Names of directors. e. Points 1a, b, c above to be expressed in terms of shares of stock: face value of share, number of shares to be retained by directors, and number to be sold (if any) to other persons. f. Times of stockholders' meetings.
3	Send articles of incorporation and application for state charter (or certificate of incorporation) to appropriate state official.	a. Official reviews papers for compliance with state laws. b. Articles of incorporation returned for revision, if necessary.
4	Charter is issued by state if articles of incorporation comply with state laws. A new corporation has thus officially come into being.	a. Shares to be sold publicly may now be marketed through an investment banking firm. b. As business grows, further financing may be carried on by new issues of common stock, and by the sale of preferred stock and bonds.

A corporation is managed by a board of directors. The management of a corporation rests with a group of directors elected by the stockholders. Each stockholder has as many votes as he has shares. Stockholders (or shareholders as they are often called) may vote for themselves as directors if they wish. An owner of a majority of the shares of a corporation, as in the case of a small company, usually would do this. Because of the number of votes he controls, he could also elect the other directors. Directors make general policies for the corporation, and decide when dividends are to be paid and the amounts per share. They also appoint the corporation's president and other principal officials. In a small corporation, directors are likely to appoint themselves as officials.

A board of directors usually must have at least three members. These three members could be the two original partners and the wife of one of them. With more than half of the stock controlled by two families, the two original partners in the clothing store mentioned above would have effective control of the corporation. If the 156,000 dollars is sufficient for the purpose, the clothier and his former partner are ready to move ahead with the new and expanded store.

In a large corporation stock ownership is

Organization chart of a typical manufacturing corporation

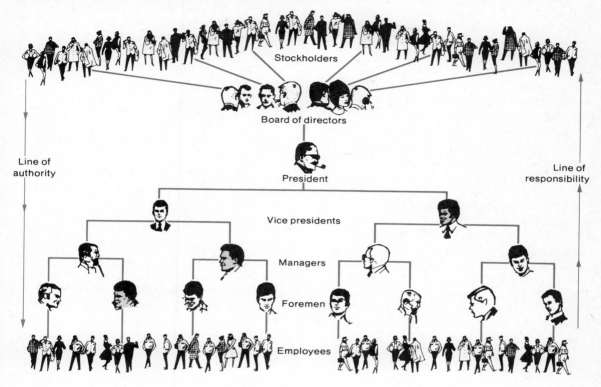

Stockholders

Board of directors

Line of
authority

President

Line of
responsibility

Vice presidents

Managers

Foremen

Employees

widely scattered. In a small corporation, a few persons are likely to own the majority of stock and to be the officers and directors. In larger corporations, however, stock ownership is likely to be scattered among many people—perhaps thousands or hundreds of thousands. Each stockholder in such cases has only a small per cent of the total number of shares. The officers of the corporation are usually employed because of their abilities as managers, and are paid high salaries.

The combined stock holdings of the officers and directors of a large corporation may be less than 5 per cent of the total shares of stock. Yet these few people often are able to main-tain virtual control of the corporation year after year. They usually manage to do this by a system of *proxies,* which transfer the voting rights of many holders of small amounts of stock to a few large stockholders or their representatives. Under this system the management asks the stockholders to give a *proxy committee* the authority to vote the way it wishes. Since the proxy committee in reality usually represents the management, this arrangement enables management to control the corporation.

If the majority of the stockholders should find fault with the way the company is being operated, they no longer would turn over their proxies to management. Instead, they might "gang up" and vote for a new management. This sometimes happens. To prevent such an occurrence, management tries to operate the company profitably, and makes sure that reasonable dividends on the stocks are paid whenever possible.

Funds can be raised in other ways than by issuing common stocks. As a business expands, more funds will be needed. Corporations may buy on credit or borrow from banks. They may also obtain funds by issuing *bonds* and *preferred stock.*

It will be recalled from Chapter 7 that a *bond* is a promise by a firm to repay at the end of a stated number of years the full amount of the money a person has loaned to the firm. Interest at a certain per cent of the stated value (face value) of the bond must be paid the owner at fixed intervals whether or not the corporation is making a profit. If a corporation is not able to pay back the full amount of the bond at the due date, or if interest is not paid

when due, the bondholders can force payment. Buildings and land, machinery, stock, and other assets of the corporation may even have to be sold to meet these payments. Bonds, therefore, usually are a much safer investment than is common stock. But bondholders do not share in profits—all they receive is the interest on their bonds. Nor do bondholders have any voting rights in the corporation.

Thus, if the new corporation which the clothier and his partner formed issued 30,000 dollars in bonds at 6 per cent interest, they would have to pay each year 1800 dollars in interest. The directors would have to determine whether the corporation's earnings could be expected to increase sufficiently to warrant this extra expense.

Preferred stock resembles bonds in that investors in preferred stock receive dividends at a fixed rate of return, usually set at the time of issue. Moreover, preferred stockholders are paid their dividends out of corporation profits *before* common stockholders receive their dividends. Preferred stock resembles common stock in that dividends out of profits, not interest, are paid to its holders. If there are no profits, preferred stockholders receive no dividends. Owners of preferred stock usually do not have a vote in the corporation.

Because the face value of bonds must be paid before any other obligations, the returns on bonds tend to be lower than on preferred stock or common stock. This may not be true, however, if the corporation's profits are small. Furthermore, income from common stock is affected by general trends in the stock market and by other factors which reduce the corporation's profits. Holders of common stock naturally look for greater returns on their investments to offset greater possible losses. If the corporation fails, bondholders will be paid first, preferred stockholders second, and common stockholders will have to settle for what is left.

It is seldom that a large corporation which fails has so many obligations that the bondholders are not paid in full. Usually holders of preferred stock are also paid. But the holders

---

NUMBER OF STOCKHOLDERS REACHES NEW PEAK

The number of people in the United States owning stocks is at the all-time high of 25 million. Below are the ten corporations having the most stockholders in a recent year.

Company	Number of Stockholders
American Telephone and Telegraph	3,142,000
General Motors	1,349,000
Standard Oil of New Jersey	774,000
General Telephone and Electronics	544,000
General Electric	541,000
International Business Machines	501,000
Ford Motor	384,000
United States Steel	349,000
Radio Corporation of America	321,000
Sears Roebuck	252,000

Source: New York Stock Exchange

Different types of securities

	common stock	preferred stock	bond
Relationship of security owner to corporation	Part owner of corporation (limited liability)	Part owner of corporation (limited liability)	Creditor of corporation
Earnings	Cash dividend or stock dividend if so declared by the board of directors	Cash dividend based on specified percentage of face value of share, if so declared by board of directors	Interest is usually paid at regular intervals, whether or not corporation earns a profit
Time Limit	Ownership ceases only when stock is sold or company ceases to exist	Ownership ceases only when stock is sold or when company "calls" it (buys it back) or converts it into common stock at a stipulated ratio	Bond must be repaid in full at its date of maturity
Value	Rises and falls as demand for stock fluctuates	Rises and falls as demand for stock fluctuates	Established at a set amount when bond is issued
Advantages	Often earns highest return; right to vote for directors of corporation	Dividend paid before that of common stock	Receives interest payment before dividends are declared; first claim on corporate assets in cases of bankruptcy

of common stock often lose part, if not all, of their investment.

Corporations have several advantages over individual proprietorships or partnerships. Besides providing adequate funds more readily than do other forms of business organization, a corporation has the following advantages:

1. Each stockholder has legal liability for only the amount of stock he holds. The value of his stock may shrink to nothing if the corporation fails, but he cannot be held personally responsible for the corporation's debts. Unlike a single owner or a partner, he has *limited liability*.

2. Corporation stockholders do not have to become involved in the actual management of the business. This is left to the corporation's board of directors, officers, and managers.

3. Shares of stock are transferable—they may be sold or given to someone else without changing the status of the corporation. The process of buying and selling shares of stock is relatively simple. One seldom has any difficulty selling the stock of a reputable corporation. The actual selling is usually handled by licensed brokers (see Chapter 7).

4. Corporations have a perpetual life (limited only by the terms of their corporate charters). Unlike individual proprietorships or partnerships, the business does not have to be closed or reorganized upon the death or withdrawal of one of the owners.

Corporations pay high income taxes. One of the most widely discussed disadvantages of the corporate form of organization is the fact that it is subject to high federal income tax rates. In 1971 a small corporation, with earnings of not more than 25,000 dollars, had to pay 22 per cent of its net income in taxes. For earnings of more than 25,000 dollars, corporate income tax amounted to 48 per cent. When the remaining profits, or a portion of them, are paid to stockholders as dividends, those receiving dividends also have to pay personal income tax on them. This is called *double taxation.*

Individual proprietorships and partnerships, as such, do not pay income taxes. The owners of these businesses do, of course, pay their own individual income taxes, but there is no "double taxation." It should be pointed out, however, that despite such higher taxes, new corporations continue to be formed and to thrive. Apparently the heavy corporate taxes are no insurmountable barrier to this type of business organization.

CHECK UP

1. What are the advantages and limitations of corporate business organization?

2. How is a corporation created? Managed? Owned?

3. In what different ways can a corporation raise needed funds?

5

What is a co-operative?

A co-operative is a jointly owned business organization operated for the benefit of its members. Members are also *patrons*—persons who utilize the services offered by the co-operative. Hence they are often referred to as "member-patrons." The benefits usually take the form of *refunds,* or payments based on the net income of the co-operative. The payments are distributed among the members much as dividends are paid to stockholders of a corporation.

Like regular stock companies (corporations), co-operatives must be chartered under the laws of the state in which they are organized. In many other respects, however, co-operative associations differ from corporations.

The co-operative idea goes back to 1844, when a group of 28 weavers met in Rochdale, England, to explore ways of reducing their cost of living. After much discussion, they decided to pool their money and organize their own retail store. The plan was to buy foods and processed goods directly from producers and wholesalers. By taking turns working in the store, they found they could reduce labor costs and realize appreciable savings.

Co-operatives are based on certain principles. The Rochdale weavers formulated three fundamental principles which still are basic to the operation of most co-operatives: (1) democratic control, (2) limited returns from capital, and (3) fair distribution of savings to member-patrons. These principles differ from the purposes of a corporation, which is organized to yield a profit to the owners from the sale of its products. They give the co-operative its distinctive character.

(1) *Democratic control.* A co-operative is an organization in which all the members work to achieve common ends. Without democratic control this is not possible. Democratic control is usually accomplished by voting on the basis of "one member, one vote." This prevents a concentration of power. The member-patrons have a voice in determining the product or service that the co-operative offers. They can help decide the policies which govern the management of their association.

(2) *Limited returns from capital.* A co-operative, like any privately owned business, needs capital. It must have buildings, equipment, and goods and funds to carry on its day-to-day operations. This capital is used to build up the volume of business for better service to members. Because of this need to expand its capital and at the same time to charge low (competitive) prices, the return on a co-op-

Dedicated Reformer

Robert Owen

(1771–1858)

In England during the early 1800's the use of machinery increased the quantity and improved the quality of textile goods. During these years living conditions in the new mill towns seemed to grow worse. An oversupply of labor allowed mill owners to pay extremely low wages. Often they replaced men with women and children who would work for less. Poverty compelled workers to live in cramped and unheated tenements where disease and malnutrition were causes of early death.

One of the successful textile manufacturers of this era was Robert Owen. Upon acquiring the mills in New Lanark, Scotland, he was shocked by conditions in the factories and by the wretched appearance and ill health of the workers. Owen believed the workers were the victims of their environment and that industrialists had an obligation to use a fair share of their profits for the betterment of their employees. Were this done, living conditions would be improved and society would be better for the change.

To put this theory into practice, Owen introduced reforms at New Lanark. He raised wages, reduced working hours, and abolished fines for spoiled work. No child under ten was employed, for all of them went to the free school. Children between ten and eighteen received some education during working hours. He built new housing for the workers and provided a store where they could buy good food and clothing at low prices. Insurance funds were established and recreation facilities were built. Soon this model community attracted attention in other lands.

Owen was an ardent supporter of trade unions as well as factory reforms. In those days factory workers in England had no vote and Parliament strongly approved *laissez faire*. Balked in his attempts to get reforms written into law, Owen turned to the co-operative association, the thing for which he is chiefly remembered. Owen believed that the profits of middlemen were the chief cause of high prices. Abolish these and prices would sink to a level that workers could afford. He helped to develop the National Equitable Labor Exchange which used "labor notes" instead of money. But it failed, as did co-operative communities which he established. One was New Harmony in Indiana. However, some of Owen's theories about a co-operative association were adopted in 1844 by a group of weavers in Rochdale, England. The Rochdale Society is usually considered the first successful co-operative. It transformed Owen's ideas into reality.

Owen, like Karl Marx, erred in thinking that the price of a good should be no more than the value of the labor used to produce it. But Owen favored peaceful methods of change and never suggested the abolition of private property.

erative's capital investment tends to be small.

The job of a co-operative store is to sell as inexpensively as possible to its members. A farmers' co-operative disposes of farm products for its members. A co-operative which lends money wants to make funds available to its members at the lowest possible interest rate. The greatest part of a co-operative's earnings are redistributed to members or are used to expand the business.

(3) *Fair distribution of savings.* Co-operatives operate on the basis of supplying service at cost. When a co-operative has more income than is needed for running the business, it is distributed to member-patrons, but not necessarily in the form of cash. Because the savings are distributed on the basis of patronage, they are usually called *patronage dividends* or *refunds.*

The division of patronage refunds may be based on the value or on the number of units of the products handled. For example, a farmer who delivers 10,000 bushels of grain to his co-operative's grain elevator has contributed ten times as much to the business of his association as the farmer who delivers only 1000 bushels. If the net income (savings) of the co-operative amounts to one cent a bushel, the farmer who delivers 10,000 bushels is entitled to $100 and the other farmer to only $10.

Patronage refunds are a convenient means of helping members finance their co-operative. Often these refunds are certificates issued to members showing that they are entitled to a stated sum. This sum may be left in the co-operative for a period of several years and then paid to members in the form of cash. It provides a "revolving fund" used in the business until paid to the member.

Certain associations pay patronage refunds only to members, although they may do business with nonmembers. Others distribute savings at a lower rate to nonmembers than to members. And some co-operatives distribute refunds to patron-members and nonmembers at the same rate.

There are four major types of co-operatives. In the United States there are four main types of co-operatives:

(1) *Purchasing co-operatives,* generally operated as retail stores to provide goods for their members. They buy for their members such items as building materials, seed, fertilizer, and feed. Sometimes they also manufacture or process some of the goods they sell. This was the type of association established by the Rochdale weavers.

(2) *Marketing co-operatives,* organized to sell agricultural or other produce of members. Such organizations eliminate middlemen's charges and pass whatever savings are made back to the producer-members. The marketing co-operative may store products and keep them off the market until prices become more favorable. These associations often process, grade, and advertise their products. Successful examples of this kind of co-operative are to be found in the citrus fruit and dairy products industries.

(3) *Servicing co-operatives,* which perform various types of services for their members. These include operating storage facilities; lending money; providing health, fire, life, and hospital insurance; and supplying gas, electric power, and irrigation services. The credit union is one example of such a service co-operative that is familiar to workers in many large companies.

(4) *Industrial co-operatives* have been least successful in the United States. In this type of organization worker-members co-operate in manufacturing, farming, mining, construction, and other large-scale industries. The Cincinnati Iron Molders, formed in 1847, was an example of such a co-operative. Members share in the operation and in the net income of their co-operative enterprise according to the Rochdale principles.

Co-operatives met with only limited early success. Co-operatives had a difficult time getting started in the United States. But within the century following the organization of the

Rochdale weavers' co-operative (1844) they became an important form of business organization. In 1922 the Congress of the United States passed the Capper-Volstead Act, which made it clear that farmers' co-operatives were not to be considered as "combinations in restraint of trade." That is, they were not subject to antitrust laws. At other times, too, the federal government has tended to encourage the co-operative movement as a form of self-help among farmers.

Some co-operatives have grown into big business concerns. Today there are many co-operatives, and some of them can be termed big-business enterprises. Marketing and servicing co-operatives have been particularly successful in agricultural and dairy-producing areas. Many of the purchasing associations originally designed to meet the needs of urban industrial workers have moved to rural areas and small towns to serve farmers.

The co-operative must depend upon its members as steady customers. If members of a purchasing co-operative are swayed by temporary lower prices elsewhere and take their business to others, the co-operative cannot function efficiently. A natural development, therefore, has been for co-operatives to unite in order to broaden the scope of their operations and to operate more efficiently. A co-operative may own stock in other businesses, just as may other corporate organizations. For example, farmer co-operatives frequently own such businesses as flour mills, packing houses, canneries, manufacturing plants, and oil refineries.

The co-operative movement in the United States reports a healthy and continuing growth. Some 32,000 consumer co-operatives, including credit unions, did a total volume of business in excess of 15 billion dollars during a recent year. Exact figures are not available for the business done by all co-operatives.

CHECK UP

1. What principles are basic to the operation of most co-operatives?

2. What are four major types of co-operatives? Which of these have been most successful in the United States?

6

What are the advantages and disadvantages of "bigness" in business?

In some types of economic activities, large businesses clearly are more efficient than small ones. But there is considerable disagreement over whether or not "bigness" in itself is "good" or "bad," and over the point at which a business may become "too big." Perhaps there are no general answers to these questions. The best that one can do is to consider the advantages and disadvantages of large and small businesses in general and then to make value judgments in particular situations.

In manufacturing, a large business can use specialized machines economically. Specialized machines are used in practically all large-scale manufacturing in the country. Each machine has been designed to perform a specific job. Such machines are expensive to own and operate, and in many industries they are likely to go out of date quickly. Because these machines are both expensive and short-lived, they must be used at or near full capacity to be profitable for their owners. When they are used to capacity, they are economical because they take the place of more costly hand labor.

In the manufacture of automobiles, for example, the labor-saving assembly-line method is used to advantage. On the automobile assembly line one worker has the job of welding certain parts, another tightens bolts, still another finishes surfaces and perhaps paints them, and so on. As the automobile moves on the assembly line past one worker after another,

The new technology: industry

Five hundred years ago, machines were used to drill holes, but they were simple ones held and turned by hand. Today, drills are automatic. These pictures of the same operation as done at different times show how technological change increases productivity.

a

About 1500, a bowstring twisted around a drill shaft, **a,** was used to make holes in beads. The operator worked the drill by moving the bow rapidly back and forth. By 1800, drilling machines were more powerful, but still hand-operated, **b.** Round weights added momentum on either end of the bar and turned the screw. An 1870 machine, **c,** was driven by an engine and a system of gears, controlled by a foot-pedal.

b

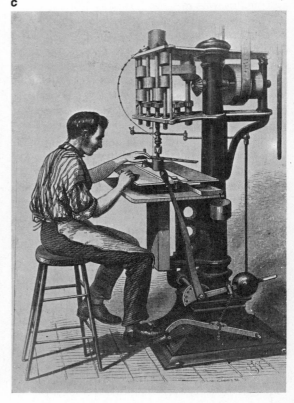
c

Modern drills can penetrate the earth to depths of thousands of feet. In **d,** 90-foot sections of an oil well drill are guided into place. Drilling operations on assembly lines are often completely automated. In **e,** one man oversees a computerized sequence at a Ford Motor Company plant.

d

e

it "grows" from a bare frame to a car that can be driven off under its own power at the end of the line. Without efficient assembly lines, automobiles would cost several times as much as they do, and relatively few people could afford to own them.

Large firms can use by-products. Large companies have been able to use by-products to a greater extent than can small organizations. For example, a small slaughtering plant might waste such by-products of livestock as the inedible parts. In the large packing plants, practically every part of an animal is used for some purpose. Such use yields financial returns to the packing house, part of which may be passed back to the farmer who produces the livestock or on to the consumer. Competition forces packing plants to pay farmers as high prices as possible, while keeping consumer prices low enough to compete with the prices of other packing plants.

Workers in large concerns may have specialized skill and training. A factory, large or small, usually has a division of labor, but this is usually carried farther in a large plant. In the large factory each worker on an assembly line concentrates on his particular task. In consequence he can do his job more rapidly and more skillfully than if he had to perform several tasks.

With division of labor, foremen and managers can make the best use of their specialized training. They can spend their time seeing that workers are qualified for their jobs and that they do them well. They can keep abreast of improvements and new inventions, and thus insure maximum efficiency in the operation of the plant.

Research is carried on by large organizations. If one compares a current model of a given refrigerator, electric food mixer, or gas range with one five years old, one will be impressed with the improvements that have been made. These improvements are the result of research and experimentation. First, a new idea occurs to an individual, usually after considerable time and thought have been given to the subject. The idea is developed in a laboratory, and experiments are carried on to see if it is workable. If the idea appears to have possibilities, additional experimental work is necessary before a finished product can be marketed, even in small quantities.

To illustrate, some years ago an automobile company devoted five years of research and experimentation to produce an engine of a new design. Several months passed before the more promising designs were converted into blueprints. From these blueprints, master craftsmen hand-built some 30 engines at a cost of about 25,000 dollars each. Modifications were made again and again as these engines underwent every conceivable laboratory and highway test. When the designers finally were satisfied that they had the best possible experimental model, the company undertook production of the new engine.

Eighteen months were required to make the machine tools needed to produce the engine in quantity. These are the tools which make possible modern mass production, but the machine tools themselves cannot be mass-produced. Each machine tool was tailored for a specific job. There was no thought of trying to do a hurry-up job; the machine tools had to be right.

On the experimental engines, 127 hours had been needed to finish a crankcase from a casting and 180 hours to turn out a crankshaft from a bar of steel. Cylinder heads took a similar length of time. It was a slow and costly process. But once the new "baby" was ready to go on the assembly line, several hundred car engines could be manufactured in the time and at the cost needed to make one such engine by hand methods.

This is only one example of the research, money, and time devoted to improving the design and performance of an industrial product. A small company would not have the financial resources to undertake this kind of project.

A large firm buys materials in large quantities. When supplies are purchased in large quantities, they can usually be bought for less than if small quantities are bought at different times. The large buyer often makes a contract with a seller to take a shipment of materials at stated intervals. Thus he has greater bargaining power than smaller competitors. The seller, in turn, benefits from being able to plan ahead of time. He can operate with a smaller sales force and maintain a smaller clerical and management staff than would be the case if he had to depend on small orders which might not be renewed regularly. The seller often passes a part of his saving on to the buyer. Moreover, a large operator often can obtain raw materials directly from their original sources rather than from nearby wholesalers or jobbers.

Large businesses have an advantage over small business in advertising their products. With large-scale production the advertising cost per unit is much lower since the costs are spread over a much larger number of units. Advertising in one of America's large-circulation magazines, or over a national radio or television hookup, tends to give a product prestige among consumers. Because a large company can afford national advertising, it generally is in a stronger position than a small one to keep the public well-disposed toward its product. This, of course, helps to increase sales.

Big business is impersonal. Workers on highly specialized jobs may feel that their work is not important or not appreciated. For example, tightening a screw on each automobile moving by on an assembly line may be boring and therefore tiring. The worker may feel no sense of accomplishment or pride of workmanship. Perhaps he also ponders the possibility that an automatic screw-tightening machine may be developed. Should this happen, the worker may be out of a job and lack the skills

"COME ANY FURTHER AND I'LL STRIKE!"

Eric in The Atlanta Journal

necessary to obtain other suitable employment.

Mass production and automation create problems. Mass production methods and mechanization in big businesses probably have improved standards of living. But they have also created uncertainties. Automation is contributing to these uncertainties at the same time that it holds out the prospect of freedom from drudgery.

Workers, faced with the possibility of losing their jobs in a shift from mechanized to automated production, tend to view automation as a curse. Some leisure is wonderful, but for a man with a family to support, the threat of unpaid leisure is disturbing. True, highly skilled workers are needed to build and service automation devices, but these workers are not necessarily the same men who were displaced.

In some industries great size is not necessarily an advantage. In such industries as spinning and weaving, a moderate-sized factory can compete with a larger one. The reason is that there is little to be gained by putting in many machines (looms for weaving cloth) which do the same job, at the same unit cost, as a smaller number of similar looms. Although the output of the factory would be increased with more looms, so must the number of people who work on them. Savings are greatest when efficient machines replace labor. Increasing the number of machines may, in fact, increase overhead costs if each machine requires the same amount of labor.

In some industries men cannot be replaced by machines. Where highly skilled hand work, such as assembling the parts in high grade watches, is required, machines cannot do all the work. Small specialized companies are still common in the United States, and more common in most foreign countries. Mass production methods cannot replace the highly specialized functions performed by skilled workers in small shops. Many businesses providing services rather than goods also operate more efficiently on a small scale.

A few firms may get a disproportionate control of output. Under conditions where big businesses are highly efficient, a few firms may get control of the major part of production. (The issue of monopoly control is discussed in Chapter 10.) Critics of monopoly say that when a few firms obtain control over the supply of a product, artificially high prices will result. This can happen if the firms deliberately fix prices. Although price-fixing is illegal, it may be hard to prove. For this reason, price-fixing has sometimes occurred.

CHECK UP

1. What are the advantages of big business?

2. What are possible disadvantages of "bigness"?

3. In what type of industry is size not necessarily an advantage?

Clinching the main ideas

Although the greatest number of businesses in this country are small, big businesses dominate certain essential industries, and account for a large part of the nation's total productivity.

There are three basic legal forms of business organization, besides co-operatives: individual proprietorships, partnerships, and corporations. Each has its advantages and disadvantages. The advantages of corporations are summarized on page 209. Co-operatives, designed primarily to serve their members at cost, are recognized legally. They are particularly effective in the agricultural sector of the economy. The co-operative retail store has become a familiar sight in many American communities.

Large businesses often have advantages over small businesses. These include: specialized equipment and specialized workers; more effective utilization of industrial by-products; greater capability for carrying on research, experimentation, and product development; bargaining power in large-scale purchases; and a lower per-unit cost in advertising.

On the other hand, there are also disadvantages to bigness. These include: the impersonality of business relations; a tendency toward drab uniformity and standardization; the possibility of a too rigid control of the market and the temptation to fix prices to insure higher profits.

In industries dealing with specialty products (handicrafts, gifts), bigness may not have any particular advantages over smallness, and may actually be a disadvantage.

There is no one "best" form or size of business organization. What is best must be determined by each businessman in the light of his own situation. Nor is there a sure formula for success in business. Imagination and intelligence, experience and hard work, plus adequate financing are among the prerequisites to success for any business venture.

Chapter 9 review

Terms to understand

1. unlimited liability
2. voting stock
3. good will
4. dividends
5. articles of incorporation
6. proxies
7. preferred stock
8. double taxation
9. patronage dividends
10. automation
11. board of directors
12. silent partner

What do you think?

1. What inference can be drawn from the fact that the average capital investment per manufacturing employee is about 23,000 dollars? From the fact that only about 1 per cent of all manufacturing firms produces nearly two-thirds of the manufactured goods as measured by value of sales?

2. "A corporation is a separate legal person in the eyes of the law." What does this mean?

3. Should a corporation pay an income tax on its net income?

4. Why are more than three-fourths of the nation's businesses individual proprietorships?

5. From the point of view of the owners, would it be desirable for most partnerships to incorporate? Why?

6. Why have other types of business sometimes claimed that co-operatives provide unfair competition?

Extending your knowledge of economics

1. What are your state's regulations for incorporating a business? The necessary forms may be obtained from the Bureau of Corporations (or a corresponding office) in the state capital.

2. The corporation income tax has an interesting history. For information about it, refer to *Federal Income Taxation of Corporations and Shareholders* by B. I. Bittker, or *The Corporation Income Tax* by Richard Goode, or any other recent book on corporate taxation.

case analysis 5

Stock market fluctuations: boom, bust, and boom

General background

Individuals and organizations buy stocks in anticipation of future income from dividends or from growth in the value of the stock. Many factors may lead one to buy a given stock but the decision to buy *some* stock is largely determined by one's estimate of future economic conditions. Expectations for the future, in turn, are influenced to a considerable extent by economic trends in the immediate past, as well as by one's understanding of what has occurred over a longer period of time.

People vary greatly in their outlook on the future. Some are optimistic; others, pessimistic. Among investors as a group, however, optimism and pessimism seem to run in waves. This is reflected in the behavior of stock market prices.

The nonprofessional investor is influenced by what others seem to be doing. For example, if stock prices have been declining, there may be a sudden rush to "sell at any price." Or if stock prices have been moving upward, small investors may rush to buy. These sudden swings in attitudes often cause sharp fluctuations in the prices of stock.

But for every sale there must be a buyer, and vice versa. Professional investors (both individuals and institutions), who deal with investments on a large scale, are well aware of the dictum "Sell when others buy, and buy when others sell." These professionals often exert a stabilizing force on the market.

The issue: swings in yields, growth, and prices

An old (pre-World War II) stock market rule-of-thumb was that a stock is likely to be a "good buy" when its *price-earnings ratio* is about 10— that is, when it is selling at a price about 10 times its annual earnings. This "rule" grew out of the experiences of the 1920's and 1930's.

The price end of the price-earnings ratio for the whole market[1] is expressed by using an index. The *Dow-Jones Industrials Average,* compiled by Dow Jones & Company, Inc. (a financial news agency) is the most well-known such index. The Dow-Jones Average is based on the price of 30 selected stocks. Originally, in 1897, the average was computed by dividing the sum of the stock prices by the number of stocks selected (originally twelve). But stock splits soon distorted this average.

Stock splits occur when the price of a company's stock rises too high to be attractive to investors. To reduce its stock price, the company declares a stock split, and offers to exchange two or more newly-created shares for one old share. A stock split brings down the price of stock dramatically, but this does not mean that the company is in trouble. To avoid lowering the stock market average, and thereby creating the impression of a retreat, a new divisor was computed. Adjustments for stock splits are thus provided for periodically in the Dow-Jones Industrials Average.

There is also a Dow-Jones Transportation Companies' Index, based on a group of railroad stocks, and a Utilities Average, based on utilities stocks. Other averages are similarly computed by other agencies; there is a New York Times Index, Standard and Poor's Index, and the New York Stock Exchange Common Stock Index.

The "earnings" part of the price-earnings ratio refers to the profits made by the company divided by the number of shares outstanding. When the price-earnings ratio is 10, for example, it might be interpreted to signify that the stock is selling for 100 dollars and earning ten dollars a share.

During the short 1949 recession, the price-earnings ratio of the stocks included in the Dow-Jones Average reached a post-World War II low of 7. Recovery was rapid, however, and the *bull market* (optimistic expectations, leading to rising stock prices) which started at that time has generally prevailed during most years since. This bull market has suffered some temporary relapses (*bear markets,* ruled by pessimistic expectations

---

1 "The market" refers here and elsewhere to the New York Stock Exchange, although there are other exchanges which operate in a similar manner.

and declining prices), but each of these relapses to date has been followed by even higher prices and higher price-earnings ratios.

For example, the ratio reached almost 12 in its 1953 peak, declined, and then exceeded 14 in 1956. There were other declines, followed by increases, in 1957–58 and 1960. Eventually the price-earnings ratio reached a level of almost 23 in December, 1961. At this point, the average *yield* (dividend income as a per cent of price) had dropped to a little more than 3 per cent, as compared to a yield of 5.3 per cent at the 1953 peak. But while good stocks were yielding an average of only a little more than 3 per cent, good corporation bonds, supposedly a safer but lower-income type of investment, were yielding considerably more than 4 per cent! Obviously the "old rules" were not being followed.

Following a gradual decline from December, 1961, stock prices took a very sharp tumble late in May and early June of 1962. Even at the "low" price levels of June, 1962, however, the Dow-Jones Industrials showed a price-earnings ratio of 16, and were yielding an average return of only about 4.3 per cent, roughly equivalent to the yield of high-grade corporation bonds at that time.

The Dow-Jones Average (remember that this is an index number) dropped from 734 in December, 1961, to 536 in June, 1962. Following this decline, stock prices again climbed upward, with some short downward swings, until late in 1968. During this period, the Average reached a level of 995 (February, 1966). In December, 1968, the stock market took a sharp downward break, which generally continued into the decade of the 1970's.

By early August, 1970, the Dow-Jones Average was at 726, some 98 points below its position one year earlier and 269 points (or about 27 per cent) below the high of early 1966. At this August, 1970, price, the stocks in the Dow-Jones Industrials were yielding a return of about 4.45 per cent, which was considerably less than the return available on good low-risk bonds at the time.

Some effects of these market fluctuations on the stocks of five well-known firms are shown in the accompanying Table 1.

THE DOW THEORY

Many investors rely on what is known as the "Dow theory" in deciding whether to buy stocks. It is based on the ideas of Charles H. Dow, editor of the *Wall Street Journal* and founder of Dow, Jones, & Co. in the late 1800's. The Dow theory has three major tenets.

1. *Stock prices tend to move up and down as a group.* The Dow-Jones Industrials Average is considered significant because the gains or losses recorded by most stocks do not vary tremendously. If they did, the Dow-Jones Average would not tell much about the market. An observer would not know if the average reflected a general trend, or if it had been distorted by the fantastic gains of a few stocks, while most others lost slightly. But in general if the average goes up, most stocks go up too.

Despite the usefulness of the Dow-Jones Average, two criticisms are often heard. One is that the stocks selected for the average are generally

Table 1. Prices, earnings, and dividends of stocks in five large corporations

corporation	1958–1969 lowest and highest stock prices		1969 earnings per share	1969 dividends per share	January-June 1970 prices per share	
	highest	lowest			highest	lowest
General Motors	$114	$ 34	$5.95	$4.30	$ 76	$ 59
American Telephone and Telegraph	75	28	4.00	2.40	53	40
E. I. duPont de Nemours	294	101	7.35	5.25	124	92
International Business Machines	375	33	8.21	3.60	387	237
Texas Instruments	145	10	3.06	0.80	134	63

stronger than the market as a whole. Their prices are generally higher and more stable. Thus they do not accurately reflect the fortunes of all the stocks listed on the New York Stock Exchange.

A second criticism is that within the average group of 30, the same percentage increase by two different companies will have different effects depending on the price of the stock, not on the relative size or importance of the corporations involved. The biggest companies do not by any means have the most expensive common stock. For instance, Company A may sell at 75 dollars a share, then increase by 10 per cent. Its $7.50 rise will be given the same weight as a 10 per cent rise in Company B's stock which sold originally at 40 dollars (a cash increase of four dollars). Thus Company A will boost the average further than Company B. Yet Company B may be much more important to the country's economy. It may employ more people and produce more wealth. Such factors are not reflected in the Dow-Jones Average, however.

2. *The stock market reflects business trends.* In general, when the stock market goes up, prosperity is on the increase. When it goes down, recession may be in the offing. Most business fluctuations can be followed by watching stock market prices, but not all.

3. *Stock market trends may be described as major, secondary, or minor.* Major stock market trends are spread over several years and reflect the business cycle. That is to say, the market follows a long term pattern. For several years, prices may go up, and then decline or stagnate for an equal length of time. Major trends can be discerned by watching the Industrials Average and the Transportation Index together. Should they both move sharply in the same direction, a basic trend in that direction is confirmed.

Secondary trends are price movements which work against the major trend. For instance, if stocks are generally on the rise for several years, there may be shorter periods of a month or two when prices fall. One job of a stock market analyst is to identify major and secondary trends correctly and not confuse the two. Trends are often the subject of great controversy.

Minor trends are sharp price variations which last only a day or two. A general increase in market prices might stop suddenly because of a discouraging piece of world news. Such items do not usually affect the market for more than a day or two, however. Experienced investors can spot such short variations easily and take advantage of them.

THE PSYCHOLOGY OF STOCK INVESTORS

No generally acceptable reason, other than "jitters" on the part of many investors has been offered for the sharp decline in stock prices during 1962. And no single satisfactory explanation for their "jitters" has been given. Business conditions and corporation profits and dividends remained good. And while stock prices were "high" and yields "low" according to earlier yardsticks, prices soon went much higher and yields even lower, without a corresponding market dip.

Analyzing another sharp decline of stock prices in January of 1970 provides a glimpse of the various factors motivating investors. When the decline began, *Business Week* stated that the "most important factor is that the economy is nearing a recession with no end in sight." The London *Economist* blamed the decline on two major factors: 1) caution on the part of investors who were fearful that prices would sink further, and 2) a continuation of unusually high returns on bonds, which drew investors' money away from stocks. The *Wall Street Journal,* a daily financial newspaper, offered more detailed explanations.

On Monday, January 26, the market is down. The *Journal* notes: "Worry about the depth and breadth of the recession apparently being produced by the fiscal and monetary restraints is what is bothering investors the most, brokers report." President Nixon delivers his State of the Union address Monday, but it fails to produce a rally. At the close of trading, 1000 stocks decline and only 306 rise in price. One hundred fifty-eight stocks hit a new low for 1969–70, while only four hit new highs. Investors are reported to be awaiting a presidential news conference Friday and an economic report on Monday.

Thursday, January 29, a rise in the wholesale price index is announced. It chilled a budding market rally because of its discouraging implications. The rise indicated that inflation was still increasing despite efforts to control it. During the day, Assistant Secretary of Commerce Harold C. Passer states that he thinks some people exaggerate the weakness of the economy. His statement, intended to buoy the market, has little effect.

On Friday, brokers blame a further decline on more news of low corporate earnings, concern over inflation and tight credit, a downturn of glamour issues,[2] and the lack of any buying incentive. Ironically, they also say a *Wall Street Journal* story about the discouraging economic situation produced even further discouragement!

More low earnings reports on February 2 keep prices down. During the day, President Nixon suggests interest rates could be relaxed—and a small market rally ensues. Analysts, however, call it a "technical" rally, which occurs when traders believe the market has declined to an unrealistically low point, and move in to snap up bargains.

Finally, a dramatic rally is sparked February 3 by (former) Secretary of the Treasury David M. Kennedy. He indicates that the administration favors a loosening of monetary restrictions. Nothing he says is especially new or different from several previous administration statements, but for some reason, investors begin to buy. At the close of the day, 946 stocks are priced higher, and 423 are lower. These figures reverse the ratio of January 26.

On the 5th, the market drifts; on the 6th, it rallies again. By the 7th, brokers predict a long period of "base-building," when the price index should "settle down" at about 740. The decline is over—for the time being.

While many explanations are possible for the market's behavior during this short period, few can be proved. To some extent, rumors, news, politics, and whim influenced the market.

Why stocks are bought

It appears that since World War II American investors have become accustomed to accept stock price-earnings ratios that are considerably higher and yields that are considerably lower than were

2 Glamour issues: stocks of companies in newer fields of endeavor, such as computer technology, which appear to offer great promise of growth.

acceptable a generation or so ago. Several explanations have been given for this change in investors' attitudes:

1. They believe that a continued high level of economic growth will eventually cause their investments to increase in value, even though present earnings and dividends are low in comparison to the prices paid.

2. They have faith that the nation's essentially stable economy will prevent serious losses from major depressions.

3. They expect some degree of inflation to continue. The ownership of common stocks generally provides more protection against inflation than does investment in bonds or other fixed-income yielding securities or assets.

4. They are influenced by income tax considerations in stock market trading. Losses made on stocks may be deducted from ordinary income, thus reducing one's income tax payments. Similarly, under certain circumstances, gains made on stocks are taxed at "capital gains" rates, which are lower than "ordinary income" tax rates. For persons in high income tax brackets, these tax factors may be much more important in determining what stocks to buy and sell, and when to buy and sell, than are prospective dividend yields or growth possibilities.

5. Many stock buyers speculate. They apparently pay very little attention to past, present, or prospective future earnings and yields. Instead, they ride the waves of optimism in bull markets, buy "hot" (rapidly selling and fast rising) stocks, with the idea of "unloading" (selling) them within the next few weeks or months at a considerably higher price. In stock market slang, this practice is called "the next sucker theory."

If these assumed investor or speculator views of the future do not change, no substantial long-term decrease in stock prices (and no substantial increase in yields) should occur within the foreseeable future. Instead, the post-1949 pattern may be expected to continue. In this pattern, stock declines, perhaps brought on by pessimism, are soon offset by recoveries. Should basic economic conditions change significantly the viewpoints of investors may be expected to change accordingly.

Unquestionably, there is a limit beyond which

price-earnings ratios cannot climb (or conversely, a limit below which yields cannot fall) if investors are to continue buying stocks. Some analysts are of the opinion that this limit is approaching, and perhaps has been reached already. Others are not so sure. This difference of opinion doubtless helps keep the stock markets active, and reminds economists that stock market analysis is more of an art than a science.

Toward better understanding

QUESTIONS TO CONSIDER IN ANALYZING THIS CASE

1. Explain these terms: price-earnings ratio, yield, Dow-Jones Industrials Average. What can one learn from each?

2. What is a bull market? A bear market? What are the causes of each? Would all stocks make the same percentage gain or loss in each type of market? Why?

3. In Table 1, compute the per cent of earnings per share distributed as dividends for the stocks listed. How do you explain the great differences? On the basis of the data provided in Table 1, which two stocks would you consider growth stocks? Why?

4. Note the reasons given in *Business Week,* the London *Economist,* and the *Wall Street Journal* for the sharp decline of stock prices in January of 1970. What factors in early February contributed to a rally? Hurt a budding rally? Explain why in each case.

5. Why are present-day investors buying stocks with higher price-earning ratios and lower yields than were acceptable a generation ago? Make sure that point #4 on page 223 is clearly understood.

THINKING ABOUT THE BASIC ECONOMIC ISSUES

1. Why is it a good rule "to sell when others buy and to buy when others sell"? How can professional investors exert a stabilizing influence on the market?

2. Why do stocks provide greater protection against inflation than bonds? Explain.

3. How people feel about the times (optimistic or pessimistic) seems to affect the stock market. Can this popular feeling also affect other prices? If so give examples and explain.

4. What are the advantages and possible disadvantages of "playing the market," that is, selling stock at higher prices than you paid for them, and buying stock when prices are low? Of purchasing good stock which you retain? Of buying good bonds?

5. Explain the three major tenets of the Dow theory. How might it influence the thinking and behavior of the manager of a large department store?

chapter ten

Competition, monopoly, and government regulation

1. **How does competition work?**
2. **What are the effects of limited competition and monopoly?**
3. **How is business regulated by government?**
4. **What is the extent of legalized monopoly?**
5. **How does government sometimes compete with business?**

After economists realize that perfect competition is not spontaneously attained or enforceable, the problem of defining and approaching "workable competition" becomes paramount. Here is the frontier for economic policy.

PAUL A. SAMUELSON,
Economics

The term "free enterprise" suggests absence of regulation and competition in business. This chapter is focused on the effects of the varying degrees of competition presently found in the American business system, and on why and how government regulation intervenes in business activities in some situations.

A few industries or situations are examples of relatively unrestricted or "pure" competition. At the opposite extremes are examples of "monopoly"—only one producer or seller in a given industry. Most business transactions fall between these two extremes, within an area of limited competition often described as "monopolistic competition" or "oligopoly."

Although pure competition may be desirable from the consumer's viewpoint in many instances, it does not always result in the best services or the lowest prices. Government, in the public's interest, encourages some types of monopolies, and also regulates monopolies and various forms of limited competition. In some instances, too, government actually competes with privately-owned businesses.

In comparison with most other countries, there is a great deal of competition and free enterprise in the United States. But the American economy is far from a purely competitive and a purely free enterprise economy. Rather, it is best described as a *mixed economy*. That is, competition and free enterprise certainly are dominant features of the economy, but the role of government also is significant.

1

How does competition work?

Competition is rivalry, whether in sports, love, or business. One person (or firm, or other kind of organization) attempts to outdo others in attaining some goal. In business, this goal is profits.

Competition often helps consumers and increases efficiency in business. Whether a person wants a tube of toothpaste, a new pair of shoes, a sweater, or even an automobile, he generally has a choice of several brands and may shop at any one of several places. Sellers of these products are rivals for this business.

Every competing firm attempts to sell the best product it can for the lowest price and still make a reasonable profit. Only by giving as much as or more than its rivals at an equivalent price can a firm expect to sell enough of its product to remain in business. Firms compete with each other not only in price but also in quality. More for the same price, of course, is the same as an equivalent amount at a lower price.

Not only merchants but manufacturers compete with each other. The manufacturer who can make a product of higher quality or at a lower price than his competitors is in a strong competitive position. He may develop a new machine which saves labor and reduces .cost of production. Or he may improve his product, or the services connected with the product. Any of these is likely to increase sales, probably at the expense of competitors. However,

this manufacturer may maintain his advantage for only a short time. As his competitors also develop better methods, they will regain lost ground or even pull into the lead. Competition is a never-ending battle which keeps businessmen on their toes.

If competition is very keen, prices will only be high enough to cover production costs and provide a firm with enough profits to induce it to remain in business. To meet or beat their competitors, businessmen must use their resources (labor, capital, land, management) as efficiently as possible. This is why it is often said that competition leads to "the most efficient allocation of resources" as well as to the lowest prices.

New business firms may be established. There are usually people who have money available for investment. If they see an opportunity to make a good profit, they will invest funds in a business. For example, if a person (or corporation) with available funds concludes that profits are high or efficiency is low in the retail grocery business in a particular location, he may start a new retail grocery store in competition with others in that area. Should the new proprietor be able to operate with

---

THE "DISCRETIONARY" DOLLAR

"Discretionary" spending is a term used to describe how a family distributes its income after paying for necessities. The distinction between "discretionary spending" and spending for necessities is not always easy to make. The average family spends one-fifth of its income for food. But if people were willing to live as frugally as their great-grandparents did, only one-seventh of the income would be used for this purpose. Only about one-half of the money spent for housing and clothing is spent for real necessities. The rest is discretionary spending.

Producers use various tactics in competing for the discretionary dollar. The most obvious of these is advertising. In addition, many companies include gift "surprises" in their packaged goods. Stores hold special sales and many of them give stamps which can be redeemed for household and personal items. This once-popular sales gimmick has ceased to appeal so widely to buyers since it became known that instead of providing shoppers with gifts or savings, stamps were being paid for through higher prices. Suburban shopping centers, branch stores, stores open in the evening, drive-in banks and theaters—all are examples of the growing competition for the consumers' discretionary spending.

greater efficiency and lower costs, or can buy his groceries at lower prices than the established retailers, he can sell at reduced prices. The older firms soon will have to increase their efficiency, lower their costs, and develop whatever methods are necessary to satisfy buyers, or else be forced out of business. The rise of new firms is a constant threat to any type of competitive business where efficiency is low, or profits unduly high. Thus, consumers tend to benefit not only from competition between established firms, but also because new firms may enter a field which offers a chance to make profits.

Second-hand products compete with new products. Not only do rivals within an industry compete with each other in the sale of new products, but used or "second-hand" products often compete with these new products. As an illustration, used automobiles or farm machinery, or perhaps rebuilt products such as washing machines, compete with new products in these fields. If prices of the new product seem too high for buyers, they may choose to purchase a substitute or second-hand product. Competition of this kind exists only for a limited number of products, however.

Different industries compete with one another. Just as one automobile company competes with another, so the automotive industry competes as a whole against other industries, such as the television industry. No consumer has an inexhaustible supply of dollars. For example, a family which wants a new car, may also wish to have a new television set, a new radio, or new living room furniture. But if the price of a new or used automobile seems high in relation to its expected utility as compared to the price and utility of a new television set, the family may decide to buy the television set and "make do" with the old car.

When many families make similar decisions, automobile dealers may be forced to reduce prices in order to attract more business. Thus it is not merely a matter of different makes of cars competing with each other, or of used cars

Sales of new and used cars

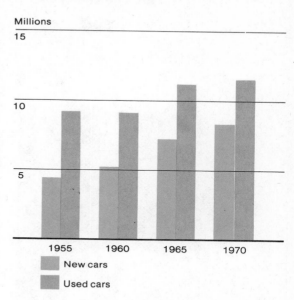

Source: Statistical Abstract

competing with new models. It is equally important to recognize that one type of consumer goods (a television set, for example) competes with other types of consumer goods (such as an automobile). Producers and sellers of entirely unlike goods and services are all competing for the consumer's dollar.

Competition covers a much wider field than one might think. In the field of transportation, the bus, the truck, the family automobile, and sometimes even the motorcycle compete with the railroads and the airplane. In communication, radio, television, movies, newspapers, and magazines compete with each other in presenting news and entertainment to the public. (Chapter 2 discusses the competition which exists among various goods or services needed or desired by an individual or a family.) Individual expenditures are made for that which consumers feel will bring the greatest amount of satisfaction.

Champion of Private Enterprise

Adam Smith

(1723–1790)

Soon after Adam Smith published *The Wealth of Nations* in 1776, he was acclaimed as the Father of Political Economy. It was mere coincidence that his outstanding contribution to economic theory was presented to the public in the same year as the American Declaration of Independence. Yet both contain protests against Britain's policy of strict regulation of trade. Smith was among the first to urge the government not to interfere with private business (*laissez faire*), and he was an early advocate of free trade between nations. Such ideas ran contrary to the economic thinking of his time, but eventually Smith's logical arguments convinced people that his views were economically sound. In the 1840's England adopted a free trade policy.

Many other ideas developed in *The Wealth of Nations* deserve attention. Smith, who lived during the early years of the Industrial Revolution, was one of the first to understand the advantage of a division of labor in manufacturing. Such a plan made possible an increased output of goods at a lower unit cost. Lower prices enabled more people to buy, thus creating a larger market. Such reasoning still holds true. In the United States, automobiles could not be purchased by the average consumer were it not for the mass production of cars through a division of labor and the use of an assembly line.

Smith considered natural resources and labor the real wealth of a country. He was one of the first to believe that labor was "the ultimate and real standard by which the value of all commodities can, at all times and places, be estimated and compared." Thus he differed vigorously with those who believed that the wealth of a nation depended on a surplus of exports. Smith was one of the first to point out how the law of supply and demand affected the price of a good and the quantity of it made available. He applied this theory to the wage rates of labor, suggesting that it was job competition between workers that kept wages low.

In urging an economy free of government influence, Smith explained his theory of the "invisible hand." The man of some economic independence (not a laborer), intent upon his own gain, frequently promotes the good of the nation more effectively than he really intends. That is because his own profit is also the nation's. This view that it was individual ambition and effort that served as the mainspring of social good has made Smith popular with the supporters of private enterprise ever since.

Smith relied upon and was greatly influenced by earlier writers. But he also had the ability to express the results of his keen observations and logical reasoning in clear language. Many of Smith's views have been adopted by modern economic theorists.

Manufacturers develop new products to improve their competitive position. Another indication that manufacturers compete sharply with each other for consumer sales and dollars is the invention and development of new products. Private industry spends large sums each year on research and the development of new products, to improve existing products, and to find ways of reducing production costs. Companies would not spend large sums of money for these purposes unless competition made it urgent for them to market the best possible product at the lowest possible price.

New products which are the outgrowth of research are constantly coming into the market to compete with older products. During recent years new models of food freezers, air conditioners, dishwashers, television sets, radios, and vacuum cleaners have been produced in large quantities. Each is battling for markets in competition with similar products as well as with other kinds of products. The same is true of clothing. New synthetic fabrics such as nylon, Orlon, and Dacron are competing with older, natural fabrics—cotton, wool, and silk. Much the same situation exists in most other industries.

Free enterprise and competition go hand in hand. American businessmen characteristically want to be free to go into whatever business they prefer. This tendency to develop their own businesses is encouraged by a free enterprise system, just as free enterprise is supported by competition.

Free enterprise permits businesses within a given industry to compete in selling the largest possible volume of goods or services to the maximum number of buyers. Usually the greater the number of firms in an industry, the keener is the competition. Under the most highly competitive conditions, sometimes called *pure competition,* any one firm controls only a very small part of the total supply of a uniform product. No single firm, therefore, can have much influence on prices. In a situation of pure competition, the price which the individual seller can receive is determined wholly by the forces of supply and demand. (Recall the wheat market discussed in Chapter 3.)

Pure competition is not widespread. Except in some phases of agriculture, and perhaps small retail and service establishments in some communities, most of the things a family buys are not produced and sold under purely competitive conditions. Most businesses do have some control over the prices they charge, and in effect competition is limited by the number of sellers.

Pure competition may be both wasteful and costly under some circumstances. Some types of business require large capital investments. Such businesses, in order to produce efficiently, must engage in mass production. This, in turn, requires mass marketing. But the total market demand for some products is not great enough to support many large producers.

The automobile industry is an example of a situation where pure competition obviously does not exist. The costs of building an efficient automobile manufacturing plant and establishing the necessary national marketing and dealer organization are very high. Unless each plant or each company has large sales, it cannot stay in business. During the past two or three generations, several dozen automobile manufacturing companies have gone out of business or have been absorbed by larger companies. Today, there are only three large companies and a few smaller ones in this field. It would be difficult to prove that automobile prices are lower with only three or four major producers than they would be with twice as many (or one-half as many) manufacturers. But most people would agree that car prices are lower under present conditions than they would be if there were several hundred or several thousand manufacturers. Pure competition, in this industry, would greatly increase consumer costs. The same principle holds true for many other industries.

CHECK UP

1. How does competition contribute to the development of better products at lower prices? Why do second-hand or rebuilt products compete with new goods? How do different industries compete with each other?

2. What can businessmen do to improve their competitive position? Why are new business firms established?

2

What are the effects of limited competition and monopoly?

Pure competition is a marketing situation in which there are so many sellers of an identical or uniform product that no one seller can have any noticeable influence upon prices. Monopoly exists when there is only one seller of

a given product. Between these is a broad area of limited competition or partial monopoly. Several economic terms are used in describing these various "in-between" situations.

Monopolistic competition is the market condition nearest pure competition. Monopolistic competition exists when a large number of sellers are offering products which, although they are not identical, are so similar in natures that they serve the same general purpose.

For example, in almost any store, one may have a choice between Shino, Kleeno, Brito, or a dozen other toothpastes. All serve the same purpose—to clean teeth. But if one has a slight preference for the taste of Shino, he would always buy that brand if the prices of competing products are the same. One might even pay a few cents more for Shino than for other brands in a tube of the same size, but probably not 25 cents more.

The sellers of Shino, then, so far as persons with similar tastes are concerned, may have a slight competitive advantage based on their slightly different product. Sellers of other brands

Economic competition versus monopoly control

	1. allocation of resources	2. economic freedom	3. economic growth	4. economic power
competition	Competition promotes more efficient allocation of resources. Output of consumer goods is limited only by the available supply of raw materials. As output increases, prices tend to go down.	Consumers have a wider range of choices in a competitive market. Producers have greater freedom of opportunity where competition is not artificially limited. Economic freedom is basic to private enterprise.	Competition provides an incentive for: 1) business efficiency, 2) adoption of new methods of production, 3) new products and services. Since competing companies tend to imitate technical improvements, the gains become widespread.	Where economic power is dispersed among competing businesses there is less danger of political power being mobilized in favor of special interests.
monopoly	Monopoly control of a market can bring about misallocation of resources thus limiting output and raising prices.	Consumers are subject to the will of a single supplier, unless substitutes for the monopolized product are available. Producers of monopolized goods are, generally, less responsive to consumer demand.	Under monopoly there are fewer incentives for efficiency, or the introduction of new methods of production. Monopolies may be a barrier to freedom of opportunity and to economic growth.	Large monopolies usually acquire political power. Too much monopoly may therefore create serious political problems, and pose a threat to a free society.

of toothpaste will also have their followings. A seller of a given brand will then compete by trying to convince buyers through advertising that his brand is "better" than other brands. This differs from the case of the purely competitive wheat farmer, who would have no reason for advertising his particular wheat.

A product may be "different" from another in the buyer's mind even though physically it is the same. Shino at the corner grocery store, one block away, differs from Shino at the uptown drug store, 30 blocks away, in that the purchaser prefers the shorter trip. Or he may prefer one storekeeper's cheery smile and "Good Morning" to another's scowl and grunt. Anything that causes a person to prefer buying from one particular retailer rather than from another, even though the product bought is physically the same, may involve an element of monopolistic competition.

Furthermore, anything that leads one to *believe* that one product or service differs from another, even though it may not actually differ, may cause him to act just as if there were actual differences. This helps to explain why there are so many similar products, and why so much advertising is devoted to emphasizing real or imaginary differences. If a seller can convince a large number of buyers that his own product is "different" (and "better"), he may be able to sell more of it, or to sell it at a somewhat higher price. Thus "product differentiation" gives a seller more control over his prices than he would have under conditions of purer competition. Almost every businessman, therefore, strives to differentiate his product if it is at all possible to do so.

Oligopoly is further removed from pure competition. An oligopolist can influence prices. Oligopoly is the situation that exists when there are only a few sellers of a product (the Greek word *oligos* means "a few"). In this case, "few" is a number small enough so that any one seller controls enough of the supply to exert a significant influence on prices. Oligopoly may be either "pure" (that is, sellers

with identical products) or "differentiated" (similar but not identical products). Producers of bulk cement or graded lumber or steel plates are what might be considered reasonably representative examples of pure oligopoly. Automobiles, cigarettes, and farm equipment, on the other hand, are examples of differentiated oligopoly. That is to say, there are differences among the various makes of cars—though all are turned out by a few major manufacturers. Most large-sized manufactured goods, such as household appliances and motor vehicles, are produced under conditions of oligopoly. A very large producer—an "oligopolist"—would be in a position to control a quantity of the total supply sufficient to influence the price of the product, while the many small manufacturers account for a mere fraction of the total production.

DEGREES OF COMPETITION

Pure competition
1. Many sellers in an industry.
2. Identical (or perfectly substitutable) products.
3. No individual seller has appreciable influence on prices.

Monopolistic competition
1. Many sellers in an industry.
2. Similar but differentiated products.
3. Sellers can vary prices within narrow limits.

Oligopoly
1. Few sellers in an industry.
2. May be "pure" (identical products) or "differentiated" (closely substitutable but not identical products).
3. Sellers can vary prices within limits, recognizing that all have influence on the overall price level.

Monopoly
1. One seller in an industry or given market.
2. (Hence no competing products.)
3. Prices established by seller.

"Differentiated oligopolists," like sellers under monopolistic competition, will strive to advertise the slight differences in their products, or to magnify these differences in ways designed to lure buyers. "Pure oligopolists," however, like sellers under conditions of pure competition, have no particular basis for advertising their individual product except by brand name. At best, they usually can engage in a form of advertising which will attract buyers to their industry as a whole, or win "good will" for themselves or their industry. For this reason, much of the advertising of pure oligopolists is conducted by associations which represent the industry as a whole. Some dominant firm or firms in pure oligopoly, however, sometimes do advertise on their own—especially if one or two manufacturers account for a very large part of the total production as in the steel and aluminum industries.

Price differences are greater in differentiated than in pure oligopoly. Under both pure and differentiated oligopoly, each of the "giants" can have a significant influence on prices. Management in these companies usually is aware of the influence their companies exert on prices. They realize that whatever actions they take on prices will lead to corresponding price reactions by other producers in the industry. For example, if an oligopolist lowers his prices significantly, he probably would expect that his competitors would do likewise—perhaps even touching off a price war. On the other hand, an oligopolist would not be likely to make large increases in his prices unless he had reason to think that his competitors would follow his lead. If his competitors did not also increase their prices, he would be likely to lose a good part of his business to them.

The prices charged by a pure oligopolist usually cannot remain significantly different from the prices of others in the industry. Somewhat larger price differences are possible in products of differentiated oligopoly because of product differences and consumer preference. For this reason, it is normally advantageous for a "pure" oligopolist to join the ranks of differentiated oligopoly (just as it would be advantageous for a "pure" competitor to differentiate his product and become a monopolistic competitor). Such moves are not always beneficial to the public, however.

Advertising and other costs of differentiation may be quite high, and certainly are reflected in prices paid by consumers. From the consumer's viewpoint, the advantages of a wider choice among somewhat similar products must be balanced against the disadvantages of higher prices. Experts, such as economists or accountants, may be able to indicate the nature of the costs (and prices) paid for differentiation. But they cannot say positively whether this is desirable or undesirable.

Competition may be keen even in the absence of "pure" competition. The fact that a particular industry is characterized by oligopoly or monopolistic competition does not necessarily mean that competition is weakened. In striving for increased sales and profits, businessmen and firms are eager to outdo their rivals whether they are two, twenty, or two hundred in number.

Actually, competition sometimes may be more keen between a few large and financially strong firms than between a much larger number of smaller and weaker sellers. Large firms must sell a large volume of goods to cover their costs. Also, they usually are better able to afford the costs and withstand the temporary losses that may accompany keen competition. Consumers frequently benefit from the lowered prices which result when a few large firms are fighting it out for a dominant position in a market.

Private monopolies are relatively few in number. "Monopoly" means "one seller." Beyond this, there is no complete agreement as to the meaning of this term. To take an extreme viewpoint, one may argue that monopoly can exist only if there is just one seller of everything in the whole world, or at least in one market. From this viewpoint, the people in Communist lands who must buy at government-owned stores are more completely subjected to monopoly than are buyers in our own country.

A practical definition of monopoly is *control by one seller of a particular product in a specific market.* Even by this restricted definition, complete monopoly in this country is very limited. It is confined largely to instances where the government has authorized one firm to provide a particular kind of public utility or transport service in an area, or to patents, copyrights, and trade-mark authorization.

A monopolist is in a favorable business position. Barring the influence of government regulations, monopolies have more control over their prices and production levels than do other forms of business. An unregulated monopolist can either set a price and produce as much as he can sell at that price, or at the other extreme he can produce all he can and sell it at whatever price he can get. Usually he takes a middle position—that is, he has the necessary flexibility to adjust both his price and his production to the levels which bring in the greatest possible profits.

There is no assurance, of course, that a monopolist will always make profits. Production costs and demand situations may be such that profits are impossible. A monopoly in the manufacture of nose-rings in this country would be worth very little. But a monopolist usually does have a better chance to make profits, or to make larger profits, than any other type of enterprise. He does not have to worry about competition from a similar product, although he does have to compete overall for the consumers' dollars. And he may even have to compete with products from other sources which can partly be substituted for his own product.

To sum up, business enterprise varies from pure competition to monopoly. There is no clear-cut division between the various stages or degrees of competition, however. One shades into the other. Aside from public utilities, there are hardly any complete monopolies, and there is little *pure* competition except perhaps in the production and sale of certain agricultural products. Instead, one typically finds a blending of elements of competition and monopoly.

Industries usually try to avoid being labelled "monopolistic." Despite the marketing advantages of monopoly, private businesses during recent years have usually been careful to conduct their general operations so that they do not force all competitors out of business. This is especially true of large businesses which are frequently in the public eye. They prefer a situation in which a small number of firms continue to compete, because a single surviving firm would be subject to prosecution for monopolizing the market. The courts might then break up the monopoly into several competing firms. Business firms do not want the public to feel that their practices are monopolistic. The very word "monopoly" seems to suggest a type of operation which is unfair or even damaging to free enterprise and which may lead to unfair prices and to demands for regulation.

Industries have tried to get control of a market in a number of ways. Businesses have employed a variety of means to expand their power and influence. Sometimes a larger market is obtained simply by being more efficient in production and selling at lower prices than competitors. A small firm, if successful at this, may grow into a dominant one.

More often, however, firms become large by *merger* with other firms, or by *acquiring the assets* and facilities of other businesses. A merger occurs when two or more firms go together and organize themselves into one. Acquisition of assets involves buying out other businesses, either for cash or by an exchange of stocks. Many of the very large businesses in this country are a result of dozens, and sometimes even hundreds, of mergers and acquisitions.

How business becomes "big" through combination

1 Mergers

Ownership and control of two or more corporations is merged into one corporation. This is the most common type of combination. It is not illegal unless "restraint of trade" can definitely be established.

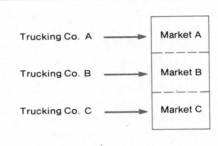

Farm Machinery Company A ⟶

Harvester Company B ⟶ AB Farm Machinery Company

2 Pools

Two or more competitors agree to limit their respective operations and to share output, territory, or profits. Pooling agreements are illegal because their purpose is to restrain competition. However, the existence of the pool must be established.

Trucking Co. A ⟶ Market A

Trucking Co. B ⟶ Market B

Trucking Co. C ⟶ Market C

3 Trusts

Several corporations are brought under a centralized control. The original trust, wherein trust certificates were issued in exchange for stock, is illegal. The interlocking directorate is not considered a violation of antitrust laws, however, unless clear evidence of "restraint of trade" can be shown.
Here, the trust directorate owns stock in companies A, B and C, and also has its members on their boards of directors.

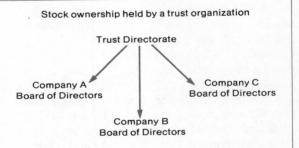

Stock ownership held by a trust organization

Trust Directorate

Company A
Board of Directors

Company B
Board of Directors

Company C
Board of Directors

4 Holding companies

A corporation (called a holding company) is set up to run several corporations in related fields of industry. Ownership of controlling stock interest in the subsidiary corporations enables the holding company to manipulate the operations of whole series of corporations.
Under the Public Utilities Holding Company Act of 1935, holding companies at the "Z" level or higher, were declared illegal in the electric power and gas industries.

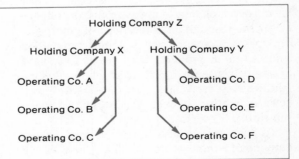

Holding Company Z

Holding Company X

Holding Company Y

Operating Co. A

Operating Co. B

Operating Co. C

Operating Co. D

Operating Co. E

Operating Co. F

Markets have been "shared" by "agreements." If several companies are in strong competition with one another, each may try to capture a bigger share of the market by lowering its prices. Such attempts to undercut one another may lead to a "price war." Of course there are limits to this type of competition. The small independent producers eventually will be forced to retire from the market, leaving the field to a few of the "big fellows." These, in turn, may decide that it is to their advantage to form a *pool,* or *pooling agreement* by which each member pledges that he will share the output, the profits, or the sales territory with his comembers. (If the agreement affects the world market, it is called a *cartel.*) Since such agreements generally are not legal in this country, a pool can be only as strong as the word of each member. Businesses usually try to avoid giving the impression that they are involved in such "gentlemen's agreements." The penalties can be quite severe if such agreements are discovered.

In the case of the *trust,* however, members were bound by more than a mere verbal agreement. In the early trusts, several different corporations surrendered their stock certificates for an equivalent value in trust certificates. The directors of the resulting new organization, called *trustees,* managed the overall operations of the member corporations.

Some corporations have circumvented the legal restrictions against trusts by means of the *interlocking directorate.* Under this arrangement the member corporations retain their separate identities. However, by obtaining a controlling interest in the stock of various corporations, a small group of men get themselves elected to the board of directors of each corporation. Thus they are in a position to control the market. In many cases, interlocking directorates have been found to be an illegal means of exercising undue control over markets.

Holding companies are widely used. A holding company is a corporation which owns stocks in other corporations. For example, Company A may own a controlling stock interest in Company B, which in turn owns controlling interest in Companies C, D, and E. As corporate control requires only a maximum of more than 50 per cent of comon stock (and usually much less), Company A may be able to control vast amounts of assets with a relatively small investment of its own. This gives great economic power to the directors of Company A. Such a device may allow an excellent group of top managers to direct and co-ordinate the activities of several firms, thus obtaining, in part at least, the "advantages" of "bigness" (see Chapter 9). Consequently, holding companies are not illegal as such—in fact, they are very numerous. But if a holding company actually is used as a method of unduly restraining competition, it may run afoul of the law in the same way as a pool, trust, or interlocking directorate.

"Conglomerate" holding companies have expanded in recent years. Prior to the 1960's, most holding companies were organized in some one industry. A *conglomerate* is a holding company which diversifies into a number of quite different industries. For example, a conglomerate may own controlling interest in railroads, mines, publishing houses, retail stores, and a variety of manufacturing firms. As a rule, the "parent" firm of the conglomerate spreads its holdings among many different types of business activities.

Conglomerates proved attractive to many investors who wished to "insure" against poor economic conditions in some one industry. It appears, however, that many of them were organized by "promoters" who were more interested in quick gains of stock prices than in long-run profitable operations. They are not illegal as such, and do not seem to pose a greater threat to competition than do other holding companies. They do, however, involve the concentration of a vast amount of economic power in the hands of a small number of people. For this reason, the Justice Department, as well as many consumers and businessmen, had become quite concerned about the trend toward conglomerates during the late 1960's. The overall economic effects of conglomerates still is a matter of dispute. (See Case Analysis 6.)

CHECK UP

1. Explain monopolistic competition, pure oligopoly, differentiated oligopoly. Give examples of each.

2. How does product differentiation help the seller? Does it help the consumer? Explain.

3. What is a monopoly? With what kind of competition does a monopolist have to contend? Why does an industry not wish to be labeled monopolistic?

4. What is the purpose of a merger? A pooling agreement? A trust? An interlocking directorate? A holding company? A conglomerate?

MERGER ACTIVITY

Gulf & Western was the most active acquiring company of the 1960's. In the words of its president, it is "a young corporation, but it is composed of some of America's long-established companies." Its two billion dollars in assets gives it the rank of 34 among *Fortune's* 500 largest industrial corporations but to this should be added some 1.6 billion dollars of an unconsolidated subsidiary, Associated Investments Co., one of its latest and, thus far, its largest acquisition.

During the period 1961–68, Gulf & Western acquired at least 67 companies and an aggregation of assets of approximately 2.8 billion dollars, more than half of which came from its single 1968 acquisition in the investment business. Gulf & Western has diversified far beyond its initial field, automotive parts, into such industries as motion pictures, sugar, cigars, zinc, fertilizer, wire and cable, publishing, paper, musical instruments, real estate, insurance and investments.

Source: Federal Trade Commission, Economic Report on Corporate Mergers

3

How is business regulated by government?

"Laissez faire" is a part of the American tradition. For many years, most business in this country was relatively free from government regulation. This was called a *laissez faire* economy. (*Laissez faire* is French for "let alone.") The American people favored such a policy. They felt that almost unlimited freedom of competition and little or no public control in business and industry was best for everyone.

A laissez faire system has some disadvantages. Under a system of complete freedom of activity, producers could manufacture, advertise, and sell anything they wished, regardless of quality. There was little likelihood of legal redress for a purchaser who discovered that the merchandise he bought did not measure up to the claims made for it. Of course, if a business concern continued to misrepresent its product, it might gradually lose buyers. But in the meantime the concern might make huge sales and tremendous profits at the expense of the public. By the time the buying public became aware that a particular item was inferior, it would be too late to do anything about it.

Certain business organizations, such as railroads, oil refineries, and manufacturers of certain products, could obtain rates, or charge prices, which many people came to feel were excessive. As these situations developed, more people became convinced that the government must take action to protect the public interest.

Control of businesses developed gradually. During the latter half of the 1800's, people in the United States began to be deeply concerned about the continued growth of large corporations. Many believed that a number of the larger firms were deliberately attempting to establish monopolistic combinations in order to charge high prices (or *rates* in the cases of

The government's response to economic emergencies

emergency	resulting economic policy
Panic of 1908	Creation of Federal Reserve System, 1913
Sharp fall in farm prices, 1920–1921	Regulation of packers and stockyards Encouragement to farm co-operatives Additional farm credit facilities Regulation of commodity exchanges
Stock market collapse, 1929	Securities Act, 1933 Securities and Exchange Act, 1934 Regulation of margin requirements, 1934
Collapse of electric holding company systems, 1929–1932	Public Utility Holding Companies Act, 1935 Additional authority to Federal Power Commission, 1935
Bank failures, 1929–1933	Federal deposit insurance Increased powers for Federal Reserve Board, 1935
Failure of banking system, 1933	Abandonment of gold standard Devaluation of dollar
Fall in crude oil prices, 1931–1933	State conservation measures
Collapse of state government finances, 1930–1932; serious unemployment and destitution	Federal emergency relief Social security
Heavy unemployment, after 1930	Federal relief, 1933 Work relief, 1934 and 1935 Unemployment insurance, 1935
Fall in farm prices, 1929–1933	Agricultural Adjustment Act, 1933
Serious deflation, 1929–1932	Reconstruction Finance Corporation; loans to banks, insurance companies, and railroads
Drought, 1936	Soil conservation payments to farmers
Economic distress in other countries, after 1945	Foreign economic aid

Source: Adapted from *Economic Policy: Business and Government* by Donald S. Watson (Houghton Mifflin Company). Used by permission.

railroads and warehouses). Fingers were pointed accusingly at the railroads, the oil refineries, and the tobacco companies.

Federal and state legislative bodies and courts eventually agreed with voters that, for the public good, a certain amount of regulation of private industry was necessary. Furthermore, it was the duty of government to see that regulatory laws were passed and enforced. After much discussion in Congress and in state legislatures, laws were passed to prevent or regulate monopolies. There was also legislation promoting fair trade practices. Prices or rates for specified services such as transportation were made subject to certain limits or "ceilings."

Industries affected by this legislation claimed

that government had no right to interfere with business. But the courts ruled that government (state or federal) had the power of control over those businesses which were "affected with a public interest"; in short, those businesses which, if unregulated, could operate in a manner harmful to the public. These controls have been extended to cover many phases of the economy. Nevertheless, American business as a whole enjoys a great deal of freedom from government supervision—certainly more than is true for private business in any other major country.

Railroads were the first major type of business subjected to extensive government regulation. Many parts of the country have only two or three railroads, and some are served by only one. In those areas the railroads might be classed as an oligopoly or even as a monopoly. Hence, it might seem that they could charge a higher rate than would be necessary to cover their costs and to make a reasonable profit. It is interesting to note, however, that the regulation of railroads was less the result of monopolistic prices than of unfair practices which grew out of bitter rivalry among competing roads.

Before they were regulated, many railroads resorted to various unfair practices in the hope of making greater profits. The most serious was the practice of discrimination—that is, giving preferred treatment to some users of the railroad.

A common form of railroad discrimination was charging different rates to different shippers. Even though the rates to all shippers were *quoted at the same figure,* some railroads gave

Milestones of antimonopoly legislation

year	law	purpose
1887	Interstate Commerce Act	Gave Interstate Commerce Commission power to regulate shipping rates charged by railroads; made railroad pools illegal. Since 1887 the powers of the ICC have been broadened.
1890	Sherman Act	Prohibits "combinations in restraint of trade," or attempts to establish a monopoly in business.
1914	Clayton Act	Forbids price discrimination among different customers and makes "holding companies" illegal when these interfere with competition.
1914	Federal Trade Commission Act	Outlaws "unfair methods of competition" in interstate commerce and empowers the FTC to enforce government regulations relating to interstate commerce.
1936	Robinson-Patman Act	Originally intended to curb pricing powers of chain stores. Tightened provisions of Clayton Act which forbade price discrimination—as when a supplier of goods to chain stores offers lower wholesale prices than those charged to individual merchants.
1944	Surplus Property Act	Required that surplus government property be disposed of in such a manner as to encourage competition among prospective buyers and sellers of the surplus goods.

refunds or rebates to favored shippers, usually those who shipped goods in very large volume.

A second form of discrimination was charging higher rates between points where there was no competition in commercial transportation. (The competition might be either with rival railroad lines or with other types of carriers, such as river barges.) This kind of discrimination was considered unfair because it favored certain cities and businesses at the expense of others.

Still another form of discrimination was the charging of different rates for products which were similar and hence required similar handling. If a railroad had a financial interest in a certain product, it might discriminate against a similar product in which it had no interest.

Government regulation has been based on the principle of public interest. In an effort to regulate railroad rates and practices, several states created railroad commissions during the 1870's. These commissions, under laws enacted by state legislatures, were given broad regulatory powers over railroads and associated businesses such as grain elevators and warehouses. The businesses involved protested, of course. But the United States Supreme Court in a series of decisions (the so-called *Granger Cases,* about 1876) upheld the rights of governments to regulate businesses "affected with the public interest." Subsequent court decisions greatly broadened the scope of the "public interest," or welfare, by increasing the number and kinds of businesses subject to regulation under this concept. Today, it would appear that legislative bodies may decide that any kind of business is "affected with the public interest."

It soon became apparent that state regulation of businesses operating in many states was impractical, as well as a violation of the "interstate commerce clause" (Article I, Section 8 (3)) of the United States Constitution. This clause gives Congress the power to "regulate Commerce with foreign Nations, and among the several States, and with the Indian Tribes." In

1887, therefore, the United States Congress established the Interstate Commerce Commission (ICC) to regulate interstate railroad operations. The ICC now regulates all forms of interstate transportation except air transport—which is regulated by the Civil Aeronautics Board (CAB). Transoceanic transportation is regulated by the Federal Maritime Commission (FMC). Transportation conducted within the borders of a single state (intrastate) generally is regulated by a state commission.

Other businesses were brought under regulation. The *Interstate Commerce Act* dealt only with the regulation of transportation. In 1890, however, Congress enacted the *Sherman Anti-Trust Act,* which applies to businesses in general, and is intended to prohibit monopolies and combinations or conspiracies "in restraint of trade." Such practices, if proved in the courts, may be punished by both fine and imprisonment.

To eliminate some weaknesses of the Sherman Act, Congress passed the *Clayton Anti-Trust Act* and the *Federal Trade Commission Act* in 1914. The Clayton Act forbids price discrimination among different customers or control of one corporation by another, in instances where such actions lessen competition in interstate commerce. The Federal Trade Commission Act declares that "unfair methods of competition" in interstate commerce are unlawful. It created a Federal Trade Commission (FTC) to serve as a watchdog for violations.

Antitrust laws are powerful. The antitrust laws are a potent tool for government regulation. They may be used in several ways. Large firms may be required to break up into smaller ones. For example, during early Sherman Act days a large tobacco manufacturing company and a large petroleum company were ordered broken up by the United States Supreme Court. More recently, DuPont was ordered to dispose of its large holdings of General Motors stock. Penalties may also be imposed on individual businesses or businessmen who conspire to set prices. During 1961, several electrical equipment manufacturing firms including officers of General Electric and Westinghouse, were found guilty of this charge. Settlements exceeded 100 million dollars and several executives of these corporations went to jail. A similar situation arose in the plumbing supply business in 1968.

Economists, attorneys, and businessmen are not in complete agreement about the effectiveness of the antitrust laws or how best to administer them. Some experts think that the laws are too strict; others, that they are not strict enough. Enforcement is made difficult because the penalties are in general smaller than the profits to be made by violation, and because of inadequate funding of the Antitrust Division of the Department of Justice. Furthermore,

there is little agreement on definitions of "monopoly," "competition," "restraint of trade," and "unfair trade practices." Even more difficult is "proving" their existence or nonexistence in a court of law.

Commissions administer much of the regulatory legislation. In addition to regulations affecting businesses in general, such as the antitrust and securities acts, several industries are subject to more specific regulations. Federal and state regulation of transportation and public utility companies already has been mentioned. Under laws passed by Congress, much of this regulation is provided by regulatory commissions. Besides those already mentioned are the *Federal Communications Commission* (FCC) for regulating radio, television, telegraph, and interstate telephone service, and the *Federal Power Commission* (FPC) for regulating interstate electric and natural gas services.

Regulatory commissions exercise a wide degree of independence. Regulatory bodies, especially at the federal level, are often called "independent" commissions. That is, as creations of the legislature (Congress or state legislatures, as the case may be) they are not subject to direct control by the President or a governor. Members usually are appointed by the chief executive with legislative approval. But after appointment, commissioners usually are fairly well protected from the administration even if commission action does not meet with administration approval. The legislative body càn refuse to appropriate operating funds. But it cannot dictate to a commission other than by changing the laws under which the commission operates.

There are both critics and defenders of commission regulation. Commission regulation has been praised as providing continuous, expert, and flexible regulation by competent full-time men. On the other hand, critics accuse some commissions of being a "rule by men" rather than a "rule by law." They also charge that the

"It's All Right–I've Got Him On A Leash"

The Herblock Book (*Beacon Press, 1952*)

existence of so many commissions makes government a top-heavy, slow-moving bureaucracy. Moreover, insofar as a commission makes and enforces its own regulations and judges violations of them, it may seem to exercise too much independent power. Such concentration of power could be a danger to private businesses and even to democratic government. Other critics argue that the commissions have been too easy on the corporations they were supposed to regulate and not sufficiently active in protecting the public interest.

Both critics and defenders of commission regulation are partly correct. Commissions operate under the federal Constitution or state constitutions and the laws passed by legislative bodies. Their decisions are subject to review by state or federal courts. Within these limitations, however, they have wide latitude in interpreting and applying the law. But in general, commissioners recognize their responsibility to see that the public gets adequate services at reasonable prices and is protected from fraudulent actions. They also recognize that regulated businesses must be allowed to earn reasonable profits under honest and efficient management if such businesses are to continue.

Perhaps the main justification for commission regulation is that a commission can interpret the broad intent of the law and can make detailed rulings which fit a wide variety of circumstances. Most serious students of government and economics agree that the commission form of regulation is usually a satisfactory device, even though commissioners are only human and do make mistakes. Such mistakes, if serious, can eventually be corrected by the legislatures or the courts.

Regulation is here to stay. In summary, while a vast majority of Americans firmly believe in free enterprise, they also believe that economic freedom, like political freedom, carries certain responsibilities, and that regulation of certain types of economic activity is necessary to insure that these responsibilities are met. Expert

Federal regulatory commissions and their functions

Interstate Commerce Commission

Regulates domestic interstate truck, bus, barge, railroad, ship and oil pipeline transportation. Approves freight rates and passenger fares, mergers, entry into business and other matters. Attempts to insure an adequate surface transport service for national commerce and defense.

Federal Communications Commission

Regulates radio, television broadcasting and telephone and telegraph industries. Under the Communications Satellite Act of 1962 it is empowered to insure fair access to Telstar or other communications satellites.

Federal Trade Commission

"The basic objective of the Commission is the maintenance of free competitive enterprise as the keystone of the American economic system." Among its activities are prevention of price-fixing agreements, and checking deceptive practices in interstate commerce.

Federal Maritime Commission

"Regulates the services, practices, and agreements of common carriers by water and other persons engaged in the foreign commerce of the United States." This includes the issuing of licenses to engage in ocean freight forwarding activities.

The Securities and Exchange Commission

Specifies the conditions that must be met before new securities can be marketed, and controls holding companies in the electric power and gas industries.

Federal Power Commission

Regulates interstate aspects of electric power and natural gas industries, including rates. Grants or withholds permits for constructing and operating private hydro electric power projects.

Civil Aeronautics Board

Regulates economic aspects of domestic and international United States air carrier operations; assists the Department of State in negotiating international air routes; investigates accidents involving civil aircraft, and recommends air safety measures.

opinion concerning the necessary amount and kind of regulation varies. But it is not likely that there will occur any substantial lessening of overall business regulation. As a society becomes more and more complex, more rather than fewer rules may be expected if the rights of all groups within the society are to be protected.

CHECK UP

1. What were the advantages and disadvantages of nineteenth-century *laissez-faire* economy? Why was a policy of government regulation adopted during the second half of the century?

2. What abuses led to the regulation of railroads? How was such regulation justified? What other forms of business have been brought under government regulation?

3. Are people generally agreed about the effectiveness of antitrust laws and how best to administer them? Why? About the desirability of commission regulation? Give arguments on both sides.

4

What is the extent of legalized monopoly?

Although Americans generally disapprove of monopoly, and the country's laws have made most of them illegal, there are some exceptions. In these few cases, it is believed the advantages of monopoly are greater than its disadvantages. Consequently, government itself encourages or requires monopoly. The monopolies concerned, of course, must operate under rigid laws or governmental controls.

Public utilities (firms supplying communications, energy, and street transit services) are often considered to be monopolies. Public utility managers will not accept this line of thinking, however. Even though an organization does have a complete monopoly in one particular commodity, the chances are that there are certain substitutes which can replace the monopoly product for at least some uses or some users. For example, plastics, wood, aluminum, and other products can in many cases be substituted for steel. Thus, even if one company controlled all steel production in this country (which, of course, is not true), it might be argued that this would not be a monopoly. It all depends on one's definition of monopoly.

By the same line of reasoning, even such services as telephones, electric lighting, and gas are not complete monopolies. Although each of these public utility services may be furnished by one company in a given area (which is not always true), there are substitutes. For example, messages can be sent by telegraph or letter as well as by telephone. Heat and light can be provided by both electricity and gas, or by kerosene. Utility firms, too, must compete for the consumer's dollar with firms selling automobiles, food, and an immense variety of other services and products.

Public utility firms, however, usually are regulated by federal, state, or local government, or by all three. This is because of the special types of services provided by such companies. If, for example, only one company is providing a certain kind of service in a locality—such as electric power—that company is said to be exercising a *natural monopoly* in the area. It is thought to be in the public interest for all local power services to be provided by one company, because in most cases, it would be both confusing and more costly to have two or more electric light, telephone, or gas companies, or street transportation systems. There may be significant cost savings associated with large-size public utility operations under some circumstances. Overhead costs per unit of service, for example, are greatly reduced as the number of customers increases. The public utility, therefore, frequently is granted exclusive rights to operate as the sole seller of its particular service throughout a designated area. Although there is some disagreement with this arrangement, most people consider it the best plan for providing privately operated public utility services.

Patents are another form of monopoly. When one invents something, he can have it *patented* by the United States Patent Office, thus obtaining exclusive rights to its manufacture for seventeen years. Also, if substantial improvements are made over the original invention during this period, new patents may be obtained. Patent laws strengthen the power of big industrial corporations by enabling them to obtain the exclusive rights to technical devices and processes.

Many patented inventions are of great value, but some are weird and impractical. For example, one person patented a device which would enable a person, if buried alive, to signal to the outside. Another patent provided for rails to be attached to the roofs of the cars of a train. The rails were to curve down over the regular railroad rails. The inventor's reasoning was that if Train A should overtake Train B which was

equipped with the rail attachment, Train A could run over the top of the other train, thus avoiding a collision.

There is a constant struggle in the economy to put out newly-patented products which give the inventor a competitive advantage. But the value of patent rights depends on how well the patented product is merchandised and how popular it is with the buying public. For example, should someone take out a patent on a new type of carburetor which would give motorists greatly improved gas mileage, it would soon enjoy an advantage in sales over its predecessor, and would perhaps gradually replace it. Practically all large manufacturers have research staffs constantly working on new ideas. In some instances a newly patented product barely gets onto the market when another and better product replaces it.

Copyrights and trademarks also create limited monopolies. Anyone who writes a book, a musical composition, a television script, a play, or a motion picture scenario, can obtain ex-

Nation's patents

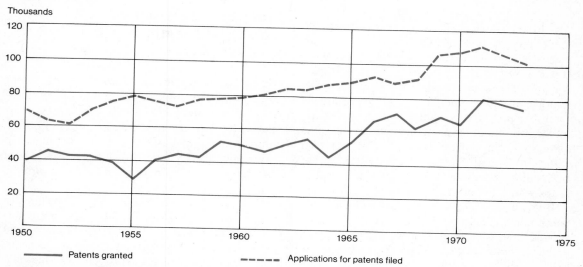

Thousands

Source: Commissioner of Patents Annual Report

clusive rights, or a *copyright,* on his work for 28 years. The copyright can then be renewed for another 28 years. The holder of a copyright has a complete monopoly for the entire copyright period. If, for example, a million copies of a book are sold, the writer will be able to collect all the royalties and the publisher will get the remaining profits from the sales. No other person has the right to reproduce a copyrighted work, wholly or in part, without first obtaining permission from the copyright owner.

There are some exceptions to this, however. Short passages from a copyrighted publication may be quoted in a review or in a scholarly treatise without securing the permission of the copyright holder. Moreover, in recent years the advent of inexpensive methods of reproducing printed or written material—for example, by the use of Xerox machines—has forced Congress to consider other modifications of the existing copyright laws. Should a scholar be permitted to reproduce for his own use pages from a copyrighted publication without first obtaining permission to do so? In this instance, new technology is threatening to undermine significant sections of the copyright laws.

Trademarks may be thought of as another form of monopoly, because their uses are limited to registered holders. When you see the familiar name of a certain soap with a particular design on a certain colored background, you know it is a given kind of soap. Buyers recognize the brand and buy on the basis of the brand name. The company manufacturing the soap has monopoly rights to that particular trademark. No other company can use the same name and design if the trademark is registered with the United States Patent Office. Other companies, of course, may produce similar soaps with different trademarks.

But just as trademarks sometimes benefit the consumer by helping him to identify quality products, so they may also work to his disadvantage. Trademarks sometimes allow firms to reap excessive profits because of the exaggerated image in the public's mind (fostered by advertising) of a particular product's quality. In this connection, some state legislatures have been considering laws requiring physicians to prescribe drugs by their *generic* (or chemical) names instead of by their patented brand names. Lobbyists for the better-known drug companies oppose such legislation, insisting that even in medicines, brand names are important indicators of quality. The argument against this is that the Food and Drug Administration itself dictates standards in the drug field, and that patients should be allowed whatever savings may be possible through the purchase of lesser-known brands of drugs.

CHECK UP

1. Are public utilities complete monopolies? Explain. Why are they regulated by federal, state, and local governments?

2. Define and explain: patent, copyright, trademark. Why are these forms of monopoly authorized by law? Do they favor big business? Explain.

5

How does government sometimes compete with business?

Some public service facilities are government owned. Public utilities owned and operated by local and state governments sometimes compete with private business enterprises. For example, there may be two bus companies in your town or city, one owned and operated by the local government, the other by a private company or an individual.

Federally owned and controlled businesses also exist in the United States. The more important ones include the United States Postal Service, numerous irrigation and power projects, and various enterprises connected with national defense.

Anyone who works for a government-owned public service, whether as an unskilled laborer or a manager, is an employee of the government unit that carries on the enterprise. The postmaster who manages the local post office is employed by the federal government. Similarly, the person in charge of the municipal water department and the people who work under him are employees of the city government.

At least part of the expense of operating a publicly owned service, such as the postal service, usually is paid by the individuals who use it. However, this may not always meet the entire expense of operation. The balance then must be paid from the state, local, or federal treasury.

Roads and highways provide a public service. Many of the nation's highways are built and financed jointly by the federal and state governments. This arrangement has produced an efficient highway system. People all over the country use highways for personal business or pleasure, and businesses use them for the transportation of large quantities of freight.

"Public corporations" are sometimes used as a technique of public ownership. The publicly-owned utility, such as the city gas and electric company, has been common in the United States for many years. But another kind of public agency has been developed more recently—mainly since the 1930's. Some economists have called this new type of public agency a *public corporation.* The federal government maintains general ownership and control of this type of corporation, but the organization is operated in much the same way as a private corporation. The most recent example of a public corporation is the United States Postal Service, which for many years functioned as a government agency, but which became a public corporation by act of Congress in 1970. Another well-known example of a public corporation is the *Tennessee Valley Authority* (TVA).

TVA is a successful public corporation. For many years a large area in Tennessee and parts of adjoining states had suffered seriously from

Five government corporations

The Tennessee Valley Authority

The Tennessee Valley Authority was established in 1933 to develop the Tennessee River and its tributaries. Its responsibilities have included navigation, flood control, electric power production, recreation, agriculture, forestry, and water quality control. It is financed through the sale of bonds and electric power, and governed by a three-member board of directors appointed by the President and approved by the Senate.

The United States Postal Service

The U.S. Postal Service is a new government corporation, although delivery of the mail has long been a function of the federal government. The corporation is designed to take politics out of the post office, which has been a source of patronage in the past. It is governed by an eleven-member board of governors which selects the Postmaster General and the Deputy Postmaster-General. The Postal Service has the power to negotiate pay increases and working conditions with unions and sell up to ten billion dollars' worth of bonds for modernization. A separate five-member commission will hold hearings to decide upon rate requests.

The Panama Canal Company

The Panama Canal Company in conjunction with the Canal Zone Government has operated and maintained the Panama Canal. The president of the company, who is also the governor of the Canal Zone, is appointed by the President and reports to the Secretary of the Army. In 1964, negotiations to redefine the status of the Canal and the Canal Zone began with the government of Panama, but the process was stalemated following a military coup there in 1968. In 1971, the United States remained owner of the Canal, receiving the revenue collected from it and in turn making rent payments to Panama.

The Federal Deposit Insurance Corporation

The Federal Deposit Insurance Corporation was set up to protect depositors from bank failures by insuring deposits in all banks covered by the Federal Deposit Insurance Act. The FDIC acts as receiver for most banks which declare bankruptcy. It is also charged with preventing unsafe and unsound banking practices. Its income is derived from investments and assessments on insured banks. It is run by a three-member board of directors. Two are appointed by the President with the advice of the Senate for a term of six years; the third is the Comptroller of the Currency.

The Export-Import Bank of the United States

The Export-Import Bank is authorized to make loans in order to encourage and aid exports and imports. It has a capital stock of one billion dollars and may borrow up to six billion from the Treasury. It may lend up to $13.5 billion. The Bank is run by a board of directors consisting of three members appointed by the President with the advice of the Senate, and the Bank's president and first vice-president. No more than three directors may be from one political party.

floods and soil erosion. People in the area urged Congress to make funds available for the construction of flood control dams. No privately owned organization could have financed or operated such an enterprise at a profit.

Finally, in 1933, funds were made available and work was started on the TVA. In part, this was done to provide employment during the Great Depression. In part it was a conservation project and an attempt to raise the low living standards in the area. Since that time many dams have been built on the Tennessee River and the smaller rivers running into it. These dams have served two main purposes: (1) they control floods and accompanying soil erosion, and (2) they generate electric power.

The tremendous amount of hydroelectric power which has been developed by those dams serves a vast area. This power is sold to the public. According to the bookkeeping methods of the government, which charge a portion of the costs involved to flood control and navigation improvement, power sales yield a profitable return to the project. TVA thus combines the functions of flood prevention, soil conservation, and navigation improvement, with the function of supplying power to the surrounding area.

During more recent years, though, a majority of TVA power has been generated from coal-burning steam plants. This has provided a much stronger argument for privately owned utilities and opponents of "big government" who have maintained from the beginning that the TVA is purely and simply a vast "socialistic" undertaking.

City ownership is quite common for some types of enterprise. While federal- and state-owned enterprises account for only a small part of the nation's economic production, a relatively large number of enterprises are owned and operated by cities. These operate under the general laws of the state in which the city is located. Among them are waterworks, electric plants, transportation facilities, public schools, and various other public services. The majority of cities, for example, own and run their water

supply systems. Many other services performed for the city perhaps *could* be municipally owned. The general practice, however, is to leave many types of city-used services in the hands of private owners.

This is consistent with this country's traditional preference for private enterprise. Generally, public ownership has not come about as a result of any strong belief in a particular political theory. Rather it has developed because of some inability or failure on the part of private enterprise to provide the public with the kinds of service it wants.

CHECK UP

1. Give examples of types of businesses (or services) owned and controlled by the federal government. By state governments. Why do they exist? What are some advantages and disadvantages of government ownership?

2. What is a public corporation? Why was TVA established? Why was the post office changed to a public corporation? What services does TVA render? Why has TVA been criticized?

Clinching the main ideas

Some degree of competition is typical in American industry. Competitive relationships may range, however, from "pure competition" through "monopolistic competition" to "pure oligopoly" and "differentiated oligopoly." "Monopoly" is the opposite of pure competition.

Generally, Americans have favored a competitive or "laissez faire" approach. They have recognized, however, that "legalized monopoly" sometimes is desirable, and that some businesses should be regulated in the public interest. Thus, laws have been enacted to permit or encourage certain types of monopolies and also to make certain businesses act in a more competitive manner. In some types of enterprise, Americans have even resorted to public ownership as a means of better satisfying their commonly-felt needs—although not everyone agrees with this principle.

Despite government regulations and government ownership, more freedom of private enterprise exists in the United States than in any other major country. And despite criticisms of government regulation and ownership, there is little likelihood that either will be lessened within the foreseeable future. One should always remember, however, that usually such regulation and control by the government reflect the wishes of a majority of citizens. Laws are enacted by the elected representatives of the people. If citizens do not like these laws, they can change them.

Chapter 10 review

Terms to understand

1. pure competition
2. product differentiation
3. monopolistic competition
4. commission regulation
5. natural monopoly
6. *laissez faire*
7. Granger Cases
8. holding company
9. public corporation
10. generic name
11. copyright
12. conglomerate

What do you think?

1. "Competition leads to the most efficient distribution of resources, as well as to the lowest prices." Is this statement true or false? Why? Why does the government strictly allocate resources during a period of national emergency?

2. Would it be in the public interest if pure competition existed in the automobile industry? Why?

3. Why would a "pure" oligopolist probably prefer to be a differentiated oligopolist?

4. Why may competition be keener between a small number of large firms than between a large number of small firms?

5. Why was a laissez faire economy more acceptable in the first half of the nineteenth century than in the second half? Do you believe that "regulation is here to stay"? Why?

6. Government regulation of the railroads began in the late 1800's. Today many railroads are operating at a loss and some are facing bankruptcy. Has government regulation caused this condition? Explain.

7. Critics of regulatory commissions hold that they combine administrative, legislative, and judicial functions. Explain this criticism. Is it just?

Extending your knowledge of economics

1. Use the card index file in your school or public library and the *Reader's Guide to Periodical Literature* to locate books and articles dealing with TVA. Summarize the chief points made by critics and defenders of TVA.

2. Interview an official of a local public utility. What taxes does it pay? What regulations are imposed on it? What are its plans for expanding services? Are rates likely to become higher or lower? Doubtless members of the class will suggest other questions for the interview. Perhaps the official would prefer to speak to the class.

case analysis 6

Conglomerate power— its sources and consequences

General background

Recent decades have witnessed the emergence of new forms of corporate power, and one of the most controversial of these is the conglomerate merger. To learn how a conglomerate operates, it will be instructive to consider first the case of Ling-Temco-Vought, Inc.

The story begins

In 1946, James Ling sold his Texas home and used his profits of 3000 dollars to begin an electrical contracting business. In 1958, Ling Electric bought a small electronics firm, and soon embarked on an ambitious program of expansion by buying up some companies and merging with others. By the mid-1960's, Ling's firm (now called Ling-Temco-Vought, or LTV) had become a giant of American industry. At the end of 1967, LTV had acquired more than 20 companies and had assets totaling 1.8 billion dollars. The price of LTV stock reached a peak of 169 dollars a share. Ling himself had personal holdings worth 54 million dollars.

Yet by 1970, LTV was in serious trouble. Its stock tumbled to 8 dollars a share. LTV was sued for antitrust violations by the Justice Department, an action which froze a large part of its assets. The financial columns of magazines and newspapers featured stories of LTV's demise. James Ling had been replaced as chairman by a Dallas banker, and his holdings were now worth only 4 million dollars. Even most of that amount was pledged against loans and could not be spent.

James Ling, still only 47 years old, was said to have remarked: "I never had any money to begin with, and I've enjoyed life with and without money. At my age, with all the economic perturbations we've gone through in the last fifteen years, we should all be professional about these things."

THE CONGLOMERATE DEFINED

James Ling had built LTV into a *conglomerate*. A report of the Federal Trade Commission (FTC) defines a conglomerate as

. . . a company engaged in a number of industrial activities serving more or less distinct markets. Some large corporations are conglomerated only to a minor degree. The great bulk of their revenues may come from a few very closely related lines having similar demand and supply characteristics. Or they may engage in many product or geographical markets having different demand and supply conditions, each contributing minor parts to the firm's total income. . . . The less a firm is dependent on one or a few lines of activity for its economic welfare and the longer and wider are its products or geographic markets, the more conglomerated it is.[1]

The report went on to characterize LTV as a typical conglomerate, in that its business is divided between widely varied fields.

The diversity of LTV's acquisition program is reflected in the fact that while once an aerospace company, by 1968 over half of its business was divided between meat packing and other foods, sporting goods, pharmaceuticals and iron and steel, with the balance in such diverse areas as aerospace, air transportation, electronics, wire and cable, floor coverings and consumer and commercial electronics.[2]

The picture chart on page 249 explains how LTV went from a profitable operation to one in serious trouble, in the space of only two years. Not all conglomerates ran into trouble as serious as LTV's, but by the beginning of the 1970's, most had lost the favor with investors which they had in the mid-1960's.

THE CORPORATE MERGER AND THE HISTORY OF BIG BUSINESS

Controversy over the combining of corporations to form ever-larger economic bodies is nothing new to American political life. Revolutions in

1 *Economic Report on Corporate Mergers: A Staff Report to the Federal Trade Commission* (Washington, D.C.: 1969), p. 295.
2 *Ibid.*, p. 278.

Drawing by Roy Doty. Reproduced by permission of the artist.

Number and total assets of manufacturing and mining firms acquired, 1948-1970

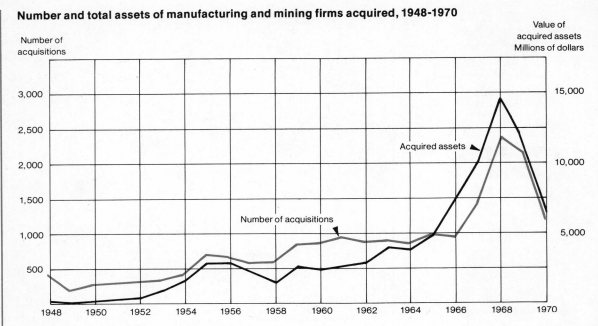

Source: Bureau of Economics, Federal Trade Commission

technology and production have produced revolutions in the organization of business as well. New methods of large-scale production required large amounts of money, and the corporate type of business organization enabled businessmen to combine resources without risking so much of their capital.

Corporations are accorded all the rights of individuals in the market place by English Common Law. They have the right to due process of law and those who own corporations are exempted from personal liability for corporate debt. Corporations are also allowed to become the owners of other corporations.[3] Large private corporations were opposed by some who thought that they could grow to an uncontrollable size. Others contended that corporations were an essential agent of economic growth.

The debate over corporate mergers is quite similar to early debates about corporations themselves. The same arguments favoring a limit on the concentration of wealth and power are offered

3 See pp. 204–210 for a discussion of corporations.

to offset the arguments in favor of bigger and more efficient business organizations which allow for greater profits and productvity.

There have been roughly three major periods of corporate merger activity. In the late 1800's and early 1900's, trusts were set up in attempts to control whole industries—such as tobacco, steel, oil and sugar. Trusts were opposed in Congress, however, and ultimately two important antitrust laws were enacted—the Sherman Antitrust Act (1890) and the Clayton Act (1914). These two laws formed the foundation of antitrust regulation. During the 1920's, another wave of mergers took place. Many were based on financial deals which collapsed with the crash of 1929. The effects of the collapse sparked a new law regulating utilities holding companies—the Wheeler-Rayburn Act of 1935.

In the post-World War II period, mergers regained popularity. (See graph above.) A new aspect was added, however; many of the mergers involved corporations engaged in widely varied kinds of production. These companies became the conglomerates defined above. Because of their growing number and size, and the new patterns they have established, conglomerates are being closely watched by students and critics of the American economy.

The issues

WHY ARE CONGLOMERATES FORMED?

Market power. Businessmen have said there are several benefits to be derived from a conglomerate merger. First, it may offer the resulting (new) parent organization an extraordinary amount of "market power." A conglomeration of interests puts the parent corporation in a favorable competitive position by putting more resources at its command. As an official of one company said:

In general, the basic purpose is not to monopolize or to pyramid financial structures, but, rather, to create and bring together logical industrial and operational empires—business entities of power, commercial position, stability, improved sales and earnings, and greater likelihood of growth and longevity of existence.[4]

Bargains. A second reason some businessmen give for merging is that a merger may offer the buyer-firm a bargain. For example, company A, which is small, may be able to earn a profit with the help of additional capital. Without such capital it is in a weak position. Company B, a large company, can buy company A at a comparatively low price, supply additional capital, and make a good profit. Or, in the words of one businessman:

Another company's manufacturing facility may be far too big for its own needs. A merger can add additional manufacturing load to the present facility and permit greater efficiency and substantial reduction in per-unit overhead charges.[5]

Growth. Third, the absorption of a small company by a larger one may enable the latter to record greater growth for the stock market. Market trends of the 1960's showed that investors preferred stocks with a high rate of growth to those paying higher dividends. They were more interested in buying stocks and selling them a short time later at a profit than in buying stocks in order to collect the dividends over a longer period. So companies interested in raising capital through the sale of stock appealed to the market by encouraging a high rate of growth. James Ling followed this method:

From my own point of view, redeploying assets in this way is building values and these values are measured on the stock market. And in turn they are useful financially as the means of building new values.[6]

In the case of LTV, the process of acquiring new companies and issuing "growth stocks" seemed to produce spectacular profits. To quote *Fortune* magazine:

The application of Project Redeployment has been imaginative. When LTV took over Wilson & Co., in a transaction that totaled about 165 million dollars, it split the company into three parts: Wilson & Co., meat and food processing; Wilson Sporting Goods; and Wilson Pharmaceutical and Chemical. A block of stock in each part was sold to the public, with total proceeds to the three new companies of some $45 million. A month ago, LTV's remaining interest in the three Wilson Companies was valued at 262 million dollars.[7]

In other words, LTV gained 45 million dollars from selling stock, and 97 million dollars from a rise in the price of the stock it retained—a total of 142 million dollars' profit.

Risk spreading. A further benefit to businessmen of conglomerate mergers is that they spread the risks of investment over many industries. If the profits of one subsidiary should drop off, the loss is absorbed by the better profits earned in a different line of production. According to the *New York Times:*

The basic idea of the conglomerate corporation was that, through a broad-based program of acquisitions,

---

4 Robert G. Dettmar, "Reasons for Mergers and Acquisitions," in *Corporate Growth Through Merger and Acquisition* (New York: American Management Association, 1963), p. 29.

5 *Ibid.,* p. 31.

6 *New York Times,* May 18, 1970.

7 *Fortune* (June 15, 1968), p. 249.

a company could diversify its operations into a variety of industries. If business conditions turned downward in one field, the theory went, the company's profits would be maintained or increased by the success of its interests in other fields.[8]

Financial and taxation benefits. Conglomerate mergers often are accomplished by exchanging stock of the conglomerate firm for the stock held by the owners of the acquired corporation. In using this device, the conglomerate does not have to make any cash outlays to acquire other firms; it simply issues more of its own stock. Furthermore, profits made by owners of the acquired company through such exchanges of stock usually are not subject to income taxes unless or until these stocks are sold. On the other hand, if the owners of the acquired company should sell their stocks to the conglomerate or to anyone else, any profits made would be taxable immediately. Thus, the device of trading one kind of stock for another makes it easier financially for conglomerates to acquire other firms, and may provide a strong tax inducement for such mergers.

A simple example of this idea would be that if one buys an apple for ten cents, a sales tax may have to be paid. But if one trades an apple for an orange, nothing is taxed.

WHAT ARE THE ARGUMENTS AGAINST CONGLOMERATES?

Criticisms of conglomerates center on three points: 1) a great concentration of wealth is in itself damaging to competition, 2) large conglomerates lend themselves to particular abuses more easily than do smaller, traditional companies, and 3) concentrations of wealth can pose a threat to American political institutions.

Oligopoly. The first criticism hinges on the question of whether competition and diversified ownership of the means of production—cornerstones of the ideal free enterprise system—are fostered or undermined by large concentrations of economic wealth. Critics contend that in a market dominated by a few large sellers of a particular product, that is, in a situation of oli-

gopoly, sellers tend to act interdependently. If one raises prices, the others follow suit, confident there is no one to undercut them, and therefore no reason to attempt to cut costs and compete. Such a situation arose in the steel industry in 1962. The leading steel producer announced a price increase, and its few competitors also raised prices instead of trying to garner new business by keeping prices stable. Their reaction was challenged by President Kennedy, and the prices were lowered, but only temporarily.

Business abuses. Critics of the conglomerate merger movement point to several practices which they believe to be abuses of proper accounting and other procedures. Three will be explained here: (1) reciprocity, (2) cross-subsidization, and (3) misleading accounting practices.

1. *Reciprocity* occurs when Company A agrees to do business with Company B on condition that Company B will agree to do business with Company A. Reciprocity eliminates open competition between suppliers and is illegal, as well as damaging to the economy since it encourages inefficiency. One example of reciprocity resulted from the merger of the Liquid Carbonic Corporation,[9] a small producer of industrial gases, with General Dynamics, a huge conglomerate active chiefly in producing Defense Department contracts. General Dynamics began a program of coercing its suppliers to buy industrial gases from Liquid Carbonic, according to the Justice Department. The Attorney General successfully sued the company for violating the antitrust laws.

2. A second abuse associated with conglomerates is the practice of *cross-subsidization.* Elsewhere, it was noted that a conglomerate may use the profits of one subsidiary to offset the losses of another. Cross subsidization is similar, except that profits of a market outlet in one area are used to sell products below cost and thus undercut competition in another area. For example, the Safeway supermarket chain once incurred a temporary loss in order to undersell its competitors in a certain city. Branches in other cities continued to make profits which offset the loss. The chain

8 May 31, 1970.

9 *Economic Report.* . . , pp. 341–344.

chapter eleven

 **Agriculture in a changing environment**

1. What are the trends in American agriculture?
2. How is agriculture influenced by geography?
3. What economic conditions affect agriculture?
4. How do farm products reach consumers?
5. How does government influence agriculture?
6. What is the outlook for American farmers?

When tillage begins, other arts follow. The farmers therefore are the founders of civilization.

DANIEL WEBSTER

Some historians assert that civilization really began when mankind started the practice of agriculture. Early primitive societies relied upon hunting, fishing, or the gathering of wild fruits, seeds and roots for their food. People in such societies could not settle down in communities, develop handicrafts, and exchange goods. As agriculture became productive, fewer workers were able to produce enough food for the group, thus freeing other people to weave cloth, or to make tools or weapons. Yet even today in many countries most of the population is engaged in agriculture.

Agriculture remains an important part of the American economy, although fewer persons are engaged in it each year. American farmers grow most of the food to supply the nation, as well as large surpluses of certain crops for export. Farmers purchase goods processed or manufactured by city dwellers, and thus help to keep city workers employed. City dwellers and farmers are closely dependent upon each other.

City consumers often blame farmers for high food prices and criticize government assistance to agriculture. Farmers believe that such complaints reflect the fact that the city people do not understand the problems of agriculture. Doubtless each group needs a better understanding of the other's problems. Such understanding would reduce friction between them and contribute to the solution of mutual problems.

1

What are the trends in American agriculture?

The farm population is shrinking. The number of American farms and of persons engaged in farming has been decreasing for more than 60 years. At the time of the American Revolution, at least 90 per cent of the inhabitants lived on farms. As late as the mid-1930's, one-fourth of the population was rural. Today, only about 5 per cent of Americans are engaged in farming.

Farm and nonfarm population in the United States

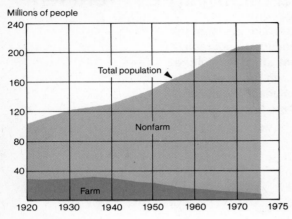

Millions of people

Source: Statistical Abstract

Most people live in a city, town, or suburb. Indeed many of those still residing in rural areas do not engage in farming. Still others are part-time farmers.

Farms are fewer in number but larger in size. At the end of World War II there were almost six million farms in this country; now there are about three million. The average farm, meantime, has increased from about 190 to about 370 acres. The total acreage devoted to agriculture has changed very little during this period. But fewer persons are operating larger farms.

Agricultural production still involves comparatively small economic enterprises. Farms are relatively small operating units (firms) compared to many other types of economic activity. In automobile manufacturing, for example, four companies produce almost all American-made cars. Many other industries also are dominated by a few firms. With so many farms, each producing only a very small part of the total output of any given agricultural product, no one farmer can have any significant control over prices.

Farmers producing certain commodities do organize co-operative marketing associations to be able to bargain for higher prices for their products. But the forces of demand and supply (discussed in Chapter 3) generally are by far the most important determiners of agricultural prices.

Farming is becoming more of a business and less of a "way of life." Even in colonial America, many farmers were interested in growing products for sale in this country or even in Europe. In this century, however, farming for the market has become increasingly important.

A century ago, a young farm couple might settle on free, or almost free, land. With a team of mules, a plow, an axe, and a few crude hand tools, plus seeds, they could build a home, clear the land, and start farming. A few staple foods, and a rifle to kill wild game for meat would tide them over until their first crop was harvested. Although they usually expected to sell a part of their crop, they were relatively self-sufficient. Very little money was necessary. For them farming was a way of life as well as a livelihood.

This is no longer true. Today, large commercial farms, often specializing in a single product,

Farms — number and acreage

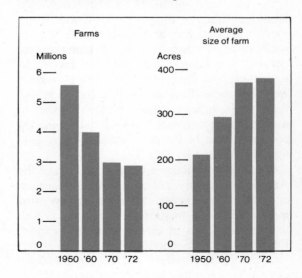

Source: U.S. Bureau of the Census; data from U.S. Department of Agriculture, Economic Research Service

account for the larger share of most agricultural commodities. About one-fourth of the farms sell more than four-fifths of all the agricultural products that reach the market. Very few commercial farms grow much of their own food. Like other businesses, they produce goods for sale on the market and buy what they need on the market.

There are many small full-time or part-time farmers. They cannot afford to buy expensive equipment, and their farms generally are too small to be operated efficiently. Small farms are steadily decreasing in number, as is their percentage of total agricultural output.

Many small farmers supplement their incomes by nonfarm employment. And many small farms are operated by elderly people unwilling to leave their homes, or perhaps unable to find other work. Young people in large numbers have left small farms for other occupations. Unfortunately, a large portion of the small farmers, struggling to make ends meet, are not eligible for farm subsidies or other forms of government assistance. It is not surprising, therefore, that a serious problem of rural poverty exists among small farmers. According to government reports, more than a half million farm families are living at, or below, the poverty level.

Agricultural productivity per man-hour and per acre has increased remarkably in recent years. During the past 20 years, total farm output in this country has increased by over one-third. (The nation's population has increased at about the same rate.) During this same period, the agricultural labor force has decreased by about 55 per cent and the number of acres tilled has decreased slightly.

Stated in another way, the average output per man-hour in farming has increased by more than 300 per cent during the last two decades, while the average per-acre output has increased by almost 40 per cent. Twenty years ago, one farm worker produced food and fiber for fourteen persons; today, one worker supplies 47 persons. At present, only about 5.5 acres of

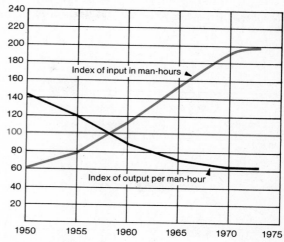

U.S. farm output per man-hour

Index of input in man-hours

Index of output per man-hour

Source: Statistical Abstract

agricultural land is required to support one person, compared to nearly eight acres twenty years ago. The increase in agricultural productivity during this period has been much greater than the increase in productivity in either industrial or distributive occupations.

Without this increase in agricultural productivity, present-day food supplies surely would be much less plentiful, and food prices would be considerably higher. Decreased use of labor in agriculture has also meant that more workers are available for other occupations.

This increased agricultural output has been brought about partly by more intensive farming. Today high-yield crops are grown on land formerly used for low-yield crops. More important, farmers today are using more and better machinery, more fertilizers, better seeds, and improved chemical sprays to control insects and weeds. Although both the large commercial and the smaller farms have increased in efficiency, the greater increase has been on the larger farms.

Increased farm productivity has contributed to economic problems. These new farming

Farm productivity has increased

Number of persons for whom food can be supplied by one farm worker

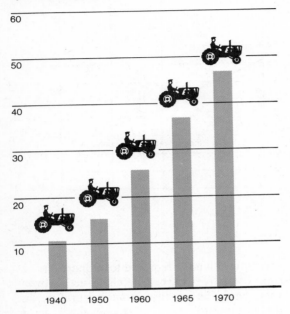

Source: Statistical Abstract

techniques require higher total expenditures, even though the expenditure per unit of crop produced may be lower. This means that small farms decrease in number, and the need for daily hired agricultural labor, migrant workers, and tenant *sharecroppers* (tenants who work owners' land for shares of the product) is declining.

Many displaced farm workers, both white and nonwhite, have flocked to large cities seeking employment and better living conditions. Unfortunately, comparatively few of them have the education or skills required to obtain good positions in the cities. Thus, they continue to live in poverty, contribute to city welfare problems, and increase the unrest and disorder in the slum areas where they are concentrated. Increased economic efficiency, at least tempo-

rarily, has been accompanied by high social costs.

Modern farming requires large investments in land and equipment. The average farm today uses land and buildings worth about 65,000 dollars and machinery and equipment worth more than 10,000 dollars. Only 20 years ago, the average farmer's investment in such assets was less than one-fifth of this amount.

Of course, averages can be misleading if they are not interpreted properly. Many large farms represent much larger investments than the average, and many more represent much smaller investments. A large part of the increased value of farm investments can be ascribed to higher price levels resulting from inflation. The fact remains, however, that a sizable investment is required to engage in farming on a scale that is likely to make one an efficient producer.

Comparatively few farmers are wealthy. The "average" farmer owes about 17,000 dollars on his land and equipment. After paying his operating expenses, he receives a net income of less than 3000 dollars from the sale of his products. This is a return of about 5 per cent annually on the net worth of his property—actually less than he could get by investing the same amount of money in sound stocks or bonds. Only the most efficient (and usually the larger) farmers receive incomes proportionate to their investments, labor, and management efforts.

Some farmers rent the land which they farm. The number of farmers owning or acquiring ownership of their land is increasing. In some parts of the country, and particularly in the north central and southern states, many of the farmers still rent all or a part of the land they farm. In the country as a whole, more than one-tenth of the acreage used in agriculture is rented. Sharecropping is quite common in the South. In other areas, tenants usually pay an agreed-upon, fixed-cost rent to the landowner each year.

Some tenant farmers, especially those paying cash rents, often have good incomes. If a capable farmer rents a relatively large and high-producing farm, he only has to buy his farm equipment and operating supplies. In such cases, his income may be considerably greater than if he had used his limited funds to purchase a smaller farm and less equipment.

Sharecroppers, on the other hand, usually have little money to invest, and little preparation for efficient farming. Thus their incomes usually are quite low. Sharecropping is rapidly being displaced by new farming methods. Mechanical cotton pickers and similar types of machinery are being used to good advantage on large commercial farms.

CHECK UP

1. What have been the trends in American agriculture during the last 40 years? Why has farming become a business rather than a "way of life"?

2. Why has farm productivity per man-hour and per acre increased during the last 20 years? What have been the results?

3. Under what arrangements may a tenant farmer rent the land he farms? What advantages may there be in paying cash rent rather than buying a farm? Why is sharecropping becoming less common?

2

How is agriculture influenced by geography?

Geographic factors influence the type of farming carried on in an area. Climate (temperature and rainfall), topography (the comparative flatness of land), and soil (texture, drainage, and fertility characteristics) limit the types of farming carried on in a region. A farmer must adjust his farming operations to them. For example, cotton requires one kind of climate, wheat another, and various fruits and vegetables still others. Mountainous areas, too hilly for cultivation, or comparatively dry areas may be suitable

for livestock grazing. Of course, dry lands can be irrigated, swamplands drained, and certain fruits and vegetables grown in hothouses. But such modifications of natural geographic conditions are expensive.

Farm production is characterized by geographic specialization and division of labor. The advantages of personal specialization and division of labor in mass industrial production were discussed in Chapter 2. The same economic principles apply to geographical specialization in agriculture. Despite the costs of transporting commodities from one place to another, a greater total agricultural output with the use of less economic resources (land, labor, capital, and management) can be achieved by a geographical (regional) division of labor.

This is not to say that only one kind of product can be produced in a particular part of the country. Some areas are well suited for general farming, involving the production of a wide variety of commodities. But in general, some one type or a few types of product tend to dominate agricultural output in most geographic areas. Such expressions as the "corn belt," the "cotton belt," the "wheat belt," or the "hog belt" refer to regions where production of the given product tend to be concentrated.

Geographic specialization is not fixed for all time. Sometimes changing economic conditions or other factors may lead to changes in regional agricultural patterns. Cotton, for example, is no longer exclusively produced in the South. Farmers in California and Arizona, by irrigating dry lands, have become large cotton producers. Citrus fruits are grown in Florida, California, Arizona, and West Texas. A century ago, sheep were raised on New York farms, but as the population in New York City increased, dairying became more profitable than sheep raising. Many western areas once used for livestock grazing are now under irrigation, and produce potatoes, sugar beets, and various kinds of fruit. Areas specializing in the production of fresh vegetables and milk often are adjacent to large cities. In some cases the advantage of lower

Major types of farming in the United States

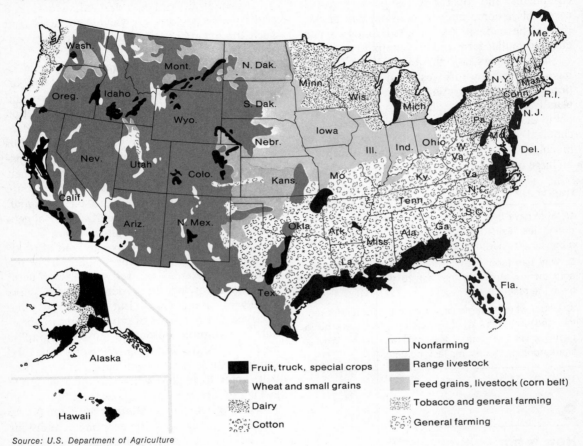

Fruit, truck, special crops

Wheat and small grains

Dairy

Cotton

Nonfarming

Range livestock

Feed grains, livestock (corn belt)

Tobacco and general farming

General farming

Source: U.S. Department of Agriculture

transportation costs for such products outweighs unfavorable geographic factors.

Geographic specialization exists in the economy in an even broader sense. The greatest concentration of population in this country is found in the Northeast. This is relatively the most important section in manufacturing. Industrial plants require a large population from which to recruit workers. But the Northeast, of course, also had other initial advantages in developing its industries. Persons engaged in industrial occupations cannot grow all of their food, even if sufficient vacant and suitable

land was available. Consequently, they must depend on other areas to provide food in exchange for manufactured products.

The less industrialized western and southern sections of the country ship large quantities of foodstuffs, raw materials, and semiprocessed products to the Northeast. In return, large quantities of manufactured goods are shipped from the Northeast to the South and West. It has been estimated that at any given time there is only enough food in New York City to feed its population for eight days.

What has been said does not imply that the

Northeast grows none of its own food, or that other parts of the country are not engaged in manufacturing. It simply suggests the broad pattern of regional specialization in the nation's economy. Such patterns, however, are not completely fixed. Actually, in relative terms, manufacturing has been growing more rapidly in some parts of the South and the West than in the Northeast for many years.

CHECK UP

1. Why is farm production characterized by geographic specialization? What factors may lead to changes in regional agricultural patterns? Give examples.

2. Why do western and southern parts of the United States sell foodstuffs and raw materials to the Northeast?

3

What economic conditions affect agriculture?

Several economic conditions and principles which earlier have been referred to in this book significantly affect agriculture. Some of these create problems not only for farmers but for the economy as a whole. Because of the interdependence between all sectors of the economy, anything which affects farmers is also likely to be felt by nonfarmers.

Constant costs of farming encourage high production. In agriculture, constant or fixed costs include land, buildings, some of the machinery and equipment, and property taxes on these items. Only a very small proportion of the costs of farming vary with level of output. In fact, fertilizer and hired labor are the only important *variable costs*. Since a large proportion of the costs are constant, the total cost of operating a given farm is almost the same

regardless of the amount produced. And when the total cost of production is spread over many units of a commodity, the cost per unit tends to be reduced. (This principle was discussed in Chapter 3.)

A farmer consequently can be expected to step up production to the level at which he will obtain the highest net income from his land, labor, and capital. This tendency contributes to *farm surpluses*. By creating a supply of products larger than the effective demand for them, farm surpluses bring about a reduction in the overall prices for farm products.

Since about 1930—except for the period of World War II—the federal government has had programs to reduce price-depressing surpluses. Were it not for these programs, surpluses might have been so gigantic and prices so low that many more farmers would have been forced out of business.

In manufacturing, two important costs—raw materials and labor—vary with the output of the manufacturer. A manufacturer, therefore, may be able to cut back production without serious loss by reducing the number of employees and the amount of raw materials used. In this way manufacturing is basically different from farming.

Diminishing returns operate in farm production. Whether he is a renter or an owner, it is usually true that the more carefully a farmer cultivates his land and the more fertilizer he applies, the greater will be the yield per acre. But after a certain point, each additional unit of fertilizer, or each added unit of labor or equipment used in cultivation, brings a smaller return than the previous unit. (This principle is similar to the principle of diminishing utility discussed in Chapter 2.)

Table 1 shows the results obtained in an experiment involving different amounts of fertilizer on four plots of land. Except for the amount of fertilizer, the methods of cultivation were identical. The table shows that by increasing the amount of fertilizer from $3 to $5 per acre, the total output was increased by 5

Table 1. An example of diminishing returns in farm production

	cost of fertilizer per acre	yield in bushels	total cost of production	cost of production per bushel	change in cost per bushel for each added amount of fertilizer
plot 1	$3.00	10	$22.50	$2.25	—
plot 2	5.00	15	24.50	1.63	−62¢
plot 3	7.00	18	26.50	1.47	−16¢*
plot 4	9.00	19	28.50	1.50	+ 3¢

* point of diminishing returns is reached

bushels and the cost of production per bushel was reduced by 62 cents. When $9 worth of fertilizer was added, 19 bushels were produced compared to 18 bushels when the cost of fertilizer was $7. The cost of production per bushel increased from $1.47 to $1.50. Up to this point of diminishing returns, additional amounts of fertilizer had resulted in a lower cost per bushel. Eventually, perhaps, additional fertilizer would bring no increase in yield. Indeed too much fertilizer might even damage the plants and actually reduce yield.

A farmer seldom performs this kind of an experiment. These are usually carried on at agricultural experiment stations, which in turn make recommendations to farmers.

Some farmers have difficulties in adjusting their outputs to changes in consumer tastes. Consumers' tastes and preferences in food change over the years. For example, Americans today are eating less starchy food (bread and potatoes) and pork per capita than formerly. Also, foreign markets for some American farm products have declined. This reduced demand has created serious problems for some farmers. A farmer accustomed to growing wheat, for example, may be reluctant to shift to fruit or milk products. Climatic, soil, or other conditions may also make such a shift difficult. Consequently, he may continue to grow wheat. As the price he receives for wheat declines, the farmer may even try to produce more wheat in order to maintain his level of income.

Adjustments are especially difficult for operators of small "family" farms. These farmers may not be as well informed about market trends or as efficient producers as large-scale farmers. Furthermore, they have neither the know-how nor the financial resources to shift to other types of farming. Thus, as large-scale farming becomes more efficient, these small ("marginal") farmers are squeezed harder and harder. This "squeeze" is an important aspect of the "farm problem."

Farmers are affected by price changes. If prices for farm products increase more rapidly than prices of the things farmers buy, obviously they benefit. If the opposite occurs, they are hurt. During recent years, farmers generally have been hurt more often than helped by price changes.

To illustrate, two young World War II veterans bought farms in 1947. One, a native of the Midwest, became a grain farmer. The other, a Southerner, became a tobacco farmer and also raised livestock for meat sales. Both are still farming.

Twenty-five years later, the prices these farmers had to pay for farm machinery as well as labor costs more than doubled. Property taxes on their land and equipment tripled. Prices of fertilizers increased by about 15 per cent. Feed for livestock declined slightly in price, however.

Family living expenses for both farmers increased by more than 40 per cent, and both

Farmers' prices

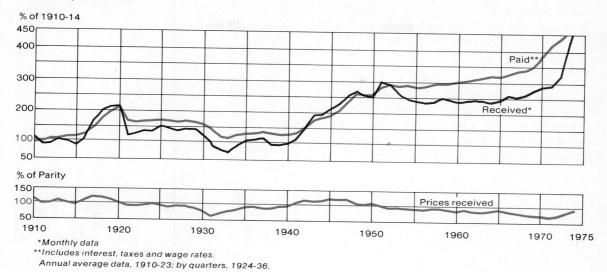

*Monthly data
**Includes interest, taxes and wage rates.
Annual average data, 1910-23; by quarters, 1924-36.

Source: U.S. Department of Agriculture

had children in college. Feed grain prices more than doubled. Prices of meat animals trebled.

Clearly, both farmers were hurt by price changes after they purchased their farms, but in different degree. To remain solvent, both had to increase their efficiency in the use of manpower, equipment, land, and supplies. Unlike many farmers during this period, they were able to remain in operation. But it is doubtful that their children will remain farmers unless economic conditions become more favorable for medium-sized farms.

CHECK UP

1. What are fixed costs in agriculture? Variable costs? How does this situation affect production? Why? What are the results?

2. Explain how the law of diminishing returns operates in farm production. How are farmers affected by market trends? Give examples. Why are small farmers most likely to be hurt?

3. How can farmers be helped or hurt by price changes?

4

How do farm products reach consumers?

Most farm products go through long stages of processing, transportation, and marketing before reaching the consumer's table. The expense of operations after the growing of agricultural products adds more to the cost of food than those involved in the actual growing. On the average, farmers receive only 38 cents of every dollar spent for food in this country. From this share of the food dollar they have to pay

New technology in agriculture: land and labor

Improved technology in farming has brought many changes. It has made possible greater crop yields per acre with less labor, but requires more investment in equipment. It has put many small farmers who cannot afford to mechanize out of business, and encouraged the creation of large, corporate-owned commercial farms. These farms need to hire labor only seasonally, leaving many farm workers unemployed. Others are migrant workers, who are forced to move from place to place as different crops mature.

a

b

c

The helicopter spraying insecticide, **a,** and the grain drill planting wheat, **b,** are two examples of the mechanization of American agriculture which has reduced farming expenses by eliminating much of the need for manual labor. Another device for reducing costs which aids small farmers is the marketing co-operative. In **c,** a farmhand tends pigs which are sold cooperatively by some Indiana farmers.

The need for migrant farm labor has always been highest during harvest time. In **d,** workers pick grapes in a California vineyard. Even children are employed; in **e,** they pick strawberries grown in Washington. The development of harvesting machines has contributed to the unemployment of many of these unskilled farm workers. The potato harvester in **f** yields 8500 bushels of potatoes a day, or seventeen acres' worth.

e

d

f

g

h

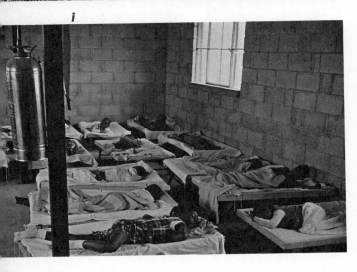

i

Living conditions for those migrant workers still needed are often deplorable. Small, rundown shacks, **g,** provide housing in one Florida migrant camp viewed by a Senate committee investigating hunger in the United States. Small children not working in the fields are frequently left without supervision, **h.** Their parents have no means of caring for them while earning a living. Some efforts are being made to improve living conditions: in **i,** children nap at a day-care center where they are served food through a program sponsored by the U.S. Department of Agriculture.

Others have proposed an alternate solution to the farm workers' plight—unionization. The United Farm Workers Organizing Committee (UFWOC) has won contracts from grape-growers in California and is now organizing workers in other crops. In **j,** UFWOC leader Cesar Chavez leads a march during the grape growers' strike. An organizational meeting of farm workers is depicted in **k.**

j

k

The marketing process in agriculture: from producer to consumer

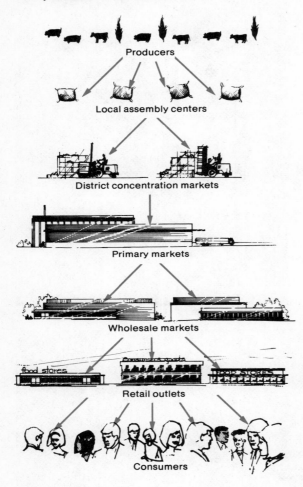

Producers

Local assembly centers

District concentration markets

Primary markets

Wholesale markets

Retail outlets

Consumers

The movement of commodities from producer to consumer suggested by this diagram emphasizes the large number of middlemen involved in the marketing process. The location and size of each market vary with the commodity.

all costs associated with owning and operating their farms.

Processing and distribution have become more efficient during recent years, but these increases in efficiency have lagged far behind similar increases in agricultural production. Today the consumer demands much more in the way of processed food—"heat and eat" TV dinners, "warm and serve" French-fried potatoes, and the like. Expressed as a percentage of consumer income, the cost of food in this country is among the lowest of any in the world. This can be attributed mainly to increased agricultural production.

Processing increases cost and adds to the spread between farm prices and consumer prices. Extensive processing of food results in higher costs for the consumer, and, usually, lower profits for the farmer. Livestock, for example, must go through at least three processes: (1) the animal is slaughtered, (2) the carcass is carved into the different cuts, and (3) the cuts may have to be wrapped, labelled, frozen, or even precooked.

All parts of the animal, of course, cannot be converted into meat for human consumption. Indeed only about half of a live steer is made into various cuts of beef. Much of the rest, however, is converted into leather, fertilizer, or other nonedible products. Some portions of the animal have no value at all.

By weight, only about three-fourths of the wheat kernel can be milled into white flour. Much of the outside, which is dark in color, has to be separated from the white particles by sieves during the process of milling. These darker and coarser parts of the wheat kernel are used as feed for livestock.

Shrinkage in fresh fruits and vegetables results from spoilage. The shrinkage in the marketing of fruits and vegetables is caused largely by spoilage while the products are being transported and marketed. Since most fresh vegetables and fruits are almost completely edible, there is little shrinkage or loss of weight in processing. But no matter how carefully products are handled as they pass from producer to consumer, there is some spoilage. This loss is a considerable part of the cost of marketing such commodities.

Cloth fibers must be extensively processed. Fibers produced on the farm—wool, cotton, and flax—go through several steps in processing before they can be used by the consumer. Workers in textile mills spin yarn from the raw product and weave the yarn into fabrics. Then dyers color the fabrics. Finally, clothing manufacturers convert the fabrics into shirts, suits, dresses, and upholstery. The producer of raw cloth fibers gets only a small part of the price paid by the person who finally buys a shirt. But then he contributes only a small part of the labor that goes into making the finished shirt.

Processed products must be packaged. Packaging is an important part of assembling, processing, and distributing food products. Eggs and butter are put in cartons, milk and cream in bottles or cartons. Bread is wrapped in colorful waxed paper. Fruits and vegetables are packed for shipment in boxes or baskets. As consumers become increasingly concerned about the appearance of food and fiber products, packaging becomes more and more important.

Farm products must be transported to consumer markets. An important step in the marketing system is the transportation of farm products from where they are produced to where they are to be consumed. In a grocery store, foods from more than a dozen different states and even from foreign countries are attractively packaged and are "farm fresh" in appearance. One may marvel at the efficiency of a marketing system that assembles so many food items from so many distant sources.

In general, farm products are "funneled in" from many farmers all over the country to a few central market points. From these centers they are "fanned out" to consumers all over the country. Between the farmers and the consumers in the marketing system are many *middlemen,* each of whom adds utility to a product.

Local assembly centers play an important part in marketing. The main job of local assemblers is to purchase small lots of different products from nearby farmers and ship these in carload or truckload lots to district markets. To illustrate, the local assembly point for wheat is the grain elevator where wheat is stored and cleaned. For butter it is the creamery where the cream is churned into butter; for cheese it is the cheese factory; and for eggs, the local produce dealer. For some products a part or all of the processing is done at these local assembly points.

Some products are "funneled in" to primary markets. A *primary market* is the principal center where one or more commodities are bought and sold. Primary markets for one or more farm products are located in many of the country's larger cities. For example, Chicago, Minneapolis, and Kansas City are primary markets for wheat and some other grains. New York, Chicago, and San Francisco are primary markets for dairy and poultry products. The primary cotton markets are in New Orleans, Memphis, Houston, and Dallas. Even though most of the wool produced in the United States comes from the West and Southwest, the primary wool market is Boston. This comes about because of New England's leadership in the manufacture of woolen textiles.

Some products, on the other hand, are shipped more or less directly from producer areas to wholesale distributing markets and from these to retail food stores. Fruits and vegetables, for example, seldom have primary markets. And most milk used in fluid form is consumed near its production center. If milk is not processed where it is produced, it is sent directly to city milk distributors who process, bottle, and deliver it to consumers.

Products are "fanned out" to consumer centers. After food products reach primary markets, they are "fanned out" to consumers by such middlemen as wholesalers, jobbers, brokers, and retailers. The wholesaler handles large quantities of a product, usually buying

Marketing channels for fresh fruit and vegetables

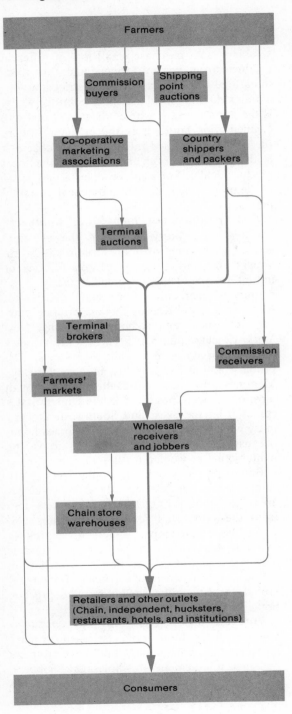

goods in carload or truckload lots and selling them in smaller lots. The *jobber* buys goods in small lots from wholesalers and sells them to retail stores, hotels, bakeries, and other businesses.

The *broker* does not buy or handle products. His function is to put sellers and buyers in touch with each other. Usually these transactions are carried on by telephone or telegraph. Since the broker does not actually own or handle a product, he obtains a commission for his service. The *commission merchant,* in a sense, is a cross between the wholesaler and the broker. He handles products in large amounts but does not actually buy them. Like the broker, he serves as a contact man and receives a commission.

The *retailer* is the final step in the marketing system. Food retailers range in size from national chains that may operate several hundred widely scattered stores, to the small corner grocery, owned and operated by a family.

Every middleman performs some service, or in economic terms, adds utility to a product and consequently increases its value (and price). Thus, from the economic point of view, those who market the nation's foods and fibers are producers just as are the farmers.

Farmers should not be blamed for high food prices. Most farmers do not have high incomes, even during periods of prosperity and high prices. In the case of most foods, the largest part of the food dollar does not go to farmers. Indeed, farmers generally have little if any control over the prices they receive. It should also be pointed out that American consumers pay less of their income for food than do consumers in any other nation.

The diagram at left for a specific category of farm products (compare chart, page 268) shows that while most of the produce is funneled through several intermediate channels, some of it may go directly to the retailer or consumer.

To bring about major economies in the cost of food, processing and distribution costs must be reduced substantially. Or the trend to demand highly processed foods which require little preparation in the kitchen must be reversed. Neither seems likely in the foreseeable future, however. It is not realistic to expect that food prices will be significantly lower than they are; indeed, the opposite is more likely to occur.

CHECK UP

1. Why is there often a great difference between the price of an original product at the farm and the finished product at the store? Consider processing, shrinkage, spoilage, packaging.

2. How are farm products brought to consumer markets? Consider local assembly points, primary markets, middlemen, wholesaler, jobber, broker, retailer. How do middlemen create utility?

5

How does government influence agriculture?

The federal government has been actively interested in agricultural problems for more than a century. Official government involvement in the concerns of farmers is not new. In 1862 Congress passed three measures of great importance to agriculture. (1) A Department of Agriculture was established as a division of the Patent Office. This Department was elevated to Cabinet status in 1889. (2) The Homestead Act enabled an adult to acquire ownership of 160 acres of western public land by paying a small fee and living on it and cultivating it for five years. (3) The Morrill Act set aside large tracts of public land for support of agricultural colleges, intended to promote research in agriculture and to provide education and assistance for farmers. Over the years, still other programs have been set up in order to aid agriculture.

Agricultural experiment stations have helped farmers. The Morrill Act provided federal assistance in establishing a college of agriculture in each state. Each of these institutions was to have an agricultural experiment station. These "land-grant" colleges prepared specialists who could study ways of controlling plant and animal diseases and of increasing crop yields and livestock production.

County agents are local representatives of the colleges of agriculture. The experimental work carried on by agricultural colleges yielded important findings. The next step was to bring research findings to the attention of farmers. To that end, the federal government in 1913 established the Agricultural Extension Service. Specialists known as *county agents* were jointly employed by the county, state, and federal governments to work with farmers. These county agents acquaint farmers with ideas developed at experiment stations. They explain to farmers how to control plant diseases and insects, and demonstrate ways of improving tillage of the soil. Their assistance enables farmers to improve the quality of crops as well as the yield per acre.

The government makes loans to farmers. Financial assistance has been made available to help farmers who were in difficulty because of conditions beyond their control, such as droughts and floods. This assistance has taken the form of loans at low interest rates. Such loans could be used (1) to purchase land and seed grain, and (2) to finance the operation of farmer-owned-and-controlled co-operatives. Loans to make possible the purchase of land have been made by the Federal Land Banks, established in 1916.

Direct financial assistance has also been provided. The government has spent much more money on direct financial assistance to farmers than on loans. Direct aid began when agriculture was thrown out of balance by World War I. During that war, and again during World War

II, agricultural output was vastly increased to meet the great demand for foodstuffs. After both wars, when demand decreased, farmers were reluctant to cut back their production. Had total output of farm products across the nation been sharply reduced, prices would have risen. *But total output represents the production of thousands of individual farmers.* It does not pay an individual farmer to reduce his output, since the reduction would be too small to influence prices. Consequently, since each farmer continues to produce at a high level, the total output of many farm products may actually increase from year to year.

As the farmer's situation grew worse, the government began to provide direct support to farm prices. Although a growing number of people, including many farmers, question the wisdom of present-day policies, it seems likely that some form of direct federal aid will be continued. The questions usually asked about this policy are: How much money should the government spend on a farm program? What type of program should be developed?

A major goal of agricultural aid has been to maintain "parity prices" for farmers. Parity means equality. As this term is used in the case of agricultural prices, it means that the prices of things that farmers buy should not increase faster than the prices of things that farmers sell. The relationships between these prices are measured by index numbers. (Index numbers are discussed in Chapter 3.) Each month the U.S. Department of Agriculture publishes a "parity ratio" showing the relationships between prices of farm products and the prices of things farmers buy. This ratio makes possible comparisons between the economic status of farmers today and in earlier years.

Parity price ratios, however, do not tell the whole story. The *total* (gross) *income* of a farmer is determined by the amount of products produced on his farm and the selling price per unit of each product. His *net income* is gross income less farm expenses. New methods of controlling weeds and insects, cultivating crops, and fertilizing the soil have increased yields per acre. Modern machinery, at the same time, has reduced the cost of production. In other words, present-day farmers are able to produce farm commodities at a lower unit cost than during the base period. This is especially true of farmers who operate the larger and more productive farms. Many of them have made a very satisfactory income even when the prices of farm products were below parity level. Inefficient farms, on the other hand, have difficulties even when prices are high.

Price supports are used to maintain parity for some products. One of the ways in which the United States government aids farmers is through price supports for certain products. First, farmers agree to limit their acreage of supported crops. Then, if prices on the open market fall below a certain level, the government lends the farmer money equal to the support price for the crop. The crop is then stored. Should the market price rise above the support level, the farmer repays the loan and sells his crop at the higher market price. If the market price does not rise to the support level within a certain period, the government keeps the crop. In effect, the farmer "sells" his crop to the government, with an "option" to "buy it back" should that be profitable for him. The effect is to prevent the market price from dropping much below the support price.

The government has many billions of dollars "invested" in agricultural products, and is spending more each year for "buying" and storing farm surpluses. Along with government price-support programs there has been a system of crop control (or reduction). In general, this consists of reducing the number of acres of crops grown. However, as acreages under cultivation have been decreased by the price-support program, farmers have increased their yields per acre. They have done this by retiring their least productive land and through more intensive cultivation of the remainder. This has been true especially in the case of the larger and better-equipped farm operators. In the past,

Payments and costs of the Commodity Credit Corporation

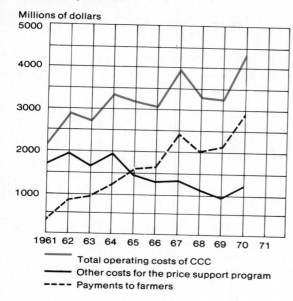

Millions of dollars

— Total operating costs of CCC
— Other costs for the price support program
- - - - Payments to farmers

While the cost to taxpayers of agricultural subsidies is clearly enormous, a large share of the total is absorbed by surplus crop storage, disposal, conservation, research projects, shipments abroad, and other programs. Thus direct payments to farmers are only a fraction of the total cost of the farm program. (The Commodity Credit Corporation is the federal agency which administers the price-support program.)

Source: U.S. Department of Agriculture

acreage controls with price supports have led to large government-held surpluses. The controls failed to reduce output substantially as planned. More recently, various relief programs, both at home and abroad, have reduced or eliminated surpluses of certain commodities. The program did succeed in keeping farm prices higher than they otherwise would have been.

Of course, not all farm products are under the price-support program. The principal supported commodities are: wheat, feed grains (corn, oats, barley, grain sorghums), cotton, tobacco, dairy products, rice, and peanuts. Meats and poultry, fruits, and most vegetables, are not supported.

The price-support program is often criticized. Many persons, including some farmers, maintain that agriculture should stand on its own feet in a competitive market. They hold that the law of supply and demand should be allowed to operate freely, and that price supports merely cause farmers to continue producing goods that consumers are not willing to buy at the price-support levels. Other critics point out that farm prices have become so high that many of this country's traditional foreign markets have been lost.

Consumers complain that food and clothing prices are higher than they would be without price supports. Some economists maintain that high support prices keep people and capital resources employed in farming which would be more productive in other occupations. Conservationists say we are exhausting the fertility of soil by growing unnecessary crops. And taxpayers cry out against the high costs of support programs.

Informed observers call attention to the fact that large payments are made to efficient large-scale farmers who could make a handsome profit without government assistance. Because some large farm operators actually were receiving several hundred thousand dollars each year in price-support payments, Congress decided to limit the amount that could be paid to one farmer for one crop. Many farms actually are so small and produce so little that even if prices of these commodities were raised by 50 per cent, the total income would not be sufficient to maintain an acceptable level of living.

The price-support program, however, has many defenders who use the following arguments in its behalf:

1. A strong and vigorous agriculture is necessary in case of war.

2. Agricultural resources (people, know-

Surpluses for three major crops

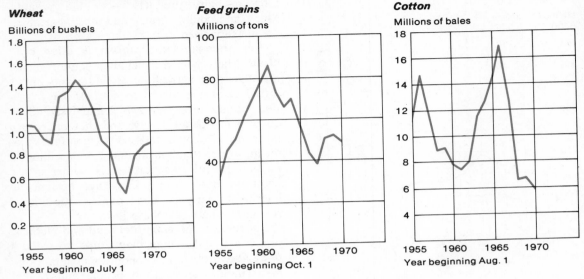

Wheat
Billions of bushels

Feed grains
Millions of tons

Cotton
Millions of bales

Year beginning July 1

Year beginning Oct. 1

Year beginning Aug. 1

Source: U.S. Department of Agriculture

how, and capital) must be maintained to provide for a rapidly growing population in the years ahead. Then there may no longer be any farm surpluses.

3. If farmers are not prosperous, they cannot buy the goods and services of other producers. A severe agricultural depression might wreck the nation's economy.

4. Acreage limitations associated with price supports conserve soil fertility for future generations.

5. Price supports assure a steady flow of essential products to consumers without the wide price fluctuations that would accompany alternate periods of shortages and surpluses under the free operation of "demand and supply."

6. The higher profits made possible by price supports have provided the financing that makes possible larger farms and mechanized production. These, in turn, have led to greatly increased output per man-hour in recent years.

7. Elimination of government aid would force many farmers off the land. This seems inconsistent with traditional beliefs in farming as a "way of life." It would also create massive unemployment. Other occupations could not easily absorb a large number of unemployed who had spent their lives in farm work.

Political realities must also be considered. Farmers vote, and in many states they are able to swing elections. Consequently, elected officials are not eager to antagonize the farm vote. Besides, farmers can point out that they are not the only subsidized group in the economy. Many manufacturers, for example, are favored by protective tariffs. Labor has unions and minimum wages. Students do not pay the full costs of their education. Why should farmers, therefore, be expected to live under an unrestricted system of "supply and demand"?

Very few people, including most farmers, are entirely satisfied with the present system of price supports. Various alternatives, including abandonment of the system, have been proposed. Congress year after year spends a great deal of time debating the farm problem. But no alternative has been suggested which is more acceptable than the present program. Until a better plan is found, or unless the economic conditions affecting agriculture substantially change, major changes in present procedures are unlikely.

CHECK UP

1. Why has the federal government long given assistance to agriculture? How has the agricultural experiment station helped the farmer? The county agent? Government loans?

2. What are parity prices? How are they determined? What are price supports? Acreage allotments?

3. On what grounds are price-support programs criticized? Defended? Are farmers the only group subsidized by government? Explain.

6

What is the outlook for American farmers?

Present trends in agriculture are likely to continue. There is no evidence to suggest that there will be a reversal of the agricultural trends discussed in the first part of this chapter, but in some cases the trends may slow down.

For example, the farm population has declined so rapidly that it may be nearing a relatively stable level. Productivity per acre and per man-hour may have reached levels that may slow the pace of further increases. In other words, the "agricultural revolution" may largely have run its course. This does *not* mean that productivity increases will cease or that farming will become less commercialized. But it does suggest that the nature of the "farm problem" will gradually change.

Total farm income

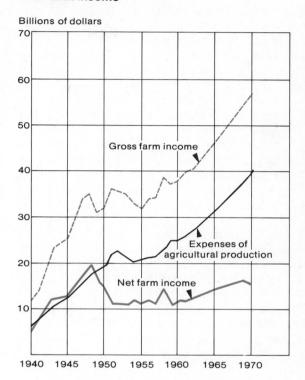

Billions of dollars

Total expenses of agricultural production, 1970

4% Interest on mortgages
3% Net rent to nonfarm landlords
8% Taxes on farms

17% Depreciation

60%

Wages paid to hired
8% farm labor
*Current farm operating expenses

*Includes purchase of feed, livestock, seed, fertilizer and lime, cost of farm maintenance and repairs, and miscellaneous expenses such as the cost of pesticides.

Source: Statistical Abstract

The demand for agricultural products will increase. Population experts suggest that the nation's population will increase by at least 50 per cent within a generation. Then some 300 million persons must be fed. Since Americans probably will have become more affluent and overcome many of the problems of poverty and low incomes, it seems probable that demands for food will increase more rapidly than the population.

The supply of land, however, is fixed in quantity. More and more of it will be required for living space (houses, roads, recreation areas), factories and businesses, and public buildings. This country has a much larger ratio of land to people than many other countries, but Americans will have to make better use of the land. This means increased productivity from presently-used lands through more intensive use and improved farming practices. Eventually some low-yielding lands that are not farmed today will be brought into production.

World hunger is a serious threat. Some experts believe that mass famine may occur in some parts of the world within a decade. World population is increasing at a rapid rate—and unfortunately, population increases are most rapid in the developing lands.

If agriculture could be made as productive in developing countries as in the United States, mass starvation could be postponed for many generations despite population trends. But poor nations, some of which have large areas suitable for agriculture, tend to be deficient in education, scientific "know-how," and capital resources. The cultures and traditions of some nations do not favor change.

There are some countries, such as Japan, which, despite the application of technical expertise to food production, find it difficult to feed their expanding population. These countries must import much of their agricultural products. Should the United States, recognizing the needs of such countries, consider taking on a greater role as an exporter of agricultural products to countries such as Japan, India, and China? A number of economists hold that it should. Such a policy might eliminate the

---

POLLUTION PROBLEMS IN AGRICULTURE

The unlimited and largely uncontrolled use of pesticides and fertilizers in commercial agriculture has recently been challenged by many scientists and citizens concerned about their effect on the environment.

The critics cite two main classes of pollution which originate with modern agriculture. One is the overuse of pesticides. Most pesticides remain chemically intact for years after application. They are absorbed into the environment where they build up dangerous concentrations in the soil and in the systems of animals. Certain kinds of birds, for example, lay eggs with such thin shells that they break, destroying the birds' offspring.

The other source of pollution is fertilizers which, when used in large amounts, increase plant nutrients in the soil to unnatural levels. These nutrients are washed into bodies of water by rain, where they increase the growth of algae. The algae use up much of the oxygen in the water, eventually killing the fish.

One step taken to correct the situation has been a Federal ban on the use of DDT, a particularly strong pesticide. The United Farm Workers Organizing Committee, a union, has negotiated an agreement with employers in California also banning the use of DDT and three other pesticides, as well as providing other safety controls and health measures. Most states and the federal government have special agencies responsible for environmental pollution, and the Department of Agriculture is responsible for special problems pertaining to farming.

Physician Turned Physiocrat
François Quesnay

(1694–1774)

During most of the eighteenth century France had grave economic problems. Her armies fought in wars on three continents, and the government piled up huge debts that undermined its financial position.

François Quesnay, a physician as well as an economist of the time, set himself to writing about this problem. He was confident that if certain basic economic principles were followed, conditions in France could be improved.

Quesnay's fundamental assumption was that a prosperous agriculture was essential to a nation which wished to have a sound economy. He and his followers, who became known as the *Physiocrats,* held that all wealth was derived from the land. Indeed, only the earth could return more than was put into it. Tiny seeds, when planted, could produce great trees.

The Physiocrats divided labor into two classes, the agricultural and the "sterile." The former was considered productive since it alone produced a surplus greater than the wealth used in growing the original product. The farming class even supplied the sterile class with products it needed to live. Quesnay maintained that the manufacturing, or sterile, class merely altered the form of products already provided by nature.

Quesnay and his group introduced the term *laissez faire.* By it they meant that the state should not interfere with what they considered the "natural order." The Physiocrats applied this idea to foreign trade, implying that a nation should not try to export more than it imported. If a country's only real wealth is its natural resources, such a policy was not illogical. The Physiocrats heaped scorn on those who approved of state subsidies and monopoly rights, for these were a violation of the "natural order."

The price of industrial goods should be the cost of the basic raw materials, plus the cost of the labor which transformed these into a manufactured good. This view anticipated the labor theory expounded by Adam Smith (see page 228). Neither the Physiocrats nor the classical economists recognized that other factors, such as the utility (usefulness) and the scarcity of a product also influence price.

Because the Physiocrats believed that surpluses could only come from the land, they argued that land should be the only basis for taxation. All other taxes interfered with the natural order. This proposal of a "single tax" on land was later adopted by Henry George.

More recent economists believe that Quesnay and the Physiocrats overemphasized the importance of agriculture compared to manufacturing. The group's extreme *laissez-faire* position has also been criticized, for who is to decide what the "natural order" is?

problem of overproduction and agricultural surpluses in the United States. On the other hand, it would also mean that this country would have to open its market more freely to manufactured goods from abroad, so that those countries could earn the dollars with which to purchase primary goods (agricultural commodities and raw materials). The United States already exports to Japan more crude materials and agricultural products than manufactured goods. But this policy is opposed by many domestic manufacturers and labor leaders. They argue that the importation on a large scale of foreign manufactured goods, which are cheaper than those produced in the United States (because of the lower wages of most foreign workers), would force domestic prices downward, causing a reduction in American wages or putting American manufacturers out of business entirely. (See Chapter 19 and Case Analysis 10 for further discussion of this problem.)

The United States cannot exist as an isle of plenty in a sea of world famine. Even if Americans could ignore the moral implications of watching other people starve, mass world hunger would affect this nation. One can be sure that if the threatened large-scale famines do occur, the hungry will attempt to force those who are better off to share their relative abundance. Hungry people will follow any leader or subscribe to any ideology that promises food.

The present problem of agricultural surpluses may be replaced by the more serious problem of shortages. For many years, the country's potential agricultural productivity has increased more rapidly than its population. But because of low incomes and inadequate distribution not all Americans have been well fed. This country has exported large quantities of food to other nations and has paid some farmers to limit their production. But if the experts are right, the present generation of high school students will face a quite different problem as adults—the problem of agricultural shortages.

In the meantime, the nation continues to have the problem of small, inefficient, low-income farmers, and of surpluses in the case of some agricultural commodities. The immediate agricultural problem, then, is to convert inefficiently used resources into more efficient use, in preparation for much larger future demands. This should be done with the least possible economic, social, and personal disruption. May the nation have sufficient time and the wise leadership and understanding needed to achieve this end.

CHECK UP

1. What trends in agriculture are likely to continue? To slow down? Why?

2. What are the implications for American agriculture of the rapid increase in the world's population? What are the implications for this country's economy if agricultural exports are greatly increased?

Clinching the main ideas

American agriculture is highly productive because the nation has large areas of fertile land, varied climates, and an increasingly more efficient technology. Fewer and fewer farmers are producing food and fibers for more and more people. This trend frees a large part of the population for other kinds of production, but it also contributes to social and economic problems, particularly in the large cities.

The processing and marketing of agricultural products involves complicated and well-organized operations. The distribution system is efficient, but increases in its efficiency have lagged behind increases in agricultural production. The combined efficiency of production and distribution gives this country the lowest "real" food costs (that is, food costs as a proportion of income) of any country in the world.

Agricultural production is surrounded by physical uncertainties and economic hazards. For these reasons, and mindful of the importance of a stable and prosperous agricultural system, the government in recent years has aided agriculture in many ways. Price supports, designed to maintain farmers' incomes, is an example. Unfortunately the farmers most in need of higher incomes receive no price supports.

The agricultural sector of the economy is in a state of rapid and often painful transition. For many years the "farm problem" receiving the most attention has been income maintenance through the control of "surplus" production of certain products. Within the near future, however, the problem of surpluses may be replaced by a shortage problem.

Meantime, there remain the social problems caused by increased pressures for weeding out inefficient operations and operators. The nature of the problems change, but the "farm problem" itself is likely to continue. All Americans—city-dwellers, factory workers, business and professional people, as well as farmers themselves—will continue to be affected significantly by the problems and the changing environment of agriculture.

Chapter 11 review

Terms to understand

1. co-operative marketing associations
2. commercial farm
3. sharecroppers
4. general farming
5. farm surpluses
6. processed foods
7. middlemen
8. primary market
9. commission merchant
10. broker
11. jobber
12. land-grant college
13. county agent
14. parity price
15. price supports
16. agricultural revolution
17. primary goods

What do you think?

1. Why is it easier for industry than for agriculture to cut back production when demand declines?

2. Prices on basic farm commodities are higher in this country than on the world market. Why? Does this fact create any problems?

3. In 1846 England repealed the Corn Laws which levied a duty on imported wheat. How did this action affect English wheat farmers and city workers? English exports? Why did England adopt this policy?

4. It has been said that support programs are not needed by most efficient producers and are not high enough really to help marginal farmers. Can both statements be true? How can the economic situation of marginal farmers be improved?

5. The productivity of the American farm worker increased from 100 in 1950 to 248 in 1965. How was this possible? Do these index numbers suggest that each worker in 1965 produced nearly 2½ times as much per hour as did each worker in 1950? Explain.

6. Many of the farm surpluses which plagued the nation a decade ago have been greatly reduced. Indeed there now is a suggestion that strategic reserves must be maintained. Why has the situation changed?

Applying your knowledge of economics

1. Use the *Statistical Abstract* to prepare a graph illustrating some important trend in farming. Explain the significance of the graph.

2. Draw an agricultural map of your state showing where principal crops are raised.

3. Various annual reference books, such as *The New York Times Encyclopedic Almanac,* contain information about per capita income. Information is provided for the nation as a whole, the major regions, and some states. Note trends and regional differences over a period of years. Changes in farm income are included. Present the facts and your conclusions. The source of the data cited in the *Almanac* is the Office of Business Economics, United States Department of Commerce.

Low farm prices and rural poverty

General background

Except for short periods during years of wartime food shortages, the average income of the American farmer has been lower than that of people in most other sectors of the American economy. Self-employed farmers must invest sizable sums of money in land, buildings, and farm equipment. They must work hard and for long hours. Yet during the prosperous late 1960's, the net cash income received by the average farm family was less than half the national average family income.

Many farm families produce part of their own food and do not pay cash rent, and many receive income from nonfarm occupations. But even including other sources of income, many farmers—especially the small or "marginal" farmers—receive a return for their farm labor much lower than current wage rates in industry and a much lower return on their farm investment than current returns on investments in good bonds and stocks or time bank deposits.

Government has long been interested in helping farmers. Many people feel that the "grass-roots" small farmer is the "backbone" of the nation. Clearly it is in the public interest to maintain the purchasing power of farm families and to insure an adequate food supply for the nation. Besides, at least until quite recently, rural areas had greater representation in Congress, in proportion to population, than did urban areas.

The chief form of direct federal aid to farmers stems from the Agricultural Adjustment Act of 1933. This law, despite amendments, retains the approaches for assisting farmers that were introduced decades ago. Key elements of the farm program are the subsidies through price supports and acreage controls for certain crops. (See Chapter 11). The original economic goal of this program was to maintain prices of basic agricultural products at a profitable (or parity) level by eliminating or reducing price-depressing surpluses. Maintaining parity prices, it was thought, would provide a fair and adequate income for farmers.

After more than a generation of experimentation, many economists as well as many farmers feel that the agricultural subsidy program has been a failure. There also has been a lack of coordination between various government programs. A 1970 article in the *New York Times* called attention to some of these shortcomings:

There is little co-ordination between government programs. The Agriculture Department spent $3.5 billion on subsidies last year, while the Interior Department's Bureau of Reclamation was spending $85 million a year for irrigation projects to bring arid lands of the West into production.

On Arlin Hartzog's farm in Parmer County, Texas, as on others across the country, both the crop-limiting and crop-increasing programs were in action at the same time. Mr. Hartzog received more than $30,000 in federal subsidies last year for limiting his acreage while the government was helping him pay for an irrigation system that enables him to make up for the production of the land he had diverted. . . .[1]

Some crops were never included in the subsidy program. Most of the farmers who participated were small operators, and received comparatively small amounts of aid. A few very large commercial farms (many run by corporations), however, received very large sums. As the number of farms and the size of the farm population continued to decline, the program actually became more expensive. Federal expenditures for various kinds of direct agricultural assistance amounted to about 20 billion dollars, 1933 to 1960, whereas expenditures, 1960 to 1970, amounted to approximately 28 billion. In 1970, the program cost 3.5 billion dollars. The contrasting economic situation of some farmers and most farm workers was brought out in the *New York Times* article:

Young Fred Salyer swung his little red and white monoplane through a bright California sky, looking down on the flat expanse of the San Joaquin Valley. His father had faced bankruptcy there in the early 'thirties. Now the land supports a thriving farm, with operations so extensive that only in an airplane can

1 William Robbins, "Farm Policy Helps Make the Rural Rich Richer," *New York Times*, April 5, 1970. © 1970 by The New York Times Company. Reprinted by permission.

they all be checked in one day.

Three thousand miles away, on a muddy road leading to a sagging house in South Carolina, Thomas Washington looked out over his 67 sandy acres [and] summed up the result of a year's work. "Mister," he said, "there wasn't nothing left."

Both men are wards of the Department of Agriculture, but both get widely different benefits. The department pays the Salyer family nearly $1.7 million a year in subsidies; it pays Mr. Washington slightly more than $300.

Trips to the major agricultural regions of the United States, interviews with economists and government officials and examination of official government budgets and documents over several months show that the stories of Mr. Salyer and Mr. Washington are not unusual.

After three and a half decades and costs of billions of dollars, the Department of Agriculture's farm programs continue to widen the gap between the rich and the poor.

During the inflation of the 1970's, urban consumers complained about high food and clothing prices, asserting that they were being heavily taxed to help pay farmers not to produce, and thus to keep prices high. At the same time, the balance of political power was shifting rapidly from rural to urban areas. Consequently, the crop subsidy program was subjected to extensive debate in Congress during 1970.

LIMITATIONS ON SUBSIDY PAYMENTS

The 1970 debate was focused largely on acreage control payments to growers of wheat, feed grains, and cotton. These crops accounted for more than four-fifths of all direct agricultural subsidy payments based on acreage control.

The debate in Congress and government reports, the latter widely reported and discussed in the news media, brought out that the great majority of the farmers received government payments ranging from a few hundred to a few thousand dollars annually. On the other hand, one large commercial farm received almost 4.4 million dollars in subsidy payments in 1969, and at least four others received more than one million dollars each. Altogether, during that year, some 1100 farms received subsidies of more than 55,000 dollars each. Of these, some 950 were cotton farmers,

most of them in Arizona, California, and Texas. Congressman Paul Findley (R.-Illinois), one of the early advocates of ceilings on subsidy payments, voiced the growing criticism of inequalities under this program:

The adoption of payment limitation would clearly make the present commodity programs less vulnerable to criticism. Taxpayers are furious over big payments to millionaire farmers and justly so. On the other hand they understand the need for income support for small farmers who are financially less able to deal with the alarming cost-price squeeze now afflicting agriculture.

Annual payments as high as $4 million to a single farmer bring these programs into such disrepute as to threaten their survival. At the same time they tend to accelerate the trend toward bigness in agriculture, handing to well-financed large operators extra money which can be used to absorb the small farmer.[2]

In response to the public outcry, the Senate voted in 1970 to place a maximum of 20,000 dollars per farm on subsidy payments. (The House had twice voted a similar 20,000-dollar limit in previous years, but the Senate had refused to concur.) The 1970 House debate, then was concerned with what maximum limitation, if any, should be imposed. Finally, this boiled down to a choice between a limit of 20,000 dollars, 55,000 dollars, or no limit at all.

Those advocating no-limit—that is, no change —pointed out that a 55,000-dollar limit would save the government only 58 million dollars despite the fact that the total subsidy called for expenditures of 3.5 billion dollars. Such a limit, they said, could create "chaos" in agriculture. A limit on the amount of subsidy might cause large commercial farms to withdraw from the crop control program altogether. Thus there would be a great overproduction of crops currently subsidized. Market prices would then plunge downward, the subsidy payments would serve no useful purpose, and many small farmers would be threatened with bankruptcy. Land withdrawn from acreage controls might be used to grow nonsubsidized crops, thus leading to depressed prices for still other agricultural products.

In a letter to a Republican on the House Agri-

2 *Congressional Record,* April 30, 1969, H3260.

cultural Committee, President Nixon stated that he felt a limit of less than 55,000 dollars "could be harmful." "Too low a limitation," he said, "will make it impossible for many farm producers to participate efficiently in the program." But in spite of his views, the President indicated that he would not veto such a bill, because it is "peculiarly within the province of Congress" to establish limits to subsidization.

Many members of the House, however, were very sensitive to the complaints of urban consumers about high prices and expensive farm subsidies, especially since 1970 was a Congressional election year. A determined effort was made to pass the 20,000-dollar limit already approved in the Senate. This fight was led mainly by representatives from urban areas, although some support came from representatives of rural districts. Of course, some members of the House voted for the 20,000-dollar limit in the hope that it would be a first step in the elimination of all farm subsidies. It was pointed out that "one way to end the program is to cut down on payments."

In August, 1970, the House, by a vote of 212 to 171, passed a compromise bill which fixed maximum subsidy payments per farm at 55,000 dollars for each of the three crops. (Very few farmers grow more than one of the three subsidized crops.) Since the Senate already had passed a bill with a lower limit, it was left to a Senate-House Conference Committee to work out a compromise acceptable to both bodies.

The issues

TO SUBSIDIZE OR NOT TO SUBSIDIZE

The present subsidy policy has helped to stabilize prices but it has not solved the problem of how to give significant help to poor small farmers. Those most in need of assistance get the least assistance, or none at all. But is the subsidy as such at fault, or is it the present *policy* of subsidization? The first question to ask about direct agricultural subsidies is whether or not they are desirable in any form. To answer that question, still another question must be asked. What would happen if the laws of supply and demand determined what was produced and what prices were paid for agri-

cultural products? Many kinds of crops are sold freely now, but in general they are crops least suitable for large-scale production.

Most observers agree that a free market in agriculture would speed the decline in small farming. The family farm, and farming as a way of life, would disappear in most sections of the country. Many farm workers and small farm owners, untrained for urban jobs, would have to move to already overcrowded cities and seek employment. Present urban economic and social problems doubtless would grow worse. The savings achieved by eliminating farm subsidies would be more than offset by appropriations needed to cope with new problems.

It might be expected that if there were no subsidies much more agricultural production would be provided by efficient commercial farms. Lower production costs might mean lower prices for consumers. But if comparatively few large farmers dominated agricultural production, it is possible that they might keep prices at artificially high levels. In some parts of the country, where food production is carried on by large corporations, there is a movement among farm workers to organize unions and press for higher wages and improved working conditions. To meet such demands, farmers may have to charge more for their produce and thus raise the prices paid by consumers. It is not at all certain, therefore, that large-scale commercial farms, despite technological and other advantages, would insure lower prices for consumers.

Thus economic and social reasons can be cited both for and against agricultural subsidies. Few persons who favor the elimination of subsidies believe that it can be done all at once. They recommend a gradual approach, so that the shock to the economy will not be too great. Some form of agricultural subsidies, therefore, will probably be continued for some time. Assuming this to be true, it is well to consider what form subsidies should take.

WHAT KIND OF SUBSIDIZATION?

With the benefit of hindsight, fault can be found with the original concept of the Agricultural Adjustment Act. It was intended to further two basic goals: (1) Agricultural prices were to be maintained by controlling supply; that is, by removing agricultural surpluses from the market through acreage controls and price support programs. (2) The income of farmers was to be raised and maintained at an adequate level.

Doing the one does not insure the other. The first goal has been achieved, at least for certain important crops, but it has not made possible the second goal. High prices do not necessarily insure high net incomes. The size of the farm and efficiency of operations frequently are as important as prices received. Moreover, the farm program never attempted directly to increase prices for some crops and kinds of agriculture.

To cope with the problem of poverty and low income among a large segment of the farming population, should one focus on *price* maintenance or on *income* maintenance? Price maintenance apparently has not assured adequate incomes. The *New York Times* article referred to earlier provides a description of the plight of what is considered a typical farm worker in Texas:

Parmer County, whose farmers received $12 million in federal payments last year, has no food program although many of its hungry are farm workers, like Reuben Gallardo, who lives with his family in a boxcar at Bovina.

Mr. Gallardo is unemployed part of every year, but for farm workers there is no unemployment pay, no compensation for accidents, no maximum to the hours they can be made to work without overtime pay, no minimum wage on most farms and no right to have a union bargain to improve their lot.

How does the problem of inadequate income for certain agricultural workers differ in principle from that of similar groups in nonrural occupations? And if problems are the same, why are completely different approaches to their solutions necessary?

If Americans believe that there are compelling economic and social reasons for subsidizing low-income farmers, can this not be done in a more efficient way than through farm subsidies? Cannot assistance be provided those who need it without also subsidizing the rich?

Alternative solutions have been suggested. These include low-interest loans, tax incentives (reduced property taxes for the farmer), educational and retraining programs, developing nonfarm jobs in poverty-stricken agricultural areas, and even direct payments to supplement the incomes of poor families. (See Case Analysis 4 on welfare.)

Most people agree that much is wrong with the present agricultural subsidy program, but there is little agreement on how to change it. Perhaps Americans have been getting the wrong answers because they have not been asking the right questions.

Toward better understanding

QUESTIONS TO CONSIDER IN ANALYZING THIS CASE

1. Less than half the nation's farmers produce 90 per cent of the farm products marketed. Most of the others are subsistence farmers. How does this fact affect a program of production control and subsidization?
2. Could farmers have solved the problem of overproduction without government control? How? What might have been the economic consequences?
3. Should the government have instituted a more rigid system of controlling production of crops and livestock to insure higher prices? Why or why not?
4. How would a program of rigid production control have affected the processors of farm products? Consumer food prices?
5. A reduction by some 20 per cent of the *number of acres planted* of certain crops has resulted in the reduction of only a few per cent in the total production. How can this be explained? (Hint: The farmers themselves, it should be remembered, determined the fields to be taken out of production, and they also determined crop cultivation practices.)
6. Why does the government spend money on irrigation projects at the same time that it subsidizes farmers who curtail production?

THINKING ABOUT THE BASIC ECONOMIC ISSUES

1. Are there basic economic differences between agriculture and other sectors of the economy (mining, manufacturing, transportation, for example)

which justify government aid to agriculture? What are they? Do other sectors of the economy also receive government aid? What kind? Why?

2. Would the best interests of the great majority of consumers (and taxpayers) be served if all government aid programs were discontinued? Why?

3. What other segments of the economy could logically use similar arguments for government aid as those used by the farmers?

4. What effect do support prices have on the sale of farm commodities on the world market? Explain.

5. Why have grain-producing countries at times found fault with this country for giving away (or selling at low cost) stored grain to developing countries suffering from a shortage of food?

6. What values underlie a policy of providing government aid to a segment of the population in economic distress? What values underlie a *laissez faire* policy in this sort of a situation?

7. Would President Nixon's suggestion for a minimum family income better meet the needs of the rural poor than the present system of subsidies and relief payments? Why or why not?

chapter twelve

Union and nonunion labor

1. How do labor markets differ from other markets?
2. How have labor unions developed?
3. What are the effects of unionization?
4. What is the role of government in labor-management relations?

It is one of the characteristics of a free and democratic modern nation that it have free and independent labor unions.

FRANKLIN D. ROOSEVELT

Until about 200 years ago, most manufacturing was carried on in the home or in small shops employing a few workers. Distinctions between "workers," "owners," and "managers" were less clearly defined than they are today. In a shop the master, a journeyman, and some apprentices worked alongside each other. Although the work may have been hard, the hours long, and the pay small, the workers took pride in what they were doing. An apprentice could expect to become a journeyman, and might hope to become a master craftsman.

Modern methods of production—including the organization and use of human labor—have changed working conditions. Today most workers are employed away from their homes and neighborhoods. They work in large factories or other business enterprises which usually are owned by giant corporations. Few workers can call themselves "their own boss," and fewer still can look forward to owning the business which

employs them. They own neither the materials they work on, nor the machines or tools used in their work. They may never see, much less meet or get to know, the owner of the company they work for. They simply sell their labor for wages. This impersonal form of selling one's labor in exchange for wages is a key feature of modern production.

In a private enterprise, or capitalist, economy, the interests of labor and management often do not coincide. On the one hand, workers are interested in job security, higher wages, shorter hours, safer and more comfortable working conditions, and increasingly expensive "fringe benefits." Management, on the other hand, is concerned about producing goods inexpensively and selling them at a profit. The strong differences between labor and management have led workers to organize themselves into labor unions. Unionization now provides labor with a protective framework in which the buying and selling of labor may take place. Big labor is thus able to negotiate with big business. However, there are many workers as yet unorganized into unions, especially in small companies and in white collar and service occupations.

The impact of technological change on American labor

1. *Technological changes have caused a firm shift in work force makeup.*

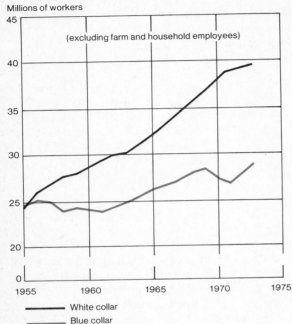

Millions of workers

(excluding farm and household employees)

White collar

Blue collar

2. *The use of new machinery has increased workers' productivity.*

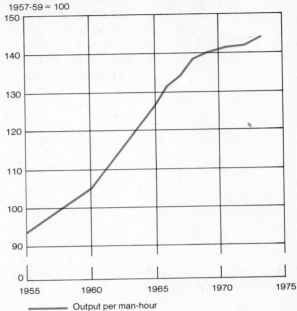

1957-59 = 100

Output per man-hour

Source: Statistical Abstract

1

How do labor markets differ from other markets?

Labor is more than a "commodity." Perhaps there have been employers who dreamed of "a standardized worker with interchangeable parts," workers who could be controlled and manipulated like lumps of coal or machines. But even though it is convenient in economics to consider labor services as a factor subject to general economic laws and principles—the laws of supply and demand, for example—in practice human behavior is too complex and unpre-dictable for workers to be treated like a commodity that is bought and sold on the market.

Labor-saving machinery may endanger a worker's job security. Talk about the nation's "general prosperity" and high wage levels is meaningless to a worker who has no job. This concern for job security is reflected in the attitude of most American workers toward technological progress. In principle, labor-saving machines are considered a good thing, but what if they displace a man from his job and lead to widespread unemployment? Can unions be expected to support the introduction of labor-saving equipment simply because it is a mark of industrial progress—regardless of other consequences? Probably most workers are also in favor of the *principle* of competition. But how

3. *Although the number of workers is rising,*
unemployment is high.

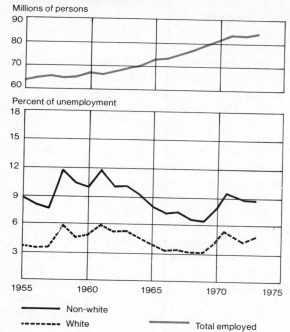

Millions of persons

Percent of unemployment

——— Non-white

------- White   ——— Total employed

4. *Nevertheless, the standard of living of workers*
is steadily rising.

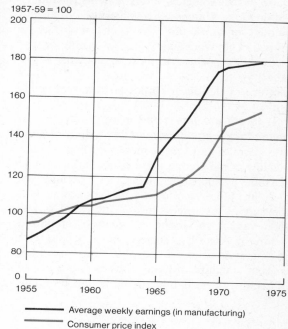

1957-59 = 100

——— Average weekly earnings (in manufacturing)
——— Consumer price index

many persons would be willing to give up their jobs to further either technological improvements or competition?

Throughout history workers have resisted technological change which threatened their jobs. When the Industrial Revolution caused skilled craftsmen to be replaced with steam-powered machines operated by unskilled women and children, many workers opposed mechanization by any means possible. They broke machinery, rioted, and even set fire to some of the factories. In the course of the violence, numbers of workers were injured or killed. Many were thrown into prison. But they failed to stem the tide of industrialization.

In more recent years a new stage of technological development has been reached, that of *automation*—the wide-scale use of automatic machines and computers in industry. In consequence, large numbers of workers have been displaced by automated factories. Labor unions have frequently opposed the introduction of automation, contending that management must first find satisfactory alternative employment or provide job retraining for the employees who would be deprived of their livelihoods. In some instances labor has accepted new technology after management has agreed to share with workers the benefits of the resulting cost savings and additional profits. These benefits may take the form of higher wages, lump-sum "separation pay" for discharged workers, and payments to union welfare and pension funds. Some union contracts contain provisions which limit the number of employees that may be laid off because of technological improvements, including automation. Unions also may insist that the amount of work done by each employee be limited. The overriding factor governing organized labor's position in these agreements is job security—the necessity to protect one's job in the face of the uncertainties of a market economy.

Workers are interested in wage levels and methods of wage determination. Almost everyone wants to make more money each year, both because of the greater number of comforts made possible by increased income and because society has long regarded a person's income as a measure of his success in life. Increased wages, then, rank high among the goals of organized labor. In American society, most people wish to maintain and, if possible, increase their present standard of living. But during a period of rising prices, living standards can be maintained only through increased income. That is why labor unions bargain for "cost of living" wage increases. Generally a *union contract* includes a provision for cost-of-living wage increases, based on an agreed formula.

Periodic unemployment is a problem in many industries. While wages may be relatively high, short lay-offs may be common for many workers. In some industries, therefore, workers have sought and obtained a *guaranteed annual wage*. This means that the employer agrees to pay a minimum amount annually to each worker even though he has not had enough hours of employment at going wage rates to earn this sum.

Various methods are used to determine how much a worker is paid. The *time wage* is most common. Under this method the worker is paid a specified amount per hour, per week, or per month. All workers doing the same work for the same employer for the same length of time usually are paid the same wage. This method takes no account of the fact that some workers may be more productive than others. Pay scales are adjusted to the worker's experience and seniority, however. The *piece* wage is based on the amount of work actually completed. A *progressive wage* combines these two methods. A worker is paid a specified time wage, but is given additional pay for doing more than a predetermined "standard" set for the job.

Workers generally favor time wages. They feel that piece wages place undue pressure on them, and benefit only the fastest workers. The average worker on piece work receives no extra pay or other benefits, and actually may receive less than under a time-rate system. Employers sometimes feel that time rates allow the inefficient or the lazy to "take advantage" of the employer without any reduction in pay.

Working hours and working conditions are very important to workers. The average worker spends about one-half of his waking hours on the job, five days a week. Naturally, he would like to have more "free time," without a decrease in pay. Thus there are movements for

---

LABOR'S CONCERN WITH TECHNOLOGY
Technology is having a revolutionary effect on productivity of American workers. Between 1955 and 1970 output per man-hour increased by approximately 48 per cent, whereas the number of workers employed increased by only 8 per cent.

Employment on the railroads has been cut by more than half since World War II. The diesel has replaced the steam engine, and the continued use of firemen has been a subject of prolonged dispute between labor and management.

Thousands of coal miners, steel workers, and farm workers have lost their jobs because of technological change. Newspaper, airline, and waterfront workers have also felt compelled to strike against automation.

These reactions to technological advances reflect the acute problem of job security facing unions. In many unions, this issue seems more urgent even than that of higher wages.

shorter workdays, shorter work weeks, more paid holidays, and longer vacations. These historic labor objectives are expressed in an old labor jingle: "Whether we work by the hour or work by the day, decreasing the hours increases the pay."

Oddly enough, many workers take advantage of short working hours and vacations to increase their incomes by "moonlighting"—that is, a second job. Sometimes short working hours are used as a method of increasing incomes by making overtime work possible at a higher hourly rate of pay.

One's working environment has much to do with his job satisfaction. People like to work in pleasant surroundings. They want proper lighting, ventilation, and comfortable temperature, as well as locker rooms, clean restrooms, water coolers, cafeterias, and the like. Workers also like to have rest periods and "coffee breaks." Every worker doubtless appreciates an agreeable boss and dislikes being badgered to work faster or harder. Poor working conditions lower morale, contribute to dissension, and adversely affect the quality and amount of work done.

Fringe benefits are becoming increasingly important to workers. A generation or two ago, workers were concerned largely with wages, hours, and working conditions. As wage levels have been raised, hours shortened, and working conditions improved, workers increasingly have made other demands.

Today there is great emphasis on retirement pension plans, employer-financed health and hospitalization insurance, paid vacations, and bonuses or profit-sharing arrangements. Some benefits paid for by the employer (such as pension or insurance contributions) in effect increase the worker's pay without increasing his income taxes. By including payments of this kind as a part of its operating costs, a business can reduce its own income taxes. Existing tax laws provide a strong incentive to expand fringe-benefits or "nonwage compensation."

The goals of workers and employers often conflict. Businesses must operate at a profit to survive. Because wages are one of the largest business costs, and because most other workers' demands are expensive, employers at times must oppose workers' demands that will sharply increase business operating costs.

Workers may sense that a business cannot operate at a loss indefinitely, and that a firm's bankruptcy is likely to cost them their jobs. But business failure is likely to seem a rather remote possibility to most workers. Besides, they may believe that they readily can get another job. Generally speaking, workers are not well-informed about the costs and profits of a business. Surveys have shown that most workers believe their employer is making much greater profits than is actually the case. Sometimes workers may know that their employer *can* afford to meet their demands.

Employers have a significant bargaining advantage over individual workers. If an individual employee loses his job or is unwilling to work for the wage offered, he soon feels a financial squeeze. Without income, his family will suffer. But the employer and his business usually are little affected by the loss of a single worker. Usually the employer will be able to hire someone else, since normally there are more persons wanting jobs than there are jobs available.

If there is a labor surplus and workers individually compete for jobs, employers can pay low wages and get by with inadequate working conditions. This was the case in most businesses and occupations for over a century after the Industrial Revolution. Employers stated terms on a "take it or leave it" basis. If a worker refused to work, his family would starve. If he did work, his family survived by living at a low poverty level.

Many workers soon realized the necessity for collective action in bargaining with employers. The recognition of this fact led to the labor union movement. But the way was not easy. Years passed before labor made any headway toward its goals. The very right to organize and

Humanist Economist

John Stuart Mill

(1806–1873)

The son of a famous economist, John Stuart Mill was a child prodigy. He studied Greek at the age of three, Latin at seven, logic at twelve, and political economy (economics) at thirteen. Meantime, he also studied mathematics, botany, chemistry, history, and classical literature. He wrote scholarly articles for publication at the age of seventeen.

Mill lived a quiet life. He served one term in Parliament. Most of his working life was spent in a comfortable position with the East India Company, which afforded him the leisure to think and write. He generally is ranked among the great classical economists, along with Adam Smith, Thomas Malthus, and David Ricardo.

Mill's interests were much broader than those of most of these earlier economists. In addition to writing brilliant works on logic, philosophy, and politics, he was an ardent supporter of women's rights, and of social and economic reform. It has been said that he "humanized" the "dismal science" of Malthus and Ricardo.

Mill accepted most of the theories of his famous predecessors, and combined and restated their ideas masterfully. He differed with them on one major point, namely that only *production* is governed by "natural" or scientific laws. *Distribution* of the product, he maintained, is determined by man-made rules. He argued that "the distribution of wealth . . . depends on the laws and customs of society" and that "the things once there, mankind can do with them as they like."

It is significant to note that Mill believed workers were not receiving an adequate reward for their labor, and advocated reforms to increase their share. He held that the workers themselves must take the necessary steps to bring about such reforms. As a result, although Mill certainly did not consider himself a Socialist, he has sometimes been claimed by Socialists to have been one.

Mill's name, unfortunately, sometimes is associated with the "wage-fund doctrine." This doctrine holds that wages are paid out of past capital accumulations, which cannot be changed by any actions on the part of workers or employers. Although he held this belief early in life, his later views, like those of present-day economists, recognized that wages and other employer costs actually are paid out of current receipts or "cash flow." But the wage-fund doctrine occasionally still reappears in some guise.

Mill's major work in economics was *Principles of Political Economy* (1848). This book was the leading textbook on the subject for more than 40 years, and still is required reading for most advanced students of economics.

bargain collectively with employers was established only after great difficulty.

CHECK UP

1. How have modern methods of production affected relations between workers and management? How does management view technological change? Labor? Why, in each case?

2. What are the goals of labor? Management? What different approaches are used in determining wages? Which are preferred by labor? Management? What other factors than income are important to labor?

3. Why do the goals of labor and management often conflict? Why is collective bargaining an important right of labor?

2

How have labor unions developed?

Today organized labor ranks with business and agriculture as one of the nation's major economic "power blocs." Unions are an important American institution and are likely to remain so. It is essential, therefore, to understand their history, objectives, and methods.

Unions, like other organizations, vigorously defend all of their hard-won rights and privileges. They may feel that to give ground on even one minor point may lead to stronger attacks on other more important fronts. Actions that at first glance may appear irrational can be understood when viewed in the light of the tribulations of labor organizations in past centuries.

Medieval craft guilds were early forms of workmen's organizations. In the Middle Ages, a *guild* was an organization of men engaged in similar work and having certain common interests. These guilds were not labor unions as these exist today, for they included both the employers and employees in a given craft. The em-

ployer was a "master craftsman" who worked in his shop side by side with "journeyman craftsmen" and "apprentices" learning his trade.

Guilds had several purposes. They maintained price levels, regulated business practices, and set standards with respect to quality of work and working conditions. They also provided a method for young men to learn a trade. Guilds fulfilled the functions now performed by government, unions, and employer associations.

Each craft guild reduced competition for jobs in two ways: (1) by limiting the number of young men accepted as apprentices; and (2) by examining the skill of men who sought to qualify as journeymen or masters. As a result, the number of persons qualified to work in a particular craft was limited. This fact tended to limit production and to keep prices high.

Under the guild system, both employers (masters) and employees (journeymen) would receive higher incomes than if there had been a labor surplus (many more craftsmen). But most workers in those days were in agriculture, whereas the guild controlled only some urban occupations. The other workers had little or no protection.

The Industrial Revolution transformed the workingman's way of life. The invention of new machines, which performed much of the work previously done by hand labor, brought about the Industrial Revolution. This replacement of hand labor by machinery in the long run provided advantages for workers, but it immediately created many difficult problems. Machines greatly increased the total output of goods. When it became possible to produce more goods in a shorter time, higher wages, shorter workdays, and a shorter workweek resulted. At first, however, the effects of mechanization were quite different.

The early benefits of the Industrial Revolution went to employers—who owned the machines and factories—rather than to employees. Skilled workmen were displaced by machines which did the work faster, more cheaply, and sometimes better than hand labor. In the textile

The growth of labor unions in the United States, 1897-1968

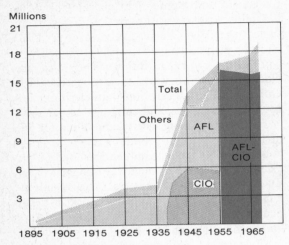

Millions

Union membership as a per cent of total nonagricultural employment

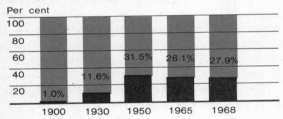

Per cent

1.0%   11.6%   31.5%   28.1%   27.9%

1900   1930   1950   1965   1968

Source: Statistical Abstract

industry, for example, skilled spinners and weavers lost their jobs to machines that could be operated by unskilled women and children. The supply of unskilled labor was so great that skilled workers were forced to accept low wages and poor working conditions in order to work at all. Not until the early 1900's was legislation passed restricting child labor and regulating the working conditions of women.

The situation depressed the general labor market for all workers. It remained difficult for both unskilled and skilled workers to earn an income that enabled them to maintain a decent standard of living. In Europe and America a depressed labor market persisted for about a century.

One point, however, should be emphasized. Even though mechanization—and more recently, automation—may have brought changes which were disadvantageous to many workers for a time, in the long run they made possible a higher general living standard. Mass-production has made goods available to consumers at significantly lower costs. Markets have expanded and more labor has been required to provide raw material, to build machines, and to operate them. New industries have sprung up. Mass production has also created jobs in marketing and services which now exceed the number of jobs in industry.

Big business and union organization developed together. The Industrial Revolution spread from the factories of England to the United States. For years American factories and business firms were relatively small, and while a few labor unions were organized in the early 1800's, their rapid growth began after the Civil War. The great demand for war materials stimulated industrial production in the North. After the war, industry continued to grow in the North and became important in the South.

Business concerns became large and impersonal. When shops and factories were small, employers and employees usually enjoyed face-to-face relationships. Owners knew "their people" and often were concerned for their welfare. As industry expanded, more money was needed to finance new machines and larger factories. Shares of stock were sold nationally, giving ownership to persons who often lived at a distance from the businesses in which they had invested. Large businesses with headquarters in distant cities bought out or merged with smaller ones.

Owners hired managers to run their businesses. Their primary concern was efficient production and higher profits—not workers' welfare. Managers were inclined to pay no higher wages than necessary. Relations between labor and management became more impersonal and less friendly. The worker was now a unit of production, not an individual known personally by his employers. Individuals could not bargain effectively. The necessity for workers to organize and bargain collectively with their employers gave rise to the union movement in this country.

For a time, the efforts of labor to organize were not very successful. Groups that did organize were too small to be effective in bargaining with employers. Labor organizations existed mostly on a local level. Workers in different occupations or in different parts of the country co-operated only to a limited extent.

Employers opposed national unions. At first employers denied workers the right to bargain collectively. They argued that since employers hired workers individually, they had the right to bargain with each worker individually. The widespread opposition to labor organizations found expression in the blacklist and the "iron-clad oath" or the "yellow-dog contract."[1]

In order to block national unions, employers established *company unions*. Company unions usually are indirectly controlled by the employer. Their existence made it less likely that workers would join independent unions.

---

[1] The *blacklist* was an employers' privately circulated catalogue or card-index of workers who were to be refused employment because they held opinions or engaged in activities thought to be contrary to employers' interests. "Iron-clad oaths" were antiunion contracts exacted by employers from workers. They were first used in the 1870's and 1880's. Applicants for jobs were told that if they wished to be hired, they must sign an agreement not to belong to any labor association while employed or aid in any strike for any change in the employer's nonunion rules. The employer, however, reserved his unlimited right to discharge workers—making it a one-sided agreement. The Supreme Court upheld antiunion contracts in its Hitchman decision of 1917. They were then called "yellow-dog contracts" by organized labor to stigmatize the conduct of individuals willing to be bound by such agreements. The Norris-LaGuardia Act of 1932 declared antiunion contracts to be contrary to public policy.

The courts were another obstacle to the formation of independent unions. The law forbidding "combinations in restraint of trade" was generally interpreted by the courts to make labor unions illegal. Only after 1914 did federal law prevent such rulings.

Immigrants increased the labor supply. Immigration was another factor that made it difficult to form effective labor unions. Each year, until legislation greatly restricting immigration was passed following World War I, hundreds of thousands of immigrants came to America in search of new opportunities. Employers were able to exploit the increased labor supply (which depressed wage scales). Immigrants were subject to deportation until they were naturalized, and this fact coupled with their inability to speak English made them hesitant to join unions. Immigrants were even used by employers as strikebreakers. And as long as employers could find workers willing to work under the conditions they imposed, they were in a better position to ignore the demands of labor unions. Eventually, however, immigrants helped build strong unions, especially in the Northeast.

Many workers hoped to become self-employed. The view that with hard work and a little luck anyone in America might "strike it rich" was another hindrance to organized labor. Many immigrants as well as the native born regarded the work that they were doing as temporary. They did not wish to work for wages all their lives. They hoped to save a little money and start a business of their own. For a time, the availability of western land was an incentive for poor men to seek a measure of prosperity through farming and small business. This "American dream" caused many workers to show little or no interest in labor unions.

However, as good free land was exhausted and American business enterprises grew larger, more and more families became dependent upon the weekly paycheck earned at the mill, the mine, or the factory. As more employees realized that they would always be employees, labor unions became much more important in the life of American workers. As this happened, antiunion forces gathered strength. In the labor struggles which followed, powerful employers did not scruple to employ spies, strikebreakers, armed guards, or "goon squads" (bands of paid terrorists) to intimidate workers and prevent them from organizing. Workers who lived in company towns, or in company-owned dwellings, or who bought provisions in the company store, could expect eviction and firing if they participated in union-organizing activities. Sheriffs and their deputies, often in the pay of the company "boss," provided workers with little or no protection from these harassments.

A short-lived labor union advocates reforms. Delegates representing a variety of crafts formed the National Labor Union in 1866. At its annual conventions various plans to aid labor were discussed, among them the eight-hour day, arbitration to settle labor disputes, the enactment of safety laws for factories, and the establishment of co-operatives. Some of its leaders showed interest in reforms of less direct concern to labor, such as women's rights, civil service reform, and inflation of the currency. Believing that the best way to bring about change was political

action, the National Labor Union in 1872 backed the Labor Reform Party. The party was charged with advocating socialism and attracted very little support. This setback, plus hard times caused by the Panic of 1873, led to the collapse of the National Labor Union.

The Knights of Labor establishes "one big union." Whereas the National Labor Union brought together existing craft unions, the Noble Order of the Knights of Labor had as its goal the enlistment of all workers, skilled or unskilled. Because this ideal did not appeal to members of craft unions, the organization's growth was slow during its first decade, 1869–1879. When Terence V. Powderly became Grand Master Workman in 1878 the Knights had fewer than 30,000 members. By 1886 Powderly had built an organization of 700,000. A former member of the Machinist's Union, Powderly had been blacklisted for his union activities. Having just been elected mayor of Scranton in 1878, he dominated a meeting called to reorganize the Knights. Powderly became that union's leader for the next fifteen years.

The goals of the Knights were much the same as those of the National Labor Union. But the

FARM WORKERS ORGANIZE

Agricultural workers were not organized into unions during the 1930's and '40's, in part because they are not under the jurisdiction of the National Labor Relations Act. In 1970, however, California grape pickers were successful in obtaining contracts for farm workers.

In 1965, the United Farm Workers Organizing Committee (UFWOC) had begun a drive to organize these workers. Farms growing wine grapes were the first target. A boycott of California table wines soon persuaded these vineyards to sign a contract. A much longer struggle ensued when UFWOC moved against the growers of table grapes.

This second drive, however, received widespread support from civil rights organizations, Catholic and other clergy, and some politicians. When a boycott reduced the price of table grapes by 15 per cent, the growers filed suit against the union for damages. They also used strikebreakers from Mexico. The first breakthrough occurred in mid-1969. Ten growers in the Coachella area signed a contract covering about 10 per cent of the state's total production of table grapes. Finally, on July 29, 1970, 26 major grape growers signed contracts with UFWOC, ending the grape boycott. The farm workers' leader, Cesar Chavez, immediately announced plans to move against the producers of other crops. The first step was a boycott of lettuce harvested by nonunion workers.

recession of 1884 increased unemployment and labor unrest. When employers took advantage of the opportunity to fire workers who belonged to the Knights, boycotts and strikes resulted. Although the public sympathized with the union in some strikes, the great railroad strike of 1886 in the Southwest was so effective that the governors of four states ordered strikers not to interfere with trains. The public strongly approved this action.

Soon afterwards some 340,000 workers took part in the May Day (1886) strikes called in many parts of the country in support of the movement for an eight-hour day. In Chicago a small group of anarchists tried to persuade the strikers and strike sympathizers that the time had come to abolish the established government. On May 3 police dispersed a crowd of strikers addressed by an anarchist newspaper editor. In the fighting several strikers were killed and some twenty wounded. At a protest meeting held the following evening in Haymarket Square the workers once again were addressed by anarchists. When police again moved in to disperse the orderly crowd, a bomb exploded. One policeman was killed; several wounded. In the savage fighting which followed, seven police and four civilians died; more than 60 police and perhaps 50 civilians were wounded.

An outraged public demanded punishment for the guilty, and eight anarchists were brought to trial and convicted, although no evidence was produced to link them with making or throwing the bomb. To the public the Knights of Labor seemed "guilty by association." Actually Powderly had opposed the idea of a strike to further the eight-hour day. But doubtless some anarchists had infiltrated the Knights and spoken at that union's meetings. Skilled workers felt that the unskilled workers belonging to the union were provoking needless conflicts and hurting the cause of labor. Consequently they withdrew to form their own craft unions. By 1890 membership had dwindled to 100,000 and the Order soon disappeared. The rapid growth of the American Federation of Labor was a major factor in the death of the Noble Order of the Knights of Labor.

The federation of craft unions was an important step for labor. Samuel Gompers launched the American Federation of Labor in 1881 and remained its leader for more than 40 years. Gompers, who had joined the cigarmakers' union at the age of fourteen, became spokesman for his local at age sixteen. Largely because of his efforts, the Cigarmakers' International Union was reorganized on a sounder basis. Gompers then turned his attention to a national labor movement, the formation of the American Federation of Labor (AFL).

As its name implies, the AFL was a *federation* and not "one big union" such as the Knights of Labor. A labor federation brings together various unions under a central authority, leaving each union in control of its internal affairs. Each AFL union was composed of workers in a certain trade or craft; hence the name *craft union*.

A craft union is composed of workers in only one trade, while an *industrial union* is made up of all the workers in an industry. In the AFL each group of craftsmen had its own organization at three levels: local, state, and national. It affiliated with skilled workers in other crafts through membership in the Federation. Gompers felt that American workmen were more interested in wages, hours, and working conditions in their own occupations than in general "social reform" or "one big union." For a long time Gompers appeared to be correct.

Members of the AFL sought to raise the living standards of labor by obtaining shorter working hours, higher wages, the abolition of child labor, and better working conditions. The AFL also sought greater security for its members by working for unemployment compensation and insurance plans financed by workers or their employers or both.

Unlike the National Labor Union and the Knights of Labor, the AFL worked to achieve immediate goals. As one leader said, "We are all practical men. We have no *ultimate ends.* We are going on from day to day. We are fighting only for immediate objectives—objectives that can be realized in a few years."

Many AFL aims were achieved through peaceful but organized pressure on state and federal lawmakers, and through collective bargaining with management. (Collective bargaining is the orderly process of reconciling the demands of labor and management through negotiation. The *union contract* is the agreement which results when negotiations are fruitful. It recognizes the rights of both sides. Strikes usually occur only in the absence of such contracts, or when a union believes its contract has been violated.) The Federation did not hesitate to back member unions when they went on strike. The AFL also supported political candidates sympathetic to its aims.

The AFL grew rapidly during the decade 1894 to 1904, having a membership of more than 1.5 million workers by the latter date.

Although the AFL had its ups and downs, its membership grew steadily, and it remained a strong influence within organized labor, even after its merger in 1955 with its younger counterpart among noncraft workers, the Congress of Industrial Organizations (CIO).

Until the 1930's, industrial unions developed slowly. The skilled craftsmen who comprised the membership of AFL unions had greater bargaining power than the great mass of unskilled workers. Millions of workers in the steel, automobile, rubber, and other mass production industries remained unorganized and unrepresented. Although Gompers and his successor, William Green, purported to speak for all labor, they represented at the most one-tenth of all the men and women working for wages.

John L. Lewis of the coal miners, Charles P. Howard of the typographers, and Sidney Hillman and David Dubinsky of the clothing industry workers strove to organize unskilled industrial workers within the AFL. Their at-

Two types of labor organizations

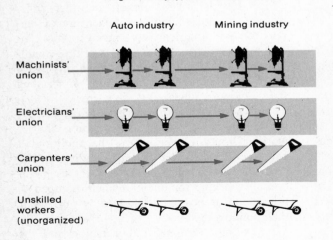

Craft unions
(Original basis of AFL)
Organized by type of work performed

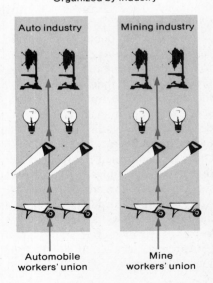

Industrial unions
(Original basis of CIO)
Organized by industry

tempts met with continued opposition from the supporters of craft unions, however. Nevertheless, in 1935 they formed the Committee for Industrial Organization, and began recruiting workers into industrial unions. Three years later, the AFL expelled unions belonging to the Committee. The latter, in turn, formed the Congress of Industrial Organizations.

By 1942 the CIO included more than 40 national industrial unions with a total membership of over five million. The successful organization of automobile and steel workers made the CIO a powerful force in economic and political affairs. The CIO initiated new tactics; for example, it conducted a vigorous campaign to educate the public and win its support. It also took an active part in politics. As a result, the CIO grew rapidly and soon rivaled the AFL in membership and power.

Conflict between craft and industrial unions led to unification. When American industrial productivity was at its peak during World War II, both the CIO and AFL tried to gain members at the other's expense. Conflict caused by "raiding" not only reduced the general effectiveness of both unions but was expensive. Finally, in 1955, the two union bodies decided to merge. George Meany, AFL president, became president of the new AFL-CIO organization. Walter Reuther of the United Auto workers, former CIO president, became vice-president.

But policy differences between the two groups persisted. After more than ten years in the AFL-CIO, the United Auto Workers, still led by Reuther, withdrew from the organization. The UAW and the Teamsters Union, which had been evicted from the AFL-CIO earlier, have since formed the American Labor Alliance. There are other unions that also were never part of the AFL-CIO, or which left that organization.

More than 19 million persons, or nearly one-fourth of the country's total work force, now belong to one of some 200 major labor unions. Four-fifths of these union members belong to

AFL-CIO unions. The combined assets of American unions at all levels exceeds two billion dollars, and annual receipts from membership dues and other sources add much more to this total. Numbers, organization, and financial strength have brought labor a long way since the days of Powderly and Gompers.

Organized labor uses united action to obtain its demands from management. Unions have several weapons. The *strike* has been the most powerful weapon of the labor unions, regardless of how they are organized. When a worker strikes, he is not giving up his job. To prevent others from working in his place and thwarting the purpose of the strike, he and his fellows maintain a watch over the plant or factory. They form a *picket line* to discourage nonstrikers from seeking employment there. Rules for picketing are established by law and by the courts. The main purpose of picketing is to publicize the union's position and grievances. People who cross such picket lines to work are called "scabs" by union members. Disagreements, and occasionally violence, occur between

Time lost from strikes in the United States

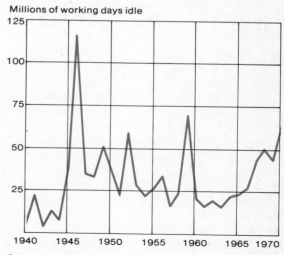

Millions of working days idle

picketers and management representatives or outsiders.

When union members go on strike without the approval of their national union, it is called a *wildcat strike*. During the 1930's, CIO strikers sometimes "sat down" and refused to leave the plant, thus preventing strikebreakers from taking their jobs. Such *sit-down strikes* have been declared illegal.

The refusal of workers and their supporters to buy goods or services from an employer is called a *boycott*. The union which has called the boycott usually appeals to the public to support its efforts. Workers who are not on strike but wish to express their solidarity with the strikers may sometimes leave their jobs. At the very least, they will respect another union's picket lines by refusing to cross them to deliver goods or provide services.

Management has used various methods to offset united actions by labor. Formerly blacklists containing the names of persons active in organizing unions were circulated among employers. Such persons were denied employment. As already pointed out, employers hired strikebreakers to break picket lines, and sent paid informers ("spies") to union meetings to learn about workers' plans.

When an employer learned that a strike was imminent, he frequently *locked out* workers until they agreed to his terms. Just as a union had to be sure that it could afford a strike, so an employer wished to know whether workers could outlast a lockout.

One of the most effective weapons of management employed against unions was the *injunction*. An injunction is a court order to an individual or group directing him or it to desist from some specific practice on the ground that it is illegal. Refusal to comply is contempt of court, and is punishable by fine or imprisonment. Prior to 1914 the courts were generally biased in favor of employers, and injunctions were easy for them to obtain. Injunctions against mass picketing and other tactics are still obtainable.

Labor and management today usually settle disagreements through collective bargaining. Strikes can cause great hardship to the public. Nationwide strikes in transportation or communication industries, for example, could paralyze the nation. For their own benefit and to further the general welfare, labor and management today are likely to discuss differences in an effort to reach a compromise rather than resort to extreme measures. Union leadership is responsible for bargaining for all members of the union. The actual bargaining is the process of arriving at compromises which reconcile the demands of workers with the concessions that employers are willing to make. The extent to which each side yields is often determined by its relative economic strength and by public opinion.

A new contract may be drawn up, or grievances resolved, by negotiation, arbitration, or mediation. When an employer and union representatives meet to discuss the demands of the strikers, they are using *negotiation* to reach an agreement. Discussion sometimes ends in a stalemate, however.

When collective bargaining fails, the negotiators may seek the help of a neutral, unbiased party in reaching an agreement. Such a process is known as *mediation* or *conciliation*. The mediator listens to the arguments of each side, and then recommends compromise measures which may or may not be accepted.

When an employer and union representatives cannot reach an agreement through either negotiation or mediation, they may take their dispute to a third party to whom they give the power to dictate the terms of settlement. This is called *arbitration*. The disputing factions must then abide by the decisions of the arbitrator, unless some special provision to the contrary has been made prior to arbitration.

Some unions have been charged with discriminating against minority groups. Nonwhite minority groups, especially Negroes, have complained that unreasonable membership requirements have excluded them from some unions.

This complaint has been made against building trades unions, which enjoy high hourly wages. These unions usually require a long apprenticeship and study in mastering the craft. Civil rights groups allege that relatives of present (mostly white) union members tend to be given preference in admission to apprenticeship programs.

These unions have denied charges of racial discrimination. They assert that membership is open to all qualified persons, but that few nonwhites have met their qualifications. Early in 1968, eighteen building trades unions having 3.5 million members officially resolved to prohibit racial discrimination and actively to recruit nonwhites into apprenticeship programs. However, when there was no significant increase in the actual number of nonwhites on the job, black workmen and their supporters decided on "direct action." Consequently, in late 1969, picket lines, demonstrations, and marches were organized. Several confrontations between union construction workers and nonwhites took place at construction sites. There was some violence, and arrests were made. One outcome of these demonstrations was a quota system which the federal government established for federally-financed construction projects, guaranteeing a percentage of jobs to nonwhites.

In the past, the success of the CIO was due in part to the way it united men and women, blacks and whites, natives and foreign-born in pursuit of better wages and working conditions. Informed observers of the labor movement are calling for a renewal of unity in the ranks of organized labor as one answer to the problem of racism in American society. Such unity, they argue, benefits whites by eliminating reserves of unorganized labor (which depress the labor market), and benefits blacks by raising wages and providing greater job security.

CHECK UP

1. How was a craft guild different from a labor union? What purposes did the guild serve? How did this system benefit employers? Employees? How did the

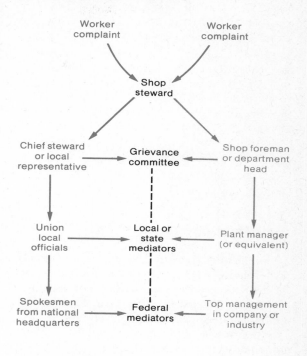

From local grievance to national dispute
Stages in collective bargaining

→ Line of referral
Neutral third party
Management
Union
- - - - Breakdown of negotiations

Industrial Revolution affect employers? Employees? The general standard of living?

2. Why did big business and larger unions develop in the United States in the last third of the 1800's? How did industrial growth affect relations between employers and employees? What practices were used by management in opposing the early unions? By these unions in fighting management?

3. What reforms were urged by the National Labor Union and the Knights of Labor? How did the two differ? Why did each collapse? How did the AFL differ from the Knights of Labor in organization? Goals? Methods?

4. How did the CIO differ from the AFL? Why was the former successful? Why did the two organizations unite? What methods were used by labor and management in post-World War I conflicts? How are disagreements usually settled?

5. Why have charges of discrimination against minority groups been directed against some unions? What has been the reaction of minorities? Unions? The federal government?

3

What are the effects of unionization?

Union membership still is concentrated heavily in a relatively few industries and occupations. In the South and in some jobs, union membership is the exception rather than the rule. But union activities clearly affect everyone.

Union wages and working conditions affect nonunion wages and conditions. When unions win benefits for their members, similar benefits tend to spread to nonunion workers. In order to keep nonunion employees satisfied, and to keep them out of unions, employers often establish wages and working conditions similar to those enjoyed by union members. If union conditions were significantly better than nonunion conditions, workers eventually would move from nonunion to union occupations and areas. Nonunion workers rarely enjoy wages and other benefits *equal* to those of union workers, however. But some people do not like to move or to change jobs, and some occupations are more readily unionized than others.

If union demands are too high compared to nonunion wages and conditions, unionized firms may lose business to nonunion firms. This has happened often in the past, and it still occurs occasionally. Some companies move their factories to nonunion areas—the South, for example—to take advantage of nonunion labor and lower wage scales. Historically union and nonunion wages in one area have moved up and down together, although at different levels.

Some would argue that wages are dependent upon productivity, and that unions cannot really influence them. There is a grain, but only a grain, of truth in this argument. While employers limit wages according to productivity, it may be that unions, by improving living standards for their members, actually cause workers to be more productive. Also, without union pressures, employers are less inclined to share productivity increases with their employees.

Unions work for social legislation. Unorganized workers are helped by most laws which establish minimum wages, maximum working hours, safe working conditions, injury and retirement payments, and similar benefits. Unions can bargain with employers on such matters, but unorganized workers have to depend upon laws for their protection. In recent decades, unions have taken an active part in supporting laws protecting all workers, just as earlier unions supported free public education and the prohibition of child labor. Social legislation

NEW SAFETY ACT PASSED

A new occupational safety act was passed in 1970 to protect workers in industry. In supporting the new legislation, labor officials called attention to the more than two million work-related accidents and close to two billion dollars in lost wages.

Initially, businessmen were opposed to any federal regulation of plant conditions, but in its final form the bill was acceptable to both the AFL-CIO and the Chamber of Commerce.

The act authorizes the Secretary of Labor to set safety standards before 1973. These will then be enforced by a three-man board appointed by the President. Fines for violations of the act are set at 1000 dollars for each violation and 10,000 dollars for each "willful" violation.

benefits union members to some extent, of course, but it is much more important to unorganized workers.

Modern technology and marketing have helped to improve wages, hours, and working conditions. Labor's demands no doubt have compelled management to seek ways of increasing productivity and lowering costs, and to share their profits with workers through higher wages. The use of capital accumulated by owners in the development of more and better machines and equipment—plus more efficient management and marketing techniques —have also increased productivity. In the long run, higher wages, shorter hours, better working conditions, and fringe benefits are paid for only out of profits. Goods and services are produced only by the combined use of all four factors of production—land, labor, capital, and entrepreneurship (including technical expertise).

Union activities may contribute to inflation. One criticism of union activity is that it may bring about higher prices. Many employers, after accepting costly union demands, raise prices to maintain profits. The gains of union members may thus be at the expense of unorganized workers, the largest group in the consuming public.

Furthermore, if prices rise with incomes, no one benefits. Workers' *real wages* (their purchasing power) would not increase. Should one's income double tonight, and the prices of everything one buys also double, the higher income could buy no more tomorrow than the lower did today. Such a spiral is called *inflation*. Inflation is hardest on persons with fixed incomes such as pensions, and puts American business at a disadvantage in foreign trade. The decreased value of the dollar is a boon, of course, to persons who have large debts to pay.

There is some truth to this criticism. But one should recall that prices in the short-time period are more controlled by demand than by costs. It may not be possible for employers to offset wage increases by price increases. Even in the

long run, increased costs from higher wages will not always result in corresponding price increases to consumers. Employers may at times take lower profits or cut other costs to offset higher wages.

Higher wages sometimes mean higher prices, but not always. It is impossible to make a general statement covering all situations. Each case must be examined in its own economic context, but even if the total amount of a wage increase is passed on to the public in the form of higher prices, workers receiving the higher wages usually will benefit. These benefits may be shared indirectly by others, for example by those who sell goods and services.

Both employers and employees have public responsibilities. Power is always accompanied by responsibilities—whether or not the persons or groups possessing power recognize this fact. If groups in the economy become careless about their responsibilities, ultimately their powers will be reduced. This has happened both to business and to organized labor.

A capitalist economy presupposes that each person or group works for his or its own best interests, but the economic competition which this involves is permitted only within limits. Businesses are allowed to make reasonable profits, labor can demand reasonable wages, and the public expects to pay reasonable prices. But definitions of what is "reasonable" vary greatly. The government—especially in wartime or other periods of national emergency— may sometimes enter into these disputes.

Neither employers nor employees can wholly disregard the public interest or public opinion. Whether this is due more to fear of repressive legislation or other forms of government pressures or to a sense of responsibility, the effect is the same.

CHECK UP

1. How have union wages and working conditions affected nonunion wages and working conditions? How have modern technology and marketing helped to improve working conditions?

2. Under what conditions may union activities contribute to inflation? What groups are hurt by inflation?

3. Why do higher wages not necessarily result in higher prices? Why can neither management nor labor afford to disregard the public interest?

4

What is the role of government in labor-management relations?

The federal government often intervenes in labor-management disputes. Congress has passed laws governing labor-management relations. These laws are interpreted by the courts. The Federal Mediation and Conciliation Service, created in 1947 under the Labor-Management Relations Act, is the principal government agency providing mediation and other services to the contending parties in a labor dispute, but it possesses no law enforcement authority. The agency relies upon techniques of persuasion to perform its duties. The federal government seeks to maintain a balance in the bargaining positions of employers and employees, while at the same time protecting the interests of the entire public.

The first national legislation affecting unions was designed to control big business. The Sherman Anti-Trust Act of 1890 was intended to "control combinations in restraint of trade" operated by big-business trusts. Anti-union employers, however, sought to have the Supreme Court rule that the law applied equally to unions. The Court did so in 1895 and again in 1908, much to the dismay of labor supporters. Injunctions against unions thereafter became more common than against business.

The Clayton Anti-Trust Act of 1914 was the first federal law to favor labor. It stated that unions were not the same as business monopolies and that labor was not a "commodity."

The courts, however, continued to grant injunctions against unions on much the same grounds as they did before the Clayton Act was passed. However, the Clayton Act broadened the powers of labor unions in other ways. It legalized peaceful assemblies (union meetings), strikes, picketing, boycotts, and the collection of benefit money by unions for the support of members during strikes.

Labor demanded further protection. During the hard times of the 1930's, low wages and great unemployment led to a growing demand for constructive labor legislation. In 1932 the Norris-LaGuardia Act limited the right of courts to issue injunctions. (The same act outlawed the "yellow-dog contract.")

In 1935 the National Labor Relations Act, often called the Wagner Act, was passed. This act prohibited employers from (1) refusing to bargain collectively with properly selected delegates of workers, or (2) dominating or interfering with a labor organization by refusing to hire or to retain union members. In order to enforce this new law, the National Labor Relations Board was established.

The growth of unions led to government regulation of their power. By the end of World War II, there was a growing feeling among employers and others that the Wagner Act gave labor too much power. They argued that unions had grown so powerful that they had to be controlled—not only protected—by government. In consequence of this feeling, Congress in 1947 passed the Labor-Management Relations Act, also known as the Taft-Hartley Act. It provides the major legal basis for government intervention in the affairs and practices of organized labor. The Taft-Hartley Act forbade (1) the *jurisdictional strike* (called by one union to assert itself over another organizing in the same shop), (2) the *secondary boycott* (boycotts by nonstriking unions), and (3) the *closed shop* (where only union members are hired). The union shop remained, but the states were given the right to prohibit union shops, and many states have done so. Such laws are frequently referred to as "right-to-work" laws.

In addition, the Taft-Hartley Act (1) outlawed strikes by federal employees, (2) gave employers and unions the right to sue for damages when contracts were broken, (3) made the unions file regular reports of their officers, membership, and finances with the Secretary of Labor, (4) prohibited unions from making contributions to political campaigns, and (5) forced the officials of unions seeking recognition under the Wagner Act to swear they were not Communists and did not support any organization advocating the forcible overthrow of the government. Finally, the law required a 60-day "cooling-off" period before strikes and lockouts, and permitted the President to invoke an 80-day injunction prohibiting strikes which seriously affected the national welfare. In general, the Taft-Hartley Act significantly tightened government control of unions.

Unions were bitter about the new legislation, calling it a "slave labor law" because it limited the right to strike. After the law was passed, union organizing declined, and during the 1950's union membership remained at a nearly constant level. The Labor-Management Reporting and Disclosure Act of 1959 (the Landrum-Griffin Act) provided for further government regulation. It required unions to conduct business according to democratic procedures, including use of the secret ballot; to submit regular reports of union finances (pension and welfare funds) to the Secretary of Labor; and to prohibit persons convicted of felonies and Communist Party members from holding union offices.

Government can intervene directly in serious labor-management disputes. In addition to mediation, existing laws allow the government to take a firm hand in strikes which threaten to cripple the nation's economy. It can order strikers to return to work, and in certain cases can impose binding arbitration.

Occasionally the President has been called upon to intervene in disputes which appeared hopelessly deadlocked. This has occurred in

Many factors determine the bargaining strength of labor

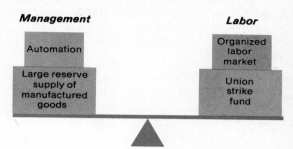

Size of labor market
A large supply of workers in proportion to the available jobs weakens labor's position.

Automation
The more easily labor can be replaced by machines, the weaker its position.

Competition
Presence of a rival union divides the loyalty of organized labor, weakens its posture

Storability of product
Labor's position is weakened if the manufactured goods can be stored.

Extent of unionization
Full union membership strengthen labor's hand.

Competition
A rival firm within the industry weakens management's position.

Financial status
A sound financial condition is essential for both labor unions and management.

times of national crisis and in strikes affecting major essential industries such as coal mining, steel, and railroads. There are legal limits beyond which government intervention cannot go. (Presidential actions in strikes have been twice declared unconstitutional by the Supreme Court.) And there is no law empowering the President to act as a final umpire. The President, however, has immense power and prestige in matters affecting the public interest.

Both labor and management prefer to settle their disputes without government intervention. (Both actively lobby for favorable legislation, however!) But sometimes a deadlock is reached, or one side or the other thinks it will gain by appealing to the government for a decision. Such occurrences are not common, however.

Most workers and employers apparently believe that substantial freedoms may be lost if it becomes customary to refer economic disputes to the government for solution.

CHECK UP

1. What is the traditional role of the federal government in labor-management disputes? How was labor affected by the Sherman Anti-Trust Act? The Clayton Anti-Trust Act? The Norris-LaGuardia Act?

2. Why did the feeling develop after World War II that labor had not accepted the responsibilities that should go with power? What were the provisions of the Taft-Hartley Act? The Landrum-Griffin Act? How did labor react to such legislation?

3. Why do labor and management prefer to settle their disputes without government intervention?

Clinching the main ideas

Less than a century ago most people worked ten to twelve hours a day, six days a week—a total of 60 to 70 hours or more each week. Today a 40-hour week is common in American industry, and there is a strong movement toward a 35-hour or even a 30-hour workweek. Work is generally easier and working conditions more comfortable and pleasant than in "the good old days."

Wages also have increased in the *real* sense (as well as in the monetary sense), so that American workers enjoy not only the bare necessities but also many comforts and luxuries unimaginable a few generations ago.

Improvements were slow at times, but over the years labor's gains, among both organized and unorganized workers, have been tremendous. The gains have been partly the result of new inventions, new methods, and the use of large quantities of capital in mass production, and partly the result of efforts by organized labor.

Modern American labor unions are a unique outgrowth of this country's industrial capitalism. Although their origins date back to the beginnings of the Industrial Revolution some 200 years ago, they were not widely successful until after the Civil War. Only after World War I and the Great Depression did unionism reach its present strength.

More and more, responsible union leaders and members, like responsible employers, are recognizing their overall obligations to the general public. But when either unions or employers lose sight of the public interest, stern legal measures may be used to force them back into line.

Chapter 12 review

Terms to understand

1. automation
2. union contract
3. time wage
4. piece wage
5. progressive wage
6. "moonlighting"
7. fringe benefits
8. craft guilds
9. guaranteed annual wage
10. blacklist
11. "yellow-dog" contract
12. Knights of Labor
13. craft union
14. industrial union
15. AFL-CIO
16. picket line
17. sit-down strike
18. secondary boycott
19. lockout
20. injunction
21. collective bargaining
22. arbitration
23. real wages
24. Norris-LaGuardia Act
25. Taft-Hartley Act
26. Wagner Act

What do you think?

1. The economic theory of *laissez faire* was widely accepted by English industrialists during the first half century of the Industrial Revolution. Why? What were the results?

2. American labor is opposed to piece work, which is commonplace in the Soviet Union. Yet ours is called a capitalist economy and theirs a Communist. Is not this a strange situation? How do you account for it?

3. During the twentieth century the productivity of the American worker has increased tremendously. What has been the effect on production? On prices? On hours of labor? On wages? On work load? Explain.

4. Has the rise of big labor in this country paralleled that of big business? Explain. Why has the increase of government controls over business and labor paralleled the growth of big business and labor?

5. Trace changes in the relations of labor and management during the twentieth century. Explain why these have taken place. How was it possible for labor to make some of its greatest gains during the Great Depression?

6. At times a President has felt that a price increase or a strike was not in the national interest. What can he do to prevent one or the other? Why may he be reluctant to take action?

Applying your knowledge of economics

1. What labor unions are active in your community? What types of workers are included in each? What industries and groups are not unionized? Report your findings in a chart or table.

2. Try to arrange an informal discussion involving a representative of management and of labor in a local industry. The subject might be union-management relations.

3. List the most important labor legislation since World War II. Use *Reader's Guide* to locate articles favorable to (or critical of) each law. Summarize points for and against. Try to discover the present views of local leaders in labor and in business and industry on the laws in question.

Strikes in essential industries: the railroads

General background

One of the most difficult problems confronting the nation is what to do about strikes in essential industries. To compel workers to work against their will ignores the "rights of labor" and conflicts with democratic ideals. Yet the various parts of this country's economy are so interdependent that a strike in an essential industry can have disastrous results for the nation. Federal legislation has been enacted to reduce the likelihood of such strikes, and to facilitate the settlement of labor-management disputes in essential industries. Management generally has hailed the enactment of such laws, but labor tends to regard regulatory legislation as a threat to its bargaining power. At present there are laws requiring employees in certain industries to stay on the job for a stipulated period beyond the expiration of their union contracts. A long-standing dispute between the railroads and the United Transportation Union (which includes the former Brotherhood of Firemen and Enginemen), for example, has set in motion the complicated machinery of the Railway Labor Act.

The vital importance of keeping the railroads running is generally recognized. Railroads haul more than 40 per cent of the intercity freight in this country. Most railroad freight is hauled for relatively long distances, and most of it is made up of heavy and bulky essential raw materials, semiprocessed goods, and manufactured products. Among such items are coal, ores, and lumber; grain and other food stuffs; steel, automobiles, and heavy machinery.

Railroads were one of the first major American industries to become almost wholly unionized and to engage in nationwide collective bargaining. The Railway Labor Act of 1926, as amended, was one of the earliest national labor laws. Basically, it provides four steps for the settlement of contract disputes:

1. *Free collective bargaining procedures.*

2. *Mediation by the National Board of Mediation.* This Board is made up of three impartial public officials appointed by the President with the advice and consent of the Senate. It takes over when management and labor cannot reach agreement on a contract through collective bargaining. This Board does not decide issues; it merely works with labor and management to help them reach an agreement.

3. *Voluntary arbitration.* If the Mediation Board fails in its efforts to help labor and management reach an agreement, a possible next step is voluntary arbitration. It would be necessary for both sides to agree in advance to abide by the decision of the arbitrators. One-third of the arbitrators would be chosen by management and one-third by labor. These two groups, in turn, would choose the other third. (If the labor and management groups cannot agree, the "neutral" arbitrators are chosen by the Mediation Board.) Neither side can be compelled to agree to arbitration, but once a dispute is submitted to arbitration by mutual agreement, the decision of the arbitrators is final and legally binding on both parties.

4. *Action by the President.* If one or both sides refuse to accept arbitration, the President is empowered to appoint an Emergency Board. This Emergency Board has 30 days in which to reach its decision. During the 30 days that the Board is deliberating, and for an additional 30 days after its decision has been announced, a strike is illegal. Neither side, however, can be compelled to accept the Board's recommendations. Thus, the appointment of the Emergency Board may merely insure that the strike is postponed for 60 days. The Railway Labor Act provides no further procedures for settling a dispute.

The Railway Labor Act was designed to provide a lengthy "cooling-off" period, during which management and labor hopefully would reach an agreement. For about 20 years this procedure worked. More recently, however, it has been less successful.

Since World War II, railroads have lost much of their profitable business to competing forms of transportation, such as trucking and air freight. Many of the lines have operated "in the red." To reduce costs, railroad management has introduced technological improvements and sought to reduce its work force. The latter has led to a long dispute over the jobs of railroad firemen.

The dispute over firemen

During the days of coal-burning steam locomotives, railroad firemen played an essential role. A fireman might have to shovel more than a ton of coal an hour to keep a locomotive running. His job was hard and dirty. When American railroads introduced oil-burning diesel locomotives soon after World War II, there no longer was a need to shovel coal. Consequently, during the middle 1950's, railroad management decided to eliminate firemen on freight trains, but not on passenger trains. Three years of fruitless union-management discussions followed. When the railroads decided to put their plan into effect in 1959, labor was outraged.

Under the "work rules" agreed upon by labor and management in 1919, three persons rode in the cab of a freight train locomotive: an engineer, a fireman, and the "head end" brakeman. On a diesel locomotive, it now was the position of railroad management that firemen no longer were needed on freight trains. Their continued employment merely increased costs for an industry already suffering from dwindling profits. Daniel P. Loomis, then President of the Association of American Railroads, expressed the view of management:

With respect to the position of firemen on diesel locomotives, . . . the duties of that position have long since disappeared. It used to be that on the old coal-burning engines the firemen had one of the toughest jobs in the country, but on the modern diesel, with all its automatic appliances, practically nothing is left except lookout duties. In freight service, the head brakeman also rides on the locomotive with the engineer, and . . . we certainly do not need three. In railroad yard service, someone from the ground crew is almost invariably on or near the locomotive, and the fireman in yard service has absolutely nothing to do. The railroads have not proposed to take the fireman off the passenger locomotives, there will still be two men in the cab. . . .

The viewpoint of the Brotherhood of Locomotive Firemen and Enginemen (since merged with three other railroad unions to·form the United Transportation Union) was that: (1) Firemen contribute to safety by helping the engineer keep watch along the track; (2) in an emergency, the fireman can stop the train; (3) firemen learn how to be engineers by riding the cab, thus assuring a supply of competent engineers; and (4) without the protection of long-established "work rules," agreed to by both management and labor, the occupation of fireman will soon cease to exist. Henry Franklyn, head of the Firemen's Union on the Long Island Railroad, presented the union point of view:

The fact that a fireman does no manual labor on a train is the reason . . . the railroads are . . . saying he's not necessary on a diesel locomotive. This we do not agree with. The accident factor would increase . . . the additional cost of the law suits and the accidents will more than pay the fireman's wages. . . . The engineer cannot see the left side of the locomotive as it nears the crossings . . . the fireman on the left side of the locomotive has that vision, and he also, on ninety per cent of the locomotives, has an emergency air brake that he can apply. . . .

Because collective bargaining and other procedures called for under the provisions of the Railway Labor Act achieved no results, President Eisenhower, in November of 1960, appointed a special Presidential Railroad Commission to deal with the question of the firemen and other matters in dispute. Both sides agreed to wait for this Commission's report.

The Presidential Commission eventually reported to President Kennedy in February, 1962. It found that firemen are not needed on freight trains, and recommended that firemen with less than ten years' service be laid off, with provisions for severance pay, retraining, and preferential hiring rights on other jobs. The Commission recommended that firemen with more than ten years' seniority should be retained in their positions. The railroads reluctantly accepted these recommendations. But H. E. Gilbert, then President of the Brotherhood of Firemen and Enginemen, called them "harsh, inhumane, and retrogressive."

After more months of deadlocked negotiations, legal proceedings, the appointment of an Emergency Board under provisions of the Railway Labor Act, and waiting for its report, the railroads decided to start dismissing firemen. The union was determined to strike. It was in this crisis that the President, in 1963, asked Congress to enact a law providing for compulsory arbitration in this case. This Congress did. In 1964, the special arbitration board established under this law ruled that 18,000 firemen were to be assigned other jobs, laid off, or retired over the next two years. "Full crew" laws, however, were on the books of six states. These required a fireman on every locomotive. The union lobbied to have these laws remain in effect. An engine crossing the border into one of these six states would have to stop to take on a fireman to comply with state law.

The agreement reached through the work of the special arbitration board expired in 1966. The debate then was resumed and it continued during the remaining years of the Johnson administration and into that of Nixon. The union demanded that the old jobs be restored. Meanwhile there was a series of legal, Congressional, and Presidential actions designed to prevent a nationwide railroad strike. Several railroads did strike during 1968. The union had adopted the policy of "whipsawing" the railroads by striking one or a few lines at a time, but avoiding a national strike. In 1968, another Emergency Board recommended that collective bargaining concerning the firemen be conducted with individual railroad lines on a crew-by-crew basis. Whatever the procedure, both sides held firmly to their earlier positions.

In July of 1970, as a result of a strike against three railroads, President Nixon appointed yet another Emergency Board. This Board recommended that the jobs of fireman and brakeman be combined, and that the old fireman's job be eliminated. Both labor and management accepted the recommendation, but they failed to agree on the seniority rights of the 21,000 firemen.

The issues

In addition to the problem of determining the facts bearing on specific disputes (for example,

whether or not firemen are necessary on freight trains for safety reasons), a number of basic questions arise with respect to labor-management disputes in any so-called essential industry. Some of these questions are:

1. What is an "essential" industry?
2. Do labor and management have a greater obligation to act with restraint in issues affecting essential industries than in those affecting less essential industries?
3. Should the rights of the general public be safeguarded by preventing strikes in essential industries? What should be the role of government in preventing such strikes? Should the President of the United States have to become involved in settling strikes?
4. Are there workable alternatives to strikes in essential industries? If so, what are they? How can management and labor be persuaded (or compelled) to accept such an alternative?
5. Should unions, union leaders, and individual union members be penalized for refusal to work? If so, how can the penalties be prescribed and enforced? Should management likewise be penalized for failure to reach an agreement with labor? Should management have to pay the wage rates set by a third party? Should labor have to accept them?

All these and many other related questions must receive thoughtful consideration from the general public. Strikes in essential industries, as well as strikes by teachers and government employees who are legally prohibited from striking (but occasionally do strike, nonetheless) have become a growing problem in this country.

Toward better understanding

QUESTIONS TO CONSIDER IN ANALYZING
THIS CASE

1. When were the work rules for the operating railroad unions established? Why did management in the late 1950's consider these rules less than satisfactory?
2. Why did the carriers in 1959 urge the appointment of a presidential commission to study work rules and wages? Why did they not negotiate directly with the unions? Why were the unions not

willing to accept the recommendations of a commission as binding?

3. The carriers held that a fireman is not needed in the cab of a diesel pulling a freight train. How did union spokesmen refute the charge of unneeded workmen?

4. Why do you think that the presidential commission made the recommendations it did in 1962? Do you agree with Mr. Gilbert's evaluation of these recommendations? Why? Why were the recommendations of the 1970 Emergency Board more acceptable to the unions?

5. The Constitution guarantees property rights. Unions hold that a worker's right to his job should be respected and safeguarded as much as property rights. Take a position on this issue and prepare a defense of it.

THINKING ABOUT THE BASIC ECONOMIC ISSUES

1. Should an industry introduce labor-saving equipment as speedily as possible in order to operate efficiently, regardless of the consequences to employees? Why or why not?

2. What should be done about workers displaced because of technological improvements?

3. How should the costs of technological unemployment be met? Consider both private and public sources of funds. Justify the use of either or both.

4. Identify the value judgments which underlie a preference for one or another solution to such questions as those asked above.

5. How would questions about wages and work rules be settled in a totalitarian state? Could management-labor conflicts take place in such countries? Why or why not?

s

a
ty
of
co-
ther
bad"
"bad"
ry as a
ividual?
ch ques-
standing
ent eco-

ction to
ional in-
ed are in
ed either
limit it

1

What are the relationships between wealth and income?

Wealth includes all material things capable of being owned and having economic value. In the *real* sense, wealth consists of such things as land and its resources, factories and their equipment, office buildings, homes and their furnishings, and other producer or consumer goods. These goods may be either privately or publicly owned. They can be exchanged for other goods or services, bought or sold, or transferred to other owners as gifts or bequests. Such property possesses economic value (utility) in that it may be used to satisfy wants.

Money enables its possessor to purchase goods (real wealth); therefore, money or the evidence of having control over money, is a claim on real wealth. Evidence of control over money may include bank accounts, the ownership of stocks or bonds, or other assets which can be readily liquidated, or converted into cash. One should bear in mind that money itself is *not* wealth in an economic sense, unless it is money made from metals which can be melted down and used for some other economic purpose. Money is, strictly speaking, a *symbol* of wealth.

In a modern economy, money is used as a medium of exchange in buying or selling economic goods and services. It is customary, therefore, to *measure* wealth in terms of money. One person may own a million dollars in cash or in a bank account, but he may possess very few material goods. Another person may own property which could be sold for one million dollars, but he may have little money in cash or bank balances. Both persons are "millionaires," however, because both have the ability to control a million dollars' worth of wealth— one through actual ownership of real wealth, the other by ownership of money which can be used to acquire real wealth.

Wealth may be privately or publicly owned. In this country, a great deal of wealth is owned by individuals and business organizations. This is called *private wealth*. Another form of wealth is that which is controlled by the government (federal, state, or local), called *public wealth*. It exists in the form of streets, highways, school and office buildings, parks, national forests, power dams, water works, military equipment, and other government-owned property which meets specific public needs. The combined total of private and public wealth sometimes is called *national wealth*.

It would be impossible to measure the national wealth accurately in monetary terms. Rough estimates have placed a current market value of about three trillion dollars ($3,000,-000,000,000) on the total amount of private and public wealth in this country. This amounts to about 15,000 dollars in wealth for every person in the country. About 80 per cent of this national wealth is privately owned; 20 per cent is in the form of public wealth.

The United States has been blessed with immense natural resources. When European settlers first came to this country they found an unbelievable abundance of minerals, timber, and fertile soil. Favorable climates made it possible to develop many kinds of agricultural activities. Rivers and lakes provided water for navigation, irrigation, and hydroelectric power. Resources of the land awaited only labor, capital, and management to make them productive. The country's natural resources have provided a basis for the development of a high level of national prosperity. But the mere existence of resources does not make a people prosperous. Knowledge of how to use resources effectively is the magic key to prosperity.

American technology promotes efficient production. When Europeans discovered the New World, they brought with them a relatively advanced technology. This technology has been

A symbol of value: money

Money can be any commodity which is in such steady demand that it can be easily exchanged at any time for other goods. Ancient peoples found that lumps of metal were a handy, lasting kind of money, but troublesome to weigh and test for purity. Reliable money encourages trade, so ancient rulers began to issue coins of a standard weight and quality. A later development was paper money, valueless in itself, but guaranteed to represent a fixed amount of value.

The copper ring, **a,** *used as money in Egypt 3000 years ago, was easy to carry and always valuable to people who needed this relatively scarce metal for tools, weapons, and jewelry. On the Malay peninsula in Southeast Asia, "tree money" made of metal was used,* **b.** *A bronze spade,* **c,** *served as currency in ancient China.*

a
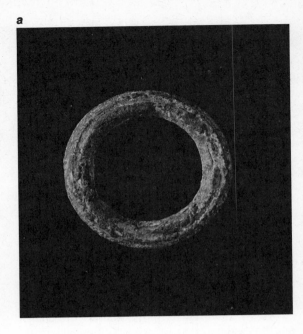

b
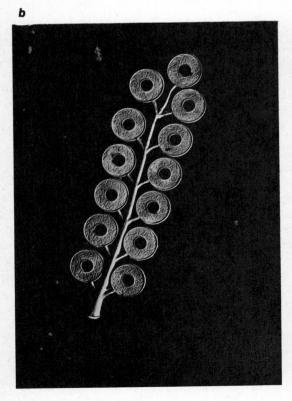

c

The value of paper money depends more on the faith of the holder and is also influenced by variations in international trade. Before the Constitution was ratified, different states, towns, and banks all issued paper money—even for only one cent, **d.** During the Civil War, Confederate dollars, **e,** became worth very little because so many were issued without enough backing. The financial panic accompanying the depression eliminated convertible gold notes, **g,** when the private ownership of gold was disallowed in the United States. Food stamps, **f,** are used as money in food stores by people eligible to buy them from the federal government because of their low income.

e

f

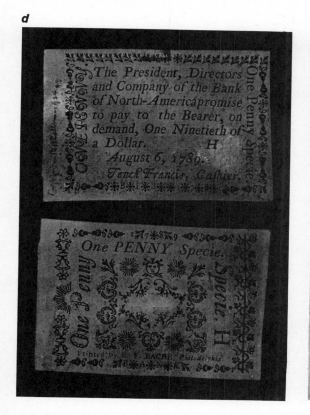

d

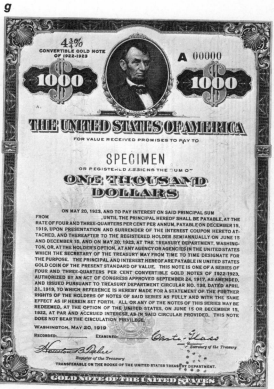

g

constantly improved by making education widely available, and through an economic and political system which encourages inventors and management to seek better ways of doing things. Americans have reduced the costs of production and sought out and used natural resources which were completely unknown to this country's original inhabitants. The result has been a great increase in productivity, wealth, and standards of living. America's problem is not a lack of productive capacity. Rather it is to make sure that all Americans receive a fair share of what is produced.

The country's economic and political system encourages productivity. The American economic system enables most individuals to prepare themselves for the occupations of their choice and permits them to reap the financial rewards of their efforts. The principle of equality of opportunity is reflected in the country's laws. These laws uphold the personal rights of individuals and guarantee property rights.

In an atmosphere of freedom, many feel inclined to try something new, to seek something better, to improve themselves.

A person who is confident that he will be rewarded for the effort and capital that he puts into a business venture is encouraged to explore new possibilities. A political system that assures people of protection under the law creates confidence. The people of America have sometimes worked night and day to develop resources or to create new inventions.

The "forty-niners" went west because they knew that the gold they found in California would be theirs. Today the same incentive governs the business corporations which send men into remote areas in search of new deposits of ore and oil. Likewise, the profit motive impels individuals and business firms to develop new products and new methods of production and distribution. Managers expect to realize gains from their hard work. But American society as a whole gains, too, when more of

Uneven distribution of the world's income and agricultural resources

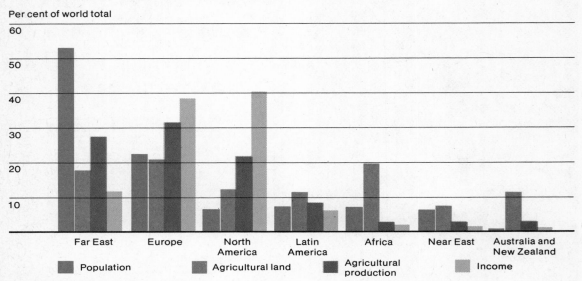

Per cent of world total

Population   Agricultural land   Agricultural production   Income

Source: Scientific American

the "good things of life" are made available to more people at lower prices. Adam Smith, "the father of economics," once said that the free-enterprise profits-seeking manager is guided by an "invisible hand" which promotes the interest of society even though this may not be his primary purpose.

Private wealth has played an important role in American society. It has already been suggested that the profit motive is at the very heart of the American economic system. Competition among businessmen for a greater share of economic wealth undoubtedly has been one of the reasons why the economy has forged ahead of those of many older nations. Such competition in the nineteenth century led to the accumulation of a number of private fortunes. As a result, the multi-millionaire emerged as a symbol of the type of "self-made man" possible in a free enterprise economy. In general, most Americans do not resent— indeed they may even admire—the successful businessman who gets ahead by dint of his own efforts, initiative, and ingenuity.

Today most citizens regard efforts to eliminate poverty from the national scene as a not impossible objective for a country so richly endowed with natural resources. The influential rich man who flaunts his wealth before those of modest circumstances is not a fashionable figure now—if indeed he ever was. Nor is the millionaire playboy who squanders riches he has inherited from his forebears' labors. Instead, Americans have come to expect that great wealth carries with it a corresponding sense of responsibility to the society and the economic and social system that made such wealth possible. It is not surprising, therefore, that many colleges and universities, hospitals, and research foundations are supported in large part from incomes produced by endowments given them by wealthy individuals.

Most people do not desire wealth for itself. Only misers want to accumulate and hoard wealth for its own sake. Greedy King Midas, according to Greek mythology, became very

Industrial production index

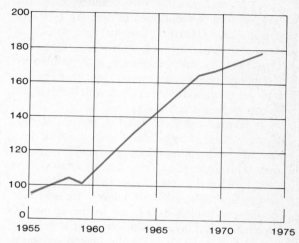

1969 and 1970 are estimates

Source: Statistical Abstract

unhappy when everything he touched turned into gold. One cannot eat gold—or land, factory buildings, or most other forms of capital or representative wealth. Usually people value wealth because it aids them in satisfying more basic desires.

Some kinds of wealth do provide direct satisfactions. A family enjoys a comfortable home with attractive furniture and modern conveniences. Some members of the family may get great pleasure from a late-model car, or may enjoy television. The younger members may get satisfaction from clothes in the latest styles. Art lovers appreciate fine paintings; music lovers, a good concert. But all of these things, as well as the essentials of food, clothing, and shelter, are acquired from income—and incomes, in turn, come either from labor (or managerial efforts) or from wealth.

Wealth is desired primarily because it brings in an income. Income in the *real* sense is a *flow of goods and services which can be used to satisfy wants.* (In contrast, wealth is a *stock* *of goods.*) In a strict economic sense, the enjoyments and satisfactions coming from the items of wealth mentioned earlier are forms of real income. Usually, however, one thinks of income as one does of wealth—in monetary terms. That is, one's income is a given number of dollars per week, month, or year, rather than all the goods or services which might be bought with these dollars.

As pointed out in Chapter 4, income is produced by and distributed among the four factors of production—labor (wages), management (profits), land (rent), and capital (interest). The last two factors, of course, are forms of wealth. All four factors are essential for the production of income in the economy. Generally speaking, persons owning the greatest amounts of wealth receive the largest incomes.

Although the greatest *percentage* of the total national income goes to labor, wealth is not equally distributed among the population. A relatively small number of people own a relatively large portion of the wealth. It has been estimated that less than 1 per cent of this country's population owns at least 30 per cent of its private wealth.

American incomes are high by world-wide standards. High and increasing productivity has made American *per capita income* (the average income, arrived at by dividing total national income by the number of people in the country) by far the highest in the world. Furthermore, the distribution of this income is more equitable than in many other countries. Some nations have a few very rich people and a large number of extremely poor. In the United States, there are both rich and poor, but the great majority are in the "middle income" brackets. That is, incomes are sufficient to provide for primary needs, and also to have something left over for comforts and luxuries. Such nations as Sweden, Denmark, and the Netherlands probably distribute their incomes more equally, even though on the average they are less affluent than the United States.

How the national income was divided in a recent year

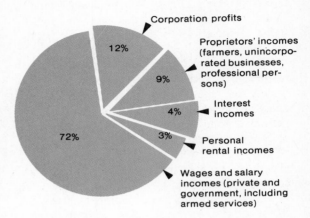

The division of national income tends to remain fairly constant.

Source: Statistical Abstract

National income *is the total of all incomes in the country.* In the real sense, national income consists of all the goods and services produced—either privately or publicly—by the four factors of production. It is more convenient to measure national income in monetary terms rather than in real terms, however, just as it is more convenient to measure wealth and personal incomes in terms of money.

National income usually is measured for the year or by quarterly periods. These measures give an indication of how well (or how poorly) the economy is performing compared to past periods and other countries. These statistics are watched closely by public officials, business and labor union leaders, and others concerned with the nation's economic health. Even newspapers and newscasters frequently refer to the status of the national income. It is important, therefore, to understand how national income is calculated and measured.

CHECK UP

1. Define these economic terms: wealth, private wealth, public wealth, national wealth, money. What are the uses of money?

2. How does a nation's wealth depend on natural resources? Advanced technology and efficient production? Its social, economic, and political systems?

3. What role has private wealth played in the development of this country? Why are men of great wealth in American society expected to display a sense of social responsibility?

4. Why is per capita income high in this country? Define the term *national income*. Is it equitably distributed? Explain

2

How is national income measured?

The United States Department of Commerce calculates national income, and its figures are released to news sources and published in government publications. Fairly reliable figures are available for each year since 1929; the figures for earlier years are less exact.

Only the final monetary value of production is included in national income measurement. In arriving at a monetary value for production, it is essential that only the final values of goods and services be included. A new automobile, for example, is included at its final selling price in the dealer's salesroom. This price includes all the costs (including profits) that went into the car, from the mining, refining, and manufacturing of its metal parts, through assembly, and delivery by the dealer to the consumer.

If a new car sells for 3000 dollars, that is the figure included in national income. The figure would be much higher if the costs incurred at all stages of the manufacture and distribution of the vehicle were totaled. For example, parts

and subassembly manufacturers might pay 600 dollars to metal producers for materials. An automobile manufacturer, then, might pay 1200 dollars for the parts and subassemblies. After assembling, the auto manufacturer might put the car into a dealer's hands for 2600 dollars. Then the dealer sells it to a customer for 3000 dollars. If all these figures are added the total is 7400 dollars. But this total includes 4400 dollars for items counted more than once. The actual increase in available economic goods is only 3000 dollars, and that is the amount included in national income measurement.

Note, however, that the $3000 final value of this car is the same as the total of the *net* values added at each stage of production. The original materials bought by the parts and subassembly manufacturers had a value of $600. These manufacturers added another $600 in value before the materials went to the auto manufacturer ($1200 minus $600). The auto company added another $1400 in value ($2600 minus $1200). The dealer, in turn, added another $400 in value ($3000 minus $2600). That is, all the net values added (or utilities created) at each stage of production add up to the total final value of a product.

Only new production is included in national income. Goods produced during earlier time periods are not included in current national income measurements. If such goods were not excluded, current production would appear to be higher than it actually is. For example, the production of a new car or the building of a new home increases national income. Something exists which did not exist before. But the role of a used jalopy or the resale of a home adds nothing new to the economy. National income is not increased (except, perhaps, by the amount of "services" involved in making the sales, as measured by the salesmen's commissions or profits)

Not all new items are included in national income measurements. Some items, especially services, cannot be valued easily in monetary terms. Thus, they are omitted in calculating national income. It is feasible to calculate the rental value of owner-occupied homes and include this in the measurement, but it would be very difficult to place a monetary value on all the services performed by a housewife in her own home. These services, although certainly valuable, are not included. If, on the other hand, a housewife pays a maid 80 dollars a week to do her housework, this sum of money is included in the calculation of national income. It can be measured in monetary terms.

National income figures are not completely accurate. Although the best possible methods are used in obtaining information and making calculations, no one pretends that the reported national income is completely precise. Estimates are necessarily involved. But if the same methods are used consistently, the mistakes and omissions of one year are not likely to differ greatly from those of another year. The figures, in other words, are useful and reliable for purposes of comparison.

Absolute precision is not necessary since the national income figures are intended to reveal economic *trends*. How well (or how poorly) is the national economy doing this year as compared to previous years? In what direction and at what speed is the national economy moving? If things are going badly, for example, the government wants to know this as soon as possible in order to take corrective steps.

Several different terms are used in referring to various measurements of national income. Economists, financial experts, businessmen, and government officials have developed a standard terminology for describing the various segments of national income. Each, therefore, has a different meaning. The following are important terms used in referring to national income:

The composition of gross national product

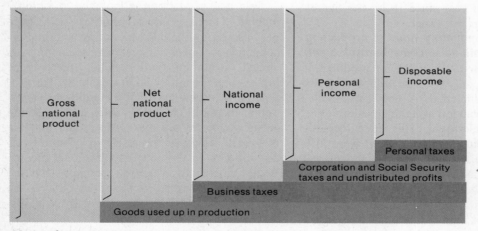

National income, or gross national product (GNP), measures the performance of the whole economy. This diagram makes clear the relationship between major components of GNP without indicating their relative size (see table on page 321). Note, for example, that net national product is GNP minus value of goods used in production.

Gross National Product (often abbreviated to GNP). This is the estimated final total dollar value of all goods and services produced in the nation. This basic national income figure is usually calculated and reported quarterly and annually.

Net National Product (NNP). This is GNP *minus* the value of goods used up or worn out in the production process. For many purposes, this is considered the most important of the national income measures. It tells how much better off (or worse off) the nation is in comparison to other time periods or other countries.

National Income (NI). This is NNP *minus* indirect business taxes (that is, minus taxes other than corporation and personal income taxes, Social Security contributions, and other personal taxes). "Indirect business taxes" include excises, gasoline taxes, and sales taxes. NI can be looked upon as the total "before tax" incomes *earned* by the factors of production, or by individuals, business firms, and government agencies involved in producing and selling goods and services.

Personal Income (PI). This is NI *minus* corporation taxes, Social Security taxes, and undistributed corporation profits, and *plus* "transfer payments" made by government to persons for various reasons. (Government payments to individuals for such things as Social Security retirement benefits, unemployment compensation, welfare, and the like, are called transfer payments because they transfer income from one source to another and are not made in exchange for any productive service—that is, they do not increase or decrease GNP.) This

Components of national income

Gross national product	$1,151.8
Net national product	1,048.1
National income	934.7
Personal income	935.9
Disposable income	795.1

(in billions)

Source: Statistical Abstract, 1973

figure shows the total "before-tax" incomes of individuals.

Disposable Income (DI). This is PI *minus* all personal taxes, and might be called "net" or "take-home" income. This is the portion of income that determines one's standard of living. This disposable income is either *spent for consumption or saved*.

The diagram on page 320 and the table on this page show the relationships between these various measures of national income.

Incomes are derived from expenditures. The "circular flow" of income (mentioned in Chapter 5) is one of the most basic, most important, and simplest of economic principles. Unfortunately, it frequently is not understood by persons who lack knowledge of economics.

Basically, the "circular flow" principle holds that every monetary *expenditure* made by anyone (individual, business organization, government agency) for consumption or investment must be monetary *income* to someone else. Or, put in another way, everyone's money income is derived from someone else's spending. What one person spends, another receives.

Expenditures and incomes, in other words, are opposite sides of the same coin. In the economy as a whole, if expenditures increase, incomes increase in like amount; that is, GNP increases. If total expenditures decrease, total incomes decrease in the same way—GNP declines. This principle has a significant effect on the national economy, and underlies national economic policy.

GNP can be viewed as a four-way measure. National income is a measure of the *final values* at each stage of production. (Recall the example of the automobile.) GNP is also made up of total dollar *expenditures,* which are the same as total dollar *incomes* in the economy. Thus, GNP is a measure of four things—final values, values added, expenditures, and incomes. All these, of course, are the same in monetary terms.

National income is measured in terms of both "current dollars" and "constant dollars."

Sales of goods and services are reported in national income statistics at their actual prices when the transactions occurred. These are known as *current dollar* figures. But since many prices constantly change, the general price level (or the purchasing power of the dollar) is also moving upward or downward. For many years the dollar's purchasing power has tended to decrease—that is, the general price level has been increasing.

If one wishes to learn from the GNP or any other measure of national income how well or how poorly the nation is doing in comparison with past years, one must make adjustments for differing price levels during the years considered. This is done by computing price index numbers (see Chapter 3). Some *base year* is chosen, and current dollar national income figures are adjusted upward or downward according to changes in the general price level since that base year. This gives a *constant dollar* figure for national income in terms of base year prices. That is, it eliminates the monetary effects of price changes and shows how much the true output of goods and services has changed.

The year 1958 is frequently used as the base in arriving at constant dollar national income. An example will show how the adjustment from current dollars to constant dollars affects the figures for GNP during selected years. In 1929, *current* dollar GNP was 103 billion dollars, but in 1958 *constant* dollar terms it would have been 204 billion dollars. This difference reflects the fact that the general price level almost doubled between 1929 and 1958. In 1968, current dollar GNP was 861 billion dollars, while

The interaction of spending and production in the economy

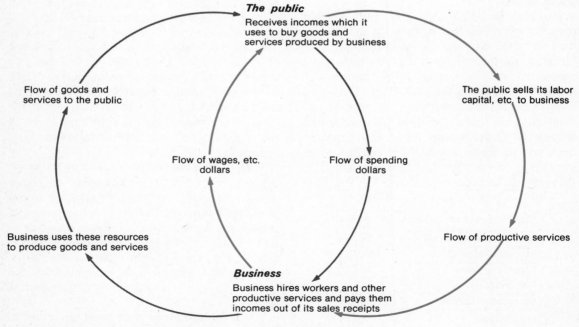

Source: Economic Education in the Schools, *Committee for Economic Development*

in 1958 constant dollars it was 707 billion. This reflects a general price level increase of about 22 per cent between 1958 and 1968. Or stated in another way, it shows that goods or services costing one dollar in 1958 cost $1.22 in 1968.

Constant dollar national income usually increases from year to year. As the population increases, more people are working. Also, because of better educated and more skilled workers, improved production methods, and greater use of capital equipment, the average productivity per worker generally increases at a rate of 2 to 3 per cent yearly.

With more people working more efficiently each year, the real output of goods and services increases. It is only during periods of severe recession or depression, when many workers are unemployed, that national income fails to increase. Between 1929 and 1969 the national income failed to increase in the years 1930 through 1933, 1938, 1945 through 1947, and 1954.

During the period 1950 to 1970 GNP has increased by about 110 per cent and DI by about 208 per cent in constant (1958) dollar terms. Meantime, the country's population increased by about 35 per cent. This means that the *average* real income or purchasing power per person during these two decades, despite price increases, has risen by about 157 per cent. Remember, though, that "average" can be misleading when applied to particular individuals. Increases in purchasing power, like incomes, are not equally distributed among all groups and individuals. In this connection, you may wish to refer back to Chapter 5.

GNP and other national income figures provide a rough measure of the country's economic "well being." GNP actually is a measure of the output of all goods and services. When constant dollar GNP is high and rising, this means that many people and large amounts of the factors of production are employed. If GNP is declining, the economy is in trouble—people are unemployed, and capital and natural resources are not being used fully. Or when con-

How the gross national product has increased

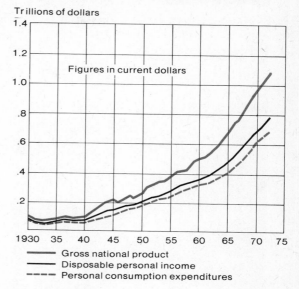

Trillions of dollars

Figures in current dollars

Gross national product
Disposable personal income
Personal consumption expenditures

Source: Statistical Abstract

stant dollar DI increases faster than population, average purchasing power is increasing. Consequently, national income figures are watched closely by economists, businessmen, labor union leaders, and government officials concerned with the country's economic health.

As has been pointed out, the national output sometimes declines. For the country to maintain its present state of economic health, the national income must keep pace with the population growth. Average living standards can increase only when real (constant dollar) national income increases more rapidly than population. It is quite possible that small increases in national income can be more than offset by larger increases in population, thus resulting in lower average living standards. This is the situation which exists in some of the developing nations.

On the other hand, current dollar national income sometimes can increase too fast for economic health. When people seeking emptoy-

Statistical Economist

William Petty

(1623–1687)

Many great economists have been successful men of affairs. One of these was William Petty. A poor English lad, he went to sea as a cabin-boy at an early age. Finding himself stranded in France, he gained admission to a Jesuit college, where he mastered French, Latin, Greek, arithmetic, geometry, and astronomy by the age of fifteen. Afterwards he served in the Royal Navy, studied medicine in Holland, France, and England, and became a "doctor of phisick" and a professor of anatomy.

Because of his services as physician-general in Cromwell's army and later as surveyor-general of Ireland, Petty acquired a large Irish estate. Here he developed iron works, marble quarries, lead mines, fisheries, and a trade in timber. He also invented, among other things, a copying machine, an "engine" for propelling ships, and a double-bottomed ship (which unfortunately sank after a few voyages). His last quarter-century was spent in writing, mainly on economic subjects.

Petty favored an inductive approach to economics. In his own words, he tried to express himself ". . . in Terms of Number, Weight, or Measure; to use only Arguments of Sense, and to consider only such Causes as have visible Foundations in Nature."

In accordance with this philosophy and with his belief that the value of any good depends upon the amount of labor necessary to produce it, he attempted to establish a fixed basic unit of value. This, he said, was the amount necessary to sustain one person for one day.

Petty's book, *Political Arithmetik,* published three years after his death, was the first attempt to measure and compare the national wealth and incomes of various countries. He was the first economist to use statistical data in combination with economic analysis.

In addition to pioneering in both the statistical approach and in the national wealth and income measurement approach to economics, Petty expressed several other "modern ideas." He recognized the circular flow of income, and discussed the importance of velocity as well as of the amount of money in circulation. He saw that public expenditures could be used to combat unemployment, and argued that such expenditures should be for "productive" rather than for "wasteful" purposes. Taxation, he felt, should be designed as far as possible to leave everyone in the same relative position as he was in before paying taxes.

Contrary to most economists of his time, Petty believed that a nation's wealth and income depends more upon production than upon foreign trade. Consequently, he saw no advantage in government efforts to prevent the export of gold, set low interest rates, or otherwise interfere with trade or production. He summed up his views on production by saying that "labour is the father and active principle of wealth, lands are the mother."

ment find it easily, and all capital and natural resources are already being used fairly efficiently, the real output of goods and services cannot be further increased substantially. During such times, some producers may bid up the prices for scarce labor and resources. This means that almost everyone—workers and owners—receives more money. But there is no additional output available to be bought with this additional money. Consumers bid up the prices of the limited available output. Prices rise, and so does current dollar national income. The result is inflation, which hurts many people, especially those whose incomes do not increase as fast as does the price level.

The same inflationary effect may develop when an unusually large portion of the nation's output ceases to be available to consumers. This happens in wartime, when almost all workers may be receiving good wages. But much of the output consists of weapons rather than consumer goods. The resulting short supply of consumer goods pushes up the prices one must pay for them. In smaller degree, the same situation may arise when large quantities of goods are sent abroad for foreign aid programs, or when substantial resources are used for space exploration or other similar purposes. With money to spend but a scarcity of consumer goods to buy, prices may rise.

During World War II and the Korean War, the federal government attempted to control the price level by fixing maximum prices for most goods and services. This kept prices lower than they otherwise would have been, but some "black markets" developed. That is, some sellers charged and received prices higher than permitted by law. During these periods, people saved more than they would if a greater abundance of goods and services had been available. During the Vietnam War, however, the government imposed no controls on prices, nor did it attempt to reallocate the nation's resources, reorder its priorities, or greatly increase taxes to pay for the war. Consumer spending continued unabated, and prices increased steadily

into the 1970's, even after the federal government ordered cutbacks in domestic programs. The curtailment of such programs as space and aid to education brought about a considerable amount of unemployment; but among those who were employed, spending did not significantly decline. Consequently, the nation was faced with the dual problem of inflationary prices and relatively high unemployment, or recession.

In summary, the economy can become "overheated" from inflation or "underheated" from recession and unemployment. Neither is desirable from the viewpoints of most people. Most Americans desire income growth sufficient to provide full employment for population and resources, with an increase in standards of living but without unduly large price increases. Such a balance is not easy to maintain.

CHECK UP

1. What is meant by national income? Why is national income expressed in money? What items are not included? Define each of the following terms: GNP, NNP, NI, PI, DI. Explain the "circular flow" principle.

2. Why is national income expressed in "constant dollars" as well as "current dollars"? Why has constant dollar income tended to increase? What conclusions can be drawn from this fact?

3. Why can current dollar income at times increase too fast for economic health? Why can a war produce a similar situation? How can the government slow the rate of inflation?

Clinching the main ideas

Wealth includes those useful material things having economic value and usually but not always owned by individuals, businesses, or governments (the public). It can be looked upon as a *stock* of goods or resources. *Income* is a *flow* of goods and services produced by that wealth. Wealth is desired mainly because it yields an income. Wealth and income usually are measured in monetary terms for convenience, although strictly speaking they consist of *real* goods or services.

A nation's wealth and income are based both upon its natural and human resources, plus the willingness and ability of its people to make productive use of these resources. This country is fortunate in having an abundance of natural resources. Americans have made their country the world's wealthiest nation and have achieved the world's highest income levels.

The important branch of economics dealing with the national economy as a whole is called *macroeconomics* (in contrast with *microeconomics,* which deals with the particular parts of the economy). Macroeconomics is approached through the study of the *national income.*

Real national income consists of all the goods and services that are produced. For convenience, this is measured both in *current dollar* and *constant dollar* terms. Constant dollar national income measurements reveal much about the general health of the economy. This knowledge provides a basis for such corrective policy actions as appear desirable.

National income is expressed in terms of *Gross National Product, Net National Product, National Income, Personal Income,* and *Disposable Income.* Each of these terms has a different meaning.

Ideally, Americans would like to see national income high, rising faster than population increases, and without rapidly rising prices—in other words, prosperity without undue inflation. Many government economic policies, which significantly affect all citizens, are directed toward this goal. These major policies will be discussed in the chapters which follow.

Chapter 13 review

Terms to understand

1. macroeconomics
2. wealth
3. private wealth
4. public wealth
5. national wealth
6. per capita income
7. economic trends
8. GNP
9. NNP
10. income
11. personal income
12. national income
13. "circular flow" principle
14. constant dollar

What do you think?

1. The Indians who inhabited what is now the United States about 1500 A.D. had a low level of living in terms of present-day standards. Why?

2. Most developing countries would like to introduce mass production of goods. Why? Why do they find this difficult?

3. Should foreign aid to a developing country be spent for consumers' goods or producers' goods? Why?

4. Contrast the allocation of productive resources in this country and in the Soviet Union. What are advantages and disadvantages in each system?

5. Since World War II such countries as France, West Germany, and Japan have had a higher average annual increase in GNP than the United States. Why?

6. If average annual increase in population is about the same as average annual increase in GNP, what does this mean for the nation in question?

7. If the great powers should adopt a program of disarmament which next year reduced all defense budgets by 50 per cent, would a worldwide depression follow? Why? What could be done with the money saved in this country?

Applying your knowledge of economics

1. Bearing in mind the meaning of GNP, check: (a) the statistics showing the number of automobiles made in 1945, 1955, and 1965, and the most recent year for which there are data; (b) the number of families which owned automobiles in those same years. Did the number of cars manufactured maintain the same percentage of importance in GNP? Why or why not? (Figures may be obtained in the *Statistical Abstract of the United States.* If you cannot locate statistics for the four years asked for in this question, take different years which you can locate.)

2. Use *Reader's Guide* and the card index in your library to find articles and books dealing with the rate of economic growth in this country and in the USSR since world War II. Is there general agreement among the authors as to the significance of these statistics? Try to summarize the points of view expressed.

chapter fourteen

Government services and taxation

1. **What government services do taxes buy?**
2. **What kinds of taxes do Americans pay?**

Everyone who receives the protection of society owes a return for the benefit, and the fact of living in society renders it indispensable that each should be bound to observe a certain line of conduct towards the rest.

JOHN STUART MILL, On Liberty

The saying, "Nothing is certain but death and taxes," points out a significant truth. Everyone pays many kinds of taxes. Some taxes are hidden in the prices of things people buy. Others are direct and clearly evident. Altogether, the various taxes paid by the average person add up to the largest single "expenditure" made during his lifetime.

Taxes are compulsory payments made to government by individuals or organizations. Although no one likes to pay taxes, everyone enjoys many of the benefits financed by the tax funds. Benefits and payments, however, are not always proportionate. Some pay much more (or less) and receive much less (or more) than others. Almost everyone thinks his own taxes are too high and his neighbor's taxes too low.

"Taxation without representation" was one of the rallying cries in the movement for American independence. Today's taxes are much higher than those paid to the British government by the American colonists, but today's taxpayers, by and large, are not without representation. Elected federal, state, and local government officials determine the kinds of taxes to be levied and the funds to be appropriated to provide the kinds of government services citizens want. (Sometimes citizens vote directly on taxes, rather than having tax laws passed by elected officials.)

Whenever a majority of voters feel that their taxes are too high or unjust, they can elect new officials. These men may or may not be able to reduce spending or to reform the tax structure. Yet to a degree, the amount and kinds of taxes levied, are determined by the people. The increased cost of government has led some cities to levy sales and even income taxes. In order to raise revenue, New York City has sponsored off-track betting. Other cities are faced with similar financial crises.

This chapter considers first the principal kinds of government services supported by tax funds. Next it examines the principal kinds of taxes and their effects.

1

What government services do taxes buy?

Americans seldom stop to think how many and varied are the services of government (local, state, and federal), and how much they receive for the taxes paid. People tend to take many of these services for granted, although they would miss them immediately were they no longer available.

Local governments perform many essential services. The largest portion of taxes paid to local governments is used to build, maintain, and operate the public schools. Because of the increasing emphasis on education in American society, and the growing population, more and more tax funds are needed for this purpose with each passing year. The building and repair of highways, roads, and streets is the next largest item in the budgets of local governments. Public welfare—care of the aged, the needy, and others unable to care for themselves and who are not aided sufficiently by other levels of government—also is costly.

Public health services, including an adequate water supply and an efficient waste disposal system, are essential functions of local government. The same is true of such protective services as police and fire departments, as well as recreation facilities such as parks and playgrounds. The salaries of local government officials and employees are also a major item in the budgets of local governments.

In addition to these basic local governmental services, some parts of the country receive additional services from local "special service" districts. These districts may be organized to provide water for irrigation, fire protection in rural areas, control over harmful plants or insects in farming areas, or to operate airports, hospitals, parks, or zoos. Altogether in the

The tax dollar in state and local government

1 Income

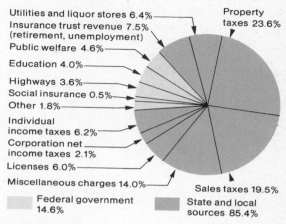

Utilities and liquor stores 6.4%
Insurance trust revenue 7.5% (retirement, unemployment)
Public welfare 4.6%
Education 4.0%
Highways 3.6%
Social insurance 0.5%
Other 1.8%
Individual income taxes 6.2%
Corporation net income taxes 2.1%
Licenses 6.0%
Miscellaneous charges 14.0%
Property taxes 23.6%
Sales taxes 19.5%

Federal government 14.6%
State and local sources 85.4%

2 Expenditures

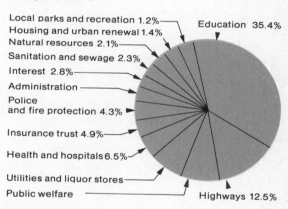

Local parks and recreation 1.2%
Housing and urban renewal 1.4%
Natural resources 2.1%
Sanitation and sewage 2.3%
Interest 2.8%
Administration
Police and fire protection 4.3%
Insurance trust 4.9%
Health and hospitals 6.5%
Utilities and liquor stores
Public welfare
Education 35.4%
Highways 12.5%

Source: Statistical Abstract

United States, there are more than 20,000 such special service districts, in addition to counties, municipalities, townships, and school districts.

State governments also provide necessary services. As is the case with local governments, the largest expenditure of state governments is for education. This includes the funds for state colleges and universities, as well as a part of the funds for local public schools. Also, as is true for local governments, the next largest state expenditure is for highway construction and maintenance.

States also spend large sums for welfare programs, unemployment compensation, and public health. Furthermore, state tax funds maintain (or help to maintain) state police, militia, and civil defense forces, as well as the courts which dispense justice and the prisons and corrective institutions where criminals are confined. The states often operate various kinds of recreational programs, maintaining state parks, forest reserves, and a variety of public buildings.

The total of all state government expenditures is not as large as that of all local governments. States spend less than one-sixth of the total tax dollars, while local government agencies spend more than one-fourth. All local and state government expenditures combined, therefore, are considerably less than total federal expenditures.

The federal government has many important responsibilities. The Preamble to the Constitution of the United States states that the basic purposes of the national government are to "establish justice," "insure domestic tranquility," "provide for the common defense," "promote the general welfare," and "secure the blessings of liberty." Specific Articles in the Constitution give to Congress the authority to do these things. For example, Article I, Section 8, states that "The Congress shall have power to lay and collect taxes, . . . to pay the debts and provide for the common defense and general welfare of the United States." These are big and expensive responsibilities.

The federal court system applies the laws enacted by Congress. A legal case involving an alleged violation of federal law is heard in a federal District Court. Decisions of these courts may be appealed to a federal Court of Appeals, and perhaps even to the United States Supreme Court. The decision of the Supreme Court is final. This Court primarily interprets how the United States Constitution should be applied. At many times in this country's history, the Supreme Court has handed down decisions which have significantly affected the economy. This Court is the ultimate legal protector of justice and liberty in the nation.

The federal government provides for national defense. By far the largest expenditure of the federal government is for the national defense. During recent years, defense expenditures have accounted for more than 40 per cent of all federal expenditures. The war in Vietnam greatly increased defense expenditures during the 1960's, but even without this increase the Department of Defense budget is much larger than that of any other department.

Defense funds are spent for (1) the purchase of military equipment and supplies for the Army, Navy, and Air Force; (2) the compensation of millions of men and women in the armed forces; (3) the maintenance of military bases in the United States and abroad; and (4) the supervision of defense-related research programs such as the development of improved missiles and other weapons, as well as communications and military intelligence systems designed to warn against possible enemy attack.

Other kinds of federal expenditures are closely related to national defense. Veteran's benefits and services amount to several billions of dollars annually, as does the conduct of international affairs (including foreign aid to friendly nations). In a sense, even the large sums spent in building major highways, developing natural resources, and carrying on explorations in outer space contribute to the nation's defense.

Were these defense-related programs included with defense expenditures, it is likely that about one-half of the total federal expenditures in a given year might be listed under "providing for the common defense." It is regrettable that so high a percentage of the total tax dollars—money sorely needed for other purposes—must be spent for protection against possible aggression. It is a fact of life, however, that Americans are living in an imperfect world. Seemingly a majority of the voters and their elected representatives believe that this country

The federal budget (1973)

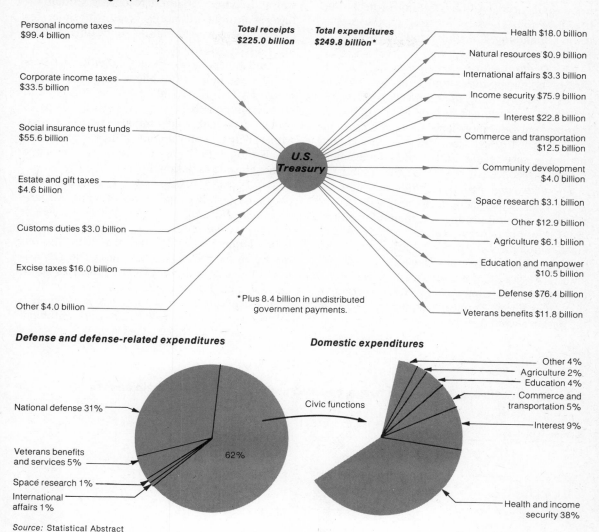

Personal income taxes $99.4 billion

Corporate income taxes $33.5 billion

Social insurance trust funds $55.6 billion

Estate and gift taxes $4.6 billion

Customs duties $3.0 billion

Excise taxes $16.0 billion

Other $4.0 billion

Total receipts $225.0 billion

Total expenditures $249.8 billion*

U.S. Treasury

*Plus 8.4 billion in undistributed government payments.

Health $18.0 billion

Natural resources $0.9 billion

International affairs $3.3 billion

Income security $75.9 billion

Interest $22.8 billion

Commerce and transportation $12.5 billion

Community development $4.0 billion

Space research $3.1 billion

Other $12.9 billion

Agriculture $6.1 billion

Education and manpower $10.5 billion

Defense $76.4 billion

Veterans benefits $11.8 billion

Defense and defense-related expenditures

National defense 31%

Veterans benefits and services 5%

Space research 1%

International affairs 1%

62%

Civic functions

Domestic expenditures

Other 4%

Agriculture 2%

Education 4%

Commerce and transportation 5%

Interest 9%

Health and income security 38%

Source: Statistical Abstract

must be militarily powerful. Large expenditures for defense are likely to continue during the foreseeable future.

Promotion of "the general welfare" calls for a variety of expenditures. Through the *Department of Health, Education and Welfare* (HEW), the national government furthers the well-being of citizens. One of the most important functions of this Department is the assistance provided older persons and their dependents through the Social Security program (see Chapter 8). HEW also administers various aid programs for the urban and rural poor, and encourages education through subsidies for various programs. The Public Health Service carries on research and seeks to bring the benefits of advances in medical knowledge to more and more people. The Food and Drug Administration protects the health of consumers by insisting on the proper testing, handling, labeling, and packaging of foods and drugs.

The *Department of Labor* promotes the welfare of both employees and employers. It enforces laws providing minimum wages and establishing maximum hours of work; publishes information on labor legislation, wages, and prices; and through its collective bargaining mediation service aids labor and management in reaching collective bargaining agreements.

The *Department of Agriculture* sponsors research and experimentation designed to improve agricultural production, maintain soil fertility, develop improved plants and farm animals, and control diseases that affect crops and livestock. The Agriculture Department also administers price supports and other kinds of aid to farmers (see Chapter 11). One of its divisions, the Forest Service, has supervision over the nation's great forests.

The *Department of the Interior* helps to control and conserve natural resources so that future generations will not be faced with shortages of essential raw materials. Among this department's many responsibilities are the construction and supervision of major irrigation projects and the regulation of public grazing and timber lands. Its Fish and Wildlife Service, working in co-operation with state governments, helps to protect fish and wild animals. Its Bureau of Mines helps in developing mineral resources; the National Park Service manages the large areas set aside as national parks.

The *Postal Service* (now a government corporation) handles mail services. The *Department of Housing and Urban Development* (HUD) is concerned with making more and better homes available, and also with improving living conditions in the cities. The *Department of Transportation* (DOT) promotes better and safer land, water, and air transportation.

The *Department of Justice* has the responsibility for seeing that federal laws are enforced.

Public and private expenditures for health, education, welfare, and income maintenance

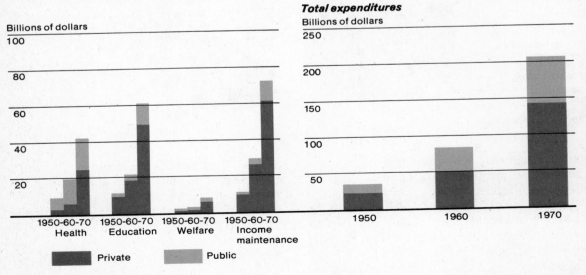

Source: Social Security Bulletin

The growing expenditure of public funds

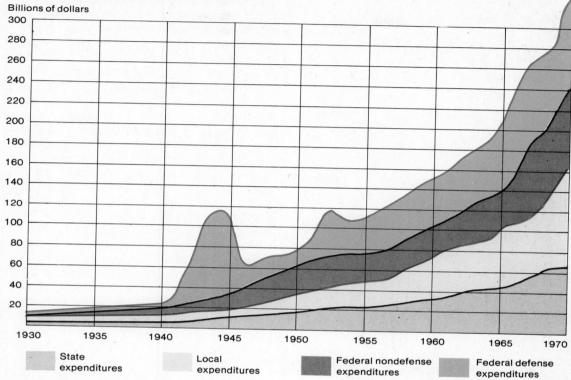

Billions of dollars

State expenditures | Local expenditures | Federal nondefense expenditures | Federal defense expenditures

Source: Statistical Abstract

It particularly watches for violations of the anti-monopoly laws, such as the Sherman Anti-Trust Act and the Clayton Act (see Chapter 10). It also works closely with the Federal Trade Commission (FTC) and the Securities and Exchange Commission (SEC) and other independent regulatory agencies. The Federal Bureau of Investigation (FBI) is an agency within the Justice Department which investigates suspected violations of federal laws.

The *Department of Commerce* engages in many activities to keep the economy running more smoothly. A few of the services provided by this department's many agencies are: (1) tabulation of population statistics—the Bureau of the Census; (2) weather forecasting—the Weather Bureau; (3) registration of patents, copyrights, and trademarks—the Patent Office and Copyright Office; (4) establishing legal standards for weights and measures—the National Bureau of Standards.

The foregoing listing of federal agencies and services is far from complete. Yet it serves to suggest why taxes are high.

The cost of government services is increasing. The costs of government more than doubled between 1960 and 1970. This increase was true both for the federal government and for state and local governments. It is easy to see why defense spending increased during the 1960's. But federal non-defense spending actually increased even more rapidly than defense spend-

Apostle of the Single Tax

Henry George

(1839–1897)

During his childhood, Henry George wondered why some people lived in poverty and others in luxury. Economic inequality in the United States and in other countries which he visited had a great effect on George's later thinking.

After prospecting unsuccessfully for gold in California, George obtained a position with a newspaper in that state. Writing for the press, he described the glaring inequalities of his day. Land values were rising rapidly in California, and those who had been able to buy land years before were making huge profits. George had a burning desire to improve conditions for the poor and his vivid style of writing caused many people to read his articles. Eventually George outlined his general philosophy as well as a tax program in a book, *Progress and Poverty,* published in 1880.

George had two basic ideas about land. The first was that the land belongs to all the people in a country, just as do air or sunlight. The second was a strong belief in man's right to own property. However, those fortunate enough to own land have certain obligations. Chief of these is that of paying taxes, since landowners profit from agricultural or manufactured goods produced on their property, or from the rents they collect. George further believed that since land is the basis of wealth, a tax on land should be the only tax collected.

Taxing rich landowners was an idea which met with an enthusiastic public response. Widespread interest in George's views about taxation continued for many years. But only a few unsuccessful attempts were made to put the single tax into operation. For various reasons the public gradually lost interest in the idea.

It is true that when an area is being developed, land values may increase rapidly. Under such circumstances the "early bird" who buys land may make large profits. But, once a region is settled, land values tend to stabilize and landowners may make no greater profit than do owners of other kinds of property. Land, obviously, is not the only kind of property which increases in value with time.

Although George's single tax on land was never put into use, his belief that surplus wealth should be taxed has been accepted. Since 1913 the United States government has levied a graduated income tax according to the size of a person's income. The federal government also taxes those who inherit wealth as well as those who profit from buying and selling securities. Such plans are all based on the principle of taxing those best able to pay.

ing during this decade. And spending by state and local governments increased even more rapidly than did federal spending.

There are several reasons why government costs are rising. Since population is increasing, it would be more expensive each year to provide even the same level of government services. Actually, new services and larger quantities of the old services are being provided each year in response to public demands. Rising price levels (inflation) naturally have made goods and services in general more expensive than they were ten years ago.

Since the Gross National Product (in current dollar terms) approximately doubled during the 1960's, government spending as a percentage of Gross National Product did not increase greatly during that decade. Actually, the percentage of Gross National Product going into taxes in the United States—almost one-third of GNP—still is lower than that in most other advanced industrial countries.

Most government revenues necessarily come from taxes. Many government agencies do sell some goods or services, and funds are received from various kinds of fees, licenses, and fines. The total revenue received from such sources, however, is very small in terms of total government expenditures.

State and local governments, as well as the federal government, from time to time, borrow money for their operations or for specific projects. This borrowing usually is done by selling government bonds to financial institutions or to the general public. At the level of local government, such borrowing usually requires a favorable vote from residents in the community concerned.

Borrowing—that is, the expansion of the public debt—reflects the fact that the right to tax enables government to pay its debts. People who lend money to the government expect to be repaid with interest. Public debt is discussed in more detail in Chapter 16.

Lowering taxes substantially is difficult. Most taxpayers doubtless would welcome a tax cut. But there is little agreement among them as to the services, if any, which should be eliminated in order to reduce government spending. In a recent election the citizens of a small community voted overwhelmingly for the candidates of a political party pledged to reduce government spending. When this party took office, one of its first budget cuts eliminated a research laboratory located in that community. Since over half the workers in that district were employed in this laboratory, the economic well-being of the community was jeopardized. Immediately the congressman from this district and the two senators from the state received a flood

---

GREATER FEDERAL SUPPORT FOR THE ARTS URGED

The visual and performing arts in the United States traditionally have received their principal financial support from private donations, with some additional funding from foundations, and small amounts of federal aid. There is growing evidence that primary dependence on the first of these sources will no longer yield sufficient funds for the performing arts to survive in this country. Those concerned with this problem point out that inflation has increased costs by about 10 per cent per year, and that most other countries subsidize the arts to a far greater extent than does the United States.

A 1970 study revealed that in this country government contributes 7½ cents per person annually to the support of the arts. In contrast, West Germany provides $2.42 per person, Sweden and Austria each contribute $2.00, and Great Britain gives $1.23. A private group called "Partnership for the Arts" has proposed that the federal government provide 200 million dollars for the support of the arts, thus raising its per capita contribution to one dollar. This group calls attention to the fact that even such a federal appropriation would amount to only 10 per cent of the two billion dollars derived from all other sources for support of the arts in the United States.

of angry telegrams and letters. "Why us? Our laboratory renders an important service to the nation. Why don't you eliminate services that are wasteful and unnecessary?" This is a typical reaction. Many people want to reduce government spending, but only if the reduction does not threaten the community where they live.

Once a government service has been established, those employed in it and those receiving benefits from it are determined to keep it from being discontinued. Frequently they lobby to promote its growth. Since government services come into being in response to demands from voters, the decision to eliminate or curtail services must also come from the people. Experts studying government reorganization have spent much time in the preparation of reports showing where savings might be made. Candidates for political office have brought to light inadequacies and have proposed improvements in the operating efficiency of government agencies and bureaus. But spending continues to increase.

Only an aroused electorate can reduce government spending. Here and there throughout the nation there is evidence that citizens are trying to reduce the cost of government. Some communities are voting against bond issues to build new schools or to raise the salaries of teachers. State-supported institutions are raising tuition for out-of-state students and even for those within the state. In some places there have even been tax strikes.

But at the same time more and more people are becoming concerned about the housing, health, and nutrition problems of the elderly, and of the poor. Large sums of money will be required for many years to aid disadvantaged groups in reaching minimum decent living standards. It seems likely that an increasing portion of public revenue will be needed in any serious campaign to wipe out poverty.

The people of the United States must decide what they want most from their various governments, and how much they are willing to pay in taxes to get what they want. To make these decisions intelligently, Americans must be determined to maintain honest and efficient government, yet willing to support spending urgently needed for the common good.

CHECK UP

1. What important services are provided by local government? By state governments?

2. What functions are assigned the national government by the Constitution? What role does Congress play in implementing these responsibilities? What is the role of the federal courts?

3. What are major items in the defense budget? What are the principal defense-related items?

4. What departments and agencies render services related to the promotion of the general welfare?

5. Why are the costs of government rising rapidly? In what ways are these costs met? Why is it difficult to reduce government spending?

2

What kinds of taxes do Americans pay?

In any discussion of taxation there is likely to be wide disagreement about "who" should pay "how much." Different taxes affect different groups and individuals differently.

There is a conflict between the principles of "benefits received" and "ability to pay." It is often argued that an individual's taxes should be proportionate to the benefits or services he receives from government. In other words, everyone should pay his own way. In an abstract consideration of fairness, this argument seems to have merit. Nevertheless, this is a principle which can be carried only so far.

Often those receiving substantial government services cannot pay high taxes. An impoverished ghetto mother with several dependent children, receiving 300 dollars per month in welfare benefits, for example, cannot be expected to pay 300 dollars per month in taxes. Sometimes taxes can be based in considerable part upon benefits received; sometimes not.

The "ability-to-pay" argument recognizes that a certain amount of revenue is needed to carry on essential government operations. The necessary funds can come only from groups with sufficiently high incomes to pay the taxes levied. The more one has, the more he can afford to pay. This type of taxation, of course, results in a "redistribution" of income. Those with high incomes pay high taxes which are used to provide government services for all Americans, including those with low incomes.

Although most taxes tend to reflect both the "benefits received" and the "ability-to-pay" principles, the latter tends to dominate. Although this principle is fairly well accepted by the American public, there is considerable debate about how far it should be carried.

Taxes may be regressive or progressive. A tax is said to be "regressive" when it bears more

heavily on low-income groups, and "progressive" when it bears more heavily on high-income groups. The "burden" is measured in terms of percentage of income required to pay the tax. The following examples illustrate differences between regressive and progressive taxes.

Suppose that one person has an annual income of 5000 dollars; another, an income of 25,000 dollars per year. Each pays a tax of 500 dollars. The first person has paid a tax that amounts to 10 per cent of his income; the second, a tax that is only 2 per cent of his income. This tax is *regressive*.

Suppose, however, that the first person pays 500 dollars, or 10 per cent of his income; the second, 5000 dollars. The second person then has paid 20 per cent of his income in taxes. This is a *progressive* tax, based largely on the "ability-to-pay" principle.

A *proportional* tax is one for which the percentage of income required to pay the tax is the same for all, regardless of level of income. Using the earlier illustration, if the first person paid 500 dollars and the second 2500 dollars, the tax would be *proportional*. Each would

Federal tax receipts for the 1970 fiscal year, by type of tax (in billions of dollars)

Progressive:	Personal income taxes		90.4
	Death and gift taxes		3.4
Intermediate:	Corporation income taxes		32.8
Regressive:	Employment or payroll taxes		39.1
	Excise taxes		18.0
	Tobacco and liquor	6.7	
	Manufacturing and		
	retail excises	1.8	
	Customs duties	2.3	
	Highway trust fund	5.0	
	Miscellaneous	2.1	
	Other taxes and receipts		9.1
	Total		192.8

"Intermediate" refers to taxes which are progressive in some respects and regressive in others.

Source: U.S. Bureau of the Budget

What taxes buy: guns and butter

The phrase "guns or butter" suggests the difficulty of maintaining a large defense establishment while meeting demands for consumer goods. Critics of recent administrations have charged that a high level of defense spending has led to the neglect of the nation's social needs.

*The impact of two federal programs are suggested in these pictures of children, **a**, using equipment purchased with funds under the Elementary and Secondary Education Act, and **b**, standing on the balcony of housing constructed with federal funds.*

High-level defense spending is frequently the subject of heated debate in Congress and in the press. Planes for the Air Force are shown coming off an assembly line in **d.** Pictured also are American tanks, **c,** and gunboats, **e,** in Vietnam.

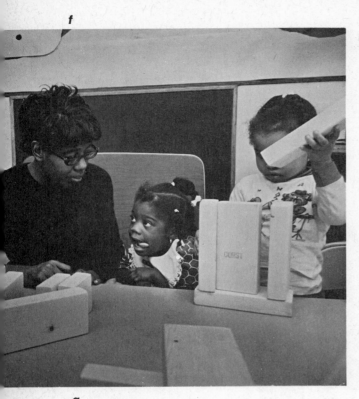

f

Many Americans are urging increased federal spending to combat poverty. A day-care center, **f,** insures good care for the children of working mothers. There is support also for federal funds to curb the steep rise in health care costs. Pictured are an expensive heart-lung machine, **g,** and a hospital construction project, **h.**

Exploration of space, **i,** calls for massive spending. It yields results of scientific importance and also provides jobs. Pictured are government-employed mission control engineers, **j,** and a rocket, **k,** the building of which provided work for various contractors and subcontractors.

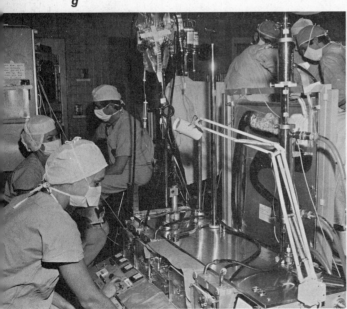

g

h

i

j

k

have paid 10 per cent of his income. Even though the burden of this tax doubtless would be heavier for the person left with an after-tax income of 4500 dollars, the tax cannot be called "regressive" according to the accepted definitions.

Tax policy may be used to influence the economy. Taxation does more than to provide government revenue and redistribute income. Taxes may, in effect, regulate, control, or promote certain kinds of economic activities. High taxes on cigarettes and alcoholic beverages, for example, are designed in part to discourage the consumption of these items. High tariffs (a form of taxation) on goods brought into this country from abroad are intended in part to discourage the flow of certain foreign products into the country. On the other hand, businesses sometimes are taxed at a lower-than-normal rate on certain kinds of "socially desirable" investments; for example, equipment to reduce air or water pollution.

In a broader sense, taxation affects the allocation of resources between public and private sectors of the economy. One cannot use the money paid in taxes to buy an automobile or a television set. The more one pays in taxes,

the less he has for private spending. Thus higher taxes increase the "public sector" of the economy at the expense of the "private sector." Today, about one-third of the Gross National Product consists of publicly supplied goods and services. Whether this is desirable or not is a personal value judgment. If the great majority of Americans found it undesirable, doubtless a greater effort would be made to halt or reduce the public use of resources.

Taxes influence many kinds of business and personal decisions. A firm gives some consideration to the levels of taxation in various communities in deciding where to locate a new plant. Similarly, a family considers local taxes in various communities before deciding where to buy a home. Large investors in securities often prefer municipal bonds—the interest payments of which are exempted from federal income taxes—to corporate stocks or bonds, whose yields are subject to taxation. The buying and selling of securities often are determined by income tax considerations; for example, losses on some sales may be used to offset gains on others, thus reducing the seller's total taxable income.

Chapter 3 brought out that people usually will buy more of most kinds of goods and services if their prices are low than if they are high. Thus, if taxes cause prices to be higher, less goods will be bought, or more low-taxed and fewer high-taxed items will be purchased. Such changes in buying would lead, in turn, to a different use of economic resources, (land, labor, capital, and entrepreneurship) than would otherwise occur.

In short, taxes affect people and all kinds of economic activities in ways that are not obvious at first glance. Little wonder that there is heated debate about what kinds of taxes are most (and least) desirable.

There are generally accepted standards for determining what is a "good" tax. Most tax experts agree that a "good" tax for revenue purposes should conform to the following standards, or criteria:

A TAXPAYERS' REVOLT?

"Taxation without representation" was the reason behind the American colonists' rebellion against Britain. But opposition to government tax policy has been a recurring theme throughout United States history. Shays' Rebellion (1786) and the Whiskey Insurrection (1794) are well-known examples of citizens' tax revolts that were put down. And most students of American literature know of Henry Thoreau's imprisonment for his refusal to pay a state tax supportive of the Mexican War. In recent years, discontent with government spending has been manifested by citizens' lobbies, demonstrations, and in a few instances by outright refusal to pay federal taxes.

1. It should provide enough money to pay for the services it was established to finance.

2. It should be easy and inexpensive to collect and difficult to avoid.

3. It should be easily understandable by those who pay it.

4. In many cases, it should be paid, at least in part, by those who benefit from the services it provides. (The gasoline tax is an example.)

5. It should be levied on the basis of the ability of taxpayers to pay it.

6. It should be reasonably stable—that is, it should provide about the same amount of revenues from year to year.

7. It should interfere as little as possible with the production of income and wealth. In other words, care should be taken not to kill the goose that lays the golden egg.

No single tax meets all the standards for a good tax. Governments must use great care and judgment in developing their tax systems. Since they are likely to rely upon more than one kind of tax, the weaknesses in one may be offset by strengths in another. Also, as already mentioned, some kinds of taxes are intended in part to do more than to raise revenue. During recent years, for example, one of the goals of tax policy has been to minimize the effects of inflation and recession in the national economy.

In reading about the most important types of taxes used in this country, consider the extent to which each meets the seven standards of a "good" tax, as already outlined. Consider also what might be the economic effects (other than raising revenue) of each of these taxes.

The property tax is one of the oldest and most widely used forms of taxation. The property tax still provides the main source of revenue for local governments. Counties obtain more than four-fifths of their tax revenues from property taxes; and cities more than two-thirds. Most local special service districts, including school districts, also rely heavily on property taxes. In former years, the property tax was a major source of income for state governments. Recently, however, most states have replaced (or supplemented) property taxes with income taxes, sales taxes, and various other types of taxation.

Property taxes are collected from the owners of *real estate* (land and buildings). In some cases they also are levied on *personal property* (for example, furniture, jewelry, automobiles, livestock, store inventories, securities, and the like).

Property taxes are based on assessed value. The government taxing agency employs *assessors* to set a value on all property subject to taxation. This *assessed* value often is less than the actual sales value of the property. Each year, the government taxing agency estimates the money needed during the coming year. Then the dollar figure representing the tax funds needed is divided by the assessed value of all the property to be taxed. This is the *tax rate* which will be levied on the taxable property.

An example will illustrate the procedure followed. A small town needs $600,000 in tax

City tax revenue

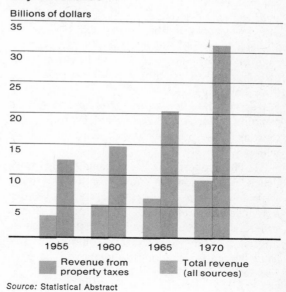

Billions of dollars

Source: Statistical Abstract

■ Revenue from property taxes   ■ Total revenue (all sources)

income during the coming year, and the assessed value of taxable property is $20 million. When $20 million is divided into $600,000, a tax rate of three cents per dollar (or $30 per $1000 of assessed value) is obtained. Some communities express their tax rates in *mills* per dollar of assessed value. (A mill is one-tenth of a cent.) In this case the millage rate would be 30 per dollar. If the assessed value of a family's taxable property is $15,000, the family must pay $450 in property taxes (that is, 15 × $30).

The property tax has several disadvantages. Even though the property tax remains one of the most common forms of taxation, it has certain disadvantages.

1. Because it is mainly a tax on real estate, much of the tax burden falls on the average home-owning family. The value of a family's residence (or even of a business property) may not accurately reflect the owner's ability to pay taxes.

2. Properties may not be assessed fairly. Consequently, some pay too high a tax; others too little. A vacant lot in the city may be over- (or under-) valued. It is only when the lot is sold that the owner discovers whether or not the assessed value was too high.

3. When personal property is included, the assessor may be unable to discover and assess all such property. Since items not assessed escape taxation, some people pay less than their just share of taxes; others pay relatively more than their fair share.

Despite its limitations, the property tax remains important. There are at least four major reasons why property taxes continue to be widely used.

1. The property tax has become firmly established. When some members of a community wish to change the tax structure, they must convince the majority of the taxpayers that a different tax structure would be better. Because any tax system has its shortcomings, people may be fearful that a new plan will be even less satisfactory.

2. The property tax produces a large and constant revenue. The taxing agency can predict fairly accurately how much money will be coming in from year to year.

3. Many people believe that the amount of property owned is roughly related to a person's ability to pay taxes. Families with annual incomes of 8000 dollars, for example, seldom own 60,000-dollar homes.

4. Many of the services provided by local governments (fire and police protection, sewers, and streets, for example) directly benefit property owners, perhaps roughly in proportion to the values of their properties. Therefore some people believe that property taxes reflect the "benefits-received" principle of taxation. No doubt this is true for many kinds of local services. It probably is not true for public education, for example, which is largely supported by property taxes in many communities.

The sales tax is an important source of revenue for state governments. Most states have a sales tax. Income from sales taxes amounts to about three-fifths of all the money brought in by state taxes. A small but growing number of local governments also have adopted a sales tax.

Sales taxes usually are levied at the retail level. When a shopper buys an item priced at one dollar, for example, he may pay an additional amount (usually two to five cents) to the merchant. The merchant, in turn, remits the sales tax money collected to the state or local government at specified periods. Sales taxes may also be levied on services, such as dry-cleaning, hotel rooms, and admissions to movie theaters and sports events. Some states exempt food, prescription medicines, and certain other essentials such as clothing from sales taxes.

The sales tax often is criticized because it "hits" families with low incomes as well as high-income groups. In fact, some critics call it a "sock-the-poor" tax! Doubtless its overall effect is regressive. Even though a family with a high income may buy more taxable items, and therefore pays more total sales tax, it typically saves a larger portion of its income which thereby escapes taxation. A low-income family, on the other hand, may spend a larger portion of its income on taxable items.

A family with an income of 4000 dollars per year in a typical state with a 3 per cent sales tax, for example, may pay 90 dollars per year in sales taxes, or 2.25 per cent of the family's income. Another family in the same state with an income of 40,000 dollars per year may pay sales taxes of 480 dollars, which is only 1.2 per cent of that family's income. Clearly, the sales tax is not based entirely on the "ability-to-pay" principle.

Defenders of the sales tax point out that it brings in large, stable, and predictable revenue. It is not expensive for the state to collect, since the initial collections are made by merchants. Also, it is said to be relatively "painless" because it is paid in small amounts throughout the year. In fact, many people do not know how much they pay each year in sales taxes. Further, it is argued that the sales tax reaches many who otherwise would pay little or no taxes. Paying a sales tax is supposed to make such persons aware of the fact that government services are not "free"!

Excise taxes are similar to sales taxes. Excise taxes are levied only on certain specified items. These items usually are taxed at a higher rate than are items covered by a general sales tax. Usually, also, excise taxes are levied on manufacturers or distributors rather than on consumers at the retail level. Thus, they often are called "hidden" taxes. Actually, some excises are paid directly by consumers. Even when this is not the case, consumers ultimately pay a substantial part of most excise taxes. That is to say, they pay higher prices for the taxed products.

Excise taxes are levied both by the federal government and state governments. A few local governments also levy some excise taxes, and other local governments share in state-collected excises. Items commonly subject to excise tax are gasoline, cigarettes, alcoholic beverages, furs, cosmetics, sporting goods, and telephone and telegraph services.

The general economic effects of excise taxes are similar to those of sales taxes. It is argued, however, that excises are not as regressive as sales taxes, that some of them are based on direct benefits received, and that some are useful from the viewpoint of regulating "undesirable" types of consumption. To illustrate, few poor people buy expensive fur coats. Excises on sporting goods are used to improve hunting, fishing, and other recreational facilities. Because many feel that consumption of tobacco and alcohol is harmful, they favor heavy "punitive" taxation to discourage their consumption. It is presumed that if the tax raises the price of such commodities, less is bought than would be the case if the price were lower in the absence of the tax. There is little evidence, however, that high taxes cause people to smoke or drink very much less.

Gasoline taxes are an important form of the excise tax. The federal and state governments, as well as some local governments, levy taxes on gasoline, amounting to eight cents or more per gallon. Generally, the large funds collected from gasoline taxes are used to build and maintain highways and streets. Thus this is a tax based largely on the "benefits-received" principle. One who does not drive a car pays no gasoline taxes. In some states gasoline taxes are used for different purposes, however.

Personal income taxes are the chief source of income for the federal government. Excluding payments into Social Security accounts by employers and employees, about 60 per cent of federal tax revenues are derived from personal income tax payments. The federal personal income tax is more nearly based on the "ability-to-pay" principle than is any other tax. Most of the required federal income taxes are *withheld* from pay checks in the case of the great majority of employees.

Everyone with an income above a given amount must file a federal income tax return. Congress passed legislation increasing this amount from 600 to 700 dollars in 1970, with a further increase to take effect in 1972. In 1970 some persons with low incomes who clearly would have no income tax liabilities no longer were required to file returns.

In calculating the actual amount of federal personal income tax to be paid, one is allowed a *personal exemption* (750 dollars in 1972). If one is filing as the head of a family, each family member gets an exemption. That is, a husband, wife, and three children would receive a total tax exemption of 3750 dollars in 1972. Additional exemptions are given the elderly and the blind. Also, an additional amount is excluded from taxation in the case of very low-income families.

Certain *deductions* also are allowed in arriving at taxable income. These include such things as the amounts paid in state and local taxes, interest payments on home mortgages and some kinds of purchases, medical and dental expenses above a certain percentage of income, union dues, and several other kinds of necessary expenses. One has the choice of *itemizing* his deductions or of taking an optional "standard" deduction.

Exemptions and deductions are totaled and subtracted from *gross income* to obtain *taxable income*. This is the amount upon which taxes are paid.

The federal personal income tax is a progressive tax. The greater one's taxable income, the larger the percentage of income going for taxes. The tax is applied in *brackets*. For example, the first $2000 of taxable income may be taxed at 15 per cent, the next $1000 at 16 per cent, the next $1000 at 17 per cent, and so on. This would result in a tax of $300 on $2000 of taxable income, $460 on $3000, and $630 on $4000. In 1970 the highest tax rate for individuals was lowered from 70 per cent to 50 per cent. The top bracket reached by the great majority of taxpayers falls within the 20 to 30 per cent range.

The progressive federal income tax is a subject of controversy. Some critics have referred to the income tax as a "soak-the-rich" tax, asserting that the high rates for upper incomes discourage individual incentive and tend to reduce funds that otherwise might be used for the expansion and modernization of industry and business. Advocates of the progressive income tax point out that, were it not for the high income taxes paid by persons with medium-sized and large incomes, it would be necessary to find entirely new sources of revenue.

Corporations also pay federal income taxes. The corporate income tax is a tax on the net incomes (profits) of corporations. This source

The effect of progressive taxation on the distribution of national income

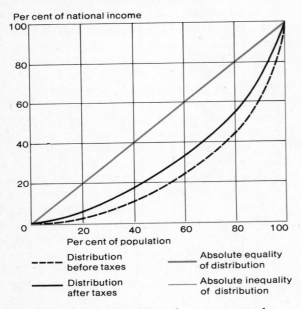

The curves on this graph have been exaggerated deliberately to emphasize the theory of progressive taxation.

provides about one-fourth of federal government tax funds (excluding Social Security taxes). Unlike the personal income tax, the corporate income tax is progressive only in a very restricted sense. On profits of more than 25,000 dollars, the current tax rate is 48 per cent. Profits of less than 25,000 dollars are taxed at 22 per cent. One should remember, however, that dividends paid out of already-taxed corporate profits are considered personal incomes for those receiving them. As such, they are again subject to income taxation if they are above a certain small amount.

On the theory that natural resources are not inexhaustible, and that companies which mine and extract them incur losses from the depletion of these resources, the tax laws permit a percentage *depletion allowance* from the corporate income taxes such companies are required to pay. In 1969, in response to growing taxpayer discontent over the "loopholes" that were eroding the tax base, this depletion allowance was lowered for oil companies from 27.5 to 22 per cent. Despite this and other reforms under the tax law, there is still much criticism of the "legal evasion" of tax payment possible under present laws.

Some states and local governments also levy income taxes. About three-fourths of the states, and a few local governments, also tax incomes. This is a particularly important source of revenue for the few states not having sales taxes (a majority of the states have both income and sales taxes). About one-fifth of all state tax revenue comes from personal and corporate income taxes. These taxes, therefore, produce about one-third as much state tax revenue as do sales taxes.

Exemptions, deductions, and tax rates vary considerably from state to state. Generally speaking, personal exemptions and deductions are as high or higher than those permitted by the federal government. In all states, the tax rates are much lower, and generally much less progressive, than is true for the federal income tax. Like the federal government, most states

require that a portion or all of the personal income taxes due be withheld from employee paychecks.

There always are suggestions for "tax reform." Although the types of taxes discussed do not include all of the taxes levied, the most important have been included. Each of these types of taxation is opposed by some individuals and groups. Some persons who do not oppose a given type of tax may find fault with the way it is administered. They criticize it for having rates that are too high or too low, or too progressive or too regressive.

Some persons argue that income taxes contain too many "loopholes" which allow individuals or corporations with high incomes to escape their "fair share" of the tax burden. Whereas some hold that property taxes should be abolished, others believe that taxes should be levied only on property owners.

The so-called *value-added tax,* used by some Western European countries, has been proposed by some economists as a substitute for existing forms of taxation. With a value-added tax applied at each stage of production or distribution, each firm concerned would pay a tax on the difference between the price it pays for its materials and the price for which it sells the product after processing, manufacturing, or otherwise handling it. Actually, the "tax base" in this case would be the same as Gross National Product. (Chapter 13 pointed out that the totals of the net values added at all stages of production add up to the total of GNP.) Consumers would then probably have to pay higher prices for goods and services, since the value-added tax would be considered as another production cost by business firms.

Proposals for tax reforms or new taxes usually are influenced more by political than by economic considerations. Persons who do not understand the economic effects of various kinds of taxes are likely to base their conclusions on "pocketbook" considerations. But even if one understands the economic effects of a tax, one's judgment of its "goodness" or "badness" compared to other taxes is likely to be influenced by personal values. It is likely that a majority of people will usually prefer the old "tried and true" methods of taxation to new and untried methods. Thus, there tends to be a great deal of discussion (but little significant action) in the field of tax reform.

CHECK UP

1. What are the implications of applying the "ability-to-pay" principle in levying taxes? Of the "benefits-received" principle? What is a regressive tax? A progressive tax? A proportional tax?

2. How can tax policy influence the economy? Business and family decisions? Give examples in each case.

3. What are the characteristics of a good tax? Why does no single tax meet all of these standards?

4. Explain the steps in determining the amount of property tax to be paid on a house in a given year. What are some disadvantages of the property tax? Why is it retained?

5. What are the characteristics of the personal income tax? The corporate income tax? On what grounds are income taxes criticized? Defended?

6. What are excise and sales taxes? On what grounds are these criticized? Defended?

7. Why are proposals for tax reform and new taxes more likely to be influenced by political than economic considerations?

Clinching the main ideas

Taxes provide the revenue used by federal, state, and local governments to provide the services desired by a majority of Americans. Governments have no source of income other than the incomes of citizens. In other words, nothing received from government is "free."

Taxes may be based on the principle of "benefits received" or "ability to pay," or both. Additionally, there are certain generally accepted standards for a desirable tax for revenue purposes. Because no tax meets all these standards, there are a variety of taxes. Taxes may be intended, in part at least, to further non-revenue objectives based on value judgments.

Although some kinds of taxes are progressive and others regressive, all taxes result in a redistribution of income, affect the allocation of economic resources, and shift resources from the "private sector" to the "public sector" of the economy.

The major types of taxes are the income tax (used by the federal and state governments), the sales tax (state governments), excise taxes (federal and state governments), and property taxes (local governments). There is some overlapping in the types of taxation used by the various levels of government. Each of these taxes has its strengths and weaknesses, its supporters and critics.

"Tax reform" is much discussed but seldom implemented. Voters, and their elected representatives, tend to be conservative about making major tax changes. Most persons would like to pay less in taxes, but are unwilling to give up services received from government.

Chapter 14 review

Terms to understand

1. special service district
2. "the common defense"
3. "the general welfare"
4. government borrowing
5. disadvantaged groups
6. regressive tax
7. progressive tax
8. proportional tax
9. tax rate
10. assessed value
11. sales tax
12. excise
13. gross income
14. taxable income
15. depletion allowance
16. value-added tax

What do you think?

1. Government expenditures more than doubled between 1960 and 1970. Spending by state and local governments increased more rapidly than federal spending, and federal nondefense spending more rapidly than defense spending. Why? What conclusions may be drawn from these facts?

2. Should taxes be used "to regulate and control" as well as to raise revenue? Why?

3. Of the various types of taxes discussed in this chapter, which most nearly meets the standards of a good tax? Why?

4. Should the "value-added tax" replace all present federal taxes? Does it meet the criteria for a good tax? Explain.

5. The fact that taxes are collected by many units of government adds to the expense of collection and makes work for taxpayers. Do you see any solution to this problem? Is it likely to be accepted? Why or why not?

6. Should the principle of capacity to pay be interpreted in such a way that even low income families pay small amounts in direct taxes to local, state, and federal governments? Why?

7. If taxpayers knew exactly what they were paying for given services, would they be less likely to demand more and better services from their government? Why?

Applying your knowledge of economics

1. Find out the current property tax rate in your community. How is property assessed (for example, as a percentage of market value)? List the major purposes for which this tax money is spent, and the amount appropriated to each. Most towns and cities prepare an annual report including this and other information. Prepare a report in which community expenditures are shown in a graph or table.

2. *The New York Times Encyclopedic Almanac* and other similar works contain information about: (1) Tax Burden: Selected Countries, (2) U.S. Budget: 1789 to the Present (receipts and outlays), (3) Effective Rates of Federal Individual Income Tax, (4) State Sales and Use Tax Rates, (5) State Income Tax Rates, (6) State and Local Government Expenditures Per Capita (for major purposes during the last half century), and (7) comparable data on revenue and expenditures for each of the 50 states. These data can be used in reporting trends in taxing and spending at the national and state levels.

3. Obtain the latest federal income tax form from the nearest Office of Internal Revenue and prepare a return for yourself (based on actual or imaginary earnings) or for a fictitious person. Use the "long form" and itemize all possible deductions.

Federal revenue sharing: boon or boondoggle?

General background

Although the United States is made up of 50 states, with more than 81,000 local governments (counties, cities, townships, school districts, special service districts, and the like), the federal government collects about 60 per cent of all taxes paid. State governments and local governments collect about 20 per cent each.

There is some sharing or transfer of funds between the different levels of government. For example, states contribute to the support of local schools and sometimes to construction of streets and roads. The federal government also contributes, under various programs, to both state and local government expenses.

During the 1960's, federal funds amounting to from 8 to 12 per cent of total federal tax receipts were returned to state and local governments. Almost all federal funds were earmarked for specific uses; that is, they were tied to particular kinds of state or local government expenditures. During 1970, for example, the largest shared amount, about one third of the total, aided public welfare assistance. In order of size, the next two were for highway construction aid and educational aid. Other tied federal grants were for assistance in airport development, regional development, model cities programs, and crime control and prevention.

For many years, state and local governments have complained that their tax revenues are inadequate to meet their needs. The federal government collects more than 90 per cent of all personal and corporate income taxes, by far the most fertile sources of tax revenues. Because federal income taxes are so high, state and local governments rely mainly upon state sales taxes and local property taxes for revenue. But in recent years taxpayers have strongly resisted increases in sales and property taxes. Faced with rising demands for public services far in excess of tax revenues, state and local governments seek relief through financial aid from the federal government.

The federal government could assist state and local governments with their financial problem in either of two ways. Federal taxes could be reduced, thereby leaving greater tax revenue sources for state and local use. Or a larger portion of federal tax income could be shared with state and local governments.

For political and administrative reasons, many elected state and local officials seem to prefer federal revenue sharing to a reduction in federal tax income. Elected officials do not like to propose higher taxes. Such a proposal makes voters unhappy. If sufficient funds could be obtained from the federal government, voters would have no reason to turn against state and local officials at election time. Besides, federal tax collection is generally considered to be more efficient (less expensive) than that of state or local governments.

Most of the discussion of federal revenue sharing has been concerned with federal grants to state governments. It would be much easier for the federal government to share its funds with the 50 states than to make separate grants to 50 states plus 3000 counties, 35,000 municipalities or townships, 44,000 school districts or systems, and perhaps other local government taxing bodies. Sharing with local governments could more easily be handled at the state level, according to the laws and established procedures of each state.

Tied grants versus block grants

As already noted, most federal grants-in-aid to state and local governments have been tied to special uses.

Categorical assistance has represented an increasing portion of both total federal outlays and state and local revenues. But, too often, it has also been accompanied by an ever growing maze of program restrictions, formulas, matching provisions, project approval requirements, and a host and variety of administrative burdens. The result has been the creation of a complicated network of intergovernmental assistance efforts with many inefficiencies and unworkable features.[1]

[1] Murray I. Weidenbaum (Assistant Secretary of the Treasury for Economic Policy), Speech before the National Conference of State Legislative Leaders, St. Louis, Missouri, August 27, 1970.

States, therefore, have advocated more "block" grants. This means that a certain amount of money would be forthcoming regularly and automatically, and could be used by a state, without matching, for whatever purposes it sees fit. (This kind of expanded revenue sharing was proposed by President Nixon in his "New Federalism" speech.) The amount to be received by each state could be determined in various ways, but one of the most commonly discussed proposals is to share on a population basis.

Opponents of block grants argue that these grants would provide a convenient way for state officials to evade political responsibility for their spending decisions. (Many people seem to consider federal money "free.") Also, many persons believe that the greatest needs for additional state tax revenues are to aid in solving the many problems of cities, to provide additional aid for schools, and to alleviate the heavy property tax burden. State governments might be tempted to spend "non-tied" federal funds for nonessential purposes.

In my judgment, the federal government is not only in a better position than the states to allocate public spending, it is in a stronger position to resist unwholesome pressures toward diversion of tax money to the *wrong* purposes. Of course, the federal government's record has not been perfect in this respect. . . .

But there is scant evidence that the states would do better if they had federally collected revenues to spend as they wished; on the contrary, the misdirection of federal efforts in this field [housing] has been due principally to too much reliance upon state and local officials.[2]

Congress has always been reluctant to make unrestricted grants to other government bodies. A supporter of this Congressional policy states:

The American people watch what their national government and its leaders are doing much more closely than they watch what their state governments are doing. Even if this could be changed—and I do not think it could be—*it violates every principle of good government that 50 states should spend without standards*

[2] Leon H. Keyserling, "Sharing Revenue with the States" in *Revenue Sharing and Its Alternatives: What Future for Fiscal Federalism?* Issued by the Subcommittee on Fiscal Policy of the Joint Economic Committee (Volume II of *Range of Alternatives for Fiscal Federalism*), Ninetieth Congress, first session, p. 945.

or "strings" the money that one government collects. To be sure, we *do* need to develop state and local responsibility. But insofar as the spending of revenues collected by the federal government is involved, this can be achieved through federal grants-in-aid. These I entirely favor, with appropriate modifications and expansion. They permit considerable flexibility, and even from the standpoint of administrative costs are at least as economical as revenue-sharing, without its attendant liabilities. . . .

Moreover, the application of the grants-in-aid principle, in contrast with revenue-sharing with the states, gives the federal government much greater leeway in deciding whether the cities, or the states, shall spend federally collected revenues. Dr. [Walter W.] Heller appears satisfied to leave the cities to the mercies of the states. Yet we know how often this has worked badly, especially because state legislatures in many instances are grossly nonrepresentative of their populations. The answer that political reapportionment will take care of all this in time is too facile. At best, it will take many years before reapportionment can achieve throughout the nation the purposes toward which it is aimed. And even then, it should be directed mainly toward improved allocation by the state of the revenues which they themselves collect.[3]

National economic stability

There has been very little discussion among either economists or government officials of the possible effects of federal revenue sharing on the national government's efforts to use fiscal policy in promoting economic stability. Should a large percentage of federal tax revenues (15 or 20 per cent) be returned to the states, will this not reduce the federal government's fiscal flexibility? Is this desirable?

If the federal government, in effect, becomes tax collector for the states, a continuing high level of federal taxation seems likely. Once states become accustomed to receiving some of their revenue from this source, political pressure will make substantial cuts in federal taxes difficult.

Similarly, should the federal government accumulate a substantial surplus fund, there will be political pressure to increase funds given to the states. Doubtless the states will tend to spend the funds received each year. Thus, even if the federal government wished to reduce government spend-

[3] *Ibid.*, p. 948.

ing to combat inflation, state expenditures would probably remain higher than if there was no revenue sharing. Thus the effect of policy would be partially offset.

Another consideration is the effect of revenue sharing on the size of the federal budget and the national debt. An analyst comments:

With federal costs soaring . . . the government can ill afford to add several billion dollars more to its outlays, bringing further dislocations in the federal budgetary situation and adding to the burden of our huge national debt.

When the idea of federal tax sharing began to receive public attention in 1964, it was believed that it should be financed out of budgetary surpluses produced by a booming economy. Now, however, . . . there is little hope of achieving a balanced budget with any excess in revenues in the foreseeable future. During the past 30 years, budgetary surpluses have been the exception rather than the general rule. In only 6 years [during] the period from fiscal year 1937 through 1966 was a surplus realized. As the Treasury closed its books on June 30, 1966, another deficit of $2.3 billion was incurred. And the President in his 1967 State of the Union message predicted even higher deficits in the years ahead. For the fiscal year 1967, he estimated a deficit of $9.7 billion. Beyond that, even assuming that his latest tax recommendations are enacted, another $8.1 billion deficit is anticipated for the fiscal year 1968. Latest statistics on the gross public debt outstanding report that as of January 17, 1967, it had reached $329.7 billion—the highest level in U.S. history and very close to the public debt ceiling of $330 billion. [*Note:* The President's budget for the fiscal year 1975 was an unbalanced one. It included a deficit of $9.4 billion.][4]

In summary, if the federal government turns over a portion of its revenues to state governments, with or without strings, it reduces its stabilizing alternatives. Those who believe that the federal government should not use fiscal policy to further stabilization would think this desirable. Others would disagree.

The proposals

The Nixon administration submitted a two-part revenue sharing plan in 1971. The first part calls

for quarterly payments to the states and local governments from federal income tax revenue. The amount would be based on population and "tax effort" (how much is collected in local taxes), and there would be no strings. The estimated amount at the outset was five billion dollars.

The second part of the Nixon plan would include one third of all existing federal aid programs in one of six categories from which less restrictive grants can be made. These new categories would be urban development, rural development, education, manpower training, law enforcement, and transportation. State and local governments would control spending from these funds, possibly amounting to eleven billion dollars per year.

The nation's mayors discussed the Nixon plan at a conference. They opposed the second part on the grounds that any tampering with present urban programs probably would make them less effective.

Organized labor and civil rights groups opposed the whole plan because they have greater trust in the federal government than in state and local governments. The proposals also seemed too drastic to many others, and alternative plans were put forward in Congress.

Wilbur Mills, chairman of the powerful House Ways and Means Committee, proposed that the federal government take over the total cost of the aid to dependent children (welfare) program. This program was most frequently cited by local and state officials as the cause of their financial plight. Many state governors gave their support to federal assumption of the cost for welfare aid, believing it a practical alternative with greater chance of success in Congress than revenue sharing.

The issues

In discussing federal revenue sharing, the first question is whether it is desirable in any form. Some argue that federal, state, and local governments should each determine the programs appropriate to its jurisdiction and levy the taxes to support them. Others argue that most major state and local problems are also federal problems. Consequently all or part of the funds needed to cope

[4] *op. cit.,* p. 727.

with these problems should come from the federal government.

Between these extremes, others favor sharing costs of problems which both federal and state-local levels of government agree are their mutual responsibility.

If the decision is in favor of revenue sharing, there remains the question whether "block" grants or "tied" grants, or some combination of the two, should be used. For years the "tied" grant has been favored by Congress, despite criticisms directed at this plan by state and local officials and some "neutral" observers. But a strong movement has developed in support of block grants as a substitute for, or a supplement to, tied grants.

If one assumes that there should be federal revenue sharing, two further questions arise. What is the total sum to be returned by the federal government? How will this money be allocated among the various states?

In thinking about federal revenue sharing, one must carefully consider (as has already been suggested) the impact of such a program on taxation and fiscal policy. But as is true in the case of most controversial economic issues, noneconomic considerations cannot be ignored. Political views and value judgments are bound to influence the conclusions reached and the action taken. Those serving in the executive and legislative branches of government scarcely need to be reminded that regardless of the level of government which collects or spends money, there is one ultimate source of all tax revenues. That ultimate source is the taxpayer.

Toward better understanding

QUESTIONS TO CONSIDER IN ANALYZING THIS CASE

1. What levels of government collect taxes? Which collects the largest amount? Is there overlap in the purpose for which tax revenue collected at different levels is spent? Why?
2. In what two ways could the federal government help local and state governments with their financial problem? Which would the latter prefer?
3. Distinguish between tied grants and block grants. Which would the states prefer? Why?
4. What arguments have been advanced in support of federal revenue sharing? Against increased dependence on it?
5. What groups have endorsed the plan advanced by the Nixon Administration? Why? Opposed it?

THINKING ABOUT THE BASIC ECONOMIC ISSUES

1. Why are local and state governments finding it increasingly difficult to raise enough revenue to meet their needs?
2. Taking into account arguments pro and con, which type of federal grant-in-aid seems most desirable? Why do you think so?
3. Why might federal revenue sharing interfere with the national government's use of fiscal policy to promote economic stability? Tend to increase the size of the national debt?
4. What would be the advantages and disadvantages of having uniform tax rates throughout the 50 states, limiting the number of different kinds of taxes collected (perhaps a value-added tax, a progressive personal income tax, a sales tax, and tariff duties), and having a single tax-collecting agency?

chapter fifteen

Economic instability: inflation and recession

1. What are the causes and effects of inflation?
2. What are the causes and effects of recession?
3. How do "automatic stabilizers" work?

It may be said that, so far as the technical and economic problems are concerned, Americans now have adequate knowledge about how to stabilize their economy: the real question is whether they have the political wisdom and the moral courage to take the necessary measures.

MAX LERNER,
America As a Civilization

The "twin evils" of inflation and recession have afflicted the economy from time to time throughout the country's history. This is not peculiar to the United States, of course. All advanced industrial countries experience some economic instability. Actually, many of them have experienced much greater extremes of "boom and bust" than the United States. Only countries relying mainly upon subsistence agriculture, and those having their economies almost completely controlled by dictatorial governments, can hope to remain relatively immune to economic fluctuations—and even they have not remained completely free from inflation and recession.

It once was thought that economic instability is an inevitable feature of a relatively free-enterprise capitalist system. Most present-day economists believe, however, that at least the extreme

fluctuations which have occurred in the past can be kept within reasonable bounds; that is, that without drastic changes in the nation's present economic system, the harshness of both inflation and recession can be reduced greatly. If the nation fails in this respect, it will not be because of a lack of expert knowledge. Rather, it will be because of a lack of will.

This chapter discusses some of the causes and effects of economic instability—inflation and recession—and some of the so-called "automatic stabilizers" which have been "built into" the economic system.

1

What are the causes and effects of inflation?

Inflation exists when prices are rising rapidly. Chapter 3 brought out that the general price level rises when spending increases more rapidly than the amounts of goods and services available for purchase. (Deflation is the opposite.) Stated in terms of Gross National Product, inflation occurs when current-dollar (or monetary) GNP is increasing faster than constant-dollar (or real) GNP.

Strictly speaking, any increase in the general price level is inflation. Minor changes in prices occur all the time, however. It is only when prices in general move upward consistently for a considerable period of time, or increase drastically within a short time, that economists become alarmed about inflation. Most consumers (and economists) probably would not worry about general price level increases of 1 or 2 per cent annually. But even at this rate of inflation, the purchasing power of money decreases substantially within a few years.

There are several reasons why spending may increase faster than do the things available to buy. The rate of spending is determined by (1) the amount of money in circulation, and (2) the average speed at which this money changes hands. In economic jargon this is known as "the velocity of circulation." If either the amount of money in the economy or the speed of its turnover increases, without a corresponding decrease in the other, spending obviously increases.

Increased spending alone does not cause higher prices. If increases in the goods or services keep up with increases in spending, general price levels will not increase. (Refer to Chapter 1, where the economic model MV = PT is described.) But if the real production of goods and services (that is, real GNP) lags behind spending, prices will increase. Also, if a substantial portion of goods and services are not available for purchase—for example, if much of the GNP is diverted into military hardware, rather than used for consumer or producer goods—the prices of those goods available for ordinary purchase can be expected to rise.

The economy has been marked by long-term general price increases. Chapter 13 brought out that the economy's general price level has approximately doubled since 1929. If these price increases had been spread fairly evenly over the more than 40 years since 1929, their economic effect would have been minor. Price increases in most countries have been much greater than in the United States during this

Volume of business activity since 1916

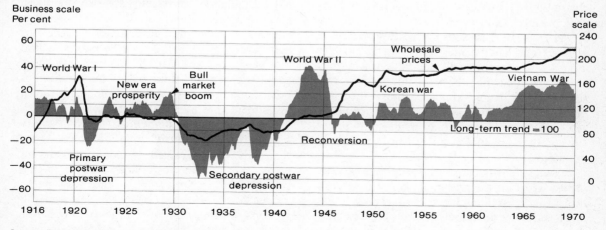

Source: The Cleveland Trust Company, Cleveland, Ohio

period. The history of money shows that the purchasing power of all forms of money tends to decrease with time.

Serious inflation usually comes in spurts. Periods of gradually rising prices, or even of declining prices, are followed by periods of unusually rapid price increases. People then become alarmed about the evils of inflation. One such spurt in this country began in the middle 1960's. (Prices had been rising gradually each year since 1949.) By the beginning of the 1970's, inflation had become one of the more serious—some thought the most serious—of this country's economic problems.

Inflation hurts many people. Unless one's monetary income increases at least as fast as the price of things one must buy, one's real income—or standard of living—declines. A pay increase of 25 dollars per month is always welcome, but the gain is more than offset should the cost of living increase by 30 dollars per month. (How inflation affects individuals in some groups was discussed in Chapters 5 and 11, and how the likelihood of inflation may affect the actions of investors in Chapter 7.) Inflation, of course, affects different groups and individuals differently.

The very high income groups suffer little from inflation. Probably few people in the 100,000 dollars per year income bracket decrease their purchases of food, clothing, or convenience and luxury items when prices rise by 10 per cent. Such persons normally save sizable portions of their incomes in any case. It is far more likely that they will put aside less money in savings than that they will lower their real standards of living. Many of those receiving high incomes have investments in common stocks whose dividends may increase as prices rise, or they are in other ways protected from inflation.

Inflation hits hardest at the middle-income group. Working people who are not in a position to increase their incomes as rapidly or as much as prices increase bear the greatest burden of inflation. This group includes most non-union workers, teachers, and other public (governmental) employees. Also included are those retired persons depending mainly on fixed incomes from private pensions or from private investments made when they were younger.

In many cases, even union workers in a wide variety of occupations cannot protect themselves from inflation. Powerful unions in some industries have been able to negotiate wage agreements which allow their members to at least maintain their standards of living. In some cases wage increases may even exceed price increases, but these are exceptions rather than the general rule. During a period of rapid inflation, wage increases usually are very soon offset by price increases. Very few middle income people benefit from substantial inflation. Since most people in this country are in the middle income group, it is easy to see why inflation is feared.

Inflation may make it easier to pay debts. During inflationary periods, the purchasing power of the dollar decreases. This means that one who has incurred debts during a lower-price, lower-income period is able to pay his debts with "cheaper" dollars—that is, with dollars which will purchase less than those originally borrowed.

It is often said that inflation benefits debtors at the expense of creditors. This is true only if the harmful effects of inflation on debtors are not greater than the beneficial. For example, a person buying a home on a long-term mortgage may find that inflation considerably reduces his *real* burden of payments. But he may also find that the real values of his life insurance policies, annuities, pension fund contributions, savings bonds, and other forms of fixed monetary return investments are likewise reduced.

Union wage settlements sometimes are blamed for "cost-push" inflation. Some argue that high wages received by union members increase production costs and lead to higher prices. Often referred to as the "cost-push" model, this like many other economic generalizations, contains some truth. If production costs *are* increased by the full amount of wage increases, and if demand conditions are such that producers *can* pass along all their increased production costs to consumers, some "cost-push" inflation will result from large wage increases. In many cases, however, these two requirements are not met.

Union representatives, in turn, often blame high profits of business firms for "cost-push" inflation. Again, this may or may not be so. Higher prices do not always mean higher profits. In other words, higher wages (or higher profits) may or may not be a major contributor to inflation, depending upon the total circumstances.

The "demand-pull" model differs from the "cost-push" explanation of inflation. The "demand-pull" model of inflation holds that for a variety of reasons, the production or availability of goods and services does not always keep up with demands. Consequently, this shortage leads to the bidding up of the prices of the available goods and services. That is, increased demand without a corresponding increase in supply brings higher prices.

When this happens, the owners of those factors of production who are able to do so, including labor, faced with higher costs of living, try to charge higher prices for their services. If successful, this increases production costs. Thus, an "inflationary spiral" is touched off, leading to succeeding rounds of price and wage increases.

This spiral continues either until spending slows down or until goods and services catch up with demand. Unfortunately, many past periods of inflation have not stopped short of a recession in economic activity, leading to widespread unemployment of people and resources. This is the hard way to stop inflation!

Both demand and supply contribute to inflation. Inflation is rising prices, and as was pointed out in Chapter 3, demand and supply act together to determine prices. Demand is determined by what people are able and willing to pay. Supply is determined by what sellers are willing to sell their goods and services for, which, in turn, is influenced by costs of production. Thus, it is incorrect to lay sole blame for

inflation at the door of either "cost-push" or "demand-pull." Both have a role. Once substantial inflation starts, it is more important to try to bring it under control than to try to assess blame.

Expectations concerning future prices may contribute to inflation. If people believe that prices will be higher next week, next month, or next year than they are today, they are likely to buy today rather than later. Some may even go into debt to do so.

When a large number of people strongly believe, for whatever reasons, that prices are going

Economic indicators show many parallel up and down movements

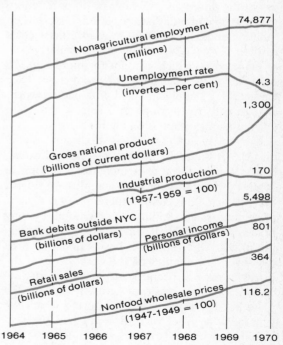

"Unemployment" is inverted because it tends to rise when the economy falls, and vice versa.

Source: Statistical Abstract, Federal Reserve Bulletin, US Department of Commerce

to rise rapidly, there is a rush to buy. This, in turn, creates scarcity and leads to higher prices. On the other hand, if people believe future prices are going to be lower than present prices, the result may be unsold merchandise, deflation (lower prices), or even an economic recession. This kind of reaction is often referred to as a "self-fulfilling prophecy."

Government economic forecasts are very cautious in speaking about inflation or recession. Government officials do not want their statements to increase economic instability. Consequently they tend to be optimistic in all situations. If inflation prevails, they suggest that it will soon be under control. If there is a recession, they may suggest that prosperity is "just around the corner."

The general price level seldom sinks back to pre-inflation levels. Most production costs, including prices of the factors of production, increase during inflationary periods. Even when inflation ends, it is difficult to reduce these costs to their former levels. This is particularly true of labor costs, which account for more than 70 per cent of the total costs of production. (See Chapter 4.) Labor unions and individual workers strongly resist wage and salary cuts even when unemployment is on the rise.

Control of inflation, then, does not usually mean a substantial roll-back of prices. Instead, it usually means that price increases are stopped, at least temporarily, or that increases are slowed down. During this century there have been years of relative price stability or of gradually rising prices, followed by fewer years of rapidly rising prices. Only during a few periods, such as the severe depression of the early 1930's, did prices in general decrease substantially for several years in succession. Actually, since 1939 there has been only one year during which the general price level was lower than in the preceding year.

Americans may be getting "conditioned" to a rising general price level. For more than a generation now, predicted general price increases have come about most of the time. It may be that many people do not ask themselves *whether* prices are going to increase, but rather *how fast* will they increase. Such an attitude may have a "self-fulfilling prophecy" effect. In other words, the rate of turnover of money (velocity of circulation) and credit buying remains high, thus bidding up the prices of available goods and services.

Most people favor control of inflation. On balance, most people probably feel that they are harmed more than they are helped by inflation. They expect government and business to "do something" about rapidly rising prices. Inflation can be controlled either by increasing the available supply of goods and services, or by decreasing the amount of spending, or both.

But if economic resources already are almost fully employed and production is high, it may not be possible to increase supply except rather slowly as new plant and equipment are constructed and brought into production. Therefore, to get quick results, spending must be reduced. Further, if individuals and business firms are not willing to decrease spending voluntarily —as may be the case if people are conditioned to expect inflation—any successful anti-inflation action may depend on government. When government action to decrease private spending is taken—raising tax rates, for example, someone usually complains of being harmed economically.

Some stabilizing features have been developed in the economic system to dampen price instability with a minimum of harmful effects. These are discussed later in this chapter. When these stabilizers do not work effectively, the government policies discussed in Chapter 16 may be brought into play.

CHECK UP

1. Explain the term "inflation." What are the basic causes of inflation? How does inflation affect the high-income group? Middle income? Poor? Debtors? Creditors?

2. What is the "cost-push" explanation of inflation? The "demand-pull" explanation? Why do both explanations have validity? How can people's expectations contribute to inflation? Recession?

3. When a period of serious inflation ends, why is it unlikely that the general price level will sink to the pre-inflation level? What probably is the attitude of most Americans toward inflation?

2

What are the causes and effects of recession?

An economic recession means that the actual production of goods and services declines, or fails to keep pace with the potential capacity of the economy. That is, people, plant, and equipment are unemployed or underemployed. Technically, for measurement purposes, economists usually agree that recession exists when real GNP declines (or fails to grow) for two calendar quarters in succession. Even if real GNP grows, but too slowly to provide jobs for the steadily growing number of persons who want to work, a very real crisis will emerge within two or three years. The difference between a recession and a depression is merely one of degree. A depression is a severe and long-continued recession.

There have been numerous periods of recession (or depression) followed by periods of general prosperity. Recessions are not unique to this country. All industrialized free enterprise economies have experienced recessions—often at the same time that they have occurred in the United States. In Communist countries, where most of the labor force is employed in government-owned enterprises, people may not be thrown out of work by recessions. But even those economies undergo some fluctuation. Only the least developed societies—where most persons gain their livings from subsistence agriculture—have escaped alternating periods of recession and prosperity. And those societies are subject to famine when crops fail or other natural disasters strike.

Alternating periods of prosperity and recession (or "boom" and "bust") have been called "business cycles." The term "business cycle"

AN INCOMES POLICY?

Many economists advocate an "incomes policy" as a means of adjusting to a high rate of inflation. An incomes policy would seek to regulate personal and corporate incomes through some form of government intervention. One proposal is to impose a surtax on the profits of companies which agree to "inflationary" wage increases in union contracts. Labor leaders generally object to this proposal. Another approach would be the enforcement of wage and price controls, a suggestion opposed by both labor and management.

The traditional method of combating inflation has been to slow down the economy, even at the cost of creating unemployment. This result was achieved in part by the 1969–70 cutbacks in federal spending and increases in bank lending rates. Yet inflation continued, despite the fact that unemployment increased. Supporters of an "Incomes policy" maintain that in order to strengthen the free market system, the government must occasionally intervene in it. (There is precedent for this action. During the Great Depression of the 1930's the government undertook many new regulatory functions in an effort to stimulate the economy.)

Some economists doubt that an "incomes policy" would insure high employment and price stability. They maintain that a policy of mild inflation is inevitable and desirable, and that interference with wage and price levels tends to weaken the market system.

The four phases of the business cycle

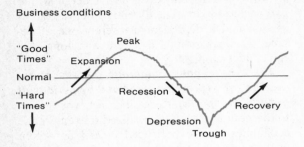

is not used as often today as it once was. It seems to imply that economic fluctuation or instability is inherent or inevitable in the economy. Most people once believed this to be true. Many of today's economists, however, believe that serious recessions can be avoided. The fact remains that the United States has had many recessions, and, although not recently, several severe depressions. These have caused much hardship and economic waste.

Recessions follow a well-defined pattern. For some reason, consumer buying declines or slows down. Businesses find themselves with lower profits and larger stocks of unsold goods. Retailers cut down on their orders. Manufacturers and processors, in turn, cut back production. Lesser amounts of raw materials and agricultural products are bought, and the prices of these products usually decline. Some manufacturing plants are closed, and others run only part-time. Workers are laid off or placed on shorter work weeks. Businesses reduce spending for new plants and equipment. Little hiring is done.

The recession feeds upon itself, or "snowballs." Because unemployment and underemployment are high, many people have less money to spend. Many who still are employed fear that they may soon lose their jobs or receive lower incomes. Consumers avoid going into debt for credit purchases, and attempt to save more of their incomes for possibly worse days ahead. Buying, especially of nonessential

items, further declines. This, in turn, leads to still lower business profits, lower production, and more unemployment. If this process continues long enough, the country is in a depression.

Older people still remember the "Great Depression" of the 1930's. The worst depression this country has experienced occurred during the 1930's. Although the country has had several recessions since that time, none has been serious enough to be a real "depression."

Persons who are over 50 have vivid memories of the "Great Depression." They are more afraid of depression and recession than are the younger generations who did not live through it. These fears no doubt tend to influence their economic actions—another aspect of the much-discussed "generation gap."

During that troubled period, more than one worker out of four throughout the country was unemployed for an extended period of time. Many others could find only part-time employment at low wages (it was not until later that a 20-cents-per-hour minimum wage was instituted for some jobs.) There was no unemployment insurance, and virtually no public welfare assistance or large-scale private charity. The suicide rate increased by 40 per cent, the rate of entry into mental hospitals tripled, the marriage rate declined by 30 per cent, and the birth rate declined even more. As the expression went, "times were tough all over."

From 1929 to 1933, real GNP declined by 30 per cent, homebuilding by 74 per cent, manufacturing by 49 per cent, and bank deposits by 20 per cent. The total annual profits of all the country's corporations declined from 10 billion dollars to a *loss* of 3 billions, a decline of 13 billion dollars. Business failures increased by 50 per cent. Real GNP did not regain the 1929 level until 1939. The loss in production of goods and services from the unemployment of people and resources during the 1930's amounted to at least 750 billions in current dollars.

Statistics alone cannot describe the effects of

Anti-Establishment Economist

Thorstein Veblen

(1857–1929)

The satirical pen of Thorstein Veblen infuriated opponents but delighted his admirers. This Wisconsin-born and Minnesota-reared son of a Norwegian immigrant farm family had an insight into the workings of economic and social institutions enjoyed by few other persons. And he did not hesitate to say what he thought.

By materialistic standards, Veblen's life was a failure. After a brilliant record in graduate school, he waited seven years for a university appointment, and then was named only to an assistantship. His peculiar mannerisms kept him from achieving high academic rank or a large salary, and caused him to lose many positions. He hated lecturing to undergraduate students. During an era of conformity, he dressed sloppily and paid little attention to grooming. He was constantly accused of carrying on love affairs with the wives of other faculty members and even with students.

Veblen savagely attacked orthodox economics and predicted a great collapse of "the system." (The Great Depression which he foresaw began with the stock market collapse in the year of his death. He did not live to see it.) He viewed big businessmen and financiers as enemies of productive efficiency, economists and churches as apologists for the existing system, universities as baby-sitters for bright young persons, and small businessmen and farmers as dupes of big business. In general, he was "against" rather than "for," but he appears to have had a vision of a rational and highly productive society in which major economic and political decisions would be made by scientists and engineers rather than by profit-seeking businessmen and office-seeking politicians.

Of Veblen's many books, *The Theory of the Leisure Class* (1899), in which he tossed his sharpest darts at the behavior of the wealthy, has remained the most popular. *The Theory of Business Enterprise* (1904) and *The Instinct of Workmanship* (1914) contain the best exposition of his economic thought. His vivid use of terminology such as "conspicuous consumption," "conspicuous waste," "pecuniary emulation," "kept classes," "captains of industry," "capitalistic sabotage," and "predatory fraud" has continued to delight generations of young (and some not-so-young) intellectual rebels.

Often the impact of a "negative" philosophy voiced by a social misfit is slight. Veblen's impact, however, was considerable among the generation of economists who took part in shaping the era of social reform which began in this country during the 1930's. His lasting influence has been much greater than that of many economists who achieved far greater recognition and rewards during Veblen's lifetime.

this tragic depression on human beings. There is no adequate way of measuring the full costs of hardship, hunger, broken families, and blighted lives. But at least statistics can give some insights into the nature of a severe depression, and some explanation of why no one wants to undergo another experience of this kind. When one who has lived through this depression hears people speak longingly of "the good old days," he may be tempted to reply that the good old days are here now.

Recession benefits few but harms many. If a person keeps his job, or maintains his income, he may not be hurt personally by a recession. In fact, if the recession leads to a lower general price level, thus increasing the purchasing power of money, his real income may even increase. In particular, retired persons receiving fixed incomes (Social Security benefits, pensions, annuities, interest on long-term bonds, and the like) may find that their purchasing power increases because of lower prices. The same is true of others not dependent upon wages, salaries, or profits for income—mainly those who receive interest or rentals based on long-term contracts.

But there is no assurance that price levels actually will be significantly lower during a recession. Prices did decline substantially during the early 1930's, but since that time recessions generally have resulted only in a temporary leveling off or slowing down of price increases. In fact, the prices of many kinds of goods and services have continued to rise during the last three recessions—1958, 1960, and 1970.

In addition to the overall economic losses from lower production, recession poses a threat to almost every worker, businessman, farmer, and professional person. Very few workers can be absolutely certain that they will not lose their jobs, or be forced to work shorter hours or take wage cuts, if a recession comes. Most businesses can expect lower profits. Farmers can anticipate lower prices for agricultural products, and professional fees may be fewer and even lower. Debtors may be unable to repay

their debts, or even to make required interest payments on debts, thus harming their creditors and hurting their credit ratings. Should a recession result in generally lower prices, debtors must repay their debts in money with greater purchasing power than the money they borrowed.

Most informed persons do not like inflation. But given a choice between mild inflation and mild recession, most people would choose inflation. The men who must choose between alternative government economic policies are well aware of this fact. No political party wants to be "blamed" for inflation, but being blamed for a recession is a sure way of being voted out of office.

Many hypotheses have been advanced to explain the causes of recessions and depressions. Economists and business and political leaders have studied the causes of recessions during the past two centuries. Many books have been written on this topic in attempts to prove or disprove various hypotheses.

About a century ago, for example, some economists thought that variations in sun spots affected the weather, and thus affected agricultural production, and perhaps people's moods. This, in turn, they felt, created economic instability. Other economists have viewed "overproduction," "underconsumption," "scarcity of money," "public psychology," "the infrequency of new inventions," and several other factors, as primary causes of recessions.

The fact is that no one has satisfactorily proved that any one cause is responsible for all recessions. Rather, it seems likely that a combination of factors may lead to recession, and that the combination, and the relative importance of the various factors involved, may differ from one recession to another. There seems little doubt, for example, that uncertainties growing out of the greatly increased military spending incident to the Vietnam War and efforts to control the resulting inflation were chiefly responsible for the recession of 1970, whereas this was not the case for the recession of 1958.

It is not necessary to have universal agreement on the causes of a recession, however, to combat its effects, any more than it is necessary for a physician to know why a boy has broken his arm in order to treat this injury. Actually, most economists and persons well-informed about the nation's economy believe that recessions can be effectively combated when they occur, and that it is possible to prevent serious recessions from occurring.

Recessions (or depressions) occur when spending declines in relationship to actual or potential production. Recession, like its twin evil inflation, is brought about directly by spending—in the one case by too little spending, in the other, by too much, in relationship to available goods, services, and resources.

It would be interesting to know *why* "too much" or "too little" spending occurs at certain times. But even without this knowledge much can be done to control economic instability (both recession and inflation) *if* the rate of spending can be controlled. And spending *can* be controlled within certain limits.

Spending is for consumption or investment. Most of the net income or take-home pay received by most individuals is spent for consumer goods and services. The major investment expenditure of individuals is for homes. Businesses (including farmers), in addition to their expenditures for wages and various operating expenses, spend to replace their inventories and facilities. If businessmen are optimistic about the future, they also spend (invest) in additional new plants, equipment, and inventories in order to increase their production. That is, they increase their *net real investments.* Conversely, if businessmen are pessimistic, they allow their investments to decrease by failing to replace all of their inventories as sales occur and by failing to replace their plants and equipment as these wear out.

In Chapter 13 it was stated that the total of all expenditures must be the same as the total of all incomes. Since expenditures can be classified as going either for consumption or for

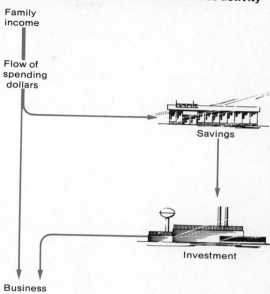

How savings may slow down business activity

Family income

Flow of spending dollars

Savings

Investment

Business

investment purposes, it is obvious that total incomes must equal total consumption spending *plus* total investment spending. In economics "shorthand" this often is expressed by the following equation:

$$Y = C + I$$

Governmental expenditures (federal, state, and local) also might be classified as for consumption or investment. Generally, however, government expenditures are placed in a separate category (called "G" in the "shorthand" terminology). Thus, the "income equation" is expanded to say that total income (GNP, or "Y") equals total private consumption expenditures *plus* total private investment expenditures *plus* total governmental expenditures; or, $Y = C + I + G$.

If spending declines, income declines. If either C, I, or G decreases, without an offsetting increase in the other factors on the same side of the equation, Y must also decrease.

Stimulus for growth: federal funds

These photographs depict government efforts to stimulate the economy through spending, or fiscal policy. They show highway construction, public works projects, urban renewal programs, and manpower training classes—all designed in the end to put more money into the hands of consumers. Chapter 16 of this book contains a discussion of the uses of fiscal and monetary policy to affect the economy.

The government first began to make large-scale efforts to stimulate the economy during the depression. All kinds of agencies were set up to run new government programs. Below, **a,** unemployed workers construct runways at the Chicago Municipal Airport for the Works Project Administration during the 1930's. In **b,** men not so lucky wait in line outside a state employment office in Memphis, Tennessee, unable to find jobs.

a

b

Today, the United States is prosperous compared to the 1930's, but problem areas remain. The government has appropriated funds for urban renewal in many cities. Old buildings have been rehabilitated and new ones constructed. In **c,** the Government Center complex built in Boston includes private buildings and government offices in a single design package. In **d** and **e,** a before-and-after comparison shows the effects of facelifting an older building.

d

c

State   Private   Federal   City

e

f

g

h

366

Major projects such as the Hoover Dam, **f,** are built by the federal government to produce power and conserve water. In **h** is the Kingston Steam Plant, built by the Tennessee Valley Authority, a public corporation. Highway construction, **g,** stimulates trade by improving transportation between producers and markets.

The Appalachian Highway System is part of a federal program to bring industry into Appalachia. In **j,** construction proceeds on a four-lane highway to replace a winding two-lane road across mountains in Virginia. Federally-sponsored job training, **i,** stimulates the economy by enabling unskilled workers to improve their earnings. In **k,** Navajo Indians work on construction of a warehouse for the federally-aided Navajo Forest Products Mill, a tribal enterprise.

i

j

k

This is what happens during a recession or depression. Chapter 13 brought out that Y (or GNP) is a monetary measure of production and employment. If total expenditures for production decrease (for any reason other than a decrease in the general price level) production will be cut back and people and resources will become unemployed or underemployed.

Increased (or decreased) spending has a "multiplier effect." The ultimate change in spending levels resulting from an initial change is much greater than the initial change. This is because every expenditure made by anyone also is income to someone else. The person receiving the income then respends the amount received or some portion of it, and so the process continues through the economy.

"Biggest Christmas Stocking You've Ever Had"

© 1970 by Herblock in The Washington Post

The following example shows how the multiplier works. In this example, it is assumed that the "propensity to spend" is 90 per cent and thus that the "propensity to save" is 10 per cent. In other words, on the average people spend 90 per cent of their incomes for consumption purposes, and save 10 per cent.

Someone spends one dollar. The person receiving this dollar spends 90 cents of it. The person receiving the 90 cents, in turn, spends an additional 81 cents. The person receiving the 81 cents then spends 90 per cent of it (almost 73 cents), and so on. Eventually, the total amount of additional spending (and income) resulting from the original one dollar expenditure will add up to ten dollars. That is, the multiplier in this case is ten. (In formula terms, $M = \dfrac{1}{1 - P}$, with M being the multiplier and P being the propensity to spend, expressed as a decimal.)

The size of the multiplier, of course, depends on the fractional amount of income spent as compared to the amount saved. If the propensity to spend is lower, the multiplier is lower, while if the propensity to spend is higher, the multiplier is higher. The length of time required for the multiplier effect to work itself out completely is determined by the velocity of circulation—that is, by the speed at which money changes hands. Most of the multiplier effects come within a fairly short period of time—normally, within one or two years.

The multiplier effect works for decreased spending as well as for additional spending. But the multiplier usually will be different for spending decreases than for increases. If one's income decreases, his expenditures may not immediately decrease by the same amount. Instead, it is likely that one will, for a time at least, draw upon savings or credit sources in an attempt to maintain one's customary living standards.

Increased (or decreased) consumption spending also may have an "accelerator ef-

fect." The acceleration principle is based on the fact that a certain level of business investment in capital goods is required to maintain any given level of consumption. When spending for consumption changes by a given percentage, investment spending may change by a much greater percentage. Again, an example can be used to illustrate the accelerator effect.

Suppose that a shoe factory operates ten machines, each of which produces 100,000 pairs of shoes per year, or a total annual production of one million pairs of shoes. Suppose also that the useful working life of each machine is ten years. This means that one replacement machine must be bought each year.

But if sales increase so that the manufacturer wants to increase his production from 1,000,000 to 1,100,000 pairs of shoes, he will have to buy one additional new machine as well as one replacement machine this year. That is, an anticipated 10 per cent increase in the demand for shoes brings about a 100 per cent increase in the purchase of shoe manufacturing machinery (two new machines, rather than one) for this year.

On the other hand, if the manufacturer believes that only 900,000 pairs of shoes can be sold, he will not replace the machine which wears out this year. The accelerator, like the multiplier, works both ways. Small percentage increases in consumption spending may encourage businesses to make much greater percentage increases in investment. Likewise, small percentage decreases in consumption may bring about much larger percentage decreases in spending for business investment.

The multiplier and the accelerator reinforce each other. When consumption spending increases, businessmen become optimistic and expand their investments in new plants, equipment, and inventories. New jobs are created, and incomes increase. Much of the additional income resulting from additional investment is spent for consumption. Businessmen become even more optimistic and invest still more. An economic "boom" develops and continues until consumer spending slows down or businessmen become less optimistic. Then, with less consumption spending there is less business investment, fewer jobs, lower incomes, and still less consumption spending. This may lead to recession.

The problem of controlling recession (like the problem of controlling inflation) is a problem of controlling expenditures. If expenditures grow steadily and in pace with the economy's ability to make goods and services available to consumers, and do not exceed this ability, there can be prosperity without inflation. On the other hand, if expenditures fluctuate violently, for whatever reasons, there will be economic instability.

Several important protective devices against economic instability (often called "automatic stabilizers") have been built into the economic system by government and private business policies during the last 40 years. These devices, which mainly lead to more stability in private consumer spending, are discussed in the next section. Chapter 16 considers government policies which may be put into effect when "automatic stabilizers" fail.

CHECK UP

1. How do economists define a recession? What are the causes of recession? How does a depression differ from a recession? What is a business cycle?

2. What were the economic dimensions of the Great Depression? What other social costs stemmed from it? Why do most people prefer inflation to recession?

3. What various explanations have been given for recessions? Why is the rate of spending in business and in government an important factor in the nation's economic health?

4. Explain the "multiplier effect" in spending. The "accelerator effect." What is the basic problem in controlling either recession or inflation?

3

How do "automatic stabilizers" work?

Some automatic stabilizers help maintain consumer purchasing power. The more purchasing power (consumer expenditures) that can be maintained during a recession, the less severe the recession will be. Several government and private business programs aid in maintaining purchasing power for certain groups.

Social Security retirement payments and private pension and annuity plans provide steady incomes for elderly retired persons. Aid to Dependent Children and public welfare programs assist many of the poor. Social Security payments, Workmen's Compensation payments, and private disability insurance provide income to disabled workers. Unemployment insurance helps tide over the temporarily unemployed. Guaranteed annual wages help stabilize the incomes of those covered by such agreements. Some workers receive a lump-sum amount of "severance pay" when they are laid off.

Most of these devices, and similar ones, were not designed expressly to combat recessions. Instead, they have been adopted mainly to prevent economic hardship and suffering. Government at all levels, as well as businesses, labor unions, and individuals have been active in bringing about such programs for humanitarian reasons. But all of these programs do in fact help maintain consumer spending, and thus to some extent "dampen down" the effects of recession.

Progressive personal income taxation also aids in stabilizing purchasing power. Chapter 14 stated that a "progressive" tax is one in which the *percentage amount* of one's income going for taxes becomes higher as his income increases. During periods of prosperity, when average incomes are high, proportionately more of one's income goes for personal income taxes

—thus, take-home pay is smaller than it would be under a "proportional" tax. But during periods of recession, proportionately less of one's total income goes for taxes, thus making take-home pay higher than it would be otherwise.

The effect of the present system of personal income taxation, in other words, as compared to a proportional tax, is to leave consumers with relatively more purchasing power when their incomes are low and relatively less when their incomes are high. Unlike the other automatic stabilizers, the income tax serves as a dampener or stabilizer both during periods of recession and periods of inflation. The income tax system was designed, to a considerable extent, to accomplish this. (There are of course other reasons for progressive taxation.)

Palmer in the Springfield Leader and Press

Finally, when corporate profits increase, dividend payments are usually expanded more slowly, and when profits fall, dividends usually are not cut back in the same proportion. Thus dividend income tends to be more stable than total profits.

The automatic stabilizers have a significant influence on the economy. Millions of persons have relatively steady (although often small) incomes because of the various government and private programs for income maintenance. Also, income tax payments are huge. These stabilizers, in addition to their other effects, help considerably in stabilizing the economy, especially in combating recession. But they cannot do the whole job when a severe recession or depression threatens. And with the exception of the income tax these measures are virtually useless in combating inflation.

CHECK UP

1. What is an "automatic stabilizer"? Give examples.

2. Why does a progressive income tax act as a stabilizer?

Clinching the main ideas

The twin evils of economic instability—inflation and recession—cause great hardships for many individuals and groups. Production and income losses due to recession, like lost time, are never found again. The loss of purchasing power, or real income, during inflation is particularly hard on middle-income groups. Most people agree that these evils of economic instability should be contained, as far as possible.

Although there is no general agreement about the basic causes—the *why*—of economic instability, there is considerable agreement about *how* it works. During inflation, spending outruns the quantities of available goods and services, and prices are bid upward. During recession (or depression) spending declines, and consequently there are declines in production, employment, and incomes.

Most informed persons no longer believe that instability is an "inherent" feature of the American economic system. Even though there is no general agreement on the basic cause or causes of instability (which may differ from time to time), the techniques of controlling it are sufficiently well known to prevent its worst consequences. These techniques consist in regulating or influencing the amount of spending.

Government and business, sometimes in response to the prodding of labor and the public, have taken various steps to offset the more serious hardships resulting from recession. These are the "automatic stabilizers," which tend to "smooth out" the extremes of instability. Most of these stabilizers (except the progressive income tax) were adopted for humanitarian reasons rather than primarily to combat instability. But their "side effects" are useful in maintaining purchasing power at a relatively stable level.

Chapter 15 review

Terms to understand
1. inflation
2. depression
3. recession
4. business cycle
5. severance pay
6. "cost push"
7. "demand pull"
8. progressive tax
9. automatic stabilizer
10. underconsumption
11. overproduction
12. net real investment
13. accelerator effect
14. multiplier effect
15. inflationary spiral
16. "propensity to spend"

What do you think?

1. What effect would a cut in federal taxes on corporation and personal income have in combating a depression?

2. The federal budget should be balanced in boom times but it might well be unbalanced during hard times. Why?

3. Why did the Great Depression cause greater hardship in agricultural states than would a depression during the 1790's?

4. Does pessimism cause depressed conditions in business or does it result from depressed conditions?

5. Some economists have suggested that what is sometimes referred to as overproduction could just as well be called underconsumption. What do they mean?

6. What groups are least likely to be hurt by inflation? Most likely to be helped? Explain.

Applying your knowledge of economics

1. Find an editorial or cartoon in a newspaper or magazine in which businessmen are urged to help the economy in some way—by not charging more for their product, by expanding their operation (thereby increasing employment) or by maintaining high standards of quality in production. Or better still, write an editorial of your own or draw your own cartoon.

2. Read *The Great Crash* by John Kenneth Galbraith to discover why the Great Depression came when it did, what efforts were made to end it, and how effective these were. Report findings to the class and bring out why different "remedies" are used now from those in the early 1930's.

3. Read the report *Distressed Areas in a Growing Economy,* published by the Committee for Economic Development. Summarize the highlights of this report in outline form for oral presentation to the class. If this publication is not available, perhaps the library has other reports dealing with distressed areas and "pockets of poverty" in this country. Or consult the book list in the Appendix for other suggested readings.

chapter sixteen

Monetary and fiscal policies for stabilization and growth

1. How does monetary policy work?
2. How does fiscal policy work?

Our system is depressive-manic;
It runs to boom, or else to panic.
In view of this it would be wise
For Government to Stabilize—
Remembering the need for both
Stability and steady growth,
And that inflation dulls the enjoyment
Even of constant full employment.

KENNETH BOULDING

One of the nation's major goals is to achieve steady economic growth. The only way for the society as a whole to have more is for production (GNP) to increase faster than population growth. Serious inflation hampers orderly economic growth. More dollars chasing the same amount of goods does not increase real income. Furthermore, the measures taken to halt inflation may lead to recession and to decreased real consumption. And inflation, like recession, harms many group in society.

Inflation results from too much spending in relation to the amount of goods and services produced; recession results from too little spending. It would seem, then, that if spending

could be controlled, the extremes of inflation and recession could be avoided, and the resulting relatively full employment and steady price levels would permit orderly economic growth.

The federal government has consciously tried to combat economic instability and to promote economic growth since the early 1930's—with greater success at some times than at others. The so-called automatic stabilizers often are reinforced by the use of *monetary policy* and *fiscal policy*

1

How does monetary policy work?

Monetary policy attempts to influence or control the amount of spending by individuals and businesses by making it harder or easier for them to borrow money. It is carried out by the

Federal Reserve System, an agency relatively independent of Congress and the President, through the influence and control it exerts over commercial banks. To understand how monetary policy works, therefore, it is necessary to understand the "money-creating" role of commercial banks, and the relationships between these banks and the Federal Reserve System.

The commercial banking system "creates" demand deposits. Chapter 6 explained the *fractional reserve* method used by modern commercial banks. That discussion may provide a clue as to how the banking system may "create money" by expanding deposits. No single bank can do this, but a number of banks working together—the banking system—can expand total deposits considerably from a single original deposit.

The Federal Reserve System is a nationwide organization. In 1913 the Federal Reserve System was established by passage of the Federal Reserve Act. Under this law, twelve Federal Reserve Banks were established. The Board of Governors of the system is appointed by the President of the United States and confirmed by the Senate. These twelve banks are located in large cities, as shown on the accompanying map. All *national banks,* that is, banks chartered and supervised by the federal government, were required to become members of the Federal Reserve System. Many of the larger state banks also joined. (There are about 5000 national banks. About 9000 other banks are chartered and supervised by the state governments.)

The Federal Reserve System exercises partial control over the nation's total supply of credit. There are three principal ways in which the Federal Reserve System can help to keep the nation's total supply of credit reasonably uniform. These three methods are explained below.

The Federal Reserve can change the percentage of bank deposits required to be held as reserve. The *Board of Governors* of the Federal Reserve System may change the reserve percentage from time to time. For example, when the reserve requirement is 20 per cent, a member bank must keep in its reserve account with a Federal Reserve Bank $20 out of every $100 of its own deposits. It then has $80 left out of every $100 to lend or invest. If reserve requirements are raised to 25 per cent, the member bank has to keep $25 uninvested and has only $75 to lend. And if requirements are reduced to 10 per cent, it needs to keep only $10 uninvested. Thus, a change in reserve requirements changes the rules under which member banks must operate. It controls the amount of money available for lending. And if banks are required to increase their reserves, there will be less money in circulation.

The Federal Reserve can change the rate of interest member banks are required to pay for loans. Suppose a bank has lent or invested all its funds above legal requirements. It may then acquire additional loan funds by depositing some of its customers' promissory notes with a Federal Reserve Bank. Or it may give its own note to such a bank.

To illustrate, Mr. Levy has borrowed $500 from his bank. He has signed a note promising to repay the $500 plus interest at the rate of 8 per cent per annum by a given date. Notes of this kind held by a bank are called *short-term commercial paper*.

If the bank wants to lend more money, it can use Mr. Levy's and other promissory notes as security in borrowing from the Federal Reserve Bank. The Federal Reserve charges member banks interest on loans made to them. Mr. Levy's bank can make a reasonable profit if it can borrow on its commercial paper at 5 per cent interest. If the Federal Reserve increased this interest rate, the member bank's margin of profit would be reduced. The member bank might then cut back on its loans or raise its own interest rates, thus discouraging borrowing. If many member banks did the same thing, credit would become tight and business activity would decline.

A Federal Reserve Bank does not have to grant credit to a member bank. Its decision is based on (1) the needs of the bank seeking a loan, and (2) the use to be made of the loan. A member bank in good standing, within limits, usually can obtain the desired credit from a Federal Reserve Bank. Clearly the interest, or *discount,* rate which member banks must pay affects the amount of such borrowing. Of course the Federal Reserve always has in mind whether or not easy credit is in the public interest.

When the Board of Governors of the Federal Reserve believes that expansion of the supply of credit money would be in the public interest, it sets a low discount rate in relation to prevailing market rates. When it believes that further expansion of credit would be harmful, it raises the discount rate. A high discount rate, or an advance in rate, indicates the danger that too much money on the market will encourage inflation. A low discount rate, or a reduction in the rate, makes clear that the Federal Reserve

The federal reserve system

■ Board of governors of federal reserve system
● Federal reserve bank cities
✳ Federal reserve branch cities

──── Boundaries of federal reserve districts
━━━━ Boundaries of federal reserve branch territories

Source: The Federal Reserve

officials believe an increased supply of money would be in the public interest.

The Federal Reserve influences the money supply by buying or selling government bonds. Bankers refer to the buying and selling of government bonds by the Federal Reserve as *open-market operations*. Open-market operations are a method of influencing the money supply undertaken at the discretion of the Federal Reserve Board. If the Board decides that there is too little credit money in circulation it proceeds to buy securities. Bonds of the United States government are the principal kind of security bought or sold in this way.

How do the open-market operations of the Federal Reserve influence the reserves of member banks? If the Federal Reserve Bank decides to buy 100 million dollars' worth of United States government bonds, it notifies dealers in securities. The dealer who supplies the securities receives in payment a Federal Reserve Bank check which he deposits in a member bank. This bank in turn deposits the check with a Federal Reserve Bank. Thus the Reserve Bank has added 100 million dollars to its holdings of United States government securities, and has added the same amount to the reserve account of a member bank. This commercial bank con-

Organization of the federal reserve system

Open market committee (7 members of the board and 5 representatives of federal reserve banks elected by directors of all federal reserve district banks).

Board of governors (7 members appointed by the president and confirmed by the senate) Appoints 3 public members to each federal reserve bank board of directors.

Federal advisory council (12 members elected from each federal reserve district bank board of directors).

12 federal reserve banks (9 directors each from banking, business, and public sectors). Directors appoint bank officers subject to approval of board of governors.

Operates 24 federal reserve bank branches.

6200 member banks divided into large, medium, and small (each category elects one federal reserve district bank board member from banking and one from business— 6 altogether). 7300 nonmember commercial banks.

Member and nonmember commercial banks owned by individual stockholders and businesses.

Source: The Federal Reserve System, Purposes and Functions, *Board of Governors of the Federal Reserve*

The federal reserve system influences the economy through the control of credit

	Credit expands Loose money policy	*Credit contracts* Tight money policy
Reserve requirements imposed by federal reserve banks on member commercial banks	The reserve requirements are lowered. Result: More deposit dollars on hand, and more money is available for loans.	The reserve requirements are raised. Result: Fewer deposit dollars on hand, hence member banks grant fewer loans.
Interest rates charged by federal reserve on credit extended to member commercial banks	Lower interest rates stimulate borrowing by the member banks and encourage loans to business. Result: Usually, increased business activity.	Raising the interest rates inhibits borrowing by the member banks and tends to discourage loans to business. Result: Usually, reduced business activity.
Open market operations of federal reserve banks	Federal reserve bank purchases government securities. The money is deposited in a commercial bank. Result: The commercial bank's supply of dollar deposits is increased and, therefore, the money that is available for loans to business.	The federal reserve bank sells government securities. It receives money payment for them. Result: Smaller supply of dollar deposits on hand in commercial banks, and, therefore, less money for loans to business.

sequently is able to increase its loans to business.

If the Federal Reserve Bank decides to reduce the reserves of member banks (and thus the country's total supply of credit money), it sells government securities to a dealer. This dealer draws a check on a member bank to pay the Federal Reserve Bank. The Reserve Bank then deducts the amount of this check from the reserve account of the given member bank. If the amount is 100 million dollars, the result is a reduction by that amount in Federal Reserve holdings or United States government securities and a corresponding reduction in the member bank's reserves. Thus the given member bank (and in time still other member banks) may have to curtail their lending.

Monetary policy can have a great impact on the economy. The policy of the "Fed" significantly affects the economic welfare of all Americans. When reserve requirements and the dis-

count rate are raised, money becomes "tight." Many businesses and individuals are unable or unwilling to pay the high interest; spending decreases, and the rate of inflation is slowed. If this trend continues, production and employment decline, and the nation may be nudged into a recession. The Board of Governors, of course, does not want to make its controls too tough or to continue them too long. But the Board may err in its efforts to "fine-tune" the economy.

The Fed seems to be less successful in pulling the country out of recessions than in curtailing inflation. If funds are not available, or are available only at very high interest rates, spending declines. But the mere availability of funds at low interest rates ("easy money") does not always insure a quick and significant increase in spending. Whether or not available funds actually are spent depends upon the public's expectations for the future.

Easy money makes possible economic expansion and growth when businessmen and consumers are optimistic. In other words, with respect to expansion, the effects of the Fed's policies are more nearly *permissive* than controlling. This is a different role than the one it assumes in combating inflation.

"Tight money" policies affect different groups and regions in different ways. Potential buyers and the builders of new homes are among the first to be seriously affected by a policy which makes it difficult to borrow money. Most new homes are financed by borrowing. The builder (contractor) borrows to buy building materials and pay his workers, and the prospective homeowner gets a mortgage to help finance his purchase.

The total amount paid by a typical middle-income home buyer on a 30-year mortgage will be increased by 6000 dollars if the interest rate is 8 per cent rather than 6 per cent. During a period of tight money, the required down payment usually is larger. This fact eliminates potential buyers who cannot raise the funds for a larger down payment. Because "money is scarce," many persons may find it impossible to negotiate loans even if they are willing to pay the high interest rates.

Construction is an important bellweather of the economy. When tight money curtails home-building, men in the building trades work fewer hours or are unemployed. The producers of building materials such as lumber, plywood, brick, and various other items are compelled to cut production and reduce their work forces. When the incomes of a substantial number of persons in a community decline, the sale of consumer items, from automobiles to haircuts, likewise decreases. Soon workers in a wide range of industries throughout the country may be faced with layoffs.

Twice during the 1960's tight money policies seriously curtailed homebuilding and other construction activities. This was at a time when a growing population and a shortage of housing created a greater need for new homes than ever before. Unemployment soared in sections of the country (especially the Pacific Northwest and some parts of the Southeast) which specialize in the production of lumber and plywood. Unemployment increased in the building trades throughout the country, and the housing situation grew even worse. Renters had to pay higher rents for less desirable houses and apartments. Landlords, of course, benefited from higher rents, as did lending institutions from higher interest rates.

Some critics propose a lesser role for the Fed. A small but growing group of economists are becoming increasingly critical of the Fed's role with respect to monetary policy. They believe that attempts to use monetary policy to stabilize the economy have been harmful rather than helpful in recent years. These men recognize the need for economic stability, but argue that present information and insight do not enable the Fed to determine just when a tight monetary policy should be adopted, or just how tight it should be. In general, they compare the Fed's attempts to "fine tune" the economy with attempts to repair a watch with an eight-inch screwdriver.

Some of these critics argue that the Fed should provide an annual increase in the country's monetary supply. This increase should be about the same as the annual increase in real productivity (GNP). A 5 per cent increase per year is often suggested. Such a policy would contribute to relatively stable prices (although it would not eliminate fluctuations in individual prices), while providing the necessary monetary funds to insure real growth in production. It would also eliminate the danger of overreaction by the Fed, which may contribute to inflation and recession, as the case may be. Finally, it would reduce the inequities which grow from efforts by the Fed to curb inflation. Invariably, tight money imposes a heavier burden upon some groups than upon others. Construction, for example, is usually cut back drastically.

It is unlikely that the Fed will surrender its discretionary authority. Most Americans favor economic stability, and monetary policy is a powerful tool in achieving this goal. It can be applied quickly, and relatively independently of action or inaction by Congress and the White House. Its effects are felt immediately, especially when a tight money policy is adopted to check inflation.

How is the policy of the Federal Reserve System related to the expansion of the money supply? This question has already been answered in part, but it is important to understand how bank deposits expand. Just as a customer maintains a checking account in a commercial bank, so this commercial bank maintains a checking account in one of the Federal Reserve Banks. A commercial bank's holdings of money, together with its checking account in the Fed are called its "reserves."

To illustrate the expansion of deposits, assume that a college student receives a gift of ten 100-dollar bills on his twentieth birthday. These bills are deposited in the student's account in a commercial bank. This bank keeps a small amount of this money in its vault, but deposits most of the bills in the Fed, thus adding to its checking account there. As money in its vault, or as deposits in the Fed, the commercial bank's reserves have been increased by 1000 dollars, as have its deposit liabilities.

The new reserves and the new deposit liabilities are in a one-to-one ratio. But the Fed requires the bank to maintain a reserve deposit ratio no greater than one to five. In other words, new deposits of $1000 legally require only $200 of new reserves. Therefore, the bank has excess reserves of $800.

The bank disposes of this excess reserve of $800 by making a loan to the local lumber dealer. The bank adds $800 to the dealer's checking account, receiving from him a promise to repay the loan with interest in three months. The lumber dealer then uses the $800 to buy lumber from a mill in Portland, Oregon. He pays by writing a check on his own bank (Bank X). The lumber mill deposits the check in its Portland bank, thus adding $800 to its account. The Portland bank returns the check via a Federal Reserve Bank to Bank X, which then subtracts $800 from the account of the lumber dealer. The local lumber dealer has now parted with the $800 loaned him by Bank X.

As this check was returned from the Portland bank to Bank X via the Federal Reserve Bank, the Fed added $800 to the reserve account of the Portland bank and subtracted $800 from the reserve account of Bank X. In other words, when the customer of Bank X pays $800 by check to the mill which is a customer of the Portland bank, Bank X's reserve account in the Fed goes down by $800 and the Portland bank's reserve account in the Fed goes up by $800.

It should be remembered that Bank X could afford to lose $800 of its reserves because its reserves were initially $800 over and above the legally required amount. Although Bank X has parted with $800 of its reserves, it will profit from interest on the $800 loan. Deposits in the banking *system* (not in Bank X, but in the Portland bank) have been expanded by $800.

Not only have the Portland bank's deposits been increased by $800, but also its reserves in the Fed. The law requires a reserve of $160 for a deposit of $800. Therefore, the Portland bank has excess reserves of $640 and can safely make a $640 loan to (i.e., add to the bank account of) one of its customers. This customer may write a check for $640 in payment for a purchase made from a firm which keeps its money in Bank Z. This continuing process explains the expansion of deposits in the banking system.

The chart on the next page shows how "money" grows. Loans and investments make possible the expansion of 1000 dollars of new reserves to 6⅔ times that amount—not in any one bank, but throughout the banking system.

Expansion of deposits under the commercial banking system

(Reserve requirement: 15%)

Through stage after stage of expansion, "money" can grow to a total of 6-2/3 times the new reserves supplied to the commercial banking system . . .

		Assets			Liabilities
	Total	Reserves (required)	(Excess)	Loans and investments	Demand deposits
Initial reserves	1,000	150	850		1,000
Expansion—Stage 1	1,000	278	722	850	1,850
Stage 2	1,000	386	614	1,572	2,572
Stage 3	1,000	478	522	2,186	3,186
Stage 4	1,000	556	444	2,708	3,708
Stage 5	1,000	623	377	3,152	4,152
Stage 6	1,000	680	320	3,529	4,529
Stage 7	1,000	728	272	3,849	4,849
Stage 8	1,000	769	231	4,121	5,121
Stage 9	1,000	803	197	4,352	5,352
Stage 10	1,000	833	167	4,549	5,549
Stage 20	1,000	961	39	5,448	6,448
Final stage	1,000	1,000	0	5,667	6,667

. . . as the new deposits created by loans at each stage are added to those created at all earlier stages and those supplied by the initial reserve-creating action.

Cumulative expansion in deposits
on basis of 1,000 of new reserves
and reserve requirements
of 15 per cent.

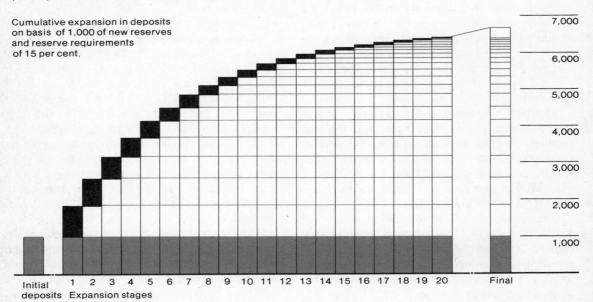

Source: *The Federal Reserve Bank of Chicago*

CHECK UP

1. How can the Federal Reserve System influence the nation's total supply of credit through changing the percentage of bank deposits required as a reserve? Changing the rate of interest charged member banks for loans? Buying or selling government bonds?

2. Why can monetary policy have great impact on the nation's economy?

3. Why would some economists limit the Fed's influence over monetary policy?

2

How does fiscal policy work?

Fiscal policy deals with government finance; that is, with government taxation, borrowing, and spending. Usually the term "fiscal policy" as used in economics refers to the policy of the federal government. It should be recognized, however, that state and local governments also have fiscal policies, which sometimes have other economic effects than those sought by the federal government.

Federal fiscal policy is determined by Congress, although Congress may be influenced by the President's recommendations. Because fiscal policy involves legislative bodies, it is more directly affected by political considerations than is monetary policy. Consequently, changes in fiscal policy are likely to be made more slowly and are more subject to compromise than are changes in monetary policy.

Fiscal policy greatly affects the economy. Although there may be lack of agreement about how fiscal policy should be managed, there is no question about its importance. Government expenditures and taxation (at all levels of government) amount to about one-third of the GNP. So great purchasing power obviously has a significant impact upon economic activities.

Most government funds come from taxes;

the remainder are borrowed. Clearly the money paid in taxes by individuals and businesses, or loaned to government, is not available for private use. Likewise, the resources, goods, and services used by government diminish the amounts available in the private economy, and thus limit private choice among goods and services.

Chapter 15 pointed out that money spent by government is income for someone. This fact suggests how fiscal policy may be used to combat economic instability. Two general principles apply:

1. If government spending increases, without a corresponding decrease in private spending, GNP will increase;

2. If government spending decreases, with-

Rate of demand deposit turnover

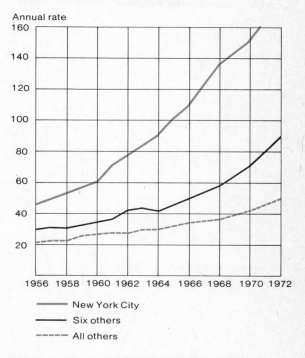

Annual rate

New York City

Six others

All others

Source: The Federal Reserve Bulletin

out a corresponding increase in private spending, GNP will decrease.

There is always a question, of course, as to the effect changes in government spending will have on private spending, and as to whether or not changes in government spending should be undertaken to bring about changes in GNP. The latter question is primarily a value judgment, but nevertheless very important.

The federal government consciously uses fiscal policy to combat inflation and recession. Prior to the Great Depression of the 1930's (discussed in Chapter 15), the government had not deliberately used fiscal policy as a stabilizing tool. Since that time, however, fiscal policy has been widely used, both in this and other countries, as a stabilization device. How is this done, first in anti-inflation measures, then in antirecession measures?

When inflation occurs, government can reduce its expenditures while maintaining current tax levels, or it can maintain expenditures while increasing taxes. Either of these measures, or any combination of them which leads to *decreased total expenditures* in the economy (that is, decreasing the sum of C + I + G, as defined in the "income equation" discussed in Chapter 15) will decrease monetary income.

The opposite steps are taken in combating recession. Recession comes when decreased expenditures for consumer goods and services (C) and producer goods and services (I) cause significant declines in production, employment and incomes (Y). At such times, government may

Federal receipts and expenditures, 1789-1950

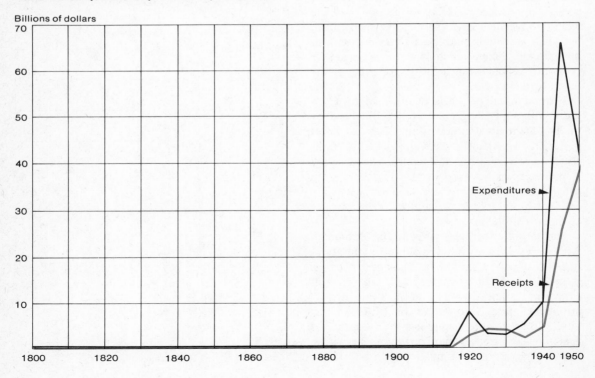

spend more than it takes in from taxes—that is, it may borrow.

This increased government spending is designed to offset low levels of private spending, and thus to increase production, employment, and incomes. Lower taxes insure that private individuals and businesses will have more funds to spend. Such government actions are designed to bring into play the multiplier and accelerator effects discussed in Chapter 15.

The federal budget provides clues to the government's fiscal policy. If government obtains more revenue from taxes than it pays out in expenditures, there is a *budgetary surplus*—an indication that the rate of overall spending in the economy is being reduced. Government is collecting money that private individuals and

business otherwise might spend, but government itself is not spending all of these funds. A budgetary surplus, therefore, is anti-inflationary. (But note that tax increases are not anti-inflationary if government spends the additional tax revenues.)

On the other hand, when government spends more than it takes in from taxes—that is, when it engages in *deficit spending* or *deficit financing* —this means that incomes (Y, or monetary GNP) will be higher than otherwise would be the case. At least this is the case unless government actions in some way lead to a corresponding reduction in private spending.

Deficit spending leads to a *budgetary deficit* and an increase in government debt (the *national debt* in the case of the federal govern-

Federal receipts and expenditures, 1951-1970

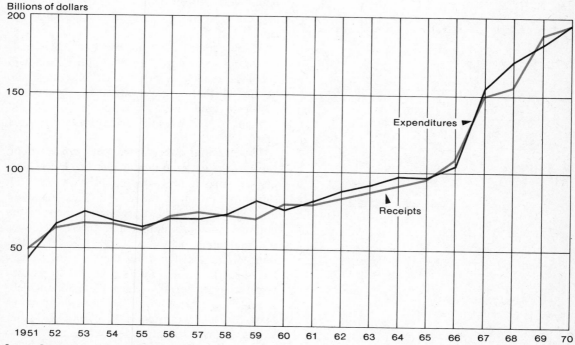

Source: Department of the Treasury (both pages)

ment). Deficit financing, or a budgetary deficit, is government's fiscal policy tool for fighting recession. Of course wars or other national emergencies may also cause deficit financing.

Such deficit spending may or may not be inflationary. If unemployed people and resources are put to work, so that the quantities of available real economic goods and services increase at least as rapidly as do monetary incomes, there is no reason to expect changes in general price levels. But if there already is relatively full employment, so that real production can increase very little—or if production efforts are diverted into goods and services not generally available to the public, as in the case of war materials or space exploration hardware—deficit spending will cause inflation.

Some people fear a large and increasing public debt. The federal government showed a budgetary deficit for 30 of the 40 years beginning in 1931. During this period, the national debt climbed from about 18 billion to over 300 billion dollars. About two-thirds of this increase resulted from military expenditures during World War II, and another sizable increase of the same kind was caused by the war in Vietnam beginning in 1965.

During this 40-year period when the federal debt increased by more than 1600 per cent, the debts of state and local governments increased by more than 800 per cent. Actually, during the decade of the 1960's, despite federal military expenditures, state and local government debt increased at a percentage rate four times that of the federal debt. Total private debts of individuals and businesses have increased by about 900 per cent during the past 25 years, and the GNP has increased by almost 500 per cent.

Many persons fear that the national debt is becoming too large, and that the nation will become "bankrupt." There is, of course, no likelihood that a government which has the power to issue money as well as to tax will become bankrupt in the same sense as does a private debtor.

The national debt differs from private debt. Most of the national debt is owed to individuals and organizations in this country. As is often said, "We owe it to ourselves." This statement does not imply that proper management of the national debt is unimportant. Interest charges on the national debt at present are about 17 billion dollars per year. This money must be collected in taxes. Tax funds collected to pay interest charges, or to reduce the national debt in effect take money from some of the nation's taxpayers and transfer it to others. In other words, a large national debt causes a "redistribution" of income within the country. Some

Comparison of U.S. national income, national debt, and interest on the national debt

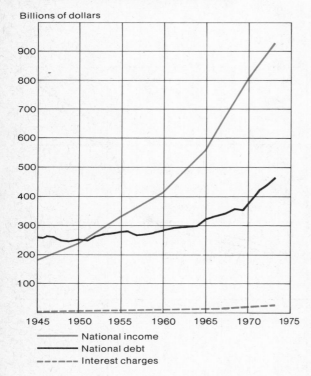

Billions of dollars

National income
National debt
Interest charges

Source: Historical Statistics of the United States *and* Statistical Abstract

Analyzer of Business Cycles

John Maynard Keynes
(1883–1946)

The influence of John Maynard Keynes (Lord Keynes) on present-day economic thought is often termed the "Keynesian Revolution." As one who influenced public policy, he must be ranked with Adam Smith and Karl Marx.

Keynes, the son of a well-known British economist, studied traditional neoclassical economics under Alfred Marshall at Cambridge. By 1918, he already was recognized as one of the ablest economists of his generation. During the 1930's, however, Keynes was to shake traditional economics to its foundations.

European nations suffered a prolonged depression during the 1920's. Hard times came to the United States during the next decade. Although millions were unemployed, classical or neoclassical economists held that the severe depression was only a temporary maladjustment. They believed that full employment and full use of resources was the normal state of the economy. To bring the economic situation back to normal or to an "equilibrium," they proposed cutting prices and lowering wages. Then employers would hire more workers and buy raw materials, and labor soon would have wages to spend.

Keynes became convinced, however, that there was no certainty that prosperity would return. He realized that an economy's "equilibrium" might be at less than full employment. He also believed that total spending must equal total income in an economy. Consequently, if spending and investment decrease, business income will decrease. The inevitable result will be less than full employment of people and resources.

According to Keynes, investment spending moves up and down much more than does consumer spending. When business investment declines, the level of economic activity also declines. Since private business does not maintain a continuous high flow of investment, some substitute must be found during periods when private investment is low. Keynes' solution was government spending. When conditions improve, and private investment again is high, government spending can be cut back.

Keynes' ideas shocked not only traditional economists but businessmen and leaders in government. But he himself felt sure that his proposals would help preserve capitalism. Keynes advocated massive government intervention ("planning") in economic affairs and deficit spending during depressions. Within a few years many leading economists and government officials had accepted Keynes' thinking. His suggested policies were already being adapted in some countries before the 1936 publication of his brilliant *General Theory of Employment, Interest, and Money.*

Gross national product and national debt

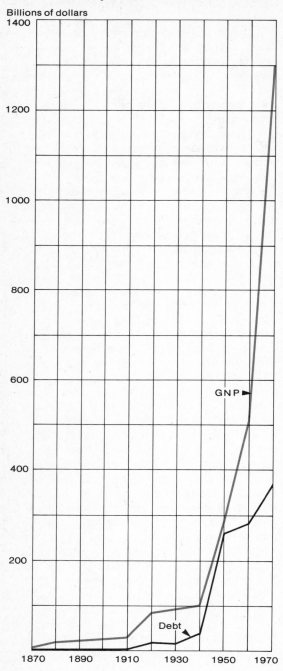

Source: Department of Commerce

individuals and organizations have more spendable income, and some less.

Actually, there are no urgent reasons for ever "paying off" or substantially reducing the national debt—or for substantially increasing it, for that matter—*except* for purposes of carrying out fiscal policy designed to meet some economic objective such as stabilization or orderly growth.

Fiscal policies affect economic growth. Everyone would agree that the elimination of the unemployment and lost production which characterize recessions contributes to economic growth. Most would agree, also, that extreme inflation, in addition to its other undesirable features, tends to lead to recession. Thus, there is little doubt that fiscal policy designed to bring about relative economic stability contributes to orderly economic growth.

Some argue that "liberal" fiscal and monetary policies also stimulate economic growth. These persons suggest that individuals and businesses will consume and invest more if money is plentiful, especially if there is little fear of recession. Thus, the argument goes, low taxes and deficit spending (combined with easy money policies) contribute to constant growth in employment and real production. This school of thought recognizes that such policies may cause some inflation, but holds that "mild" and controllable inflation is a small price to pay for continued economic growth and full employment. It is not clear, however, how mild inflation could be held in check—apart from establishing strict price controls.

On the other hand, those who are "conservative" with respect to fiscal policy fear that both inflation and a possible "loss of confidence" in the economic system will result from "liberal" policies. They say that such policies will lead to a "worthless" (low purchasing power) dollar, and a loss of foreign markets to producers in other countries. Generally they advocate a sound dollar, a reduction in the national debt, and as little government intervention in the workings of the economy as possible. This, they argue, would encourage confidence in the economic system, thus insuring the individual and business savings necessary for investments and economic growth.

Apparently valid arguments, and some historical evidence, support both the "liberal" and "conservative" positions. Perhaps the answer is somewhere between the two extremes. If policies are too "liberal" for too long, runaway inflation could result. But if policies are too cautious and "conservative," the nation will doubtless be plagued by periods of high unemployment. The crucial problem continually facing government is how to strike a happy medium. For more than a generation the federal government has tended to favor the "liberal" course. Elected officials, like most of the people who elect them, are not as afraid of mild inflation as they are of a recession.

Some economists advocate a "cyclically balanced" budget. Although some people do not worry about the size of the national debt, there are others who strongly believe that the budget should be "balanced" (meaning that expenditures should be no greater than tax receipts) almost every year, with reduction of the national debt whenever possible. Still others have advocated that the budget be balanced over the period of a business cycle, that is, that deficits incurred during periods of low economic activity be offset by surpluses (and reduction of the debt) during prosperous periods. Although this seems to be a reasonable compromise, it has not worked very well in practice. Political pressures for deficit spending during economically depressed periods always are much stronger than pressures for increased taxes or decreased spending during periods of prosperity.

The national debt can be reduced only by cutting expenditures, or by increasing taxes, or some combination of these. There always is strong opposition to increasing taxes or to reducing expenditures. Elected officials, who want to be re-elected, cannot ignore this opposition. Fiscal policy is determined by political decisions, hopefully based in part upon economic facts and goals. But politics has been described

Per capita GNP and national debt

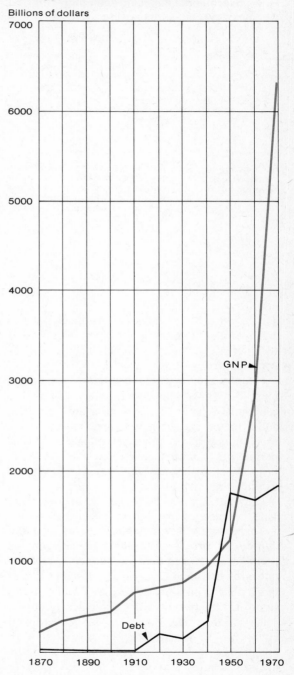

Billions of dollars

Source: Department of Commerce

How government taxing and spending (fiscal policy) may affect business cycles

Fluctuations in the absence of government action.	Fluctuations when government operates with a budgetary surplus during periods of high business activity and with a budgetary deficit during periods of low business activity.

as "the art of the possible." Fortunately, at any given level of tax rates, government tax revenues will increase as long as national income (GNP) continues to increase.

Fiscal policy cannot be neutral. Americans must recognize that fiscal policy affects the economy. Whether tax revenues are less than, equal to, or exceed government expenditures, fiscal policy has a powerful impact. The important questions to be answered are:

1. What do citizens want fiscal policy to do for the economy?

2. What kind of fiscal policy, at any given time, best accomplishes these objectives?

There are both "ideological" objections and "practical" problems to using fiscal policy as a deliberate tool to achieve economic stability and growth. Some object to a conscious use of fiscal policy simply because they do not understand it. Others object on ideological grounds. That is, they feel strongly that government ought not to attempt conscious direction or "planning" of the economy. Still others oppose its use as an economic tool for a variety of practical reasons.

One major objection to the deliberate use of fiscal policy for stabilization or growth—the potential danger of inflation—already has been mentioned. Other objections include the following:

1. *The difficulty of getting agreement on economic goals.* How much stability and growth do Americans want, and how much are they willing to pay for it? This is largely a personal value judgment rather than an economic judgment.

2. *Lack of agreement on the specific methods to be used.* This is mainly an economic judgment, but even so, "experts" may disagree on the answers.

3. *Inability to forecast economic conditions so accurately that the proper remedies may be applied in the right amount at the right time.* Again, this is an economic judgment, but the fact that future economic events may be influenced by noneconomic factors cannot be ignored.

A BALANCED BUDGET?
Traditional economics holds that the national budget should be balanced at all times. In recent years, however, there has been increased acceptance of the view that a budget deficit aids recovery during a period of recession. The assumption is that where the economy is sluggish there is little danger of inflation from an unbalanced budget and increased spending.

The practice of a planned deficit in times of recession was further refined during the Nixon administration. Advisors to the President devised two kinds of deficits—"full employment balance" and "full employment deficit." For a full-employment balance, spending is not compared with current income, but with what income would have been under full employment. A full-employment deficit would call for even greater spending than during boom times. The term "full employment" in this context assumes 4 per cent unemployment.

4. *The differing reactions of private individuals and business to government policies.* If increased government spending, for example, is offset by decreased private spending, the economy may be simply spinning its wheels. The same is true if personal savings from a tax cut are hoarded rather than spent.

5. *Political realities.* Any proposed government economic program will be influenced by existing institutions, prejudices, and pressure groups. Major decisions usually are made slowly and reflect a compromise between many differing viewpoints. The public may get "too little, too late," or "too much, too soon," when what it really needs is "just enough, at the right time."

6. *The question of how large a budgetary surplus or deficit is needed to reverse a trend toward inflation or recession.* With a trillion-dollar GNP, some economists seriously question whether or not a small surplus or deficit will have any noticeable effect on the overall economy. Under "normal" or nonemergency conditions it is politically unrealistic to expect very large surpluses or deficits.

7. *Fiscal policies of state and local governments which offset federal fiscal policies.* More than one-fourth of government taxation and spending occurs at the state and local level, and the percentage is increasing. Few state or local governments make deliberate use of fiscal policies for purposes of stabilization or economic growth. Sometimes their policies run counter to the policies of the federal government. Little can be done about this at the federal level, although some state and local expenditures depend on the availability of federal funds (highway and airport construction, for example).

In spite of these objections and problems, the federal government has made conscious use of fiscal policy (and its twin, monetary policy) for many years. It has been used more often and more effectively in combating recession than in combating inflation or promoting growth, but at least some attempts have been made to do the latter.

CHECK UP

1. What is fiscal policy? How does it differ from monetary policy?

2. How does the government's fiscal policy affect the economy? How can fiscal policy be used to combat inflation? Depression?

3. What is a balanced budget? A "cyclically balanced" budget?

4. What are arguments for using fiscal policy to achieve stability and growth? Against it?

Clinching the main ideas

Monetary policy and fiscal policy are powerful devices for combating economic instability and promoting economic growth. The first has to do with the *availability* of money for consumption and investment, and the *price* (interest rate) charged for money. The second is concerned with government *revenues* and *expenditures,* particularly at the federal level.

Generally, monetary policies and fiscal policies are directed toward the same economic goals. *Easy money* policies are compatible with *budgetary deficits,* while *tight money* policies are used in conjunction with *budgetary surpluses.* Each policy reinforces the other, and both are reinforced by *multiplier* and *accelerator* effects.

Both monetary and fiscal policy have their own weaknesses and strengths, and practical problems arise when they are used. Ideological objections to one or the other are raised by some. Nonetheless, both have been used widely for more than a generation. These policies have been less effective at some times than at others. But it is reasonable to expect that greater effectiveness will result from increased knowledge and experience.

Monetary and fiscal policies affect everyone. A decision by the Federal Reserve Board concerning interest (discount) rates, or a decision by Congress concerning federal taxation or spending, may determine whether or not a youth will be able to find a job or go to college after graduation. It is important, therefore, that all citizens know as much as possible about how monetary and fiscal policies work and what is current thinking about their use. In that way, Americans will be better able to influence decisions that affect their lives, and perhaps to protect themselves from the effects of extremes in economic change.

Chapter 16 review

Terms to understand

1. monetary policy
2. fiscal policy
3. fractional reserve
4. national bank
5. Federal Reserve System
6. short-term commercial paper
7. open-market operations
8. deficit spending
9. inflation
10. discount rate

What do you think?

1. Why were there so many bank failures in the early 1930's? Why were banks unable to meet the demands for cash made by their customers?

2. What can the Federal Reserve System do to slow down inflation? To help end a recession?

3. Some hold that the federal budget should be balanced each year. How could this be done?

4. Why does the government tend to be more successful in pulling the country out of a recession than in slowing inflation?

5. Should the United States have a "cyclically balanced" budget? Why?

Extending your knowledge of economics

1. Between 1955 and 1965 taxes as a per cent of GNP declined from 17.2 to 14.4 in China (Taiwan); increased from 24.9 to 27.3 in the United States; increased from 21.9 to 31.0 in Canada. What conclusions may be drawn from these figures?

2. What views about federal, state, and local taxing and spending are expressed in current newspapers and magazines? About inflation and ways of coping with that problem?

3. The United States experienced a number of serious depressions during the 1800's. Why did these occur? What did the federal government do about them? Why did the economy in each case experience an upturn?

4. To understand reasons for the Great Depression and why government policies failed to improve economic conditions, read John Kenneth Galbraith's *The Great Crash* and summarize the book's conclusions for class consideration.

part five

The international economy

chapter seventeen

 American capitalism and alternative economic systems

1. **Why has capitalism flourished in the United States?**
2. **What are the characteristics of socialism?**
3. **What are the characteristics of communism?**
4. **Why do so many people fear communism?**

It is the Soviet view that when the Communist system has demonstrated its superiority, other nations will voluntarily abandon their opposition to communism and will come to embrace it of their own accord. The democratic countries of the West . . . interpret peaceful coexistence to mean that it is possible for fundamentally different political and economic systems to continue to exist side by side indefinitely and on peaceful terms.

ALLAN G. GRUCHY,
Comparative Economic Systems

Every society throughout history has faced the problem of how to allocate and manage its resources. Geographic conditions, cultural heritage, states of economic and political development, and the accepted "way of life" are among the factors which influence the way a society orders its economy. No two countries are exactly alike either with respect to these factors or to the way they seek to solve economic problems.

Economic ideas from various sources, like economic goods, compete with each other. This competition has greatly increased as methods of communication and transportation have become more efficient. It is only when the followers of a given ideology seek to impose their views and ways of life on others that civilization is threatened. Americans need a better understanding of other ideologies and the economies shaped by them. This is especially true in the case of the Soviet Union and the Communist People's Republic of China. The former is one of the world's two superpowers; the latter country has by far the largest population in the world. Both are Communist dictatorships. There are, of course, countries which have an economy different from both the capitalism of the United States and the state-controlled Communist systems.

American capitalism is a decentralized system of ownership, economic planning, and management of resources. It relies mainly (although not entirely) upon the enterprise of individuals and profit-motivated business firms to satisfy most economic wants. Communism relies mainly (but not entirely) upon centralized planning by the government. Socialism falls between these two extremes. It espouses public ownership of utilities and other major industries.

1

Why has capitalism flourished in the United States?

Advocates of capitalism believe that an individual will make his most productive and useful contribution to society if he is free to choose the field of economic activity in which he thinks that he will be happiest and most successful. Of course, freedom of enterprise does not sanction activity of an antisocial nature or one which poses a threat to the public welfare.

Under American capitalism most property is privately owned. In the United States, individuals and private businesses are entitled to control the economic wealth which they acquire. An individual may enter into contracts concerning the use of his property and can count on the government to protect his contractual rights. He may also provide for the distribution of his property after his death. The uses of private property are limited only if the owners violate the rights of others or operate in a monopolistic manner. The Fifth and Fourteenth Amendments to the Constitution forbid federal and state governments to deprive any person of his property without "due process of law."

Of course the *right of eminent domain* enables government to take property needed for the public good—to build a highway, a public building, or even a factory which manufactures goods essential to national security. In such cases the government has the power to buy *at a fair price* property needed for public use, whether or not the owner wishes to sell it.

Competition is a basic factor in capitalism. In 1776 Adam Smith stated that competition acts like an "invisible hand," controlling the economy for the benefit of an entire nation. In his book, *The Wealth of Nations,* he contended that each producer and worker, eager to improve his economic status, would naturally strive to surpass the performance of others. For example, one who wished to sell a product would: (1) provide a better good or service than his competitor, (2) provide goods or services at a lower price, or (3) provide a new product or service not offered on the market. In these ways competition in a *laissez faire* economy would tend to insure product quality, determine prices, and stimulate inventions and new products and services.

Smith's laissez faire economy had some obvious weaknesses. Earlier chapters have brought out that uncontrolled economic activity has not always resulted in optimum well-being for all citizens. During periods of economic depression, large numbers of unemployed people have suffered hardships, and even during prosperous times far too many people have incomes that are too low to maintain a decent standard of living.

In some cases, monopolistic practices have controlled production and prices and withheld new inventions from production, to the disadvantage of the public. As the need for restraint and control was recognized, the government, representing the will of the people, passed legislation to regulate business practices that were harmful to the public. Competition, however, operates more fully under the capitalist system than in any other type of economy.

The American economic system has undergone many changes. This country does not now have (and never has had) a pure capitalist economy. Like all economic systems, the American economy continually adapts to changing conditions and social ideas. Perhaps best described by the term "mixed economy," it approximates capitalism more closely than does the economy of any other leading country. But the economy is much farther from pure capitalism today than it was in earlier periods of the nation's history.

Most of the early European immigrants to this country became farmers. They produced most of the goods they needed on their own land with family labor. Surplus products were exchanged at the nearest town for the few commodities people could not produce for themselves. Government interfered very little with their activities, and taxes were low. These pioneers believed in "rugged individualism," a tradition which was maintained for several generations.

This philosophy no longer characterizes American life. Modern society does not permit anyone to use his property entirely as he wishes. Taxes are high. Legislation and court decisions, in response to changing economic conditions and social ideas, have modified capitalism by introducing a significant amount of government control. A way of life appropriate for a population of 20 million is less suitable for a population of over 200 million. The needs of a technologically advanced urban society are not the same as those of a simple agricultural economy.

Capitalism puts a premium on working. Most people invest their time, labor, and money in order to live better. They want good homes, adequate diet and medical care, attractive clothes, and the time and means to enjoy life. By striving to improve their knowledge and skills, Americans hope to increase their earnings. They invest their savings, hoping to get a reasonable rate of return and thus increase their income. The prospect of greater material reward has encouraged the development of agriculture, manufacturing, commerce, and transportation. It urges Americans on to achieve new goals.

The necessity to earn money is only one of several factors making claims on a person's time, resources, and labor. Many citizens give a great deal of time to unpaid activities. And many men and women choose their life's work in the expectation of getting personal satisfaction from helping others.

"Mixed" capitalism has brought Americans the world's highest living standards. America's per capita production of goods and services, computed by dividing real GNP by population, is at least one-third higher than that of any other country. The standard of living of the average family in the United States is the highest in the world. Even most of the American poor live better than those classified as "poor" in other parts of the world.

The number of millionaires in the United States is small compared with the tens of millions of middle-income people. Many countries have some very rich families, comparatively few in the middle-income brackets, and a large number of very poor. The great bulk of Americans fall within the middle-income group. That is, they have incomes sufficiently large to buy most of the necessities of life, as well as some luxuries denied most peoples elsewhere.

No one can prove that the high average standard of living in this country is due solely to the capitalist system. Compared to much of the rest of the world, the United States still is thinly populated and has abundant natural resources. But neither can anyone prove that living standards would be higher under a different economic system. "Mixed" capitalism has worked reasonably well in this country and is approved by a majority of citizens.

Some Americans favor drastic changes in the economic system. A comparatively small minority is critical of the economic system. Some have been very vocal in finding fault with the way wealth is distributed in this country. This group includes members of nonwhite minorities, many of whom have experienced economic hardship. But most of those who feel oppressed by the economic system want no part in its overthrow through violence. What they want is a larger share of the system's benefits through peaceful changes.

CHECK UP

1. What are the characteristics of American capitalism?

2. What is the role of competition in a *laissez-faire* economy? In the American economy today?

3. How has the American economy changed since 1790? Has "mixed" capitalism proved successful in this country? Why or why not?

2

What are the characteristics of socialism?

Under a system of "pure" socialism, most manufacturing and the basic industries such as steel, mining, utilities, banking, and transportation are publicly owned and run by the government. But most present-day countries considered Socialist combine the systems of public and private ownership. Depending on which kind of ownership predominates, countries are classified as capitalist or Socialist. On that basis, almost one-fourth of the world's population live under Socialist systems. A little more than one-tenth of the world's people live under economic systems roughly similar to that of this country, and one-third live under communism. Most of the rest live in developing nations, still not firmly committed to any particular economic system. These countries, however, are leaning toward some kind of socialism rather than toward either capitalism or communism.

Modern socialism is a product of the Industrial Revolution. Although many persons earlier had talked about utopias, it was not until about 1750 that present-day Socialist thought began to emerge in Western Europe. This was about the time that the Industrial Revolution made possible greatly increased production. Surplus workers from rural areas flocked to the cities to work in the new factories. In most of the industrial towns, workers received low pay, worked long hours, and could afford only crowded and unhealthful housing.

When it was discovered that children could operate the machines, the textile mills began to employ boys and girls as young as seven. These children often worked twelve hours per day, six days a week, for less than 10 cents per hour. Child labor and the extremely low wages paid adult workers enabled manufacturers to grow wealthy. This was *laissez faire* at its worst. Naturally discontent among workers mounted.

Karl Marx was the founder of modern socialism. Among the many nineteenth-century writers who called attention to the misery of the working class was Karl Marx. Asserting that workers had been exploited over the centuries, Marx urged the adoption of a new economic system called "scientific socialism."

The basic question Marx repeatedly asked was: "Why are laborers the poorest of all classes of people, when wealth is the product of their work?" He argued that the "capitalist" class (by which he meant the employers of labor) was enriching itself by withholding from labor its rightful share of the profits of production. Because of the conflicting interests of labor and capital, he argued that a *class struggle* between them was inevitable. To him, the solution was for socialism to replace the existing economic system. Marxian Socialists argue that no man should be permitted to employ other men and thus profit from their labor.

Under "pure" Marxian socialism, land and all means of production and distribution would be owned by the government. Socialism is generally thought of as an economic system under which land and other wealth-producing property are owned in common by all the people—by "society." Management is a function of the state (actually the government).

"The collective ownership and control of the means of production and exchange" would insure that the people (collectively through their government) would own farms, mines, factories, wholesale and retail stores, and transportation and communications systems. In short, the people would own *all property used to produce additional property.* Under "pure" socialism, the formula that would govern production and distribution would be: "From each according to his ability, to each according to his need." Socialism, in common with capitalism, recognizes the right of individuals to enjoy exclusive ownership of personal property, including consumer goods. Under socialism, however, the production and distribution of these goods may be limited and controlled.

"Pure" Marxian socialism has been adopted in no country. Great as Marx's influence has been, no nation has yet developed a pure Marxist society. The economies of Great Britain, most other nations in Western Europe, Israel, Australia and New Zealand, and India, among others, may be considered a mild form of socialism. In these countries, the principles of socialism have been modified in the light of the cultural backgrounds and economic conditions of the peoples concerned.

The Scandinavian countries have achieved a high standard of living under Socialist governments. Scandinavian socialism was strongly Marxian when it took root in the third quarter of the nineteenth century. But socialism in the Scandinavian countries soon became dominated by reformist elements which advocated a gradual approach to the solution of economic problems. By the end of the Second World War, Socialist leaders in Norway, Sweden, and Denmark were much less enthusiastic about the nationalization of industry than, for example, the leaders of the British Labor Party.[1] They decided, instead, that a policy of nationalization would be followed only when an established private industry was of crucial importance to the nation's economy, or when it was impractical to have private industry provide a service of vital importance to society. In some instances, when too many small and inefficient

firms operated in an industry, a policy of nationalization was followed to insure more efficient utilization of labor and of the country's natural resources. Defense or other public considerations also made public ownership of some industries desirable.

Industry in the Scandinavian countries must be operated in the national interest. Although the people of Norway, Sweden, and Denmark decided against nationalization for the sake of nationalization, they wanted to make sure that private industry would be operated for the social good of all. Were control of shipping companies, export firms, and private domestic enterprises to remain in private hands, they must operate in such a way as to further the national interest as determined in long-range economic plans. This meant that the state could exercise some control over prices, wages, interest rates, capital expansion, and still other things which affect production, sales, and employment. Close collaboration between private business and government has emerged over the years. It has been accepted that the private market system can be relied upon to allocate scarce resources efficiently and to meet consumer preferences. (Consumer co-operatives are a widely favored means of achieving these goals.) Basic economic policies, such as determining the rate of economic growth, are established by the government after consultation with private economic interests.

Another goal of Scandinavian socialism is the *democratization of private industry.* The workers' share in the management of private business is enlarged through joint production committees in individual businesses and through development councils for each major industry. Overall problems such as research, technological progress, insuring a supply of skilled labor, and maintaining quality control are the concern of these committees and councils.

As early as 1930 the Scandinavian Socialists had abandoned the goal of transforming Scandinavia into a "worker's state." Their aim was

[1] After 1951 the British Socialists had second thoughts about the goal of nationalization and moved closer to the Scandinavian Socialists on this issue.

rather to make it a "people's home." The Scandinavian Socialist parties ceased to be "class parties" and became instead "people's parties" with broad support from members of professional and "white collar" classes as well as from factory workers, farmers, and fishermen. Noneconomic goals received equal emphasis with economic, and thus insured that workers would enjoy a larger share of cultural benefits. Socialist theoreticians continually stressed the importance of "cultural democracy," which they said could be achieved by providing an education that afforded each individual a sense of personal responsibility for the functioning of society. Torolf Elster, a well-known Norwegian Socialist thinker, put it this way:

[Our] task is to create a higher grade of consciousness such that we can co-operate in freedom to solve our problems. This is socialism . . . to organize so that it stimulates all to develop themselves, and it creates in them a sense of personal responsibility . . . to secure for all a general and technical education up to the limit of their personal capacities. In this manner we shall effectively break down class divisions.[2]

Many of this country's welfare and public services are consistent with Socialist principles. Although the United States is an outstanding example of capitalistic free enterprise, about one-third of its GNP is found in the "public sector" of the economy. Such municipal services as public education, fire and police protection, disposal of wastes, water supplies, electric power, and street transportation, are often provided by local government. The states help to finance education, highways, and various other services. The federal government, in addition to providing Social Security and welfare programs, sells electric power from government-owned-and-operated dams, rents public lands

[2] Torolf Elster, *Socialism before the Year 2000* (Oslo, 1956), pp. 12–14. Quoted in Allan G. Gruchy, *Comparative Economic Systems* (Boston: Houghton Mifflin Company, 1966), pp. 279–280.

for grazing, operates parks, and the like. This list of public services provided by various levels of government is representative rather than complete. It should be recalled also that government consciously uses monetary and fiscal policies to give direction to the economy.

In this country public services have not been forced on a reluctant public by an irresponsible government. It is rather that the elected representatives of the people have attempted to provide the public with desired services. The overwhelming majority of Americans are not Socialists. Most Americans are much less concerned with ideology than with what seems to work well for them.

CHECK UP

1. What are the world's major economic systems? About what per cent of the world's population lives under each?

2. Why did socialism develop following the Industrial Revolution? Explain the basic beliefs of Marxian socialism.

3. How has socialism been introduced in certain countries through legislative action? What are the characteristics of Scandinavian socialism?

4. To what extent are Socialist principles reflected in this country's government and economy?

3

What are the characteristics of communism?

Because many people equate communism with socialism, it is important to consider carefully the goals of each. Karl Marx believed that oppressed workers would overthrow capitalist oppressors and take over the means of production.

Alternative systems: socialism and communism

Communism and socialism are the major economic systems in the world in addition to capitalism. The Soviet Union, eastern Europe, and China are the strongholds of communism. In these countries, the economy is organized by the state under the direction of the Communist Party. Pictured are various aspects of economic life in Communist lands. Sweden and Israel are among the countries with Socialist features. In Sweden, the emphasis is on welfare services and co-operatives; in Israel agriculture is frequently a communal venture.

c

a

d

b

Hungary is still famous for paprika, which this man grows under a state contract for export, **a.** In Romania, people vacation at a state-run resort, **b.** In **c,** workers have exceeded plant goals set by the state for the production of coiled wire. A young Soviet woman, **d,** is serving her apprenticeship in a machine shop.

In Mongolia, another young woman inoculates cattle against disease, **e.** Motorcycles, **f,** await shipment in the Soviet republic of Byelorussia. In **g,** children attend a school built by a collective farm. The farm resembles a planned town in many respects.

e

f

g

h

In China, life is highly organized. School girls help harvest tea in **h.** In **i,** a worker produces silk-screen banners of Mao Tse-tung that will be displayed all over the country. Members of a commune transport bricks for a construction project, **j.**

Sweden is known as a model welfare state. In **k,** a father on his way to work leaves his child at a day-care center. The fees charged vary according to family income. In **l,** shoppers buy at a Consumer's Co-operative Society Store. The Society has one and a half million members and 246 stores. In Israel there are many kibbutzim, or voluntary agricultural communes. Much desert land is reclaimed, **m,** eventually to become fertile farmland, as in **n.**

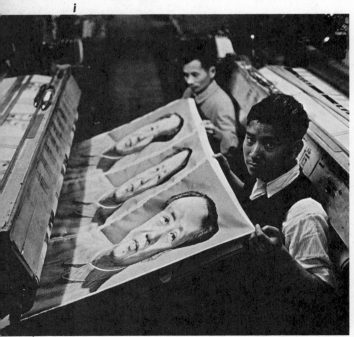

i

j

k

l

m

n

Once this was done, the need for government and its services would gradually disappear. The state would "wither away." Under pure socialism there would be no conflict within a nation or between nations. In this ideal world each person would produce according to his ability, and each would receive what he needed. It is hardly necessary to say that this situation exists no place on earth.

When communism was introduced in Russia, a small revolutionary group, the Bolsheviks, took over the government and used force to put down all opposition. The Communist dictatorship took over the means of production, "liquidating" groups that stood in the way, whether rival political leaders, industrialists, or farmers. Workers worked for the state on jobs to which they were assigned and at hours and wage rates determined by the state. What the economy should produce and how much was determined by the government. Because consumer goods were held to be less important than producers' goods, the former were scarce, expensive, and rationed. Obviously communism had not created the worker's paradise envisioned by Marx nor had it caused government as such to disappear. Planning committees and bosses in the Communist Party exercised the functions of "capitalists." Most workers were not even members of the Communist Party and hence had little chance to be heard or to get ahead.

Russia is a union of several states under a strong central government. The Union of Soviet Socialist Republics (USSR) is made up of fifteen so-called federated states (or "republics"). These states range in size from the Russian Soviet Federal Socialist Republic, which is larger than the entire United States, to the Armenian Soviet Socialist Republic, approximately the size of Massachusetts. The country's total population is about one-fourth greater than that of the United States.

All the Soviet "republics" have similar governments, and all are dominated by the Council of Ministers of the Supreme Soviet in Moscow (the central government). Within this Council of Ministers, there has been intense rivalry for personal political power. The first Soviet leader after the Revolution was Nikolai Lenin. Joseph Stalin pushed aside Leon Trotsky and exercised dictatoral power until his death in 1953. For a short time after Stalin's death a committee form of government made decisions, but Nikita Khrushchev soon emerged as the new leader. After a few years other Soviet leaders forced Khrushchev to resign. He was replaced as the First Secretary (now General Secretary) of the Communist Party by Leonid Brezhnev and as Premier by Aleksei Kosygin.

The economic system of the USSR is based on government control. When the Bolshevik Revolution of 1917 brought Nikolai Lenin to power he introduced changes that squared with Marxist ideology. But he recognized that the highest priorities were peace with Germany, an end to civil war, and increased industrial production. The last of these goals seemed to call for measures that Marx would never have approved. But in the Soviet Union Marxist theory has always had to yield to measures that promise to meet the country's needs. Today, land, factories and other means of production, and the transportation and communication systems are owned and operated by the state. This is true also of all housing facilities except farmsteads and a very few homes in the cities.

The new order envisioned by Marx was a "classless society." Each person was to produce according to his ability and receive goods and services according to his needs. A temporary political dictatorship would wither away once people understood the advantages of this new social and economic order that would insure true democracy for all the people. Present conditions in the Soviet Union fall far short of this ideal.

The economic choices of Soviet workers are limited. Russian workers may enter occupations of their choice, but they will always have the same employer—the state. The government owns nearly all wage-paying enterprises. In theory, workers may move from one job or one

How industry is administered in the USSR

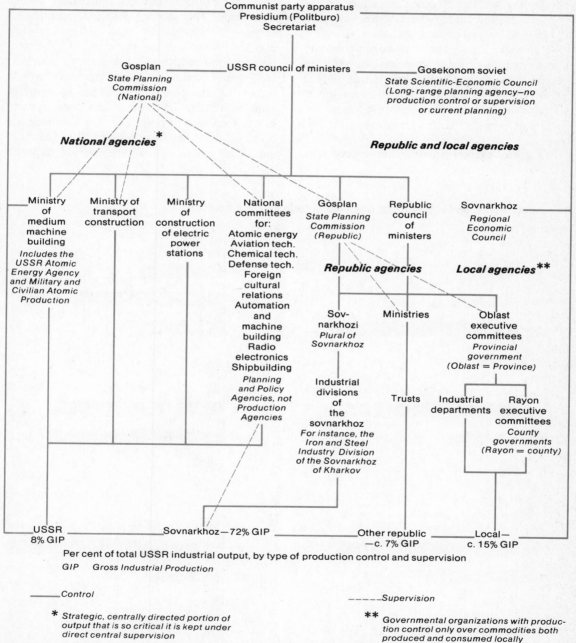

Per cent of total USSR industrial output, by type of production control and supervision

GIP   Gross Industrial Production

————Control   - - - -Supervision

* *Strategic, centrally directed portion of
output that is so critical it is kept under
direct central supervision*

** *Governmental organizations with produc-
tion control only over commodities both
produced and consumed locally*

Reprinted by permission of the Committee for Economic Development and The Saturday Review

city to another. But in practice these rights cannot be exercised. A worker cannot move to another city without advance assurance of living quarters and employment, both of which are assigned by government officials.

To be sure, Russia's state-managed economy guarantees jobs of some kind at some place to everyone able to work. But this is true only if the worker is willing to take whatever job is offered, wherever that may be. Most Americans would not consider such conditions economic freedom.

The Soviet system provides some economic rewards for workers. Prior to 1917, when Russia was ruled by the Romanov tsars, there was little political freedom and most people were poor. The average Russian doubtless is better off economically than before the Bolshevik Revolution. He is better fed, housed, clothed, and educated, and enjoys comforts and luxuries unknown to his ancestors. But in comparing the economic rewards of communism with those of another economic system, it is not enough to point out that Russians are better off than they were before 1917. The more important question is whether or not they are

The United States, Soviet Union and Communist China — a comparison

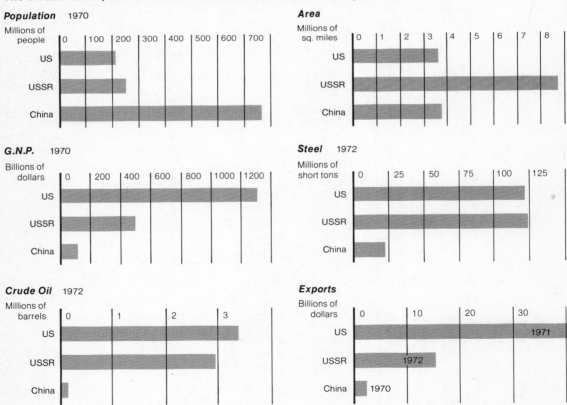

Source: The 1973 Encyclopaedia Britannica Book of the Year *and* Statistical Abstract

Foremost Foe of Capitalism

Karl Marx

(1818–1883)

The theories of Karl Marx have sparked social and political revolutions all over the world. Marx was a German political exile who wrote his socialist theories in the British Museum in London. Today, considerably modified, these theories guide the thinking of leaders in Communist countries all over the world. The beliefs of Socialist political parties, including, for example, the British Labor Party, also reflect Marxian ideas.

Historical materialism or "economic determinism" are terms used to describe Marx's concept of history. He believed that social and political institutions are shaped solely by economic forces and that man's behavior is shaped by his material interests.

Marx traced history from slavery through feudalism to capitalism, pointing out that at each stage of development there had been conflict (class struggle) between the ruling and the oppressed classes. As the oppressed workers (*proletariat*) became more numerous, more miserable, and better organized, he expected them to rise against their rulers and employers and overthrow capitalism. Government, as such, would disappear in time, and the "classless society," based on voluntary co-operation, would finally emerge.

For the "capitalist" law of supply and demand Marx substituted the *labor theory of value.* This means that a good is worth only as much as the amount of labor needed to produce it. (This concept was not original with Marx. It goes back to Aristotle and was accepted by Adam Smith and other classical economists.) However, Marx pointed out that the nineteenth-century laborer was being paid bare subsistence wages by his capitalist employer although the goods which labor produced were sold at the highest obtainable price. The difference between the selling price of the good and the workers' earnings Marx called *surplus value.* By pocketing this surplus value, capitalists "live off the sweat of the workers." By reinvesting these surpluses, or profits, capitalists become increasingly wealthy and powerful, and force less successful employers out of business. Eventually, Marx believed, the proletariat would unite to overthrow this oppressive system.

Marx's best-known writings are his *Communist Manifesto* (written with Friedrich Engels who frequently gave Marx financial support) and *Das Kapital* ("Capital"), the basic text of the Communists.

Despite Marx's predictions, capitalism has not disappeared, Communist standards of living have not outstripped those of Western Europe and the "oppressed" workers of "capitalistic America" show no signs of rising in revolt against their "exploiting masters." In short, Marx's theories did not correctly interpret man's nature nor make allowances for changes that might transform the economic conditions that prevailed in his day.

better off under communism than they would have been under another system.

Because cultural, environmental, and economic factors differ greatly among nations, it is difficult to make valid comparisons between economic systems. But it is possible to describe existing conditions in the Soviet Union. The student should bear in mind that the Soviet Union, like the United States, is a very large country with abundant natural resources and a variety of climates. It is populated by a vigorous and fairly well-educated people.

Compared to this country, most wages in the Soviet Union are low and most prices high. In general the standard of living in the Soviet Union is much lower than in the United States. Economists estimate that real GNP in the USSR is about one-half this country's real GNP. But as the graph on this page shows, there is a wide range of estimates with respect to future growth rates of the two economies. Even the most generous estimates would suggest that the Soviet Union is unlikely to overtake this country's GNP before 1985.

One-third of the Soviet population is engaged in agriculture on *state farms* or on *collective farms*. Workers on state farms are paid wages by the government. Collective farms are owned by the farmers living on them, and the income is shared by the farm workers and the state. Collective farmers are permitted to till small plots of land on which they raise food for their own consumption or for sale. Crop yields are much higher per acre on these plots than on the fields of state or collective farms.

Since medical services are provided by the government, they are within the reach of all. (Some would argue that the quality of medical treatment for the average Russian may be lower than in this country.) Education through the eighth grade is free and compulsory. Beyond the eighth grade most students who continue their educations attend technical or vocational schools. University education is inexpensive, but entrance requirements are very high.

Russia recently has introduced some incentives and management practices similar to those of capitalism. In recent years, decisions with respect to production and distribution have been decentralized somewhat. Bureaucratic controls have been relaxed so that factory managers have a voice in determining what and how much will be produced and how it will be priced and distributed. If their judgments are correct, these

Relative growth rates, USA and USSR

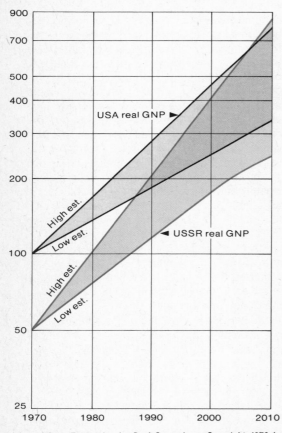

Adapted from Economics by Paul Samuelson. Copyright 1970 by McGraw-Hill Book Company. Used with permission of McGraw-Hill Book Company.

managers, like businessmen in private-enterprise economies, receive higher pay and bonuses for themselves and their workers. If their judgments are faulty, they are in for trouble.

This trend away from rigid centralized economic controls is called "Libermanism," for Professor Yevsei Liberman, a Soviet economist who has been its most outspoken advocate. Other Communist states in Eastern Europe also have experimented with Libermanism, some more extensively than has the Soviet Union.

The Communists will not admit that they have borrowed ideas from "decadent capitalism," and experiments with Libermanism are watched closely. It seems that leading Party officials have not made up their minds (or perhaps they disagree among themselves) about the extent of economic decentralization to be permitted.

Wide differences in income have created a "class structure" in the Soviet Union. The Marxian ideal of "from each according to his ability, to each according to his need" has not been achieved in the Soviet Union. Top-level scientists, professors, authors, factory managers, and military and political leaders receive much higher pay—commonly 20 times that of the average factory or farm worker. These "rich men" also enjoy more spacious and better housing, often including second homes in the country or in resort areas, free automobiles with drivers, government-paid servants, and various other benefits. Top Party officials, with real incomes perhaps 400 times that of the average worker, are wealthy by any standard.

Russians do not deny that wide differences in income exist. They make the point, however, that these differences have nothing to do with social class. A worker's child has the same opportunity to reach the top as does the child of a great scientist or a Party official. One cannot help wondering, however, whether differences in the home environment and in access to superior education do not in fact make for inequality of opportunity and class distinctions.

The USSR is a powerful nation. Among the nations, the Soviet Union ranks first in land area, third in population, and second in GNP. It has immense natural resources, and its GNP and per capita income are increasing rapidly. The Soviet Union is also one of the world's two great military powers.

According to reports, many Russians desire greater political freedom and less censorship. But doubtless the average Russian is convinced that his economic system is better than free enterprise. Consequently, despite whatever relaxation time may bring in political controls, the great majority of Soviet citizens doubtless will remain "sold" on communism. Americans

---

A DIFFERENT KIND OF COMMUNISM

All Communist economies do not operate in exactly the same way. Some retain more "capitalist" practices and provide greater involvement of workers in planning than do others.

Yugoslavia, as early as 1950, introduced workers' councils to share in the management of economic enterprises. To stimulate production, enterprises were encouraged to compete for sales, and profit-sharing for workers and managers was also instituted. Advertising is widely used in Yugoslavia, and the importation of goods from non-Communist countries is encouraged. Private farms still exist.

Parallel developments on the political scene have accompanied these changes. A wide range of opinion can be found in the Yugoslavian press, and foreign publications are readily available. The national parliament has not been reduced to the role of "rubber stamping" the Party's program. Emigration from the country is permitted. The greater freedom in Yugoslavia may stem in part from the need to accommodate the many nationalities and ethnic groups which lived in the six republics of the Yugoslavian federation.

and Russians, therefore, must make every effort to further "peaceful coexistence" as the only realistic policy for the two superpowers.

Mainland China is the world's second powerful Communist nation. Communist China has the world's largest population (more than one-fifth of the total world population), the third largest land area, and immense natural resources. Most observers agree that China still lags behind other great nations; they also agree that its organizational efficiency, production, and world influence are increasing.

China's economic development lagged far behind that of modern Western nations. During ancient and medieval times, as these terms are used in the history of the Western world, China enjoyed an advanced civilization. Emperors held sway over China, and the government was administered by a highly-developed bureaucracy. But during the 1800's and early 1900's, the Chinese economy and government were somewhat like those of medieval Western Europe. During the early 1900's, powerful "warlords" controlled much of the land, levied high taxes, and fought among themselves. Poverty was the lot of the mass of the people, and famine was not uncommon.

By the late 1800's, China had become too weak to resist the demands of the Western powers and nearby Japan. These countries, therefore, were able to acquire "spheres of influence" and to obtain profitable trade treaties. During the early 1900's, Dr. Sun Yat-sen and other Western-educated Chinese led a revolution which resulted in the establishment of a republican government. But two World Wars and civil wars in China itself blocked attempts to establish a Western-style democratic government and to introduce a more efficient economic system.

The Chinese Communist Party led a second revolution. By 1950, the Chinese Communists had managed to drive the Chinese Nationalist leader, Chiang Kai-chek, and his army from the mainland. The Nationalists took refuge on the island of Formosa. Mao Tse-tung then became head of the government of Mainland China and began a drastic reorganization of Chinese society.

The Chinese Communists introduced sweeping changes. Increased production was desperately needed to feed, clothe, and house the growing population. Order had to be restored and Communist ways imposed upon the people. Many Chinese traditions were scrapped, and those who clung to the old ways were ruthlessly destroyed.

All land was taken by the state and men and women were assigned whatever tasks were needed to implement long-range plans. Traditional small family farms were consolidated into large farming communities (communes). For a time most farm workers lived in barracks, ate food prepared in a common kitchen, and worked under the direction of government supervisors. However, when agricultural production dropped because of floods and drought, and also because of low morale among workers, the largest communes were broken up.

Producers' goods and military supplies received highest priority in production plans. Soviet technical aid helped to build China's heavy industry, develop electric power, and exploit its mineral resources more efficiently. Even more so than in the Soviet Union, the production of consumer goods became secondary. Tractors, trucks, trains, and tanks came before homes, utensils, and even adequate diets.

Growing differences between Soviet and Chinese Communists in the late 1950's led to a sharp reduction in Soviet economic aid. Soviet technicians returned home, and their exodus from Communist China slowed China's industrial development. Another reason for the decline in industrial output was that workers had to be shifted from the cities to the farms in order to help farmers raise more food to stave off the threat of famine.

China's "cultural revolution" hampered her economic progress. In 1966 and 1967, an internal power struggle created further problems. Leaders critical of Mao Tse-tung urged greater emphasis on production for private consumption, while those loyal to Mao believed that as in the past highest priority should be given to heavy industry and armaments. Mao gave his blessings to the millions of students and young people who began roaming the country, chastising those who had lost the "revolutionary spirit."

In the course of this ideological struggle, many persons with valuable technical skills were ousted. The youths (known as the "Red Guard") and older pro-Mao followers carried forward what they called the "Proletarian Cultural Revolution"—a movement to return to the "pure" ideas of Mao. Armed conflicts occurred between them and urban workers and peasants. Frequently military forces had to intervene to restore order. The lasting effects of China's internal upheavals are not yet fully known, but agricultural and industrial production unquestionably suffered.

By the late 1960's, Chinese Communists were clashing with Russians. The Chinese Communists have accused the Soviet Union of being "soft" in failing to adhere closely to Marxist dogma and in becoming too friendly with Western nations. The Chinese also have a memory of Chinese territories acquired by Russia in the time of the tsars. Armed clashes between Chinese and Soviet border troops have taken place along the border in recent years.

Following President Nixon's historic visit to China in February, 1972, there were increased efforts to normalize relations between our two countries. But China continued to be suspicious of the Soviet Union's intentions.

Most Mainland Chinese probably feel that the Communist regime has made gains. China now is ruled by Chinese and not by "foreigners." The country has produced nuclear weapons and space satellites, and has become a formidable military power. Western economic experts believe that official Chinese claims of increased production and prosperity are exaggerated, but concede that substantial progress has been made.

The Chinese masses, accustomed to hardship, turmoil, and restrictions on their freedom, continue to endure these conditions. Food, housing, and consumer goods are far from adequate by Western standards. Too great centralization of decision-making hampers agricultural and industrial production, and has hampered the attainment of announced economic goals. Yet many neutral observers and some recent American visitors feel that the Chinese masses are better off materially than before Mao came to power.

CHECK UP

1. How was a Communist dictatorship established in Russia? How is the nation governed? How does the Soviet economy differ from that envisioned by Marx?

2. Contrast the Soviet economy with that of this country. What economic changes are being considered in the Soviet Union?

3. What problems confronted the Chinese in the late 1800's and early 1900's? How did the Chinese Communist Party come to power? What changes did it introduce? What problems have the leaders of Communist China had to face?

4

Why do so many people fear communism?

Few Americans would want to live under communism even when they criticize the present economic system. There is little reason to believe that Russia or China could impose communism on the United States. Why, then, is there great fear of communism in the United States and in many other Western lands?

Dedicated Communists are determined to make the world Communist. Marx advocated a working-class revolution. Communist leaders from the time of Lenin have reaffirmed the long-range goal of communism to "liberate" the world's "oppressed" workers by whatever means necessary, and whether or not the workers want to be "liberated." These statements reflect acceptance of the "party line," and may be intended mainly for home consumption.

But the fact remains that both the Soviet Union and Communist China have taken advantage of every opportunity to extend their influence over neighboring lands by subversion, revolution, and military invasion. Rebellions against Soviet domination have been ruthlessly crushed in East Germany, Poland, Hungary, Czechoslovakia, and elsewhere. The Chinese Communists have done the same in Tibet.

Two former "satellite" states have managed to break away from the Soviet orbit but still retain communism. Yugoslavia has a large, well-equipped, and well-trained army, mountainous terrain unsuitable for Soviet tanks, and an intensely patriotic population. Albania may seem too small and too distant to be worth coercing.

Both are at some distance from the Soviet Union. Yugoslavia follows a policy of "independent communism," whereas Albania has allied itself with Red China.

Recently the Soviet government has proclaimed the "Brezhnev Doctrine." It provides that Soviet troops may be used to put down "disorders" and "counterrevolutions" in any Communist nation. This doctrine doubtless has served to intimidate some countries in Eastern Europe. On the other hand, it was denounced by Communist parties in West European countries and by the People's Republic of China.

Both the USSR and Communist China have powerful armed forces. The Soviet Union spends a much larger percentage of its GNP for military purposes than does this country, and the same appears true for China. The Soviet armed forces have modern weaponry, including nuclear missiles, a large air force, and a rapidly expanding navy. China's armaments are less modern but its huge population provides an almost inexhaustible supply of ground troops.

Both countries seem to believe that huge armed forces are needed to protect them from outside aggression—or, perhaps, from internal disorders. Both speak of themselves as "peace loving" and denounce their current ideological opponents as "warmongers."

The United States and the Soviet Union have been negotiating for mutual nuclear and other arms reductions for several years. But despite their improved relations with the United States, neither the USSR nor China have reduced their military spending substantially.

Tensions between Soviet and Chinese Communists and this country have lessened somewhat. Since World War II, serious confrontations with Communists have occurred in Iran, Greece, Korea, Southeast Asia, Africa, the Middle East, Cuba, and elsewhere. Tens of thousands of American servicemen were killed in Korea and Vietnam. The cost of maintaining United States armed forces in readiness has amounted to considerably more than one trillion dollars. Since 1972, however, there has been more co-operation and less confrontation between the United States

The heavy burden of national defense

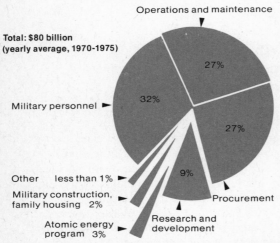

Total: $80 billion
(yearly average, 1970-1975)

Operations and maintenance
27%

Military personnel ►
32%

27%

9%

Other   less than 1%
Military construction, family housing 2%

Atomic energy program 3%

Research and development

Procurement

Source: Statistical Abstract; President's Budget Message (1974)

and the two Communist superpowers. There is hope that this spirit of peaceful co-operation can be maintained and expanded.

The Soviets and Communist Chinese distrust the motives of "foreigners." Communist doctrine stresses the class war between capitalism and communism. Unfortunately comparatively few Russians and Chinese have traveled widely outside their own countries. What they have read or heard about the rest of the world has been screened by censorship and colored by propaganda. Throughout history, both Russia and China have frequently been invaded and have lost territory to neighbors whenever they were weak militarily. These experiences and limited access to travel and unbiased information help to explain attitudes held in these countries.

International problems might arise with the Soviet Union and Mainland China even if they were not Communist nations. Throughout their history, both Russia and China have followed a policy of expansion. The international policies of Russia under the tsars and of China under its great emperors were much like those of their twentieth-century leaders. There is one difference, so far as this country is concerned. During these earlier conflicts the United States was not yet a nation with worldwide interests.

It may be an oversimplification to blame so many of this country's international woes on communism. Over the years the United States had had differences with such non-Communist nations as Britain, Mexico, Spain, Germany, Italy, and Japan. Is it possible, therefore, that recent problems with the Soviet Union and China were not primarily ideological?

CHECK UP

1. How successful has the Soviet Union been in extending its influence?

2. Why have tensions developed between the Soviet Union and the People's Republic of China?

3. Why have tensions developed between the two Communist giants and the United States?

Clinching the main ideas

The world is divided into competing economic and political systems. The United States is the leading example of capitalism, but there are some 20 other advanced western-style economies. In most of these government intervention is more pronounced than in the United States. Norway, Sweden, and Denmark are of all European nations the most committed to socialism, which in those countries is combined with a democratic political system. Others, notably the Soviet Union and the People's Republic of China, practice a system of state socialism generally known as communism, in which individual economic freedom is subordinated to national policy, and political democracy as Americans know it is nonexistent.

The American system offers private ownership of property, freedom of occupational choice, and economic competition subject to restrictions voted by Congress. It also provides opportunities for citizens to improve their economic position through their own efforts.

Communism is based on a highly centralized and planned economy and allows very little economic or political freedom. Most persons in the Communist countries, and many peoples in developing countries, appear to be strongly attracted to communism. The fact that communism as an ideology has wide appeal cannot be ignored. At present, however, communism as an ideology poses no threat to the American economic system.

Whether as "nationalists" or as Communists, the leaders of the Soviet Union and China have used communism as a tool to weaken the United States. By helping developing peoples to overcome economic and political conditions which makes communism seem attractive, the United States is helping itself. This policy doubtless must be continued until lasting international co-operation, or at least peaceful coexistence, replaces international tensions and power struggles in the community of nations.

Chapter 17 review

Terms to understand

1. class struggle
2. socialism
3. "Libermanism"
4. commune
5. Brezhnev Doctrine
6. Marxian socialism
7. "mixed" capitalism
8. classless society
9. Proletarian Cultural Revolution
10. *Wealth of Nations*
11. *Das Kapital*
12. democratization of private industry
13. collective farm
14. state farm
15. independent communism

What do you think?

1. Why do present-day Americans place a higher value on security than did their ancestors in the early 1800's? Is this point of view characteristic of an industrialized society? Why?

2. Compare incentives for working hard in this country and in the Soviet Union. What conclusions may be drawn from the fact that only about ten million Soviet citizens hold membership in the Communist Party?

3. Karl Marx was aroused by the plight of workers in European industrialized countries during the mid-1800's. He predicted that communism would replace capitalism in industrialized nations. Why has this not happened? Actually communism was established in Russia and China, countries which had a predominantly agricultural economy at the time of the Communist take-over. Why?

4. What is the difference between the way socialism was introduced in Russia and in the Scandinavian countries? Is this difference important?

5. In what ways have the Soviet Union and Mainland China co-operated? Failed to see eye to eye? Explain why in each case.

Extending your knowledge of economics

1. Do some research on similarities and differences in the Chinese and Russian approaches to communism. Report your findings to the class.

2. Consult books on communism to learn how the Communist Party controls the Soviet Union and how a few leaders control the Party. (Refer to the book list at the back of this book.) Three excellent titles, available in paperback, are Rodger Swearingen, *Focus: World Communism* and Hyman Kublin, *Russia* and *Russia: Selected Readings.*

3. Pretend that you are a Soviet citizen working on a collective or state farm. You have a friend or relative in the United States with whom you are permitted to correspond. Write an imaginary letter in which you describe your work.

chapter eighteen

Aid to the developing economies

1. **What is life like in an "underdeveloped" economy?**
2. **What is the purpose of foreign aid?**
3. **What is the economic outlook for the developing nations?**

The upshot for those who live in contemporary transitional societies is clearly not predetermined either by the patterns of history or by the nature of the technical tasks of growth or by the balance of the Cold War. The historical stage at which their societies stand, the pool of unapplied and relevant technology, and the world setting in which they find themselves set the limits and the possibilities of their problems. But like other peoples at great moments of decision, their fate still lies substantially within their own hands.

WALT WHITMAN ROSTOW,
The Stages of Economic Growth

Following World War II, the United States provided about 150 billion dollars in economic aid to developing and war-torn countries. Never before had a people been so generous in sharing its resources.

This country's "foreign aid programs" have been widely discussed in Congress, in the news media, and at the "grass roots." Some Americans argue that this country has too many problems at home to be giving away billions to other countries. Others hold that United States

aid saved the world from anarchy and suggest that developing countries continue to need assistance. Still others approve the principles underlying economic aid, but feel that its administration should be entrusted to international agencies.

Value judgments obviously underlie decisions on such questions as: Should developed nations aid developing nations? How much? How? Decisions about the kinds of aid provided certainly also reflect economic considerations.

1

What is life like in an "underdeveloped" economy?

Per capita production and average standards of living vary greatly both among developed countries and among those that are developing. The Mexican economy, for example, may seem "underdeveloped" when compared to that of the United States. But compared to Bolivia,

India, or Sudan, Mexico must be considered a nation with a developed economy. In reaching a precise judgment, one would need to look at various measures of economic development.

The average amount of production of goods and services per person (annual per capita GNP) is one measure of economic development. This country's per capita GNP is the world's highest. Only about a dozen countries reach half the level of the United States. At the other extreme, at least 65 countries have per capita GNP's of not more than *one-fourth* that of the United States. And at least ten countries have per capita GNP's less than *one-fortieth* that of this country.

The average amount of food available per person may be used as a measure of economic development. A minimum amount of food is necessary to sustain life. In very poor societies, people have to do without many comforts and conveniences—indeed all less essential things—in order to get this necessary minimum nourishment. At least 24 countries have an average daily food consumption (measured in calories) of less than three-fourths the United States average. Experts in health and nutrition state that this is not enough food intake for people to work efficiently. To make matters worse, diets in these countries typically are extremely unbalanced from a nutritional standpoint, as well as lacking in variety.

The availability of medical care may be a measure of a nation's stage of economic development. The rate of infant mortality (the per cent of children dying before reaching one year of age) is often used as a standard in evaluating medical care. In about one-fifth of the world's countries the infant mortality rate is at least twice as high as in the United States. In some countries it is six or seven times as high. The poorest people in the countries least developed in an economic sense live under very primitive sanitary conditions. Most of them never see a medical doctor and must rely on folk medicine when injured or ill.

Generally, birth rates are high in the less developed economies. Despite high infant mortality and high general death rates, grossly inadequate sanitation, extreme poverty, and dearth of medical services, population continues to increase rapidly in many comparatively poor countries. In Indonesia, India, Pakistan, Colombia, El Salvador, Ghana, and Morocco, for example, the birth rate (number of births per year per 1,000 population) is from two to three times that in the United States. Although many infants die, so many children survive that the total number of poor people increases each year.

Mounting population pressure strains the resources of developing economies. Many poor nations have areas of fertile lands, or forest or mineral resources, that are not being used efficiently. Some, of course, have very scanty resources. But in most developing countries, population increases tend to absorb productivity increases.

To illustrate, the density of population in the United States is about 60 persons per square mile, and the annual rate of population increase is just over 1 per cent. In India, the world's second most populous nation, the average number of persons per square mile is more than 400, and the annual rate of population increase is about 2½ per cent. This country's annual per capita GNP is over 6000 dollars; India's is below 100 dollars. In terms of average availability of food, the United States has 3200 calories per person per day; India has just over 1800. The seriousness of this situation becomes clear when one considers that 2500 calories per day commonly are accepted as the minimum necessary to insure health for the average active person.

A high percentage of the work force in most developing countries is engaged in agriculture. Because people must eat, food must be grown. Unfortunately, in most developing countries a very large proportion of the population is engaged in agriculture—mainly in "subsistence agriculture." That is, each family grows very little more than the food it consumes.

Generally, the amount of land available to a family is small; tools may be similar to those used hundreds of years ago; fertilizers and improved seed are not available. With little or no knowledge of scientific agriculture, and no resources for introducing it, agricultural yields remain low and the threat of hunger is ever present. These are the conditions under which half of the world's population lives.

If most of its labor force is engaged in subsistence agriculture, a country finds it difficult to develop industry. Very little can be done about industrialization until agriculture becomes more efficient, and produces a surplus that can be sold on the world market. Indeed, if agricultural output increases no faster than the rural population, there is no surplus to

feed an industrial work force. In short, to raise either industrial output or living standards substantially, developing nations need to: (1) increase their agricultural productivity, and (2) reduce their rate of population growth.

Most economically underdeveloped societies are bound by custom and tradition. A large part of the population in an underdeveloped economy has never attended school. Many have never traveled ten miles from the village where they were born. Their work habits and day-to-day life are governed by ancient customs and traditions, handed down from generation to generation. Ideas of progress and change—of different and perhaps better ways of doing things—either are unheard of or are mistrusted and resisted. Doubtless most people in such societies would like to have more of the material things of life. But cherished traditional

AID THROUGH INTERNATIONAL AGENCIES: THE WORLD BANK

Much of United States foreign aid is channeled through international agencies such as the World Bank. The Bank receives funds from developed countries and makes loans to developing countries. In 1969, lending by the World Bank and its affiliate, the International Development Association, passed the two-billion-dollar mark—thus outstripping the U.S. foreign aid budget.

Views differ on the role played by the Bank. Although its profits set a record, rising 25 per cent last year, the Bank was criticized by both left and right. Some claim that the bank is increasing the burden of public debt in many countries by lending them too much money. They point out that the external public debt of the developing countries has tripled since 1960.

Another criticism is that there is a gap between the Bank's commitments to lend money and the disbursement of the funds. Even after the Bank authorizes loans, it requires the borrowing country to submit a detailed statement of the use to which it plans to put the funds. The Bank must then approve the statement, and it is at this point where there has been a logjam. This fact has suggested to some critics that not enough planning is done on projects when they were originally approved for funding.

Officials of the Bank point out that projects approved yield at least a 10 to 15 per cent return, and that the returns from social projects are as difficult to measure as they are necessary. Meanwhile, many developing countries complain that loans are still too hard to obtain, and that the Bank is not doing enough in the fight against world poverty.

values, lack of education, and environmental factors, prevent them from taking the necessary steps to raise living standards.

Capital is very scarce in underdeveloped economies. To bring about the increased production needed to raise standards of living, large amounts of real capital must be combined with skilled workers and sound management methods. Factories, transportation systems, and fuel or power supplies must be provided. Workers, managers, and professional personnel must be educated. Getting these things done is beyond the resources of most underveloped economies.

When most workers are raising food crops, and the yield barely meets their own needs, there is no "surplus" to support either the education or industrialization. Without a surplus ("savings"), either from inside or outside the economy, little headway can be made. The vicious circle that blocks progress in underdeveloped economies can be stated briefly: no savings equals no capital accumulation equals no increased productivity equals no savings.

The expectations of peoples in developing economies are growing. No one wants to be hungry, cold, or ill. Parents do not want their children to die young from lack of food and health care. Workers want greater economic rewards for their labor. This is true of people in any economy. Dissatisfaction multiplies once people realize the great inequalities that exist in the world.

Although a great many of the world's very poor are illiterate and have never traveled far from their village, they realize that better conditions obtain in other lands. They reach these conclusions from programs on their village radios, and word-of-mouth reports, and from observing foreign visitors and well-to-do people in their own country. Their knowledge about the United States, Western Europe, the Soviet Union, or Japan, may be vague, but they feel sure that people in these countries, compared to themselves, are wealthy.

No one can blame the peoples in developing nations for wanting a better way of life, and for wanting it *now*. Present-day developed and prosperous nations once were poor. The work and savings of many past generations have made possible this country's present standard of living. But the hungry peasant in a developing nation has no knowledge of conditions in America 100 or 200 years ago. All he knows is that Americans live in an affluent society, a way of life which he would like to share. And he does not want to wait 200 years for this to happen.

Communist influence has increased in many developing lands. Communism thrives on poverty and despair. To the poor it holds out the promise of taking from the rich and sharing with the poor. Many of the developing countries were colonies of European nations until World War II. People in these countries expected that their economic lot would improve quickly once they were free from the "exploitation" of colonialism. Generally, this has not happened, or progress has been much slower than was expected. In some cases, economic and political conditions may have worsened. In many of the young nations, the disappointed and the disillusioned grasp at the promises of communism.

As was pointed out in the preceding chapter, developing nations, which have about one-third of the world's population, are not yet firmly committed to any one type of economic system. But they seem more inclined toward socialism than either capitalism or communism.

CHECK UP

1. What are some measures of the comparative economic development of a country? Which seem especially significant? Why?

2. Why is economic development a relative matter?

3. Why are the expectations of peoples in developing countries increasing? Why may communism appeal to them?

2

What is the purpose of foreign aid?

Since World War II, the government of this country has provided economic aid and encouraged American investments in developing countries. During the 1960's, it also sponsored the Peace Corps and other programs designed to help people in developing countries help themselves. The programs stressed a person-to-person rather than nation-to-nation approach. Programs of this kind, in a sense, are also a form of foreign aid. But the present discussion is focused on outright grants or loans designed to strengthen a country's economy, or to meet an emergency such as famine, or to improve general health and sanitation. Funds have also been provided to strengthen a nation's defense against invasion or internal unrest. The last

example of aid is usually referred to as "military assistance"; the others are commonly called "economic assistance."

The first goal of economic aid after World War II was to speed the recovery of war-torn nations. As early as 1945, the United States began to provide aid to both allies and former foes. Two years later, Congress approved the "Truman Doctrine," a policy of helping free nations resist Communist attack or subversion. The "Marshall Plan" in 1948 was an instrument for channeling aid into Western Europe, and the "Point Four Program" in 1949 stressed programs of technical assistance to developing lands.

Since the mid-1950's, appropriations for military aid have become relatively more important. With the outbreak of the Korean War, large-scale military assistance received high priority. Currently the State Department's Agency for International Development (AID) administers nonmilitary assistance programs; the Defense Department administers military aid. Both

Economic assistance under the foreign assistance acts

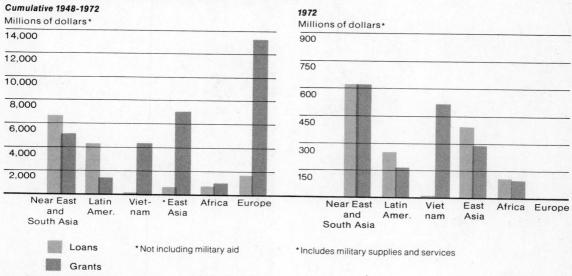

Cumulative 1948-1972
Millions of dollars*

1972
Millions of dollars*

Loans
Grants

*Not including military aid

*Includes military supplies and services

Source: Statistical Abstract; *Bureau of Economic Analysis, U.S. Department of Commerce*

Developing economies: a changing "third world"

The development of agriculture and education are two primary concerns of the developing countries. Agricultural production especially must be modernized not only to feed each country's population, but also to provide a surplus which may be exchanged for much-needed capital.

*In **a,** a Brazilian refuels a tractor on an experimental farm, and in **b,** an Indian plant pathologist inoculates corn against bacterial stalk rot. Production of flour from millet grain, **c,** is carried out at the first millet processing plant in the world, in Niger. A schoolboy, **d,** uses charcoal ink to write on his slate in an Indian village. Indian women welcome trainees arriving from a Home Economics Training Center to begin a nutrition program, **e.** At a college in Nigeria, **f,** future teachers study chemistry in a laboratory.*

a

b

c

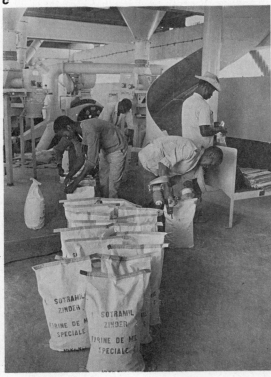

d

e

f

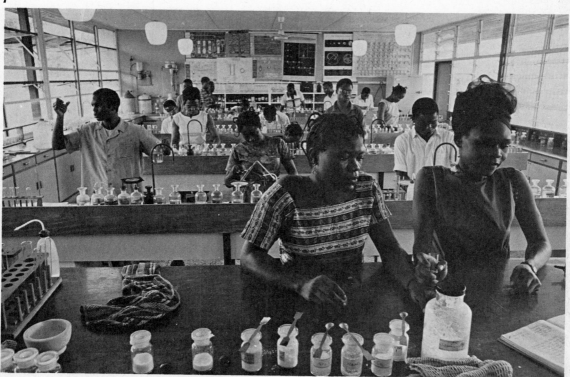

g

h

i

Industrial and scientific progress is yet another aim of the "third world" countries. Mexico has completed a new, ultramodern subway in Mexico City, **g,** which will speed urban transit. In Bolivia, oil and gas production has become increasingly important; at the drill site shown, **h,** gas has been discovered in large amounts. When modernization sets in, old and new are found side by side. In **i,** an atomic energy research center flourishes in India, while illiteracy there is 72 per cent and the average life expectancy is 50 years.

Growing cities are characteristic of a developing economy. In **j** a view of Kinshasa, Congo, shows much modern construction. Urban centers are often the chief marketplaces; in **k,** produce is brought to the "farmers' market" in Guatemala City. A new supermarket in Brazil provides a different outlet for farm products, **l.**

programs, of course, are controlled by Congress, which appropriates the necessary funds.

To date, of the more than 150 billion dollars spent on aid programs, about 30 per cent has been allotted to Western Europe. The Near East and South Asia have received about one fourth of the total amount, East Asia (including Vietnam) another one third. Latin America has received about 8 per cent of the total, African nations about 3 per cent, and Eastern Europe less than 2 per cent.

Most of the funds "given" to foreign lands have been "spent" in this country. The types of aid just mentioned have seldom involved outright cash grants. Most of these funds were used to pay American producers and workers for goods provided the various countries. Some of the funds, of course, were used to pay the salaries of American supervisors and technicians on foreign assignments, and also to pay the wages of citizens in these countries who did work connected with the projects. In this country, the economic effect of foreign aid has been to provide employment for Americans in the production of goods sent to other countries.

Foreign assistance: Aid expenditures for commodities in a recent year

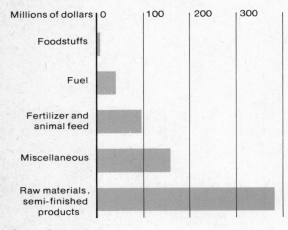

Source: Statistical Abstract

Doubtless foreign aid programs have contributed to high employment and to higher prices in this country.

Nations receiving economic assistance have a good deal to say about what is done with it. United States economic aid has gone into projects such as dams, irrigation or drainage systems, transportation networks, school buildings and teacher training, fertilizer factories, improved roads, and the like. Some aid has been used by the countries receiving it to finance economically questionable "prestige" projects such as large steel mills, international airlines, and superhighways when secondary roads are urgently needed. At times funds have been eroded by graft and black market operations. Instances of undesirable uses of foreign assistance have received much attention in the American press and have given a bad name to a highly useful program.

Americans must understand that the customs and practices in nations which receive economic aid may differ from those in this country. Human nature being what it is, public funds are not always spent wisely in the United States. Why expect greater perfection of others? In evaluating foreign aid, certain questions should be asked: Why was the program undertaken? What are its economic or other merits? What evidence is there that it has been successful?

Foreign aid has been provided for humanitarian reasons. When a nation has been threatened with mass starvation or mass deaths from epidemics, the United States has made available food and medical supplies. This kind of short-term assistance was made available to war-torn countries following World War II. It has also been used in cases of crop failures or natural disasters.

Such emergency aid has been reasonably effective. Thousands of persons in many parts of the world are alive today because of "gifts" of food or medicine from the United States. But there can be no question of attempting to feed *all* the world's hungry and cure all its sick.

Even the United States does not have the resources needed for such an undertaking.

Foreign aid has been undertaken to increase economic productivity and to stimulate trade. No nation can produce everything it needs, and each nation can produce certain goods more efficiently than others. If each country produces surpluses of the goods it can produce most efficiently, and exchanges these surpluses for needed goods that other nations can produce most efficiently, all the nations involved in the exchange of goods will be more prosperous.

Unfortunately, developing nations produce few surplus products. One of the goals of United States foreign aid programs has been to break the vicious circles stemming from low production and low savings. If the United States can help developing nations to establish export industries, they eventually can earn the money needed to buy machinery further to industrialize their economies.

United States foreign aid contributed greatly to restoring the economies of Western Europe and Japan, which had suffered severe damage during World War II. But these countries had developed economies before the war. Massive aid has made possible extensive and rapid change in the economies of Taiwan and South Korea. In many countries, however, gains in productivity have been largely offset by population increases.

One reason for foreign aid was to check the spread of communism. This country was alarmed by the spread of communism and the imperialist expansion of the Soviet Union following World War II. American statesmen realized that poverty and an uncertain future provided fertile soil for communism. A major goal of foreign aid, therefore, was to help nations build economies that would increase contentment among their peoples and make them less open to subversion.

The threat of communism seems much less great today. During this generation very few nations have had communism imposed by force.

And some countries that once appeared to be turning toward communism have become less receptive to it.

This country's efforts to check the spread of communism have led to heavy spending for armaments and to involvement in "hot" as well as "cold" wars. Resources used for these purposes could have been used to improve productivity and living standards in this and other lands had there been no power struggle. The same can be said for the Soviet Union.

CHECK UP

1. What various kinds of aid did this country contribute to war-torn and developing nations following World War II? Why?

2. How did foreign aid affect this country's economy? Why? Why have some aid programs been criticized in this country?

3. Why have some aid programs been more successful than others in increasing the economic productivity of the recipient nations?

3

What is the economic outlook for the developing nations?

Economic development is relative. In time differences between per capita GNP may diminish, but some nations still will have relatively underdeveloped economies.

The economic future for today's developing regions is not necessarily bleak. West Europeans and Americans have no permanent monopoly of natural resources, skilled manpower, and imaginative managerial personnel. The developing nations that were short of capital and technological skills have made great progress since World War II. Many others doubtless will make substantial gains within a generation or two. Skills can be developed quickly through education. Sufficient capital to break out of the rut of low-level production doubtless is a critical factor in many lands. Capital may have to be acquired from outside the country in many cases. But it is necessary also strictly to allocate a developing nation's resources to where they can do the most good. In any event, the rate of population growth must be lower than growth in productivity.

Culture patterns may block economic development. The age-old desire for large families, and traditional ways of producing and exchanging goods, tend to restrict productivity and to slow the rate of saving in developing countries. These patterns are beginning to change, however, as more people begin to realize that "old ways" must be modified if a people are to enjoy the economic benefits of the "new ways."

The economies of developing nations may not be patterned after that of the United States. Every society has its own value preferences, styles of life, and ways of doing things. It is not realistic, therefore, to expect that every "friendly" developing nation will adopt the political and economic institutions of the developed nation that provides it with aid. It is becoming increasingly clear that all Communist states are not carbon copies of the Soviet Union (or Mainland China). Economic assistance that tends to force a developing nation into a pattern which conflicts with its culture and traditions will not win friends for the donor nor prove helpful to the receiver.

The "wealthy" nations must help the "poor" nations. Humanitarian motives aside, the developed nations have no choice but to continue to help developing nations. The poor greatly outnumber the wealthy, and their populations are increasing at a far faster rate. Poverty and hopelessness breed discontent and may lead to violence that might impair or destroy the economic relations that contribute to the prosperity of developed nations. To insure the good life for Americans, the United States must continue to aid and encourage the developing countries. This, too, must be the policy of all the world's relatively prosperous nations.

CHECK UP

1. Why may economic conditions in some developing countries be expected to improve during the next quarter century? What obstacles must be overcome for this to happen?

2. Should Americans expect developing countries to pattern their economies after the American economy? Why or why not? Why should developed nations help developing lands?

Clinching the main ideas

The United States is the world's wealthiest nation, and its people have the world's highest average standard of living. In contrast, a large and increasing majority of the world's peoples live in dire poverty.

Since World War II, the United States government has spent large sums in attempts to raise living standards in developing countries. These "foreign aid" programs have been undertaken for humanitarian reasons as well as to make possible increased production and the expansion of international trade and to contain the spread of communism.

Developed nations such as Japan and countries in Western Europe, stimulated by economic aid from the United States, quickly recovered from the ravages of World War II. That the spread of communism has been slowed during the past two decades can be ascribed in part to United States economic and military assistance. In some developing countries, economic assistance has improved living standards. But in others the greater amount of production has been offset by substantial population increases.

The populations of "poor" countries are increasing much more rapidly than the populations of "rich" countries. Increasingly the peoples of developing nations are demanding their share of the "good things of life." Lasting peace cannot be achieved unless peoples in developing nations have hope of living better. It is in the interest of the developed nations, therefore, to narrow the economic gap between their ways of living and those in the emerging nations. Constructive programs of economic assistance provide the best assurance for peace and a happier and better life for the peoples of the world.

Chapter 18 review

Terms to understand

1. foreign aid
2. colonialism
3. Point 4 program
4. developing nations
5. per capita GNP
6. Marshall Plan

What do you think?

1. What are the major differences between a developed and a developing economy?

2. Why have communism and socialism had an appeal for peoples in developing countries?

3. How can an economy based on subsistence agriculture break away from the limitations inherent in that system?

4. Why are present-day peoples in poor countries more dissatisfied with their lot than they were a century ago?

5. What are the comparative advantages of aid programs administered by donor countries and by an international agency?

6. Why is it to the advantage of developed nations to aid developing countries?

Extending your knowledge of economics

1. Barbara Ward in *Five Ideas That Changed the World* (Norton) discusses the impact of nationalism, industrialism, colonialism, communism, and internationalism. What conclusions can be drawn from this book about desirable relations between developed and developing countries?

2. Max F. Millikan, Director of the Center for International Studies at the Massachusetts Institute of Technology, in *American Foreign Aid: Strategies for the 1970's* (No. 196 in the "Headline Series" published by the Foreign Policy Association), argues that no change in the world environment "has been more dramatic or more far-reaching in its implications than the emergence of two-thirds of the world's people into a process of economic, social, and political transformation without parallel" in history. A committee of students can report on the policy he recommends for the United States and other developed nations. Discussion can bring out why he holds these views and provide an opportunity for students to suggest other courses of action.

chapter nineteen

 **International trade and finance**

1. What benefits stem from international trade?
2. How are payments made in international trade?
3. Why do governments levy tariffs on imports?

It is not therefore the keeping of our money in the Kingdom, but the necessity and use of our wares in foreign countries, and our want of their commodities that causeth the vent and consumption on all sides which makes a quick and ample Trade.

THOMAS MUN, England's Treasure by Foreign Trade, 1630

International trade involves the exchange of products between the peoples of different nations. The reasons for such trade are (1) that different kinds of resources are found or can be produced most efficiently in different parts of the world, and (2) the fact that the economic principle of "specialization" works in the same way between countries as between individuals or between regions in a single country. Foreign trade is a method by which the demands of people for more and better goods can be satisfied at lower costs.

Small countries, with only a few kinds of economic resources or products, cannot hope to maintain adequate standards of living without engaging in international trade. Large na-

tions, such as the United States or the Soviet Union, which have diversified resources, are less dependent upon international trade than small nations. But even these large nations fare much better with international trade than without it. Every country depends on international trade to supply some of its material goods or to sell some of its raw materials or manufactured products.

1

What benefits stem from international trade?

Trade was an important reason for the settlement of this country. In the sixteenth and seventeenth centuries, many European nations were eager to get from the New World raw materials and foodstuffs which were not available in Europe. These nations also hoped to sell their own products, especially manufactured goods, to their New World colonies.

Even after this country won its political independence, this form of trade continued. For many years the United States was, in effect, an "economic colony" of Europe. For about a century after the Revolutionary War, the international trade of the United States was based largely on the export of raw materials and foods to Europe in exchange for European manufactured or processed goods.

America's role in international trade has changed. Today this country is primarily an exporter of manufactured goods and an importer of raw materials. The United States, however, still exports large amounts of raw materials and foodstuffs and imports sizable quantities of manufactured items. A century ago, three fourths of this country's foreign trade was with Europe. Today, in dollar values, more than 40 per cent of United States trade is with Western Hemisphere countries, a little less than one third is with Western Europe, more than one fifth is with Asia, and the remaining approximately 7 per cent with the rest of the world.

Most international trade occurs between the economically developed nations. About 70 per cent of this country's international trade is with the economically developed free-world nations of Western Europe, and with Canada, Japan, Australia, New Zealand, and South Africa. More than half of this country's trade is with five nations—Canada, Japan, West Germany, Britain, and Mexico. The first four of these countries are economically developed and industrialized countries much like the United States. And Mexico has the second highest total GNP and the fourth highest per capita GNP among the 20 Latin American countries.

Poor countries are not good international trading partners. Because they have very little to sell they cannot buy very much. This country's annual investments in many of the developing nations, in the form of economic aid and private business investment, far exceed the annual dollar returns from investments. Chapter 18 brought out that one objective of foreign economic assistance is to speed economic development in the nations helped. An expanding economy would enable these nations to expand their international trade.

International trade makes possible higher standards of living. Without international trade Americans would not have many of the goods they take for granted—or, at best, these goods would cost so much that few could afford them. For example, coffee, tea, cocoa, bananas, spices, and silk are imported from other countries. This country also imports substantial quantities of food, beverages, and clothing materials. Although Americans could exist without such imports, most people surely would miss some of them.

International trade provides raw materials for industry. This country produces neither rubber nor tin. Most of the manganese (used in making steel) and bauxite and aluminum ores (used in making aluminum products) come

Composition of U.S. exports with four major industrial areas

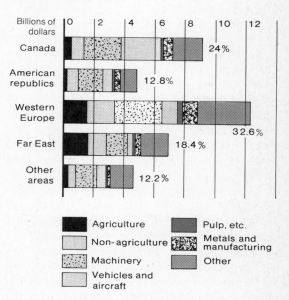

Source: Statistical Abstract

from other countries. Large quantities of iron, mercury, and uranium ores, petroleum, and even of some kinds of forest products are imported each year. Additionally, many kinds of finished manufactured goods and parts of semi-processed materials are purchased abroad.

It has been said that 48 materials imported from 18 different countries are used in a telephone receiver. Likewise, it has been estimated that 38 of the 148 materials essential to the production of automobiles are largely imported. Much the same is true for radios, television sets, and many other kinds of manufactured products. Clearly, an end to international trade would severely disrupt the economy and the American way of life.

International trade provides important markets for many American products. During a recent typical year, the United States exported machinery and vehicles worth eighteen billion dollars, agricultural products worth five billion dollars, chemicals valued at three billion, and various other productions to the amount of nine billion dollars. American workmen received wages for the production and distribution of all these products. Were this nation not able to sell large quantities of goods abroad, the jobs of millions of American workmen would be affected.

The United States leads the world in international trade. This country accounts for more than one-seventh of the world's total international trade as measured in monetary value. Among other leaders in international trade are West Germany, Japan, Britain, France, and Canada.

The total value of this country's annual exports and imports total less than 8 per cent of its GNP. This percentage has increased slightly in recent years.

Many countries are far more dependent on international trade than is this country. About one fifth of Japan's GNP is derived from exports and imports. Comparable figures for the GNP's of West Germany and the Netherlands

are one third and two thirds, respectively. A considerably smaller percentage of the Soviet Union's GNP stems from international trade than is true for this country.

Most international trade is carried on between exporters and importers. Except for trade between Communist nations, the exchange of goods is not carried on directly between nations. Most international trade involves transactions between private business firms. Those who sell to firms in other countries are called exporters; those who buy from firms in other countries are called importers. Businesses operate in international trade much as in domestic commerce, and for the same purpose—to make profits.

To make the profits needed to remain in business, importers and exporters must perform a useful service. To illustrate, an American jewelry store may buy Swiss-made watches through an American importer. The manager of the jewelry store believes that the Swiss watches are the best buy. He expects to make a higher profit from handling those watches than he could from selling the same number of comparable American watches. A French merchant who sells washing machines may be able to buy American machines at a lower price than machines of the same quality made in France. Consequently he will buy the former through a firm that imports goods from the United States.

How can Swiss watches on which there are import duties compete with American-made watches? The main reasons are that Swiss watchmakers are highly skilled and efficient, and may be willing to work for lower wages than American workers receive. Thus the Swiss watches can be manufactured at a lower cost than comparable American-made watches. On the other hand, mass-production methods are used in the manufacture of washing machines in this country. Highly efficient mass production reduces production costs so much that American machines can compete with European made machines despite the fact that the former must be shipped across the Atlantic and pay import duties at the French port of entry.

The "law of comparative advantage" determines what a nation exports and imports. From the examples just cited, it does not follow that the profits of Swiss watchmaking firms are as high as those of American washing-machine manufacturers. But it would be safe to assume that the Swiss—because of the availability of highly skilled watchmakers and their tradition of excellence in this craft—make a greater profit by producing watches than they could by manufacturing washing machines. This is an illustration of the economic *law (or principle) of comparative advantage.*

The principle of comparative advantage states that one person (or firm, or region, or nation) benefits most by doing those things in which he (or it) has the *relatively* greatest productive efficiency. This *does not* mean doing something more efficiently than anyone else—that would be *absolute advantage*. The following examples illustrate both comparative advantage and the difference between comparative advantage and absolute advantage.

Suppose an imported shirt can be bought at a price of $3, and a shirt of the same quality produced domestically for $6. This means that a $6 package of domestic resources is required to produce the shirt domestically. However, a $6 package of resources to produce $6 of exports would earn enough money abroad to buy two of the $3 foreign shirts. In other words, if the price of an imported good is less than the price of a domestically produced equivalent good, the quantity of resources required to "produce" the imported article *indirectly* (by first producing exports) is smaller than the quantity of resources required to produce the domestic article. *More products can be obtained if each one is produced by the method involving the smallest real resource cost.*

A lawyer may be an excellent typist as well as a competent lawyer. He can probably earn an average of $45 per working hour by practicing law, and he can hire a secretary to do his typing for $3 an hour. Although he can type even better than the secretary he hires (that is, he has an *absolute advantage* over his employee both in typing and in practicing law), it is to his financial advantage to concentrate on legal work. His *comparative advantage* is greater in the practice of law.

Similarly, it pays nations to specialize in those forms of production in which their comparative advantage is greatest. Perhaps one

How foreign investment stimulates trade

Developing countries borrow capital which leads to:

More production

Higher incomes

Higher living standards

Investment capital

Two-way trade

Developed countries lend capital which results in:

Bigger export market

More raw materials for industry

More employment in industry

Higher standards of living

country can manufacture both watches and washing machines at a lower cost than any other country. But its advantage is so much greater in the production of washing machines that the greater profit can be made by producing washing machines and trading some of these for watches. Through such specialization, all producing firms in all countries can produce larger quantities of goods at lower prices than otherwise would be possible.

CHECK UP

1. What was the nature of trade between mother country and colonies in the New World? Between the United States and other countries today? Why does most international trade take place between developed countries?

2. In what different ways does international trade benefit this country? What are the roles of importers and exporters? How does the law of comparative advantage influence exports and imports?

2

How are payments made in international trade?

Every country prints the money used within its own boundaries, but generally this money does not circulate freely in other lands. The fact that money from different countries has different values (differing purchasing power per monetary unit), would seem to create a problem in international trade. Actually there is a workable method for handling this problem.

Most international payments are made by using the services of a foreign exchange dealer. International commercial banks handle international payments and collections for their customers in much the same way that domestic banks handle checking account transactions. In other words, most payments in international trade are simply bookkeeping entries (or "clearing-house" transactions), in which funds are transferred from one account to another.

Suppose, for example, that a Japanese importer buys coal worth five million dollars from an American mine. The importer has no dollars, and he cannot pay the American exporter in yen (Japanese money) that cannot be spent in this country. But about the same time an American importer buys from a Japanese manufacturer transitor radios valued at about five million dollars in United States money. The international trade department of the bank (or banks) handling the payments for these two transactions can offset one purchase against the other at the current *exchange rate* (the rate at which dollars and yen are exchanged.) Thus the Japanese buyer pays in yen and the Japanese seller is paid in yen, while the two Americans pay and receive dollars. There is no actual exchange of money between the two countries.

Should there be a difference between the monetary values of goods exported from and imported into a country, there will be a *deficit* balance on the accounts in one country and a surplus *balance* in the other. It is only when a country's overall foreign exchange balance shows a deficit that money has to be sent to cover the balance. The "money" used in most cases is gold bullion. The bullion itself usually is not transported; instead, the right of ownership to stored gold may be transferred.

The international exchange rate (the value of one nation's money in terms of the money of other nations) tends to fluctuate. In a perfectly free market, the international value of every nation's money would be self-adjusting and determined by the forces of demand and supply. If Americans export a large volume of goods to Japan, the Japanese will require a large amount of dollar exchange to make payment. But if Americans import very little from Japan, a comparatively small sum of yen will be required to pay the Japanese. Consequently, the value of the dollar will rise relative to the value of the yen. Therefore more yen will be required to "buy" a given number of dollars, a given number of dollars will "buy" more yen. In other words, as dollars become more "expensive" to the Japanese, yen become less "expensive" to Americans. Doubtless the Japanese will buy fewer United States products, whereas Americans will tend to buy more of theirs. In this way, the flow of international trade in each direction will be brought into balance.

This simplified illustration has involved only two countries. In reality the demand for both dollars and yen is worldwide, and exchange rates and the volume of trade are influenced by all the nations engaged in international trade. But the economic principle operates in the same way in the example dealing with the transactions between two nations.

Today many countries set the exchange rates for their money. Following World War I, many governments intervened in the foreign exchange market to set the rates at which their money is exchanged for the money of other countries. Thus, a country might hope to increase its exports or to reduce imports. Such a policy would also affect employment and the country's resource use. It also creates some problems.

If a country sets the exchange value of its money too high in relation to the money of other countries (say a British pound is valued at $4 when world market conditions otherwise would value it at $3), that country's exports will decrease. People in other nations will not buy at such high prices. On the other hand, if the exchange rate is low, people in other nations will rush to buy more. This would increase production and employment in the exporting industries of the "low price" country. And it would also reduce production and employment in the same industries in the countries which are importing more goods from the "low price" country. Other countries, therefore, will also devalue their money, thus touching off an international "price war."

To eliminate instability in international exchange rates, the International Monetary Fund was established in 1944. The International Monetary fund, supported by contributions from member nations, makes short-term loans of whatever kind of money a country may need to stabilize its exchange rate during a period when it is experiencing a *temporary* balance of payments deficit. Such a deficit would require devaluation of the nation's currency if the International Monetary Fund did not extend a loan to finance the deficit. Member nations agree to vary their exchange rates only under certain conditions and within certain limits. The International Monetary Fund has not been quite as successful as had been hoped, but it has maintained much more stable conditions than otherwise would have been possible.

Each nation is concerned about its "balance of trade" and "balance of payments." An excess of exports over imports, as measured in monetary values, is called a *favorable balance of trade*. This means that a country is selling more abroad than it is buying. (One might question whether the balance really is "favorable" when other nations obtain more American products than the United States receives of theirs. But this is the meaning of the term in economics.) The reverse—that is, buying more from abroad than is sold abroad is called an *unfavorable balance of trade*. Note that these terms refer only to the purchase and sale of *goods*.

The *balance of payments* refers to the flow of funds between nations. A *favorable* balance of payments exists when more funds come into a country from abroad than go out; an *unfavorable* balance of payments is the opposite. "Payments" includes payments for goods, and also includes the expenditures of tourists, sums spent for various services (ocean transportation and insurance, for example), foreign loans, interest and dividends on foreign investments, and military and economic assistance. It is quite possible for a country at the same time to have a favorable trade balance and an unfavorable payments balance, or the reverse.

The United States generally has had a favorable balance of trade for about a century. The United States generally had an unfavorable balance of trade before the Civil War (1861–1865). Since that time, however, the nation's trade balance generally has been favorable, and there were no deficits from 1888 until 1971, when a $3 billion deficit occurred.

During the decade of the 1960's, the total surplus in this country's balance of trade (the difference between the dollar values of exports and imports) amounted to more than 42 bil-

lion dollars. However, whereas the total volume of United States international trade more than doubled, imports increased much faster than exports. By the end of the decade, the annual favorable balance had dropped to a little more than one billion dollars.

This shrinking in the annual trade balance can be attributed at least in part to the inflation (higher production costs and prices) which has plagued this country since the mid-1960's. Continued inflation reduced the volume of goods the United States sells abroad, and encouraged increased American buying of relatively less expensive foreign products. It also contributed to the United States balance of payments problem abroad.

The United States balance of trade is favorable

Value of U.S. imports and exports with seven major areas

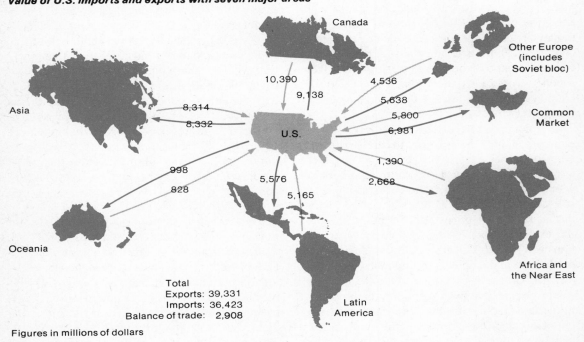

Canada

Other Europe (includes Soviet bloc)

Asia

10,390
9,138

4,536
5,638
5,800
6,981

Common Market

8,314
8,332

U.S.

998
828

5,576
5,165

1,390
2,668

Oceania

Africa and the Near East

Total
Exports: 39,331
Imports: 36,423
Balance of trade: 2,908

Latin America

Figures in millions of dollars

Source: U.S. Department of Commerce, Bureau of International Commerce

Payment balance — the key factors

1. The U.S. has had an unfavorable balance of payments for many years.

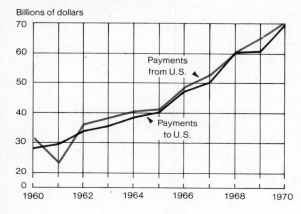

2. Many factors contribute to the adverse balance of payments.

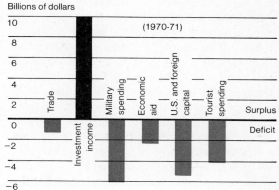

3. The deficit has resulted in a decline of the U.S. gold stock.

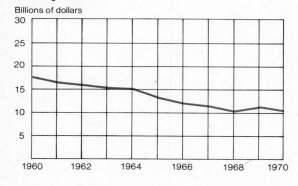

4. Dollar devaluation and the world energy crisis have affected the balance of trade.

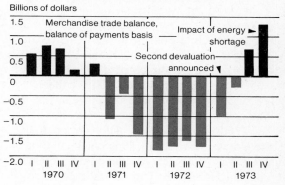

Source: Statistical Abstract; Federal Reserve Bulletin; *Bureau of Economic Analysis, U.S. Department of Commerce*

Recently the balance of payments situation has differed from the balance-of-trade situation. Since World War II, the United States has provided large-scale economic and military aid to many countries. American business firms also have made many loans and investments abroad, and American citizens have traveled in other countries. Thus there has been an outward flow of funds (or total of payments of all kinds) larger than the incoming flow (total receipts from exports and other sources). During the decade of the 1960's, this country's net balance-of-payments deficit amounted to almost twelve billion dollars. Seven out of the ten years showed a deficit.

The international value of a country's money declines if the country continues to have a large unfavorable balance of payments. Many citizens as well as the government became alarmed about this situation during the late 1960's. Steps were taken to discourage foreign travel and to reduce the number of American civilians employed by this country abroad, to persuade friendly nations to buy more from the United States, and to encourage American business firms to try to sell more in international markets. Also, new American business investments in other countries were limited by law. These steps resulted in some improvement in the country's balance-of-payments position.

American dollars have been widely used as an international form of money since World War II. If a fixed number of dollars always can be exchanged for a fixed weight of gold, there is no need for the actual physical transfer of gold bullion between countries to settle payments balances. Foreigners have been willing to accept dollars instead of gold in payment for this country's balance-of-payments deficit.

To support the stability of the dollar and its acceptance as an "international money," an International Gold Pool, with the United States as a major participant, "guaranteed" that the market price of an ounce of gold will always be 35 United States dollars. This dollar-gold relationship was maintained by either buying or selling gold for $35 an ounce on demand.

By 1967, the dwindling gold stocks of the United States, caused by large and continued unfavorable balance of payments, created doubts abroad that the United States could continue to sell gold on demand at $35 an ounce. There were fears that inflation caused by large budgetary deficits growing out of the Vietnam conflict would seriously reduce the purchasing power of the dollar in the United States.

Speculators consequently bought gold frantically in late 1967 and early 1968. They hoped that the exhaustion of United States gold stocks and persistent payments deficits would eventually require a devaluation of the dollar. Such action would make American exports more attractive to foreigners and reduce American im-ports. But a devaluation of the dollar would also mean that other currencies and gold would be more valuable. That is, the price of gold would be above $35 per ounce, and would yield a profit to speculators who had bought gold at $35.

The United States made additional gold available by removing its "gold backing" for Federal Reserve Notes. But attacks on the dollar continued. In 1971, official gold prices were raised to $38 an ounce, and in 1973 to $42.22. This was an international dollar "devaluation" of about 18 per cent. That is, dollars bought less in foreign countries, while American exports were cheaper to foreign buyers.

Meantime, most major nations abandoned their attempts to keep exchange rates set at the old fixed levels. Relative values were set by market forces ("floating" rates). Later in 1973, national central banks announced that they would buy and sell gold at going prices on the open market (free gold prices then were around $100 an ounce). Because of devaluation, exchange rate changes, and other factors, United States' trade and payments balances improved substantially by 1973.

The International Monetary Fund is now sponsoring *Special Drawing Rights* (SDR's) as a new method of settling payments balances. This "paper gold" is transferred between nations by bookkeeping entries. SDR's help to reduce the reliance on gold or dollars in international trade, and thus discourage speculation and wild exchange rate fluctuations.

CHECK UP

1. How are payments made in international trade? Why does the international exchange rate tend to fluctuate? Why do some countries set the exchange rates for their money? How has the International Monetary Fund tried to stabilize exchange rates?

2. What is a favorable balance of trade? An unfavorable balance of payments?

3. Why were dollars widely used after World War II to settle balance of payments? What problem arose from the use of dollars? Why? What is the function of "paper gold"?

3

Why do governments levy tariffs on imports?

There are times when a country for political reasons may wish to prohibit its citizens from trading with other countries. The United States has such a policy regarding Cuba, and only recently abandoned such a policy related to mainland China, and to the USSR for some kinds of goods. Sometimes, when a country's avail-

able foreign exchange is dwindling, it may impose restrictions on what can be imported or upon the purposes for which foreign receipts may be used. At other times, a country may establish import "quotas" to protect the domestic producers of given products from outside competition. These and other similar devices are barriers to free international trade. The most commonly used barrier, of course, is the *tariff* (a tax or "duty" assessed against imported products).

Tariffs may be levied for revenue or for protection. If a tariff is so high that it prevents or significantly reduces imports, it is called a *protective tariff*. This means that it protects the country's producers from foreign competition by making the prices of imported goods as high as (or higher than) domestically produced goods. A lower tariff, which permits foreign goods to be sold in competition with domestic products, and which is intended mainly to raise

The tariff wall — average tariff rates on dutiable U.S. imports since 1821

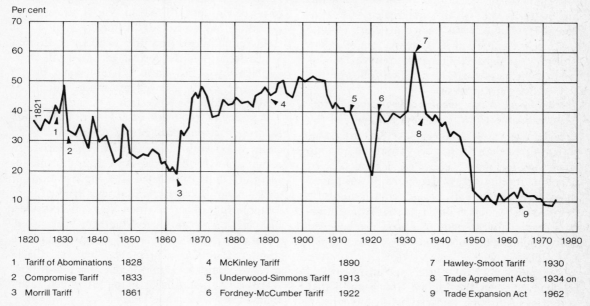

1	Tariff of Abominations	1828	4	McKinley Tariff	1890	7	Hawley-Smoot Tariff	1930
2	Compromise Tariff	1833	5	Underwood-Simmons Tariff	1913	8	Trade Agreement Acts	1934 on
3	Morrill Tariff	1861	6	Fordney-McCumber Tariff	1922	9	Trade Expansion Act	1962

Source: Statistical Abstract

revenue, is known as a *revenue tariff*. This kind of tariff may be levied even on goods which are not produced in a country. Of course, even a revenue tariff leads to higher prices, and thus reduces the consumption of imported products.

At certain periods in its history the United States has had protective tariffs. During President Washington's administration, Alexander Hamilton advocated a policy of protecting "infant" industries from the competition of foreign goods. He wished to make tariffs so high that there would be a large increase in American manufactures.

New England manufacturers supported this program. Southern planters and farmers, compelled to pay higher prices for manufactured goods imported from England, favored low tariffs or none at all (free trade). After the Civil War, and until the early 1900's, Congress enacted high tariffs to protect American industry. The "McKinley Tariff" of 1890 was at that time the highest tariff in the nation's history. During President Wilson's administration substantial tariff reductions were made. But the highest tariff wall of all was erected when the Smoot-Hawley Act was passed in 1930. Doubtless many members of Congress thought at the time that a higher tariff might relieve the depressed business conditions which followed the 1929 stock market crash.

Reciprocal trade agreements increased foreign trade. In 1934, Congress empowered the President to raise or lower specific tariff rates by not more than 50 per cent from the existing level, and also gave the President power to negotiate foreign trade agreements. It was hoped that these agreements would contribute to a world-wide reduction of tariffs that would stimulate trade between nations. It was also believed that would help to create a world outlook favorable to peace.

Altogether, 21 of these agreements were reached between the United States and other countries. Although the trade with any one of these nations was not large, the total amount of trade under these treaties amounted to about a third of the nation's total international trade. The most important treaty, the one with Canada, covered 180 commodities imported from that country.

By January, 1939, these treaties had brought about a reduction of rates in about one-third of this country's tariff schedules. Nearly one half of these changes were reductions of 40–50 per cent in the earlier rates. Because of worldwide depressed conditions, this program produced limited results. The chief reason why this country could not sell more goods abroad was the low level of incomes during the Great Depression of the 1930's. The main reason why the United States did not buy much more abroad was the low level of incomes in this country.

With the outbreak of World War II, American foreign trade policies were geared to the war effort of providing supplies to this country's allies. These countries could export little to the United States while they were engaged in all-out war. Following the war, however, this country again became interested in lower tariffs. As a result of various post-World War II agreements, including the so-called "Kennedy Round" of tariff reductions during the 1960's, the United States today has the lowest general tariff rates in its history. But there still are some purely protective tariffs, as well as import quotas or similar restrictions on certain products.

A policy of free trade or of lower tariffs tends to arouse opposition. Many Americans dread competition with "low-wage" foreign labor. In recent years, for example, American shoe manufacturers have protested the importation of shoes from European countries. Producers of hatters' fur, filberts, dried figs, motorcycles, bicycles, textile products, lumber, beef, wool, radio and television sets and components have registered similar complaints. They ask, "How can we compete with foreign workers whose wages and standards of living are much lower than ours?"

There is, of course, a factor which compensates at least in part for cheap foreign labor. If the productivity of the American worker is much greater, the higher wages paid him will not boost the price of American products above those of competing foreign goods. A highly mechanized industrial plant, by turning out goods on a mass-production basis, reduces the unit cost of production. Doubtless one reason the American shoe industry has suffered from foreign competition is that many of the American plants were small and inefficient. Of course there are countries, such as West Germany and Japan, in which a lower wage scale combined with a relatively high degree of mechanization make possible the production of certain goods more cheaply than in the United States.

As nations become more highly industrialized, standards of living are likely to rise. This implies rising wages. Such nations are likely to become better customers than they were before.

Some industrial leaders favor unrestricted foreign trade. Some leaders in American industry favor a program to stimulate foreign trade. A leading automobile manufacturer, for example, has urged the reciprocal elimination of the tariff on imported automobiles. Still other changes in tariff laws have been urged to enable foreign countries to sell more goods here.

Many economists consider *free trade* between nations, such as this country has among the 50 states, the best solution for the problems of world trade. This assumes free operation of the law of comparative advantage and the abolition of tariffs.

Free trade sometimes is opposed on grounds of military security. Economic goals may conflict with noneconomic goals, and this may be true in discussions of protective tariffs. For example, if American watch manufacturers cannot compete in quality and price with Swiss manufacturers, the latter, under a free trade policy, would capture much of the American market. Some American watch manufacturers would be forced out of business. Doubtless

many of their highly skilled employees (watchmakers) would be compelled to take other jobs which do not require the same skills. In the event of war, watch manufacturers and their highly skilled employees are well qualified to produce precision instruments for military purposes. Were its watchmaking industry wiped out, the United States might no longer have the craftsmen needed for precision work in war-related industry. The nation's security might be endangered if the country became dependent upon foreign countries for the production of precision instruments in wartime.

From an economic point of view in peacetime, most nations (not necessarily all) may be better off under a policy of free trade. But in wartime, every country needs to be as self-sufficient as possible. There may be other ways than protective tariffs to preserve industries of vital importance to the nation. But trade barriers have been widely used for this purpose.

There are some good arguments against free trade. If the nations of the world trusted each other and were willing to live in peace, one could justify free trade between nations for much the same reasons as between the 50 states. But there also are arguments in favor of re-

CONTROVERSY OVER IMPORTS
In 1963, a round of international tariff negotiations called the "Kennedy Round" began which resulted in a significant lowering of tariff rates for imports into the United States. The new rates met with little opposition until the late 1960's. Then the flood of inexpensive shoes and textiles from Europe and Japan led American manufacturers to press for import quotas.

A bill introduced in Congress in 1970 reflected considerable support for import quotas, not only for shoes and textiles, but for other products as well. The bill was opposed by President Nixon, who thought it too restrictive. His view was consistent with that of presidents since Franklin D. Roosevelt.

taining tariffs. These usually run as follows:

1. Protective tariffs promote national economic independence, an advantage in the event of war.

2. A tariff protects "infant" industries which may eventually "grow up" and no longer need protection. This is often a valid argument in the case of developing countries seeking to industrialize.

3. Tariffs may be needed at times to prevent "dumping." This implies that a country may sell goods at below-cost prices to kill possible future competition or simply to get rid of surpluses.

A country must take all relevant factors into account in shaping its tariff policy. A highly industrialized country may not fear foreign competition in manufactured goods, and it may need to import raw materials. Such a country may favor free trade, both to increase its sale of manufactured goods and to obtain raw materials as cheaply as possible.

On the other hand, a country producing raw materials may wish to industrialize. To that end, it may need to exclude some foreign manufactured goods, at least for a time, and to use more of its raw materials in its own industrial plants. Such a country may favor high protective tariffs.

Despite the fact that free trade may result in more efficient production of goods on a worldwide basis, most nations are primarily interested in their own welfare. From the viewpoint of a given nation, the "best" tariff policy can be determined only in the light of its present situation and what it wants for the future.

Trade barriers are being lowered in Western Europe. During the late 1950's, six West European nations agreed to form the European

1970 Chicago Daily News

WITH FRIENDS LIKE THIS...

Source: Fischetti in The Chicago Daily News, Courtesy Publishers—Hall Syndicate.

Champion of Increased Trade
Thomas Mun
(1571–1641)

Some 500 years ago, nation-states developed in western Europe. Rulers of these nation-states were eager to strengthen their powers of government and to acquire more land. For both purposes they needed greater sources of taxable wealth. Consequently rulers encouraged manufacturing and commerce. It is not surprising that the merchant class in the cities tended to support rulers in their struggles against powerful nobles. The word *mercantilism* is used to suggest policies designed to strengthen the economy of a state by encouraging manufacturing and export trade.

Under mercantilism, industry, trade, the monetary system, and even consumption are subject to government regulation. Colonies were sought as sources of raw materials and as markets for finished goods. The paramount goal of each nation was to maintain a favorable balance of trade by exporting more than it imported.

Some of the basic ideas of mercantilism were clearly stated in the writings of a wealthy London merchant named Thomas Mun. Mun was also a director of the East India Company, a corporation which traded with the Far East. When it was discovered that this company had been exporting bullion from England, there was a loud outcry. If the purpose of mercantilism was to increase the nation's wealth and thus to increase the supply of money, should not the export of gold and silver be prohibited? Mun defended the company's policy in a book called *A Discourse of Trade,* written in 1621. Showing himself to be far ahead of his time, he pointed out that gold was needed to pay for goods purchased in the East. When these goods later were resold in foreign markets, more gold flowed into England than the amount originally exported. Thus in the end, the nation's wealth was increased.

In a later work, *England's Treasure by Foreign Trade,* Mun pointed out that the nation's chief economic goal was a favorable balance of payments. This could be attained by (1) the production in England of goods formerly imported, (2) high tariffs to discourage imports, (3) laws limiting the consumption of foreign luxury goods, (4) charging high prices on goods which foreign countries could buy only from England, and (5) underselling competing nations in the trading of common items. Mun also stressed the importance of "invisible imports" in achieving a favorable balance of payments. These included such items as freight expenses, commissions, insurance charges, travel expenditures, and interest and profits from foreign investments. To increase income from such sources, he advocated the expansion of English shipping and said the government should forbid English commerce to travel in anything but English ships. This would do away with paying freight charges to foreigners. Munn regarded restrictions on the international flow of bullion as harmful.

Mun even argued that keeping too much money within the nation is detrimental to its economy, since "plenty of money in a Kingdom doth make the native commodities dearer, which as it is to the profit of some private men in their revenues, so is it directly against the benefit of the Public in the quantity of the trade; for as plenty of money makes wares dearer, so dear wares decline their use and consumption."

Mun saw more clearly than most men of his age the goals to be sought through government controls if a nation were to prosper. His was a far more sophisticated understanding of the true purposes of mercantilism than was possessed by most advocates of that policy. It is unfortunate that no likeness of so shrewd a thinker as Mun seems to have survived.

Economic Community (EEC), usually referred to as the *Common Market*. The original countries involved were Belgium, France, West Germany, Italy, Luxemburg, and the Netherlands. Britain, Ireland, and Denmark joined the EEC during the early 1970's.

The goal of the Common Market is to unify its member nations into one big producing, trading, and consuming area. Tariffs will be eliminated completely between member nations, and a common tariff policy (involving some protectionism) will be applied toward non-member nations. Agricultural, mining, manufacturing, and transportation technology will be improved, and more efficient merchandising and financial methods developed. In 1970, a plan for a single uniform system of money throughout the Common Market within ten years (by 1980) was announced.

The Common Market countries expect to become much more self-sufficient economically, and to improve the per capita incomes and living standards of their citizens. Substantial progress has been made in this direction, although many difficult problems remain. Eventually, it is anticipated that the EEC will be joined by most other Western European nations, including those countries belonging to the more loosely organized European Free Trade Association (EFTA). This latter association consists of Norway, Sweden, Austria, Switzerland, and Portugal. (Britain and Denmark formerly belonged to EFTA before joining the EEC.)

It is contemplated that the Common Market nations, and any other nations joining with them in the future, will retain their political independence. But by acting in concert on economic matters, they become more nearly the economic equal of the two superpowers. Should the EEC and the EFTA unite, the members would have one-fourth as much territory and 40 per cent more population than the United States. The combined GNP of the EEC and EFTA nations is about two-thirds that of this country.

Whatever form the Common Market eventually may take, American international trade will be affected significantly. Producers in Common Market countries can sell in a mass European market with unrestricted movements of materials, capital, and labor between countries. They will be able to produce more efficiently. Also, they will have a common tariff against products from the outside. This means that American products moving into Europe, as well as into other parts of the world, may expect to face keener competition.[1]

The idea of regional economic co-operation has stimulated the development of international associations in other parts of the world. The "common market" idea is being tried outside Europe. For example, the Latin American Free Trade Association (LAFTA) includes Mexico and most South American countries. The Central American Common Market (CACM) is made up of Costa Rica, El Salvador, Guatemala, Honduras, and Nicaragua. These regional associations of developing nations are making progress toward breaking down tariff and other international trade barriers. Common market arrangements in some ways are perhaps more important to these countries than even to Western Europe. "Infant" industries will not develop into efficient low-cost "mature" industries unless they can serve a market large enough to insure the economies of large-scale production. The protection of infant industries on a national rather than a continental basis seems doomed to failure. Most national markets will always be too small to permit the economies stemming from large-scale production.

[1] It should be pointed out, however, that American corporations already have made substantial investments in these countries, and that profits from such sources are not affected by the tariff policies of the nations concerned. And of course the goods made by the European subsidiaries of United States corporations move freely within the Common Market.

CHECK UP

1. Why may a country have a revenue tariff? A protective tariff? What is the purpose of reciprocal trade agreements?

2. What are arguments in favor of lower tariffs? Against free trade? What progress has been made in reducing tariff barriers in Western Europe? In Latin America? What are the advantages of regional economic co-operation?

Clinching the main ideas

Foreign trade in the non-Communist world, like domestic trade, is conducted by private businesses for the purpose of making profits. Payments are made mainly by offsetting payments and receipts. The ownership of gold or currency is transferred only to settle the net difference between a country's total payments and total receipts. Some governments protect their exchange balances by closely regulating imports and exports. But in general the best way to equalize payments and receipts is by adjusting the exchange rates.

The United States has had a "favorable balance of trade" (exports exceeding imports) for many years. During several recent years, however, its "balance of payments" has been unfavorable. This resulted partly from an overvaluation of the dollar relative to other currencies, and also from huge expenditures for foreign military and economic aid programs. This unfavorable balance caused serious concern in the United States and abroad. International devaluation of the dollar in relation to foreign currencies, however, seemed to have brought substantial improvements by 1974.

Tariffs impede the flow of trade. Free-trade policies promote the exchange of the larger quantities of goods which can be produced and enjoyed if each country specializes in those goods which it can produce at lowest cost. Although United States tariff policies have varied over the years, this country by and large has pursued a low-tariff policy.

Many economists favor free trade in principle. Noneconomic factors (such as national defense) must be considered, however. From an individual nation's viewpoint, there is no one "best" tariff policy for all times and under all conditions. Protection of infant industries is often a legitimate policy for the developing nations, however, especially when they can join with neighboring nations to provide a potentially larger market for their goods.

There are at least three strong reasons why foreign trade is important to the United States:

1. This country needs many things which it cannot produce (or which it can produce only in small amounts at high cost) to maintain and improve standards of living. The *law of comparative advantage* recognizes that the cost of producing certain goods may be less in some nations than in others. This law influences trade policy to a large extent.

2. Many basic agricultural and industrial producers are dependent upon foreign markets for the sale of a large part of their output.

3. Many developing countries desperately need machinery to modernize their industries. But purchases of such machinery are possible only if the United States permits them to earn dollars by selling their exports to this country.

In recent decades, important free-trade agreements have been concluded among European and Latin American nations. These agreements have resulted in the formation of the European Economic Community, the European Free Trade Association, and the Latin American Free Trade Association. If these common market arrangements prove successful, they may bring about radical changes in existing world trade patterns. But common market systems may also be expected to contribute to the improved living standards for the nations involved in them.

Chapter 19 review

Terms to understand

1. law of comparative advantage
2. International Monetary Fund
3. Special Drawing Rights
4. European Economic Community
5. Latin American Free Trade Association
6. Central American Common Market
7. exchange rate
8. balance of trade
9. balance of payments
10. revenue tariff
11. protective tariff
12. free trade

What do you think?

1. Asia has the largest population of any continent. Yet Asia's share of this country's international trade is smaller than that of Europe or Canada. Why?

2. The Common Market's tariffs provide protection for French agriculture. Why? Would this policy pose a problem for Britain if that country were to become a member of the Common Market? Why?

3. This country's unfavorable balance of payments has been a problem for recent administrations. What steps could be taken to correct this situation? Give arguments for and against each.

4. Why are American industrialists divided on the question of tariff protection for American industry? What arguments are offered on each side?

5. This country raised its tariffs after World War I but not after World War II. In each case was the action taken wise? Why?

Extending your knowledge of economics

1. From your reading in this chapter and elsewhere, write a report giving your opinion of the "Buy American" slogan.

2. Small farmers in France, Germany, and Italy feel that the Common Market favors industry at the expense of agriculture. They oppose its policy of creating larger farms that can make effective use of farm machinery. Why do the farmers feel as they do? For information about the Common Market, have a member of the class write to the European Community Information Service, 155 East 44th Street, New York, N.Y., 10017.

3. Hold a panel discussion on the subject, "What Should Be This Country's Tariff Policy?" Have one student play the role of a labor union official in an industry facing heavy foreign competition, another student the role of a businessman who sells his product in foreign markets, and a third the role of a consumer. Participants should prepare brief statements, followed by informal discussion.

Conflicting interests in international trade: Pacific Northwest lumber

The overall national interest, as well as a variety of conflicting regional and local interests and particular group interests, always are involved in international trade policy disputes. Various regions of the country, as well as groups such as resource owners, manufacturers, laborers, transportation firms, and consumers are affected by decisions concerning trade. The Constitution provides that Congress shall have the power "to regulate commerce with foreign nations. . . ." The President usually tries to coordinate trade policy with foreign policy. Each conflicting group presents its case in the legislative arena and attempts to muster support to influence the final decision. Usually the result is a political compromise in which no one wins a clear-cut victory, but which may at least be an attempt to minimize dissatisfaction throughout the nation as a whole.

Examples of the kinds of issues and controls involved in international trade policies are found in the continuing disputes over imported Canadian lumber and the export of logs to Japan.

General background

More than one-half of the nation's softwood (fir, pine, and similar species) lumber is produced in the Pacific Northwest. Forest industries have long dominated the economy of this region in terms of employment and value of output.

Much of the lumber produced in the Pacific Northwest is consumed in the heavily populated, industrialized, and timber-short northeastern states. Lumber producers traditionally have competed for business in these large northeastern markets. A price difference of only a few cents, or at most a few dollars, per thousand board feet of lumber may determine whether producers from the Pacific Northwest or the Southeast will win out in a particular market. In order to sell at a profit, producers from competing regions must watch their costs very closely. They cut costs wherever possible.

Southeastern producers, because of smaller and less dense stands of timber, have higher production costs for logging their timber and milling it into lumber than do their competitors in the Pacific Northwest. But Pacific Northwest producers, since they are located much farther from principal northeastern markets have higher transportation costs to northeastern markets.

Southeastern producers ship their lumber to the Northeast by rail or truck (sometimes by barge) for distances ranging from 600 to 1200 miles. Inland producers in the Pacific Northwest rely on rail transportation to move lumber for distances ranging from 1800 to 3000 miles. Rail transportation costs for these producers frequently are from one fourth to one third of the delivered market price of their lumber. "Tidewater" mills (located near the Pacific Ocean) in the Pacific Northwest historically relied on low-priced intercoastal water transportation to move their lumber to the North Atlantic seaboard. This form of transportation virtually ceased during World War II and was never revived.

Because of their competitive situation, Pacific Northwest lumber producers are very alert to anything which may increase their production costs or enable their competitors to obtain a delivered price advantage in their principal markets. And because the economic welfare of the region is closely tied to conditions in the forest industries, the entire Pacific Northwest is deeply concerned whenever serious competitive threats arise. This concern has been aroused twice during recent years because of issues related to international trade.

Canadian lumber imports

During the early 1960's, softwood lumber imports from Canada (coastal British Columbia) began to cut heavily into Pacific Northwest lumber producers' markets along the North Atlantic seaboard. In some of these northeastern markets whose needs had largely been met with Pacific Northwest lumber, Canadian lumber accounted for as much as 70 per cent of total sales during 1962.

Pacific Northwest lumbermen claimed that

Canadian competition was responsible for the closing of 200 mills and the unemployment of thousands of workers in the region in 1961. They stated that unless Canadian lumber imports were greatly reduced the domestic lumber industry would continue to decline. The Pacific Northwest lumbermen launched a campaign to check Canadian imports in 1962.

Spokesmen for the Pacific Northwest lumber industry held that two factors contributed to their problem. (1) The Canadian dollar had recently been devalued to about 92 cents in United States currency. These "cheaper" Canadian dollars lowered Canadian production costs compared to those in the United States. (2) Canadian producers used foreign-owned steamships which charged low rates to transport lumber to the Northeast. United States producers under the Jones Act had to use American ships which charged higher rates.

Pacific Northwest lumbermen realized that they could do nothing about the devaluation of the Canadian dollar. But they urged the national government to help their industry: (1) by modifying the Jones Act, (2) by establishing import quotas, and (3) by raising the tariff on Canadian lumber.

THE JONES ACT

The Jones Act (Merchant Marine Act of 1920) had been passed by Congress to aid United States steamship lines and shipbuilders, and their employees. Among other things, it prohibits the use of foreign-owned or foreign-built ships to transport goods from one United States port to another. Canadians are free to use ships from any country in transporting goods between Canadian and United States ports. Consequently Canadian producers enjoy a transportation cost advantage of $8 to $12 per thousand board feet of lumber over their Pacific Northwest tidewater mill competitors. The advantage was even greater when these tidewater mills had to use higher-priced rail transportation (as increasingly was the case).

Pacific Northwest tidewater lumbermen, therefore, sought to have Congress repeal the Jones Act port-to-port restrictions. Competing southeastern lumbermen and even some inland Pacific Northwest producers, however, opposed this move. They feared that lower transportation costs for tidewater lumber would lead to lower prices and more competition for their own output. Obviously, the railroads which hauled lumber from the Pacific Northwest did not look with favor on attempts to lower the costs of water transportation. Lower water rates would obviously hurt their business.

Modification of the Jones Act was also opposed by the United States steamship industry (which has its foreign operations subsidized by the federal government) and by maritime unions. Both feared that any tampering with merchant marine laws and policies might set precedents which could lead to the repeal of other special benefits.

The controversy continued into 1963, but no action was taken on the bill Senator Maurine Neuberger of Oregon had introduced to repeal Jones Act restrictions. The Pacific Northwest lumbermen had to look for other remedies.

IMPORT QUOTAS

Pacific Northwest lumbermen sought to have the United States Tariff Commission impose a quota on foreign lumber that would limit imports to not more than 6.5 per cent of the nation's total lumber consumption. The Commission, however, found that the Pacific Northwest lumbermen were disadvantaged because Canadian producers had more readily accessible timber and because United States transportation policies and regulations increased transportation costs in this country. In view of these findings, and because the national policy favored less restriction on international trade, the Tariff Commission refused to impose a quota.

Next, a petition drafted by former Congressman Jack Westland (R-Washington) and signed by 105 other Congressmen was presented to the President. The petition urged the President to impose a temporary quota, and went on to say that "there appears to be no other alternative but that the Congress enact legislation to provide a quota." Neither the President nor Congress took the requested action.

It should be mentioned, however, that even in the Pacific Northwest there was no general agreement on the desirability of a quota. The *Eugene (Oregon) Register-Guard,* a daily newspaper in the city which long has called itself "the lumber capital of the world," stated in an editorial:

> However popular it might be locally, this newspaper cannot support the notion that Canadian competition for our lumber mills should be curbed through use of import quotas. Not only would such trade-restricting action be contrary to the free-trading pattern this nation has been advocating for all the Free World, it would be completely contrary to the spirit of free enterprise and to the overall interests of this nation. .--. . Trade barriers benefit no one in the long run. They simply reduce the real purchasing power of every man's labor, in every country where they are imposed.

HIGHER TARIFFS

Pacific Northwest lumbermen also attempted to have tariffs on imported lumber increased from $1 to $6 per thousand board feet. The United States Tariff Commission denied this request for the same reasons that earlier had led it to deny import quotas. An effort was made to have Congress enact legislation overriding the Commission's decision, but nothing came of it. Most concerned members of Congress believed that even if such legislation was enacted, it would be vetoed by the President.

THE RESULTS

Pacific Northwest lumbermen were unsuccessful in all their efforts to reduce Canadian competition through government actions. Finally, they became reconciled to living with conditions as they were. This was made easier by increasing countrywide prosperity during the middle 1960's which, in turn, led to increased prosperity in the Pacific Northwest forest industries and in the region as a whole.

By 1968, total Canadian softwood lumber imports into the United States were about 60 per cent above the 1960 level. During these years, the country's total consumption of softwood lumber increased by only about 17 per cent. This meant that Canadian softwood lumber imports accounted for a little more than 16 per cent of total United States softwood lumber consumption in 1968, compared to about 12 per cent in 1960.

Meantime, despite an average price increase of about 30 per cent for softwood lumber between 1960 and 1968, lumber production in the Pacific Northwest areas most affected by Canadian competition (western Oregon and Washington) continued to decline slowly. Lumber production, however, was increasing in other regions of the country.

By 1968, the Pacific Northwest lumber industry had become involved in still another international trade controversy.

Log exports to Japan

JAPANESE NEEDS AND PURCHASES

Japan, next to Canada this country's foremost partner in international trade, is a large importer of timber products. Historically, much of Japan's imported softwood timber had come from the Pacific Northwest. Other sources of supply were Alaska, Canada, and the Soviet Union.

Lumber needs increased greatly in Japan during that country's unprecedented economic expansion in the late 1950's and into the 1960's. The Japanese policy was to import logs that were milled into lumber in their own country. They were not satisfied with the quality of lumber milled abroad and then exported to Japan. Of course the Japanese also wanted their country to enjoy the benefits of the additional employment and value added by the milling process. Substantial investments were made in lumber mills in various Japanese seaports.

Japanese log purchases from the Pacific Northwest increased by about 675 per cent between 1962 and 1968. These purchases were made both from large forest industries which owned their own timber supplies, and from logging contractors who bought timber from public forests and logged it for resale.

Industry projections suggested that by 1970 a volume of logs equivalent to more than 15 per cent of the total annually milled into lumber in the Pacific Northwest would be exported to Japan. By 1980 a volume equivalent to more than 18 per cent of local milling would be exported to that country. Increased demand helps to explain why the average price of sawlogs on the open market in western Oregon and Washington increased from $57.40 to $82.00 (almost 43 per cent) from

1962 to 1968. Thereafter prices continued to rise.

OPPOSITION, SUPPORT, AND ACTIONS

The trends just described alarmed small lumber mill operators in the Pacific Northwest. They were largely dependent upon buying logs on the open market or from public forests. Their trade group, the Western Forest Industries Association, Portland, Oregon, supported by the Lumber and Sawmill Workers Union, attempted to stop the increasing flow of logs to Japan. They alleged that log shortages and high log prices resulting from Japanese purchases were driving small mill operators out of business. They argued that exporting logs to Japan was equivalent to exporting American jobs. A study by the United States Forest Service revealed that 7.47 man-hours of labor per 1000 board feet were spent, on the average, in logging and handling exported logs, while from 12.47 to 14.22 man-hours (depending upon the size of the mill) were spent on logs processed into lumber in the Pacific Northwest.

Many political leaders in the Pacific Northwest, including senators, congressmen, and governors, supported the anti-export movement, as did various regional newspapers and conservation groups. On the other hand, those who were engaged in selling logs to Japan (mainly large private timber owners), and others who profited from these exports (Pacific Northwest seaport managers, stevedores and longshoremen, and loggers employed in cutting and hauling for exporters) opposed any restrictions.

No one seriously considered a policy of prohibiting private timber owners from selling their own logs to the Japanese. The anti-export group, however, attempted to have the federal government establish a quota on the export of logs bought from public forests. But the Johnson administration vehemently opposed restriction on international trade in general, and did not wish to antagonize Japan. Income earned from the sale of logs to Japan also helped this country's balance of payments position. Nothing was done.

In Congress, Senator Wayne Morse of Oregon introduced an amendment to a pending Foreign Aid Bill. The Morse amendment proposed a three-year limitation, 1969 through 1971, on the annual export to Japan of logs from publicly owned lands. The number of 350 million board feet mentioned in the bill was a little more than what had been exported from both public and private lands in 1962. The bill also included safeguards to prevent private timber owners from selling their own logs to the Japanese and replacing them with logs from public lands. Despite opposition from the Administration and other sources, the Oregon Senator obtained enough political support to pass his measure. The President did not veto this amended bill, since that would also have involved a veto of the entire Foreign Aid bill.

The anti-export group, although not completely satisfied, had achieved a partial victory. But private log exports to Japan continued to increase, reaching a new quarterly high of more than 575 million board feet (from both private and public timberlands) during the second quarter of 1970. Although the Morse amendment does not expire until the end of 1971, anti-export forces already have made plans to secure its extension or to obtain even greater restrictions.

Summary

In international trade, as in other economic matters, groups of similarly-situated individuals are very sensitive to developments which directly affect them. Buyers like to buy at low prices; sellers wish to sell at high prices. Producers want to keep their costs low, in order to meet or beat their competitors' prices and thus stay in business and make profits. Workers want their employers to stay in business (so that they will have jobs), but they also want high wages. Even a person who believes in free trade as a matter of principle is not likely to welcome the prospect of being "free traded" out of his means of livelihood.

Imported Canadian softwood lumber probably has led to lower prices for many purchasers. It is clear, however, that imported lumber also has lowered profits and employment in some areas of the Pacific Northwest. Unfortunately, plans which might be used to restrict Canadian imports, or to aid Pacific Northwest lumbermen in other ways, would harm certain persons and businesses.

Similarly, the export of logs obviously benefits

businesses and workers outside the forest industries. But it also has harmed some producers and workers, and may have contributed to higher lumber prices in this country. Again, government action or failure to act has benefited some at the expense of others.

In considering what to do in such cases, Congress and the President must carefully weigh the advantages and disadvantages of various policies. They must not only weigh the arguments advanced by interest groups, but must consider the best interests of the nation as a whole. Whatever is done, many people are likely to be dissatisfied, and any solution reached is likely to be only a temporary one.

Toward better understanding

QUESTIONS TO CONSIDER IN ANALYZING THIS CASE

1. Why is the northeastern section of the United States a heavy consumer of lumber brought from other regions? Why are the Pacific Northwest and the Southeast leading producers of softwood lumber, despite their distance from principal markets?

2. How is it possible that northwestern producers, located farther away from the northeastern markets and with consequent higher transportation costs to market, are able to compete with nearer southeastern producers in these markets? What effect might differing kinds of timber stands in the two regions have on this competition? What role do transportation costs play? Explain fully.

3. Why would a devaluation of the Canadian dollar enable Canadian producers to compete more effectively in the United States markets? What might be expected to happen if the Canadian dollar became more valuable than our dollar? Why?

4. How is a law giving our ships a monopoly on intercoastal steamship transportation supposed to aid United States steamship companies and their employees? How can such a law be justified on economic or other grounds? Who bears the cost of this aid? Do similar laws apply to other industries? Do you favor such laws? Why, or why not?

5. Would you favor a higher tariff, or import quotas, on Canadian lumber? Why, or why not? What might be the viewpoint of a United States lumber mill employee? Of a grocery merchant or a used car dealer located in the Pacific Northwest or in the Southeast? Of a northeastern consumer? Of a midwestern building materials salesman?

6. Why did Japan import logs rather than milled lumber from the Pacific Northwest? Could the Southeast compete for this market?

7. In the best interests of the total United States public (which includes lumber producers and consumers in all sections of the country), what would you propose as the most satisfactory "solution" to the Canadian lumber import "problem"? Consider your answer carefully and be prepared to defend it.

THINKING ABOUT THE BASIC ECONOMIC ISSUES

1. The problem of foreign competition is not unique to the lumber industry. What other industries are faced with similar problems? Are any of these industries aided by subsidies? Are there contrasting viewpoints with respect to "solutions" held by various groups within these industries? Explain.

2. What relationships, if any, exist between the lumber import controversy and the conservation and wise use of national resources? Explain.

3. Does the principle of comparative advantage provide any "answers" for the American lumbermen's problems? Why, or why not?

4. In the European Common Market, member countries enjoy a free trade area among themselves, but have a common tariff policy in trading with nonmembers. If the United States and Canada were members of a Common Market, what would be the effect on lumber exports to the United States from Canada? On log exports to Japan?

chapter twenty

The future of the American economy

1. **What makes a problem primarily economic?**
2. **What is the outlook for the economy?**
3. **How should young citizens prepare themselves to cope with economic problems?**

The future is like heaven—everyone exalts it but no one wants to go there now.

JAMES BALDWIN, Nobody
Knows My Name

The young people of today are highly critical of the values and life-style of their parents. Each generation tends to believe that the older generation has "messed things up." The "generation gap" is nothing new. Today's older generation once blamed the generation before it for the Great Depression of the 1930's and World War II. When students now in high school are married and have teen-aged children of their own, that "younger generation" doubtless will point an accusing finger at those who left them a less-than-perfect world.

The truth is that some problems are never solved. Other problems can be solved only at great cost and over a long period of time. Sometimes the solution of one problem creates unforeseen new problems which, in turn, must be tackled. These statements should not be interpreted as a suggestion to throw up one's hands in despair. Human intelligence enables people to overcome many obstacles, and to adapt themselves to situations for which there is

no immediate remedy or none that is apparent.

Change is ever-present, in economic affairs as in other areas. The very fact of change provides stimulation and may contribute to the solution of a persistent problem. But change also brings new problems. The purpose of this chapter is to focus information and insights from economics on some major problems of today and of the decade ahead.

1

What makes a problem primarily economic?

When a problem is solved a goal has been reached. A goal is some desirable end that one wishes to reach. A problem is an obstacle blocking the attainment of a given goal. There may be more than one way of solving an economic problem and of attaining an economic goal. But before these can be explored, it is necessary to reach general agreement with respect to the goal and the problems that must be overcome. This done, one must reach agreement on the most promising course of action.

In a democracy, social and economic goals are determined by the will of the majority. In a free society, people tend to act in a manner consistent with their beliefs and values. Because differences exist, it may prove difficult to reach agreement on *precise* goals. Compromise may be necessary. But in the United States most people can agree, most of the time, on *general* goals—that is, the general direction in which they wish American society to move. Once there is agreement on direction, it becomes possible to judge whether a proposed course of action is likely to facilitate attainment of the desired goal.

To illustrate, sometime in the future most Americans may agree that a larger percentage of the GNP should be spent by private businesses and individuals. The goal, in other words, would be to reduce expenditures in the public sector. There might be lack of agreement as to the amount of change but consensus that reduction in public spending is desirable. The problem in this case involves change in fiscal policy. Increased private spending becomes possible with a lowering of taxes and reduced government expenditures. However, there may be wide differences about what taxes to cut and what government expenditures to reduce or eliminate. But once there is agreement on the general goal and the general approach to solving the problem, compromise solutions can be worked out that are acceptable to the majority. Even if comparatively few are completely satisfied, the majority are convinced that the changes made are in the right direction.

Only some social goals and problems are primarily economic. Two questions shed light on whether a problem is primarily economic in nature: Can the problem be resolved by the tools of economic analysis? Can the solution be put into effect by material means?

Most citizens would agree on the desirability of such goals as maximum personal freedom, equal justice under law, racial and religious equality, and good schools. These goals are in some way related to economics, but personal values and national ideals enter into their attainment as much as (or more than) economic considerations.

On the other hand, a decent standard of living and a healthful physical environment for everyone are distinctly economic goals. Not everyone will agree on the specifics for either of these goals, and certainly each of them has its noneconomic aspects. But it is possible to move toward their attainment through the implementation of appropriate economic policies.

In summary, some social goals can be reached and some problems solved largely by economic methods; others cannot. Most problems involve other factors than economic, and their solution will involve techniques and policies that are noneconomic in nature. In coping with social problems it may be as important to know what will not work as to know what will work. When a citizen reads about a proposed economic solution to a social problem, he should ask himself whether the proposed plan squares with sound economic principles.

CHECK UP

1. What is a social goal? Why is it necessary to define such goals in general terms?

2. Why may there be more than one way to achieve a social goal? Give examples.

2

What is the outlook for the economy?

The older generation has not been a "do-nothing" group. Those who belong to what is now called the "older generation" lived through the Great Depression and World War II. Their outlook on life has been influenced by the human tragedy and economic waste which they witnessed. They did their utmost to insure that the present generation lived in a better world than theirs was when they were young. Much has been accomplished, but much remains to be done.

Poverty still exists in the United States. Since the early 1930's, programs of public welfare, aid to dependent children, old-age benefits, and unemployment insurance have helped millions of people. Private and public pension plans also have been developed for retired workers. Fewer people live in dire poverty, and each year more people attain middle-class standards of living. Nevertheless, an estimated 40 million Americans still live at a level which the Bureau of Labor Statistics terms below the "poverty line." There are millions of people, both urban and rural, white and nonwhite, who lack adequate food, clothing, housing, and education,

and who do not receive the medical care they need. In an affluent society, the gap between "haves" and "have-nots" should be narrowed.

Solving the problem of poverty will involve increased production, more equitable allocation of goods and services, and a rethinking of government taxing and spending policies. Anyone able to work must be educated or trained so that his skills may be used to best advantage. Minimum wages and payments to those unable to work must be tied to the cost of living.

Many people cannot afford adequate health care. Medicare and government-sponsored health insurance have brought hospitalization, medical treatment, drugs, therapy, and home health care within the reach of most elderly citizens. Public welfare provides some hospital and medical benefits to others, while private hospitalization and medical insurance (Blue

---

HIGH UNEMPLOYMENT RATE FOR TEENAGERS
In recent years, the unemployment rates for sixteen-to nineteen-year-olds has remained the highest of any age group. The following table, based on statistics from the Labor Department, suggests the scope of this problem.

	males	females
1950	12.8	12.0
1955	11.7	10.6
1960	15.3	14.2
1965	14.3	16.5
1970	14.6	12.3
1973	14.0	10.7

It seems likely that the high unemployment rate for teenagers will continue. Thirty-four million new young workers looking for jobs will enter the labor market in the 1970's. While the proportion of teenagers will decline slightly from 8.7 to 8.3 per cent, their numbers will continue to rise. In 1960, there were 5.2 million teenagers in the work force. By 1968 there were 7.1 million, and by 1980 there will be 8.3 million.

The rise in the teenage population during the 1960's is attributed to the post-World War II "baby boom." Whereas the annual growth rate has been 3.9 per cent, it is expected to drop to 1.3 per cent by 1980. Thus the teen-age population will gradually decline.

Most teenagers are unemployed because they lack work experience and education, and because there are too few jobs available for unskilled workers.

Changes in output per man-hour in selected industries

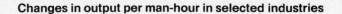

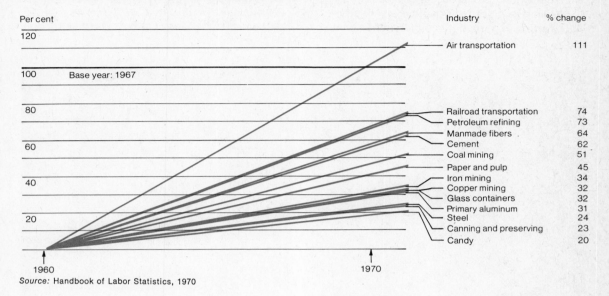

Industry	% change
Air transportation	111
Railroad transportation	74
Petroleum refining	73
Manmade fibers	64
Cement	62
Coal mining	51
Paper and pulp	45
Iron mining	34
Copper mining	32
Glass containers	32
Primary aluminum	31
Steel	24
Canning and preserving	23
Candy	20

Base year: 1967

Source: Handbook of Labor Statistics, 1970

Cross, Blue Shield, and various other private plans) cover millions of Americans. These programs provide some form of medical or hospital insurance for about half of the population, but even for this half the amount may not be adequate to cover serious or prolonged illnesses.

Many dreaded diseases, such as polio, smallpox, diphtheria, typhus, scarlet fever, malaria, typhoid, and tuberculosis have almost been eliminated in this country and greatly reduced in other parts of the world. Even the "childhood diseases" of measles, mumps, and whooping cough no longer present serious problems, and ways of preventing or treating many other ailments have been much improved. The average life-expectancy of a newborn child in this country is more than half again that of a child born in India. Today an American is more likely to die of ailments associated with old age than with youth.

Social progress has lagged far behind technological advances. Achievements in science

In 1985, most young adult workers will be high school graduates

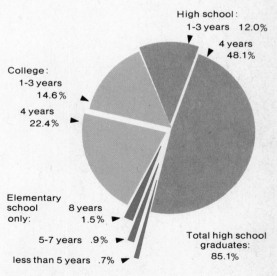

Source: Handbook of Labor Statistics

The urban crisis: challenge of the seventies

Cities today are beset by crises in housing, transportation, pollution, and recreation. Increasing numbers of people are on welfare. Many urban experts believe that unless these problems are solved, only the very rich and the very poor will remain in the city—the rich because they can afford to stay and the poor because they cannot afford to move.

a

b

c

Air pollution affects everyone, everywhere. At
left, *a,* smoke pours from an electric power plant
in New York City, and in *b* vehicle exhaust fumes
reduce vision and endanger health in Los
Angeles. Ecologists have been urging manufacturers to package their products in recyclable
(reusable) containers, pointing out that existing
methods of packaging add greatly to the
accumulation of trash, *c.* Waste disposal has
become a formidable problem in most cities.

Finding decent housing at reasonable rent poses
a serious dilemma for most urban dwellers.
Large apartments suitable for families are particularly difficult to obtain. Dilapidated tenements,
such as exist on the lower east side of New
York, *d,* and overpopulation, *e,* are aspects of
this problem. To alleviate the shortage, many
more new housing units, like those shown in *f,*
will need to be built for people of low and
moderate income.

e

f

d

g

Space which has been developed for recreation is particularly scarce. In **g,** a yard outside a housing project is totally lacking in play equipment. Even where equipment exists, children must often avoid broken glass, tin cans, and other trash; in **h,** surrounding buildings have been abandoned. In new towns such as Columbia, Maryland, **i,** community needs have been incorporated into an overall plan.

Public transportation needs have increased as more people commute and highways become clogged. Large cities have subways, **j** and **k,** which provide the most rapid transit, although they are not the most comfortable means of conveyance. Buses are found in most cities of any size at all, **l.** Cars, **m,** are still favored by many for their door-to-door advantage—that is, if there is any parking space! For long-distance travel, airplanes, **n,** have replaced railroads in almost every case.

h

i

j

k

l

m

n

and technology have been notable. In addition to advances in medical and biological sciences, the past half-century has witnessed the development of computers, transistors, lasers, synthetics, nuclear energy, jet-driven air transport, space navigation, and many other examples of applied technology which people take for granted. But during this period also were developed atomic-powered submarines, hydrogen bombs with multiple warheads, and long-range missiles for delivering the bombs.

Technological advances and better educated workers have greatly increased per capita output while reducing the average work week. On the other hand, greatly increased production has created shortages of some natural resources, and has contributed to the pollution of air, land, and water. The great migration from rural to urban areas has helped bring about traffic congestion, slums, and housing problems and high crime rates in the cities. Only a beginning has been made toward correcting many of these social ills.

High productivity and consumption create problems as well as affluence. Critics of the American way of life often point out that this country, with but 6 per cent of the world's population, uses about one-third of the world's resources. But they often neglect to point out that this country also accounts for one-third of the world's production (as measured by GNP's). It might be argued that instead of "exploiting the rest of the world" by its high level of consumption, the United States is being exploited by the rest of the world. The nation's long-sustained favorable balance of trade shows that more goods are shipped out of this country than into it. Americans are not living "high on the hog" at the expense of other nations. Quite the contrary. Peoples in many lands would live less well if the United States produced less.

Yet there is another side to this coin. In any discussion of the consumption of the world's resources, it should be recognized: (1) that some resources are not renewable; and (2) that

as developing countries increase their production, each of them will increase its consumption of these resources. One might ask what would happen if people in many other lands began to produce and consume at the same rate as people in the United States. Would not greatly increased worldwide production and consumption lead to the depletion of important natural resources and create serious ecological problems?

Racism continues to plague American society. Racial discrimination and prejudice exist in this country, as they do in all countries having large racial minorities. This is one of mankind's most deeply-rooted and troublesome social problems. In this country, the older generation has broken down the principal legal barriers to integrated education and minority voting rights. Some progress has been made also with respect to housing and employment. But much more remains to be done.

In 1968, the President's National Advisory Commission on Civil Disorders (the Kerner Commission) issued a report about the racial crisis in American cities. Subsequently the Commission issued follow-ups of its original report confirming its earlier observations. The report concluded:

1. The nation is rapidly moving toward two increasingly separate Americas.

Within two decades, this division could be so deep that it would be almost impossible to unite: a white society principally located in suburbs, in smaller central cities, and in the peripheral parts of large central cities; and a Negro society largely concentrated within large central cities. . . .

2. In the long run, continuation and expansion of such a permanent division threatens us with two perils.

The first is the danger of sustained violence in our cities. The timing, scale, nature, and repercussions of such violence cannot be foreseen. But if it occurred, it would further destroy our ability to achieve the basic American promises of liberty, justice, and equality.

The second is the danger of a conclusive repudiation of the traditional American ideal of individual dignity, freedom, and equality of opportunity. We will not be able to espouse these ideals meaningfully to the rest of the world, to ourselves, to our children. . . .

3. We cannot escape responsibility for choosing the future of our metropolitan areas and the human relations which develop within them. It is a responsibility so critical that even an unconscious choice to continue present policies has the gravest implications.[1]

The report made specific recommendations for arresting the process of alienation between the races. Most of their recommendations were economic in nature. They included:

Consolidating and concentrating employment efforts.
Opening the existing job structure.
Creating one million new jobs in the public sector in three years.
Creating one million new jobs in the private sector in three years.
Developing urban and rural poverty areas.
Encouraging business ownership in the ghetto.[2]

Methods of implementing each of these recommendations were also proposed.

The environment must be cleaned up. Pollution of air, water, and land has gotten out of hand in many parts of the country. The great majority of communities have not solved the problem of disposing of garbage, sewage, and solid waste materials. Rats thrive in dumps. Chimneys and cars spew noxious and dangerous fumes that threaten the lives of trees, plants, and humans. Unsightly billboards and junkyards and a growing amount of litter deface highways and recreational areas. Industries, government agencies, and individual citizens continue to pollute Planet Earth as though they believed living space to be unlimited and the environment indestructible. The long-range economic

[1] *Report of the National Advisory Commission on Civil Disorders* (Washington, D.C.: U.S. Government Printing Office, 1968), pp. 225–226.
[2] *Ibid.*, p. 233.

and social costs of this neglect may be catastrophic.

Cities are confronted with difficult environmental problems. In the large cities a great many people are crowded together, often in substandard housing. City sanitary services, geared to smaller communities, often are inadequate. There are, therefore, serious problems of pollution, traffic congestion, and fire hazards, as well as risks of epidemics—all aggravated, if not caused, by overcrowding. Schools find it difficult to meet the needs of all pupils, and there are high rates of crime and delinquency. Because high-income families and many businesses have moved to suburbs, city income from taxes is not sufficient to meet growing urban needs.

A leading newspaper provided a frightening account of what a breakdown of public services would mean to New York City. The sidewalks were strewn with rubbish because the men who operate the municipal sanitation service were on strike. They had asked for money which the city could not pay. Fires were breaking out in various parts of the city. Alarms sounded in the fire stations, but no apparatus moved because firemen were also on strike. Crimes and looting spread even more quickly than the fires. Where were the police? On strike. The article went on to point out that the only exaggeration in this description of a big city threatened with anarchy and collapse was the timing of the strikes. They did not occur simultaneously. Moreover, the article suggested that still other public services were similarly deteriorating in the nation's largest cities, including telephone, postal, and public transportation systems.

The situation in rural areas also needs to improve. Poor environment, poor people, and poor public services are problems in rural America as well as in the cities. There are rural slums and rural poor, less visible only because they are less concentrated. Many farmers do not have enough land for a profitable operation, and many rural workers lack the education and work skills needed to make a living in the cities.

Moving to the city is often a will-o'-the wisp.

Big farmers make a good living from their crops, livestock, and government subsidies, whereas small farmers and agricultural laborers make up the rural poor. Only recently have some farm workers been unionized. Unprofitable farming eventually should be eliminated (along with government agricultural subsidies), but the persons involved in such operations must be provided with opportunities for necessary retraining to earn a living in other occupations.

There is a danger that economic power will rest in too few hands. In any free enterprise system, the successful tend to drive out or to take over the less successful. Corporations grow larger and some of them become amazingly diversified. Economists and Presidents have warned against a "military-industrial complex" and the influence it exerts over government spending. Both the economy and the lives of most Americans may be increasingly controlled by the "Five Bigs" of contemporary society— Big Agriculture, Big Business, Big Government, Big Labor, and Big Military.

"Bigness" in itself is not necessarily either good or bad. In some operations, efficiency increases with size; in other operations, being small may be an advantage. Bigness should evolve in business when it is efficient, provided that it does not ignore and threaten the rights of the smaller business.

Big Labor implies that it needs bigness to bargain effectively with Big Business. Big Military seems necessary for the nation's security; Big Government to cope with the ever-growing problems and needs of society. At times consumers of goods and services may feel that they too need to organize and grow big!

Developing countries must be helped to raise their standard of living. For humanitarian as well as other reasons, the inhabitants of the world's less-developed nations must live better. World peace depends upon international good will and trust, and the hope for a better way of life. Anarchy may well characterize the behavior of people who know that others live well while they themselves starve. Military adventures may be used by dictators who seek to unify their underprivileged subjects by directing their hatred against a scapegoat.

As citizens of the world's richest nation, Americans necessarily must play a leading role in furthering international prosperity and peace. This goal, however, cannot be achieved by one nation. All the economically developed countries of the world must somehow be united in an effort for the common good of mankind. And the developing nations themselves must be encouraged to co-operate in the task of helping themselves.

This may be the next generation's most important and most difficult problem. The very future of civilization, and even of mankind itself, may depend upon how successfully the problem of helping developing nations to achieve economic maturity is solved.

Too rapid population growth is a major contributing factor to many difficult problems. Economic reasons help to explain why peoples in developing countries tend to have large fami-

Public costs soar as U.S. population grows

Per cent increase 1965-1972

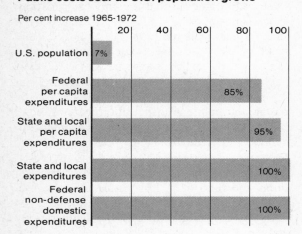

Source: Statistical Abstract

lies. Many hands may be needed to do the work. Parents can look forward to a more secure old age if several grown-up children can look after them. And in earlier times, deaths among children were so high that comparatively few survived to maturity.

In developed countries social values and religious beliefs are factors that influence the size of families. But whatever the reasons, too rapid population growth carries important economic implications for any society, whether developing or developed.

Gloomy predictions have been made that the world's population may double three times within a century. Some experts predict that such population growth will exhaust food, fuel, and other resources. Optimistic statements have also been made that the world can easily support several times its present population. Which is right? The truth probably lies somewhere between these two extremes.

Certainly some habitable regions are thinly populated, and the underwater resources of the oceans have barely been tapped. Increased scientific knowledge, better production methods, and perhaps different consumption habits should make possible a much more efficient use of food and other resources.

Yet the earth's resources, including usable land, are limited. Already many parts of the world are so overpopulated (and underproductive) that hunger and want are the constant companions of millions of people. Most of these poor people cannot move to more hospitable lands. Some form of population control seems to be the best path towards a better way of life. This approach already is being encouraged in India. In the United States, a "thinly populated" country, some people feel that such problems as poverty, pollution, and urban congestion grow out of this country's "population explosion."

CHECK UP

1. Why is there poverty in this country? What can be done about it? About health care?

2. Why are high productivity and consumption a boon for a nation? What problems may they create?

3. What problems were identified in the Kerner Commission Report? What economic recommendations were made in it?

4. What causes contributed to the current problems of this country's big cities? To the pollution of the environment?

3

How should young citizens prepare themselves to cope with economic problems?

Economic problem-solving occurs at many levels. Economic problems such as those just mentioned, and many that were not mentioned, are of concern to all citizens. Such problems cannot be ignored, and they must be dealt with at different levels. Federal, state, and local governments and international organizations all have a role to play. So do business, agriculture, and organized labor.

The individual citizen can make important contributions. He can refrain from littering sidewalks, roadsides, and recreation areas. He can prepare himself to be a productive worker. He can keep well-informed on economic issues and seek to influence public opinion. By his vote he can support political leaders who seem to have a grasp of economic realities and show concern for the common good. Because constructive programs for solving difficult problems are likely to be expensive, the good citizen will not grumble about high taxes. His chief concern should be, "Has the money been well spent?"

Each person is responsible for his own economic success. This country provides citizens with optimum opportunities for a formal education and continuing means for keeping informed. The American political and economic system allows each person to choose his occupation. It gives the greatest rewards to those who produce most. If one *produces* less than he is capable of producing, one should not be surprised at *earning* less than he is capable of earning. This country does not "owe a living" to anyone who is able to work but unwilling to do so. The "old-fashioned" virtues of honesty, hard work, and thrift have not gone out of style. The surest road to economic success is determination to work hard at one's chosen occupation.

Responsible citizenship calls for an understanding of trends. Change takes place constantly. By understanding the direction of change, one can make necessary adjustments and even to some extent control its direction and rate. Obviously no one can foretell the future with certainty. But through careful observation and analysis of past developments and present conditions, he can acquire a better understanding of major economic trends. Barring all-out war or other cataclysmic event, the following trends seem likely to continue.

1. *Big business will be increasingly involved in programs of social betterment.* Business may be expected to become increasingly responsive to social "value judgments" and will undertake socially beneficial projects now handled by government or not handled at all. The production of goods and services will continue to increase, but what is produced and how much will be influenced by considerations of public good as well as private needs.

2. *Opportunities for creative leisure will increase.* Computers, automation, and machines will reduce the number of workers needed for hard manual labor and routine clerical tasks. Education and high skill will become increasingly important. The resulting displacement of labor will necessitate retraining programs to upgrade personnel and to qualify them for skilled positions. The workday and workweek will become shorter.

3. *Economic conditions will improve throughout the world.* Increased industrialization in most countries will lead to increased exchange of raw materials and finished products. Tariffs and other trade barriers will tend to be reduced substantially. Greater international monetary co-operation will reduce exchange rate instability. Living standards will continue to rise in the developed nations, several present-day developing nations will move away from this classification, and developing nations will continue to move ahead.

It has been said that the past is history and that projection into the future is sheer speculation. This chapter has used information about what has been happening to establish trends. Then it has listed some socially desirable goals, suggested problems that must be overcome to achieve these goals, and indicated what needs to be done to overcome the problems. Each student who reads this book will have his own views about these goals, the problems to be overcome, and ways of coping with them. He may wish to add to and subtract from what has been said. That is all to the good. For few goals are ever fully achieved, and comparatively few social problems are solved once and for all. To create the better world hinted at in this chapter there will be work for all!

Median income of males, 25 years of age and older, by years of school completed

Total income in thousands of dollars

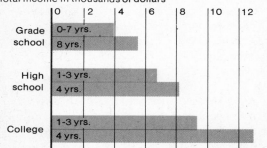

Source: Handbook of Labor Statistics

The outlook for the U.S. economy

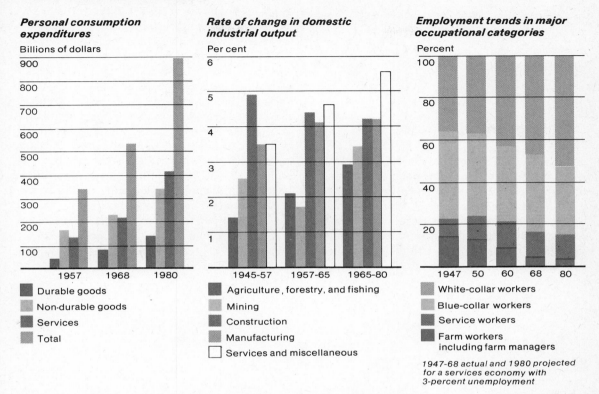

Personal consumption expenditures

Billions of dollars

- Durable goods
- Non-durable goods
- Services
- Total

Rate of change in domestic industrial output

Per cent

- Agriculture, forestry, and fishing
- Mining
- Construction
- Manufacturing
- Services and miscellaneous

Employment trends in major occupational categories

Percent

- White-collar workers
- Blue-collar workers
- Service workers
- Farm workers including farm managers

1947-68 actual and 1980 projected for a services economy with 3-percent unemployment

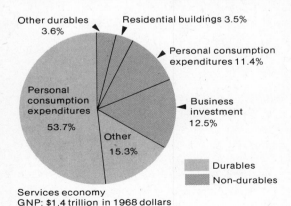

Demand structure in a services economy, 1980

Other durables 3.6%
Residential buildings 3.5%
Personal consumption expenditures 11.4%
Business investment 12.5%
Personal consumption expenditures 53.7%
Other 15.3%

- Durables
- Non-durables

Services economy
GNP: $1.4 trillion in 1968 dollars

Both 3- and 4-percent unemployment levels

Source: Bureau of Labor Statistics

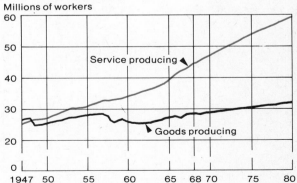

Employment trends in goods-producing and services-producing industries

Millions of workers

Service producing

Goods producing

1947-68 actual and 1968-80 projected for a services economy with 3-percent unemployment
Wage and salary workers only, except in agriculture, which includes self-employed and unpaid family workers.

CHECK UP

1. How can a person further his own economic success?

2. What are economic trends? What are the implications of each of those listed?

Clinching the main ideas

Goals represent the general directions in which society wishes to move. Problems are roadblocks which must be overcome in moving toward the goals. There may be several satisfactory ways to overcome a problem, but to be most effective, there should be some agreement on methods. It is important to be able to identify those problems which are susceptible of economic solution.

The "older generation" has made some progress in coming to grips with present-day economic problems. But much remains to be done by individuals acting alone as well as co-operatively through private, governmental, and even international organizations.

In this country, the problems of poverty, racism, environment, energy and raw materials shortages, technological change, and economic concentration persist. In the international sphere, widespread underdevelopment exists, and the population growth threatens to outstrip the supply of food and natural resources. Overriding all these problems is the question of how to establish an enduring world peace.

The youth of today face tremendous challenges and opportunities. It is everyone's responsibility to prepare himself as thoroughly as he possibly can for his place in the world of the future.

Chapter 20 review

Terms to understand

1. generation gap
2. social goal
3. "poverty line"
4. alienation
5. Kerner Commission
6. military-industrial complex
7. economic trend
8. value judgment

What do you think?

1. On the whole, has the tendency toward bigness in business benefited or harmed the economy of the United States? Give reasons.

2. Why is compromise necessary in arriving at decisions affecting economic policy?

3. Why has the United States provided a greater amount of economic aid to developing countries than has the People's Republic of China? Why have some developing countries sought help from the latter?

4. Why is the "younger generation" likely to be critical of the "older generation"? Give examples.

5. Why does social progress fail to keep pace with technological and scientific progress?

6. Is "bigness" bad in agriculture? In government? Industry? Labor? The military establishment? Explain.

Extending your knowledge of economics

1. Analyze in detail a problem in the public sector, such as traffic control or air pollution, and suggest possible solutions.

2. In 1971 the *Christian Science Monitor* ran a series of nine articles dealing with what it called the "nine crucial problems of the decade." The problems were: Crime, The Aged, Business Ethics, Peace, Poverty, Television Quality, Race Relations, and Pollution. Which of these problems are primarily economic? Only secondarily related to economics? Explain why in each case.

amounts of land. Compare with *intensive farming*.

face value: in insurance, the maximum amount, as stated on the policy, that the company will pay the insured in case of loss.

factors of production: land, labor, capital, and enterpriser (management) are combined to produce wealth.

farm surpluses: a supply of farm products larger than that for which there is effective demand. Also, products purchased by the federal government or taken as security for loans in order to maintain higher price levels.

fascism: a political-economic system such as that established in Italy by Mussolini. Private property and private production are retained, but are subjected to close governmental control. Labor also is subject to strict governmental control.

favorable balance of trade: a term used in international trade to describe a country whose exports are greater (in money value) than its imports.

FDA: Food and Drug Administration—the federal agency which regulates the sale and distribution of food and drugs.

featherbedding: labor union rules allegedly provide easy jobs by restricting employees' output or requiring the assignment of more workers than are needed for a given task.

Federal Communications Commission (FCC): government regulatory agency concerned with radio, television, telegraph, and interstate telephone service.

Federal Deposit Insurance Corporation (FDIC): a public corporation created by the federal government in 1933. It insures a depositor's first 20,000 dollars in any member bank, thus protecting him against loss if the bank fails.

Federal land banks: twelve banks administered by the Farm Credit Administration. Their chief function is to provide long-term first-mortgage loans to farmers.

Federal Maritime Commission (FMC): government regulatory agency which controls American firms engaged in overseas and offshore water transportation.

Federal Reserve note: U.S. paper money issued by Federal Reserve Banks, secured by gold certificates, by commercial paper held by these banks, and by government bonds.

Federal Reserve System: a system of twelve Federal Reserve banks, a Board of Governors appointed by the President, and hundreds of member banks. The latter include all national banks plus state banks and trust companies which have applied for membership and been admitted.

Federal Trade Commission (FTC): government regulatory agency established to serve as watchdog for violations of the Federal Trade Commission Act. The Wheeler-Lea Act authorizes FTC also to prevent unfair trade practices in the advertising of foods and drugs.

Federal Trade Commission Act: an act passed by Congress in 1914 which established the FTC to prevent "unfair methods of competition," boycotts, and price-fixing agreements in interstate commerce.

federation: in organized labor, a grouping of unions under a central authority, but with each union in control of its own internal affairs.

fiat money: paper money which is not redeemable in gold or silver. The government issuing it, however, states that this money is legal tender. Its value depends on the taxing power of the government and the faith of the people in the financial stability of their country.

firm: a company within an industry; any privately-owned productive unit.

fiscal policy: government policy for achieving certain goals for the nation's economy. The policy concerns legislation and administrative practices with respect to taxation and the public debt, appropriations and expenditures.

Five Year Plan: in the Soviet Union, the overall allocation of the nation's resources and productive efforts during a five-year period. The nation's goals and the needs of the economy, as seen by government (Communist Party) officials, determine production quotas.

fixed cost (overhead): a cost which remains comparatively constant whether the total volume of production increases or decreases, such as interest on borrowed capital.

fixed expenses: in a family budget, such items as rent or mortgage payments, utilities, and loan payments, which remain relatively constant from month to month.

fixed income: income not likely to change, such as Social Security, welfare, pensions, etc.

floor: a minimum price level, usually guaranteed by the government, below which prices of a commodity will not be permitted to drop.

foreign exchange: the process of settling debts between persons or businesses in different countries. Bills of exchange (claims for payment in a foreign currency) are used for this purpose.

form utility: satisfying a human want by changing the shape or composition of some good, as in the conversion of wheat into bread.

foundation: a special type of corporation, operated

for charitable or educational purposes, and often administered by a trust company. It is not operated for profit and does not have to pay taxes.

fractional reserve system: a plan that permits commercial banks to hold only part of their deposits as bank reserves. This plan enables commercial banks to make loans, thus creating deposit currency.

franchise: a right granted to an individual, partnership, or corporation by a government, to render a given service, e.g., a local bus line; also the right (generally exclusive) to sell a product of a producing company.

free enterprise: see *capitalism*.

free good: anything external to man and inherently useful, which exists in such large supply that no conscious effort is necessary to secure as much as is desired. Example: air. An *economic good,* on the other hand, is relatively scarce. See *good*.

free market economy: free enterprise; privately-owned business is operated with a minimum of government restrictions.

"free rider": a labor union term for workers who do not belong to a union. Working with union workers, they enjoy many benefits brought about by union activity without paying the cost of membership.

free trade: international trade unrestricted by import and export duties or by regulations designed to limit or channel trade.

fringe benefit: compensation other than regular wages, such as paid vacations and holidays, or company contributions to pensions and insurance plans.

garnishee: a court order requiring an employer to pay to the court for the benefit of a creditor a designated part of a debtor-employee's wages until the debt is paid.

general farming: farming in an area where a number of different kinds of crops may be grown under a system of crop rotation.

general partnership: each partner is legally responsible for all financial obligations of the business. See *partnership* and *silent partner*.

general sales tax: a form of consumption tax imposed at retail or consumer level.

general strike: a strike involving more than a single firm or industry; an extended work stoppage throughout the country, which may be directed against the government.

"the general welfare": a clause in Article I, Section 8 of the Constitution, in which Congress is directed to enact legislation and appropriate money for the general well-being of the population.

generic name: the chemical rather than the patented brand names of drugs prescribed by a physician.

geometric ratio: mathematical term for a series of numbers, each of which is double the one before, e.g., 2,4,8,16.

gold standard: a monetary system in which a nation's unit of money is defined as being equal to a given weight of gold. Gold coins are legal tender and circulate freely. The value of other forms of money is maintained at a par with gold coins.

good: anything external to man that is wanted by people.

good will: the earning power of a going concern in addition to what it might normally expect to earn from its tangible assets; its reputation and customer relations.

government borrowing: usually done by selling bonds to the public or to financial institutions.

Granger Cases: series of decisions of the United States Supreme Court during the 1870's upholding the right of government to regulate businesses "affected with the public interest."

gross income: in a business the total income, determined by the amount of goods and services times the selling price per unit of each commodity, before deductions, expenses, or costs. For an individual, his total income before the amounts for Social Security, taxes, health insurance, etc., are deducted.

gross investment: net or new investment expenditures plus expenditures for replacing existing facilities.

Gross National Product (GNP): the total value of all goods and services produced by the nation's economy; based on market prices and reported annually and quarterly; the broadest available measure of the rate of economic activity.

group insurance: term insurance which covers all members of a given group, such as a labor union, and which normally is issued without a medical examination.

growth stocks: stocks purchased despite low yield in expectation of larger returns later.

guaranteed annual wage: a plan which stipulates a given number of weeks of employment, or the equivalent in wages, during the year.

guaranteed price level: point at which government will step in to buy certain products whose prices are declining. See *floor*.

guild: formerly an organization of men engaged in similar work and having common interests. It included both employers and employees in a given skilled trade. The guild performed regulatory, educational, and social service functions now performed by government, unions, and employer associations.

hard goods: consumer goods with a relatively long

life, including such items as washing machines, refrigerators, furniture, appliances, and automobiles.

high price level: a condition of the consumer market that prevails when the buying power of the dollar is low.

holding company: a corporation holding sufficient stock in other companies to be able to control their operations.

hypothesis: an untested statement suggesting a possible cause and effect relationship between observed facts.

importer: a representative who handles transactions related to the importation of products from foreign countries; also, a firm which brings in goods from foreign countries for its own use.

impulse buying: buying things spontaneously without consideration of one's long-range financial situation.

incentive pay: a wage policy providing a bonus for increased production or production in excess of the norm or standard.

income: the return or material benefits, expressed in money equivalents, arising from the services of people or from the use of wealth.

income tax: a federal (and sometimes state or local) tax levied upon corporate and individual incomes above specified amounts. Certain deductions are permitted by law.

independent communism: a national policy independent of the Soviet Union followed by some Communist countries; for example, Yugoslavia.

index numbers: averages obtained from prices of a number of commodities; used to measure overall changes of the price level of similar products or services from one period of time to another. The index number of the base period usually is 100. See *base period*.

individual proprietorship: a business having a single owner, who manages the business, is responsible for all debts of the business, and receives all the profits.

industrial bank: (Morris Plan System) makes small loans to persons of sound character who have limited assets. Weekly or monthly installment payments are arranged until the loan has been liquidated.

industrial co-operative: a co-operative in which worker-members co-operate in such operations as manufacturing, farming, mining, or construction, sharing in the operation and net income.

industrialized economy: a society in which the production and distribution of goods and services is highly organized and mechanized, and in which most of the inhabitants live in urban communities and do nonagricultural work. Because of division of labor, workers are largely dependent on others to produce their food, clothing, and shelter.

industrial union: a union whose membership includes all the workers in a given industry, e.g., the United Auto Workers.

inelastic currency: the supply of money in circulation cannot readily be expanded or contracted to meet the changing demands of the economy; held to be a contributing factor in depressions or panics. The opposite of *elastic currency*.

infant industry: newly established industry. Tariff protection often is provided to protect the industry from foreign competitors.

inflation: sharply increased prices for goods and services; may occur when the purchasing power of the general public is high compared to the amount of goods and services offered. The public's increasing desire to convert money into goods through stepped-up buying may, in turn, reflect a lack of confidence in the nation's currency.

inflationary spiral: succeeding rounds of price and wage increases.

injunction: a court order requiring an individual or group to refrain from some specific practice (such as striking); violation constitutes contempt of court.

"in restraint of trade": phrase referring to price fixing, monopoly, or other practices which may inhibit the free exchange of goods and services; usually refers to a violation of anti-trust laws.

installment contract: agreement between seller and purchaser calling for payments for goods or services at regular intervals over a specified period of time.

insurance: protection against risk.

intensive farming: the use of relatively large amounts of labor and capital on relatively small farms; the production of high-yield crops; the opposite of *extensive farming*.

interest: a percentage (called the *interest rate*) of the face value of a loan paid periodically to the lender until the principal is repaid; also, the return on the use of capital as a factor of production.

interlocking directorate: persons who, by acting as directors of companies which are natural competitors, control prices and company policies in a given field even though the companies retain their separate identities, thus circumventing legislation passed to restrain trusts, pools, or monopolies.

International Monetary Fund (IMF): a fund supported by contributions from member-nations which makes short-term loans of whatever kind of money a country may need to stabilize its exchange rate.

interstate commerce: commerce between the states; business transactions involving firms or persons in more than one state.

Interstate Commerce Clause: that section of the Constitution (Article I, Section 8, §3) which gives power to Congress to regulate commerce with foreign nations, and among the several states.

Interstate Commerce Commission (ICC): an independent administrative agency of the U.S. government which regulates many aspects of interstate transportation except by air.

investment: exchanging money for some form of property with the expectation of making a profit, and with the expectation of retaining this property for a longer period of time than is the case in *speculation*.

investment bank: purchases and resells large blocks of new securities, in expectation of a profit; is not permitted to accept money for deposit or perform other services usually associated with banking.

investment club: group of people generally with moderate incomes, who pool their money, time, and knowledge in order to purchase shares of stock and thus acquire diversified holdings.

investment trust: an institution that invests its capital in other corporations, selling its own securities to make stock purchases. The income covers operating expenses and yields a profit to shareholders.

Iron Clad Oath: see *yellow-dog contract*.

jobber: a "middleman" in the marketing process who buys goods from importers, manufacturers, or wholesalers and sells them to retailers.

journeyman: a skilled worker who has learned his trade by serving an apprenticeship.

jurisdictional strike: a strike which grows out of a dispute between two labor unions about which of them should perform a service over which each claims jurisdiction.

Kerner Commission: a commission appointed by President Lyndon Johnson and headed by former Illinois Governor Otto Kerner which issued a report on civil disorders, focusing on the racial problems of the United States.

Knights of Labor: the first really successful American labor union. It was organized in 1869.

labor: all persons engaged, or capable of being engaged, in the production process, except for the enterpriser himself; one of the four factors of production.

labor force: "persons over fourteen who are gainfully employed or who are working at least 15 hours per week without pay on a family farm or business." (Definition of the United States Bureau of the Census.) See also *labor; factors of production*

Labor-Management Relations Act: see *Taft-Hartley Act*.

labor market: market for a particular kind of labor in a given location at a given time.

labor union: an organization of employees; its representatives negotiate with employers to promote and protect the interests of members.

laissez faire: French for "let alone," an economic system advocated by Adam Smith in which government regulation of or interference with private enterprise is kept at an absolute minimum.

land: one of the major factors of production; usually any economic good supplied by nature without the aid of man. See *free good, good*.

land grant college: an institution of higher learning which benefited from the land grants provided under the Morrill Act. The institution was expected to provide instruction in "agriculture and the mechanic arts."

Latin America Free Trade Association: a regional association of governments dedicated to lowering barriers to trade within the association.

law of comparative advantage: see *comparative advantage*.

law of demand: economic principle which states that the higher the price, the less of a product people will buy; the lower the price, the more of a product people will be willing to buy.

law of diminishing utility: economic principle which states that each succeeding unit of any good satisfies a less intense desire than the previous one.

law of supply: economic principle which states that an increase in the price of any good tends to bring a larger quantity to the market; a decrease in price tends to reduce the quantity coming to the market.

lease: a contract by which one person, for a consideration, turns over the use of specified property to another person for the period stipulated in the contract.

least-cost combination: the one combination of land, labor, and capital which insures the lowest production cost (measured in money terms) for a given volume of output.

legal liability: see *liability*.

legal tender: money that must be accepted at its face value in settlement of any public or private debt.

liability: a legal obligation or a debt, usually stated in terms of money.

"Libermanism": the trend away from centralized economic control in Communist economies, advocated by Yevsei Liberman, a Soviet economist.

life expectancy: the estimated number of years that a

person of given age may be expected to live. This figure is derived from the average length of life of great numbers of persons in various occupations.

life insurance: in return for premiums paid by the insured on a straight life policy, the beneficiary (should the insured die) receives the face value of the policy in a lump-sum settlement or the equivalent.

life underwriter: an insurance representative whose earnings often depend on the amount of insurance he sells; also the insurance company.

limited liability: should a corporation fail, a stockholder has no legal responsibility for its debts beyond the sum he has invested in the corporation.

limited payment life insurance: the stipulated sum is paid the beneficiary upon the death of the insured in return for premiums paid by the insured within a specified number of years.

list price: a manufacturer's suggested price on a product, such as a car.

loan shark: an unlicensed moneylender who charges excessive interest on loans to persons unable to obtain loans from another source.

loan value: in life insurance, the amount which a policyholder can borrow from an insurance company on his policy.

location (or space) value: the worth of a piece of land that results from its location rather than its fertility. The land with the highest location value in the United States is in the heart of New York City.

lockout: closing a plant and thus putting pressure on employees to accept the terms offered by management.

low price level: the overall prices of representative commodities are low, and the buying power of the dollar is relatively high. See *price level*.

macroeconomics: the study of the characteristics and performance of the national economy.

Malthusian theory: theory of Thomas Malthus that population increases by a geometric ratio whereas the food supply increases by an arithmetic ratio. He argued that the resulting food shortages would lead to famine. Starvation, war, and disease, according to Malthus, were nature's way of eliminating the surplus population.

management: sometimes considered one of the factors in production, it directs the use of land, labor, and capital in production. Management usually is the enterpriser in the case of small firms. Large corporations, however, usually are managed by persons hired by the stockholders (owners).

margin: (1) in establishing prices, the difference between the wholesaler's (or manufacturer's) price and the price set by the next seller to insure himself a profit. (2) The minimum down payment permitted in the purchase of corporate stock.

marginal farmer: lack of know-how, inadequate capital, and marginal land restrict income to near the subsistence level.

marginal productivity theory: theory which states that if all workers are interchangeable, no worker gets a higher wage than the value of the output of the marginal worker (the last worker it pays the employer to hire).

market place (or market): an area where buyers and sellers meet for the purpose of buying or selling given commodities.

market pricing situation (or market time period): determination of prices purely by market forces, after all the costs of production have been fully incurred.

marketing co-operative: a joint enterprise established to sell agricultural or other products for its members, thus eliminating certain middlemen's charges. Examples are Sunkist Growers, Inc., and Land o'Lakes Creameries.

marketing research: research done by businesses in order to provide information about future demand.

markup: see *margin*.

Marshall Plan (or European Recovery Program): a plan to speed the economic recovery of Europe after World War II. Proposed by Secretary of State George Marshall in 1947, it called for an inventory of European resources and needs, and for financial aid from this country. Co-operating countries were to use their own resources to best advantage and to seek to overcome barriers to trade. USSR and satellite countries remained aloof from the plan.

Marxian socialism: the theoretical economic system advocated by Karl Marx and his followers, in which all means of production would be owned by the workers. Each person would contribute according to his ability and receive what he needed.

mass production: the production of goods on a large scale, using division of labor, machinery, and standardized parts.

master craftsman: member of a medieval guild who had achieved recognized proficiency in his trade and directed the work of journeymen and apprentices; a position still retained by some craft unions.

maturity: in the case of securities, the date when the principal is due to be paid.

median: the central or middle number in a distribution of numbers in descending order; in any group, one-half is above the median and one-half below.

mediation (or conciliation): the method generally used after the failure of collective bargaining; each side states its case to the mediator who makes recommendations on the points at issue.

medium of exchange: money or any commodity generally accepted in exchange for goods and services.

membership raid: encouraging the members of a union to shift to another union.

merger: the purchase of all the capital stock of a corporation by another corporation.

middleman: anyone who deals in a product between its production and its acquisition by the consumer, such as a wholesaler, retailer, or broker.

mills per dollar valuation: for example, a tax rate of 30 mills per dollar of assessed valuation, which is the same as $30 per $1,000. In other words, one mill is one tenth of a cent.

"mixed" capitalism: see mixed economy.

mixed economy: an economy which combines private enterprise with government-owned enterprise.

model: a brief way of stating key relationships between the facts being studied; commonly written as a mathematical equation.

monetary income: income as measured by the face value of money received.

monetary policies: government actions regulating the availability of money and credit. Compare *fiscal policy*.

money: anything generally accepted in exchange for property, goods, or services. Today our currency includes both cash (coins, paper dollars) and credit money (bank checks, postal money orders, express checks, etc.).

monopolistic competition: the market condition that exists when a large number of sellers are offering products which, although not identical, are so similar in nature that they serve the same purpose.

monopoly: a complete monopoly exists if there is only one seller of a product, who therefore can set his own price. The combined action of several companies who control the supply of a product also results in monopoly because no competitor can enter the field.

moonlighting: taking a second job, usually at night.

Morrill Act: legislation passed in 1862 providing federal assistance to states to establish colleges teaching agriculture and the "mechanic arts."

Morris Plan System: see *industrial bank*.

mortgage: property pledged as security for the repayment of a debt.

mortgage loan: loan from a bank or other lending institution to an individual, in which the borrower's house or other real estate is put up as security for the repayment of the principal and interest.

multiplier effect: the process through which an initial change in spending produces greater change in spending, because money spent is income to someone who in turn respends it, so that it is spent over and over, adding up to many times the initial amount.

mutual funds: see *investment trust*.

mutual insurance company: a type of insurance company in which each policyholder is a part owner of the company.

national bank: an incorporated commercial bank chartered by the federal government and belonging to the Federal Reserve System.

national bank note: paper money issued by a national bank during the period 1863–1935.

national debt: in the United States, debt which the national (federal) government owes those holding its securities. The national debt plus the debts of state and local governments make up the *public debt*.

National Income (NI): total net income from all factors related to the production of goods and services.

National Labor Relations Act (or Wagner Act): gave employees the right to organize and to choose representatives for purposes of collective bargaining; made practices which curtailed the right of collective bargaining unlawful.

National Labor Union: the first labor union federation of any significance; founded in 1866 by William H. Sylvis and composed of workers from several crafts and occupations.

national union: a nationwide union with local affiliations.

national wealth: the total money value of all net claims and assets owned by the residents of a country and by its government.

nationalization: government take-over and operation of a formerly privately-run enterprise such as transportation.

natural monopoly: a monopoly resulting from natural conditions, as when a rare mineral is controlled by a single enterprise. Also, a monopoly (such as telephone service in a given city) which results from the fact that competition would not be in the public interest.

natural resources (or land): all fields and soil fertility, water and potential waterpower fish and wild life, minerals and timber, which constitute the natural wealth of a country.

negotiable property: any good which has utility and can be traded or sold for some other good or service. Securities and real estate are examples.

negotiation: discussion of current problems and demands between the representatives of labor and management, often in contract terms. See *contract*.

net income: see *profit*.

net investment: spending for additional facilities, rather than for the replacement of existing assets.

Net National Product (NNP): Gross National Product minus the value of goods used up or worn out in the production process; the net value of commodities and services produced by the entire nation. See *Gross National Product*.

net real investment: investment in plants, equipment, and inventories.

net worth: the difference between one's assets and one's liabilities.

no-fault automobile liability insurance: plan whereby insurance company pays policyholder for his personal injury without regard to who was at fault in an accident.

noncontributory plan: a payment system in which the employer assumes the entire cost of pensions and other "fringe benefits" for workers. In a contributory plan sums for these purposes are also deducted from an employee's wages.

Norris-LaGuardia Act: federal legislation in 1932 which limited the right of courts to issue injunctions against labor unions and outlawed the "yellow-dog contract," thus providing protection to labor.

note: a type of contract in which the borrower promises to repay a loan, plus interest, at a stipulated rate, by a specified date or on demand. See *promissory note*.

Old Age, Survivors, and Disability Insurance (OASDI): a system of social insurance financed by equal contributions from the employer and employee; provides old-age benefits to the insured at age 65 and also to the employee's family in the event of his death. See *Social Security Act*.

oligopoly (or partial monopoly): the fact that there are only a few sellers of a given product creates a market situation in which the supply offered by any one of them greatly influences the market price.

open market operations: the buying and selling of various securities (chiefly those of the government), bills of exchange, and bankers' acceptances eligible for discount by Federal Reserve Banks. By this method, the Federal Reserve Board attempts to regulate the supply of money and to stabilize the supply and cost of credit throughout the nation.

open shop: a factory in which union membership is not required for employment.

opportunity cost: the value of whatever must be given up in order to acquire something else.

option: an agreement permitting one to buy or sell the thing named within the time and on the terms stipulated.

overdraw: to issue checks for a greater amount than one has on deposit in the bank on which the checks are drawn.

overhead: see *fixed cost*.

overproduction: when total production in the economy exceeds total demand.

over-the-counter market: buying and selling of securities of companies not listed on a stock exchange, through a broker.

over-the-counter securities: securities which are not listed or traded on registered stock exchanges.

package policy: an insurance policy which covers a variety of risks, such as liability insurance, water damage, fire, theft, etc.

paid-up policy: a life-insurance policy with all its premiums paid.

par value: the stated value printed on a share of stock or a bond.

parity: the condition of being equivalent; a policy of maintaining prices on agricultural commodities at a level comparable to those of products which the farmer must buy.

parity price: in agriculture, a price at which farmers are able to sell their produce and which keeps pace with the prices of things farmers must buy.

partnership: an agreement of two or more persons to share the ownership, management, financial responsibilities, and profits of a business enterprise.

patent: a grant of the United States Patent Office which gives an inventor exclusive rights to the manufacture of his invention over a specified period of years.

patronage dividend (or patronage refund): income received by a member of a co-operative. The amount of the dividend is usually figured on the basis of the co-operative's net profits, and as a percentage of the member's total purchases during a given period.

pawnbroker: a person who makes small loans secured by personal property such as jewelry or clothing. If the loan is not repaid within a definite period of time, the collateral is forfeited and sold by the pawnbroker.

pension: payments at regular intervals to a former employee after his retirement.

per capita income: an average income, computed by dividing the total national income by the number of people in the country. See also *National Income.*

personal income: technically, the total "before-taxes" income of all individuals in the nation.

personal liability insurance: insurance policy which protects, up to a designated amount, the insured and his family against claims for personal injury or property damage.

picket line: striking workers marching in front of a factory or place of business to persuade workers or potential customers not to enter (or do business with) the plant or store.

piece wage: wage based on number of articles produced.

place utility: making goods available at a place where they are wanted. Transporting Florida citrus fruit to New York creates place utility.

Point Four Program: a 1949 foreign aid program which stressed technical assistance to developing lands.

policyholder: the buyer of an insurance policy; the person or firm which is insured.

political economy: term formerly used for economics, implying close connection between political (or governmental) and economic activity.

pool (or pooling agreement): an arrangement, illegal when in restraint of trade, whereby corporations that normally would compete with each other reach an agreement for dividing the market or maintaining prices at a given level.

postal savings: a banking service of the United States Post Office Department which pays a specified rate of interest on savings deposits.

poverty line: the income figure below which a family is deemed by the federal government to be too poor to live with adequate food and shelter.

preferred stock: shares in a corporation which have a prior claim (compared to common stock) on the net assets and on a specified amount of the profits.

premium: in insurance, the amount the policyholder pays for protection against the risk specified in the policy.

price ceiling: see *ceiling.*

price concession: a favorable allowance on a customer's used product; a reduction in price in order to sell quickly the remaining cars before new models are delivered.

price control (or price fixing): (1) wartime government policy of setting maximum prices on commodities; (2) an attempt by corporations to create artificially high prices by controlling the supply of a product.

price level: the prices of a selected list of commodities at a given time, considered as a group, and expressed in a composite figure called an *index number.*

price support: a government plan of financial aid to producers to keep prices of commodities from falling below a given minimum level. The prices are maintained by subsidies, and by government purchases from (and government loans to) producers at higher-than-market prices. Efforts are made to restrict production and to keep commodities off the market by storing them.

primary goods: agricultural commodities and raw materials.

primary market: the principal center where a given commodity is bought and sold. For example, the primary wool market in the United States is Boston.

primary want: the basic physical need for food, clothing, and shelter, and the basic social desire for association with others.

principal: the original amount invested. (Interest rates are based on the amount of the principal.)

principle: a theory which has stood the test of time.

private enterprise: economic activities undertaken with the expectation of profit by private individuals (as individual owners, partnerships, corporations), but with the risk of loss.

private (or individual) wealth: economic wealth owned by individuals, partnerships, or corporations.

processed goods: goods which are no longer in their original state, but have gone through one or more alterations, such as wheat being milled into flour.

processing center: point to which products are transported from their original source for further processing before being sent to the consumers' market.

producer: anyone who increases the usefulness of a good, idea, or service, including those who sell or transport.

product differentiation: the emphasis placed by advertising on real or imagined differences between competing products.

production: the creation of economic value; making goods and services available to satisfy human wants; creating time, place, form, or possession utility.

profit: in economics, the share of the product remaining after deducting all payments for interest, rent, and wages.

profit and loss statement: annual listing by a corporation of all income and all expenses.

profit sharing: a system by which employees receive part of the profits of the business in addition to their regular wages.

progressive tax: a tax, such as the federal income tax, which applies higher rates of taxation to higher levels of income.

progressive wage: wage which in addition to regular compensation provides piecework payment for production above the norm set for the job.

Proletarian Cultural Revolution: an ideological struggle in China in 1966–67, marked by violence, over the future course of Chinese political and economic development.

promissory note: a written promise by the borrower to pay the lender the specified amount of money at a given time and place, with interest (if any) at a specified rate.

propensity to spend: the inclination to spend a certain portion of income, expressed in a percentage, which measures how much income will re-enter the economy as spending, and how much as savings.

property tax: a tax levied on real or personal property; a major source of revenue for local and state governments.

proportional tax: one in which the percentage of income required as a tax is the same for all.

protective tariff: a tariff sufficiently high to protect domestic producers against effective competition from foreign-made products.

proxy: a stockholder's authorization for someone else to vote his stock.

public corporation: a corporation organized by government to perform the service of a public agency, such as TVA. (The federal government owns and controls TVA, but otherwise it is run in much the same way as a private corporation.)

public liability insurance: a protection for property owners, especially of income-producing property, who may be sued for injuries suffered by persons on their property.

public sector: those parts of the nation's economy which are the common property of all citizens, such as schools, roads, and parks. The term is also used to describe governmental expenditures for public purposes.

public utility: an enterprise producing something of such basic importance to the public that it is regulated by law, such as water, electricity, and telephone.

public wealth: see *public sector*.

public works: construction of highways, bridges, and public buildings at government expense; often used as a means of providing work for the unemployed.

purchasing co-operative: the earliest form of co-operative; operated as a retail store to provide goods for members.

purchasing power: the ability to buy; that is, the amount of money an individual has to spend.

pure competition: see *competition*.

railroad commissions: agencies created in the 1870's by state legislatures, and given broad regulatory powers over railroads and associated businesses, such as grain elevators and warehouses. Their purpose was to prevent rate discrimination and other undesirable practices.

rate: (1) a term describing a relationship between two quantities. It may be a formula for calculating wages, unit prices, interest, or discount; as 3 per cent—meaning $3 per $100; (2) price charged by a transportation or utility company.

rationing: government limitations on the number or amount of scarce items to be sold to one person.

real estate: land and permanent buildings erected on land.

real income: income measured by the purchasing power of the money received.

real investment: expenditures which create new and additional capital assets; for example, new plants and new machinery.

real property: see *real estate*.

real wage: the purchasing power of money received as wages.

rebate: the generally illegal business practice of giving favored customers a refund.

recession: a period of declining business activity; a phase of the business cycle which follows prosperity.

reciprocal trade agreements: a lever used by the United States in negotiating with foreign countries to increase mutually profitable trade; the President has the power to cut or raise present rates on imported goods as much as 50 per cent.

recovery: an upward movement in economic activity; a phase of the business cycle which follows depression.

regressive tax: a tax which bears more heavily on low-income groups, because it specifies either a set amount of cash or a set percentage of income from all taxpayers.

regulatory commissions: bodies established by Congress to safeguard the public interest in such fields as transportation, public utilities, communications, and the buying and selling of securities. The ICC, the SEC, and the FTC are examples.

rent: payment for the use of land and improvements on it; also, payment for the use of a capital good such as machinery or other plant equipment.

repossess: to take back an article bought on the installment plan because the buyer fails to make the regular payments called for in the conditional sales contract.

representative money: money which has little or no value as a commodity but which represents (or can be exchanged for) commodity money. Example: silver certificates.

reserve: (1) money set aside to cover depreciation of capital assets such as machinery in a factory; (2) money kept by a bank to meet day-to-day needs.

retailer: a person or business firm selling directly to consumers.

revenue: (1) the total income of the government from taxes and other sources; (2) the receipts of a business.

revenue tariff: a tax on imported goods for the purpose of raising money rather than to discourage the use of foreign goods. See *protective tariff*.

"right to work" laws: state laws making the union shop illegal.

Rochdale principles: the three principles still basic to the operation of co-operatives; namely: (1) democratic control, (2) limited returns, and (3) fair distribution of savings. The Rochdale weavers of Lancashire, England, established the first successful co-operative in 1844.

run on a bank: a sudden demand by depositors to withdraw their money, especially when banks' fractional reserves often were inadequate to meet this demand.

"runner": in investments, a person who carries messages from a brokerage firm to the firm's agent at the trading post in the stock exchange.

safe-deposit box: space rented in a bank for the safe-keeping of important papers, securities, and valuable personal property.

salary: in popular usage, pay at regular intervals for services (other than physical labor) rendered. In economic terminology, a salary would be considered a wage.

sales tax: see *general sales tax*.

savings: accumulation of wealth through the postponement of consumption.

savings account: bank account in which money usually remains for a long time and collects interest at rates from two to five per cent. Money can be withdrawn at any time, but checks cannot be written against this type of account.

savings-and-loan association: a special type of savings institution which pays dividends on money deposited, through purchase of investment share certificates. It makes loans secured by first mortgages on residential property.

savings bank: a bank which accepts time deposits. Depositors leave their money in savings accounts to collect interest. Most commercial banks are also savings banks.

scientific method: procedure used in determining cause and effect relationships through logical reasoning, observation, and experimentation.

scientific socialism: the economic system proposed by Karl Marx to improve the condition of the working classes.

seasonal price fluctuation: the rise and fall of prices due to the large or small amount of a commodity on the market according to the season of the year. Agricultural products are especially subject to these price variations.

secondary boycott: boycotts of goods by non-striking unions in support of striking unions.

secured credit: granting of credit after collateral has been presented as insurance against failure to pay.

Securities and Exchange Commission (SEC): federal government regulatory agency which must give approval before any large amount of stock can be issued. It imposes penalties for misleading or incomplete information about stocks.

security: a corporate stock certificate or bond.

service utility: utility created by the performance of a personal service, such as the services of a physician.

servicing co-operative: a co-operative which helps its members by lending money, operating storage facilities, and providing insurance; or by supplying gas, electric power, and irrigation services.

severance pay: sum of money paid to an employee who is laid off; payment may be made in a lump sum or spread over a period of time.

share: a stock certificate representing a proportionate ownership in a given corporation. One share represents one vote in the control of the business.

sharecropper: a tenant farmer who receives land, living quarters, tools, and seed from the owner, and who repays the landlord with part of his crop.

shareholder: see *stockholder*.

Sherman Anti-Trust Act: a law passed by Congress in 1890 which prohibits monopolies and combinations "in restraint of trade."

short-run prices: prices based on the need to cover one's variable costs.

short-term commercial paper: a promissory note for a short-term loan from a bank.

short-time price changes: those changes in prices that occur from day to day or week to week; usually due to changes or expected changes in quantities available.

silent partner: member of a business partnership who takes no part in its management and is not subject to unlimited liability. See *general partnership* and *partnership*.

silver certificate: paper money issued by the federal government, representing silver coin or bullion.

simple interest: interest calculated on the principal but not on the accumulated interest.

single-member family: for census purposes, an individual who maintains separate living quarters.

sit-down strike: an illegal type of strike in which the workers remain in the plant but do no work.

six-for-five plan: borrowing plan run by loansharks; the borrower receives five dollars on Monday and must repay six dollars on Saturday.

slowdown: a deliberate slowing down of production by employees.

small-loan law: state law limiting the interest which banks and finance companies may charge for loans.

social insurance: various types of insurance designed to provide security for low income workers and their families; usually refers to plans offered by the government. Examples are retirement and unemployment insurance, and workmen's compensation.

social sciences: studies dealing primarily with relationships between people and people (that is, with society), or between people and their environments.

Social Security: nationwide system of social insurance created by the Social Security Act of 1935 and its amendments.

Social Security Act: a law passed by Congress in 1935 to provide old-age and survivors' insurance to help people finance their retirement. Deductions are made from workers' wages during their earning years and equal amounts are contributed by their employers. Later amendments have increased both the types of benefits provided and the number of people covered.

Social Security tax: deductions collected from employees and self-employed people to finance old-age, survivors', and disability insurance, and unemployment compensation. Employers are required to match the contributions of employees.

socialism: a plan for collective ownership and operation of the means of production.

social want: desire not based on physical needs, but on preferences, such as the desire to eat with friends or keep up with the Joneses.

"sound" dollar: dollar with high purchasing power (as opposed to a dollar with low purchasing power during times of inflation).

space value: see *location value.*

speculation: buying securities or commodities with the hope of selling at a higher price. The speculator is more interested in a rapid rise in price than in the dividend return which attracts the more conservative investor.

standard of living: the level of consumption of individuals, groups, or an entire country, determined by the variety, quantity, and quality of goods and services to which they are accustomed, and/or to which they aspire if increased goods and services are available.

state farm: farm owned by the government which pays wages to farm-workers.

state income tax: tax levied by a state on personal or corporate income.

status symbols: luxury items such as a second car or a mink coat; examples of conspicuous consumption which are evidence of one's wealth or position in the community.

stock: shares of stock (stock certificates) representing ownership in a corporation. See *common stock* and *share.*

stock exchange: a central location for buying and selling securities. Members trade in securities for themselves and in behalf of customers.

stockholder: owner of shares of stock in a corporation. Holders of common stock are entitled to one vote per share at the stockholders' meeting; holders of preferred stock usually cannot vote.

stored value: representations of wealth, such as money and securities.

straight life insurance: in return for a fixed annual premium paid by the insured during his lifetime, the insurance company pays a stipulated sum to the beneficiary upon the death of the insured. Also known as "ordinary life," "whole life," and "permanent life."

strike: an organized work stoppage by employees intended to persuade the employer to grant the demands made by the workers.

strikebreaker: man hired by an employer to take the job of a man out on strike.

subsidiary coin: coins such as dimes, quarters, and fifty-cent pieces which contain silver, though not in amounts equal to their value in relation to the dollar.

sunk cost: an initial cost in production which is not repeated as additional units are manufactured or grown. See *fixed cost.*

supply and demand: often called the "law of supply and demand," the assertion that price varies directly with demand and inversely with supply. See *law of demand; law of supply.*

supply schedule: graph or table which shows the quantity of a good which will be offered for sale at various prices. See table on page 65.

Taft-Hartley Act (Labor-Management Relations Act):

a law passed by Congress in 1947; the following union practices were declared illegal: the jurisdictional strike, the boycott, and the closed shop.

tariff: a tax or duty imposed on goods imported from another country or exported to it. In the United States, the Constitution prohibits a tax on exports.

tax: a charge levied by government to obtain revenue for public purposes. The most common forms are the property tax, income tax, and sales tax.

tax rate: computed on property by dividing the sum that the taxing unit wishes to raise by the total assessed value of the property to be taxed.

technical assistance programs: governmental and United Nations' projects which provide information to the developing nations on ways to increase agricultural output and to improve manufacturing and marketing techniques.

technological unemployment: unemployment resulting from the adoption of machine methods to increase production. See *automation.*

Tennessee Valley Authority (TVA): a public corporation established in 1933 to develop the Tennessee River Valley. By building locks and dams, floods were eliminated, hydroelectric power was generated, and the river was made navigable. Improvements were made in farm practices and living standards raised in an area of over 40,000 square miles.

term insurance: see *term life insurance.*

term life insurance: a life insurance policy which provides the greatest protection at the lowest cost for a limited number of years, but has no cash or loan value.

theory: hypothesis which has been verified by testing; a conclusion which satisfactorily explains cause and effect relationships.

ticker tape: the tape used in a machine which automatically prints stock and bond transactions made across the country.

"tight" money: a situation of money scarcity, brought about by monetary and/or fiscal policies; interest rates become higher.

time deposit: money in a savings account which can be withdrawn only after the specified number of days' notice.

time wage: a payment for work done by hour, day, week, or month.

title search: examination to determine whether the seller holds a clear title to the property he wishes to sell, or whether there are claims against it such as unpaid taxes.

token coins: coins, such as pennies and nickels, made from base (not precious) metals.

totalitarian: refers to a government which restricts individual liberties and has almost complete control over the economy.

trade-in allowance: reduction in the price of a new product based on the value of the old product which is taken in trade.

trademark: a name or symbol used to identify a given manufacturer and his product; registered in the United States Patent Office, it can be used only by the given manufacturer.

trading post: a position in a stock exchange where a broker's representative, on orders from his firm, buys or sells securities.

transferable note: a note which can be endorsed and passed from one person to another.

transfer payment: payments such as retirement benefits and veterans' pensions, which move income from one source to another but are not payments for current productive services.

trough: the lowest point in a business cycle. See *business cycle.*

trust: a large corporation or combination of corporations which has a monopolistic (or semimonopolistic) control over the production or distribution of a product or service.

trust company: a financial organization which usually performs customary banking services, and specializes in the management of estates and investments for special funds.

truth-in-packaging laws: laws which prescribe strict standards for packaging and labeling consumer products.

"turnover" of money: increased "turnover" of money (money changing hands) without a corresponding increase in goods and services leads to inflation or higher prices; the opposite situation leads to deflation or lower prices.

underconsumption: a condition in which total consumption in the economy falls short of production.

underdeveloped nation: a country in which food shortages, rapid population growth, inadequate transportation and communication, low levels of industrial production and of per capita income create problems.

underwriter: (1) an investment banker who markets large blocks of new securities for corporations; see *investment bank.* (2) An insurance company (or agent) which sells insurance contracts.

unemployment compensation: see *unemployment insurance.*

unemployment insurance: state programs providing payments to unemployed workers, financed by state funds.

unfavorable balance of trade: condition in which the money value of a nation's imports is greater than that of its exports.

union contract: contract between employees organized into a union and their employer, covering salaries, benefits, and working conditions.

union shop: a plant in which all employees must join the union within a specified time.

unlimited liability: the requirement that the owner or owners must assume full responsibility for all losses or debts incurred in their business.

unsecured credit: a loan for which collateral is not given.

unweighted (or simple) index: an index number computed merely by finding the average of all items; there is no weighting of items to reflect their relative importance.

utility: the amount of satisfaction one gets from a good or service.

value: the quantity of money or something else given in exchange for another thing.

value judgment: a judgment of the worth or importance of one thing over another.

value-added tax: applied to producers on the difference between the amount they pay for something and the amount they sell it for.

variable cost: see *direct cost*.

volume of business activity: total amount of production and business transactions during a given period.

voting stock: usually common stock in a corporation entitling the owner to one vote per share in the corporation's business.

wage: the money paid a worker for service rendered. In economics, the term refers to the share of the nation's wealth paid to labor, as distinct from other forms of income—rent, interest, profit.

Wagner Act: see *National Labor Relations Act*.

wealth: all material things that have economic value as well as their representations in money, stocks, and bonds.

Wealth of Nations: book by Adam Smith in which he contended that economic competition was the "invisible hand" controlling the economy for the benefit of an entire nation.

weighting: in establishing index numbers, the taking into account of the relative importance of each item included. Thus, items such as bread, sugar, or milk would be given weights in proportion to the expenditure for each in a representative budget.

wholesale market: the distribution point between the producer and the retailer, at which large quantities of goods are sold to buyers representing retail stores, hotels, and restaurants.

wholesaler: a "middleman" in the marketing system, who buys goods in large quantities and sells them in smaller lots to retailers.

wildcat strike: a strike in a local plant or service which has not been approved by the parent union.

workmen's compensation: payments by employers to employees who have been injured or have contracted an illness on the job. State laws are increasingly supplementing common-law rules of liability.

yellow-dog contract: workers' term for the Iron Clad Oath. Agreement, now illegal, between a worker and an employer that the worker will not join a union.

yield stock: stock purchased because it regularly pays comparatively high dividends.

For further reading

Readings for the course

General

Allen, Frederick L., *The Big Change: America Transforms Itself, 1900–1950,* Harper, also later edition in paperback (Bantam). A fascinating account of social and economic changes in the American scene since the turn of the century.

Bach, George L., *Economics: An Introduction to Analysis and Policy,* Prentice-Hall. A college introductory text designed to give an understanding of the fundamentals of economic analysis.

Chamberlain, John, *The Enterprising Americans: A Business History of the United States,* Harper, also in paperback (Perennial Library). An interesting and concise history of American business and business leaders from colonial times to the present, written in a popular style.

Cochrane, James L., *Macroeconomics Before Keynes,* Scott, Foresman. Paperback. Concise analysis of macroeconomic theories of leading schools of economic thought from the Physiocrats to the 1930's. A background in mathematics is necessary for full understanding.

Crane, Burton, *Practical Economist,* Simon, revised edition in paperback (Collier). Basic elements of today's economics analyzed in everyday language.

Dillard, Dudley, *The Economics of John Maynard Keynes,* Prentice-Hall. An old but excellent discussion of Keynesian economics. Reasonably sophisticated, but mathematics not necessary.

Economic Report of the President, United States Government Printing Office. Annual analysis of current economic problems, including an index of statistical material.

Heilbroner, Robert L., *The Making of Economic Society,* Prentice-Hall, also in paperback. Essentially a history of economic thought, it traces the development of economic institutions.

Heilbroner, Robert L., *The Worldly Philosophers,* Simon, also in paperback. A survey of the ideas of leading economic thinkers, from Adam Smith to the present. Written in a popular style.

Joint Economic Report, United States Government Printing Office. Annual analysis of the *Economic Report of the President* with recommendations by the Joint Economic Committee for realizing the suggested economic goals.

Lancaster, Kelvin, *Introduction to Modern Microeconomics,* Rand McNally. A concise text covering the key theoretical concepts of basic microeconomics. Some mathematical background helpful.

Lekachman, Robert, *A History of Economic Ideas,* Harper. Summarizes economic thought; provides biographical and historical background.

Levy, Lester S., and Sampson, Roy J., *American Economic Development,* Allyn. A history of the development of economic thought and institutions from ancient times, with special reference to the American scene.

McConnell, Campbell R., *Economics: Principles, Problems, and Policies,* 4th ed., McGraw-Hill. A widely used standard college textbook for introductory economics courses.

Mulcahy, Richard, ed., *Readings in Economics from Fortune Magazine,* Holt, also in paperback (Newman Press). Compilation of economic articles from *Fortune,* each prefaced by a summary of main ideas developed in it.

Orr, John A. and Savage, Donald T., *Economics in American Society,* Wadsworth. An introductory text which grew out of a series of university-sponsored television lectures on economics.

Reynolds, Lloyd G., *Economics: A General Introduction,* Irwin. A standard text for introductory economics courses.

Robinson, Marshall A., Morton, Herbert C., and Calderwood, James D., *Introduction to Economic Reasoning,* The Brookings Institution, also published in paperback (Doubleday Anchor). The purpose of this book is to show how to "think through" an economic question.

Samuelson, Paul A., *Economics,* 8th ed., McGraw-Hill. The most widely used college introductory economics textbook for more than 20 years.

Samuelson, Paul A., with Felicity Skidmore, *Readings in Economics,* McGraw-Hill. A collection of 97 short readings from leading past and present economists. Includes topics on basic economic concepts, national income and its fluctuations and distribution, pricing, international trade, and a wide variety of current problems, such as poverty and the cities.

Singer, Leslie P., *Economics Made Simple,* Doubleday Made Simple Books. Paperback which provides a survey of economic thought and the contemporary economic scene.

Soule, George, *Ideas of the Great Economists,* Mentor. A clear presentation of major economic ideas from past to present.

Ulmer, Melville J., *Economics: Theory and Practice,* Houghton. Introductory survey.

United States Department of Commerce, *United States Income and Output,* United States Government Printing Office. Contains statistics showing the nation's economic growth and provides information about how estimates are made.

Whittaker, Edmund, *Schools and Streams of Economic Thought,* Rand McNally. Comprehensive history of economic thought. Quotations from original sources. Annotated bibliography provided.

Milestones in economic thought

Epstein, Ralph C., and Butler, Arthur D., eds., *Selections in Economics,* vols. 1 and 2, Economica Books, Smith. Readings from Keynes, Mitchell, Taussig, Lerner, Chamberlin, Ricardo, Johnson, Ely, and Bye.

Keynes, John Maynard, *The General Theory of Employment, Interest and Money,* Harcourt. The major theoretical work underlying Keynes' "new economics." For advanced students. (See also selections from this work included in the Marshall anthology below.)

Marshall, Alfred, *Principles of Economics,* Macmillan. Major work of the 19th century economist who attempted to restate the whole body of economic thought.

Marshall, Howard D. and Marshall, Natalie J., *The History of Economic Thought: A Book of Readings,* Pitman. A judiciously selected and edited anthology, consisting of important extracts from economics "classics" by Adam Smith, Thomas Malthus, David Ricardo, John Stuart Mill, Karl Marx, William Stanley Jevons, Alfred Marshall, Joan Robinson, and John Maynard Keynes.

Marx, Karl, *Capital,* Modern Library, also in paperback (Gateway). Marx's principal work, which sets forth his analysis of capitalism and his reasons for believing that it ultimately would be superseded by a socialist economic order.

Smith, Adam, *Wealth of Nations,* Methuen, also in paperback (Gateway). Major work of the great classical economist.

Tawney, R. H., *Acquisitive Society,* Harcourt, also in paperback (Harvest Books). Argues that we are too concerned with economic activity as an end in itself rather than as a means to serve society.

Weber, Max, translated by Frank H. Knight, *General Economic History,* Collier. Weber's economic analysis of history in which he finds that the forces giving birth to the Industrial Revolution were largely social.

Reference

Economic Almanac, National Industrial Conference Board. Statistics on national income, spending, production, trade, and other areas of the economy.

Economic Report of the President. United States Government Printing Office. Published each January or February. The first part of this document is the economic report of the President to Congress, in which he summarizes economic developments of the past year, discusses prospects for the year ahead, and offers recommendations for dealing with economic problems. The second part, much longer than the first, is the annual report of the Council of Economic Advisers, which deals with various aspects of the economy. The last part consists of statistical tables on income, employment, and production.

Facts and Figures on Government Finance, The Tax Foundation, New York. Data on the collection of taxes and their expenditure.

Hacker, Louis M., *Major Documents in American Economic History,* 2 vols., Van Nostrand. Contains useful source material for a course in economics.

Landsberg, Hans H., Fischman, Leonard L., and Fisher, Joseph L., *Resources in America's Future: Patterns of Requirements and Availabilities 1960–2000,* Johns Hopkins. Comprehensive and detailed study of America's natural resources. Projections of future requirements in areas of human needs and wants.

Sloan, Harold S., and Zurcher, Arnold J., *Dictionary of Economics,* Barnes, also in paperback. Defines terms used in works on business and economics.

United States Bureau of the Census, *Historical Statistics of the United States, Colonial Times to 1957,* United States Government Printing Office. Useful statistics on various sectors of the American economy.

United States Bureau of the Census, *Statistical Abstract of the United States,* United States Government Printing Office. An annual publication giving statistical data on the American economy.

United States Department of Commerce, *Survey of*

Current Business. A monthly bulletin containing latest official statistics on the state of the national economy. Also has articles on specialized topics such as personal income, American investment abroad, and capital expansion in industry.

United States Department of Labor, *Monthly Labor Review.* Reports on all matters affecting labor and employment, including rates of pay in various industries, hours lost through strikes, and the job situation.

Periodicals and newspapers

Barron's. A weekly magazine which reports on current trends in industry.

Business Week. A weekly business magazine reporting on stock market and other developments of interest to businessmen.

Challenge. Published six times a year, with articles by leading economists on various facets of the American economy.

Forbes. A semimonthly business magazine of special interest to investors.

Fortune. A monthly magazine which contains authoritative articles on business and the nation's economy.

Newsweek. A weekly newsmagazine which includes reports on the state of the nation's economy.

The New York Times. Contains an excellent daily financial section.

Time. A weekly newsmagazine with coverage of financial and business trends.

U.S. News & World Report. A weekly newsmagazine which uses many excellent graphs and charts to describe economic developments.

Wall Street Journal. The daily newspaper of business; also treats related news.

Readings for each chapter

chapter 1: *What economics is all about*

McConnell, Campbell R., *Economics: Principles, Problems, and Policies,* 4th ed., McGraw-Hill. Chapter 1.

Samuelson, Paul A., *Economics,* 8th ed., McGraw-Hill. Chapter 1.

Chase, Stuart, *The Proper Study of Mankind,* rev. ed., Harper, also in paperback. A survey of what the social sciences have contributed to help us under-

stand our culture and its problems. Very readable.

Faulkner, Harold U., *American Economic History,* Harper. Standard economic history, stressing economic causes and their results.

Galbraith, John Kenneth, *The Affluent Society,* Houghton. Provides an interesting analysis of current economic, social, and political problems in the United States, and of how to cope with them.

Heilbroner, Robert L., *The Quest for Wealth,* Simon. A study of man's efforts to amass wealth.

chapter 2: *How wants lead to production*

McConnell, Campbell R., *Economics: Principles, Problems, and Policies,* chapter 4.

Samuelson, Paul A., *Economics,* chapters 2 and 3.

Britt, Steuart Henderson, *The Spenders,* McGraw. The influence which consumer behavior and motivation have upon markets. Challenges views expressed in *The Waste Makers* (see below).

Chase, Stuart, *Men and Machines,* Macmillan. A balanced view of the effect of machines on modern life.

De Bell, Garrett, ed., *The Environmental Handbook,* Ballantine (paperback). A collection of essays by ecologists and others concerned about the threat to the environment posed by pollution, waste, and noise.

Fenn, Dan H., Jr., ed., *Managing America's Economic Explosion,* McGraw. Businessmen and economists estimate our probable economic growth, and consider issues which management must face in the coming years.

Katona, George, *The Powerful Consumer,* McGraw. Analyzes the psychological factors which motivate the consumer and their effect on the economy.

Lee, Maurice W., *Economic Fluctuations: Growth and Stability,* Irwin. Theory, analysis, and history of economic fluctuations and their effect on growth and stability.

Mayer, Martin, *Madison Avenue, U.S.A.,* Harper. A journalist describes the "advertising capital" of the world.

Packard, Vance, *The Hidden Persuaders,* McKay. A one-time best seller which explores some of the subtler techniques used in advertising.

Packard, Vance, *The Waste Makers,* McKay. Describes how our resources may be wasted by manufacturers in their attempts to stimulate consumer spending.

Wilhelms, Fred T., and Heimerl, Raymond P., *Consumer Economics, Principles and Problems,* McGraw. An explanation of our economic system with particular emphasis on personal and family finance.

Woytinsky, Wladimir S. and Emma S., *World Popula-*

tion and Production: Trends and Outlooks, Twentieth Century Fund. Published in 1953, this massive book presents a statistical picture of collective resources, and their potential use.

chapter 3: *Prices in a free market economy*

McConnell, Campbell R., *Economics: Principles, Problems, and Policies,* chapter 5.

Samuelson, Paul A., *Economics,* chapter 4.

American Capitalism, An Introduction for Young Citizens, CASE Economic Literacy Series #1, Council for Advancement of Secondary Education. Analysis of the solution of economic problems through the operation of free markets. Useful chapter on modifications of free enterprise in the United States.

Bloom, Clarke C., *How the American Economy Is Organized, Primer of Economics #2,* Bureau of Business and Economic Research, State University of Iowa, Iowa City. Describes the part played by market mechanisms in the American economy.

Competitive Prices in Action, The Industrial Relations Center, University of Chicago. Pamphlet discussing the purpose of competitive prices, how they work, and the competitive price system as a whole. Written in nontechnical language.

Galbraith, John Kenneth, *American Capitalism: The Concept of Countervailing Power,* Houghton, also paperback (Sentry). Challenges accepted economic positions, for example, the idea that private enterprise is necessarily unstable.

The National Income and Its Distribution, A Study in Economic Principles and Human Well-Being, The American Competitive Enterprise Economy, No. IV, Chamber of Commerce of the United States. Discussion is based on the circular flow of funds.

Wages, Prices, Profits and Productivity, The American Assembly. The historical pattern of wages, prices, and productivity, and the relationship of each to specific areas of analysis.

Why Prices? Chamber of Commerce of the United States. A simple forthright presentation of the role of prices under conditions of relatively perfect competition.

chapter 4: *Uses and rewards of the factors of production*

McConnell, Campbell R., *Economics: Principles, Problems, and Policies,* chapter 5.

Samuelson, Paul A., *Economics,* chapters 28–31.

Anderson, Martin, *The Federal Bulldozer,* MIT Press. Raises interesting questions about land use as it is affected by urban renewal projects.

Blaug, Mark, *Ricardian Economics,* Yale University Press. A detailed analysis of Ricardo's theory of economic rent.

Bulloch, Paul, *Standards of Wage Determination,* Institute of Industrial Relations, University of California, Los Angeles. A booklet which describes seven major standards used to determine wages—comparisons, cost of living, ability to pay, productivity, family budgets, purchasing power, and technical and miscellaneous factors.

Capital: Key to Progress, The Industrial Relations Center, University of Chicago. An explanation of how money is invested in capital equipment, inventories, buildings, and the improvement of human beings, and how such investment makes modern methods of production possible.

Galbraith, John Kenneth, *The New Industrial State,* Houghton. A liberal economist suggests that the rise of the large modern corporation has changed traditional concepts of entrepreneurship.

Perlman, Richard, ed., *Wage Determination—Market or Power Forces?* Heath. A book of readings which marshals the arguments for two different theories of how wages should be determined.

chapter 5: *The family as a consuming unit*

McConnell, Campbell R., *Economics: Principles, Problems, and Policies,* chapter 38.

Samuelson, Paul A., *Economics,* chapters 6 and 39.

Batchelder, A.B., *The Economics of Poverty,* Wiley. One economist's analysis of why poverty exists in this country.

Berger, Robert, and Teplin, Joseph, *Law and the Consumer* (Justice in Urban America Series), Houghton. Delves into advertising, contracts, and credit, and evaluates ways of buying goods and services.

Hamilton, David, *The Consumer in Our Economy,* Houghton. Discusses spending patterns and suggests ways of improving them; the subject of government protection for the consumer is also treated.

Harrington, Michael, *The Other America: Poverty in the United States,* Macmillan (also a Penguin paperback). An analysis of poverty which influenced the government in first starting antipoverty programs.

Levitan, Sar A., *Programs in Aid of the Poor for the 1970's,* Johns Hopkins. A description of existing and proposed programs to alleviate poverty.

Magnuson, Warren G., and Carper, Jean, *The Dark Side of the Marketplace: The Plight of the American Consumer,* Prentice-Hall. Deceptive selling practices and their effects on modern society.

Margolius, Sidney, *The Innocent Consumer versus the Exploiters,* Trident. A survey of consumer problems and protection agencies; cites many abuses.

Meissner, Hanna H., *Poverty in the Affluent Society*, Harper. Describes the plight of the poor in this country and recommends measures to eliminate poverty.

Trump, Fred, *Buyer Beware: A Consumer's Guide to Hoaxes and Hucksters*, Abingdon. Tells how to avoid being taken in.

chapter 6: *Managing the family's finances*

Commission On Money and Credit, *Money and Credit: Their Influence on Jobs, Prices and Growth*, Prentice-Hall, also in paperback. A panel of experts presents recommendations in the field of monetary practices. For advanced students.

Consumer Beware, AFL-CIO Publication. The hidden costs of credit.

Hart, Albert G., and Kenen, Peter B., *Money, Debt and Economic Activity*, (3rd ed.), Prentice-Hall. Describes the U.S. monetary system, including recent trends.

Jacoby, Neil H., ed., *United States Monetary Policy*, The American Assembly, Columbia University. Collection of articles on monetary policy by leading economists.

Thal, Helen M., *Your Family and Its Money*, Houghton. Deals with money management in terms of the needs of the total family. Presents financial planning in a problem-solving context.

Understanding Money and Banking, The Industrial Relations Center, University of Chicago. Explains the importance of money and its function in our economy.

Welfling, Weldon, *Money and Banking in the American Economy*, CASE Economic Literacy Series #3, Council for the Advancement of Secondary Education. Clear and comprehensive treatment of this field.

chapter 7: *Investing for family security*

Crane, Burton, *The Sophisticated Investor*, Simon (paperback). A guide to stock market profits, with specific suggestions on what to look for to make money.

Editors of *Fortune*, *Markets of the Seventies*, Viking (paperback). A look at the state of the economy, with some educated guesses about investment prospects in selected fields.

Engel, Louis, *How to Buy Stocks*, Little. A successful investor offers helpful guidelines on stocks and bonds for the beginner.

Epstein, Ralph C., *Making Money in Today's Market*, Doubleday paperback and Smith Economica Books.

Suggests a set of principles for obtaining the highest yield consistent with a certain degree of security.

Institute of Life Insurance, *A Discussion of Family Money: How Budgets Work and What They Do*, Women's Division of The Institute, N.Y. Pamphlet discussing how to prepare a budget and the importance of budgeting.

Mayer, Martin, *Wall Street: Men and Money*, Collier. A former reporter describes Wall Street and its role in the economy.

Understanding the New York Stock Exchange, The New York Stock Exchange. An elementary description of what happens on the stock exchange.

chapter 8: *Insurance against family hardships*

Economic Security for Americans, An Analysis, Joint Council on Economic Education. Pamphlet discusses major approaches to problems of economic security —through individual savings, industry and union-sponsored pension plans, and government programs of public assistance and social security.

Individual and Group Security, Chamber of Commerce of the United States. Advocates restricting government welfare programs and stresses importance of self-reliance.

Johnson, Robert H., *Some Economic Implications of Welfare Programs*, State University of Iowa. A study of the economic effects of welfare measures on the use of resources, the distribution of income, and economic growth and stability.

To Meet the American People's Needs, AFL-CIO. Position of organized labor on tax-supported services.

United States Department of Health, Education and Welfare, *Social Security in the United States*, The United States Government Printing Office. Background and function of social security programs.

chapter 9: *How business is organized for production*

McConnell, Campbell R., *Economics: Principles, Problems, and Policies*, chapter 8.

Samuelson, Paul A., *Economics*, chapter 9.

Cochran, Thomas C., *Basic History of American Business*, Van Nostrand. Traces the problems with which American business has had to cope from the days of colonial trade to present-day marketing and management-labor problems, and government-business conflicts. Includes documents.

Drucker, Peter, *Concept of the Corporation*, Day, also in paperback (Beacon). A study based on General Motors.

How a Corporation Works, Good Reading Rack

Service Division, Koster Dana Corporation. Brief pamphlet describing the corporate form of organization.

Joskow, Jules, and Stelzer, Irwin, *The Consumer and Anti-Trust,* Consumer Problem Series #4, Council on Consumer Information, Colorado State College. Easy-to-read, comprehensive survey of antitrust laws.

Kaplan, Abraham D. H., and Kahn, Alfred, *Big Business in a Competitive Society,* The Brookings Institution. The nature and strategy of competition between big businesses and their contribution to the whole economy. For advanced students.

Korey, Edward L., *Business and the American Way,* Oxford. Lists the size and distribution of firms by industry groups, and the size of firms in different areas. Discusses the place of corporations and the role of profit-seeking enterprise in our economy. Considers some of the difficulties associated with large corporations.

Lamott, Kenneth, *The Moneymakers: The Great Big New Rich in America,* Bantam. A lively account of the "new breed" of millionaires who came to prominence after World War II. Includes such figures as Jean Paul Getty, Howard Hughes, H. L. Hunt, Norton Simon, and James J. Ling.

Mitchell, Wesley Clair, *Business Cycles and Their Causes,* University of California Press. A detailed analysis of a complex subject. For advanced students.

Smith, Richard Austin, *Corporations in Crisis,* Doubleday. Woes experienced by corporations, ranging from court cases to mismanagement and overexpansion.

chapter 10: *Competition, monopoly, and government regulation*

McConnell, Campbell R., *Economics: Principles, Problems, and Policies,* chapter 23.

Samuelson, Paul A., *Economics,* chapter 26.

Anderson, Ronald A., *Government and Business* (2nd ed.), South-Western. Describes some of the historic legal cases involving the government and business.

Kefauver, Estes, and Till, Irene, *In a Few Hands: Monopoly Power in America,* Pantheon. Findings of the Senate subcommittee hearings on antitrust and monopoly.

Mintz, Morton, and Cohen, Jerry S., *America, Inc.: Who Owns and Operates the United States,* Dial. Argues that too great a concentration of economic power leads to anticompetitive behavior that is bad for the consumer, and, equally, bad for industry.

Mund, Vernon A., *Government and Business* (3rd

ed.), Harper. Description of the many ways in which business and economic life are shaped and directed by the government. Includes case histories and background data.

Rogers, Jack, *Automation: Technology's New Face,* Institute of Industrial Relations, University of California. Considers the probable rate and ultimate extent of automatic processes. Views problems of both labor and management.

Watson, Donald Stevenson, *Economic Policy: Business and Government,* Houghton. Deals with government policy in the regulation of business and its effect on growth, stability, and redistribution of income. Covers a wide range of topics and includes excellent reading references. For advanced students.

chapter 11: *Agriculture in a changing environment*

McConnell, Campbell R., *Economics: Principles, Problems, and Policies,* chapter 36.

Samuelson, Paul A., *Economics,* chapter 21.

An Adaptive Program for Agriculture, Committee for Economic Development. Focuses on the role of government in encouraging the movement of labor and capital out of agriculture along with the appropriate cushioning effects upon people and property.

Barr, Wallace, *The Farm Problem Identified,* National Committee on Agricultural Policy, Ohio State University. Brief, readable discussion of the farm problem.

Black, John D., *Agricultural Reform in the United States,* McGraw-Hill. A detailed treatment of agricultural issues.

Dexter, Wayne, *What Makes Farmers' Prices,* United States Government Printing Office. The factors influencing farm prices.

The Farm Problem—What Are the Choices? National Committee on Agricultural Policy, Ohio State University. A series of leaflets on twelve policy proposals.

Smith, Marvin G., and Christian, Carlton F., eds., *Adjustments in Agriculture,* A National Basebook, Iowa State University Press, Ames, Iowa. Up-to-date analysis of various sides of the agricultural problem.

Wilcox, Walter W., and Cochrane, Willard W., *Economics of American Agriculture* (2nd ed.), Prentice-Hall. Analyzes the operation of the farm economy in the context of modern economic life.

Wilcox, Walter W., *The American Farmer in a Changing World,* and Johnson, Glenn L., *Agriculture's Technological Revolution,* Graduate School of Business, Columbia University. These two papers give an excellent review of the problems and progress of

American agriculture during the last few decades.

chapter 12:   *Union and nonunion labor*

McConnell, Campbell R., *Economics: Principles, Problems, and Policies,* chapter 37.

Samuelson, Paul A., *Economics,* chapters 7 and 29.

Bakke, Edward W., Kerr, Clark, et al., *Unions, Management, and the Public Policy* (2nd ed.), Harcourt. Collection of readings on labor problems, policies, and relations.

Barbash, Jack, *The Labor Movement in the U.S.* (Public Affairs Pamphlet No. 262), Public Affairs Committee. A good description of union goals, problems, and contributions to American society.

Bernstein, Irving, *The Lean Years,* Houghton. Report on the conditions in America between 1920 and 1933 which brought a resurgence of the labor movement.

Bloom, Gordon F., and Northrup, Herbert R., *Economics of Labor Relations,* (4th ed.), Irwin. The goals of labor and the unions' problems in achieving them.

Brief History of the American Labor Movement, U.S. Department of Labor, Bureau of Labor Statistics. A useful pamphlet which lists highlights in the development of the labor movement.

Doherty, Robert E., *The Employer-Employee Relationship,* Booklet No. 25, Grass Roots Guides on Democracy and Practical Politics, Center for Information on America, Washington, Connecticut. Identifies interests common to management and labor, areas of agreement and disagreement, and the changing nature of management-labor relationships.

Laslett, John, ed., *The Workingman in American Life,* Houghton. Readings which trace the rise of the labor movement and the problems it has faced.

Petro, Sylvester, *Power Unlimited,* Ronald. Report of the McClellan Committee hearings, which produced evidence of wrong-doings in unions.

Randle, C. Wilson, and Wortman, Max S., Jr., *Collective Bargaining: Principles and Practice,* Houghton. A text survey of past uses of collective bargaining, with a thoughtful discussion of its future possibilities.

Richardson, Reed C., *American Labor Unions,* Bulletin 30, School of Industrial and Labor Relations, Cornell University. A summary of labor history, with emphasis on current collective bargaining responses and the legal framework for collective bargaining which exists at the federal level.

United States Department of Labor, *Labor Information Bulletin,* Bureau of Labor Statistics. Monthly publication of current labor statistics.

Widick, B. J., *Labor Today,* Houghton. Recent developments in the field of organized labor. Includes sketches of labor leaders.

chapter 13:   *National wealth and income*

McConnell, Campbell R., *Economics: Principles, Problems, and Policies,* chapter 10.

Samuelson, Paul A., *Economics,* chapter 10.

Federal Economic Policy, Congressional Quarterly Service. Economic developments including legislation, budgetary controversies, and the President's Economic Report are analyzed. Presupposes some knowledge of economics.

How Everybody Makes a Living, Koster-Dana Corporation. Easy-to-understand explanation of GNP and "national income" concepts.

The National Income and Its Distribution, Chamber of Commerce of the United States.

Wagner, Lewis E., *Measuring the Performance of the Economy,* State University of Iowa. Study of the elements of a national budget.

chapter 14:   *Government services and taxation*

McConnell, Campbell R., *Economics: Principles, Problems, and Policies,* chapter 9.

Samuelson, Paul A., *Economics,* chapters 8 and 9.

Bator, Francis M., *The Question of Government Spending, Public Needs and Private Wants,* Harper. Public and private spending considered in relation to the economy as a whole.

Bureau of the Budget, Executive Office of the President, *The Federal Budget in Brief,* United States Government Printing Office. Condensation of the budget document, with the President's budget message, sources of revenue, and objects of expenditure.

A Fiscal Program for a Balanced Federalism, Committee for Economic Development. Booklet. Discussion of ways for improving the financing of state and local government, including possible actions of the federal government.

Government and the Economy, Understanding Economics Series, No. 7, United States Chamber of Commerce. Booklet. A description of the federal tax system with some consideration of the burden of taxes and the federal budget.

Handbook of State and Local Government Finance, Tax Foundation, Inc. A well-written analysis of why state and local governments exist and of the services they provide. Treats such services as education, highways, welfare, health and hospitals, and protection.

Rolph, Earl R., and Break, George F., *Public Finance*

(2nd ed.), Ronald. Analysis of government finance and its role in the United States economy. Comparisons with other countries.

Seligman, Ben B., *Poverty as a Public Issue,* Free Press. Issues relating to the financing and administering of antipoverty programs.

Taxes in the United States, The Industrial Relations Center, University of Chicago. A pamphlet which presents a simplified and clear discussion of the subject of taxes.

chapter 15: *Economic instability: inflation*
           and recession

McConnell, Campbell R., *Economics: Principles Problems, and Policies,* chapter 11.

Samuelson, Paul A., *Economics,* chapters 11–14.

Buckingham, Walter, *Automation, Its Impact on Business and People,* Harper. Fundamental principles and history of automation reviewed in nontechnical language.

Business Ups and Downs, U.S. Chamber of Commerce. A simple explanation of the causes of instability and ways of combating it.

Galbraith, John Kenneth, *The Great Crash,* Houghton, also in paperback (Sentry). The story of 1929.

The Mystery of Economic Growth, Federal Reserve Bank of Philadelphia. A pamphlet which sets forth clearly the distinction between "real" growth and money growth.

Silk, Leonard S., *The Research Revolution,* McGraw. An analysis of the changes taking place which will greatly affect our economy.

Unemployment in Prosperity—Why? Series for Economic Education, Federal Reserve Bank of Philadelphia. Pamphlet which serves as a concise introduction to developments in the economy producing unemployment.

Unemployment: Is Permanent Prevention Possible?, Center for Information on America, Washington, Connecticut. Distinguishes between various types of unemployment.

Wagner, Lewis E., *Income, Employment and Prices,* Bureau of Business and Economic Research, State University of Iowa. Analyzes the causes of economic instability. Written for high school students.

chapter 16: *Monetary and fiscal policies*
           for stabilization and growth

McConnell, Campbell R., *Economics: Principles, Problems, and Policies,* chapters 15 and 18.

Samuelson, Paul A., *Economics,* chapters 15–17 and 19.

The Federal Reserve System: Purposes and Functions, Board of Governors of the Federal Reserve System. Organization, purposes, and objectives of the Federal Reserve System and its contribution to stable economic progress.

Friedman, Milton, and Heller, Walter W., *Monetary vs. Fiscal Policy: A Dialogue,* Norton. Fascinating debate between two leading economists who differ on the role of fiscal and monetary policy to achieve economic growth.

Harriss, C. Lowell, *Money and Banking,* Allyn. Comprehensive coverage of the topics of money and commercial banking.

Heller, Walter W., *New Dimensions of Political Economy,* Norton (paperback). The former chairman of the Council of Economic Advisers discusses the importance of strong fiscal policies for strengthening the national economy.

Madden, Carl H., *The Money Side of "the Street,"* Federal Reserve Bank of New York. Behind the scenes on Wall Street.

Modern Money Mechanics, Federal Reserve Bank of Chicago. Workbook on deposits, currency, and bank reserves.

Prochnow, Herbert V., ed., *The Federal Reserve System,* Harper. Description of the nature and history of the Federal Reserve System by nineteen prominent bankers. Also deals with its relation to the economy in general.

Ratchford, B. U., and Black, R. P., *The Federal Reserve at Work,* Federal Reserve Bank of Richmond. Booklet which describes in simple terms the operations of the "Fed" and explains the tools of monetary policy.

Ritter, Lawrence S., *Money and Economic Activity: Readings In Money and Banking,* Houghton. Each article is prefaced by a short introductory summary, highlighting the general points stressed.

chapter 17: *American capitalism and*
           alternative economic systems

McConnell, Campbell R., *Economics: Principles, Problems, and Policies,* chapter 44.

Samuelson, Paul A., *Economics,* chapter 42.

The British Economy, British Information Services. Pamphlet describing the British experiment with their unique brand of democratic socialism.

Campbell, Robert W., *Soviet Economic Power, Its Organization, Growth and Challenge,* Houghton. An economic analysis of the Soviet system.

Capitalism and Other Economic Systems, CASE Economic Literacy Series #2, Council for the Advancement of Secondary Education. A comparison of the market economy with Communist and Socialist systems, written for high school students.

Gruchy, Allan G., *Comparative Economic Systems,* Houghton. Evaluates accomplishments of capitalism, socialism, and communism.

Hacker, Louis M., *American Capitalism: Its Promise and Accomplishment,* Van Nostrand. Highlights American economic development from colonial times to present.

Kovner, Milton, *The Challenge of Coexistence, A Study of Soviet Economic Diplomacy,* Public Affairs Press. Explains how the Soviet government controls Russian economy and uses it to influence relations with other lands.

Monsen, R. Joseph Jr., *Modern American Capitalism: Ideologies and Issues,* Houghton. A discussion of values underlying the free enterprise system and issues which it must solve.

Oxenfeldt, Alfred R., *Economic Systems in Action: The United States, The Soviet Union, The United Kingdom,* Holt. Surveys the chief differences between the capitalist, Socialist, and Communist economic systems.

Röpke, Wilhelm, *A Humane Economy, The Social Framework of the Free Market,* Regnery. Describes the bases of the free market economy and social and ethical problems which challenge its existence.

Swearingen, Rodger, *The World of Communism,* Houghton. Contains information about the Soviet economic system, Soviet trade and aid, and standards of living.

Wagner, Lewis E., *Methods of Organizing Economic Activity in the United States and the Soviet Union,* Joint Council on Economic Education. Contrasts the two economies.

chapter 18: *Aid to the developing economies*

McConnell, Campbell R., *Economics: Principles, Problems, and Policies,* chapter 43.

Samuelson, Paul A., *Economics,* chapter 38.

Heilbroner, Robert L., *This Growing World: Development and the World Bank,* Public Affairs Pamphlet No. 237-A, Public Affairs Committee. A well-written pamphlet focusing on the problems of economic development and the role and functions of the World Bank in assisting it.

Hoffman, Paul G., *World Without Want,* Harper (paperback). A former UN relief director offers proposals for alleviating hunger and poverty in the developing countries.

How Low Income Countries Can Advance Their Own Growth, Committee for Economic Development. A realistic appraisal of the economic requirements for per capita income of Latin American citizens to rise rapidly enough to approach expectations. Argues that prime emphasis must be placed on increasing agricultural productivity.

Isenberg, Irwin, ed., *Developing Nations* (Reference Shelf Series, vol. 41, No. 1), Wilson. A collection of readings on various problems confronting the developing economies.

Johnson, Harry, *Economic Policies Toward Less Developed Countries,* Brookings. An examination of the options available to this country in arriving at a policy of providing aid to developing nations.

Murden, Forrest D., *Underdeveloped Lands, 'Revolutions of Rising Expectations,'* Foreign Policy Association, Incorporated, New York. Considers the economic factors which contribute to "underdevelopment." Discusses United States and international programs for helping underdeveloped lands.

Myrdal, Gunnar, *International Economy: Problems and Prospects,* Harper. The famed Swedish economist suggests that a sense of urgency is needed in assisting the poorer nations of the world.

Shonfield, Andrew, *Attack on World Poverty,* (rev. ed.), Random House, published also as a paperback (Vintage). Concerned with the need for increased and more effective economic aid.

Ward, Barbara, *Lopsided World,* Norton (paperback). A well-known British economist points out the polarities existing between the affluent and poorer nations, and proposes ways of overcoming them.

Zimmerman, Louis J. *Poor Lands, Rich Lands: The Widening Gap,* Random (paperback). A useful study of the problem of the developing nations.

chapter 19: *International trade and finance*

McConnell, Campbell R., *Economics: Principles, Problems, and Policies,* chapters 40–42.

Samuelson, Paul A., *Economics,* chapters 33–35.

America and the World Economy, Basic Economics Series, The Industrial Relations Center, University of Chicago. Pamphlet which presents in nontechnical language the basis of international trade.

The Balance of Payments Crisis, Public Affairs Pamphlet No. 378-A, Public Affairs Committee. Discusses the implications of the balance of payments deficit.

Calderwood, James D., *International Economic Problems,* Curriculum Resources Incorporated, Minneapolis. Illuminates the principles underlying international trade. For advanced students.

Calderwood, James D., and Jones, Hazel J., *World Trade,* Curriculum Resources. A less advanced treatment of the principles underlying world trade.

Diebold, William, Jr., *The Schuman Plan*, Praeger. An analysis of the European Coal and Steel Community.

Gardner, Richard N., *New Directions in U.S. Foreign Economic Policy*, Foreign Policy Association, New York. Analyzes trade, investment, and foreign aid.

Gordon, Wendell C., *International Trade: Goods, People and Ideas*, Knopf. Studies all aspects of trade between nations.

Kenen, Peter B., *Giant Among Nations*, Harcourt. Considers this country's policies with respect to foreign aid, investments, and trade. Points out the importance of more efficient use of resources.

Kramer, Roland L., et al., *International Trade, Theory, Policy, Practice*, South-Western. Clear presentation of all sides of international trade, both technical and practical.

Krause, Walter, *International Economics*, Houghton. Thorough treatment of the theory and practice of economic relations among nations. Topics include cartels, balance of payments, foreign aid.

Understanding the International Monetary System, Headline Series No. 182, Foreign Policy Association. Explains, in layman's terms, the problem of international monetary reserves.

Wasserman, Max J., Hultman, Charles W., and Zsoldos, Laszlo, *International Finance*, Simmons-Boardman Publishing Corporation. Chapters 4–6 explain a balance of payments statement in clear terms.

chapter 20: *The future of the American economy*

Samuelson, Paul A., *Economics*, chapter 40.

Biegeleisen, J. I., *How to Go About Getting a Job with a Future*, Grosset. Vocational guidance, written for students, with helpful bibliography.

The Challenge to America: Its Economic and Social Aspects, Rockefeller Brothers Fund, Doubleday. Report on policies to promote growth in the American economy. Deals with means for promoting stability, tax reform, trade expansion, development of science and technology, and advances in education.

Economic Growth in the United States—Its Past and Future, Committee for Economic Development. Pamphlet contains factual and statistical descriptions of economic growth.

Economic Report of the President, United States Government Printing Office. Issued yearly by the Council of Economic Advisors.

The Goals of Economic Policy, Chamber of Commerce of the United States. Brief discussion of each of the five basic goals of the economy—economic freedom, efficiency, growth, stability, and security.

The Promise of Economic Growth: Prospects, Costs, Conditions, Chamber of Commerce of the United States. Distinguishes between various growth measures in discussing the costs of growth. Assesses prospects for the future. Recommended for advanced students.

Acknowledgments

The authors and publisher wish to express their appreciation to persons and organizations listed below for their courtesy in making pictures available for reproduction.

ii	Mobil Oil Corporation
x	Stock, Boston
16	Black Star (middle left); RCA (lower right); Stock, Boston (all others)
112	Robert C. Lautman
196	United Nations
310	Jean-Claude Lejeune

Pioneers in Economic Thought

9	Brown Brothers
44	Bettmann Archive
80	Rand Corporation
93	Bettmann Archive
99	Culver Pictures
211	Historical Pictures Service
228	Bettmann Archive
277	Bettmann Archive
290	Rand Corporation
324	Bettmann Archive
334	Bettmann Archive
361	Rand Corporation
385	Brown Brothers
407	Bettmann Archive

Picture Essays

46–49,	The environmental crisis; natural resources
a, c	United States Forest Service
b	Soil Conservation Service, USDA
d	International Paper Company
e	American Forest Products Industries, Inc.
f	Nancy Hays, Monkmeyer
g	Federal Water Pollution Control Administration
h	United Press International
i	Kennecott Paper Corporation
j, k	Jean Martin Warholic
68–69,	Setting a price: markets
a, b	New York Stock Exchange
c	Culver Pictures
d	Claus Meyer, Black Star
e	Bettmann Archive
f	American Tobacco Company
102–105,	From grain to bread: production
a	J. C. Allen and Son
b, c, e–i, k	American Bakers Association
d, j, l	Continental Baking Company
m	USDA
125–128,	For the consumer: protection
a	Brown Brothers
b	USDA
c	FDA
d	Ford Motor Company
e	Chas. Pfizer and Company
f	Corn Products Company
g	United Press International
h	Commonwealth of Massachusetts
i	Consumers Union
214–215,	The new technology: industry
a–c	Bettmann Archive
d	Standard Oil Company of California
e	Ford Motor Company
264–267,	New technology in agriculture: land and labor
a	Shel Hershorn, Black Star
b	John Deere Company
c, i	USDA
d, j	George Ballis, Black Star
e, h	Doug Wilson, Black Star
f	Soil Conservation Service, USDA
g	Paul Barton, Black Star
k	Bob Fitch, Black Star
314–315,	A symbol of value: money
a–e	Chase Manhattan Bank Museum
f, g	U.S. Department of the Treasury
338–341,	What taxes buy: guns and butter
a	National Education Association
b	Diane Koos, Black Star
c	U.S. Defense Department
e	U.S. Department of the Navy
g	Massachusetts General Hospital
h	Susan Mirin, Mount Auburn Hospital

496

81–82; family expenditures for, *82,* 82–83; consumer tastes in, 262; distribution of, 263–271, *268, 270;* processing of, 268, 269; cost of, 268, 270–271, 273; availability of, as measure of economic development, 416; in U.S. and India, 416; aid expenditures for, *424*

Food and Agricultural Organization (FAO), 45

Food and Drug Administration (FDA), *125,* 129, *130,* 244, 332

Food and Drug Act (1906), *125, 130*

Food, Drug, and Cosmetic Act (1938), *130*

Food stamp program, 77, 119

Ford Motor Company, *208,* 253

Foreign aid, emergency, *237,* 424; and national defense, 330; costs of, 415, *419,* 424, *424;* and World Bank, 417; purpose of, 419–425, *424*

Foreign exchange, 432–433

Forest products, imported, 430; and international trade disputes, 445–449

Forest resources, *46–47,* 53–54

Forest Service, *54,* 332, 448

Form utility, 31–32

Forty-niners, 316

Fractional reserve system, 151, 374

France, economic problems of, in 18th century, 277; as leader in international trade, 430; in Common Market, 442

Franklin, Benjamin, 7–8; quoted, 142

Franklyn, Henry, quoted, 307

Freedom, of movement, and home ownership, 162; economic, with competition and monopoly, *230*

Free enterprise, in American economic system, *5,* 5–6; decision-making under, 38; anti-pollution action by, 59–60; profits in, 198, 317; the term, 225; and competition, 229; labor-management conflict in, 285; and concentration of power, 460. *See also* Capitalism

Free good, 29

Free market, 70; in agriculture, 282

Free trade, 438–440; arguments against, 439–440; and Common Market, 442

Friedman, Milton, 137

Fringe benefits, 188, 289

Front-end load, 170

Fruits and vegetables, geographic production of, 259, *260;* spoilage of, 268–269; marketing of, 269, *270*

Fuels, transported by pipeline, *35,* 36; and economic expansion, 50–52, *51;* for automobiles, and pollution, 59; aid expenditures for, 424. *See also* Coal; Electricity; Gas; Oil

Full employment balance; full employment deficit, 388

Galbraith, John Kenneth, quoted, 106, 114

Garnishment of wages, 149

Gas, transported through pipelines, *35,* 36; conservation of, 50; in Bolivia, *422,* 423

Gasoline, lead-free, 59, 60; tax on, 345

General Dynamics, 252

General Electric Company, *208,* 240

General Motors Corporation, 199, *208, 221*

General Telephone and Electronics, *208*

General Theory of Employment, Interest, and Money (Keynes), 385

Generic names, 244

Gentlemen's agreements, 235

George, Henry, 277, 334, *334*

Gilbert, H. E., 307

Glamour issues, 223

Gold, as money, 76; decline in U.S. stock of, *435;* market price of, 436; "paper," 436

Gold standard, abandoned, *237*

Gompers, Samuel, 295, 296

Goods, defined, 29; free, 29; consumer and producer, 32; surplus of, 98; primary, 278

Good will, in business, 205

Good will advertising, 232

"Goon squads," 294

Government, role of, in economic affairs, 5, 6; receipts and expenditures by, 31, 174, *329,* 330, *331,* 331–333, *332, 333, 337, 343,* 381–382, *382, 383,* 385, *412, 440, 460;* control of pollution by, 60; intervention of, in pricing process, 70–71; anti-poverty measures of, 115, 117, *119,* 119–121, *120, 121;* consumer protection by, 124–131, *130,* 132; assistance to poor by, 135–141, *137;* investments of, 174; sources of revenue of, 175, 335; social insurance provided by, 191–194; regulation of business by, 202, 205, *206,* 236–242, *237, 238, 241,* 250, 395; in business, 244–246, *245;* and agriculture, 271–275, *273;* and price support program, 272–274, 280–283; and labor-management relations, 302–304, 306, 307–308; transfer payments made by, 321; services supplied by, 329–336, *331, 332,* 399; support of the arts by, 335; taxes levied by, 342–348; monetary policy of, 373–379, *375, 376, 377, 380;* fiscal policy of, 381–389, *388;* economic role of, under socialism, 397–398; of Soviet republics, 404, *405;* economic role of, under communism, 404, 406. *See also* Expenditures; Federal aid; Local governments; States; Taxation; Welfare programs

Government bonds, 162, *162, 165,* 167, 169, 172, 175

Graduated income tax, 334

Grains, *260;* storing of, 269; surpluses of, 273, *274*

Granger Cases, 239

Grants-in-aid, 350–353

Grants to foreign countries, *419. See also* Foreign aid

Grape boycott, 294

Graphs, interpretation of, 17–24

Great Britain, government support

PEARSON   ALWAYS LEARNING

Community Relations
PAD 3874

Second Custom Edition for St. Petersburg College

Taken from:
Police-Community Relations and the Administration of Justice,
Eighth Edition
by Ronald D. Hunter and Thomas Barker

Community Psychology: Guiding Principles and Orienting Concepts
by Jennifer Kofkin Rudkin

*Investigating Difference: Human and Cultural Relations in
Criminal Justice*, Second Edition
by The Criminology and Criminal Justice Collective of
Northern Arizona University

ISBN 10: 1-323-12986-3
ISBN 13: 978-1-323-12986-9

CONTENTS

MODULE 1

CHAPTER 1

The Administration of Justice and the Police

"Injustice anywhere is a threat to justice everywhere."
—Letter from Birmingham Jail, April 16, 1963.
—Martin Luther King, Jr.

KEY CONCEPTS

Civil Justice	Distributive Justice	Restorative Justice
Civil Liberties	Equality	Rule of Law
Common Law	Federalism	Social Justice
Commutative Justice	Human Rights	Social Stability
Criminal Justice	Justice	Symbolic Reassurance

LEARNING OBJECTIVES

Studying this chapter will enable you to:

1. Discuss the need for justice in order for nations and their governmental components to survive.
2. Define human rights and describe their importance to people living throughout the world.
3. Explain the importance of the Bill of Rights in protecting the civil liberties of American citizens.
4. Identify the different agencies responsible for protecting the civil rights of U.S. citizens.
5. Define justice and describe the different types of justice.
6. Explain the mission of a justice system.
7. Identify the four kinds of justice systems found around the world.
8. Discuss the challenges of administering justice within a democratic society.
9. Explain how federalism affects the administration of justice in America.
10. Present and discuss the various components within the U.S. justice system in addition to the police.
11. Describe how America's police system is structured.
12. Understand where the police fit within the U.S. justice system.
13. Be familiar with the "Four C's" of police–community relations.

Police-Community Relations and the Administration of Justice, Eighth Edition
by Ronald D. Hunter, Thomas Barker

INTRODUCTION

The majority of those reading this text have completed other courses about the criminal justice system and its processes. However, we are of the opinion that a brief refresher is in order to remind law enforcement students that the police do not exist in a vacuum. The myriad of agencies that comprise the "police" are integral components of a vital system of justice upon which social order and stability are dependent. The purpose, roles, and functions of the police within every nation on earth are interdependent with those of other governmental entities. To understand the police, one must understand the other components of the criminal justice system. To understand the criminal justice system, one must understand the concept of justice.

THE IDEA OF JUSTICE

To many of us, the concept of justice is relatively straightforward; the large numbers of people that comprise our societies require regulation to ensure peace and stability. Otherwise, competing interests and differing perspectives on what constitutes acceptable behavior would lead to chaos. The weak would be victimized by the strong, violence would become the social norm, and civilization would cease to exist. We often simplify this idea of justice into two words: "law and order." However, as we may easily note when viewing current world events, who determines what constitutes the law, who defines the nature of order, and how their views are imposed on the populace are not as clear-cut.

The Need for Justice

Nations and their components (states, territories, provinces, cities, counties, etc.) cannot exist without established systems of justice. These systems must not only ensure that domestic peace and tranquility are preserved, they must do so in a manner acceptable to those who are governed. This is true even in totalitarian societies. While those subject to governmental edicts may have little or no say in how laws are enacted and enforced, there must be a belief that subservience to their government is preferable to disorder. The reader may challenge this assertion by pointing to the arbitrariness and unfairness that may be found within the brutal dictatorships that have existed (and that unfortunately still exist) within our world. We agree. But even in those countries, one will find that those in power must present an appearance of justice. While these justice systems may be backed by repressive force, the masses of people must still feel that they and their families can reasonably exist. Otherwise, rebellion will take place.

Regardless of the nature of a society, social stability is not enough. Citizens must also feel that they are being treated "properly." What is viewed as proper is determined by historical and cultural influences. Governmental actions that would be totally acceptable in one nation would not be seen as such in others. As humankind has developed, its expectations have likewise developed. Two key components in evaluating the world's justice systems are the provisions for basic human rights and the extent of civil rights granted to citizens.

HUMAN RIGHTS **Human rights** in its simplest term may be defined as a person's right to the basic necessities for survival. These include adequate food, shelter, medical care, and not being the victim of a government's or government-condoned group's efforts to commit genocide. Efforts on the part of the U.S. Army during the 1800s to annihilate Native Americans and by the Iraqi government during the rule of Saddam Hussein to eliminate the Kurds are clear examples of human rights violations. Modern human rights organizations would also charge that the existence of poverty and famine within third-world nations is another example. As this is being written, the United Nations is calling for the closure of the U.S. prison at Guantanamo Bay, Cuba, where terrorist suspects are being held, citing that these incarcerations are violations of human rights.

On December 10, 1948, the General Assembly of the United Nations adopted and proclaimed the Universal Declaration of Human Rights. Following this historic act, the Assembly called upon all member countries to publicize the text of the Declaration and "to cause it to be disseminated, displayed, read and expounded principally in schools and other educational institutions, without distinction based on the political status of countries or territories." (See Figure 1.1) This figure is the longest within the entire text, but we feel it warrants inclusion because (despite the fears of opponents of "world government," including the authors') the justice system in America will increasingly be held accountable to the edicts of international organizations.

CIVIL RIGHTS   As the reader can see within Figure 1.1, the U.N. Declaration goes beyond our definition of basic survival necessities to incorporate equal rights, freedom of speech, and protection from government abuse. In reality, many of the world's 191 nations do not adhere to

FIGURE 1.1   The U.N. Universal Declaration of Human Rights.

Preamble

Whereas recognition of the inherent dignity and of the equal and inalienable rights of all members of the human family is the foundation of freedom, justice and peace in the world,

Whereas disregard and contempt for human rights have resulted in barbarous acts which have outraged the conscience of mankind, and the advent of a world in which human beings shall enjoy freedom of speech and belief and freedom from fear and want has been proclaimed as the highest aspiration of the common people,

Whereas it is essential, if man is not to be compelled to have recourse, as a last resort, to rebellion against tyranny and oppression, that human rights should be protected by the rule of law,

Whereas it is essential to promote the development of friendly relations between nations,

Whereas the peoples of the United Nations have in the Charter reaffirmed their faith in fundamental human rights, in the dignity and worth of the human person and in the equal rights of men and women and have determined to promote social progress and better standards of life in larger freedom,

Whereas Member States have pledged themselves to achieve, in co-operation with the United Nations, the promotion of universal respect for and observance of human rights and fundamental freedoms,

Whereas a common understanding of these rights and freedoms is of the greatest importance for the full realization of this pledge,

Now, Therefore THE GENERAL ASSEMBLY proclaims THIS UNIVERSAL DECLARATION OF HUMAN RIGHTS as a common standard of achievement for all peoples and all nations, to the end that every individual and every organ of society, keeping this Declaration constantly in mind, shall strive by teaching and education to promote respect for these rights and freedoms and by progressive measures, national and international, to secure their universal and effective recognition and observance, both among the peoples of Member States themselves and among the peoples of territories under their jurisdiction.

Article 1.

All human beings are born free and equal in dignity and rights. They are endowed with reason and conscience and should act towards one another in a spirit of brotherhood.

Article 2.

Everyone is entitled to all the rights and freedoms set forth in this Declaration, without distinction of any kind, such as race, color, sex, language, religion, political or other opinion, national or social origin, property, birth or other status. Furthermore, no distinction shall be made on the basis of the political, jurisdictional or international status of the country or territory to which a person belongs, whether it be independent, trust, non-self-governing or under any other limitation of sovereignty.

Article 3.

Everyone has the right to life, liberty and security of person.

Article 4.

No one shall be held in slavery or servitude; slavery and the slave trade shall be prohibited in all their forms.

Article 5.

No one shall be subjected to torture or to cruel, inhuman or degrading treatment or punishment.

Article 6.

Everyone has the right to recognition everywhere as a person before the law.

Article 7.

All are equal before the law and are entitled without any discrimination to equal protection of the law. All are entitled to equal protection against any discrimination in violation of this Declaration and against any incitement to such discrimination.

Article 8.

Everyone has the right to an effective remedy by the competent national tribunals for acts violating the fundamental rights granted him by the constitution or by law.

(continued)

FIGURE 1.1   **Continued**

Article 9.

No one shall be subjected to arbitrary arrest, detention or exile.

Article 10.

Everyone is entitled in full equality to a fair and public hearing by an independent and impartial tribunal, in the determination of his rights and obligations and of any criminal charge against him.

Article 11.

(1) Everyone charged with a penal offence has the right to be presumed innocent until proved guilty according to law in a public trial at which he has had all the guarantees necessary for his defense.

(2) No one shall be held guilty of any penal offence on account of any act or omission which did not constitute a penal offence, under national or international law, at the time when it was committed. Nor shall a heavier penalty be imposed than the one that was applicable at the time the penal offence was committed.

Article 12.

No one shall be subjected to arbitrary interference with his privacy, family, home or correspondence, nor to attacks upon his honor and reputation. Everyone has the right to the protection of the law against such interference or attacks.

Article 13.

(1) Everyone has the right to freedom of movement and residence within the borders of each state.

(2) Everyone has the right to leave any country, including his own, and to return to his country.

Article 14.

(1) Everyone has the right to seek and to enjoy in other countries asylum from persecution.

(2) This right may not be invoked in the case of prosecutions genuinely arising from non-political crimes or from acts contrary to the purposes and principles of the United Nations.

Article 15.

(1) Everyone has the right to a nationality.

(2) No one shall be arbitrarily deprived of his nationality nor denied the right to change his nationality.

Article 16.

(1) Men and women of full age, without any limitation due to race, nationality or religion, have the right to marry and to found a family. They are entitled to equal rights as to marriage, during marriage and at its dissolution.

(2) Marriage shall be entered into only with the free and full consent of the intending spouses.

(3) The family is the natural and fundamental group unit of society and is entitled to protection by society and the State.

Article 17.

(1) Everyone has the right to own property alone as well as in association with others.

(2) No one shall be arbitrarily deprived of his property.

Article 18.

Everyone has the right to freedom of thought, conscience and religion; this right includes freedom to change his religion or belief, and freedom, either alone or in community with others and in public or private, to manifest his religion or belief in teaching, practice, worship and observance.

Article 19.

Everyone has the right to freedom of opinion and expression; this right includes freedom to hold opinions without interference and to seek, receive and impart information and ideas through any media and regardless of frontiers.

Article 20.

(1) Everyone has the right to freedom of peaceful assembly and association.

(2) No one may be compelled to belong to an association.

Article 21.

(1) Everyone has the right to take part in the government of his country, directly or through freely chosen representatives.

(2) Everyone has the right of equal access to public service in his country.

(3) The will of the people shall be the basis of the authority of government; this shall be expressed in periodic and genuine elections which shall be by universal and equal suffrage and shall be held by secret vote or by equivalent free voting procedures.

Article 22.

Everyone, as a member of society, has the right to social security and is entitled to realization, through national effort and international co-operation and in accordance with the organization and resources of each State, of the economic, social and cultural rights indispensable for his dignity and the free development of his personality.

Article 23.

(1) Everyone has the right to work, to free choice of employment, to just and favorable conditions of work and to protection against unemployment.

(2) Everyone, without any discrimination, has the right to equal pay for equal work.

(3) Everyone who works has the right to just and favorable remuneration ensuring for himself and his family an existence worthy of human dignity, and supplemented, if necessary, by other means of social protection.

(4) Everyone has the right to form and to join trade unions for the protection of his interests.

Article 24.

Everyone has the right to rest and leisure, including reasonable limitation of working hours and periodic holidays with pay.

Article 25.

(1) Everyone has the right to a standard of living adequate for the health and well-being of himself and of his family, including food, clothing, housing and medical care and necessary social services, and the right to security in the event of unemployment, sickness, disability, widowhood, old age or other lack of livelihood in circumstances beyond his control.

(2) Motherhood and childhood are entitled to special care and assistance. All children, whether born in or out of wedlock, shall enjoy the same social protection.

Article 26.

(1) Everyone has the right to education. Education shall be free, at least in the elementary and fundamental stages. Elementary education shall be compulsory. Technical and professional education shall be made generally available and higher education shall be equally accessible to all on the basis of merit.

(2) Education shall be directed to the full development of the human personality and to the strengthening of respect for human rights and fundamental freedoms. It shall promote understanding, tolerance and friendship among all nations, racial or religious groups, and shall further the activities of the United Nations for the maintenance of peace.

(3) Parents have a prior right to choose the kind of education that shall be given to their children.

Article 27.

(1) Everyone has the right freely to participate in the cultural life of the community, to enjoy the arts and to share in scientific advancement and its benefits.

(2) Everyone has the right to the protection of the moral and material interests resulting from any scientific, literary or artistic production of which he is the author.

Article 28.

Everyone is entitled to a social and international order in which the rights and freedoms set forth in this Declaration can be fully realized.

Article 29.

(1) Everyone has duties to the community in which alone the free and full development of his personality is possible.

(2) In the exercise of his rights and freedoms, everyone shall be subject only to such limitations as are determined by law solely for the purpose of securing due recognition and respect for the rights and freedoms of others and of meeting the just requirements of morality, public order and the general welfare in a democratic society.

(3) These rights and freedoms may in no case be exercised contrary to the purposes and principles of the United Nations.

Article 30.

Nothing in this Declaration may be interpreted as implying for any State, group or person any right to engage in any activity or to perform any act aimed at the destruction of any of the rights and freedoms set forth herein.

Source: Adopted and proclaimed by General Assembly resolution 217 A (III) of December 10, 1948.

these standards. Even Western democracies have been slow to adopt them in their totality. Despite the protections of the Bill of Rights (the First Ten Amendments to the U.S. Constitution, written 150 years before the U.N. Declaration), it was not until the 1960s that full enforcement of civil rights began within the United States.

We view civil rights as moving beyond the basic necessities for survival to include equal participation in democratic elections, equal access to legal institutions, and equal protection by the government from both governmental and private abuse. Freedoms from government oppression or intrusive practices are also known as **civil liberties** (we will discuss them in more detail in a later section). The extension of these rights, based on gender and physical disabilities, was interpreted as being covered by the Bill of Rights during the 1970s (see Figure 1.2). Sexual orientation was included during the 1990s.

Federal civil rights violations may be investigated by the Civil Rights Division of the U.S. Department of Justice, by the Federal Bureau of Investigation (FBI), by civil suits filed by

FIGURE 1.2 **The Bill of Rights.**

Amendments 1–10 of the U.S. Constitution

The Conventions of a number of the States having, at the time of adopting the Constitution, expressed a desire, in order to prevent misconstruction or abuse of its powers, that further declaratory and restrictive clauses should be added, and as extending the ground of public confidence in the Government will best insure the beneficent ends of its institution.

Resolved, by the Senate and House of Representatives of the United States of America, in Congress assembled, two-thirds of both Houses concurring, that the following articles be proposed to the Legislatures of the several States, as amendments to the Constitution of the United States; all or any of which articles, when ratified by three-fourths of the said Legislatures, to be valid to all intents and purposes as part of the said Constitution, namely:

Amendment I

Congress shall make no law respecting an establishment of religion, or prohibiting the free exercise thereof; or abridging the freedom of speech, or of the press; or the right of the people peaceably to assemble, and to petition the government for a redress of grievances.

Amendment II

A well regulated militia, being necessary to the security of a free state, the right of the people to keep and bear arms, shall not be infringed.

Amendment III

No soldier shall, in time of peace be quartered in any house, without the consent of the owner, nor in time of war, but in a manner to be prescribed by law.

Amendment IV

The right of the people to be secure in their persons, houses, papers, and effects, against unreasonable searches and seizures, shall not be violated, and no warrants shall issue, but upon probable cause, supported by oath or affirmation, and particularly describing the place to be searched, and the persons or things to be seized.

Amendment V

No person shall be held to answer for a capital, or otherwise infamous crime, unless on a presentment or indictment of a grand jury, except in cases arising in the land or naval forces, or in the militia, when in actual service in time of war or public danger; nor shall any person be subject for the same offense to be twice put in jeopardy of life or limb; nor shall be compelled in any criminal case to be a witness against himself, nor be deprived of life, liberty, or property, without due process of law; nor shall private property be taken for public use, without just compensation.

Amendment VI

In all criminal prosecutions, the accused shall enjoy the right to a speedy and public trial, by an impartial jury of the state and district wherein the crime shall have been committed, which district shall have been previously ascertained by law, and to be informed of the nature and cause of the accusation; to be confronted with the witnesses against him; to have compulsory process for obtaining witnesses in his favor, and to have the assistance of counsel for his defense.

Amendment VII

In suits at common law, where the value in controversy shall exceed twenty dollars, the right of trial by jury shall be preserved, and no fact tried by a jury, shall be otherwise reexamined in any court of the United States, than according to the rules of the common law.

Amendment VIII

Excessive bail shall not be required, nor excessive fines imposed, nor cruel and unusual punishments inflicted.

Amendment IX

The enumeration in the Constitution, of certain rights, shall not be construed to deny or disparage others retained by the people.

Amendment X

The powers not delegated to the United States by the Constitution, nor prohibited by it to the states, are reserved to the states respectively, or to the people.

Amendment XIV

All persons born or naturalized in the United States, and subject to the jurisdiction thereof, are citizens of the United States and of the state wherein they reside. No state shall make or enforce any law which shall abridge the privileges or immunities of citizens of the United States; nor shall any State deprive any person of life, liberty, or property, without due process of law; nor deny to any person within its jurisdiction the equal protection of the laws.

Note: The Fourteenth Amendment warrants inclusion here because it is the mechanism by which the Bill of Rights became applicable as protections from state and local governments in addition to the national government.

FIGURE 1.3   Mission of the U.S. Commission on Civil Rights.

To investigate complaints alleging that citizens are being deprived of their right to vote by reason of their race, color, religion, sex, age, disability, or national origin, or by reason of fraudulent practices.

To study and collect information relating to discrimination or a denial of equal protection of the laws under the Constitution because of race, color, religion, sex, age, disability, or national origin, or in the administration of justice.

To appraise federal laws and policies with respect to discrimination or denial of equal protection of the laws because of race, color, religion, sex, age, disability, or national origin, or in the administration of justice.

To serve as a national clearinghouse for information in respect to discrimination or denial of equal protection of the laws because of race, color, religion, sex, age, disability, or national origin.

To submit reports, findings, and recommendations to the President and Congress.

To issue public service announcements to discourage discrimination or denial of equal protection of the law.

individuals, or by complaints filed with the U.S. Commission on Civil Rights (see Figure 1.3). They may also be enforced by lawsuits and criminal prosecutions filed under the constitutional protections of the states.

JUSTICE DEFINED

While everyone has his or her own concept of justice (usually determined by what we think is best for us), it is not as easily defined as one might think. According to Crank (2003), efforts at clarity tend to conflict with concerns over inclusiveness. Definitions are also determined by the perspective of the viewer. Reiman (2007) argues that our system of justice is biased against the poor and is, therefore, not just. Lawyers tend to view justice as the obligation that the legal system has toward the individual citizen and society as a whole. A common definition views justice as a concept involving the fair, moral, and impartial treatment of all persons (Wikipedia, 2007). To ensure that justice is seen from the relevant perspective of policing, we define **justice** *as the fair and equitable application of the rule of law by agents of social control regardless of the socioeconomic status of the individuals concerned.* While we admit that this is a rather idyllic view, we argue that it is, indeed, what a free society should strive for.

To accomplish justice, we feel that there are six components that the administration of justice must contain:

- *Compliance with the **Rule of Law**.* Codified legal standards must exist and must be followed. As noted in the Fourteenth Amendment of the U.S. Constitution, citizens can be deprived of life, liberty, or property only by due process of law.
- *Equity.* Laws must be applied in an equal manner to everyone subject to them. In addition, every person must be allowed equal access to the legal system. This is a subject of great debate in regard to the U.S. criminal justice system, and even greater debate in regard to the U.S. civil justice system.
- *Fairness.* Laws, as well as their application, must be fair and not single out groups or individuals for arbitrary or unfair treatment. As with equity, fairness is not easily monitored and can often become lost in legalities and legalese that govern the system's operations.
- *Accessibility.* There must be allowances for those individuals who do not have financial recourse to receive competent legal advice and support. This is dealt with in the criminal justice system by provisions for indigent defense. However, this is one component in which the U.S. civil justice system is very much lacking.
- *Effectiveness.* The system must work for common citizens in actuality as well as on paper. Like beauty, effectiveness is in the eye of the beholder. How well the U.S. justice system accomplishes this need is even more hotly debated than the previous components.

BOX 1.1

Alternative Definitions of Justice

Some satirical views of justice from Webster's online dictionary:

Justice. A commodity which in a more or less adulterated condition the State sells to the citizen as a reward for his allegiance, taxes and personal service.

Justice. Fair play; often sought, but seldom discovered, in company with Law.

Justice. A mythological character whose statue has been frequently erected. She had eye trouble.

Source: www.websters-online-dictionary.org/definition/justice.

- *Oversight*. There must be remedies for failures or misapplications of justice to be corrected. The checks and balances of the federal system, and judicial oversight in particular, are the mechanisms designed to correct injustices that occur. While far from perfect and frequently yielding unsatisfactory results, this process is as functional as any other that may be found within the world community.

Critics may correctly cite examples to argue that the above components are more idealistic than accurate. Indeed, the administration of justice (particularly within a democratic society of more than 300 million) will always be a subject of debate.

Types of Justice

Understanding the administration of justice is further complicated by the different types of justice found within our society and the meanings attached to them. While the police are predominately linked with criminal justice, the other types of justice impact on both how the police are perceived by others and how they function within society. Brief overviews of these other types of justice follow:

SOCIAL JUSTICE   **Social justice** is rendering to everyone that which is his or her due as a human being. Social justice is seen by its proponents as not just emphasizing equity and fairness in the application of jurisprudence but in regulating how a society's resources are allocated (Crank, 2003). Redistribution of wealth by the use of progressive tax systems, strict regulation of business, and extensive use of social interventions by government are principles embodied within social justice. Social justice seeks to see that people are treated both fairly and "morally" within all areas of society. Social justice may be either distributive or commutative.

Distributive justice seeks to distribute rewards and punishments so that neither equal persons have unequal things, nor unequal persons equal things. In other words, need is considered, but merit is rewarded. The U.S. system of welfare capitalism is based on distributive justice. Protections exist to ensure that the tenets of civil and human rights are provided but individual successes or failures are allowed.

Commutative justice seeks to ensure **equality** among citizens so that no one may be a gainer by another's loss. The fair and moral treatment of all persons, especially as regards social rules, is the part of a continued effort to do what is "right" (Crank, 2003; Reiman, 2007). Commutative justice places a greater emphasis on need rather than individual merit. Proponents of this perspective argue that biases due to class, ethnicity, gender, or other distinctions make capitalist society inherently unfair. Therefore, greater efforts by government in the redistribution of wealth and the enhancement of life for minorities and the lower class must be implemented to address social inequities. Until these occur, true justice is not attainable (Cole, 2004; Reiman, 2007).

CIVIL JUSTICE   **Civil justice** is the legal system that regulates the relationships between individuals. Distributive and commutative aspects do exist within the civil law system. However, the focus of civil law is to regulate noncriminal behaviors within society. Redress for harm from another's actions is not by criminal prosecution but by seeking legal intervention to regain that which was lost due to another's improper actions and/or to prevent further harm. Monetary compensation may be for the harm that was incurred. Punitive damages may also be awarded. Due to the complexities and costs of successful litigation, it is in the areas of civil law that the poor and the middle class are more likely to experience inequitable treatment.

The civil legal system is concerned with torts (private wrongs that are not deemed to be criminal). However, in cases of evictions and foreclosures, police officers (especially deputy sheriffs) may find themselves involved. Ill feelings and frustrations from civil actions may also lead to criminal activities on the part of those who feel that they have been wronged. Administrative law, rules, and regulations followed and/or enforced by governmental agencies are also dealt with by the civil law system. Some behaviors (such as cheating on your income tax, violating another's civil rights, and insider trading) may have both civil and criminal components.

RESTORATIVE JUSTICE   Yet another type of justice that may or may not involve the criminal justice system is the practice of restorative justice. As the name implies, **restorative justice** seeks to mitigate adverse relationships between individuals as well as certain behaviors that could be deemed to be criminal. Instead of seeking to punish based on criminal sanctions or imposing legal compensation, restorative justice seeks to avoid formal adjudication by using arbitration to resolve conflicts (Van Ness and Strong, 2006). Because it emphasizes the use of alternative means to restore relationships, this concept is also known as peacemaking (Fuller, 2005). Efforts at restorative justice usually involve issues of lesser monetary import and/or minor offenses. Restorative justice may take place in lieu of civil litigation, and it may also be used as an alternative to criminal prosecution.

CRIMINAL JUSTICE   **Criminal justice** is the system that the readers of this text are interested in. As we have noted above, it is not truly separate from the other systems of justice and actually interacts with them. We utilized Rush's (2004) definition of the criminal justice system as the "process of adjudication by which the legal rights of private parties are vindicated and the guilt or innocence of accused persons is established." Please note that the *criminal justice system is concerned not only with the enforcement of laws but with the protection of legal rights as well.* To ensure that laws are not arbitrarily imposed, the criminal justice system relies on procedural law as well as substantive law.

Substantive law defines behaviors (and in some cases, failures to act) that are deemed to be unlawful and establishes sanctions for their commission (or omission). Procedural law regulates how substantive law may be applied. The famous *exclusionary rule* (see Box 1.2) is one mechanism by which American courts ensure that a defendant's due process rights are protected.

BOX 1.2
The Exclusionary Rule

In 1914, the U.S. Supreme Court ruled in *Weeks* v. *United States* that evidence illegally obtained by federal officers must be excluded from admission at trial. In 1960, this rule was extended to state and local officers in the *Mapp* v. *Ohio* ruling. The exclusionary rule not only prevents evidence obtained from unreasonable searches and seizures from admission in trials, it also ensures that judicial integrity and the faith of citizens are upheld.

The protections of the Fourth Amendment as enforced by the exclusionary rule are also known as the "Fruits of the Poisonous Tree Doctrine." Searches, arrests, confessions, and other evidence-gathering activities that are obtained through improper or illegal techniques are deemed to be poisonous and must, therefore, be suppressed to keep the entire legal process from becoming tainted.

There are exceptions to the exclusionary rule. In *United States* v. *Leon*, the U.S. Supreme Court ruled that "evidence seized on a search warrant that was subsequently invalidated could not justify the substantial costs of exclusion." The key to this exception is that the efforts were, indeed, reasonable and in good faith. Good intentions are not enough.

Another exception to the exclusionary rule is the "Inevitable Discovery Rule." This rule was established by the U.S. Supreme Court in *Wong Sun* v. *United States*. This rule allows the admission of evidence if it would have been found and discovered legally at a later time.

Source: Adapted from Roberson, Wallace, and Stuckey (2007).

THE MISSION OF A CRIMINAL JUSTICE SYSTEM

Having reviewed several pages pointing out the complexities of justice, the reader may legitimately ask, "What then is the purpose of a criminal justice system?" The answer is simpler than our previous discussions may suggest. In a nutshell, *the U.S. criminal justice system exists to apply the rule of law as a means of providing social stability.* As we discussed previously, citizens must feel that their government is protecting them from crime and disorder. While the system need not be flawless, the public as a whole must have confidence in it.

The Rule of Law

Rule of law may be defined as government's establishment and imposition of legal processes to protect society from crime. It may also be defined as the mechanism by which government ensures the protection of individual rights. In order to accomplish these tasks, laws must provide for the following:

VENGEANCE/RETRIBUTION   When civilization evolved from tribal states to nation-states, government assumed responsibility for exacting vengeance on behalf of victims of crime. No longer would the strong be allowed to prey on the weak. Nor would victims or their families be permitted to conduct blood feuds to avenge themselves on those by whom they had been harmed. To keep citizens from "taking the law into their own hands," agents of social control must exact vengeance on behalf of victims.

ATONEMENT   Under the rule of law, those who commit crimes against others are seen as committing crimes against the state. In order to be allowed readmission to law-abiding society, offenders must atone for their crimes. The crime justice process is the means by which criminal offenders "pay their debt to society." While many ex-convicts may rightly argue otherwise, having been punished theoretically enables offenders to resume their place in society.

DETERRENCE/PREVENTION   The fundamental premise of the classical system of justice is that the imposition of punishment prevents further crime from occurring. Specific deterrence is the idea that by having received punishment, the offender will decide that the crime was not worth it. General deterrence is the concept that others contemplating similar crimes will be dissuaded from doing so by seeing the punishment of previous offenders (Hunter and Dantzker, 2005). Experienced police officers can point to the recidivism of offenders to question how well these premises work, but deterrence remains as the mainstay of the U.S. justice system.

TREATMENT   As part of the system's concerns to rehabilitate offenders so that they may reenter society and live productive lives, treatment is also an important component of justice in America. Like deterrence, the impacts of treatment are often disappointing, but fundamental fairness and social justice require that treatment be provided. Whether the treatments provided are appropriate or adequate will continue to be subjects of debate.

INCAPACITATION   In many cases, incarceration, as well as other means of incapacitation, is seen as legitimate goals of the U.S. justice system. Proponents of incapacitation argue that while offenders may return to crime later (except in the case of capital punishment—the ultimate incapacitation), they are prevented from doing so while under correctional control. A more correct version may be that they are impeded from committing crimes on the general public.

REPARATIONS   Lastly, a more humane means of applying the rule of law is to focus on the victim rather than society. Instead of punishing the offenders based on the harm they caused to society, they are ordered to make reparations to the victims of their crimes. This "restorative technique" is seen as not only helping those who have been harmed but also helping the offender.

Social Stability

Social stability is defined as the maintenance of order and the continuation of equitable social control by government. This requires government to not only repress criminal behaviors but to provide services (regulation of the private sector and the provision of public services) and to promote activities (such as public education and social programs) designed to benefit society as a whole.

MAINTENANCE OF ORDER   The maintenance of order involves many activities. Providing for democratic elections, collecting taxes, enforcing zoning regulations, collecting garbage, operating public utilities, providing crowd control at public events, enforcing parking regulations (including the issuing of parking tickets to students), and providing emergency services are but a few of the multitude of activities by government, many of which are performed by the police.

EQUITABLE SOCIAL CONTROL   One of the more controversial aspects of government is the need to address social inequities. While we may grouse at increasing government intrusion into our lives, providing social stability within a diverse nation of 300 million requires proactive government actions. As civil libertarians, the authors believe that citizens should be grudging in their tolerance of government interventions. However, we are also quick to note that these actions are necessary to ensure that all citizens are able to enjoy "life, liberty, and property." Government requirements such as progressive taxation, compulsory education, mandatory minimum wages, and protection of minority rights are examples of controversial government intrusions that are now seen as vital to public stability.

SYMBOLIC REASSURANCE   The last requirement of a justice system is what Hunter (see Hunter and Dantzker, 2005, p. 213) refers to as symbolic reassurance. **Symbolic reassurance** is the view that the criminal justice system not only provides guidelines for society to follow, it also punishes evil-doers to affirm law-abiding citizens' belief in the system. Universal conformity is not attained through threats of prosecution, but by reassuring law-abiding citizens that the system of justice is working. As long as a few offenders get occasional punishment (the more severe, the better), the public, especially the middle class, will remain compliant, even if they are not totally satisfied. Taken to an extreme, this concept implies that as long as the public perceives that "something is being done," even if it later proves to be faulty, the public will, for the most part, remain supportive.

THE CHALLENGES OF ADMINISTERING JUSTICE IN A FREE SOCIETY

We have discussed the protections of the Bill of Rights and the necessary components of a justice system within previous sections. This section will not repeat those arguments. However, we will stress the fundamental challenge that faces criminal justice practitioners within the United States. That challenge is quite simple: In a democratic and freedom-loving nation, how do we control crime while ensuring due process of law?

Crime Control versus Due Process

Crime control is the emphasis of justice system resources on the suppression of crime through the speedy enforcement of criminal laws. Advocates of the crime control model argue that the rights of society to be protected from crime should be the primary focus of the criminal justice system. Efficiency and effectiveness in criminal prosecutions are emphasized. In this model, the adjudication process is viewed as being an "assembly line." The counterpart to the crime control model is the due process model. In this model, the emphasis of the justice system is formal, adjudicative fact-finding that emphasizes the rights of the accused. The administration of justice is a slow and deliberate process that may be viewed as being an "obstacle course" (Packer, 1968).

BOX 1.3
Other Justice Systems

When seeking to study the U.S. system of justice, it is helpful to understand that our system is but one of many that exist within the world. While widely divergent in how they are comprised, most justice systems can be categorized into four distinct typologies:

Common Law Justice Systems

The common-law tradition evolved from the United Kingdom. Nations such as the United States that were formerly British Colonies tend to follow this legal tradition. Key elements of this tradition are the protection of individual liberties, concerns for equity, reliance on legal custom, and adversarial prosecution.

Civil Law Justice Systems

The civil law tradition (not the same as what is referred to as civil law in the United States) developed in Europe from Roman law and Catholic canon law. These systems are found in continental Europe and in nations around the world that emerged from European colonization. Key elements of this tradition are codified law, an emphasis on the protection of society, and inquisitorial prosecutions. France and Germany are leading exemplars of this tradition.

Islamic Justice Systems

The Islamic legal tradition is based on the Shari'a, law based on the Qur'an (the holy book of Islam) and the Sunna (the writings of the Prophet Mohammed). Varying interpretations of this system are found in Muslim nations. How strictly the Shari'a is applied within individual nations depends on cultural influences as well as the religious perspectives of the dominant Islamic sect within those nations.

Socialist Justice Systems

The socialist legal tradition evolved from the merger of Russian law and Marxist-Leninism following the revolution that led to the creation of the Soviet Union. This tradition viewed the law as artificial (meaning that rather than viewing the rule of law as binding, the edicts and rulings of the communist party, as well as adherence to Marxist philosophy, held precedence). Despite the breakup of the Soviet Union and the spread of democratic practices within its former satellites, the influence of this tradition may still be found in many of these nations. Currently, the Peoples Republic of China would be the leading example of this tradition.

Source: Adapted from Reichel (2005) and Dammer, Fairchild, and Albanese (2006).

RIGHTS OF SOCIETY   According to Bohm and Haley (2005), the crime-control perspective is a reflection of traditional conservative values. Conservatives would probably agree with this assessment but argue that they are not seeking to deemphasize the protections of due process but to eliminate burdensome legal technicalities that neither protect individual rights nor protect society from crime. They point to other Western democracies that utilize the Civil Law System, in which the rights of society are deemed more important than those of any one individual. They may also accurately argue that most courts of limited jurisdiction in the United States operate in this manner.

RIGHTS OF INDIVIDUALS   Bohm and Haley (2005) characterize the due process model as being a reflection of traditional liberal values. They point to the **common law** tradition of emphasizing the rights of individuals as safeguards from government oppression. They further argue that the protection of individual rights actually serves to protect societal rights.

Balancing the Rights of Society with Those of Individuals.   As with most debates, the truth lies somewhere in the middle. Due process as defined by Roberson, Wallace, and Stuckey (2007, p. 454) is: "Those procedures that effectively guarantee individual rights in the face of criminal prosecution and those procedures that are fundamental rules for fair and orderly legal proceedings." In actual practice, individual rights are protected within the U.S. justice system, but the sheer volume of cases require that fair and orderly proceedings be expedited in lower-level courts and on less serious offenses. Capital cases and cases in which lengthy prison terms could be imposed rightly receive the greatest scrutiny.

This debate will continue as long as there is a U.S. justice system. During times of unrest and tension, the public will demand greater protections for society (the current dispute over the

BOX 1.4
The Civil Rights Act of 1871

The Civil Rights Act of 1871 (42 U.S.C. § 1983) is one of the most important federal statutes in force in the United States. It was originally enacted a few years after the American Civil War and consisted of the 1870 Force Act and 1871 Ku Klux Klan Act. One of the main reasons behind its passage was to protect Southern blacks from the Ku Klux Klan by providing a civil remedy for abuses then being committed in the South. The statute has been subjected to only minor changes since then but has been the subject of voluminous interpretation by courts.

Section 1983 does not create new civil rights. Instead, it allows individuals to sue state actors in federal courts for civil rights violations. To gain federal jurisdiction, that is, access to a court, the individual must point to a federal civil right that has been allegedly violated. These rights are encoded in the U.S. Constitution and federal statutes.

The statute reads:

Every person who under color of any statute, ordinance, regulation, custom, or usage, of any State or Territory or the District of Columbia, subjects, or causes to be subjected, any citizen of the United States or other person within the jurisdiction thereof to the deprivation of any rights, privileges, or immunities secured by the Constitution and laws, shall be liable to the party injured in an action at law, Suit in equity, or other proper proceeding for redress, except that in any action brought against a judicial officer

for an act or omission taken in such officer's judicial capacity, injunctive relief shall not be granted unless a declaratory decree was violated or declaratory relief was unavailable. For the purposes of this section, any Act of Congress applicable exclusively to the District of Columbia shall be considered to be a statute of the District of Columbia.

For most of its history, Section 1983 had very little force. The legal community did not think the statute served as a check on state officials and did not often litigate under the statute. However, this changed in 1961 when the Supreme Court of the United States decided *Monroe* v. *Pape*, 365 U.S. 167. In that case, the Court articulated three purposes that underlay the statute: "1) 'to override certain kinds of state laws'; 2) to provide 'a remedy where state law was inadequate'; and 3) to provide 'a federal remedy where the state remedy, though adequate in theory, was not available in practice.'" Blum & Urbonya, Section 1983 Litigation, p. 2 (Federal Judicial Center, 1998) (quoting *Monroe* v. *Pape*). *Pape* opened the door for renewed interest in Section 1983.

Now the statute stands as one of the most powerful authorities with which federal courts may protect those whose rights are deprived. It is most often used to sue police and other state officials who allegedly deprived a plaintiff of constitutional rights within the criminal justice system.

Source: Adapted from Wikipedia (2007).

Patriot Act as a means of combating terrorism is a prime example). Civil libertarians see the Patriot Act as an encroachment on individual liberties. Advocates argue that it does not negatively impact law-abiding citizens and provides needed societal protections. Regardless of where you stand on the Patriot Act, the fact remains that the U.S. justice system will always have to juggle efficiency and effectiveness in protecting society from criminals with our traditional concern for individual rights. By the nature of their law enforcement responsibilities, the police will remain at the forefront of this debate (Walker, 2002).

THE COMPONENTS OF THE U.S. JUSTICE SYSTEM

The Federalist System

When discussing the U.S. justice system, one must be aware that there are in actuality several types of justice systems. The U.S. Constitution establishes a federalist system of government in which the national government shares power with the states and the states' political subdivisions (municipalities, townships, special districts, and counties). The magnitude of these systems may be realized by the knowledge that there are more than half a million elected officials within the United States. In addition to the state and national governments, these officials serve in more than 74,500 local governments, 20,000 municipalities, 16,500 townships, 3,000 counties, and more than 35,000 special districts (Fiorina et al., 2005: Chapters 1 and 3). At every level of government, you will find legislative bodies that make laws, executive agencies that enforce those laws, courts that interpret and apply the laws, and correctional organizations that carry out adjudicated sanctions. The criminal justice process utilized by every governmental level is displayed within Figure 1.4.

LAWMAKING When we think of lawmaking within the United States, we generally think of the U.S. Congress or the 50 state legislatures. These legislative bodies (including the legislatures of American territories of the Virgin Islands, Guam, and American Samoa, as well as the Commonwealth of Puerto Rico and the council of the District of Columbia) enact laws that are known as statutes. The decisions of these bodies have considerable impact on the lives of their citizens. But it is at the local levels (among the approximately 74,500 local governmental bodies mentioned above) that most citizens have direct contact on a regular basis. Each of these entities has legislative bodies (usually referred to as councils, commissions, boards, or authorities) that enact lesser laws known as ordinances or codes (property taxes, sales taxes, zoning and building regulations, liquor sales and consumption, garbage collection, animal control, noise and nuisance abatement, etc.) that influence your daily life.

LAW ENFORCEMENT In the following section, we will describe the police system in America in more detail. Suffice it to say at this point that if you are in need of police services, it is most likely that the officers that respond will be employed by a local government.

PROSECUTION At the national level, the U.S. District Attorneys are responsible for the prosecution of federal cases within their respective jurisdictions. The numbers of cases that they prosecute are a mere fraction of those dealt with by state-level prosecutors. Depending on the state in which they serve, these prosecutors (known as District Attorneys or State's Attorneys) may deal only with violations of state laws, or they may also be responsible for enforcing local ordinances within their jurisdictions. In many states, local ordinances (as well as lesser state offenses delegated to them by the state legislatures) may be prosecuted by local attorneys (either the city attorney, an assistant city attorney, or a local attorney employed part-time), often known as solicitors. In many jurisdictions, this responsibility may actually extend to the police officers who made the arrests or issued the citations.

ADJUDICATION At every level within the U.S. justice system, trial courts exist to adjudicate the cases within their respective jurisdictions. Ninety-four district courts try federal cases within the 50 states and territories. State trial courts of general jurisdiction try violations of state laws and civil cases within their judicial circuits or districts. These courts also try cases that are transferred or appealed from lower courts. Courts of appeal exist at both the state and federal levels. The U.S. Supreme Court is the highest court of appeal in America. While these courts are the ones that receive the greatest amount of media attention, it is in the courts of limited jurisdiction in which the vast majority of cases are tried. These courts may be lower-level state courts assigned to try lesser offenses and ordinance violations for the counties and municipalities within their area, or they may be separate county or municipal courts operated by those governmental entities. It is within these courts that the previously discussed "assembly line" may be found, with dozens of cases being tried within a single session.

CORRECTIONS Correctional institutions exist at every level within the U.S. system. Federal prisons of every security category house convicted prisoners. State courts do the same. Municipal and county jails house prisoners awaiting trial, convicted prisoners awaiting sentencing, convicted prisoners awaiting transfer to state or federal facilities, and prisoners convicted of lesser crimes and ordinance violations. Community corrections programs are also found at every governmental level. Due to their costs, many counties and municipalities use private correctional organizations to provide community supervision. Local police agencies may find themselves supervising offenders assigned to community service and/or inmate work programs.

THE CRIMINAL JUSTICE SYSTEM

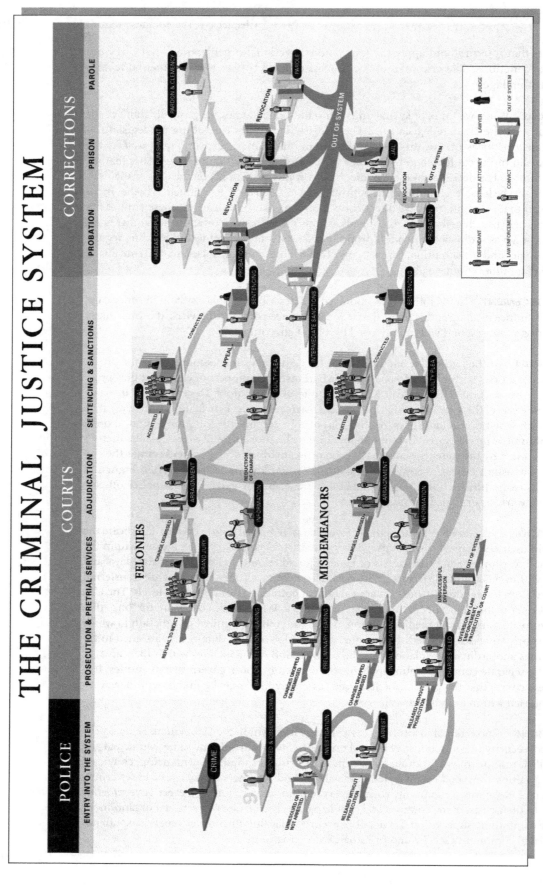

FIGURE 1.4 The Criminal Justice Process in the United States.

Source: www.ojp.usdoj.gov/bjs/flowchart.htm#efiles.

THE STRUCTURE OF THE POLICE SYSTEM IN AMERICA

In America, we have many important police organizations at the state and national levels. However, we are actually a nation of local police forces. There are approximately 18,760 separate police agencies in the United States, with approximately 940,275 employees and a combined annual budget of about $51 billion. As noted earlier, the Tenth Amendment of the Constitution reserves police powers to the states, and both **federalism** and American tradition have resulted in a fragmented police structure at lower levels of government; this fragmentation is exemplified by the separation of local police into four levels: municipal, township, county, and special districts.

Count totals are further compounded by problems of classification at the local level. Some local governments are true municipalities, while others are classified as townships or villages that may or may not have qualifying police agencies. There are a surprisingly large number of housing districts and transit authorities in the United States (34,684 at last count), which obviously do not all consider themselves as having their own police agencies. A large number of independent school districts also exist (13,726), which are independent of any other government authority, and can have or not have their own police agency. Many colleges and universities, both public and private, have their own police departments, although there is a tendency to not count the private college agencies. With multibranch campuses, the problem becomes one of whether you count the police agency at every academic site as a separate police agency. Railway police agencies are generally counted at the county level, but hospital, port, airport, and tunnel police agencies are often counted at the municipal level. Tribal police agencies also exist at many of the nation's 567 federally recognized reservations, and it is unclear if they should be considered state, county, or local police (O'Conner, 2006).

Federal Police Agencies

By including all units that have arrest and firearm authority, there are approximately 100 different federal police agencies. The largest agencies are formally located within the Justice and the Treasury Departments. Since the creation of the Department of Homeland Security, several agencies have been moved (see Box 1.5).

DEPARTMENT OF TREASURY AGENCIES   The Treasury Department was established in 1789, and its enforcement function revolves around the collection of revenue. Its four primary law enforcement agencies were the Bureau of Alcohol, Tobacco, and Firearms; the U.S. Customs Service; the Internal Revenue Service; and the U.S. Secret Service. With the creation of the Department of Homeland Security on November 25, 2002, three of these large agencies were transferred from the Treasury Department: The U.S. Secret Service and the U.S. Customs

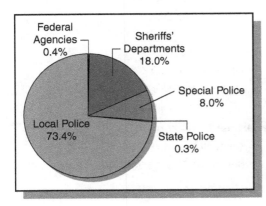

FIGURE 1.5   Public Law Enforcement Agencies in the United States (From approximately 18,760 federal, state, and local law enforcement agencies).

Sources: O'Conner (2006); Reaves and Bauer (2002); and Reaves and Hickman (2003).

BOX 1.5
Federal Law Enforcement Agencies

Administrative Office of the U.S. Courts
  Federal Corrections Supervision Division

Amtrak Police

Central Intelligence Agency
  Office of Security

Civil Aeronautics Board

Department of Agriculture
  Office of Inspector General
  U.S. Forest Service
  Division of Law Enforcement and Investigations

Department of Commerce
  Bureau of Industry and Security
    Office of Export Enforcement
  National Institute of Standards and Technology
    Office of Security
  National Oceanic & Atmospheric Administration,
    National Marine Fisheries Service
    Office of Law Enforcement
  Office of Inspector General

Department of Defense
  Defense Criminal Investigative Service
  National Security Agency
  Office of Inspector General
  Pentagon Force Protection Agency
  U.S. Air Force
    Office of Security Police
    Office of Special Investigations
  U.S. Army
    Criminal Investigation Command
    Intelligence and Security Command
    Military Police Corps
    Provost Marshall
  U.S. Marine Corps
    Military Police
  U.S. Navy
    Naval Criminal Investigative Service

Department of Education
  Office of Inspector General

Department of Energy
  Transportation Safeguards Division

Department of Health and Human Services
  Food & Drug Administration
    Office of Criminal Investigation
  National Institutes of Health
    Division of Public Safety
  Office of Inspector General

Department of Homeland Security
  Customs and Border Protection
    Border Patrol
  Federal Emergency Management Agency
    Security Division
  Immigration and Customs Enforcement
    Federal Protective Service
  Transportation Security Administration
  U.S. Coast Guard
    Intelligence and Law Enforcement Branch
  U.S. Secret Service
    Uniformed Division

Department of Housing and Urban Development
  Fair Housing and Equal Opportunity Division
  Office of Inspector General

Department of the Interior
  Bureau of Indian Affairs
    Division of Law Enforcement Services
  Bureau of Land Management
    Office of Enforcement
  Bureau of Reclamation
    Hoover Dam Police
  National Park Service
    Division of Ranger Activities & Protection
    U.S. Park Police
  Office of Inspector General
  U.S. Fish and Wildlife Service
    Division of Law Enforcement

Department of Justice
  Antitrust Division
  Bureau of Alcohol, Tobacco, Firearms, and Explosives

(continued)

Bureau of Prisons
Civil Rights Division
Drug Enforcement Administration
Federal Bureau of Investigation
Office of Inspector General
U.S. Marshals Service

Department of Labor
Occupational Safety and Health Administration
Office of Inspector General
Office of Labor-Management Standards

Department of State
Bureau of Diplomatic Security, Diplomatic
   Security Service
Bureau of Diplomatic Security, Protective
   Liaison Division
Office of Inspector General

Department of Transportation
Federal Aviation Administration, Police
Office of Inspector General

Department of the Treasury
Bureau of Engraving and Printing, U.S. Mint Police
Internal Revenue Service
   Criminal Investigation Division
   Inspection Service
   Office of Inspector General
   Office of the Regional Inspector

Department of Veterans Affairs
Office of Inspector General
Veterans Health Administration
   Office of Security and Law Enforcement

Environmental Protection Agency
Office of Criminal Investigations
Office of Inspector General

Federal Communications Commission

Federal Maritime Commission

Federal Trade Commission

General Services Administration
Office of Inspector General

Interstate Commerce Commission

Library of Congress
Police

National Aeronautics and Space Administration
Office of Inspector General

Nuclear Regulatory Commission
Office of Enforcement

Office of Personnel Management
Compliance and Investigations Group
Office of Inspector General

Securities and Exchange Commission
Division of Enforcement

Smithsonian Institution
National Zoological Park Police
Office of Protection Services

Social Security Administration
Office of Inspector General

Tennessee Valley Authority
Office of Inspector General
Public Safety Service

U.S. Capitol Police

U.S. Government Printing Office
Police

U.S. Mint
Police

U.S. Postal Service
Postal Inspection Service
Postal Security Force

U.S. Supreme Court Police

Sources: Barker, Hunter, and Rush (1994); Conser et al. (2005, pp. 91–92); Fuller (2005, p. 164); Reaves and Bauer (2003); and federal agency Web sites.

Service are now located within the Department of Homeland Security, and the Bureau of Alcohol, Tobacco, and Firearms is now located within the Department of Justice. While there are some smaller units that continue to have law enforcement authority, the only large federal police agency remaining within the Treasury Department is the Internal Revenue Service, which employs approximately 2,855 federal officers (Reaves and Bauer, 2003).

DEPARTMENT OF JUSTICE AGENCIES   The Justice Department was created in 1870 and is responsible for enforcing laws passed by the U.S. Congress (federal crimes). The largest Justice Department agency is the Bureau of Prisons. Since this is primarily a corrections organization, we will not discuss it. Other justice units having law enforcement authority are the Antitrust Division, the Civil Rights Division, and the Office of Inspector General. The organization of the Department of Justice is displayed in Figure 1.6. The four primary law enforcement agencies within the department are the Bureau of Alcohol, Tobacco, Firearms and Explosives; the Drug Enforcement Administration; the U.S. Marshals Service; and the FBI.

Bureau of Alcohol, Tobacco, Firearms and Explosives.   The Bureau of Alcohol, Tobacco, Firearms and Explosives (ATF) performs the dual responsibilities of enforcing federal criminal laws and regulating the firearms and explosives industries. ATF's duties are to investigate and reduce crime involving firearms and explosives, acts of arson, and illegal trafficking of alcohol and tobacco products. Effective January 24, 2003, the Bureau of Alcohol, Tobacco, and Firearms (ATF) was transferred under the Homeland Security bill to the Department of Justice. The law enforcement functions of ATF under the Department of the Treasury were transferred to the Department of Justice. The tax and trade functions of the former ATF remained in the Treasury

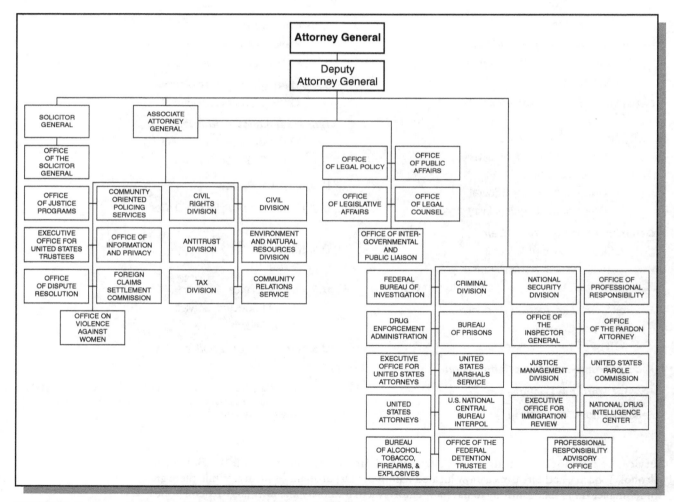

FIGURE 1.6   Organizational Chart of the U.S. Department of Justice.

Source: www.usdoj.gov/dojorg.htm.

Department with a new Alcohol and Tobacco Tax and Trade Bureau. At the time of its transfer to the Department of Justice, the agency's name was changed to the Bureau of Alcohol, Tobacco, Firearms and Explosives (ATF) to reflect its new mission in the Department of Justice.

In order to accomplish its mission, the Bureau of Alcohol, Tobacco, Firearms and Explosives works with local law enforcement to identify, arrest, and prosecute the most violent criminals in designated cities. ATF investigates fire and explosives incidents throughout the United States. ATF is also responsible for enforcing federal criminal laws relating to alcohol and tobacco diversion and trafficking. In addition, ATF's investigative efforts are directed at reducing the source of funding to criminal and terrorist organizations, and stemming the loss of revenue to affected states and the federal government.

Drug Enforcement Administration.   The Drug Enforcement Administration (DEA) was created in 1973 with the merger of the Bureau of Narcotics and Dangerous Drugs with several other federal drug regulation and investigative agencies. It is currently one of the larger federal law enforcement agencies, with 10,894 employees of which 5,296 are special agents. The mission of the DEA is to enforce the controlled substances laws and regulations of the United States and bring to the criminal and civil justice systems of the United States, or any other competent jurisdiction, those organizations and principal members of organizations involved in the growing, manufacture, or distribution of controlled substances appearing in or destined for illicit traffic in the United States; and to recommend and support nonenforcement programs aimed at reducing the availability of illicit controlled substances on the domestic and international markets (Drug Enforcement Administration, 2006).

In carrying out its mission as the agency responsible for enforcing the controlled substances laws and regulations of the United States, the DEA's primary responsibilities include:

Investigation and preparation for the prosecution of major violators of controlled substance laws operating at interstate and international levels.

Investigation and preparation for prosecution of criminals and drug gangs who perpetrate violence in our communities and terrorize citizens through fear and intimidation.

Management of a national drug intelligence program in cooperation with federal, state, local, and foreign officials to collect, analyze, and disseminate strategic and operational drug intelligence information.

Seizure and forfeiture of assets derived from, traceable to, or intended to be used for illicit drug trafficking.

Enforcement of the provisions of the Controlled Substances Act as they pertain to the manufacture, distribution, and dispensing of legally produced controlled substances.

Coordination and cooperation with federal, state, and local law enforcement officials on mutual drug enforcement efforts and enhancement of such efforts through exploitation of potential interstate and international investigations beyond local or limited federal jurisdictions and resources.

Coordination and cooperation with federal, state, and local agencies, and with foreign governments, in programs designed to reduce the availability of illicit abuse-type drugs on the U.S. market through nonenforcement methods such as crop eradication, crop substitution, and training of foreign officials.

Responsibility, under the policy guidance of the Secretary of State and U.S. Ambassadors, for all programs associated with drug law enforcement counterparts in foreign countries.

Liaison with the United Nations, Interpol, and other organizations on matters relating to international drug control programs.

U.S. Marshals Service.   The U.S. Marshals Service is the oldest federal law enforcement agency, having been created by Congress in 1789. While the 94 U.S. Marshals are appointed by the president and approved by Congress, in 1969, the agency's regulations, training, and duties were standardized to ensure uniformity and professionalism among its offices. The Marshals Service is one of the more diverse law enforcement agencies, with a variety of duties that once included conducting the U.S. Census. Today, the U.S. Marshals Service is responsible for apprehending fugitives, protecting federal judges and courts, managing and selling seized assets, transporting prisoners, managing prisoners, protecting witnesses, and serving court documents (United States Marshals Service, 2006).

Federal Bureau of Investigation.   The Federal Bureau of Investigation (FBI) is the primary investigative agency of the federal government and arguably the most famous of the federal law enforcement agencies. The primary responsibility of the FBI is to investigate violations of federal criminal law and to assist local and state agencies in investigations. These include crimes such as kidnapping, bank robbery, art and cultural property crime, jewelry and gem theft; white-collar crime, and organized crime. The FBI is also responsible for investigating corporate fraud, health care fraud, mortgage fraud, identity theft, insurance fraud, telemarketing fraud, Internet fraud, and money laundering.

In addition to the above crimes, the FBI is engaged in counterterrorism activities, counter-intelligence activities, and cyber crime investigations (including stopping those behind serious computer intrusions and the spread of malicious code as well as identifying and thwarting online sexual predators who use the Internet to meet and exploit children and produce, share, or possess child pornography). The FBI also counteracts operations that target U.S. intellectual property and endanger national security and competitiveness.

The FBI's other duties include investigating public corruption at all levels of government; investigating all allegations regarding violations of applicable federal civil rights laws (its Civil Rights program consists of the following subprograms: Hate Crimes, Color of Law/Police Misconduct, Involuntary Servitude/Slavery, and Freedom of Access to Clinic Entrances); and suppressing violent street gangs, motorcycle gangs, and prison gangs. In addition, the FBI has federal law enforcement responsibility on more than 200 of the nation's 267 Indian reservations.

DEPARTMENT OF HOMELAND SECURITY AGENCIES   The Department of Homeland Security was created on November 25, 2002, in an effort to better coordinate efforts to protect the United States from terrorism. Twenty-two federal agencies were either created or transferred into what immediately became the largest federal justice organization. The organizational chart for the Department of Homeland Security is displayed in Figure 1.7. The largest agencies transferred into the Department of Homeland Security were the U.S. Secret Service and the U.S. Customs Service (from the Treasury Department), the Immigration and Naturalization Service and U.S. Border Patrol (from the Department of Justice), the Federal Emergency Management Agency (formerly independent), and the Transportation Security Administration and the U.S. Coast Guard (from the Department of Transportation).

Customs and Border Protection.   U.S. Customs and Border Protection (CBP) is the unified border agency within the Department of Homeland Security (DHS). CBP combined the inspectional workforces and broad border authorities of U.S. Customs, U.S. Immigration, Animal and Plant Health Inspection Service, and the entire U.S. Border Patrol. CBP includes more than 41,000 employees to manage, control, and protect the nation's borders, at and between the official ports of entry. CBP's priority mission is preventing terrorists and terrorist weapons from entering the United States while also facilitating the flow of legitimate trade and travel.

U.S. Customs and Border Protection assesses all passengers flying into the United States from abroad for terrorist risk. The CBP regularly refuses entry to people who may pose a threat to the security of our country. This was not a focus prior to 9/11, but a shift in priorities and the formation of U.S. Customs and Border Protection have made this the top priority of the agency: keeping terrorists and terrorist weapons out of the country (Bureau of Customs and Border Protection, 2006).

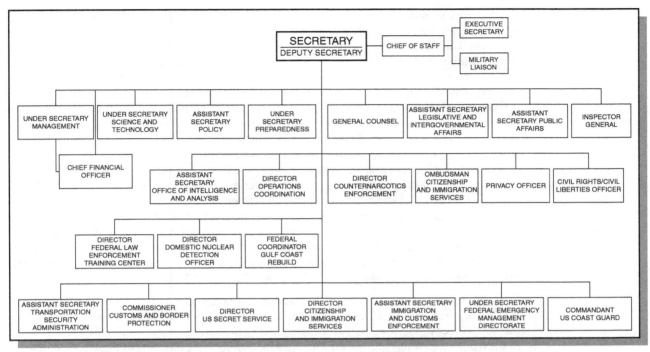

FIGURE 1.7 **Organizational Chart of the Department of Homeland Security.**

Source: Department of Homeland Security (2006).

Immigration and Customs Enforcement.   Created in March 2003, the Immigration and Customs Enforcement (ICE) is the largest investigative branch of the Department of Homeland Security (DHS). The agency was created after 9/11, by combining the law enforcement arms of the former Immigration and Naturalization Service (INS) and the former U.S. Customs Service to more effectively enforce immigration and customs laws and to protect the United States against terrorist attacks. ICE does this by targeting illegal immigrants: the people, money, and materials that support terrorism and other criminal activities.

The ICE mission is to protect America and uphold public safety. ICE attempts to fulfill this mission by identifying criminal activities and eliminating vulnerabilities that pose a threat to our nation's borders, as well as enforcing economic, transportation, and infrastructure security. ICE seeks to eliminate the potential threat of terrorist acts against the United States, creating a host of new systems to better address national security threats and to detect potential terrorist activities in the United States (Bureau of Immigration and Customs Enforcement, 2006).

Transportation Security Administration.   The Transportation Security Administration (TSA) was created in response to the terrorist attacks of September 11, 2001, as part of the Aviation and Transportation Security Act that was signed into law by President George W. Bush on November 19, 2001. TSA was originally in the Department of Transportation but was moved to the Department of Homeland Security in March 2003.

TSA's mission is to protect the nation's transportation systems by ensuring the freedom of movement for people and commerce. In February 2002, TSA assumed responsibility for security at the nation's airports and by the end of the year had deployed a federal workforce to meet congressional deadlines for screening all passengers and baggage (Transportation Security Administration, 2006).

The U.S. Coast Guard.   The U.S. Coast Guard is a military, multimission, maritime service and may be considered one of the nation's five armed services. Its mission is to protect the public, the environment, and U.S. economic interests—in the nation's ports and waterways, along the coast, on international waters, or in any maritime region as required to support national security.

Its numerous cutters, aircraft, and boats carry out these functions. In wartime, the Coast Guard operates under the aegis of the U.S. Navy.

The U.S. Coast Guard is the nation's leading maritime law enforcement agency and has broad, multifaceted jurisdictional authority. The specific statutory authority for the Coast Guard Law Enforcement mission is given in 14 USC 2, "The Coast Guard shall enforce or assist in the enforcement of all applicable laws on, under and over the high seas and waters subject to the jurisdiction of the United States." In addition, 14 USC 89 provides the authority for U.S. Coast Guard active duty commissioned, warrant, and petty officers to enforce applicable U.S. law. It authorizes Coast Guard personnel to enforce federal law on waters subject to U.S. jurisdiction and in international waters, as well as on all vessels subject to U.S. jurisdiction.

The Coast Guard is responsible for protecting the U.S. Exclusive Economic Zone from foreign encroachment, enforcing domestic fisheries law, and developing and enforcing international fisheries agreements. It is the lead federal agency for maritime drug interdiction and shares lead responsibility for air interdiction with the U.S. Customs Service. As such, it is a key player in combating the flow of illegal drugs to the United States. The Coast Guard is also tasked with enforcing immigration law at sea. It conducts patrols and coordinates with other federal agencies and foreign countries to interdict undocumented migrants at sea, denying them entry via maritime routes to the United States, its territories, and possessions (United States Coast Guard, 2006).

U.S. Secret Service.   The U.S. Secret Service Division began on July 5, 1865, in Washington, D.C., to suppress counterfeit currency. In 1867, Secret Service responsibilities were broadened to include "detecting persons perpetrating frauds against the government." This appropriation resulted in investigations into the Ku Klux Klan, nonconforming distillers, smugglers, mail robbers, land frauds, and a number of other infractions against the federal laws. In 1902, the Secret Service assumed full-time responsibility for protection of the president. In the years since, Secret Service protections have been extended to include former presidents, the president's family, candidates for president, the president-elect, and the vice president.

The passing of the Patriot Act in 2001 (Public Law 107-56) increased the Secret Service's role in investigating fraud and related activity in connection with computers. In addition, it authorized the Director of the Secret Service to establish nationwide electronic crimes task forces to assist law enforcement, private sector, and academia in detecting and suppressing computer-based crime; increased the statutory penalties for the manufacturing, possession, dealing, and passing of counterfeit U.S. or foreign obligations; and allowed enforcement action to be taken to protect American financial payment systems while combating transnational financial crimes directed by terrorists or other criminals. In March 2003, the Secret Service was transferred from the Department of the Treasury to the Department of Homeland Security (United States Secret Service, 2006).

Uniformed Division.   The Secret Service Uniformed Division, initially a force comprised of a few members of the military and the Metropolitan Police Department, began formalized protection of the White House and its grounds in 1860. This unit was under the direction of the White House Military Aide until 1922 when President Warren G. Harding prompted the establishment of a White House police force.

In 1930, Congress placed the supervision of the White House police under the direction of the Chief of the Secret Service. In 1970, Public Law 91-217 expanded the role of the White House police, newly named the Executive Protective Service, to include protection of diplomatic missions in the Washington, D.C., area. Congress later added the protection of the vice president's immediate family as an Executive Protective Service's responsibility in 1974. After several name revisions, the force officially adopted its current name, the United States Secret Service Uniformed Division in 1977. While protection of the White House complex remains its primary mission, the Uniformed Division's responsibilities have expanded greatly over the years.

It now protects the following: the White House complex, the main treasury building and annex, and other presidential offices; the president and members of the immediate family; the temporary official residence of the vice president in the District of Columbia; the vice president and members of the immediate family; and foreign diplomatic missions in the Washington, D.C., metropolitan area, and throughout the United States and its territories and possessions, as prescribed by statute (United States Secret Service, 2006).

STATE POLICE AGENCIES   In the United States, state police are a police body unique to each state, having statewide authority to conduct law enforcement activities and criminal investigations. State police agencies exist in some form in all U.S. states except Hawaii. In general, they perform functions outside the normal purview of the city police or the county sheriff, such as enforcing traffic laws on state highway and interstate expressways, overseeing the security of the state capitol complex, protecting the governor, training new officers for local police forces too small to operate an academy, providing technological and scientific support services, and helping to coordinate multijurisdictional task force activity in serious or complicated cases.

Twenty-three states actually call their state police by the term "State Police." In this case, state police are general-power law enforcement officers with statewide jurisdiction who conduct patrols and respond to calls for service and perform all the other aforementioned duties. These states are Alaska, Arkansas, Delaware, Idaho, Illinois, Indiana, Kentucky, Louisiana, Maine, Maryland, Massachusetts, Michigan, New Hampshire, New Jersey, New Mexico, New York, Oregon, Pennsylvania, Rhode Island, Vermont, Virginia, and West Virginia.

In the other 25 states (Alabama, Arizona, Connecticut, California, Colorado, Florida, Georgia, Iowa, Kansas, Minnesota, Mississippi, Missouri, Montana, Nebraska, Nevada, North Carolina, North Dakota, Ohio, Oklahoma, South Carolina, South Dakota, Tennessee, Texas, Utah, Wisconsin, and Wyoming) the state police are limited-function traffic enforcement agencies known by any of the following: State Highway Patrol, Highway Patrol, State Patrol State Troopers, or Department of Public Safety. These agencies are usually complemented by limited-function investigative agencies. Examples of such and their divergent names are the Arizona Criminal Investigations Bureau, Colorado Bureau of Investigation, Florida Department of Law Enforcement, Minnesota Bureau of Criminal Apprehension, Mississippi Criminal Investigation Bureau, North Carolina State Bureau of Investigation, Ohio Bureau of Criminal Identification and Investigation, the Oklahoma State Bureau of Narcotics and Dangerous Drugs, South Carolina State Law Enforcement Division, Texas Rangers, and the Utah Bureau of Organized Crime and Criminal Information.

There are also many other special-purpose state police agencies, such as those devoted to wildlife, fire, and alcoholic beverage control. Regional special-purpose task forces (e.g., for drug, gang, or terrorist control) exist at all levels of government. New task forces are constantly being created and old ones eliminated based on changes in criminal activity, political expediency, and/or available resources. States that have highway patrols rather than general-service state police have tended to create investigative agencies patterned after the FBI to investigate violations of specific state laws and to assist local law enforcement agencies in complex or multicounty investigations (Conser et al., 2005; O'Conner, 2006).

County Law Enforcement

When people think of county law enforcement, they usually think of a sheriff's office, and there are about 3,100 sheriffs in the United States (Reaves and Hickman, 2002). Most of them are elected officials who exercise political control and influence and go to a county board for money. Some counties (like Orleans Parish in Louisiana) have two sheriffs: one criminal and the other civil. Sheriffs, in general, have other duties besides law enforcement, such as running a jail, collecting taxes, serving papers, and courthouse security. A contract system also exists where cities contract with the sheriff's office for police services.

Not all counties have sheriff's offices. In many states, the larger counties have county police departments run by a chief of police. In some metropolitan areas, city and county departments have been consolidated. When such cases occur, there are usually funding problems in continuing to maintain the sheriff's office, the workload becomes too much for the sheriff, or county officials want to exert more power over law enforcement. Some counties have both a sheriff's office and a county police department. In those counties, the sheriff's departments focus on running the

TABLE 1.1 State and Local Law Enforcement Agencies in the United States

Type of Agency	Number of State and Local Law Enforcement Agencies, June 2000
Total	17,784
Local Police	12,666
Sheriff	3,070
Primary State	49
Special Jurisdiction	1,376
Texas Constable	623

Source: Adapted from Reaves and Hickman (2002).

jails and serving civil process and warrants in a manner similar to those states that have general-service state police agencies (O'Conner, 2006).

Municipal Police

There are more municipal police departments (approximately 13,000) in the United States than any other kind of agency (Reaves and Hickman, 2002). This number includes transit, school, and housing police. There are about 800 departments that have only one officer, but NYPD is in a class by itself with about 40,000 regular officers and 13,000 special-purpose transit, school, and housing officers. A complete list of all "special-purpose" police agencies would include animal cruelty, beach, harbor, hospital, housing, port, railroad, sanitation, school, transit, and transportation authorities. These are usually separate municipal-level agencies and should not be confused with specialized units belonging to a single department, such as airborne, band, bicycle, bomb, D.A.R.E., detective, forensics, gang, graffiti, HAZMAT, intelligence, internal affairs, K9, marine, motorcycle, mounted, narcotics, operations, organized crime, sex crimes, SWAT, or traffic.

The vast majority of municipal departments are small, having 10 or fewer officers. The great number of these "micro" agencies helps keep the average size of all police departments in the United States around 25 sworn officers, not counting civilians, a measure of police strength (counting the civilians is a measure of professional growth). Larger, "macro" agencies with 1,000 officers or more usually have many specialized units. More "medium"- to "large"-size agencies with 26–999 (average 150) officers usually maintain extensive order/maintenance functions, assigned to municipal "peacekeeping" agencies in general.

TABLE 1.2 Ten Largest Police Departments by Number of Full-Time Sworn Personnel

Agency	Number of Sworn Officers, June 2000
New York City	40,435
Chicago	13,466
Los Angeles	9,341
Philadelphia	7,024
Houston	5,343
Detroit	4,154
Washington, D.C.	3,612
Nassau Co. (NY)	3,038
Baltimore	3,034
Miami-Dade Co.	3,008

Source: Adapted from Reaves and Hickman (2002).

WHERE THE POLICE "FIT" WITHIN THE U.S. JUSTICE SYSTEM

Where the police fit within the U.S. system of justice depends on who is making the determination. Americans are rightly jealous of their civil liberties, and allowing designated persons to have the authority to make arrests and carry firearms makes many people uneasy. For these reasons, police officers live in "glass houses." They are held to higher moral standards, and their professional actions are scrutinized on a daily basis by the legal community as well as laypersons. How the police are regarded is often influenced by factors over which they have little or no control.

Many citizens tend to view the police as heroes who risk their lives to protect and serve the public. These views are reinforced on those occasions when an officer actually loses his or her life while on duty. There are many others who see the police as abusive and corrupt villains who help maintain an unjust society. Unfortunately, these views are reinforced whenever a corrupt or brutal action on the part of a police officer becomes public knowledge. Fortunately, more enlightened citizens tend to view police officers as ordinary people doing a demanding, often thankless, and occasionally dangerous job.

The roles assigned to various police agencies affect how they are perceived. Local law enforcement agencies have the greater impact on the lives of larger portions of the populace than do state and federal officers. They also tend to be held in less awe than officers at the state and federal levels. How police officers are perceived is also determined by their roles. State and federal agencies generally perform duties that are considered "law enforcement" more than do local police agencies. At the local level, crime fighting is only a portion of a patrol officer's duties. Order maintenance and service responsibilities take up most of his or her time.

Because of their diverse duties, local agencies often have officers with the least experience, education, and training exercising greater discretion and performing some of the more challenging and dangerous duties. This is just one of the realities of police work. Another reality is that the nature of police work will naturally lead to conflict with certain groups of people. Civil libertarians, social activists, trial lawyers, and journalists will always provide challenges for the police. Members of the lower and working classes, young people, and ethnic minorities also provide challenges due to cultural factors as well as social and civil justice issues independent of the police.

The police are necessary for the success of the criminal justice system. As such, they are also vital to the stability of society as a whole. How well they perform as individual officers and as police organizations is determined by many issues that will be discussed within subsequent chapters. As we begin this journey, we wish to address four factors that will ultimately determine where the police fit within the administration of justice in the United States. These factors may be referred to as the *"Four C's" of police–community relations*. They are as follows:

Communication between the police and their communities must be two-way and continuous.

Cooperation between the police and their communities is crucial for success.

Competition between the police and their constituents is detrimental to success. And,

Complacency leads to corruption and cannot be tolerated.

BOX 1.6
To Protect and Serve

Perhaps the most commonly used cliché regarding police work is "to protect and serve." Along with the American flag, this adage may be found on police and sheriff's stationery, logos, and vehicles across the United States. If you wish to engage in an interesting classroom discussion, ask the following questions: Who is being protected? How are they being protected? Who are they being protected from? You will find that the responses are no longer so common. Then ask the following: Who is being served? How are they being served? And lastly, are the services rendered the same for every police organization? We think that you will find that once you move beyond the jargon, there is not as much agreement or understanding as one would suppose.

REALITY CHECK

The Murder of Derwin Brown

Police Captain Derwin Brown was a 23-year veteran of the DeKalb Police Department when he was elected to the position of Sheriff of DeKalb County, Georgia. The sheriff in DeKalb County runs the largest jail in the South, with a budget of $51 million. Brown had run on a platform of cleaning up the corruption and graft that had historically troubled the DeKalb Sheriff's Department. During the period between his election and his assuming office, Brown had announced plans to fire 38 jail employees, most of them appointed by the incumbent sheriff Sidney Dorsey. He had also vowed to conduct an investigation into allegations of racketeering and corruption on the part of Sidney Dorsey and many of his subordinates.

On the evening of December 15, 2000, Brown was shot in front of his home. He was hit 11 times with bullets fired from a Tec-9 handgun and died on the scene. For nearly a year, the investigation stalled and sputtered. But on November 30, 2001, investigators charged three men with his murder. The arrests came just days after former deputy Patrick Cuffy agreed to cooperate and pleaded guilty to a lesser charge in an unrelated shootout at his home in March that left one man dead. Cuffy and Paul Skyers—who worked for a security company owned by incumbent DeKalb County Sheriff Sidney Dorsey—told investigators that they and two other men spent several Friday nights rehearsing Brown's killing, making practice runs to the neighborhood to prepare for the attack and the getaway.

According to Cuffy and Skyers, they had drawn straws with ex-deputy Melvin Walker and David Isaiah Ramsey to determine who would be the triggerman. Walker drew the short straw. On the night of the assassination, Walker stepped from the shadows and opened fire with a Tec-9 semiautomatic pistol. Even more compelling was that Cuffy and Skyers told investigators the men took their orders from Sidney Dorsey, who was angry about losing the election to Brown. Cuffy told investigators that Dorsey had a hit list that included a district attorney and at least four others, and that Dorsey promised the men promotions and jobs if they helped him.

In an acrimonious trial, attorneys for Walker and Ramsey denied that the defendants had anything to do with Brown's death. They accused Cuffy and Skyers of concocting lies about their clients and Dorsey's involvement in order to avoid prosecution for a murder that they themselves actually committed. On March 25, 2002, Walker and Ramsey were acquitted. Dorsey's supporters hailed the verdicts as a victory and predicted that Dorsey would also be acquitted. The district attorney stated that he would honor the immunity deals that he had made with Cuffy and Skyers.

On June 10, 2002, the murder trial of Sidney Dorsey began. The trial was moved to Albany, Georgia, due to pretrial publicity. Jury selection was completed on June 14, 2002. Over the next four weeks, a bizarre story of corruption, extortion, racketeering, thefts, coerced sex, bribery, and misuse of office would emerge. The prosecution would present Sidney Dorsey as a bitter man who had sought revenge against the man who had defeated him and who also wanted to obstruct Brown's expected probe into corruption that occurred during his own tenure as sheriff.

During the trial, the jury learned that Dorsey routinely used deputies to conduct his personal business. He was said to have required deputies to work for his private security business while on duty. He coerced female subordinates and females seeking business contracts with the Sheriff's Department to have sex with him. He had employees run personal errands, including delivering "happy meals" to his son at school and driving his daughter to and from Tennessee, as well as driving family members on a Florida vacation. He also required employees to perform legal work for him and a woman with whom he was having a sexual relationship. According to District Attorney J. Tom Morgan, once he had proven to the jury that Dorsey was a thief, it was much easier to convince them that he was also a murderer.

On July 10, 2002, nearly 19 months after Derwin Brown's death, Sidney Dorsey was convicted of ordering Brown's assassination, two counts of racketeering, one count of violation of oath of office, and eight counts of theft by taking. He was sentenced to life in prison for the murder of

Derwin Brown and an additional 23 years for the other convictions. On May 12, 2004, Dorsey's attorney appealed his convictions. On July 1, 2005, the Georgia Supreme Court upheld the murder and racketeering charges against Dorsey.

On March 30, 2004, Melvin Walker and David Ramsey were indicted on federal civil rights charges of "depriving Derwin Brown of his life without due process of law" as well as gun possession charges. Their federal trial began on July 8, 2005. On August 3, 2005, Walker and Ramsey were convicted on all charges. On November 21, 2005, Walker and Ramsey were each sentenced to life in prison with no chance of parole.

Conclusions

Nations must demonstrate to their citizens that they are able to provide justice in order for their governments to survive. While we may not feel that the justice systems of many nations are actually "just," they must not become too abusive or revolution will occur. Human rights and civil liberties are interpreted differently among the nations of the world. The Western democracies and the United States in particular have justice systems based on the protection of civil liberties that utilize due process of law to deprive individuals of their lives, liberties, and properties. The mission of the U.S. justice system is to provide protection from crime and maintain social stability while respecting individual rights. Compliance with the rule of law, equity, fairness, accessibility, effectiveness, and oversight is a fundamental component in achieving justice. We also noted that in order to administer criminal justice, nations must also promote social and civil justice.

The administration of justice in the United States is further complicated by the common-law traditions of individual liberties, rule of law, and an adversarial legal system. These due process considerations make crime control more difficult for the United States than in other nations. The federalist system also complicates the administration of justice in America. The impacts of federalism and the common-law tradition are felt within all components of the U.S. system of justice. They have particular impacts on the structure and practices of America's police. They also influence where and how the police fit within the U.S. justice system.

Student Checklist

1. Understand why debates regarding the meaning of justice are relevant to students of the police.
2. Why should the police be concerned about protecting the civil rights of American citizens?
3. Explain the impact of the Civil Rights Act of 1871 on actions of police in America.
4. Describe the functions of a justice system in addition to providing "law and order."
5. Describe how the common law system of justice differs from other justice systems.
6. Provide an overview of how America's police system is structured.
7. Identify the more important federal police agencies and describe their responsibilities.
8. Describe how the police "fit" within the U.S. justice system.
9. Explain why the "Four C's" are relevant to police–community relations.

Topics For Discussion

1. Discuss the impact of the U.N.'s Declaration of Human Rights on the nations of the world.
2. Why must students of the police in America understand the importance of the Bill of Rights?
3. Should police officers in America be held criminally liable for violations of citizens' civil liberties?
4. Would the United States be better served by a more centralized system of policing, such as that found in other Western democracies?
5. Has the creation of the Department of Homeland Security enhanced or hindered the coordination of federal law enforcement efforts?

Bibliography

Barker, T., Hunter, R. D., and Rush, J. P. (1994). *Police Systems and Practices*. Upper Saddle River, NJ: Pearson/Prentice Hall.

Bohm, R. M., and Haley, K. N. (2005). *Introduction to Criminal Justice*, 4th ed. Boston, MA: McGraw-Hill.

Bureau of Customs and Border Protection. (2006). www.cbp.gov

Bureau of Immigration and Customs Enforcement. (2006). www.bice.immigration.gov

Bureau of Justice Statistics. (2006). www.ojp.usdoj.gov/bjs/

Cole, D. (2004). *No Equal Justice: Race and Class in the American Justice System*. New York: The New Press.

Conser, J. A., Russell, G. D., Paynich, R., and Gingerich, T. E. (2005). *Law Enforcement in the United States*, 2nd ed. Sudbury, MA: Jones and Bartlett.

Crank, J. P. (2003). *Imagining Justice*. Cincinnati, OH: Anderson Publishing.

Dammer, H. R., Fairchild, E., and Albanese, J. S. (2006). *Comparative Criminal Justice Systems*, 3rd ed. Belmont, CA: Thomson/Wadsworth.

Department of Homeland Security. (2006). www.dhs.gov

Drug Enforcement Administration. (2006). www.usdoj.gov/dea

Federal Bureau of Investigation. (2006). www.fbi.gov/hq.htm

Fiorina, M. P., Peterson, P. E., Johnson, B., and Voss, D. S. (2005). *The New American Democracy*, 4th ed. New York: Pearson/Longman.

Fuller, J. R. (2005). *Criminal Justice: Mainstreams and Crossroads*. Upper Saddle River, NJ: Pearson/Prentice Hall.

Grant, H., and Terry, K. J. (2005). *Law Enforcement in the 21st Century*. Boston, MA: Pearson/Allyn and Bacon.

Hess, K. A., and Wrobleski, H. M. (2006). *Police Operations, Theory and Practice*, 4th ed. Belmont, CA: Thomson/Wadsworth.

Hickman, M. J., and Reaves, B. A. (2002). *Local Police Departments, 2000*. NCJ 196002. Washington, D.C.: Bureau of Justice Statistics.

Hunter, R. D., and Dantzker, M. L. (2005). *Crime and Criminality: Causes and Consequences*. Monsey, NY: Criminal Justice Press.

King, M. L., Jr. (1963). *Letter from Birmingham Jail*, April 16.

O'Conner, T. (2006). http://faculty.ncwc.edu/toconnor/polstruct.htm

Packer, H. E. (1968). *The Limits of the Criminal Sanction*. Stanford, CA: Stanford University Press.

Reaves, B. A., and Bauer, L. M. (2003). *Federal Law Enforcement Officers, 2000*, NCJ 199995. Washington, D.C.: Bureau of Justice Statistics.

Reaves, B. A., and Hickman, M. J. (2002). *Census of State and Local Law Enforcement Agencies, 2000*, NCJ 194066. Washington, D.C.: Bureau of Justice Statistics.

Reichel, P. L. (2005). *Comparative Criminal Justice Systems: A Topical Approach*, 4th ed. Upper Saddle River, NJ: Pearson/Prentice Hall.

Reiman, J. (2007). *The Rich Get Richer and the Poor Get Prison*, 8th ed. Boston, MA: Pearson/Allyn and Bacon.

Roberson, C. R., Wallace, H., and Stuckey, G. B. (2007). *Procedures in the Justice System*, 8th ed. Upper Saddle River, NJ: Pearson/Prentice Hall.

Rush, G. (2004). *The Dictionary of Criminal Justice*, 6th ed. Guilford, CT: McGraw-Hill/Dushkin.

Transportation Security Administration. (2006). www.tsa.gov

United Nations. (2007). www.un.org/overview/rights.html

United States Coast Guard. (2006). www.uscg.mil

United States Commission on Civil Rights. (2007). www.usccr.gov

United States Department of Homeland Security. (2007). www.dhs.gov/interweb/assetlibrary/DHS_OrgChart.pdf

United States Department of Justice. (2007). www.usdoj.gov/dojorg.htm

United States Marshals Service. (2006). www.usdoj.gov/marshals

United States Secret Service. (2006). www.secretservice.gov

Van Ness, D., and Strong, K. H. (2006). *Restoring Justice: An Introduction to Restorative Justice*, 3rd ed. Cincinnati, OH: LexisNexis.

Walker, J. T. (2002). "Laws of the state and the state of the law: The relationship between police and law," in Walker, J. T. (Ed.), *Policing and the Law*. Upper Saddle River, NJ: Pearson/Prentice Hall.

Webster's Online Dictionary. (2007). www.websters-online-dictionary.org/definition/justice

Wikipedia. (2007). http://en.wikipedia.org/wiki/Justice

CHAPTER 2

Police Role Concept in a Changing Society

The Policeman is a "Rorschach" in uniform as he patrols his beat. His occupational accoutrements—shield, nightstick, gun, and summons book—clothe him in a mantle of symbolism that stimulates fantasy and projection.

—NIEDERHOFFER, 1967

Variation is basic to all human beings. We might fight less quickly if we looked at it this way and also we might put more energy into finding more harmonious ways to incorporate the differentness.

—SATIR, 1978

KEY CONCEPTS

Crime Control Role	Generalization	Perception
Crime-Fighting Model	Objectivity	Role Concept
Deletion	Order Maintenance	Service Role
Distortion	Role	Subjectivity

LEARNING OBJECTIVES

Studying this chapter will enable you to:

1. Define *perception* and *role conflict*.
2. Identify and explore conflicting perceptions that exist regarding the role of police officers in the community.
3. Identify major elements necessary to the success of programs designed to assist officers in achieving realistic role concepts and improved service to and participation in the community.
4. Describe the factors and conditions of change in our society.
5. Identify and describe some of the paradoxes and dilemmas that our changing society creates for the police officer.

In the previous chapter, we discussed where the police fit within the American system of justice as well as within society as a whole. The nature of police officers' relationships with members of various communities will be detailed in the following chapters. This chapter will examine how the police view themselves within our constantly changing and increasingly complex society. We will also discuss how individuals, groups, and organizations within society may view the police. These views of who officers are and what they do (or are supposed to do) may be defined as the roles of the police.

Roles are distinct behavior patterns acted out in connection with a particular social position. Roles are either *ascribed* (not under the person's control) or *achieved* (attained voluntarily). Examples of ascribed roles include male, female, and infant; examples of achieved roles include husband, wife, and teacher. Roles provide us with ways of categorizing and anticipating the behavior of others. They assist us in deciding how to act in relationship to others and help to give order to our world. One person plays many roles, and sometimes these roles conflict. The Hispanic American police officer, for instance, may be faced with role conflict because he or she is both Hispanic American and an officer, and he or she has difficulty in reconciling the two. Conflict might also occur in other ways: (1) the expectations of others regarding behaviors appropriate to a role may be different from the expectations of the role incumbent; (2) the expectations of others might vary widely, making it very difficult for the role incumbent to be successful in that role; or (3) the "official" and working definitions of the role are contradictory. The police role includes all of these contradictions.

Ask anyone. A police officer is a "crime fighter," or a "human service worker," or a "knight in blue," or the "power arm of the Establishment," or a "dumb cop," or a "competent professional." Ask a police officer. What will he or she say they are? This chapter identifies and accounts for some of the conflicting perceptions that exist regarding the police role.

GREAT EXPECTATIONS

Police officers in today's society are expected not only to apprehend bank robbers and murderers, but they are also expected to direct traffic, transport the sick and injured to the hospital, help schoolchildren cross streets, patrol polling places on election day, provide shelter and care for drunks and drug abusers, investigate accidents, settle family disputes, locate missing and runaway children, and a host of other things. They must be all things to all people. They are the only all-purpose emergency service in society (Doerner, 2004). As such, they respond to all situations in which "something-that ought-not-to-be-happening-and-about-which-someone-had-better-do-something-now!" (Bittner, 1970). They are expected not only to enforce the law, maintain order, and resolve disputes but also to do so in a scrupulously fair manner, no matter what sort of verbal or physical abuse might be directed toward them.

When they gather evidence or apprehend criminals, police must never violate an offender's constitutional rights under penalty of having the evidence suppressed in court. They must be professionally detached from the violence and tragedy that they encounter on their daily tour of duty. They are expected not only to be honest and fair in fact but also to give a constant appearance of honesty and fairness. They must have a professional knowledge of criminal law in order to ensure that the rights of those they apprehend are protected. They must be prepared to manage conflicts and to deal swiftly and appropriately with almost every manner of crisis our society has invented.

The relationship between police and the citizens they are sworn to serve is a close one. As the President's Commission on Law Enforcement and the Administration of Justice observed:

> It is hard to overstate the intimacy of the contact between the police and the community. Policemen deal with people when they are both most threatening and most vulnerable, when they are angry, when they are frightened, when they are desperate, when they are drunk, when they are violent, or when they are ashamed. Every police

action can affect in some way someone's dignity, or self-respect, or sense of privacy, or constitutional rights. As a matter of routine, policemen become privy to, and make judgments about, secrets that most citizens guard jealously from their closest friends: relationships between husbands and wives, the misbehavior of children, personal eccentricities, peccadilloes, and lapses of all kinds. Very often policemen must physically restrain or subdue unruly citizens. (President's Commission on Law Enforcement and the Administration of Justice, 1967, pp. 91–92)

Perhaps that is why the officer often is viewed so subjectively. The perception of what the role of a police officer in society is and should be varies considerably depending on who is doing the perceiving and under what circumstances judgment is made.

PERCEPTION

Seeing and Perceiving

Man is not disturbed by events, but by the view he takes of them.

—Epictetus

How often have you heard such statements as these?

Well, this is the way I see it.

I suppose that is just the way he sees it.

I have to respond the way I see it.

I suppose you have to act in accordance with the way you see it.

Perception is more than receiving visual stimulation, or sensing something. It is actually a process of creating meaning out of what we hear, see, smell, taste, and feel (our sensations, or sensory experience) and using the sense that we make of the world as the basis for our actions. As used in the examples above, the word "see" also implies more than a visual sensation. "To see" can mean to believe, to understand, and to make sense of, as well as to view. Sometimes we use the word "see" when we actually mean "perceive."

Perception Is Personal

It is unlikely that two people, even at a given time and place, will perceive the same event in exactly the same way. Every police officer knows that eyewitness accounts, however sincere, may vary widely and be inaccurate (Loftus, 1996; Zalman and Seigel, 1999). On occasion, mistaken eyewitness testimony can lead to wrongful convictions. In 1999, the Innocence Project examined the 62 DNA exonerations that had taken place up to that time and concluded that mistaken eyewitness testimony was a factor in 84 percent of those wrongful convictions (Poveda, 2001, pp. 689–708).

Creating meaning from sensations requires a judgment call. Several elements combine to set the context, or the frame of reference, within which a person makes such a judgment call. Attention, knowledge, past experiences, and present motives or needs all help to shape the way a person perceives (or perhaps misperceives). The relatively stable and predictable set of habits by which the person manages day-to-day living under ordinary conditions (personality) influences perception.

Behavior is closely linked to perception. Our actions are based on the world as we believe it to be.

Donna Allen pulls her van over to the curb and steps out to the sidewalk to ask directions from Joan Patrick, who is walking toward her. Before Joan finishes giving Donna the directions she asked for, both women look up simultaneously and see a huge lion approaching them. "A lion!" screams Joan, as she turns and runs in the opposite direction as fast as she can. "Stop!" yells Donna, but Joan is soon out of earshot. Donna then walks to the lion, gently strokes his mane to indicate that all is well, takes the lion to the back of the van, and orders him to leap into the van, which the lion does. Donna then closes the tailgate of the van, climbs into the driver's seat, and continues on her way, regretting that Joan did not take time to give her sufficient directions to reach her destination. She would undoubtedly have to stop again and ask directions, which might make her late for her performance at the circus.

In this example, the objective experience of the two women was the same, but they had different perceptual experiences. Objective experience can be standardized and agreed upon by most people. Donna and Joan would agree that they saw an animal approach and the animal was a lion. The lion's appearance on the sidewalk as the two women talked was an objective experience. The perceptual experiences of the two women can be implied by observing their behavior as the lion approached them. Joan saw the lion as dangerous and a threat to her well-being and ran away in fright. Donna did not see the lion as a threat but showed affection toward the lion and concern that the lion might be upset. Her behavior was to comfort the lion, and her most outstanding concern was to get to her destination as soon as possible.

It is possible to analyze this situation in terms of *knowledge, past experience,* and *need.* Donna was acquainted with the lion, and since she was the lion's trainer, she knew that the lion was not dangerous and was no threat to either of the two women. Joan did not have this knowledge and was therefore afraid of the lion. Donna had obviously had experience with this particular lion and perhaps other lions and probably tended to "see" lions in general in a different way than did Joan. Joan's past experience with lions primarily consisted of indirect experiences, such as seeing lions in the zoo, in movies, and on television; in most of those instances, the lions she had seen were portrayed as being dangerous and threatening. Those in the zoo were locked up, and those in the movies and on television were always attacking someone or some other animal. Joan had no need in relationship to the experiencing of the lion other than the need for survival. She perceived that her survival was threatened at that moment; thus, her need for survival was really why she chose to run. Donna's most outstanding need of the moment was related to her desire to put on a good performance at the circus and to reach the circus in time for that performance. Consequently, the temperament of the lion was very important to her, so she proceeded to comfort the lion, to load him back into the van, and to drive off as rapidly as she could, hopefully in the direction of the circus.

Richard Bandler and John Grinder theorized how perception comes about. They claim that **generalization, deletion,** and **distortion** are psychological processes common to all people. These are ways in which we make sense of and survive in the world. "The processes which allow us to accomplish the most extraordinary and unique human activities are the same processes which block our further growth if we commit the error of mistaking the model for the reality" (Bandler and Grinder, 1975, p. 14).

Generalization is the psychological process whereby a person detaches some part of one model from an original experience and then applies this model to represent an entire category. A common example is experiencing an ice cube. When a person touches an ice cube for the first time, he or she learns that ice cubes are cold. As part of learning about the world, it will be helpful to this person to generalize that other ice cubes are also cold. However, if he or she refused to touch ice cubes after that original experience, generalizing that cold is painful to touch, the generalization could be a hindrance.

"*Deletion* is a process by which we selectively pay attention to certain dimensions of our experience and exclude others" (Bandler and Grinder, 1975, p. 15). People have the ability to filter out experiences while concentrating on a model. The coach, for example, watching the video replay of his basketball team's victory, screens out (deletes) all the activity on the basketball court except the behaviors of the team members and the opponents. He deletes the behavior of the cheerleaders and everyone else in the gym. Although through deletion the coach is able to pinpoint specific information that he might have otherwise missed, he loses the flavor added by the spectators, the band, and the cheerleaders, because he has deleted this dimension of his experience. The coach's perception could get him into trouble when his wife, the band director, asks him later how he enjoyed the victory song played by the band and the coach has no recollection of the experience.

Distortion is the third modeling process, and it allows us to make shifts in our experience of sensory data (Bandler and Grinder, 1975, p. 16). An actress onstage distorts as she exaggerates her movements and sounds. This is a useful form of distortion because it allows the audience to experience the performance in a rich and fantasized fashion. If, however, once offstage, the same actress rushes to the telephone and tearfully reports to the police an exaggerated version of a disagreement between her and her husband, the shift in her experience of sensory data will not be positively useful.

Perception issues exist between police and community groups. In most cases, the officer on the beat perceives the behavior of citizens differently from the way they perceive their own situation, circumstances, and behavior. Citizens may perceive the police officer's role, purpose, and behavior quite differently from the way the police officer does. The factors responsible for such differences in perception are the same as outlined in the previous discussion:

1. Differences in past experience, and sets of habits.
2. Knowledge.
3. Individual needs relative to the situation in question through the modeling processes of generalization, distortion, and deletion.

Consider another example:

John, age twenty-five, has lived all of his life in a suburban area near a large U.S. city. Roy, also age twenty-five, has lived all of his life in an inner-city neighborhood of that same large U.S. city where confrontations between police and youth have escalated to violence several times in the last few years. John and Roy are walking together on a sidewalk within that inner-city area when they see a police officer, on foot, approaching them. As the officer draws nearer, he nods his head in greeting and smiles. John responds, "Good morning, Officer," and returns his smile. As the officer passes, John becomes aware that Roy looks uncomfortable. He recalls that Roy at first did not look at the officer. But after he had said, "Good morning," Roy had looked up at the officer with a tremendous frown on his face and a look of contempt in his eyes. Roy neither spoke to the officer nor returned his smile. John is puzzled; he cannot understand Roy's reaction. To John, the officer was obviously trying to be pleasant. He did not offend John or Roy, and he showed no indication of ill will toward them. Yet Roy finds it very difficult to understand John's behavior because just as Roy was beginning to trust John, John demonstrated to Roy that he was inclined to be friendly with police officers. John feels that Roy now believes John is "not to be trusted"; when the chips are down, John is on the side of the cop.

Is John's perception of Roy in this instance "true"? Or is Roy's perception of John "true"? Whether these perceptions are true or not, the perceptual experiences of the two men in this instance are nevertheless quite real, and capable of affecting their attitudes toward each other, their ability to trust each other, and the way they behave toward each other in the future.

Another question to be asked is this: Why did Roy and John react differently toward the same objective experience—the approaching of a police officer who greeted them with a friendly smile? First, although the police officer was looking at both of the men when he gave his nod of greeting and smiled, Roy perceived that he was not smiling at him at all. Throughout his life, Roy's only relationships with police officers have been negative ones. Roy has generalized from these experiences to avoid police officers at all costs. He has distorted reality and perceives that "the only purpose of the police is to control, not to protect." Roy perceives that what the police mean by control is to "keep people from the inner city in their place," "prevent them from expressing themselves," "deprive them of most of the nicer things in life," and so forth. Roy's past experiences with police officers have included their frequent questioning of him about crimes committed—crimes that he knew nothing about. In fact, Roy has never committed a crime in his life. In the past, however, police officers have taken him down to the precinct station and applied pressure to get him to "finger" friends who have been accused of crimes. On several occasions, when Roy indicated to them that he knew nothing about whether or not the person involved had committed a crime, he was told that if he did not cooperate, little or no mercy would be shown to him by the police when they caught him in a crime (which they seemed to feel was inevitable).

The police officers who have taken Roy down to the station to question him may be distorting objective reality in much the same fashion that Roy does. The officers may be generalizing from past experience, assuming that Roy's behavior will be similar to the behavior of others in their experience. The officers may be deleting the objective reality about Roy (that he is a law-abiding citizen, for instance) and, instead, be distorting the scowl that appeared on Roy's face when he saw the officers approaching to mean that Roy is guilty. In fact, Roy may be in the process of generalizing from his own past experience about police officers.

Moreover, Roy has never heard any of his friends indicate that they had ever been protected by police officers. His friends always talked about the police as the "enemy." Roy is often afraid as he walks down a street after leaving the movies. He is afraid of other people who might rob or take advantage of persons walking alone on the street late at night. Roy has caught himself on many occasions wishing that there were a police department that would protect him from such hoodlums. Yet, he has never felt that any police officer saw this as his role. Through his own experiences and conversations with his friends, Roy has come to view the police as the most definitive instrument of an oppressing society, deployed not only to protect the rest of society *from* him but to keep him *down* in every way.

In contrast to Roy's past experiences with the police, John had always been taught that police officers were his friends. John read about the helpful police in storybooks; police officers came to his schools, and even one of his father's best friends was a police lieutenant who lived in the area. John remembers the time when his family returned from a vacation and discovered that their house had been burglarized. They called the police, and after the house had been searched, it was discovered that the only missing item was $50, which John's mother had placed in an envelope and left on the coffee table before leaving. After the police had talked to John's parents, one of the officers said, "Don't worry, Mr. and Mrs. Jones, we have sufficient evidence. We will get the thief, and your $50 will be returned." As John grew up, he became friends with a few police officers, who went out of their way to be nice to him. On a few occasions, he had been stopped by police officers for speeding or committing some minor traffic violation. However, he seldom received a ticket, only a warning that usually ended in "I'm going to let you go this time, but be careful. We want you to get wherever you are going safely." In general, John has always thought of police officers as his friends and that the chief role of the police in the community is to protect citizens.

Because of these past experiences, John and Roy responded differently to the smiling policeman as he approached them on the sidewalk. Their different behaviors were obviously based on their different perceptions. Their different perceptions were in turn based on the differences between them in terms of past experiences with the police, their habits, knowledge of the situation that they were in at the moment, personal needs, distortion, generalization, and deletion.

John and Roy were both reacting to reality as it impinged upon them. Each person's perceptual experience is "reality." Because perceptual experience is not altogether a conscious phenomenon, many individuals would be at a loss if they were asked to explain why they understand life the way they do. In the case of the smiling police officer, Roy could not have readily explained to John why his perception of the officer's behavior was negative. Similarly, John could not have readily explained to Roy why he perceived the officer's behavior to be positive. Still, each one acted in what he believed to be his own best interest, based on his understanding of reality.

Perceptions of the police function differ in the ghetto, the middle- and upper-middle-class suburbs, the political arena, the police briefing room, and so on. Some people see the police as their personal instruments for ending or reducing crime on the street to ensure their personal safety. Others see police as an instrument of society with the somewhat broader aim of maintaining a degree of harmony, consistency, and peace (whatever the latter has come to mean in today's world). Some people have a more restricted view of the police, seeing them as an agency to suppress underprivileged and minority segments of society. Still others perceive the police as an agency by which dominant society confines and reinforces the boundaries of ghettos and minority groups. The police are also viewed as being so helplessly caught within social class, racial, and political factions that they are utterly stymied in their work but are made scapegoats for the ills that are inevitable in a society torn by conflict. It is doubtful that any two people selected at random would completely agree as to what a police officer does (or should do).

ROLE CONCEPT

A role may be defined as a set of behavioral expectations and obligations associated with a position in a social structure or organization (Cox and Fitzgerald, 1999). These expectations can be framed in an objective, dispassionate manner; a subjective, totally personal manner; or in some modification of these two approaches.

Objectivity as an approach requires the observer to determine, study, and weigh facts in an unbiased, scientific manner, setting aside preconceived notions and personal prejudices and preferences. In this approach, conclusions are drawn from the facts. Any conclusion not borne out by evidence that is objectively based is not acceptable.

Subjectivity, on the other hand, is not concerned with objective fact, and even an awareness by the subjective observer of such fact does not guarantee an objective conclusion. Facts are redefined by the observer in terms of his or her personal life experiences, biases, assumptions, dreams, and fears. Individual judgment is based on how a person feels about what he or she sees and how the person believes what he or she sees relates to him or her. Although others may consider his or her view unrealistic, given the world as he or she understands it, his or her expectations are logical. Most expectations held by most people are, to some degree, subjectively derived.

THE POLICE OFFICER'S ROLES

Crime Control

> Ask a retiring officer to tell you about his best memories. He'll probably recall stories of high-speed pursuits, shoot-outs, fights, or chasing someone on foot. Ask a new rookie what he likes about being a cop, and he'll say things like "putting the bad guys in jail." The fact is, most officers see their role as a crime fighter. (Trautman, 1991, p. 16)

Very few, if any, would argue with the statement that a core mission of the police is to control crime. The police do have, and we expect them to perform, a crime control role. However, the police and the public often see crime control as the total responsibility of the police. Furthermore, the police and the public see the crime control role of the police as the only role the police should perform. This myopic view of the police and their role has a significant impact on policing as an occupation and on the performance of individual officers as actors in the criminal justice system.

The exclusive image of the **crime control role** of the police embodied in the "crime fighter" image has serious consequences on the police and their behavior. Crime and its control are not the sole responsibility of the police. The police did not create nor can they control the social conditions that create crime. At best, the law and the criminal justice system are poor controllers of human behavior. As long as we see crime control as the primary role of the police, we fail to recognize that crime is a social phenomenon and that crime prevention is the responsibility of society, communities, and a host of other social institutions. In addition to creating unrealistic expectations about the police's ability to contend with crime, this narrow view prevents an informed analysis of the other important roles assigned to the police (Walker and Katz, 2002).

Order Maintenance

The crime control role involves all those functions of arrest and detection of law violators as well as those behaviors devoted to crime prevention (e.g., preventive patrol). However, as Wilson (1968, p. 4) pointed out, less than one-third of all police radio calls involve criminal matters that may result in an arrest, and only about 5 percent of all cases actually result in an arrest. It is the **order maintenance role** that is more central to the modern police officer's job than any other aspect of his or her behavior. Most recent studies support the assertion by Wilson that the role of a patrol officer "is defined more by his responsibility for maintaining order than by his responsibility for enforcing the law" (Wilson, 1968, p. 16).

Order maintenance activities may consist simply of officers being seen so as to provide a sense of security or as an aid in promoting the public peace. It may consist of monitoring the activities of individuals engaging in behavior that, if allowed to "get out of hand," could result in inconvenience or annoyance for other citizens. It can involve restoration of order in disorderly or potentially disorderly situations. It can be actual intervention into disputes between individuals or groups that, if unchecked, could lead to serious violations of the law. Most of these activities do not involve actual enforcement of laws. Those situations in which legal conditions for arrests do exist are dealt with through mediation or warnings in lieu of arrest (Wrobleski and Hess, 2006).

Service

In addition to their crime control and order maintenance roles, the police spend a great deal of time performing service activities. This role is second only to order maintenance in importance. The duties and responsibilities that fall within this category include many activities that may appear to be only peripherally related to the direct police services of patrol, investigations, traffic control, and the police mission of preventing crime and disorder (Barker, Hunter, and Rush, 1994). Providing emergency rescue services, working traffic accidents, unlocking locked cars, jump-starting stalled vehicles, and helping people in distress are but a few of the many services routinely provided by the police. Also, the police as first responders provide numerous services to special populations, particularly the elderly. The **service role** is vitally important to the police in an era of community policing because it shows that the police and the law-abiding community can work together to solve problems and meet needs.

Many of the services performed by the police are not inherent to the police mission but have become police services by default. Because the police are available 24 hours a day and no one else has emerged to perform a specific task, that task may come to be seen within a particular community as a police responsibility. In addition to being the only 24/7 (hours/days), 365-days-a-year general emergency service public agency, they are society's only 24/7, 365-days-a-year all-purpose social service public agency.

Other Roles

In addition to the three roles discussed above, other duties are also performed by the police (see Table 2.1). Whereas Cordner (1992) argues that information gathering could legitimately be classified as a law enforcement duty, others argue that it is more appropriately a service or even an order maintenance function. Still others (Barker, Hunter, and Rush, 1994) consider information gathering to be a separate role that falls partially within all three. Since the majority of police reports are taken primarily for insurance purposes, we will classify information gathering as a distinct role.

Yet another police role that is contained partially within the duties of crime control, order maintenance, and service is that of protection of individual rights. The police in the United States and other democracies are responsible not only for protecting society from individual behavior but also for ensuring that the constitutional rights of all citizens are upheld (Conser et al., 2005).

TABLE 2.1 Twenty-Five Most Frequent Types of Calls for Service

Type of Call for Service	Frequency	Percent
1 Suspicious Activity Calls	13,436	10.2
2 Burglary Alarm Calls	8,867	6.7
3 Loud Music/Noise/Party Calls	8,586	6.5
4 Traffic Accident Calls	8,311	6.3
5 Check Welfare Calls	7,708	5.8
6 9-1-1 Hangup Calls	5,990	4.5
7 Theft/Burglary from Vehicle Calls	5,948	4.5
8 Criminal Information Calls	5,185	3.9
9 Agency Assist Calls	4,320	3.3
10 Theft Calls	3,888	2.9
11 Illegal Parking Calls	3,825	2.9
12 Criminal Damage Calls	3,228	2.4
13 Stolen Vehicle Calls	3,161	2.4
14 Family Fight Calls	3,128	2.4
15 Burglary Calls	2,974	2.3
16 Stranded Motorist Calls	2,852	2.2
17 Fight Calls	2,066	1.6
18 Subject Disturbing Calls	2,039	1.5
19 Trespassing Calls	1,697	1.3
20 Shoplifting Calls	1,509	1.1
21 Assault Calls	1,498	1.1
22 Incorrigible Juvenile Calls	1,449	1.1
23 Unwanted Guest Calls	1,304	1.0
24 Threat Calls	1,198	0.9
25 Traffic Hazard Calls	1,189	0.9
All Other Calls	26,692	20.2
	132,048	**100.0**

Source: What Police Do (Police Workload in Tempe, Arizona, 2003). Tempe Police Department, 2006
(http://www.tempe.gov/police/AnnualReport2003/CallsForServiceInfo03.htm).

POLICE ROLE CONFLICT

In the preceding section, we discussed the various roles assigned to police officers within a typical police agency. The extent to which these complex and often contradictory roles are carried out varies considerably among police agencies, due to their nature, tradition, size, location, mission, and the orientation of the community served. In addition, considerable variation within agencies is due to different role outlooks among individual officers. As discussed earlier, the police are affected by both external and internal groups. Individual perceptions and political ideologies also influence the behavior of police officers (Walker and Katz, 2002).

Traditionally, the literature on policing has focused on four individual styles that were derived from Wilson's (1968) departmental roles. This typology consists of *crime fighters, social agents, law enforcers*, and *watchmen* (Peak, 2006). The *crime fighter* or "cowboy" is an officer who views himself or herself as primarily a serious crime investigator. Lesser offenses and noncriminal duties are seen as trivial and not worthy of police attention. The *social agent* views policing as a combination of crime control, order maintenance, and provision of services; law enforcement duties are considered an important but only a minimal portion of their overall duties. The *law enforcer* or "legalist" is similar to the crime fighter in that he or she tends to emphasize crime control. However, the law enforcer differs from the crime fighter in that all statutes, ordinances, and regulations are felt to be important and require strict enforcement. The *watchman* is dedicated to preserving social and political order within the community. He or she will enforce the laws to the extent necessary to maintain the peace.

The four categories described above are not believed by many police scholars to adequately present the variations among individual officers in regard to role perceptions. In response to such criticisms, Broderick (1987) developed a classification scheme that attempts to categorize officers based on personality type rather than on a particular police style. His typology is useful in assessing individual behavior patterns but is less rigid in predicting performance. Broderick's categories include *enforcers, idealists, realists,* and *optimists.*

Enforcers are concerned primarily with keeping the streets "clean" and ensuring that citizens behave properly. They see themselves as protecting the "good people" from the "bad people." Most enforcers would be considered authoritarians who perceive citizens as either hostile or apathetic toward them. *Idealists* are committed to the law and the rights of citizens. They see themselves as professionals who better serve the public than do their more authoritarian and/or less dedicated colleagues. Frustration with the "system" often drives these individuals into other careers or causes them to become realists. *Realists* tend to be cynical and dissatisfied with society and the criminal justice system. As a defense mechanism, they have stopped caring about their role as police officers and generally do only what is required to stay out of trouble. Realists often seek transfers to assignments where they can "hide out" and be left alone by both the public and other police officials. *Optimists* see themselves as service providers who are performing an important societal function. They view themselves, their colleagues, and the public in a positive manner. Although aware that they alone cannot change the world, they are willing to do their part. Officers often do not fit in any one of these categories and may occasionally shift categories during their careers.

As if the contradictory perceptions on the part of individual officers were not complicated enough, debates regarding the role of the police in a democratic society confuse the issue further. As seen by Roberg, Novak, and Cordner (2005), these debates include the following:

> Do rigid bureaucratic rules or responsiveness to political demands best serve the public interest?
> Should police be concerned with preserving community norms or strict compliance with laws?
> Is the police occupation a professional activity or a craft?
> Are officers to emphasize their duties as crime fighters or social service workers?
> Should the police be more concerned with crime prevention or the apprehension of criminals?
> Should police activities be of a proactive or reactive nature?

The manner in which public officials, community leaders, and police officials resolve their differences in regard to these debates influences the organization's values and goals and determines those tasks and activities that will be emphasized by that police agency.

The consequences of contradictory views on the part of individual police officers, police administrators, public officials, and community leaders cause more confusion (and often conflict) than consensus in regard to the role of the police.

FORMATION OF ROLE CONCEPTS

The Sources of Role Concepts

Role concepts have their sources in needs and past experiences. Because both of these can vary widely from group to group and individual to individual, so can role concepts.

Three major factors affect the way individuals and groups in society perceive the role of the police officer:

1. The individual's or group's specific needs and problems.
2. The individual's or group's personal experiences with police officers.
3. The image of police officers created by various media.

If expectations are unrealistic, so is the role concept, and it will become further distorted if the unrealistic expectations are repeatedly unmet.

Some people, for instance, have often experienced oppression by the police. If a particular neighborhood has a severe crime problem and the police are not solving it, residents will conclude that police either cannot or do not want to fulfill the community's needs—in other words, unfulfilled needs and past experience have induced the community to expect little of the police. Based on that expectation, residents may withhold community cooperation from law enforcement, thus compounding the problem and further strengthening the negative role concept.

Lack of Information

Sometimes, lack of accurate citizen information regarding police efforts can lead to unreasonable expectations on the part of an individual or a group in the community. For example, an area of a city might be plagued with assaults and robberies. The police in that area may respond by increasing routine patrol, increasing foot patrol in business areas, and generally focusing most of their efforts on that current problem. Personnel shortages may prevent ideal service to other, less immediate problems, such as juveniles racing cars in the streets. The citizens may not be aware of the increased efforts of the police in the assault and robbery areas. When complaints are made about juveniles racing cars in the streets, the citizens may conclude that the police are negligent if they take longer than usual to respond to the call.

How Police Respond

To understand the problems involved in creating and maintaining positive role expectations for the police, consider the three outcomes that are possible when a law enforcement problem arises:

1. *The problem is confronted and solved.* This creates the expectation that the police will do the same again, if and when necessary. Note, however, that in the familiar area of enforcing traffic laws, the police often are attributed with a negative role concept due to their effective actions.
2. *The problem is confronted but not solved.* Naturally, this often has a negative impact on the police role concept, but the police may have no way of preventing certain problems (ranging from murder to domestic arguments); citizens who believe otherwise have unrealistic expectations.
3. *The problem is not confronted.* The usual reason is that the problem (trash removal, street and light maintenance, etc.) is the responsibility of some other agency. Nevertheless, the citizen may feel it is due to police failure to provide service.

Thus, in at least two of the three cases just described, observers are likely to adopt a negative role concept of the police, even though the expectations on which that concept is based are unrealistic or mistaken.

THE MEDIA AND ROLE CONCEPTS

In the United States today, the media play a very important part in forming expectations about the police. Thus, many people evaluate the actions of police officers against criteria formed by TV or movie scriptwriters. If preconceived ideas regarding the police role are challenged by a reality that contradicts what people believe to be true, will they choose to believe the reality? Unfortunately, the answer is not always yes.

The police officers of Hollywood lore are fictional images of police stereotypes that have been exaggerated to provide entertainment to a bored public. That public (and indeed, the police themselves) tend to accept the images created by scriptwriters and portrayed by actors and actresses who have little or no knowledge of what police officers actually do. The result is the creation of mythical police roles that have only a limited basis in reality.

Holden (1992) identified six police stereotypes that have either been created or perpetuated by the entertainment media. The first and perhaps oldest media image of the police is that of the buffoon. This characterization began in early movies such as *The Keystone Kops* and continues in present-day television and movie depictions. A second image is not as extreme as the buffoon but tends to present police officers as slow-witted and unprofessional dullards who need the guidance of smart citizens (à la Sherlock Holmes, Mrs. Columbo, or Jessica Fletcher of *Murder, She Wrote*) to solve crimes. A third type, the sadist, abuses his or her police authority to perpetuate evil acts. Such characters were aptly portrayed by Richard Gere in *Internal Affairs*, Ray Liotta in *Unlawful Entry*, and Michael Chiklis in *The Shield*. A fourth image is that of the hero who fights the bad guys (and often police superiors and the criminal justice system) to protect the innocent from evil. Mel Gibson in the *Lethal Weapon* series and Bruce Willis in the *Die Hard* series exemplify such heroes. A fifth character is the *wizard*, a supercop who solves challenging cases utilizing his or her superior intellect and/or technical expertise. These images are exemplified in the several *CSI* television shows in which individuals perform the tasks of investigators and forensic scientists. Finally, we are presented with the harassed professional who is highly competent but overworked and underappreciated. The characters of *NYPD Blue* and *Law and Order* would fall within this category.

In addition to the foregoing roles depicted by the entertainment media, the public is influenced considerably by the news media. Media attention (TV, newspapers, radio, and magazines) comes to police agencies for the police's crime-fighting role rather than its service role (the former makes better copy). Depicting the police negatively as misusing deadly force, police prejudice, or police corruption is also newsworthy. The amount of emphasis given to police actions and the media's interpretation of these actions as either proper or improper have a tremendous effect on the public's perception of the police. It has been argued that media coverage can transform a local incident into a national crisis (Grant and Terry, 2005). We doubt that anyone watching the media coverage of the 1999 murders of several students at Columbine High School in Littleton, Colorado, would question that assertion.

FACTORS AND CONDITIONS OF CHANGE

Reassessing the Dimensions

Traditionally, obedience to the law, ethical behavior, and moral decisions have been bound and intertwined into an absolute adherence based on extremes of legal versus illegal, good versus bad, and right versus wrong. Situations were black and white, or at least they appeared to be. In small rural, agriculturally based communities, a police officer could make decisions based on the relatively fixed value system of the majority. It was not that minorities did not exist, but rather that they were usually not vocal and, for the most part, not counted separately.

Since the end of World War II, however, the continuing struggle between tradition and change, between fixed values and no values, and between simple lives and complex living has seen tradition slowly dying. At the same time, people have not been able to adapt as quickly as the technology surrounding them. They are somewhat bewildered by a growing shrinkage of space and time and a negative relationship between the two. They find the so-called knowledge and information explosions threatening to overwhelm them. They find that the emergence of electronic controls creates what might be called "electronic amorality." The struggle for survival takes on new dimensions, and fixed value systems are seriously questioned and sometimes abandoned.

Never before have philosophers and peace officers, politicians, and the public been so carefully and sincerely reexamining the dimensions and limits of liberty, freedom, and democracy as living entities. Some years ago, George Orwell stated this:

> The point is that the relative freedom which we enjoy depends on public opinion, the law is no protection. The governments make laws, but whether they are carried out, and how the police behave, depends upon the general temper of the country. If large numbers of people are interested in freedom of speech, there will be freedom of speech even if the law forbids it; if public opinion is sluggish, inconvenient minorities will be persecuted, even if laws exist to protect them. (Orwell, 1963)

Milton Mayer, a philosopher and commentator on humankind in a democracy, in his *Liberty: Man versus State* commented on the many perceptual facets of liberty: "Plainly, what one man calls justice another man calls expropriation; and one man's security is another man's slavery, one man's liberty is another man's anarchy" (Mayer, 1969, p. 41). Mayer wondered if in our time the rule of law is not becoming the enemy of liberty.

Values have become relative to one another and to situations. "Policies" help to "bend" the law, and social conditions tend to confuse and confound the search for simple solutions and answers. From a quiet, relatively simple rural life with fixed values, we have moved to an involved, complex urban community where any sense of common union is difficult to find and where all groups wish to be counted. Increasingly in the last several decades, many of the formerly powerless groups in our society (African Americans, Hispanic Americans, Asian Americans, Native Americans, women, the elderly, and gays, to name a varied few) have demanded that their wants and needs be addressed (Figure 2.1). The influences of minority groups on policing are in evidence

FIGURE 2.1 An officer in Chinatown.

Courtesy of the New York City Police Department.

both inside and outside police organizations. Although most of the media and public attention regarding the police and minorities focuses on external relations, advocacy groups representing the views of minority officers are becoming commonplace.

In determining the will and consent of the people, all these factors must be considered in a given community, and absolutes are very difficult to find.

A World of Infinite Choices

A new era of development is occurring in the world. Changes are overwhelming and rapid. This time has been dubbed the "Information Age," and it is developing out of television, cable networks, microcomputers, the Internet, satellites, and other related information and entertainment resources. In many ways the tiny microprocessor (a silicon chip) has been at the center of the storm. Every field of human endeavor and most leisure activities have been or will be affected by it. Combined with various other scientific advances (particularly biomedical ones), this new era promises to move us into a world of choices we have never even imagined.

Those who attempt to predict the future disagree on whether the greatest impact of this new age will be positive or negative. Everyone agrees, however, that it will be great—perhaps greater than any revolution we have yet known.

Life is already being changed by these new technologies, and with change comes new opportunities and new problems. Some jobs are disappearing and others appearing as industries computerize. Social isolation, already a problem in our society, may be a by-product of our changed lifestyles as more work is done without ever leaving home. Intense interaction with machines is new to most of us. It will be a very different kind of communication. Some people will find the promised increase in leisure time satisfying, whereas others will find it boring. Boredom can bring about frustration, anger, and depression.

Biomedical advances have changed our lives for the better—and, in the opinion of some, for the worse. Artificial organs, prosthetic devices, birth control pills, test-tube babies, genetic engineering, and microsurgery at the level of DNA have all moved us into the twenty-first century.

New ethical problems must be confronted. When does life begin and end? What is "quality of life?" What limits are appropriate on creating and ending human life? How can we protect rights to privacy in an information age? Who is to monitor information systems? Can we prevent the dehumanization effect that so many people fear? Will private and governmental monitoring of our lives and activities take away or add to our freedom? What values are we modeling as the TV screen becomes an all-purpose display, and even a two-way communication instrument? What values do we wish to model?

These changes can make the job of police officers easier and more scientific. They can also bring new cooperation and integration among members of the justice community. Already new technologies have made it possible for officers to predict where and at what time crime will occur, match crime characteristics to offender characteristics quickly, increase the information that can be gathered and used from a crime or crisis scene, improve surveillance techniques, record calls and responses, and benefit from research in all areas of criminal justice training and function.

These same advances are changing the nature of the role of the police officer and the skills that an officer needs on the job. New technologies, especially the use of computers, will change policing in the twenty-first century. In 1999, all local police departments serving 25,000 or more residents used computers for administration purposes (Bureau of Justice Statistics, 2001). Seventy percent of these departments had computerized arrest records, 45 percent used computers for criminal investigation purposes, and 38 percent used computers for crime analysis. In the field, 31 percent used in-field computers, primarily laptops. The officers used these in-field computers to produce field reports and to access driving records, criminal histories, prior calls for service, and reports of stolen property. The improved skills in sorting and using the available information, problem solving, and knowledge of utilizing new technologies and resources may be just the beginning in the changing role of policing (Conser et al, 2005; Grant and Terry, 2005).

Although important to effective police function, technological sophistication cannot take the place of daily, one-on-one interactions between officers and the citizens they serve. As the trend toward computerization increases, police administrators will need to ensure that positive police–community relations, in the form of daily interaction between officers and the citizens they serve, continue to be a departmental priority.

THE PARADOXES OF POLICE PRACTICE

Individuals involved in our criminal justice system have to face paradox after paradox: They are very often confronted with situations in which they are "damned if they do and damned if they don't." This paradox is illustrated by the fact that society is just starting to recognize the contradictions and burdens placed on the police. They are expected to represent heritage in a changing time. They are expected to represent the controls of authority and the controls of tradition, yet they are faced with a hierarchy of ethical decisions in which they often must decide which law they may or may not allow the individual or criminal or the youngster to break or not break. The police are faced with the ethical problem of how far one can bend the law before it will break. In keeping with these paradoxical concepts, we find that police are expected to have a definite, if somewhat vague, role in society—a role tainted and tinged by stereotyping, prejudice, and an aura of unreality concerning this stressful profession.

Within this framework, in which police are considered to be on the side of our heritage and yet are expected to cope with change, we find that there is not just one "police officer"—a person involved in various aspects of law enforcement. Rather, we find that there are many "police officers" and that there are many emerging roles, styles, and skills involving the police. These include the police officer as a counselor, as a human services representative and member of the human services team, as a human relations expert, as a decision maker, as an agent for change, and as a trust builder between police agencies on the one hand and the various increasingly hostile segments of society on the other. The police officer is not only expected but is mandated to transmit, carry forward, control, and enforce those aspects of human existence that individuals, societies, nations, and civilizations have considered worthwhile, and which they have put into codes of law.

Community Relations: Residue from the Past

Often compounding the individual officer's problems is the police department's problem of poor community relations. Looking back into the recent history of policing, we can find many practices that were seemingly brutal and abusive, but which had the open or silent approval of most of the members of the community. Even though these practices of misconduct have been eliminated or greatly curtailed, the residents of the community may still have a tendency to view their police as somewhat less than sensitive, as well as unfair, oppressive, and perhaps even unaware of social needs and changes.

New officers who rid themselves of prejudicial attitudes or master their personal prejudices so that they do not affect their jobs are still perceived by the community as being insensitive, unfair, oppressive, and unaware of social needs and changes. The members of the community respond only to their perceptions of the uniform. As a group, they generally do not consider any officer's professional attributes. Members of the community may therefore act in a hostile manner, regardless of the individual officer's professional behavior. Some community members apparently have been conditioned to the concept that everyone who wears the uniform has certain prejudicial attitudes. Because the new officer is responded to with what he or she considers to be hostility, he or she is not given a chance to demonstrate to the community that he or she is an unbiased professional. Older officers will warn the new officer that his or her professional considerations are not the appropriate response for dealing with certain groups or individuals in the community, and that "There's only one way to handle those people." The typical response for the new officer is to become more and more like the experienced officers.

The chance the police department had of beginning a new era of excellent community relations is then stifled. The incoming officer is socialized to the standards of the past. Thus, the cycle of poor police–community relations seems to continue unbroken, even when the department has been fortunate enough to recruit an officer who did not bring unfavorable attitudes to the job or could control the negative attitudes he or she did have.

TOWARD A REALISTIC ROLE CONCEPT

The Police Officer's Working Personality and Reality

Skolnick's analysis of the police officer's "working personality" highlights three elements of the officer's task: danger, authority, and efficiency. According to Skolnick, these elements in turn generate three personality characteristics: suspiciousness, feelings of isolation, and police solidarity (Skolnick, 1975, p. 44). This context is supported by the paramilitary structure of the police organization, which discourages innovation and flexibility and encourages dependency (Doerner, 2004). As the rigidity of the structure increases, the degree to which these characteristics are emphasized also increases.

If more than 80 percent of the officer's time is spent in service-related duties, role concepts that stress danger, authority, and efficiency should be joined or replaced with one more in keeping with the service function.

Service versus Crime Fighting

Clearly, role concepts based on crime fighting and on the service model of police work will be quite different. Some of the most important contrasts between the two are presented below:

Crime Fighting	**Service**
Focus on law breakers	Focus on law abiders
Specialization	Decentralization
Strong hierarchical authority	Neighborhood involvement
High mobility	Foot patrol
Strict procedures	Wide discretion
Close surveillance and readiness to make arrests	Tolerance and willingness to handle problems by means other than arrest

Which model is more appropriate for police work? Many citizens and police officers would choose the **crime-fighting model**. Yet the objective realities of police work suggest that the service model must be given at least equal emphasis.

TOWARD A CONGRUENT ROLE

Police roles must be defined within the legal limits of authority and in relationship to the needs of the public. The National Advisory Commission on Criminal Justice Standards and Goals recognized the following list of functions that police agencies perform:

- Prevention of criminal activity
- Detection of criminal activity
- Apprehension of criminal offenders
- Participation in court proceedings
- Protection of constitutional guarantees
- Assistance to those who cannot care for themselves or who are in danger of physical harm
- Control of traffic
- Resolution of day-to-day conflicts among family, friends, and neighbors

(a)

(b)

(c)

FIGURE 2.2   Differing Police Roles (a) A SWAT Team posing during training; (b) Sergeant Kent Davis delivering food items to North Carolina families displaced by flooding from Hurricane Floyd; (c) Jackson County Sheriff's Deputies taking needy children shopping during their annual "Shop with a Cop" activities.

Courtesy of Jackson County Sheriff's Department (photos [a] and [c]) and Western Carolina University Police Department (photo [b]).

- Creation and maintenance of a feeling of security in the community
- Promotion and preservation of civil order (National Advisory Commission on Criminal Justice Standards and Goals, 1973, p. 72).

How much emphasis each function should receive is often a matter of controversy and varies from jurisdiction to jurisdiction. In every instance, however, working out the optimum mix of functions and priorities will require the active cooperation of local government, the police, and the community.

ELEMENTS OF CHANGE

The police–community relationship is vital to obtaining a realistic and mutually satisfactory role concept for police officers. For their part, police administrators must take steps to overcome the distrust and misunderstandings of the past and to develop internal and external programs that help officers to achieve the following: (1) serve the community more effectively, (2) view their

FIGURE 2.3 **The Rome Police Department appreciates the congruent roles of policing.**

Courtesy of Rome Police Department.

own roles in more favorable terms, and (3) participate in developing community relations. This will require sound planning based on the following elements:

1. Absolute commitment on the part of the police organization.
2. A law enforcement philosophy that recognizes that about 80 percent of police activity involves noncriminal matters.
3. Attempts to instill a professional service concept in existing personnel and in new recruits.
4. Proper balance between the academic and practical aspects of police education and training.
5. Using nonpolice personnel to teach police wherever appropriate (e.g., in areas such as sociology, psychology, and criminal law).
6. An organizational philosophy based on a behavioral approach to law enforcement goals (i.e., on modifying attitudes and behavior).
7. A reevaluation of recruitment methods.
8. Use of such methods as problem simulation, role playing, and group work to modify attitudes and behavior.
9. The realization that change is lasting only if it occurs at all organizational levels.

CRITERIA FOR CHANGE

The following criteria can be used to evaluate police education and training programs. These must be designed to promote needed change:

1. The education and training process should be lively and creative—an arena where ideologies, ideas, and points of view may clash and compete.

2. Attention must be given to a wide range of personal and institutional behavior. Being an effective and professional police officer involves at least the following attributes:
   a. a sophisticated understanding of the moral, social, political, and legal framework of the society.
   b. an intensive understanding of the community—its values, aspirations, difficulties, needs, and resources.
   c. considerable personal strength, autonomy, and self-understanding.
   d. the ability to understand, empathize, and communicate with others.
   e. a deep commitment to the basic ideals of justice and freedom within our society.
   f. a deep understanding and knowledge of the policies and practices of law enforcement organization.
3. Stress should be placed on the development of programs designed to give insight into the personal, social, legal, and cultural context of law enforcement service. The education and training function should be able to develop more sophisticated mechanisms for field training and greater articulation between the classroom and the real world.

POLICING IN A CHANGING SOCIETY

The conditions that affect society have their potential effect on the police officer as an ethical practitioner and as a human being. Police officers are not immune to the situations they must face. They are influencers and controllers of those situations. Whether they are facing problems of deadly force, problems of mixed ethical decisions, or problems involving the fundamental privacy of individual citizens, it all rubs off on them.

The alienation resulting from loneliness, inadequacy, despair, and helplessness found among many of the persons with whom they are in contact every day is bound to have its effect on the personality and psychological stability of every police officer. Many police officers sense that they are becoming withdrawn and distant because of the situations they have to face. There is no greater irony in law enforcement than to find attrition in the ranks of competent police officers as they paraphrase the adage "We have faced the enemy, and he is us."

Yet if this is a time of growing public and private cynicism and changing values, it is particularly challenging for people in law enforcement to avoid attempts to manipulate and distort daily police practice. Indeed, now more than ever before, it is essential for those sworn to represent and uphold the law to do exactly that.

The police officer is, for most people, their only contact with the law. What the officer says, thinks, and does reflects on the total community. A successful police department must be attuned to and have the respect and support of the community. The misuse of office or denial of justice to even one person, like ripples on a pond, spreads wider and wider until all are touched.

The National Advisory Commission's assessment of the situation remains as relevant today as it was in 1973:

> The communities of this Nation are torn by racial strife, economic chasms, and struggles between the values of the old and the viewpoints of the young. These circumstances have made it difficult for the policeman to identify with and be identified as part of a community of citizens. As communities have divided within themselves, there has been a breakdown in cooperation between the police and the citizens.
>
> The problem is particularly acute in large urban population centers. Here, the fibers of mutual assistance and neighborliness that bind citizens together have grown precariously thin. (National Advisory Commission on Criminal Justice Standards and Goals, 1973, p. 72)

The prescription recommended for improving the situation described is cooperation between police and community. As an essential element of cooperation, the police agency must constantly

FIGURE 2.4   An officer with children in a public housing area.
Courtesy of Rome Police Department.

seek to improve its ability to determine the needs and expectations of the public, to act upon those needs and expectations, and to inform the people of the resulting policies developed to improve the delivery of police services. This cooperation is a partnership between the community and its police agency. The partnership extends to mutual problem identification and problem solving.

On the other side of the relationship, the public must be informed of the police agency's roles so that it can better support the police in their efforts to reduce crime.

REALITY CHECK

A Lighter Side of Reality

A young patrol officer serving with the Tallahassee Police Department found himself assigned to do an "officer friendly" visit with a group of first graders at a local elementary school. At first unhappy that he would not be available for serious crime-fighting duties within his beat, the officer warmed up considerably when he met the excited students who had been eagerly anticipating his arrival. He spent a great deal of time telling the students how police officers were their friends and that they (the children) should feel free to talk to police officers and should never hesitate to contact the police if they became lost or frightened. During his presentation, the young officer described the many things that the police do for the public.

After talking to the children for about half an hour, the young officer asked if the children had any questions. He then spent the next several minutes answering a variety of questions about his uniform, his equipment, and his experiences, as well as listening to a myriad of comments and stories the children had heard about police officers. Reveling in the adoration of his young admirers, the officer was beginning to feel very good about himself and his role as a police officer.

During his interaction with the children, the officer had noticed that one young boy had hung back from the other students when they had crowded around to talk with him and that he had not participated when the other children were asking questions. Feeling very much the hero and wanting to make sure that every child had the opportunity to interact with him, the officer made a point of talking to the boy before he left the classroom. He walked over to the child and asked, "How are you?" The child replied, "Okay." The officer asked, "Is anything wrong?" The child sullenly responded, "No." The officer then said, "You didn't come up to talk to me. Do you know who I am?" To which the boy retorted, "My daddy says you're a son of a bitch!" Taken by surprise, the officer said, "Oh. Well, tell your daddy I said, Hi." He then made a hasty exit to resume his patrol duties. Reality had been restored.

Conclusions

Law enforcement often becomes the object of animosity against the establishment. Because of the police officer's traditional role, this may be an expected sociological or psychological occurrence. It seems clear that if new methods of reducing tensions are not found, an increased polarization in society will take place, which can only lead to more violence and retaliation. In an atmosphere of fear and distrust, the problems themselves lose proportion and cooperative solutions become impossible.

Police agencies generally reflect the community. If the community is progressive, its police agencies become progressive. If the entire community is belligerent, police agencies become belligerent. If a community has racist tendencies or is indifferent to the plight of minority groups, police agencies will almost always reflect the same tendencies. If the community is apathetic, police agencies become apathetic.

The police must make every effort to understand the needs and aspirations of all members of the community. There is also a great need for the public to understand the proper role to be played not only by police agencies but also by the entire criminal justice system within the community in our changing society. Such an understanding is impossible to achieve if it is forgotten that the police are essentially a service agency.

If progress is to be made, changes must be sought and initiated by all segments of the community, including the police. The progress of change always seems to begin with small things. Change must be based on an understanding of the community and an appreciation of what the community can be tomorrow and the day after.

Student Checklist

1. Define the terms *perception* and *role concept*.
2. How does a citizen's perceptions of the police affect the way the citizen acts toward a police officer?
3. List three factors responsible for differences in perception.
4. Describe the processes of generalization, deletion, and distortion.
5. Describe objective and subjective approaches to framing role expectations.
6. Identify and account for some of the conflicting perceptions that exist regarding the role of a police officer in the community.
7. Name several factors and conditions of change in our society.
8. Identify some of the paradoxes and dilemmas our changing society creates for the police officer.
9. What are some of the elements necessary to the success of programs designed to assist officers in achieving realistic role concepts and improved service to and participation in the community?

Topics for Discussion

1. What is your perception of the police in your community? What life experiences have brought you to that perception?
2. From your own community, suggest some specific examples of destructive perceptions between police and citizens (individuals or groups) that lead or could lead to poor police–community relations.
3. Suggest some ways to modify these destructive perceptions (see topic 2).

4. Survey students in the class individually as to their concepts regarding the role of police officers. Is there a consensus of views? To what degree are the concepts subjective? Objective?

Are the views expressed representative of the views of identifiable groups in your community?

Bibliography

Bandler, R., and Grinder, J. (1975). *The Structure of Magic*, Vol. I. Palo Alto, CA: Science and Behavior Books.

Barker, T., Hunter, R. D., and Rush, J. P. (1994). *Police Systems and Practices: An Introduction*. Upper Saddle River, NJ: Prentice Hall.

Bittner, E. (1970). *The Functions of Police in Modern Society*. Rockville, MD: National Institute of Mental Health.

Broderick, J. J. (1987). *Police in a Time of Change*, 2nd ed. Prospect Heights, IL: Waveland Press.

Bureau of Justice Statistics. (2001). *Law Enforcement Management and Administrative Statistics: Local Police Departments 1999*. Washington, D.C.: U.S. Department of Justice.

Conser, J. A., Russell, G. B., Paynich, R., and Gingerich, T. E. (2005). *Law Enforcement in the United States*, 2nd ed. Boston, MA: Jones and Bartlett.

Cordner, G. W. (1992). "The police on patrol," in D. J. Kenney (Ed.), *Police and Policing: Contemporary Issues*, 2nd ed. New York: Greenwood Press.

Cox, S. M., and Fitzgerald, J. D. (1999). *Police in Community Relations: Critical Issues*, 4th ed. New York: McGraw-Hill.

Doerner, W. G. (2004). *Introduction to Law Enforcement: An Insider's View*, 2nd ed. Dubuque, IA: Kendall/Hunt.

Grant, H. B., and Terry, R. J. (2005). *Law Enforcement in the 21st Century*. Boston, MA: Pearson/Allyn and Bacon.

Greene, J. R., and Klockars, C. B. (1992). "What police do," in C. B. Klockars and J. R. Greene (Eds.), *Thinking about Police: Contemporary Readings*. New York: McGraw-Hill.

Holden, R. N. (1992). *Law Enforcement: An Introduction*. Upper Saddle River, NJ: Prentice Hall.

Loftus, E. (1996). *Eyewitness Testimony*. Cambridge, MA: Harvard University Press.

Mastrofski, S. D. (1990). "The prospects of change in police patrol: A decade in review," *American Journal of Police*, Vol. XI, No. 9, pp. 1–79.

Mayer, M. (1969). *Liberty: Man versus State*. Santa Barbara, CA: Center for the Study of Democratic Institutions.

National Advisory Commission on Criminal Justice Standards and Goals. (1973). *A National Strategy to Reduce Crime*. Washington, D.C.: U.S. Government Printing Office.

Niederhoffer, A. (1967). *Behind the Shield*. New York: Doubleday.

Orwell, G. (1963). *1984*. New York: Harcourt Brace Jovanovich.

Peak, K. J. (2006). *Policing in America: Methods, Issues, and Challenges*, 5th ed. Upper Saddle River, NJ: Pearson/Prentice Hall.

Poveda, T. G. (2001). "Estimating wrongful convictions," *Justice Quarterly*, Vol. 18, No. 3, pp. 689–708.

President's Commission on Law Enforcement and the Administration of Justice. (1967). *The Challenge of Crime in a Free Society*. Washington, D.C.: U.S. Government Printing Office.

Roberg, R. R., Novak, K., and Cordner, G. W. (2005). *Police and Society*, 3rd ed. Los Angeles, CA: Roxbury Press.

Satir, V. (1978). *Your Many Faces*. Millbrae, CA: Celestial Arts.

Skolnick, J. H. (1975). *Justice without Trial*, 2nd ed. New York: Wiley.

Trautman, N. (1991). *How to Be a Great Cop*. Dallas, TX: Standards and Training, Inc.

Walker, S. (1997). *Sense and Nonsense About Crime and Drugs: A Policy Guide*, 4th ed. Belmont, CA: Wadsworth.

Walker, S. (1998). *The Police in America: An Introduction*, 3rd ed. New York: McGraw-Hill.

Walker, S., and Katz, C. M. (2002). *The Police in America: An Introduction*, 4th ed. Boston, MA: McGraw-Hill.

Wilson, J. Q. (1968). *Varieties of Police Behavior*. Cambridge, MA: Harvard University Press.

Wrobleski, H. M., and Hess, K. M. (2006). *Introduction to Law Enforcement and Criminal Justice*, 8th ed. Pacific Grove, CA: Thomson/Wadsworth.

Zalman, M., and Seigel, L. (1999). "Psychology of perception, eyewitness identification, and the lineup," in L. Stolzenberg and S. J. D'Alessio (Eds.), *Criminal Courts for the 21st Century*. Upper Saddle River, NJ: Prentice Hall.

MODULE 2

CHAPTER 3

Police–Community Relations: An Overview

The police are the public and the public are the police.

—PEEL'S PRINCIPLES

KEY CONCEPTS

Community–Police
Relations
External Communities

Feedback (information flow)
Internal Communities
Overlapping Communities

People's Police
Police–Community
Relations

LEARNING OBJECTIVES

Studying this chapter will enable you to:

1. Provide an overview of police–community relations and their impact on the police system.

2. Explain how police–community relations are complex interactions among a multitude of internal and external communities.

3. Define the *people's police* and *community*.

4. Describe the evolution of police–community relations programs in the United States.

5. Identify the current status of and prospects for police–community relations.

I n the last few years, American law enforcement has accepted (begrudgingly at times) the notion that community relations is an important and even indispensable part of police work. In doing so, it has recaptured the old belief that a police force can and should be "the people's police"—an agency that is responsive to the public it serves.

Philosophically, not every officer agrees, and practically, the nature of community relations varies widely from agency to agency, community to community, but change has occurred. Awareness and acceptance of community relations—the process of developing and maintaining meaningful communication among the agency, its service area, and specific populations served, aims to identify, define, and resolve problems of mutual concern—have increased.

Police-Community Relations and the Administration of Justice, Eighth Edition
by Ronald D. Hunter, Thomas Barker

THE POLICE–COMMUNITY ENVIRONMENT

Of all the issues that affect the police in the United States, none is more important than the manner in which the police and the public interrelate. Despite our democratic traditions (or perhaps because of them), we in the United States have been slow to accept the concept that "police are the public and the public the police." Yet the police and the community are not only interdependent, but are in fact inseparable from one another.

Readers, both police and civilian, may find it difficult to accept the assertion that police and community are inseparable. If one adheres to the traditional concept of police–community relations (as shown in Figure 3.1), such a statement may actually seem ludicrous. Typically, the police have responded to pressure from politicians and others who have reacted to complaints from groups or individual citizens regarding police procedures. Such an isolationist view has perpetuated an "us against them" mentality that has detracted from police–community interaction.

However, if one adheres to the more contemporary view that the individuals within various police organizations are but a microcosm of the general society and that this society is composed of numerous interrelated communities, the previous assertion is valid. Today's police organizations are not isolated monoliths that are impervious to the communities they serve. The police organization is not a unified community, nor is there a single community to which they respond. There are in actuality a myriad of sometimes cooperating, often competing communities that are constantly influencing and being influenced by one another.

Police organizations are in truth very responsive to this rapidly changing "community environment." To understand police–community interaction, it is necessary for the student of police to realize that there are constant exchanges among the various communities that exist both inside and outside the police organization. Figure 3.2 demonstrates how these "exchange relationships" (Cole and Smith, 2007) between communities occur.

As displayed in Figure 3.2, the police organization comprised a number of **internal communities** engaged in constant interaction with one another. These internal communities are engaged in numerous individual and group exchanges with a myriad of **external communities**. Within the **overlapping communities** displayed are those groups from which both the internal and external communities are comprised.

DEFINING POLICE–COMMUNITY RELATIONS

As argued in the preceding section, there is no one "community" that is served by the police. Instead, there are numerous communities that make up an often indefinable "public." As a result, "public opinion" is usually not a clear consensus of viewpoint within a nation, state, county, or municipality but a chorus of differing opinions from various communities.

Police–community relations are complicated and constantly changing interactions between representatives of the police organization and an assortment of governmental agencies, public

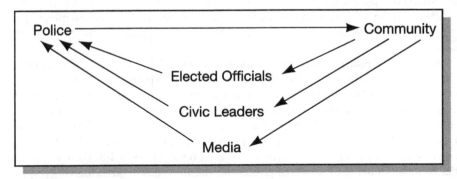

FIGURE 3.1 **Traditional police–community relations.**

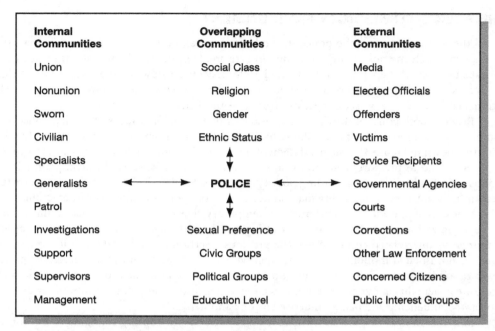

Internal Communities	Overlapping Communities	External Communities
Union	Social Class	Media
Nonunion	Religion	Elected Officials
Sworn	Gender	Offenders
Civilian	Ethnic Status	Victims
Specialists	↕	Service Recipients
Generalists	←→ **POLICE** ←→	Governmental Agencies
Patrol	↕	Courts
Investigations	Sexual Preference	Corrections
Support	Civic Groups	Other Law Enforcement
Supervisors	Political Groups	Concerned Citizens
Management	Education Level	Public Interest Groups

FIGURE 3.2   **Contemporary police–community relations.**

groups, and private individuals representing a wide range of competing and often conflicting interests.

Throughout this book we focus our discussion of police and community interaction on both the external communities outside the police organization and the internal communities within the police organization. Our primary contention is that successful police–community relations must take into account exchange relationships among community groups located both inside and outside the police organization. To be successful, these exchange relations depend on feedback from the internal and external community groups. Feedback leads to improvement and goal attainment. The isolated police agencies of the past failed to recognize that their success, however defined, required feedback from the community and the citizens served.

ACCEPTANCE OF THE CONCEPT OF POLICE–COMMUNITY RELATIONS

Secrecy and institutional separation have ceased to be defensible positions for police agencies to take in relation to the communities they serve. Although secrecy and institutional separation have not totally disappeared, it is valid to state that in less than two decades the most insular of all institutions in American society is becoming committed, at least in principle, to programs of ongoing exchanges with the community and with other agencies about its mandate and practices.

The concept of police–community relations has gained a secure level of acceptance in the law enforcement establishment and in urban government. Acceptance, in a working sense, means that proposals to establish and maintain such programs have a fair chance of success. There are no longer any organized factions publicly opposing police efforts to open and cultivate channels of communication with the public in general and with civic groups and social movements in particular. Whether those who were aligned against such attempts are now merely silent for the time being, or whether they have changed their views, is an open question. But there is no doubt that activities included under the heading of police–community relations are achieving respectability, and that a large and growing number of police officials in positions of responsibility have come to view them as indispensable for effective law enforcement and peacekeeping.

ACCEPTANCE AS A SIGN OF PROGRESS

This acceptance alone is a sign of progress, a remarkable achievement. It is, however, only a first step toward implementation. It is much easier to agree with the reasonableness and justice of a proposal than to implement it and live with the consequences of its implementation. Above all, when the task is to decide what must and can be done, it is important to measure aspirations against resistance, inertia, and regression. For example, despite the acceptance of the principle of police–community relations, few, if any, actually functioning police–community relations programs are fully deserving of the name. In an assessment that remains accurate, Moore (1992, p. 102) stated that "no police department in the United States can today be accurately characterized as community policing or problem-oriented policing departments."

A positive statement of present circumstances is that although newly functioning programs have been accepted in principle, the kinds of activities that total acceptance would lead one to expect have yet to be implemented. However, as we shall see, there is definitely reason to be optimistic. American policing in the twenty-first century has come a long way since it was transplanted from England. Nevertheless, the current "War on Terrorism," brought on by the 9/11 attacks on the United States, and the resulting economic crisis have had effects on American policing, particularly in the area of funding. Recent events also will increase the need for good police–community relations between the police and certain minority communities.

TIGHT FINANCES AND THEIR EFFECTS

In times of tight finances, new and existing programs must compete for reduced funding and for human resources with other programs that meet long-established police obligations (e.g., crime, traffic, and vice control). In such circumstances it becomes necessary to demonstrate a high level of cost-effectiveness in meeting police goals. Often, community relations programs become locked into quick and relatively safe ways of demonstrating success: (1) "busywork" activities, which show that something is happening and presumably goals are being accomplished and (2) solving easy problems and postponing (sometimes indefinitely) the more difficult ones (e.g., maintaining contact with civic and political groups that are receptive to the police and failing to reach out to those that are not receptive).

Such difficulties can arise with virtually any kind of program in which success is expected. The way police–community relations programs have developed seems to pose some unique difficulties for these programs in particular.

A HISTORICAL PERSPECTIVE

Nineteenth-Century Origins

The concept of police–community relations is not new. When Sir Robert Peel undertook the reorganization of the London police forces with the Metropolitan Police Act of 1829, he and the two key commissioners that he appointed, Charles Rowan and Richard Mayne, emphasized that the police should work in cooperation with the people and that members of the office should protect the rights, serve the needs, and earn the *trust* of the population they policed (Critchley, 1967; Reith, 1952).

Writing at the turn of the century, Melville Lee discussed Peel's principles of law enforcement. The following excerpts from Lee's text retain the flavor of the period in which they were written. They also reflect many of the concepts of police–community relations that are being proposed today. According to Lee, police officers are "public servants in the fullest sense of the term."

> It should be understood at the outset that the principal object to be attained is the prevention of crime. To this great end every effort of the police is to be directed.
>
> The absence of crime will be considered the best proof of the complete efficiency of the police.

. . . There is no qualification more indispensable to a police officer than a perfect command of temper, never suffering himself to be moved in the slightest degree by any language or threats that may be used; if he does his duty in a quiet and determined manner, such conduct will probably induce well-disposed bystanders to assist him should he require it.

. . . What is wanted is the respect and approval of all good citizens.

The wisdom of fostering cordial relations between the people and the civil defenders of their lives and properties seems so obvious, that it is a source of wonder that so little attention has been given to the study of how best to promote this desirable *entente cordiale.*

The police . . . are simply a disciplined body of men, specially engaged in protecting "masses" as well as "classes," from any infringement of their rights on the part of those who are not law-abiding.

. . . It is necessary also that they [the public] should be acquainted with the conditions that govern the mutual relationship.

We are well served by our police because we have wisely made them personally responsible for their actions.

. . . That is to say, the modern system rests, as the ancient one did, on the sure foundation of mutual reliance. (Lee, 1971)

These principles were imported into U.S. police departments. In a way, they had to be: There was strenuous opposition to establishing organized police forces on the grounds that they would be the exclusive organ of executive government and indifferent to public influence. They would function against the people, resulting in a "police state." Opposition was in part silenced by assurances that the new institution would be "the people's police" (Astor, 1971).

In many ways the institution focused on the needs of the people. Engaging in community service activities is a part of the American police heritage (see Figure 3.3). As Zumbrun (1983) noted, "During the early part of the 20th century, the New York City Police Department engaged in such non-stereotyped activities as massive Christmas parties for poverty-stricken children and their families, engaging in job hunts for released prisoners from Sing Sing prison and other non-crime fighting endeavors."

The "police state" issue did not die. World War II and many wars and cold war struggles before and since have been waged against so-called police states. In many European countries and

FIGURE 3.3 **Service is part of the American police heritage.**

in the United States, the police worked hard to disassociate themselves from such a label in the aftermath of World War II. Still, many Americans found adequate evidence to support the view that during their first century of existence in the United States, the police were often corrupt agents of boss-dominated urban governments (Berkley, 1969).

SELLING THE POLICE TO THE PEOPLE

The reformers of the 1950s felt that it was necessary to overcome the attitudes of contempt that middle-class citizens held toward police and, literally, to sell the police to the people. This was done by sending speakers to high schools, to business luncheons, to meetings of civil organizations, and so on. These speakers argued that the police are the "thin blue line," the last bulwark of defense against the dark forces of crime and disorder.

Three key elements were notable in these efforts:

1. At their best, the police employed highly sophisticated techniques of advertising, selling, and, of course, public relations.
2. To police the "public" in a public relations sense, meant, essentially, policing middle-class adults and youth ("solid citizens" and their offspring).
3. No attempt was made to improve the "product"; the programs were designed solely to improve the police "image"; there was little or no provision to recommend or effect needed changes in departmental policy or procedures.

Although these police–community contacts were chosen very selectively, in the 1950s they did constitute a movement away from the exclusive dominance of police departments by city-hall bosses.

The 1960s: From Public Relations to Community Relations

At the beginning of the 1960s, the police had reason to believe their public relations programs had been successful. But then minorities, disaffected young people, the poor, recent immigrants, antiwar activists, and street people made new claims and demands. Their quarrel was with the "system," or with society as a whole, but their confrontations were often with the police, who usually responded with force. One lesson should have been clear: Public relations programs designed to appeal to "solid citizens" were ineffective in dealing with the disadvantaged and the aggrieved—many of whom were openly hostile to the police.

Something else was needed—police–community relations—where *community* was defined realistically to include, as one anonymous reviewer of this text stated, all of the "stratified, segmentalized, unintegrated, and differential environments where police work." This focus includes precisely those segments of society ignored by the earlier public-relations approach. New police–community relations programs were built on the foundations of already existing public relations programs.

The San Francisco Community Relations Unit

In the mid-1950s, the Metropolitan Police Department of St. Louis, Missouri, established a public relations division that became known as one of the best-functioning programs of its kind in the country (School of Police Administration, 1967). The division contained a speakers' bureau, published a newsletter, organized citizens' councils, and maintained school contacts, all of which were considered to be effective in accordance with their aims. There were also police and community relations committees in housing projects, which, in the department's own estimate, did not function well even as late as 1966. Nevertheless, the undertaking as a whole had an enviable reputation. In 1962, Chief Thomas Cahill of San Francisco visited St. Louis to help obtain answers to his own problems. Chief Cahill realized that it was important to use other resources, not just physical force, to deal with outbreaks of discontent. His department was faced with student protests against hearings being conducted in San Francisco City Hall by the House Un-American Activities Committee. Chief Cahill took the new director of his community relations program, Lieutenant Dante Andreotti, to St. Louis to study that city's methods. Cahill and

Andreotti went to St. Louis to learn because they had a problem on their hands; their problem, however, was quite different from the situation that had motivated the St. Louis department. The St. Louis program was formulated primarily to address the "solid citizens." No one considered the program seriously impaired by the fact that the project that was directed toward working with the disadvantaged and the aggrieved did not function.

In the ensuing years, Lieutenant Andreotti developed a program in San Francisco that was vastly different from the St. Louis program. The direction of work that was permitted to lie fallow in St. Louis became the central interest of the San Francisco community relations unit. While Andreotti commanded the unit, "community relations" meant working primarily with the disadvantaged and the aggrieved segments of the population. The unit's officers were attached to organizations such as the Youth Opportunity Center, which served ghetto youngsters, and the Office of Economic Opportunity. They also exerted themselves to meet with, talk and listen to, and help people living in the Tenderloin, the city's skid row, and its ghetto. The activities of the San Francisco unit are illustrated by the following example:

> A robbery and beating of a white grocery store operator in a minority group neighborhood resulted in community-wide concern, and tension. As a result of the efforts of the police and the community relations unit, together with minority group leaders, a group of youngsters (many of whom had juvenile records) were organized into a picket line which marched back and forth in front of the store carrying signs condemning violence and stating that they were ashamed of what had happened. Although the boys picketing were not involved in the robbery or the beating, they offered verbal apologies to the family of the victim for the act done by members of their race. The publicity given this parade by the various media communications resulted in an almost immediate lessening of tensions. (School of Police Administration, 1967, p. 49)

This incident should not be taken as indicating the scope of the unit's program nor even its focal concerns. The routine work of the officers assigned to the unit concentrated much more on everyday kinds of predicaments, such as protecting persons who were not resourceful on their own or helping persons with police records find employment or lodging. The officers acted upon the realization that life in the city comprises many conditions, circumstances, and troubled people. They worked on the assumptions that ex-cons without jobs are likely to commit crimes again; intergroup tension may lead to violent confrontations; children without recreational facilities tend to get into mischief; and so on. When such potential is not checked, it leads to consequences that will sooner or later have to be handled by detectives, riot squads, or juvenile officers, depending on the specific situation.

Those in the San Francisco community relations unit were not the first police officers ever to help a former criminal find a job, nor were they the first to succeed in preventing a public disorder. Their innovation was in two additional aspects of their work. First, they did not simply go out to solve some problem; rather, they always dealt with problems in conjunction with other community resources. In the previous example, they worked together with minority group leaders. Cooperation was not simply a convenient expedient; it involved an established and ongoing mutually cooperative arrangement between members of the police and members of the community. Second, persons in the unit felt that providing services to citizens was their primary job. In the past such services were rendered on rare occasions and only after the officers took care of more demanding crime control problems.

The establishment of the community relations unit in San Francisco meant that personnel resources were specifically assigned to the task of working cooperatively with the people. More important, the chief of the department referred to the existence of the unit with pride. He claimed credit for creating it and gave weight to its importance by having its commanding officer report directly to the office of the chief, rather than through the chain of command. Nevertheless, some commanding officers and several line officers did not like the unit. Yet even without total acceptance within the department, the unit gained momentum. It soon was regarded locally and nationally as conspicuously successful.

Although others considered the unit to be a success, its commander, Lieutenant Andreotti, recognized the problems that still had to be faced and spoke about them at a law enforcement conference in 1968:

> It is my belief that there isn't a successful police-community program anywhere in the country today, in terms of commitment by all members of the law enforcement agency. There have been successful police-community relations units, but practically all of them have been frustrated in their efforts to get the rank and file involved to the point of a genuine, personal interest and commitment. (Andreotti, 1971, p. 120)

Police–Community Relations since the 1960s

The themes of the 1970s were Vietnam, the Watergate scandal of the Nixon administration, inflation, and the energy crisis. Compared with the 1960s, the 1970s were relatively subdued, except for a notable and disturbing increase in violence. It was a period of "finding" oneself, or, as it was called, the "Me Decade."

Out of turmoil of the 1960s, and based on the findings of several presidential commissions, funding was made available through the Federal Law Enforcement Assistance Administration for research, education and training, and projects of criminal justice agencies designed to reduce crime. Law enforcement agencies had the opportunity to develop and implement new programs— and they did. Many were described as community relations projects, and some of those were innovative and elaborate. Many, in practice, were simply public relations activities. Few were carefully evaluated. As federal funding for them ended, many projects ended. Others, not necessarily as originally conceived, are still part of agency function today.

During the 1980s, the increasing fear of crime throughout U.S. society resulted in a transition of focus from enhancing relations with minority communities to providing reassurances to the general public that crime was not running rampant. Crime prevention units became popular with police agencies throughout the nation. These units served not only as a means of educating the public about crime prevention strategies but also became valuable tools for enhancing public perceptions of the police.

In addition to developing crime prevention units, the police also sought to enhance their relationships with the media. Specialized public information units sprang into existence across the country in agencies that previously had sought to suppress information. These units not only made information more accessible to the media and civic groups but also promoted support for police programs.

The results of the previous strategies led progressive police administrators to seek out new programs in which the public could become more actively involved with their police agencies. An array of community liaison units, school resource programs, joint police–community activities, and enhanced civilian oversight of police operations were experimented with. The culmination of these efforts is community-oriented policing.

Despite the advances in police–community relations since the 1960s, few programs receive the total support of their agencies. Andreotti's concern, first voiced in 1968, continues to be a community relations concern as we enter the new century. In terms of commitment by all members of law enforcement agencies, the status of police–community relations has not changed dramatically since 1968.

The rise of gangs in the inner cities and their rapid spread to suburban America, the detrimental effects of a flourishing illicit drug trade, the dramatic increase in hate crimes by both right-wing extremists and frustrated minorities, as well as the fear and instability produced by a declining economy demonstrate the need for enhanced police–community relations. The riots in Los Angeles and other major cities during the 1960s served to motivate police agencies to begin police–community relations. The distrust and resentment of police expressed in many U.S. cities following the Los Angeles riot of 1992, provoked by the acquittal of police officers charged with beating an African American motorist, also served as the catalyst for new developments in police–community relations.

A strong economy, a decline in violent crime, and more responsiveness on the part of the police to citizen complaints yielded positive results as the 1990s ended. However, the 1999 shooting death of an African immigrant by the New York City Police and the reactions of African American activists to that shooting have reignited tensions, in that city and elsewhere. The three-day riot (April 7–10, 2001) in Cincinnati, Ohio, following a police shooting of an unarmed black male demonstrates that there are still fragile relationships between the police and certain community groups. Currently, one of the major issues facing U.S. policing are claims that police officers and police departments are engaged in racial profiling or racially biased policing, particularly in the areas of traffic stops and searches. These events demonstrate that we still have far to go.

The Police and Social Work

Even under the best circumstances, community relations programs suffer both from neglect and from being given low priority by police departments. Many police officers have little interest in community relations programs, and even resist and condemn them. Social problems, as the thinking in police circles sometimes goes, are best left to social workers; they are not "proper" police business (i.e., they have little to do with preventing people from committing crimes and with bringing them to justice when they do). This view persists. Academy training often continues to focus predominantly on "crime fighting" behavior, even though it is generally known that the major portion of police work (some references note as high as 80 percent) is social service–related rather than "crime fighting" behavior.

To say that only social workers should deal with these problems is similar to arguing that a champion swimmer should not pull a drowning person from the water unless the swimmer has a Red Cross life-saving certificate. Commitment to the principles of police–community relations means acting on the assumption that the police are a service organization dedicated to keeping the peace, to the defense of the rights of the people, and to the enforcement of laws. In all these fields, they are not merely independent instruments of government; rather, they must work with individuals, community groups, and community institutions to achieve desired objectives.

It was this latter attitude that governed the intervention of the San Francisco community relations unit in the incident mentioned previously. This incident is a good example of commitment to the principles of police–community relations on the level of departmental organization. It is not clear in this case at which point community leaders would be told to stay out of it and let the experts take over (and the community relations unit would move on to the next case). Typically, that would be most likely to occur as procedures leading to the apprehension and trial of the assailants were set into motion.

Such a move may seem appropriate. Citizens are not expected to be involved in "catching criminals." In fact, when they insist upon becoming involved, police believe that they are likely to cause more harm than good. This is also the view of many judges, public prosecutors, city council members, and citizens. Thinking in terms of isolated offenses, it is difficult to reason otherwise.

Thus, even those who are in favor of genuine police–community relations are forced to agree that the work must be assigned to special units that work independently while the rest of policing takes its ordinary course. In other words, progressive departments establish external units to deal with their communities, but these units must follow the department's conditions. In still different terms, it appears that accepting the principles of police–community relations in its presently exclusively outward-oriented direction (somewhat in the way nations send envoys to other nations) does not mean that two-way police–community relations are the norm (or, to continue the analogy, that the other nations send them envoys).

This situation is not unique. The police are not alone in thinking that they can communicate adequately with the people by means of external ambassadors. Indeed, they have done better with this approach than have other institutions. The educational system, for example, keeps parents at arm's length while pretending to allow involvement by letting assistant principals of schools deal with the PTA. Similarly, institutions that deliver medical services often do not even pretend to communicate with the people they serve. In each of these cases, it is argued that lay people could not possibly contribute to solving the problems of a slow-learning child or a diabetic patient, just as it is said that lay people could not be helpful in solving a robbery.

All communities have educational needs, health needs, and law enforcement and peacekeeping needs. It is neither proper nor efficient for the specialists alone to define the nature of these needs nor the way in which they will be met. Specialists bring competence and skills to bear on meeting these needs, but they must communicate with lay citizens to determine what those needs are.

The Success of Police–Community Relations

The establishment of police–community relations units is a first, long step in recognition of the usefulness of bringing needs and special resources together in a harmonious relationship. Nevertheless, it is just that—a first step. The establishment of **community–police relations**, in a much broader sense, is a logical next step. An example might help in making clear what this involves.

It is commonly accepted that the ghettos of our cities produce a disproportionately large number of people who are arrested for criminal activities and that people living in these ghettos are exposed to a far greater risk of being criminally victimized than are other citizens. Finally, it is no secret that people living in these areas distrust the police and often are reluctant to help officers in their efforts to control crime. What would be more sensible, for the police to consider these three facts, together with their present ways of dealing with suspects and victims, as systematically related? Joint consideration of the larger problem suggests that a successful attack on the problem can come only from the establishment of a program of trusting and fully cooperative relations between ghetto communities and the police.

The reversal of terms—from police–community relations to community–police relations—was not done simply to coin a new term. It does not matter what the arrangement is called. What matters is that the full effectiveness of the program cannot be attained merely by having a special unit to implement it. At best, such units can succeed only in doing an occasional good deed and putting out an occasional fire, while leaving the rest of the police department's work unaffected by even these accomplishments. Creating a special unit that has the responsibility for effective community relations has four adverse consequences (Moore, 1992, p. 135):

> First, by isolating the function in a special unit, the unit becomes vulnerable to organizational ridicule. The community relations units become known as the "grin and wave" or "rubber gun" squads.
>
> Second, after a special unit is formed, everyone else in the department is seemingly relieved of responsibility for enhancing community relations.
>
> Third, if the community relations unit should obtain important information about community concerns or ways in which the community might be able to help the department, it is difficult to make those observations heard in the department. Department members are not receptive to bad news or unwelcome demands; after all, that is the responsibility of the unit to stamp out dissent in the community.
>
> Fourth, the organization no longer looks for other ways to improve community relations.

Success of community–police relations requires a "people's police" attitude. Rank-and-file officers need to recognize that the police are a service organization dedicated to keeping the peace, defending the rights of the people, and enforcing the laws. Community–police relations is a broad, two-way program that involves every officer, not just a special unit.

INTERNALIZING COMMUNITY RELATIONS

Perhaps it would be easiest to explain the concept of incorporating community relations into police work by first discussing what it does *not* mean.

What "Community Relations" Does Not Mean

- *Making entire departments do what police–community relations units do now.* Special programs would remain the responsibility of the units, just as other units in police agencies also have special responsibilities. Although support for programs needs to be broadly based, it would be inefficient to have all units specializing in all programs.
- *Weakening law enforcement.* Viewing crime as a social problem does not imply that crime control would be "soft." Actually, police might become more strongly dedicated to crime control than they are now, and possibly become more effective in that task. Improved community relations would be a tool, or organizational strategy, used in crime control.
- *Close involvement with partisan politics.* Mobilizing support for police–community relations at state, county, and community levels may involve working with "political" figures and organizations, but it is a position that is not partisan, conservative, or liberal. It is a method for doing police work that considers the distribution of political forces in any community and seeks the cooperation of all.
- *"Bending" to community pressures.* Clearly, this is a danger in the face of conflicting demands, but risks can be contained provided that responsiveness to community needs and demands is not interpreted as bargaining away the police mandate. Because openness is reciprocal, the risk can become an opportunity for citizens to understand and respect the police mandate in society.
- *Turning police officers into social workers.* Social interaction is a critical part of police work, and police perform "social" work as part of their everyday tasks. The basic functions of social work are to develop, maintain, and strengthen the social welfare system so that it can meet basic human needs; to ensure adequate standards of subsistence, health, and welfare for all; to enable people to function optimally within their social institutional roles and statuses; and to support and improve the social order and institutional structure of society (Farley, Smith, and Boyle, 2006). Police also are involved in such a function as part of the overall mission of a service organization, dedicated to keeping the peace, defending the rights of the people, preventing crime, and enforcing laws. The common interests are apparent, but the professional specialty and the context within which each functions may vary (see also Morales, Sheafor, and Scott, 2007). Improving police–community relations in all aspects of police work will allow officers to be more effective public servants while exercising the full range of their proper police duties and service responsibilities.

What "Community Relations" Does Mean

- *Reviving the ideas of "the* **people's police.***"* This is the basic notion on which modern, urban police departments were founded. Needs for police service must be determined on the basis of ongoing communication between the people and the police.
- *A more reasoned basis for police work.* Police officers usually operate with a repertoire of responses determined by penal codes, municipal ordinances, and demands of the often recurrent types of situations and emergencies with which they deal. The police–community relations concept encourages police to deal with complex problems in complex ways, going beyond traditional constraints and procedures where necessary (see Bittner, 1970).
- *A deeper, more comprehensive interest in human life.* To some, this phrase may sound sentimental, and to others, unnecessary, because many effective police officers now operate with humanity and compassion. Still, many police officers do not find it improper to adopt cynical attitudes toward human life. The police–community relations approach, by contrast, stresses that police are both entitled and required to take an interest in and help to resolve human problems.
- *An acceptance of the view that "relations" is a process, not a product.* It is vital, ongoing, and constantly changing. It requires mutual respect and mutual exchange and cannot be compartmentalized if it is to be effective. Feedback is a necessary ingredient of this process. The community and its groups must be encouraged to provide feedback to the people's police, and the police in turn must provide feedback to the community.

FIGURE 3.4 An example of good police–community relations.

Michael Newman, Photo Edit Inc.

SYSTEMS AND COMMUNITIES

A system is a set of elements, or components, interacting with each other. These elements may be physiological—as in organic systems in the human body, individuals within a family, groups of individuals as in a police department—or groups of systems, as in the criminal justice system. Systems, according to systems theory, are guided by major principles, which include the following:

1. The whole is greater than the sum of its parts.
2. Elements of a system interact in repetitive patterns.
3. A change in one part of the system will reverberate throughout the system (transactional reciprocity).
4. Interactions are governed by a set of rules.
5. Systems tend to maintain a balance among the elements.
6. Open systems exchange energy, or information flow, with the surrounding environment (Norgard and Whitman, 1980).

Feedback/Input

Important to the systems analogy, and the theme throughout this book, is the element of **feedback, or information flow** (mentioned in 6 above). Feedback/input separates public relations from police–community relations (discussed in Chapter 4) and is essential for improving the relationships between the police and their communities. As systems interact with their environments (internal and external), they receive feedback from these environments. In the past, police agencies ignored or set up shields to protect themselves from this feedback, not realizing the potential it had

FIGURE 3.5 Another example of good police–community relations.
Courtesy of Rome Police Department.

for system improvement or giving their "clients" the opportunity to act with and not merely be acted on. This feedback can be very useful in evaluating the operation or goal achievement of the system, particularly a social system such as a government agency. Feedback/input operates to allow the community or service clients to impact the operation and goal setting of the government agency, creating what the authors of the national best-selling book *Reinventing Government* called "Community-Owned Government" (Osborne and Gaebler, 1993). As an example of community-owned government, Osborne and Gaebler cite the efforts of Lee Brown when he became police chief of Houston, Texas, in 1982. In setting up "neighborhood-oriented policing," Brown believed that the police should do more than respond to incidents of crime by also helping neighborhoods solve problems that create crime and crime conditions. The police, particularly beat officers, solicited input from neighborhood residents because Brown recognized that police officers are the boundary spanners between the police department as a system and the community as the external environment. Good police–community relationships demand that feedback from the community is constantly solicited and evaluated by the police. Efforts to solicit feedback, to name a few, come in the form of community surveys, customer follow-ups (contacting and surveying those who have requested the police), customer contacts (beat patrol), customer councils (regularly scheduled community meetings), focus groups, involvement in police activities (ride-alongs and citizen academies), and complaint-tracking systems. As cited in the book, many police agencies are involved in these activities.

The police must also solicit and involve themselves in providing feedback/input to other systems. Police agencies are a part of several systems and are also a system within a system. They are part of the criminal justice, the human services delivery, and the community social systems. Each person in the police agency is part of a family system and of the police agency system. Police agencies and police officers are affected by systems principles in all of these contexts. They help to shape the systems in which they participate, and they are shaped by them. Each of these systems is, in effect, a community with which the police must relate. Community is defined as a group of people sharing common boundaries, such as common goals, needs, interests, and/or geographical location. The task of police–community relations appears more complex as each community is considered.

THE MANY COMMUNITIES IN COMMUNITY RELATIONS

In future chapters, each of these communities, and others, will receive individual attention. At this point, however, it is important to recognize a few of the many communities that make up the environment in which police work. Each has a distinct identity of its own; each has its own elements, and each interacts in some distinct way with police and with each other. Each community must be part of police–community relations if it is to be truly effective.

External Communities

THE JUSTICE COMMUNITY   Other police agencies, jurisdictions, courts, and corrections departments existing at many levels of government are part of the justice community with which police must interact. The nature of the relationship between police and members of the justice community has a direct impact on police effectiveness in achieving goals. A lack of coordination, communication, and mutual respect within this community, or system, is legendary. Community relations includes relations with this community as a whole and with its individual members.

THE POLITICAL COMMUNITY   As we stated, the early police reformers worked to extricate the police from domination by political bosses and their partisan politics. It is proper that partisan politics, in the form of interference in police personnel decisions and enforcement decisions, be eliminated. However, the police can never divorce themselves completely from politics and elected officials. Our current system of decentralized policing ensures that police departments "are closely tied to political and community interests, and that they be held politically accountable for their actions" (Cordner, Scarborough, and Sheehan, 2004). The political community— in the form of elected officials—is one of the ways that democratic societies keep police power

FIGURE 3.6   The best police–community relations is a product of caring: Deputies assisting with the local Special Olympics.

Courtesy of Jackson County Sheriff's Department.

in check. The political community also provides funding and other resources. Many police executives have failed to recognize the importance of the political community to their, and their agencies', success. The legendary battle between Los Angeles P.D. Chief Daryl Gates and Mayor Bradley is well known (Gates, 1992).

THE HUMAN SERVICES COMMUNITY   The human services umbrella includes many public and private social service resources: mental health and general medical services; media, civic, and religious groups; and educational services. These also form a community, and sometimes multiple communities, with which police officers and agencies interact. Mutual support and availability of services may be lacking because of poor police–community relations. Keeping the peace may depend on access to and coordination of such resources.

CITIZENS AND THE POLICE   Peel's principles state that (Critchley, 1967; Reith, 1952) "the police must secure the willing cooperation of the public in voluntary observance of the law to be able to secure and maintain public respect." Part of police–community relations is understanding the public that police serve and having the public understand police. That is no easy task. The public is many people, with many varying needs and hopes, who live in a changing society and bring to that society conflicting values and cultural rules. The police agency is relatively closed, somewhat secretive, and vague as to what the police role and the citizen role should be. Citizen participation in policing, particularly in crime-prevention aspects, has increased in recent years. The business community actively participates in police-designed crime-prevention programs. Neighborhoods operate effective block watches. Many of these efforts are models in cost-effective crime prevention. Citizen volunteers now participate in many areas of police work. Even those efforts that have been focused on little more than public relations could be redefined and expanded in the context of community relations.

Thus far, however, much of this redefinition and expansion is rhetorical rather than practiced, and those communities and neighborhoods most in need of improved police–community relationships are the ones least likely to be involved in such projects. The cooperation and support of other groups are much easier to gain and maintain.

Internal Communities

THE PERSONAL SUPPORT COMMUNITY   The officers' support groups, both in the sense of a family system and close personal relationships, affect the officers' perspective and effectiveness. Each officer has an impact on the support groups as well. This relationship may be one of the most critical in determining an officer's ability to cope with the human experience of being a cop. It also may determine to a large degree how the individual officer will relate with other communities.

THE POLICE COMMUNITY   The police officer must also be considered as a member of the police agency and police structure. It is this community that can determine whether police–community relations outside the agency will be supported or undermined both as a matter of policy and practice. The first positive relationship that must be formed in effective community relations is accomplished within the agency itself (Fischer, 1981, pp. 54–55).

REALITY CHECK
The Need to Emphasize Membership in Communities

As young police officers (which we freely acknowledge to have been many years ago), the authors found themselves increasingly socializing with officers with whom they worked. They also found that parties they attended were increasingly "cop parties" in which everyone present either was in, or affiliated with, law enforcement. The tendency for police to socialize within their own "comfort group" is very natural in that this can prevent them from confrontations with others who are biased against police officers, as well as avoiding unpleasant situations (such as parties where drugs are present) in which they might be forced to intervene.

Although this socialization phenomenon is not unique to policing, it can become a major impediment to good police–community relations because it helps to perpetuate the view on the part of many police officers that they are separate and distinct from "the public." This can lead to an "us versus them" perspective that Barker, Hunter, and Rush (1994) labeled as "Blue Blindness." This perspective not only creates a potential for abuse and intolerance on the part of the police, but leads to suspicion and distrust of the police by citizens. The dilemma faced by police administrators is how do they combat these views from developing? Common strategies are to ensure diversity in hiring and implement training programs that promote tolerance and understanding.

The uses of hiring to ensure minority representation and training to promote awareness are not only wise but necessary to comply with legal and social expectations. However, these strategies are not enough to prevent officers from becoming isolated from the many communities they serve. What is needed is to intervene during the early socialization of new officers to prevent blue blindness from occurring. This is done by encouraging officers to maintain their ties with people who are not in law enforcement (contrary to what some may think, there are plenty of "normal people" within the communities that an officer may belong to who do not engage in unlawful behavior). In addition, during their initial training, both at the academy and in field training, officers should be encouraged to engage in social and recreational activities that enable them to interact with people from other professions. Becoming involved in "external communities" is beneficial for both the officers and agencies in which they serve.

Conclusions

Police–community relations programs were built on the foundations of already existing public relations programs and, like those programs, involved working with the community in ways that leave little or no room for recommending or effecting changes in departmental policies or procedures. In other words, there was no allowance for essential feedback.

Police–community work concentrated on precisely the segments of the community (e.g., blacks, lower-class youth, and poor) that were most neglected by the earlier public-relations approach, a change that called for new attitudes and procedures.

Police–community relations (following a familiar tendency of our age and bureaucracies everywhere) has become a specialized function to be carried out by special units.

Programs were begun in the 1970s because it was apparent that some response to injustice, discrimination, and poverty was needed, but the response was rarely the result of careful analysis and planning.

Police–community relations work to date has revealed the isolation of the police in society, particularly their isolation from what is going on in ghettos, universities, hospitals, union halls, various government agencies, and, most important, other institutions of the criminal justice system.

If police wish to maintain ongoing dialogues with all members of society, community relations must be a part of every officer's job and the department's mission.

A police agency is part of several systems and is also a system within a system. Each of these systems is, in effect, a community with which the police must relate. These include the justice community, the political community, the human services community, the personal support community, the system within a system, and citizens and the police. The task of police–community relations appears increasingly complex as each community is considered. However, understanding the concept of police–community relations, the people who are involved in its processes, the systems in which they function, the problems they encounter, and the successes they achieve provides a basis for improving police–community relationships in all communities.

Student Checklist

1. Describe the different views of communities utilized within "traditional" police–community relations and "contemporary" police–community relations.
2. What is police–community relations as described in this chapter?
3. Define the *people's police* and *community*.
4. Describe briefly the impact of police–community relations on the police system.
5. Why is feedback necessary for effective police–community relations?
6. Describe briefly the evolution of police–community relations programs in the United States.
7. List some of the difficulties surrounding a new police–community relations program.
8. Identify several "communities" within which the police play important roles.
9. Describe the current status of and prospects for police–community programs in the United States.

Topics for Discussion

1. Describe some of the difficulties that might be encountered by a new police–community relations program in your community.
2. How can police, psychiatrists, social workers, and teachers be mutually helpful and yet not intrude into each other's professions?
3. Discuss the merit of formal meetings between police administrators and presiding judges, and compare this with the need to change attitudes in these areas of the criminal justice system.
4. Demonstrate that a police–community relations program is a process, not a product.
5. Discuss how overlapping memberships in various internal and external communities could facilitate both conflict and cooperation.

Bibliography

Andreotti, D. A. (1971). "Present problems in police-community relations," in C. R. Chromache and M. Hormachea (Eds.), *Confrontation: Violence and the Police*. Boston, MA: Holbrook Press.

Astor, C. (1971). *The New York Cops: An Informal History*. New York: Scribner.

Barker, T., Hunter, R. A., and Rush, J. P. (1994). *Police Systems and Practices: An Introduction*. Upper Saddle River, NJ: Prentice Hall.

Berkley, G. E. (1969). *The Democratic Policeman*. Boston, MA: Beacon Press.

Bittner, E. (1970). *The Functions of the Police in Modern Society*. Washington, D.C.: U.S. Government Printing Office.

Cole, G. F., and Smith, C. E. (2007). *The American System of Criminal Justice*, 11th ed. Pacific Grove, CA: Wadsworth.

Cordner, G. W., Scarborough, K., and Sheehan, R. (2004). *Police Administration*, 5th ed. Cincinnati, OH: Anderson Publishing.

Critchley, T. A. (1967). *A History of Police in England and Wales, 1900–1966*. London: Constable.

Farley, O. W., Smith, L. L., and Boyle, S. W. (2006). *Introduction to Social Work*, 10th ed. Boston, MA: Pearson/Allyn and Bacon.

Fischer, R. J. (December 1981). "Administration in law enforcement: Management in law enforcement viewed as a system of systems," *The Police Chief*.

Gates, D. F. (1992). *Chief: My Life in the LAPD*. New York: Bantam Books.

Goldstein, H. (1977). *Policing a Free Society*. Cambridge, MA: Ballinger.

Lee, M. (1971). *A History of Police in England*. Montclair, NJ: Patterson Smith. (Originally published in 1901 by Methuen and Co.)

Moore, M. H. (1992). "Problem-Solving and Community Policing," in M. Tonry and N. Morris (Eds.), *Modern Policing*. Chicago, IL: The University of Chicago Press.

Morales, A. T., Sheafor, B. W., and Scott, M. E. (2007). *Social Work: A Profession of Many Faces*, 10th ed. Boston, MA: Pearson/Allyn and Bacon.

Norgard, K. E., and Whitman, S. T. (1980). *Understanding the Family as a System*. Phoenix, AZ: Arizona Department of Economic Security.

Osborne, D., and Gaebler, T. (1993). *Reinventing Government*. New York: Penguin Books.

Reith, C. (1952). *The Blind Eye of History*. London: Faber & Faber.

School of Police Administration and Public Safety, Michigan State University. (1967). *A National Survey of Police and Community Relations*. Washington, D.C.: U.S. Government Printing Office.

Zumbrun, A. J. T. (June 1983). Manuscript comments.

CHAPTER 4

Public Relations and Community Relations: A Contrast

I think it is important for the police officer who works a beat to be involved in going to meetings of neighborhood associations and civic clubs, getting to know the people so they can know him. It is important for the managers (police supervisors) to do the same thing. Oftentimes there is a historical tendency to have kind of a one-way communications system. It's equally important for the police to receive feedback.

—L. P. BROWN, INTERVIEW IN THE *NATIONAL CENTURION*, AUGUST 1983

KEY CONCEPTS

Community Advisory
  Councils/Committees
Citizens Police Academy
Community Crime Watch
Community Relations
Crime Prevention

Foot Patrol Programs
Neighborhood Team
  Policing
Neighborhood Watch
Operation Identification
Police Auxiliary Volunteers

Problem-Oriented
  Policing
Ride-Along Program
Rumor Control
Speakers' Bureau
Storefront Centers

LEARNING OBJECTIVES

Studying this chapter will enable you to:

1. Describe the origin of police–community relations as a separate operational concept.
2. Distinguish between police–public relations and police–community relations.
3. Identify the major purposes of community relations activities.
4. Provide examples of existing programs.
5. Describe community relations issues regarding crime-prevention programs.

P olice–community relations programs in the United States have been built on already exist-ing public relations programs. However, though community and public relations may be related, they are by no means the same. The differences become especially apparent when the two are compared with reference to their purposes, the activities they involve, and the type of citizen reaction or interest they presuppose. Public relations activities are designed to create a favorable environment for agency operations by keeping the public informed of agency goals and operations and by enhancing the police image; the target is a citizen who passively accepts (and approves) what the police department is doing. There is no feedback or input. **Community relations,** on the other hand, seeks to involve the citizen actively in determining what (and how) police services will be provided to the community and in establishing ongoing mechanisms for resolving problems of mutual interest to the community and the police—feedback and input.

PUBLIC RELATIONS AND/OR COMMUNITY RELATIONS?

During the short history of police–community relations, there has been little agreement on what it actually is. This lack of agreement among law enforcement professionals has resulted in the development of programs and approaches to community relations that reflect the personal views of local administrators more than they reflect any widely accepted body of knowledge. As a result, considerable confusion exists as to what community relations efforts should accomplish, and how they should do so.

It is generally accepted that police–community relations as a separate operational concept originated in the St. Louis Police Department in 1957. Since that time, the police–community relations concept has experienced sporadic growth throughout the nation. Although the need for community relations is widely accepted today as a crucial part of police administration, its current prominence is of short duration.

The rapid growth of community relations programs resulted from the violent confrontations of the mid- to late 1960s. In larger cities and urban centers, law enforcement administrators realized that they were confronting problems that traditional police tactics were not capable of solving. Administrators in smaller cities, usually on the urban fringes, recognized the possibility that violence might spill over into their communities. In both cases, the creation of specialized units, or the assignment of so-called community relations duties to specific officers, was the response. It was widely felt that such specialized responsibilities could help improve communications between increasingly activist minority groups and the police. In fact, the primary goal of such units at the outset was usually to serve as go-betweens, interpreting the attitudes, desires, and intentions of minority citizens and police agencies to each other.

Over the years, additional duties have been assigned to the community relations specialists. Thus, the community relations function has been variously described as a problem-avoidance methodology (International City Manager's Association, 1967), an "art" that is embodied in police administrative philosophy (Earle, 1980), a way of integrating police operations with community needs and desires (Brown, *n.d.*), and a way of accommodating the reality that the police are part of the political system (Attorney General's Advisory Commission on Community-Police Relations, 1973). In the early 1980s, it was often described as synonymous with police-organized community crime prevention. The concept of community policing has now added new meaning to the traditional understanding of police–community relations in the 1990s and beyond (Trojanowicz et al., 1998). The community policing philosophy broadens the scope of police–community interactions from a narrow focus devoted exclusively to crime to an examination of community concerns, such as the fear of crime, disorder of all types, neighborhood decay, and crime prevention. The philosophy seeks to change police–community relations from the traditional reactive approach of police agencies dealing with community problems as they define them to a proactive approach by partners in the definition and solving of community problems.

These diverse views have resulted in police involvement in remedial educational projects, employment counseling, encounter groups, intensive training in human relations, teaching school, inspecting residences for antiburglary campaigns, organizing block meetings, and dozens of other activities. This dispersion of effort both reflects and intensifies the lack of agreement on just what community relations is. However, most theoreticians and practitioners agree on one point: What community relations should not be. The President's Commission on Law Enforcement and the Administration of Justice stated that community relations is:

> not a public relations program to "sell the police image" to the people. It is not a set of expedients whose purpose is to tranquilize for a time an angry neighborhood by, for example, suddenly promoting a few Negro officers in the wake of a racial disturbance. (President's Commission on Law Enforcement and the Administration of Justice, 1967)

Despite this warning, and despite the fact that most professionals recognize that community relations must go further than mere image improvement on the part of law enforcement, there is still considerable confusion between the concepts of public relations and community relations.

The Relationship

There is a definite relationship between community relations and public relations. It is important, however, to recognize their differences and to practice both concepts in a way that will meet the needs of the contemporary police agency most effectively. Doing so requires (1) developing an acceptable definition of each; and (2) developing an analytical framework within which they can be examined and measured, which is no easy task in an area generally considered to be intangible.

Defining Community Relations

We have already noted the problems involved in defining community relations. However, for purposes of the following discussion, it is necessary to construct a definition that includes the most significant characteristics of those definitions discussed earlier. We also need a definition that can generally be applied to a wide range of police efforts. The following definition is suggested by the Attorney General's Advisory Commission on Community-Police Relations (1973):

> Community-police relations is a philosophy of administering and providing police services, which embodies all activities within a given jurisdiction aimed at involving members of the community and the police in the determination of: (1) what police services will be provided; (2) how they will be provided; and (3) how the police and members of the community will resolve common problems.

Such a definition includes the key characteristics of community relations. It must incorporate the following:

- Be a philosophy of police administration and service.
- Integrate police operations with community needs.
- Involve the police and community in problem solving.
- Be reciprocal.
- Be ongoing.

Defining Public Relations

Admittedly, the preceding definition is not too specific. It must be as broad as it is, however, to include the many activities that make up community relations. Any definition of public relations is also broad. It, too, must include the wide variety of operations carried out in its name. For example, *Webster's New Collegiate Dictionary* (2003) defines public relations as "The business of inducing the public to have understanding for and goodwill toward a person, firm, or institution."

A review of various texts on public relations reveals a variety of definitions. They all have one element in common: Each holds that public relations includes those activities that attempt to explain agency goals and operations to the public and to gain public support for those goals and operations.

These two definitions should not lead to the conclusion that either community relations or public relations can be isolated or explained easily. Neither concept is as simple as a basic definition might imply. Rather, the two are complex and can be understood only when several of their individual characteristics are examined.

COMMON FRAMEWORK FOR ANALYZING COMMUNITY AND PUBLIC RELATIONS

Because they are related and both properly part of police activity, the differences between community and public relations should be understood. A useful analytical framework for this purpose focuses on three characteristics of their activities:

1. The *purpose* of the activity.
2. The *processes* involved in the activity.
3. The extent of *citizen involvement*.

The Purpose of the Activity

All police operations have, or should have, a stated purpose or goal. The purpose of an activity generally embodies the values that the police agency intends to live by. Purpose is an administrative guide. It answers this question: Why has this activity been designed? Purpose, in this sense, is largely philosophical. It describes a hoped-for end. In practice, an activity may serve several purposes. Some activities may be given great administrative importance and others very little.

Why an activity actually takes place and what it accomplishes may have little to do with its stated purpose. Suppose that in an agency, fewer than 7 percent of the agency goals are to "improve the police image," yet some 30 percent of all programs described by the agency fit into a public information category in which most public relations or image-enhancement activities are contained. Officers who participated in the programs probably would rate their programs as highly successful. Their own goals for the programs have been met. The values that the police agency intended to adhere to have not. Understanding the purpose of an activity requires careful observation of what is actually being accomplished versus what was expected.

Public Relations

One common purpose of public relations activities is to develop and maintain a good environment in which to operate. For the police, this involves influencing attitudes in three areas of the environment. They must influence the public, from whom they need support (or, at least, noninterference). They must influence politicians, who are the source of funds. They must influence staff in other elements of the justice community who process those people the police usher into the system. Public information through the media can increase the preventive activity of the mass media when they cover security topics important to the public.

In order to achieve this purpose, the police must minimize obstacles and encourage support. The obstacles result from conscious opposition to what the police have done, are doing, or plan to do. They can include anything from subtle refusal to cooperate to overtly undermining police function. Support for police, on the other hand, could mean anything from passive acceptance to active support and cooperation. Passive acceptance may not be helpful, but neither is it harmful. Active support, such as that required for a campaign to target-harden a residence, is helpful to both the citizen and the police.

In general, the police have employed two ways of achieving their public relations purpose: public information and image enhancement. Public information is perhaps the most routine and widely applied public relations activity in which the police and most other organizations engage. Image enhancement is a logical extension of the public information effort.

PUBLIC INFORMATION   A strongly held value in our culture is that the informed and educated citizen is the best participant in democratic government. Applied to police performance, the theory is that if people understand why an agency (such as the police) performs as it does, they will be supportive of their performance. Information received by the public, however, often is misinformation, fostered in part by the popular entertainment media, which frequently spotlights and glamorizes the police crime-fighting role.

A check of TV listings for a one-week period in November 1982 revealed that 39 hours of prime-time (4:00–10:00 P.M.) scheduling were dedicated to police or police-related shows. The listings came from four major networks, one independent station, and one pay-TV station. In the six-hour period covered by the study, at least one hour was dedicated to newscasts (sometimes crime drama in themselves, but not counted as part of the 39 hours). Omitting that hour, a person conceivably could have watched police or police-related shows for the entire prime-time period on Saturday, Sunday, Tuesday, and Thursday, and for four hours on Wednesday. Mondays and Fridays offered less than three hours of this type of material. These shows ranged from serious drama/adventure to light, humorous entertainment programming. A reexamination of TV listings for a one-week period in April 1999 revealed similar results. In a check of TV listings from 5:00 to 10:00 P.M., 43 hours were devoted to police or police-related shows.

Complicating the effect of these programs on public information is the fact that the image portrayed is often distorted. Officers are most often white and criminals and suspects shown are more likely to be black or Hispanic. Police aggression is overplayed. Popular shows like *CSI, Law and Order, Without a Trace, Cold Case*, and *NCIS* exaggerate the occurrence of violent crimes such as stranger murders, kidnappings, and serial killings. The programs leave the impression that crimes are easily solved and justice always prevails. Many of the technologies portrayed are more fiction than fact. There is concern that jurors often have a distorted image of police evidence gathering because of television portrayals.

News coverage of police activities focuses on their crime-related duties because these are the most newsworthy. Such emphasis is understandable: Because much public information activity by police is in response to media inquiries about crime, police public information campaigns may underwrite misperception by stressing criminal themes, rather than the totality of the police job, which actually consists mainly of noncriminal responsibilities. Los Angeles Police Chief William Bratton has asked the media to stop providing real-time coverage of police chases because some run from the police to seek fame in the media spotlight. Television executives declined the request because police pursuits were newsworthy and popular.

IMAGE ENHANCEMENT   Promoting a positive image is a logical extension of public information activity. Police realize that community-wide respect and cooperation are difficult goals to achieve. There are many negative aspects to the role that society has assigned to the police. Police are charged with seeing that large numbers of people adhere to sometimes unpopular standards, and even the fact that a police force is necessary is distasteful to many citizens. Police need to promote a positive image of themselves whenever possible. In most cases, this is done by stressing the "helping" and "emergency" attributes of the police role. Public information campaigns that focus on an officer rescuing lost children, capturing armed robbers, and providing assistance at the scene of an automobile accident serve the image-enhancement purpose well.

Community Relations

Community relations programs can (and often do) share purposes and subpurposes with public relations efforts. In this context, however, public relations is a part of a broader, more complex goal. Community relations efforts are geared toward integrating community forces and law enforcement agencies into active partnerships for dealing with the many social and criminal problems assigned to the police. Within this framework are the following specific objectives of community relations programs:

- To determine the appropriate range of services the police will provide to the community.
- To determine how these services will be provided (in the sense of appropriate tactics and procedures).
- To identify and define potential problem areas and move to correct them.
- To establish ongoing mechanisms for resolving problems of mutual interest to the police and the community.

The philosophy of community relations stresses the interrelationships and mutual dependencies of police agencies and citizens. Community relations seeks to involve citizens actively in determining what (and how) police services will be provided to the community and establishes ongoing mechanisms for resolving problems of mutual interest. The police must depend on the community as a source of their legitimacy. If they cease to be the "people's police," they no longer achieve their basic mission. Protecting and serving must be defined in terms of the community's needs and wishes in order for the police function to be legitimate. The community is in turn dependent on the police to provide services essential to maintaining an atmosphere of stability. Ultimately, then, community relations serves to create and maintain mutually supportive relationships between police and citizens—something that is needed by both.

PROCESSES INVOLVED IN THE ACTIVITY

Several interesting differences arise when public relations and community relations activities are compared with respect to a set of process questions that apply to both:

1. To what degree are the activities standardized?
2. Is the activity agency oriented, community oriented, or both?
3. What is the direction of information flow?
4. What is the hierarchical level of police agency involvement?
5. What is the breadth of agency involvement?

Public Relations

STANDARDIZATION Public relations activities tend to be routinized and specialized wherever possible. This makes them easier to control, facilitates their repetition, and prevents wasteful duplication or diversion of staff energy from other more highly valued tasks. An excellent example is the agency-initiated press release, which is the basic tool of the public information function. Preparing such a release is largely a matter of following a standardized form, taking clearly defined steps to obtain administrative sanction, and using regular distribution channels. These steps guarantee a logical, predictable base for the information function.

AGENCY ORIENTED, COMMUNITY ORIENTED, OR BOTH Public relations activities are agency oriented. They include a range of services designed primarily to serve agency needs. Even services to those outside the agency are designed around the benefits that can be gained by the agency. The agency press release, for example, serves the news media by providing newsworthy information in a readily digestible form. The selection of material and its initial presentation, however, are structured to maximize their image-building or support-gathering potential for the agency.

INFORMATION FLOW In public relations activities, information flows outward. This one-way pattern reflects the belief that if those in the agency's environment are properly informed about police operations, they will support them.

HIERARCHICAL LEVEL OF INVOLVEMENT   Because virtually all police agencies are hierarchical in nature, it is relatively easy to pinpoint management responsibility for agency activities once that responsibility has been assigned. Assignment is generally made in direct relationship to the importance given to a specific program by top administration. In other words, if the program is regarded as important, a high-ranking officer will be in charge of it.

BREADTH OF AGENCY INVOLVEMENT   Agency involvement in public relations is narrow. Public relations is a tool of police management, not an essential component of operating philosophy. It is an easily compartmentalized function, even though it attempts to represent all segments of departmental activity. Public relations activities are generally assigned to a specific unit, and they do not require heavy commitments from other elements of the department.

Community Relations

STANDARDIZATION   In general, community relations activities are difficult to routinize and standardize. Some of their elements may become routine, but the function they are supposed to perform—linking the police to a wide array of publics and interests—usually requires flexibility and capacity for rapid change. Police administrators who prefer the familiar "standard operating procedures" find the concepts of flexibility and capacity for rapid change difficult to understand and accept—and sometimes difficult to permit.

AGENCY ORIENTED, COMMUNITY ORIENTED, OR BOTH   If the function of the police is to protect and serve, then to be community oriented ultimately serves the needs of the agency, too. The aim of community relations is to provide services that are considered important (not by some police administrator but by the people) to the public served. For example, a police storefront center in an urban neighborhood can serve the police by being a place to collect information on criminal activity and by functioning as a complaint center, thereby improving communication with area residents. If the center is truly a community relations activity, it also will provide citizens with services that they identify as crucial, such as liaison with other government agencies, assistance in domestic crises, conflict mediation, and referral and counseling services. In this way, an intentional balance of self-serving and citizen-serving processes is achieved.

INFORMATION FLOW   Two-way information flow is critical to community relations. The communication process must publicize the police point of view, stimulate discussion of issues, and solicit feedback from members of the community or communities involved. In practice, many agencies continue to emphasize the outward flow of messages, sometimes undermining their own community relations efforts.

HIERARCHICAL LEVEL OF INVOLVEMENT   As in the case of public relations, the hierarchical setting of responsibility for community relations activities is so varied that it defies generalization. If community relations activities are specialized, their responsibility would undoubtedly be that of a ranking agency person. But if the activities are expected to pervade the entire organization or involve only specific, line-level units, responsibility might be assigned to lower levels. Each instance is evaluated independently.

BREADTH OF AGENCY INVOLVEMENT   The breadth of agency involvement is a different matter. Although certain aspects of community relations may be assigned to specific departmental units, involvement generally crosses divisional boundaries. This requires a distinction between *specialized programs*, which may have relevance only to a certain geographical or functional unit, and *general practices* aimed at accomplishing community relations objectives across the department and the community. The former are likely to be successful on a long-term basis only if the latter are part of the department's operating philosophy. Here, a reliable system of internal communication is essential in ensuring that the agency presents a "united" community relations philosophy, particularly in areas where news media take special interest in discovering and publishing contradictions among units of the department.

CITIZEN INVOLVEMENT

Although the police have either assumed or have been assigned responsibility for dealing with many of our more complex social problems, it is folly to think that they alone can solve any of them. In reality, the police are only able to provide limited specialized attention to the most crucial problems, usually in a crisis-reactive fashion. Real solutions require much broader efforts by many segments of the community. Even effective crisis reactions often require the involvement of nonpolice resources. In terms of citizen involvement, public relations and community relations activities provide a definite contrast.

Public Relations

In most public relations activities, citizen involvement is kept to a minimum. It is generally passive; the citizens receive information dispensed by the law enforcement agency or utilize services that primarily serve agency purposes. In most cases, citizens are reasons for, but not participants in, the activity.

Community Relations

Community relations activities often rely heavily on citizen involvement. The citizen is, by definition, an active participant. The police agency does not relinquish responsibility for administering agency programs or practices relating to community relations. It does, however, ensure that citizen resources are properly accommodated, both to provide assistance in accomplishing police goals and to stimulate feedback on issues and problems. Table 4.1 summarizes the characteristics of public relations as compared to community relations.

WHY PUBLIC RELATIONS IS NOT ENOUGH   Public relations activities can and should be part of a properly applied community relations program, but they cannot substitute for it. The analysis in the following section pinpoints some very real weaknesses of public relations programs.

TABLE 4.1 Characteristics of Public Relations as Compared to Community Relations

	Public Relations	Community Relations
Purpose	Attain/maintain good environment	Develop police–community partnership
	Inform public	Integrate community needs with police practices
	Enhance image	
	Minimize obstacles	
	Stimulate support	
Process	Routinized functions comprise activities	Flexible and adaptable functions comprise activities
	Agency-oriented services	Community-oriented services
	One-way (outward) information flow	Two-way information flow
	Responsibility compartmentalized	Responsibility dispersed throughout agency
Citizen Involvement	Consciously kept to a minimum	Actively sought and stimulated

BOX 4.1
Police–Community Relations Must Involve Citizens!

Philosophical Framework

To achieve its mission, a police agency needs the support and active participation of the citizens served. Such a mission requires that the agency seek to develop the following:

- A high level of police–community understanding and trust.
- Effective and meaningful two-way communication.
- Increased community awareness of crime problems and ways to reduce the probability of being victimized.
- Alternative resources for the agency that will increase productivity and more effective use of certified officers.

The list above constitutes the mission of the community relations section of the Pima County Sheriff's Office. Programs developed to fulfill this mission meet nationally recognized criteria for crime-prevention practices. They are also unique. They meet the specific needs of the agency and population served. They are innovative in recruitment, training, and utilization of citizen volunteers. The Pima County Sheriff's Office has received national recognition for seeking meaningful participation of citizens in almost every agency function.

Specific Projects and Programs

As Lewis and Salem (1981) stated, "Community crime prevention strategies prevent crime by altering the relations between the criminal, victim, and environment, reducing the opportunity for victimization." Programs developed seeking to apply these strategies with the help of citizen volunteers in the sheriff's office are listed below. Some of these exist in similar form in many communities in the United States. Others are unique to this agency.

- *Suspicious activity cards.* All sheriff's auxiliary volunteers participate by documenting their observations, which are then routed to the appropriate agency (see Figure 4.2).
- *Business identification program.* Citizen volunteers maintain a cross-indexed file of businesses and their owners or managers, allowing officers quick access to relevant information in the event of a fire or crime on the premises after business hours.
- *Emergency response program.* Certain volunteers have developed additional skills and have citizen band radio

FIGURE 4.1   Volunteer auxiliary teams involve citizens of all ages in police support activities.

Courtesy of Buffalo Police Department.

(continued)

SUSPICIOUS ACTIVITY CARD

SUSPICIOUS PERSON # ONE:			☐ DRIVER		☐ PASSENGER		☐ PEDESTRIAN	
Sex	Race	Hgt	Wgt	Hair	Eyes	Skin	Approx. Age	

SUSPICIOUS PERSON # TWO:			☐ DRIVER		☐ PASSENGER		☐ PEDESTRIAN	
Sex	Race	Hgt	Wgt	Hair	Eyes	Skin	Approx. Age	

Manner of Dress & Identifying Marks (Person # One)   ☐ Glasses   ☐ Moustache or Beard

Manner of Dress & Identifying Marks (Person # Two)   ☐ Glasses   ☐ Moustache or Beard

Possible Occupation or Activity of Subject(s)

Location of Suspicious Activity	Sub-Division	Time	Date

Type Veh	Make	Model	Year	Color	Lic No.	State or Color Plate

Additional Information:

Submitted by: C. Bear #

FIGURE 4.2 Suspicious activity card used by volunteers to report suspicious activity to appropriate agency.

Courtesy of Pima County Sheriff's Department.

capability. They have a call-out system devised to put "eyes and ears" into specific areas on request of the department.

- *Neighborhood Watch program.* The backbone of community involvement with crime prevention. Neighborhoods are organized into manageable groups that meet four times per year. Members are given initial and follow-up information on crime-prevention techniques. Neighbors are encouraged to be more observant and involved in their areas (Figure 4.3).
- *Home security survey.* All residential burglary victims are contacted by mail and offered a personalized survey of their home to help prevent being victimized again (Figure 4.4).
- *Operation Identification.* Normally included within home security checks or Neighborhood Watch presentations. Citizens who demonstrate compliance with suggested procedures receive free Operation Identification stickers.
- *Crime watch program.* A minicourse of instruction for public nonpolice officials and private/commercial organizations that have radio-equipped vehicles operating in the community. The course is aimed at making the operators more efficient observers and reporters of criminal or suspicious activity (Figure 4.5).
- *Interdepartmental people power assistance program.* Many volunteers have provided support to the depart-

ment by assisting with administrative duties. Help has been provided to the records section, burglary detail, auto theft detail, district level administration, and management services division, which is where the volunteer program is coordinated. The burglary and auto theft units use volunteers to maintain their multi-indexed intelligence files of stolen property.

Public Awareness Programs

The volunteers have participated in various crime-prevention awareness shows or programs. They have worked closely with other local crime-prevention groups, including the Crime Prevention Fair and Crime Resisters. At the crime fair, volunteers staff an informational display. This fair is a highly successful, countywide awareness event held for one week each October. At the annual county fair, held each spring, the volunteers staff and maintain an informational and recruitment display. Volunteers also assist local shopping malls in presenting specific crime-prevention themes during weekend expositions. Topics typically include auto theft, burglary prevention, and child safety.

Recruitment

The minimum age for adult citizen volunteers is 18. No upper age limit or restriction exists. A separate county volunteer program exists for teenagers through Explorer Scout posts.

FIGURE 4.3   Neighborhood watch sign.
David R. Frazier, Folio, Inc.

Sheriff's Auxiliary Volunteers
of Pima County, Inc.
P.O. BOX 910 • TUCSON, ARIZONA 85702

INFORMATION FOR ALL NEIGHBORHOOD WATCHES:

The Sheriff's Auxiliary Volunteers has a program in
which we video tape the property inside of your home.
This service is free and you are given the tape to be
put in safety deposit box or in a safe place.

We also have home inspections. An inspector comes to
your home and checks locks, windows, doors, etc.

We have an engraver to loan so you may etch your
drivers license number on the TV, microwave, etc.

For more information call the phone numbers listed
below.

George Meyers--741-4972
Home Inspections

Isabel Powers--741-4685
Crime Prevention

FIGURE 4.4   Sheriff's Auxiliary Volunteers information sheet regarding its home security survey.
Courtesy of Pima County Sheriff's Department.

(continued)

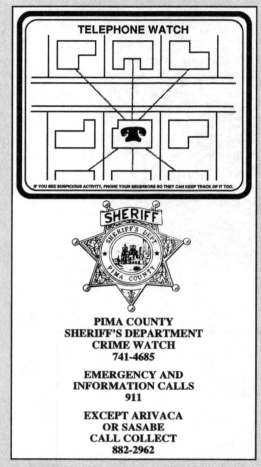

FIGURE 4.5   Pima County Telephone Watch program.

Courtesy of Pima County Sheriff's Department.

Recruitment is countywide. Both officers and volunteers are involved in recruiting efforts. There are no physical requirements for admission. Screening is thorough. A background check for arrest or prior contact with law enforcement is routine. Prior arrest does not automatically bar an applicant from participation. Circumstances surrounding the event and lapse of time since the offense are considered. The agency seeks responsible volunteers who are sincere in their service goals and who will fulfill the citizen volunteer standard of conduct.

Training

The foundation of a successful volunteer program is training. In addition to an orientation to the agency and crime prevention (four to six hours), each sheriff's office volunteer is trained in basic civil liability; the goals, structure, and procedures of

the volunteer programs; introduction to law enforcement systems and agencies; cardiopulmonary resuscitation; basic medical first aid care; identification of criminal or suspicious activity and reporting methods; and traffic accident scene assistance (20 hours).

Advanced skills training is offered in specialized areas. For example, a 44-hour advanced course is required for volunteers who wish to be crime-prevention instructors and program facilitators. This training includes the history and theory of crime prevention and risk management; the concept of creating barriers; security lighting; locks; alarm systems; how to do home security surveys; how to develop Neighborhood Watch programs; public speaking and instruction skills; how to facilitate citizen emergency response training; and civil liability for instructors.

Class members must demonstrate proficiency through oral board and written examination prior to certification by the department.

Identification

All volunteers who successfully complete the training are issued identification cards that remain the property of the department. Volunteers in specialized support programs may also wear identifying patches when on duty (Figure 4.7a).

Supervision of Volunteers

Effective supervision is critical to program success. Supervision is required to accomplish the following:

- Ensure that the skills and interests of the volunteer are matched to departmental needs.
- Facilitate acceptance of the volunteer by departmental personnel.
- Identify any problems early and work toward their solution.
- Encourage cooperation and teamwork among volunteers and between volunteers and agency personnel.
- Effectively coordinate the many volunteer programs and projects.
- Continue to challenge the interest and support of volunteers.
- Maintain the flexibility necessary to meet changing community and departmental needs.

Communication Connections

Information exchange, support, and recognition, always necessary to the success of volunteer programs, are facilitated through a regular newsletter. The *Community Connection* is published at least bimonthly.

Comments

The Volunteers in Prevention, Prosecution, Probation, Prison and Parole (VIP) division of the National Council on Crime

FIGURE 4.6 Citizen Volunteer Standard of Conduct.

Members shall conduct their private and professional lives in such a manner as to avoid adverse reflection upon themselves or this department.

Members shall obey all federal, state, and local laws as well as the rules and regulations listed herein.

Members knowing of any other member violating any laws shall report such violation to their District Volunteer Liaison Officer (DVLO) or District Commander.

Members shall treat their peers and associates with respect. They shall be civil and courteous at all times in their relationships with one another.

Members shall make no false reports or knowingly enter or cause to be entered in any departmental report or record any inaccurate or false information.

No member shall willfully misrepresent any matter. Members shall not release any official business of the department without the direct consent of the District Commander or their DVLO.

While acting in an official Sheriff's Auxiliary Team capacity, members shall not recommend to any person the employment of a particular attorney, bail bondsman, towing company, or any other service for which a fee is charged.

Members shall not solicit or accept any personal gift, gratuity, or reward for services rendered in the line of volunteer duty. No member shall purchase, consume, or be under the influence of any alcoholic beverage while acting in the capacity of a Sheriff's Auxiliary Team volunteer.

Members shall not possess or use any controlled substance, narcotic, or hallucinogenic except when prescribed by a physician or dentist.

Members shall keep their liaison deputy informed of any unusual activity, situation, or problem with which the department would logically be concerned.

Source: Pima County Maternal: Deputy L. R. Sacco, SAU Coordinator, Pima County Sheriff's Department.

FIGURE 4.7 Special identification for auxiliary volunteers.
Courtesy of Pima County Sheriff's Department.

(continued)

and Delinquency (NCCD) estimates that at least 350,000 volunteers are currently active in direct-service juvenile and criminal justice programs. If volunteers in all capacities of criminal justice are included, the total number would be closer to 750,000 volunteers.

Not every justice agency has had the positive experience with volunteer programs that Pima County has had. What are the ingredients that make this and other volunteer programs successful? A study of programs in a variety of justice agencies in the United States suggests that the critical ingredients for success of volunteer programs are as follows:

1. Strong administrative commitment to the concept.
2. Clearly defined program goals and functions that relate to community and agency need.
3. Careful screening of volunteers.
4. A strong training program, including ongoing training in specialized areas.
5. Assessment of volunteer interests and skills and assignment of volunteers to meaningful tasks.
6. Sensitivity to the needs and fears of agency personnel regarding volunteer services and early resolution of problems in this area.
7. Development of support of agency personnel for the volunteer concept.
8. Effective supervision of volunteers and monitoring of volunteer activities.
9. Involvement of volunteers in recruiting and supervisory activities.
10. Feedback system that encourages recognition, evaluation, and recommendations for change from volunteers and staff.
11. Sensitivity to the needs of volunteers.
12. Willingness to encourage and accept change within the program that is necessary for its vitality.
13. Application of group dynamics principles in strengthening volunteer cooperation and coordination.
14. Strong personal commitment on the part of those who supervise the project.
15. Inclusion of line personnel in every phase of the program development and implementation.

Failing to Provide True Problem-Solving Mechanisms.   Public relations techniques aim to preserve and enhance a department's image, not cope with operating problems. In contrast, community relations programs make a point of identifying problems and working with the community to prevent or resolve them.

Reaching the Wrong Targets.   Public relations efforts are often directed at intermediaries, usually respected, organized groups whose members are likely to support the agency in any case. For example, providing public speakers is a common public relations device. The department thoughtfully provides informed officers to speak to civic groups, business concerns, clubs, schools, and so on, in basically an educational effort. The target group is generally already supportive of the police. The speaker may talk "at" the audience, answer a few questions, and return to headquarters. In most instances, everyone is pleased. No dialogue has taken place, however, and the citizens have rarely been encouraged to take an active part in solving police–community problems. The department hopes that group members will act as intermediaries, carrying the department's message to others, thus building support to avert future problems. In contrast, community relations programs are directed both to groups that are supportive of the police and groups that are not. Active citizen assistance and feedback are sought from both.

Alienating Concerned Citizens.   The pure public relations approach alienates concerned citizens by convincing them that the department is merely interested in image building, not in dealing with problems or in effective communication with the community. Similar feelings may disenchant intermediaries with their role. The community newspaper, for example, receiving only superficial news releases that fail to discuss significant issues of concern, will soon refuse to print them. Only limited descriptive material about training courses, medal-of-valor awards, and number of arrests made during a month will be printed if real problems of rising crime rates, citizen dissatisfaction with police performance, or similar issues are ignored. Alienating concerned citizens is one of the greatest inherent dangers of a pure public relations concept.

Dealing Ineptly with Crucial Issues.   The purpose of public relations is essentially to change perceptions, not to solve substantive operational problems. Thus, when internal change or real communication between police and community is needed, the superficiality of the public relations approach may simply aggravate matters.

Limited Decision-Making Power.   Public relations is a secondary element of police management, and it is compartmentalized. Those in charge of its activities have little power to influence policy or procedural decisions; their responsibility is merely to secure acceptance of the decisions others make.

How Public Relations Can Strengthen Community Relations

The public relations concept has a distinct and valuable place in agency operations as an element of an overall community relations program when the latter is truly part of administrative philosophy. There are at least five functions that are essentially public relations in thrust but which complement community relations efforts.

INFORMING THE PUBLIC ABOUT CRUCIAL ISSUES   The public relations purpose of informing the public can be valuable to both police and citizens if it extends to critical issues. The "whys" of police policies and procedures can be explained to the public. Alternatives to current practice, as seen by the agency, can be explained and any trade-offs outlined. These explanations must be straightforward and honestly portray the police intention to inform, not to sell the status quo. This is the point at which the public relations effort supports the community relations effort. Proper performance of police tasks, not public relations techniques, must do the selling.

DEVELOPING COMMUNITY SUPPORT   Public relations can work to stimulate active citizen support, including cooperation in crime control and prevention activities. This is a change from the traditional public relations orientation. Generating support must be part of an overall mission of involvement, and it must be done with scrupulous honesty. The agency will need to be wary of passive lip service that has characterized purely public relations approaches in the past. Stimulating true citizen involvement can secure the strongest support any criminal justice agency can promote.

SUPPLEMENTING AGENCY OPERATIONS AND PROGRAMS   As an outgrowth of a balanced community relations philosophy, police agencies may implement special operations and programs. Public relations techniques can be used to explain the reasons for and goals of these activities, to stimulate discussion, and to elicit feedback about them.

For example, both public and community relations techniques are useful in initiating a Neighborhood Watch program. The former can help to sell the concept, and the latter can help to define a specific neighborhood's needs and develop and maintain community feedback and support.

PRESENTING AN ACCURATE PICTURE OF THE AGENCY AND ITS FUNCTIONS   The modern police agency performs a confusing variety of tasks, from catching criminals to providing on-site assistance in serious emotional crises. The mundane and sensational, the dull and controversial—and how they relate to one another—are important aspects of agency function. By presenting an accurate and balanced picture of the police organization, public relations efforts can promote true public understanding of the police role and mission. This is perhaps the most important function that public relations can perform as part of a community relations effort.

ENHANCING THE AGENCY'S IMAGE   Public relations can continue to perform many of its traditional functions, even when operating in a community relations mode, but these functions become subordinated to the principles of the broader concept. For example, it is unrealistic to ask any bureaucratic organization to abandon its efforts to achieve support for its programs. The realities of competing for scarce operating resources—money, personnel, and material—preclude such simplistic proposals. Nevertheless, the achievement of support, including image enhancement, must be accomplished in accordance with a strict set of guidelines requiring honesty and integrity in the tactics used. Building the agency's image should be a conscientiously controlled means of providing better service, not the ultimate goal of the agency's community relations program.

PROGRAM EXAMPLES

Thus far, this chapter has focused on the differences between the concepts of public relations and community relations as they are commonly applied by the contemporary law enforcement agency. In this final section, attention will turn to examining several public relations and community relations programs. There are few "pure" programs, just as there are few agencies that embody only the characteristics associated with the concept in the preceding pages. Any evaluation of an agency's orientation must be made by examining the total structure of its operations. Some representative examples of community outreach efforts are described in the following pages.

PUBLIC RELATIONS PROGRAMS   Whether or not a program is purely public relations oriented or is part of a larger community relations thrust is often determined by its long-range goals and the population it seeks to reach. Although most of the programs listed below as public relations could possibly be incorporated into community relations, they frequently exist for short-term enhancement and reach a population that is already supportive of the police.

SPEAKERS' BUREAU   Most law enforcement agencies are ready on request to provide speakers to civic groups, business concerns, schools, and other organizations. The speakers usually give a short, informative talk on a topic such as drug abuse, traffic safety, or crime and protection. They may also distribute descriptive literature to an audience.

RIDE-ALONG PROGRAM   Another common program is the citizen ride-along. This program allows members of the general public to accompany a police officer on routine patrol. Although some jurisdictions place few restrictions on the **ride-along program**, many require that the rider be free of a criminal record or meet requirements of age, occupation, or other significant conditions. The ride-along program does have elements of mutual education for both citizen and police officer, but its primary purpose is to help the citizen "understand" the difficulties of modern police work.

POLICE STATION TOURS   Guided tours of police stations have become standard fare for civic organizations and school groups. Depending on the size and sophistication of the agency, such tours include visiting the jail, crime lab, lineup room, communications center, records center, and various operating bureaus or divisions. Tours are often arranged in conjunction with "police week" ceremonies.

SAFETY LECTURES   Lectures on traffic laws, crossing streets, and other safety topics—usually geared toward children—are conducted in shopping centers and schools and are often accompanied by films and demonstrations.

CITIZEN RECOGNITION   Many agencies give awards to citizens who provide particularly helpful services to the police. Such awards may be given for bravery or merely for reporting a suspicious person who turns out to be a burglar or armed robber. In either case, the agency makes a formal presentation of a plaque or some other suitable award to show its appreciation for an informed and involved citizenry.

CITIZENS ACADEMIES   One of the most popular public relations programs at all levels of police agencies in the United States, Canada, and the United Kingdom are citizens academies.

They are, like many U.S. police innovations, a cultural transplant from Great Britain. In 1977, the British Constabularies of Devon and Cornwall established a "Police Night School" to familiarize citizens with their police agencies. Today, citizens academies are found in the United States in state police agencies, sheriff's agencies, and local police agencies of all sizes. The Royal Canadian Mounted Police (RCMP) also has citizens academies throughout Canada. All citizens academies have the common purpose of creating a better understanding and communications between the agency and the citizens through education. Citizens academies produce informed citizens. They show how police officers perform their duties and serve the community. In many communities, they are strictly public relations efforts, although the departments refer to them as community relations; in others they are a part of the overall community relations strategy of the agency.

Programs with a Major Community Relations Focus

Successful community relations programs also serve a public relations function. Improved public relations is a by-product of these programs, not the sole or even primary goal of these (Trojanowicz et al., 1998, p. 15). The following programs were designed as community relations programs. Although they are not universally implemented in ways that realize their optimum effectiveness, the dominant focus of each is community relations. They generally share the common characteristics of community partnership and reciprocal police community feedback/input.

RUMOR CONTROL   The **rumor control** program is most often used during violent street confrontations, generally between the police and residents of racial and ethnic minority neighborhoods. It involves developing networks for gathering, sorting, and clarifying information. Unfounded or exaggerated rumors are identified and exposed. Facts are provided before the rumors can precipitate disturbances. Local civic leaders such as businesspeople, teachers, and religious leaders usually assist in this process. In some communities, the rumor control operation has been used ineffectively simply to provide information to the community by the police. Where it has been optimally used, however, the control network has developed into a useful forum for discussing common police problems in many neighborhoods. The prevention of civil disorder requires that police leadership and management recognize rumors and the problems that caused them in order to put into place a speedy and effective response through their community networks.

COMMUNITY ADVISORY COUNCILS/COMMITTEES   Community Advisory Councils/Committees are known by several names in the United States, Canada, and the United Kingdom but they all have the common purpose of offering community groups and individuals a forum to discuss community issues with the police. Community groups with members on these councils include representatives from all ethnic and cultural populations, as well as business and social welfare agencies depending on the diversity of the community. The groups provide input and feedback on the policies, programs, and practices of the police agency.

STOREFRONT CENTERS   **Storefront centers**, a well-publicized method of bringing the police officer closer to the people, have been complaint reception centers, mini-precinct houses, and meeting places and have served many other purposes. Their effectiveness depends on whether they embody the one-way principles of public relations or the two-way principles of community relations.

NEIGHBORHOOD TEAM POLICING   Community-based teams, under a team commander, have been used to deliver police services to particular neighborhoods. The team has responsibility for deployment, assignments, methods of operations, and other organizational and operational decisions, and offices for team members are located within the policed area. This policing style provides several community relations opportunities. These opportunities include closer, more stable ties with neighborhood residents; citizen participation in planning and delivery of services; and participation and input from all team members with regard to team management and activities. Effectiveness of community-based teams varies widely. Those that are most effective work as a team and consider themselves part of the community they serve.

BOX 4.2
Neighborhood Policing in the United Kingdom and the United States

Neighbourhood Police Teams (United Kingdom)

Neighbourhood Policing is provided by teams of police officers and Police Community Support Officers (PCSOs) [nonsworn constables who assist police officers and handle incidents not requiring full police powers] often together with Special Constables, local authority wardens, volunteers, and partners.

It aims to provide people who live or work in a neighborhood with:

- **Access**—to local policing services through a named point of contact.
- **Influence**—over policing services through a named point of contact.
- **Influence**—over policing priorities in their neighbourhood.
- **Interventions**—joint action with partners & the public.
- **Answers**—sustainable solutions & feedback on what is being done.

This means that neighbourhood teams:

- publicize how to get in touch with them
- find out what the local issues are that make people feel unsafe in their neighbourhood and ask them to put them in order of priority
- decide with partners and local people what should be done to deal with those priorities and work with them to deliver the solutions
- let people know what is being done and find out if they are satisfied with the results.

Source: National Policing Improvement Agency, www.neighbourhoodpolicing.co.uk/

Neighborhood Police Teams (United States)
Ferguson, Missouri Police Department (54 sworn officers)

The Neighborhood Enforcement Team (N.E.T. squad) formed in 2004, identifies neighborhood public safety concerns and crime problems. Policing strategies and action plans are then developed to address these concerns and problems. . . . Citizen input, data analysis, and interdependent communication help the N.E.T. Squad concentrate their enforcement activities to make Ferguson neighborhoods safer and minimize crime. The N.E.T. Squad engages in numerous policing activities from traffic enforcement to criminal arrests to quality of life issues, such as issuing summons or taking suspects into custody for noise violations, manner of walking in the roadway, and other disruptive behaviors.

Source: www.fergusoncity.com

Spokane, Washington Police Department (300 sworn officers)

Starting in 2008, the Spokane Police Department will begin its implementation of a Neighborhood Policing Plan. In a series of several phases, the current north/south patrol response format will be separated into four precincts, each composed of two districts. Partnering with local Community Policing Services (COPS) Shops, patrol officers will be permanently assigned to these smaller geographical areas, creating the opportunity to build lasting partnerships with community members. Each precinct will have at least one Neighborhood Resource Officer (NRO) and each precinct will have one crime analyst specifically examining crime trends for that precinct.

Source: www.spokanepolice.org/patrol/beats

St. Louis County, Missouri Police Department (465 sworn officers)

Neighborhood Policing is a philosophy—one of a partnership between police and law-abiding citizens to create permanent solutions to problems that lead to crime. . . . Neighborhood policing is a partnership of the police, the community, and other agencies of St. Louis County government. Armed with the philosophy of neighborhood policing, these groups come together to identify, analyze, and solve the crime and disorder problems that are unique to each area neighborhood . . . a knowledgeable team of neighborhood beat officers is formed, to serve and provide service 24 hours a day, 7 days a week. This team is assigned to each of the St. Louis County Police Department's police beats. Each beat is grouped together to form a neighborhood policing sector.

Source: www.co.st-louis.mo.us/police

FOOT PATROL PROGRAMS The reestablishment of police foot patrol in many cities has reintroduced a traditional method for intensifying the interaction between citizens and police. A strict reliance on motorized patrol creates a situation where there is little or no face-to-face interaction between citizens and the police and prevents the development of communication and trust. Skolnick and Bayley reported that their observations of foot patrol and research studies pertaining to it revealed four meritorious effects:

1. Since there is a concerned human presence on the street, foot patrol is more adaptable to street happenings and thus may prevent crime before it begins.
2. Foot patrol personnel may make arrests, but they are also around to give warnings either directly or indirectly, merely through their presence.
3. Carried out properly, foot patrol generates goodwill in the neighborhood, which has the derivative consequence of making other crime-prevention tactics more effective. This effectiveness in turn tends to raise citizen morale and reduce citizen fear of crime.
4. Foot patrol seems to raise officer morale (Skolnick and Bayley, 1986, p. 216).

PHYSICAL DECENTRALIZATION OF COMMAND Many police organizations are decentralizing the police bureaucracy to provide for quality interaction between the police and the community and, as in neighborhood policing, a heightened identification between the police and specific areas. This has led to the creation of fixed substations, ministations, and the creation of additional precincts.

Although these programs share some of the characteristics and objectives of neighborhood team policing, they are quite different, in that they provide for the creation of small autonomous commands and involve the assignment of police personnel to specific areas for long periods of time.

PROBLEM-ORIENTED POLICING **Problem-oriented policing**, which includes a number of different programs undertaken in a large number of police agencies, provides for a new approach to the delivery of police services. In this approach the police go beyond individual crimes and reactions to calls for service by attacking the problems that caused them. It moves the police from a reactive response to individual incidents to a proactive approach to citizen concerns.

In practice, police examine the reasons why particular crimes or calls for service occur in certain locations or at particular times and then map out a strategy for dealing with them. The strategy for dealing with these events involves active participation by the community members affected. The following are four features of problem-oriented policing:

1. As part of their work, officers identify groups of similar or related events that constitute problems.
2. Then they collect, from a variety of sources, information describing the nature, causes, and consequences of each problem.
3. Officers work with private citizens, local businesses, and public agencies to develop and implement solutions.
4. Officers evaluate solutions to see if the problems were reduced (Spelman and Eck, 1986, p. 4).

Crime Prevention: Another Name for Community Relations?

Almost all of the program examples mentioned could be included under a broad crime-prevention umbrella, and many others could be added to the list. Several hundreds of millions of federal and local funds have been spent on crime-prevention projects in recent years. There is no doubt that **crime prevention** is a well-advertised, whether or not a well-executed, focus of police function. Citizen demand for crime-prevention programs continues to grow. A National Crime Prevention Institute has been established to provide specialized prevention training and consultation.

Some of these programs are oriented toward community relations and have become citizen action–centered. In these, citizens and police are involved in defining what crime problems exist in a particular area and population and what actions can be taken to prevent such crimes from occurring. Implementation and evaluation are part of the prevention program.

Most programs that are tagged as "crime prevention," however, continue to be, at least in practice if not in original purpose, almost entirely informational—from the police to the citizen. As Krajick stated, "in what some crime prevention experts term a 'knee-jerk reflex,' popular programs like brochure distribution and security surveys are picked up by police departments without any study as to whether those programs address a particular problem in their jurisdictions" (Krajick, 1979, p. 7).

Some programs are considered very successful, and their success is defined in terms of several criteria. These include (1) the number of neighborhood crime watch teams formed; (2) number of volunteers in the program; (3) measurable decrease in a particular type of crime in a given neighborhood; (4) number of brochures distributed; (5) number of presentations made; and (6) number of households following the security advice of police representatives.

Some projects have not been successful by the most generous, short-term criteria for success. Even the design or methodology of program evaluations are sometimes suspect.

Do successful crime-prevention programs also meet long-range community relations goals? The answer is difficult to determine from the short-term rationale used to test for a program's success. Involving the community in an ongoing program of crime prevention requires an underlying community relations perspective. The characteristics of neighborhoods and their problems must be considered. Two-way communication must exist, and a structure must be provided that will encourage continuing involvement of the community.

Even this level of crime prevention will be easier to achieve when working with neighborhoods that already have a positive view of the police. It is much more difficult (and therefore seldom attempted) to build the same relationship in neighborhoods that have had more negative confrontations with police. However, it has been found that police efforts that help minority parents protect their children (DARE, McGruff, Safe Kids, etc.) are more positively received.

In recent years, many agencies have defined police–community relations in terms of their crime-prevention activities. Given the criteria discussed in this chapter for true community relations programs, for prevention services to qualify, they would have to be broadly based, meet long-range goals, and be set up to address far more than just "crime-specific" problems. Rarely is this the case in practice. Therefore, where crime prevention has been substituted for community relations, the community relations concept has usually been narrowed. Crime-prevention activities can support a total police–community relations effort, but they are only part of it.

The following are crime-prevention programs that are among the most public relations oriented:

- *Security surveys* in which the police, by invitation or request, visit a home or business and suggest ways in which security can be improved.
- *Clinics* in which individual citizens and businesses are advised how to prevent specific types of crime (e.g., rape, shoplifting, bank robbery, and burglary).
- *Awareness-alertness programs* in which bulletins about particular crime problems occurring in the community are issued. During the holiday season, many police agencies will issue to businesspeople circulars pointing out various shoplifting techniques. Some agencies also insert burglary-prevention messages in public utility billing statements or bank statements. Although these awareness notices often call upon the citizen to help the police by making it hard for the criminal to consummate an unlawful act, they seldom follow up on such requests, nor do they provide any realistic means for helping the citizen to do so.

Under the umbrella of crime prevention are several programs that include both the elements of public relations and community relations. The ultimate impact of these programs depends on the emphasis placed on the various elements and on the context in which they are applied.

Neighborhood Watch

The many varieties of area watch programs range from those in which residents of a neighborhood are asked to watch for strange activities at their neighbors' homes to those in which citizens are mobilized into committees to work with local police units in identifying local problems and developing responses to them. In the first instance, the police ask citizens to report any suspicious activities occurring in the neighborhood. The citizen merely becomes an extension of the police patrol apparatus. In the latter instance, the police officer on the beat and the citizen endeavor to perfect their partnership responsibilities in identifying those problems that can ultimately be corrected by police intervention. Neighborhood Watch programs can successfully reduce crime. For example, a Neighborhood Watch program was created in the Korbow subdivision in Fayetteville, North Carolina, in 2006. In the initial month of creation, the subdivision reported 63 crimes; in their first anniversary month, five crimes were reported; and in the second anniversary month, only two crimes were committed (Barksdale, 2009).

OPERATION IDENTIFICATION   In an **operation identification** program, police encourage citizens to mark their possessions with their Social Security numbers or other identification recognizable as belonging to them, in order to discourage theft and to increase the possibility of apprehending the offender and restoring the goods to the original owner. Usually, citizens can bring items to the station for identification marking or they will be provided with an etching tool so that they can mark items at home.

POLICE AUXILIARY VOLUNTEERS   The elderly are a prime target of crime today. Senior volunteer programs combine police expertise and elderly citizen volunteers, who work together to find ways in which the elderly can assist in preventing crime and in providing support and assistance to elderly victims. Many volunteer auxiliary programs involve citizens of all ages in a broad range of police support activities. (See Reality Check for a discussion of this project.)

FIGURE 4.8   A crime-prevention billboard.
Joe Rowley, AP Wide World Photos.

COMMUNITY CRIME WATCH   In some communities, public utilities, such as telephone, gas, and electric companies, have been trained and organized as part of a crime-watch team. Because of the extent of their community access and their frequent opportunity for "patrol," employees of such agencies can provide a unique community service. Once trained in what to look for, they become an excellent police support group. If they observe suspicious behavior or circumstances, they are asked not to intervene but to report.

CRIME STOPPERS   The programs included in this category are known by several names: Crime Stoppers, Crimes Solvers, Secret Witness, Crime Line, and so on. These programs join the news media, the community, and the police in a concerted effort to enlist private citizens in the fight against crime. The program is based on the premise that some citizens who know of or observe crimes will not report them because of apathy or fear but will report them for a cash reward.

The first Crime Stoppers Program was begun by police officer Greg MacAleese in Albuquerque, New Mexico, in 1976. Since that time the number of such programs has steadily increased in the United States and in Canada and New Zealand. In 1985 there were 600 programs, resulting in 92,000 felony arrests, 20,000 convictions, and the recovery of $500 million in stolen property (Rosenbaum, Lurigio, and Lavrakas, 1987).

REALITY CHECK

The Need for Discretion within Community Programs

Within this chapter, and throughout this text, you will see examples of numerous citizen and community programs that police agencies are encouraged to utilize in order to enhance police–community relations. We wholeheartedly endorse the programs discussed within this text. However, as with everything in life, discretion is necessary. There must be adequate screening mechanisms for these programs to ensure they do not create liability and/or embarrassment for the agency. In addition, if citizens are going to be involved in positions of trust, background checks and training should be mandatory. Three examples of good intentions that went awry follow:

1. When a Florida police department first began ride-along programs, any interested citizen was invited to participate. They merely had to complete a card that freed the agency from liability if they were injured during their ride-along. One young man (who had stated that he was interested in becoming a police officer when he graduated from college) became a frequent rider with the midnight shifts. He was good company on slow nights and did as he was told when required to stay back from hazardous or delicate situations. This came to a halt several months later after he was arrested for burglary. At his booking we learned that he had an extensive record of thefts and burglary that a background check would have revealed. When questioned about his activities, he stated that he had really enjoyed his interactions with the police officers and also had gained very useful information for his occupation.

2. In an effort to help the families of police officers gain insights into their loved ones' occupations, children and spouses were encouraged to participate in the (now more restrictive) ride-along program with their wives or husbands. One officer brought his wife to ride with him almost every weekend. All went well until one night when the officer was injured in a traffic accident. His wife accompanied him in the ambulance to the hospital where he was treated for minor injuries. Not knowing that his wife was riding along, a dispatcher called

his home to inform his family that he had been injured. Imagine the surprise of the police supervisor when the officer's real wife showed up at the hospital and found another woman by the officer's bedside. Clearances to participate in ride-alongs suddenly became even more restrictive.

3. Another Florida agency developed a senior volunteer program somewhat like the examples provided from Pima County, but without the training and oversights that they utilize. One elderly lady was found to be quite useful within the Records Section where her typing and filing skills were greatly appreciated. She volunteered several hours each week and was quickly accepted into the police "internal community." Unfortunately, after confidential information from a controversial child abuse case became public knowledge, it was learned that the dear lady had seen nothing wrong with regaling the members of her quilting club with the inside information that she gained from her access to police reports.

Conclusions

The difference between public relations and community relations is not always clear-cut. The guidelines presented in this chapter can help an observer to make informed judgments about the nature and purpose of police activities, but only if the activities are studied in the context in which they occur. To what extent do primarily self-serving principles and practices affect a police agency's receptivity to community input? The answer to this question ultimately determines whether the agency is operating under a public relations or community relations philosophy.

Public relations by itself can often prove valueless and even harmful to police agencies because its activities are agency oriented (and thus basically self-serving). Public relations officers are not agents of change and may gloss over or misrepresent crucial issues. On the other hand, every police agency must rely on public relations to some extent to help ensure its position in relation to other forces at work within the community. Public relations activities can play a valuable role in community relations programs provided they follow strict guidelines of honesty and integrity and make a goal such as image enhancement subordinate to providing better service.

Crime prevention has become a household phrase, although not necessarily a household effort. For crime prevention to be synonymous with police–community relations, crime-prevention efforts will need to meet police–community relations goals, something that seldom occurs in practice.

Student Checklist

1. Describe how police–community relations originated as a separate operational concept.
2. Describe the difference between police–community relations and police–public relations.
3. What is the major purpose of police–community relations activity?
4. List three examples of police–public relations programs.
5. List three examples of crime-prevention programs.
6. List three examples of programs with a major community relations focus.
7. Describe the characteristics of a crime-prevention program that meets police–community relations goals.

Topics for Discussion

1. Discover what activities and programs your local police agencies participate in. Are these oriented predominantly toward public relations or community relations? Whom do they serve and involve?
2. Devise a community relations project in crime prevention that could be initiated in your community. What are the characteristics that make your project oriented toward community relations rather than toward public relations?
3. What are the disadvantages of community relations programs?

Bibliography

Attorney General's Advisory Commission on Community-Police Relations. (1973). *The Police in the California Community*. Sacramento, CA: State of California.

Barksdale, A. (April 5, 2009). Fayetteville police chief to unveil plan to fight crime. *The Fayetteville Observer*, www.fayobserver.com

Brown, L. P. (*n.d.*). Police-community evaluation project (unpublished manuscript).

Earle, H. H. (1980). *Police-Community Relations: Crisis in Our Time*, 3rd ed. Springfield, IL: Charles C Thomas.

International City Manager's Association. (1967). *Police Community Relations Programs*. Washington, D.C.: ICMA.

Krajick, K. (1979). "Preventing crime," *Police Magazine*, November, pp. 7–13.

Lewis, D. A., and Salem, G. (1981). "Community crime prevention," *Crime and Delinquency*, July, pp. 405–421.

Merriam-*Webster's 11th New Collegiate Dictionary*. (2003). Springfield, MA: Merriam-Webster.

President's Commission on Law Enforcement and the Administration of Justice. (1967). *The Challenge of Crime in a Free Society*. Washington, D.C.: U.S. Government Printing Office.

Rosenbaum, D. P., Lurgio, A. J., and Lavrakas, P. J. (1987). *Crime Stoppers: A National Evaluation of Program Operations and Effects*. Washington D.C.: National Institute of Justice, U.S. Department of Justice.

Skolnick, J. H., and Bayley, D. H. (1986). *The New Blue Line: Police Innovation in Six American Cities*. New York: Free Press.

Spelman, W., and Eck, J. E. (1986). *Problem-Oriented Policing*. Washington, D.C.: Police Executive Research Forum.

Trojanowicz, R. C., Kappler, V. E., Gaines, L., and Bucqueroux, B. (1998). *Community Policing: A Contemporary Perspective*, 2nd ed. Cincinnati, OH: Anderson.

CHAPTER 5

The Public and the Police: A Consortium of Communities

The criminal justice system is, in reality, if not in appearance, a system. . . . You are most likely to accept [it] as a system if you recognize that society is in the process of imposing the system concept on an existing criminal justice apparatus that for years has been loosely tied together.

—CHAMELIN, FOX, AND WHISENAND

I pick up a guy for car theft; he kicks me and calls me everything but an upstanding citizen all the way to the jail. While I'm still doing the paperwork, he's on his way home, free to steal another car. I don't know why I bother.

—A FRUSTRATED COP

KEY CONCEPTS

Civic Organizations
Community Interest
    Organizations
Economic/Business
    Organizations

Ethnic/Racial
    Minorities
External Communities
Government Agencies
Internal Communities

Labor Unions
Political Organizations
Public Service
    Organizations
Religious Organizations

LEARNING OBJECTIVES

Studying this chapter will enable you to:

1. Discuss how relations between the police and the public are in reality complex relations among many overlapping communities.

2. Identify and describe the external communities that comprise the public.

3. Identify and describe the internal communities that comprise the police.

4. Describe how exchange relationships among various communities affect police–community relations.

In Chapter 3, we stated that "police–community relations are complicated and constantly changing interactions between representatives of the police organization and an assortment of governmental agencies, public groups, and private individuals representing a wide range of competing and often conflicting interests." In these interactions, those communities that are most vocal, like the proverbial squeaky wheel, often receive more attention and wield more influence. Some receive moderate attention and have moderate influence. Still others are seemingly neglected. Due to constant variations within society, the attention given to individual communities by the police and the influence they have on the police vary considerably over time.

In this chapter, we focus our discussion of police and community interaction on both the external communities outside the police organization and the internal communities within the police organization. Our primary contention is that successful police–community relations must take into account exchange relationships among community groups located both inside and outside the police organization (Figure 5.1).

In the following sections, we introduce many of the communities, both external and internal, which exert influence on and are in turn influenced by the police. Understanding the complexity of the interactions among the many communities that comprise the public and the police will enable the reader to better grasp the difficult challenges involved in establishing and maintaining true police–community relations.

EXTERNAL COMMUNITIES

Ethnic/Racial Minorities

The difficulties that the police and various ethnic groups have had in relating to one another are not of recent origin. Long before the New World was discovered, police forces were being used to control dissident groups. Usually, these groups were comprised of individuals whose homelands had been conquered by another group. The fictional warfare between the Sheriff of Nottingham and Robin Hood was based on actual difficulties that the Normans had with the Saxons following their conquest of England. Today, similar difficulties are all too apparent in

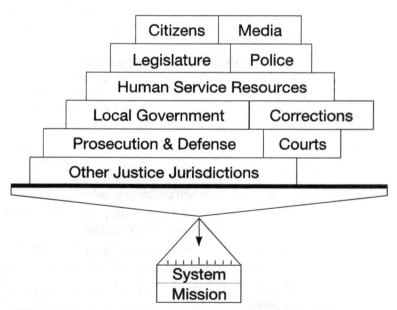

FIGURE 5.1   Achieving the mission of the criminal justice system depends on the functioning of many external and internal communities.

Israel, Northern Ireland, and Eastern Europe. However, one need not leave the United States to explore this phenomenon.

There are many ethnic minorities within the United States. With the exception of Hispanics (defined by heritage and language), ethnic concerns in the United States focus primarily on racial rather than national, cultural, or religious memberships. The numbers and the extent to which ethnic minorities differ from the white majority affect how these minorities are treated within society. Interestingly, discrimination against minority groups is often perpetuated by other minority groups. The worst urban riots that took place in the United States during the 1980s occurred in Miami, Florida, and pitted African Americans against Hispanic Americans, and the Los Angeles riot of 1992 produced bitter conflicts between African Americans and Asian Americans.

BOX 5.1
Operationalizing the System Concept

Assessing a Local System

This process may be used for assessing either the local justice system, including all key components, or one local agency as a subsystem, or system within a system of that larger system.

I. System Mission
   A. What is the mission of the system?
      1. As defined by legislative and judicial guidelines
      2. As defined by written policy statements
      3. As defined by present agency administrators
      4. As defined by line personnel
      5. As defined by the communities served
      6. As defined by those whose lives are directly affected by the system, the victims and offenders
   B. Assess the mission in system terms.
      1. Is there agreement among these definitions?
      2. If agreement does not exist, what is the nature of the disagreement and where does it exist?

II. System Components
   A. Identify the key internal system components.
   B. Identify the key functions of each component.
      1. As defined by policy
      2. As defined by procedure
      3. As defined by practice/perception of line personnel
   C. Analyze the ways in which these functions accomplish or undermine system mission.

III. Interaction in Repetitive Ways
   A. Identify ways that each component interacts with each other.
   B. Identify the written (explicit) rules that guide the interactions of each component with other components.
   C. Identify the unwritten (implicit) rules that guide interactions.
   D. Analyze the ways in which these rules for interaction are constructive or destructive to the system mission.

IV. Structural Variables
   A. Use of power
      1. How is power manifested in the system and in components?
      2. Where is power centered?
      3. What influence do individual components and individuals have on the system?
      4. What sort of leadership evolves from the power structure?
      5. How is power achieved?
      6. How is influence maintained?
      7. How is power balanced among system (or subsystem) components?
   B. Autonomy
      1. How much autonomy (to be self-directing) is given to each component in the system?
      2. How much autonomy is given to each individual?
      3. How is interdependence affected by the autonomy existing in the system?
   C. Coalitions
      1. How do components and individuals within a system form alliances for joint action?
      2. Are the alliances rigid or flexible?
   D. Negotiation
      1. How are agreements made and mutual problems solved within the system?
      2. Is negotiation open and goal oriented?

(continued)

E. Syntax: The Quality of Connections
(This aspect is difficult to evaluate. Some key questions relating to affect, empathy, respect, and bonding might include the following.)
1. Is the prevailing mood in an agency or the system trusting, affectionate, hopeful, cynical, or depressing?
2. Do system members demonstrate a willingness to understand the functions and problems of other system members?
3. Do police extend positive regard to corrections (and vice versa)?
4. Are emotional bonds among system members strong or weak?
5. Are existing emotional bonds healthy or destructive?

V. Internal Process
A. System communication
1. Permeability
a. To what degree are system members open to messages from others?
b. Do system members make certain that messages are mutually understood?
c. Do system members discount messages from others?
2. Communication style
a. Do system members balance consideration of personal needs, the needs of others, and the requirements of the situation?
b. Is anyone discounted or omitted?
3. Information processing
a. Is there congruence in the way different members/components process information?
b. Are misunderstandings expressed and resolved?
4. Coherence and flow
a. Are messages confused in transmission?
b. Is attention among members focused or scattered?
c. Does communication flow or is it chaotic and disjointed?
B. The change process
1. Impose change, or select an example of imposed change. Analyze the impact on other components of change in one component based on this example.
2. How do system components deal with change?
C. Self-esteem
1. How do members (candidly) value others within the system?
2. How do members (candidly) value themselves within the system?

VI. External Relationships
A. The external systems
1. Identify local systems that impinge on (have major influence on) this system.
2. What is the function of each as it relates to the system?
B. The relationship
1. What is the nature of the relationship of the system/system components with external systems in general (open or closed)?
2. What is the nature of the relationship of the system/system components with each external system?
C. How do system relationships with external systems/ individuals affect the achievement of system goals?

VII. Summary of Strengths and Weaknesses
A. In what ways is this system working effectively as a system?
B. In what ways is this system working ineffectively as a system?
C. Given the legal structure, where can change be best applied to effect positive change in the total system?

VIII. System Planning
Robert Cushman (1980) states:
Local criminal justice decision-making should be guided by planning efforts at three levels: criminal justice agency planning, city or county level criminal justice planning, and comprehensive interagency and intergovernmental planning for the criminal justice system as a whole. Planning can help individual criminal justice agencies become more efficient, more productive, and more effective. Planning can help officials of general government—the city mayor, the board of supervisors, and county commissioners—evaluate and make decisions about the criminal justice system and its cost and performance. Many local governments also are finding that comprehensive system-wide planning (interagency and cross-jurisdictional) can help to streamline the entire system of criminal justice, eliminate duplication and fill service gaps, and generally improve the quality of service while minimizing costs.
A. Based on your analysis of the system mission and the reality of systems practice, determine what agencies/individuals should be involved in system planning.
B. Determine an approach to resolving system weaknesses and building on system strengths.

Regardless of the minority group in question, the primary issues that are faced by police are the same. First, police must provide services to all communities in a fair and equitable manner. Second, they must convince each community that they are actually doing so. Often, the second portion of the community relations formula is more difficult to attain than the first. The best means of enhancing relations with minority communities is not slick public relations programs presented by specialized units but the development of police forces that are carefully selected, well trained, highly disciplined, and representative of all communities served (Shusta et al., 2005).

Women

Sexism, like racism, has led the police into conflict with a sizable portion of the American populace. The treatment of women has differed historically from the treatment of minority groups, in that they were not necessarily the targets of physical brutality or verbal abuse. However, they have suffered as a gender group from discrimination in the forms of condescension and insensitivity on the part of a male-dominated occupation (Fuller, 2006).

The women's movement and the resulting assertion of women's rights in the workforce and the political process have brought about tremendous changes within a relatively short period of time (Peak and Glenser, 2004). Male police are becoming highly sensitized to issues that affect females as clients (whether as victims, witnesses, offenders, or concerned citizens) and as colleagues. The increasing number of women in law enforcement is accelerating this awareness as police forces become more representative of their communities.

Gays and Lesbians

Homosexuals have long experienced discrimination from police officers. Police have zealously enforced laws against homosexuality, which have existed in every state. As those laws have been eliminated (or ignored), gay people no longer suffer from such blatant persecution but in many areas continue to be treated as second-class citizens (Carter and Radelet, 2002). Contempt and derision for the gay lifestyle have led to difficulties in providing the police services to which all citizens are entitled. Confrontations with gay-rights protesters have further heightened tensions between police communities and gay communities. This issue is being addressed through training and regulations that promote equitable treatment for gay citizens. Some cities, such as San Francisco, actively recruit gay people to join their police forces in order to become more representative of the communities they serve. However, as long as the status of homosexuals in the United States remains unclear, the tensions between gays and police will continue.

Youth

Although most young people never experience any actual difficulties with the legal system, as a group they come into conflict with police at a higher rate than do middle-aged or older people (Walker and Katz, 2002). Much of this conflict is nothing more than the age-old dispute that naturally occurs between youths and adults. As young people mature from childhood into adolescence, their potential for conflict increases. Teenagers who are mobile and interested in having fun become even more likely to experience difficulties with police (as well as with other authority figures). Young adults become more conforming as they mature and find their place within society. The greatest challenge for the police is to allow youth to enjoy being young but to keep them from doing harm to themselves or others.

The Elderly

"Persons sixty-five and older comprise the largest part of the nation's live-alone population, and this proportion is growing steadily" (Carter and Radelet, 2002). As the number of elderly Americans increases, they are all too frequently becoming the victims of serious crimes. The living conditions of our elderly citizens and their relative susceptibility to crime have caused many to find that their "golden years" are filled with terror. Law enforcement must rise to the challenge of providing services that, along with other governmental assistance, will enrich the lives of our older citizens. Enrichment programs are necessary not only to reduce the victimization of elderly citizens but also to halt the increasing number of elderly engaged in drunkenness, drunken driving, and theft. Public awareness of the needs of the elderly has increased, but there is much to do to alleviate the impact of crime and the fear of it among older Americans.

The Poor

Members of the lower class often view police in a different light than do members of the middle and upper classes. Rather than seeing police officers as protectors of their rights and property, the poor tend to see police as the protectors of others' rights and property. In short, many lower-class people think of the police as their oppressors rather than their defenders. This perspective is easily understood. Although the lower class comprises predominantly honest and hardworking individuals, it is dramatically overrepresented within the ranks of lawbreakers. People who feel they have been wronged by society have less commitment to the laws of that society. People who are in desperate situations are more likely to commit desperate acts. Those who feel they have nothing to lose are more willing to risk being arrested (Reiman, 2001).

No matter how fair our society becomes—whether we adopt socialistic programs comparable to those of several European nations or whether the standard of living for all Americans greatly improves—there will always be a sizable lower class and members of this class will be overrepresented within the criminal community. Therefore, we cannot eliminate conflict between the police and the lower class. However, we can reduce the amount of conflict by developing procedures and regulations that ensure that lower-class citizens receive fair and equitable treatment and services from the police.

The Media

The relationship between the police and the media is a complicated one. The police are interested in serving the public and protecting their reputations. The media are interested in serving the public and making profits. The police are obligated at times to withhold information that they feel would be detrimental to the public good (names of victims, case specifics, etc.). The media are obligated to release information that they feel the "public has a right to know." Too often, though, deciding what information should be released or withheld is based on self-interest on the part of the media or the police rather than on what is in the public interest (Grant and Terry, 2005).

Because of conflicting views on what is best for the public and because of self-serving motives, the media and the police are often adversaries. How this adversarial relationship is handled is of the utmost importance for the police, the media, and the public. Quite frankly, some secrets must be kept, and the media grudgingly realize this. However, the police must also realize that only those secrets that would cause public harm (this does not include embarrassment of police officials or concealment of improper practices) can be legitimately withheld from the media. Therefore, the relations between media and police personnel should be based on openness, honesty, and accessibility. Anything less will only exacerbate an already difficult relationship.

Religious Organizations

The influence of **religious organizations** may be seen throughout U.S. society. Historically, the United States has been viewed as a Christian country, with most religious disputes occurring between Catholics and the various Protestant denominations. Minority religions were (and are) protected by the U.S. Constitution but have not necessarily been tolerated by its peoples. "Blue laws" were passed in many states and communities to force Catholics and non-Christians to comply with Protestant practices. Religious groups, such as Jews, Muslims, Hindus, and Buddhists, often found themselves the objects of hatred and intolerance. During the nineteenth century, Mormons were driven out of several states before finding a safe haven in what would become the state of Utah. At that time also, Native Americans were prevented from practicing their religions.

Today, the relationship between the police and religious organizations is, for the most part, amicable. Most of the traditional religions are supportive of police efforts to provide "law and order" for their communities. However, some nontraditional religions are built around practices that might bring them into conflict with law enforcement, and religious organizations are often split on social issues such as civil rights, war, and abortion. In the resulting conflicts, police officials may be placed in the unpopular position of arresting community members who are convinced that they are doing "God's will." As with ethnic minorities, fair and equitable treatment is the key to building and/or maintaining positive relations.

Civic Organizations

Civic organizations such as the Kiwanis, Rotary, Exchange, Civitan, Masons, Shriners, Jaycees, and Lions are less likely to come into conflict with law enforcement than are religious organizations. They, along with the many other reputable organizations dedicated to community service, often comprise persons who are thought to be "mainstays" of a community. However, as with any organizations, individual members may engage in unlawful behavior, and local organizations may be created under the guise of civic service that are actually fronts for illegal activities. Police officials should take care to ensure that their membership (or lack of membership) in these organizations does not affect any dealings they may have with them.

Public Service Organizations

Public service organizations are nonprofit associations directed toward accomplishing community goals. The Salvation Army, Goodwill Industries, and the American Red Cross are three of the better-known charities. The Boy Scouts and Girl Scouts are two of the better-known youth-development associations. Many local groups that offer family support, crisis counseling, and emergency aid can be valuable allies for the police in rendering assistance to people in need. Police officials need to identify and establish communications with those organizations to enhance their ability to serve the public.

Political Organizations

Politics and policing have been difficult bedfellows for many years. The linkage between politics and police corruption has been a problem not only within the nation's larger cities (Reppetto, 1978; Walker, 1977), but among rural law enforcement as well (Bopp and Schultz, 1977; Johnson and Wolfe, 2003). To "get politics out of the police and the police out of politics" (Walker and Katz, 2002) has been a goal of reformers for more than a century.

Unfortunately (or perhaps, fortunately) the simple truth is that politics cannot be eliminated from policing or any other governmental agency (Carter and Radelet, 2002). Efforts to regulate police membership in opposition parties or to prohibit their involvement in political campaigns have traditionally resulted in abuses on the part of "reformers" (Walker, 1977). As citizens, police officers are entitled to belong to political parties and other political organizations. However, their behavior can be regulated through clear and concise policies and procedures to ensure that their political outlook or activity does not affect their job performance.

Labor Unions

The historical relationship between police organizations and **labor unions** has been one of hostility and mistrust. The police were frequently used as strikebreakers in the labor disputes of the early twentieth century (Reppetto, 1978). Today, the police are prohibited by state and federal laws from violating the rights of striking workers. However, this does not mean that tensions between the police and union members are eliminated. The police are still responsible for the property and safety of industrial management. They must also see that the rights of those workers who do not participate in union activities are protected. Fair and impartial law enforcement remains essential.

Economic/Business Organizations

The relations that the police have had with the business community have not been as physically violent as with labor unions, but they have not always been pleasant. Often, business leaders have felt that they are "above the law" and should be exempt from police "intrusion" into their affairs. Similarly, many expect preferential treatment when they do need police services. Cooperative relations with business organizations such as the local chamber of commerce, builders' associations, food services, and the trucking industry are necessary. But the neutrality of the police organization in enforcing laws must be stressed.

Community Interest Organizations

The number of watchdog organizations dedicated to maintaining surveillance over governmental agencies continues to increase. Organizations such as the American Civil Liberties Union and Common Cause are nationally known and respected. Others may consist of only one or two people within a specific community. These organizations may exist for a variety of reasons: to ensure that individual rights are protected; to guard against governmental waste and inefficiency; to protect citizens from hazardous conditions; to attract attention to a particular issue; or just to satisfy individual egos. Regardless of their motivation, law enforcement agencies are advised to cooperate with them to the extent that departmental procedures, governmental regulations, and state laws will allow.

Clients

The interrelationships between the police community and the **external communities** are vitally important. However, most individuals hold memberships within several communities at the same time. Furthermore, there may be additional factors that influence how they interact with various police communities.

Many citizens may never have direct contact with police officials. The latest figures from a 1999 national survey show that only 21 percent of U.S. residents had a contact with the police (see Table 5.1). Individual perceptions of the police are based on citizens' memberships within their respective communities. Those perceptions may be reinforced or altered if and when direct contact occurs. A victim who feels that his or her case received only minimal attention from police may be very understanding or very dissatisfied. A victim who feels that he or she was treated with respect and the case handled properly may become an enthusiastic supporter. The same holds true for witnesses, concerned citizens, and sometimes even offenders. Courteous and professional treatment by a police officer can overcome many preconceptions about police. Similarly, one inconsiderate or rude officer can undermine the efforts of many. Once again, fair and equitable treatment of all people with whom the police come into contact, regardless of the situation or the person's station in life, is the key to good relations.

Governmental Agencies

Law enforcement agencies are but one group out of a myriad number of organizations at all levels of government. The police must interact on a daily basis with representatives of these **government agencies**: elected officials, top administrators, midlevel bureaucrats, and frontline employees. These agencies may be subunits of the same political entity as the police organization, such as agencies charged with maintaining the streets, utilities, public housing, educational

---

TABLE 5.1 Contacts between Police and the Public—2005

In 2005:

19 percent of U.S. residents age 16 or older had contact with the police

56 percent of contacts were in traffic stops

24 percent of contacts were to report a problem

1.6 percent of contacts involved police use or threat of force

83 percent of those who had force used against them thought it was excessive

White, black, and Hispanic drivers were stopped at similar rates, although blacks
and Hispanics were more likely to be searched

11.6 percent of all searches found evidence of criminal wrongdoing

Male drivers were three times more likely than female drivers to be arrested, and black
drivers were twice as likely to be arrested.

86 percent of stopped drivers thought they were pulled over for a legitimate reason.

Overall, 9 out of 10 persons who had contact with the police thought they acted properly.

Source: Duprose, M. R., and Langran, P. A. Contacts between Police and the Public: Findings from the 2005 National Survey, Bureau of Justice Statistics, U.S. Department of Justice, 2005.

facilities, parks, and public transportation. They may be emergency organizations such as fire departments, ambulance services, and civil defense. They may be local, state, or federal regulatory agencies. They may be legislative bodies: city councils, county commissions, state or federal legislatures that pass laws these agencies are responsible for abiding by and enforcing. In short, the police do not operate in a governmental vacuum (Cole and Smith, 1997). They are dependent on and are depended upon by many other governmental organizations equally dedicated to serving their respective publics.

FOR BETTER, FOR WORSE The concept of "system"—a set of communities interacting with each other—is imposed on the fragmented, sometimes chaotic and dysfunctional process of justice in which the police are active participants. No one has ever suggested that the justice system works efficiently as a system. As a committee of the American Bar Association observed:

> The American criminal justice system is rocked by inefficiency, lack of coordination, and an obsessive adherence to outmoded practices and procedures. In many respects, the entire process might more aptly be termed a nonsystem, a feudalistic confederation of several independent components often working at cross purposes. (American Bar Association, Committee on Crime Prevention and Control, 1972, p. 7)

Even in a dysfunctional system, system principles apply. The members of the justice system are interdependent and interrelated in their mission and their functions. If police dramatically increase their arrests, other components of the system will feel the strain. If corrections does not correct, other components of the system will have to process repeat offenders. If police do not investigate thoroughly (sometimes even if they do), their efforts will be wasted because the case will be dismissed. If prosecution is not adequate, even a perfect investigation will be of little benefit. There are times that police might understandably wish for divorce from this system. Even in the case of murder, the crime that is most likely to be reported in our society and for which police are most likely to make an arrest (86 percent of the cases), only 64 percent of those apprehended are actually prosecuted, and only 43 percent of these are convicted.

For better or worse, open or closed, functional or dysfunctional, exchange will occur among members of this system. Each may declare at times to be an independent agent within the system, owing loyalty and consideration to no one, but this is more an exercise in self-deception than fact. Worse, the deception itself increases the problem of fragmentation. The greater the fragmentation, the less likely system goals will be achieved. Understanding how system principles relate to the justice community will help us to gain a better understanding of this community, assess its needs, and improve its relationships.

INTERNAL COMMUNITIES

Minorities

Initially, minority representatives, regardless of their race or ethnicity, were treated as "tokens" by both police and public (Dulaney, 1996). The few minority officers who were employed often had restricted powers and served only in "their" communities. Nevertheless, the employment of the first black police officer in Atlanta, Georgia, in 1948 was the occasion for a parade in the black community. However, the great reform police chief, Herbert Jenkins, had to assure Atlanta citizens that "the Negro policemen would arrest only Negro persons" (Jenkins, 1970, p. 26). Since the 1960s, as a result of the Civil Rights Movement, Affirmative Action requirements, federal lawsuits, increased political activities on the part of minorities, and heightened awareness on the part of the white majority, minority representation has increased. Although U.S. policing is still dominated by whites (76.4 percent), blacks (11.7 percent) and Hispanics (7.8 percent) are now represented within the system. Other groups, such as Asians and Native Americans, appear to remain underrepresented (Bureau of Justice Statistics, 2006).

Despite having achieved more equitable membership within the ranks of the police organization, minorities within supervisory and administrative positions have progressed at a slower rate. However, progress is occurring. As of 1996, former chief Reuben Greenberg—a black Jew—of the Charleston Police Department in South Carolina, reported that blacks had held "the top positions in most of the largest cities in the nation: New York, Chicago, Houston, Dallas, Washington, D.C., Los Angeles, Philadelphia, Detroit, Miami, New Orleans, Baltimore, Oakland, Atlanta, and Memphis" (Dulaney, 1996, p. ix). In addition, two blacks have served as president of the International Association of Chiefs of Police. Lee P. Brown, the former mayor of Houston, Texas, has been the police chief in Atlanta, Houston, and New York City, as well as National Drug

FIGURE 5.2 A police check-on that reflects modern ethnic and gender diversity.
Courtesy of Birmingham Police Department.

Czar for the Clinton administration. When he was the chief in Houston, the legendary police reformer Patrick M. Murphy said that Brown was "the best police chief in the nation" (Dulaney, 1996, p. 94). At this writing, minority (African American and Hispanic American) members hold many leadership positions within law enforcement at the local, state, and federal levels.

Although there has been substantial progress in racial and ethnic representation within law enforcement, it has not been easy or without pain. Resentments have occurred within the police ranks. Charges of discrimination by minorities often have been answered with charges of reverse discrimination by white officers (Roberg, Kuykendall, and Novak, 2002). Addressing past inequities has created stressful situations for all concerned. These concerns can be dealt with only through organizational policies and procedures that are fair to both minority and majority members.

Gender

Many of the issues discussed in the preceding section are also applicable to women. Actually, female representation in law enforcement has progressed at a slower rate than has that of ethnic minorities. In 1999, females accounted for 6.3 percent of white officers, 2.5 percent of black officers, and 1 percent of Hispanic officers in local police departments (BJS, 1999). In 2000, women comprised 13 percent of all sworn law enforcement positions nationwide (National Center for Women and Policing, 2001). The National Center for Women and Policing (2001, p. 2) reports "that [13 percent] is a paltry four percentage points higher than in 1990, when women comprised 9 percent of sworn officers." In 2001, there had not been substantial improvement. Women accounted for 12.7 percent of all sworn law enforcement officers in large police agencies (i.e., those over 100 sworn officers). In agencies under 100 sworn personnel, women accounted for 8.1 percent of all sworn personnel. The combined figures show that women represent only 11.2 percent of all sworn police personnel, even though they are 46.5 percent of the total workforce (National Center for Women and Policing, 2002). It was not until the 1972 Amendments to the Civil Rights Act of 1965 that women obtained the opportunity to choose law enforcement as a profession (Martin, 1989, pp. 312–330). Prior to those amendments, female representation in law enforcement was minimal, and assignments were usually to positions thought to be "properly suitable" by their male supervisors.

Only through legal actions and the perseverance of a group of exceptional pioneers did women break down the barriers within this traditionally male occupation. The first woman police chief in a major police force, Portland, Oregon, suffered personally and professionally as she shattered the bulletproof glass ceiling (Harrington, 1999).

Today, women have long since proven that they can perform well in all areas of law enforcement. Like ethnic minorities, they have experienced discrimination, resentment, and allegations of preferential treatment. In addition, they have endured the difficulties of sexual harassment from police and public alike. Despite these challenges, women have earned their place in policing.

Sexual Preference

Just as gay men and women have struggled for equitable treatment within the external communities, so too have they struggled within the law enforcement communities. Previously, gay police officers were required to keep their sexual preferences secret, not only to avoid ostracism but to avoid prosecution for violating laws against homosexuality. This has changed in many cities and police departments. The Gay Officers Action League (GOAL) was recognized in New York City in 1992 (Goalne, 2006; Goalny, 2006). Since then it has expanded to chapters throughout the nation and overseas.

As the nation has become more enlightened, laws regulating sexual relations between consenting adults have become more permissive. However, attitudes toward gays and lesbians in general and in law enforcement have softened only slightly. Whether gay people deserve the special protections accorded to ethnic minorities and females is a matter of debate (they are, after

FIGURE 5.3 **A sign at the front entrance of the Southern States PBA, a police labor organization that provides protections similar to yet distinct from a police union.**

Courtesy of Southern States Police Benevolent Association, Inc.

all, not recognizable as gay unless they indicate their sexual preference). That their private lives may be infringed upon by others who may disapprove of their sexual preference is not a debatable issue. Like religion, sexual preference should have no bearing on how people do their jobs or how they are treated while on the job. Gay officers must be accorded the same protections from harassment and discrimination as are accorded heterosexual police employees.

Police Unions

Employee organizations have a variety of names, such as leagues, fraternal organizations, federations, and benevolent associations, and differing degrees of employee representation (Whisenand and Ferguson, 1989). Whatever their name or their affiliation with external employee groups, their mission is to protect and promote the interests of their constituents. While they are categorized as an internal community due to their membership and influence within the police organization, they are often perceived by police administrators as being an external community (Cordner, Scarborough, and Sheehan, 2004).

REALITY CHECK

Harmless Spoof or Insult?

In February 2006, a video made by officers of the San Francisco Police Department's Bayview Station was posted to the Internet and immediately caused a major controversy. Some of the scenes within the video depicted a homeless African American woman being run over by a patrol car, officers receiving simulated sex within an Asian massage parlor, officers making homoerotic advances to one another, female officers dressed provocatively, and a male officer dressed as a transgendered person.

The major television networks included portions of the video on their national newscasts. Civil rights activists in San Francisco and around the country decried the video and called for its participants to be punished. Declaring the video to be racist, sexist, and homophobic, Mayor Gavin Newsom ordered an investigation not just by SFPD, but by the city's Human Rights Commission and the city's Commission on the Status of Women. He also created a blue ribbon commission to study the SFPD's personnel policies and standards of conduct and training. Police Chief Heather Fong declared the video "a dark day in the history of the department" and immediately suspended 20 officers for misuse of city resources.

The officers involved in making the video argued that it was a spoof of the stresses of police work that was made for private showing at a party. Officer Andrew Cohen, who made the video, declared that the film was satire and should be viewed as such. San Francisco Police Officers Association president Gary Delagnes called the responses to the video to be hypocritical in a city that allegedly promotes freedom of expression and the tolerance of others' rights. He also pointed out in his argument that among the officers who willingly participated in making the video were gays, females, African Americans, and Asians.

The consensus among San Francisco police officers from other stations who were interviewed appeared to be that although they did not condone the video, they understood it as an attempt to mock the pressures that officers face on a daily basis, and they felt the reactions by city officials were extreme. One openly gay officer, who had previously worked at the Bayview Station, stated that he personally wasn't offended and that the video should not be used to judge a very progressive department. However, local gay and transgender activists did not share his opinion.

What do you think?

Conclusions

In this chapter, we have proposed that police–community interaction is not a simple relationship between a police organization and the community it serves but is instead a series of complex and constantly changing relationships between internal police communities and external communities. These communities influence and are influenced by one another on a daily basis. The relationships that exist among various communities are usually competitive, often cooperative, and frequently conflictive.

External communities include ethnic minorities, women, gays, youth, the elderly, the poor, religious organizations, civic organizations, public service organizations, labor unions, business groups, community interest groups, governmental agencies, the courts, corrections, legislative bodies, the other law enforcement agencies, the media, citizens directly served by the police, and a myriad of other community groupings.

The internal police communities consist of the following: administrative personnel, support personnel, operational personnel, management, civilians, political groups, minorities, males, females, gays, religious groups, college graduates, union members, and other typologies by which individuals and groups may be categorized.

To deal effectively with this complex hodgepodge of humanity, the police organization must be managed in a fair and competent manner that provides equal access and equitable treatment to all communities. Communication is the key not only to the police organization's success in police–community relations but also to its survival.

Student Checklist

1. Discuss how relations between the police and the public are in reality complex relations among many overlapping communities.
2. Identify and describe the external communities that comprise the public.
3. Identify and describe the internal communities that comprise the police.
4. Describe how exchange relationships among various communities affect police–community relations.

Topics for Discussion

1. Identify and describe all the communities of which you are a member. Which could be considered a subsystem of others?

2. Identify and describe all the communities of which a police officer might be a part. Could these overlapping memberships result in conflict for the officer?

Bibliography

American Bar Association, Committee on Crime Prevention and Control. (1972). *New Perspectives on Urban Crime*. Chicago, IL: American Bar Association.

Bopp, W. J., and Schultz, D. O. (1977). *A Short History of American Law Enforcement*. Springfield, IL: Charles C Thomas.

Bureau of Justice Statistics. (2006). *Sourcebook of Criminal Justice Statistics*. Washington, D.C., Table 1, p. 53.

Carter, D. L., and Radelet, L. A. (2002). *The Police and the Community*, 7th ed. Upper Saddle River, NJ: Prentice Hall.

Cole, G. F., and Smith, C. E. (1997). *The American System of Criminal Justice*, 8th ed. Belmont, CA: Wadsworth.

Cordner, G. W., Scarborough, K. E., and Sheehan, R. (2004). *Police Administration*, 5th ed. Cincinnati, OH: Anderson Publishing Co.

Cushman, R. C. (1980). *Criminal Justice Planning for Local Governments*. American Justice Institute, Washington, D.C.: U.S. Department of Justice (LEAA).

Dulaney, W. M. (1996). *Black Police in America*. Bloomington, IN: Indiana University Press.

Fuller, J. R. (2006). *Criminal Justice: Mainstream and Cross Currents*. Upper Saddle River, NJ: Pearson/Prentice Hall.

Goalne. (2006). Gay Officers Action League of New England, http://www.goalne.org

Goalny. (2006). Gay Officers Action League of New York, http://www.goalny.org

Grant, H. B., and Terry, R. J. (2005). *Law Enforcement in the 21st Century*. Boston, MA: Pearson/Allyn and Bacon.

Harrington, P. (1999). *Triumph of Spirit*. Chicago, IL: Brittany Publications.

Jenkins, H. (1970). *Keeping the Peace: A Police Chief Looks at His Job*. New York: Harper & Row.

Johnson, H. A., and Wolfe, N. T. (2003). *History of Criminal Justice*, 3rd ed. Cincinnati, OH: Anderson Publishing.

Martin, S. E. (1989). "Female officers on the move? A status report on women in policing," in R. Dunham and G. P. Alpert (Eds.), *Critical Issues in Policing: Contemporary Issues*. Prospect Heights, IL: Waveland Press.

National Center for Women and Policing. (2001). *Equality Denied*. Los Angeles, CA: Feminist Majority Foundation.

National Center for Women and Policing. (2002). *Equity Denied*. Los Angeles, CA: Feminist Foundation.

Peak, K., and Glenser, R. W. (2004). *Community Policing and Problem Solving*, 4th ed. Upper Saddle River, NJ: Prentice Hall.

Reiman, J. (2001). *The Rich Get Richer and the Poor Get Prison: Ideology, Class and Criminal Justice*, 6th ed. Boston, MA: Allyn and Bacon.

Reppetto, T. A. (1978). *The Blue Parade*. New York: Free Press.

Roberg, R. R., Kuykendall, J., and Novak, K. (2002). *Police Management*, 3rd ed. Los Angeles, CA: Roxbury Press.

Shusta, R. M., Levine, D. R., Wong, H. Z., and Harris, P. R. (2005). *Multicultural Law Enforcement: Strategies for Peacemaking in a Diverse Society*. Upper Saddle River, NJ: Pearson/Prentice Hall.

Walker, S. (1977). *A Critical History of Police Reform: The Emergence of Professionalism*. Lexington, MA: Lexington Books.

Walker, S., and Katz, C. M. (2002). *The Police in America: An Introduction*, 4th ed. Boston, MA: McGraw-Hill.

Whisenand, P. M., and Ferguson, F. (1989). *The Managing of Police Organizations*, 3rd ed. Upper Saddle River, NJ: Prentice Hall.

MODULE 3

CHAPTER 6

Police–Community Relations and the Media

The media represents a powerful mechanism by which to communicate with the community. They can assist with publicizing community concerns and available solutions, such as services from government or community agencies or new laws or codes that will be enforced in addition, the media can have a significant impact on public perceptions of the police, crime problems, and fear of crime.

—OFFICE OF COMMUNITY ORIENTED POLICING SERVICES

It is the philosophy of the Boise Police Department to respond to media inquiries as quickly, completely and accurately as possible. This media policy is only part of the department's general philosophy to operate in an open, cooperative partnership with the community [emphasis added].

—BOISE POLICE DEPARTMENT—MEDIA GUIDE

KEY CONCEPTS

Commitment to Crime Coverage	Crisis Guidelines	Restricting Coverage Argument
Competing Rights of the Media	Exploitation of Crime News	Heavy Coverage Argument
	Police Information Officer/ Public Information Officer	Marketing Police Community Relations

LEARNING OBJECTIVES

Studying this chapter will enable you to:

1. Overview media commitment to the reporting of crime news.
2. Contrast the responsibility of the press and the police.
3. Justify the need for guidelines in reporting.
4. Establish police–media guidelines for routine information release, crisis situations, and hostage situations.
5. Identify ongoing blocks to positive police–media relations and strategies for resolving them.

Police-Community Relations and the Administration of Justice, Eighth Edition
by Ronald D. Hunter, Thomas Barker

6. Contrast individual constitutional rights and the public's right to know.
7. Recognize the importance of the media in police–community relations.

The police and the media need each other. The police want a positive public image and the media want quick and reliable crime information. The media represent a principal link between police agencies and the public they serve. This link provides the police with a means to communicate successfully with, not to, its external environment. Again, as we said earlier, police–community relations is what the police do with, not to, their community. Whether or not that relationship is successful often depends on the relationship that the police department has with its local media representatives. Media impact on virtually every citizen is enormous, and crime news is a major media topic. Except for the relatively few people who become directly involved with the police, private citizens learn of police activity, of crime prevention, of the pursuit and apprehension of criminals and their disposition in the courts by what they read in their newspapers and see and hear on television and radio. True or not, positive or negative, what a citizen reads, hears, and observes in the local media largely defines the citizen's perception of the police.

The relationship between the police and the media is sometimes one of conflict and contention. Efforts of the press to transmit the truth as they see it may help or hinder the efforts of the police. They may endanger an individual or group; increase public fear, the intensity of riots, and the credibility of terrorists; and according to some observers, create a criminal environment. They may invade privacy or defame character of individuals. They may interfere with the rights of defendants to a fair trial. On the other hand, efforts of the press may uncover crimes and criminals, exonerate those convicted unjustly, protect the public from corruption in public service, encourage public involvement in crime prevention and other special emphasis programs, decrease danger to individuals or groups, and allay excessive public fear, usually through education.

COMMUNITY RELATIONS CONTEXT

Any discussion of the mass media involves the print and electronic media, including the newspapers, magazines, television, movies, radio, and the Internet. Each separately and collectively has an impact on police–community relations. In this chapter, we address police–media relations, something that is rarely hidden from the public. Some approach police–media concerns in a narrow public information or public relations context and that does have its place. We approach it, instead, in the broader context of community relations because the nature of the police–media relationship in a community is integrally related to the nature of the larger police–community relationship. The average citizen's secondhand experience of crime and the police through the media affects their attitudes toward and expectations of the police (Morgan and Newburn, 1997, p. 109).

COMMITMENT TO CRIME COVERAGE

Statistics on massive media impact would be of little interest to police if it were not for the fact that media **commitment to crime coverage** is great. Some difference of opinion exists as to how much news about murder, robbery, rape, and larceny the public really wants or demands. Yet there can be little doubt that, with or without clear public demand, maximum coverage of crime is offered. Recent surveys place the proportion of crime news to total newspaper space at anywhere from 3 to 10 percent. In an individual issue, crime news may represent 30–35 percent. Moreover, this news often is given priority space.

The Subjectivity Factor

Newspapers can emphasize crime (grossly overemphasize, the critics of the press argue) by the placement of stories on page one; by large, black, and often lurid headlines; and by other attention-getting devices. "In weighing the effect on justice," Lofton, author of *Justice and the Press*, wrote, "The play and the slant of crime news are even more important than the amount of space allotted to the subject. . . . The large and dramatic headline on the front page gets more attention from readers than a small, unprovocative item buried on the back pages" (Lofton, 1966). In large-city newspapers in particular, sensational crimes are often given more space than significant news of national and international events. The story of a $15 robbery in a small community often occupies more space in the local newspaper than the expenditure by the local government of hundreds of thousands of dollars.

Some people question whether or not a news story can ever be totally objective. Paul Harvey, the well-known radio commentator, was asked on ABC television's *Good Morning, America*, why he chose to call his newscasts commentaries rather than news reports. He explained that news reports are assumed to be objective, yet, realistically, all such reports include some elements of subjectivity (in what is reported and omitted, what is accented, the tone in which it is reported, etc.). Saying that a report is objective, then, may be misleading. Paul Harvey would rather not mislead his listeners. Because news commentary makes no claims to objectivity and is, by definition, a subjective comment on the news, Mr. Harvey stated that he felt more comfortable with that format (1983). For the same reason, Dan Abrams, NBC News legal analyst and the CEO of Abrams Research, says that there is no need for him or any citizen to presume that the swindler Bernie Madoff or Caylee Anthony's mother, Casey, is innocent (Abrams, 2009). The facts as reported in the news would suggest otherwise in both cases. However, this may complicate both cases when they go to trial, where the presumption of innocence is objective, not subjective. Anyone who watches Nancy Grace on CNN TV knows that she appears to presume that every defendant is guilty.

Restricting Coverage Argument

Although some media sources choose individually to restrict crime coverage in some specific category of crime for a specific period of time, rarely has a general policy to restrict crime coverage been made and adhered to.

In the 1930s, Curtis H. Clay, editor of the *Post-Tribune* of La Salle, Illinois, made such a policy. Although crime news was not entirely omitted from the newspaper, it was relegated to less than front-page priority for a period of two or three years. Ownership of the paper has changed. It is now called the *Daily News-Tribune*, and this policy no longer exists. Mr. Clay's rationale for his restrictive policy is instructive, however:

> The intelligent criminal enters his career deliberately, with eyes open to chances of beating the law. He believes he is smarter than the police. Publicity encourages him; he likes to see his name in the headlines. He laughs at the "dumb cops" and continues his outlawry, glorying in his notoriety. If and when he gets caught, he is ready to face the music. Wasn't his name on the front page for weeks, months? . . . Publicity can't stop him. It will not injure his reputation. It will enhance it. (MacDougall, 1964, p. 389)

The above rationale continues to have merit today. Within a few days of the media sensationalization of the April 1999 massacre at Columbine High School in Littleton, Colorado, a copycat incident occurred in Alberta, Canada, as did a rash of bomb and gun threats across the United States.

Heavy Coverage Argument

Using Al Capone as his central character, Thomas S. Rice, a student of the press, argued an opposite view—that of sensationalizing crime in order to fight it:

> It is far, far better for the safety of our citizens and their families that we should have too much crime news instead of too little. . . . Every improvement in police adminis-tration and methods has followed newspapers playing up crime. Constant harping on Al Capone, with the definite object of bringing him to book, was not making a hero out of him. The Chicago newspapers which led the fight against that contami-nation of their city had the definite purpose of causing his fall. . . . Capone and other lawbreakers have come to grief from systematic sensationalizing of their personalities as well as their deeds until the public rose in revolt. (MacDougall, 1964, p. 391)

Rice claimed that what he called "systematic sensationalizing" led not only to Capone's downfall but also to the creation of the Chicago Crime Commission, which helped improve the administration of criminal justice in that city. Similar "sensationalizing" by newspapers, Rice said, led to the creation of similar commissions in Cleveland, Baltimore, and Philadelphia.

Certainly the press often can cause public outrage that, in turn, will bring about political pressures needed to motivate appropriate police action (Barker and Carter, 1994). The media and anti-gun forces argue that the Columbine High School incident warrants heavy coverage so that the nation can show its sympathy and develop strategies to prevent the future occurrence of similar events.

EXPLOITATION OF CRIME NEWS

Whatever one thinks of the relative merits of the conflicting arguments of Clay and Rice, it is the latter's views that are practiced by virtually all publishers, editors, and reporters of the daily news-papers of America. Newspaper coverage that followed the 1946 arrest of a 17-year-old Chicago youth, William Heirens, for several brutal murders was reasonably typical: The five Chicago newspapers gave, in total, much more coverage to the Heirens case, from arrest to sentencing, than to critical national events. A study of 85 issues of Chicago newspapers during that period revealed 62 banner headlines for the Heirens case, 11 to the operations of the Office of Price Administration (which affected the pocketbooks of virtually every person in America), and only 4 to atomic bomb tests.

Whether or not the readers of U.S. newspapers share this preoccupation, a favorite topic of the media, newspapers in particular, is violent crime. And although the degree of sensational-izing in American newspapers has diminished in the last 50 years, there is more than enough evidence that the press relies heavily on crime news. There is also evidence to suggest that some newspapers exploit what they claim to be public interest in crime in order to sell their newspa-pers. Ed Murray, managing editor of the *Los Angeles Mirror*, wrote of the Marilyn Sheppard murder case, "This case has mystery, society, sex, and glamour," thus explaining the massive cov-erage U.S. papers gave to an event that was really a rather ordinary homicide (Lofton, 1966, p. 182). Herbert H. Krauch, editor of the *Los Angeles Herald and Express* (2,000 miles from the murder and trial site) said of the trial of Sam Sheppard, "It's been a long time since there's been a murder trial this good."

There are other editors who, like Murray and Krauch, are convinced that crime news sells, and there is evidence to support them. In 1956, for example, two sisters were raped and mur-dered, and the resultant stories boosted total circulation of the city's daily newspapers by 50,000 copies. One year later when a rapist ran wild in San Francisco, that city's four newspapers had a field day. The *Chronicle* called the attacker the "Torture Kit Rapist" (the victims had been mana-cled and tortured by the rapist who had used a knife, adhesive tape, manacles, and scissors). The

News called the murderer the "Fang Fiend" because he had been described by one would-be victim as having "canine teeth, which protruded fang-like over his lower lip." A 23-year-old warehouse clerk was arrested as the rapist-murderer; when another man confessed, the press abandoned the case, but the coverage had been profitable. During each day of the almost two-week coverage of the case, each San Francisco newspaper sold about 15,000 more copies than normal.

Crime news is the most frequently reported news and there are several reasons for this (Chermak and Chapman, 2007). Newspapers must attract and maintain a pool of readers, and crime news is uncomplicated and can be easily lengthened or shortened to fill needed space. Furthermore, it can be gathered from police organizations at little cost.

Along this same line, many argue that the current fascination with reality-based television programs, such as *Cops, First 48, Dallas SWAT, FBI,* and *American Detective,* leads to the beliefs that policing is an action-packed profession and criminals are predominantly violent; that crime is the work of minorities, particularly African Americans; and that the police are regularly successful in their crime-fighting activities (Worral, 2000). Equally disturbing are the incidents of questionable practices (e.g., unreasonable force and violations of constitutional rights) shown being committed by real police officers as they execute warrants and make arrests during these pseudo news events.

Morgan and Newburn (1997) state that in both Great Britain and the United States "crime is our major source of entertainment" (p. 108). The film industry relies on crime stories; the more violent the better. Newspapers, television, and radio news broadcast crime accounts. Television dramas, particularly serial programs such as *CSI* and *Law & Order,* are very popular. "True crime" reconstructions are popular in Great Britain and the United States; every night, citizens of both countries can be entertained by flashing lights and wailing sirens.

An interesting phenomenon has occurred in recent years: As serious crime has decreased, media coverage has increased. Staszak (2001) says that three reasons are responsible for this paradox:

> First, for years the media has given priority to this type of news, and old habits are hard to break. Second, consumers of electronic and printed media still follow crime coverage. Polls show that this information still holds people's interest. Third, crime coverage is easy, loaded with good visuals and sound bites, and relatively inexpensive to cover. (p. 10)

PUBLIC REACTION TO MEDIA COVERAGE

Much has been said about the impact of television programming—sometimes including the news—particularly on young members of the viewing public. This impact is behind the recent move of the television networks to restrict the amount of violence shown on TV. This voluntary movement by the television networks came about because Congress was going to examine the issue. The average American child watches more than 20 hours of TV a week, and studies have shown that youths exposed to violence and aggression on television and in the movies are more likely to copy that behavior (Siegel and Senna, 2007). Controlled laboratory studies have not confirmed this link, however, so there is a need for more research on this issue.

The media, particularly television, has been criticized by citizens, acting independently of these organizations, for what the citizens have perceived as exploitation of crime coverage. For example, a television documentary on the life of Gary Gilmore, the convicted murderer who made national news for choosing to be executed, was angrily denounced by many as a poor use of airtime. It was suggested that the time and money spent developing and airing such a product could be better spent on documentaries about people who had made positive contributions to our civilization.

NBC's 1983 program *Special Report* generated even more anger among many citizens. *Special Report* was actually a work of fiction realistically portrayed on television, using NBC's

Special Report format. The story was a modern version of H. G. Wells's *The War of the Worlds*. It ended depicting massive destruction by terrorists in South Carolina. Although disclaimers were broadcast frequently, many people believed that the story was a special news report. The anger directed at the network, however, was for what citizens viewed as network irresponsibility in presenting a realistic model for terrorists to follow.

Coverage by media of the Tylenol poisonings in Chicago in 1982 received mixed reviews by the public. Some people seemed to feel that the coverage sensationalized events and encouraged "copycat" crimes. Others expressed an appreciation of the coverage, calling it restrained and geared toward the protection of the public because the cause of the problem was not immediately apparent.

The 1992 Pepsi tampering scare led to more than 50 complaints in 23 states within days of the first complaint in Tacoma, Washington. By the end of the first week, many of these complaints had been exposed as hoaxes, and at least a dozen people had been arrested. Forensic psychiatrist Park Dietz, consultant to the FBI, states that "each nationally publicized incident generates on average 30 more seriously disruptive crimes," and asks that news organizations limit their coverage of tampering (Toufexis, 1993). N. G. Berrill, a psychologist with the New York Forensic Health Group, states that the classic tamperer is an angry, antisocial person who "gets a real sense of power from devising a plan and seeing it blossom in the media" (Toufexis, 1993).

When ABC undertook its 1983 *Crime in America* series, the network demonstrated awareness of crime coverage issues by taking great care to avoid sensationalism. The series was presented with documentation and reserve. Balance was provided by presenting issues from many points of view. The current interest in such shows as *America's Most Wanted* and *Cops* would be open to charges of crime exploitation, especially when they portray actual victims and witnesses, if it were not for their crime-fighting credentials.

The coverage of crime-related issues by the media (both print and television) is often filled with irony. Efforts to condemn and exploit crime may actually appear within the same publication or presentation. As an example, the day after the Columbine High School assault, *The Anniston Star* had a detailed story on what had transpired, along with an editorial expressing support for the citizens of Littleton and concern as to how such a tragedy could occur. In that same edition of the newspaper was an article telling how funny MTV's *Death Match* (a show in which caricatures of celebrities fought to the death) was to watch.

CONFLICT BETWEEN MEDIA AND POLICE

It is clear that accounts of sensational, violent crimes sell newspapers and draw attention to radio and television news. But do attempts by the media to report crime help or hinder police efforts to fight crime? The record does not supply a clear answer.

BOX 6.1

How TV Creates Better Criminals and Unrealistic Juries

According to a story carried in the September 30, 2005, issue of *The Week*, shows like *CSI* and *Law & Order* are teaching criminals how to avoid being caught. British police have experienced cases in which car thieves dumped bins full of cigarette butts into cars they had abandoned, effectively flooding the crime scene with DNA samples. American police have found that suspects are using gloves, condoms, and other protective gear to avoid leaving physical evidence behind. Suspects also are wiping crime scenes down and removing items they once would have overlooked.

As if savvier criminals weren't enough of a problem, prosecutors are finding that jurors have heightened expectations about the evidence presented at trials. The oversimplification of evidence collection and forensic analyses on shows such as *CSI* has created unrealistic expectations on the part of jurors. It appears that jurors who watch crime dramas expect every case to have forensic evidence to support the charges. Even in relatively straightforward cases, juries are citing the lack of physical evidence in acquitting defendants.

A Hindrance and a Help

From the point of view of the police, overcoverage and sensationalizing of crime may not in themselves produce law enforcement problems. Occasionally, however, the press works at cross-purposes with the police, and law enforcement is hindered. This is particularly true in kidnapping cases, where the relationship between press and police is the most critical; the safety of the victim often depends on the cooperation given by the press to the police. Former FBI Director J. Edgar Hoover once compiled a list of cases in which he claimed the media had seriously hindered the work of his agency. One such case cited by Hoover was the Mattson kidnapping. Newspaper reporters prevented contact with the kidnappers of young Charles Mattson by refusing to leave the neighborhood of the Mattson home in Seattle. The boy's father received a letter from the kidnappers containing a newspaper picture of reporters around the house and said there would be no contact until they left. The Mattson boy was later found dead, obviously murdered by the kidnappers. In the kidnapping of Peter Levine, a reporter who was trying to verify rumors that the boy was missing phoned the boy's father who, caught off guard, admitted that his child was missing and said that he was willing to pay ransom. Warned by the kidnapper to prevent publicity, the father tried to persuade the newspapers to suppress the story, but the papers refused. Later, the headless body of the kidnapped boy was found floating in Long Island Sound.

A more recent case demonstrates how the media can hinder police operations and endanger the lives of others. In 1998, in Tampa, Florida, a three-time cop killer was chased to a convenience store, where he took a hostage. The police were unable to contact the hostage taker because a radio reporter had called the store and was conducting a live interview on the air. To further complicate matters, live television coverage of the event was describing the movements of the tactical unit, and there was a TV in the store (Rosenthal, 2001a). The event was finally resolved when the cop killer released the hostage and committed suicide. This event led to a voluntary agreement between the police and the local media (described later).

In another recent hostage case, news stations in Baltimore, Maryland, refrained from revealing information, conducting interviews, or showing images while the police conducted a four-day effort to resolve the situation and free three hostages, including a 12-year-old boy (Trigoboff, 2000). Agreements between the police and the media, whereby the media agrees not to provide live coverage of incidents involving hostages and barricaded suspects, have been in place in Portland, Oregon, since 1998 and in Boston, Massachusetts, since 1999 (Rosenthal, 1999a). Media cooperation with the police has also drawn criticism from some in the media. During a potential suicide attempt in Denver, Colorado, two television stations provided equipment complete with station logos and allowed two police officers to pose as TV journalists to talk a mentally disturbed person off a downtown statue (Sotelo, 2000). The TV stations were criticized by some in the media.

In other cases, the press has shown restraint and cooperation with the police. In the Lindbergh baby kidnapping case, the press voluntarily suppressed the contents of the original ransom note and the fact that the U.S. Treasury Department had sent the serial numbers of the bank notes used as ransom to banks across the country. The press also refrained from following Lindbergh on his futile trips to meet the kidnapper and deliberately misled the kidnapper by publishing false information about police activity. However, such cooperation did not save the Lindbergh infant. The media cooperation eventually led to the capture, trial, and execution of Bruno Richard Hauptmann for the kidnapping and murder of young Lindbergh.

Generally, the press has become more sensitive in kidnapping cases. In 1954, a 60-hour "conspiracy of silence" by all San Francisco newspapers, wire services, and broadcasters was credited with saving the life of a kidnapped realtor. A year later, however, the *New York Daily News* was widely, and properly, condemned by police and others for failing to go along with other New York–area newspapers that had refrained from publishing accounts of the kidnapping of one-month-old Peter Weinberger (MacDougall, 1964, p. 395). Frightened by the crowd at the site selected for the transfer of the ransom money, which had been reported in the *Daily News*, the kidnapper killed the baby.

The press has occasionally thwarted police work in other cases as well. By reporting detailed clues discovered by the police or announcing the time and place of a planned investigation, the press can—and in some cases actually does—tip off the criminal, who may destroy the evidence and avoid capture. Again, though, the record of the press is mixed, for persistent, imaginative reporters have helped the police to solve crimes and, in some cases, have solved the crimes themselves. The brutal murder of Bobby Franks in Chicago in 1923 was solved by the detective work of two reporters of the *Chicago Daily News*, whose suspicions led to the arrest and conviction of Nathan Leopold and Richard Loeb. In 1930, the *Kansas City Star* solved the murder of Mrs. A. D. Payne by her husband. Ku Klux Klan leader D. C. Stephenson went to prison for the murder of Madge Oberhalzer as a result of the investigative efforts of the *Indianapolis Times* and the *Vincennes Commercial*. The *Chicago Daily News* won a Pulitzer Prize for uncovering the stealing of millions of dollars from the Illinois State Treasury by the state auditor, Orville Hodge.

Other media exposés include the Watergate findings that ended the presidency of Richard Nixon and brought charges against his aides, and the revelation of President Bill Clinton's affair with Monica Lewinsky that ultimately led to his 1999 impeachment trial for perjury and obstruction of justice. The media's coverage of the Clinton presidency and its several scandals has led to charges by Clinton supporters that he, his wife, and staff have been harassed by the media. Interestingly, the coverage of leaks of a CIA operative's identity and the investigation of payoffs by lobbyists led to similar allegations by supporters of former president Bush.

The complete list of similar exposés of crime is long, evidence that the press and police are not necessarily natural adversaries.

Champions of the Innocent

The press has uncovered crime and criminals, and it can point to a long record of exonerating people already convicted of crime. In 1932, Joe Majczek was sent to prison for life for a murder he insisted he had not committed. Twelve years later, a series of articles in the *Chicago Times* revealed that he had been convicted largely on the testimony of a witness who had been threatened with prosecution for violating the Prohibition law unless she identified Majczek as the murderer. Majczek thereupon was freed from prison, fully pardoned, and compensated by the state for his twelve years in prison. The same year that Majczek was freed, a young, inarticulate black, Willie Calloway, was sentenced to life imprisonment for murder. His case came to the attention of reporter Ken McCormack of the *Detroit Free Press*, who wrote a series of articles that helped to exonerate Calloway. Calloway was then released after eight years in prison for a crime he did not commit. The scathing attack on death penalty convictions in Illinois by the *Chicago Tribune* from January 10 to 14, 1999, is widely believed to have led to Illinois Governor George Ryan's moratorium on executions until the state's death penalty procedures were reviewed. The highly successful Innocence Project owes much of its success to investigative reporters who have pursued witnesses and uncovered evidence. Barry Scheck, the cofounder of the Innocence Project, was recently quoted as saying: "When procedural mechanisms begin to fail, the press is the last resort for the public to find out the truth" (Arango, 2009).

A CLEAR NEED FOR GUIDELINES

The Background

Essentially, police and the media have different functions, and the difference can bring them into conflict. The police's task is to prevent crime, maintain law and order, protect the citizens of the community, and apprehend lawbreakers and bring them to justice. The media in a free society have an obligation to seek out and report the truth, even though the truth may embarrass or hinder the police. The information becomes a product that they package and sell in competition with other media. Nevertheless, the Society of Professional Journalists has had a Code of Ethics since 1926 (see Figure 6.1). This code does not specifically cover all the incidents that may arise in the reporting of crime-related information (protection of rape victims, juveniles, hostage and

Code of Ethics

SOCIETY OF PROFESSIONAL JOURNALISTS.

Preamble

Members of the Society of Professional Journalists believe that public enlightenment is the forerunner of justice and the foundation of democracy. The duty of the journalist is to further those ends by seeking truth and providing a fair and comprehensive account of events and issues. Conscientious journalists from all media and specialties strive to serve the public with thoroughness and honesty. Professional integrity is the cornerstone of a journalist's credibility.

Members of the Society share a dedication to ethical behavior and adopt this code to declare the Society's principles and standards of practice.

Seek Truth and Report It

Journalists should be honest, fair and courageous in gathering, reporting and interpreting information.

Journalists should:

▶ Test the accuracy of information from all sources and exercise care to avoid inadvertent error. Deliberate distortion is never permissible.

▶ Diligently seek out subjects of news stories to give them the opportunity to respond to allegations of wrongdoing.

▶ Identify sources whenever feasible. The public is entitled to as much information as possible on sources' reliability.

▶ Always question sources' motives before promising anonymity. Clarify conditions attached to any promise made in exchange for information. Keep promises.

▶ Make certain that headlines, news teases and promotional material, photos, video, audio, graphics, sound bites and quotations do not misrepresent. They should not oversimplify or highlight incidents out of context.

▶ Never distort the content of news photos or video. Image enhancement for technical clarity is always permissible. Label montages and photo illustrations.

▶ Avoid misleading re-enactments or staged news events. If re-enactment is necessary to tell a story, label it.

▶ Avoid undercover or other surreptitious methods of gathering information except when traditional open methods will not yield information vital to the public. Use of such methods should be explained as part of the story.

▶ Never plagiarize.

▶ Tell the story of the diversity and magnitude of the human experience boldly, even when it is unpopular to do so.

▶ Examine their own cultural values and avoid imposing those values on others.

▶ Avoid stereotyping by race, gender, age, religion, ethnicity, geography, sexual orientation, disability, physical appearance or social status.

▶ Support the open exchange of views, even views they find repugnant.

▶ Give voice to the voiceless; official and unofficial sources of information can be equally valid.

▶ Distinguish between advocacy and news reporting. Analysis and commentary should be labeled and not misrepresent fact or context.

▶ Distinguish news from advertising and shun hybrids that blur the lines between the two.

▶ Recognize a special obligation to ensure that the public's business is conducted in the open and that government records are open to inspection.

Minimize Harm

Ethical journalists treat sources, subjects and colleagues as human beings deserving of respect.

Journalists should:

▶ Show compassion for those who may be affected adversely by news coverage. Use special sensitivity when dealing with children and inexperienced sources or subjects.

▶ Be sensitive when seeking or using interviews or photographs of those affected by tragedy or grief.

▶ Recognize that gathering and reporting information may cause harm or discomfort. Pursuit of the news is not a license for arrogance.

▶ Recognize that private people have a greater right to control information about themselves than do public officials and others who seek power, influence or attention. Only an overriding public need can justify intrusion into anyone's privacy.

▶ Show good taste. Avoid pandering to lurid curiosity.

▶ Be cautious about identifying juvenile suspects or victims of sex crimes.

▶ Be judicious about naming criminal suspects before the formal filing of charges.

▶ Balance a criminal suspect's fair trial rights with the public's right to be informed.

Act Independently

Journalists should be free of obligation to any interest other than the public's right to know.

Journalists should:

▶ Avoid conflicts of interest, real or perceived.

▶ Remain free of associations and activities that may compromise integrity or damage credibility.

▶ Refuse gifts, favors, fees, free travel and special treatment, and shun secondary employment, political involvement, public office and service in community organizations if they compromise journalistic integrity.

▶ Disclose unavoidable conflicts.

▶ Be vigilant and courageous about holding those with power accountable.

▶ Deny favored treatment to advertisers and special interests and resist their pressure to influence news coverage.

▶ Be wary of sources offering information for favors or money; avoid bidding for news.

Be Accountable

Journalists are accountable to their readers, listeners, viewers and each other.

Journalists should:

▶ Clarify and explain news coverage and invite dialogue with the public over journalistic conduct.

▶ Encourage the public to voice grievances against the news media.

▶ Admit mistakes and correct them promptly.

▶ Expose unethical practices of journalists and the news media.

▶ Abide by the same high standards to which they hold others.

Sigma Delta Chi's first Code of Ethics was borrowed from the American Society of Newspaper Editors in 1926. In 1973, Sigma Delta Chi wrote its own code, which was revised in 1984 and 1987. The present version of the Society of Professional Journalists' Code of Ethics was adopted in September 1996.

FIGURE 6.1

terrorist incidents, etc.). However, as we have seen, the police and the media have entered into voluntary agreement (described later).

Competing Rights

Conflict between police and media often arises because the police are caught in the crossfire of competing rights under two key amendments to the U.S. Constitution. On one hand, the First Amendment guarantees an almost absolute right to print virtually anything, free of legal restraint. The Sixth Amendment, however, guarantees every person the right to a fair trial, which means a trial by peers who have not been influenced by prejudicial publicity before or during trial. Individuals in our society have a right to privacy and, within limits, not to have their character defamed. How can these competing rights be resolved fairly?

According to the U.S. Supreme Court in *Branzburg* v. *Hayes* [408 U.S. 665, 682–685, 92 S.Ct., 2646, 2657–2658, 33 LEd 2nd. 626 640–642 (1972)], "Newsmen have no constitutional right of access to the scenes of crime or disaster when the general public is excluded and they may be prohibited from attending or publishing information about trials if such restrictions are necessary to ensure a defendant a fair trial before an impartial tribunal."

Recognizing the Need for Guidelines

The necessity for developing guidelines for resolving or controlling conflicts involving the responsibilities or rights of the media, the police, and citizens (victims and defendants) has not always been recognized. However, four sensational cases were largely responsible for spotlighting or demonstrating this need.

THE BRUNO HAUPTMANN TRIAL Before 1935, there was comparatively little concern for the rights of suspects and defendants, some of whom were badly treated by the police or the press, or by both. Then came the trial of Bruno Hauptmann for the kidnap-murder of the Lindbergh infant. The press, which had shown such commendable restraint before Hauptmann's capture, treated the trial at Flemington, New Jersey, as a combination circus and passion play, as did the prosecution, the defense, and the public. The prosecutor told a reporter that he "would wrap the kidnap ladder around Hauptmann's neck," a threat that was duly carried in the newspapers of the day. The defense counsel ordered stationery for Hauptmann to answer his "fan mail"; the letterhead carried a facsimile of the kidnap ladder. The press allied itself with the prosecution, charging once that the defendant was making "senseless denials" and, on another occasion, with being "a thing lacking in human characteristics." Although photographs had been forbidden in the courtroom, not only still pictures but motion pictures as well were taken and displayed to the public.

It was the Hauptmann trial that first compelled the organized bar to consider the need for a code of conduct that might prevent the improprieties and excesses of that trial. An 18-member committee of newspaper reporters, broadcasters, editors, publishers, and lawyers agreed on a general code of conduct to guide prosecutors, defense counsel, and the press in future criminal trials. The code drawn up by this committee was accepted by the American Bar Association but, except for Canon 35 (which prohibited photographs in the courtroom), the guidelines were generally ignored until two events many years later—the assassination of President John F. Kennedy and the Supreme Court decision in the Sam Sheppard case.

THE ASSASSINATION OF PRESIDENT JOHN F. KENNEDY The aftermath of the Kennedy assassination in 1963 did more than anything since the Hauptmann trial to spur new remedies for the injustices of pretrial publicity. "From the moment of his arrest until his murder two days later," the American Civil Liberties Union concluded, "Lee Harvey Oswald was tried and convicted many times over in the newspapers, on the radio, and over television by the public statements of the Dallas law enforcement officials. Time and time again, high-ranking police and prosecution officials stated their complete satisfaction that Oswald was the assassin. As their investigation uncovered one piece of evidence after the other, the results were broadcast to the public" (Lofton, 1966, p. 130). The Warren Commission reached similar conclusions in its 1964 report and also criticized District Attorney Henry Wade and Police Chief Jesse E. Curry for their statements to the press which, the commission believed, were potentially harmful to both the prosecution and the defense. The commission criticized the press, too, for its lack of self-discipline, which created general disorder in the police and court buildings in Dallas. The events in Dallas that weekend, the commission said, "are a dramatic affirmation of the need for steps to bring about a proper balance between the right of the public to be informed and the right of an individual to a fair and impartial trial" (Lofton, 1966, p. xii).

THE TRIAL OF DR. SAM SHEPPARD   The need for definitive guidelines did not become critical until 1966 when the Supreme Court, in the Sam Sheppard decision, told the bench, the bar, the police, and the press that every defendant in a criminal case was entitled to a trial unpolluted by prejudicial pretrial publicity. It is widely held that the 1955 trial of Dr. Sheppard is one of the most flagrant examples of irresponsible behavior, not only by the news media but by the judiciary and law enforcement officials as well. The Supreme Court, in reversing Sheppard's conviction, agreed.

In its Sheppard decision, the Court offered explicit guidance on how trial courts and police should seek to preserve the defendant's right to a fair and impartial trial, preventing interference by the press. Many of these strictures were incorporated into guidelines that were later drawn up by joint bench–bar–press committees in various states, although many of the Supreme Court "rules" were already contained in such guidelines established prior to 1966.

THE TRIAL OF O. J. SIMPSON   The 1995 trial of former football star O. J. Simpson for the murder of Nicole Brown Simpson and Ronald Goldman received extensive media coverage. The nation was to a large degree divided along racial lines. African Americans celebrated when the defense's allegations of police incompetence and possible planting of evidence by a racist police officer led to an acquittal. Many European Americans felt that Simpson's $10 million legal "dream team" had used race to defeat compelling hair, fiber, and blood evidence that proved him guilty. Ultimately, both critics and supporters complained about the media's coverage.

MORE RECENT CASES   Due perhaps to the media's attention to the "War on Terror," political unrest, and the impacts of natural disasters such as Hurricane Katrina, there have not been as many sensational trials that received national attention in recent years. However, there have been at least three cases that have received scrutiny from the nation's media.

The first case is the murder of Jonbenet Ramsey. On December 25, 1996, 6-year-old Jonbenet was abducted from her bedroom, sexually assaulted, and murdered in the basement of her parents' home. Media from across the country followed the investigation for months. Speculation ran rampant as to who had committed the hideous crime. The use of the Ramsey's writing utensils in the preparation of a ransom note and references within the note that only a family insider would have been aware indicate that the killer was someone with intimate knowledge of the family. The hiring of an attorney and their perceived lack of cooperation with the police and district attorney's office created a cloud of suspicion that follows the Ramsey family to this day. The Boulder Police Department worked for years interviewing hundreds of witnesses to no avail. At the time of this writing, despite a series of books, television specials, and the employment of some of the nation's foremost investigators and forensic scientists, the case remains unsolved.

The second case has a much happier ending. On June 5, 2002, 14-year-old Elizabeth Smart was abducted from her bedroom in Salt Lake City, Utah. Her younger sister, who was in the same bedroom and witnessed the abduction, reported that a man with a gun had taken Elizabeth. Despite a thorough investigation on the part of the police, efforts to find Elizabeth or even determine what had happened to her were futile. The national media closely followed the case, and many comparisons were made to the Ramsey case. The willing cooperation from the child's parents did help dispel the type of suspicions raised in that case. Initial investigative efforts focused on a young drifter from West Virginia who had a history of bizarre behavior and who had been in the area. He was later removed from the list of likely suspects. Handyman Richard Ricci, who died in prison while serving a sentence for having burglarized the Smarts' home at another time, would remain a suspect. In October 2002, the younger sister would tell her parents that she thought she might know who the kidnapper was. She stated that he resembled a transient whom the family had employed for a few hours in 2001. The man had called himself Emmanuel. On March 12, 2003, police received calls that "Emmanuel" had been seen in the nearby city of Sandy, Utah, accompanied by two women. Police located Emmanuel and discovered that Elizabeth Smart, disguised in a wig, sunglasses, and an overcoat, was one of the women with him. Emmanuel, actually self-described prophet Brian David Mitchell, and his wife, Wanda Eileen

Barzee, had kept the child with them through threats of death if she attempted to escape. Elizabeth, was happily reunited with her family.

The third case, the murder of Caylee Anthony, is still in the news and has the potential for becoming the most publicized in U.S. history. The child's mother, Casey, is the chief suspect in the case, and several crime news commentators, such as Nancy Grace, appear to be convinced of her guilt as are many members of the public due to the media coverage. The broad Florida public-records laws have allowed thousands of pages of legal documents to be released to the media (Edwards, 2009). Those documents have included forensic-evidence reports, transcripts of detectives' interview, and details about parties and clubs she frequented, as well as information about her family's financial difficulties. Every aspect of the 22-year-old mother's life has become public. The authors cannot recall a case that has received this much media attention. The outcome of all this media attention on future court action is unpredictable at this time.

In addition to the issues raised earlier about reality-based television programs (overemphasis on violence, misrepresenting the nature of police work, overrepresentation of minorities, etc.), there are numerous constitutional issues involved. At issue in a U.S. Supreme Court decision in 1999 (*Wilson* v. *Layne*, U.S. Lexis 3633) was whether or not police–media ride-along programs violated the Fourth Amendment rights of parties inside private areas. The Supreme Court ruled that the presence of the media at the invitation of law enforcement officers during a search violated the Fourth Amendment rights of the Wilsons (Crawford, 2000). This decision will cause a reexamination of police–media ride-alongs and the presence of other third parties during police operations.

Complicating Issues

CONCERNS OF VICTIMS AND WITNESSES Publication of a victim's name and address may increase potential danger to that person and lessen his or her ability to resolve the personal emotional trauma related to the event. This is especially true for rape victims. There are times when witnesses also may be endangered in much the same way by media coverage. Media restraint in these areas requires guidelines. Only recently have the concerns of victims and witnesses been considered in any organized way by the media.

The highly publicized 10-day rape trial of William Kennedy Smith in 1991 raised two issues concerning media coverage: the use of TV cameras in the courtroom and media protection of the privacy rights of the rape victim. The legal community was deeply divided over the issue of TV coverage (*USA Today*, 1991). Nevertheless, TV coverage was allowed in this trial, and the privacy issue became a source of controversy. CNN News hid the face of the alleged rape victim, but it was not long before she was identified. The same issues were raised in the highly publicized 1992 rape trial of heavyweight boxing champion Mike Tyson. The state of Indiana, which normally does not allow courtroom TV coverage, allowed the use of closed-circuit TV to accommodate more than a hundred news organizations that covered the trial.

It is easy to imagine the horror of learning of the death of a loved one by way of the media news. Because the news may be broadcast or published before next of kin can be notified of the death of a family member, guidelines for release of the name and address of the deceased are necessary.

THE NEED TO GET THE FULL STORY A counterargument to the above is the need for the media to get the story right. Although the need to protect victims and witnesses is of vital importance, so is the need to see that justice is being carried out correctly. If the media publishes only what they are provided by the police and prosecutors, miscarriages of justice, systemic problems, and questionable practices could be overlooked. Sometimes the suspect's story needs to be told as well.

Crisis Situations

DISTURBANCES AND UNREST The advent of militancy in the 1960s, urban guerrilla warfare, student unrest and demonstrations, civil rights protests, riots, and fire bombings have created new problems for the police. Effective working arrangements with the mass media in these situations are critical.

One commentator said, "Nothing, but nothing, ever happens the same way after you put a television or movie camera on it." Television, with its capacity for instantaneous reporting, has often incited violence, usually unintentionally, by attracting those who seek attention. Both rioters and police have been known to perform for the media. Occasionally the media has manufactured the news. During the riots in Newark, New Jersey, for example, a newspaper photographer from a New York newspaper was seen urging, and finally convincing, a young black boy to throw a rock for the benefit of the cameras. In Chicago in the late 1960s, a television camera crew was seen leading two "hippie" girls into an area filled with National Guardsmen. As the cameras started rolling, one of the girls cried on cue, "Don't beat me, don't beat me!" Virtually all the media outlets have their own rules against this sort of staging, but occasionally the rules tend to be forgotten during a major upheaval.

A less violent confrontation was described by an observer in the 1960s after a three-man television crew arrived at a labor picket line. Although the crew chief was disappointed because, from a pictorial standpoint, it was not much of a demonstration, he decided to film it anyway ("We may as well get it."). As the observer related, "The light man held up his 30-foot lamp and laid a 4-foot beam of light across the picket line. Instantly, the marchers' heads snapped up, their eyes flashed. They threw up their arms in the clenched-fist salute. Some made a V with their fingers, and they held up their banners for the cameras." The event was transformed into something substantially different than it would have been had not the television crew arrived to record it.

Immense damage can result during a civil disturbance as a result of a lack of restraint by press or police, by inaccurate reporting, by journalistic sensationalizing, by police overreaction, or by a breakdown in communication between the press and the police. A false rumor that police had killed a black cab driver in Newark, New Jersey, and an unfounded report of the killing of a 7-year-old boy in Plainfield, New Jersey, fanned major disturbances in those cities. In Tampa, Florida, a deputy sheriff died in the early stages of a riot that intensified after both the Associated Press and United Press International reported that he had been killed by rioters when, in actuality, he had suffered a heart attack.

Much concern was expressed by the media and the public regarding a man who "performed" a suicide for the camera. Many observers believed that no suicide would have taken place if the media had not covered the "event." Some local television stations, acknowledging that "acting" for the camera during disturbances adds to existing problems, use unmarked units on the scene, and thus maintain a low profile (Figure 6.2).

Although television coverage does provide incentive to violence, police should realize that coverage can also have the opposite effect. No one, including demonstrators, wants his or her unlawful acts recorded on camera (Figure 6.3). The presence of cameras can also have a restraining influence on overzealous police authorities; during the late 1950s and early 1960s, the U.S. Justice Department encouraged media coverage of civil rights demonstrations in the belief that it would inhibit violence by unsympathetic police in the Southern states.

Except in the rare instance when police intend to engage in improper conduct, it is in their interest to have reporters present. In Chicago in the 1960s, comedian Dick Gregory complained that police had been "brutal" in arresting him. Station WMAQ-TV carried Gregory's statement without comment, then reran the film showing Gregory being arrested, a film that did not bear out his claim. The Chicago Police were grateful.

Media representatives have long been aware of their grave responsibilities during riot situations. As far back as June 1963, in anticipation of confrontations in Selma, Alabama, Richard Salant, president of CBS News, sent a memorandum to his news personnel at Selma. He warned of "the unsettling effect on a stimulated crowd that the TV camera has" and requested that personnel and equipment be as unobtrusive as possible and that cameras be turned away or covered when there was any danger that their presence might aggravate tensions. In the 1980s in Miami, Florida, the media helped both to increase and decrease tensions in that already tense community.

FIGURE 6.2   How could press coverage help or hinder police efforts in resolving this crisis?

Getty Images, Inc.-Stone Allstock.

In December 1979, Arthur McDuffie was involved in a high-speed chase with the police in the streets of Liberty City, a ghetto area of Miami. When he was stopped, a struggle ensued from which McDuffie emerged in a coma. He died four days later from massive skull injuries. Four officers were charged with his death and were acquitted in May 1980. In the riot that followed this decision, 18 more deaths occurred in the Liberty City ghetto. The media in this instance helped to increase the tensions in Liberty City. The case became a major national media event, and many officials believe that the coverage contributed to the problems that already existed (Katzenbach, 1980). In contrast, in early 1983, when blacks were again prepared to riot over another incident, media coverage helped to prevent more violence. Leaders were televised advising restraint. Community administrators were covered promising an investigation that was forthcoming. This strategy has been emulated in other cities during the 1980s and 1990s with positive results. A noted exception is the Los Angeles riot of 1992 (discussed previously).

Hostage and Terrorist Activity

Of growing concern is the disturbing frequency of hostage and terrorist activity involving mass media and local police in almost free-for-all, three-sided confrontation. This has been exacerbated by technological advances in communications such as satellites, microwave relays, and portable cameras and recorders. Most disturbing of all is the occurrence of the "media events" that are staged by various terrorist groups or lone psychotics solely to attract mass public attention to their particular demands or problems. A particularly disturbing event of this nature took place in Berkeley, California, in 1990. Mehrdad Dashti held 33 hostages in a hotel bar while he

FIGURE 6.3 Although television coverage of scenes of potential disorder may provide an incentive to violence, it may also deter violence, since neither demonstrators nor police wish to have unlawful acts recorded on camera.
Courtesy of Birmingham Police Department.

made a series of barely coherent demands and statements defining his purpose. Even though there was a television set in the bar, TV crews broadcast the event live and reported on what the police were doing outside. The hostage situation was finally resolved with eight hostages shot, one fatally, and Dashti shot dead by the police. This event resulted in a debate over media disclosures of police operations (Goodman, 1990).

Vetter and Perlstein (1991) stated that the 1977 Hanafi Muslim siege in Washington, D.C., is a good example of how the media can be used to make a big story out of a minor terrorist incident. On March 9, 1977, Hamaas Abdul Khaalis, a Hanafi Muslim leader, and 12 members of his religious sect seized 134 hostages. Khaalis's demands were that the murderers (rival religious sect) of his family members be handed over to him so that he could exact justice. He also wanted the movie *Mohammed, Messenger of God* banned in the United States because it was blasphemous. Television reporters began broadcasting live from the scene, and journalists tied up telephone lines by interviewing the terrorists. According to Schmid and DeGraaf (1982), during the three days of the incident, NBC spent more than 53 percent of its evening news on the story, CBS spent more than 31 percent, and ABC spent 40 percent. One news reporter, seeing the police bringing food to the terrorists, reported erroneously that the police were preparing to assault the building. Another reporter called Khaalis and told him that the police were trying to trick him.

In 1993, the entire world was mesmerized by the siege of the Branch Davidian compound in Waco, Texas, and the deaths of four federal officers during the initial siege. There are allegations that the cult members were tipped off about the assault by media representatives. However, no evidence has been found to support these charges.

Of major concern and frustration to the police in these events is the apparent erosion of police control over the situation as a result of the presence of an aggressive, emotion-charged press corps. At times, the terrorist–media contact becomes more amiable than the police–media contact. The obvious presence of physical danger to hostages, police, and others heightens the frustration felt by police.

Since the 1977 Washington, D.C., situation occurred, many attempts have been made to resolve differences between police and press. Negotiations have taken place in many cities between news media and police in an effort to establish workable guidelines for both "sides," should such crisis occur in their city. At the time of this writing, the authors are aware of four police–media agreements that establish voluntary guidelines for live media coverage of critical incidents (Portland, Oregon; Tampa, Florida; Miami/Fort Lauderdale/Palm Beach, Florida; and Sahuarita, Arizona). Such agreements set out guidelines for the media and the police. They are not, nor can they be, one-sided restrictions on either party.

SETTING GUIDELINES

Information Release

Guidelines—or statements of principles, as they are called in some states—do exist. Some examples include a Bar-Press-Broadcasters Joint Statement of Principles in Oregon; in Massachusetts, a Guide for Bar and News Media; in Kentucky, a Press Association Statement of Principles for Pretrial Reporting; in New York, a Code on Fair Trial and Free Press of the New York County Lawyers Association; and in Philadelphia, a Statement of Policy of the Philadelphia Bar Association. In 1965 the U.S. Department of Justice adopted rules, later to be known as the Katzenbach Guidelines (after the then attorney general), which dealt with release of information relating to criminal proceedings by police personnel of the department and its agencies, such as the Federal Bureau of Investigation.

Most such guidelines, particularly as they apply to police, are basically similar. The following discussion is of two sets of guidelines. The first was developed in 1968 by the Wisconsin Advisory Commission on Pretrial Publicity (including a local police chief, a county sheriff, a district attorney, newspaper reporters and broadcasters, several academicians, and a trial judge). The second set was first developed in 1975 by the Professional Standards Division of the International Association of Chiefs of Police, with input from public information officers from all regions of the United States. These are relatively typical of those developed by other states and in local communities.

The Wisconsin Guidelines

These guidelines acknowledge that the media have the right to publish, and the public has the right to have, the truth about the administration of criminal justice. On the other hand, law enforcement officials have the right and responsibility to protect the individual's right to a fair trial. The guidelines, therefore, were to aid these officials in deciding what information should or should not be released.

WHAT CAN BE RELEASED   After arrest, the police can make public the following information under the Wisconsin guidelines:

- The text or substance of the charge.
- The name of the investigative and arresting agency.
- The length of the investigation.
- The defendant's name, address, age, employment, and marital status.

In most states, the police cannot by law release the name of a juvenile defendant. During an investigation, the police can release photographs of suspects' "wanted" posters and other information deemed necessary to the investigation or the apprehension of suspects.

WHAT CANNOT BE RELEASED   The Wisconsin guidelines advise that the police not release the following kinds of information:

- Any confessions, admissions, or incriminating statements by the suspect.
- The results of investigative procedures (e.g., polygraph tests, fingerprint identification, and ballistics tests).
- Any statement by police officers that might reflect on the credibility of witnesses and expected testimony.
- Any expression of opinion by police officers regarding the character or the guilt or innocence of the accused.

PROBLEM AREAS   On some matters, guidelines have been somewhat difficult to formulate, and different codes take different positions on what is to be done.

1. *Interviews.* Under the Wisconsin guidelines (and most others) the police will allow the media to interview a defendant only if the person in custody requests it and has been advised of the right to counsel. If the defendant already has an attorney, that attorney must be advised of the request for interview.
2. *Photographs.* Should the police grant media requests to photograph or televise suspects while in custody? The Wisconsin guidelines position is that the practice should neither be encouraged nor discouraged. The police should not deliberately pose the suspect, but they may give out a current photo of the suspect.
3. *The circumstances of arrest.* Like most guidelines, those in Wisconsin allow the police to make *a factual, unadorned* statement of the circumstances surrounding an arrest (e.g., possession of contraband or weapons, and resistance to arrest).
4. *Previous criminal record.* The appearance of a suspect's prior record in the press could influence a potential juror; on the other hand, the record is supposed to be public. The Wisconsin guidelines (and most others) resolve the dilemma by instructing police not to volunteer the information, but to make it available on specific inquiry about it.

Police Operational Response

Guidelines like those adopted in Wisconsin indicate what information should or should not be released to the media, but they do not indicate who in police agencies should make the relevant decisions. Nevertheless, the following rules seem sensible:

1. Statements relating to crime should be made by the ranking member of the department who is present before representatives of the media.
2. If no ranking officer is present, the police officer at the scene of the crime should be entitled to supply "basic and unelaborated information."
3. Where there is doubt as to whether information should be released or withheld, police officers should always choose to withhold it. (If the decision proves wrong, it can be corrected later; a decision to release, on the other hand, cannot be corrected later.)

Advantages of Guidelines

Measures to restrict the flow of prejudicial pretrial publicity may be implemented as a result of statute or court order. The police, press, and members of the bar, however, are free to take such measures on their own as the four departments mentioned earlier have done with critical incidents. Of course, such voluntary guidelines are not legally binding; nevertheless, by properly disciplining violators, a police agency can ensure that members of the department observe the guidelines.

BOX 6.2
CALEA Guidelines on Public Information

54.1 Public Information

54.1.1 A written directive states that the agency is committed to informing the community and the news media of events within the public domain that are handled by or involve the agency.

Commentary: To operate effectively, law enforcement agencies must obtain the support of the public they serve. By providing the news media and the community with information on agency administration and operations, the agency can foster a relationship of mutual trust, cooperation, and respect. (Mandatory for all agencies)

54.1.2 A written directive establishes a public information function, to include:

- assisting news personnel in covering routine news stories, and at the scenes of incidents;
- being available for on-call responses to the news media;
- preparing and distributing agency news releases;
- arranging for, and assisting at, news conferences;
- coordinating and authorizing the release of information about victims, witnesses, and suspects;
- assisting in crisis situations within the agency; and
- coordinating and authorizing the release of information concerning confidential agency investigations and operations.

Commentary: The agency's written directive should address how the agency will handle potential situations in which the news media are interested in agency operations, as well as situations in which the agency wishes to generate media interest. (Mandatory)

54.1.3 A written directive specifies a position in the agency responsible for the public information function.

Commentary: The intent of the standard is to ensure that the agency has a point of control for disseminating information to the community, to the media, and to other criminal justice agencies.

In smaller agencies these activities may be assigned as part-time responsibilities; in larger agencies the activities may be assigned to a full-time public information officer or component.

The directive should also establish procedures to guide the actions of the public information officer in daily operations, as well as at the scene of crimes, catastrophes, special events, and unusual occurrences. (Mandatory)

54.1.4 A written directive establishes the procedures for press releases, to include:

- frequency of press releases;
- subject matter; and
- media recipients.

Commentary: The agency should have procedures that address the criteria to be used in determining (1) the need for press releases on a daily or weekly basis, or as necessitated by specific occurrences in the agency's service area, and (2) the content and the extent of coverage of agency activities.

The directive should also include policy on disseminating material in such a manner as to ensure that first-release information is equally available to all news media. Press releases may be issued in bulletin form or through tape-recorded messages, as long as the agency has addressed the equal-access issue. (Optional)

54.1.5 A written directive identifies—by name or position held—those within the agency who may release information to the news media:

- at the scene of an incident;
- from agency files;
- concerning an ongoing criminal investigation; and/or
- at any time that the public information officer is not available.

Commentary: Situations may arise when the agency's public information officer is not available or events at the scene of an incident or other fast-breaking event require an immediate agency spokesperson. (Mandatory)

54.1.6 A written directive establishes criteria and procedures for issuing and revoking credentials to news media representatives.

Commentary: Because of the unique relationship between agencies and news media personnel, agencies should develop procedures governing the issuance and the revocation of credentials, as well as criteria for the conduct of news media representatives. The agency policy should not attempt to limit the number of credentials issued but should make media representatives aware of their obligations and responsibilities as they cover daily assignments and special events. Credentials should be revoked only when the criteria governing conduct have been violated. If credentials are revoked, a statement should be sent to the concerned individual's employer citing the specific violation. (Optional)

54.1.7 A written directive governs the access of news media representatives, including photographers, to the:

- scenes of major fires, natural disasters, or other catastrophic events; and
- perimeter of crime scenes.

Commentary: News media representatives should not be in a position to interfere with law enforcement operations at the scene of an incident. The guidelines for news media access, including access by photographers, to the scene should be communicated to the media to help ensure their cooperation. (Mandatory)

54.1.8 A written directive establishes procedures for involving the news media in the development of changes in policies and procedures relating to the news media.

Commentary: By allowing media representatives to participate in the process of developing policies and procedures relating to the news media, agencies can demonstrate that they value good rapport with the media and appreciate the problems such persons confront in their daily work. (Optional)

54.1.9 A written directive specifies the information held by the agency regarding ongoing criminal investigations that may be released to the news media.

Commentary: The intent of the standard is that the agency provide specific guidance to personnel regarding the release of information about (1) the prior criminal record, character, or reputation of the accused; (2) mugshots of the accused; (3) the existence of any confession, admission of guilt, or statement made by the accused or the failure or refusal by the accused to make a statement; (4) the results of any examinations or tests conducted or refusal by the accused to submit to any examinations or tests; (5) the identity, testimony, or credibility of any prospective witness; (6) any opinion of agency personnel regarding the guilt or innocence

of the accused; (7) any opinion of agency personnel regarding the merits of the case or quality of evidence gathered; (8) personal information identifying the victim; (9) information identifying juveniles; and (10) information received from other law enforcement agencies without their concurrence in releasing that information. (Mandatory)

54.1.10 A written directive requires that information released under standard 54.1.9 be reported to the agency's public information officer as soon as possible.

Commentary: The person responsible for the public information function should not have to rely on the media to be informed of newsworthy events involving the agency that occur within the agency's service area. Moreover, such information should be conveyed in a timely fashion. (Optional)

54.1.11 A written directive establishes agency procedures for releasing information when other service agencies are involved in a mutual effort.

Commentary: The word *agencies* as used above is meant to refer to all public service agencies (e.g., fire departments and coroners' offices). In instances in which more than one agency is involved, the agency having primary jurisdiction should be responsible for releasing, or coordinating the release of, information. (Optional)

Source: From the Commission on Accreditation for Law Enforcement Agencies (1991, pp. 54–1 to 54–3).

In criminal cases police officers at all levels may face a great deal of media or public pressure to release information that should be withheld. If joint press–bar–police guidelines are in effect, they relieve pressure by pointing to what the police and the press have both agreed to. If only the police have adopted the guidelines, the individual officers can still take themselves "off the hook" by emphasizing that they are only following "policy."

CRISIS GUIDELINES FOR THE MEDIA

As a result of evidence that the presence of the news media, especially television, can encourage violence, the National Advisory Commission on Civil Disorders urged news organizations to develop guidelines for responsible coverage of riots. Some of the results are listed below with the news agencies that had them at the time. (The initials used indicate the three major networks—NBC, CBS, and ABC.)

1. Use of unmarked or camouflaged cars and equipment (NBC and CBS).
2. Extreme care in using inflammatory words and phrases (e.g., "police brutality," "angry mob," "racial," and "riot") and in estimating the size and intensity of crowds (all three networks).
3. Prohibitions against giving the exact location of disturbances or specifics about weaponry; "capping" cameras and lights if they seem to be contributing to disorder or interfering with the police (all three networks).
4. No "live" coverage of disturbances (ABC and CBS).
5. Agreement that media representatives would ask for police protection when needed and that the police are entitled to ask for special credentials from press representatives (all three networks).

Local stations and network affiliates may have individual policies that vary from these guidelines. Police officials need to work closely with local media.

Some suggestions made by a committee of the Northern California chapter of the Radio and TV News Directors Association fill some of the gaps in the network codes:

1. Competition between broadcasters should continue, but the focus should be changed from dynamic impact to calm reporting of vital information to the public, with maximum assistance in reestablishment of control as the primary goal.
2. Police authorities should take necessary steps to ensure that adequately informed staff members will be on duty at command posts and available to supply properly identified broadcast newspeople with pertinent information about the disorder.
3. Reports should be calm and objective and should present the overall picture. They should be devoid of sensationalism, speculation, and rumors that could incite or further extend disturbances or stir news breaks.

A Common Interest

The interests of the police and the media sometimes conflict, but they both want to see order restored as quickly as possible in riot situations. The media need the police to get the facts, and the police need the help and the restraint of the media. Thus, they have a second basis for cooperation and for working out, together, plans for dealing with disorders.

A Proposal for Hostage–Terrorist Situations

The following specific guidelines were first suggested by District of Columbia Police Chief Maurice J. Cullinane in 1977 after several major incidents. These suggestions give increased authority and discretion to the police negotiator.

1. Live minicamera broadcast should be limited to distance shots.
2. Media should remain in a special "broadcast area" apart from the police line, where they could receive briefings from police. (The police negotiator might allow the press into the command center where negotiations are conducted, if circumstances allow.)
3. Telephone calls to people holding hostages should be banned.
4. Live broadcasts showing police stationed around a hostage situation would be barred.

POLICE–COMMUNITY RELATIONS

We have discussed the general aspects of police–media relations; now we turn our attention to police–community relations and how its link with the media fits in. Police–community relations is a complicated and changing relationship between the police internal communities and its external communities. The media is the primary link between the police organization and its external environment. The media is instrumental to the police as they attempt to manage their image and create support for programs and strategies. Community- and problem-oriented policing initiatives to be successful must have the support and involvement of community members. The public must know about the programs and the problems addressed, and then must be willing to give up their time and participate. Support and involvement once created are maintained by a steady flow of information. Unfortunately, information on police–community relations topics, particularly on community policing, does not receive the same media attention as crime topics. Furthermore, it appears that police agencies are not adequately publicizing their community- and problem-oriented efforts, or if publicizing them, many citizens do not receive the publicity (Chermack and Weiss, 2006). Also, the police–community relationship may be so strained that the public do not believe that the police are serious. The media is in the position to be an important partner in assisting the police to identify problems and communicate community and problem-solving efforts to the public and community leaders. The success and growth of "Crimestoppers" programs mentioned earlier is evidence of a successful police–media partnership. Therefore, the police turn to proactive strategies to involve the media as a partner in building and sustaining good police–community relations. One of those strategies is the appointment of public information officers (PIOs) (Chermak and Weiss, 2005).

Public Information Officer

Most large agencies, those serving over 100,000 population, have chosen to communicate with the media through a designated public information officer (Chermak and Weiss, 2005). A **public information officer** (PIO) maintains liaisons with the media, thus relieving department administrators of some of the burden of working with reporters. The duties of PIOs include responding to media inquiries, developing media releases, scheduling press conferences, and conducting training throughout the organization (Surett and Richard, 1995). PIOs as one of several "gatekeepers," others include crime reporters and newspaper editors, determine which crimes become news (Chermak and Chapman, 2007). They do so while performing a public relations role in promoting the best image of the department. PIOs also respond proactively to scandals, create public and political support for new department activities, and satisfy media requests for information. The PIO is not necessarily a sworn police officer. In the Chermak and Weiss (2005) study of 239 law enforcement agencies, over 50 percent of the departments used sworn personnel as PIOs, 17 percent used personnel who had other duties along with public information responsibilities, 14 percent used civilians, and 16 percent used a combination of sworn and civilians acting as PIOs. The PIOs in the study were very busy individuals meeting daily with the chief and were contacted by approximately 15 reporters daily and 13 different media agencies each week. Their busy schedule often prevents them from conveying information on police initiatives. Some departments have decentralized the publications of community policing and crime prevention programs to the units involved. The media also had reasons for not publicizing community policing stories. Crime stories were easier to produce than stories evaluating community policing programs. The reporter would have to interview community-policing officers, residents, and community leaders. The majority of the police and the media personnel in the study agreed or strongly agreed that the relationships were cordial but had the potential to change dramatically because of unpredictable events such as scandals or misrepresentations by either party. Nevertheless, the study concluded that police agencies should consider other marketing strategies to increase public awareness and involvement in community policing activities. The study also pointed to a need for additional personnel and resources to market community policing.

BOX 6.3
Fort Lauderdale, Florida, PD Office of Media Relations

Media Relations Coordinator

The duties of the Media Relations Coordinator include, but are not limited to, preparing written news releases on incidents that are of public interest, meeting with media personnel on the scene of high profile incidents, responding to media and public inquires, and publishing information related to progressive programs established to enhance relations between the community and its police department.

Source: www.fortlauderdale.gov/police/media.html

Seattle PD-Media Relations Office

The Seattle Police Department believes a responsible and effective partnership with the media is vital to our mission. We depend on that partnership—as well as community trust and confidence—in carrying out our responsibilities. There is one sergeant and three media relations officers assigned to this office, who respond to media requests as early as possible, release public safety information in a timely manner, and accommodate other media requests when needed.

Source: www.seattle.gov/police/contact/media.htm

The PIO's skill is a critical factor in moving the agency from an adversary position to one of cooperation. The PIO is a critical person during demonstrations and protests who should not condemn the cause, which is usually protected by the U.S. Constitution, but should denounce illegal tactics and acts if they occur (King, 2000). In a newsworthy event, the PIO frequently use a news briefing to disseminate the facts to the public as quickly as possible, allowing the media to report the facts accurately (Sparks and Staszak, 2000). Sparks and Staszak state that a well-conducted news briefing conveys information and assures the citizens that the department serves the community. Anyone who watched television during the Columbine High School massacre in Colorado is familiar with Deputy Steve Davis, the PIO for the Jefferson County Sheriff's Office. He arrived on the scene eighteen minutes after the call went out, and for the next two weeks, he held news briefings every hour (Rosenthal, 1999b).

The PIO office is also the ideal unit in which to set up internal training programs in press relations. The Fairfax County (Virginia) Office of Public Information established in 1974 has a field PIO program that provides four weeks of training for selected officers (Rosenthal, 2001b). The trained officers fill in for the Office of Public Information (OPI) as needed. All Fairfax County Police Department first-line supervisors receive a one-day orientation on the department's media and public information policies. In recognition of the area's cultural diversity, the department communicates information in Spanish, Korean, Farsi, Vietnamese, and English. The OPI is also a member of the Metropolitan Washington Public Safety Media Relations Council. This association of public safety and media professionals established in 1968 meets monthly to air grievances and exchange information.

The National Association of Public Safety Information Officers (NAPSIO), set up by PIOs in 1974, became a major forum for exchanging ideas and programs. NAPSIO has conducted training workshops in all facets of professionalizing police–press liaison and maintains a network of correspondence among PIOs throughout the country, with beneficial results.

NAPSIO no longer exists as an organization. PIOs now are associated through the Public Information Office Section of the International Association of Chiefs of Police (IACP) and through that affiliation have worked together to develop international standards for police–media relations. PIOs from various criminal justice agencies have formed regional associations, such as the Lake County (Indiana) Public Information Officers Association, founded by the PIO of the Lake County Prosecutor's Office (Rosenthal, 2001a). There is a statewide PIO association in Colorado. The Emergency Services Public Information Officers of Colorado had 80 members in 1999 (Rosenthal, 1999a).

Marketing Police–Community Relations

Publicizing police efforts in order to create a partnership between the police and the community and to involve community members in community policing, problem solving, or crime prevention programs is not the same as producing crime statistics and traditional crime reports for the media. Police agencies have to go beyond the media and traditional outreach strategies. The agency's outreach strategies must be designed to compliment and supplement the media (Chermak and Weiss, 2003). In other words, police departments must be creative in marketing police–community relations.

Chief Mark Fazzini, College of DuPage Police Department in Glen Ellyn, Illinois, has a unique approach to reaching citizens in the community and educating them to available police services that has implications for public relations and police–community relations. He calls his plan Marketing Available Police Services (MAPS). Marketing, he says, consists of understanding, creating, communicating, and delivering services to obtain members' satisfaction. For police purposes, this begins with understanding the communities and the need and expectations that citizens have of their police services. This includes meeting with the diverse community entities and have them provide input into problem identification and problem-solving strategies. The department then communicates the developed initiatives to affected groups. Chief Fazzini realizes that if the department has services but the community does not know of them, they are a waste of resources. Communication between the police and the community is the key to the MAPS concept and can develop positive relationships between the police and the community.

Creative outreach programs have been successful in other police agencies according to Chermak and Weiss (2003). Chicago PD, when they began their community policing program, used multimedia and multilingual initiatives such as brochures, newsletters, billboards, and television and radio ads and set up informational hotlines. The New Haven, Connecticut, community policing outreach effort included a public TV program, workshops for residents, and a documentary film profiling the city's police and community policing. The Corcoran, California, a city of 26,000, created Amigos de la Comunidad, a Spanish-language police academy which led to a Spanish-language unit in the department's volunteer community patrol. These examples and the other presented throughout the book demonstrate creative marketing of programs through the media and other outlets to improve police–community relations.

REALITY CHECK

The Media Comes Through

In Rome, Georgia, the District Attorney is Leigh Patterson. Ms. Patterson has been accused of zealously prosecuting people without power or influence, while overlooking felonies committed by those who are affluent or politically connected (and in at least one case, employed by her). Despite her reputation, Ms. Patterson is strongly supported by the local Democratic Party and influential members of the local bar. She also has been astute enough to employ one of the better attorneys in the area in responding to recall efforts.

On February 10, 2003, Marcus Dixon (then 18) had sex with Kristie Brown, a 15-year-old girl at a local high school. Two days later Dixon was arrested on charges of statutory rape and sexual battery. Dixon is African American; the alleged victim is white. At the time of his arrest, Dixon claimed that the sex was consensual and that the victim claimed rape when it was discovered that she had lost her virginity to a black male. On March 14, 2003, Dixon was indicted on the rape and sexual assault charges as well as an additional charge of aggravated child molestation. On May 15, 2003, he was acquitted of rape, false imprisonment, sexual battery, and aggravated assault. He was convicted of aggravated child molestation and misdemeanor statutory rape. On May 23, 2003, he was sentenced to 15 years in prison, to serve at least 10 behind bars.

Some of the jurors in the case later indicated that they were not convinced that the sex was not consensual but had convicted Dixon on what they understood to be lesser charges because of the three-year age difference. At least one juror indicated that she was shocked to learn that the child molestation charge carried a mandatory prison sentence. Dixon appealed the child abuse conviction on the grounds that the law (which was created to deal with sexual predators that had harmed children) was wrongly applied to his situation.

Civil rights groups took up the case as an example of racial injustice. An Atlanta attorney, David Baltzer, took up the appeal at no charge to Dixon. Ms. Patterson claimed that the vaginal bruising and tearing from the loss of virginity constituted injury and the statute was correctly applied. On January 22, 2004, oral arguments were heard before the Georgia Supreme Court.

Media coverage of the case intensified after the case was discussed on the *Oprah* broadcast of February 26, 2004. During this time local African American leaders sought to initiate a recall petition of Ms. Patterson. Her attorney successfully argued that the recall document was improperly worded and had to be dismissed. Under Georgia Law it could not be brought back up for six months (this time frame was extended due to another portion of the law that prohibits recall petitions during apolitical campaigns).

On May 3, 2004, the Georgia Supreme Court ruled that the aggravated child molestation charge was inappropriate. Following the decision, Superior Court Judge Walter Matthews ordered Dixon to be released on recognizance while the statutory rape charge was reviewed. He later noted that Dixon had served a longer period in prison than the maximum required for the statutory rape conviction and ordered him released. Ms. Patterson criticized the Georgia Supreme Court for making a bad decision and turning a "sexual predator" loose. She also criticized Judge Matthews because he allowed bond before receiving written confirmation of the higher court's ruling. She indicated that she would file a motion for reconsideration and would also seek charges against Dixon on another case. Her motion was denied, and additional charges against Dixon were not pursued.

There is no doubt in the minds of Marcus Dixon's family, friends, and supporters that if the media had not provided intense coverage of his case, he would still be sitting in prison on wrongful charges by a racist, malicious, and unscrupulous prosecutor.

Conclusions

The media represent a principal link between police agencies and the public they serve. Media impact on virtually every citizen is enormous, and crime news is a major media topic. Except for the relatively few people who become directly involved with the police, private citizens learn of police activity, crime prevention, the pursuit and apprehension of criminals, and their disposition in the courts by what they read in their newspapers and see and hear on television and radio. What a citizen reads, hears, and observes in the local media largely define the citizen's perception of the police.

Easy generalizations about whether the media help or hinder law enforcement and "heat up" or "cool off" civil disorders should be avoided: It is too easy to cite evidence on either side of the issue. However, both the police and members of the media have an interest in the security of all citizens and the preservation of order. The U.S. system has a built-in conflict between the freedom of the press guaranteed by the First Amendment to the U.S. Constitution and the right to a fair trial guaranteed by the Sixth Amendment; there is often accurate information that could prejudice jurors if it were known to them. The police are in the center of this conflict, and therefore should develop—with or without the cooperation of the media—guidelines for disseminating information about crime.

During the crisis situations (e.g., riots, demonstrations, and terrorist actions) that have become so characteristic of today, the police and the media have sometimes found themselves working at cross-purposes; here again, guidelines are needed so that neither party tramples on the rights or responsibilities of the other. Fortunately, several means exist for improving police–media relations, including regularly scheduled police–media meetings; press councils; working with a press, radio, or TV ombudsman; mutual education programs; and mutual projects and goals.

The police–media–community link is a critical one. The nature of a community's police–media relationship helps to define police–community relations in that community.

Student Checklist

1. Overview media commitment to the reporting of crime news.
2. Contrast the responsibility of the press and the police.
3. Justify the need for guidelines in reporting.
4. Establish police–media guidelines for routine information release, crisis situations, and hostage situations.
5. Identify ongoing blocks to positive police–media relations and strategies for resolving them.
6. Contrast individual constitutional rights and the public's right to know.
7. Describe the duties and responsibilities of a public information officer.

Topics for Discussion

1. Should there be a code of conduct for all the media, not just professional journalists? Support your answer.
2. What information, in your opinion, should police not volunteer to the media about a crime?
3. How responsible is the press in your community?
4. How is information disseminated to the press by police agencies in your community?
5. How could your local police department market its community policing programs?

Bibliography

Abrams, D. (2009). "Presumed Innocent? Bernie Madoff?," *The Wall Street Journal*. http.//online.wsj.com/article.

Arango, T. (2009). "Death Row Foes See Newsroom Cuts as Blow," *The New York Times*. www.nytimes.com

Barker, T., and Carter, D. L. (1994). *Police Deviance*, 3rd ed. Cincinnati, OH: Anderson.

Chermak, S., and Weiss, A. (2003). *Marketing Community Policing in the News: A Missed Opportunity?* U.S. Department of Justice Office of Justice Programs, National Institute of Justice.

Chermak, S., and Weiss, A. (2005). "Maintaining legitimacy using external communications strategies: An analysis of police-media relations," *Journal of Criminal Justice*, Vol. 33, pp. 501–512.

Chermak, S., and Chapman, N. M. (2007). "Predicting crime story salience: A replication," *Journal of Criminal Justice*, Vol. 35, pp. 351–363.

Crawford, K. A. (2000). "Media ride-alongs," *FBI Law Enforcement Bulletin*, Vol. 69, No. 7, pp. 26–31.

Edwards, A. L. (2009). "Florida laws upon book on Casey Anthony's life," *OrlandoSentinel.com*. www.orlandosentinel.com/news.

Goodman, W. (October 29, 1990). "How much should t.v. tell and when?" *New York Times*.

Katzenbach, J. (September 1980). "Overwhelmed in Miami," *Police Magazine*, pp. 7–15.

King, T. R. (2000). "Managing protests on public land," *FBI Law Enforcement Bulletin*, Vol. 69, No. 9, pp. 10–13.

Lazin, F. A. (1980). "How the police view the press," *Journal of Police Science and Administration*, Vol. 8, pp. 148–159.

Lofton, J. (1966). *Justice and the Press*. Boston, MA: Beacon Press.

MacDougall, C. D. (1964). *The Press and Its Problems*. Dubuque, IA: W. C. Brown.

Morgan, R., and Newburn, T. (1997). *The Future of Policing*. Oxford, England: Clarendon Press.

Rosenthal, R. (1999a). "Portland cements media agreement," *Law & Order*, Vol. 33, No. 11, pp. 22–23.

Rosenthal, R. (1999b). "Lessons from Littleton: Managing the media in a crisis," *Law & Order*, Vol. 47, No. 6, pp. 25–26.

Rosenthal, R. (2001a). "Chicago trains the media," *Law & Order*, Vol. 49, No. 8, pp. 20–21.

Rosenthal, R. (2001b). "Winning media strategies," *Law & Order*, Vol. 49, No. 6, pp. 23–24.

Rosenthal, R. (2001c). "One of the best PIOs," *Law & Order*, Vol. 49, No. 3, pp. 21–22.

Schmid, A. P., and DeGraaf, J. (1982). *Violence as Communication: Insurgent Terrorism and the Western News Media*. Beverly Hills, CA: Sage.

Siegel, L. J., and Senna, J. J. (2007). *Essentials of Criminal Justice*, 5th ed. Pacific Grove, CA: Thomson/Wadsworth.

Sotelo, M. (2000). "Exploring police, media's vexing problem of relationships," *New Photographer*, Vol. 55, No. 2, pp. 12–14.

Sparks, A. B., and Staszak, D. D. (2000). "Fine tuning your news briefing," *FBI Law Enforcement Bulletin*, Vol. 69, No. 12, pp. 22–24.

Staszak, D. (2001). "Media trends and the public information officer," *FBI Law Enforcement Bulletin*, Vol. 70, No. 3, pp. 10–13.

Surette, R., and Richard, A. (1995). "Public information officers: A descriptive study of crime news gatekeepers," *Journal of Criminal Justice*, Vol. 23, pp. 325–326.

Trigoboff, D. (2000). "Stations restrained, or manipulated," *Broadcasting & Cable*, Vol. 130, No. 3, p.14.

Toufexis, A. (June 28, 1993). "A weird case baby? Un huh," *Time*, p. 41.

USA Today. (December 12, 1991). "Smith trial offers mixed message about date rape," Editorial, p. 10A.

Vetter, H. J., and Perlstein, G. R. (1991). *Perspectives on Terrorism*. Pacific Grove, CA: Brooks/Cole.

Worral, J. L. (2000). "Constitutional issues in reality-based police television programs: Media ride-alongs," *American Journal of Criminal Justice*, Vol. 25, No. 1, pp. 41–64.

Walsh, M., Vice-Chairman, Public Information Officers Section, International Association of Chiefs of Police (April/May 1983). Interview.

MODULE 4

Chapter 7

Community Psychologists:
Who We Are and What We Do

⌘ Introduction

Chapter One described the field of community psychology: where it came from and what it is. Now let's look at the people in the field—who we are and what we do. Community psychologists assume a plethora of different roles. We are organizers, consultants, teachers, program directors, politicians, educators, co-learners, service deliverers, writers, evaluators, activists, mediators, analysts, fundraisers, facilitators, administrators, managers, planners, documenters/historians, workshop leaders, researchers, advocates, policymakers, technical assistants, ambassadors, problem solvers, healers, visionaries, and troublemakers. Community psychologists perform these roles in a wide variety of settings. We work in and with schools, hospitals, correctional facilities, mental health centers, research institutes, businesses, colleges and universities, non-profit agencies, grassroots organizations, neighborhood associations, advocacy groups, and governmental offices at the local, state, and federal level. Despite this vast array of job descriptions and environments, there are commonalities that unite us all.

⌘ Who Are Community Psychologists?

Community psychologists are united by our shared belief in the tenets of the field. Our guiding principles attract people with certain qualities, and our training and experiences strengthen these qualities. Several community psychologists have specified the characteristics necessary for work in our field, most notably, James Kelly.

KELLY'S QUALITIES FOR THE COMMUNITY PSYCHOLOGIST

In 1971, when community psychology was a young and burgeoning field, James Kelly outlined seven important qualities for the community psychologist. Since that time, others have constructed lists of their own (e.g., Iscoe, 1997; Wolff, 1987). Kelly's original seven qualities and one additional quality are described below.

CLEARLY IDENTIFIED COMPETENCE

Kelly argued that in order to solve pressing problems, a community psychologist must have a recognizable area of competence. He saw this as the key attribute, the quality on which all other qualities built. Although some area of competence is necessary, the exact nature of the competence can vary. In 1971 Kelly's list of possible competencies included the abilities to be therapeutic with individuals, to organize a community service, to study a complex social problem, or to create a sense of community. A list of competencies for community psychologists compiled today might differ from this original list. Therapy with individuals appears less often in the

In the arena of human life the honors and rewards fall to those who show their good qualities in action.

—Aristotle

job descriptions of community psychologists, while the analytical competence of a researcher has gained importance.

Most people trained as community psychologists conduct research as part of their postgraduate work (Nemec, Hungerford, Hutchings, & Huygens, 2000; O'Donnell & Ferrari, 2000). One study followed graduates from three types of academic programs: community-clinical psychology; applied social psychology; and community psychology (Feis, Mavis, Weth, & Davidson, 1990). The clinical psychology programs focused on imparting human service skills, and program graduates found jobs in which they provided direct services to clients. Applied social psychology programs centered on developing administrative and organizational skills, and graduates tended to find consulting jobs. Graduates of community psychology programs most often obtained jobs in which they conducted research.

The most obvious components of research competence are knowledge about methodology and statistics. All researchers need to know how to design studies, collect data, and analyze information. Equally important to community psychologists, however, is an understanding of the *context* of research. In reviewing lessons learned as researchers in the field, Geoffrey Nelson (1998) and his colleagues observed that their "notions of what it means to be a good researcher have changed from an emphasis on expertise in research design and measurement to more of an emphasis on the interpersonal and political dynamics of the research process" (p. 894).

Research is not the only competency important to community psychologists today. A recent study of community psychology program graduates cited the importance of written and oral skills, since many jobs required reports and presentations (Nemec, et al., 2000). Program graduates also reported using their organizing and consultation skills. Perhaps most importantly, the unique perspective of community psychology was viewed as a competence in and of itself (see also O'Donnell & Ferrari, 2000). The principles of the field allowed community psychologists to approach problems from multilevel, interdisciplinary, and strengths-based perspectives, a skill valued by numerous employers.

CREATING AN ECO-IDENTITY

Kelly believed that community psychologists must identify with the communities in which they work. This means creating an **eco-identity** by stepping out of one's professional role and becoming emotionally involved in the social setting. The community psychologist Julia Green Brody recognized the importance of an eco-identity in her work for Texas Agriculture Commissioner Jim Hightower. When she began her work, the U.S. Department of Energy was deciding which of nine sites to choose as the locale for a nuclear waste depository. Two sites in Texas were among the final nine. Brody's job was to ensure that the dump would not be located in either of the two Texas panhandle counties that produced 10 billion bushels of wheat and a half billion head of cattle each year.

In her work, Brody (1986) came into frequent contact with farmers whose livelihood depended on beef. She recounted the story of a representative from the U.S. Department of Energy who declared his vegetarianism to an audience of ranchers. She wrote:

> I am a vegetarian, too. But when I go to Tulia, I eat at K-Bob's Steakhouse. . . You do not have to be a community psychologist to know that it is unsafe to tell a roomful of cattleman that you are a vegetarian. But it does help to have a conscious sense that learning about the community where you work is more than a common courtesy: It's part of doing your job well. (p. 142)

Brody, like other community psychologists, followed the sage advice of her teacher, Ira Iscoe: "If you want to be invited in, be prepared to share the food" (Brody, 1986, p. 142).

According to Kelly, creating an eco-identity involves caring enough about the community to explore all its sectors: the interrelationships among subcommunities, the politics of the area, the needs and resources of different physical localities.

Community psychologists need "to sense the range of behavior, styles of life, and conflicts, without becoming immune to the diversity and seeing only chaos" (Kelly, 1971, p. 900). The ability to recognize and appreciate the community's diversity constitutes Kelly's third key quality.

TOLERANCE/APPRECIATION OF DIVERSITY

In 1971 Kelly cited the importance of honoring a community's diversity, although in today's language the term *appreciation* would replace his word *tolerance.* For community psychologists, appreciating diversity means recognizing and responding to various **stakeholders** in the community—the legislators, politicians, community leaders, citizens, and others who have an investment in the issue at hand. These stakeholders often have conflicting perspectives that stem not only from social roles (e.g., agency director versus service recipient) but also from **social position.** Social position refers to those salient aspects of identity, such as race, gender, and socioeconomic status, along which a given society is stratified (e.g. García Coll, Lamberty, Jenkins, McAdoo, Crnic, Wasik, & Vásquez García, 1996). These two sources of diversity, social role and social position, are confounded. The targets of social programs often occupy subordinate social positions (e.g. poor, ethnic minority), while the people with the most decision-making power tend occupy dominant social positions (e.g. White, financially secure, male).

Kelly (1971) asserted that appreciating diversity means not only acknowledging a community's heterogeneity, but also searching out what these differences mean. This exploration should be guided by the maxim "There is something valid in each example, yet something incomplete in all of them" (p. 900). Differences among people easily lead to misunderstandings, breakdowns in communication, and entrenchment in opposing camps. Too often the potential for diverse perspectives to expand our understanding of an issue remains unrealized.

Consider, for example, the struggle for women to overcome gender-based oppression. Historically, many women have been left out of the women's movement. In 1851 attendees of a women's convention in Akron, Ohio, tried to keep the ex-slave Sojourner Truth from speaking for fear that the women's movement would lose credibility if confused with the abolition movement. Truth spoke all the same and changed the terms of the debate on women's rights when she proclaimed, "Nobody ever helps me into carriages, or over mud-puddles, or gives me any best place! And ain't I a woman? I could work as much and eat as much as a man—when I could get it—and bear the lash as well! Ain't I a woman?" (Schneir, 1972, p. 94–95). Similarly, leaders of the women's movement in the 1960s silenced and disavowed lesbians at the movement's vanguard for fear that alignment with gay rights would impede the progress of the women's movement (Marotta, 1981). Poor women have also remained on the fringes of the modern women's movement.

Nevertheless, the perspectives of diverse women add to the arsenal of those battling for women's equality. Gender oppression hurts *everyone*. As Sojourner Truth proclaimed, equal rights for women are about much more than chivalrous behavior. The concerns highlighted by Black women's experiences also merit consideration (see also Lorde, 1984), and lesbian activists know that rigid gender roles contribute to both women's oppression and gay oppression (Pharr, 1988). Johnnie Tillmon, an early leader of the welfare rights movement declared, "Welfare is a women's issue," since many "women are one man away from welfare" (West, 1990, p. 149). More recent research on the disproportionate number of female-headed households living in poverty and the declines in income following divorce gives credibility to Tillmon's assertion (e.g., Sherman, Amey, Duffield, Ebb, & Weinstein, 1998).

The perspective of any one group is limited, and consideration of multiple viewpoints allows insights that would not be possible otherwise. Indeed, men have recently recognized the ways their own development has been compromised by social constructions of gender (Garbarino, 1999; Levant & Pollack, 1997; Pollack, 1998; Silverstein, & Rashbaum, 1994). The social problems of interest to community psychologists are complex and multifaceted. The more community psychologists honor diverse voices, the more complete our understanding.

COPING EFFECTIVELY WITH VARIED RESOURCES

A diversity of people means a diversity of resources. One job of the community psychologist is to assess and mobilize the resources available to tackle problems of interest. By searching out the skills and talents of community members and organizations and pointing out the relevance of these resources to the challenges at hand, the community psychologist promotes innovative ways of addressing entrenched problems.

Interventions have traditionally focused on deficits rather than strengths. They have sought to correct what went wrong rather than build on what went right. Community psychologists take a different tack. We seek to enhance capacities by identifying and supporting individual and community assets. All communities have untapped resources. For example, community psychologists might develop new opportunities for involvement that utilize senior citizens, youth, artists, people with disabilities, and members of other marginalized groups whose capacity to contribute to the social good is underappreciated (Kretzmann & McKnight, 1993). In addition, to creating new roles, existing roles might be reinforced. Emory Cowen (1982) tried to enhance community resources by improving the helping capabilities of "informal" or "natural" helpers such as bartenders and hairdressers (see Classic Research box on p. 141).

In addition to people, local organizations and institutions (e.g. religious groups, libraries, schools) may also constitute untapped resources. For example, in the era of megabookstores and the internet, public libraries across the country have become more essential to neighborhoods by shifting away from strictly scholarly pursuits toward functions once associated with community centers and community colleges. Some libraries now offer meeting places, lectures, and a variety of classes, from aerobics for older adults to English classes for immigrants (Murphy, 2001). As another example, Edward Zigler,

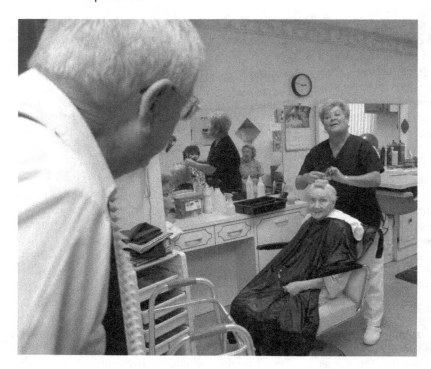

"Natural helpers," such as hairdressers, often play important roles in the lives of their clients. *Kevin Seifert/ Durham Herald Sun.*

a principal architect of Head Start, proposed the concept of *21st Century Schools*. He suggested that school buildings could serve as hubs for comprehensive and affordable family support services, such as preschool child care, before- and after-school care for older children, information and referral services for families, and support and training for child care providers (Zigler & Finn-Stevenson, 1999; see also New York City's Beacon schools reported in Schorr, 1997).

COMMITMENT TO RISK-TAKING

Community psychologists seek to create change. Change entails risk. First and foremost is the risk of failure. Kelly advised that a high probability of "failure" should not act as a deterrent because "losing" often allows for invaluable learning opportunities. N. Dickon Reppucci and four colleagues demonstrated the truth of this notion in a chapter entitled

We Bombed in Mountville: Lessons Learned in Consultation to a Correctional Facility for Adolescent Offenders (1973). This "failed" intervention resulted in much new learning. It offered the authors numerous insights into the dynamics of community consultation (some of which will be examined later in this chapter). It also led four of the five clinically trained consultants to pursue careers in a new field: community psychology.

Not only do challenges to change efforts often fail, success brings new risks as counterforces seek to resist changes in the status quo. The applied community psychologist Thomas Wolff found this out when he taught a course on planned organizational change strategies to university students. The training program enjoyed considerable success, and one year a number of campus activists enrolled, each with a goal she or he hoped to achieve. The president of Student Government wanted to turn that organization into a union. The leader of the

CLASSIC RESEARCH

Emory Cowen
Helping Helpers to Help

As the 1950s gave way to the 1960s, three insights about the nature of mental health service delivery led to new ways of thinking about how to help. First, there was a growing awareness that professional helpers could not be trained in numbers sufficient to meet the demands for help (e.g. Albee, 1959). Second, only a small percentage of people in need of mental health services ever sought help from mental health professionals (Joint Commission on Mental Illness and Health, 1961). Finally, doubt existed as to whether trained professionals were even capable of helping people. The efficacy of the most prestigious techniques of the time remained unproven (Eysenck, 1961), and some treatments, particularly hospitalization, seemed to make clients *less* able to function in society (Goffman, 1961).

Community psychologists elaborated on these early findings. Some warned that professional helping relationships exacerbated problems by fostering the help-seekers' dependence on expert helpers (e.g. Tyler, Pargament, & Gatz, 1983). Some conducted research to show that informal helpers may be as effective, perhaps even more effective, than professional helpers (e.g. Durlak, 1979. See Christensen & Jacobson, 1994 for a more recent review, and Halpern, 2000 for a dissenting view). One of the leaders in community psychology, Emory Cowen, conducted a classic study entitled, *Help Is Where You Find It* (1982), to explore the nature and extent of nonprofessional helping channels. He studied four informal help-givers: hairdressers, bartenders, divorce lawyers, and industrial supervisors.

As one might expect, the nature of the assistance given by these informal helpers differed in systematic ways. The numbers of people helped varied substantially across categories of helpers. On average, divorce lawyers assisted 20 clients each year, while hairdressers saw 55 customers per week, and bartenders served an impressive 104 patrons in a day. The types of problems raised by clients also varied. Hairdressers most often heard about clients' difficulties with their children. Bartenders and supervisors most often heard about job problems. Divorce lawyers heard about problems with spouses. In addition, the help-givers responded in different ways. Hairdressers and bartenders listened, offered support and sympathy, or tried to be light-hearted. Lawyers asked questions, gave advice, and pointed out the consequences of bad ideas.

Cowen found that helpers from these four groups enjoyed giving assistance, felt reasonably competent in the help-giving role, and saw help-giving as part of their job. Nevertheless, they wanted to improve their ability to help. Thus, Cowen and his colleagues organized ten workshops on such topics as listening and attending skills, and referral resources and mechanisms.

Cowen attempted to use his professional competencies to build community strengths. Although he found that his workshops changed the ways in which the helpers offered assistance, the larger question of whether they became more or less helpful remained unanswered. When Cowen conducted his groundbreaking study, community psychologists were less aware of the potential for interventions to have unintended negative consequences. Today, community psychologists would likely evaluate the effectiveness of such an intervention.

Black Studies Action Office hoped to double the Office's budget. The head of the Women's Center sought to effect several campus-wide changes. The university administration unexpectedly canceled Wolff's course. Upon hearing the news, Wolff reported regaining perspective by rereading Kelly's article on the qualities of the community psychologist (Wolff, 1987). A commitment to risk-taking means expecting some measure of opposition—indeed it can be a testament to one's effectiveness.

METABOLIC BALANCE OF PATIENCE AND ZEAL

Community psychologists are concerned about pressing social problems. A sense of urgency fuels many of our activities. At the same time, entrenched problems are not easily solved and perhaps can never be solved once and for all (Sarason, 1978). The status quo is perpetuated by ingrained ways of thinking and behaving at all levels of society, including individual minds, institutional practices, and cultural worldviews.

Thus, the importance of both patience and zeal. Leonard Jason reported sitting on the Chicago Lung Association's Smoking and Health Committee for three years, waiting patiently for the right opportunity to launch a media-based smoking cessation project (Jason, 1998). Balancing patience and zeal means attending to timing, persevering in the face of obstacles, and maintaining a realistic sense of how much time and energy is required to make a difference. Community psychologists need to remember long-term goals while working to achieve short-term objectives Although not a community psychologist per se, Wallace Lambert (1992) exemplifies a researcher balancing patience and zeal, as the following example shows.

In the late 1950s, French speakers comprised 80% of the population of Quebec, but English speakers owned most of the businesses. Thus, a condition of "one-way bilingualism" existed. Success required that French speakers know English, but English speakers did not need to know French. While riding on a bus in the winter of 1958 Lambert overheard a conversation between two anglophones in which they disparaged the francophones who were laughing behind them. Lambert hypothesized that the English speakers feared that the francophones, whom they could not understand, were laughing at them. This hypothesis led to a thirty-year research program geared toward social change.

In his initial studies, Lambert found that when unseen bilinguals spoke English, they were rated as taller, better looking, more intelligent, more dependable, kinder, and more ambitious than when these same bilinguals spoke French. Interestingly, French Canadians evaluated the French speakers even *more* negatively than the English Canadians did. Lambert challenged the widespread assumptions of inferiority by demonstrating that bilingualism actually corresponded with an increased proficiency in one's first language, higher school achievement, and greater facility in concept formation.

Lambert and his colleagues used this information to launch a social experiment. In collaboration with a group of English Canadian parents who wanted their children to gain the academic edge bilingualism offered, they instituted an immersion language program led by teachers who spoke only French. During the next twenty-five years, Lambert and his colleagues demonstrated the efficacy of these programs. Not only did the English Canadian students learn a second language, they demonstrated an increase in IQ scores, more proficiency on measures of divergent thinking, and greater competence in their first language (English, in this case). Perhaps most importantly, immersion students developed a deeper appreciation and affection for French Canadians. They had learned about French Canadian culture from their teachers, and their ability to speak French afforded them the opportunity to interact with francophones. If they overheard French speakers laughing on a bus, they did not need to hypothesize about the reasons for laughter. These English Canadian students could understand what the francophones were saying and could join them in conversation.

GIVING AWAY THE BYLINE

Kelly asserted that the hallmark of a community psychologist is her or his satisfaction in realizing the six qualities outlined above. He contended that our main goal should be to foster the development of the people and communities with whom we work. Visibility and congratulations for our accomplishments should not be motivators. Indeed, they are counter-productive to the nonhierarchical, collaborative relationships needed for the tasks at hand. Kelly stated that if one's professional vanity required recognition and appreciation, short-term pseudo-solutions would be attractive and real change impossible. The reward of community psychology is the improvement of the community, not the gratitude of community members (Kelly, 1971; see also Iscoe, 1974).

One challenge for community psychologists is how to develop community resources without fostering dependence. We have a competence to bring but do not want to be solely responsible for community change. The notion of **planned obsolescence** offers a solution. In the business world, planned obsolescence means sustaining a market for one's products by ensuring that they do not last too long—designing cars to break down upon reaching the 100,000 mile mark, for example, even when technology exists to build engines that last much longer. In community psychology, the goal of planned obsolescence is just the opposite—we plan our *own* obsolescence. We find ways of ensuring that the competence we bring to (or bring out of) any community can eventually be realized by that community alone. And then we move on.

Kelly recognized that an orientation toward giving away the byline runs counter to the reward systems of the universities and colleges where many community psychologists work. Indeed, several of the qualities outlined by Kelly do not fit into academic merit systems. Community efforts require time as settings must be entered carefully, eco-identities forged slowly, and work conducted in a collaborative, and therefore time-consuming fashion. This is inconsistent with university requirements for individual achievement in the form of multiple publications in academic journals, large research grants, and national reputations.

Since Kelly's article, the need to remodel the ivory tower has been recognized by many. As one example, the Society for the Teaching of Psychology's Task Force on Defining Scholarship in Psychology (1998) recommended a definition of scholarship that extends beyond the production of original research. They noted the importance of integrating knowledge into a larger body of concepts and facts, and translating knowledge for legal, popular, and community audiences (see also Boyer, 1990; Gray, Froh, & Diamond, 1992). Community psychologists, led by Kelly, recognized the need for a redefinition of scholarship years ago. Kelly wrote that the community should be the final judge of what is 'good,' and that effective community workers are rewarded by being "invited to work on still tougher problems" (Kelly, 1971, p. 903).

AN ADDITIONAL QUALITY: TOLERANCE FOR AMBIGUITY

One additional characteristic has frequently appeared as a quality for community psychologists since Kelly constructed his list in 1971. I first heard about this quality in 1986. As a first year graduate student, I was overcome with confusion. I wasn't sure how best to become a community psychologist. There seemed to be an overabundance of possible research topics for my master's thesis, a myriad of community concerns to tackle in my fieldwork, and countless courses in related disciplines that would enrich my education. Which would be the best path, and how would I know? During a particularly angst-filled meeting, my mentor, N. Dickon Reppucci, conveyed this memorable piece of advice: "Jennifer, if you want to be a community psychologist, you have to have a tolerance for ambiguity" (see also Bond, 1999; Iscoe, 1997).

My appreciation for the wisdom of these words increased in the years that followed. As Dick forewarned, I have conducted numerous job searches and have never once come across an employer looking for community psychologist. Only a handful of colleagues have even heard of the field.

Many other community psychologists echo this experience. After using community psychology principles in a mental health agency for over a decade, John Morgan (2000) reported that "few of my colleagues in the agency or the community know that I am a 'community psychologist'; fewer still would know what one was" (p. 745). Similarly, Judith Meyers (2000) observed that "Nowhere, neither in my job description nor in my everyday work in various policy positions from 1986 through 1989, have I been identified as a community psychologist" (p. 761).

Community psychologists redefine themselves in accordance with the demands of each new position. And there may be many. One study of 38 community psychology program graduates found that only 7 people had worked in a single job, and 6 of these had graduated just one year prior. Most study respondents spent only one to three years in each position, and several juggled multiple part-time jobs or contracts at the same time (Nemec, et al., 2000). Community psychologists, especially those affiliated primarily with applied settings, spend their careers "carving out jobs, incomes, and support systems in order to follow a belief in the value of applied community psychology" (Wolff, 2000, p. 772). When we tolerate ambiguity we can (in our more reflective moments) see the lack of prescribed roles as an opportunity to affirm the value of community psychology in unlimited ways.

The routes to becoming a community psychologist are varied. After graduation, we rarely encounter employers looking specifically for community psychologists. In addition, throughout our careers we will likely walk the line between academia and practice, science and values. Perhaps most importantly, the community problems on which we work are often entrenched and multifaceted. The process of change is unpredictable, and change efforts do not always lead in a direct way to observable results. For all of these reasons, tolerance for ambiguity is a key characteristic of community psychologists.

⌘ What Do Community Psychologists Do?

So now we have some sense of who community psychologists are—key qualities that help us to do our work. Next, let's look at what this work consists of.

The work of community psychologists bridges the domains of scientific research (conducted primarily

in academic settings) and applied practice (conducted primarily in the field). Academia and practice have traditionally been construed as different, even diametrically opposed, domains. Indeed one definition of *academic* is "having no practical or useful significance" (Merriam-Webster, 2000). This dichotomy, like all dichotomies, is false. Science is not removed from the "real world." The questions, methods, and findings of research are all shaped by the surrounding context, and the research process is itself an intervention, regardless of whether or not the researcher intends to effect changes (Swift, 1990). Similarly, practitioners continually gather evidence about whether or not their actions led to the desired results and elaborate their theories of why things happen as they gather evidence.

For community psychologists, research and practice are inextricably linked (e.g. Galano, 1996). Early in community psychology's history, Richard Price and Cary Cherniss (1977) delineated four characteristics of community research, each of which emphasizes the link between research and practice. They posited that community research should 1) be stimulated by community needs, 2) drive action, 3) result in products that are useful to the community—a new program or training manual rather than publication in an esoteric journal or a new line on the researcher's vitae, and 4) be evaluated to ensure that good intentions did indeed lead to positive effects. Several years later, Irma Serrano-García (1984, 1990) proposed an Intervention within research model that viewed the processes of research and intervention as simultaneous and interdependent, though also distinguishable. This model recognizes participants as integral to the research process and views the researcher/intervener as needing competencies not only in research, but also in community organizing and political analysis.

Although community psychology brings academia and practice together, tensions remain. One tension for academic community psychologists is the often-lamented inverse relationship between rigor and social relevance—as one increases, the other decreases (e.g., Fawcett, 1991; Lounsbury, Leader, Meares, & Cook, 1980; Novaco & Monahan, 1980). Robert Reiff proposed that the only distinction between community psychologists and citizens seeking change is that the "professionals" attempt to bring greater order into change efforts (1977; see also Kelly, 1970). This order can be burdensome as community researchers struggle to balance a commitment to the scientific methods with a desire to effect change. Attempts to study phenomena rigorously may lead academic psychologists to ask small questions, focus on methodological details, and delay action.

A challenge for community practitioners, on the other hand, is to maintain ties with a profession that seems oriented toward science and research. A review of the published literature on community psychology would likely lead to the conclusion that the field is primarily an academic one. Applied community psychologists do not always see themselves and their concerns reflected in the field's formal institutions and publications (Wolff, 2000). In a study designed to elucidate the differences between academic and nonacademic community psychologists, Maurice Elias and his colleagues identified "exemplary" community psychologists whose work embodied significant elements of the field's paradigm. These "exemplars" were nearly all affiliated primarily with academic settings (Elias et al., 1984).

One reason for the imbalance in representations of academic and applied perspectives may relate to time. For academics, reflection and writing are part of the scholarship required in research settings, while practitioners may be too busy *doing* community psychology to write about it. Regardless of the reasons, the "promise of community psychology is half filled without defined practices" (Chavis, 1993, p. 179). Academic community psychologists who lead the field's institutions have tried to right this imbalance, but it is difficult to transcend one's own perspective. Before the 2001 SCRA Biennial Conference, several postings on the community psychology listserv promoted sessions focusing on nonacademic perspectives. Gloria Levin caused a stir when she objected to the very use of the term "NONacademic" to describe community psychology practitioners. How would academics feel, she asked, if they were always referred to as "NONpractitioners" (Levin, June 6, 2001)?

Although academic psychologists work to improve communities and practitioners conduct research and develop theory, researchers and practitioners have different priorities, face different challenges, and receive different rewards. In the next section we will look at the work of community psychology through the lens afforded by an academic perspective and then turn to a more explicit examination of practice. The academic perspective is better documented in the community psychology literature on which this textbook is based. Thus, I will outline issues that flow from the five guiding principles that will frame the discussion of research that occurs in subsequent chapters. I will also review two forums through which academic researchers often engage in practice. The practice section will examine three important roles for applied community psychologists.

THE ACADEMIC SIDE OF COMMUNITY PSYCHOLOGY

Psychology, like other sciences, rests on the tradition of **logical positivism**. This tradition views knowledge as grounded in objective, incontrovertible facts that accumulate through scientifically rigorous study. In these studies, hypotheses about how the world works are generated, tested, and either retained or rejected based on their ability to survive experimental tests. The logical positivist tradition presents challenges to each of the five guiding principles of community psychology.

RESEARCH AND THE GUIDING PRINCIPLES

Table 7.1 summarizes characteristics of community research that flow from the guiding principles. Each principle has important implications for academic psychology, which inherits notions of scientific integrity from a logical positivist tradition.

Research and the Importance of Values. The logical positivist tradition attempts to eliminate biases, which are construed as "highly personal and unreasoned distortions of judgment" (Merriam-Webster, 2000). In psychology, an agreed-upon set

Table 7.1   How Community Psychology's Guiding Principles Affect Research

Guiding Principle	Challenge to Traditional Research
VALUES: Knowledge develops within a value system.	Research is not objective and value free.
CONTEXT: Individuals are embedded in a many-leveled social context.	Research should capture processes that occur beyond the level of the individual.
DIVERSITY: The voices of diverse groups must be honored.	Researchers should be culturally sensitive.
SOCIAL CHANGE: People's lives should be improved through social change efforts.	Research should not simply add to the body of scientific knowledge, but be socially useful.
PEOPLE'S STRENGTHS: The strengths of those we seek to help should be emphasized rather than their deficits.	Respect for people's competence should be reflected in what we study and how we study it.

of scientific procedures has developed to remove personal biases from the process of inquiry. For example, scientists try to establish **reliability**, which means that findings from one study can and should be replicated in other studies that different researchers conduct at different times with different people.

The objective scientific observer who removes himself or herself from the fact-finding process has long been an ideal in science. In the modern era, however, even the "hard" science of physics has found that the observer inevitably affects the process of inquiry (as described in Heisenberg's uncertainty principle). Few contemporary philosophers of science believe that scientific endeavors can exist untouched by value-laden personal, political, and social forces (e.g., Kane, 1998). Indeed, researcher bias has become a topic of study in and of itself (e.g., MacCoun, 1998).

Some scholars suggest that the impartial observer is not only impossible, but undesirable as well. Research is, after all, a human endeavor. Does our humanity weaken our science? Is our ability to understand reality necessarily enhanced by a stance that is impersonal, reasoned, dispassionate, and

distant? Parker J. Palmer (1998) warned that the effort to be objective prevents us from truly relating to the world around us. "When we distance ourselves from something, it becomes an object; when it becomes an object, it no longer has life; when it is lifeless, it cannot touch or transform us. . ." (pp. 51–52).

Despite advances in the philosophy of science, positivism remains in many ways the unspoken gold standard for good science. Ironically, even though logical positivism rejects the importance of values, its elevation to the purest and best way of knowing is itself a value that can be questioned... and rejected. Often, this questioning does not occur. The "influence [of logical positivism] is so pervasive as to be unrecognized by those enmeshed in its web of meaning" (Moke & Bohan, 1992, p. 7). Community psychologists, too, get caught in the web of logical positivism, and despite our guiding principles, most of our research studies have embodied this approach (Speer, Dey, Griggs, Gbson, Lubin, & Hughey, 1992; Tolan, Chertok, Keys, & Jason, 1990; Walsh, 1987).

At the same time, Ana Marie Cauce (1990) warned against "logical positivism bashing," which results in the summary dismissal of everything associated with this tradition (p. 205). Under the rubric of community psychology there is room to for many research approaches, including logical positivism (see also Dokecki, 1992). Nevertheless, researchers in this tradition must still recognize that values determine what is studied, how it is studied, and how results are interpreted.

David Chavis and his colleagues (1983) suggested that one mechanism for remaining aware of and accountable for our values is to collaborate with the community members who are consumers of our research. The myth of neutral objectivity is quickly dispelled as researchers "clarify their expectations, values, and priorities with the nonscientific community. Conflicts may arise, but they are conflicts not between science and nonscience but between alternative values, priorities, and ways of problem solving" (1983, p. 425).

Research and the Context Beyond the Individual. The logical positivist tradition views science as value free. It also assumes that context does not matter (Moke & Bohan, 1992). The goal of science is to isolate single causes with universal effects. If A then B. Always. Everywhere. With everyone. To community psychologists, however, the context is all important. We do not believe that we can understand individuals independent of their multilevel environments.

In order to isolate single causes with universal effects, the positivist tradition depends on experimental control. The scientist seeks to demonstrate that the manipulation of one variable of interest (the **independent variable**) causes the predicted effects on another variable of interest (the **dependent variable**). All extraneous factors are **confounding variables** that must be nullified through experimental design or statistical analysis. Attempts to gain control have led many researchers into the laboratory to conduct elegantly designed studies.

The developmental psychologist Urie Bronfenbrenner, who has had a large impact on community psychology warned against the scientific practice of putting research subjects in unfamiliar and artificial situations for exceedingly short periods of times in order to elicit unusual behaviors. He questioned whether results obtained under such controlled and contrived conditions could be generalized to people in normal environments. He coined the term **ecological validity** to indicate the extent to which the research environment contained properties relevant to the real-world settings that the experimenter hoped to elucidate (Bronfenbrenner, 1977). The philosopher, educator, and psychologist John Dewey (1899) recognized the tradeoff between control and applicability a century ago.

> The great advantage of the psychological laboratory is paid for by certain obvious defects. The completer the control of conditions, with resulting greater accuracy of determination, demands an isolation, a ruling out of the usual media of thought and action, which leads to remoteness, and easily to a certain artificiality. (p. 145)

The "media of thought and action" are not the source of confounds, but the all-important context of behavior of interest to community psychologists.

To further complicate the task for community researchers, this context is multileveled. Our thoughts and actions are affected by dynamic processes that occur within our hearts and minds, in interaction with the people around us, and also at higher levels of analysis that are more difficult to study. A researcher interested in child abuse, for example, might consider the abuser's mental health status, the interaction patterns in families where abuse occurs, the existence of neighborhood support systems, the contributing stress of poverty or unemployment, and the role of cultural norms with regard to violence (Belsky 1980; Phillips 2000).

Research and the Appreciation of Diversity. In the logical positivist tradition, lack of attention to real-world environments has led to a de-emphasis of the cultural context of research (Gergen, Gulerce, Lock, & Misra, 1996; Sue, 1999). In the search for universals researchers assumed that scientific findings applied to all people. As a result, the unique experiences of minority group members went un-studied, a situation aptly captured in the book enti-tled *Even the Rats Were White* (Guthrie, 1998; see also Bohan, 1995). Many researchers have hesitated to consider social position in a conscious and criti-cal way. Analyses of the impact of race, ethnicity, gender, and other dimensions of difference have often occurred either as an afterthought (Scarr, 1988) or as an attempt to control for "nuisance" variables (Spencer, 1990). Community psychology attempts to "overcome this tradition and replaces it with the intention to understand different groups and individuals on their own terms," (Rappaport, 1984c, p. 360). This intention brings many chal-lenges. Let's consider a few of them.

The Difficulty of Obtaining Samples. When we no longer assume universal effects we can no longer rely on samples of convenience. Undergraduate psychology students who receive course credit for participation in research may be readily available, but not necessarily representative of diverse voices (Sears, 1986). Reliance on convenient samples has led to theories of human behavior based primarily on White and middle class people (Graham, 1992; see also Reid, 1994; Rogler, 1999; Segall, Lonner, & Berry, 1998). To rectify this situation, more research is needed on the life experiences of members of dis-enfranchised groups. Such samples are more diffi-cult to obtain for a variety of reasons, however. Researchers have less access to and credibility with people of different social positions, and members of marginalized groups may have less time and energy to devote to activities from which they do not di-rectly benefit. Disenfranchised people may not see research as advancing their own causes, a percep-tion that has too often been accurate.

Our Ability to Interpret the Thoughts and Behav-iors of Others Must Be Questioned. Marginalized groups have historically been studied in comparison to mainstream groups and observed differences ex-plained in terms of minority group deficits (e.g., Be-tancourt & Lopez, 1993; McHugh, Koeske, & Frieze, 1986; Moghaddam & Studer, 1997; Vega, 1992). Majority group behavior has served as the norm—the "gold standard" for understanding the behavior of all other groups (Vega, 1992, p. 381; see also Katz & Kofkin, 1997). These standards are often inappropriate as different groups live in different contexts. For example, keeping a 12-year-old under constant supervision may seem over-restrictive (i.e. negative parenting) in low-crime areas. In high crime areas, however, it may constitute responsible and necessary (i.e. positive) parenting (Hughes, Seid-man, & Williams, 1993).

Appropriate Measures and Methodologies May Not Exist. Measurement issues pose additional challenges (e.g., Caldwell, Jackson, Tucker, & Bow-man, 1999; Cauce, Coronado, & Watson, 1998). Many standard measures have been developed and tested on samples of convenience and do not reflect the experiences of people who are not White and middle class (e.g., Manson, Shore, & Bloom, 1985; Prelow, Tein, Roosa, & Wood, 2000; Rogler, 1999). This is true not only in terms of scale content (e.g., what behaviors constitute positive parenting), but also in terms of scale usage. When completing rat-ing scales, African American and Hispanic respon-dents endorse more extreme response categories as compared to Euro-American respondents (Bachman & O'Malley, 1984; Hui & Triandis, 1989; Marín, Gamba, & Marín, 1992).

While some culturally sensitive researchers seek to adapt existing measures and methodologies for use with under-represented groups (see Caldwell, et al., 1999), others call for new epistemologies—new ways of seeking knowledge. For example, William Vega advocated the **emic approach** used by an-thropologists. In the emic approach, research meth-ods allow the systems of meaning inherent in the group under study to guide the research process (Vega 1992; see also Berry & Kim, 1993; Kim & Berry, 1993; see Belenky, Clinchy, Goldberger, & Tarule, 1986, for a woman-centered approach). This contrasts with the **etic approach**, which as-sumes universality in human experience, therefore disregarding ethnicity and culture. In this approach, structures for understanding the experiences of the people under study are predetermined by re-searchers (who often belong to dominant social groups) and imposed from the outside.

Attention to Broad Categories Is Only the Tip of the Diversity Iceberg. Cultural insensitivity is also reflected in researchers' willingness to reduce complex groups into single categories based on superficial similarities (e.g., Bernal & Enchautegui-de-Jesus, 1994; Helms, 1994; Hughes et al., 1993; Vega, 1992). This has been most evident with regard to ethnic background. All people from Spanish-speaking countries (Mexico, Puerto Rico, Cuba) are considered Hispanic, and people from such diverse countries as Japan, China, Korea, Cambodia, Vietnam, and India are grouped together as Asian. These groupings may facilitate statistical analyses that require a minimum number of people in each group examined, but they fail to account for differences among subgroups along socially and theoretically meaningful variables, such as socioeconomic status and level of acculturation (e.g., Linville, Fischer, & Salovey, 1989). Multiethnic people add further to the challenge of categorization (see Root, 1996; Kerwin & Ponterotto, 1995; Williams, 1999). In recognition of biracial and multiethnic people, the 2000 U.S. census allowed respondents to check *all* ethnic categories to which they belonged, an option chosen by 7 million people, or 2.5% of the population (U.S. Bureau of the Census, 2001). This change makes quantitative analysis of the census data much more complex.

The challenges of accounting for diversity are significant. The perspectives of women, people of color, individuals with disabilities, and others have been under-represented not only in mainstream scientific publications, but in community psychology journals as well (e.g., Angelique & Culley, 2000; Serrano-Garcia & Bond, 1994; Loo, Fong, & Iwamasa, 1988). Community psychologists have proposed guidelines to facilitate research with disenfranchised populations, such as involving diverse stakeholders in the research process from beginning to end, attending to the meaning behind group categorization, and choosing from (and developing) a wide variety of methods (Hughes et al., 1993; Vega, 1992).

Research and Social Change. Community psychology's emphasis on social change also puts researchers at odds with a strict positivist view of science. In the words of Seymour Sarason (1986), "because community psychology reflected and required, in part at least, an activist stance, it would not be viewed by academic psychology as fitting in with psychology's picture of the neutral, objective, fact-finding, theory-building researcher" (p. 405).

Community psychologists generally do not conduct **basic research,** which is designed to test hypotheses and add to the body of scientific knowledge. Some favor **applied research,** which has clear and purposeful implications for social intervention. Others advocate more radical approaches. In his presidential address to Division 27, Ed Seidman (1988) held that community psychologists should conduct **action research** that, unlike either applied or basic research, challenges the status quo and promotes social change.

The term *action research* is often traced to the influential work of social psychologist Kurt Lewin (Lewin, 1948; Lewin, 1951; see also Argyris, Putnam, & Smith, 1985; Dewey, 1946). Lewin posited that researchers do not learn best by objectively studying the world from a distance. Rather, we gain insight by rolling up our sleeves, trying to make a difference in the world, and documenting the change process as it unfolds. Knowledge accumulates through continuous cycles of planning, acting, observing the effects of one's actions, and using the observed results to plan anew (see Figure 7.1). Lewin's research model challenged prevailing perspectives that pitted science against practice. Lewin saw the two as complementary.

Research and a Strengths-Based Approach. "Action research" has become an exceedingly popular term to describe a variety of applied research projects. These projects do not necessarily challenge the status quo and may even proceed from traditional paradigms that objectify the people who provide data. In the logical positivist tradition, the individuals studied are not seen as unique and competent contributors to the research process. They are, instead, a necessary means to the data, and the data are what *really* matter. Research subjects are anonymous, interchangeable, silent, and subservient to the experimenters (Fawcett, 1991; Madigan, Johnson, & Linton, 1995). Such a view is

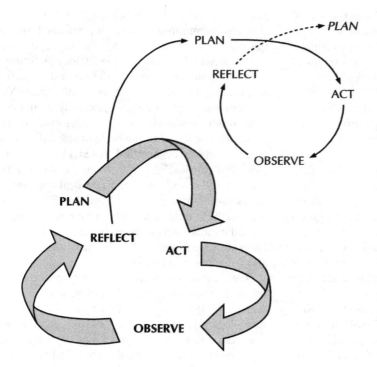

Figure 7.1

The cycle of research and action: plan, act, observe, reflect, then plan again.

inconsistent with the fifth guiding principle of community psychology—a focus on the strengths and capabilities of the people we seek to understand and assist.

In psychology, the term *research participant*[1] has replaced the term *subject*. (American Psychological Association, 1994). The new term suggests that people in studies are active contributors—*participants* in the research process. Those who take this notion most to heart advocate **participatory research**. Participatory research has been defined as more radical than action research (Brown & Tandon, 1983). The approach emerged in the 1970s from work with oppressed people in developing countries and was greatly influenced by the writings of

South American philosopher and educator Paulo Freire (Smith, 1997; Yeich, 1996). It was designed to enhance the psychological and political power of oppressed people by providing a forum for members of dominated or subordinated populations to articulate their own points of view (Hall, 1993). Participatory research entails a democratization of information. Knowledge is no longer under the purview of learned professors in white lab coats and other members of the educated elite, but belongs to everyone—stay-at-home mothers concerned about the potability of their drinking water or youth in high-crime neighborhoods determined to make their streets safer (Gaventa, 1993; Park, 1993).

Participatory research overlaps conceptually with *empowerment research* (e.g., Rappaport, 1990; Fetterman, Kaftarian, & Wandersman, 1996) and *feminist research* (e.g., Bond, Hill, Mulvey, & Terenzio, 2000). All of these types of research appeal to community psychologists in that they reject the myth of scientific objectivity, appreciate the complexity of social reality, advocate social action, attend to the voices of

[1]The term *research participant* is also used in this text, but it is not an ideal term. It refers only to the people of interest to researchers and not to the researchers themselves, who are co-participants in the research process. Distance between the examined and the examiner is therefore retained.

Calvin and Hobbes   by Bill Watterson

Unlike traditional academic researchers, participatory researchers do not exclude community members through esoteric jargon. CALVIN AND HOBBES © Watterson. Reprinted with permission of UNIVERSAL PRESS SYNDICATE. All rights reserved.

disenfranchised people, and foster community ownership of the research process (e.g., Yeich, 1996).

In participatory research, the disenfranchised people of concern to researchers do not simply supply the data or comment on questionnaires. They set the research agenda, define the research questions, interpret the findings, and disseminate results (Gaventa, 1993). This requires a shift in perspective for everyone involved. The research participants, who have been imbued with traditional ideas about science as a professional activity, may hesitate to take ownership of the research process (Serrano-Garcia, 1990). Meanwhile, the researcher must learn to relinquish control and the expert role. Geoffrey Nelson and his colleagues suggested numerous mechanisms for promoting participatory research, including:

- Establish research steering committees that include those affected by the research.
- Hire those affected by the research to conduct the studies.
- Locate and collaborate with group(s) who can use the research findings for education and advocacy.
- Encourage the development of authentic and supportive relationships among all participants. (Nelson et al., 1998)

General Implications of the Guiding Principles. The guiding principles affect how community psychologists conduct research. We recognize the need for methods that embrace subjectivity, honor the voices of diverse participants, consider ecology at multiple levels, have the potential to build individual and community strengths, and encourage more just social relationships. Although methodologies based in the logical positivist tradition have their place, new methodologies or ways of studying issues of interest are of paramount importance (Denzin & Lincoln, 2000; Speer et al., 1992; Tolan et al., 1990; Walsh, 1987).

Many community psychologists have come to rely on qualitative research techniques (see Guba & Lincoln, 1994; Miller & Banyard, 1998). **Qualitative research** attempts to capture the richness and complexity of people's lived experience (Gilbert, 2001; Miles & Huberman, 1984; Patton, 1987). This contrasts with logical positivism's emphasis on **quantitative research,** which reduces complex phenomenon to numerical values that are statistically analyzed in order to support or refute predetermined hypotheses. Quantitative techniques are preferable when all the cases studied "fall in line," a requirement that is often not met in community research where the particularities of context and social position are integral to our questions of interest (Rapkin & Luke, 1993). Another way of distinguishing qualitative and quantitative research is that quantitative research is about counting while qualitative research is about conversing (Stewart, 2000). Many alternative methodologies employed by community psychologists, such as ethnographies (Fetterman, 1998), oral histories (Kelly, 2001), narratives (Rappaport, 1990, 1995), and dialogic methods (e.g., Keiffer, 1984; Bond, Belenky, & Weinstock, 2000) rely on conversation and story telling (see also the *Promise of Community Psychology* section on page 352).

WHERE SCIENCE MEETS ACTION

The preceding discussion highlights the challenges community psychology's guiding principles present to the science of psychology. Academically based community psychologists not only put the guiding principles into effect by pursuing science in a new way, but they also have one foot firmly planted in the world of action. There are many forums for academic psychologists to engage in community practice. Two common applied activities are developing and evaluating community programs and using social science research to inform legal and policy decisions.

Program Development and Evaluation A common applied activity for many academically oriented community psychologists is program development and evaluation (e.g., O'Donnell & Ferrari, 2000). Community psychologists have implemented and assessed countless research-based intervention programs. Several books examine effective interventions in detail, such as *14 Ounces of Prevention: A Casebook for Practitioners* (Price, Cowen, Lorion, & Ramos-McKay, 1988) and *Primary Prevention Works* (Albee & Gullotta, 1997). Many programs summarized in these books are described throughout this textbook. For example, I describe the STEP program, which organized school structures to facilitate students' transition to high school, and the ICPS program to teach interpersonal problem-solving skills to preschoolers. The Community Intervention boxes that appear in each chapter also describe innovative programs, many of which have

been developed and/or evaluated by community psychologists (in this chapter, for example, I describe the development and evaluation of George Fairweather's program for people with mental illness).

Program evaluation is conventionally seen as falling into two categories (e.g., Scheirer, 1994; Wholey, Hatry, & Newcomer, 1994). **Process evaluations** (also called *formative evaluations*) monitor and measure the delivery of the program during implementation. **Outcome evaluations** (also called *summative evaluations*) occur at the end of a program cycle and assess the program's success in meeting its goals. Program evaluations may also include a **cost-benefit analysis**, which determines whether the planned intervention was a fiscally sound one. Do the benefits of the program in comparison to other possible interventions justify its costs?

Evaluations hold the program accountable to funders and to the larger community (Brown, 1995). They can also build a setting's capacity. Dialogues among researchers, setting members, and community stakeholders that occur during the course of a program evaluation can help staff gain insight about how to intervene effectively. Setting capacity is also increased when the staff learns to conduct its own evaluation research.

Program evaluation also adds to the larger body of knowledge about community change. A strong research base generated from a multitude of evaluations has allowed scholars to draw conclusions about what makes an intervention effective. Successful programs offer a broad spectrum of services, transcend traditional professional boundaries, remove bureaucratic barriers to service delivery, consider the contexts in which individuals live, provide comprehensive and easy-to-use services, are run by skilled staff members who truly care about and respect the people served, and have a clear mission and long-term goals (Schorr, 1988, 1997).

Because community evaluations serve several functions, evaluators cannot rely on research skills alone. Effective program evaluators need to have several competencies. They must have pedagogical skills so that they can teach setting members to become their own evaluators. Political skills help community researchers assess and address the multiple and potentially conflicting interests of various stakeholders. Interpersonal skills are needed to gain the stakeholders' trust and sustain their commitment to the program development and evaluation process (Brown 1995).

Research with Policy Implications. Many community psychologists who work in academic settings (as well as applied community psychologists in various settings) become involved in policymaking (e.g., Melton, 1995, 2000; Perkins, 1988; Phillips, 2000; Solarz, 2000; Wilcox, 2000; Wursten & Sales, 1988). Often, this means conducting research with legal and policy implications. For example, Deborah Phillips and her colleagues (1992) assessed how the stringency of state childcare regulations and compliance with these regulations affected the quality of caregiving environments. Leonard Jason and colleagues (1999) studied how the enforcement of laws prohibiting youth access to tobacco affects the prevalence of smoking. Psychologists who conduct policy-relevant research may have opportunities to offer expert testimony in Congress or in the courtroom, as Jason did (Jason, 1999; see also Greenberger, 1983).[2] Community psychologists involved in policy arenas may not only conduct original research but also summarize the legal and policy implications of other people's research. The Public Policy Office of the American Psychological Association (APA),[3] for example, prepares policy-relevant briefs on a wide variety of issues—mental and physical health, education, and poverty to name a few. For example, Allison Rosenberg and her colleagues summarized a policy agenda to combat homelessness (e.g., Rosenberg, Solarz, and Bailey, 1991).

Psychologists interested in influencing policy must translate research into a form usable by public officials (e.g., Fiske, Bersoff, Borgida, Deaux, and

Heilman, 1991). First, we must learn to be brief. Academic audiences want to know about sample composition, methodology, confounding variables, and other factors that could affect results. Policy audiences do not. Meticulous and verbose professional reports are not read by public officials who have only minutes—even seconds—to review briefs or hear testimony (e.g., Lawrence, Phillips, & Rundquist, 1993). In addition, social science research is based on probabilities and is bound by its reliance on particular samples, methods, and theories. Thus, psychologists are trained to present both sides of issues and not to take stands (i.e. to be "objective"). Public decision-makers, however, need to make decision and want to hear what the research suggests they do (Perkins, 1988).

In order to bridge the gap between research and action, psychologists in policy and legal worlds need to make brief, engaging, and memorable research presentations with the major points clearly identified and recommended actions specified (Wursten & Sales, 1988). They must also realize that one-shot briefings are unlikely to be effective. "Ideas must percolate in the policy process before they obtain enough support from relevant interest groups and key decision makers to result in action" (Melton, 1995, p. 769; see also Lindblom and Cohen, 1979). Social policy is a diffuse, imprecise, and largely unpredictable process (Loftus, 1991; Seekins, Maynard-Moody, & Fawcett, 1987; Vincent, 1990). Deborah Phillips (2000) described it as a human drama with the requisite unfolding plot and diverse cast of characters.

Social science research can affect legislative decisions, however. The research of Kenneth and Mamie Clark played a prominent role in the Supreme Court's 1954 ruling that segregation in the schools was unconstitutional. This decision signaled the potential role of psychological research in legal decisions (e.g., Haney, 1993; Perkins, 1988). Since the 1960s, conservative and liberal judges alike have recognized the importance of social science data (Melton, 2000).

Some community psychologists engage in the policy process in order to broaden the impact of their research. They believe that intervening at higher levels is more effective because "working strictly

---

[2]Some community psychologists leave academia to spend time on Capitol Hill, often through the APA Congressional Fellowship Program. On the Hill, academic psychologists assess and summarize research that bears on policy decisions and work to get desired legislation passed (e.g., Wilcox, 2000).
[3]The website of APA's Public Policy Office is *http://www.apa.org/ppo/*.

within the confines of a community may ultimately limit the scope of an intervention" (Wursten & Sales, 1988, p. 488). The notion that top-down policy interventions inspire more wide-ranging changes is arguable (e.g., Fox, 1993; Haney, 1993) as is the assumption that policy does indeed operate in a top-down fashion. Phillips (2000) noted that policies around domestic violence, for example, occur at all levels, from court-mandated treatment of individual offenders to income support legislation and public education campaigns.

Social problems are multiply determined. Thus, effective interventions can address the problem at a variety of levels. One can, for example, volunteer to help a battered woman obtain her GED, fundraise for the local shelter, and/ or lobby for anti-violence legislation. Top-down and bottom-up approaches are by no means mutually exclusive. Michael Fullan (1999) noted that

> you can't mandate local commitment and capacity, but mandates do matter. They put needed pressure on local reform, and they provide opportunities for legitimizing the efforts of local change agents working against the grain. . . Top-down mandates and bottom-up energies need each other. (p. 19)

All levels of the social context affect behavior, and community psychologists in courtrooms and hearing rooms open up new opportunities for social change.

THE APPLIED SIDE OF COMMUNITY PSYCHOLOGY

Although the published literature of community psychology emphasizes the academic side of the discipline, it is our work in the field that makes us community psychologists. In receiving a Division 27 award for his applied work, David Chavis (1993) observed that, "If we are a profession, then we must define our place of action" (p. 179). He advised that our values, theories, and research do not house families, provide teenage mothers with daycare and

jobs, or prevent young men of color from crowding the jails. "Only a practice of community psychology can show the difference our field can make" (1993, p. 179). Although academically based community psychologists engage in applied activities as part of their professional work, community psychology practitioners are based in applied settings and focus on the practice side of community psychology.

There are almost as many job descriptions for applied community psychologists as there are applied community psychologists. In this section, we explore three commonly identified roles for community psychologists in applied settings: consultant, creator of new settings, and community organizer/coalition builder. Although academic community psychologists may assume these roles as part of their professional work, these three roles provide opportunities for employment outside of academia.

The three roles are both overarching and overlapping. For example, in 1971, Ira Goldenberg wrote a classic book on his efforts to establish a Residential Youth Center (RYC) for low-income adolescents. RYC was an innovative center that employed a nonprofessional staff and utilized a horizontal, nonhierarchical organizational structure. It promoted close relationships among youth, families, and staff, and emphasized the development of community resources. Initially, Goldenberg worked as a creator of this setting but later operated as a consultant.

CONSULTATION

In 1970 Gerald Caplan distinguished four models of consultation (see also Mannino & Shore, 1972). *Client-centered* consultations help individuals better meet the needs of other individuals. A client-centered consultant might help a teacher design a learning program for a student with reading difficulties, for example, or help a clinical psychologist work more effectively with a client in an abusive relationship. Consultee-centered consultations help an individual meet the needs of an entire group of similar clients. A *consultee-centered* consultant might help a teacher identify and plan for learning-disabled students in general or sensitize clinical psychologists to the issues of women living with domestic violence. The remaining types of consultation, program-centered administrative consultation and consultee-centered administrative consultation,[+] fall under the rubric of **community consultation.** Community consultation is of central interest to community psychologists. In this type of consultation, the "client" is not an individual (e.g., teacher or psychologist), but an entire program, group, staff, or agency.

A community consultant is sought out and hired by a setting because she or he has some expertise that the setting needs in order to achieve its goals. Community consultants have a variety of competencies. They may be skilled in diagnosing organizational problems and promoting organizational functioning (O'Neill & Trickett, 1982). This might entail, for example, altering the decision-making processes or restructuring organizational charts. Community consultants may have expertise in reducing conflict among subgroups, perhaps helping agencies address racial and other tensions. As one of many examples, the Public Conversations Project in Watertown Massachusetts is a nonprofit organization that uses consultation as a way of facilitating conversations across people's differences (Madsen, 2001; see also ***http://www.publicconversations.org***).

Regardless of the problem of focus, community consultants strive to create change by contributing to the efficacy of an existing setting. Thus, they provide indirect support rather than direct services to clients (Trickett, Barone, & Watts, 2000). Community psychologists consult to a variety of settings: schools, police departments, mental health centers, neighborhood associations. The possibilities are vast. Edward Lichtenstein and his colleagues (1996) described a tobacco control consultation to Northwest Indian tribes. Stephanie Reinharz (1983) described a community consultation to an alternative bakery whose collectivist values of fairness, cooperation, and tolerance interfered with the goal of operating a profitable business.

[+]The main difference between these two types of consultation is that former attempts to address problems around a program or organization while the latter focuses on the professional functioning of the staff.

Characteristics of Community Consultation. The most important feature of community consultation is its system orientation. A community consultant must be sensitive to group processes and networks of relationships within the setting and across settings. The awareness of multilevel contexts promoted by community psychology can serve community consultants well. For example, Edison Trickett and his colleagues (Trickett & Birman, 1989; Trickett et al., 2000) described a consultation with a public school focusing on problems associated with its many foreign-born students. As teachers become more aware of the challenges the students faced, they became more compassionate. Sleeping in class and incomplete homework assignments were no longer attributed to laziness, but to the exhaustion of students who worked long hours after school and on weekends to support themselves and their families. Teachers also became more cognizant of their own pressures, such as the national movement for excellence and accountability in teaching. These pressures augmented the teachers' investment in test scores and reduced their willingness to tolerate poor performance. As a result of community consultation, teachers became more interested in individual students, classroom dynamics, school-wide challenges, and also district policies that impinged on them. Thus, the effects of a community consultation can radiate throughout interrelated systems (Trickett et al., 2000).

On the other hand, the larger ecology of the consultation can also limit effectiveness. Based on their "failed" consultation to a program for adolescent offenders, Dick Reppucci and his colleagues (1973) recommended viewing the target system in broad terms. The small Mountville Camp for offending adolescents, the setting with which the consultants contracted, actually had little authority to enact recommended changes. In retrospect, the consultants believed that they would have achieved more success if the central governing office of the Corrections Department had been involved in the consultation from the beginning.

A second important characteristic of community consultation is that the setting is in charge. Consultants do not issue orders, they dispense advice.

Ideally, this advice should help settings identify, nurture, and develop indigenous resources (Trickett, et al., 2000). The consultant is generally not a regular employee of the agency, and his or her involvement in the setting is usually time-limited. As an outsider, the consultant has a fresh perspective from which to view the organization. Outsider status also allows the consultant a level of honesty in presenting criticisms of policies and practices that insiders in ongoing relationships with each other may not be able to afford.

Stages of Community Consultation. Community consultations generally proceed through four broad stages: entry, diagnosis, implementation, and disengagement (Dougherty, 1990, 2000). Entry activities include negotiating a contract and forming a working alliance. During this stage the setting and consultant establish a foundation of trust from which to build a working alliance. Cultural differences along such dimensions as language, need for personal and professional boundaries, time orientations, and criteria by which "legitimacy" is established can affect the building of rapport (Gibbs, 1980).

Diagnosis involves defining the problem to be addressed by the consultation. Not all members of a setting will agree about what the problem is, why it exists, and how best to address it (perhaps questioning whether the consultant should have been hired at all). A community consultant needs to be aware of varying viewpoints and the possibility that her or his arrival on the scene has been construed as a sign of failure. The community consultant also needs to recognize people's tendency to cast problems in individual or small group terms and ignore

important processes at higher levels (Lachenmeyer, 1992). In the earlier example, teachers' intolerance of foreign student failure stemmed from their framing of the problem at the individual level, such as student laziness. School personnel did not initially see the economic pressures faced by students or the pressures teachers faced as a result of district emphases on test scores (Trickett & Birman, 1989; see also Rappaport, 2000a).

After identifying the problem on which the consultation will focus, consultants help to devise possible solutions. The consultant helps the setting establish a process for evaluating the effects of implemented changes, and making adjustments based on results. Finally, the consultant orchestrates her or his departure, ensuring that the mechanisms to sustain effective changes exist within the setting.

Challenges of Community Consultation. Perhaps the most talked about challenge in community consultation is the conflict between the consultant's values and the values of the setting (e.g., O'Neill & Trickett, 1982). The goal of consultation is to help the setting operate more effectively, and the community consultant must assess whether she or he can do this in good conscience. In some cases the mismatch in values is obvious. Community psychologists would most likely not consult with the Ku Klux Klan. But even when the goals of the setting and the consultant initially seem compatible, different value orientation may later emerge that can undermine the consultation.

A second challenge pertains to the consultant's time commitment. The community consultant's job is to build the setting's strength and reduce its reliance

Community consultants are not distant experts who frame problems in terms of individual deficits. DILBERT reprinted by permission of United Feature Syndicate, Inc.

on outside assistance. This brings up the critical issue of the length of involvement. Edison Trickett (1994) argued that considerable time is required before the helper can understand the local ecology from the inside out and develop the necessary trust. Similarly, Irma Serrano-García (1984) advised that a community psychologist's involvement with settings must be long enough to learn about the local environment, show our commitment, convey our skills, share important information, and perhaps help raise consciousness. She warned, however, that it must not be so long as to foster the setting's dependence on the consultant or burnout in the change agents. One important factor in deciding on length of involvement is the distance between the consultant and the setting. When the consultant and setting differ in terms of race, gender, socioeconomic status (SES), educational background, cultural background, or other important variable, more time may be needed to build an eco-identity and gain trust.

Community consultants work with existing systems. They hope to better social conditions by improving the services provided by settings already in operation. Another potentially more radical approach to community change is the formation of alternative settings (Cherniss & Deegan, 2000).

CREATION OF ALTERNATIVE SETTINGS

In 1972 Seymour Sarason established the creation of alternative settings as an important activity for community psychologists with his influential book entitled, *Creation of Settings and the Future Societies.* Sarason's (1972) notion of a setting was broad. He defined a setting as "any instance in which two or more people come together in new relationships over a sustained period of time in order to achieve certain goals" (p. 1). Setting creation could include everything from marriage to revolution. Community psychologists have helped create settings at different levels—a new program, such as a high school transition program, a new agency, such as an alternative school or woman's shelter, or even a new planned community. A classic example of setting creation in the community psychology literature is George Fairweather's lodge societies, which were

independent residences for people with mental illness (see Community Intervention box). As more recent examples, Susan Yeich and Ralph Levine (1994) helped create a union for homeless people as a vehicle for political action, and Lynne Bond and her colleagues (2000) established support groups for rural mothers of young children who felt unheard, undervalued, alone, and powerless.

Characteristics of Alternative Settings. Not every new setting can be described as an *alternative* setting. Cary Cherniss and Gene Deegan (2000) contended that alternative settings are inherently radical as they propose new and untried ways of addressing social problems. An organization can be radical in a number of ways—organizational structure, goals, ideologies—and so "alternativeness" is best viewed as a multidimensional construct. According to this definition, fundamentalist, authoritarian, and oppressive cults and societies may also be seen as alternative settings (Cherniss & Deegan, 2000). *Alternative* is not synonymous with *progressive.*

Seymour Sarason (1972) identified numerous stages in the creation of settings. A setting's shape is outlined long before its inception by the before-the-beginning context. In the early stages of existence, the setting is shaped by the group's mission. New settings are collectives bound together by a core group's vision and sense of purpose (Sarason, 1972; Senge, 1994). The group's mission defines the existing problem of interest and the preferred means of addressing that problem. New settings form out of dissatisfaction with existing settings, coupled with optimism about the possibility of having a positive effect (Goldenberg, 1971). Subsequent stages in setting creation include the departure of the founding members, the transfer of leadership, the search for a physical space to house the group (which Sarason calls "the tail that wags the dog"), and the setting's possible demise. Many alternative settings do not survive their first year (Cherniss & Deegan, 2000).

Challenges of Alternative Settings. A key challenge for alternative settings that survive is how to become established while remaining radical (Cherniss & Deegan, 2000; Heller, Price, Reinharz,

COMMUNITY INTERVENTION:

George Fairweather's Lodge Societies
Designing, Implementing, and Disseminating Alternative Settings

In the 1960s (no surprise about that time frame!) George Fairweather helped create an alternative setting for formerly institutionalized psychiatric patients. His goal was to develop community living arrangements, called **lodge societies,** where ex-patients lived in self-governing and self-sustaining homes. Before entering the lodges, future residents were taught basic survival skills, such as meal planning and home maintenance, as well as skills for making group decisions, such as how to initiate and carry out vote taking. Residents were also helped to find and maintain jobs in the community, often doing janitorial and gardening work. After this period of preparation, lodge members came together to make a home. Fairweather found that residents were indeed able to take charge of their daily routines, rotate responsibility for the upkeep of the lodge, and support themselves within the community.

According to Fairweather, three groups needed to be involved in any effort to address a social problem: representatives of the "problem" population, social administrators who represented the larger society, and social scientists who had the skills to help these two groups create and evaluate the effort (Fairweather, 1979). He contended that only with careful study could the target populations and administrators know that the alternative social programs accomplished what they intended. Fairweather's work with lodge societies is remarkable not only because he helped devise and implement an innovative approach to working with people with mental illness, but also because he went further and both evaluated his effort *and* attempted to disseminate this innovation.

In evaluating the lodge societies, Fairweather and his colleagues adhered to strict scientific standards (e.g., use of a control group that did not live in lodge societies, random assignment to treatment or control group conditions). A comprehensive 40-month follow-up of the lodge program documented striking improvements over other residential settings for people with mental illness (Fairweather, 1979; Fairweather, Sanders, Maynard, & Cressler, 1969). Lodge participants were more likely to remain in the community. They spent, on average, 80% of their time in community settings, as compared to less than 20% for residents of the other settings. Lodge members returned less often to institutional care. In addition, lodge residents were frequently employed (between 40% and 80% of the time) while members of the control group were rarely employed (less than 5% of the time). Although implementation of the lodge program required funds initially, the lodge members' employment enabled the lodges to become self-sustaining. All other intervention strategies for people with mental illness entailed substantial costs—even at that time, psychiatric hospitalization cost as much as $55 per day per resident. Fairweather and his colleagues assessed a variety of other important outcomes, as well. For example, they surveyed the attitudes and actions of community neighbors as well as lodge participants and found that each group evaluated the other more positively over time.

Fairweather and his colleagues then went one important step further. They used research to increase the chances that this new and successful alternative setting would serve as a model in other locales. Fairweather knew that organizational change was difficult and that "all organizations are established to maintain the status quo" (Fairweather, 1979; p. 323). Thus, it was no surprise that despite overwhelming evidence of the efficacy of lodge societies, widespread adoption of the model did not occur automatically. Only two initial attempts were made to replicate Fairweather's lodges, and these replicas were found to be even *more* effective than the prototype lodge Fairweather had developed.

Thus, Fairweather launched a campaign to disseminate his findings and encourage the adoption of the lodge model by others. Once again, he carefully documented his efforts. The dissemination experiment involved 97% of all mental hospitals in the United States (255 hospitals) and lasted for five years. Various persuasive techniques were assessed, such as written information, workshops, and demonstrations. Fairweather (1979) concluded that:

- The social status of the gatekeeper initially approached in the hospital made little difference. Nurses could be as influential as managers, provided they had a positive view of the program.
- Social action consultants knowledgeable about the program were essential in order to help interested hospitals succeed in adopting the program.
- Active demonstration of the program was more persuasive than any written communication.

Many professionals limit their role to developing model programs and assessing their efficacy. They spend relatively little energy trying to understand and overcome the numerous barriers to the adoption of model programs (Schorr, 1997). Inspiring visions and a sense of hope do not inevitably lead to change. George Fairweather provided an excellent model of how one's commitment to social change requires active efforts to counteract the tendency for societal structures to preserve the status quo.

Riger, Wandersman, & D'Aunno, 1984; Woliver, 1996). Many alternative settings that survive the first year lose their radical edge as they confront the need to establish reliable sources of funding, coexist with other settings, and develop structures that promote organizational functioning.

Survival requires the generation of a secure funding base. In their enthusiasm about meeting individual and community needs in new ways, members of alternative settings may initially fail to attend to important, if seemingly mundane organizational tasks, such as fundraising. If alternative settings do not have funding, they cannot hire qualified staff or enough staff to provide the needed services. In order to obtain funding, settings may need to engage in activities that threaten their status as alternative. For example, Stephanie Riger (2001) described her efforts to help domestic violence and sexual assault programs attract funding by documenting their efficacy. This led programs to focus on outcomes that were readily measured and easily improved. They concentrated, for example, on ensuring that women developed safety plans and on increasing the number of counseling hours. This personal change orientation, while easily documented, detracted from the original and more radical social change mission of reducing the incidence of violence against women.

Coexistence with other settings provides additional challenges to alternative settings. An independent attitude may be helpful early in the settings history, but in later stages collaboration with other agencies correlates with legitimacy, support, and longevity (Trickett, 1991). A superior or hostile attitude toward existing groups (e.g., welfare agencies, the police) may initially inspire a setting's creation and fuel a sense of mission, but it ultimately fosters competition and can contribute to the setting's demise (Sarason, 1972; Cherniss & Deegan, 2000). From a practical perspective, foundations and government funders now require collaborative ties with other agencies (Chavis, 2001). From a more visionary perspective, alternative settings may find that larger social change goals, such as ending domestic violence or homelessness, are best achieved in coalition with others.

The third challenge to sustainability is developing an organizational structure that allows the setting to survive and thrive. Research suggests that setting members appreciate formal structures (Wandersman & Florin, 2000). This contrasts with the "consensual anarchy" that often dominates in the early phases of the setting's life span (Holleb & Abrams, 1975). Some organizations retain a feeling of anarchy. Some activist-led AIDS organizations, for example, strive to be democratic and share leadership to the extent that they fail to work toward clear goals or have a meaningful identity.

The good news is that some alternative settings survive and succeed in maintaining their radical edge. A study of rape crisis centers found that centers formed at the peak of the antirape movement (1978 or earlier) remained more radical than those formed in the more politically conservative era that followed. The older centers were more often freestanding collectives that espoused social change values, engaged in social change activities, and adopted participatory decision-making processes at all levels of operation (Campbell et al., 2000). Factors that affect the likelihood that settings remain antibureaucratic may include a view of the setting as transitory, a definition of the setting as opposing the status quo, a sense of belonging to a larger social movement, and established opportunities for reflection and criticism (Rothschild-Whitt, 1979).

COMMUNITY ORGANIZING AND COALITION BUILDING

To paraphrase Bill Berkowitz, **community organizing** consists of intentional activities to bring community residents together in joint action designed to improve the context of their lives both locally and in the broader society (Berkowitz, 2000a). This has traditionally involved confronting external powers, though it has come to entail strengthening existing resources or developing new community structures (Rothman, 1995).

Bill Berkowitz (2000a) argued that community organizing, as a process for enhancing community life and establishing more equitable social relations in the larger world, ought to spark the interest of community psychologists. It is, however, neither dominant nor even prominent in the field's research, theory, training, or practice. Saul Alinsky's classic primer *Rules for Radicals* (1971) is required reading in many community psychology classes, but community organizing is rarely discussed as a career option in today's world.

Saul Alinsky helped existing community settings (e.g., churches, labor unions) trace the injustices they experienced to a visible enemy and organize confrontational encounters that compelled the enemy to behave more equitably. For example, a store that only hired Blacks for menial jobs was targeted in one of Alinsky's efforts. Alinsky threatened to have three thousand Black people enter the main floor of the store, occupy the attention of all the salespeople, order merchandise COD, and ultimately refuse delivery. The department store responded to this threat by requesting a meeting to discuss personnel changes.

Community organizing traditionally seeks to redistribute social power through confrontation with individuals and social systems that wield control (Speer & Hughey, 1995). In recent decades this approach has changed (e.g., McKnight, 1995). Rates of participation in existing community settings have decreased (e.g., Putnam, 2000), and so they less often serve as a hub for organizing activities. In addition, enemies are less visible and tangible in this era of globalization (e.g., Gamson, 1989). Community organizing around resistance to a common enemy has given way to collaborative efforts that augment neighborhood and community capacity (McKnight, 1995; Gittell & Vidal, 1998). Traditional community organizing has given way to building **community coalition building.** This currently popular community-level change activity brings together groups of diverse community members, organizations, and constituencies to resolve local problems and meet resident needs (Feighery & Rogers, 1989; Wolff, 2001a).

As an early example of community coalition building, Michael Morris and Linda Frisman (1987) described their efforts to establish networks among community groups in Connecticut in order to facilitate the reintegration of youth into the community after the federal government mandated deinstitutionalization of juvenile status offenders. Morris and Frisman held meetings for individuals representing a variety of agencies affected by the new legislation. The meetings were facilitated by a networker who could respond to questions about the legislation, steer the group away from unproductive "gripe sessions," and encourage the exchange of information. These meetings also provided a forum for the recognition of connections that already existed among participants (e.g., "You did a good job with that family I referred to you last month," or "It's nice to match a face with a voice on the phone" [p. 32]).

Morris and Frisman identified several obstacles to the commitment, communication, mutual awareness, and collaborative spirit necessary for community coalitions to function competently. First, individuals within an agency or organization often pursued their own agency's mission with dedication but lacked a broader imperative that would sensitize them to community-wide concerns and the perspectives of other agencies. The lack of identification with the local community and focus only the agenda of one's own agency disrupted the flow of information within the community. For example, a community educator was more likely to discuss the new legislation with a fellow educator who lived in another part of the country rather than with a police officer in her own town. In addition, agencies often saw themselves as competing with other agencies for scarce resources, which further reduced the community's ability to work together as a whole.

The inherently controversial and political nature of community organizing may help explain its neglect as a topic of study in community psychology, but coalition building is not inherently controversial, and this change strategy also remains an understudied example of community psychology practice. Bill Berkowitz (2000a, 2001) proposed that these practices are understudied because they involve complex and multilevel processes that are exceedingly difficult to document. As a result, most of what we currently know about community organizing comes from homemade manuals, booklets, tip sheets, anecdotal accounts, and the popular press (Berkowitz, 2000a; Wolff, 2001b).

It is also true that in these necessarily community-based endeavors, tensions between academia and practice become evident. Alinsky (1971) asserted that professional training makes community organizers less radical; "they organize to get rid of four-legged rats and stop there; we organize to get rid of four-legged rats so that we can get on to removing two-legged rats" (p. 68). Recently, the tension between academia and practice emerged in a special issue of the *American Journal of Community Psychology* dedicated to the Block Boosters Project (see also the Classic Research box on page 337). In addition to articles by the researchers involved in this project, practitioners were invited to present their observations. A block association president wrote of his frustrations over the researchers' emphasis on data collection (Burgess, 1990). A grassroots community organizer noted that tensions, feuds, and

issues of 'turf' arose often (Kaye, 1990). In commenting on this special issue, Richard Price (1990) wrote: "One cannot read these articles without a breathtaking sense of how wide the gulf is between the culture of social science and the culture of community organizing and block leadership" (p. 165).

For community psychologists, however, the gulf between science and practice constitutes a worthy challenge, not an insurmountable stumbling block. Community organizing and coalition building remain largely unexplored, but potentially powerful professional activities for applied—and academic—community psychologists.

⌘ The Promise of Community Psychology: Putting the "Work" into Network

Early in this chapter I discussed the various competencies useful for the work of community psychology. Not explicitly mentioned in that list was an acute interest and investment in human relationships. The desire to spend time with, talk to, learn about, and learn from different people facilitates all that we do as community psychologists.

This is true for academic community psychologists and practitioners alike. Community research, unlike traditional research, requires close relationships between the researcher and the researched. Meg Bond (1990) described community research as a pooling of resources between researcher and participant. These resources are not equivalent, however. The researcher's most important resource is scientific knowledge. The participants' major contribution is their lived experience. Scientific knowledge is viewed by society as more valuable. It is also less personal. The more intimate information contributed by the participants results in a vulnerability that can reinforce the unequal power relationship between researcher and participant (Bond, 1990).

Thus, the community researcher must work to deconstruct the barriers that separate the examiner and the examined (Nelson et al., 1998). More equal and intimate research relationships present new challenges (Perkins & Wandersman 1990; Wicker & Sommer, 1993; Stewart, 2000), but the rewards are immense. Our data are more accurate and more complete, and our research is better valued and utilized. In addition, reciprocal relationships with research participants are often personally rewarding and help us to integrate our personal, professional, and political selves (Nelson et al., 1998).

Community psychology practitioners, too, recognize the importance of deconstructing professional boundaries. Dick Reppucci (1973) and his colleagues advised community consultants to disclaim "the magical aura professionals often either intentionally or unintentionally carry with them" (p. 149). Lisbeth Schorr (1997) noted that "[i]nterventions that are successful with high-risk populations all seem to have staffs with the time and skill to establish relationships based on mutual respect and trust" (p. xxii). In addition, psychologists involved in advocacy activities repeatedly find that networking and personal connections shape the course of a bill or the ruling of a judge (e.g., Greenberger, 1983).

For community psychologists, the boundaries between professional and personal life blur, and the most effective way of entering a community setting may not be a formal display of scholarly knowledge through written or oral presentations. It might be preferable to find ways to let community members get to know the "outsider" a bit and develop a basis for personal relationships *before* focusing on the tasks at hand (Gibbs, 1980).

Effective community psychologists need to develop professional competencies. We also need to take advantage of invaluable opportunities to catch a bite to eat, go for a walk, carpool, or simply tell a joke. Eco-identities may be forged over dinner (e.g., Brody, 1986) and working alliances developed on a fishing trip (Jeffrey & Reeves, 1978; cited in Trickett et al., 2000). As Thomas Wolff (2001b) advised, "post-meeting 'schmoozing' is as critical as the meeting itself" (p. 187), and the community psychologist Kurt Ribisl (2000) resolved, "when I attend conferences, I am committed to always attending the happy hour" (p. 99).

Action Agenda

Qualities Inventory

Review the eight qualities for a community psychologist described in this chapter. Which ones come easiest to you? Which ones present challenges? What ideas do you have about how best to capitalize on your strengths? What ideas do you have about how best to compensate for or eliminate your weaknesses? What can you do personally? What can you do in your collaborations with others? Think about the sorts of community psychology jobs that appeal to you. How do your areas of strengths and challenges match the demands of potential jobs?

What Kind of Job?

People who study community psychology are often asked, "What kind of a job would you get?" The job title "community psychologist" rarely appears in classified advertisements. Jobs do exist, of course, but community psychologists need to think creatively about where our skills and interests can best be utilized.

Conduct a mock job search to identify the range of jobs appropriate for someone trained in community psychology. This exercise might take place across the semester. Clip and copy classified advertisements and position announcements from various sources. What sorts of titles and settings would you look for? How would you locate job openings (newspapers, on-line directories, personal networking)? What experiences would you stress on a job application for each of the potential jobs you find? What additional educational experiences do you think would strengthen your application to those jobs that most appeal to you?

Here are a few job descriptions that I have clipped:

> COMMUNITY SERVICES REPRESENTATIVE: This highly visible and challenging position acts as a liaison between the State Hospital and the local community. . .
>
> COUNSELOR: A non-profit agency seeks energetic individual to co-facilitate drop out prevention/leadership program for high school females. . .
>
> PARENT INVOLVEMENT COORDINATOR: Parent involvement coordinator wanted to implement the parent involvement component of a Head Start program. . .
>
> EXECUTIVE DIRECTOR: Needed for developing Children's Advocacy Center to provide services relating to child abuse including outreach and family support services, volunteer management, team leadership, and grant writing. . .

Students in community psychology who are conducting or are about to conduct real job searches might read the article *Practicing What We Preach: Integrating Community Psychology into the Job Search Process* (Campbell, Angelique, BootsMiller, & Davidson, 2000). This chapter describes a job club formed to support community psychologists in their search for employment after graduation.

Shadow a Practitioner

Identify someone whom you believe embodies the characteristics of a community psychologist and/or does the kind of work community psychologists do. Arrange to follow that person throughout the day. You might want to call on the networks of classmates, friends, and teachers in identifying and approaching possible candidates to shadow. If possible, arrange to observe this person at work and also interview him or her with regard to the issues raised in this chapter: What personal characteristics help the person to succeed at work? Are there any key experiences that made him or her want to do this job (such as Lambert's overheard conversation on the bus, [see section on *Metabolic Balance Between Patience and Zeal*])? How does the person's current job fit into his or her career path (educational background, job history, future goals)? Which, if any, of the five principles of community psychology guide this person's work? Do you think you could (or would want to) do what this person does? Why or why not?

Key Terms

action research

applied research

basic research

community coalition building

community consultation

community organizing

confounding variables

cost-benefit analysis

dependent variable

eco-identity

ecological validity

emic approach

etic approach

independent variable

lodge societies

logical positivism

outcome evaluation

participatory research

planned obsolescence

process evaluation

qualitative research

quantitative research

reliability

social position

stakeholders

CHAPTER 8

Conceptualizing Difference

Nancy A. Wonders

Despite the critical role that difference plays within the criminal justice system, it is rare for either practitioners or scholars to spend time investigating difference. It is often taken for granted that the differences between people are natural and obvious and, therefore, uncontroversial. Yet, little about difference is actually either natural or obvious. And difference is far from uncontroversial. Over the last decade, there has been an explosion of work on difference and identity. This scholarly work has highlighted the complex nature of difference; it also contains lessons that are invaluable for those seeking to understand the place of difference within the criminal justice system.

In this chapter, I outline some of the important insights about difference that have emerged from the contemporary literature on difference and identity. My objectives are to explore "difference" as a topic of study, to forge conceptual links between the concept of difference and justice issues, and to introduce some of the common themes regarding difference that are discussed in the chapters in this volume. The subsections that follow offer answers to these questions: What is difference, and where does it come from? Why do some differences matter, while others do not? What is the relationship between law and difference? Why study difference within the field of criminal justice?

DIFFERENCE IS SOCIALLY CONSTRUCTED

Most people think that the most important differences between individuals are fundamentally biological. Race, ethnicity, sexual orientation, gender, age, and even social class are frequently viewed as inherited traits—what sociologists call *ascribed characteristics*. In this view, people are "black" because they were born with dark skin; "white" because their skin is lighter in color. People are designated "female" or "male" because they are born with particular genitalia. What is most interesting about biology, however, is not how different we all are from each other, but rather how remarkably similar most people are in both design and function.

Indeed, the biological differences that do exist between people rarely matter in themselves; instead, they are made to matter through the process of social interaction. To say that *difference is socially constructed*, then, is to say that the meaning attached to difference, including biological difference, is created by people in interaction with each other. From this perspective, difference is a social process that can be understood only historically, contextually, and culturally—we are all "doing difference" all the time (West and Fenstermaker, 2002). To reiterate an earlier point, "difference" is the term used to describe the social and cultural *meanings* attached to human variation.

Of course, there are biological differences between us. Some people have larger noses, smaller feet, larger breasts, or lighter skin. However, biological differences do not come with instructions telling us how to deal with or respond to them. In fact, if biology were destiny, we probably would not spend so much time and money dressing our boys in blue and our girls in pink, because boys would be "naturally" masculine and girls "naturally" feminine, regardless of the color of their clothes or other markers used to signify their sex to the rest of the world. Nor would Jews have been made to wear yellow stars during World War II so that they could be identified easily. Nor would we emphasize the importance of eating certain kinds of traditional foods or engaging in particular cultural celebrations. Instead, we put enormous energy into constructing and enforcing gender, ethnic, sexual orientation, race, and other differences as a kind of insurance against "nature." Race, ethnicity, social class, sexual orientation, and even age reflect the *meaning* we give them rather than natural facts about our biology. Some additional examples may help to illustrate this point.

Today, it is frequently assumed that women are naturally more interested than men in fashion and beauty, and that these interests are associated with femininity and femaleness. It is important to remember, however, that in Victorian England, it was men who wore wigs, high heels, stockings, and frilly blouses. Instead of exhibiting femininity, this set of differences was strongly associated with masculinity and power. Only "real men" wore wigs! Biology is clearly not destiny. For this reason, many scholars (e.g., Lorber, 2007) find it useful to make a distinction between "sex" and "gender": *sex* refers to human variations in bodies, hormones, genitalia, and reproductive abilities (which have relatively limited consequence since reproduction directly affects only a small portion of the human life cycle), whereas *gender* refers to the social characteristics, statuses, and legal identities that have come to be loosely associated with sex (e.g., femininity and masculinity). Sexual variation exists, but it is the meaning that is made out of that variation through the construction of gender that has the greatest consequence for individual life chances. Importantly, children must be taught how to act in gender-appropriate ways. The behaviors associated with each gender, however, have changed over time as society has changed, and are not determined by biological differences. History reveals that:

> Sex categorization involves no well-defined set of criteria that must be satisfied to identify someone; rather, it involves treating appearances (e.g., deportment, dress, and bearing) as if they were indicative of an underlying state of affairs (e.g., anatomical, hormonal, and chromosomal arrangements). The point worth stressing here is that, while sex category serves as an "indicator" of sex, it does not depend on it. Societal members will "see" a world populated by two and only two sexes, even in public situations that preclude inspection of the physiological "facts." . . . Gender, we argue, is a situated accomplishment of societal members, the local management of conduct in relation to normative conceptions of appropriate attitudes and activities for particular sex categories. From this perspective, gender is not merely an individual attribute but something that is accomplished in interaction with others. (West and Fenstermaker, 2002: 65)

In other words, we are all constantly "doing gender" by acting in ways that signal to others how we ought to be categorized and by reacting to others in ways that define them as "male" or "female" (Fenstermaker and West, 2002). We "do" gender every day by dressing, sitting, talking, and acting in ways that create and reinforce gendered patterns of behavior. In fact, we are often confused and bothered by individuals who do not act consistently with our own expectations of appropriate "female" or "male" behavior, or whose dress or physical features seem inconsistent with their gendered behavior; for example, women who are unusually tall or masculine or men who are unusually petite. Indeed, such inconsistencies have often led to prejudice and discrimination against individuals in the justice system and in the larger society for their failure to communicate their sex and gender "appropriately" and consistently with dominant expectations (Belknap, 2007).

Similarly, it was often assumed historically that race reflected biological differences between people. Yet, the anthropological evidence is clear that race is not a biological difference; there are no genetic markers that clearly differentiate where "white" or "black" begins. Instead, *race* is a social construction, given meaning by people in the context of social interaction and history (Ore, 2008; Winant, 2004). Pieter-Dirk Uys (1988), a satirist from South Africa, illustrates the historic flexibility of race in the following remarks, which appeared in the *New York Times*:

> Let me quote from one of our few remaining daily newspapers, the Government Gazette: "Nearly 800 South Africans became officially members of a different race group last year, according to figures quoted in Parliament and based on the Population Registration Act. They included 518 colored who were officially reclassified as white, 14 whites who became colored, 7 Chinese who became white, 2 whites who became Chinese, 3 Malays who became white, 1 white who became an Indian, 50 Indians who became colored, 54 coloreds who became Indian, 17 Indians who became Malay, 4 coloreds who became Chinese, 1 Malay who became Chinese, 89 blacks who became colored, 5 coloreds who became black." I couldn't make it up if I tried.

This example illustrates the changing nature of race over time and the fact that racial categorization depends heavily upon who is doing the defining. A person considered black in the United States may not be considered so in South Africa or in Brazil; "indeed, some U.S. blacks may be considered white in Brazil" (Telles, 2006:79). Throughout history, race as a category of meaning has changed to fit changing circumstances. Like gender, the meaning of race is constructed through human interaction.

Ethnicity, or socially constructed cultural affiliation, is similar in this regard, as evidenced by the historical process by which immigrants to the United States, particularly non-Hispanic whites, were able to transform themselves from Italian, Irish, or Japanese ethnic groups into "Americans" and more specifically into "White" Americans (Roediger, 2006). The fact that ethnic and racial identities reflect a long process of historical construction was explicitly recognized in the year 2000 when the U.S. Census, our national strategy for counting race and ethnicity, moved beyond the six racial categories listed and allowed individuals to check more than one category of identification, creating a new "multiracial" category. Research has found that individuals who self-identify in one racial group but who are routinely misclassified by others experience adverse psychological consequences (Campbell, 2007). Thus, because ethnicity and race have been made to matter in our society, it is important to respect how individuals *self*-identify.

Even social class differences cannot be explained merely by external variation in wealth or income. *Social class* is also a social construction linked to history and culture, and one's class identity can be understood only in relationship to others. Social class is evidenced through barometers such as material success and social location in the economic system, but it is also characterized by the presence or absence of particular styles of speech, behaviors, and attitudes. As Langston (2004:141) argues, "class is also culture":

> . . . class is how you think, feel, act, look, dress, talk, move, walk; class is what stores you shop at, restaurants you eat in; class is the schools you attend, the education you attain; class is the very jobs you will work at throughout your adult life. We experience class at every level of our lives; class is who our friends are, where we live and work even what kind of car we drive, if we own one, and what kind of health care we receive, if any. Have I left anything out? In other words, class is socially constructed and all encompassing. When we experience classism, it will be because of our lack of money (i.e., choices and power in this society) and because of the way we talk, think, act, move—because of our culture.

Because class is cultural, individuals who are poor have a difficult time becoming middle class even when they obtain more money. Being middle class means learning how to "act" middle class—to "walk the walk" and "talk the talk." Growing up poor creates a distinct cultural disadvantage given that "proper" behavior, dress, and linguistic style in much of the world of work and within the justice system is determined by those from higher social classes. There is a well-documented history of discrimination against lower-class individuals within the criminal justice system, beginning with the creation of laws specifically designed to control the "dangerous classes" and affecting virtually every stage of the criminal justice system (Reiman, 2006; Shelden, 2007). As will be illustrated later in this volume, the price for class differences can be high.

As these examples illustrate, the construction of difference reflects an historical process of human interaction and negotiation. All differences have a cultural component that carries enormous weight in shaping attitudes and behavior. In this sense, who others "think" we are may matter more than who we "really" are. This is a particularly important point for justice workers. Police officers may think of themselves as caring citizens trying to help others, but this matters little if citizens "think" police officers are "pigs" and, therefore, act toward them with hostility. A young man wearing baggy pants and a bandanna may think of himself as a hardworking student, loving son, or good friend, while others consider him to be only a gangbanger. Being regarded as "black" or "white," "gay" or "straight," or "female or male" carries the weight of the culture behind it. For this reason, it is important to realize that saying that difference is socially constructed is not the same thing as saying that individuals construct their own identities. We each have some control over how we will be viewed in the world, but mostly the identity choices available to us result from *structured social inequality*-which is to say that our choices are constrained and structured by our culture, the historical time period into which we are born into, previous patterns of inequality, social institutions, and where in the society we are located. You might think of yourself as without a race or gender, for example, but try getting everyone else to treat you that way and see how far you get!

Understanding that difference is socially constructed is a critical first step toward ensuring justice in a democratic society. We all bear some responsibility for the differences between us, and for the real consequences those differences have for human lives. It is especially important for those who work in the justice system to understand the role they play in giving differences meaning and making some differences matter.

DIFFERENCE ASSUMES A NORM OR STANDARD THAT REFLECTS POWER RELATIONS AND PRIVILEGE WITHIN THE CULTURE

Because differences are socially constructed though a process of human interaction, power plays an important role in determining how differences will be defined and which differences will be made to matter. Not surprisingly, some people have more *power* to define differences than do others. In general, history evidences a process whereby those with greater power become the standard of comparison against whom everyone else is measured. It is through this process that difference comes to have meaning.

Difference can only exist where there is a *norm* or standard against which everyone else is compared. Difference always implies a contrast and frequently it depends upon the construction of a two-part *dichotomy*.

Difference is constructed when a continuum is turned into a dichotomy, such that one part of the dichotomy is represented as better than the other. So we take the continuum of age, create the categories of "adult" and "child," and privilege adults over children. We take the continuum of skin color, invent racial categories based on how closely skin color resembles blackness or whiteness, and then privilege whiteness. Difference is a linguist construction in which the *relationship* between two halves of the dichotomous construction is ignored, while the binary construction is elevated in importance . . . (Wonders, 1998: 117)

So we can understand the concept "man" only by understanding the concept "woman." We can understand "black" only because we can conceptualize "white." Over time, these dichotomies come to take on a life of their own—to seem "natural," even biologically based.

Yet, social scientists have provided compelling evidence that virtually all human variations fall along a continuum rather than into two (or more) discrete boxes. People are not "black" or "white" but instead exhibit a huge range of skin colors, making racial designations based on skin color exceedingly arbitrary. People are not just "heterosexual" or "homosexual," since a large number of individuals have same-gender sexual experiences at some point during their lives without ever considering themselves gay or lesbian. Indeed, ". . . contemporary youths are increasingly adopting alternative labels . . . or rejecting sexual identity labels altogether, in an explicit acknowledgement of these labels' arbitrary nature . . ." (Diamond, 2003:491). Similarly, biological genitalia and body function provide a relatively weak basis for dichotomizing either sex or gender, since physical variation, even on such narrow criteria as breast size, the capacity for menstruation, and the size of one's external genitalia, is very high among humans and over the life course (Fausto-Sterling, 2000).

Not only is dividing social reality into dichotomies fundamentally inaccurate, it can have very harmful consequences. This is especially true when one half of the dichotomy is valued while the other half is devalued, a tendency that is all too common. *Devaluation* of social identities is expressed in a myriad of ways, through structural barriers to housing and employment, neighborhood segregation, interpersonal violence, and hate crime (Perry, 2001). The destructive impact of this devaluation has been well documented in research. For example, "Blacks and those in lower socioeconomic positions are less satisfied with their personal lives, housing, incomes, jobs, free time and standard of living. They also tend to be less satisfied with the way things are going in the country" (Hurst, 2004:236). Another example of this devaluation can be found in research on girls, which sadly has found that "even by the end of grade school, girls begin to evaluate themselves more negatively than do boys" (Chesney-Lind and Irwin, 2008:70). This *internalization* of negative societal messaging also has adverse consequences for justice in the United States. Some scholars, for example, argue that citizen perceptions that justice workers regard women and people of color as second-class citizens may reduce reliance on the police by the very groups most likely to experience certain kinds of personal victimization (Belknap, 2007; Gabbidon and Greene, 2005).

Clearly, dichotomizing differences into two parts or groups does not mean that each part is viewed as equal. Not only is one group often devalued, the other group obtains greater privilege, in part because it comes to be viewed as somehow more "normal." This phenomenon, known as *normative privilege,* ensures that the standard for evaluation reflects and maintains the already existing privilege of the more powerful group. As a result, we have a tendency to focus on only one portion of the dichotomy when discussing difference. The more privileged groups often remain invisible. When we discuss "race," most people assume we are only talking about people of color. When the issue of "gender" is raised, people assume it is a women's issue. But to the extent that a society divides people into categories, then *everyone* is subject to the impact of categorization. Some people benefit, some do not, but everyone is affected.

In this volume, the authors have chosen to devote relatively more time to description and analysis of groups within the United States that have historically been disadvantaged and marginalized within our culture and within the justice system. The increased attention to these groups is regarded as a needed antidote to the lack of attention to these groups within the criminal justice literature. However, the chapters that follow also investigate the behavior of those groups who have historically been privileged by justice practices in the United States. We believe that issues of difference do not belong to only one group; they are human issues that ought to concern us all.

DIFFERENCE MATTERS

Although the meanings attached to differences are socially constructed (rather than natural or biological), once differences are created they have real consequences for human lives and for the justice system. Because difference construction is a historical process, the place and time period into which we are born will have a lot to do with defining which characteristics will matter to the larger society. To be born with dark skin in the United States means something different today than it did during most of the 1800s, when slavery was commonplace. Those born without eyesight earlier in the twentieth century had significantly different life chances than those born without eyesight today. But in every case, once society has decided that a particular characteristic or set of characteristics warrants differential treatment, those viewed as having those characteristics will have a difficult time escaping categorization, prejudice, stereotyping, and discrimination.

Categorization is the process by which society decides which individuals fit into the boxes used to create difference. Once categories are created and given significant societal consequence, it becomes extremely important to decide who fits into which category. That is why so many individuals in South Africa had their race changed—different racial categories are linked to different privileges and opportunities in South African society. It's also why we work so hard to be sure that "boys will be boys." Research has evidenced that males experience greater privilege in our society in numerous areas, including in employment, education, and economic opportunity (Levit, 2000). Once society has created categories, enormous effort goes into forcing people into one category or another. Through the process of *socialization*, children are taught which categories they fit into, as well as how to behave consistently with those identities. Key agents of socialization, including parents, the media, schools, peers, and important social institutions, such as religion, all participate in socializing children to internalize the differences that are assigned to them from birth. Socialization is a form of *soft social control* that helps to ensure that cultural attitudes about difference will be internalized and passed down from generation to generation. As will be seen shortly, the justice system and other agents of *hard social control* also have played an active role in defining and maintaining differences in our society, sometimes through force, but also via the law and justice institutions.

Two other processes that help to ensure the continuation of difference are prejudice and discrimination. Prejudice and discrimination are different, though related phenomena. *Prejudice* is a set of beliefs and attitudes about people based on their group membership. Stereotyping is closely linked to prejudice and helps to reinforce it. *Stereotypes* are based on the assumption that all individuals who belong to a particular group share the same characteristics. It is important to point out that stereotypes and prejudices can be "good" or "bad" in intent, but they are much more often bad than good in their consequences. For example, it may be that Asian Americans are stereotyped as being especially good at academics (presumably a "good" trait), but this assumption can be devastating for the Asian American youth who does not fit the stereotype, even though it is an apparently positive stereotype.

While prejudice is a set of attitudes about individuals and the groups they belong to, *discrimination* is a *behavior* whereby individuals are treated adversely because of their group membership. Discrimination serves to privilege some characteristics over others by linking particular characteristics with either positive or negative consequences. Prejudice ensures that those on one side of the dichotomies we create—male/female, dark/light, straight/gay—are viewed as "less than" those on the other end. Discrimination is the behavioral component of prejudice. When people discriminate, they act toward others in positive or negative ways based upon real or imagined group membership.

Although some people argue that people are discriminated against because they are different, it is more plausible to argue that people come to be viewed as "different" because they are discriminated against. Because privilege and opportunity often result in greater power in the society, it is in the interests of those who are privileged by the construction of difference to perpetuate differences so that they, their children, and others like them can continue to receive dispropor-tionate benefit. Said differently, we all want to avoid the negative consequences attached to preju-dice and discrimination, and at the same time we desire the advantages offered to us by our privileged statuses; thus, there is a built-in incentive to try to maintain categories that privilege some individuals and groups over others. Thus, one way to reduce the power of difference is to eliminate the discriminatory and/or privileging effects attached to a particular difference. Merely having blue eyes rather than brown eyes is a difference that does not "matter" because neither privilege nor negative consequences accrue to those with different eye colors. Other dif-ferences might matter less if we could successfully alter the dichotomous nature of the rewards attached to them.

LAW PLAYS A CRITICAL ROLE IN CREATING AND MAINTAINING DIFFERENCE; IT CAN ALSO BE USED TO AMELIORATE THE NEGATIVE CONSEQUENCES OF DIFFERENCE

Historically and contemporarily, law has played a central role in the construction and mainte-nance of difference. In some cases, it is obvious that law works to categorize people in ways that artificially construct difference. One good example is age. Everyone is one age or another, but the social meaning attached to age has varied over time and from culture to culture (Stearns, 2006). Less than 100 years ago in the United States, children were expected to take on the responsibilities of adulthood as soon as they were able. Until relatively recently, people of all ages worked on farms or in factories—everyone performed the work of society. This is still true in many cultures and, indeed, in some neighborhoods in the United States.

Childhood as a separate category does not exist "naturally." The meaning of childhood must be created, and this is often accomplished through legal mechanisms, such as the creation of laws regarding the age of majority. In the United States, the age of majority has fluctuated over time, ranging between the ages of 18 and 21 in the last two decades; those younger than this age were considered to be "children" under the law, with limited rights and responsibilities. The arbi-trary nature of this boundary is highlighted by the contradictions it creates, such as the fact that an individual 18 years old cannot drink alcohol but can be tried as an adult in a court of law or drafted into military service. The definition of childhood and the rights and responsibilities attached to that definition also vary cross-culturally. For example, in many states in the United States, a 17-year-old can drive but not drink alcohol, while in many European countries, such as the Netherlands, the opposite is true—young people are permitted to drink well before they gain the privilege of driving.

The meaning of race and ethnicity has also been shaped by the law. Historically, legal defi-nitions often sought to facilitate the social exclusion or social control of particular groups. During the period of slavery, the United States developed a law saying that individuals with even one drop of black blood were to be considered black (Doob, 1999). Similarly, laws passed to define who constituted an American Indian rested on "blood quantum" or "degree of Indian blood," a measure that became useful in reducing the official number of Native Americans. At the turn of the twentieth century, this standard facilitated the federal government's strategy of forced assimilation for American Indians via land seizure and acceptance of the ideology of private property (versus collectively held property). Land seized was reallocated to individuals; "each Indian identified as being those documentably of *one-half or more Indian blood*, was entitled to receive title in fee of such a parcel; all others were simply disenfranchised altogether" (Jaimes, 1992). Today, federal laws continue to set standards that define who may be considered a member of a particular Native American tribe. The rigid, legal definition of identity may one day define Native Americans out of existence, because intermarriage with other groups will ensure a dilu-tion of the percentage of "Indian-ness" the next generation can claim. As these examples illus-trate, law plays a critical role in defining difference.

Law also plays an important role in maintaining differences once they are created, and helps to ensure that differences will "matter." For example, when one man hits another man, this behavior may be prosecuted as assault in every state. However, if a husband hits his wife, in many states this behavior is defined as "domestic violence." Not only does the phrase "domestic" make the violence sound less serious, but extensive research has evidenced that the widespread attitude that violence between intimates is less serious than violence between strangers slows police response, reduces the likelihood of arrest, and reduces penalties if the perpetrator is convicted (Belknap, 2007). This differential treatment of violence against women reinforces the differences between men and women and helps to ensure that the category "woman" will be less valued than the category "man." Historically, legal restrictions on voting rights, marriage rights, and property rights for women, certain racial and ethnic groups, children, the differently abled, and for individuals with particular sexual preferences have helped to ensure that socially constructed differences would privilege some and disadvantage others.

A great deal of scholarly work has explored the link between law and difference. This work has evidenced the way that law has been used to maintain and perpetuate ageism, racism, ethnic discrimination, gender discrimination, classism, and many other differences between people as well.

It is important to point out that law is not just a vehicle for creating and maintaining difference; it can also be used to ameliorate the negative consequences associated with difference in our society. It is evident that law served to restrict the rights of huge segments of the U.S. population when the country was founded. For example, when the Constitution was written, those who did not own property, as well as women and people of color were all precluded from voting in the newly created "democracy" (Parenti, 2007). However, the law has also been used to extend rights to groups formerly disenfranchised. Although some would argue that law is a limited method for creating social change because it may not change deeply held attitudes and beliefs, it can provide important protections to those who experience inequality. As Martin Luther King (as cited in Ayers, 1993:135) said,

> The law cannot make an employer love an employee, but it can prevent him from refusing to hire me because of the color of my skin. The habits, if not the hearts of people, have been and are being altered by legislative acts, judicial decisions, and executive orders.

Although efforts to use the law as an instrument of social change are often controversial, it is clear that laws and policies like affirmative action, busing, and hate crime legislation will continue to have an important impact upon the meanings and consequences attached to difference in our society. For this reason, later in the book, substantial attention will be devoted to the role of law in promoting social changes and ensuring greater justice.

DIFFERENCES OVERLAP AND INTERSECT WITH ONE ANOTHER

For the most part, the chapters in this book address difference by describing the historical and contemporary experiences of particular social groups in our society: African Americans, religious minorities, women, lesbians and gays, and so forth. Yet, identity is a complex construct for most people. Although it is possible to talk generically about "women" or "Hispanics" or "heterosexuals," most people would deny that their membership in a single group defines who they are as individuals. Nor can we simply add identities together if we want to understand the complex identity of a particular individual. Understanding the experience of "blacks" in the justice system and then analyzing the experience of "women," is not the same thing as understanding the experience of "black women." Similarly, men are never just "men" or children just "children"; they always occupy many categories simultaneously. People differ from one another in many ways and they belong to many groups at the same time—in other words, individuals reflect the *intersectionality* of multiple identities.

Most of the work that has been done to understand difference within the justice system analyzes only one difference at a time, focusing on race *or* gender *or* social class. Only recently has research been conducted that tries to analyze more complex relationships between differences and the way that differences intersect with one another to shape our experience of justice. For example, in their research on the criminalization of pregnant drug users, Rector and Wonders (2004) illustrate the way that race, class, and gender inequalities intersect to ensure that poor African American women will be much more likely to be criminalized for their drug use than others because they are much more likely to seek treatment in public hospitals, to come under the scrutiny of disproportionately white caregivers, and to be held responsible for the health problems of their unborn/newborn children (in marked contrast to drug-using fathers). This research is just one example of a new wave of research that explores how differences intersect to shape the experience of justice.

The organization of this book uses specific historic group identities as a heuristic device for exploring differences. However, to the extent that it is possible, each chapter will touch on some of the ways that differences overlap to affect justice experiences and outcomes as a way to remind readers that lived experiences are always a product of unique intersections between individual biographies and the larger social world.

DIFFERENCES AND THEIR CONSEQUENCES CAN BE CHANGED

Perhaps the most hopeful aspect of studying difference is realizing that because differences are constructed by people, they can be changed by people. However, this is often more easily said than done. Even if we choose to live as though our race, sex, and ethnicity are irrelevant to who we are, these characteristics will still be important in our lives if the rest of the world links arrest decisions, employment decisions, educational opportunities, and so on to our membership in certain groups. In other words, attitudinal change toward difference is often very difficult to achieve in the short run; constructing difference differently often requires a great deal of patience. However, changing behavior is often easier to accomplish. We may not be able to easily change how others will perceive us, but we can restrict their ability to use differences as a basis for discrimination. The authors of this volume are convinced that those who work in the justice system have a special obligation to ensure that their behavior promotes justice rather than injustice.

Some people today claim that focusing on differences is actually part of the problem since dividing the world into separate groups-even for analytic purposes- reinforces the differences further. This is a serious danger. When we study "race" or "ethnicity," we make them "real" for the purpose of our study. When we divide people into "Hispanic" or "female" or "white" groups, we give the meaning attached to group membership greater weight. However, an even more serious risk occurs when differences that have real consequences are ignored. This is a risk criminal justice professionals cannot afford to take. For instance, claiming that race does not "really" exist in nature does little to help us explain why the majority of those incarcerated in U.S. jails and prisons are people of color (Sudbury, 2005). For those who work daily in justice occupations, misunderstanding or ignoring difference can be a matter of life and death. Assuming that the only danger in our society comes from people who look a certain way may make us vulnerable to serious harm from those who do not fit the stereotype.

Much research, for example, has shown that the crime committed by white collar and corporate offenders is far more harmful to the public than the crime committed by traditional street offenders (Michalowski and Kramer, 2006; Reiman, 2006). Partly because white-collar offenders and government officials do not fit our stereotypic image of the "criminal," we have failed to respond effectively to a wide range of extremely harmful behavior, including environmental pollution, consumer fraud, and occupational injury. This is a mistake that can be remedied only by careful attention to the construction of difference and the consequences of privileging some groups over others within a democratic society.

Part of what makes talking about difference a difficult task is that there is a tendency to assume that acknowledging differences must be a bad thing. But it is too simplistic to say, "Let's just do away with difference!" Indeed, if we could do away with difference, the world would be an extremely boring place. The problem is not with difference *per se*; the difficulty arises in the meaning we make out of difference. It is not a problem that some people have lighter skin and some darker, or that some people hold one set of religious beliefs but not another. The problem is that some societies treat those with one set of characteristics or beliefs as valuable and those with another set as less worthwhile. It is this process of giving meaning to and placing value on differences that requires our attention. This is especially critical within the justice system.

DIFFERENCE AND THE PURSUIT OF JUSTICE IN A GLOBALIZED WORLD

Ultimately, the goal of studying difference within the justice system is to ensure that, as a democratic society, we do not penalize people for the differences they exhibit and that we create a justice system that does more to foster human diversity rather than to constrain it. This has never been more important than it is today, given how rapidly globalization is changing our society and our world. Globalization has brought into sharp relief many of the cultural, religious, ethnic, and social differences that divide the planet. At the same time, it has created new opportunities for cooperation, collaboration, and global engagement. The next generation of justice professionals will have to understand much more about cultural diversity, global and comparative criminology, transnational crime and justice, and human rights issues than any generation thus far if they are to effectively foster the pursuit of justice in a globalized world. The new and pressing problems of our time—terrorism, cross-border migration, identity theft, genocide, and human trafficking, just to name a few—simply cannot be understood without broad intercultural and global knowledge.

Indeed, it is our job to *investigate difference* in order to protect the rich diversity of identities, groups, and individuals on the planet, and to guarantee that justice is available to all. The authors of this book recognize that this can be difficult to accomplish on a practical level. The goals of the justice system are often contradictory, and there is no clear standard of "fairness" with which we all agree. Too often, justice practitioners lack the knowledge and skills needed to ensure that justice prevails in an increasingly multicultural society and global world. Surely, one book cannot analyze, let alone overcome, all of the challenges associated with "difference" in the criminal justice system. However, by investigating how identity and difference affect the justice process, we do hope that this book will provide a useful starting point for those committed to creating a just society.

Reference

Ayers, Alex. 1993. *The Wisdom of Martin Luther King, Jr.* New York: Meridian.

Belknap, Joanne. 2007. *The Invisible Woman: Gender, Crime and Justice.* New York: Wadsworth.

Campbell, Mary E. 2007. The Implications of Racial Misclassification by Observers. *American Sociological Review* 72 (5): 750–765.

Chesney-Lind, Meda, and Katherine Irwin. 2008. *Beyond Bad Girls: Gender, Violence and Hype.* London: Routledge.

Diamond, Lisa M. 2003. Special Section: Integrating Research on Sexual-Minority and Heterosexual Development: Theoretical and Clinical Implications. *Journal of Clinical Child and Adolescent Psychology* 32 (4): 490–498.

Doob, Christopher Bates. 1999. *Racism: An American Cauldron.* New York: Longman.

Fausto-Sterling, Anne. 2000. *Sexing the Body: Gender Politics and the Construction of Sexuality.* New York: Basic Books.

Fenstermaker, Sarah, and Candace West. 2002. *Doing Gender, Doing Difference.* New York: Routledge.

Gabbidon, Shaun L., and Helen Taylor Greene. 2005. *Race and Crime.* Thousand Oaks: Sage Publications.

Hurst, Charles E. 2004. *Social Inequality: Forms, Causes, and Consequences*. Boston, MA: Pearson.

Jaimes, M. Annette. (Ed). 1992. Federal Indian Identification Policy: A Usurpation of Indigenous Sovereignty in North America. In *The State of Native America: Genocide, Colonization, and Resistance*, 123–138. Boston: South End Press.

Langston, Donna. 2004. Tired of Playing Monopoly? In *Race, Class and Gender: An Anthology*, ed. Margaret L. Anderson and Patricia Hill Collins, 140–149. New York: Wadsworth.

Levit, Nancy. 2000. *The Gender Line: Men, Women and the Law*. New York: New York University Press.

Lorber, Judith. 2007. *Gender Inequality: Feminist Theories and Politics*. New York: Oxford University Press.

Michalowski, Raymond J., and Ronald C. Kramer. 2006. *State-Corporate Crime: Wrongdoing at the Intersection of Business and Government*. New Brunswick, NJ: Rutgers University Press.

Ore, Tracy E. 2008. *The Social Construction of Difference and Inequality: Race, Class, Gender and Sexuality*. Boston, MA: McGraw-Hill.

Parenti, Michael. 2007. *Democracy for the Few*. Belmont, CA: Wadsworth.

Perry, Barbara. 2001. *In the Name of Hate: Under-standing Hate Crimes*. London: Routledge.

Rector, Paula K., and Nancy A. Wonders. 2004. Intersecting Identities and Pregnant Drug Users: Victimization and Vulnerabilities to Criminalization. In *Victimizing Vulnerable Groups: Images of Uniquely High-Risk Crime Targets*, ed. Charisse Tia Maria Coston, 107–116. Westport, CT: Praeger.

Reiman, Jeffrey. 2006. *The Rich Get Richer and the Poor Get Prison*, 8th edn. Boston, MA: Allyn and Bacon.

Roediger, David R. 2006. *Working Toward Whiteness: How America's Immigrants Became White–the Strange Journey from Ellis Island to the Suburbs*. New York: Perseus Books.

Shelden, Randall G. 2007. *Controlling the Dangerous Classes: A Critical Introduction to the History of Criminal Justice*. Boston, MA: Allyn and Bacon.

Stearns, Peter N. 2006. *Childhood in World History*. London: Routledge.

Sudbury, Julia. 2005. *Global Lockdown: Race, Gender and the Prison-Industrial Complex*. London: Routledge.

Telles, Edward Eric. 2006. *Race in Another America: The Significance of Skin Color in Brazil*. Princeton, NJ/Oxford: Princeton University Press.

Uys, Pieter-Dirk. 1988. Chameleons Thrive Under Apartheid. *New York Times* Friday, September 23. pp. 27(N) pA35(L).

West, Candace, and Sarah Fenstermaker. 2002. Doing Difference. In *Doing Gender, Doing Difference*, ed. Sarah Fenstermaker and Candace West, 55–80. New York: Routledge.

Winant, Howard. 2004. *The New Politics of Race: Globalism Difference Justice*. Minneapolis, MN: University of Minnesota Press.

Wonders, Nancy A. 1998. Postmodern feminist criminology and social justice. In *Social Justice/Criminal Justice*, ed. Bruce Arrigo, 111–128. Belmont, CA: Wadsworth.

MODULE 5

CHAPTER 9

Community Relations in the Context of Culture

I have a dream that one day my children will be judged by the strength of their character and not by the color of their skin.

—MARTIN LUTHER KING JR., 1963

Racial classifications of any sort pose the risk of lasting harm to our society. They reinforce the belief, held for too much of our history, that individuals should be judged by the color of their skin.

—SANDRA DAY O'CONNOR, 1993

KEY CONCEPTS

Cognitive Scripts
Community Relations Service
Cross-Cultural Factors
Cultural Citizens Police
    Academies
Cultural Diversity

Cultural Relativism
Cultural Universals
Discretionary Decision
    Making
Ethnocentrism
Multiculturalism

Police Multicultural Advisory
    Committees
Stereotyping
Xenophobia
Xenophiles
Xenocentrism

LEARNING OBJECTIVES

Studying this chapter will enable you to:

1. Define *cultural context*.

2. Describe the cultural context of community relations.

3. Contrast characteristics of different cultural groups.

4. Analyze several cultural factors that may be misunderstood by police.

5. Describe several community relations strategies for improving community relations in the context of culture.

Police-Community Relations and the Administration of Justice, Eighth Edition
by Ronald D. Hunter, Thomas Barker

T his chapter examines the impact of culture in the United States, and how cultural considerations affect police–community relations.

Culture is the way of life shared by members of a society. It includes not only language, values, and symbolic meanings but also technology and material objects (Brinkerhoff, 1998). When applied to the United States, this definition would allow for individual and group differences according to region, ethnicity, religion, political orientation, class, and gender but would hold that, despite these differences, Americans share a common culture based on a national heritage of personal freedom and democratic principles. While encouraging individuality, U.S. citizens and resident aliens are expected to adhere to basic societal values and beliefs.

Other definitions of culture are not as inclusive. Rather than seeing a society in which there is great consensus despite regional, ethnic, religious, political, class, and gender diversity, these definitions stress the conflicts that occur within such a broad-based nation. They tend to see culture as all that human beings learn to do, to use, to produce, to know, and to believe as they grow into maturity and live out their lives in the social groups to which they belong (Tischler, 2007). Such a definition would view the United States not as a cultural melting pot but as a complex mixture of diverse groups engaged in competitions that too frequently boil over into cultural conflicts.

Both of the definitions are accurate and both are somewhat misleading. U.S. culture may be distinguished from European, African, or Asian cultures. The American people, however (as is true of most large social groups, including European, Asian, and African), are not culturally homogeneous. In fact, the United States is culturally diverse. There are numerous ethnic groups, religious groups, and many age and sex attributes of communities across the United States that help to make them unique. Immigrants—newcomers who may have difficulty in understanding the common characteristics shared by U.S. citizens (particularly our traditions and norms)—comprise still another culturally diverse group.

In this chapter, we seek to understand how culture influences human behavior, on the part of both the police and the communities they serve. Our view is that neither the common values and beliefs of U.S. society as a whole nor the competing views produced by **cultural diversity** within it can be ignored. Both the commonality of the former and the distinctions of the latter contribute to our strength as a nation.

Understanding and appreciating individuals within a cultural context—within the framework of the way their language and behavior express their feelings and beliefs as part of a cultural group—will provide new opportunities for police and citizens to increase the effectiveness of their interpersonal communication, open avenues for increased mutual respect, and form a realistic base for clarifying common values and areas of mutual concern.

THE CULTURAL CONTEXT OF COMMUNITY RELATIONS

A *context* is a framework for understanding meaning. It is the environment, or the conditions in which something is said or done. Contexts are very important. Without them, what people mean by what they say and do would rarely be clearly understood. The media is often accused of quoting people "out of context," that is, of selecting some portion of a speech and using it in a way that infers a meaning that the speaker did not intend. Because people usually behave in culturally defined ways, culture is a part of the meaning of every interpersonal interaction.

Being Culturally Appropriate

It is possible to have excellent counseling skills and yet apply them in culturally inappropriate ways (see Weaver, 1992). It is possible to make decisions precisely by the letter of policy and procedure and to commit acts that are inappropriate and inhumane. Understanding the cultural context of our own beliefs and actions and the beliefs and actions of others can help to prevent such tragedy.

In order to understand how to deal with people of different cultures (or of divergent sub-cultures within a dominant culture), one must seek to examine the context of that particular culture. Weaver (1992) demonstrated that failure to understand the dynamics of another culture could cause police officers to misinterpret the intentions of others. The seeking of contextual understanding of different cultures is defined by sociologists as cultural relativism. **Cultural relativism** means that we seek to understand different cultures from their particular perspectives or on their own terms rather than imposing preconceived standards from our own cultural development (Tischler, 2007).

Achieving cultural relativism is not an easy task. We all have biases and preconceptions that we bring to every situation we encounter. Psychologists use the term **cognitive scripts** to refer to the application of past experiences to new situations or encounters (Bartol, 1998). How we approach these situations is thus colored by our personal development, which is largely influenced by our own cultural environment. How we respond to influences from our cultural environment shapes how we respond to other cultures. When we perceive cultures other than our own as flawed or inferior, we are being *ethnocentric*. People within a nation who see all other nations as inferior, individuals who see other races, religions, or regions as having lesser morality or intellect, are practicing **ethnocentrism** (Bucher, 2004; LeMay, 2005). Ethnocentrism is a form of **xenophobia** in that those things with which we are familiar and therefore perceive as preferable are influenced by cultural considerations. Catholics who have contempt for Baptists, African Americans who hate Hispanics, Northerners who perceive Southerners as inferior, and upper-class elitists who consider those of other classes to be unworthy are all examples of ethnocentrism.

Cultural biases are not always to the detriment of those who are different from us. Frequently, people are so concerned about being fair to others that they discriminate against their own kind. **Xenophiles** are people who are ashamed of who or what they are. They feel that people who are different from them are either superior or warrant preferential consideration. When these feelings are applied to other cultures they are referred to as **xenocentrism** (Bucher, 2004; LeMay, 2005). If we have come to perceive our culture as flawed or inferior to others, we are being *xenocentric*. Such perceptions can be just as detrimental to cultural relations as those of ethno-centrists. Americans who are anti-American, Southerners who are anti-Southern, Native Americans who are ashamed of their ancestry, and individuals who are ashamed of their social class are examples of xenocentrism.

To deal fairly and objectively with other people within a culturally diverse society, one must be both accepting and understanding of his or her own culture, as well as others. We must be sensitive to the norms and traditions of others, but we must also understand that there are **cultural universals** that are dictated by the overall society in which we live (Popenoe, 2000). Determining and applying those behaviors or values that are appropriate universal standards (i.e., U.S. ideals of individual freedoms, social equality, order under law, and democratic values) can be extremely difficult. People must come to terms with their own moral and social perspectives, as well as understand how compatible their views are within society as a whole. There is considerable disagreement on what behaviors are culturally appropriate. What is often perceived as being a societal standard is "often only a common strand found among the diverse elements of which it is composed" (Popenoe, 2000).

In the following sections we discuss many of the cultural influences that the police must consider to properly enforce universal standards in a diverse U.S. society.

Understanding Crime

In order to understand crime in minority communities we must take into account the ideas, feelings, and experiences of the people in the community (Shusta et al., 2005). Weis and Sederstrom (1981) stated, "In essence an individual learns criminal behavior, particularly within social groups or social areas where there is a culture conflict or inconsistency surrounding the violation of the law." They argue for getting families, schools, peer groups, youth gangs, local officials, and social organizations involved in healthier social development opportunities for young people, and effectively organizing the community against crime. Accomplishing such a goal requires an understanding of cultural contexts.

Providing Services to the Community

New immigrant communities and other communities in transition need special police attention. Officers can help to ease the shock of entering a new culture by offering protection and informal education. But such work requires close personal contact, not remote observation through the windows of patrol cars (Shusta et al., 2005). Services to any community must be matched to the citizen's perception of need and to the resources of the community. Distrust of established agencies, expectations of community members, different languages and different symbols, and many other factors must be considered in planning and providing for effective services (Colvard, 1992; Pitter, 1992). Many new immigrants, both legal and illegal, suffered abuses at the hands of government officials in their native lands. A product of those abuses is a strong distrust of government institutions in general and the police in particular (Pitter, 1992). These immigrants tend to perceive the police as oppressors rather than public servants (Colvard, 1992). Their fears are heightened by cultural conflicts and language barriers that block effective communication between the police and many ethnic communities.

These blocks to effective communication are experienced not only in immigrant communities but are also observable within communities comprising English-speaking ethnic minorities. In those areas, the language may appear on the surface to be the same, but cultural variations in linguistic patterns and semantic meanings impair understanding and heighten tensions between officers and citizens. The results are police–citizen encounters in which individuals "talk at" one another rather than communicating.

FIGURE 9.1   Cultural diversity is not pleasing to everyone.
Courtesy of Birmingham Police Department.

Overcoming Stereotypes

Stereotyping of police by the community and of the community by the police interferes with effective community relations. Stereotyping is often based on prejudice. Prejudice creates and is created by hostility and mutual fear, and distrust is intensified in the process.

Officers and community members who can appreciate and respect cultural differences are less likely to be fearful and judgmental of people from cultures other than their own. They can be more open to assessing their own biases and achieving mutual respect.

Understanding beliefs and behavior in a cultural context may help to debunk stereotypes about members of that culture, but even in the process of gaining understanding, a new danger exists. Because characteristics must be generalized to place them in a cultural context, we must take care not to replace the old stereotypes with new ones.

Discretionary Decision Making

Three major factors that influence decision making in the field are space, time, and appearance (Greenlee, 1980, p. 50). Perception and use of these are often culturally defined.

SPACE   The suspect's use of physical and personal space both during an alleged offense and during questioning influence decision making by the officer. Finally, the officer's decision is usually based on his or her own cultural definition of the proper use of space in such a situation, even though that definition may not be understood by the suspect.

TIME   Time of day, elapsed time, and use of time on the part of the suspect are decision-making factors. "Proper" use of time usually is culturally defined. Time may be perceived specifically or globally, depending on the cultural context of the perceiver.

APPEARANCE   Males are more likely than females to commit some types of crimes (e.g., rape and voyeurism). Age, too, may be a factor in determining who to stop and question about a specific crime. The person who looks "out of place" in a neighborhood may be considered a primary suspect, as may a person who is stereotyped as a potential problem. Care must be taken not to mistake poverty and its impact on a group of people for culture.

As Greenlee states, "a discretionary decision resulting in a just action depends on the officer's ability to assess cultural norms accurately and to be, in effect, the cultural and social engineer at that moment" (Greenlee, 1980, p. 51).

Characteristics of Culture

Culture comprises all of the following characteristics:

- *It is organic and supraorganic.* It depends on people acting, thinking, and feeling to exist, but it outlives individual people and generations.
- *It is overt and covert.* Overt parts of culture, such as language and houses, can be observed, but attitudes, philosophies, and spiritual elements are inferred.
- *It is explicit and implicit.* Explicit culture can be described by the people who perform the behavior that is a part of it (e.g., playing football, brushing teeth). Implicit culture is more difficult to describe objectively (e.g., adults speak a common language but may not be able to explain objectively its grammar and syntax).
- *It is ideal and manifest.* The ideal culture is what people believe their behavior should be; manifest culture is how people really behave.
- *It is stable and changing.* System principles apply to cultures. Both change and a need for structure and predictability are constants.

No person adheres to all the values in a given culture; socialization is seldom complete. Within every culture there are distinctive subcultures (Popenoe, 2000). As a result, diversity within a culture is common. Hispanic culture includes Cuban, Puerto Rican, Mexican, Spanish, and other subcultural groups. Southeast Asian culture includes Laotian, Vietnamese, and Cambodian groups. It is possible to describe basic traditions and standards, or touchstones, of a culture because these are less subject to area variation. It is not possible, however, to define a culture precisely, nor to find a person who perfectly represents a given culture.

CROSS-CULTURAL FACTORS

The following factors should be viewed only as examples of the variety of **cross-cultural factors** that lead to cultural understanding and misunderstanding.

African Americans

The term *African American* has supplanted *black* as the preferred terminology by which to refer to Americans who fall within the Negroid categorization of racial groups. This terminology can be misleading, in that there are Americans of African descent who are not black and there are blacks residing in the United States who are neither American nor of direct African descent. Despite those distinctions, in this book the term *African American* is used to refer to U.S. residents who are Negroid or identify themselves as being African American, Afro-American, Negro, or black.

African Americans are no longer the majority minority within the United States; they have been surpassed by Hispanics or Latinos. However, African Americans number 34,658,190 (U.S. Bureau of the Census, 2001), and comprise 12.3 percent of the U.S. population. The majority of African Americans reside within urbanized areas of the nation. They also represent 22.1 percent of all persons living below the poverty level (U.S. Bureau of the Census, 2001). These figures may be interpreted to mean that African Americans are overrepresented both within the lower class and within inner cities. The products of these findings are that large numbers of African Americans live under both economic and social hardships. The existence of such hardships places a direct burden on the relations between African Americans and the police who serve them.

Despite considerable progress in regard to race relations within U.S. society, African Americans continue to be dramatically overrepresented within U.S. correctional institutions. At the end of 2000, there were 1,381,892 black prisoners in federal and state prisons (Bureau of Justice Statistics, www.ojp.usdoj.gov/bjs/prisons.htm). This translates into 3,457 imprisoned black males per 100,000 black males in the United States. This overrepresentation will continue until such time as economic and social conditions for African Americans improve. Although African Americans have for the most part become *culturally assimilated*—adopted behaviors, customs, language, dress, and values consistent with the norms of the overall society—large numbers are still striving to be *structurally assimilated*—integrated into the common institutional and social life of the country (Rothman, 2005; Schaefer, 2007). This resistance to structural assimilation is a product of lingering ethnocentrism among both the white majority and African Americans.

African Americans have experienced more difficulty in becoming assimilated into U.S. society than have many other ethnic minorities, for two primary reasons: (1) clearly notable racial characteristics, and (2) the legacy of slavery. The first difficulty has been reduced as U.S. society has become less color conscious due to the civil rights movement, laws barring racial discrimination, and the continued deepening of human understanding. The second difficulty is actually more challenging. Even in a society committed to social equality that utilizes governmental programs to redistribute wealth and enhance the quality of life and opportunities for the lower class, change comes slowly. The change is hindered by political disagreements with regard to the appropriateness of change strategies utilized by governments and individuals.

FIGURE 9.2 **The Birmingham Police Department, which once symbolized racial intolerance toward African Americans, is now reflective of cultural diversity.**
Courtesy of Birmingham Police Department.

Within both African American communities and U.S. society as a whole, constant disagreements occur over what should be done to enhance the quality of life for African Americans (LeMay, 2005). Should we follow the model of Martin Luther King Jr., who sought an integrated, color-blind society in which all citizens were treated equally? Or, do we follow the Malcolm X model, which demands enhanced economic opportunities while maintaining separation of the races? Is racism only a white problem? Or is anyone who dislikes members of other races or seeks treatment distinctive from other races guilty of racism? Are affirmative action programs still beneficial? Or have they become more divisive than beneficial? These are but a few of the complex and difficult questions with which we as a society continue to wrestle.

Within the ranks of African Americans, the perspectives are as varied as those found within American society as a whole. Many African Americans call for continued understanding and cooperation among the races. They stress mutual respect and opposition to racism and bigotry on the part of both blacks and whites. Others, such as the National Coalition of Blacks for Reparations in America, argue that peaceful coexistence cannot be achieved until "white society" atones by apologizing for the enslavement of African American ancestors and subsequent injustices that have continued to the present and then pays reparations to every African American. Still others hold more moderate positions as to what is best for both African Americans and other Americans (Healey, 2003; Macionis, 2006).

The end result of the foregoing debates is that the police will continue to be seen by many African Americans as representatives of an unjust and oppressive society (Cole, 1999). Unfortunately, African Americans will continue to be a large part of the police clientele (both as victims and offenders). The police must therefore seek to understand the perspectives and problems of African Americans, and they must do so with true concern and sensitivity. This is best achieved through the enhanced selection, training, disciplinary, and accountability strategies discussed in previous chapters. It is also supported by continued emphasis on equitable minority representation at all levels within police agencies and increased community involvement in the police decision-making process. Hopefully, the successful implementation of these strategies will prevent racial riots such as those experienced in Los Angeles in 1992 and Cincinnati in 2000.

NEW IMMIGRANTS   The complexity of African American relations within U.S. society (and with the police in particular) is further compounded by the diversity of immigrants (both legal and illegal) who have begun arriving in the United States from Africa and the Caribbean. Most Africans have little in common with African Americans beyond racial similarities. The cultural norms, values, history, and traditions differ significantly. Tribal and family influences, language difficulties, religious differences, and divergent attitudes regarding democracy and legal order make assimilation into both U.S. society as a whole and within African American communities quite challenging for all but the better educated Africans.

The influx of Caribbean refugees who are Negroid is creating a similar dilemma. Although many refugees speak English, most are poorly educated and can neither read nor write. Like African immigrants, they have distinctive cultural traditions and values that conflict with U.S. societal norms. This has led to heated debates as to what immigration policies should be regarding specific island nations. Haiti, where many of the poorly educated, French-speaking populace seek to escape abject poverty and political turmoil by entering the United States is a classic example (Macionis, 2006).

Hispanic Americans

Hispanic Americans comprise the majority ethnic group in America. The 2000 census found 35,305,818 residents of Hispanic descent, comprising 12.5 percent of the total population (U.S. Bureau of the Census, 2001). It is thought that this number is grossly underrepresentative due to the fact that many Hispanics are undocumented aliens who avoided contact with census takers and many individuals did not identify themselves as Hispanic.

Hispanic Americans are unique among U.S. ethnic minorities in that they are categorized not by race but by ethnic heritage. Hispanics are a very diverse ethnic group whose racial membership includes individuals who could be racially classified as Negroid, American Mongoloid, or Caucasoid, with most being varied mixtures of Caucasoid and American Mongoloid, or Caucasoid and Negroid. According to the U.S. Census Bureau, Hispanics are those persons who identify themselves as being of Mexican, Puerto Rican, Cuban, Central or South American, or other Spanish-culture origin. Many do not choose to identify themselves under the umbrella of Hispanic, which they consider to be too broad, preferring designations more specific to their particular origins (Schaefer, 2007). Others prefer to be referred to as Latinos. Still others prefer to be identified solely as Americans.

There are many differences among the ethnic subgroups that Hispanic Americans comprise. However, they share several common difficulties that set them apart from others in U.S. society. The most notable distinction for many Hispanics who have recently immigrated to the United States or have lived their lives within segregated enclaves is that of the Spanish language. There are many Hispanic dialects, some so different from others that they may appear to be another language. However, except for some variations in the definition and use of specific terms, they are similar enough to be mutually understood. Unfortunately, to those who do not understand the language's subtle nuances and reliance on nonverbal gestures, the different use of surnames and last names to indicate heritage, the closer proximity of communications, the greater use of touching, and its heightened expressiveness, the Spanish language may appear to be both foreign and threatening. This can lead to serious misunderstanding between Spanish-speaking citizens and English-speaking police officers (Colvard, 1992; Shusta et al., 2005; Weaver, 1992).

While language is a major distinction for Hispanics, other important cultural differences deserve comment. Hispanic males tend to exhibit a strong sense of *machismo*, in which they place great emphasis on their personal honor and their position of power within traditionally male-dominated families (Tischler, 2007). Hispanics have very strong commitments to family and often live within large familial groups that include three or more generations. Religion (predominantly Catholicism) plays an important role in their lives, and many have a fatalistic view of life ("If it is God's will, it will occur") (Bucher, 2004). Like other ethnic minorities, Hispanics place a greater emphasis on the welfare of the group rather than of individuals. Hispanics have traditionally been less materialistic than other U.S. ethnic groups, which combined with discrimination contributes to their being overrepresented within the lower class. Like other ethnic minorities, their frustration with limited social and economic opportunities has frequently led to negative relations with the police.

There are more than five million Hispanics from Central America, South America, or other Spanish cultures or origins. However, we confine our discussions to the three largest categories of Hispanic Americans: Mexican Americans, Puerto Ricans, and Cuban Americans.

MEXICAN AMERICANS   Mexican Americans are by far the largest Hispanic group in the United States. There were 20,640,711 Mexican Americans identified by the 2000 Census, comprising 7.3 percent of the total population (U.S. Bureau of the Census, 2001). Like African Americans, Mexican Americans (or Chicanos) have a long history of oppression in U.S. society. While we may tend to think of Mexican Americans as being recent (often illegal) immigrants from Mexico seeking better economic conditions, many have historical connections within the United States that are far older than those of all other ethnic groups except Native Americans (Rothman, 2005). They became Americans because their homelands were forcibly annexed by American colonialism. As a Chicano living in New Mexico informed one of the authors, "My family never moved. The United States moved." This perspective is also held by many Mexican immigrants who feel that they have merely moved to lands that rightfully belong to their people (LeMay, 2005).

Mexican Americans see themselves as quite distinct from other Hispanics both in racial composition and cultural history (Schaefer, 2007). They are a racial amalgamation of European and Native American, which while distinctly different from "Anglos" is the least divergent of all non-Caucasian groups. Their cultural development was shaped by early Spanish and Native American historical events that took place in Mexico and the American Southwest.

Mexican Americans have not created nationwide political organizations to promote their group interests as have African Americans and some other ethnic groups (Schaefer, 2007). Nor have they been quick to use social unrest as a weapon against injustice. The 1977 drowning of a handcuffed Chicano by six white Houston police officers led to demonstrations by Mexican Americans and calls for reforms but did not lead to riots. Chicanos have seemed more content to use the established political process to address their grievances than have other ethnic groups. It has been argued that this is due to successful assimilation on the part of many Mexican Americans (Shusta et al., 2005).

PUERTO RICANS   Puerto Ricans make up the second-largest grouping of Hispanics within the United States. In the 2000 census, 3,406,178 Puerto Ricans (1.2 percent of the total population) were identified (U.S. Bureau of the Census, 2001). This figure does not include people living in Puerto Rico, which is a U.S. possession. Like many Mexican Americans and all Native Americans, Puerto Ricans are Americans because their lands were incorporated into the United States (Mobasher and

Sadri, 2004). Puerto Rico became a U.S. possession in 1899 following the Spanish-American War. All Puerto Ricans are considered U.S. citizens who may freely move back and forth from the island to the continent, which many frequently do (Kitano, 1996). The privileges and responsibilities extended to Puerto Ricans (i.e., voting in presidential elections and paying federal income tax) vary depending on whether they reside in Puerto Rico or elsewhere in the United States.

Approximately one-third of all Puerto Ricans are black, with the majority being varying mixtures of Caucasoid, American Mongoloid, and Negroid (Schaefer, 2006). As a result of this ethnic and racial mixture, white Puerto Ricans may suffer from discrimination against Hispanics, while black Puerto Ricans also may suffer from racial discrimination. Due to discrimination and other cultural influences that make assimilation into society on the U.S. mainland difficult, many Puerto Ricans move back to Puerto Rico.

The attitudes of Puerto Ricans toward the United States varies considerably. Many Puerto Ricans view the United States as a colonial power that wrongly holds their island. They feel that Puerto Rico should be granted independence from the United States. Others feel that Puerto Rico is a distinct region within the United States and that as such it should be granted statehood. Still others feel that Puerto Rico is best served by being an American possession but having a degree of autonomy as currently provided by its status as a commonwealth. This debate has raged for several years, and at this writing it appears that the status quo will continue into the foreseeable future.

CUBAN AMERICANS   Cuban Americans numbered 1,241,685 persons, or 0.4 percent of the total population in the 2000 census (U.S. Bureau of the Census, 2001). They are mostly concentrated within southeast Florida near their original homeland. While there was some migration to the United States during the 1800s and early 1900s due to the close proximity of Florida to Cuba, most did not immigrate until Fidel Castro took power in 1959. The initial Cuban immigrants were predominantly well-educated members of the upper and middle class who were light skinned and either spoke English or readily learned to do so. These individuals maintained their Cuban identity but were easily absorbed into southeast Florida society. Later immigrants fleeing from Cuba's Communist society were less affluent, and more racially diverse; few spoke English, but they were able to adapt due to American acceptance of refugees from Communism and resources provided by previous immigrants. As the Cuban American community grew in the Miami area, many immigrants were able to adapt without learning English or adopting "American" customs (Rothman, 2005).

In 1980, Castro agreed to allow more than 100,000 Cubans to leave Cuba from the port of Mariel. In addition to political refugees, most of whom were poor, lacking in job skills, and unable to speak English, the Cuban government included several thousand people who had been imprisoned for committing nonpolitical crimes, being mentally ill, or being homosexual. The inclusion of this relatively small number of individuals resulted in a negative reaction toward the "Marielitos," which previous Cuban immigrants had not experienced. This negativism also heightened discriminatory attitudes by other ethnic groups toward Cuban Americans in general. Today, the Miami region is an ethnically and racially diverse area in which Cuban Americans comprise almost half of the populace (U.S. Bureau of the Census, 2001).

The political and social influence wielded by Cuban Americans in southeast Florida has provoked considerable resistance on the part of non-Cubans living there. Relations with lower- and middle-class whites, African Americans, and other Hispanics not of Cuban descent have frequently become strained. Twice during the 1980s, riots occurred as the result of police actions that led to the death of African Americans. One was precipitated by the death of a motorcyclist at the hands of a predominantly white group of police officers. The second occurred after an African American was killed by a Cuban American officer. In 1991, another riot occurred after a Hispanic officer of Colombian descent shot an African American motorist. The fact that riots did not occur following the officer's acquittal on manslaughter charges in 1993 is testimony to enhanced efforts to mediate grievances within Miami's multicultural community.

Asian Americans

Asian Americans are a highly diverse group made up of persons of Chinese, Japanese, Filipino, Korean, Vietnamese, Cambodian, Hmong, Laotian, Thai, Asian Indian, Bangladeshi, Burmese, Indonesian, Malayan, Okinawan, Pakistani, Sri Lankan, and other nationalities. In 2000, Asians comprised 3.6 percent of the American populace or 10,242,998 persons (U.S. Bureau of the Census, 2001). As categorized by the U.S. Census Bureau, Asians include persons classified both by racial characteristics (i.e., individuals displaying Mongolian features) and geographic origin (areas in which the inhabitants reside are considered to be a part of Asia, but like Asian Indians, the residents do not display Mongolian features).

Like other immigrant groups, Asian Americans have suffered from discrimination due to differences in race, religion, culture, language, and social organization (Popenoe, 2000). During the 1800s, Asian immigrants were used when cheap labor was desirable but abused when they and their children were perceived as being in economic competition. In California, citizenship was denied to immigrants who were not white. As recently as 1952, the California constitution forbade the employment of Asian workers. This "fear" of Asians flooding the country led the U.S. government to impose restrictive immigration laws that severely limited the number of Asians that could enter the country (Schaefer, 2006).

In addition to discrimination based on fear of economic competition by both whites and other ethnic groups, Asian Americans suffered from the view that they had unbreakable ties with their homelands that were stronger than any attachments they might have for the United States. This view was erroneous in that descendants of Asian immigrants had readily adopted mainstream American customs (including the use of English as a primary, if not a single, language) (Farley, 2005). Their adherence to cultural traditions and heritage was in effect no stronger than what might be found among white ethnic groups. Another difficulty faced by Asian Americans is that members of other ethnic groups who have had little exposure to Orientals (other than Hollywood stereotypes) tend to look upon all Asians as being the same. This has often led to spillover bigotry from persons who dislike an Asian nation or another Asian American group (Henslin, 2007). Such bigotry caused the 1982 beating death of a Vietnamese American by unemployed autoworkers who thought he was Japanese (Tischler, 2007).

The largest Asian groups in American society are Chinese Americans, Filipino Americans, Japanese Americans, Asian Indians, Korean Americans, and Vietnamese Americans. Other Americans of Asian descent make up only a small percentage of U.S. ethnic minorities. The following sections focus on the larger categories of Chinese Americans, Filipino Americans, Japanese Americans, and to a lesser degree, Asian Indians, Vietnamese Americans, and Korean Americans.

CHINESE AMERICANS Chinese Americans were the earliest of the Asian groups to begin immigrating to the United States. They were first imported in the 1850s to work in mines, to help build railroads, and to perform duties that were considered inappropriate for white males (LeMay, 2005). Today they remain one of the largest groupings of any new immigrants. There were approximately 2,432,585 Chinese Americans identified in 2000 (U.S. Bureau of the Census, 2001). Many of these citizens are descendants of immigrants who came to this country more than 100 years ago. Others (both legal and illegal) are recent arrivals. The majority of Chinese Americans reside in California and Hawaii, but they may be found living throughout the United States.

Like other Asian Americans, Chinese Americans tend to have strong family ties, strict discipline, and a deep-seated respect for heritage and traditions. As mentioned earlier, Chinese Americans have historically experienced severe oppression within American society. They were denied both citizenship and work because of their race (Popenoe, 2000; Schaefer, 2007). They were specifically excluded from immigration to the United States (Tischler, 2007). They were also barred from testifying against whites. Despite these handicaps, Chinese Americans as a whole have persevered, in large part, because of strong commitments to both educational and economic success.

Despite the successes of many upper- and middle-class Chinese Americans, large numbers continue to live in poverty in racially segregated "Chinatowns." Racial discrimination and cultural conflict continue today. Although current stereotypes depict Chinese Americans as having economic affluence and political influence, large numbers (particularly recent immigrants) have not been assimilated into U.S. society.

FILIPINO AMERICANS   Filipino Americans numbered 1,850,314 in the 2000 Census, making them the second-largest grouping of Asian Americans (U.S. Bureau of the Census, 2001). Like other Asian Americans, their numbers tend to be clustered in California and Hawaii. Unlike other Asian American ethnic groups, Filipinos are more racially diverse. They are predominantly of Malayan descent with varying mixtures of other races, due to various times during which the Philippines were controlled by other nations (i.e., Spain, the United States, and Japan). Indeed, Filipino Americans are frequently mistaken for Hispanic Americans due to their physical appearance and Spanish surnames (Mobasher and Sadri, 2004).

The Philippines were annexed by the United States following the Spanish-American War. Like Puerto Ricans, they had a unique status as both U.S. nationals and subjects. This ended when the Philippines was officially granted independence in 1934. Easy immigration to the United States was halted following independence, but a large number of Filipinos had already migrated in search of better economic conditions in Hawaii and California. Their lives as workers on Hawaiian plantations and West Coast farms were harsh, and they were paid meager wages (Popenoe, 2000). They were also segregated from other ethnic groups due to cultural differences and discrimination (Healey, 2003).

Following World War II, restrictions on Filipino immigration were loosened, and a second wave of immigrants came to the United States (Popenoe, 2000). Like other immigrants they experienced hardships both in adjusting to and being accepted into U.S. society. Despite these obstacles, Filipino Americans have been able to achieve a median family income that is one of the highest among Asian American groups (Popenoe, 2000).

ASIAN INDIANS   Asian Indians comprised the third-largest Asian group according to the 2000 census, which found residents of Indian ancestry. Like neighboring Pakistan, Bangladesh, Burma, and Sri Lanka, India is populated by people with a very complex mixture of racial, ethnic, and religious groups who are in constant competition and, frequently, open conflict with one another. These conflicts are exacerbated by the population density of India. In addition, widespread poverty may be found within the rigid class system that still exists within Indian society (Mobasher and Sadri, 2004). Due to these conditions, many Asian Indians have immigrated in search of a better life.

In that they have dark skins but Caucasian features, Asian Indians are an "in-between ethnic group" that differs from other racial classifications (Henslin, 2007). This means that they are not readily assimilated into other groups that tend to have predominantly Caucasoid, Mongolian, or Negroid features. In addition, their religious beliefs (Hinduism, Islam, Sikhism, Buddhism, and Jainism) and traditions are seen as threatening by many Americans. This has led to segregated communities and limited opportunities for Asian Indians of less affluence.

VIETNAMESE AMERICANS   The fourth-largest Asian group in American society is that of Vietnamese Americans. In a manner similar to that of Korean Americans, the immigration of Vietnamese to the United States was largely the product of U.S. involvement in an Asian conflict. Unlike Korea, war immigrants were not limited to American brides, orphans, and students. The fall of South Vietnam to Communist North Vietnam led to thousands of Vietnamese citizens seeking asylum in other countries (Popenoe, 2000). The initial wave of Vietnamese refugees immigrating to the United States consisted primarily of upper- and middle-class individuals, predominantly Catholic, who left Vietnam to escape reprisals from the Communists (Schaefer, 2006; Schaefer, 2007). Assimilation for this group, while challenging, was not as difficult as for those who came later.

The second wave of Vietnamese refugees began arriving in the United States after 1975. As a whole they were less educated, poorer, younger, Buddhist, and less prepared for entry into American society (Schaefer, 2006; Schaefer, 2007). Many of these refugees were "boat people" who had endured extreme hardships to escape Vietnam and eventually gain entry in the United States. The combined number of Vietnamese Americans that resulted from these immigration processes was 1,122,528 in the 2000 census (U.S. Bureau of the Census, 2001).

Like some other Asian groups, those Vietnamese who spoke English, were better educated, and had economic assets and/or marketable skills experienced considerably less difficulty in gaining acceptance in the communities in which they settled. The poorer, less affluent refugees have experienced challenges more similar to those of earlier Asian immigrants. Prejudice and hostility toward Vietnamese immigrants have been extremely severe in areas in which Vietnamese customs and economic competition have brought them into direct conflict with working-class persons of other races.

The outcome of the Vietnam War did not result only in mass immigration from Vietnam. Other Asian groups who had supported U.S. involvement in Southeast Asia also fled their countries as political refugees. These groups were predominantly Cambodians, Hmong (a separate ethnic group living in Laos), Laotians, and Thais. Their immigration added greatly to the numbers of Cambodians, Hmong, Laotians, and Thais living in the United States.

KOREAN AMERICANS Korean immigration has taken place in three waves. The first began in 1882 with the signing of the Shufeldt Treaty and ended in 1905 when Japan took control of Korea. The second took place during and after the Korean War (between 1950 and 1953) when

FIGURE 9.3 Sgt. Cheng Her of the Western Carolina Police Department.

Courtesy of Western Carolina Police Department.

immigration policies were relaxed for war brides, war orphans, and students. The third wave began following the Immigration and Naturalization Act of 1965 and continues today (Bucher, 2004). The product of these successive waves is that there were 1,076,872 Korean Americans identified in the 2000 census (U.S. Bureau of the Census, 2001).

Korean Americans have experienced difficulties similar to those of other Asian immigrants. Like Chinese Americans and Japanese Americans, Korean Americans have been relatively success-ful in adapting to American society (Tischler, 2007). A willingness to learn English and adopt Christianity has aided their success. Some may even argue that they have been too successful. These "hardworking, striving, studious people living in closely knit families" have begun to suffer from the same domestic problems (divorce, abuse, alcoholism, etc.) that plague the white major-ity (Henslin, 2007). It should be further noted that the success of Korean Americans has led to strained relations with other minorities, as evidenced in the Los Angeles riot of 1992.

JAPANESE AMERICANS   Japanese Americans began arriving in the United States in fairly large numbers during the 1870s. Their experiences were very similar to those of Chinese Americans in regard to mistreatment and prejudice at the hands of the white majority and other ethnic groups (Popenoe, 2000). Although they were the objects of bigotry and discrimination, Japanese Americans were more readily adaptable to American society than were many other immigrant groups. Like Chinese Americans, they were industrious and sought to attain both educational and economic success. Unlike Chinese Americans and other Asian groups, the Japanese are less likely to segregate themselves within ethnic communities (Schaefer, 2007) and are more likely to intermarry outside their ethnic group (Farley, 2005). As a result, they have been more easily assimilated than Chinese Americans.

Due to the war with Japan, one of the more shameful exhibitions of racism in U.S. history was perpetrated upon Japanese Americans during World War II, when more than 110,000

FIGURE 9.4   Officer with a citizen in front of a community police ministation.

Courtesy of Delray Beach Police Department.

Americans of Japanese descent were forcibly removed from their homes and placed in "relocation camps" (LeMay, 2005). Included were people whose families had lived in the United States for nearly a century. Anyone of one-eighth or greater Japanese blood was considered a potential Japanese sympathizer (Henslin, 2007). It was not until 1988 that survivors of the Japanese relocation programs received an official apology and partial compensation from the U.S. government (Tischler, 2007).

Although they did not arrive in the United States in large numbers until after 1900, the Japanese American population has grown steadily. Today they comprise the fifth-largest group of Asian Americans, numbering 796,700 in the 2000 census (U.S. Bureau of the Census, 2001). As a group, Japanese Americans have been very successful in both economic and educational achievements (Henslin, 2007), yet they continue to suffer from discrimination and bigotry. Much of this discrimination is based on racism, but a great deal may also be attributed to envy by other groups. Japanese Americans are resented not just because of their (exaggerated) success within American society but also because of Japan's success in the world economy (Farley, 2005).

Native Americans

The previous sections focused on those persons who have immigrated to the United States and the difficulties they have experienced in adjusting to and being accepted into American society. The racial and cultural distinctions among those ethnic minorities have significantly influenced how they interact with one another and with the white majority. Ironically, the challenges those groups have faced are overshadowed by those endured by the indigenous peoples of the lands that now comprise the United States.

PACIFIC ISLANDERS   Until 1980, Pacific Islanders were classified among "Other Races" within the U.S. census. In the 1980 and 1990 censuses, Pacific Islanders were grouped with Asians. We have not classified them as such for two reasons. The first is that such a grouping was based more on geography than on race or culture. Pacific Islanders are predominantly Polynesians, Micronesians, or Melanesians (Mobasher and Sadri, 2004). These racial groups are distinct from

FIGURE 9.5   Tribal police officers at the San Juan (New Mexico) Pueblo.

others discussed previously. The second reason is that the vast majority of Pacific Islanders residing within the United States are not immigrants from other nations but from lands that are part of the United States. In that these peoples are Americans due to American imperialism rather than to immigration, they are more correctly classified as Native Americans.

HAWAIIAN AMERICANS   The majority of Pacific Islanders residing in the United States are Hawaiian Americans. Hawaii was a separate kingdom until 1893, when American businessmen, aided by the U.S. Navy, led a successful revolt against the Hawaiian monarchy. In 1900, Hawaii became a territory of the United States despite considerable opposition by native Hawaiians. Efforts to make Hawaii a state were resisted by Congress until 1959, primarily due to fears of its heavily Oriental population, which had been imported during the late 1800s and early 1900s to work on the plantations (Lind, 1980). Today, Hawaii is a prosperous state noted for its natural beauty, its mild climate, its friendly treatment of visitors, and its cultural diversity. However, the negative impact of the American experience on native Hawaiians tends to be overlooked.

Hawaiian Americans numbered 140,652 in the 2000 census (U.S. Bureau of the Census, 2001). True Hawaiian Americans are of Polynesian descent. Today they are a minority population in the state of Hawaii. That few pure Hawaiians remain is the result of diseases transported to the islands by visitors, which nearly decimated the native populace during the 1800s, and Hawaiian intermarriage with Asian and white immigrants. The social product is a "melting pot" of diverse cultures and traditions (Schaefer, 2006). Unfortunately, within this "multicultural society," native Hawaiians have suffered discrimination and abuse at the hands of both white Americans and Asian Americans. Native Hawaiians (who were traditionally friendly and trusting) discovered that their lands had been taken over, their economic opportunities limited, and their cultural heritage repressed by other ethnic groups. Many native Hawaiians residing in the "American Paradise" today are currently experiencing economic and social adversities similar to those of other ethnic minorities.

SAMOAN AMERICANS   The Samoan Islands were an independent kingdom in the South Pacific until 1899, when they were partitioned by the United States and Germany. The western islands, which had been seized by Germany, were administered by New Zealand following World War I. In 1962, Western Samoa became an independent nation. American Samoa, as the smaller group of eastern islands is known, has remained under the control of the United States since 1899 (Schaefer, 2006).

The residents of American Samoa are of Polynesian descent and are predominantly Catholics. They are not U.S. citizens, but as U.S. nationals they are free to travel to the United States. As the result of unrestricted immigration, mostly in search of better economic conditions, there were 91,029 Samoan Americans included in the 2000 census (U.S. Bureau of the Census, 2001). Many Samoans immigrate to Hawaii, where they are more readily assimilated than on the U.S. mainland (Schaefer, 2007). The Samoan American experience has been similar to that of other ethnic minorities.

GUAMANIAN AMERICANS   Guam is located within the Marianas Islands and is now a part of the Commonwealth of the Northern Marianas. The United States obtained control of Guam in 1898 at the conclusion of the Spanish-American War. Most Guamanians are "Chamoros," a mixture of native Guamanians, Filipinos, Mexicans, Anglos, and Japanese (Bucher, 2004). Increased economic competition caused Guamanians to begin immigrating to the U.S. mainland in 1970 after the U.S. government opened immigration to Guam for other Asian groups. The 58,240 Guamanian Americans identified in the 2000 census (U.S. Bureau of the Census, 2001) have encountered difficulties similar to those of other Pacific Islanders.

AMERICAN INDIANS   We use the term *Native American* as an umbrella under which all the indigenous peoples of America are categorized. To distinguish others from Pacific Islanders,

Eskimos, and Aleuts, we use the term *American Indian* to refer to the 308 tribes of Native Americans residing within the continental United States (Magleby et al., 2006). Some Native Americans object to the label *American Indian,* citing its derivation from the erroneous assumptions of early European explorers (Cummings and Wise, 2005). However, in that the term is still in use by the U.S. Census Bureau, the Bureau of Indian Affairs, and the American Indian Movement, we shall utilize this terminology. (The authors of this current edition are one-sixteenth Sioux and one-quarter Chickasaw, respectively, so we assure the reader that no disrespect is intended.)

Thus far we have discussed American Indians as if they are a homogeneous group (a practice that the U.S. government too frequently followed). Nothing is further from the truth. Like Asian Americans and Hispanic Americans, American Indians are comprised of culturally diverse peoples who have little in common. The depiction of "bloodthirsty" half-naked warriors riding across the Plains made great Hollywood hype but bore little resemblance to reality. To discuss the diversity among the many tribes and their various cultures and traditions would require volumes. However, the reader should be aware that American Indians had (and continue to have) many different lifestyles that were greatly influenced by their tribal traditions and geographical area. Many were fishermen, farmers, shepherds, ranchers, and craftsmen who lived in permanent and well-governed communities (Bucher, 2004). In fact, the model used by Benjamin Franklin in drafting the Articles of Confederation, which originally governed the United States, was based on the League of the Iroquois (Tischler, 2007).

American Indians are the most disadvantaged minority group in the United States. They have suffered harsher and more prolonged discrimination than has any other minority group. Almost every ethnic group in America has been grievously exploited but none to the degree of American Indians. The enslavement of Indian tribes began in New England prior to the importation of African slaves and continued in the Southwest for several years after the freeing of African slaves (Barker, Hunter, and Rush, 1994). Entire Indian tribes were driven from their lands, confined to lives of poverty on dreary reservations, and/or massacred at the hands of white settlers and the U.S. government. The "Trail of Tears," in which members of the Eastern tribes were forcibly removed to lands west of the Mississippi River, the 1864 Sand Creek Massacre of peaceful Indians in Colorado, the 1890 Massacre at Wounded Knee in South Dakota, and countless other acts of wanton aggression against American Indian men, women, and children (Farley, 2005) exemplify one of the more shameful periods in the history of the United States.

Even in today's enlightened society, which seeks to promote ethnic harmony and which vigorously enforces laws prohibiting discrimination against ethnic minorities, approximately half of American Indians live on government reservations (Schaefer, 2007). Conditions on those 278 reservations are predominantly poor, with most residents living in poverty and lacking decent health care (Magleby et al., 2006). Of those who live off reservations, nearly one-fourth live in poverty (Cummings and Wise, 2005).

American Indians are estimated to have numbered as high as 10 million at the time that Europeans began settling in North America. By 1850 their numbers had declined to approximately 250,000 as a result of starvation, disease, and deliberate massacre (LeMay, 2005). It has only been within the latter portion of this century that the number of American Indians has experienced sizable growth. In the 2000 census, American Indians and Alaskan Natives numbered 2,475,956, or 0.9 percent of the U.S. population (U.S. Bureau of the Census, 2001). This increase has been attributed to high birth rates and somewhat improved living conditions (Popenoe, 2000). It is also due in part to a greater willingness on the part of respondents to identify with their American Indian heritage (Tischler, 2007).

Due to increasing awareness of the continued plight of American Indians and the efforts of organizations such as the American Indian Movement and the National Indian Youth Council, it is hoped that the economic and social conditions of American Indians will improve. But when one realizes that these first Americans were not granted U.S. citizenship until 1924, it appears that change will come slowly.

ESKIMOS AND ALEUTS   Like American Indians, Eskimos and Aleuts are considered Native Americans. These groups have distinct racial and cultural features similar to those of Siberian Asians, which distinguish them from American Indians (Cummings and Wise, 2005). In the 1990 census, when they were classified apart from American Indians, there were 57,152 Eskimos and 23,797 Aleuts residing in the United States (U.S. Bureau of the Census, 1991). Due to their segregation from most of American society in the Alaskan Arctic, Aleuts and Eskimos did not share the long history of oppression experienced by American Indians. However, with the coming of white settlers in the late 1800s and the development that has followed, they have experienced difficulties similar to those of other ethnic minorities.

White Americans

Based on the preceding sections, the reader might assume that all ethnocentric wrongs have been perpetuated on minorities by the "white majority." This view is incorrect for two reasons:

1. All peoples tend to be somewhat xenophobic. The products of this xenophobia are racism, bigotry, intolerance, and discrimination against other groups. Just as minorities have suffered from these social evils, so have they imposed them on one another, as well as on whites. Historically, those within positions of power in the United States have been predominantly white. This has led to the false impression that all whites have power and that all minorities are powerless. It has also led white xenophiles and minority xenophobes to overlook, or too readily excuse, minority misconduct.
2. There is no cohesive "White America." White Americans are as culturally diverse as any other racial category. Indeed, white Americans are varying mixtures of many Caucasoid ethnic groups. To classify all whites as Anglo Americans would be equivalent to labeling all Asians as Japanese, all Hispanics as Chicano, all Pacific Islanders as Samoan, or all American Indians as Cherokee. "European American" is a more accurate designation but still fails to note that many whites, while predominantly of European descent, also have the blood of other races.

In the 2001 census, whites listing one race numbered 274,595,678 or 97.63 percent of the U.S. population. Those listing race in combination with one or more races were 216,930,975 or 77.1 percent (U.S. Bureau of the Census, 2001). There has been an increasing interest in ethnic heritage among white Americans during the past decade, which ironically gained impetus due to the televised presentation of Alex Haley's *Roots*, a history of an African American family. Later films, such as Ron Howard's *Far and Away*, have aided in keeping white ethnic interests alive. Heightened awareness of cultural heritage among whites has also resulted from the current push for multicultural education by minorities and white liberals.

Due to the past success of "Americanization," which emphasized learning to speak English and abandoning national origin or cultural identity in favor of becoming an American (Tischler, 2007), many whites have only limited knowledge of their cultural heritage. Despite this loss, the majority of white Americans are still able to identify their national, if not specific area of, origin.

EUROPEAN AMERICANS   The original European immigrants to America were primarily from the colonial powers of England, France, Holland, and Spain. By 1700, the English culture was dominant along the East Coast (Schaefer, 2007). Later immigrants (both before and after the American Revolution) were expected to adopt the social standards of this earlier group of White Anglo-Saxon Protestants (WASPs). Affluent WASPs controlled the political and social environment of early America (many non-WASPs argue that they still do). As non-English immigrants from western Europe arrived, they were indoctrinated as to how to conduct themselves. For Protestants from Scotland, Wales, Ireland, Sweden, Norway, Germany, France, and Switzerland, this was not a particularly difficult task. For Catholics from those same nations, the adjustment was more difficult due to religious persecution. Irish Catholics, in particular, were the recipients of severe harassment and oppression at the hands of the WASP power structure (LeMay, 2005).

As masses of non-Protestant immigrants began arriving in America from southern and eastern Europe, they also suffered from bigotry and discrimination. These "White Ethnics," as they are called (Healey, 2003), did not assimilate as readily as had previous white immigrants. Even in the 1990s, despite the constant pressures of Americanization, strong cultural identification can be found among their descendants. In addition to their cultural identification, one can also find a resentment among this group toward those who would declare that their "whiteness" has made for easy assimilation into American society. This resentment appears to be well founded if one considers that 66.5 percent of the nation's poor are white (U.S. Bureau of the Census, 1992, p. 12).

JEWISH AMERICANS Approximately 6,500,000 Americans identify themselves as being Jewish (Schaefer, 2007). Unlike the other non-Protestant ethnic groups identified above, Jewish Americans did not identify with a common homeland. Nor can Jews be identified as a distinct racial group (despite the efforts of anti-Semites to do so). Their intermarriages with other ethnic cultures and the adoption of Judaism by members of diverse racial groups preclude such a racial identity. However, being Jewish transcends mere religious identification. Many people who do not practice Judaism still strongly identify with being Jewish. This strong cultural identification has been both beneficial and detrimental to Jews. Their adherence to a specific ethnic identity has enabled them to preserve their unique cultural heritage. Unfortunately, it has also led to their being targeted by others for being "different."

Jewish immigration to America began during the colonial period and continues today. The earliest Jewish immigrants came from Spain and Portugal. They were followed by immigrants from Germany and later from eastern Europe. In recent years, Jewish immigration into the United States has been primarily from Russia. As a group, Jewish Americans have achieved economic success and considerable political power, yet they have suffered from prejudice and discrimination throughout American history (Macionis, 2006). Anti-Semitism is no longer as common in the United States, but it continues.

Middle-Easterners and Northern Africans

Another cultural grouping that may be found in the United States is that of Middle-Easterners and Northern Africans. Members of this group either immigrated from or are descendants of immigrants from the Middle East or Northern Africa. Included in this grouping would be Arab Americans, Iranian Americans, and Turkish Americans. The exact number of Americans of Middle Eastern or Northern African descent is difficult to ascertain in that some members of this grouping are categorized as "Other Asian," others are classified within the general category of "White," and still others may be found within the category of "Other Race." However, utilizing data from the 2000 census (U.S. Bureau of the Census, 2001), it appears that their numbers would exceed 1 million. While many practice other religions, the majority are Muslim.

Immigration from Northern Africa and the Middle East has been a fairly recent phenomenon. Northern Africans and Middle-Easterners did not begin arriving in the United States in large numbers until the relaxing of immigration restrictions by the Immigration and Naturalization Act of 1965. Although their numbers are relatively small in comparison to other ethnic groups, they have received considerable attention in recent years due to the hostile relations that the United States has had with Iran and Iraq, and due to terrorist activities by a variety of Arab and Middle Eastern groups. The product of this attention has been a dramatic increase in hostility, discrimination, and assaults on U.S. citizens and resident aliens of Arab and Middle Eastern descent, particularly since the events of September 11, 2001.

A Perspective on Diverse Cultures

The United States is comprised of numerous ethnic groups that are actively engaged in social and economic competition in a pluralistic society. Racism, ethnocentrism, and discrimination continue. Too frequently, we experience racial unrest in our urban areas. "Hate crimes" are perpetuated by frustrated individuals who act out against groups or persons who differ from them. A casual observer may wonder why outright cultural conflict such as that currently found in regions of eastern Europe and Africa does not break out.

Although the authors cannot assure the reader that such incidents will never take place in the United States, we can offer hope that they will not. We will always have individuals who fear and hate peoples who are different from them, and there will always be individuals and groups who will play on those fears and hatred for their own political and/or economic gain. Some will blatantly preach their bigotry, others will seek to conceal it within noble-sounding rhetoric. Despite the existence of those who harbor resentment and animosity toward other races or ethnic groups, the majority of Americans are actually quite tolerant of one another. The reason for this is quite simple: *We are more alike than we are different.*

IMPROVING COMMUNITY RELATIONS IN THE CONTEXT OF CULTURE

Generally, the following elements must exist in order for strategies designed to improve community relations in the context of culture to be successful, especially since we have such diverse cultural groups in most U.S. cities.

Appreciating Culture

Understanding and appreciating the cultural patterns and characteristics that exist in the community are prerequisites to making positive decisions in a cultural context. Developing a strategy in which the community can participate and retain a sense of community ownership and self-help must begin with this step.

Understanding Language

Lack of a common language creates the likelihood for misunderstanding, increased fear, and increased distance in interpersonal relations. It is not possible to be fluent in each of the many languages and ethnic dialects that exist in our larger, multicultural cities. It is possible, however, to learn key street-applicable phrases in the language, to have translators available in major language groups, and to appreciate some of the cultural values expressed in language. As members of the community teach new language skills to police officers, they may also learn from the officers some of the same elements of English.

Getting Involved in Meaningful Ways

Getting involved can reduce isolation and stereotyping and increase community morale and participation in policing. Those who live outside the community and spend little free time there are outsiders, even if they once were community residents. Face-to-face contact is important. A new immigrant may come to the United States with a view of the police based on an old-country value, which is one of fear and distrust. Police must understand that view and appreciate its cultural context if change is to be possible.

In another sense, the community will have to make the same commitment in reverse and seek to understand the police view and appreciate its cultural context. Rather than leading to stereotyping and distrust, such efforts could lead to helping both officers and the community achieve their goals. If it is true that the values of police officers are lower in context than the communities they serve, this understanding of context can be used by police and the community to build cooperation. Reward can be attached by the agency and the community to community relations projects, gaining social recognition for the officers. The challenge of confronting barriers and building a legacy of cooperation can be both exciting and lead to inner harmony. In this way, meeting community needs can also meet the needs of the officers.

Affecting Public Policy

Community members can be encouraged by police officers to get involved in the formation of public police policy that affects their lives. Police can help build a supportive network that involves the leadership of more than one cultural group.

Making a Firm, Full Commitment

The agency and its officers must make a firm, full commitment to improving relations in the context of culture if the effort is to be successful. It must be firm in the sense that what is promised is what is delivered; the commitment is not just rhetoric but real. It must be firm also in the sense that it will be supported over a long period of time and will not be abandoned at the first sign of problems. It must be full in the sense that energy, money, and time must be committed to the effort. This includes rewards for officers and enough flexibility within the program to meet new challenges as they arise.

Multicultural Advisory Committees

Multicultural advisory committees that form partnerships with the diverse ethnic communities and their police agencies are examples of community policing in action and should be put into place by police agencies at all levels of government. Our neighbor to the North, Canada, is a nation of diverse cultures. Canadian police agencies practice community policing at all levels and have multicultural advisory committees in them. The Royal Canadian Mounted Police (RCMP), an agency similar to the FBI and Canada's federal police, are committed to serving the needs of their diverse communities. For example, the Richmond, British Columbia, RCMP state on their Web site that they are "reaching out to and partnering with a cross section of Richmond's diverse multicultural groups to strengthen existing partnerships and build positive relationships with representatives from local cultural organizations" (www.richmond.ca/safety/police/cprograms/multicultural.htm). The agency's multicultural advisory committee is the vehicle for this outreach effort and its mission is to "advance and promote positive relations between the Richmond RCMP and Richmond's diverse multicultural community by:

- creating an open, equitable, and sensitive organization, and
- encouraging an effective RCMP response to diversity issues and to reaching the goals of our national Bias-free Policing policy."

Bias-free policing involves decisions based on reasonable suspicion or probable grounds (probable cause) rather than on stereotypes about race, religion, ethnicity, gender, or other prohibited grounds.

The Canadian police agencies at the local level also have multicultural advisory committees. The Victoria and Vancouver Police Departments have police diversity committees. The Vancouver Diversity Advisory Committee, created in 1996 and composed of police and community members, meets monthly to discuss and implement improvements with respect to the relationships between the police and the community. The Greater Victoria Police Diversity Committee is a consultative and advisory committee to police departments in the Greater Victoria area. Their Web site says that the goal "is to help police members better understand the diverse cultures, value systems, unique perspectives, and conditions and religious beliefs" of the minority groups they serve (http://vicpd.ca/diversity.html).

Australia, another country that practices community policing and has widely diverse groups, has a long history of police–community multicultural advisory committees. The first

Australian police multicultural advisory unit (MAU) was established by the Victoria police in 1983. The unit within the police department is staffed by bilingual/bicultural sworn and unsworn members who are responsible for the following:

- Advising police on multicultural issues
- Providing cross-cultural training for police members
- Providing information on the role of police to Victorians from culturally and linguistically diverse backgrounds (www.police.vic.gov.au).

In 1985 the Police and Community Multicultural Advisory Committee (PACMAC) was established. This is a joint committee between the Victoria police and the Victorian Multicultural Commission. The members for this advisory committee are drawn from the Victoria police and Victoria's culturally and linguistically diverse communities. In 1993 the National Police Ethnic Advisory Bureau was established. This bureau recommends to all the police commissioners of Australia national policies, programs, and initiatives for improving police–ethnic community relations in Australia. This has led to state and local agencies forming their own police ethnic advisory groups made up of police and members from the multicultural communities.

In the United States, at the federal level, regional office of the Federal Bureau of Investigation establishes multicultural advisory councils composed of community representatives from ethnic and religious groups and law enforcement agencies. The goals of these councils are to build relationships and intergroup knowledge to improve community safety. The Los Angeles FBI office with their multicultural advisory committee (MCAC) holds town hall meetings to discuss community issues. In 2008, the New Orleans Field Office created a multicultural advisory council composed of community leaders and representatives from the diverse groups in the city to promote understanding and communication between the New Orleans community and the FBI (http://new orleans.fbu.gov/pressrel/2008/no073008.htm). Among the participating groups are representatives of the City of New Orleans Human Relations Commission, Children's Bureau of New Orleans, the Human Rights Campaign, the Anti-Defamation League, Catholic Charities Archdiocese of New Orleans, the Hispanic Chamber of Commerce, Reaping the Harvest Church, Unity of Greater New Orleans, the Loyola Center for Intercultural Understanding, the Better Business Bureau, Mary Queen of Vietnam Church and the Vietnamese community, the Jewish Federation of Greater New Orleans, Advocacy Center, the Times Picayune-Asian Affairs, the Indian community, the Ninth Ward community, and the Mid-City Neighborhood Organization.

Local police multicultural advisory committees are not as numerous and well developed as those found in Canada and Australia. However, there are some good examples: The Richfield, Minnesota, police multicultural advisory committee "will provide advice, suggestions, and assistance to the Richfield Police Department to aid them in better serving, communicating with, and understanding the many cultures that reside in, work in, or visit the Richfield area" (www.ci.richfield.mn.us).

Specific Targets

RECRUITMENT It is generally accepted that recruitment of officers must reflect the racial/cultural makeup of the community. The agency must seek the best candidates within these groups and then assist them to be culturally appropriate and to translate their understanding of their culture into positive action.

A three-year national advertising campaign to support local police recruitment, especially women and ethnic minorities, was undertaken in the United Kingdom (England and Wales) in 2000. The campaign sought to demonstrate the challenges the police face and to raise the status of policing in the public's eye and among the police themselves (Anonymous, 2000). Advertisements by celebrities and others ran on TV, in newspapers, on radio, and in theaters. The first year results showed a 77 percent increase in police recruits (Anonymous, 2001a). Such a national advertising program might work well in the United States, especially in conjunction with the federal COPS program.

The minority recruiting efforts of many police departments have dramatically changed the demographics of the departments. Shifting demographic patterns and an aggressive recruitment program have changed the New York City Police Department from 86.6 percent white in 1979 to 52.3 percent white in 2005 (Lee, 2005). The rest of the department in 2005 was 17.4 percent black, 25.5 percent Hispanic, and 3.8 percent Asian. In fact Asian Americans are the fastest growing group in the department. The 2005 academy graduating class of 1,750 recruits was the first time that minorities made up the majority of recruits (www.nyc.gov). More than half of the class, 54.06 percent were minorities—28.17 percent Hispanic, 17.7 percent black, 8 percent Asian, and 0.22 percent other. The graduating class was also the most educated in the department's history, with 57 percent having either an associate's or baccalaureate degree; 68 recruits had a master's degree and three were attorneys. The fire department is still 92 percent white, demonstrating that changing demographics is not solely responsible for the shift in the NYPD.

Progressive U.S. police departments like the NYPD, and those in many other countries, no longer hire at the minimum level—that is, they pursue a process of screening in, not screening out applicants (Cordner, Scarborough, and Sheehan, 2004). Basically, the screening-out process considers all applicants who meet the basic qualifications of high school diploma or GED, background checks, and so on. In the screening-in process, the department considers all those who meet the minimum qualifications, but only hires those who meet identified needs. For many departments these needs include ethnic diversity. Therefore, many police departments are specifically targeting minority/ethnic communities to ensure that women and men recruited by such efforts come from various racial and ethnic backgrounds (Prussel and Lonsway, 2001). Targeting minority communities is the best, and maybe the only, way to increase diversity in policing. In Long Beach, California, community leaders assist in recruiting efforts by training cultural groups to qualify for positions with the police department and other city agencies. In addition, several police departments are paying language incentive pay. The Dallas Police Department pays an additional $75–100 per month to officers fluent in Spanish, Cambodian, or sign language. San Jose, California, gives hiring preferences to applicants who speak eight certified foreign languages (Bennett, 1999). Regular officers who speak these languages receive incentive pay.

TRAINING　The United States has become more multicultural and it is necessary that all police training (preservice and in service) must reflect the demographics of the community served. To accomplish that, training must reflect the following six principles (Himelfarb, 1991, pp. 53–55):

1. Respect for and sensitivity to the diverse communities served is essential for effective policing.
2. Respect for and sensitivity to ethnocultural communities can best be achieved through a broad-based multicultural strategy.
3. Training must be an essential element of such a strategy.
4. Training must be ongoing and built into the experience of policing; that is, it must be more than a course or two on **multiculturalism**.
5. A multicultural strategy that supports it will be most effective if perceived as integrated aspects of the philosophy and operations of policing.
6. A multicultural strategy and training program must be created in consultation with the ethnocultural communities served by the police.

The training must emphasize that the police are not "apart from" the community but are "a part" of the community (Coderoni, 2002).

The Santa Ana Police Department was instrumental in setting up the Task Force on Police–Asian Relations (TOPAR) in Orange County, California. Several departments joined to produce a series of videotapes for both officers and immigrants. They held a series of seminars explaining Southeast Asian culture with the goal of increasing communication and understanding between refugees and police. Problems still exist, but most feel that progress has been made (Taft, 1982, pp. 17–21).

Language skills may be taught through the use of key words, role-play situations depicting cross-cultural incidents, and case studies that demonstrate values, beliefs, and lifestyles. Involvement of community members and practice are critical to the success of language training. Crash courses usually have little long-term use.

The Houston Police Department's academy and in-service program incorporates many of the key strategies discussed in this chapter in an effort to improve community relations with the Hispanic population. The program includes information about Hispanic culture and its variations and information and activities regarding stress—what causes it and how to recognize it. Part of the training also includes discussion about Hispanic culture and cultural differences at Ripley House, a community center in a Hispanic area. This encourages communication between police officers and members of the Hispanic community. Confronting stereotypes through asking and answering anonymous questions of officers and learning a basic system of communication in Spanish that is geared toward street use are also part of the overall program. Input from officers is an important part of the training. A fiesta attended by officers and community members concludes one part of the training. Attendance is supported by the department. Each officer is rewarded with points toward certification, an insignia, and an opportunity to make changes in the program.

Rockland County, New York, because of its borders (Connecticut, New Jersey, and Westchester County, New York) and its proximity to New York City, has 15 different cultures (including Jamaican, Korean, Hasidic, Filipino, Cambodian, Haitian, Chinese, and Ramapo Mountain Indians) within its borders. With input from individuals from each culture and assistance from the Rockland County Chief's Association, the sheriff's office developed a 200-page sensitivity training manual (Merla, 1996). The manual, used in the police academy, provides information on each culture's religion, language, characteristics, and community dynamics. The manual also contains cultural taboos (e.g., a female officer touching an Hasidic male is considered offensive).

Since early 1990, the California cities of San Jose, Long Beach, Stockton, and Garden Grove have provided cultural diversity training to their officers. Stockton and Garden Grove provide such training to all employees. African Americans, Asian Americans, and Hispanic Americans make up almost 50 percent of each city's population (Bennett, 1995). The Roanoke, Virginia, Police Department has made efforts to build relationships with the Vietnamese community. An integral part of this program is cultural awareness training for Roanoke police officers (Coventry and Johnson, 2001).

PUBLIC INFORMATION BULLETINS FOR LANGUAGE MINORITIES   The U.S. Department of Justice has published a brochure containing ideas for developing materials for people who do not speak fluent English. The materials are geared toward involving such people in the nation's social, political, economic, and legal mainstream to avoid isolation and frustration.

ONGOING COMMUNITY PARTICIPATION   Involving the community in training programs and in volunteer and citizen review efforts helps to secure continuing input. Police can be personally involved in community activities, particularly in outreach activities with youth. Foot patrol and/or team policing in designated areas may also be helpful. Close personal connections with the community must be maintained both on duty and off. The Los Angeles Police Department storefront center in Korea Town is the joint effort of the department and the community.

In St. Paul, Minnesota, the police chief meets with leaders of the Hmong, a group of 10,000 Laotian hill people who have settled there. His goal is to stay up to date on community developments and provide meaningful in-service training in the police department on Hmong culture (Taft, 1982, p. 17). On July 12, 2001, the Houston Police Department held its ninth Multicultural Reception at a local restaurant (Anonymous, 2001b). Citizens representing African American, Hispanic American, Asian American, and other ethnic and cultural groups attended. All were encouraged to wear attire that represented their culture or ethnicity.

Cultural Citizens Police Academies

The success of citizens police academies (CPA) has led many police departments to offer the same instruction in the group's native language or special topics that affect the minority groups. The Orlando, Florida, Police Department has offered a citizens police academy in Spanish since 2003. The Corcoran, California, Police Department offers a Spanish-language CPA entitled "Amigos de la Comunidad" or "Friends of the Community." The instruction is translated from the English-language CPA. In 2002, there were 20 Spanish-language CPAs in 12 states (Walker, Herbst, and Irlbeck, 2002).

Sacramento, California, is the most racially and ethnically integrated major American city, with 48 different cultures, including Hmong, Vietnamese, Slavic, and Mien (www.policevolunteers.org). The Sacramento Police Department conducts cultural academies for the Mien, Hmong, and Slavic communities. These academies are held once a week for three hours over a six-week period. The topics are more or less the same as in the English-language CPA and include additional topics of concern to the cultural group.

THE COMMUNITY RELATIONS SERVICE (CRS)   CRS is an agency of the U.S. Department of Justice, created by the Civil Rights Act of 1964. The purpose of the agency is to assist in resolving community racial conflict, and the method is through noncoercive, third-party intervention. The service has regional offices in Atlanta, Boston, Chicago, Dallas, Denver, Kansas City, New York, Philadelphia, San Francisco, and Seattle. CRS conducts formal negotiations and offers informal assistance to facilitate resolution of conflicts, frequently assisting communities in resolving disputes arising from alleged police use of excessive force.

ADVOCACY   "Action" committees can be formed that work with community social and legal services, civil rights, and other groups to promote police–citizen communication and citizen participation in formulating and monitoring police policies and practices that reflect the cultural needs of the community. For example, Hispanic Americans are becoming increasingly involved in and committed to influencing public policy in justice areas.

POLICE–COMMUNITY RELATIONS COMMITTEES   Whenever minority groups voice concern that they are not receiving fair treatment form their police force, police–community relations committees can be established that include representatives from these alienated groups. This is exactly what happened in New London, Connecticut, in 1984 when complaints came from the black and Hispanic residents about the lack of fair treatment by a predominately white New London Police Department. A nine-member committee was formed with representatives from the NAACP and the Hispanic community, at least one woman, a council member, two nonvoting representatives for the high school, a member of the police union, and a police member designated by the chief. Recently, a member from the gay community was added. The original purpose of the committee "was to recommend to the city administration and City Council methods and programs designed to foster better understanding between citizens and police officers." The committee has had a rocky past but it is still functioning.

REALITY CHECK

Coping with Cultural Diversity

In light of the many racial and ethnic groups in the United States, how do we as a nation deal properly with cultural diversity? In the 1990s, three distinct perspectives were held by Americans in regard to cultural diversity. Each of these three perspectives offers a solution for coping with cultural diversity that is contradictory to the solutions offered by the others.

Leftist advocates of cultural pluralism claim that since the United States is a multicultural society, the political, economic, and educational systems must reflect that diversity. This "politically correct" group argues that straight, white, Anglo males have wrongly dominated American society (Gates, 1993). This wrong must be corrected by providing preferential treatment for females, ethnic minorities, and homosexuals until true equality of results has been achieved.

Political correctness (PC) calls for downplaying traditional studies of Western culture in favor of studies that emphasize the views of ethnic minorities, non-Christian religions, females, and gays (Eshleman, Cashion, and Basirico, 1993). PC advocates also support bilingual education by asserting that forcing immigrants to learn English is demeaning to minorities. Quotas designed to achieve equal results are considered both appropriate and necessary. They respond to allegations of reverse racism, sexism, and "straight bashing" by declaring that these actions are needed to pay back white males for their past oppressions of others. In short, not only must equality of results be accomplished, but atonement for past injustices must be made.

Conservative proponents of Americanization claim that PC is racist, sexist, anti-Christian, and heterophobic. These "fundamentalists" see the overemphasis of multiculturalism and discrimination against white males as harmful to all of society in that they promote separateness, bigotry, and intolerance. Actions that took place in the past cannot be undone in the present, particularly when those now targeted either had nothing to do with past injustices or were themselves victims of injustice. This group argues that English must be the official language of the United States in order to maintain the American culture (Eshleman, Cashion, and Basirico, 1993). They argue further that traditional American values must be upheld to protect our national identity, thwart moral decline, and prevent society from breaking down into cultural enclaves such as those currently found in eastern Europe and Africa.

Americanization proponents partially agree with the concept of equal opportunity for individuals but oppose the use of quotas or other mechanisms to ensure equality of results. They state that ethnic minorities and females are being assimilated into the economic and political power structure, and that time will eventually remove any inequities. Stressing multiculturalism is seen as rewarding activists who are motivated by selfish desires for economic and political gain rather than contributing to society. They further argue that efforts to redistribute wealth and expand welfare programs stifle individual initiatives and lead to overreliance on government (Brookhiser, 1993). Finally, these American fundamentalists view homosexuality as a deviant lifestyle that should be repressed rather than accepted by society. Critics of this extreme conservatism argue that it is close-minded, racist, sexist, classist, and homophobic.

A third view is held by *moderates, joined by a mainstream coalition of both liberals and conservatives.* This group disagrees with the extremism of the two other perspectives. Multiculturalism is seen as reasonable and healthy, but it is felt that societal norms and shared values must be preserved to protect all groups and maintain order within a pluralistic society. Affirmative action programs designed to provide equality of opportunity by ensuring a "level playing field" for women and minorities are felt to be appropriate. However, absolute guarantees of equal results are viewed with skepticism. Bilingual education is seen as beneficial in preserving ethnic identity as long as it does not ignore the competency in English needed to be competitive in American society (Tischler, 2007). Homosexuality is seen as a personal matter that should be used neither for nor against gays.

This moderate approach to multiculturalism is based on a desire to create an equitable, color-blind nation that is tolerant of differences among its diverse population. All groups, regardless of cultural heritage, gender, or sexual persuasion, are seen as contributing to American society. In this perspective, past injustices should be acknowledged in order to guard against similar unfairness in the future. However, efforts to exact vengeance for past evils (real or imagined) are seen as meaningless and divisive. Instead, cooperation based on education, tolerance, and a desire for a common good is seen as the appropriate means for coping with cultural diversity. Both left- and right-wing critics of moderation tend to see it as being allied with their ideological opponents at the opposite extreme.

Which of the foregoing perspectives is most compatible with your own views on culture? Why?

Conclusions

People usually behave in culturally defined ways, and their behavior can often be understood in the context of culture. Positive police–community relations are easiest to achieve in a community that is relatively culturally integrated. They are most difficult to achieve in fragmented communities that are culturally diverse and where cultural rules are in transition and unclear.

We rarely have the ideal as an option, but even in the most fragmented community an aggressive ongoing program for improving community relations in the context of culture can be effective. The key elements of a successful program include appreciating the culture(s); understanding the language(s); getting involved in meaningful ways; making a firm, full commitment; and creatively overcoming barriers.

It is important to remember that we are one culture as well as many. We have some basic values and goals in common. We share common feelings of anger, sadness, happiness, and fear. We also wish to be valued and to belong. Ruth Benedict (1934) wrote this:

> What really binds men together is their culture— the ideas and the standards they have in common. If instead of selecting a symbol like common blood heredity and making a slogan of it, the nation turned its attention rather to the culture that unites its people, emphasizing its major merits and recognizing the different values which may develop in a different culture, it would substitute realistic thinking for a kind of symbolism which is dangerous because it is misleading. (p. 16)

Student Checklist

1. Define *cultural context.*
2. Describe the cultural context of community relations.
3. Contrast characteristics of different cultural groups.
4. Analyze several cultural factors that may be misunderstood by police.
5. Describe several community relations strategies for improving community relations in the context of culture.

Topics for Discussion

1. List five values that you share with other members of your family. Are these values commonly held by all members of your community?
2. Discuss the cultural contexts that exist in your community. How has your community worked to resolve conflicts in values among these contexts?
3. What training is offered to police officers in your community that could improve community relations across cultures?
4. What are the possible benefits to be obtained from forming police multicultural advisory committees?
5. Does your local police department have any special minority recruitment programs? If so, what are they?

Bibliography

Anonymous. (August 30 2000). "UK Government: Home secretary launches first ever national advertising police campaign," *M2 Presswire*, Coventry.

Anonymous. (April 23 2001a). "UK Government: Police recruits up 77%," *M2 Presswire*, Coventry.

Anonymous. (2001b). "HPD recognizes diversity at multi-cultural reception," *The HPD News*, Vol. 1, No. 8, p. 1.

Barker, T., Hunter, R. D., and Rush, J. P. (1994). *Police Systems and Practices: An Introduction.* Upper Saddle River, NJ: Prentice Hall.

Bartol, C. R. (1998). *Criminal Behavior: A Psychosocial Approach*, 5th ed. Upper Saddle River, NJ: Prentice Hall.

Benedict, R. (1934). *Patterns of Culture.* Boston, MA: Houghton Mifflin.

Bennett, B. R. (1995). "Incorporating diversity: Police response to multicultural changes in their communities," *FBI Law Enforcement Bulletin*, Vol. 64, No. 12, pp. 1–6.

Bennett, B. (1999). "Beyond affirmative action: Police response to a changing society," *Journal of California Law Enforcement*, Vol. 33, No. 2, pp. 10–15.

Brinkerhoff, D. B. (1998). *Essentials of Sociology*, 4th ed. St. Paul, MN: Wadsworth.

Brookhiser, R. (March 1, 1993). "The melting pot is still simmering," *Time*, p. 72.

Bucher, R. D. (2004). *Diversity Consciousness: Opening Our Minds to People, Cultures and Opportunities*, 2nd ed. Upper Saddle River, NJ: Pearson/Prentice Hall.

Coderoni, G. R. (November 2002). "The relationship between multicultural training for police and effective law enforcement," *FBI Law Enforcement Bulletin*.

Colvard, A. L. (1992). "Foreign languages: A contemporary training requirement," *FBI Law Enforcement Bulletin*, Vol. 61, No. 9, pp. 20–23.

Cole, D. (1999). *No Equal Justice*. New York: The New Press.

Cordner, G. W., Scarbourgh, K., and Sheehan, R. (2004). *Police Administration*, 5th ed. Cincinnati, OH: Anderson Publishing.

Coventry, G., and Johnson, K. D. (2001). "Building relationships between police and Vietnamese community in Roanoke, Virginia," *Bureau of Justice Assistance Bulletin*, Washington, D.C.: U.S. Department of Justice.

Cummings, M. C., Jr., and Wise, D. (2005). *Democracy under Pressure: An Introduction to the American Political System*, 10th ed. Pacific Grove, CA: Thomson/Wadsworth.

Farley, J. E. (2005). *Majority-Minority Relations*, 5th ed. Upper Saddle River, NJ: Pearson/Prentice Hall.

Gates, D. (March 29, 1993). "White male paranoia," *Newsweek*, pp. 48–53.

Greenlee, M. R. (February 1980). "Discretionary decision making in the field," *Police Chief*, pp. 50–51.

Healey, J. F. (2003). *Race Ethnicity and Gender*, 3rd ed. Thousand Oaks, CA: Pine Forge Press.

Henslin, J. M. (2007). *Sociology: A Down-to-Earth Approach*, 8th ed. Boston, MA: Pearson/Allyn and Bacon.

Himelfarb, F. (November 1991). "A training strategy for policing in a multicultural society," *The Police Chief*, pp. 53–55.

King, M. L., Jr. (August 28, 1963). "I have a dream" speech, in Washington, D.C.

Kitano, H. H. L. (1996). *Race Relations*, 5th ed. Upper Saddle River, NJ: Prentice Hall.

Lee, J. (2005). *In Police Class, Blue Comes in Many Colors*. www.michaelsaray.com.

LeMay, M. (2005). *The Perennial Struggle: Race, Ethnicity and Minority Group Relations in the United States*, 2nd ed. Upper Saddle River, NJ: Pearson/Prentice Hall.

Lind, A. W. (1980). *Hawaii's People*, 4th ed. Honolulu, HI: University Press of Hawaii.

Macionis, J. J. (2006). *Society: The Basics*, 8th ed. Upper Saddle River, NJ: Pearson/Prentice Hall.

Magleby, D. B., O'Brien, D. M., Light, P. C., Burns, J. M., Peltason, J. W., and Cronin, T. E. (2006). *Government by the People*, 21st ed. Upper Saddle River, NJ: Pearson/Prentice Hall.

Merla, M. (March/April 1996). "Fair treatment for all: Equal opportunity police training," *Community Policing Exchange*, p. 3.

Mobasher, M., and Sadri, M. (2004). *Migration, Globalization and Ethnic Relations: An Interdisciplinary Approach*. Upper Saddle River, NJ: Pearson/Prentice Hall.

O'Connor, S. D. (June 28, 1993). Supreme Court majority opinion written by Justice O'Conner, in *Shaw v. Barr* 92–357.

Pitter, G. E. (1992). "Policing cultural celebrations," *FBI Law Enforcement Bulletin*, Vol. 61, No. 9, pp. 10–14.

Popenoe, D. (2000). *Sociology*, 11th ed. Upper Saddle River, NJ: Pearson/Prentice Hall.

Prussel, D., and Lonsway, K. A. (2001). "Recruiting women police officers," *Law & Order*, Vol. 49, No. 7, pp. 91–96.

Rothman, R. A. (2005). *Inequality and Stratification: Race, Class and Gender*, 5th ed. Upper Saddle River, NJ: Pearson/Prentice Hall.

Schaefer, R. T. (2006). *Racial and Ethnic Groups*, 10th ed. Upper Saddle River, NJ: Pearson/ Prentice Hall.

Schaefer, R. T. (2007). *Race and Ethnicity in the U.S.*, 4th ed. Upper Saddle River, NJ: Pearson/Prentice Hall.

Shusta, R. M., Levine, D. R., Wong, H. Z., and Harris, P. R. (2005). *Multicultural Law Enforcement: Strategies for Peacemaking in a Diverse Society*. Upper Saddle River, NJ: Pearson/Prentice Hall.

Taft, P. B., Jr. (July 1982). "Policing the new immigrant ghettos," *Police Magazine*, pp. 10–26.

Tischler, H. L. (2007). *Introduction to Sociology*, 9th ed. Pacific Grove, CA: Thomson/Wadsworth.

U.S. Bureau of the Census. (1992). *Income, Poverty, and Wealth in the United States: A Chartbook*. Washington, D.C.: U.S. Government Printing Office.

U.S. Bureau of the Census. (2001). *2000 Census of Population: General Characteristics of the United States: 2001*. Washington, D.C.: U.S. Government Printing Office.

Walker, S., Herbst, L., and Irlbeck, D. (2002). *Police Outreach to the Hispanic/Latino Community: A Survey of Programs and Activities*. A Report by the Police Professionalism Initiative University of Nebraska at Omaha and the National Latino Peace Officers Association.

Weaver, G. (1992). "Law enforcement in a culturally diverse society," *FBI Law Enforcement Bulletin*, Vol. 61, No. 9, pp. 1–7.

Weis, J. G., and Sederstrom, J. (1981). *The Prevention of Serious Delinquency: What to Do?* Reports of the National Juvenile Justice Assessment Centers. Washington, D.C.: U.S. Department of Justice.

CHAPTER 10

Undocumented Immigration as Moral Panic
Casting Difference as Threat

Michael Costelloe

INTRODUCTION

Public discourse concerning immigration and immigration policy often relies on the characterization and universalization of the threats that are posed by increasing immigration. That is, rather than engaging in rational discussions that acknowledge that immigration reform must strike a balance between the interests of current citizens and a recognition of the needs of those who risk their lives coming to the United States for a better existence, those who favor restrictive immigration policies tend to engage in rhetoric that refers to the widespread personal, social, and economic threats posed by undocumented immigration.[1] It is the specification of and reference to these threats that allows one to consider undocumented immigration as an ideologically driven "moral panic" and to examine how framing undocumented immigration in terms of threat influences public policy. Moreover, this chapter will examine how policies developed out of moral panics are often ineffectual and at times harmful and even deadly.

MORAL PANIC

Although the term "moral panic" was first used by Jock Young in 1971, Stanley Cohen (1972) is credited for analytically applying the concept in his seminal work on Mods and Rockers. Cohen noted that at certain times:

> a condition, episode, person or group of persons emerges to become defined as a threat to societal values and interests; its nature is presented in a stylized and stereotypical fashion by the mass media; moral barricades are manned by editors, bishops, politicians and other right-thinking people; socially accredited experts pronounce their diagnosis and solutions; ways of coping are evolved or (more often) resorted to; the condition then disappears, submerges or deteriorates and becomes more visible. Sometimes the subject of the panic is quite novel and at other times it is something which has been in existence long enough, but suddenly appears in the limelight. (Cohen, 1972:9)

In short, the term "moral panic" defines the exaggerated social reactions to perceived deviance from and threats to societal values.

Based on Cohen's definition of moral panics, Kenneth Thompson (1998:8) outlines five significant aspects of moral panics:

- Something or someone is defined as a threat to values or interests.
- This threat is depicted in an easily recognizable form by the media.
- There is a rapid build-up of public concern.
- There is a response from authorities or opinion-makers.
- The panic recedes or results in social change.

Implicit in the term "moral panic" is the belief that "the threat is to something held sacred by or fundamental to the society" (Thompson, 1998:8). That is, what distinguish moral panics from other forms of public concerns are both the intensity with which the threat is felt and its potential effect on societal values and morals. The problem, left unchecked, portends to tear at moral fabric. In the United States, threats to such values as family (particularly aimed at children), culture, personal safety, and religion tend to have a greater probability of becoming moral panics than other types of concerns.

The term "moral panic" is a sociological concept; it is not itself a theory (Goode, 2000). It is a tool that can be employed by any number of diverse theories to aid in the examination of the similarities between seemingly different phenomena (Critcher, 2006; Goode, 2000). Moral panics have been employed within a number of different theoretical frameworks, including quite disparate theories such as Marxist theory (e.g., Hall et al., 1978) and structural functionalism (e.g., Lauderdale, 1976). However, if the term "moral panic" is to be a useful conceptual tool and not stretched to meaninglessness, then it should be applied to only those situations that commonly exhibit most of Thompson's previously mentioned five aspects of moral panics.

Goode and Ben-Yehuda note that "the concept of moral panics expands our understanding of social structure, social process, and social change." They argue that moral panics work to clearly define normative behaviors and the moral boundaries of society and to demonstrate that there are limits to how much diversity a society can endure (1994:29). Moreover, the study of moral panics demonstrates that development and implementation of suitable policies and responses to perceived deviance do not develop from rational discourse that draws on objective assessments of the potential harm. Instead, social reaction to moral panics springs forth from the real or imagined threat to certain "positions, statuses, interests, ideologies and values" (Cohen, 1972:191).

Those involved in the creation and maintenance of moral panics include the "five powerful Ps of moral panics" (Critcher, 2006:4):

- The press and broadcasting
- Pressure groups and claim seekers
- Politicians and government
- Police and law enforcement agencies
- Public opinion

When these entities come together on a particular issue, their power to arouse intense reaction is remarkable and often results in the creation of legislation that provides for oppressive social control measures to address the problem (Critcher, 2006). In other words, a "signification spiral" occurs where the actions of and interactions between these groups take a public concern and exaggerate it until it becomes disproportionate to the true threat.

A key component of moral panics is the identification of perpetrators as evil "folk devils," or those labeled as outsiders, deviants, and threats to entrenched and cherished values of society (Cohen, 1972). In moral panics, they are often identified as the source of concern and fear. These individuals or groups are perceived as being not only problematic, but also as at odds with the normative values and morals of the society in which the panic takes place. A core component of this process involves the use of stereotypes to paint quite disparate individuals with a broad brush simply based on group membership. The result is the creation of the perception that all group members have the same problematic characteristics, which then serve to accentuate and exaggerate the differences between "us and them" (Critcher, 2006:8). This process of demonization is an important stage in the development of expanded social control measures and punitive policies founded on difference.

Moral panics are generally a response to some newly perceived problem or a previous problem that is perceived as reemerging (Cohen, 1972). They tend to develop during times of increased uncertainty and anxiety. During these times there is support, and at times demand, for increased social control measures as we attempt to redefine moral boundaries, which have arguably become blurred because of rapid and dramatic social and economic changes. Political elites, the media, and special interest groups often then exploit these generalized anxieties in an attempt to define and frame particular problems. Problems are generally defined in overly simplistic and sensationalistic terms that suggest clear policy implications. For example, past moral panics over daycare centers in the United States suggested that our children were in danger at the hands of evil day care workers. Many have argued that this was a product of anxiety concerning women who were perceived to be forsaking their familial duties for increased participation in the labor force. Unfortunately, because the problem is exaggerated, distorted, misrepresented, or misunderstood, the responses that are initiated are rarely appropriate. In the case of daycares, many individuals were wrongly prosecuted and convicted based on the unreliable testimony of children, whose accounts of bizarre and harmful behaviors were often the product of highly inappropriate and suggestive interviewing techniques by supposed experts. Children were encouraged—in some cases even coerced—to provide statements about events and behaviors that never occurred, resulting in an amplification of deviancy that was not based in reality. It is this exaggeration and/or distortion of the problem that accompanies moral panics and illustrates the link between moral panics and ideology.

MORAL PANICS AS IDEOLOGY

Referring to two forms of ideology as explicated by Gouldner (1976) and Larrain (1983), Chiricos (1996) notes that moral panics are ideological in two senses. First, they are ideological in that they involve rational, partisan discourse that attempts to mobilize public action in the pursuit of some particular interest (1996:26). That is, a problem is identified, outlined, and explained in ways that intend to encourage public concern and demands for effective responses. This corresponds to what Gouldner (1976:23–66) regarded as the "positive" or neutral form of ideology. Moral panics are also ideological in that they involve reports about a problem that are accompanied by commands to do something of a public nature, and that there is a distortion or misrepresentation of the problem in pursuit of that objective (Chiricos, 1996). This is what Larrain (1983) referred to as the "negative" form of ideology. It is this distortion that links ideology and moral panics. Moral panics exaggerate the scope of the problem, and the media, politicians, and special interest groups attempt to exploit these events in order to achieve a particular end, which generally serves a narrower interest than is publicly acknowledged.

In regard to discussions concerning unauthorized immigration, both the positive and negative forms of ideology are readily noticeable. First, the discourse surrounding immigration involves reports about the problem that attempt to justify doing something about it, whether it is building a wall between the Arizona/Mexico border, involving local and state law enforcement in the enforcement of federal immigration statutes, or implementing a guest worker program. We can also readily note the negative aspect of ideology in that often the discourse about undocumented immigration is rooted in a distortion of the problem. One common distortion seems to entail the universalization of threat. That is, a great deal of immigration discourse attempts to describe, explain, and demonstrate the general nature of the risks that are posed as a result of a failure to control our national borders. The reference to the ubiquity of threat is an important component in ideological discourse. In fact, there are those who argue that all forms of ideology are negative in the sense that they attempt to mobilize public action and reach the greatest number of people by presenting the problem in overly generalized terms (Larrain, 1983). It is critical to convince as much of the public as possible that this problem in some way affects them or at least has the potential to affect them. In terms of immigration, then, it may be important to universalize the dangers that are thought to be posed by undocumented immigration. One way this is accomplished is by referring to and describing multiple types of threat such as cultural threat, economic threat, political threat, and criminal threat. The more threats referred to, the greater saliency for a broader social audience.

A DISCOURSE OF THREAT

In attempting to characterize the discourse of threat that surrounds immigration dialogue, it is important to note that this discourse is diverse and is expressed at a number of different institutional sites, by numerous groups and individuals, and for a range of purposes. However, because anti-immigration discourses exhibit similar patterns and support comparable policies, they are considered to belong to the same discursive formations (Thompson, 1998).

Currently, the estimated percentage of the total U.S. population that is undocumented stands at approximately 4%. In other words, 96% of the U.S. population is documented. These figures are important in that they provide some context in considering the description and extent of the problems that a relatively small number of undocumented migrants are purported to present.

Critcher (2006:2) notes that moral panics are, by definition, disproportionate reactions to perceived threats. As previously mentioned, a rather effective way to mobilize public action is to create a sense that the problem is more widespread and threatening than evidence would support. Anti-immigration discourse readily relies on descriptions of the threats that are the result of porous borders and that emphasize the generalized extent of these threats. References to these threats are expressed by a broad range of individuals that include politicians, political pundits, the media, and members of a variety of special interest groups. This section examines some of the more commonly referred threats, which include cultural, economic, and criminal threats.

Cultural threats involve the belief that immigrants somehow threaten "our way of life." That is, immigrants imbued with distinct cultural patterns, norms, values, and morals infiltrate our country, drastically altering American culture. These cultural concerns include the belief that undocumented immigrants, particularly Latinos, possess an inability to assimilate, are unintelligent, and lack proper work ethics and, thus, consequently live in habitual poverty. Furthermore, it is believed that these immigrant groups are less patriotic and remain more closely tied to their homeland rather than the United States. These supposed characteristics are then deemed to contribute to the demise of an "American identity." Perceived cultural threats also include concerns and opposition to such things as bilingual language, education, street signs, and election ballots or to the importance of making English the "official language." A reference to the cultural threat posed by undocumented immigration is aptly illustrated in the comment by noted Harvard political scientist Samuel P. Huntington (2004: 221), who describes the problem of Mexican immigration as "the leading cause of the deterioration of American society, because the constant influx of immigrants has socially, linguistically, and economically diluted American unity and identity."

What seems problematic about these arguments is that what is truly distinctive about U.S. culture is that its "identity"—assuming there is some distinct American identity—cannot be easily separated from its immigration past. Unless you are a member of an indigenous population or your family was brought here against their will as slaves, your family can be traced back to an immigrant population. Therefore, U.S. culture has, in part, been developed through a process of negotiation and accommodation between different ethnic and racial groups, who often have come to the United States (or who were already here) with distinct cultural patterns and beliefs that have eventually all contributed to the "American culture." The stance of anti-immigration groups is that Latino immigration is somehow different—that their size, shared language, and religion, and the fact that they tend to be concentrated in close proximity to the border, all mean that assimilation is more unlikely (Citrin et al., 2007:31). Citrin et al. (2007) also note that this argument suffers from the assumption that assimilation is more preferable than pluralism, which rather than eradicating difference, as assimilation attempts to do, accepts and celebrates it.

Additionally, recent research concludes that available data does not seem to support the assertion that Latino immigration poses a threat to American identity. A study undertaken by Jack Citrin and his colleagues (2007) attempted to "ground the debate over Huntington's prognosis . . . in a sustained empirical analysis of recent immigrants." Using data from the U.S. Census and several large national and Los Angeles opinion surveys, the study concludes that Hispanics acquire English and lose Spanish quickly starting in the second generation; they also are as religious and as committed to the work ethic as native-born whites. Furthermore, it found that Hispanics largely reject simple ethnic identification and demonstrate levels of patriotism that grow yearly and by the third generation are equivalent to native-born whites.

Immigrants are also portrayed as representing an economic threat. This threat can be described as being applicable at an individual level whereby people are encouraged to perceive the presence of undocumented individuals as a threat to their own or familial economic prosperity. This concern is expressed in a number of different ways, which may include references to increased competition for desirable jobs and the reduction in wages. Threats to individual economic security also manifest in concern for tax increases to pay for welfare, medical care, and education for undocumented immigrants. For many, immigration is seen as a zero-sum game, whereby the acquisition of benefits for some means a loss for others. Immigrants who get jobs, educational opportunities, and social services are seen as taking away the same resources from citizens.

Economic threat can also be couched in terms of broader concerns about the overall well-being of the U.S. economy. It is believed by some that undocumented immigrants are detrimental to the U.S. economy because they are often perceived as placing strains on jobs, resources, housing, and as disproportionately benefitting from social welfare programs (Espenshade and Hempstead, 1996).

It is not surprising that this threat seems to resonate with many people. There are two plausible explanations for this fact. The first is simply that we live in a society that overemphasizes wealth as a measure of success. Therefore, we are always concerned about how policies and behaviors may affect our overall economic well-being. The second reason that the economic threat posed by recent undocumented immigrants tends to resonate with many Americans, and the reason which helps make the terrain fertile for moral panics, is the economic changes, which have led to a general sense of anxiety and insecurity. That is, over the last 40 years, corporate attempts to recoup profits in the face of expanded global competition have involved a number of strategies, which have included deindustrialization, disinvestment, and downsizing (Barlett and Steele, 1996). The result has been a reduction in wages and benefits for many American workers and an increasing sense of economic insecurity.

There is little conclusive evidence about the effect of undocumented immigration on individual economic security or the well-being of the national economy. However, one study done by the Pew Hispanic Center, using Census Bureau state-level data from 1990 to 2004, found that increases in foreign-born populations are not correlated with negative effects on the employment of native-born workers (Kochhar, 2006). While the jury is still out as to the overall effect of undocumented immigration on the economy, what is probably true is that arguments about undocumented immigrants taking a disproportionate share of social services such as welfare and food stamps is highly suspect because recipients of these services are required to provide proof of citizenship. We should also remember that many undocumented immigrants pay into the pools that are used to subsidize such services through their payment of sales and property taxes.

The American public has long suspected that newly arriving immigrants are inherently crime-prone. Historically, immigrants have been thought to be disproportionately involved in drugs and violent crimes. Pat Buchanan (2006:27) echoes this perception of criminal threat in his recent book when in reference to inadequate controls at the border, he states, "How many

American women must be assaulted, how many children molested, how many citizens must die at the hands of criminal aliens . . . before our government does its duty?" However, these threats are not strongly supported by empirical evidence. On the contrary, 2000 U.S. Census data of incarcerated males demonstrate that foreign-born people commit fewer crimes per capita than U.S. citizens, regardless of race and ethnicity. Those born in the United States commit crimes at a rate that is approximately four times that of their foreign-born counterparts. In fact, one study found that among men aged 18–40, native-born men were more likely to be incarcerated than immigrants (Butcher and Piehl, 1998a). In another study, the researcher found that recent immigrants had no significant effect on crime rates, and youth born abroad were less likely than native-born youth to be criminally active (Butcher and Piehl, 1998b). Additionally, according to Ramiro Martinez, (2002) research confirms that immigrants actually provide a stabilizing effect on their communities, reducing crime rates and increasing the area's economic viability.

A number of additional threats have been noted but have primarily played a more minor role in immigration discourse. For example, there have been references to environmental threats associated with undocumented border crossings, namely litter, destruction of the natural environment, and danger to wild animals. Medical threat has also been presented and includes stories about the spread of diseases such as AIDS, tuberculosis, and hepatitis.

One threat, however, that is notably missing in the above discussion and deserves greater attention is racial threat. Racial threat, which was expressed most aptly by Hubert Blalock (1967), who suggested that as the number of racial minorities within a particular area increases, opposition in various forms—including violence—also increases. However, rarely does public discourse about undocumented immigration explicitly refer to the racial characteristics of immigrants. This may be due not to a lack of concern about the racial ramifications of immigration, but may result from a desire to cloak racial concerns in more socially acceptable terms. Some, for example, have suggested that words like "welfare" and "crime" are simply code words for race. That is, instead of directly discussing race, which has become socially taboo, many use "race coding" to allude to perceived negative aspects of different races and ethnic groups (Gilens, 1996). Because of a perception of disproportionate minority involvement, words like "crime" and "welfare" and even references to "cultural dissimilarity" allow those who are so inclined to articulate negative feelings for minority groups without ever specifically mentioning race. Some suggest that these "code words" for race are particularly useful to political and economic elites who wish to tap and exploit negative racial perceptions and resentments among whites in the implementation of what are essentially race-based policies. In short, references to economic, cultural, criminal, and political threats of undocumented immigration may simply be serving as referents to racial concerns.

In describing the above threats, it is not suggested that these threats are entirely baseless or without some evidence. It would be difficult to argue that the presence of undocumented immigrants has had no effect on the economic and personal security of at least some Americans. In fact, ideologically based moral panics are always rooted in some form of evidence. As Cohen (1972:274) notes, it is not that there is nothing there but because the scope of the problem is distorted, exaggerated, or misunderstood, societal responses are primarily inappropriate. There is little doubt that some U.S. workers have been displaced by immigrant workers, some citizens have been criminally victimized by undocumented immigrants, and that American culture is changing (as it always has and will continue to do) in the face of changing demographics. It is the exaggerated degree to which these threats are presented as being problematic and the extent to which these threats are portrayed as universal that characterizes such discourse as an example of negative ideology.

Finally, it is worth remembering that the casting of immigrants in terms of threatening "others" is not new. Few immigrant groups (legal and illegal) were readily accepted when first arriving on U.S. shores, and most, in fact, were demonized as representing a threat to our culture, economy, and personal security in the same way that undocumented immigrants are today.

IMMIGRATION POLICY

Attempts at controlling (as well as punishing) undocumented immigration have resulted in a number of public policies as well as actions on the part of private citizens and interest groups. Some of these policies, because they are rooted in a misrepresentation or distortion of the problem, not only fail to address the problem in some meaningful and humane way, but have also had (or have the potential to have) rather dire consequences. This section examines some of these policies.

Historically, immigration control has been under the jurisdiction of the federal government. However, in light of the events of September 11, 2001, the perceived failure of the federal government to adequately control undocumented immigration, and the supposed criminality of undocumented immigrants, there has been a recent push for greater involvement of state and local law enforcement in controlling immigration. As a result, some states like Arizona require that police officers who apprehend undocumented immigrants for law violations turn them over to federal immigration officials (Menjivar and Bejarano, 2004). This sometimes results in the deportation of individuals for relatively minor offenses. Moreover, the role of local and state law enforcement in immigration control may be expanding even more to allow officers to ask about the residency status of those they come into contact with regardless of the reason.

In 2007, the Clear Law Enforcement for Alien Removal (CLEAR) Act (HR 842) was introduced in the U.S. House of Representatives (Library of Congress, 2007). This bill offers financial incentive for the involvement of local law agencies in the enforcement of federal immigration statutes. The consequences of increased involvement by local and state law enforcement have not been evaluated as this is still a relatively new phenomenon. However, there is fairly good reason to believe that while this may result in somewhat more effective immigration control, it will also have potentially detrimental effects. For example, due to the complexity of immigration law, it is more than likely that civil rights violations will occur. It often goes unnoticed that the U.S. Constitution, and the rights that it provides, applies to everyone on U.S. soil, regardless of their legal status. These types of policies are likely to increase the instances of racial profiling and police stops for "driving while Hispanic."

Perhaps even more worrisome is the effect of such enforcement on crime and public safety. These policies will seemingly undermine the efforts of police to gain the trust of the communities that they serve. Over the past few decades, there has been a strong move toward community policing. A core component of these policies is the development of trust and cooperation between the police and community members in developing joint solutions to crime problems. The concern is that if local and state police begin actively enforcing federal immigration statutes, then, those who are undocumented or may have friends and family who are undocumented may become reluctant to have any contact with police because of fear of the possible consequences, which may include deportation for themselves and/or their families. This would not only reduce the effectiveness of community policing, especially in communities with a greater proportion of immigrants, but also will presumably decrease the reporting of crime and suspicious behavior in certain neighborhoods. Criminals, therefore, may come to see undocumented immigrants and the neighborhoods in which they reside as easy and vulnerable targets.

The militarization of the border is another policy that has been adopted and widely supported. This involves the escalation of military involvement and technology in law enforcement. In 2006, President Bush detailed a series of enforcement measures including the deployment of 6,000 National Guard members to the border. These troops now provide support to the border patrol along the southern borders of Texas, Arizona, New Mexico, and California.

Strengthening of the border, either through its militarization or the construction of an 800-mile wall, is unlikely to deter those who are desperate to come to the United States. Instead, what is more likely to occur (and is occurring) is that immigrants will simply find different points of entry. Often this involves crossing the desert in areas that are less populated and more perilous.

These border policies are, therefore, likely responsible for recent increases in the number of injuries and deaths that have occurred on the U.S.–Mexico border. The U.S. Government Accountability Office (2006) reported that since 1995, the number of border-crossing deaths increased and had more than doubled by 2005. The total number of border-crossing deaths increased from 241 in 1999 to 472 in 2005. The report goes on to note that this increase in deaths occurred despite the fact that there was not a corresponding increase in the number of unauthorized border crossings. The analysis also shows that more than three-fourths of the doubling in deaths along the southwest border since 1995 can be attributed to increases in deaths occurring in the Arizona (U.S. Government Accountability Office, 2006).

Another consequence of the militarization of the border is that more immigrants will simply turn to "coyotes" (human smugglers) as a means of crossing the border. This not only increases the peril of those who pay for this method of entry; it also means an increase in crime and a decrease in public safety that often accompanies organized criminal enterprises such as these. It is estimated that coyotes are a "two billion dollar a year" business that is often accompanied by violence, kidnapping, and human slavery (Wagner, 2006).

In addition to explicit policies meant to strengthen the border, numerous other policies have been suggested, or actually developed and implemented, in an effort to either deter those who aspire to come to the United States or punish those already here. Arizona's 2006 election provides a laundry list of policies that are unlikely to effectively direct immigration reform. In this election, Arizona residents overwhelmingly supported a variety of policies that speak to their concern over immigration. Some of the propositions that were passed included denying bail in certain situations to undocumented immigrants who are charged with crimes; barring those not in this country from legally collecting punitive damages for personal injuries; prohibiting undocumented immigrants from enrolling in adult education classes, receiving state-subsidized childcare, receiving scholarships, grants, tuition assistance, or in-state tuition rates at Arizona public schools and universities; and declaring English as the state's official language.

Some of these policies deserve some discussion. For example, declaring English as the official language has no practical impact. It is merely a symbolic gesture that does little more than accentuate the difference between "us and them," and to reassert an overly restrictive definition of American culture and identity. Denying educational opportunities also seems counterproductive. This would only serve to increase the societal problems that tend to accompany a lack of education, such as crime and poverty.

To cast immigration concerns in terms of threat serves two purposes. The first is to overgeneralize the problem in an effort to mobilize public action, and the second is to cast undocumented immigrants as "others" and often as "dangerous others." Such portrayals allow us to more easily deny or ignore the humanness of those who risk their lives to seek a better life in the United States. In such instances, then, we more easily succumb to what Dario Melossi (1985) called "vocabularies of punitive motive." Melossi suggests that during certain periods, a "discursive chain" of punitiveness and severity spreads across society, linking the attitude of "moral panic" expressed by business leaders and "moral entrepreneurs" to the ways in which citizens, police, courts, and correctional authorities perceive behavior as deviant and/or criminal (1985:183). These vocabularies of punitive motive then provide the justification for lawmakers to pass legislation that expand social control measures which are often punitive and harmful with little or no public opposition.

To couch immigration discourse in terms of these threats and others simply runs the risk of developing policies that are based on stereotypes, and that attempt to scapegoat certain populations, which in turn justify punitive responses. As long as we continue to frame these discussions in terms of threat and otherness, in terms of our dissimilarities rather than what we have in common, we will continue to fail to progress toward rational and commonsense solutions to this critically important issue.

Endnote

1. The choice to use the term "undocumented immigrants" rather than "illegal immigrants" is not an arbitrary one. The term is used so as to not attach the negative and subjective connotations that accompany the word "illegal."

References

Barlett, Donald L., and James B. Steele. 1996. *America: What Went Wrong?* Kansas City, MO: Andrews and McMeel.

Blalock, Hubert M. 1967. *Toward a Theory of Minority Group Relations.* New York: John Wiley and Sons.

Buchanan, Patrick J. 2006. *State of Emergency: The Third World Invasion and Conquest of America.* New York: St. Martin Press.

Butcher, Kristen, and Anne Morrison-Piehl. 1998a. Cross-City Evidence on the Relationship Between Immigration and Crime. *Journal of Policy Analysis and Management* 17: 457–493.

Butcher, Kristen, and Anne Morrison-Piehl. 1998b. Recent Immigrants: Unexpected Implications for Crime and Incarceration. *Industrial and Labor Relations Review* 51 (4): 654–679.

Chiricos, Ted. 1996. Moral Panics as Ideology: Drugs, Violence, Race and Punishment in America. In *Race with Prejudice: Race & Justice in America*, ed. M. J. Lynch and E. B. Patterson, 19–48. New York: Harrow & Heston.

Citrin, Jack, Amy Lerman, Michael Murakami, and Kathryn Pearson. 2007. Testing Huntington: Is Hispanic Immigration a Threat to American Identity? *Perspectives on Politics* 5 (1): 31–48.

Cohen, Stanley. 1972. *Folk Devils and Moral Panics.* St. Albans: Paladin.

Critcher, Charles. 2006. *Critical Readings: Moral Panics and the Media.* Maidenhead: Open Press University.

Espenshade, Thomas J., and Katherine Hempstead. 1996. Contemporary American Attitudes Toward U.S. Immigration. *International Migration Review* 30: 535–570.

Gilens, Martin. 1996. "Race Coding" and White Opposition to Welfare. *American Political Science Review* 90: 593–604.

Goode, Erich. 2000. No Need to Panic? A Bumper Crop of Books on Moral Panics. *Sociological Forum* 15 (3): 543–552.

Goode, Erich, and Nachman Ben-Yehuda. 1994. *Moral Panic: The Social Construction of Deviance.* Oxford: Blackwell.

Gouldner, Alvin. 1976. *The Dialectic of Ideology and Technology.* New York: Oxford University Press.

Hall, Stuart, Charles Critcher, Tony Jefferson, John Clarke, and Brian Roberts. 1978. *Policing the Crisis: Mugging, the State and Law and Order.* London: Macmillan Press.

Huntington, Samuel. 2004. *Who Are We? The Challenge to America's National Identity.* New York: Simon and Shuster.

Kochhar, Rakesh. 2006. Growth in the Foreign-Born Workforce and Employment of the Native Born. *Pew Hispanic Center, Executive Summary.* August 10, 2006.

Larrain, Jorge. 1983. *Marxism and Ideology.* London: Macmillan Press.

Lauderdale, Pat. 1976. Deviance and Moral Boundaries. *American Sociological Review* 41: 660–676.

Library of Congress. 2007. *Thomas: Legislative Information from the Library of Congress.* http://thomas.loc.gov/

Martinez, Jr., Ramiro. 2002. *Latino Homicide: Immigration, Violence and Community.* New York: Routledge.

Melossi, Dario. 1985. Punishment and Social Action: Changing Vocabularies of Punitive Motive with a Political Business Cycle. *Current Perspectives in Social Theory* 6: 169–197.

Menjivar, Cecilia, and Cynthia L. Bejarano. 2004. Latino Immigrants' Perceptions of Crime and Police Authorities in the United States: A Case Study from the Phoenix Metropolitan Area. *Ethnic and Racial Studies* 27 (1): 120–148.

Thompson, Kenneth. 1998. *Moral Panics.* London: Routledge.

U.S. Bureau of Census. 2000. *Law Enforcement, Courts, and Prisons.* Washington, DC: U.S. Government Printing Office.

U.S. Government Accountability Office. 2006. *Border-crossing Deaths Have Doubled Since 1985; Border Patrol's Efforts to Prevent Deaths Have Not Been Fully Evaluated.* GAO-06-770, August.

Wagner, D. 2006. Phoenix's Hidden $2 Billion Industry – Human Smuggling. *The Arizona Republic* (Phoenix, AZ) 23, July 2006, A1.

Young, J. 1971. The Role of Police as Amplifiers of Deviancy, Negotiators of Reality and Translators of Fantasy: Some Aspects of Our Present System of Drug Control as Seen in Notting Hill. In *Images of Deviance*, ed. Stanley Cohen, 27–61. Harmondsworth: Penguin.

MODULE 6

CHAPTER 11

The Communication Process

More powerful than mace, the night stick, or the gun, effective rhetoric is an officer's most useful tool in the field.

—THOMPSON, 1982

KEY CONCEPTS

Articulation	Jargon	Proxemics
Discrimination	Kinesics	Scapegoating
Distortion	Nonjudgmental Listening	Symbolic Cues
Effective Listening	Personal Space	Tabloid Thinking
Empathy	Prejudice	

LEARNING OBJECTIVES

Studying this chapter will enable you to:

1. Define the communication process.
2. Contrast modes of communication.
3. Demonstrate effective listening skills.
4. Describe the communication process in police practices.
5. Identify several common blocks to effective communication in police–community relations.

Communication is basic to the world we know. We transmit and receive information in our world, often without even being aware that we are doing so. Because communication is a process that is shared by everyone and is constantly with us, it is easily taken for granted. Communication skills supposedly just "come naturally."

Yet it is faulty communication that generates misunderstanding and helps to build social barriers among people. The result of poor communication can be anything from poor job performance to war. Effective communication encourages healthy relationships between two

Police-Community Relations and the Administration of Justice, Eighth Edition
by Ronald D. Hunter, Thomas Barker

people, within a family, between the police and the community, between employer and employee, among nations, and so on.

It is the function of this chapter to define and describe the process of communication in action and to identify some specific ways whereby persons, such as police officers, can increase the effectiveness of their communication with others. The ultimate aim is to describe the relationship between communication and police–community relations.

COMMUNICATION IN ACTION

Communication is a process through which messages are exchanged. It is effective only when these messages are mutually understood by the sender and receiver.

Communication operates in many dimensions, the most commonly recognized being intrapersonal, interpersonal, and person to group. Because the nature of work in the administration of justice process requires volumes of written reports (many of which will become legal records of the system), we include an additional dimension in this chapter: official communications.

Intrapersonal communication takes place within the person. We "talk to ourselves" as we solve problems or perform tasks. We may even write messages to ourselves. The academic community has just begun to speculate about the intrapersonal communication of criminal justice professionals. What happens to the thinking processes of the new recruit? Some suppose that the stresses of the occupation may distort the intrapersonal process, resulting in cynical, tough patrol officers; high divorce rates; and even illness.

Interpersonal communication takes place person to person. Whether or not we are able to form and maintain caring connections with others depends largely on our effective interpersonal communication skills. Police officers may stop or start fights, increase or decrease tension, gain or lose the cooperation of a witness, victim, or suspect through the exercise of interpersonal communication skills. This is the dimension to which most discussion regarding communication skills is addressed and to which definitions of the communication process most directly refer. This dimension is a major focus of this chapter. Much that is said in this context, however, can be generalized to other dimensions of communication in action.

Person-to-group communication implies a structured situation in which one person addresses a group on a predetermined subject. Public speaking engagements, a witness before a jury, and a minister before a congregation are all examples of person-to-group communication.

Some specific skills concerning group dynamics, presentation, and public speaking are related to this dimension of communication. To the extent that a group response is sought and received, people in the group reflect a group identity as they hear and respond to the message sent. In addition to this group dimension, however, every individual–group communication is also a person-to-person communication. The speaker is actually communicating individually with each person in the group, and the message received by one person will differ to some degree from the message received by any other person. This is true even though group consensus regarding some of the elements of the message may exist, and group response may provide feedback to the sender that the message sent was (or was not) received.

Official communication is usually written and can appear to be person to person or person to group. Actually, however, it usually is a "public" documentation of policy or procedure, or an official report or evaluation of events. It may be an in-house memo or a formal communication with other agencies. Lack of effectiveness in this dimension of communication has a sometimes subtle but very high cost. Administrators may lose the cooperation of staff members; agencies and individual officers may lose community support; prosecutors may lose convictions in court; and children and adults may be mislabeled, misdiagnosed, and mistreated. Official communication is an important part of communication in action. Some of the specific basic writing skills involved in this dimension of communication are not within the scope of this chapter. Official communication is discussed here in the context of effective police–community relations.

THE PROCESS OF COMMUNICATION

Achieving Effective Communication

Communicating effectively requires ongoing effort to sharpen communication skills. It does not happen by chance, nor is it something that can be tucked away in a uniform pocket and pulled out at the appropriate opportunity. Skills learned must be applied in many different ways and in as many different situations. What works best in one situation may not be the best choice in another.

One thing is certain, however: Effective communication is essential to positive police–community relations. Its power can scarcely be overestimated. Its success is incredible; its failure disastrous.

The Elements of Communication

The process of communication, as described in Figure 11.1, begins with a source who has an idea (meaning) that he or she wishes to transmit to a receiver. The idea cannot be transmitted as an idea. It must be encoded into symbols (spoken or written words, gestures, pictures, etc.). Once encoded, the message is transmitted and received. The receiver must decode the message (the symbols) into meaning. The receiver's response, or feedback, to the source is based on the receiver's perception of the meaning of the message sent. Feedback is encoded, transmitted, and decoded, and so the process continues.

Sources of Distortion

Distortion can occur at any and all stages of the process. Perhaps the symbols used were not mutually understood. Perhaps the message sent was confused at the source. Perhaps the receiver received only a part of the message or, because of distorted perception, was not open to receiving a clear message.

Because messages are sent and received in some situational context, other elements outside the source and the receiver may contribute to or distort the message. A noisy room, a crowd of people, poor lighting, interruptions in the sending or receiving elements of the process, and even the passage of time (particularly if the message is written) can affect what is sent and received.

A Continuing Process

Communication has no beginning or end; it is a continuing process. As we analyze the process and provide its "elements" with names and functions, we may sometimes give the false impression that the communication process does have a beginning and an end and that only one message is dealt with at any given time. As a matter of fact, communication in action does occur in sequence but never so simply as it may appear in a diagram. Messages are received and sent simultaneously. Messages

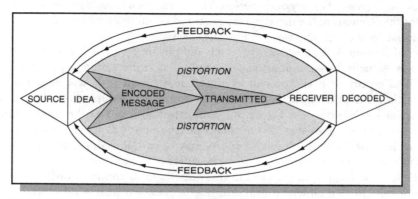

FIGURE 11.1 The process of communication.

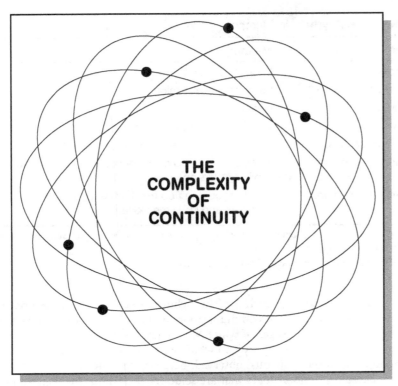

FIGURE 11.2   **With so many messages bouncing around at once, effective communication is a miracle.**

from other sources are received in addition to the message received from the identified source, and these other messages may influence the transmission or reception of the original message.

A single message may be received by one receiver, by several individual receivers (some of whom neither the source nor the receiver knew were receiving), or by a group receiving as a group and/or as individuals. Several messages may be sent at once by one source and received as one or many messages by all or some of the above-mentioned receivers. Considering the opportunities for distortion of the message and the number of messages bouncing around at any given time, it is a miracle that we are able to communicate effectively with one another at all (see Figure 11.2).

MODES OF INTERPERSONAL COMMUNICATION

There are three interpersonal channels or modes of communication: verbal, nonverbal, and symbolic.

Verbal communication refers almost totally to the words and combinations of words used in the message transmitted (or in feedback, which may again be a message transmitted). Words have no meaning in and of themselves. Meaning is derived from the person and from the context in which words are used.

The nonverbal mode can be divided into three subgroups: paralanguage (vocal characteristics), kinesics (body language), and proxemics (personal and social space). Paralanguage includes such elements as diction, the rate and pitch at which a person is speaking, the loudness or softness of speech, and changes in these characteristics during communication (Table 11.1). Kinesics includes gestures, body positioning, facial expressions, and movement. Proxemics becomes a mode of communication in the manner in which **personal space** is used. Space may become a territorial issue, an intrusion into privacy; how it is used can increase or decrease social distance.

TABLE 11.1 Tone, Rhythm, and Tempo

Statement	Meaning
"I don't care what you do."	Personally, I don't care.
"*I* don't care what you do."	But someone else might.
"I *don't* care what you do."	I really *don't*.
"I don't *care* what you do."	Just do as you please, will you?
"I don't care *what* you do."	You have the choice, do what you want.
"I don't care what *you* do."	It doesn't matter to me what you do, but I care about what others do.
"I don't care what you *do*."	It's what you don't do that I'd like to talk about. Just get out of here and leave me alone.

Note: Tone, rhythm, and tempo of speech provide nonverbal cues to the listener as to the meaning being expressed by the speaker. The same words may have a wide variety of meanings.

Source: Adapted from materials developed by Cynthia Roed, Tucson, Arizona.

Symbolic communication, which is often included as a category of the nonverbal mode rather than as a separate channel of communication, occurs continuously at a passive level. We send and receive symbolic messages of which we are not always aware. We make judgments regarding other people based on symbols to which we have assigned meaning and which may have nothing to do with the individual observed. Because symbolic communication is passive, judgments are based on symbolic data that are seldom checked out for their validity. Almost anything can be a meaningful symbol to an individual, but usually symbolic communication includes messages relating to style of dress, place of residence, place (and type) of employment, type of car driven or transportation preferred, jewelry worn (or not worn), and so on (he wears a beard; all persons who wear beards are . . .; therefore, he is . . .).

VERBAL AND PARALANGUAGE CUES

Articulation

Ralph Waldo Emerson wrote, "I learn immediately from any speaker how much he has already lived, through the poverty or the splendor of his speech." Lazy speech can be corrected. Pronunciation depends primarily on correct **articulation**. Articulators are the teeth, tongue, lips, and hard palate. Sounds to pay particular attention to are those of *f, p, b,* and *v*. These sounds are hard to pronounce correctly. As our society becomes more educated, police begin to deal with a larger population possessing a certain standard of pronunciation. Each of us lapses into an occasional "yeah," and there may be situations in which more casual diction or word usage would be appropriate. However, as a norm, sloppy articulation can be annoying, and it is extremely unprofessional. Words such as "Kinda," "jist," "gonna," "cause," and "dere," or sentences filled with "you know," "and uh," or "sorta," are examples of sloppy articulation that can be easily corrected if the speaker is aware of the problem. As students among a captive audience, we notice these patterns in an instructor, but it is more difficult to examine our own speech habits objectively and to change them.

Volume and Rate

Everyone has an "Aunt Maude." When she calls, you hold the telephone six inches from your ear, and every word is still clearly audible. Coupled with a military uniform, a loud voice will prolong the "redneck cop" stereotype. What is your reaction to a raised voice? If you are like most people, you raise your own, but the police officer has the power to declare a citizen's raised voice disorderly conduct. What if the police officer begins a transaction with a louder tone than normally used socially and the situation escalates into a shouting match? Is the citizen really at fault?

Our society equates fast speech with excitement. Fight narratives delivered in a staccato nonstop rate add excitement to even a dull match. For police officers, consideration of this fact makes the rate of their speech all-important. As an example, consider this hit-and-run accident: The victim's motorcycle was demolished, and the victim lay sprawled in the middle of rush-hour traffic, bleeding profusely from the head. Despite the obvious necessity for speed, the veteran sergeant at the scene communicated slowly and calmly with witnesses before calling in a report. Therefore, he did not heighten an already excited situation. He slowed down the witnesses' rates of speaking and increased the intelligibility of the communication he was receiving. Rate of speech can also be too slow, in which case words may sound disconnected. When this occurs, the listener may lose both interest and the trend of the thoughts expressed.

Language

Human beings have the almost unconscious ability to turn thoughts into words. The words we choose and how we string them together to express our thoughts are very important to effective communication. Meanings are in people, not in the words themselves. Unless the people involved in interpersonal communication have common meaning for the language used, the message will not be mutually understood. Language, then, can become a barrier to communication as well as a tool for effectively achieving it.

Language and its meaning vary from culture to culture. Traditionally, to say that a person is "multilingual" has meant that the person can communicate in several languages, such as Spanish, English, Chinese, or German. Today we also include sign language and computer languages in this list. We also recognize (painfully sometimes) that Spanish is not Spanish and that English is not English. Meaning and phrasing vary from locale to locale, profession to profession, street to agency, children to adults.

Jargon, the special or technical language used by a group or discipline, probably impedes communication more often than it helps. Officers who employ police jargon when communicating with citizens are likely to confuse and annoy them. They may even create problems for themselves at home. Erma Bombeck chose the topic of "Fluent Law Enforcement" for one of her columns. She humorously envisioned the following conversation begun by a wife as she greets her police officer-husband at the door:

> "Hi, honey. Dinner will be ready in a few minutes. Who was that I saw you waving to?"
> "The white Caucasian adult, approximately 62 inches tall, weighing 119 pounds, green eyes, brown hair, and no visible distinguishing marks?"
> "That's the one."
> "She has been identified tentatively as our new neighbor, but we'll have to check it out. By the way, where is 11–83?"
> "I wish you'd stop referring to our son as the code number for 'accident.' "
> (Bombeck, 1982, p. 16)

Profanity can be useful for gaining attention or expressing verbal hostility, but, in the final analysis, it reduces the user's power to negotiate. Those who want their profanity to upset hearers (or readers) should remember that the more they use a profane expression, the less shocking it is.

Research has shown that the use of profanity by police officers occurs almost exclusively during interactions with certain citizens or categories of citizens (e.g., racial and ethnic minorities, lower- and working-class citizens, and other powerless and devalued persons). The use of such language is likely to be restrained and controlled in the presence of persons of power and influence (White, Cox, and Basehart, 1994). The use of such language is deliberate and represents previously learned tactics and strategies for the performance of their duties with such categories of people. White, Cox, and Basehart also point out that simplistic explanations of officer profanity, such as "lack of verbal skills" or "loss of personal control," do not fit reality because it is inconceivable to believe that a police officer would use profanity or obscenities during a deposition or in court testimony when tensions, stress, frustration, or anger-provoking conditions are high (White, Cox, and Basehart, 1994).

There are at least three interactive contextual dimensions in which the officer might use profanity in his or her dealings with citizens. The first is a personal dimension. That is, an officer uses profanity or obscenity to satisfy his or her own psychological or personal agenda. The officer may build up tensions, frustrations, and anger on the job and find catharsis in verbal expressions. A second dimension is a situational one. Officers use profanity or obscenities as a means of dealing with a variety of stressful situations, such as perceived danger, provocation, and resistance.

The third dimension involves the socialization experiences of the officers. It may be that the socialization experiences of the officer, including his or her training, provides formal and informal definitions of persons or groups as deserving of less-than-civil treatment. Van Maanen (1978) suggested that some citizens are labeled as "assholes" by the police and treated accordingly.

Intercultural distortion of words can cause great harm. In Spanish *tu madre* means "your mother." In colloquial (street) Spanish, it is an offensive phrase. A better choice of terms would be "mama" (Quintanilla, 1983, p. 5). There are many other similar examples. Perhaps the best distortion example involves the Japanese response to our warning in 1945 that we possessed a powerful new weapon, the atomic bomb. The response contained the word *migugostu*, which can mean either abrupt dismissal or "We shall consider it." The American interpreter read it as a rebuff, perhaps wrongly, with tragic consequences for Hiroshima and Nagasaki.

Tone of Voice

In situations where communication is repetitive, it is easy to present a bored, monotonous tone. This insulates the speaker from other people and produces a feeling of coldness. Clergy repeating the same ritual each week encounter this, as do actors in a long run of a play.

Television viewers can affirm that there are many tones of voice in which the Miranda rights can be delivered. The police dispatcher sighing, "Yesss, lady," into the telephone communicates a very clear but nonverbal message to her of exasperation.

If we feel depressed, angry at the world, or hungover, our voice patterns will reflect our feelings in inflection and intonation of words. A professional police officer deals largely with a "captive" clientele. However resistant clients may feel, they must relate in some way to the officer. What the officer expresses in paralanguage may not be reported to superiors but may have great impact on the police department's image in the community.

Telephone Cues

Victor Strecher, discussing police conduct on the telephone, states, "Voice, diction, reaction to the citizen's call, approach to the problem, and basic etiquette are the criteria of judgment. Here again, negative evaluations cannot be reversed. The police telephone response can easily predispose a complainant to a favorable or unfavorable reception of the radio-car officers who later respond to this request. Those who neglect telephone courtesy will not overcome the deficiency in police image through the correctness of their uniform and their approach to service calls" (Strecher, 1971, p. 104).

Listening to one's own voice over a tape recorder is effective feedback for analyzing presentation. Objective self-criticism is difficult but necessary. Just as officers must check their uniforms and equipment, a periodic evaluation of voice is equally important. It is a matter of training the ear to hear what is and is not of value.

The telephone voice characterized as bad is expressionless, mechanical, indifferent, impatient, and inattentive. Although the officer may come across as "tough" in the station, in turn, the receiver of the communication may come across as a bristly, hostile citizen the next time he or she encounters an officer. The police officer seeking information by phone might find citizens more receptive to providing it if positive telephone communication techniques are used by the officer.

Following are the basic rules of police telephone conduct:

1. Be courteous at all times, especially when things are a mess.
2. Avoid slang.
3. Be brief, but clear and concise. Use complete sentences. Organize your thoughts in advance, particularly if you are initiating the call.
4. Speak clearly in as relaxed a voice as possible, directly into the mouthpiece.
5. Do not eat or drink when making a phone call to a client or receiving one.
6. Picture the person at the other end of the line sympathetically. Talk to that person, not to the telephone.
7. Keep the receiver close to your ear, and listen to what is being said verbally and nonverbally.
8. If you must consult with someone, put the client on hold if such equipment is available. Nothing is more aggravating, nor presents a more unprofessional image, than monitoring a shouted conversation.
9. Letters and numbers will obviously play a crucial part of police phone communication. Take care when pronouncing them, thus avoiding incorrect spelling, misunderstanding, and repetition. Effective enunciation requires that every sound be given its proper value.
10. As much as humanly possible, refrain from interrupting the other person; allow the person to finish what he or she wants to say. However, emergency phone calls that involve agitated citizens may require firmer guidance to get the proper information.

KINESICS AND PROXEMICS CUES

Correct interpretation by officers of cues communicated by suspects through body language and use of social and personal space has saved many police lives and prevented many crimes. Without the use of such cues, a major police function that is sometimes taken for granted—directing traffic—could not be accomplished.

Best-seller lists have featured several books on nonverbal cues. These books concentrate primarily on three concepts: body motion and positioning (**kinesics**) as a communication device; the use of personal and social space (**proxemics**); and the influence of certain clothing (symbolic) on ourselves and on others. Much of how we perceive ourselves is modeled in these ways.

Body Language

Julius Fast, author of *Body Language*, noted that sometimes our body cues reinforce our words, and at other times, they may contradict one another. For example, a calm, emotionless face that is accompanied by active arms, hands, legs, and feet is a distinctive feature of deception no matter what is said (Brougham, 1992, p. 16). The human body is the least controllable nonverbal channel of communication.

The Kinesic Interview Technique—taught at seminars throughout the country; the former U.S. Army Military Police School at Fort McClellan, Alabama; numerous police academies; and law enforcement agencies at the local, state, and federal levels—relies on unconscious verbal and nonverbal behaviors to reveal deception (Link, 1993). The first rule of this technique is to watch for breaks in eye contact as an indication that the interviewee is lying. This body language cue is hard to control when one is talking to another.

THE MEANING OF THE MESSAGE   Stress is often demonstrated in nonverbal ways, particularly in body language. Anger, too, denied verbally, may be "clearly" stated in kinesics (and proxemics) through clenched fists, muscle tautness, abruptness of manner, perspiration in the palms, and shaping of personal space (becoming very territorial, pacing back and forth, etc.). Many interrogators and polygraph examiners suggest that some of the same symptoms may occur in the person who is lying—willingly and knowingly relating something other than the truth. They also describe other changes in physiological and biological processes, such as change in pulse rate, perspiration flow, and change in skin color (Abrams, 1989).

Although changes in body language do have meaning, the meaning is not always apparent. What may seem to be evidence of a lie may be concern for a loved one; what may appear to be staggering and falling from drunkenness may instead be caused by a physiological disorder. We may accurately recognize a symptom, but not correctly assess what it is a symptom of. Lie detection through the use of the polygraph is supported by psychophysiologist David Raskin and challenged by psychologist David Lykken. Both agree, however, that in verifying the truthfulness of innocent subjects, "The lie detector turns up more innocent people found guilty—false positives—than guilty people found innocent" (Meyer, 1982, p. 26). As discussed in earlier chapters, what we see, hear, and smell is personalized through our perception process. Officers should not only be very aware of kinesics but also be very cautious in drawing conclusions regarding the meaning of messages received without checking out their hunches through other feedback options.

THE OFFICER'S MESSAGE   In addition to being aware of messages received through the body language of others, police officers need to be very aware of the messages transmitted through their own body language. Police officers may express boredom, interest, disgust, disrespect, anger, frustration, acceptance, authority, nervousness, and any number of other emotions through body language alone. An officer's body language may calm or ignite a situation. A youth gang member

FIGURE 11.3   The art of communication.
Courtesy of Birmingham Police Department.

may act on what he interprets in an officer's body language to be an insult. It is a rare veteran offender who does not guess, before any words are exchanged, who the new police officers and correctional service officers are and then proceed to test those people.

Personal Space

A TERRITORIAL IMPERATIVE   Nonverbal cues are probably displayed most prominently in Western peoples' use of proxemics, personal space. People tend to establish, or stake out, their own territory. Robert Ardrey (1966) traced this concept to biological inheritance, examining how animals establish certain territories. Fast (1981) relates a delightful anecdote in his book in which he experimented with a friend in a restaurant by moving his silverware and dishes, piece by piece, as if inadvertently, into the other man's table space. His friend became noticeably upset. Establishing territorial space is also illustrated by the behavior of students in the classroom: After high school, the "assigned-seat–alphabetical-order" arrangements cease, but notice how students tend to occupy the same territory in college classrooms. You may find yourself slightly irritated when someone occupies "your space."

IDENTIFYING TERRITORY   We identify territory as ours by spreading our books or dishes over a table, putting our pictures on the wall, putting our name on the mailbox, or displaying graffiti on a neighborhood boundary. Even on the job, we attempt to maintain a work area that is ours; if it is not respected, we are uneasy, somewhat confused, and at least mildly annoyed.

Territory in police work is identified in many ways: jurisdictional boundaries, district boundaries, the agency's organizational structure, job description, and so on. Territory can also be defined in the sense of level of discretionary decision making, or which car an officer drives.

The very need for territory sometimes interferes with the need for change. Change can be viewed as territorial infringement, and it may require that new boundaries be set. The issue of territory and change may become a major problem of police–community relations. It can be an issue for an individual officer or team, for two warring youth gangs, or for a neighborhood threatened by new freeway construction.

Interpersonal Space

Generally, the rules that regulate our use of personal space are implicit. Formal business requires a different use of distance than does friendship. What is comfortable and acceptable may depend both on the nature of the activity and the relationship. Hall (1966) identified four basic personal space zones:

1. *Intimate distance*, extending to about 18 inches from the skin. This is reserved space. Intimate activities include lovemaking, cuddling, and massaging.
2. *Personal distance*, about 11/2–4 feet from the body. Interactions with friends and people we care about are allowed in this space.
3. *Social distance*, about 4–12 feet. Impersonal and casual business is conducted at this distance.
4. *Public distance*, more than 12 feet. Formal interactions, lectures, and speeches take place at this distance.

THE MESSAGE OF PROXEMICS   Police officers violate, or invade, a person's space, sometimes deliberately and sometimes without intending to, causing the invaded person to move away or become (sometimes act) defensive. Brougham (1992, p. 16) reports that successful police interviewers create a high level of anxiety in a suspect by beginning an interview at a comfortable distance when discussing general information. Then the interviewer will move closer to the suspect when questioning on key points and will back off during desired responses. Brougham states that this practice serves to program a person to cooperate with the interviewer's line of questioning.

Physical obstacles may prevent effective communication. The authority figure sitting behind a desk places an obstacle between self and client. This use of proxemics says, "You must obey me. I am your superior." As Fast observed, "We learn certain tricks of domination to control a situation. We can arrange to be higher than our subordinates, or we can allow our boss to be higher than we are. We can be aware that we dominate our children when we hover over them" (Fast, 1981, p. 90). The act of stopping a vehicle is structured to place the police officer in an authoritative position. The citizen remains seated in his or her car, while the officer occupies "territory" over the individual.

Movement across social distances in our culture also distorts communication and causes feelings of anxiety. Huseman and McCurley (1972), in a study of police communication behaviors, found that police officers experience most of their problems in communicating with minority groups.

SYMBOLIC CUES

From birth we are taught to attach great importance to **symbolic cues**. A symbol is something that stands for something else. They carry a meaning that is recognized by members of a culture (Macionis, 1993, p. 65). Virtually all interactions among human beings involve the use of symbols. We are constantly looking for "clues" about the appropriate behavior in social situations.

The criminal justice system makes use of a number of symbols. The scales of justice convey the meaning that the system is blind to personal distinctions as it goes about evaluating evidence and judging guilt or innocence. Flashing blue or red lights signal the presence of an emergency vehicle. Traffic signs present various symbols that tell us what to do as we drive. Police officers use a variety of socially understood symbols, uniforms, nightsticks, other weapons, badges, and so on.

FIGURE 11.4   Sometimes words aren't necessary: It is obvious without written explanation that Deputy Holder and Sonja had a "good day."

Courtesy of the Jackson County Sheriff's Department.

Generally speaking, the police uniform is a symbol of authority. In situations where the officer is regarded as the person who can take command of a situation and solve a crisis, the uniform speaks positively in the police–citizen interaction. In situations where the officer is regarded as the enemy or as the scapegoat, the uniform becomes a negative symbolic cue, interfering with positive interaction between the officer and citizen. A veteran officer in a police–community relations class remarked, "If I approach a citizen to give a ticket, and push my hat back on my head, hook my thumb in my belt buckle, and smile, I'm in for trouble."

Realizing that the uniform itself is sometimes a negative symbolic cue to citizens, some departments have experimented with dressing officers in blazers, thus softening their image. Although studies regarding the practice have been inconclusive, interviews with police administrators indicate that street experience in most areas has led them to vary the use of the blazer and uniform depending on a number of factors. Key factors mentioned include (1) type of activity and (2) characteristics of citizens involved (e.g., age and level of initial hostility to police).

OFFICIAL COMMUNICATION

Verbal, nonverbal, and symbolic cues have relevance in the dimension of official communication. Awareness of language, its usage, and its impact are very important in written communication. The opportunity to gain immediate feedback (and therefore to determine whether or not the message received was the one sent) is not available. Certain words carry more importance than others in writing.

Paralanguage, the power of what is not said, is also critical in official communication. Written words are read without the sender's inflection. They should be reviewed carefully by the sender for any unintended ambiguity and fragmented statements.

Proxemics, in the sense of social space, may be expressed or challenged implicitly or explicitly in official communication. Territorial issues may be generated or resolved in intradepartmental memos. Reports may make positive or negative use of jurisdictional power and limitations.

Symbolic meaning is attached to whether or not official communication is written on letterhead (or on which letterhead) and in a proper format, as well as its length, the quality of paper it is on, whether it is an original or a copy, by whom it is signed, and so on.

EFFECTIVE LISTENING

Listening as a Mental Exercise

Hearing is the act or power of perceiving sound. Hearing with normal ears is an automatic process, but listening is a mental exercise. Radio and television broadcasters are continually concerned with how many people are hearing their programs. However, the question "Does anybody listen?" seems immaterial to them. This is a radically different question. It asks this: Does anyone understand my idea, my intention, my message? Does anybody care?

Americans are not effective listeners. In general they talk more than they listen. As one theorist states, "It is really not difficult to learn to listen—just unusual." Many of us, while ostensibly listening, are actually preparing a statement to "stun" the company when we gain the floor. A good relationship between listener and speaker is necessary in a conversation—in fact, an effective *listener* leads the conversation. John F. Kennedy was famous for the incisive questions he asked and the way he listened to replies. Robert Saudek, who conferred with him at the White House while producing "Profiles in Courage" for television, later told friends, "He made you think he had nothing else to do except ask you questions and listen—with extraordinary concentration—to your answers. You knew that for the time being he had blotted out both the past and the future. More than anyone else I have ever met, President Kennedy seemed to understand the importance of *now*." We all crave good listeners. Sporadic or half-attentive listening is easily detected through nonverbal feedback cues received by the source.

Effective listening is important in any occupation. However, it is especially important in police–community relations. Miscommunication between citizens and police officers can have disastrous, if not fatal, consequences.

Nonjudgmental Listening

Carl Rogers outlined the idea of **nonjudgmental listening** in his book, *On Becoming a Person*: "I would like to propose, as an hypothesis for consideration, that the major barrier to mutual interpersonal communication is our very natural tendency to judge, evaluate, to approve or disapprove the statement of the other person or the other group" (Rogers, 1961, p. 328). Rogers goes on to state that real communication occurs when one listens with understanding, trying to place oneself in another listening's position. This is most difficult in highly emotional situations—the kinds of situations often dealt with by criminal justice personnel. When a police officer encounters similar situations, such as quarrels in the same family again and again, the officer may have a strong desire to "tune out." It is precisely that behavior that is ineffective.

In many Wisconsin communities, suburban police departments employ a "court officer" who serves as liaison between the district attorney and the police department. One such officer encountered continued friction with a fellow officer over the matter of ticket dismissals. "The law is the law," the second officer adamantly stated. It did not matter to him whether or not the defendant had good reason for clemency from the judge; he would not listen to explanations but merely delivered lengthy tirades. Suddenly the duty roster rotated the men, and this officer became—you guessed it—the court officer. In a few weeks, his attitude changed completely. He learned to listen to complete explanations.

Weaver summarizes, "All this really means is that in order to understand a verbal message well, you must understand the talker to some degree. This makes communicating with a total stranger somewhat difficult when you get above the level of asking or giving directions or talking about the weather" (Weaver, 1972, p. 88). In *Future Shock*, Toffler (1970) spoke of the increasing number of short-duration relationships, particularly in service occupations, and pointed out the difficulty of a professional attempting to listen and communicate with increasingly large numbers of people.

Listening Efficiency

Tests on listening show repeatedly that people have an average listening efficiency of only 25 percent. (This varies—some people can retain up to 70 percent and others only up to 10 percent.) Listening is not an easy, passive process. It is hard work, characterized by faster heart action, increased circulation of the blood, and a small rise in body temperature.

Most people talk at a speed of about 125 words a minute. Strong evidence exists that indicates if thought were measured in words per minute, most of us could think easily at about four times that rate. It is extremely difficult to slow down thinking time; thus we normally have about 400 words of thinking time to spare during every minute a person talks to us. What do we do with that excess thinking time while someone is speaking?

In interpersonal relationships, we too often prepare our next comment; in formal situations, as the speaker bores us, we become impatient and turn our thoughts to something else. Soon the side-thought trips become too enticing, and when we attempt to return to the speaker, we are lost. Effective listeners use their thought speed to advantage, not for side trips. They constantly apply their spare thinking time to what is being said.

SOME EFFECTIVE LISTENING FACILITATORS

1. Be prepared to listen. Rid yourself of as many distractions as possible.
2. Be an attentive listener. Observe the speaker for verbal and nonverbal cues that will increase your understanding of the speaker and the subject.

3. Be willing to risk becoming involved as a participant in, not just as an observer of, the communication.
4. Avoid prejudging what is being said and interrupting to offer criticism or advice.
5. Genuinely accept the other person's feelings and recognize his or her right to have views that differ from yours.
6. Offer feedback to the speaker, not in the form of judgments as to the "rightness" or "wrongness" of what was said, but in the form of a restatement and clarification of what was said both in terms of objective reality and in terms of the speaker's perceptions of and feelings about that reality: "What I am hearing is. . . ." "Are you saying that . . . ?"

EMPATHY

The squad car is repeatedly cited as the great insulator in police work, as are heavy caseloads for probation and parole officers. Given the police officer in the squad, the changing nature of neighborhoods, and the number of people dealt with in human relations occupations, people in these professions will need to develop high degrees of trust quickly, as will society. In reply to a questionnaire, one police officer answered, "I do my work impartially and without emotion."

Imagine that you are an elderly woman. Your only income is your social security check, which is very small. As you are walking to the grocery store, a man attacks you from behind and takes your purse, containing the only money you have. You are knocked to the ground. You sit there, dazed and bewildered. Someone calls the police, and soon two officers arrive. They begin immediately to fill out their report. They take information from you, asking you short and specific questions. The officers are doing their job impartially and without emotion. They are not sharing themselves with you, and were they to take the time to understand your feelings, they would not only have to spend more time with you, but they would also have to deal with their own feelings. The method used by the police officers insulates them from their own emotional involvement with you and is expeditious and efficient. But how are you feeling about their humaneness?

People entering the criminal justice profession need to possess a very special communication quality. Unlike the development of voice or listening skills, this concept has a rather vague aesthetic nature. It is called **empathy**, and theorists maintain that those entering people-oriented professions need to have large amounts of it. It is a caring attitude, the developed capacity to understand another, and to comprehend another's feelings, attitudes, or sentiments.

In its most extreme example, those persons who are unable to comprehend another's feelings, attitudes, or sentiments are sociopathic or psychopathic personalities. They are incapable of experiencing normal amounts of love or empathy (Levin and Fox, 1985, pp. 71–72). Psychologists speculate that some people become sociopaths because they have been rejected in their family relationships and cannot form social bonds. They often engage in various forms of misbehavior, cheating, lying, and, among the most severely affected, rape and murder (Ressler, Burgess, and Douglas, 1988).

BLOCKS TO EFFECTIVE COMMUNICATION

When community relations efforts fail, at least one of the following blocks has contributed to that failure: (1) community distrust of the police; (2) police distrust of community members; (3) poor training of police; (4) the organizational structure of the police agency; and (5) scapegoating.

Community Distrust of Police

If the citizens do not trust the police, they will avoid police contact and they will not talk to them. Therefore, if distrust causes avoidance and failure to communicate, the implications for the police organization are very dramatic. Citizens will not report crime; they will not give statements to officers who are investigating crimes; and they will not testify in court. The result is inefficiency and an unsafe community.

Police Distrust of Community

If the police view the community or some geographical part of the community they have sworn to protect as dangerous and full of people who are hostile to them, police will react in a negative way. They will not feel free to communicate with the community and will be guarded and cautious when they come in contact with those they are protecting. As a result, police officers will contribute to widening the gap between themselves and the rest of the community. Their belief system will be reinforced by negative community contacts. Eventually police officers will become fearful and hostile toward the very people they are supposed to be protecting and serving.

Poor Training

The training of police officers has significantly improved in recent years. However, the training curriculum of most police academies is heavily weighted on those skills necessary to perform the law enforcement task, a task that occupies a small portion of the officers' time. The majority of the time is often spent on police procedures, law, weapons training, driver training, self-defense, and first aid. These topics will still need to be taught. However, in the twenty-first century, law enforcement is facing a changed society—one that has become more culturally diverse—and police training must incorporate these changes. Training must develop interpersonal skills, such as active listening and de-escalation techniques, and proactive problem-solving skills. The training must stress cultural diversity and the need for the police to become part of the community not apart from the community (Coderoni, 2002). The police must incorporate community policing into their training. The police officer of the twenty-first century will be someone capable of critical and independent thinking and who can work with other agencies and culturally diverse community members to solve community problems.

Organizational Structure

The majority of U.S. police departments are paramilitary organizations, with chains of command, defined areas of responsibilities, volumes of rules and regulations, and a clear hierarchy of membership. Police organizations have chiefs, deputy chiefs, captains, sergeants, and patrol officers, and many large police organizations carry the military tradition even further, using the ranks of colonel, major, and corporal in the organizational structure.

The results of the paramilitary structure being used for a police service organization are well described by Egon Bittner:

> Another complex of mischievous consequences arising out of the military bureaucracy relates to the paradoxical fact that while this kind of discipline ordinarily strengthens command authority it has the opposite effect in police departments. This effect is insidious rather than apparent. Because police superiors do not direct the activity of officers in any important sense, they are perceived as mere disciplinarians.
>
> Contrary to the army officer who is expected to lead his men into battle—even though he may never have a chance to do it—the analogously ranked police official is someone who can only do a great deal to his subordinates and very little for them. For this reason supervisory personnel are often viewed by the line personnel with distrust and even contempt. (Bittner, 1970, p. 59)

An even more important consideration is that the paramilitary organizational structure not only blocks effective communication within the organization because of the superior–subordinate relationship, but the same working relationship inevitably is transferred to contacts between patrol officers and citizens.

Scapegoating

Allport (1954) defined **scapegoating** as "a phenomenon wherein some of the aggressive energies of a person or a group are focused upon another individual, group or object; the amount of aggression and blame being either partly or wholly unwarranted."

In more specific terms, police have often focused their attention on particular groups or individuals when such attention was really unwarranted.

A number of steps precede scapegoating. If we are aware of the progression, we will be able to spot the danger signs and take action before a serious problem occurs. These steps are (1) simple preferences; (2) active biases; (3) prejudice; (4) discrimination; and (5) full-fledged scapegoating.

SIMPLE PREFERENCES   We all have preferences—we like people who agree with us, who have similar backgrounds, and who share our value system. Our socialization process in many overt and subtle ways teaches us to prefer spaghetti or curry, gefilte fish or soul food, blondes or brunettes, Cadillacs or Fords. This simple preference for one food or one type of person is both natural and inevitable. A technical term for this simple preference is *predilection*.

ACTIVE BIASES   Here the simple preference turns stronger. People state their preference in negative terms. Instead of saying "I prefer spaghetti to curry," the statement might be "I don't like curry" or "I don't like Jewish food." An active bias is the stepping-off point toward a closed mind, an ineffective person, and an uninformed person. It immediately precedes a full-blown prejudice.

PREJUDICE   Many people have **prejudices**, which means that they have a tendency to prejudge certain groups, persons, or events. A prejudice is a prejudgment that is rigid and inflexible. Although a prejudice does no great social harm as long as it is not acted out, in the case of people involved in public service, it is extremely difficult not to let a prejudice affect judgment.

DISCRIMINATION   **Discrimination** is an act of exclusion prompted by prejudice. The most commonly accepted examples are discrimination against blacks and Hispanics by white society. This discrimination has manifested itself in different areas, including employment, housing, health care, and other social institutions. Although significant progress has been made, discrimination is one of the most significant social problems in the United States and one that profoundly affects U.S. police and their level of professionalism.

Racial and ethnic groups have, in the past, been systematically excluded from police service and from promotional appointments. Affirmative action programs have had an impact on this systematic exclusion. According to a study commissioned by the Police Executive Research Forum (PERF), estimates of blacks, Hispanics, and other racial/ethnic groups in 486 police agencies serving populations of 50,000 or more were very close to the current U.S. Census Bureau estimates for the population (Carter, Sapp, and Stephens, 1989, p. 39). Although this is cause for optimism, it does not signal an end to discrimination in the hiring practices of police agencies or in discriminatory behavior on the part of individual officers. Some police officers still look upon minorities as unworthy, unwanted, and unacceptable as human beings. The shooting of an unarmed African immigrant by New York police and allegations of arbitrary traffic stops by the New Jersey State Police again raise the specter of police discrimination against minorities.

FULL-FLEDGED SCAPEGOATING   Scapegoating manifests itself after all the preceding steps are fulfilled. It consists of concentrated aggression in both word and deed. The victim is abused both physically and verbally. The persons or groups being scapegoated are often given credit for astounding power and evil, as in the following examples: "The Jews are ruining America"; "Ship all blacks back to Africa and crime will stop"; "Wetbacks (Mexicans) are responsible for all of California's labor problems"; and "All teenagers are inherently lazy." When such statements are seen in print they are easily identified as simplistic statements by anyone with average intelligence. Yet many people make these statements day after day and, unfortunately, believe what they are saying.

Why Scapegoating Occurs

Allport (1954) identifies a number of reasons for the phenomenon of scapegoating. Among them are "tabloid thinking," self-enhancement, peer pressure and conformity, fear and anxiety, and displaced aggression. Some of these are discussed in more detail in the following sections.

TABLOID THINKING   This is the process in which people simplify a problem by blaming a group or class of people. For example, some people blame crime on illegal drug abuse; they feel that most crime is committed by drug-dependent people trying to get money to feed their habits. Although these people do commit crime, in reality they are responsible for only a small percentage of the crime rate. This tabloid-thinking process allows people to overlook real issues while they focus on the wrong cause.

Illegal drugs are sometimes scapegoated by **tabloid thinking.** Illegal drugs are those that we frequently define as dangerous substances. These substances include heroin, cocaine, LSD, ECTASY, angel dust, marijuana, certain prescription drugs, and many others. These represent a wide assortment of substances with many different sources, prices, and resulting behaviors. However, the most damaging, commonly abused drug in our society is not included in the list: It is alcohol. Under most circumstances, alcohol is not illegal to use; in tabloid thinking, it is not even recognized as a drug.

Considering the extent of the problem, efforts to prevent the crime, injury, and death caused by alcohol are very limited in the United States, with the exception of a recent tightening of laws relating to DWI/DUI (driving while intoxicated/driving under the influence) behavior. We are more likely to use our resources fighting illegal drug use. Tabloid thinking is a type of tunnel vision that, by omitting all the facts, may encourage us to focus all our energies on the wrong battle.

SELF-ENHANCEMENT   Some people have inferiority complexes. People who are experienced in interviewing police applicants often discover individuals who want to join the police department because they feel that having a badge and a gun will make them something they are not—that is, strong, more respected, or allowed to exercise control or authority over other people. Such applicants are serious liabilities to the police profession if they slip through the screening process. They will cause many communication blocks with the community through their scapegoating of others to cover their own feelings of inferiority. This type of person is also dangerous because he or she is often afraid; this personal fear often results in the use of excessive force. The use of such force when it is not warranted leads to a breakdown in communication between the police and the community.

PEER PRESSURE AND CONFORMITY   The need to belong to a group or organization is very strong in most people. New officers who join an organization that engages in scapegoating will find themselves joining with their fellow officers just so they can be part of the group. This is particularly evident when a new officer is coupled with an old-timer. Too often the officer ends up acting like the trainer.

STRATEGIES OF CHANGE

Achieving Mutual Respect

Mutual respect is achieved best in an atmosphere in which everyone counts. If I make promises that I cannot keep or make decisions that affect your life without considering your needs or your views, I am discounting you. If you treat me as if I am a category rather than a person, you discount me.

Strategies for overcoming blocks in the area of mutual respect include establishing programs that encourage honest, open exchange and positive personal contact between citizens and officers. Some of the options include the following:

- Increasing the number of walking police beats.
- Decentralizing functional police units.
- Implementing police–community projects in which shared decision making actually occurs.
- Ensuring that ride-along programs involve not only the youth and adults who already have respect for the police but also those who are distrustful.
- Establishing and supporting creative educational liaison projects.
- Initiating projects that survey citizen input and make changes based on the results of the survey.
- Participating in a community communication network designed to decrease problems with rumors and misunderstandings.
- Participating in a proactive social service action program.
- Involving volunteers in most areas of the police process.
- Assisting individual officers to increase their skills in analyzing the factors existing in each situation and selecting an interpersonal communication approach that is most congruent with existing needs.

In 1997 the police department of Roanoke, Virginia, began an outreach project to build relationships between the police and the community's growing Vietnamese community. Sponsored by the Bureau of Justice Assistance, the project was designed to provide services to the Vietnamese community and cultural awareness training to police officers. Criminal justice terminology was translated into Vietnamese and 22 different legal and criminal justice brochures were produced and distributed to the community. Police officers continue to conduct sessions at community meetings and 250 police officers have participated in a four-hour cultural awareness training program (Coventry and Johnson, 2001). It is anticipated that the project will lead to Vietnamese joining the police department. This is a program that could be replicated in other police departments with expanding immigrant populations.

Improving Training

Police training is an intense experience that has improved immensely over the years. Ways in which training can change to improve effective communication in police–community relations include the following:

- Building the academy and in-service training content upon a basic humanistic philosophy.
- Incorporating the teaching of more effective communication skills in ongoing workshops for officers.
- Placing a greater emphasis and more academy hours on service concepts and issues.
- Encouraging educational goals of officers, especially in seeking professional and liberal arts and sciences degrees.
- Ensuring that street training experience for new officers supports the philosophy and content of the academy.
- Increasing cultural awareness training, especially training centered on identifiable community groups.

Rethinking Police Organization

Realistically, reorganization in police agencies is traumatic, and it is difficult to conceive, achieve, and retain. Some communication blocks seem inherent in the organizational structure. Small system changes, however, can help to reduce the number and influence of these blocks. Suggestions include the following:

- Requiring management training seminars for all key management personnel.
- Using noncertified personnel in some key positions.

- Developing a reward system that places a high agency value on effective individual communication efforts.
- Increasing opportunities for exchange between line officers and top administration.
- Incorporating a "quality-circle" concept into the organization to ensure that all personnel in the organization are valued.
- Committing the organization to a single (rather than a contradictory) philosophy that encourages personal growth and community service.

Preventing Scapegoating

Efforts that will increase mutual respect also will help to decrease scapegoating. Humanistic training efforts help, sometimes by screening out recruits whose actions already demonstrate discrimination and scapegoating attitudes. Organizational changes that encourage personal growth and community service help to discourage scapegoating. Other strategies that focus on the individual officer might include the following:

- Providing opportunities for the officer to become more self-aware.
- Increasing opportunities for personal values clarification.
- Rewarding actions that demonstrate a lack of bias.
- Providing counseling opportunities.
- Providing opportunities for the officer to experience exceptions to stereotypes.

BOX 11.1
Fact or Inference? A Communication Game

A *statement of fact* is an observation that is verifiable. An *inference* is a conclusion or opinion; a subjective evaluation. Both are a necessary part of police work. Some of our greatest problems occur when we confuse the two. This exercise* will help you learn the difference between statements of fact and inferences and gain a better understanding of the ways in which inferences are made.

In this game, you will read three reports and answer questions about them. Then you will have an opportunity to check your answers.

Testing Your Skills

Directions: After reading each report twice *and without returning to the report for review,* answer the questions related to that situation below by circling the correct response. Mark "T" if the statement is definitely true on the basis of the information given in the report. Mark "F" if the statement is definitely false. Mark a "?" if you cannot be certain on the basis of the information given in the report. If any part of the statement is doubtful, mark "?".

Situation A

John and Betty Smith are awakened in the middle of the night by a noise coming from the direction of their living room. Smith investigates and finds that the door opening into the garden, which he thought he had locked before going to bed, is standing wide open. Books and papers are scattered all over the floor around the desk in one corner of the room.

Statements about Situation A

T	F	?	**1.**	Mrs. Smith was awakened in the middle of the night.
T	F	?	**2.**	Mr. Smith locked the door from his living room to his garden before going to bed.
T	F	?	**3.**	The books and papers were scattered between the time Mr. Smith went to bed and the time he was awakened.
T	F	?	**4.**	Mr. Smith found that the door opening into the garden was shut.
T	F	?	**5.**	Mr. Smith did not lock the garden door.
T	F	?	**6.**	Mr. Smith was not awakened by a noise.
T	F	?	**7.**	Nothing was missing from the room.
T	F	?	**8.**	Mrs. Smith was sleeping when she and Mr. Smith were awakened.
T	F	?	**9.**	The noise did not come from their garden.
T	F	?	**10.**	Mr. Smith saw no burglar in the living room.
T	F	?	**11.**	Mr. and Mrs. Smith were awakened in the middle of the night by a noise.

Situation B

A businessperson had just turned off the lights in the store when a man appeared and demanded money. The owner opened a cash register. The contents of the cash register were scooped up, and the man sped away. A member of the police force was notified promptly.

Statements about Situation B

T F ? **1.** A man appeared after the owner had turned off the store lights.

T F ? **2.** The robber was a man.

T F ? **3.** The man did not demand money.

T F ? **4.** The person who opened the cash register was the owner.

T F ? **5.** The store owner scooped up the contents of the cash register and ran away.

T F ? **6.** Someone opened a cash register.

T F ? **7.** After the man who demanded the money scooped up the contents of the cash register, he ran away.

T F ? **8.** Although the cash register contained money, the report does not state how much.

T F ? **9.** The robber demanded money of the owner.

T F ? **10.** The report concerns a series of events in which only three persons are referred to: the owner of the store, a man who demanded money, and a member of the police force.

T F ? **11.** The following events were included in the report: someone demanded money, a cash register was opened, its contents were scooped up, and a man dashed out of the store.

Situation C

Members of the 12th Street Gang are planning an assault on the 4th Avenue Gang. Two days ago a 4th Avenue Gang member was in 12th Street territory. Tires on a car were slashed.

Statements about Situation C

T F ? **1.** One of the boys from the 4th Avenue Gang was in 12th Street territory.

T F ? **2.** The 4th Avenue Gang is a youth gang.

T F ? **3.** The leaders of the 12th Street Gang are planning an assault.

T F ? **4.** Three tires on a car were slashed.

T F ? **5.** The car in the story was in 12th Street Gang territory.

T F ? **6.** One of the 12th Street Gang members was in 4th Avenue territory.

T F ? **7.** The tires were slashed by a 4th Avenue Gang member.

T F ? **8.** The car belongs to a 12th Street Gang member.

T F ? **9.** The 12th Street Gang is a youth gang.

T F ? **10.** The slashing of the tires was a deliberate attack on the 12th Street Gang.

T F ? **11.** The member of the 4th Avenue Gang was in 12th Street territory to challenge the 12th Street Gang.

*This exercise is based on a game entitled "Inference versus Observation," in *Interpersonal Communication: A Guide for Staff Development*. Athens, GA: Institute of Government, University of Georgia, 1974.

REALITY CHECK

Correcting a Wrong Perception

While residing in a small Georgia town, I served as the part-time municipal judge for seven years. One of many cases I dealt with during that time involved a local who felt that he needed to drink at least a quart of beer each day in order to keep his kidneys functioning. Unfortunately, this medical precaution had not served him well when he had been arrested for DUI (driving under the influence). It had been exacerbated in that he was stopped by the police while hauling off the body of a neighbor's dog that he had shot after another neighbor had complained to him that it had chased her chickens. I had dealt with this situation as leniently as possible, allowing him to pay his fine over an extended time and placing him under the supervision of a local businessman who had interceded on his behalf.

A couple of years later, I was working in my backyard when I heard a gunshot and then observed a dog run yelping through the yards behind my house. The dog collapsed while running and then lay totally still, obviously dead. I turned to see several small neighborhood children watching what had happened. Indignant that someone had committed such an atrocity in the middle of our neighborhood, I immediately went over to the neighboring street to find out what was occurring. Upon my arrival, I saw my former dog-shooting friend sitting in his truck with a rifle beside him. He stated to me, "I'm watching that dog there."

I asked, "Haven't you been in enough trouble for shooting dogs? You'd better not shoot another one."

He stated, "I haven't shot any dog."

To which I replied, "Really, what about the one that just ran from here and died across from my house?"

He repeated, "I haven't shot any dog."

I replied that I was going to have to contact the police and that he better not shoot the dog he was watching.

As I was going to the police station, I saw that a patrol car had pulled up beside the dead dog. An officer was trying to distract the children while the body was loaded into a county truck. I asked the officer how he had responded so quickly, to which he replied that he had been with "them" when the dog was shot. I asked what he meant by them. I added that I had seen Bill (not his real name) with a gun in his truck on the next street and assumed that he had done the shooting. The officer replied with some distaste, "No, animal control had complaints on this dog and shot him when they couldn't catch him. That's them hauling him off."

Aware that I had wrongly accused Bill of shooting the dog, I went looking for him. I located him at the local grocery store where he had gone to seek help from his son. In front of his son and several customers, I said, "You were telling the truth, and I was wrong. I apologize for wrongly accusing you."

Bill was stunned. Then he stuck out his hand and thanked me for being "big enough" to apologize to him. Bill's son and the bystanders smiled and nodded in agreement.

This incident reinforced two things that I already knew. Don't jump to conclusions even if they appear to be obvious. And it really doesn't hurt to apologize when you are wrong.

Conclusions

The quality of police–community relations depends on the quality of police–community communication, and vice versa. This chapter has focused on the continuous, ongoing communication process and possible blocks to this process. Communication occurs on many levels: intrapersonal, interpersonal, person-to-group, organizational, and written. It includes the elements of sender, receiver, and message in a situational context.

The three basic modes of interpersonal communication are (1) verbal; (2) nonverbal (paralanguage, kinesics or body language, and proxemics or communication through the use of personal or social space); and (3) symbolic (the messages conveyed by style of dress, personal appearance, one's possessions, etc.). Cues exist for each mode that an effective communicator must learn to recognize and use. For example, a police officer who wants to use language and paralanguage well must pay attention to articulation of words, volume and rate of speech, tone of voice, choice of language, and (when necessary) telephone manner. The officer must also be aware of the effect of body positions, use of personal space, clothing, and personal appearance on communications.

An effective communicator is someone who not only sends but also receives messages well. Unlike hearing, listening is a mental exercise. People can "think" words much faster than they can speak or listen to them; effective listeners are those who apply their spare thinking time to what is being said—and who try to place themselves "in the speaker's shoes" in a nonjudgmental way.

Effective communicators are aware of themselves and others in a situational context. They determine what messages are appropriate to send and then couch them in an approach they feel will most effectively achieve their goals. A communication quality that is especially important in the administration is empathy. Free, open communication with other members of the community is possible only for the person who can empathize with others.

There are five common blocks to effective communication in police–community relations: community distrust of the police, police distrust of the community, poor training, police organizational issues, and scapegoating. There also are strategies for change that can eliminate or lessen these blocks to communication. Many of these strategies will be further explored in later chapters.

Student Checklist

1. Identify and describe three levels of communication.
2. Define and diagram the communication process.
3. Identify and give examples of the modes of communication.
4. What is effective listening?
5. What is the role of empathy in communication?

6. List the blocks to effective communication most frequently encountered in police–community relations.
7. List the strategies for change that could eliminate or lessen the blocks to effective police–community communication.

Topics for Discussion

1. Why is nonjudgmental listening an important skill for police officers to have?
2. When would it not be useful to be an effective listener?
3. How can you be ensured of getting feedback in the communication process?
4. Discuss the common blocks to effective communication between police and citizens mentioned in this chapter in relationship to your own community.

5. What programs identified in strategies for change might remove the blocks to effective communication that exist in your community?
6. Discuss the difference between active bias and simple preference.

Bibliography

Abrams, S. (1989). *The Complete Polygraph Handbook.* Lexington, MA: Lexington Books.

Allport, G. W. (1954). *The Nature of Prejudice.* New York: Doubleday.

Ardrey, R. (1966). *The Territorial Imperative.* New York: Atheneum.

Bittner, E. (1970). *The Functions of the Police in Modern Society.* Bethesda, MD: National Institute of Mental Health.

Bombeck, E. (August 1982). "He spoke fluent law enforcement," in *Vanguard, Official Publication of the San Jose Peace Officers Association II.*

Brougham, C. G. (July 1992). "Nonverbal communication: Can what they don't say give them away?" *FBI Law Enforcement Bulletin,* pp. 15–18.

Carter, D. L., Sapp, A. D., and Stephens, D. W. (1989). *The State of Police Education: Policy Direction for the 21st Century.* Washington, D.C.: Police Executive Research Forum.

Coderoni, G. R. (November 2002). "The relationship between multicultural training for police and effective law enforcement," *FBI Law Enforcement Bulletin.*

Coventry, G., and Johnson, D. (2001). "Building relationships between police and the Vietnamese community in Roanoke, Virginia," *Bureau of Justice Assistance Bulletin.* U.S. Department of Justice.

Fast, J. (1981). *Body Language.* New York: Pocket Books.

Hall, E. T. (1966). *The Hidden Dimension.* Garden City, NY: Doubleday.

Huseman, R., and McCurley, S. (December 1972). "Police attitudes toward communication with the public," *The Police Chief,* Vol. 39, No. 12, pp. 68–73.

Institute of Government. (1974). *Interpersonal Communication: A Guide for Staff Development.* University of Georgia, Athens, GA.

Levin, J., and Fox, J. A. (1985). *Mass Murder: America's Growing Menace.* New York: Plenum Press.

Link, F. (1993). *The Interrotec® Kinesic Interview Technique: A Short Course in Detecting Deception Behaviorally,* February 27 seminar at Fort McClellan, AL.

Macionis, J. (1993). *Sociology,* 4th ed. Upper Saddle River, NJ: Prentice Hall.

Meyer, A. (June 1982). "So lie detectors lie?" *Science,* Vol. 82, pp. 24–27.

Quintanilla, G. (February 1983). "Cross-cultural Communication: An Ongoing Challenge," *FBI Law Enforcement Bulletin,* pp. 1–8.

Ressler, R. K., Burgess, A. W., and Douglas, J. E. (1988). *Sexual Homicide: Patterns and Motives.* Lexington, MA: Lexington Books.

Rogers, C. (1961). *On Becoming a Person.* Boston, MA: Houghton Mifflin.

Strecher, V. (1971). *The Environment of Law Enforcement.* Upper Saddle River, NJ: Prentice Hall.

Toffler, A. (1970). *Future Shock.* New York: Random House.

Van Maanen, J. (1978). "The asshole," in P. K. Manning and J. Van Maanen (Eds.), *Policing: A View from the Street.* Santa Monica, CA: Goodyear Publishing Co.

Weaver, C. H. (1972). *Human Listening: Processes and Behavior.* New York: Bobbs-Merrill.

White, M. F., Cox, T. C., and Basehart, J. (1994). "Theoretical consideration of officer profanity and obscenity in formal contacts with citizens," in T. Barker and D. L. Carter (Eds.), *Police Deviance,* 3rd ed. Cincinnati, OH: Anderson.

CHAPTER 12

Talking Through Our Differences

Intercultural and Interpersonal Communication

Marianne O. Nielsen

Rebecca Maniglia

In contrast to the diversity in the offender population, on the whole, criminal justice practitioners are members of privileged groups. On average, they are white, male, physically able and middle class. This lack of commonality means that intercultural and interpersonal communication skills take on a special significance in providing justice services, especially when coupled with the power differential between criminal justice practitioners and their clients.

For example, police officers are the gatekeepers to the criminal justice system. It is "an accepted fact" for most officers that citizens will be uncomfortable communicating with them (Womack and Finley, 1986:145). Many citizens see the police as representatives of the dominant society and as authority figures who have the power to determine their security, peace of mind, freedom, and even their chances of dying. This power is not limited to the police. Lawyers, prosecutors, judges, correctional officers, and parole and probation supervisors make decisions daily that can have the same impact.

Criminal justice practitioners, like ordinary citizens, often feel uncertainty and anxiety in communicating with strangers, particularly when those exchanges cross the boundaries of difference (i.e., race or gender). The power they wield, however, gives them an added responsibility in dealing with their own negative reactions. They must ensure they have the skills to communicate effectively with those in the diverse systems in which they serve. Equally important, they must communicate with enough competence that understanding becomes a two-way street. This chapter, or indeed any book on intercultural or interpersonal communication, cannot provide "the" answer for handling all intercultural interactions effectively and appropriately;[1] it does, however, provide useful information about the knowledge and skills needed to do so, and the issues that can arise in communication.

Interpersonal communication is usually understood as verbal and nonverbal exchanges between two or more people on a specific topic. Improving intercultural communication skills can be a vital strategy for maintaining effective interpersonal communication. This is usually done through two kinds of intercultural communication training: culture-specific and culture-general (Hammer, 1989). Culture-specific training focuses on building communication competence in just one culture, as when an American Drug Enforcement Agency officer studies Colombian culture. In contrast, culture-general skills are ones that can be generalized to intercultural interactions regardless of the culture (Hammer, 1989). While intercultural communication is the focus of this chapter, most of the skills described are equally applicable to interpersonal communication with members of other groups (see Milhouse, 1993).

COMMUNICATION COMPETENCE IN CRIMINAL JUSTICE

Communication is the process that occurs between two or more individuals who use words and/or nonverbal signals to construct the reality of their interaction and to attach meaning to the messages they transmit (Gudykunst, 2003). Competent communication is about developing a shared reality or negotiating "mutual meanings, rules, and outcomes that are 'positive'" (Gudykunst and Nishida, 1989:36). It has been said that effective communication is primarily about minimizing misunderstanding (Gudykunst, 2003), but communication is seldom perfect. Both partners in the interaction bring to it their individual personalities, life experiences, and social and cultural roles. This means they may misinterpret the meaning of the other's words or actions (Gudykunst, 2003). One common area of misinterpretation is culture.

Many people are unaware of, uncomfortable with, or unable to discuss the dynamics and implications of cultural differences. This lack of knowledge or interpersonal comfort can lead to tension or conflict as people interpret others' words and behaviors incorrectly, become frustrated, make negative judgments about others, and eventually cut off the interaction. They may even end up avoiding situations of intercultural communication in the future (Cushner and Brislin, 1996). In the case of criminal justice members, they may even choose to become aggressive in their interactions with those outside of their own culture (Gundersen and Hopper, 1984). One way to avoid these scenarios is to develop the knowledge and skills to operate effectively and appropriately in intercultural interpersonal interactions or to become competent communicators.

Rewards of Competent Communication

Competent communication has many rewards. First, competent communicators learn about someone else's cultural concepts and gain insight into a world very different than their own. For example, the Cree Indians, one of the largest indigenous groups in Canada, have no word for or concept of "guilt". What does this suggest about their view of crime? What might be the repercussions of this when they appear as an accused in court? Similarly, the Cree have no gender pronouns. What might be the impact of this linguistic difference if a Cree is asked to give testimony about the identity of an offender?

Second, competent communicators may gain a new perspective on their own culture. For example, if the Japanese have many words for rice because of its centrality to their diet, what might this say about all the words Americans have for guns? Similarly, what does it mean that Americans have gender pronouns when the Cree don't? Do Americans attach status and prestige to gender in ways that are different from other cultures? How does this affect how women are treated in the criminal justice system?

Third, competent communicators are more likely to make decisions that take into account the perspectives of all parties to the interaction. Actions taken by a police officer, for example, in handling a domestic violence dispute will be more likely to calm the situation than inflame it if the police officer has some knowledge of the culturally defined domestic roles of the spouses, their attitude toward authority figures, and their normal tone of verbal and nonverbal communication.

Womack and Finley (1986) believe that good communication has a number of other benefits to the criminal justice system generally, including allowing for better community relations, a decrease in misunderstandings, tensions, and conflicts among coworkers from different backgrounds, and increased self-esteem among criminal justice members as they become better able to handle intercultural interactions.

CRITICAL KNOWLEDGE ABOUT COMMUNICATION

In order for criminal justice personnel to achieve intercultural communication competence, it is important to have knowledge about certain key influences on communication, including the impact of diversity on communication, the power of nonverbal communication, and the importance of the situational context.

The Impact of Diversity on Communication

There are many kinds of diversity that can influence communication. In this section we will look at just three: gender, culture, and power/status. While these three are among the most important for criminal justice personnel, it should be recognized that many kinds of diversity influence communication, including race, education, physical abilities, and age. Similarly, categories of diversity intersect with one another to create an even broader form of influence.

GENDER   Communication research across settings and populations has found communication differences between men and women. Aries (1996: 189) says these findings include

> [m]en show a greater task orientation in groups, women a greater social-emotional orientation; men emerge more often as leaders in initially leaderless groups; men interrupt more; women pay more attention to the face needs of their conversational partners; women talk more personally with their close friends.

The meanings connected with these differences are socially constructed and often based on gender stereotypes. For example, a man's statement might be interpreted as assertive whereas the same statement from a woman may be interpreted as aggressive or even "bitchy."

According to Aries (1996:195), "gender differences cannot be understood without putting them in the context of gender inequalities in society." Women in American society are still perceived and treated as having a lower status than men, and dominant–subordinate status can have a great deal of influence on communication. Interestingly, when men and women are given the same status, few gender differences in communication emerge. In criminal justice, the few that do exist may have positive consequences. For example, female police and correctional officers are more willing to use reason, less likely to provoke hostilities, more likely to diffuse tensions, and more likely to mediate conflict than their male counterparts (Martin and Jurik, 2007).

Verbal and nonverbal communication can be difficult to interpret. There are a wide array of variables that can influence an interaction, including the class and status of the partners, sexual orientation, age, ethnicity, and individual style. Situational factors such as the relationship between the partners, the setting, the topic, and the length of the interaction can also influence the degree to which gender differences have impact (Aries, 1996). In addition, there are cultural variances in the proper tone of conversation, the kind of touch allowed (if any), and the appropriate personal distance between men and women. There are also cultural differences in the level of appropriate intimacy in the topic and in the expectations of response. These differences could lead to misunderstandings or even to accusations of sexual harassment if one of the partners in the interaction is seen by the other as "stepping over the line" (Cushner and Brislin, 1996).

In order to deal competently with communication differences, people need to learn as much as possible about the expectations of the groups with which they interact. They also need to learn to recognize indicators of power differences and understand that they have evolved as the result of group history. Communicators should not take such changes personally and should always keep their interactions respectful and professional. Finally, competent communicators need to recognize that job-related differences in male and female communication may even be advantageous to the criminal justice system.

CULTURE   Cultural groups can be differentiated along a number of standard dimensions. While various typologies have been developed to describe these,[2] probably the best known is Hofstedes' (2005). Hofstede and Hofstede differentiate cultures by their individualism/collectivism, their high and low power distance, their uncertainty avoidance, and their approach to masculinity and femininity.[3] As they explain,

> Individualistic cultures emphasize the individual's goals while collectivistic cultures stress that group goals have precedence over individual goals. High power-distance cultures value inequality, with everyone having a "rightful place," and the hierarchy reflects existential inequality. Low power-distance cultures, in contrast, value equality. Uncertainty avoidance involves the lack of tolerance for uncertainty and ambiguity. Cultures high in uncertainty avoidance have high levels of anxiety, a great need for formal rules, and a low tolerance for groups that behave in a deviant manner. Masculinity involves valuing things, money, assertiveness, and unequal sex roles. Cultures where people, quality of life, nurturance, and equal sex roles prevail, on the other hand, are feminine (Gudykunst and Nishida, 1989:21–22).

Another important typology differentiates between high context and low context cultures (Hall, 1976). In high context cultures, much of meaning is implicit and is communicated by context and nonverbal nuances or signals. In low context cultures, meaning is given directly, with little reliance on context or nonverbal signals. African American, Native American, and Latino/a subcultures within the United States are relatively high context, while European-based cultures (i.e., the dominant "white" culture) are low context. As most criminal justice personnel are trained to be low context in their communication, knowing where a group fits in this typology can be useful for trying to anticipate and prevent cultural conflict.

POWER AND STATUS DIFFERENCES   Groups with subordinate status have developed specialized ways of communication based on their past interactions with members of the dominant group. Orbe (1998:16–17) presents a long list of these, including diverting communication away from potentially dangerous topics, remaining silent when offensive statements are made, downplaying or ignoring differences, ridiculing self, confronting, educating others, imposing a psychological distance through verbal and nonverbal strategies, and avoiding communication altogether. The individual strategy used will depend on the perceived gain or cost for the subordinate member of the interaction (Orbe, 1998).

Individuals employed within the criminal justice system may experience an instantaneous change in status that may affect how communication is perceived and carried out. There may be potential differences in naming, respect, and nonverbal communication. For instance, a Latina lawyer may be treated with more deference in court than she receives in the supermarket. Likewise, a native African employed within the system may experience black–white discrimination in ways that are unfamiliar.

The Importance of Nonverbal Communication

According to Henderson (1994), about 70 to 80% of communication is nonverbal. Knowledge of what nonverbal communication conveys, while not always reliable, is an important tool for criminal justice personnel. Most nonverbal communication is spontaneous, unconscious, and subtle (Andersen, 1994:229). The manner of speaking communicates as much as the words; it just does not communicate the same thing in every culture. Characteristics that may vary across cultures and between groups include: tone, placement of emphasis, volume, pitch, quality (e.g., clear versus slurring), and duration (Henderson, 1994). The following are seven key areas for understanding nonverbal communication.

Silence makes many Americans nervous. Citizens from the northeast are taught to finish other people's sentences, to interrupt, and to leap immediately into any space in a conversation. Similarly, some racial or ethnic populations, such as African Americans or Italians, are known for loud, expressive dialogues. Rather than being markers of impoliteness, these represent speech patterns or learned cultural behaviors. In contrast, many Native American and Asian peoples are taught to wait a space after another person has stopped talking. The length of the silence reflects the importance they give to the other person's words. In a meeting between individuals from these cultures, we might observe a significant cultural clash in communication, with some populations feeling they have no room to present their concerns because others are imposing their point of view through aggressive communication.

Gestures and movements are among the most important aspects of nonverbal communication. There are over 100,000 different gestures used around the world, and most have meanings that vary from culture to culture. A simple example is the head nod used in the United States to signify agreement. In Greece, depending on the exact movement, a nod might actually mean "no" (Henderson, 1994).

Personal space or "zones of territory" also vary across cultures, class, and gender. Generally, if a person invades the space of another, it may cause discomfort, but people in some cultures prefer to stand closer than others. High contact is desirable in Latin American, African, Arabian, and southern European cultures, while noncontact or low contact is preferred by Asian and northern European cultures (Henderson, 1994).

Touching is also viewed differently by low contact and high contact cultures. Touching includes kissing, embracing, hugging, hand shaking, and general touch. Touching varies not only by culture but by the gender and status of the persons in the interaction, the timing of the interaction, and the private or public location of the interaction (Henderson, 1994).

Eye contact standards can also vary. Cultures vary in how long people make eye contact, how intensely, when, what part of the body is looked at, and how much blinking is done (Henderson, 1994). Some cultures consider extended direct eye contact as a sign of honesty while others see it as disrespectful.

Movement while speaking can also vary. In some cultures people may walk away and return to emphasize agreement (Henderson, 1994). In others, individuals talking to authority figures are expected to stand still and upright.

Symbols are a special category of nonverbal communication. Examples include flags, ankhs, crosses, Stars of David, badges, uniforms, jewelry, scout patches, head coverings, colored ribbons, political cartoons, and thousands of others. Each group has symbols that have special meanings to its members. Some of these are easy to recognize and understand; others are not. Some are used to draw a group together (flags), while others divide or exclude (swastikas). In the criminal justice system, much gang identification relies on the colors and styles of clothing worn. Police uniforms are also symbolic—of assistance to some, while of oppression and tyranny to others.

Competent communicators must learn the nonverbal signals of cultures or cocultures that they interact with frequently but must be very careful in using them as they may not have a full appreciation of the subtleties.

Situational Context

To understand each other, partners in an interaction must know something about social, cultural, and personal context. Without context, "behavior is just noise" (Cushner and Brislin, 1996:13). Each participant in an interaction operates within the context of their own life experience, status, motivations, culture, and group history. This means that a wide range of factors can affect an interaction, including the physical and emotional setting in which the interaction occurs (i.e., in a dark park late at night or in a crowded mall) or the characteristics of the participants (i.e., their numbers, attractiveness, prototypicality, personality, temperament, and mood) (Giles and Franklyn-Stokes, 1989). The historical relations between the groups the participants represent can also matter as can personal status or power. If one group is or has been dominant and the other subordinate, power and status can influence the context of the interaction.

The participants' knowledge of the language is also an important factor. It may be taken for granted that both parties understand the meanings of words, when they may not. Words and concepts can have subtly different, slightly different, or even drastically different meanings (Cushner and Brislin, 1996:289). For example a "date" with a prostitute is not the same as a "date" to the movies, and "snow" as in precipitation differs from "snow" as in heroin. The nonverbal communication that accompanies words may also completely change their meaning. For example, "mother" can change meaning depending on the tone of voice or hand gesture that accompanies it. While a nonnative English speaker may possess a working knowledge of the language, there is a chance that they are not familiar with the nuances of English words and expressions. The English phrase "see you later," for example, has led to accusations of American insincerity, since it does not necessarily express the intent to see you later, but is simply a ritual parting phrase (Cushner and Brislin, 1996).

The purpose of the interaction can also affect communication. Some cultures have high regard for the ability to debate, while others use silence to communicate respect. Some have a great enjoyment of small talk, while some have very little use for it. Some use talk as a form of social control; others use it as a means of establishing affiliations. Even knowing how to agree or disagree may be an important skill.

What each participant considers appropriate behavior or presentation of self is also important (Henderson, 1994). This may include greetings (e.g., handshakes versus bowing), showing affection, covering the head or legs, the formality or informality of dress, removal of shoes on entering a room, how to sit "properly," how to criticize, how to give and receive compliments, and recognizing symbols of marriage (jewelry, hairstyle, clothing style).

CRITICAL ISSUES IN COMMUNICATION

There are many communication issues that may lead to difficult situations for criminal justice members. We will look at five that have had a great deal of impact on the system.

Stereotyping

In order to psychologically process all the information they receive, people learn to place others in abstract social categories based on easily identified characteristics (Gudykunst and Gumbs, 1989). In this country, these characteristics include skin color, sex, presence or absence of disabilities, and apparent age, but stereotypes can also be based on accent, social class, and/or ethnicity. Stereotypes attribute certain behaviors to all members of a certain category, allowing for no individual variation. Positive stereotypes are formed about in-groups such as family, friends, and members of the same class or race (i.e., they are all intelligent, talented, and kind), while negative stereotypes are formed about out-groups (i.e., they are all criminal, lazy, and greedy) (Gudykunst and Gumbs, 1989). Categories and placements in them are learned through jokes, ethnophaulisms (rude names), epithets (expressions), stories, and the media.

Stereotypes can prevent individuals from interacting with each other or even cause them to be afraid of each other. People are often concerned that if they try to learn more, they will embarrass themselves by saying or doing something "stupid." Yet, they may also find that the "Other" is an individual just like them, with similar family problems and career hopes. The only way to understand this, however, is to see people as individuals, overcome stereotypes, and not see others as homogeneous members of some group of strangers. This requires true, meaningful communication.

Ethnocentrism

Ethnocentrism is the tendency to judge others by the standards of one's own group and to form a negative opinion as a result of such comparisons (Hofstede and Hofstede, 2005). Often when individuals are faced with cultural practices different from their own, their reaction is to compare the practice unfavorably with what they are familiar and, therefore, not participate. Not surprisingly, such negative responses may be interpreted as disrespectful. Similarly, if someone criticizes what is perceived to be American culture, Americans may react poorly, while in these situations it is best not to assume disrespect was intended (Argyle, 1982).

Naming

Meanings of names change over time and in different regions of the country or the world, and the process of naming is influenced by the power dynamics present. Oppressed groups that have historically been named by those in power may have strong feelings about labels. For instance, the labels "African American" and "black" are often used interchangeably, while they may have particular connotations to those in that racial group. Likewise, the term "Hispanic" is commonly used to group individuals whose roots may be in countries as varied as Mexico, Argentina, Puerto Rico, and Spain. The fact that members of the dominant group do not understand why the name they use for the minority group is offensive or limiting is a sign of the social distance between members of the minority and dominant groups. It symbolizes the traditional indifference of the dominant society to the concerns of minority groups (Herbst, 1997:258).

Members of named groups may also choose to use naming as a means of "talking back" to the dominant society, for example using names like "gringo" or "round eyes" for Americans, who are members of the privileged white group. Oppressed groups may also adopt the derogatory names for their own purposes-"self-definition, solidarity, or irony" (Herbst, 1997:256, xii; Orbe, 1998:16–17)-such as the use of the term "queer" by the GLBT (Gay, Lesbian, Bisexual, and Transgender) community.

Further, many people have trouble understanding that words and expressions (such as "acting like a wild Indian" in reference to a rambunctious child) have connotations which can make them ethnic, racial, or gender slurs. Connotations are the "emotional and cognitive associations of words" (Herbst, 1997:256), and it is the connotations that are offensive more so than the words themselves. The words "restrict, misrepresent, or distort how people are known" (Herbst, 1997:ix) and as such, they are an element of stereotyping. Names reveal societal and individual attitudes about groups. They develop in response to the changing needs of their users and the evolving needs of the society in which they are used. "In the United States the vast array of abusive ethnic words reflect the society's complexity, increasing ethnic diversity and fast-paced social change" (Herbst, 1997:255). Derogatory names may hinder the political interests of groups, are ideologically loaded, mark boundaries between "us" and "them", create distance between the speaker and the group spoken of, "keep people in their place" and justify discrimination in the minds of the people discriminating (Herbst, 1997:ix, 256). They are also used to chastise people who are perceived as straying from acceptable intercultural behavior or who are assimilating too far into the dominant society of which they are not a part (Herbst, 1997:x).

Humor

Humor can be used for many social purposes, including as an information-gathering tool, as a means of giving information, as a means of anxiety management, for social control, and as a means of preserving the status quo (Foot, 2006). The first three purposes suggest that humor can be a vital strategy for criminal justice personnel developing intercultural and interpersonal communication. It can be used as a means of diffusing tense situations, as a means of coping with embarrassment, or for gathering information. It can, however, also be a risky tool. Humor targeting group membership, such as ethnicity, race, or gender can lead to serious problems. These jokes are based on stereotypes and serve (perhaps unintentionally) as a means of social control and of preserving the status quo. Jokes reinforce the characteristics and "place" of some groups within society; that is, they reinforce prejudice. As Foot (2006:271) states, "Because the joke is a socially acceptable form, the message it conveys is extremely powerful and the recipient or target, however much offended, can hardly denounce it without standing accused of the greatest crime of all-lacking a sense of humor."

In terms of using humor, it is important to remember that a great deal of humor relies on shared cultural and linguistic experiences. It is often not the words that are funny, but the understanding that goes with them. In other words, humor is highly culture-specific (Hofstede and Hofstede, 2005). It is probably best to follow the advice given by Hofstede and Hofstede, (2005:329) who suggest, "In intercultural encounters the experienced traveler [or criminal justice practitioner] knows that jokes and irony are taboo until one is absolutely sure of the other culture's conception of what represents humor."

Translation

Translation is an intervening variable in communication between two primary parties. Because translation is an active process in which the translator must make a series of decisions and judgments, it has the potential to affect the decisions or knowledge of criminal justice personnel. Cultural orientation can make direct translations meaningless or alter their meaning. Many legal concepts cannot easily be translated into some languages, and translating the underlying ideology of concepts is even more difficult. In these cases, the translator must not only translate, but also interpret. As a result, the translation has the potential to influence the results of the interaction (Banks and Banks, 1991).

With the changing population demographics in this country, the need for translation has increased geometrically for criminal justice service providers (Banks and Banks, 1991). Sanders (1989) reported that over 43,000 requests for translation services in 60 languages were made annually in federal courts and that New York City courts alone needed interpreters about 250 times *a day*. Translators trained in legal terminology can be invaluable; however, there is no standard certification required by the U.S. justice service (Banks and Banks, 1991) even though some individual states have language skills tests for translators.

CRITICAL SKILLS

Which skills are important and how to develop them has been the subject of many publications on improving intercultural and interpersonal communication (Hammer, 1989; Henderson, 1994). Gudykunst (2003) suggests that competent communicators must have the motivation, knowledge, and skills to communicate. They are motivated by the fulfillment of certain needs that arise in interaction. These include a need for predictability, a need to avoid anxiety, and a need to sustain self-concept. Knowledge means knowing about the other person's group and knowing what needs to be done in order to communicate in an effective way. Gudykunst describes six skills that are particularly important. In order to reduce anxiety, communicators must have the ability to be mindful, tolerate ambiguity, and manage anxiety; in order to reduce uncertainty, communicators must be able to empathize, adapt their behavior, and make accurate predictions about and know explanations for others' behavior (2003:253–270). Listening, asking questions, and conflict management are subsumed among these skills, but because of their importance to criminal justice personnel, they are discussed separately.

Being mindful means that communicators must be aware of their own communication behavior and the process of communication, rather than focusing on their feelings or on the outcome. It also means being open to new information and other people's perspectives. *Tolerating ambiguity* means having the skill to deal successfully with situations in which a lot of information needed for effective communication is missing. People with a low tolerance for ambiguity may try to find information that supports their previous conceptions, while people with a high tolerance try to gather objective information. *Managing anxiety* means being able to control bodily symptoms of anxiety, as well as control worrying thoughts. People who are involved in an interaction with unfamiliar, "weird" people may feel uneasy, tense, and worried. They may fear that their self-concept will be damaged, that there will be negative behavioral consequences (e.g., that they will be exploited or be harmed), and that they will be negatively evaluated by their group or the other group. It is important to remember that a moderate amount of anxiety actually aids performance while too much or too little hinders communication.

Practicing empathy means trying to take the perspective of the other in order to understand the other's feelings and point of view. This is not to be confused with sympathy, which is trying to imagine how *you* would feel in the other's situation. *Adapting* is being able to perceive different situational contexts and choose the verbal and nonverbal communication strategies that are most appropriate and effective. *Making accurate predictions and explanations* for others' behavior requires knowing that all cultures have rules of thought, feeling, and behavior, but that these vary from group to group. Effective communicators do not assume the other is using a particular set of rules but try to determine what rules are underlying the communications and use these to predict and explain behavior.

Listening, according to Gudykunst (2003), is a process in which individuals take in new information, check it against what they already know, and select information that is meaningful. It is a skill that does not come naturally and needs to be practiced. This is a particularly important skill for criminal justice personnel who must gather information and make decisions about how to deal with people. In the dominant American culture, "active listening" is the recommended strategy. *Active listening* involves three skills: attending skills comprised of the nonverbal body language, posture, and eye contact we maintain in interactions; following skills, which are the verbal and nonverbal ways we indicate to the person we are listening; and comprehending skills, which comprise the ways we ensure that we are understanding the speaker. Active listening may not be appropriate with all groups, however. Some cultures find asking questions disrespectful. Also, verbal indicators of "following" may be seen as interruptions and lead to the cessation of talk, while the "attending" skill of maintaining eye contact might be interpreted as a challenge.

In American culture, *asking questions* is the simplest way of gathering information. However, within some cultures, it is considered rude. This can be especially problematic for criminal justice personnel with investigative roles. For instance, in some Native American cultures, asking questions, especially of elders, is impolite and will not likely elicit a response. These situations require alternative ways of requesting information, such as saying, "I wonder if . . . " or "someone told me . . . ," pausing, and allowing the person time to offer information if they wish to do so. Other times it is the content of the question that is unintentionally rude as each group has topics that are not acceptable in conversation. For instance, most Americans are uncomfortable talking to casual acquaintances about their sexual relations. Finally, who is asking the question may also be an issue. In many Australian Aborigine cultures, there is "men's" knowledge and "women's" knowledge, and it is inappropriate for a man to share men's knowledge with a woman no matter what her occupation, and vice versa.

Conflict management is another important skill for criminal justice personnel. Conflict is handled differently by various cultural groups. Individualistic and collectivistic cultures, for example, handle conflict differently. Members of collectivistic cultures are more likely to try to smooth over the conflict or to avoid it altogether, whereas members of individualistic cultures are likely to try to control the conflict situation and/or treat conflict as a problem to be solved (Gudykunst and Nishida, 1989). Criminal justice practitioners need to know the appropriate strategies for different groups.

TRANSLATING COMMUNICATION COMPETENCE INTO ORGANIZATIONAL SUCCESS

Criminal justice organizations employ and must provide services to a diverse population. The cultures represented in the organization will influence management and leadership styles and overall organizational culture (Tayeb, 1996:101; Hofstede and Hofstede, 2005). Some cultural values and behaviors will have more impact than others. For instance, Tayeb (1996) suggests that organizations are particularly affected by their employees' attitudes toward power, tolerance of ambiguity, individualism, collectivism, commitment, and interpersonal trust.

Issues in intercultural and interpersonal communication within organizations are similar to those between individuals. Not surprisingly, the prejudices found in society at large are also present in the work place (Henderson, 1994). Coworkers may act in a discriminatory manner, or managers may refuse to recruit, hire, or promote members of various categories of difference.

There are, of course, also problems in communication. Racial groups interacting within the workplace, for example, may assign different meanings to verbal and nonverbal communication (Asante and Davis, 1989). Some occupations also have specialized argots that act as a communication code for practitioners (e.g., police officers using radio codes in casual conversation). These may be very difficult for new staff members to understand, especially if they come from a group that has been traditionally excluded from the occupation. There are also language usages that are exclusive to one category of individuals, leaving others out. For instance, the use of sports metaphors during planning meetings may isolate those without such knowledge.

Organizations have three options in managing their diverse workforce: they can ignore its diversity; they can recognize its diversity but not use it; or they can use its diversity as a rich resource for the provision of services. Organizations that ignore or resist diversity will find that they are denied the benefits of a fully productive diverse workforce. Further, discrimination is against the law, and companies that allow discrimination will not only lose offended customers and staff, but may well find themselves the target of lawsuits. Organizations which actively use their workforce diversity are more competitive and are more creative in problem solving and have fewer internal conflicts (Tayeb, 1996). This means that effective interpersonal and intercultural skills are valuable not only for the individuals, but also for their organizations. As a result, many organizations, including criminal justice organizations, are suggesting and even requiring that their employees take part in initiatives that will develop their communication skills.

A number of strategies can help organizations develop and make better use of the communication skills of their employees. First, management's encouragement or discouragement of diversity affects the behavior of everyone within the organization. If competent intercultural and interpersonal communication is to be part of the organizational culture, it must occur with the cooperation and active participation of senior administration (Henderson, 1994). Second, managers must learn both verbal and nonverbal communication skills in order to teach others. These managers use their skills to learn about their employees' values, motivations, communication styles, attitudes, and needs (Henderson, 1994). Third, intercultural and interpersonal communication initiatives must be based on the objectives and commitments of the organization. Policy must provide clear direction for the initiatives' objectives and how they are to be reached. Employees should be part of planning these initiatives and must feel there will be personal benefits for participation (Henderson, 1994). Fourth, policies concerning bias-free written and spoken language should be implemented. Terminology used should reflect the occupation or task, not the personal characteristics of the staff member; for example, referring to "the secretary" instead of "the girl." Similarly, proper titles or proper names should be used rather than slang names.

Finally, organizations can create programs that develop employee competency in language proficiency, negotiation, and general communication (Tayeb, 1996). Ideally, training programs should meet the needs of the trainees and their organization. There is a wide range of training programs from which to choose (Cargile and Giles, 1996). One of the most effective is the "culture-general assimilator," which presents a series of critical incidents in which intercultural communication did not work. Participants choose from a set of answers until they find the correct explanation for the failure (see Cushner and Brislin, 1996). This training method is particularly appropriate for criminal justice personnel, who must provide effective services in a wide range of job scenarios every day. Hargie (2006) recommends that training in communication skills is best carried out through "microtraining"-that is, carried out in small groups over short periods of time and focusing on only one skill at a time. Skills are identified, training sensitizes staff to those skills, and then participants are given opportunities for skill practice and to receive feedback. Evaluation of the program focuses on the impact of the new skills on client groups.

Other training methods include lectures, role plays, field trips, and experiential games (Cargile and Giles, 1996).

Organizations can evaluate the intercultural competence of their employees based on three very straightforward criteria: whether or not employees feel comfortable and satisfied with intercultural or interpersonal interactions; whether the employee is rated as a competent communicator by members of various difference categories; and whether the employees are rated by a supervisor as effective in dealing with members of other groups (Argyle, 1982). Being able to establish meaningful interpersonal relationships with members of other groups has also been suggested as an indicator of competence.

In summary, to be effective, intercultural communication initiatives must be well planned, must occur organization-wide, must be coordinated from the top, must be on-going, and must include nonverbal communication (Henderson, 1994). In this diverse world, there is little doubt that increased competence in intercultural and interpersonal communication skills is of benefit to both individuals and organizations within the criminal justice system.

Endnotes

1. It should be noted that while this chapter discusses the aggregate-level characteristics of some groups, there is a great deal of individual variation within each group. It should also be noted that most of the work in intercultural and interpersonal communication has been done from a Eurocentric point of view (Martin, 1993).
2. See Gudykunst and Nishida (1989) for an overview of theoretical frameworks for intercultural communication.
3. It should be noted that some theorists find Hofstede and Hofstede's use of the terms "masculine" and "feminine" sexist and stereotypical, and substitute the term "gender," which is still a questionable term (see Hecht, Andersen, and Ribeau, 1989).

References

Andersen, Peter. 1994. Explaining Intercultural Differences in Nonverbal Communication. In *Intercultural Communication: A Reader*, ed. Larry A. Samovar and Richard E. Porter, 7th edn., 229–239. Belmont, CA: Wadsworth.

Aries, Elizabeth. 1996. *Men and Women in Interaction.* New York: Oxford University Press.

Argyle, Michael. 1982. Intercultural Communication. In *Cultures in Contact*, ed. Stephen Bochner, 61–79. Oxford: Pergamon Press.

Asante, Molefi K., and Alice Davis. 1989. Encounters in the Interracial Workplace. In *Handbook of International and Intercultural Communication*, ed. Molefi Kete Asante and William B. Gudykunst, 374–391. Newbury Park: Sage Publications.

Banks, Anna, and Stephen P. Banks. 1991. Unexplored Barriers: The Role of Translation in Interpersonal Communication. In *Cross-cultural Interpersonal Communication*, ed. Stella Ting-Toomey and Felipe Korzenny, 171–185. Newbury Park: Sage Publications.

Cargile, Aaron C. and Howard Giles. 1996. Intercultural Communication Training: Review, Critique, and a New Theoretical Framework, In *Communication Yearbook 19*, ed. Brant R. Burleson, 385–423. Thousand Oaks: Sage Publications.

Cushner, K., and Richard W. Brislin. 1996. *Intercultural Interactions: A Practical Guide*, 2nd edn. Thousand Oaks, CA: Sage Publications.

Foot, Hugh C. 2006. Humour and Laughter. In *The Handbook of Communication Skills*, ed. Owen D. W. Hargie, 3rd edn., 259–285. London: Routledge.

Giles, Howard, and Arlene Franklyn-Stokes. 1989. Communicator Characteristics. In *Handbook of International and Intercultural Communication*, ed. Molefi Kete Asante and William B. Gudykunst, 117–144. Newbury Park: Sage Publications.

Gudykunst, William B. 2003. *Bridging Differences*, 4th edn. Thousand Oaks, CA: Sage Publications.

Gudykunst, William B. and Lauren L. Gumbs. 1989. Social Cognition and Intergroup Communication. In *Handbook of International and Intercultural Communication*, ed. Molefi Kete

Asante and William B. Gudykunst, 204–224. Newbury Park: Sage Publications.

Gudykunst, William B., and Tsukasa Nishida. 1989. Theoretical Perspectives for Studying Intercultural Communication. In *Handbook of International and Intercultural Communication*, ed. Molefi Kete Asante and William B. Gudykunst, 17–46. Newbury Park: Sage Publications.

Gundersen, D. F., and Robert Hopper. 1984. *Communication and Law Enforcement.* Lanham, MD: University Press of America.

Hall, E. T. 1976. *Beyond Culture.* New York: Anchor/Doubleday Books.

Hammer, Mitchell. 1989. Intercultural Communication Competence. In *Handbook of International and Intercultural Communication*, ed. Molefi Kete Asante and William B. Gudykunst, 247–260. Newbury Park: Sage Publications.

Hargie, Owen D. W. (Ed.). 2006. Training in Communication Skills: Research, Theory and Practice. In *The Handbook of Communication Skills*, 3rd edn., 473–482. London: Routledge.

Hecht, Michael L., Peter A. Andersen, and Sidney A. Ribeau. 1989. The Cultural Dimensions of Nonverbal Communication. In *Handbook of International and Intercultural Communication*, ed. Molefi Kete Asante and William B. Gudykunst, 163–185. Newbury Park: Sage Publications.

Henderson, George. 1994. *Cultural Diversity in the Workplace.* Westport, CT: Quorum Books.

Herbst, Philip H. 1997. *The Color of Words.* Yarmouth, MA: Intercultural Press.

Hofstede, G. and Hofstede, G. J. 2005. *Cultures and Organizations*, 2nd edn. New York: McGraw-Hill.

Martin, J. N. 1993. Intercultural Communication Competence: A Review. In *Intercultural Communication Competence*, ed. R. L. Wiseman and J. Koester, 16–29. Thousand Oaks: Sage Publications.

Martin, S. E. and Jurik, N. C. 2007. *Doing Justice, Doing Gender*, 2nd edn. Thousand Oaks: Sage Publications.

Milhouse, V. 1993. The Applicability of Interpersonal Communication Competence to the Intercultural Communication Context. In *Intercultural Communication Competence*, ed. R. L. Wiseman and J. Koester, 184–203. Thousand Oaks, CA: Sage Publications.

Orbe, M. P. 1998. *Constructing Co-Cultural Theory.* Thousand Oaks: Sage Publications.

Sanders, A. L. 1989. Libertad and Justicia for All. *Time,* May 29, 65.

Tayeb, M. H. 1996. *The Management of a Multicultural Workforce.* Chichester: John Wiley and Sons.

Womack, M. M. and Finley, H. H. 1986. *Communication: A Unique Significance for Law Enforcement.* Springfield, IL: Charles C. Thomas.

MODULE 7

Chapter 13

Stress and Coping

....

⌘ Introduction

Community psychology is a rich and diverse area of study. Thus, numerous theoreticians have sought ways of unifying the multitude of activities and viewpoints that fall under its rubric. Some have argued that community psychology is what community psychologists *do* (e.g., Spielberger & Iscoe, 1977). This tautological definition does not adequately capture the unique perspective and mission of the field.

I have described what community psychology *is* by identifying and examining each of its guiding principles. These principles are the foundation for the field's practice and research. They are stable, generally agreed-upon precepts that give the field its identity.[1] The next two chapters center on orienting concepts. Orienting concepts both reflect and influence what community psychology *does* (Novaco & Vaux, 1985). They are frameworks that summarize extant research, theory, and practice; give meaning to current efforts; and guide new inquiries. They bridge past knowledge, present practice, and future accomplishments.

As our knowledge base evolves and the context of inquiry changes, so do our orienting concepts.

[1]To be exact, the guiding principles do not describe what the field *is* but what the field *strives to be*. They embody the ideals of practice and research toward which we aim.

Indeed, orienting concepts, unlike fundamental principles, are *supposed* to change. We need new concepts to inspire novel insights, renew our energy, and shake us out of our collective intellectual complacency.

We begin our exploration of orienting concepts shortly after community psychology's birth. Five years after Swampscott, Betty Kalis (1970) noted that the concept of stress had begun to appear with increasing frequency in the community psychology literature. She proposed that crisis theory serve as an orienting concept to help shape and direct community psychology, arguing that it provided a user-friendly and open-ended conceptual model that suggested new and diverse directions of investigation.

In presenting her preferred orienting concept, Kalis (1970) recognized that a variety of other concepts might and should emerge. She observed, "As the field of community psychology develops, a number of conceptual models are appropriately being invoked in understanding and guiding research and practice" (p. 69). She reasoned that a field with such a complexity of concerns required a variety of theoretical approaches to meet the formidable challenge of synthesizing information.

As Kalis predicted, crisis theory and the closely related stress-and-coping framework did become a major orienting concept for community research and practice beginning in the 1970s and extending into the 1980s. Although Kalis laid the groundwork, the establishment of stress and coping as an orienting concept for the field is most often linked to another community psychologist, Barbara S. Dohrenwend. In 1978, Dohrenwend was elected president of Division 27 along with her husband Bruce P. Dohrenwend. In her presidential address, Barbara Dohrenwend proposed a model of stress and coping that could "provide a framework within which the apparently disparate activities of community psychologists takes on a satisfying coherence and directedness" (Dohrenwend, 1978, p. 2). We will examine Dohrenwend's framework in more detail later in this chapter.

Although the bulk of research and theory using a stress and coping paradigm occurred in the 1970s and into the 1980s, Barbara Dohrenwend was not the last to advocate for this orienting concept. In 1985, Raymond Novaco and Alan Vaux again lamented the lack of coherence in the field and echoed the previous calls by Kalis and Dohrenwend to use a stress-and-coping framework to organize the work of community psychology. More recently, in their 1997 community psychology textbook *Principles of Community Psychology: Perspectives and Applications*, Murray Levine and David Perkins affirmed the utility of stress and coping as an orienting concept. While other orienting concepts have gained favor in the past few decades and have, to some degree, displaced the stress-and-coping framework, this early orienting concept remains a useful map for those of us navigating our way through the vast and complex landscape that is community psychology.

⌘ The Concept of Stress

One reason for the appeal of the concept of stress is that it is a familiar concept to which most of us can relate. The trials of Job described in the Bible are but one example of an ancient accounting of stress (Hobfoll, 1998). Through no fault of his own Job experienced a variety of stressful life events—his oxen, donkeys, and camels were carried off, his sheep and servants burned in a fire, his brother's house collapsed on his children, and his body became covered with boils. Job lost his family, his wealth, and his health. As he tried to make sense of his misfortune, he received support from three friends who came to comfort him.

All compelling heroes in literature and mythology, from Hercules to Harry Potter, confront major challenges that change the protagonist in fundamental ways. This is true in most people's life stories. Challenging events become defining moments in life as turmoil opens the door for insights and untried ways of behaving that would never have occurred otherwise. With the wisdom of hindsight, events that seemed threatening, harmful, or even tragic when they occurred (e.g., break up with first love, death of close family member) actually come to be seen as the experiences that made us who we are, sometimes changing our lives for the better.

Stress is broad concept. Many events and circumstances qualify as stresses—extraordinary events such as Hercules' attack from a many-headed serpent or Harry Potter's encounter with an escaped prisoner of Azkaban. More mundane events, such as the loss of one's first love, also qualify as stressful events. The breadth of the concept has both advantages and disadvantages. When a concept refers to such a wide variety of events and situations, it is difficult to know if all stress researchers are actually studying the same phenomenon. Attempts to draw conclusions across studies must therefore proceed tentatively. At the same time, the advancement of knowledge does not require unanimous agreement on precise definitions. Indeed, advancement may depend on generality as well as precision. Although each study requires an explicit definition of how the researchers define and measure key concepts (that is, their **operationalization**), a more complete understanding of the concept emerges when a multitude of researchers each approaches their studies from a somewhat different perspective. All of psychology's important constructs (stress, aggression, and intelligence, to name a few) have differing definitions that capture layers of meaning.

Still, our understanding depends on some agreement about what it is we are studying. **Stress** is a disturbance in the homeostatic balance of a person's life. It is induced by environmental demands that exceed the individual's (or system's) coping resources. Thus, stress is taxing and has adverse cognitive, behavioral, and physiological effects. The nature of these effects varies, however, because stress results from a transaction between the person and the environment. Its effects are mediated by individual and social factors. As we track the development of stress-and-coping frameworks, the relevance of these characteristics should become increasingly clear.

EARLY STRESS RESEARCHERS

Modern research on stress is often traced to the work of Erich Lindemann. In 1942, a tragic fire at the Coconut Grove nightclub killed 500 people. Lindemann (1944) studied how relatives of those who perished adjusted to the deaths of their loved ones. He found that family members needed to do "grief work," which entailed letting go of the relationship with the deceased person, accepting life without that person, and forming new attachments. If people did not grieve adequately, they suffered psychological impairment. If, however, they succeeded with their grief work, they could become psychologically stronger than they had been before the trauma. Interestingly, Lindemann predated many community psychologists in warning that psychiatrists and other mental health professionals could never assume responsibility for ensuring that grief work occurred due to the vast number of people who experienced loss. He recommended training other service providers (e.g., social workers, ministers) to help people deal with losses.

Lindemann's groundbreaking work focused on the psychological effects of a stressful event. A decade later, another early stress researcher named Hans Selye (1956) focused on physiological responses to the experience of stress. In order to elucidate the mind–body link, Selye studied a variety of different stresses, including overcrowding and everyday hassles. He found that diverse events triggered similar defensive reactions, which he called the **general adaptation syndrome (GAS)**. The GAS consists of three stages. First is the *alarm* stage, during which the experience of stress activates the sympathetic nervous system. This stage is characterized by a short-lived physiological reaction, as indicated by an increase in heart and respiration rates. In the second stage, the *resistance* stage, the body attempts to defend against the chemical changes triggered during the alarm stage. If the stress persists, the third stage, *exhaustion*, occurs. This stage is characterized by physical depletion and can ultimately result in death. When multiple stresses occur, they take a cumulative toll on already-taxed individuals. Selye asserted that by helping people manage their responses to stress, psychological and physiological impairment could be avoided.

This early work inspired a colleague of Lindemann's, Gerald Caplan (1961, 1964; see also Golan, 1978), to delineate the dynamics of **crisis theory** (McGee, 1980). Caplan's theory drew on several of Selye's premises. Caplan believed that different types of crises resulted in similar responses. He also agreed that the experience of stress led to an initial, short-term response that paved the way for long-term adjustment. Caplan drew on Lindemann's work, as well. Caplan saw crises as events that disrupt a person's equilibrium and require some sort of effort to restore homeostasis. And like Lindemann, he believed that the crisis could result in either new vulnerabilities *or* new strengths. The word *crisis* comes from the Greek word meaning "to decide" and suggests a choice point—a situation that might be resolved in more than one way. Depending on how the crisis is resolved, people can grow as a result of their experience, or their functioning can be compromised. Crises entail both danger and possibility.

Developmental psychologists have long understood the role crises play in inspiring growth. Erik Erikson's stage model holds that crises at different ages lead to growth or problems in development. Jean Piaget highlighted the role of disequilibrium in motivating development. "Every classical theory of development has held—whether implicitly or explicitly stated, whether empirically or intuitively derived—that challenge and disequilibrium are harbingers of growth" (Gist, Lubin, and Redburn, 1999, p. 16). The growth potential of stress outlined by Caplan was largely forgotten, however, in the wave of research that followed.

What does not destroy me, makes me stronger.
—Friedrich Nietzsche

In the 1970s, interest in stress burgeoned. Provocative theories and research brought the concept to the attention of many, but the development of a simple user-friendly research tool revolutionized the field. A decade after Selye's work, Thomas Holmes and Richard Rahe (1967) constructed a list of major life events called the **Schedule of Recent Events (SRE)** and a companion list of event weights, the Social Readjustment Rating Scale (SRRS). The list of events resulted from the examination of the medical records of 5,000 patients. The forty-three events included on the SRE were the ones that frequently occurred in the months preceding the onset of illness (Brown, 1986). The SRE requires respondents to check any listed events that they experienced in the preceding year. Total stress scores were obtained by multiplying each event the respondent reported experiencing by the corresponding weight from the SRRS (see Table 13.1). The SRE quickly became the predominant research tool for assessing stress (Holmes, 1979).

Research using the SRE and similar instruments confirmed the link between stress and both physical health and psychological adjustment. The occurrence of major stressful events has been associated with heart problems, cancer, depression, anxiety, isolation, suicide, paranoia, aggression, and a host of other difficulties (Byrne, & Whyte, 1980; B. S. Dohrenwend, 1973; Jacobs & Charles, 1980; Gersten, Langner, Eisenberg, & Orzeck, 1974; I. Sarason, Johnson, & Seigel, 1978; Theorell, 1974; Vinokur & Selzer, 1975; see also Kessler, 1997). The wealth of studies inspired by the SRE focused on the link between stress and maladjustment. Throughout the 1970s, the potential for growth as a result of stressful incidents was largely ignored.

STRESS, COPING, AND COMMUNITY PSYCHOLOGY

As community psychology began to take shape in the 1970s, researchers and practitioners were drawn to the concepts of stress and coping for

📄 Table 13.1   Social Readjustment Rating Scale

Life Event	Weight	Life Event	Weight
Death of spouse	100	Son or daughter leaving home	29
Divorce	73	Trouble with in-laws	29
Marital separation	65	Outstanding personal achievement	28
Jail term	63	Wife begin or stop work	26
Death of close family member	63	Begin or end school	26
Personal injury or illness	53	Change in living conditions	25
Marriage	50	Revision of personal habits	24
Fired at work	47	Trouble with boss	23
Marital reconciliation	45	Change in work hours or conditions	20
Retirement	45	Change in residence	20
Change in health of family member	44	Change in schools	20
Pregnancy	40	Change in recreation	19
Sex difficulties	39	Change in church activities	19
Gain of new family member	39	Change in social activities	18
Business readjustment	39	Mortgage or loan less than $10,000	17
Change in financial state	38	Change in sleeping habits	16
Death of close friend	37	Change in number of family get-togethers	15
Change to a different line of work	36	Change in eating habits	15
Change in number of arguments with spouse	35	Vacation	13
Mortgage over $10,000	31	Christmas	12
Foreclosure of mortgage or loan	30	Minor violations of the law	11
Change in responsibilities at work	29		

Reprinted from *Journal of Psychosomatic Research, 11,* Holmes, T. H., & Rahe, R. H., The social readjustment rating scale, 213–218, Copyright 1967, with permission from Elsevier Science.

several reasons. First, stress centers on the interface between the person and her or his context. An event happens in the environment, and the affected individual must find a way to respond. Thus, stress implicates *both* people and environments. In addition, community psychologists were drawn to the opportunities for intervention. If people could be helped to cope during the period of disequilibrium, maladjustment could be prevented. Third, community psychologists were attracted to the stress framework's departure from the deficit perspectives. Stressful events could pave the way for enhancement as well as impairment.

In 1978, Barbara Dohrenwend highlighted the appeal of a stress framework to community psychologists when she presented her model of psychosocial stress to Division 27 (see also Sandler, 1979). She noted the link between stress and psychopathology that research using the SRE demonstrated so persuasively and asserted that if community psychologists wanted to reduce the incidence of psychopathology, we needed to focus our attention on the stress process.

Figure 13.1 depicts the model of stress outlined by Dohrenwend in her presidential address. This influential model will help organize the information presented in the remainder of this chapter.

The boxes in bold represent the previously discussed relationship between stress and adjustment. After the stressful event takes place, an initial response occurs, which affects the individual's long-term adjustment. Long-term adjustment can reflect impairment, growth, or a return to the previous level of functioning. The boxes that are not bolded reflect the individual and environmental contributions to the stress process. The circles at the periphery of the diagram represent avenues for intervention. Let's begin exploring this model by looking at the three

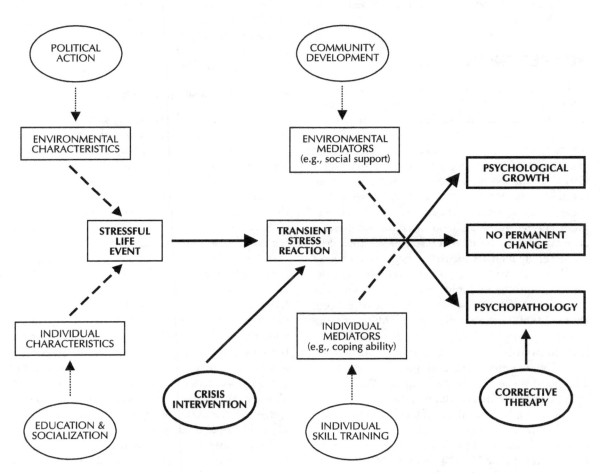

Figure 13.1

Dohrenwend's model of psychosocial stress. *Adapted from Dohrenwend, B. S. (1978). Social stress and community psychology.* American Journal of Community Psychology, 6, *1–14. Reprinted with permission.*

domains that affect adjustment to stress: the stress itself, the individual, and the environment. Although these three components are discussed separately in the following sections, they are all interrelated—the role of each is defined in part by the other two.

⌘ Event Variables

What aspects of life events affect the degree to which they cause upset or enable growth? Many features of stressful events have been examined in the stress literature.

NUMBER OF EVENTS

One of the most important findings of early stress researchers was that life events exert a cumulative impact on mental and physical health. The more stress a person experiences within a limited time frame, the more that person's resources are taxed and the greater the risk for maladjustment. Michael Rutter (1979) examined how major stresses, including severe discord between parents, overcrowding, low socioeconomic status, and maternal psychiatric disorder affected the likelihood of childhood psychiatric disorder. He found that one isolated stress does not generally increase the risk of negative outcomes for children. Two stresses entail a fourfold increase, however, and the multiplicative effect is even more marked when four stresses co-occur. In a more recent study of 9,500 members of a large HMO, exposure to four or more adversities in childhood entailed a four- to twelve-fold increase in risk for alcoholism, drug abuse, depression, and suicide attempts in adulthood (Felitti, Anda, Nordenberg, Williamson, Spitz, Edwards, Koss, & Marks, 1998).

The multiplicative effects of stress would be less troublesome if stresses generally occurred in isolation, but stresses tend to co-occur. Look again at the events listed on the SRE (Table 13.1). Many of these events are interrelated. Trouble with one's boss may lead to a different line of work, financial troubles, and a loan. Divorce may lead to a change in residence and social activities.

SEVERITY OF THE EVENT

In the earliest version of the still-popular SRE, total stress scores were derived by simply counting the number of events experienced (Hawkins, Davies, & Holmes, 1957). In the early era of stress research, investigators focused on identifying generic stress reactions (e.g., Selye's "general adaptation syndrome"). Thus, the commonalities among different types of stresses were emphasized. It soon became evident, however, that different events had different effects. A vacation, for example, would not take the same toll as the death of a spouse. This led Holmes and Rahe (1967) to develop their companion list of weights based on the severity of each event. Assessing the severity of events is not, however, as straightforward as one might initially think.

NORMATIVE AND INDIVIDUAL WEIGHTS

Holmes and Rahe (1967) established a weight for each event based on the amount of change or *social readjustment* it required. A group of 394 individuals assigned weights to each event based on an anchor value of 500 for marriage (later recalibrated to a weight of 50). Holmes and Rahe then averaged these ratings to obtain normative weights.

Subsequent researchers argued that a meaningful life-event scale must account for individual differences in perceptions of life events. Knowledge of how events are perceived *on average* tells us little about how any individual views an event (e.g., Lazarus, 1991). The death of a parent may affect someone from a close, nurturing family very differently than someone from a distant family in which the parent had been psychologically or physically absent. Researchers interested in accounting for subjective perceptions adopted methodologies that allowed respondents to assign self-determined weights to events (Byrne & Whyte, 1980; Sarason et al., 1978; Vinokur & Selzer, 1975).

Several studies have assessed which type of stress scores best predicts adjustment: simple counts of events, scores based on normative weights, or scores using individually determined ratings. Not all studies have found significant differences among techniques (Kale & Stenmark, 1983; Meuse, 1985;

Newcomb, Huba, & Bentler, 1981; Rahe & Arthur, 1978; Swearingen & Cohen, 1985a), but when differences are found, they generally favor individually determined weights (Chiriboga, 1978; Hurst, Jenkins, & Rose, 1978).

While the use of individual ratings avoids some of the problems encountered with normative weights, this methodology brings problems of its own, notably the possible confounding of subjective perceptions and adjustment. In other words, people who tend to rate events more negatively may be less well-adjusted to begin with. Thus, the stronger relationship between stress and adjustment obtained using individually determined weights is not really capturing the effect of events on later adjustment, but the effects of prior adjustment on perceptions of events (see Lazarus, DeLongis, Folkman, & Gruen, 1985; B. P. Dohrenwend & Shrout, 1985; Mueller, Edwards, & Yarvis, 1977; Rabkin & Struening, 1976).

MAJOR EVENTS AND EVERYDAY EVENTS

Most stress researchers have focused on major traumas. Richard Lazarus and Susan Folkman (1984) observed that traumatic events are fairly infrequent, yet most of us do not consider our lives to be stress free. They argued that everyday events, or **daily hassles** such as having concerns about one's weight or home maintenance concerns, constitute stresses that affect people's sense of well-being on an ongoing basis. Thus, Lazarus and his colleagues (Kanner, Coyne, Schaefer, & Lazarus, 1981) developed a measure of daily events.

Lazarus (1984) found that not only do hassles affect well-being, these daily irritants have a stronger relationship to well-being than exposure to life traumas. There are a number of possible explanations for this finding. It may be that daily hassles are manifestations of major events (e.g., Pillow, Zautra, & Sandler, 1996). Someone is more likely to gain unwanted weight when distressed about a failing marriage, for example. It is also possible that reports of daily hassles actually tap personality variables that are themselves related to health. Some suggest that minor hassles may be more subject to personal

interpretations than major events (see Hobfoll, Briggs, & Wells, 1995). A highly reactive and anxious person might experience traffic congestion as profoundly frustrating while easy-going drivers barely notice the delay. Regardless of the mechanism, research on daily hassles has encouraged stress researchers to rethink the literature's focus on large, infrequent events.

EVENT VALENCE

Holmes and Rahe derived event weights according to the amount of life change required "*regardless of the desirability of the event* (Holmes & Rahe, 1967, p. 213, italics in the original)." This strategy of ignoring event valence has been widely debated. Some researchers supported the view that the important dimension of a stressful event is the amount of readjustment required (e.g., B. S. Dohrenwend, 1973; Lloyd, Alexander, Rice, & Greenfield, 1980; Meuse, 1985; Rahe, 1974). Many others believed that the crucial component was the amount of *negative* change required or the event's *undesirability* (e.g., Gersten, et al., 1974; Gersten, Langner, Eisenberg, & Simcha-Fagan, 1977; Paykel, Prusoff, & Uhlenhuth, 1971; Ryff & Dunn, 1985; Sarason, et al., 1978; Swearingen & Cohen, 1985b; Vinokur & Selzer, 1975). Studies that compare the readjustment and undesirability views directly have generally found support for weights based on event undesirability rather than undifferentiated change (Chiriboga, 1978; Kale & Stenmark, 1983; Mueller, et al., 1977; Ross & Mirowsky, 1979).

What about desirable events? Holmes and Rahe (1967) included seemingly positive events on their list: marriage, vacation, gaining a new family member. Similarly, Lazarus and his colleagues assessed both daily hassles (as discussed previously) and daily uplifts (e.g., completing a task, visiting a friend). Do desirable events have an impact on adjustment? Research suggests that positive life events have little or no effect on physiological dysfunction or other indices of negative adjustment (e.g., Hirsch, Moos & Reischl, 1985; Mueller et al., 1977; Vinokur & Caplan, 1986). However, both desirable *and* undesirable events correlate with measures of positive adjustment (Block and Zautra, 1981; Ryff & Dunn, 1985; Vinokur & Caplan, 1986; Zautra & Reich, 1980; Zautra & Simons, 1979).

CONTROL, PREDICTABILITY, AND NORMATIVENESS

Another important event characteristic is the degree to which the event can be controlled. There are events in life we can control to a large degree (such as failing a test) and events that we cannot control at all (such as lightning strikes). Studies that differentiate controllable versus uncontrollable events find that events viewed as uncontrollable correlate much more highly with subsequent illnesses than controllable events (Stern, McCants, & Pettine, 1982; Suls & Mullen, 1981). This has led some stress researchers to develop measures in which events are classified as being within or beyond a person's control (e.g., B. S. Dohrenwend, Krasnoff, Askenasy, & B. P. Dohrenwend, 1978).

In general, people feel more control over events they can foresee. Sudden deaths, accidents, and illnesses, unexpected job losses, and natural disasters often occur with little or no warning. Thus, we cannot prepare for them emotionally or take proactive measures to mitigate their effects. Some events *can* be anticipated. One class of events that occurs on an expected timetable is **normative events**. Normative events are life experiences that generally occur during particular periods in the life span. Examples of normative events include puberty, high school graduation, and retirement. **Nonnormative events**, on the other hand, are not age-linked such as natural disasters or death of a close relative. Many researchers and theoreticians have noted the importance of distinguishing normative and nonnormative events, which have also been called *differentiated-maturational* versus *situational* crises (Aguilera & Messick, 1974), *accidental* versus *developmental* events (Morrice, 1976), and *idiosyncratic* versus *generic* crises (Jacobsen, Strickler, & Morley, 1968). Normative events differ from nonnormative events in two important respects: we can foresee them, and our peers experience them along with us. Thus,

normative events are particularly conducive to intervention. Researchers and practitioners can devise preventive efforts around these anticipated crises, such as programs to ease school transitions. Furthermore, we can simultaneously intervene with entire groups of people, such as an entering freshman class.

Research shows that normative events generate more stress when they occur out of their normal time frame—early retirement, for example, or the death of one's spouse at a young age (e.g., Borque & Back, 1977). We can hypothesize several reasons for this finding. Sense of control might come into play—if we have time to prepare for an event, we feel more in control. Off-time events also lack the sense of normalcy that exists when other people we know are going through the same experience. Research shows, for example, that being jobless at time of high unemployment is less detrimental to one's sense of well-being than joblessness at a time when rates of unemployment are low (Cohn, 1978). Experiencing a stress with others may also make it less threatening and confusing. Others can help us make sense of the event and provide models for how to cope.

CHRONIC VERSUS ACUTE STRESS

Life events, traumas, and daily hassles constitute stressful episodes in one's life. Some have argued that the stress literature has overemphasized episodic stresses and underemphasized enduring stressful conditions (e.g., Novaco & Vaux, 1985).

One source of chronic stress is the physical environment (Sigal, 1980; Stokols, 1978). For example, a naturalistic study of elementary school children in the flight path of Los Angeles International Airport found that children in high-noise schools suffered from signs of stress (Cohen, Evans, Stokols, & Krantz, 1986; see also Bronzaft & McCarthy, 1975). Some stress symptoms, such as high blood pressure, attenuated over time, but prolonged exposure continued to interfere with children's test performance. Chronic stress arises from the social

⬛ CLASSIC RESEARCH

Holmes and Rahe's Legacies
Influences on Studies Large and Small

Holmes and Rahe's (1967) simple, easy-to-use measure of stress, the SRE, revolutionized psychology and related fields. It had a broad impact on our knowledge of stress, coping, and adjustment, and also on our thinking about assessment techniques. Countless studies were inspired by their seminal work.

In the earliest version of the SRE, life events were simply counted to derive a stress score (Hawkins et al., 1957). The later versions used event weights that reflected the amount of social readjustment required, which was defined as "the intensity and length of time necessary to accommodate a life event *regardless of the desirability of the event*" (Holmes & Rahe, 1967, p. 213, italics in the original). Subsequent researchers found that undesirability was more important than change per se, and so events were then classified as either positive or negative. But does this dichotomy go far enough? Are events best classified as *either* negative *or* positive?

Some studies in the community psychology literature have attempted to tie Holmes and Rahe's research on life events to crisis theory. You will remember that crisis theory built on the belief that events have, at least potentially, positive as well as negative outcomes—they can lead to growth or maladjustment. The SRE's roots in the medical literature and goal of predicting illness led to an emphasis on pathological outcomes. In 1974, Norm Finkel switched attention to the growth-enhancing potential of events. He asked research respondents to report on their experiences with traumatic events and with events that he called *strens*. A stren was defined as the opposite of a trauma, that is, "an experience in an individual's life that builds strength into his [or her] personality" (Finkel, 1974, p. 266). One of the most interesting findings from Finkel's (1974, 1975) research was that individuals sometimes had difficulty deciding which category best described specific experiences in their lives. People described single events as *both* strens and traumas.

Finkel (1974) proposed the existence of three types of events: strens, traumas, and stren/traumas, which have elements of both. These stren/trauma events may be the same as those other researchers categorized as "ambiguous" (e.g., Kale & Stenmark, 1983) or "mixed" (Block & Zautra, 1981). Recognizing three types of events may be an advance over a negative–positive dichotomy, but it ignores the wisdom of one respondent in Finkel's (1994) study who wrote, "I cannot see how a stren experience if it is to have an influence on your life, can be devoid of trauma" (p. 268). Certainly seemingly positive events, such as the long-awaited birth of a child, inspire negative as well as positive life changes. Participation in the miracle of birth, feelings of overwhelming love, and the daily discoveries of childhood are among the unparalleled joys of parenting. And then there are the sleepless nights, worries about illnesses, lack of time for simple chores, and the continuously interrupted conversations with adult friends and relatives.

A stress study of my own grew from the conviction that *all* important life events contain, at least potentially, both positive (strenful) and negative (traumatic) elements. I assessed ninety-one events in a college student sample using a rating scheme that allowed respondents to rate each event twice, first based on how much negative change it caused and then on how much positive change it inspired. For some events the positive aspects predominated (e.g., success at an extracurricular activity), for some the negative aspects predominated (e.g., death of a close friend) and for others, the negative and positive aspects were comparable (e.g., remarriage of parents after a divorce). But *no event* was consistently viewed as purely negative or purely positive by the people who had experienced it (Kofkin & Reppucci, 1991).

I also compared my assessment technique (C below) with two parallel forms of the measure that corresponded to either Holmes and Rahe's social readjustment view (A below) or the undesirability view (form B). One third of the research participants received each version of the measure. I found that the assessment technique that allowed respondents to rate events as both negative and positive (form C) captured more of the variability in adjustment than the others (Kofkin, 1989).

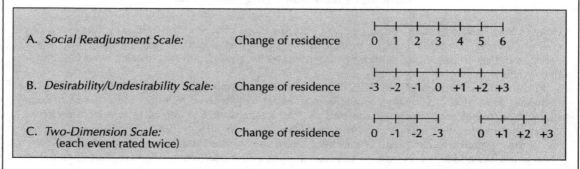

A. *Social Readjustment Scale:*	Change of residence	0 1 2 3 4 5 6
B. *Desirability/Undesirability Scale:*	Change of residence	-3 -2 -1 0 +1 +2 +3
C. *Two-Dimension Scale:* (each event rated twice)	Change of residence	0 -1 -2 -3 0 +1 +2 +3

Holmes and Rahe's innovative research technique has influenced many people's thinking about stress and research. It has inspired countless studies of the impact of stress, both large and small, including one of my own.

as well as physical environment. For example, work environments can be stressful if bosses behave in arbitrary and coercive ways, if intense time pressures exist, or if tasks are extremely repetitive (see Novaco & Vaux, 1985).

Social position variables, such as minority status, have also been framed as chronic stresses (e.g., Moritsugu & Sue, 1983). Of course, it is not minority status per se that generates stress, but the conditions that surround it. Ethnic minority status may correlate with problems of adjustment because of its association with context-shaping events and conditions, many of which are outside individual control. People of color are more likely to be poor, live in violent neighborhoods, experience the challenges of migration and acculturation, and encounter racism and discrimination (GarcíaColl, Lamberty, Jenkins, McAdoo, Crnic, Wasik, & Vásquez García, 1996; Gonzales & Kim, 1997; see also Clark, Anderson, Clark, & Williams, 1999; McLoyd, 1990).

Some research suggests that chronic stress is more deleterious to health and well-being than acute stress (e.g., McGonagle & Kessler, 1990). A number of mechanisms might account for this finding. Chronic stress does not end, and so there is no

relief for the psychological and physical taxation it causes. To use Seyle's (1956) language, people under chronic stress enter the exhaustion phase. Not all researchers agree that chronic stress exerts a larger toll, however. Stevan Hobfoll's (1998) Conservation of Resource (COR) theory suggests that the most critical aspect of a stress experience is the loss of resources (Hobfoll, et al., 1995). People strive to obtain, retain, and protect their resources, which include homes, health, and jobs. Stress occurs when resources are threatened, lost, or not gained when gains were expected. Acute stress, which is associated with an identifiable loss, might therefore be perceived as more stressful than chronic stress.

Although COR theory posits a direct relationship between acute events and stress, chronic conditions such as poverty enter into the stress process through two avenues. First, they increase the chances that acute stresses occur (see Ennis, Hobfoll, & Schröder, 2000). A lack of access to reliable transportation and daycare can lead to job loss. Poorly heated homes and unsanitary living conditions increase health risks. A lack of resources also increases the stressfulness associated with acute stresses.

For example, money shortages increase the difficulty of coping with such events as a family health crisis, job loss, and even such minor hassles as a parking ticket.

RECENCY OF THE EVENT

Early researchers recognized that people pass through different stages as they cope with stress. Selye (1956) outlined an adaptational process that involved alarm, resistance, and exhaustion. Lindemann (1944) proposed three stages of mourning: shock and disbelief, awareness, and resolution of the loss. Other prominent researchers and theoreticians have outlined stages in adaptation. John Bowlby (1961) hypothesized that the loss of a loved one is followed by shock, yearning for the lost person (accompanied by anger), giving up the hope of seeing the person (accompanied by depression), and recovery and reintegration. These stages are similar to the five stages outlined by Elizabeth Kübler-Ross (1969) in her classic work on death and dying: denial, anger, bargaining, depression, and acceptance.

The stage view of stress and coping suggests that reactions to crises follow an expected pattern. Initially crisis theorists believed that these stages followed one another quite quickly. They proposed that the psychological issues associated with the occurrence of any stressful event would be resolved, either positively or negatively, within about eight weeks (Bloom, 1963; Caplan, 1961; Caplan, 1964; Darbonne, 1967). Subsequent research showed that the adjustment process often lasts much longer. One study found that the effects of undergoing surgery for cancer endured for up to 28 weeks (Lewis, Gottesman, & Gutstein, 1979). The Buffalo Creek flood in West Virginia had a persistent influence on a subgroup of survivors fourteen years after its occurrence (Green, 1995). The Holocaust continues to affect survivors more than half a century later and reverberates in the lives of survivors' children as well (Lomranz, 1995).

The disequilibrium and stress of major events do appear to be most marked in the earlier stages of adjustment, and stress measures that weight events differentially according to their remoteness in time can improve the researcher's ability to predict outcomes (e.g., Kale & Stenmark, 1983). Nevertheless, events in the distant past may continue to have a significant impact later in life. Major life events are best construed as influences that alter one's life course rather than episodic events that impact our lives only during a discrete period of adjustment (Felner, Farber, & Primavera, 1983; Hetherington, 1979).

⌘ Individual Factors

A number of event qualities influence the stress experience, including their number, severity, valence, controllability, predictability, and recency. Event characteristics alone do not determine event impact, however. We saw, for example, that individual circumstances affect the perceived severity of an event, with the death of a parent exacting a larger toll on someone from a close family. Stress represents an intersection between event characteristics, characteristics of the individual experiencing the event, and characteristics of that individual's surrounding environment. Let's look now at individual characteristics that affect the stress process.

Dohrenwend's model (Figure 13.1) shows that individual factors affect the stress-adjustment relationship in two ways. First, individual characteristics affect the occurrence of events (box on the lower left). In addition, individual mediators affect the way stress is resolved once it occurs (box in the lower middle of the diagram). These two avenues of influence are examined below.

INDIVIDUAL CHARACTERISTICS AND THE OCCURRENCE OF EVENTS

Different groups of people experience different life events (see Hurst et al., 1978; Kilmer, Cowen, Wyman, Work, & Magnus, 1998; Pine, Padilla, & Madonado, 1985). As described above, social position affects the likelihood of a variety of stressful events. For example people in lower socioeconomic classes and African Americans more often occupy high-stress and unstable jobs and live in violent and conflictual environments (e.g., Taylor, Repetti, & Seeman, 1997).

Consider again the events that appear on the SRE (Table 13.1). Although the SRE has been used with a variety of populations, the events are most relevant to a particular group—young adult Christian men. Many of these events focus on the workplace, and so this list would not be applicable to children in school or older people who have retired. A list of events for children might include not being picked for a sports team, while a list for seniors might include no longer being able to drive. The relative lack of family-related events on the SRE suggests the inappropriateness of the SRE for women. Research shows that women are more aware of and more affected by events that occur to important others, a child's illness for example (B. S. Dohrenwend, 1977; Kessler & McLeod, 1984; Lowenthal, Thurnher, Chiriboga, Beeson, Gigy, Lurie, Pierce, Spence, & Weise, 1975; Thomae & Lehr, 1986). The inclusion of Christmas on the SRE suggests a religious bias.

In addition to differences based on group membership, individual differences also affect what events occur. One source of individual differences that has received considerable attention in recent years is genetic make-up. Studies show that the occurrence of life events in the second half of the life span is largely determined by genetic factors (Plomin, Pederson, Lichtenstein, McClearn, & Nesselrode, 1990). How might genetic factors, which are decided before birth, influence the occurrence of events in later life?

It may be that genetically linked characteristics affect the likelihood that people experience certain events. For example, genetics help determine IQ, and people who score higher on intelligence tests are more likely to work in lucrative professions, as doctors, lawyers or engineers. Thus, they may be less likely to experience stresses stemming from economic crises. Genetics also influence personality characteristics, such as risk taking. People who take more risks may be more likely to experience personal accidents and injuries as a result, for example, of driving too fast in the rain or snowboarding on

treacherous slopes. Genetic components of diseases, such as alcoholism and schizophrenia, may also increase the likelihood of experiencing some life events, such as divorce or job loss.

INDIVIDUAL MEDIATORS: COPING STYLES

Individual factors affect which events occur. They also influence the impact stresses have once they happen. Barbara Dohrenwend used the term "mediator" to refer to qualities of people and situations that define the context of stress and influence adjustment (this differs somewhat from the current usage of the term, see Baron & Kenny, 1986).

In the 1970s and 1980s, stress research and theory focused on the direct link between stress and adjustment. The finding that stress scores could explain only about 10% of the variability in adjustment led researchers to search for better ways of measuring stress. Researchers devised assessment techniques that accounted for event characteristics such as severity, valence, and controllability. Some of these innovations led to improvements in predicting adjustment, but the improvements were usually small.

The modest relationship between stress and adjustment may be due not to imprecision in measuring stress, but to the fact that a variety of individual and environmental characteristics affect the impact of stress on adjustment. Since the 1970s, individual and environmental mediators of the stress–adjustment relationship have been studied. A vast literature has developed around one particular individual mediator: coping style (Holahan, Moos, & Schaefer, 1996).

Coping has been defined as "constantly changing cognitive and behavioral efforts to manage specific external and/or internal demands that are appraised as taxing or exceeding the resources of the person" (Lazarus & Folkman, 1984, p. 141). Simply put, coping is an attempt to reduce the negative impact of stress.

TYPES OF COPING

Several researchers have described different coping styles. Susan Folkman and Richard Lazarus (1988;

Lazarus, 1966) distinguished **problem-focused coping** and **emotion-focused coping**. Problem-focused coping directs attention to the stressful situation. This often involves evaluating possible responses and deciding on the best course of action. If one is fired from a job, is it best to try to appease the boss in order to get rehired, appeal the decision to a higher authority, or decide to look for another job? Emotion-focused coping directs attention not to the situation, but to the subjective experience of stress. Emotion-focused coping efforts that improve adjustment include positive reappraisal, in which the person focuses on the potential benefits of the events, and emotional expression, which involves talking about the event in order to come to terms with it. Escapism, denial, and wish-fulfilling fantasy are examples of emotion-focused coping efforts that may not be helpful as they seek to avoid the reality of the situation.

Which brings us to a second distinction between coping strategies: **approach** versus **avoidance coping**. Approach coping involves facing the stress and dealing with it directly (e.g., Holahan, et al., 1996). Avoidance coping involves distancing oneself from the stress by trying to forget the whole thing, occupying oneself with other activities, or seeking escape in alcohol and drugs. Avoidance coping has been associated with poorer psychological adjustment (e.g., Felton & Revenson, 1984).

People can respond to stress in a variety of ways. They can try to prevent the stress, alter the stressful situation, change the psychological meaning of the stress, or manage the symptoms of stress (Pearlin & Aneshensel, 1986). The appropriateness of different coping strategies depends, in part, on the nature of the stressful situation (e.g., Pearlin & Schooler, 1978). Strategies useful in resolving problems with one's boss would not necessarily be helpful in dealing with a diagnosis of cancer. Lazarus and Folkman (1984) found that while work-related events elicited more problem-focused coping, health-related events elicited more emotion-focused coping. This may be because concrete actions can alter work situations, whereas health conditions may be less amenable to change through action. An accurate appraisal of what can realistically be done in a stressful situation allows the stressed person to choose the most appropriate coping strategy.

COPING AND PERSONALITY

Individuals may find that different coping strategies are useful in different situations. In addition, individual characteristics affect the likelihood of engaging in particular coping efforts. A variety of personality characteristics have been studied in relation to coping, including anxiety, reactivity, and introversion versus extroversion (e.g., Costa, Somerfield, & McCrae, 1996; Strelau, 1995). One of the most researched aspects of personality as it relates to coping is negative versus positive thinking.

Many problems of adjustment stem from negative thinking about the events in our lives (e.g., Ellis, 1969). For example, some people catastrophize events so that disappointments, hassles, and setbacks are blown to gigantic proportions. Some people perseverate about events and prevent their resolution. Prolonged brooding can increase the detrimental effects of an event (Novaco & Vaux, 1985). Ideas about the causes of events also affect negative and positive thinking.

Attribution theory is a way of understanding how people think about an event's cause. People explain events with reference to either internal (dispositional) factors or external (situational) factors. Martin Seligman and his colleagues (e.g., Abramson, Seligman, & Teasdale, 1978) saw this distinction as one important aspect of people's *explanatory styles*. There are two additional components. People vary in their perceptions of the duration of the event's cause. Events can be seen as resulting from stable, long-lasting factors or unstable, short-lived factors. Finally, people differ in their perceptions of the generalizability of the event's cause. The cause can be seen as local and specific to the particular situation, or global and likely to occur in a variety of contexts. If a person makes internal, stable, and global attributions for negative events, then **learned helplessness** may result (Abramson, et al., 1978). When learned helplessness occurs, people believe themselves incapable of altering their fate, even if they can, and so do not cope well with adversity.

Consider, for example, students seeking to explain a bad test grade. One student might attribute the bad grade to having gone to a party the night before instead of studying. This is a dispositional attribution, but it is neither stable nor global. Thus, a decision to stay home and study before subsequent tests can lead to improvements in one's grade. A second student might attribute the bad grade to a lack of intelligence. Such explanations are internal (the student's cognitive abilities are innately inferior), stable (intelligence does not change from day-to-day), and global (intelligence affects performance in a variety of domains). The student sees bad grades as inevitable, and the belief in her or his incompetence dooms this student to failure.

Martin Seligman and his colleagues initially focused on the pathway from negative explanatory styles to depression. More recent research has looked at how positive explanatory styles facilitate healthy adjustment. People who explain events in optimistic ways cope more effectively with events (e.g., Holahan, et al., 1996; Peterson & Seligman, 1984; Peterson, Seligman, & Vaillant, 1988; Scheier & Carver, 1985; Scheier, Weintraub, & Carver, 1986; Schwarzer & Jerusalem, 1995). For example, Michael Scheier and his colleagues (1989) found that optimists as compared to pessimists recovered more quickly from heart surgery and had better long-term prognoses.

Another related personality construct that affects coping responses is sense of control (Cohen & Edwards, 1986; Rotter, 1966). People with an **internal locus of control** believe that their actions affect the occurrence and course of events. People who believe that their lives are controlled by outside forces have an **external locus of control.** An internal as opposed to external locus of control is associated with more positive outcomes following stress (Johnson & Sarason, 1978). For example, women diagnosed with cancer may actually lived longer if they believe they can control their cancer (Taylor, 1989).

OTHER INDIVIDUAL MEDIATORS

Research suggests that individual coping styles affect how people adjust to stress. It is not, however, the only important individual-level determinant of adjustment in the face of stress. Let's consider a few more.

Health behavior also affects the stress-adjustment relationship. One study showed that stress has a less deleterious effect on people who are physically fit (Brown, 1991), exercise (Kobasa & Maddi, 1985), and play sports (Danish, 1983; Reppucci, 1987). In addition to physical activity, relaxation techniques (e.g., meditation, hypnosis, biofeedback, and music therapy) affect the stress-adjustment relationship (Lehrer & Woolfolk, 1993).

Previous exposure to stress is another individual-level variable that helps determine adjustment. People who have already experienced similar stresses may have had a chance to find meaning in and adapt to the event; thus they may be less vulnerable to future stresses. Alternatively, previous exposure to stress may deplete resources so that the experience of one stress can increase vulnerability to future stresses. We do not yet know precisely what determines whether stress inoculates against or sensitizes to future stress (e.g., Block & Zautra, 1981; Hobfoll et al., 1995). The spacing of the stresses and their relative severity are probably relevant factors.

Yet another individual-level factor that affects the stress-adjustment relationship is religious involvement. A growing literature finds a positive relationship between involvement in religion and adjustment to stress (Pargament, Ensing, Falgout, Olsen, Reilly, Van Haitsma, & Warren, 1990; see also Levin, 1994; Levin & Chatter, 1998; McIntosh, Silver, & Wortman, 1993; Pargament & Maton, 2000; Smith, Pargament, Brant, & Oliver, 2000; Thorson, 1998). Religious involvement encourages healthy living and positive thinking, promotes self-actualization, and addresses the human need to comprehend suffering and injustice. The rituals of religion also facilitate adjustment. They provide structure, stability, and a coherent meaning system during times of crisis (Vernberg & Vogel, 1993). Rituals and common beliefs also unite people and sustain connections among them. As we will see in the section on environmental mediators of stress, connections among people play an important role in buffering the effects of adversity.

PERSON–ENVIRONMENT FIT

As community psychologists know, we cannot understand stress and coping by studying individuals apart from their context. In considering individual factors that affect the stress–adjustment relationship, one must also consider the person–environment fit.

Suzanne Kobasa (1979) introduced into the stress literature, the construct of **hardiness**. People vary with regard to their ability to thrive in the face of stress. In an attempt to find out why some people handle stress better than others, Kobasa studied executives who experienced high levels of stress but did not suffer from stress-related illnesses. She identified a personality type that she labeled "hardy." Hardy individuals have a clear sense of direction, a sense of personal control, commitment to self and to work, and a tendency to see change as challenging rather than threatening. It seems, however, that hardiness may not only be a personality variable, but also an indication of person–environment fit. A sensation-seeking person who enjoys being tested by challenging situations would likely fare better in stimulating and demanding work environments (e.g., Smith, Johnson, & Sarason, 1978).

Consider, for example, air traffic controllers. Air traffic controllers continually make decisions about the flow of traffic that could have potentially disastrous consequences. This is a stressful job. Compared to pilots, air traffic controllers suffer from hypertension at six times the rate, develop diabetes at three times the rate, and experience peptic ulcers at twice the rate (Cobb & Rose, 1973, cited in Novaco & Vaux, 1985). Although most people would find controlling air traffic stressful, some people are better able to thrive under these work conditions than others. Imagine Sean Connery as an air traffic controller. Now think of Woody Allen.

⌘ Environmental Factors

The environment is the third and final player in Dohrenwend's (1978) model. Environmental factors, like individual factors, affect the stress-adjustment relationship in two ways. First, environmental characteristics affect the occurrence of events (box on the upper left in Figure 13.1). Second, environmental mediators affect the way stress is resolved once it occurs (box in the upper middle of the diagram).

ENVIRONMENTAL CHARACTERISTICS AND THE OCCURRENCE OF EVENTS

It is within our social environments that most stresses occur. Membership in families opens the door to the possibility of family conflict, the death of a relative, divorce, domestic violence, and a variety of other important events. The workplace is the source of firings, pay cuts and raises, and troubles with the boss. It is within our neighborhoods that we may be exposed to crime, gang activity, overcrowding, and physical hazards, such as noise, air, and water pollution (Taylor et al., 1997; Wandersman & Nation, 1998).

While unhealthy environments are associated with the occurrence of stressful events, healthy environments can help people to avoid stress. Families can provide the support needed to avoid school failure, resist substance abuse, and refrain from other problem behaviors that increase the likelihood of encountering stress. Consider again the events listed on the SRE (Table 13.1). There are numerous ways friends and families could help prevent many of negative events from occurring. Families and friends can discourage driving during a rainstorm and provide a safe harbor until the storm clears, thereby averting serious injuries. They can support marital relationship, thereby preventing a divorce. They can lend money that forestalls foreclosure on a loan. They can help troubleshoot about work experiences *before* difficulties develop that lead to being fired or provide emergency daycare that allows attendance at an important meeting.

Other microsystems can also help people to avoid stress. The workplace can help employees gain valuable skills, solve work-related problems, and enable them to remain employed and well paid. Religious settings can encourage healthy lifestyles and support family life (e.g., by offering marital counseling and child care). Neighborhoods provide infrastructures through which residents can satisfy their basic needs. For example, residents health and security can be fostered by the presence of food banks and crime watches (Sandler, 2001).

In understanding how environments affect the occurrence of stress, we also need to look beyond the proximal environment to larger systemic forces that exert their influences through microsystems. For example, a family's ability to meet basic needs increases in the context of robust economies and high employment rates (Long & Vaillant, 1984).

ENVIRONMENTAL MEDIATORS: SOCIAL SUPPORT

Just as the research on individual-level mediators of the stress-adjustment relationship has centered on one factor (coping styles), so too has research on environmental mediators focused on a single construct—**social support**. Although social support is a broad concept with varying definitions, it is generally viewed as interpersonal connections and exchanges that are perceived as helpful by the provider and/or the recipient. Research has clearly demonstrated a relationship between social support and health, both mental and physical (Caplan, 1974; Cassel, 1974; Cobb, 1976; Cohen & Syme, 1985). Indeed, social support plays an important role in sustaining life itself. Major studies in the United States, Scandinavia, and Japan find that socially disconnected people are two to five times more likely to die from all causes (Berkman & Glass, 2000).

The presence of supportive others during crises increases the chances that people will adjust well (e.g., Cohen & Wills, 1985; Cohen, Underwood, & Gottlieb, 2000; Kessler, Price, & Wortman, 1985). Social support cushions the impact of a variety of harmful stresses for people of all descriptions. One persuasive experiment assigned women with advanced breast cancer to either a social support condition or a no-support control condition (Spiegel, Bloom, Kraemer, & Gottheil, 1989). Women in the social support condition met weekly with other

patients and with doctors to discuss their concerns. They felt better than women in the control group and lived an average of eighteen months longer. Let's launch our exploration of social support by considering why it is helpful, then move on to an examination of who provides support, and end with a consideration of negative aspects of social support.

WHY SOCIAL SUPPORT HELPS

Support people can help in a number of ways, both directly and indirectly. The distinction between perceived and enacted support demonstrates that regardless of whether a stressed person actually receives social support, simply belonging to a web of human relationships can facilitate adjustment.

Perceived and Enacted Support. Some definitions of social support focus on enacted support, the actual exchange of resources between people. In times of stress, people call on friends and family members to lend an ear or a hand. Supportive transactions are not, however, the only way social support buffers stress. Some definitions of social support focus on perceived support—the belief that one is loved and valued (e.g., Cobb, 1976).

People have generalized ideas about the supportiveness of their social environment and the availability of support. People also have expectations about specific people in their social environments and their willingness to help. These feelings and expectations constitute perceived support (e.g., Pierce, Sarason, & Sarason, 1996). Interestingly, perceived support and enacted support do not necessarily coincide (see Lakey & Lutz, 1996). In one study, people who had been classified as either high or low in perceived support were observed interacting with friends following exposure to a stress. The individual's perceived support status was unrelated to the actual support provided by friends (Heller & Lakey, 1985).

Some researchers argue that perceived support affects adjustment to stress more than enacted support (e.g., Barrera, 1986, Cohen & Wills, 1985). If people believe that others are available to them in a crisis, the event takes less of a toll, regardless of whether support people are actually called upon or volunteer to help. This has led to the notion that social support may not be an environmental variable at all and that perceptions of support actually reflect personality variables, such as interpersonal sensitivity or the desire for intimacy (e.g., Gottlieb, 1983; Pierce et al., 1996). Personality likely plays a role in social support as well as in coping styles. For example, personality characteristics that promote positive coping (e.g., optimism, a sense of control) can also attract supportive social relationships. Social support is likely rooted both in the environment *and* in individual personalities (Lakey & Lutz, 1996). As described earlier, the characteristics of events, individuals, and environments work together to determine adjustment to stress.

Types of Support. In the section on individual mediators, coping responses were described as focusing either on managing the emotions generated by stress or addressing the stressful situation itself. Similarly, social support can help people cope with their emotional responses to stress or help ameliorate the actual effects of the stress.

Emotional Support. Social support fulfills a variety of emotional needs. First and foremost, it provides a sense of companionship (e.g., Mitchell & Trickett, 1980; Shumaker & Brownell, 1985). Companionship offers opportunities to engage in enjoyable activities and diversions that can be rejuvenating during times of stress. Perhaps more importantly, during periods of stress we benefit simply from feeling accompanied. I am reminded of the joke about the patient who advised his well-meaning therapist, "Don't just do something, stand there."

Social support also provides opportunities for stressed people to receive reassurance and encouragement. Stressed people benefit from the sense of being understood, respected, trusted, and valued (Gottlieb & Todd, 1985). Emotional support that bolsters self-esteem and self-confidence may be particularly important under conditions of stress when the stressed person's sense of control, and even their sense of worth, may be threatened (e.g., Cohen & Wills, 1985; Gottlieb, 1983; Holahan et al., 1996;

Sandler, Wolchik, MacKinnon, Ayers, & Roosa, 1997; Shumaker & Brownell, 1984). If social support enhances the stressed person's sense of mastery and efficacy, he or she may also cope more effectively with the demands presented by the stress.

In addition, supportive people provide opportunities for the stressed person to talk. Research shows that expressing feelings about a traumatic experience has therapeutic value (Pennebaker 1990; Pennebaker, Colder, & Sharp, 1990). For example, college students who wrote repeatedly about traumatic events found the writing to be upsetting in the short term but were less likely to visit the student health center and reported fewer illnesses in the six months that followed (Pennebaker & Beale, 1986). In another study, Holocaust survivors who disclosed the most about their experiences during World War II showed the greatest improvements in health over subsequent months (Pennebaker, Barger, & Tiebout, 1989). Self-expression may release the physical strain of holding back negative thoughts, allow the sufferer to gain perspective on the event, and foster close relationships with others.

Tangible Support. The emotional sustenance of social support is vitally important (e.g., House & Kahn, 1985), but it is not the only valuable aspect. Supportive others may also offer direct assistance. This may come in the form of material support (e.g., Cohen & Wills, 1985; Mitchell & Trickett, 1980). If someone is suddenly fired from a job, support people can supply food baskets to help tide the person over or even pay the next month's bills. If someone needs to spend time at the bedside of an ill family member, support people can babysit, mow the lawn, or walk the dog. Food, transportation, shelter, home repair—there are numerous types of tangible support that can help see people through stressful times.

Supportive others can also direct stressed people to relevant information and resources that enable them to cope (Gottlieb & Todd, 1985; Mitchell & Trickett, 1980; Sandler et al., 1997). They might, for example, refer a person who was fired to a local employment agency, a web-based job bank, or a recent magazine article on employment trends. Social support people can also help the stressed person assess the threat and gain a clearer and more complete understanding of the event's meaning and ramifications (Gottlieb, 1983; Gottlieb & Todd, 1985; Holahan, et al., 1996; Mitchell & Trickett, 1980; Shumaker & Brownell, 1985). They can, for example, help the person determine if the firing occurred because of individual factors ("You *did* always show up late."), characteristics of the work setting ("Your boss was such a tyrant."), or because of larger environmental factors ("Small businesses are closing all over the city."). They can then assist in planning a course of action and offer direct instruction on how to cope (Holahan, et al., 1996; Shumaker & Brownell, 1985), or serve as models of effective (or ineffective) coping (Gottlieb, 1983; Gottlieb & Todd, 1985; Sandler et al., 1997).

A third way in which support people can act as a resource is in using their skills or networks to intervene in the environment. A supportive co-worker might talk the boss into giving you another chance. A supportive neighbor might convince his aunt to interview you for another job.

Beyond Dyadic Interactions. Some researchers have focused on the functions of social support, in particular the ability of support people to provide emotional succor or tangible assistance. While the functional view of support centers on the level of the dyad, a structural analysis helps us to look at the larger support system.

How many people could you turn to in times of stress? Would these people also turn to you? How often do you see these people? How many of these people know each other? Are these people similar to you in terms of sex, age, ethnicity, profession? These questions tap structural aspects of social support networks.

Researchers focusing on social support networks assess such characteristics as the number of support people, the degree of reciprocity, the frequency of contact, social network density (interrelatedness of members), and the demographic homogeneity of network members. For example, some people have small, dense networks in which everyone knows each other. Other people have large diffuse networks

that correspond to segmented life domains (e.g., work friends don't know neighborhood friends, who don't know friends from the synagogue, and no one has ever met your family). Robert Putnam (2000) posited that a tightly knit community characterized by dense networks fosters honesty and trust. Reputations matter because network members are likely to encounter each other in the future and hear about one another through the grapevine. At the same time, dense communities exert pressure for homogeneity among members and tend to be distrustful of outsiders.

Different types of support may be required at different times. As an example, people in the early stages of grieving benefit from emotional support but at later stages need support that aids reintegration into normal social life (Shinn, Lehman, & Wong, 1984). When a spouse first dies, a small, close network of people can step in and sit by your bedside. Later on, when trying to adopt a new social identity as single person, a wider, less structured network can help introduce you around and involve you in a variety of activities (Walker, MacBride, & Vachon, 1977). This suggests the importance of broad social networks that have areas of density and also more dispersed network members. Putnam (2000) characterized the strengths of dense versus diffuse networks in this way: "Strong ties with intimate friends may ensure chicken soup when you are sick, but weak ties with distant acquaintances are more likely to produce leads for a new job" (p. 363).

WHO PROVIDES SUPPORT

Thus far, we have examined why social support helps without attention to the sources of support. Does it matter who does the helping?

Many people facing stressful situations turn to family members. Indeed, Gerald Caplan (1976) used the "ideal family" as a prototype for understanding social support more generally. An ideal family collects and disseminates information about the world, offers feedback and guidance, and grounds actions in value systems and codes of behavior. It mediates difficult situations—sharing in the problems and providing assistance in solving them. Families also furnish material aid—financial help, shelter, and so on. Ideal families are havens— a place to go when one is tired, hurt, or in need of nurture. When you knock, ideal families always take you in.

For many people, family members constitute the first line of defense against adversity. Based on her work with elderly populations, Marjorie Cantor (1979) proposed that the choice of support provider proceeds according to the primacy of relationships. For adults, spouses are the preferred source of assistance, and in their absence, support seekers turn to other relatives, and then to friends or neighbors. Formal organizations constitute a last option. For children, parents rather than spouse are the most important sources of support (see Garmezy & Rutter, 1983; Haggerty, Sherrod, Garmezy, & Rutter, 1994; Hetherington & Blechman, 1996; Wolchik & Sandler, 1997). Thus, developmental age affects where one turns for support.

Culture also play a role. Cultural norms about who should provide support to whom under what circumstances have a substantial impact on the shape of social support (e.g., Dilwoth-Anderson & Marshall, 1996; Dunkel-Shetter, Sagrestano, Feldman, & Killingsworth, 1996; Maton, Teti, Corns,

Vieira-Baker, Lavine, Gouze, & Keating, 1996; Sinha & Verma, 1994). A number of researchers have noted the crucial importance of family, including extended family, in the lives of ethnic minority group members. The impact of culture on social support is not simple, however. For example, respect of elders and strict gender hierarchies influences the flow of support between spouses and between generations in many Asian families (Dilsworth-Anderson & Marshall, 1996). As another example, despite the importance of family embodied in the cultural concept of *familism*, some research finds that Latinos are actually reluctant to seek support from family members (Kaniasty & Norris, 2000). Cultural norms affect the dynamics of support in numerous ways. As additional examples, some cultural traditions encourage emotional expression, and some do not; some foster interdependence and reliance on others, and some do not.

In the U.S. and many other countries women engage in more social support activities than men (e.g., Dwyer & Coward, 1991). Shelley Taylor and her colleagues (2000) have recently contrasted the commonly known "fight-or-flight" response to stress with the less-known "tend-and-befriend" response that characterizes women's reactions (see also Hobfoll, Dunahoo, Ben-Porath, & Monnier,

Calvin and Hobbes   by Bill Watterson

When you knock, ideal families let you in. Sometimes they even come to you. CALVIN AND HOBBES © Watterson. Reprinted with permission of UNIVERSAL PRESS SYNDICATE. All rights reserved.

1994). Women's inclination to care for others leads us to nurture and protect people in times of stress, while the propensity to befriend leads us to create and maintain supportive networks. Women's concern about relationships comes with benefits and costs; women are likely to have intimate relationships that can provide support but also have a greater number of people expecting help in times of stress (Belle, 1982; Hobfoll, 1986). The burdens of support fall disproportionately on the shoulders of women who are, for example, more likely to become the caretakers of disabled children and aging parents.

The nature of the support seekers' stress also affects who is approached (Litwak, 1985). Exceptions to the stereotype notwithstanding, women may be called upon for emotional support (a shoulder to cry on after the break up of a relationship, for example) while men might be called upon to help provide tangible assistance (help with home repairs, for example). Some challenges (e.g., the birth of triplets) require ongoing assistance from people in close proximity. Other problems (e.g., a cash flow problem) might require help from multiple friends across the miles (see Messeri, Silverstein, & Litwak, 1993).

One reason we approach different people to help with different stresses is that different people tend to offer different sorts of support. Remember the study by Emory Cowen (1982), that examined natural help-givers reported in Chapter Seven. Cowen found that hairdressers and bartenders listened, offered sympathy, and tried to be light-hearted, while lawyers asked questions, gave advice, and pointed out the consequences of bad ideas. Other research shows that professionals, such as lawyers and doctors, tend to talk more and provide more information (Toro, 1986). Not only do different categories of people offer different types of support, but our willingness to listen also varies by category. In one study, cancer patients found offers of advice helpful if they came from professionals, but not from friends or family members (Dunkel-Shetter, 1984).

Given the different types of support that people offer, and our different ideas about the utility of this support depending on such variables as the source

and the timing, it would make sense that people benefit from having a variety of support givers. For example, one study found that although family members are important sources of support, women adjusted more poorly to divorce if their support networks consisted *primarily* of family members (Wilcox, 1981). Is there a place for professional helpers in one's support network?

One of the most important findings of the 1961 report of the Joint Commission of Mental Health was that the vast majority of the population did *not* seek out professionals for help with mental health problems. Instead, they turned to family members, friends, neighbors, physicians, and religious leaders (see also Howard & Orlinsky, 1972). A more recent figure that points to the same conclusion is that only 1% to 5% of bereaved people seek professional help (Jacobs, 1993). Lindemann (1944) and others (e.g., Albee, 1959) have warned that there could never be enough professional helpers to meet the needs of all grieving and stressed people. Perhaps these scholars need not have worried about such shortages as the public has hardly been beating a path to our office doors.

There are many reasons why people do not approach professional helpers when faced with a crisis including the cost, the stigma of using professional services, and the lack of congruence between one's own background and that of most therapists (therapists are primarily White, middle class, and highly educated). Professional helpers may be most helpful when people have taxed their support networks or are dealing with crises that friends and family are ill-prepared to handle. Professional helpers are over represented, for example, in the support networks of people with major mental illnesses. Friends, neighbors, and acquaintances cannot always supply the quantity and quality of support that people suffering from depression or schizophrenia need (e.g., Schoenfeld, Halvey, Heemley-van der Velden, & Ruhf, 1986).

NEGATIVE ASPECTS OF SOCIAL SUPPORT

Although people most often turn to those closest to us in times of stress, these friends and relatives are not always the people most able to support us effectively. Camille Wortman and her colleagues (1995) found that bereaved people benefit from sharing their feelings of loss, but members of support networks may discourage this, saying, for example, that crying does no good. Support people may minimize the loss or promote a too-quick recovery, encouraging grieving people to date before they are ready, for example. They might also dispense inappropriate advice, perhaps telling someone to move to a new house without all the memories or to get a pet as a companion. Unhelpful exchanges can cause stressed people to withdraw from social relationships at a time when they need them most.

Well-intentioned members of a support network may also criticize grieving people for coping improperly—expressing too little or too much emotion, grieving for too long or not long enough (Coyne, Wortman, & Lehman, 1988; Shinn et al., 1984). Popular misconceptions about the universality of stages in grieving may lead people to believe they are being helpful when they are not. A review of five longitudinal studies, found that a substantial number of people who lost a spouse or child (as many as 78%) did not show what is believed to be the "typical" pattern of coping—intense upset in the initial weeks or months following the loss, and decreasing distress over time. Furthermore, some people never reach the resolution stage (Wortman & Silver, 1990). In a study of the loss of a child or spouse in a car accident, most bereaved people still reported painful thoughts and a lack of a sense of meaning many years after the loss (Lehman, Wortman, & Williams, 1987).

In additions to misconceptions about stages of adjustment, belief in a just world can also interfere with a support person's ability to be helpful. When we respond to misfortune by blaming the victim we do not help them cope. For example, a study of young women who had been raped found that unsupportive responses from others (e.g., criticisms for not being careful enough) far outweighed helping attempts that were perceived as supportive (Davis, Brickman, & Baker, 1991).

And the list of ways in which support network members impede positive adjustment goes on.

Indeed, psychological health sometimes is served by reconfiguring one's support network (e.g., Humphreys & Noke, 1997). Social networks can encourage unhealthy coping responses—encouraging people to deny problem or abuse substances. Support people also prevent positive adjustment if they foster emotional or material dependence. People have a basic need for relatedness and also a basic need to feel volitional and self-determined. The term *autonomy support* has been coined to describe the importance of encouraging of a strong self within the context of interpersonal relationships (R. Ryan & Solky, 1996).

Unhelpful comments and unsupportive reactions may stem from the strain suffering places on those closest to the stressed person. Support network strain may result from members of the support network also being affected by the stress. When a family matriarch dies, for example, the grief experienced by the matriarch's children might prevent them from being present for their own children who are simultaneously grieving the loss of their grandparent. In addition, providing support can be emotionally, physically, and financially exhausting. Caregiving can become a stress in itself (see Schulz, Visintainer, & Williamson, 1990). A study of homelessness found that people struggling financially often live with friends and relatives for extended periods of time and only become homeless after wearing out their welcome with supportive others (Shinn, 1992). Stressful experiences change the availability and quality of social support (e.g., Coyne et al., 1988). An interactive spiral often exists such that illnesses and other major stresses increase the need for, but decrease the availability, of helpful social support (e.g., Lane & Hobfoll, 1992).

⌘ Interventions

Now that we have discussed characteristics of events, individuals, and environments that affect adjustment to stress, let's discuss the implications of these characteristics for interventions. Consider once again the stress process outlined by Barbara Dohrenwend (1978; see Figure 13.1). In the first part of this chapter, we discussed the bolded boxes and the arrows connecting them. A stressful event occurs, which leads to a transient stress reaction and eventually a regained equilibrium that reflects growth, impairment, or no permanent change. We have discussed the three factors that affect this process: the stressful event or condition, the person, and the environment.

Now that we have looked at all the boxes in Dohrenwend's figure, let's begin to examine the circles on the periphery of the diagram. The circles represent means of intervention. Dohrenwend identified six. Only two of the six circles, however, impact the stress process directly: crisis intervention and corrective therapy. I have depicted this by connecting these two circles to the stress process with solid arrows. The next two sections of this chapter will focus on these two types of interventions. The interventions depicted in the remaining four circles exert their effects indirectly, through their effects on individuals and environments.

The interventions Dohrenwend labeled "corrective therapy" come into play during the last stage of the stress process, after the stressful event has run its course. Community psychologists today would no longer use the term Dohrenwend chose in 1978. Our goal is not to "correct" what is wrong with people, nor do we rely on "therapy" as a means of helping. We do, however, still attempt to assist people who have experienced problems as a result of adversity. In the ensuing discussion we will examine mutual help groups as an important context for gaining mastery over the ill effects of stress.

Crisis intervention also occurs immediately after the event happens, while the person (or group) is still in the midst of adjusting. Dohrenwend's term *crisis intervention* also hints of medical models and one-on-one helping exchanges, such as suicide prevention telephone hotlines (McGee, 1980). In recent years, community psychologists' interest in crisis intervention has extended beyond the individual level. We study, for example, how entire communities respond to crises that affect all community members. The literature on disaster responses will serve as an example of crisis intervention.

INTERVENING AFTER THE EVENT: MUTUAL HELP GROUPS

In the 1960s, researchers and practitioners became increasingly aware that most people experiencing stress did not seek professional help. They tended to rely on informal support networks instead: friends, family, clergy, or even hairdressers and bartenders. Sometimes people experiencing problems join together to offer each other support in **mutual help groups (MHGs)**[2].

Mutual help groups (MHGs) are established when ordinary people who share a common concern come together in settings they control to discuss their problems and learn from one another how to cope (Lieberman & Snowden, 1993; Salem, Reischl, Gallacher, & Randall, 2000). Mutual help groups are generally voluntary, democratic, nonprofessional, no-cost, and often spiritually based (Kingree & Thompson, 2000). MHGs are of great interest to community psychologists. They embody a view of people as capable of transforming their own lives and creating social change by joining together in community.

The most familiar mutual help group, Alcoholics Anonymous, began seven decades ago, and now claims two million members in the United States alone (Alcoholics Anonymous, 2000a, 2000b). Alcoholics Anonymous has served as a model for countless other groups formed by overeaters, gamblers, and others struggling to cope. Alcoholism, like other problems of living, may be seen as a maladaptive effort to cope with stress. In addition, substance abuse inspires additional stresses. Thus, Alcoholics Anonymous and similar groups may constitute as a sort of "corrective therapy," whereby people help each other to improve their mental and

[2]The term *mutual help group* is used in lieu of the term *self-help group* to emphasize that participants both give and receive help.

physical health and devise better ways of coping with future stresses.[3]

Mutual help groups have become increasingly popular in recent years (e.g., Putnam, 2000). Across the country, people gather together in church basements, office buildings, living rooms, hospitals, and even shopping malls to improve their ability to function in a challenging world. In the United States, estimates suggest that 3% to 4% of the population participates in mutual help groups in a given year, and approximately 25 million people are likely to participate at some point in their lives (Kessler, Mickelson, & Zhao, 1997; Lieberman & Snowden, 1993).

Despite the popular view that MHGs are run by members, some, perhaps as many as 60%, are professionally led (Lieberman & Snowden, 1993). Thus, the boundaries between mutual help and therapy may blur. Nevertheless, the reach of mutual help groups extends further into the community than traditional psychotherapy. While psychotherapy is most attractive to young, verbal, intelligent, and financially successful people, MHGs appeal to the more "typical" American (Kessler et al., 1997; Lieberman & Snowden, 1993). This is not to say that all citizens use MHGs in equal numbers. Mutual help groups are most popular among women, Caucasians, and singles or divorcees as compared to married people (Katz & Bender, 1976; Kessler et al., 1997; Lieberman & Snowden, 1993).

Participation rates also vary by problem area. The most common focus of support groups is, by far, alcoholism. In research on support groups in four cities, AA groups constituted 87% of the 12,596 groups studied (Davison, Pennebaker, & Dickerson, 2000). Support groups most often form around problems viewed as stigmatizing or embarrassing (e.g., alcoholism, breast cancer, and prostate cancer more than heart disease, ulcers, or chronic pain). AIDS patients were 250 times more likely to participate in support groups than hypertension patients.

---

[3]Mutual help groups can also serve as a kind of crisis intervention in which people experiencing a stress seek help from similar others while they are still in the midst of responding to that stress.

Given the finding that participation in MHGs is highest for people dealing with stigma, it is not surprising that these groups are an important source of support for people coping with marginalized social identities (e.g., Kingree & Thompson, 2000; Wuthrow, 1994). Exposure to people with the same identity who are coping well reduces self-stigma and allows insight into the public dimensions of private troubles (Gottlieb, 1983; Kingree & Thompson, 2000). As a result, adjustment to stress may improve (e.g., rates of depression and substance abuse may decline, see Kingree & Thompson, 2000). In addition, social change efforts may be launched as group members join forces to combat the environmental factors that make membership in a stigmatized group stressful.

Mutual help groups fulfill many of the functions of social support described earlier. They provide opportunities for emotional expression, companionship, insight, problem solving, a sense of belonging, and the exchange of resources (e.g., Humphreys, Finney, & Moos, 1994). Members both receive and provide knowledgeable support, advice, and information that can increase people's ability to cope actively and productively (Humphreys et al., 1994; Salem et al., 2000). Research suggests that providing help may be more beneficial to members than receiving help (Roberts, Salem, Rappaport, Toro, Luke, & Seidman, 1999).

Not all the news about mutual help groups is positive however. Some research suggests that they are not as helpful as many of us believe (e.g., Hinrichsen, Revenson, & Shinn, 1988; see also Levy, 2000). In addition, MHGs may not strengthen the larger social fabric. Robert Putnam (2000) suggested that support groups serve as a substitute for the intimate family and community ties that have weakened over time in our increasingly fragmented society. He observed that most forms of social participation co-occur. People who vote also join clubs and engage in community service. Of the twenty-two types of voluntary associations he studied, only mutual help groups were *not* associated with group affiliations in other realms. Putnam quoted Robert Wuthrow's (1994) statement that, some "small groups may not be fostering community as effectively as many of their proponents would like. Some small groups merely provide occasions for individuals to focus on themselves in the presence of others" (p. 152). As Judith Jordan (1992) observed, psychological perspectives that center on people's need to *receive* support may fail to acknowledge the broader need for mutuality and involvement in concerns that transcend narrow self interest.

INTERVENING WHEN THE EVENT OCCURS: DISASTER RELIEF

Crises are time-limited and anxiety-producing occasions that inspire feelings of uncertainty and highlight the inadequacies of existing personal and social resources (e.g., Miller & Iscoe, 1963). Immediately following a crisis, the affected person (or community) actively copes with the event by trying to determine its meaning and decide how best to respond. During the "transient stress reaction" (to use Dohrenwend's term) people demonstrate a heightened willingness to examine their situations and make changes (e.g., McGee, 1980). For example, a study of a stress management intervention found that people who had recently experienced significant negative events were most responsive to the new ideas and techniques presented in the intervention (Jason, 1998).

Crises are turning points that require those affected to do something new. Therefore, interventions occurring at this time have the potential not only to forestall pathology, but also to enhance competence (e.g., Rahe & Arthur, 1968; B. S. Dohrenwend, 1978). Many community psychologists recognize that in the immediate aftermath of a crisis, interventions can have profound effects.

Crisis intervention has its roots in the community mental health movement of the 1960s (McGee, 1980), and it experienced a revival of sorts in the 1980's, after post-traumatic stress disorder (PTSD) became an official diagnostic category (van der Kolk, van der Hart, & Burbridge, 1995). PTSD describes individual-level pattern of responses to life threatening experiences and extreme stress that includes:

re-experiencing the trauma (e.g., intrusive thoughts, recurring dreams); persistent avoidance and numbing (e.g., feelings of detachment, avoidance of activities); and arousal (e.g., sleep disturbance, anger outbursts). The reinvigoration of the concept of trauma inspired by the entry of PTSD into the *Diagnostic and Statistical Manual* (DSM) also augmented an interest in community-wide traumas such as such as floods, hurricanes, and nuclear disasters (Ginexi, Weihs, & Simmens, 2000; Green, 1995; Kaniasty & Norris, 1995, 2000).

A plethora of new acronyms emerged to describe crisis intervention with distressed communities. People involved in Disaster Mental Health Services (DMHS) coordinated responses to community disasters by organizing community response teams (CRTs). Critical incident stress debriefing (CISD) was developed to assist emergency medical personnel, search and rescue workers, law enforcement agents, and other response team members cope with their exposure to stress. Richard Gist and his colleagues (1999) commented that, "[r]ecent large-scale disasters have found communities literally besieged by counselors and would-be counselors clamoring to serve anyone even tangentially connected to the circumstances of the event" (p. 3). In some cases, the rescue workers descending on a stressed community may outnumber the affected residents. Gist and his colleagues coined the term "trauma tourism" to refer to the influx of professional outsiders to stricken communities where they offer expert knowledge and charge themselves with fixing the problems people experience.

The infusion of outside help immediately following a community disaster may prevent communities from mobilizing their own resources. **Overhelping** refers to highly visible attempts to assist stressed people who would have succeeded in overcoming their challenges without that assistance (Gilbert & Silvera, 1996). At the individual level, overhelping interferes with a person's sense of self-efficacy. It sabotages autonomy and fosters dependency. Similar processes occur at the community level. Accumulating evidence suggests that professional-led community disaster relief efforts may actually worsen outcomes (e.g., Gist et al., 1999; Foa & Meadows, 1997).

When disasters occur, community members rally. The high level of community helping that follows a visible and devastating event has been labeled "the altruistic community" or "postdisaster utopia" (Jerusalem, Kaniasty, Lehman, Ritter, & Turnbull, 1995; Kaniasty & Norris, 1999). When community leaders attempt to marshal community resources, they may be surprised to find blood donation lines that extend for blocks or traffic jams consisting of people bringing flashlights to rescue workers. Disasters can bring diverse people together. Distinctions in social status may matter little when wealthy landowners line up with migrant farm workers to receive food rations. The need for cooperation and the sense of shared trauma may transcend superficial differences when community disasters occur (Bravo, Rubio-Stipec, Canino, Woodbury, & Ribera, 1990; Yates, Axsom, Bickman, & Howe, 1989).

At the same time, disasters do not have equivalent effects on everyone. Research suggests that members of dominant ethnic groups and citizens with more economic resources receive more support following a disaster (Jerusalem et al., 1995; Kaniasty & Norris, 1999). Indeed, some disasters that affect *only* marginalized subcommunities may not even be acknowledged as disasters at all. An event that threatens the homeless poor may receive minimal response at the larger community level (Jerusalem et al., 1995). Governmental responses to the AIDS crisis occurred only after the disease became a rampant epidemic that affected upstanding citizens like Rock Hudson.

Given the current state of our knowledge about disaster relief, how best can community psychologists help? We might assist in identifying common goals around which diverse segments of stricken communities could mobilize, and encourage the equitable distribution of resources (e.g., Hobfoll et al., 1995). It should be noted, however, that attempts to promote egalitarian distribution patterns may be seen as attempts by outsiders to interfere with the traditional social order (Kaniasty & Norris, 1999; see also O'Neill, 1999 for a discussion of conflicting interests and other ethical challenges in disaster relief).

Shortly after a killer tornado hit Tupelo, Mississippi, the disaster relief center filled with donations from community members. *AP/WIDE WORLD PHOTOS*

Despite community psychology's emphasis on prevention and early intervention, we might also resist the temptation to help too much too soon. Postdisaster utopias are usually short-lived. Conflict, competition, increased politicization and fragmentation may replace the mutual help and interdependence that immediately follow community traumas (Bolin & Stanford, 1990; Kaniasty & Norris, 1999). Some residents' need for support outlives the initial period of altruism. For example, four weeks after the Loma Prieta earthquake, t-shirts appeared on the streets proclaiming, "Thank you for not sharing your earthquake experience" (Pennebraker & Harber, 1993). Over time individual and community resources are drained, energies are redirected to other pressing needs, and people still suffering the ill effects of the disaster may find themselves without listening ears and shoulders to lean on.

The number of people in need of intensive support services is likely to be relatively small, however.

A wealth of research suggests that even the severe psychological suffering associated with major community traumas resolves over time (Gist et al., 1999). A review of longitudinal studies on stress responses showed that the overwhelming majority of disaster victims recover quickly—sometimes within days or weeks (Salzer & Bickman, 1999). Certainly the scale of the disaster bears on the time needed for recovery, but disaster responses too often operate from an *abnormalcy bias* in which the pathological consequences of disasters are assumed (van den Eynde & Veno, 1999). This might actually create self-fulfilling prophesies in which people who are coping normally learn to label their responses as pathological.

Converging research and theory argue for intervention efforts that help stricken communities build their resources and so become more competent (Bravo et al., 1990; Ginexi et al., 2000). Indeed, a working group of twelve internationally recognized experts in community stress from the United States, the Netherlands, Greece, and Italy emphasized the importance of building community capacities following a disaster (Figley, Giel, Borgo, Briggs, & Haritos-Fatouros, 1995). They advised reliance on local resources and held that survivors should do as much as possible for themselves. Community psychologists and others may best help by quietly supporting the community's own efforts to provide for the needs of its residents and to use the crisis as an opportunity to find unforeseen reservoirs of strength within the community.

⌘ The Promise of Community Psychology: Community-Level Frameworks

In proposing stress and coping as an orienting concept for community psychology, Betty Kalis (1970) recommended that we adopt a community-level perspective. She observed that most investigators limited their analyses to "the individual and his immediate life space, or to a family and its interactions." She recommended focusing instead "on interlocking crises in various community ecologies" (p. 86). Although the work on mutual help groups and community disasters hint at ways in which stress and coping has importance beyond the individual level, the potential of this reconceptualization has not yet been fully realized.

An individual-level perspective permeates most of the thousands of stress studies conducted thus far. Stress is not an individual-level phenomenon, however. Stresses generally affect multiple system members simultaneously, however. Look again at the SRE (Table 13.1). Which of these events occur to individuals in isolation? Gaining a family member, changing work hours, vacation—virtually all of the listed events affect entire systems. Brian Thompson and Alan Vaux (1986) posited that events vary in "bandwidth," that is, the number of people affected by the event. Some events (e.g., failing a college exam) have small bandwiths while others (e.g., a school shooting) have large ones.

Even events with small bandwiths reverberate throughout systems. Members of systems are interdependent, and so events that affect one member affect all others. This effect can be direct, as when an event impacts multiple system members simultaneously, or indirect, through the effect of an individual's coping efforts on other system members. If I react to a poor grade on a test by determining to study an extra six hours every day, people with whom I share a household might object to my absence from dinner or shirking of daily chores. Research suggests that the coping efforts of one system member can contribute to the stress experienced by others (Cronkite & Moos, 1984).

The concept of social support, too, would benefit from a systems-level perspective. Social support does not consist solely of one-to-one exchanges between specific relatives and friends. Even social network methodologies, which try to account for the multiple sources of support available to individuals, tend to view social support as various disconnected links to a target person rather than a system of interrelationships (Felton & Shinn, 1992). An appreciation of support *systems* would lead to different methodologies. For example, in assessing support networks we might allow research participants to

COMMUNITY INTERVENTION:

The Library at Columbine High School
Rituals of Recovery

In the 1990s one community after another confronted the trauma of school shootings. In many cities newscasters issued emergency reports from behind police barricades as paramedics wheeled gurneys to and from school buildings. Shocked students and teachers gave their accounts of gunfire reverberating through hallways. One after another, small towns and cities across the country became the center of national attention: Pearl, Mississippi; West Paducah, Kentucky; Jonesboro, Arkansas; Edinboro, Pennsylvania; Springfield, Oregon; Santee, California.

The deadliest of these tragic shootings took place on April 20, 1999. Two high school students opened fire on their teachers and classmates at Columbine High School in Littleton, Colorado. In a matter of minutes, thirteen students and teachers were killed and twenty-one were wounded (Jefferson County Sheriff's Office Report, 2000).

In the immediate aftermath of the shooting, diverse communities seemed to pull together. Before long, however, fractures were in evidence. Some divisions stemmed from efforts to lay blame. Did the police respond quickly enough or in the right way? Should school personnel have identified problems between the two young men and their classmates before they reached such tragic proportions? Should the parents of the killers be held accountable for their sons' actions? Were the killers victims as well? One early debate centered on whether a spontaneous memorial erected near the school should include 15 crosses—one for each person who died—or only 13 crosses—one for each of the murdered people but none for the killers who committed suicide.

The need for memorials was clear, however. Countless people from around the world sent flowers, stuffed animals, cards, and other tokens of sympathy that became an expansive altar on the school grounds. Those affected by the tragedy wandered through the spontaneous memorial, making their own contributions and witnessing the offerings of others.

Not long after the tragedy, the families of the murdered students and teachers formed a group called HOPE (Healing of People Everywhere) with the goal of establishing a permanent memorial. Most of the killings occurred in the school library, and HOPE organized to raise funds to tear down the existing library and replace it with a new library and atrium. The school board approved this initiative in a 4–1 vote. Others joined the dissent expressed by the lone school board member who voted no. The estimated cost of the project was close to $3 million. A Columbine graduate and witness to the rampage wrote a letter to a local newspaper arguing that the money should be spent on counseling, intervention, and increased security in school buildings, not new buildings (Kohler, 2000).

The question of how best to promote community healing is an important one. Formal memorials, in their attempt to meet the needs of diverse victims, can be controversial. The documentary, *Maya Lin: A Strong Clear Vision* is a compelling case study of contention arising from the building of the Vietnam Memorial in Washington, D.C. (Sanders, Norton, & Mock, 1994). Despite initial resistance, this memorial now receives praise from people around the world, including those who originally stood in opposition. The process of memorial-making might be a topic of interest to community psychologists dedicated to finding innovative ways of helping communities heal from crises. Disaster scholars and community psychologists have recognized the need for symbols of survival that solidify the historical and cultural significance of community tragedies (e.g., Contos, 2000; van der Kolk, van der Hart, & Burbridge, 1995). Might there be a role for community psychologists in developing and carrying out rituals of recovery, such as the design and construction of memorials?

It took only six months for HOPE to raise more than $3.1 million from thousands of families, children, schools, libraries, businesses, and individuals throughout the country (HOPE Columbine, 2001). In the summer of 2001, the library was completed.

nominate support groups (e.g., religious organizations, bridge clubs, and bowling leagues) as well as individuals (Felton & Shinn, 1992). Neighborhoods, schools, churches, and clubs help people adjust to stress by reinforcing individual skills, modeling positive values, bringing individuals into contact with supportive adults, assisting families in raising their children, and providing opportunities for people to realize their strengths.

Stress, coping, and social support are systems-level phenomena. Not only do these phenomena occur within microsystems, they are also shaped by larger macrosystemic forces. Shelley Taylor and her colleagues (1997) stated that individual and family characteristics must be considered in relation to the larger systems in which these behaviors are learned and expressed. For example, a sense of control over events is not simply an individual-level personality variable (e.g., locus of control). The degree to which control is possible for a person in a given situation varies, and marginalized groups often have fewer options available to them. Thus,

the use of emotion-focused versus problem-focused coping may reflect, at least in part, the relative lack of control some groups (e.g., women) have over the social world (Jordan, 1992). Under the threat of AIDS, for example, women may be less able than men to cope actively by negotiating safer sexual practices (Ortiz-Torres, Serrano-García & Torres-Burgos, 2000).

By framing orienting concepts in ways that allow us to explore phenomena at a community level, we may find new pathways for understanding and intervention. With regard to stress-and-coping frameworks, a heightened awareness of the microsystems and macrosystems in which stress, coping, and social support take place may enable us, as individuals and communities, to turn crises into turning points that lead to new growth, better health, and a greater sense of well-being.

Action Agenda

Community Events in Your Community

What important community stresses have occurred in your community? You might want to learn more about these community events by reading articles in local newspapers papers and talking to community leaders. What were the coping responses of people at different levels: residents, community and professional groups, government? How has this event affected community health? Are there ways that the event strengthened the community? Are there ways in which community health was compromised? As a community psychologist, what might you have done (might you do) to facilitate coping with this event?

"Community Hassles and Uplifts"

Richard Lazarus and his colleagues (Kanner, et al., 1981; Lazarus, 1984) proposed that major stressful events exert their influence through daily hassles and uplifts. This notion has been explored at the individual level but not at the community level. What sorts of events would make up a community hassles scale? What about community uplifts? As a class, develop these lists. How do you think community hassles and up-lifts affect well-being at both the individual and the community level? Does your list of community hassles and uplifts suggest ways of intervening to make your commu-nity a better place? Who, other than community psychologists, might be able to use information about community hassles and uplifts?

Assessing Social Support

Social support can be assessed in a variety of ways. Here are two. Try each of them.

1. Consider the following four life events: a) failing an important exam; b) car engine trouble in the middle of the night; c) learning of a close friend's diagnosis with cancer; d) a water main break that leaves everyone within a mile radius without water for a week. List each of these events in a column on the left hand side of a page. For each event, list the first person you would call first after the event oc-curred. Now list all the other people you might consider contacting in the event's aftermath. Who are these people—family, friends, co-workers, neighbors? How do they differ in terms of age, physical distance from you, and other potentially important variables? What kind of support might you expect from each (e.g., emo-tional, material, informational, problem-solving, direct intervention)? Do you think each of these people would call on you if they had been the one experienc-ing the stress? Why or why not? Are there people you did not list who would con-sider you part of their network? Does your thinking about stress and support change if you also consider groups you might contact in the aftermath of the event (e.g., church groups, book clubs, sports teams)? What conclusions would you draw about your social network from this exercise?

2. Draw a large circle on a piece of paper. Put a dot in the middle to represent your-self. Next, think about how many settings contain people who give you support and divide the circle into that many sections (like slicing a pie). Fill each section with dots that represent people within each of those settings who are part of your support network. You may want to put initials next to the dots to keep track. Now draw lines between pairs of people who know each other. After completing this diagram, think about the number of people in your network, network density (de-gree of interconnectedneses among members), segmentation between life sectors, and the existence of boundary spanners—people in different segments who know each other. What conclusions would you draw about your social network from this diagram?

What are the strengths and weaknesses of each of these approaches? Do you have ideas on how to capture the phenomenon of social support more completely? You might work in small groups to devise new measures, perhaps three-dimensional rep-resentations that use colored materials.

 **Key Terms**

approach coping

avoidance coping

coping

crisis theory

daily hassles

emotion-focused coping

external locus of control

general adaptation syndrome (GAS)

hardiness

internal locus of control

learned helplessness

mutual-help groups (MHGs)

nonnormative events

normative events

operationalization

overhelping

problem-focused coping

Schedule of Recent Events (SRE)

social support

stress

Prevention

....

⌘ Introduction

Champions of prevention often tell some variation on the following story. One beautiful day you decide to picnic by the side of a river. You find a nice spot, shake out the checkered blanket, and arrange all your gear—lawn chair, sunscreen, paperback, sunglasses, and of course your lunch. Just as you reach into the picnic basket, you hear a call for help and see someone struggling in the water. You run to an overhanging branch, reach out your hand, and pull the person out of the river. After making sure that all is okay, you return to your picnic. You shake your head, take some deep breaths, and try to get back into the relaxing mood of a day in the park. You unwrap a sandwich, bring it to your mouth and . . . uh-oh, another cry for help! Wait, now there are *two* people struggling in the water. You rush again to the river, pull off your shoes, jump into the water, and manage another rescue, this time dragging two people to shore. Eventually you make your way back to the blanket, and lie down to let the sun dry your clothes. Not the restful day you had anticipated! All that rescuing has made you *really* hungry. You reach into the picnic basket for your long-awaited lunch and . . . yup—more cries for help. How many people this time? There are *three* people in the water.

Depending on the storyteller's penchant for long tales, your uneaten lunch may continue to languish in the late afternoon sun as your picnic is interrupted by cries from groups of four, then five, then six people struggling in the water. At some point, you can no longer keep up with the demands for help and reluctantly allow a struggling swimmer to slip by. More follow. Finally, the story ends with a question: How long do you keep pulling people out of the river before deciding to go upstream and see who, or what, is pushing them in?

Prevention efforts are based in the belief that actions taken now can avert more serious problems in the future. Prevention has existed as an orienting concept in community psychology from the very beginning. Even at Swampscott prevention served as "an orientation, philosophy, and set of activities central to the identity of community psychology" (Elias, 1987, p. 540).

The orienting concepts of stress and coping and of prevention both emerged early in community psychology's history, and each has informed the development of the other. Nevertheless, I began the chronology of the field's orienting concepts with stress and coping because this concept exploded more quickly in the literature. It also faded more quickly. Although the stress-and-coping framework continues to inform the work of many community psychologists, it no longer guides the field. Stress-and-coping research peaked in the late 1970s to early 1980s. Interest in prevention, however, has continued to grow. In 1999, Sheppard Kellam and his colleagues wrote, "There are periods in scientific development that arouse intense excitement and a sense of optimism that things are on the right track. This is such a time in prevention research" (p. 479).

⌘ Brief History

Interest in prevention is rooted in the public health movement of the nineteenth century (Bloom, 1979). During that time, modern scientific innovations allowed doctors and scientists to control or eradicate the major infectious ailments that plagued human society. Researchers found that the spread of physical diseases could be prevented by measures aimed at individuals (e.g., vaccinations for small pox and measles) and at the environment (e.g., improved sanitation to prevent cholera and dysentery). During the first half of the twentieth century, mental health researchers and practitioners began to explore the applicability of the prevention paradigm to mental disorders. Erich Lindemann (1944), whom we encountered, was among the first. By the 1960s, many researchers and practitioners touted prevention as the best means of combating mental as well as physical health problems.

By the time clinical psychologists convened in Swampscott to establish the new field of community psychology, prevention had taken hold as an important mental health concept. The Zeitgeist of the

---

Better guide well the young
than reclaim them when old,

For the voice of true wisdom is calling.

"To rescue the fallen is good, but 'tis best
To prevent other people from falling."

Better close up the source
of temptation and crime

Than deliver from dungeons or galley;

Better put a strong fence 'round
the top of the cliff

Than an ambulance down in the valley

—Joseph Malins (1895)
Excerpt from "A Fence or an Ambulance"

1960s fueled interest in prevention. The Joint Commission on Mental Health (1961) recommended a preventive approach to reducing mental disorders, and John F. Kennedy sang praises to prevention in his landmark address to Congress two years later. In 1965 the rhetoric of prevention was put into practice with the establishment of Head Start, one of the most popular and widespread prevention programs of all times.

Interest in prevention can be traced to a number of trends in society. During the 1960s, aspects of the environment, especially social inequality and injustice, were seen as important contributors to the development of mental illness. This view corresponded with prevention's emphasis on the environmental causes of disease. Interest in prevention was reinforced by the awareness that mental health professionals could never be trained in sufficient numbers to meet the mental health needs of the populace (Lindemann, 1944; Albee, 1959, 1982). Prevention programs held the promise of reaching far more people than one-on-one therapy. Many hoped that prevention programs would be more effective and ethical as well as more far-reaching. In the 1960s, questions arose about whether psychological and psychiatric treatment had delivered on its promises of cure (e.g., Eysenck, 1961) and whether the diagnosis of mental illness was anything more than a myth designed to keep marginalized people on the margins (e.g., Szasz, 1961). Prevention held the promise of promoting new and better paradigms for mental health intervention.

By the mid-1970s, talk of prevention occurred around many tables. Several influential bodies, including The President's Commission on Mental Health, the Mental Health Association, and the National Institute of Mental Health, began to take prevention seriously (Lamb & Zusman, 1979). Researchers, practitioners, legislators, and others jumped onto what Emory Cowen (1996) called the "glitzy bandwagon" of prevention (p. 239). Everything from legalized abortion to Sesame Street to yogurt appeared under prevention's shimmering banner. As a result, prevention's proponents (e.g., Cowen, 1977) and critics (e.g., Lamb & Zusman, 1979) alike bemoaned the fuzziness of the concept and the lack of empirical support for programming.

While proponents called for the sharpening of definitions and a rigorous research agenda, critics recommended abandoning the concept completely.

In a frequently cited treatise against prevention, Richard Lamb and Jack Zusman (1979) maintained that although prevention programs sought to reduce the number of seriously ill, hospitalized, and disabled people, they did little more than help a few individuals lead happier lives. They questioned whether programs that simply prevented general emotional distress merited scarce funding. The authors also objected to the social change agenda of many preventionists, asserting that no proof existed that difficult life circumstances led to mental illness. They admitted a relationship between mental illness and "social disintegration" (e.g., crime, poverty, broken homes), but claimed that a *causal* link had not been established. And even if the link *was* causal, they argued, there was no proof that prevention programs could have a significant enough impact on the social environment to prevent mental illness. Lamb and Zusman claimed that intraindividual factors (e.g., genetics and biochemistry) probably caused major mental illnesses, and prevention programs might modify but could never prevent these causes.

George Albee (1982) spoke for many community psychologists when he disputed each of these objections. In particular, Albee justified prevention's focus on the environment and its social change agenda. He argued against the medical model of mental disorder in which illness was attributed to personal defects. According to Albee, psychiatrists and other defenders of the status quo promoted such models in the hope of avoiding the widespread, expensive, and tumultuous social reform required to eradicate racism, poverty, and other social conditions that sabotaged mental health.

Despite the criticisms of a few detractors, the concept of prevention gained favor throughout the 1970s and 1980s (Cowen, 1983; Elias, 1987). Two journals on the topic appeared, *Journal of Primary Prevention* and *Prevention in Human Services*. Influential books described effective prevention programs, notably *14 Ounces of Prevention: A Casebook for Practitioners* (Price, Cowen, Lorion, & Ramos-McKay, 1988). Conferences, conventions, and policy groups were organized to explore the potential of prevention. Definitions became more precise and research more sophisticated. Indeed, half of all outcome studies that used control groups, an ingredient many see as crucial to rigorous prevention research, occurred after 1980 (Durlak & Wells, 1997a).

By the 1990s, prevention had become a respectable area of inquiry. Several comprehensive reviews of the literature documented the efficacy of preventive interventions. Notably, Joseph Durlak and Anne Wells (1997a, 1998) conducted two **meta-analyses** that assessed research on more than 300 preventive interventions. A meta-analysis is a research technique that collapses data across many studies in order to obtain an overview of the magnitude of effects. Durlak and Wells' (1997a) first study focused on prevention programs geared to people who did not yet show any signs of disorder. They found that participants in these programs usually surpassed the performance of 59% to 82% of the people in the control groups. Such improvements were striking because the program participants functioned in the normal range to begin with, and so dramatic changes in behavior would not be expected. In their second study, Durlak and Wells (1998) analyzed prevention programs that targeted people who showed initial signs of maladjustment but did not yet suffer from full-blown problems. In this study, the average program participant outperformed 70% of the people in control group. In sum, Durlak and Wells found that most preventive interventions significantly reduced problems and were at least as effective as the more well-established treatment-oriented interventions.

The studies of Durlak and Wells appeared in community psychology journals, but favorable reviews of prevention programs also occurred in broader realms. In the 1990s, the federal government issued two influential reports summarizing the state of prevention. The NIMH Prevention Research Steering Committee (1993) published *Prevention of Mental Disorders: A National Research Agenda*. Many of the points made in this document were echoed in an even more exhaustive review of federally-sponsored research in prevention. A 1990 mandate by the U.S. Congress led the Institute of Medicine (IOM) to conducted a review that resulted in the 605-page **IOM Report**. This report concluded that prevention programs were effective and merited additional federal funding and support (Mrazek & Haggerty, 1994; summarized in Muñoz, Mrazek, & Haggerty, 1996). In the 1990s, prevention research came of age and was embraced as legitimate governmental policy (Reppucci, Woolard, & Fried, 1999).

Researchers, practitioners, politicians, and the general public have embraced prevention for a number of reasons. It promises proactive efforts that reduce the total suffering of the population. It is potentially cost effective, in that people who might have drawn on collective resources through public assistance, hospitalization, or incarceration become contributing members of society instead. Even among prevention proponents, however, disagreement remains as to what makes prevention effective.

Despite the common goal of assessing the efficacy of extant prevention efforts and their conclusions about the merits of preventive approaches, the meta-analyses of Durlak and Wells and the IOM Report differed substantially (Cowen, 1997a). The two reports were based on a different set of studies—there existed only a 7% overlap between the 209 core citations in the Durlak and Wells meta-analysis and the 233 core citations in the IOM Report (Cowen, 1997a), and as we will see throughout this chapter these reviews resulted in very different ideas about how best to pursue a prevention agenda.

⌘ Typologies of Prevention

Over the years, there have been numerous attempts to clarify the definition of prevention, and several taxonomies have resulted. A review of these taxonomies illustrates the ways in which thinking about prevention has evolved over the past few decades.

PRIMARY, SECONDARY, AND TERTIARY PREVENTION

Because prevention has its roots in public health, public health terminology shaped the early thinking of mental health scholars. Public health distinguishes between the **incidence** and the **prevalence** of a disorder. The incidence is the number of new cases that arise in a population during a specified period of time, usually one year. The prevalence of a disorder is the total number of cases in a population at a given time. It reflects both the incidence and the duration of the disorder. Common colds only last a few days, and so the incidence over a year is much higher than the prevalence at a given time. Schizophrenia, on the other hand, generally affects individuals throughout their lives. Thus in a given year, the incidence of new cases is for lower than the total number of people who have schizophrenia (i.e., the prevalence). The distinction between incidence and prevalence differentiates the three types of prevention programs outlined in an early and still popular prevention taxonomy.

You may remember from the previous chapter that Gerald Caplan helped develop crisis theory. He also figured prominently in the early work on prevention. In 1964, Caplan introduced the distinction between tertiary prevention, secondary prevention, and primary prevention into the mental health literature. These three types of prevention programs have different effects on prevalence and incidence rates.

Tertiary prevention occurs after the disorder has developed. It seeks to alleviate the harmful, long-term effects of the problem. Tertiary prevention programs reduce the severity, discomfort, or disability associated with a disorder. George Fairweather's lodge societies, which helped people with mental illnesses live within the community, exemplify tertiary prevention (see the Community Intervention box in Chapter Seven). Lodge residents continued to suffer from mental illnesses but became better able to live productively in spite of them.

Caplan (1964) originally applied the term tertiary prevention to large-scale community interventions rather than individual rehabilitation. Nevertheless, tertiary prevention reflects the traditional treatment approach of most mental (and physical) health professionals. It targets people's existing deficits (Rappaport, 1977). Tertiary prevention reduces neither the incidence nor the prevalence of a problem. Indeed, tertiary prevention programs may actually increase the prevalence because improvements in the lives of individuals with disorders may help them to live longer (Bloom, 1979).

While tertiary prevention corresponds to treatment, **secondary prevention** consists of early intervention. Secondary prevention decreases the prevalence of a disorder by reducing its duration through early case finding and prompt intervention. It does not, however, reduce the incidence. Problems still occur at the same rate, they are simply "nipped in the bud." Emory Cowen's efforts to assist natural helpers, such as hairdressers and bartenders, may be seen as an example of secondary prevention (see the Classic Research box in Chapter Seven). Clients still experience the same problems, but natural helpers were taught to offer support more effectively so that the problems could be resolved more quickly.

Primary prevention differs from the other two types of prevention in that it targets people who do not show signs of disorder. The goal of primary prevention is to keep healthy people healthy. Primary prevention reduces the incidence of a disorder—new cases that would have occurred without the intervention do not develop. For example, the goal of Healthy Communities initiatives is to develop a community's economic, political, and social capacities, thereby reducing the likelihood of various problems. Although these initiatives may form in response to a community problem, the goal is to create healthy contexts in which the incidence of crime, educational failure, housing shortages, and other problems declines.

Although the distinction between primary, secondary, and tertiary prevention served mental health practitioners for many years, problems with this taxonomy emerged. Boundaries among prevention types often blur. Tertiary prevention for one disorder may constitute primary prevention for another. Mutual help groups for postmastectomy patients, for example, may constitute tertiary prevention with regard to breast cancer but may be primary prevention with regard to depression or other emotional disorders that could result from the cancer diagnosis and treatment (Bloom, 1979). The distinction between primary and secondary prevention also blurs. When should "at-risk" populations be considered healthy (and so targets for primary prevention) and when do we see them as evidencing early indicators of a problem (and so requiring secondary prevention)? Is Head Start a primary or secondary prevention program?

The prevention activities of psychologists and other helping professionals do not fall neatly into the categories adopted from public health. Thus, the IOM Report promoted a new taxonomy of prevention activities for mental health (Mrazek & Haggerty, 1994).

INDICATED, SELECTIVE, AND UNIVERSAL PREVENTION

The IOM taxonomy, like the public health taxonomy, identifies three different types of prevention that fall along an intervention continuum (see Figure 13.2).

In the IOM taxonomy, tertiary prevention no longer qualifies as prevention. The IOM Report echoed Emory Cowen's (1983) sentiment that although the goals of reducing the adverse consequences of disorder "are neither unworthy nor unneeded, they are simply *not* prevention" (Cowen, 1983, p. 11).

A second innovation of the IOM taxonomy is the division of secondary prevention into two types. **Indicated prevention** targets people who have detectable signs of maladjustment that foreshadow more significant mental disorders or who have biological markers that are linked to disorder. **Selective prevention** targets people who are at high risk for

the development of a disorder (as evidenced by biological, psychological, and/or social risk factors) but do not yet show any indication of disorder.

The final type of prevention, **universal prevention**, corresponds to primary prevention. It targets all the people in a given population (e.g., school, neighborhood, country). Universal prevention programs generally reach large numbers of people, few of whom are at imminent risk for the problem of interest. Because of its wide net, universal prevention programs ideally cost little per individual, are of demonstrated effectiveness, are acceptable to the general population, and entail little risk of negative outcomes (Mrazek & Haggerty, 1994). In order to better understand the IOM taxonomy, let's consider an example of each type of prevention.

INDICATED PREVENTION EXAMPLE

One of the best-known and best-researched indicated prevention programs is the Primary Mental Health Project (PMHP) begun in 1957 by Emory Cowen and his associates in Rochester, New York (Cowen, 1997b; Cowen & Hightower, 1989; Cowen, Izzo, Miles, Telschow, Trost, & Zax, 1963; Cowen, Pederson, Babigian, Izzo, & Trost, 1973; Cowen, Trost, Izzo, Lorion, Dorr, & Isaacson, 1975; Cowen, Zax, Izzo, & Trost, 1966). After forty years in operation, PMHPs had been established in 2000 schools across 700 districts (Cowen, 1996).

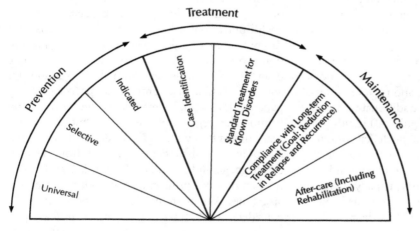

Figure 13.2
The Mental Health Intervention Spectrum for Mental Disorders.
Reprinted with permission from Reducing risks for mental disorder: Frontiers for preventive intervention research. *Copyright 1994 by the National Academy of Sciences. Courtesy of the National Academy Press, Washington, D.C.*

The idea for PMHPs grew from Cowen's observation that many older children with behavioral problems had experienced difficulties in school when they were much younger. He reasoned that intervention efforts directed at primary-aged children with school difficulties might prevent the development of more serious behavioral problems in later life. Based on classroom observations, interviews with parents, and psychological tests, children in a Rochester elementary school were classified as either at risk or not at risk for psychological problems. Because the PMHP targeted children who were already showing beginning signs of disorder, this was an indicated prevention program (despite its title *Primary* Mental Health Project).

The program originally consisted of informal conferences and education for the parents, and after-school groups for the children. The outcomes for children in the targeted school were then compared to outcomes for children in two similar schools where no intervention had occurred. Although PMHP professionals succeeded in identifying children at risk for problems, they did not successfully prevent the onset of disorder (Cowen, et al., 1963). Thus, the intervention program was revised. A staff consisting of homemakers, college students, and other nonprofessionals was carefully selected and trained to provide one-to-one and small group support for at-risk children. This support took place under the supervision of mental health professionals. In addition, school mental health counselors were encouraged to reduce their direct services to children and engage in prevention-oriented activities. Subsequent evaluations showed that the children in schools where PMHP was implemented fared better than children in control schools, as indicated by teacher ratings and school achievement (Cowen et al., 1966).

SELECTIVE PREVENTION EXAMPLE

An example of a selective intervention program is the School Transitional Environment Project (STEP), developed by Robert Felner and his colleagues (Felner & Adan, 1988; Felner, Farber & Primavera, 1983). As described in the previous chapter, some stressful life events (e.g., puberty, retirement) are predictable—they occur at particular stages of development. Because these normative events, or life transitions, represent important turning points that cohorts of people experience simultaneously, they present a promising opportunity for preventive intervention. The STEP program targeted the normative transition from middle school to high school. Research shows that this transition coincides with increased absenteeism, lower academic performance, and declines in well-being. These outcomes in turn, are, associated with more serious problems, such as school dropout, academic failure, and emotional dysfunction. These more serious problems may have lifelong consequences, including disenfranchisement from society, unemployment, and poor mental health (see Felner & Adan, 1988; Reyes, Gillock, Kobus, & Sanchez, 2000 for reviews).

STEP was a selective intervention program because the people targeted were at increased risk for the development of problems but did not yet evidence any signs of disorder. Program participants were at risk not only because they were about to undergo a school transition, but also because they attended large, urban schools predominantly serving students of low socioeconomic status. These schools tend to have higher rates of school dropout, as well as absenteeism, school failure, and a number of the other problems cited above.

For the STEP intervention, students entering high school were randomly assigned to an experimental or a control group. The intervention experienced by students in the experimental group consisted of two parts. First, the social system of the students was reorganized. Schedules were simplified and groups of new students took their core classes together in rooms located near to each other. Thus, students did not have to establish new peer relationships in each class or face threats and intimidation by older students when walking through the hallways to distant classrooms. They had more opportunities for informal interactions with classmates, and perceived the school as more stable, organized, and understandable than students in the control group.

The second aspect of the intervention involved restructuring the homeroom. STEP students were assigned to the same homeroom, and the homeroom teachers' role was modified to include administrative and counseling functions previously performed by other school personnel. For example, STEP homeroom teachers contacted family members to follow up on absences, helped students decide on elective classes, and provided information about educational and other resources. In order to fulfill these expanded roles, STEP teachers received training in such topics as academic and socioemotional counseling, listening skills, identification of emerging problems, referral processes, adolescent development, and college preparation. They also participated in teambuilding activities to enhance communication with other STEP teachers and personnel.

After one year, students who had been randomly assigned to the STEP program had higher grades, better attendance records, and more stable self-concepts than youth in the control group. While control group students saw teachers as less supportive as the year progressed, STEP students did not. A long-term follow-up showed that the dropout rate for STEP participants was less than half the rate of the students in the control group (21% versus 43%).

The STEP program appeals to community psychologists for numerous reasons. First and foremost, it focused on environmental rather than individual change. In addition, it cost little to implement—the intervention consisted of reorganizing existing resources, rather than obtaining new ones. The community psychology literature has described numerous school transition studies and programs that elaborate on the success of STEP (e.g., Compas, Wagner, Slavin, & Vannatta, 1986; Elias, Gara, Schuyler, Branden-Muller, & Sayette, 1991; Elias, Gara, Ubriaco, Rothbaum, Clabby, & Schuyler, 1986; Jason, Weine, Johnson, Danner, Kurasaki, & Warren-Sohlberg, 1993; Reyes et al., 2000; Seidman, Aber, Allen, & French, 1996; Weinstein, Soule, Collins, Cone, Mehlhorn, & Simontacchi, 1991).

UNIVERSAL PREVENTION EXAMPLE

While community psychologists designed and tested the Primary Mental Health Project (PMHP) and the School Transitional Environment Project (STEP), academic researchers do not spearhead all prevention programs. As an example, consider Project Venture, a program identified by the Western Regional Center for the Application of Prevention Technologies as a "best practice" intervention. Best practice interventions are strategies and programs that scientists at influential organizations (e.g., National Institute for Drug Abuse, Center for Substance Abuse and Prevention, and Centers for Disease Control and Prevention) deem promising based on the results of high-quality research (see ***http://www.open.org/~westcapt/bestprac.htm***).

Project Venture was developed by the National Indian Youth Leadership Development Project specifically for American Indian youth in Pueblo and Navajo communities (Hall, Levis-Pilz, Pilz, & DeJong, No date). Although Project Venture was designed to reduce substance abuse, it did not feature explicit antidrug messages or target youth at highest risk. The program stressed personal and group wellness and emphasized leadership skills, confidence, problem-solving abilities, teamwork, and community commitment for all youth. The program consisted of a five- to ten-day summer camp and follow-up intergenerational activities. While at the camp, youth engaged in experiential adventures, such as hiking, mountain biking, canoeing, rappeling, and rock climbing. They also participated in a service component, designing and implementing community projects, such as the establishment of a community greenhouse.

Project Venture was designed to be culturally appropriate for Indian youth. It included intertribal activities, appropriate spiritual content, and an ethic of service to Indian communities. Youth were encouraged to forge connections with supportive elders and to invest themselves in their cultural heritage. Graduation from the camp program was marked by a rite of passage that built on traditional coming-of-age ceremonies.

In order to assess the impact of this intervention, the American Drug and Alcohol Survey (ADAS) was administered to 850 program participants and to a control group over a three year period. Overall, program participants were less likely than control youth to abuse alcohol, tobacco, and other drugs.

PRIMARY PREVENTION
AND PROMOTION

To review, early mental health preventionists distinguished three types of prevention: primary, secondary, and tertiary. A more recent typology classified tertiary prevention as treatment rather than prevention, and refined the meaning of secondary prevention which now included indicated and selective prevention. In these two typologies, the meaning of primary prevention remained relatively consistent: efforts to reduce problems by preventing their occurrence. There is however, some debate about what activities should be included under the rubric of primary prevention, a debate highlighted by the contrasting conclusions drawn by Durlak and Wells in their meta-analyses and the IOM in their report.

DEBATE ABOUT PROMOTION

Some scholars, including many community psychologists, identify two different approaches to primary prevention (Albee, 1982; Bloom, 1979; Cowen, 1977, 1996, 1997a; Durlak & Wells, 1997a; Ford, 1985). The first approach, which virtually all preventionists embrace as primary prevention, attempts to reduce the likelihood of disorder. A second avenue for primary prevention is the enhancement of health. Health promotion programs seek to build resistance to a variety of disorders. They are based in the belief that interventions can reduce risk levels by helping people to develop skills and competencies.[1]

Relatively early in the history of community psychology, Bernard Bloom (1979) observed that there was "a substantial body of research from a variety of domains that appears to converge on competence building as perhaps the single most persuasive preventive strategy for dealing with individual and social issues in most communities" (p. 184). Many subsequent community psychologists concurred that prevention goals could be achieved through

the promotion of competence (e.g., Albee, 1982, 1996; Cowen, 1977, 1991, 1996; Seidman, 1987). Other scholars have been less positive. At the same time Bloom lauded competency-based prevention efforts, Lamb and Zusman (1979) argued against health promotion as a form of prevention, stating that "there is no evidence that it is possible to strengthen 'mental health' and thereby increase resistance to mental illness by general preventive activities" (p. 13).

This criticism may seem to carry little weight in that Lamb and Zusman discounted *all* forms of prevention. The NIMH (NIMH Prevention Research Steering House, 1993) and IOM Reports (Mrazek & Haggerty, 1994), though positive toward the concept of prevention in general, also argued against the utility of health promotion. They advocated for interventions aimed at the prevention of the specific mental disorders identified in the *Diagnostic and Statistical Manual* (DSM). Community psychologists have continued to challenge a "risk driven" view of prevention in which the most important criterion for acceptable prevention activities is the extent to which diagnosable psychiatric illnesses can be reduced (Cowen, 1996; see Albee, 1996; Durlak & Wells, 1997a). A number of programs have been cited in support of health-based prevention efforts.

PROMOTION EXAMPLE

In their meta-analysis of primary prevention programs, Durlak and Wells (1997a) identified training in interpersonal problem solving as an important competence-building approach to prevention. Interpersonal problem-solving interventions are based on the groundbreaking work of George Spivack and Myrna Shure (Shure, 1997; Shure & Spivack, 1988; Spivack & Shure, 1974).

Spivack and Shure noted that some inner-city preschool children act impatiently and are overly emotional, aggressive, or shy, behaviors that contributed to a number of problems. Further, Spivack and Shure found that children who evidenced these behaviors often lacked certain problem-solving skills. Thus, they developed a competence building intervention called Interpersonal Cognitive Problem Solving (ICPS), which the children called "I Can

---

[1]One can conceive of indicated and selective interventions based on a health-promotion model of prevention, but promotion models are usually associated with primary prevention efforts

Problem Solve." Instead of targeting aggression, shyness, or other problem behaviors, ICPS programs teach children useful skills, such as:

- *Alternative thinking:* The ability to generate different solutions to interpersonal problems
- *Consequential thinking:* The ability to foresee the results of one's actions
- *Causal thinking:* The ability to see events as the causes of other events
- *Sensitivity:* The awareness of the interpersonal nature of problems
- *Means/ends thinking:* The ability to conceptualize the steps necessary to reach a goal

ICPS programs build these skills through the use of fun activities conducted by teachers or parents. The goal is to teach children *how* to think, rather than what to think. Evaluation research showed that children who received this intervention gained in the relevant problem-solving skills. After two years, they were rated as better adjusted than children in a control group.

DOHRENWEND'S MODEL REVISITED

In considering the meaning of prevention, we have thus far examined two prevention typologies and the debate about prevention versus promotion. Before moving from conceptual maps to an examination of the issues involved in doing prevention work, let's consider one more way of thinking about prevention.

The stress-and-coping framework and the prevention framework both emerged as important orienting concepts when community psychology was founded. Several scholars, including Erich Lindemann and Gerald Caplan, helped develop both concepts. Given this close association, it is not surprising that Barbara Dohrenwend's (1978) stress model, described in this chapter (see Figure 13.1) had important ramifications for prevention. Indeed her model could serve as yet another typology for organizing prevention research and practice.

Dohrenwend identified six types of interventions (the circles on the periphery of Figure 13.1). In this chapter, we consider two of these circles. Mutual help groups were examined as an example of corrective therapy. Corrective therapies take place after a stressful event has run its course, and adjustment to the event, positive, negative, or unchanged, has occurred. In this way, corrective therapies exemplify tertiary prevention, or treatment.[2] Second, we examined disaster relief as a form of crisis intervention. Crisis intervention takes place soon after a stressful event occurs and before long-term adjustment to the event is achieved. Thus, crisis intervention constitutes a form of secondary prevention (usually selective, but also indicated).

Corrective therapy and crisis intervention target the stress process directly. The remaining four types of interventions in Dohrenwend's model do not depend on the occurrence of stress. They affect the context of stress, either at the individual or environmental level (see Table 13.2). These interventions can either prevent the occurrence of stress or facilitate the capacity to adjust after stresses occur. Let's look briefly at each.

The first type of individual-level intervention is skill training. In this chapter, we just discussed one example—the ICPS program. These programs build an individual's ability to adjust to interpersonal stresses by teaching interpersonal problem solving. As another example, Sharlene Wolchick and her colleagues (1993) developed an intervention aimed at facilitating adjustment to divorce. It sought to improve mothers' communication skills and help them to develop positive routines and enriching family activities. This program resulted in improvements in mother–child interactions and the quality of the home environment.

The second type of individual-level intervention identified by Dohrenwend was education and socialization. Although these interventions target individuals, they hold the potential to actually prevent stresses from occurring, as opposed to preventing

---

[2]It should be noted that mutual support groups, examined here in the context of corrective therapies, have also been conceptualized as primary and secondary prevention (e.g., Levy, 2000).

Table 13.2	Four Interventions that Occur outside of the Stress Process	
Level of Intervention	**Facilitate Adjustment (Target Stress Mediators)**	**Prevent Stress (Target Enduring Characteristics)**
Individual	Skill training	Education and socialization
Environmental	Community organization and development	Political action

Based on Dohrenwend, B.S. (1978). Social stress and community psychology. *American Journal of Community Psychology, 6,* 1–14.

the problems that result from stress. Mental health education aims to help people gain the knowledge, attitudes, and behaviors that support psychological well-being. People might learn how to protect themselves from sexually transmitted diseases or how to talk to their children about resisting peer pressure to use drugs. One important vehicle for education and socialization is the media (see the Community Intervention box).

The remaining two circles in Dohrenwend's model target the environment rather than the individual. Just as individuals can be helped to develop skills, so too can communities. Community organization and development may be seen as skill building at the community level. Every community has untapped resources that can be developed to help the community meet the needs of its residents (e.g., Kretzmann & McKnight, 1993). Emory Cowen's (1982) workshops to strengthen the skills of informal helpers is an example of a small-scale community development intervention that builds the community's capacity to meet the needs of stressed residents.

The final intervention outlined by Dohrenwend is perhaps the most controversial: political action. If one believes that such factors as economic inequality and discrimination account for the occurrence of many stresses, than these stresses can best be prevented through social change efforts. Support for this type of prevention has not grown over the decades. In the 1960s and 1970s, prevention

researchers were clearly concerned about the mental health consequences of social ills such as poverty, racism, and sexism. As the sociopolitical Zeitgeist changed, the revolutionary zeal of early preventionists dissipated (Albee, 1996). Change efforts through sociopolitical action do occur, but not as often as they once did. In 1996, George Albee lamented the loss of interest in social change over the past few decades. He contended that the civil rights movement should be considered one of this country's most effective prevention programs.

⌘ Targeting Prevention Efforts

Now that we have considered some different ways of thinking about prevention programs, let's explore ways of maximizing the chances that these programs actually have a preventive effect. Which type of prevention works best, and how can we maximize program efficacy?

IS PRIMARY PREVENTION BEST?

Community psychologists sometimes hail primary (or universal) prevention as a particularly desirable form of prevention (e.g., Bloom, 1979; Cowen, 1977, 1980; Felner, Felner, & Silverman, 2000;

COMMUNITY INTERVENTION:

The Stanford Heart Disease Prevention Program
Media as a Means to Prevention

In the 1960s, half of all deaths in the United States could be attributed to coronary heart disease. Moreover, the victims of heart disease were often relatively young. Research evidence suggested that heart disease in people under the age of 60 resulted from three risk factors: smoking, high serum cholesterol, and hypertension. John Farquhar and his colleagues at the Stanford Medical School designed an intervention to reduce heart disease by improving diet and reducing smoking (Maccoby & Alexander, 1979; Farquhar, 1991).

The researchers decided to launch a media campaign targeting all community members between the ages of 35 and 59. Because random assignment of individuals to intervention and control groups is not possible in a community-wide intervention, they used a quasi experimental design. Similar Northern California communities received either a media intervention alone, a media intervention combined with an intensive interpersonal instruction program (ten group sessions for high-risk people and their spouses) or no intervention at all.

The Three-Community Study began in 1972 with a baseline survey. The intervention began in 1973, and follow-up surveys were administered on a yearly basis for three years. Researchers used both self-report and physiological data to assess such variables as knowledge of risk factors, smoking rates, and eating habits.

The researchers knew that previous attempts to modify behaviors through the media had been disappointing. Based on extant research, they decided to deliver risk reduction messages through a variety of means: television and radio spots, direct mail, print advertisements, newspaper articles, and bus placards. Other innovations incorporated into their media campaign, which continued for 18 months, included:

- Establishing specific objectives before the start of the campaign
- Targeting a circumscribed segment of the population
- Constructing clear and useful messages that related to clear objectives

- Utilizing creative scheduling (not relying on free television or radio spots during hours when few people were awake)
- Making the message salient to the individual in order to create motivation for change
- Attempting to stimulate interpersonal communication among community members
- Regularly assessing the effectiveness of the campaign through process evaluation
- Obtaining long-term commitments for the support of the campaign (Maccoby & Alexander, 1979)

Researchers also tailored messages to community subgroups. Between 10% and 15% of the targeted communities were Spanish speaking, and the researchers found that the risk factors in this population differed from the Anglo population. For example, Spanish speakers smoked less but were more overweight often. Thus, a second campaign was designed that differed not only in language, but also with regard to message content and message delivery. Media-use patterns revealed that radio would be the most effective means of reaching the Spanish-speaking population of interest, and three local stations with Spanish programming were used in the campaign. The Spanish campaign engaged bilingual English and Spanish speakers not merely in translating the messages, but in transforming them in ways that would increase their appropriateness to the Spanish-speaking communities.

Research showed that the risk of coronary disease was reduced by 17% to 18% in the treatment communities, while the risk level in the control community increased 6% during the same time period. Knowledge about coronary risk, attitudes toward risk behaviors, and actual behaviors also changed in the intervention communities. Furthermore, the positive changes were maintained and sometimes increased during the second year of the study. Although the effects in people receiving mass media plus high-risk group intervention occurred more quickly, the two intervention communities

Rappaport, 1977; Seidman, 1987). Primary prevention programs reach everyone while stigmatizing no

one, emphasize health rather illness, and generally target groups as opposed to individuals. The does

showed comparable results after two years. After three years, however, results in the media-only community appeared to have faded more. After the three-year follow-up, risk-reduction materials were made available to the community that had served as the no-intervention control. The success of this program led Stanford researchers to continue to use media as a means of preventing coronary disease, and it served as a model for other media campaigns aimed at preventing mental and physical health problems (e.g., Jason, 1998).

not mean that primary prevention is the preferred approach in all situations, however. The nature of the problem of interest and the preventionist's goals may call for secondary (indicated or selective) and even tertiary prevention (e.g., Winnett, 1991).

In primary prevention, resources are not targeted. Everyone receives the intervention, whether they are at risk or not. A primary preventionist might argue that the behaviors promoted by these interventions are good for everyone. *Any* person can benefit from eating healthier, exercising more, abstaining from tobacco, or becoming a better parent or friend. On the other hand, might people with high cholesterol benefit *more* from adopting low-fat diets? Isn't information on effective parenting best directed to people who are socially isolated or have other risk factors for child abuse and neglect?

Some scholars assert that people at highest risk for a problem should be targeted for prevention programs (e.g., Coie, Watt, West, Hawkins, Asarnow, Markman, Ramey, Shure, & Long, 1993). In order to be affordable, a population-wide intervention program may not be intense enough to benefit the people who need it most. By opting for primary prevention rather than selective or indicated prevention, practitioners sometimes trade scope for intensity. The danger is that far-reaching programs will become so diluted as to have no meaningful effect. N. Dickon Reppucci, Preston Britner, and Jennifer Woolard (1997) found that child abuse prevention programs in the form of parent education were only effective if they consisted of at least six sessions. A one-shot program geared to all parents might reach everyone but help no one. Interestingly, more long-term programs may have better effects even if the content does not expand. One study found that the same 10.5 hours of programming relating to the prevention of sexual risk-taking had greater effects on adolescents if spread over seven sessions rather than compacted into three sessions (Rotherman-Borus, Gwadz, Fernandez, & Srinivasan, 1998).

In addition to the issue of intensity and program length, base rates also bear on decisions about the preferred type of prevention. Primary prevention programs for low frequency disorders need to cast an extremely wide net in order to reach even a few of the people who might be at risk. Even secondary prevention programs that target high-risk people may serve many people who would have turned out fine without the program. If a widespread program helps only a few people, can it be justified?

Sometimes the answer is yes. One reason for the appeal of early education programs such as Head Start is their promise of long-term payoffs for short-term investments. The Perry Preschool Project followed 123 low-IQ children who had lived in low-income African American families from the age of three or four to age twenty-seven. Program participants as compared to people in the control group scored higher on achievement tests, graduated from high school more often, pursued post-graduate education at higher rates, were arrested less often, had reduced rates of teenage pregnancy, earned more money as adults, and less often received welfare. These effects resulted in substantial savings—a seven-dollar return on every dollar spent on the program (Barnett, 2000). Not every preschooler had a "successful" outcome: some participants were arrested for crimes or became teen parents. In addition, some of the children in the control group thrived without the intervention. Still, the benefits of this secondary prevention program justified its expense.

Leonard Jason (1998) demonstrated that a primary-prevention program that reached only a small number of high-risk people could be cost effective. He reasoned that an antismoking media campaign broadcast to 450,000 people might reach only 150,000 smokers. Even if only 10% of these smokers achieved long-term abstinence, the lifetime savings in health care costs for these 15,000 people would approach $600,000,000.

In some cases, preventionists do not choose from among prevention approaches, but combine the best of different approaches. They might, for example, launch a large-scale primary prevention program in conjunction with a smaller-scale indicated or selective prevention effort. This was the approach taken in one of the communities in the Stanford Three Community Study (see the Community Intervention box). A primary prevention media campaign was supplemented by support groups targeting high-risk people. Leonard Jason (1998) also combined primary and targeted programming in his multilevel smoking cessation interventions. One intervention involved a televised self-help component to mass audiences, self-help manuals for all interested audience members, and a support group that specifically targeted smokers. At the end of the three-week program, 21% of the smokers who received the manuals and watched the television broadcast quit smoking, but 41% of those who participated in the support group meetings as well, were able to quit.

ASSESSING RISK

Our ability to implement effective programs requires consideration of the benefits of different prevention approaches. In some cases, limited funds, specificity of program content and other factors may lead preventionists to opt for indicated or selective (secondary) rather than primary prevention. The question then becomes how do we decide whom to target for intervention?

In the public health paradigm, specific disorders developed from single causes. A solitary virus or bacteria or contaminant led to a particular disease. Thus, the preventionists' task was straightforward: remove the pathogen from the environment or build resistance to it in the individual. If swamp-dwelling mosquitoes carry malaria, drain the swamps or develop antimalaria drugs. Mental health preventionists face different challenges. The problems of interest to us (from schizophrenia to delinquency to homelessness), cannot be traced to a single pathogen. They result from complex interactions of multiple factors, both individual and environmental. Because there is no one-to-one correspondence between problem and cause, we must instead talk about *risk* for problem development.

RISK FACTORS

Selective and indicated prevention programs require knowledge of what leads to disorder (or strengthens health) under what circumstances. At present, few or no signs or symptoms predict the onset of mental health and behavioral problems with certainty. Instead, researchers have rounded up a group of usual suspects—**risk factors** associated with a higher likelihood for the onset of a problem, and greater severity and longer duration of the problem once it occurs (see Table 13.3).

Risk factors can reside primarily within individuals (e.g., neurochemical imbalances, social incompetence) or in the environment (e.g., family disorganization, social isolation). Various individual and environmental risk factors act together as accomplices of sorts. There may be a ringleader, but rarely does one factor operate alone. A person with poor work skills is more likely to live in a low-income, disorganized neighborhood. A child with neurochemical imbalances may suffer more in a disorganized family.

In addition to risk factors, the development of disorder is also affected by **protective factors**—variables that improve people's resistance to risk factors and disorder. Protective factors can modify the disorder directly or influence the disorder by affecting risk factors—either preventing their occurrence or buffering their effects (Coie et al., 1993). Prevention efforts tend to focus on risk factors more than protective factors because preventionists (outside the realm of community psychology) tend to focus on disorder rather than health. Protective factors are more often studied by scholars interested in promoting competence.

▤ Table 13.3   Generic Risk Factors

Family Circumstances
  Low social class
  Family conflict
  Mental illness in family
  Large family size
  Poor bonding to parents
  Family disorganization
  Communication deviance

Emotional Difficulties
  Child abuse
  Apathy/emotional blunting
  Emotional immaturity
  Stressful life events
  Low self-esteem
  Emotional dyscontrol

School Problems
  Academic failure
  Scholastic demoralization

Ecological context
  Neighborhood disorganization
  Racial injustice
  Unemployment
  Extreme poverty

Constitutional Handicaps
  Perinatal complications
  Sensory disabilities
  Organic handicaps
  Neurochemical imbalance

Interpersonal Problems
  Peer rejection
  Alienation and isolation

Skill Development Delays
  Subnormal intelligence
  Social incompetence
  Attentional deficits
  Reading disabilities
  Poor work skills and habits

Coie, J. D., Watt, N. F., West, S. G., Hawkins, J. D., Asarnow, J. R., Markman, H. J., Ramey, C., Shure, M. B., & Long, B. (1993). The science of prevention: A conceptual framework and some directions for a national research program. *American Psychologist, 48*, 1013–1023. Copyright © 1993 by the American Psychological Association. Reprinted with permission.

STRESS AND RISK: PRECIPITATING AND PREDISPOSING FACTORS

Many risk factors are long-standing characteristics of a person's make-up or environment. Thus, they correspond to what have been called **predisposing factors.** These longstanding characteristics may be individual traits that likely have a genetic component (e.g., neurochemical imbalances or subnormal intelligence) or personal background factors relating to social position (e.g., socioeconomic status) or family history factors (e.g., childhood abuse). While

predisposing factors increase vulnerability, the onset of disorder often requires a **precipitating factor**. Precipitating factors are stressful occurrences that trigger the disorder. (In Table 13.3, Coie and his colleagues included stressful events under "Emotional Difficulties," subscribing to the notion that stresses are often seen as individual-level phenomena.)

The interaction between predisposing and precipitating factors reflects a conjoining of prevention and stress-and-coping frameworks and is evident in the prevention equation presented by George Albee in 1982.

$$\frac{\text{Incidence of}}{\text{Psychological Disorder}} = \frac{\text{Stress + Physical Vulnerability}}{\text{Coping Skills + Social Support + Self-Esteem}}$$

This equation influenced people's thinking about prevention for many years. The numerator reflects the joint operation of intra-individual predisposing factors and a precipitating event. The denominator includes the two mediators of the stress-adjustment relationship.

Five years after Albee's article, Maurice Elias (1987) reformulated the equation to deemphasize the individual-level and highlight environmental contributions to disorder. Elias included only environmental-level predisposing factors in his numerator, along with the occurrence of a precipitating event. He also emphasized system-level dynamics and structures in his denominator.

$$\frac{\text{Likelihood of Disorder}}{\text{in Population}} = \frac{\text{Stress + Risk Factors in Environment}}{\text{Socialization Practices + Social Support Resources + Opportunities for Connectedness}}$$

Today, most preventionists agree that an understanding of the development of disorder requires consideration of individual and environmental factors, both longstanding and episodic. For example, a parent lacking in social competence (individual factor) living in a low-income and violent neighborhood (environmental factor) might be at particularly high risk for child abuse. She or he may, however, actually harm her or his child only in the presence of a precipitating stressful event—after being fired from a job, for example, or ending a romantic relationship.

ATTRIBUTABLE RISK

Theoretically, one can calculate the amount of risk associated with a given factor. Consider tobacco use. Smoking is an important risk factor for lung cancer. People who smoke cigarettes develop lung cancer at higher rates than nonsmokers. But even if interventionists completely eradicated smoking—not a single cigarette ever puffed again—some people would still fall victim to lung cancer. Other risk factors remain, such as genetic makeup and exposure to pollutants. **Attributable risk** is the proportion of new cases of a disorder (lung cancer in this example) that would be prevented if an intervention completely eliminated a risk factor (in this case, smoking) (Muñoz, Mrazek, & Haggerty, 1996). Assessments of attributable risk can help interventionists target programs by identifying which factors lead most directly to a problem.

The inability to eliminate a problem by removing known risk factors illustrates the limited effectiveness of interventions, no matter how powerful. Given the fact that social and behavioral problems are multiply determined, even the total eradication of a major risk factor will not reduce the incidence of the targeted problem to zero. The multiplicity of risk factors comes with good news, too. Just as one disorder is affected by multiple risk factors, a single risk factor can lead to a variety of disorders. Thus, reducing a single risk factor has a beneficial effect on many problems. If no one ever smoked again, not only would the incidence of lung cancer decrease, but the incidence of emphysema and throat cancer would decrease, as well. There would be fewer injuries, deaths, and property loss from accidental fires set by careless smokers. And the overall health and fitness of millions of people would improve. As Bernard Bloom (1979) observed two decades ago, prevention programs can have specific and nonspecific effects; smoking cessation has a specific effect with regard to lung cancer, as well as nonspecific effects with regard to general health.

Some risk factors play a role in only a few social and behavioral problems, and others are implicated in many. Poverty, for example, plays a role in virtually every problem that psychologists study: domestic violence, school failure, criminal behavior, mental illness, substance abuse. It is the "greatest risk factor of all" (Schorr, 1988, p. xxii). If preventionists could engineer a significant reduction in poverty, imagine the radiating effects throughout society.

READINESS TO CHANGE

One way to target prevention efforts is to direct them to high-risk people or environments. A second approach is to target the people and environments most likely to be receptive to change efforts. Some research suggests that a relatively small segment of any population (about 10% to 20%) is ready to change key behaviors at a given point in time (Winett, 1991). If we could reach those people, our chances of success would improve.

I once worked in a program for homeless people with a man who had previously been homeless himself. When asked how he turned his life around after years of substance abuse and a marginal existence on the streets, he explained that he finally got sick and tired of being sick and tired. At that point, he was ready to try something different. Waiting until people have exhausted their resources and hit rock bottom hardly represents a preventive approach, however.

There are ways of assessing the likelihood of benefiting from programs that are more in keeping with a preventive approach. For example, preventive interventions are best directed to people who are likely to develop the problem of interest or people already experiencing beginning the stages of the problem who are ready to change. So, for example, interventions designed to prevent the health problems associated with smoking need not direct anti-smoking messages to nonsmokers who have no intention of smoking or to smokers who have no intention of quitting.

Some interventions further quantify readiness to change (e.g., the seriousness of intentions to quit smoking) utilizing the *stages of change* approach developed by James Prochaska and Carlo DiClemente (Prochaska & DiClemente, 1992; Prochaska, DiClemente, & Norcross, 1992). These authors identified five stages of change:

- *Precontemplation:* People are not thinking seriously about changing and are not interested in any kind of intervention.
- *Contemplation:* People are thinking seriously about changing but not anytime soon.

- *Preparation:* People are preparing to change in the near future.
- *Action:* People are actively changing or have recently changed their behavior.
- *Maintenance:* People have made changes and have successfully avoided temptations to return to the problematic behavior

One smoking cessation program using this stages of change model did find that readiness to change predicted program effectiveness (Turner, Morera, Johnson, Crittendon, Freels, Parsons, Flay, & Warnecke, 2001). Consideration of people's readiness to change also suggests that interventions can have two positive outcomes. They can either reduce the problem behavior or increase people's readiness to reduce that behavior in the future—a readiness that other interventions can build upon. Research suggests that people cycle through the various stages of change several times before terminating the problematic behavior (Prochaska et al., 1992).

Another approach to targeting people most likely to benefit from intervention is to focus on people who are experiencing a crisis. People in crisis may be receptive to significant and potentially life-enhancing changes they might not have embraced otherwise. For example, Leonard Jason (1998) found that people who had recently experienced significant negative events were most responsive to the new ideas and techniques presented in a stress management program. Yet another approach is to try to foster receptivity as a part of the program. For example, meditation or other relaxation techniques might increase openness to messages about change.

Readiness to change is not simply an individual-level phenomenon. In recent years the concept of **community readiness** has emerged (e.g., Edwards, Jumper-Thurman, Plested, Oetting, & Swanson, 2000; Kumpfer, Whiteside, Wandersman, & Cardenas, 1997; Pentz, Rothspan, Turner, Skara, & Voskanian, 1999). Communities go through different stages with regard to their willingness to embrace prevention programming. In general, the continuum of community readiness proceeds from a lack of awareness of the target problem to problem recognition and finally to action. E. R. Oetting and colleagues (1995) identified nine stages of community readiness. Using this framework, the National Institute of Drug Abuse (1997) described strategies to enhance community readiness at each stage. The nine stages and related strategies appear in Table 13.4.

Within any individual or community, readiness to change varies with respect to each problem. Someone might be ready to find alternatives to violence in a close relationship but be unwilling to stop smoking. At the community level, as well, the willingness to confront one problem, such as smoking, might surpass the willingness to confront another, such as violence.

In 1965 smoking prevalence in the U.S. was about 52% for men and 34% for women. By 1996, the rates had dropped to about 28% for men and 23% for women. This contrasts with the trend for violent crime. During roughly the same period, violent

Table 13.4 Community Readiness: Stages and Strategies

Stage	Characteristics	Strategies
Stage 1: Community Tolerance/ No Knowledge	Community (or subcommunity) norms either tolerate or encourage the problem behavior.	Small group and one-on-one discussions with community leaders about the problem, its costs (health, psychological, social), and the norms that support it.
Stage 2: Denial	Recognition that the behavior can be problematic but no perceived need to tackle it locally.	Education and outreach programs to community leaders and groups that might sponsor programs. Use of local incidents to illustrate harmfulness in one-to-one discussions and educational outreach programs
Stage 3: Vague Awareness	General sense that the problem exists and should be tackled locally but understanding is vague and stereotyped, and the motivation to act is low. No identifiable leadership.	Educational outreach programs on the problem's national and state prevalence rates, and rates in similar communities. Use of local incidents to illustrate harmfulness. Local media campaigns to illustrate consequences of the problem.
Stage 4: Preplanning	Clear recognition of problem and general knowledge but vague or stereotyped ideas about etiology and risk factors. Leaders are identifiable but no intervention plans have been developed.	Educational programs that identify prevalence rates, correlates, and causes of the problem for community leaders and sponsorship groups. Educational outreach to introduce concept of prevention and describe programs in similar communities. Local media campaigns on consequences of the problem and the promise of prevention.

Stage	Characteristics	Strategies
Stage 5: **Preparation**	Planning exists and focuses on practical details. Programs may have begun on a trial basis but are not grounded in formal data collection. Leadership is active and funding may be sought or has been obtained.	Educational outreach programs to general public on specific prevention programs. Educational outreach to community leaders and sponsorship groups that describes the prevention programs and their startup needs. Media campaigns on consequences of the problem and the promise of prevention.
Stage 6: **Initiation**	Trial program is up and running. Staff is in training or has just finished. Enthusiasm is high as limitations and problems have not yet occurred. Knowledge of risk factors remains stereotyped.	Inservice training for program staff on problem consequences, correlates, and causes. Publicity efforts to kickoff program. Meetings to update and inform community leaders and sponsorship groups.
Stage 7: **Institutionalization/** **Stabilization**	One or two programs are running and accepted as valuable routine activity. Limitations of programs known but little perceived need to change or expand.	Inservice training on evaluation process, new trends associated with the problem, and new prevention initiatives. Periodic review meetings and recognition events for program supporters, with local publicity.
Stage 8: **Confirmation/** **Expansion**	Standard programs are viewed as valuable, and new initiatives are being planned. Expansion funds are sought, data are obtained regularly on extent of local problem, and efforts are underway to assess risk factors and etiology.	Inservice programs on local need. Periodic review meetings and recognition events for program supporters. Results of research and evaluation of programs presented to public though local media and/or public meetings.
Stage 9: **Professionalization**	Detailed and sophisticated knowledge of risk factors and etiology exists. Staff is trained, authorities are supportive, and community involvement is high. Effective evaluation is used to test and modify programs.	Continued inservice training, assessment of the problem, and program evaluation. Continued updating of community leaders and public through local media and/or public meetings.

Adapted from National Institute of Drug Abuse (1997). *Community readiness for drug abuse prevention: Issues, tips, and tools.* (publication # PB#97-209605). Washington, D.C.: National Institute of Drug Abuse. Available at: *http://www.open.org/~westcapt/crstages.htm.*

crimes such as murder, rape, and assault increased by approximately 550% (Biglan & Taylor, 2000). Anthony Biglan and Ted Taylor (2000) argued that the readiness to tackle violent crime has lagged behind readiness to reduce smoking for several reasons. First, consensus exists about what causes smoking and how to reduce it, while problem definitions and intervention approaches with regard to violence are more varied. In addition, formal and informal antismoking organizations work together at all system levels, while there are fewer antiviolence organizations, especially nongovernmental organizations at the national level, and coordination among these organizations is less likely. Biglan and Taylor recommended that behavioral scientists interested in increasing community readiness for violence prevention articulate the progress that has been made in this domain and advocate for empirically supported violence prevention programs.

⌘ Assessing Effects

Prevention science has made great strides in the past decades. We have better typologies to guide our work and increased knowledge about how to target our efforts wisely. Let's turn now to important considerations in assessing the effects of preventive interventions.

THE BASICS OF PREVENTION RESEARCH

The IOM Report delineated a **preventive intervention research cycle** (Mrazek & Haggerty, 1994). It held that research is an ongoing cycle in which theories and methods are put into practice, tested, and revised based on their documented effects. This exemplifies Lewin's action research model described in Chapter Seven (see section entitled *Research and the Guiding Principles*).

The research cycle proposed in the IOM Report has undergone some modifications, but its essential elements remain the same (Kellam, Koretz &

Moscicki, 1999; Valente & Dodge, 1997). The cycle requires a theoretical and empirical basis, ongoing testing, and dissemination. These requirements are met through five central tasks. First, identify the problem or mental health outcome, its prevalence, and its course over the life span. Second, review relevant research (across disciplines) on risk factors and protective factors with regard to the problem of interest. Third, develop and implement innovative pilot interventions and test the efficacy of those interventions. Fourth, design, implement, and analyze the effectiveness of promising interventions in large-scale field trials with different populations and in different settings. Fifth, implement and continually evaluate prevention programs in the community, and disseminate these findings.

In carrying out this research agenda, preventionists are likely to encounter a number of challenges. Emory Cowen (1983) delineated some of the "research-weakening vicissitudes" of community-based prevention efforts (p. 21). They include difficulties in finding appropriate control groups, antagonism between researcher and community needs, attrition of participants (i.e., participants leave the study before it is over), and changes during the course of the intervention that are not attributable to the program. Additional challenges identified in the IOM Report include difficulties in maintaining strict randomization in assigning people to intervention versus control groups and insufficient long-term follow up (Muñoz et al., 1996).

Considerable progress has been made in meeting these research challenges over the past few decades. In their meta-analysis, Durlak and Wells (1997a) found that most of the 177 primary prevention interventions they studied had little subject attrition (10% or less in 80% of the studies), relied on multiple outcome measures (90%), and used random assignment to experimental and control groups (61%).

The use of control groups is particularly notable. Change occurs over time, and events unrelated to the intervention can influence the behaviors of interest. For example, between 1981 and 1993, people reduced the number of cigarettes smoked by about 108 per person each year. In the mid-1990s, however, the yearly declines slowed to about 12 cigarettes. These changes in cigarette consumption reflected fluctuations in the cost of cigarettes. Thus, antismoking interventions implemented during periods when cigarette costs changed would need to factor in the effects of cost changes on smoking rates (Levine, 1998). Similarly, AIDS prevention interventions have been affected by a variety of historical events—Magic Johnson's announcement that he was HIV positive, for example (Hobfoll, 1998). Such historical events are one reason why control groups are helpful. If experimental groups and control groups consist of similar people who are tested in similar contexts at similar times, better outcomes for people in the experimental group can be attributed to the intervention rather than to other nonprogram factors, such as historical events.

THE CHALLENGE OF FOLLOW-UP

Intervention effects, even when documented in studies using a control group, do not necessarily mean that the program worked. The possibility remains that the intervention simply postponed rather than prevented the problem of interest. When can researchers say with confidence that a problem was actually *prevented?* Based on their meta-analysis, Durlak and Wells (1997a) concluded that research projects rarely continue long enough to ensure that a targeted problem was truly prevented and not merely delayed. Although the studies included in their meta-analysis evidenced methodological sophistication in several domains, they lacked long-term follow-up. A substantial minority of the studies (25%) collected *no* follow-up data. Studies that did follow participants rarely assessed outcomes more than one year after the intervention.

Long-term follow-up is not always easy. The academic institutions where many prevention researchers work reward multiple, short-term studies and continual publications. Funders and politicians want to see quick results that justify continued support of programs. How can preventionists meet the demands of their employers and funders while conducting methodologically sound research? In particular, how long must researchers follow program participants before concluding that the problem of interest was truly prevented? Researchers have responded to these questions in two different ways: by assessing short-term outcomes that are expected to lead to the long-term results of interest and by studying the development of the disorder over the life course in order to pinpoint when follow-up should occur. These two approaches are described below.

PROXIMAL AND DISTAL OUTCOMES

One way in which prevention researchers have tried to limit the length of time necessary for follow-up is to assess **proximal outcomes** rather than **distal outcomes**. Program effectiveness is established by showing that the intervention reduces the risk behaviors that lead to the problem of interest (proximal outcomes) rather than preventing the problem itself (distal outcome). For example, researchers developing a substance abuse prevention program for first graders might assess post-intervention levels of poor achievement, aggression, or other precursors of substance use. Thus, assessments of program efficacy can occur when children are still in primary school, and researchers need not wait until middle school or high school to see if actual substance abuse rates were lowered (e.g., Ialongo, Werthamer, Kellam, Brown, Wang, & Lin, 1999).

A number of the interventions described earlier have relied on proximal outcomes. For example, implementers of high school transition programs have assessed academic achievement at the end of the year, rather than drop out rates three years later or unemployment in adulthood. Sometimes proximal outcomes are assessed in the interim between intervention and long-term follow-up. More often, proximal outcomes are assessed in lieu of long-term follow-up.

The relatively small number of intervention programs that do evaluate long-term outcomes speak to the dangers of relying only on proximal outcome data. Consider again Emory Cowen's well-researched

Primary Mental Health Project (PMHP). You will remember that PMHP targeted young children and was designed to prevent serious problems of adjustment in later life. In a long-term follow-up study, Cowen and his colleagues (1973) found that although the PMHP did reduce proximal outcomes, it did not succeed in preventing the problem of primary interest: serious maladjustment as indicated by treatment for psychological disorders at local clinics thirteen years after children's involvement in the program. Thus, the assessment of proximal outcomes can suggest that a program is promising but cannot replace long-term follow-up as a means of ensuring the program did indeed prevent the problem of central interest.

LIFE SPAN DEVELOPMENT AND PROBLEM DEVELOPMENT

Although long-term follow-up is necessary, knowledge about problem development can streamline research efforts by pinpointing exactly when long-term assessments should occur. An understanding of how problems develop over time and across the life span can help prevention researchers accomplish three important tasks: 1) identify the appropriate risk behaviors to target at particular ages and stages in problem development, 2) identify the most effective time to intervene, and 3) determine when long-term assessments will be most informative.

Julian Rappaport (1977) noted that early intervention takes two forms. It can either occur early in the life cycle, which generally means targeting infants or children, or it can occur early in the disease process. Intervening early in the disease process does not always mean intervening early in the life cycle. Researchers interested in the prevention of Alzheimer's disease, for example, would not necessarily target preschoolers. Both developmental knowledge and knowledge of **etiology** (i.e., how a condition or disorder develops over time) can help researchers decide whom to target, what outcomes to assess, and when to assess them.

Consider the importance of developmental knowledge. Preventionists need to understand the form disorders take at different ages in order to target interventions appropriately. Different behaviors mark risk at different developmental periods. It is developmentally normative for five- and six-year old boys to establish social dominance using physical aggression, but most children have developed more mature methods of interpersonal influence by the time they reach the age of eight or nine (Coie et al., 1993). Thus, physical aggression in six-year olds would not indicate a likelihood of later problems, but the same behavior in older children might signal risk.

Etiology also matters. Consider the interrelated factors of interpersonal communication, marital satisfaction, divorce, and domestic violence. How are these factors interrelated? Where should one intervene? Does marital distress disrupt communication patterns, or does poor communication lead to marital distress? Howard Markman (1991, cited in Coie et al., 1993) compared couples who received communication training with couples who did not and found that the trained couples interacted more positively and had a 50% lower divorce rate seven years later. Program participants also evidenced lower rates of marital violence. This suggests that marital communication is a cause of divorce and violence rather than the result of marital distress.

We need to know which behaviors occur first in a chain of problematic behaviors in order to intervene proactively. Knowledge of the timeline of the development of disorders also provides valuable information about when to assess outcomes.

Consider the different etiologies of depression and antisocial personality disorder presented by Ricardo Muñoz and his colleagues (1996). Fifty percent of people who develop depressive disorders have their first symptom by 25.8 years, and 50% meet the criteria for diagnosis by 38.8 years of age. In comparison to depressive disorders, antisocial disorders tend to appear at relatively early ages. Fifty percent of people who develop antisocial disorders evidence their first symptoms by 14.7 years of age and 50% are diagnosed by 25.0 years. Thus, an indicated preventive intervention might succeed in identifying people at risk for antisocial disorder during adolescence. Unlike those who develop antisocial disorders, most people prone to depression have not yet evidenced any symptoms by age fifteen. Thus, indicated prevention programs for depression could not identify people at risk until they reached adulthood. When could we best assess the efficacy of prevention programs? We might have some idea of a program's efficacy in preventing antisocial disorders by the time participants reach the age of 25, but at that age we would not yet know if a program prevented depression. To assess the efficacy of a depression prevention program, we would need to wait until participants passed the age of 38.

IATROGENESIS

Not only do researchers need to know when to assess outcomes, they also need to consider which outcomes to assess. As described earlier, risk factors can lead to a variety of problem behaviors, and so program efficacy might best be assessed by considering a number of outcomes associated with the risk factor(s) targeted. In addition, although the goal of prevention research is to document reductions in the prevalence and incidence of disorders, in some cases prevention programs may cause or exacerbate problems. Even well-meaning interventions can have negative repercussions. Raymond Lorion (1983) warned that assuming that interventions based in good intentions can have only positive or at worst neutral effects is both naïve and irresponsible. Thus researchers must assess negative as well as positive outcomes that could be associated with the intervention. The occurrence of unintended but deleterious effects is termed **iatrogenesis**.

LABELING, OVERREACTING, AND NET WIDENING

There are numerous sources of iatrogenesis. Perhaps the most frequently cited cause in prevention programming is labeling. In both selective and indicated prevention programs, program participants are often marked to themselves and to others as "in need of help." As labeling theory suggests, placing a person already evidencing vulnerability into a special program that defines them as at risk may create self-fulfilling prophesies.

In addition, the perception that a problem needs immediate, aggressive, and large-scale intervention can inspire reactionary programs and policies that do not help and potentially hurt. When people feel a compelling need to take action, the effects of these actions are not always considered carefully. Consider responses to the rash of school shootings in one community after another at the end of the twentieth century. These events were well covered in the media and led to the popular perception that school violence was epidemic. In fact, juveniles were three times as likely to be killed by an adult as by another juvenile, and during the same time period, lightning strikes killed twice as many children as gun violence in schools (Donohue, Schiraldi, & Zeidenberg, 1998). Nevertheless, the perceived need to act decisively led hundreds of schools nationwide to adopt zero tolerance policies in which *any* sign of violent intent was met by strict disciplinary action, often expulsion from school (e.g., Donohue, et al., 1998; Razzano, 2001). Zero tolerance led to the suspension of one eleven-year old for wielding a Tweety Bird key chain. In a New Jersey district, no children were suspended in the year prior to the zero-tolerance policy, while 50 children, mostly in kindergarten through third grade, were suspended in the two-weeks following the policy's adoption (Zernike, 2001). Such extreme policies often do more harm than good. In addition to problems associated with laebling, suspending and expelling youth increases their opportunities to engage in negative behaviors.

Another source of iatrogenesis is the **widening of the net**. When programs become available, more people may be identified as in need of services, whether they really need them or not. This increases dependence on service systems. Fear of net widening led Julian Rappaport and his colleagues (1985) to develop an intervention for juvenile offenders that targeted *only* those youth most likely to become repeat offenders. Minimal involvement in criminal behaviors is a normative part of adolescent development. Thus, programming for adolescents who committed only minor offenses brought youth who presented little or no risk for committing future crimes into the correctional system. Furthermore, involvement in correctional systems holds the risk of actually increasing the likelihood of future crime by bringing youth into contact with career criminals who could pass on crime techniques, provide criminal contacts, and reinforce antisocial values (Rappaport et al., 1985; Biglan & Taylor, 2000).

INSENSITIVITY TO CONTEXT

Inattention to context, including cultural context and marginalized status, may also interfere with program effectiveness and open the door to iatrogenesis. Preventionists might focus on problems that are not of primary concern to participants and therefore craft irrelevant programs. One intervention program offering prizes to Mexican American parents and children for improvements in school attendance failed because it did not understand the real reasons for absence—the need for youth to help support their families by working. Given the reality of their lives, two-cent candies and star stickers on a classroom chart did not constitute an adequate reinforcement for sustained behavior change (King, Cotler, & Patterson, 1975).

As Stevan Hobfoll (1998) put it, "male prostitutes do not risk their economic livelihoods to preserve self-esteem" (p. 139). One woman in a battered woman's shelter observed, "the staff come in here smelling of perfume and wanting me to talk about my feelings when I don't have a place to live with my kids" (Riger, 2001, p. 71).

Interventions that are insensitive to context not only risk irrelevance, they can cause harm as well. Is articulation of feelings the best priority with victims of domestic abuse? A relatively powerless person in an abusive relationship might suffer from a lack of voice, but interventions that succeed in helping people speak out without first ensuring that speech is safe can do more harm than good.

As yet another example, interventions that promote behavior changes in disenfranchised groups

"Thank God! A panel of experts!"

The Panel of Experts: Always ready to shed light on your problem. © The New Yorker Collection 1978 Brian Savage from cartoonbank.com. All Rights Reserved.

can leave program recipients marginal in two cultures (Dumas, Rollock, Prinz, Hops, & Blechman, 1999). If AIDS prevention programs convince individual program participants to practice safer sex, they may become alienated from their lovers, friends, family members, and their larger community if these important others do not affirm the importance of safer sex (Hobfoll, 1998). The resulting increase in isolation is not likely to improve the life circumstances of people at risk for AIDS, who may already suffer from social marginality. Interventions may increase the likelihood of succeeding and decrease the likelihood of alienating people from their sociocultural environment if they target people *within their social systems*.

Cultures define what is normal, socially acceptable, and valued (Dumas et al., 1999). Preventive interventions may seek to create behavior change by altering what behaviors are deemed acceptable by the social environment (e.g., Levine, 1998). This can be achieved by changing the social norms that prevail in the surrounding context or by relocating at risk people to new contexts where "better" norms prevail. Let's look at each of these approaches.

Attempts to change cultural norms are inherently risky and value laden. Decisions about "good" and "bad" norms and values are problematic. One might hope to bypass this inherently value-laden area by deciding simply to support those cultural norms that aid prevention efforts and counter norms that exacerbate the problem of interest. Such an overly simplistic approach may open the door to iatrogenesis, even as the program achieves its goals.

Blanca Ortiz-Torres, Irma Serrano-García, and Nélida Torres-Burgos (2000) described cultural norms relevant to HIV/AIDS prevention efforts with Puerto Rican and Dominican women. The researchers identified several norms that hindered the practice of safe sex, including the following beliefs: women should not speak about sexuality; reproduction-linked sexual practices are more moral than other practices; pleasurable and complete sexual relations require penetration; and women need to please their male sexual partners. The researchers also found norms that facilitated the practice of safer sex, such as the beliefs that abstinence and virginity are moral choices, women should not be promiscuous, and women need to care for themselves in order to care for others.

The authors noted that decisions to reinforce risk-protective norms and discourage risk-promoting norms are complicated by two factors. First, norms are contradictory. Women cannot retain their virginity *and* please their partners sexually. Second and perhaps more importantly, these norms have meaning within a larger value system that community psychologists may not endorse. Is it ethical for researchers and practitioners who believe in the equality of all people to frame interventions within value systems that promote such double standards as the belief that only women should be virgins and that the man's sexual pleasure matters more than the woman's?

Changing the goals that prevail within a social system can be ethically questionable and also very difficult. A second approach to changing prevailing norms is to remove at risk people from high-risk environments. Thus, the severing of social ties is the explicit goal. As a recent example, problematic adolescents may be removed from their family and peer groups and sent to "camps" or wilderness survival schools where an entirely different code of conduct is required. Such "shock" strategies may enjoy political and popular support but do not have demonstrated effectiveness (e.g., Portwood, 2001). Even if they lead to improvements in behavior within the new setting, these improvements are not often maintained after the program ends and participants return to environments that support the prior set of norms.

Furthermore, social values taint our visions of which settings promote "better" norms. In the latter half of the nineteenth century, the federal government of the United States adopted the view that Indians could best be incorporated into White society by removing Indian children from their families and communities and teaching them in off-reservation boarding schools hundreds or thousands of miles away. This form of "child-saving" was believed to be in the best interest of the Indian children because the weaker Indian society was seen as doomed to extinction. Attempts to "civilize" Indian children, which is to say to inculcate them into Western

Tom Torlino (Navajo) as he appeared 1) upon arrival to the Carlisle Indian School October 21, 1882, and 2) three years later. *Photo courtesy of the Cumberland County Historical Society, Carlisle, PA.*

norms, often brought them into the homes of White families. Army Officer Richard Pratt, a key proponent of off-reservations schools wrote

> "I believe if we took one of those Indians—a little papoose from his mother's back, always looking backward—into our families, face it the other way, and keep it under our care and training until grown, it would then be Anglo-Saxon in spirit and American in all its qualities" (quoted in DeJong, 1993, p. 110).

This is yet another example of how planned behavior changes in disenfranchised groups can leave people marginal in two cultures (Dumas et al., 1999).

ENSURING PROGRAM INTEGRITY

Prevention is an inherently value-laden endeavor because it requires assessments of what constitutes desirable behaviors and how best to promote such behaviors. Unintended negative consequences often occur. One important mechanisms for ensuring both the efficacy and integrity of prevention programming is the use of rigorous evaluations.

THE IMPERATIVE OF EVALUATION

The meta-analyses conducted by Durlak and Wells (1997a, 1998) found little evidence of iatrogenesis. Only 9 of 177 primary prevention programs and 7 of 130 secondary prevention programs yielded negative effects. Furthermore, the magnitude of these effects was small. Although the lack of evidence of iatrogenesis could mean that prevention programs do little harm, it could also mean that study authors do not always look for evidence of iatrogenesis as thoroughly as they mght. The McCord Study (see the Classic Research box) makes clear that the possibility of negative consequences must be taken seriously by all preventionists.

ETHICAL GUIDELINES

Prevention scholars have identified several ethical responsibilities for preventionists, which are summarized in the following list.

1. The first ethical responsibility accounts for the possibility of iatrogenesis. In accordance

📑 CLASSIC RESEARCH

The McCord Study
The Need for Evaluation

No study has highlighted the importance of program evaluation more clearly than the McCord study. In the late 1930s, an imaginative and exciting prevention program was designed to reduce the incidence of juvenile delinquency in young boys. It was a large-scale, comprehensive, and carefully designed intervention (McCord,1978; McCord & McCord, 1969; Powers & Witmer, 1972). Schools, welfare agencies, churches, and the police recommended "difficult" and "average" youngsters between the ages of 5 and 13 to take part in the program. These children were randomly assigned to either a control or intervention group. Participants in the intervention group were visited by counselors twice each month and were offered a variety of services. Some youth obtained academic tutoring, some received medical and psychiatric attention, some participated in summer camps, and some enrolled in community programs, such as the Boy Scouts.

In a 30-year follow-up, almost all of the original participants were located, and the majority agreed to participate in the study. Results showed that most of the men who had taken part in the program—about two-thirds—reported feeling favorably about their participation, and many recounted fond memories of their counselors. Respondents wrote of being diverted from a life of crime and "put on the right road" (McCord, 1978, p. 287) Such was the self-report data. But the evaluators did not rely solely on what participants said. They sought additional evidence of the program's effectiveness by examining official records, such as those kept by the Crime Prevention Bureau.

Here's where the plot thickens. Men who had been in the program were compared to similar men who had not been in the program along 57 dimensions. Seven of these comparisons showed significant differences between the two groups of men and *every comparison favored the men who had **not** been part of the program.* Men who had taken part in the intervention were more likely to:

- commit two or more crimes;
- abuse alcohol;
- become seriously mentally ill;
- die at an earlier age;
- suffer from stress-related illnesses;
- work in less prestigious occupations; and
- find their work unsatisfying.

The probability that all seven significant comparisons would favor the control group by chance is less than 1 in 10,000! (McCord, 1978).

These results are certainly disturbing. Well-intentioned people used the best knowledge available at the time to design and implement a thoughtful and comprehensive prevention program. Not only was the program ineffective, it seems to have had quite serious unintended negative effects.

What can one conclude from the McCord study? One conclusion is that researchers must not rely solely on self-report data. The data obtained from official records stand in stark contrast to the picture that would have emerged had the evaluators relied only on participants' subjective assessments of the program. Self-report data, especially data on client satisfaction, may be the easiest and most obvious way of evaluating interventions, but it does not tell the whole story. A second conclusion to be drawn from the McCord study is that preventionists must adhere to the ethical imperative of carefully evaluating program effects—both negative and positive.

with the Hippocratic oath, preventionists must do no harm. Even well-intentioned and well-designed prevention programs can have negative consequences, and it is incumbent on researchers to account for this possibility in their evaluations. As an additional safeguard, preventionists should intrude as little as possible into those aspects of the program recipients' lives that are not problematic.

2. Program should not be designed for the preventionist's gain. The primary purpose of preventive intervention is to improve the lives of others. The preventionist's own career advancement matters, but threats to pet theories, a reduced chance of publishing, possible loss of funding, and other potential difficulties cannot stand in the way of careful program development, rigorous evaluation, and proper dissemination of results.

3. Prevention programs should be piloted in small-scale studies to ensure their effectiveness before expanding. Pilot testing allows researchers to assess the efficacy of the program, address unforeseen problems, determine whether iatrogenesis has occurred, and estimate program costs.

4. Program participants should be treated with respect and should be active participants in planning, implementing, and evaluating the prevention effort. This means program participants should help define the problem to be prevented, identify program goals, agree on the means for achieving those goals, and assist in gathering and interpreting information on the program. Ownership on the part of program participants and stakeholders is not only an ethical responsibility, it also promotes the development of context-sensitive and effective interventions, and aids in the adoption of these programs.

5. Program planners, participants, and other involved people are entitled to professional courtesies. In particular, confidentiality must be maintained. This is essential if the program is to be developed, run, and evaluated honestly.

6. Informed consent should be obtained before implementation of the program. Informed consent is not always feasible, especially in large-scale efforts. Few of us were consulted about the fluoride in our water or antismoking billboards on our commuting routes. Nevertheless, it is incumbent on the researcher to acknowledge the importance of informed consent and live up to this ethical requirement to the greatest extent possible.

7. The prevention program should promote equity and justice. Programs require sensitivity to cultural differences and the dynamics of oppression. A long-term vision will help program planners to assess the degree to which the program contributes to positive and fundamental social change.

8. The preventionist is accountable for the impact of the program and must resolve any problems that result, intended or not.

Evaluation research is critical. It helps preventionists to identify any unintended consequences of the program. As described in the next section, it also provides evidence of which programs work with whom and under what circumstances.

PROGRAM POPULARITY AND EFFICACY

More than a decade ago, N. Dickon Reppucci and Jeffrey Haugaard (1989) emphasized the importance of evaluating the school-based sexual abuse prevention programs that were popular at the time. They feared that these programs did little good and might inflict harm, such as undue fear and worry in young children and negative influences on their trusting relationships with adults. Furthermore, a sense of accomplishment accompanies the establishment of *any* intervention, which reduces the perceived need to act. If the programs had no impact (or a negative impact), the perception that the problem was being addressed when it was not would mean a reduced likelihood of improving the situation for abused children (Reppucci & Haugaard, 1989; Reppucci et al., 1999).

Popular and political support for prevention programs do not depend on evidence of efficacy. Boot camps for juveniles, zero-tolerance school violence policies, and school-based sexual abuse programs have all enjoyed widespread support without evidence of program efficacy. The lack of relationship between popularity and efficacy is nowhere more apparent than in the example of DARE (Drug Abuse Resistance Education). DARE is a prevention program begun by the Los Angeles Police Department in 1983. Children in late elementary school receive 17 one-hour sessions designed to keep them from using drugs, tobacco and alcohol (Ennett, Tobler, Ringwalt, Flewelling, 1994). The DARE curriculum is presented by uniformed police officers who have undergone 80 hours of specialized training at a cost of more than $2,000 per officer (Wysong, Aniskiewicz, & Wright, 1994).

DARE's popularity skyrocketed after President Reagan declared his "War on Drugs" in 1986. In 1990 DARE programs were in place in more than 3,000 communities in all 50 states and reached an estimated 20 million students (Wysong et al., 1994). As of February 1994, DARE existed in at least half the public schools in the U.S. (Ennett et al., 1994), and the nationwide expenditures for DARE reached approximately $700 million per year (Wysong et al., 1994).

This price-tag has not seemed prohibitive, however; an interrelated network of organizational ties link DARE programs to local, state, and federal funding sources, as well as to private corporations. Police departments, law enforcement agencies, and politicians at every level of government have lobbied in support of the program. Congressional proposals have been crafted to earmark government funds for DARE, and corporate sponsors emerged—small local businesses and huge conglomerates such as McDonald's, Kentucky Fried Chicken, and Security Pacific National Bank. The extent of support for DARE became clear on September 10, 1992, the day U.S. Congress and former President George S. Bush designated as National DARE Day (Wysong et al., 1994).

It was into this context that reports of DARE's ineffectiveness emerged. In the early 1990s, numerous research studies and meta-analyses concluded that DARE had, at best, only a very small and very short-term effect on drug use (Ennett et al., 1994; Lynam, Milich, Zimmerman, Novak, Logan, Martin, Leukefeld, Clayton, 1999; Wysong et al., 1994). Other drug prevention programs existed that were more cost-effective and yielded better results.

Program evaluation often occurs in a political atmosphere. Since the 1960s, the federal government has slashed funding for most social programs but not Head Start, and so program evaluators face the challenge of providing accurate (and sometimes unfavorable) evaluation information without challenging the congressional faith and support that make early education programs possible (Hauser-Cram, Warfield, Upshur, & Weisner, 2000).

After about a decade of debate about the merits of studies that showed DARE to be ineffective (which DARE discounted) and about the worthiness of DARE as an intervention strategy (which evaluators questioned), common ground emerged. The widespread support and far-reaching influence of DARE constituted an important foundation for prevention programming, a foundation on which researchers and scientists could help to build an effective program. DARE, in turn, has heeded calls to base programming on sound research and evaluate program efficacy. In the twenty-first century, DARE. They have developed several principles of effectiveness, such as:

- Grounds activities in a thorough review of available data on drug and violence problems in the local community;
- Establishes local or regional advisory councils, on which community representatives serve, to set program goals and determine activities necessary to meet those goals;
- Designs activities based on research into the effectiveness of the strategies used in preventing or reducing drug use, violence, or disruptive behavior
- Conducts periodic program evaluations to determine success in meeting goals and to improve program efficacy. (DARE, No date)

⌘ Creating Long-Lasting and Widespread Change: From Demonstration to Adoption

The ultimate goal of prevention programs is to reduce problems and enhance wellness. Although prevention science has made great strides in the past few decades with regard to conceptualizing prevention, targeting efforts, and assessing outcomes, these strides have not translated into substantial improvements in health. Rates of mental disorders, substance abuse, violence, poverty, and other indicators of individual and community maladjustment remain high (e.g., Fleming, 1996; Weissberg, Gullotta, Hampton, Ryan, & Adams, 1997). One reason why innovative and effective prevention programs have not led to widespread improvements in health is that preventionists have not ensured that successful trial programs continue and are adopted in other settings (e.g., Schorr, 1997).

Many prevention programs begin as **demonstration projects.** A demonstration project is an intervention designed, implemented, and researched in the hope of developing an effective program that can be maintained in the original setting and replicated in other locales. In order to extend the reach of successful demonstration projects, researchers must understand the characteristics of programs, people, and organization that lead to program adoption. There are numerous challenges that must be surmounted in "scaling up" from small successes (Schorr, 1997, p. xiv).

George Fairweather was one of the first researchers dedicated to identifying the factors that promote the adoption of innovative programs. His active efforts contrast with the more common "publish and hope" approach (Stolz, 1984) in which prevention researchers seek to disseminate programs by describing their successes in esoteric journals that community-based professionals rarely read (Elias, 1997). Prevention programs will have a better chance of improving people's lives if researchers

attend to the numerous factors that affect the adoption of prevention programs within communities and then use these findings to encourage program adoption.

ATTENDING TO CONTEXT

A review of the literature on social support interventions concluded that few interventions document any success, and successes that do occur are generally short-lived (Lakey & Lutz, 1996). The reviewers observed that most interventions train staff and volunteers to provide support to individuals, which may help people during a crisis, but this approach does not translate into enduring changes in participants' social support networks. They argued that improvements would not continue beyond the lifetime of the program unless changes transpired in the natural environment of program participants. Maurice Elias (1997) echoed this concern in calling for preventionists to challenge the prevailing view of people-as-program-recipients, and work to create enduring changes in both people *and* their natural settings.

Prevention programs often target individuals without attending to their social context. Reppucci and his colleagues (1999) warned that prevention programs disappoint if they fail to consider the surrounding community (see also Weissberg, Caplan, & Harwood, 1991). As an example, they cited research showing that smoking cessation programs for adolescents are more effective when they target the environmental context; cigarette-seller behavior, for example, or tobacco industry advertising, rather than the teens themselves.

Attention to natural settings also means tailoring interventions to fit the microsystems in which they occur: families, schools, workplaces, neighborhoods. This was evident in a study of successful program implementation within high-risk (i.e., low-income) schools. The researchers found several important preconditions for program adoption. Prevention programs that took hold were consistent with the goals and missions of the school and became part of the culture of the school as evidenced by incorporation of prevention activities into the schools ongoing practices (Gager & Elias, 1997).

OVERCOMING RESISTANCE TO CHANGE

Issues involved in moving from program demonstration to adoption have been studied under the terms "diffusion of innovation" (e.g., Rogers, 1983) or "dissemination of innovation" (e.g., Mayer & Davidson, 2000). These terms emphasize the notion that new programs represent changes in the status quo, and change inspires resistance. Resistance is more likely when individuals affected by the change do not have enough information about what is entailed, experience a lack of control, fear losing influence over or status within the setting, do not see personal benefits in changing, already feel overloaded by existing demands, perceive the change as a criticism of their previous efforts, fear being unable to handle the new responsibilities, or expect the change will disrupt their routines (K. Ryan, 1993). Certainly prevention programmers can work to counter these individual-level sources of resistance. In addition, they can try to make the context more conducive to change.

The settings in which people work shape individual responses to change. Some organizational forms support innovation. "Organic" organizations, which have flexible structures and decentralized decision-making processes, may adopt new programs and strategies more easily than "mechanistic" organizations, which are formal and hierarchical (Mayer & Davidson, 2000).

In addition, organizational support for specific changes also matters. This was well illustrated in a recent study by Pennie Foster-Fishman and her colleagues (1999). They surveyed 186 personnel in 32 human service agencies with regard to two reform movements: the increasing push toward interagency cooperation and the growing emphasis on strength-based service delivery (Foster-Fishman,

Salem, Allen, & Fahrbach, 1999). The providers' receptivity to change depended on support for reforms in their host agency (e.g., perceptions of the director's agenda), as well as the larger social context (e.g., interagency views on the reform movements, funder mandates). Receptivity to change at any level of analysis depends on perceptions of support for that change at other levels. The proliferation of DARE programs can be attributed, in large part, to the cooperation of community leaders, politicians, corporate sponsors, and governmental agencies from the local to federal levels.

Preventionists can increase the likelihood of adoption by ensuring (or building) community support before implementation. For example, Robert Slavin has widely disseminated his school-based *Success for All* program. This program operates on the principles that 1) learning problems can be prevented by using the best available classroom strategies with the support of parents (primary prevention) and 2) by implementing immediate and intensive corrective interventions when learning problems appear (secondary prevention). Slavin only implements this program when 80% of a school faculty agrees to invite it into the school (reported in Schorr, 1997). The more broad-based the support, the better the chances of program adoption.

Diplomacy is needed in promoting change efforts. People and systems resist new programs if they are seen as requiring fundamental change. Maurice Elias (1997) warned that innovative agendas are not best advanced through social change rhetoric. He proposed that the language of preventionists in the 1960s and 1970s, which emphasized ending social ills by disrupting the existing social order, might work against the adoption of innovation in more recent times. Preventionists might promote new programs as efforts to help settings become more effective rather than attempts to subvert the status quo. Most people and systems strive to adapt incoming information to fit within existing structures (**assimilation**) rather than using that information as an impetus to change the structures (**accommodation**).

The likelihood of program adoption increases when preventionists package programs in appealing ways. Innovations are more accepted when potential adopters clearly see the relative advantages of the new program, view the intervention as easy to implement, appreciate the cost savings, easily observe the key features of the intervention, and can easily understand the program and describe it to others (Mayer & Davidson, 2000).

MANIFEST VERSUS TRUE ADOPTION

Convincing service systems to adopt programs is only part of the challenge. Equally important is ensuring that the programs remain true to the demonstration project. Julian Rappaport, Edward Seidman, and William Davidson (1985) distinguished **manifest** and **true program adoption**. They developed an indicated prevention program targeting adolescents on the brink of involvement with the legal system. Their program was adopted by the setting and continued after the demonstration ended, but the program was not adopted as intended. It soon began to serve adolescents who were only superficially involved in criminal activities—a population purposely *not* targeted in the program as initially conceived and evaluated. Thus, true adoption did not occur.

Preventionists need to help program adopters understand and embrace the key tenets of programs. Some correspondence among critical features of the program across sites is necessary to maintain the integrity of the program and to ensure the relevance of the evaluation data. This is not to say that prevention programs should be identical across settings. Programs are more effective and their adoption more likely if participants and service deliverers have ownership of the project and adapt the program to the local culture. Consequently, researchers must clearly identify **core features** of the program, that is to say crucial and defining program elements, and **adaptive features**, program characteristics that may be altered to meet the needs of the local culture (Elias, 1997; Schorr, 1997; Valente & Dodge, 1997)

ACCOUNTING FOR "OPERATOR DEPENDENCE"

Even when settings agree to adopt a program, understand the core features, and work to fit the program into the local culture, success is not guaranteed. Peter Rossi (1978) argued that model programs often do not become enduring programs because researchers fail to consider the extent to which programs are "operator-dependent."

Researchers who implement demonstration programs differ from the community-based professionals who adopt and sustain programs in important ways (Kendall & Southam-Gerow, 1995). Areas of difference include theoretical perspectives, training, rewards for prevention work, and demands on time. A researcher implementing a demonstration project has generally received special funds for materials, training, consultation, and ongoing evaluation—luxuries that service delivery settings cannot always afford (Elias, 1997). In addition, demonstration programs benefit from the excitement of novelty that may occur when a new program is developed (see S. Sarason, 1972). For these reasons, the context of demonstration often differs substantially from the context of adoption.

Another important aspect of operator dependence that cannot be programmed is leadership. Not all sites have inspiring leaders who are willing and able to ensure program success by networking with diverse people and groups, fostering cooperation, building coalitions, and mobilizing varied resources (Elias, 1997; Reppucci et al., 1999; Schorr, 1997; see also S. Sarason, 1972 for discussion of the dynamics of leadership). Individuals with unique qualities carry out interventions within particular organizational settings.

I recently had lunch with a colleague from Great Britain who told me that in England, the word "program" does not exist as it does in the United States. The notion that one can export a prepackaged, presumably universal set of operating instructions from one setting to another setting that has a completely different history, set of values, staff, and community niche would make little sense. Prevention programs today less often rely on one-size-fits-all implementation "kits" (RMC Research Corporation, 1995), but they continue to be conceived as discrete packages that exist apart from a social context. A more holistic view of prevention programs as a process rather than a package might foster the dissemination of innovation and ultimately lead to more widespread and long-lasting improvements in individual and community health.

⌘ The Promise of Community Psychology: Planning for Synergy

The NIMH and IOM Reports signaled the growing acceptance of prevention as a legitimate research and intervention activity whose potential has not yet been realized. These reports both cited the need to attend to program setting, but neither report centered on the dynamics of community context. In these reports, as in most prevention studies, ecological perspectives help explain findings, but they are not the basis for developing programs, do not shape research methodologies, and do not inform evaluations (e.g., Hobfoll, 1998). Community psychologists may contribute to the larger field of prevention by underscoring the importance of attending to social context at *all* phases of intervention.

Consider, for example, the issue of random assignment. Prevention researchers frequently cite the need for strict randomization (e.g., Cowen, 1983; Mrazek & Haggerty, 1994). Often this means that a pool of potential program recipients is identified, and individuals are randomly assigned into treatment and control conditions. Preventive interventions may have a greater chance of success, however, if they target entire cohorts of people and the settings in which they reside, rather than individuals in isolation. Murray Levine (1998) observed that an experimental approach that requires "random assignment of individuals within a cohort to treatment conditions may dilute if not destroy the impact of the intervention" (p. 192).

The interactions among program participants can lead to synergistic effects that enhance prevention agendas. **Synergism** means that when discrete agents act in cooperation, the effects are not simply additive, but multiplicative—the whole is greater than the sum of its parts. A number of preventive interventions described in this chapter try to capitalize on this synergism. Researchers in the Stanford Heart Disease Prevention Program (see the Community Intervention box) crafted media messages with the explicit goal of stimulating conversations among community members. They also invited high-risk participants to attend group workshops with their spouses. These efforts support the view that when interventions target people within their social contexts, synergism becomes possible. Similarly, one likely reason for the success of the STEP program described earlier is that it targeted an entire cohort of youth and teachers, that is to say the social system of the youth (Barrera & Prelow, 2000). Thus, group norms could emerge that reinforced the goals of the program. Indeed, the synergistic effects of community not only shape the behavior of community members, they also can have radiating effects on people outside that system. Research suggests that women whose social network promotes safer sex not only get tested for AIDS more often, but their male partners are also more likely to use condoms (Ortiz-Torres, Serrano-García, & Torres-Burgos, 2000).

Preventive approaches that capitalize on synergism are more the exception than the rule. Indeed, popular conceptualizations of prevention frame synergy as an impediment to methodological rigor. Ernest Valente and Kenneth Dodge (1997) conveyed this perspective when they characterized interventions in the context of existing classrooms and school as entailing a "major problem." They held that "[r]andom assignment of children within a classroom (or school) to intervention versus control conditions could lead to contamination of the control group children, because they might indirectly benefit from intervention with the teacher or peers" (pp. 201–202). From a community perspective, synergism is not seen as a "problem," but a gift to preventionists. If community synergy "contaminates" our research, we need to find new ways to do research.

Not only do we fail to account for the synergistic potential of communities in designing programs, we also fail to account for it when documenting program impact. Edison Trickett (1997) observed that the ecological impact of prevention programs is rarely assessed as outcomes are almost exclusively measured at the individual level. In response to this criticism, Durak and Wells (1997b) noted that 10% of the interventions they assessed in their meta-analysis of primary prevention programs did include indices of ecological impact that *could have* been evaluated. Among these indices were changes in parent and teacher attitudes, changes in parent and teacher interactions with children, and effects of the intervention on the social climate of the school.

The recognition that prevention effects radiate through social systems shifts our thinking about how to measure program effectiveness. A program that convinces each participant to reduce his or her use of illegal substances may be effective, but a program that does this and also inspires the individuals to confront the social norms that promote substance abuse in their microsystems may be more effective. And a program that does all this, and helps program participants (and all their friends) recognize and confront the larger social conditions that impact substance abuse (e.g., community poverty, drug laws) could be a really powerful prevention program.

Synergism occurs not only among people in face-to-face interaction, but also across different levels of analysis. This led Ed Seidman (1987) to advocate mesosystem-level preventive interventions—interventions aimed at connections among systems. The recent interest in community coalitions as a base for prevention activities offers an opportunity to study synergistic effects across systems. In community coalitions, groups of individuals from diverse organizations and community constituencies work together toward a common goal (Feighery & Rogers, 1989). Community coalitions generally target factors at multiple levels and across multiple groups (e.g., Butterfoss, Goodman, & Wandersman, 1996,

Mitchell, Stevenson, & Florin, 1996). The Healthy Communities movement is one example.

As another example, consider the ecologically oriented prevention initiatives supported by the National Center on Child Abuse and Neglect (reported by Earls, McGuire, & Shay, 1994). Although goal of the initiatives was to prevent child abuse and neglect, it did not focus on parents or families in isolation, but on system relationships within the broader community. Intervention efforts concentrated on building caring communities for families by providing families with a network of services, such as food pantries, home health visitors, literacy training, respite care, and mutual-help opportunities. Interventions directed to entire communities require assessment methods that do not rely solely on individual-level outcomes. New methods must become more complex to account for changes at multiple levels of analysis (Goodman, Wandersman, Chinman, Imm, & Morrissey, 1996).

Long-term multipronged interventions that converge around important goals can have a broad social impact (Levine, 1998). Leonard Jason (1998) incorporated the lessons learned in the Stanford Heart Disease Prevention Program (Maccoby & Alexander, 1979; Farqhar, 1991) into new media-based interventions. The creative multilevel interventions he devised used various voluntary associations, community groups, and for-profit agencies, as well as the media. One such program sought to reduce the incidence of smoking among African-American adolescents in Chicago. The Board of Education supplied an antismoking curriculum to 472 elementary schools. At the same time, a local newspaper with a large African American readership agreed to publish an antismoking series in their weekly children's page. A radio station popular among African American listeners ran a series of smoking prevention public service messages and aired a call-in talk show to help parents discuss smoking with their children. The radio station also played the five winning entries of a smoking prevention rap contest, and the overall winner appeared as a guest DJ. The owners of several local billboards agreed to display the winners of a smoking prevention poster contest. The contest winners also received a certificate and prizes for their schools at a special assembly. This multifaceted intervention, which targeted individuals-within-contexts, led to a decrease in student use of tobacco *and* in family use of cigarettes, alcohol, and marijuana.

Jason's interventions, like the Stanford heart disease interventions, drew on the notion of synergy (see also Schooler, Flora, & Farquhar, 1993). As Nathan Maccoby and Janet Alexander (1979) stated early in the development of the Stanford Heart Disease Prevention Program, "We tentatively attribute much of the success of the community education campaigns to the synergistic interaction of multiple educational inputs and to interpersonal communication stimulated by application of these inputs in a community setting" (p. 81). When interventions target entire groups of individuals and the systems where they reside, synergistic effects can ensure that the intervention as a whole is more than the sum of its parts.

Action Agenda

Community Readiness for Prevention

Assess your community's readiness to tackle a problem of interest to you. Clip newspaper articles. Talk to community leaders. Assess the quantity and quality of existing programs. You can use Table 13.4 as a starting point, or you might ask knowledgeable community leaders to complete the Community Key Leader Survey, devised by Robert Goodman and Abraham Wandersman, that appears on the website of the Western Region Center for Application of Preventive Technologies (*http://www. open.org/~westcapt/survey.html*) (see also Goodman et al., 1996). Additional tools are available at the Center for Substance Abuse Prevention web page (*http://www. preventiondss.org/*).

After deciding where on the scale of community readiness your community lies with regard to a particular problem, devise an intervention that you believe would increase community readiness. What would be a first step in implementing your intervention?

Taking the McCord Study Seriously

One understandable reaction to the McCord study is an attempt to attribute the findings of iatrogenesis to methodological problems—their control group was not well chosen, the outcomes assessed were not appropriate, and so on. The ethical principle of doing no harm requires, however, that preventionists take seriously the possibility that an intervention may well have unintended negative side effects. Choose a prevention study (perhaps one from *14 Ounces of Prevention*, Price et al., 1988) and list, individually or in groups, all the possible negative outcomes that *might* result. How would you assess these possible effects? What actions do you think you would be ethically obligated to take should these negative outcomes occur?

Norms, Values, and Prevention

Consider a problem that exists in a context with which you are familiar (e.g., smoking in your high school peer group, ethnic group tensions at your college, high employee turnover at your workplace). What norms that exist within these contexts help perpetuate the problem? Are there also norms that have, or potentially could have, a preventive effect? Can you think of interventions that would address the relevant norms (either changing norms that perpetuate the problem or strengthening norms that prevent it)? If you decided to implement such an intervention, what would be a first step, and what would be the ethical implications of that step?

 **Key Terms**

adaptive features

attributable risk

community readiness

core features

demonstration project

distal outcomes

etiology

iatrogenesis

incidence

indicated, selective

IOM report

manifest program adoption

meta-analysis

precipitating factors

predisposing factors

prevalence

preventive intervention research cycle

primary prevention

protective factors

proximal outcomes

risk factors

secondary prevention

synergism

tertiary prevention

true program adoption

universal prevention

widening of the net

Empowerment

⌘ Introduction

The Dudley Street neighborhood lies just two miles from downtown Boston. In the early 1980s, a downtown high-rise overlooking the neighborhood would have glimpsed a landscape of urban blight. Dudley Street was a patchwork of vacant lots, burned-out office building, and abandoned houses. Rusting cars and litter dotted the pothole-ridden streets. Decades of disinvestment, redlining,[1] abandonment, and arson-for-profit had turned a thriving commercial and residential district into a virtual wasteland (Medoff & Sklar, 1994; Negri, 2000). The diverse denizens of Dudley Street, African Americans, Latinos and Latinas, Cape Verdeans, and Euro-Americans, were united primarily in their despair.

[1]Redlining is the discriminatory practice, once popular among financial institutions, of identifying the borders of low-income minority communities and refusing to do business with residents in those areas.

Community Psychology: Guiding Principles and Orienting Concepts by Jennifer Kofkin Rudkin

Such was the view of Dudley Street in the early 1980s. In 1984 residents formed the Dudley Street Neighborhood Initiative (DSNI) and determined to turn the dilapidated neighborhood into the community of their dreams. Members worked together to create a shared neighborhood vision that coalesced around the image of an urban village. A village is a wellspring fed by the communal energy of the villagers, and the villagers, in turn, draw sustenance from the well. A village provides food, goods and services, employment, opportunities for socialization, and recreational activities (DSNI, No Date a). The residents' shared vision of an urban village guided community organizing and development on Dudley Street.

Less than twenty years later, DSNI accomplishments inspire awe. About 13% of the community's 24,000 residents belong to this vibrant voluntary organization, and countless resident-driven plans have been realized in cooperation with local businesses, banks, nonprofit organizations, and religious groups, with supplemental assistance from government agencies and foundations (notably the Riley Foundation, which catalyzed the neighborhood revitalization). Since 1984, 600 of the 1300 vacant lots have been converted to affordable homes and common spaces, including community gardens, greenhouses, parks, playgrounds, and a town commons. Three hundred new homes have been built, and another 300 renovated. Dudley Street has cleaned up its streets, closed hazardous and illegal trash transfer centers, rehabilitated parks, established low-income and cooperative housing, restored rail service, formed daycare networks, founded a high school, begun youth recreation programs, opened a community center, and organized multicultural festivals (DSNI, No Date b).

The list of accomplishments only begins to give a sense of the urban village. Let's look at life on Dudley Street more closely. It is an innovation-embracing neighborhood that pursues community self-sufficiency and resident inter-reliance. Imagine a three-acre farm in the heart of an urban neighborhood! The fruit and vegetable farm, community gardens, and a local fish farm provide fresh food year round. This food is sold in small grocery stores

that are walking distance from every home. No one needs a car on Dudley Street because almost everything is within walking distance. Residents stroll to drug stores, newsstands, tailors, dentists, beauty parlors, coffee shops, hardware stores, parks, concerts, and the authentic ethnic restaurants that enjoy widespread popularity—requests for Gladys' Splendid Sofritos have come from as far away as Puerto Rico. Dudley Street continues to look forward. The most recently built homes are solar powered and superinsulated (as well as affordable), virtually eliminating the need for gas, oil, and electric heat. Residents are currently assessing the feasibility of a stand-alone wastewater treatment system that would use aquatic plants and animals to treat sewage at a fraction of the cost of traditional systems (DSNI, No Date a).

The transformation of Dudley Street exemplifies empowerment. Demoralized residents of a devastated and largely abandoned neighborhood came together to create an urban village so vital and attractive that it now counts as one of Boston's major tourist attractions (DSNI, No Date a). People from around the world come to enjoy Dudley Street's culturally diverse food, specialty shops, music, theater, and festivals. How did this happen? Can it happen anywhere? How do the experiences on Dudley Street inform the theory, research, and practice of community psychology? Can community psychologists help bring similar transformations to other neighborhoods? Can the lessons and insights of Dudley Street guide change efforts on an even larger scale? These are some of the questions addressed in this chapter.

⌘ Brief History

The concept of empowerment has its roots in the 1960s. Empowerment was the goal of freedom fighters who turned their shared sense of identity and common understanding of the sociopolitical roots of their oppression into mandates for social change (Prilleltensky, 1998; Trickett, 1994). The ideology of empowerment figured prominently in the influential writings of Saul Alinsky (1971) and Paulo Freire (1970/1992). These two activists described how change agents (community organizers and educators, respectively) could join forces with members of disenfranchised communities to transform social relationships and redistribute social power (e.g., Shefner-Rogers, Rao, Rogers, & Wayangankar, 1998; Strawn, 1994). The term "empowerment" was not used to describe such activities until the mid-1970s, however.

Barbara Bryant Solomon (1976) was one of the first to articulate a theory of empowerment. She contended that the "devaluation" of African Americans in U.S. society resulted in widespread feelings of powerlessness among Black people in Black communities. She proposed empowerment as an antidote to the negative valuation—a way for social workers to engage African American clients and communities in efforts to reconstitute their lives. At about the same time, Peter Berger and Richard Neuhaus (1977) also used this new term and proposed that people become empowered through **mediating structures**—the systems that stand between the large impersonal institutions of public life and the private lives of individuals. Berger and Neuhaus posited that mediating structures, especially neighborhoods, families, churches, and voluntary associations play a vital role in a democratic society. They are expressions of people's collective needs and values and the means to citizen empowerment. Consequently, Berger and Neuhaus argued that public policy should actively support mediating structures, not undercut them, and utilize these structures to realize social goals.

A few years after this early work on empowerment in social work and public policy, Julian Rappaport (1981) outlined the relevance of the concept to community psychology. He noted that empowerment focuses on people's inherent strengths and directs attention to social change. Rappaport (1981, 1987; Wiley & Rappaport, 2000) asserted that community psychology's current orienting concept (prevention) failed to promote either of these central values of the field.

According to Rappaport, *prevention* evoked all the wrong symbols, images, and meta-messages.

Prevention highlights dysfunction—it targets at-risk people in order to save them from themselves. It focuses on what is currently going or soon will go wrong rather than on what is going right. It reinforces traditional models of unidimensional helping in which experts develop, package, operate, disseminate, and generally control interventions. Furthermore, despite its debt to public health, prevention seeks to improve *individual* mental health and pays insufficient attention to social contexts.

Empowerment, Rappaport argued, emphasizes strengths. It attempts to build competencies rather than correct deficiencies. It also suggests new paradigms of helping. Professionals are not distant experts but collaborators who work side by side with community members in efforts to change their social worlds. Rappaport asserted that empowerment promoted a new image of people as citizens with rights and choices that balanced the dominant images of people as needy. Members of helping professions too often viewed poor, physically disabled, mentally ill, retarded, elderly, and other marginalized people as child-like and dependent on professionals for socialization, training, and skill development. He warned that such a perspective blinded us to more productive ways of helping.

Several years after his initial treatise, Rapport (1987) clarified that his endorsement of empowerment was not a condemnation of prevention. Prevention could be seen as a strategy through which empowerment goals might be realized. Nevertheless, Rappaport asserted that community psychology could best remain faithful to its fundamental values by adopting empowerment as its primary orienting concept.

Rappaport's seminal articles placed him at the forefront of a groundswell of interest in empowerment. In the late 1980s and 1990s, talk of empowerment exploded. A search of Psycinfo, a psychological literature database that encompasses journal articles and books, revealed only twenty-two references to the root word *empower* between 1958 and 1980. The same search conducted for 1981 through 1995 revealed an incredible 4280 instances of the same word (search conducted October, 2001). Databases for education and sociology experienced similar explosions. The term also became ubiquitous in political parlance. The root word *empower* appeared in 360 different press releases between 1992 and 1994, and over 7000 state bills from 1991 to 1994 (Perkins, 1995; Perkins & Zimmerman, 1995). This is not to say that the multitude of articles, chapters, press releases and bills agreed on the meaning of the newly popular term. As we will later see, the term has taken on very different, even diametrically opposed, meanings by different factions. Let's begin our discussion by looking more closely at what community psychologists mean by empowerment.

⌘ Definitions

Definitions of emerging terms require time to consolidate. The lack of clarity in definition that hindered early prevention work also characterized early work on empowerment. Edison Trickett (1994) proposed that the evolution of any new concept not only requires, but benefits from, ambiguities in definitions. The initial ambiguity allows a concept to generate novel perspectives on what we need to do and how to do it.

Nevertheless, definitions need to solidify over time. Shortly after hailing empowerment as an orienting concept, Rappaport (1984c) voiced concern that if different people continued to use the term to advance different agendas, "empowerment" would become simply a new dressing for old ways of doing things. A decade later, community psychologists continued to call for care and precision in defining the construct, fearing that the term would otherwise "forever remain a warm and fuzzy, one-size-fits-all, concept with no clear or consistent meaning" (Perkins & Zimmerman, 1995, p. 572).

Numerous community psychologists have heeded these calls and elaborated the concept of empowerment with thought and insight. Rappaport's simple and concise definition provided a solid base. He defined empowerment as "a process, the mechanism by which people, organizations, and communities gain mastery over their affairs" (1987, p. 122). The Cornell Empowerment Group (1989)

expounded on Rappaport's initial work and developed one of the most widely used definitions:

> Empowerment is an intentional, ongoing process centered in the local community, involving mutual respect, critical reflection, caring, and group participation, through which people lacking an equal share of valued resources gain greater access to and control over those resources. (p. 2)

Community psychologists generally agree on these conceptual definitions, but as we will see, the operationalization of the term varies considerably. Empowerment may be exemplified by residents of blighted neighborhoods building vibrant villages, female dairy farmers in India gaining control over milk production or Native Americans resisting the construction of a dam on their land. Despite the diverse operationalizations of the term, defining features of empowerment can be identified.

MARC ZIMMERMAN'S KEY COMPONENTS

Marc Zimmerman, one of the most active scholars of empowerment (and a former student of Julian Rappaport), identified three key components of empowerment. They are: 1) efforts to gain access to resources; 2) participation with others to achieve goals; and 3) a critical understanding of the sociopolitical context (Perkins & Zimmerman, 1995; Zimmerman, 2000; see also Keiffer, 1984). Let's look at each of these components.

ACCESS TO RESOURCES

Basic to the concept of empowerment is the notion that resources are not distributed equally across segments of society and change is required to right this injustice. Thus, how we understand empowerment depends in large part on how we understand resources.

In general, **resources** are the elements available for the satisfaction of human needs and desires. Many community psychologists have made more fine-grained distinctions among types of resources.

Irma Serrano-García (1994) distinguished two types; **instrumental resources** actually fulfill human needs and aspirations, while **infraresources** facilitate access to instrumental resources. Stevan Hobfoll (1988, 1989) distinguished four types of resources that exist at individual and community levels (see Table 13.5). Serrano-García's infraresources correspond to what Hobfoll called *energies*—resources that help people obtain and protect other resources. Disenfranchisement coincides with a lack of resources of all descriptions—food, housing, health care, job opportunities, transportation, recreational activities, and so on.

Resources are often a battleground for power. Efforts to control resources lie at the root of struggles on small scales and large, from toddlers engaged in a tug-of-war over a coveted toy to the mutual destruction of Israelis and Palestinians battling over a homeland.

Struggles over resources often proceed on the assumption that for one person or group to gain control of a resource, another must lose control. In his groundbreaking work on empowerment, Richard Katz (1984) explored an alternative to this zero-sum approach. He proposed that competition over resources exists when **scarcity paradigms** prevail, as they do in Western society. Scarcity paradigms view resources as limited. Other societies operate from an

alternative **synergy paradigm**, in which valued resources are viewed as renewable and expandable. To show how synergy paradigms operate, Katz described the distribution of the resource of healing in two synergistic communities: the !Kung of the Kalahari Desert and the rural indigenous people of the Fiji islands.

Among the !Kung, the central healing tradition is the all-night healing dance which occurs up to four times each month. The goal of the dance is for community healers to generate healing energy, called *n/um.* As the healers dance they experience *!kia,* a form of enhanced consciousness. *!Kia* allows the healer to experience the sickness of the community members and negotiate with spirits on behalf of those who suffer. Although only the community healers generate *n/um,* everyone in this egalitarian society shares in it. In addition, almost everyone is encouraged to become a healer, and all young boys and most girls try. Only about half of the men and 10% of the women succeed, however. Healers must have strength and resolve as *n/um* is a painful, mysterious, and feared energy.

The indigenous people of the Fiji islands are more hierarchically organized than the !Kung, and healing in their culture is more specialized. Nevertheless, the synergy paradigm operates. Healing is available to anyone in the community who needs it.

Table 13.5   Types of Resources

Type of Resource	Examples at Individual Level	Examples at Community Level
Objects	Home, clothing	Roads, emergency equipment
Conditions	Secure work, good health	Employment opportunities, emergency services
Personal characteristics	Self-esteem, job skills	Sense of community, community competence
Energies (to obtain and protect resources)	Food, money	Government financing, fuel reserves

Based on Hobfoll S. E., (1988). *The ecology of stress.* New York: Hemisphere Publishing Corp. and Hobfoll, S. E. (1989). Conservation of resources: A new attempt of conceptualizing stress. *American Psychologist, 44,* 513-524.

Any person in need can present the yagona plant to a healer, and spiritual power called *mana,* is released as soon as the healer accepts this ritual offering. Again, healing requires strength and is seen as a responsibility more than a privilege. The healer's character makes healing possible, and the healer must follow a righteous path that includes living the truth, love for all, humility, respect for tradition, single-mindedness, and service to others. All healers in the Fijian community know each other and even though they have different ideas about the causes of illnesses and pathways to cure, they regularly refer clients to each other. Thus, power is shared and community members can make use of each healer's area of expertise. Katz observed that this contrasts with the U.S. approach, in which healing paradigms are often seen as mutually exclusive. Psychoanalysts, members of mutual help groups, and proponents of Eastern-based meditation practices generally do not refer clients to each other on a regular basis.

Katz's work on empowerment encourages creative thinking about resources. The following principles derive from his understanding of the !Kung.

- Valued community resources (such as healing) may be expanding and renewable.
- Valued resources are released by the community.
- Valued resources can be distributed equitably and made accessible to everyone in community.

The Fijian approach to empowerment provides two additional principles.

- Community members can more effectively use resources if they have extensive information about the variety of resources available.
- Extensive collaboration among the custodians of resources and the seekers of resources promotes the flexible and varied (i.e., empowered) use of resources.

Although the approaches of the !Kung and Fijian people seem appealing, Katz warned that they could not take hold in U.S. society without a radical paradigm shift. Synergistic communities see the embeddedness of self in community as highly desirable and the pursuit of individual gain as objectionable, two perspectives that oppose the dominant Western worldview.

PARTICIPATION WITH OTHERS

The first key feature of empowerment identified by Marc Zimmerman is that it requires equal access to resources. The second key feature is that the pursuit of a more equitable distribution of resources requires the coming together of disenfranchised people (see also Speer & Hughey, 1995). For empowerment to occur, disenfranchised people must create common cause. Initially, they may unite around their shared experience of stress and the desire to exchange social support in order to face challenges. Eventually, they may come to see the stress as resulting from a lack of resources and the lack of resources as resulting from inequities in society. This paves the ways for transformation in the group members' sense of self—no longer are they unfortunate people coping individually with their lot in life, but members of an oppressed group who can work together to create social change.

When individuals come together, change becomes possible (see the sections entitled *Awakening to Injustice* and *Creating Common Cause*). Dialogue and the exchange of information enhance people's understanding of their environment and can lead to transformative changes in society (Friere, 1970/1992). Although some authors conceive of empowerment as individual advancement through personal skill development (e.g., Fine, 1999; Caroselli, 1998), that is not the conceptualization consistent with community psychology (e.g., Watts, Griffith, & Abdul-Adil, 1999). For community psychologists, skill building relates to empowerment only to the extent that it inspires a confrontation with the existing sociopolitical context, and this confrontation requires joining forces with others.

UNDERSTANDING THE SOCIOPOLITICAL CONTEXT

When marginalized people come together to discuss their shared concerns, they become aware of shaping forces that exist beyond the individual level.

They identify with similar others, cease to blame themselves for problems stemming from social injustice, and assume responsibility for making changes (Gutiérrez, 1994). Thus, participation with others is inextricably linked to Zimmerman's third essential component of empowerment: an understanding of the sociopolitical context.

The development of sociopolitical understanding occurs in stages (Ander-Egg, 1980; Serrano-García, 1994; Watts & Abdul-Adil, 1994; Watts et al., 1999). In the *acritical* or *submissive stage*, social asymmetries remain unquestioned. If they are noticed at all, they are seen as part of the natural order. In the second, *adaptive stage*, power asymmetries are acknowledged but seen as immutable. Consequently, the task for oppressed people is to find ways of adapting to the status quo. In the next stage, called the *precritical stage*, awareness of asymmetries grows, as does dissatisfaction with the status quo. In the fourth stage, the *critical* or *critical-integrative stage*, the social and historical roots of asymmetries are understood, which generally leads to the conclusion that power asymmetries are unjust and should be changed. In the final stage, the *liberation stage*, oppressed people reject the status quo and demand social transformation.

WHAT ABOUT POWER?

In summary, Zimmerman proposed that the three key features of empowerment are access to resources, participation with others, and understanding of the sociopolitical context. These three components hint at, but do not explicitly grapple with the issue of power. Power is, however, the root of the term em*power*ment. A consideration of power adds to our understanding of empowerment. In this section we consider different ways of thinking about power, and then tackle a central

---

Self-empowerment is the most deeply political work there is, and the most difficult.

—*Audre Lorde (1984, p. 170)*

---

question in community psychology: Do we (does anyone) have the power to empower anyone else?

WHAT IS POWER?

Power is complex and value-laden term. Let's examine the concept of power from three perspectives: the distinction between perceived and actual power, *power over* versus *power to*, and the different sources of power.

PERCEPTION OF POWER VERSUS ACTUAL POWER

Zimmerman (1995) characterized actual power or control over resources as "not necessary for empowerment because in some contexts and for some populations real control or power may not be the desired goal" (p. 593). Perhaps this is one reason why Zimmerman identified the importance of *understanding* the sociopolitical context, but not necessarily *influencing* it.

Some scholars of empowerment have criticized conceptualizations of empowerment that ignore actual power (e.g. Gruber & Trickett, 1987; Riger, 1993; Serrano-García, 1994; Speer & Hughey, 1995; Swift & Levin, 1987). In an influential article entitled, *What's Wrong with Empowerment?* Stephanie Riger (1993) asserted that people may *feel* empowered while remaining quite powerless. For example, Judith Gruber and Edison Trickett (1987) described a failed empowerment effort in which a school policy council was formed to involve teachers, parents and students in decision-making (this case study is examined in more detail later in the chapter). According to Gruber and Trickett, the council failed because the teachers retained control over decisions. The parents and students generally *felt* empowered, but power was not redistributed. "It is still *not* enough for the transformation of society, this *feeling* of being free" (emphasis in original, Shor & Freire, 1987, p. 109–110; also cited in Strawn, 1994).

"Power Over" versus "Power To". Resistance to embracing the importance of actual power may stem from a view of power as requiring hierarchy or dominance. This seems antithetical to the goal of establishing equity. Stephanie Riger (1993) stressed the importance of distinguishing "power over," which implies dominance, and "power to," which consists of the opportunity to act more freely.

An emphasis on "power over" may reflect a traditionally masculine view of power. It views power as an *object* that can be possessed by an individual or group, and transferred willingly or unwillingly to other people or groups (Serrano-García, 1994). "Power to" (or "power with") may be seen as a more feminist way of thinking about power (Deutchman, 1991; Miller, 1986; Surrey, 1991; Watts, 1997).

Feminists often frame power as *receptive* rather than *active*. Power may come from openness (Rosenwasser, 1992b) or even vulnerability (Jordan, 1992). The activist Flor Fernandez conceptualized power as "*allowing* rather than controlling" (Rosenwasser, 1992c). To her, assuming a position of power meant being "in synchronicity with the energies around us" in order to "make a decision based on choices rather than on the need to control other people..." (p. 130). Katz (1984) also referred to receptive power, noting that when !Kung healers entered *!kia*, they reported feeling as if they were "opening up" or "bursting open" like a ripe pod (Katz, p. 210). This conception of power may be more in keeping with empowerment ideologies.

SOURCES OF POWER

A consideration of the sources of power also has implications for our understanding of empowerment. Katherine Klein and her colleagues (2000) explored ideas about power sources developed in the organizational literature. Of particular interest was French and Raven's (1960) enumeration of five sources of workplace power.

The first type, *legitimate power*, stems from an individual's position in the organization. Subordinates obey legitimate power because of the authority bestowed by position. Placement within the organizational hierarchy is the sole determinant of legitimate power. *Reward power* is based on the individual's ability to bestow rewards such as praise, recognition, or pay. Reward power is offered in return for compliance and depends on the other's desire for the reward. *Coercive power* is the inverse of reward power. One person obeys another out of fear of reprimand or other punishment. People higher in the organization's hierarchy have more authority to bestow rewards or punishments, but they may also inspire people to seek their praise or avoid their reprimands for personal reasons. A subordinate may simply like the more powerful person and want to gain her or his respect. Thus, reward power and coercive power blend positional and personal power. Two additional types of power stem from personal characteristics alone. *Referent power* is based on the individual's personality, attractiveness, or charm. *Expert power* refers to the special skills or knowledge the individual possesses, and is obeyed because the expert's directives are likely to be informed and helpful. Organizations can confer neither referent nor expert power.

This analysis of power from the workplace literature has important implications for the construct of empowerment more generally (Klein et al., 2000). Positional power may derive not only from one's position in the workplace, but from one's position in society as well. Members of disenfranchised groups do not have authority bestowed by social position, and so personal power (i.e., referent power and expert power) may be more critical in their efforts to access and control resources. The importance of referent power may be one reason why social movements often look toward charismatic leaders, such as Martin Luther King, Jr., to advance their cause. Personal charm is not easily acquired, however, and so interventions crafted by community psychologists (and others) often focus on helping disenfranchised people develop expert power as an instrument of empowerment. Many empowerment-oriented interventions seek to teach skills, such as leadership skills, problem solving skills, and also skills in analyzing the sociopolitical environments.

Participatory research is one vehicle for the cultivation of expert power. An example often cited in the community psychology literature occurred in a town called Love Canal where Lois Gibbs lived as a homemaker and mother in the 1970s (Biklen, 1983; Center for Health and Environmental Justice, 2000a; Berkowitz, 1987; Gibbs, 1982). Love Canal had been built on a toxic waste site, and when chemical leakage began to make residents sick, Gibbs and others were dismayed to find that those with positional power (i.e., government officials) were in no hurry to help them out. The Love Canal Homeowners Association, with the 27-year old Gibbs as founder and president, launched a comprehensive and systematic study that yielded some startling statistics: 25% of pregnancies in the affected areas ended in miscarriage, and 56% of the children born in the area had birth defects. Moreover, homes with ill family members clustered along pathways of underground drainage ditches where several hundred tons of dangerous chemicals had been dumped during World War II. The townspeople took it upon themselves to collect data that clearly showed the compromised health of residents and traced it to toxic wastes. They became more informed than anyone else about the local situation and used their expert power to leverage change.

THE POWER TO EMPOWER

Although an analysis of power suggests strategies of potential use to community psychologists, a more basic question remains. Can community psychologists, or anyone else, bring about empowerment? I referred earlier to Judith Gruber and Edison Trickett's (1987) case study of an alternative public school interested in new models of governance. Their analysis of this failed empowerment effort led them to recognize a "fundamental paradox in the idea of people empowering others because the very institutional structure that puts one group in a position to empower also works to undermine the act of empowerment" (p. 353). Let's look at Gruber and Trickett's work more closely.

The social experiment in empowerment occurred in the early 1970s in an inner-city public high school in New Haven, Connecticut. Shortly after the school was founded, personnel established a governing council with an equal representation of parents, students, and teachers. Gruber and Trickett studied verbatim notes of the council meetings and conducted yearly interviews with all council members. They also interviewed every teacher in the

school on their perceptions of the council. As a result of this research, Gruber and Trickett sought to find out if the council succeeded in its empowerment goals, that is to say, if the council actually wielded significant decision-making power and so controlled resources within the school.

The context of this school was ripe for empowerment efforts. It sought to decentralize power in numerous ways. The school encouraged self-directed learning among students. Teachers paid personal visits to parents during which they emphasized the importance of parental involvement and input. Indeed, the school itself had been established without a principal, and teachers took responsibility for decision making through consensus rather than voting.

Teachers embraced the idea of a governing council as another way of eliminating traditional authority. The council was comprised of five parents, five students, and five teachers, each with one vote in all policy decisions. During its first year, the council played an active role in developing school policy. For example, the council decided not to admit ninth graders, a decision that went against the wishes of the teachers. Over time, however, the influence of the council diminished. The issues discussed became more trivial, and the faculty dominated discussions more. A new pattern emerged: faculty members made decisions on their own and then presented them to the council for feedback. Eventually, the council came to be seen as irrelevant. Interviews conducted four years after the council formed revealed that teachers did not trust parents to make good decisions, and neither parents nor teachers trusted the students' maturity of judgment. Attendance at the meetings decreased, as did the frequency of the meetings. Gruber and Trickett identified two constraints that limited the influence of the council. First, important *inequalities in power* existed among the council subgroups. The egalitarian group structure, as epitomized by equal voting power among the three constituencies, did not eliminate the pre-existing power differences among these groups. The teachers had founded the school, oversaw day-to-day operations, responded to district administrators, sought outside funding, and were generally more committed to the success of the school. Teachers knew more about and were more responsible for the school and also had greater familiarity with larger educational issues. For the council to function effectively, teachers would have had to equalize these imbalances by bringing relevant issues to the attention of the council, facilitating the informed participation of all group members and putting council decisions into effect. This did not occur. Parents and students often felt the need to defer to teachers with regard to important decisions, such as hiring personnel and allocating budgets. On the rare occasions when parents and students joined forces and outvoted the teachers, the teachers ultimately controlled the implementation of council decisions and so could effectively undo them.

The *organizational dynamics* contributed further to the failure of the empowerment effort. Paradoxically, the school's commitment to egalitarianism contributed to the demise of the council. By eschewing formal group structures (e.g., clear leadership, differentiated roles for council members), a **tyranny of structurelessness** resulted. Incessant group time and energy was spent on the group's internal process. No one was in charge. Grievances and suggestions were lost, resolutions were abandoned as quickly as they were formed, and promised reports were never delivered. To the extent that the group was led at all, leadership was informal. Informal leaders, no matter how ineffective, cannot be voted out. The structurelessness of the council precluded proactive efforts to minimize existing power differences among the three constituencies, and so the status quo of faculty power remained unchallenged.

The inability of the council to succeed led Gruber and Trickett to some pessimistic conclusions about empowerment. They suggested that if empowerment could occur anywhere, it should have occurred at that school. The school was committed in ideology and practice to egalitarian goals and to the empowerment of students and parents. In addition, the council began when the school was still a new organization. Entrenched power structures did not yet exist and standard operating procedures had not yet emerged. The idea for the council took

shape organically—it was not an intervention imposed by outside forces but an idea formulated by the stakeholders themselves. Despite all of these conditions that would seem to support empowerment, the council failed. Gruber and Trickett (1987) saw this failure as indicative of the fundamental obstacles in the empowerment process. They wrote, "Virtually all empowerment efforts involve a grant of power by a favored group to others in the organization. Unless the favored group changes the very circumstances that have given it power in the first place, the grant of power is always partial" (p. 370). As we will see throughout this chapter, this fundamental paradox of empowerment presents on ongoing challenge to those seeking to equalize imbalances in social power.

⌘ Levels of Analysis

Thus, far we have considered definitional issues in empowerment. We examined the three components Marc Zimmerman identified as crucial, as well as the often-overlooked construct of power. These conceptual issues create backdrop for a fuller discussion of empowerment theory, research, and practice.

Since the term *empowerment* first emerged in the social science literature in the mid-1970s, it has been used to describe a wealth of research, theory, and practice. In order to examine this vast literature, let's consider empowerment at three levels of analysis: the individual, the microsystem, and beyond the microsystem.

INDIVIDUAL LEVEL

Marc Zimmerman's work on empowerment centers on the individual. He recognized, however, the importance of considering the individual-in-context and proposed a distinction between individual empowerment, and **psychological empowerment** (Zimmerman, 1990). Individual empowerment remains at the level of the person. Empowerment is seen as an individual trait. Psychological empowerment, on the other hand, considers the person–environment interaction. Zimmerman identified three aspects of psychological empowerment: intrapersonal, interactional, and behavioral (Zimmerman, 1995; 2000).

THE INTRAPERSONAL ASPECT

The intrapersonal aspect of empowerment focuses on intrapsychic dynamics. A number of constructs in the psychological literature overlap with intrapersonal empowerment. That is to say, the concept of intrapersonal empowerment casts a wide **nomological net**. The nomological net is the universe of concepts related to a target construct that can inform our understanding of that construct. Many of the concepts caught in the nomological net of intrapersonal empowerment have long histories and rich traditions in psychology (Price, 1990).

Self-esteem, or assessment of personal worth, is one concept that relates to empowerment. If a marginalized person does not feel worthy of the good things in life, she or he will not seek change. Roderick Watts (1997) noted that the construct of *internalized oppression* puts self-esteem into a sociopolitical context. Members of oppressed groups may come to believe society's negative images of that group, leaving them with feelings of low self-worth. If they feel that they deserve inferior treatment, they will not seek empowerment.

Sense of control is another long-standing psychological concept that bears on the construct of empowerment. In particular, *locus of control* refers to one's beliefs about the causes of life experiences. People with an internal locus of control believe that they can affect the events that occur in their lives, while someone with an external locus of control views their life experiences as determined by outside forces (Rotter, 1966). People who feel a sense of control tend to enjoy better mental and physical health.

Of course, a sense of control does not develop independent of the context in which one lives. Disenfranchised people may have a more external sense of control because they actually *have* less control. Julian Rappaport (1981) observed that

empowerment confronts the paradox that even the people who seem most incompetent, in need, and unable to function benefit from more rather than less control over their lives. Consider the work of the social psychologists Ellen Langer and Judith Rodin (1976).

Some institutions, such as nursing homes and hospitals, contain people who have been placed there against their will. Moreover, the institutions control many aspects of the residents' life—what they eat, whom they see, and when they see them. Langer and Rodin (1976) reasoned that residents of such total institutions would benefit from an increased sense of control. They designed a simple intervention in which residents of a nursing home in Connecticut were placed in one of two groups. The director of the home called the first group of residents together and told them that they needed to make more decisions about their lives. In the future, they would be allowed to arrange their rooms as they saw fit, have input into the choice of movies, and generally make more decisions. The director gave each resident the gift of a houseplant to symbolize their control over the future—they could nurture the plant or allow it to die. A comparison group heard a speech that did not emphasize control over decisions, and although they too received houseplants, they were told that nurses would take care of them. Residents in the first group became happier, healthier, and lived longer than residents in the second group (Rodin & Langer, 1977). A follow-up study found that twice as many people in the group without control had died. Interestingly, additional research suggests that if conditions changed so that control was gained and then lost, residents who suffered the loss were worse off than those who never gained control in the first place (Schulz & Hanusa, 1978).

The related concept of *self-efficacy* also overlaps with empowerment. Self-efficacy refers to our judgments about the degree to which our behaviors can affect desired outcomes (Bandura, 1997). If people feel that they *can* control events through individual effort, they are more likely to take action. Researchers interested in linking notions of self-efficacy with the larger social context have coined an additional term: **political efficacy**. Political efficacy reflects a person's perceived ability to participate in and influence the political process. In studying the formation of a union for homeless people, Susan Yeich and Ralph Levine (1994) proposed that political efficacy includes three components: 1) feeling capable of entering into political arenas; 2) knowing how to get the system to respond to demands; and 3) recognizing collective action as the appropriate vehicle for change.

The willingness to work toward change derives from one's expectations. Repeated experiences of failure can reinforce a belief that efforts are futile, leading to *learned helplessness* (Abramson, Seligman, & Teasdale, 1978). Marc Zimmerman (1990) proposed *learned hopefulness* as an alternative to the deficit side of the expectation–effort relationship. He argued that when individuals gain control and mastery over their lives, they feel hopeful and become empowered. Where there is hope, there is the possibility of change.

At an individual level, hope (as well as fear) is evident in our beliefs about our future. Hazel Markus and Paula Nurius (1986) coined the term **possible selves** to describe what people believe they can become. Possible selves embody both ideals and fears. Hoped-for selves might include the happy self, the athletic self, the parent self, the doctor self, and the admired self. Feared selves might include the alone self, the depressed self, the unemployed self, the overweight self, and the smoker self.

The selves we see as possible do not emerge and take shape in isolation. Theoretically, a person could create any number of possible selves for herself or himself. The *actual* universe of any person's possible selves is bounded by that person's sociocultural and historical setting. Our ideas about who we might become depend on the models, images, and symbols invoked by our context, notably the people with whom we interact and the media that surrounds us. Stereotypes, false assumptions, and labeling can constrain our sense of personal potential. In his original treatise on empowerment, Rappaport (1981) wrote

> it makes a great difference if you are viewed as a child or as a citizen, since if you believe

it you are quite likely to act the part, and if those in power believe it they are likely to develop programs, plans, and structures that will help you to believe it. (p. 11, embedded references deleted)

While negative possible selves can imprison us and stifle empowerment, positive possible selves can liberate and offer the hope of a better future. Role models and support people can foster the development of positive possible selves. It is easier today than it was fifty years ago for little girls to see themselves as astronauts and African American youths to believe they can be elected to high office. At the individual level, empowerment-based interventions may be seen as inspiring new possible selves.

Many of the concepts that fall within the nomological net of intrapersonal empowerment have higher level analogs that merit increased examination. For example, Albert Bandura (1997) devoted a chapter of his recent book on self-efficacy to the concept of *collective efficacy*. Jennifer Crocker and colleagues (e.g., Crocker & Luhtanen, 1990) have examined the notion of *collective self-esteem*. We might also think about *possible communities* (ideal and feared), as well as possible selves.

As another example of higher level analogs, Irma Serrano-García (1984) noted that learned helplessness exists at a societal level in the form of *colonialism*. In her country of Puerto Rico, colonialism means that the U.S. functions as the parent state, exercising control over Puerto Rican affairs such as foreign trade, citizenship, immigration, military service, transportation, currency, and postal services. Colonialism leads to self-debasement, alienation, loss of cultural identity, dependency, and internally directed hostility. Perhaps we need to coin a term for community-level learned hopefulness, as well.

THE INTERACTIONAL ASPECT

The intrapersonal aspect of empowerment includes such psychological factors as self-esteem, locus of control, sense of efficacy, and hope. The interactional component pertains to how people understand and seek to influence their social environment

(Zimmerman, 1995, 2000). Intrapersonal and interactional empowerment do not always co-occur. Disenfranchised people may feel in control, worthy of respect, and hopeful without understanding how to bring about needed changes, or they may know what is needed to create change but feel personally unwilling or unable to act on that understanding (Speer, 2000).

The interpersonal skills required for empowerment fall into two categories: skills needed to work in coalition with others and skills needed to obtain control from powers that be. The first category of skills may be seen as internal to the group (or groups) seeking change. Whether participation entails working within coalitions, community development initiatives, environmental action groups, neighborhood associations, or mutual help groups

(Perkins, 1995; Speer & Hughey, 1995), members must know how to function effectively as a group. After a thorough literature review, Pennie Foster-Fishman and her colleagues (2001) devised an exhaustive list of core skills needed to work in partnership with others. They include conflict-resolution skills, knowledge about the norms and perspectives of other members, propensity to share power, valuing of diversity, and willingness and ability to forge links with others. To maintain participation, individuals must also know how to recruit, train, organize, motivate, utilize, and retain group members (e.g., Wandersman & Florin, 2000).

The second type of interactional skill is externally focused and pertains to the relationship between members of the change-seeking group and those who control the desired resources. Effective groups

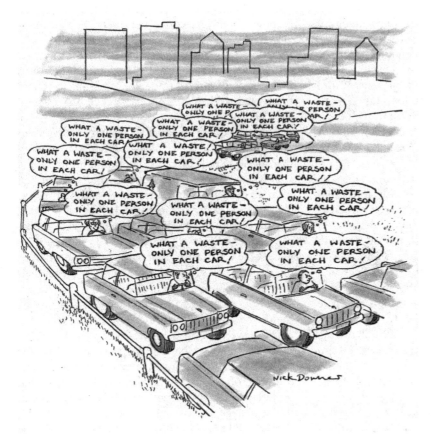

Individual insight may mean little without collective action. Copyright © 2002 by Nick Downes.

must know how best to use their resources to create change and what barriers to change exist or can be erected at different levels to block them (Zimmerman, 1995). Empowerment-oriented interventions may focus on increasing the interactional skills of people in change-seeking groups by promoting problem-solving around critical questions, such as Who ultimately controls the resources? How do the controlling people and groups operate? and What points of leverage can be used in order to gain influence? (e.g., Shefner-Rogers et al., 1998).

THE BEHAVIORAL ASPECT

Personal characteristics and interpersonal skills set the background for psychological empowerment, but empowerment hinges on a third component: taking action in an effort to access and control resources. Although the psychological literature has focused on the intrapsychic aspect of psychological empowerment (perhaps because of its relatedness to familiar constructs), some have argued that the behavioral component should be of central interest. Empowerment behaviors can be more reliably and directly measured than the intrapsychic dimensions (e.g., Perkins, 1995). In addition, to the extent that one is interested in actual as opposed to perceived control, empowerment behavior is of primary importance.

In the nomological net of empowerment, the construct that corresponds most closely to the behavioral aspect of empowerment is citizen participation. **Citizen participation** has been defined as "a process in which individuals take part in decision making in the institutions, programs, and environments that affect them" (Heller, Price, Reinharz, Riger, & Wandersman, 1984, p. 339). Like empowerment, citizen participation can be seen as a vehicle for improving people's lives. It increases people's feelings of control over their lives and enhances a sense of belonging (e.g., Wandersman & Florin, 2000; Zimmerman, 1990). Citizen participation also enables people to create environments that better meet their needs. Citizen participation is both a cause and an effect of empowerment (Perkins, Brown, & Taylor, 1996). That is to say, citizen

participation leads people to empowerment: citizen participants gain an understanding of the sociopolitical context and seek the redistribution of resources in participation with others. At the same time, empowered people are more likely to become citizen participants and so work for changes in the environments that affect them. In the next sections, we will examine the process by which people become citizen participants and the reasons why people do or do not become involved.

The Life Paths of Citizen Participants. The notion that empowerment both leads to and results from citizen participation suggests that empowerment evolves over time. It is a process rather than an end state, and one does not necessarily *achieve* empowerment (e.g., Gutiérrez, 1994).

Charles Keiffer (1984) adopted a life span developmental perspective in his study of how individual empowerment develops over time. Keiffer interviewed fifteen committed grassroots activists and identified four stages of development. Prior to their journey toward activism, the people he interviewed had a strong sense of pride and determination and felt rooted to their community. In the first stage of their journey, the *era of entry*, individuals experienced some direct threat to their own or their family's self-interest that provoked outrage. Keiffer noted that mobilization did not grow from an intellectual analysis of a problem or an outside intervention, but from an immediate and physical violation of the future activists' sense of integrity. This threat provided an impetus to confront authorities, which Keiffer saw as the hallmark of activism. According to Keiffer, people learned to speak with confidence in their own voice only after the symbolic (i.e., positional) power of authority was demystified.

In the next stage, the *era of advancement*, the budding activists became more connected with others who were engaged in similar struggles. During this stage, mentors, supportive peers, and collective organizational structures fostered a critical understanding of the social and political realities that underlay the threat the activists had experienced. In the next stage, the *era of incorporation*, self-concept, strategic abilities, and critical comprehension became mature. Finally, in the *era of commitment*, the transformation from uninvolved community member to social change activist was complete. The individual had become competent in identifying and transforming power relationships. Keiffer found that this journey generally required at least four years.

A failure to consider empowerment as a developmental process can impede interventions and lead to iatrogenesis (i.e., unintended negative consequences). For example, Irma Serrano-García (1984) wondered if it was appropriate to foster consciousness raising before citizens had the skills necessary to act upon their newly discovered reality. Similarly, Douglas Perkins and Marc Zimmerman (1995) observed that efforts to exert control can create more problems than they solve. People must have the skills to consider various strategies towards change and assess the risks and benefits associated with each. They offered the example of an urban teenager interested in reclaiming his neighborhood from gangs. Ill-considered strategies could well result in retaliation from gang members. Thus, at earlier stages of empowerment, people may need assistance in developing skills. At later stages, they might benefit more from help in managing the stress and strain that result from social change responsibilities (Keiffer, 1984).

People who do find pathways to empowerment report benefits from their participation in community action. Lois Gibbs was not the only resident of Love Canal who became an activist as a result of the threat hazardous wastes posed to the community. One study of 39 Love Canal residents, 24 of whom became activists and 15 of whom remained relatively uninvolved, found benefits to activism (Stone & Levine, 1985). Activists felt better about themselves and reported greater belief in their political efficacy. Although activists had lost some friends, presumably as a result of their social change efforts, they had gained new friends as well. This research cannot rule out the possibility that people who ultimately became activists were willing to get involved because they *already* enjoyed a sense of well-being and felt efficacious. The strong possibility remains, however, that involvement in the citizen movement led to improvements in their sense of self.

Why Individuals Do and Don't Participate. The literature on citizen participation consistently finds a relationship between involvement in community action and feelings of personal and political efficacy and well-being (e.g., Stone & Levine, 1985; Wandersman & Florin, 2000; Zimmerman, 1990; Zimmerman & Rappaport, 1988). This led Abraham Wandersman and Paul Florin (2000) to ask, "If citizen participation is so beneficial, why don't more people get involved?" Certainly some of the variables discussed earlier come into play. People with low self-esteem, an external locus of control, little desire or hope for change, and a lack of appreciation of the social causes of personal problems will not become activists. A costs–benefits perspective also bears on this question. People get involved when they stand to gain more (e.g., in terms of neighborhood safety) than they stand to lose (e.g., in terms of lost time with family) (Prestsby, Wandersman, Florin, Rich, & Chavis, 1990). "Suprapersonal" factors also play a role—altruism, a sense of civic responsibility, and community-mindedness promote citizen participation (Perkins, et al., 1996; Stewart & Weinstein, 1997).

The existence of an external trigger is also a factor. Charles Kieffer (1984) found that citizen participants became interested in social change after encountering a threat they could not ignore. Similarly, David Chavis and Abraham Wandersman (1990) found that voluntary organizations tend to form in response to a precipitating event. These events often come from the physical environment—discovery of a hazardous waste site, the experience of a shocking crime, or an unwanted development project. External triggers do not always come from environmental events, however. Outside agents did not lead to activism for any of the fifteen people Keiffer studied, but the seminal works of Alinsky (1971) and Freire (1970/1992) are based on the notion that community organizers and educators can bring people to social action. A study of community organizing with women dairy farmers in India also showed that outside agents can inspire citizen participation (see the Community Intervention box).

COMMUNITY INTERVENTION:

Empowering Women Dairy Farmers in India
Community Organizing for Empowerment

In Latin America, Africa, and Asia, countless activists are working to increase women's awareness of their disadvantaged social position in order to effect change. They seek to help women gain access to education, employment, and health care, and to free them from physical, sexual, and emotional abuse. Corinne Shefner-Rogers and her colleagues (1998) described how community organizers in India have instigated the empowerment of female dairy farmers in rural villages.

Although women comprise 85% of the seven million dairy farmers in India, they are excluded from the male-dominated milk marketing industry and often do not reap the rewards of their hard work. In an attempt to rectify the existing inequities, the National Dairy Development Board devised a Cooperative Development (CD) program that reaches about 250,000 women in 4,000 Indian villages each year, making it one of the largest scale empowerment efforts in the world.

Here is how the CD program works. A five-member CD team approaches a village and conducts a survey to assess local needs. They present the survey results to the dairy cooperative leaders, who are almost always men and ask permission to conduct the CD program. Team members educate the men about advantages that would accrue from women's empowerment, notably an increase in family financial and social strength. With their husbands' permission, women can attend CD sessions without fear of being beaten upon their return home. CD team members then visit the homes of the women, often accompanied by village leaders, such as midwives, and invite them to attend a two-day education program. The program consists of group discussion and question–answer sessions. The women learn important skills, such as farm hygiene and how to artificially inseminate milk animals. They are also made aware of their inferior social position. "Who goes to bed last in your house?" they are asked. The reply: "We do."

"Who gets up first in your house?"

"We do." The questions and replies continue. Who works hardest, who hands over the milk to their husbands to sell? We do, we do. The final question: "Who are fools?"

"We are!" (Shefner-Rogers et al., 1998, p. 329).

The CD program attendees learn that women on dairy farms contribute 70% of the work hours, earn 10% of the national income, and own 1% of the land, milk animals, and other resources. They then discuss pathways to empowerment: ways for women to gain control of milk production and distribution and to become members in dairy cooperatives. Meetings conclude with group sings and inspirational sayings.

After the training, the CD team helps organize women's clubs, or support groups, to sustain conscientization and encourage income-generating activities. In these clubs women have taught each other how to make and sell detergents, how to start saving plans, and how to run antiliquor campaigns (many of the village men spend money from the women's work on alcohol). Although men may feel a loss of power as a result of the women's empowerment, marked improvements in the family's economic situation usually compensate for the perceived loss.

Shefner-Rogers and her colleagues (1998) conducted a study to assess the efficacy of the CD program. They interviewed ninety-six women in four villages that received CD training and 88 women in four villages that did not. They found that average scores on eleven of their twelve indicators of empowerment were higher among villagers who had received CD training. These items include:

The female respondent . . .

1. owns the milk animals.
2. belongs to the dairy cooperative.
3. gets the money made from milk sales.
4. controls the milk animals' reproduction.
5. determines if animals are vaccinated or not.
6. decides how to spend income generated from the milk animals.
7. believes that women should have the final say in how many children they bear.
8. believes in equity in formal education for boys and girls.

9. believes that girls should decide when they will be married.
10. has a bank account for saving money.
11. determines which animals to buy when.
12. has joined the dairy cooperative's board of directors.

The researchers corroborated these self-report data with measures of actual change. In the four villages where the CD training occurred, the dairy cooperatives experienced a greater increase in the number of women members, greater attendance of women at annual meetings, and greater increases in overall cattle-feed sales and milk production. Men as well as women benefited from the empowerment activities. When the women became empowered, their families and their villages also prospered.

While threats, community organizers, or other catalysts may be necessary to spur citizen involvement, supporting social conditions may be required to sustain it. Douglas Perkins and his colleagues (1996) found that more citizens participated in block associations if they lived on blocks high in neighboring behaviors. Another study found that while individuals with strong beliefs in their own efficacy may initiate actions designed to improve collective situations, they are often encouraged by "less confident" neighbors on whom they depend for moral support and tangible aid (Saegert & Winkel, 1996).

Citizen participation can be promoted not only by the support of friends and neighbors, but also by organizational structures. A study of resident participation in three cities (Baltimore, New York, and Salt Lake City) found that the variables that most consistently predicted citizen involvement were informal neighboring and involvement in religious and other community organizations (Perkins et al., 1996). People who participate in social organizations more often participate in change efforts. Indeed, the formation of organizations that support social involvement can provide needed outlets for budding citizen participants. Susan Yeich and Ralph Levine (1994) found that unions for homeless persons provided a needed forum for citizen action.

In considering citizen participation thus far, we have moved from a consideration of individual factors to a recognition of the importance of microsystem supports (e.g., neighborhood social networks and voluntary associations, such as religious organizations and unions). Larger macrosystem forces also come into play. Robert Putnam (2000) painstakingly documented the powerful trend toward ever-deeper engagement in community life that swept the nation during the first two-thirds of the twentieth century and the dramatic reversal of this trend beginning in the 1980s. In the 1980s, citizens became less and less likely to participate in virtually all voluntary organizations, including neighborhood groups, religious fellowships, and workplace associations. Putnam examined a number of possible causes beyond the individual and microsystem levels that might account for this reversal in citizen's willingness to become participants.

Putnam found that busyness, mobility, suburbanization, and the growth of two-career families were not very important factors. From the 1960s to 1990s, civic participation diminished almost equally for men and women, married and single people, the financially stressed and the comfortably well off, workers and non workers, residents of cities and denizens of rural communities. He found that television viewing and other forms of electronic entertainment had a somewhat more powerful effect. People spent more of their discretionary time watching television and surfing the net in lieu of interacting with other community members and building consensus for action. In addition, television presented endless images of suffering in the guise of entertainment that dulled people's sense of outrage and perceived need to act (Pilisuk, McAllister, & Rothman, 1996). Of the variables Putnam studied, however, generational change played the largest role. As earlier generations of highly involved people died off, they were replaced by new generations of disconnected and uninvolved citizens (see Figure 13.3).

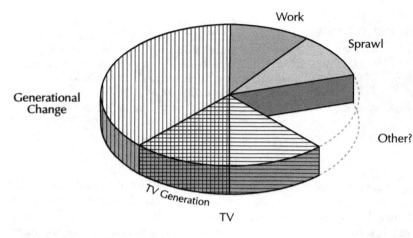

Work

Sprawl

Generational Change

Other?

TV Generation

TV

Figure 13.3

Guesstimated explanation for civic disengagement, 1965–2000. *Reprinted with the permission of Simon & Schuster Adult Publishing Group from BOWLING ALONE: The Collapse and Revival of American Community by Robert D. Putnam. Copyright © 2000 by Robert D. Putnam.*

MICROSYSTEM LEVEL

Although the majority of empowerment research and theory elaborates individual-level dynamics, most scholars agree that all levels of analysis must be considered in a comprehensive model of empowerment. As described above, the understanding of psychological empowerment eventually takes us through the microsystem and to the realm of macrosystemic forces that affect an individual's willingness to engage in empowerment activities. One cannot truly understand empowerment at one level without also considering other levels. Let's now consider how our understanding of empowerment is enhanced if we *begin* our analyses at the microsystem level.

In their seminal work on empowerment, Peter Berger and Richard Neuhaus (1977) posited that microsystems drive empowerment efforts as they link individuals with higher-level systems. They analyzed four microsystems: families, churches, voluntary associations, and neighborhoods. Bill Berkowitz and Thomas Wolff (1996) proposed that neighborhoods warrant much more attention as a structure for empowerment. First, neighborhoods are close to home—in fact, they *are* home. They provide a basis of commonality on which interpersonal relationships can build (even if the starting point is merely an exchange of "hellos" on the street). In addition, the payoff of neighborhood vitalization is great in terms of both psychological and environmental well-being (e.g., a deeper sense of community, safer

streets, more beautiful settings). The Classic Research box describes one notable effort to promote empowerment by improving the capacity of neighborhood associations.

In addition to neighborhood associations, some community psychologists have identified mutual help groups as an important locus of empowerment work (e.g., Reissman & Bay, 1992; Rappaport, Reischl, & Zimmerman, 1992). Others have studied empowerment in the workplace (e.g., Bond, 1999; Klein et al., 2000; Spreitzer, 1995), schools (e.g., Gruber & Trickett, 1987), or religious institutions (e.g., Maton & Rappaport, 1984). Many of these interventions are described in this and other chapters. For now, let's look at a conceptual issue that emerges across these setting types, and then consider setting characteristics that are associated with empowerment.

MICROSYSTEMS AS AN EXPRESSION OF INDIVIDUALS

As seen throughout this text, behavior is a function of individuals and environments. Thus, the shape empowerment takes depends on the interaction of individual characteristics and setting properties. In one study, Marc Zimmerman (1995) compared and contrasted the concerns of people in two different microsystems: voluntary service organizations and mutual help groups. Voluntary service associations tend to advocate community change, and so setting

CLASSIC RESEARCH

The Block Boosters Project
Sustaining Voluntary Associations

The Block Boosters Project was an action research effort that began in the mid-1980s and continued for two and a half years. The study involved over 1000 residents of 48 blocks in three culturally and ethnically different New York City neighborhoods. The Project attempted to assess the organizational characteristics of vital and active block associations and build these characteristics into other associations (Florin, Chavis, Wandersman, & Rich, 1992; Wandersman & Florin, 2000).

As the researchers began their longitudinal analyses, they quickly learned how difficult it is to keep block associations active. Data were collected on 28 active associations in February through May of 1985, and by May of 1986, almost one-third of these associations had lapsed into inactivity. When compared to associations that folded, associations that survived were found to have:

1. Maximized incentives to participate and minimized the costs of participation;
2. Mobilized a greater proportion of residents to join and moved nominal members into active membership more often;
3. Offered a greater number of activities that provided varied opportunities for participation;
4. Had more officers, more committees, and more formalized rules of operation;
5. Performed more outreach activities, which included direct and proactive approaches to recruiting new members, diverse methods of communicating with existing members (newsletters, personal contacts, phone calls), active preparation of new leaders, and delegation of responsibilities to a greater proportion of membership (i.e., decentralization);
6. Fostered ties and so could receive help from a variety of external organizations (Wandersman & Florin, 2000).

After obtaining information on characteristics related to association viability, the Block Boosters Project field tested a "Block Booster Process." Randomly chosen block associations received a capacity-building intervention. Scientist-practitioner teams evaluated each association and prepared an individual profile delineating the organization's strengths and weaknesses as they related to the characteristics found to enhance association viability. The association leaders received the profile along with a handbook containing suggestions on how to improve organizational functioning. Leaders also participated in neighborhood workshops to discuss how to use the information they had received. Follow-up studies showed participation in the intervention increased the likelihood that the association remained active ten months later. Half as many block associations that received the "boost" became inactive during that period (22% as compared to 44% of the control organizations).

Douglas Perkins and his colleagues (1996) revisited the Block Booster Project seven years later. In 1992, they interviewed current and former block leaders and residents on forty-four blocks that had been involved in the original research. Interestingly, the factors that enhanced organizational viability in the short-run did not seem to increase long-term survival. Over time, demographic variables became more important. For example, viable associations more often occurred on blocks with long-term residents. Perkins and his colleagues also looked at the results of the New York City block association research in comparison to findings from similar studies in Salt Lake City and Baltimore. Across all three studies, the predictors of sustained citizen action varied greatly, depending on both the time frame and the local conditions. The variables that most consistently predicted citizen involvement were informal neighboring and participation in religious and other community organizations. Thus face-to-face interactions among individual residents, and involvement in a network of community structures can help sustain citizen participation in neighborhood associations.

members assumed an outward orientation. Mutual help groups, on the other hand, are internally oriented. Thus, different microsystems foster different types of psychological empowerment. Voluntary associations might foster a sense of political efficacy (intrapersonal development), an awareness of barriers to change (interactional development), and lobbying capabilities (behavioral development). Mutual help groups might promote self-efficacy rather than political efficacy, positive relationships within the group as opposed to awareness of outside forces that control resources, and outreach to current or potential members as opposed to member activism.

In another study of person–environment transactions in the context of empowerment, Eric Stewart and Rhona Weinstein (1997) identified three types of AIDS organizations in the San Francisco Bay Area: social change associations, information/referral settings, and individual support agencies. Different organizations attracted different people and engaged them in different activities. The social change setting was comprised mostly of gay and bisexual men and focused on halting the spread of HIV through community and political involvement. The information/referral setting contained more heterosexuals and women and sought to slow the spread of HIV/AIDS through the dissemination of frank information about safer sex practices and referrals to HIV-related programs and resources. The individual support setting, which had a mixed membership, provided emotional and tangible support to people living with HIV or AIDS.

The authors of both of these studies concluded that each setting was empowering in its own way. Others might disagree. Does a setting that maintains an exclusively internal focus (such as many support groups) really promote empowerment?

EMPOWERING AND EMPOWERED MICROSYSTEMS

Marc Zimmerman (1995; 2000) argued that organizational empowerment can be conceptualized in two ways: the extent to which the organization empowers its members, and the extent to which the

organization itself works toward empowerment. An **empowering organization** offers opportunities for members to gain control over their lives. Members have the chance to develop skills, such as leadership and resource management, and they might enjoy a boost in self-esteem. **Empowered organizations**, on the other hand, engage in change efforts. They may, for example, mobilize community resources, influence policy decisions, or establish alternative systems of service delivery.

Some organizations are both empowered and empowering. The Black church, for example, is one of the few organizations built, financed, and controlled by African Americans. It has fostered the empowerment of its members, providing them with leadership opportunities, a psychological sense of community, and a positive sense collective identity and efficacy. The church has also served as a hub from social change efforts, most notably during the civil rights movements of the 1960s and 1970s (Brashears & Roberts, 1996).

Empowered organizations are not always empowering, however. For example, many large lobbying organizations (such as the American Association of Retired People and the National Rifle Association) have long membership lists and may frequently request donations but do not enhance the psychological empowerment of their members. Similarly, organizations that foster the psychological empowerment of members may not work to alter the status quo (Zimmerman, 1995; 2000). Alcoholics Anonymous (AA), for example, encourages personal growth and mutual support but is avowedly apolitical (Reissman & Bay, 1992). Robert Putnam (2000), in his cogent analysis of the decrease in civic participation, suggested that there has been an increase in the number of organizations that encourage personal growth in the presence of others but do not foster the social responsibilities on which communities depend. He also documented an increase in organizations that allow citizens to express demands in ways that demand less of them. Organizations' mailing lists grow, but member involvement does not. As Putnam (2000) put it, we "kibitz, but we don't play" (p. 183). Although Putnam did not use the terms "empowering" and empowered" organizations, I think he would agree that the main problem of the turn of this century is that people participate in fewer organizations that are *both* empowering and empowered.

ELEMENTS OF ORGANIZATIONAL SUCCESS

There are a number of organizations that have managed to swim against the tide described by Putnam (2000). Some microsystems bring people together to create change in themselves *and* the world around them. For the sake of convenience, let's call them *empowerful* organizations. What can we learn from these organizations? Insights in this section are gleaned from a number of studies described earlier, and three additional sources. Kenneth Maton and Deborah Salem (1995) identified common elements of success across three community contexts for empowerment—a religious fellowship, a mutual help group for people with serious mental illness, and an educational program for African American college students. Greg Watson (1999) drew ten lessons about organizational success from his tenure as executive director of the Dudley Street Neighborhood Initiative (DSNI), described in the opening of this chapter. The activist Thomas Wolff identified several guiding principles for creating competent community coalitions (Berkowitz & Wolff, 1996). Elements of success that converge across various analyses are described below.

Inspiring Belief System. One of the key characteristics of empowerful organizations identified by Maton and Salem (1995) is a belief system that inspires growth, emphasizes strengths, and encourages considerations that extend beyond the self. Settings can bring out the best in people by calling on them to answer to a higher cause. For some settings, this means incorporating a spiritual dimension into empowerment work, but the higher goal need not be overtly religious or spiritual. The guiding vision of an urban village developed by residents of Dudley Street constituted a strength-based, growth-inspiring belief system that transcended the self-interest of the individual residents involved.

Watson (1999) noted the importance of organizations investing whatever it takes up front in terms of time and effort to develop a shared vision. Visioning is not always easy. Lisbeth Schorr (1997) described the difficulties of a group charged with visioning health goals for a community development project in Baltimore. They aimed no higher than shortening the wait in emergency rooms from all day to a few hours. The harsh realities of life for disenfranchised people can make it difficult to "dream big," and service providers' ability to dream may be similarly constrained by the context of their lives—ongoing encounters with budget constraints, bureaucratic barriers, and political mandates.

Opportunities for Involvement. Maton and Salem (1995) also cited the importance of opportunities for organization members to assume multiple and meaningful roles. Indeed, one of the groups they studied purposely created underpopulated settings to encourage the involvement of ever-larger numbers of people (Zimmerman, Reischl, Seidman, Rappaport, Toro & Salem, 1991).

According to Julian Rappaport (1987) one goal of empowerment is the creation of formal roles and responsibilities for every member of the setting, regardless of the person's level of functioning, Empowerful organizations find a niche for anyone who wants to belong. Thomas Wolff (Berkowitz & Wolff, 1996) held that successful coalitions operate on the assumption that everyone in the community has a role to play, and it is only a matter of time before they are brought into the collaborative. On Dudley Street, local residents are seen as a reservoir of community wealth. Watson (1999) described the collective wisdom of *all* residents as an invaluable and expandable resource that must be continually tapped. DSNI has formed numerous committees to utilize resident wisdom (DSNI, No Date c). Similarly, the Block Booster Project (see the Classic Research box) confirmed the importance of opportunities for involvement. Block associations that stood the test of time had more officers, twice the number of committees, and sponsored more activities as compared to those that ceased operations. (Florin, et al., 1992; Wandersman & Florin, 2000).

In considering the importance of creating opportunities for involvement, attention should be paid to

Calvin and Hobbes   by Bill Watterson

Successful organizations offer multiple opportunities for involvement. CALVIN AND HOBBES © Watterson. Reprinted with permission of UNIVERSAL PRESS SYNDICATE. All rights reserved.

ensuring that disenfranchised people have a voice. This includes youth. Watson (1999) argued that youth involvement keeps a community's vision alive because young people are the most valuable renewable resource.

Leadership. A paradox of organizational empowerment is that strong leadership enhances the full participation of setting members. Research shows that group members prefer leaders who actively direct the group and enforce rules (Wandersman & Florin, 2000). Leaders must, however, lead with flair. Organization members do not simply want to be told what to do. Empowerful leaders provide direction, but also inspire community participation. The civil rights activist Dianne Nash noted that, "Charismatic leadership has not freed us and it never will, because freedom is, by definition, people realizing that they are their own leaders" (Ingram, 1990; pp. 221–222). DSNI has established a Leadership Development Committee devoted to cultivating leadership skills in residents (DSNI, No Date c).

Maton and Salem (1985) found that empowerful organizations relied on the shared, visionary leadership of interpersonally and organizationally talented people who were committed to the growth of members and the setting as a whole. This characterization of leaders coincides with the notion of *collaborative*

leadership (Chrislip & Larson, 1994). Collaborative leaders inspire a commitment to action, lead as peer problem solvers, foster broad-based involvement, and sustain hope.

Leadership may be particularly important when power differentials exist among setting subgroups. In their study of the failed policy council in an alternative school, Judith Gruber and Edison Trickett (1987) hypothesized that formal leaders could have minimized the pre-existing power differentials among members that contributed to the council's downfall. Checks on leadership are also important. DSNI established a Board Development Committee to ensure that the leadership operates as intended and that residents ultimately make decisions about policies that have neighborhood implications.

Organizational Structure. Gruber and Trickett (1987) found that resistance to formal structures (including elected leaders) led to a "tyranny of structurelessness." Research strongly suggests that setting members prefer formal as opposed to informal group structure (Wandersman & Florin, 2000). Formal structure is associated with greater member involvement and increased satisfaction with the group. Structure reduces ambiguities. Clear roles, tasks, responsibilities, and operating procedures allow group members to work together to achieve their goals.

Organizational structures, like visionary leadership, can also balance pre-existing power differences among setting subgroups. Meg Bond and Chris Keys (Bond, 1999; Bond & Keys, 1993) described the tensions between parents and nonparents on a community board seeking responsive and appropriate services for children with developmental disabilities. Tensions stemmed, in part, from the parents' subordinate social position. Parent board members came from predominantly working class backgrounds, while nonparents were almost exclusively middle class. Two formal group structures were instituted to reduce tensions and promote parent empowerment. First, group composition was changed so that parent status and socioeconomic status no longer intertwined. Board members who spanned the two categories (i.e., middle class parents and working class nonparents) enabled each subgroup to hear the other more willingly. Second, power differentials were balanced by the creation of bylaws that dictated a majority representation by parents at all times. DSNI has similar bylaws to ensure that all the diverse voices of the neighborhood have a say in the neighborhood organization (DSNI, No Date d).

Innovation. As described in the chapter opening, Dudley Street embraces innovation. Watson (1999) noted the importance of challenging conventional wisdom. It was business as usual that allowed disempowerment to occur in the first place, and so new paradigms are needed to promote empowerment. As the poet–activist Audre Lorde (1984) put it, "the master's tools will never dismantle the master's house" (p. 110).

For example, Dudley Street residents recognized that traditional urban planning is inherently flawed and biased. It focuses on functional urban designs without consideration of human values and the local community. Watson (1999) recounted that the plans for rebuilding Dudley Street crafted by planning professionals called for hotels, office towers and historical parks that would gentrify the area, displace current residents, and obliterate local culture. Watson noted that the willingness to explore new ways of doing things allowed DSNI to become

the first community-based nonprofit organization to be granted power of eminent domain. Dudley Street activists convinced the Boston city government to take the unprecedented step of allowing the community to acquire empty lots and use them for affordable housing and other development projects as the residents saw fit. On Dudley Street, the community ultimately decides what gets built. The importance of this power becomes clear to me when I think of the local coffee shops, hardware stores, and other businesses in my own neighborhood that have closed in the past three years as yet another Starbucks, Home Depot, and SuperTarget opened nearby.

Celebration of Identity. In reviewing the literature on effective community organizations, Abraham Wandersman and Paul Florin (2000) found that members appreciate team spirit and camaraderie. Similarly, Maton and Salem (1995) found that empowerful organizations have peer-based support systems that foster a shared sense of identity. The possibilities for empowerment increase when group members feel connected to each other, and when this connection constitutes a reason to rejoice. Thomas Wolff (Berkowtiz & Wolff, 1996) noted the importance of celebrating hope, having fun, and affirming the strengths of the community. On Dudley Street, the multicultural festival was one of the first organizing efforts of DSNI and continues to be a popular, community-building event.

BEYOND THE MICROSYSTEM

Empowerment links individuals, local settings, and the larger social structure (e.g., Chavis & Wandersman, 1990; Florin et al., 1992; Wandersman & Florin, 2000). It provides opportunities for individuals to join groups where they can develop new competencies, grow in confidence, gain a sense of control, decrease feelings of social alienation, and become hopeful about the future. People working in coalition can improve their neighborhoods—reclaim vacant lots, combat crime, ensure a better education for their children. Ideally, individual and organizational empowerment also lead to changes in the larger structures that shape our lives.

Change at the macrosystem level is difficult to effect, however. Thomas Wolff (Berkowitz & Wolff, 1996) acknowledged that the community coalitions with which he has worked have succeeded in creating local changes but not larger-scale social and economic transformations. At the same time, Stephanie Riger (1993) questioned whether a view of empowerment as a lower-level phenomenon can ever address the all-important systemic causes of disenfranchisement that necessitate empowerment in the first place.

INFLUENCE OF THE MACROSYSTEM ON LOWER-LEVEL CHANGE EFFORTS

Can interventions that enhance perceived or even actual control of resources solely at the individual level, or even at the microsystem level, be considered empowerment? Let's look briefly at examples of "empowerment" interventions at the individual level and microsystem level and then consider two in-depth examples of how well-conceived empowerment efforts can be undone by higher-level processes.

As an individual-level example, Emily Ozer and Albert Bandura (1990) described an intervention they labeled as empowerment that targeted forty-three women, many of whom had previously been assaulted. These women were taught self-defense skills, including physical strategies (eye strokes, biting, kicking), verbal defense techniques, and ways of projecting a confident demeanor that might protect them from attack. The researchers found that women who participated in the intervention reported an enhanced perception of self-efficacy and an improved quality of life. As testimony to the effectiveness of the intervention, the researchers quoted a participant who recounted, " 'I feel freer and more capable now than ever. I now make choices about what I will or won't do based on whether or not I want to, not whether or not it's frightening me' " (Ozer & Bandura, 1990, p. 484). Can this intervention be considered an example of empowerment if the psychological transformation of individual

women did not coincide with a reduction in violence against women through improved social conditions? Even if program participants learned to stave off attacks, is the program successful if would-be assailants simply go off in search of easier targets?

At a microsystem level, consider an example from the workplace literature. Meg Bond (1999) observed that "worker empowerment" reached the status of buzzword near the end of the twentieth century. In the 1980s and 1990s, *quality circles* were an extremely popular means of "worker empowerment," used by 80% of Fortune 1000 companies (Klein et al., 2000). Quality circles consisted of groups of workers, usually numbering between six and twelve, who met regularly to address work-related problems. Although workers were authorized to make suggestions, they generally did not make final decisions. Thus, they did not have actual power. Managerial commitment to quality circles was often limited, and their adoption often stemmed from a desire to boost employee morale (and improve organizational performance!) rather than a true interest in redistributing organizational power. Can workplace programs be considered empowering if they support or even promote worker exploitation?

Questions remain as to whether individual-level or microsystem-level interventions that do not target injustices in the larger social system can be considered empowerment. In addition, even enlightened empowerment interventions that consider the sociopolitical context can be undone by higher-level processes. As Gruber and Trickett (1987) observed, the creation of an egalitarian structure does not ensure the equal distribution of power because these structures exists as part of larger systems in which the distribution of resources is not equal. In reading the following two examples, consider with the wisdom of hindsight what program planners *might* have done to increase the likelihood of true empowerment.

TWO EXAMPLES

Let's now look at two examples of how larger systems can undo empowerment-oriented interventions, one in the United States and one in Puerto Rico.

The Perinatal Outreach Program. Clare Strawn (1994) described the Perinatal Outreach Program (PNO), an outreach and education program designed to improve the perinatal care of low-income women in several ethnic communities in California. Using participant observation, analysis of program documents (e.g., grant proposals, evaluation reports, case files) and ethnographic interviews, Strawn showed that although the crafters of PNO articulated a philosophy of empowerment, the actual intervention did not match their objectives and philosophy.

The PNO goals implicitly and explicitly endorsed an empowerment approach. The program founders sought to provide outreach, case management, and support services in a nonjudgmental, culturally appropriate, respectful, and supportive manner to pregnant women and new mothers. They sought to assist women within their natural social support systems and aimed to encourage clients' self-determination and participation in decision-making and problem-solving. They explicitly sought to "facilitate the empowerment and autonomy of the client" (Strawn, 1994, p. 164).

Gradually, program features that would foster client empowerment disappeared. The idea of creating mutual support groups among women was one of the first ideas to go. It was eliminated from the final contract as it did not coincide with the priorities of the funding agency (the California Health Department). Information on the clients' natural support systems was gathered as intended, but these networks were not integrated into the interventions as the program developers originally planned. Caseworkers used these networks only to spread the word of the program After establishing contact with clients, the caseworkers adopted traditional models of helping that fostered dependency. PNO staff positioned themselves as the primary support givers. Their resources—cars, driving ability, knowledge of English, and direct connections to organizations of power—were on loan to the women, temporarily expanding their access to services. The women remained isolated from each other, however, and had no opportunity to develop their personal and communal resources.

The ethnic diversity and disenfranchisement of the clients received attention by PNO staff. The directors hired bilingual and sometimes bicultural caseworkers. No one attended, however, to the political, economic, and social context of disenfranchisement. An individualized notion of empowerment placed responsibility for the problem of poor prenatal care on the shoulders of the mothers-to-be and ignored such social conditions as the fragmentation of services, inadequate transportation, shortage of childcare and lack of employment opportunities.

Strawn showed that during this intervention, opportunities for real change occurred. An individual-level ideology enveloped the program, however, and opportunities for collective empowerment were not seized. For example, at one PNO meeting, a staff person asked residents what they most needed. Transportation emerged as the most pressing concern, but caseworkers dismissed it as a low priority because the original grant proposal did not address transportation issues. On another occasion, a group of Southeast Asian women requested a PNO class on birth control. Once again, PNO workers did not follow through. The expression of the felt needs of the community for transportation and birth control created openings for dialogue in which outside agents could have supported the clients as agents of the changes they viewed as necessary.

As yet another example, a Russian caseworker working with Russian clients in PNO learned that her community contained no medical practitioners. This shortage was traced to policies that prevented health care providers trained in Russia from practicing in the U.S. The caseworker devised an individual-level rather than system-changing solution to this problem—she decided to enroll in nursing school. Contrast this decision with the social change solution developed by immigrants from Cambodia in Lowell, Massachusetts, when faced with a similar situation (Silka & Tip, 1994). As a result of immigration, the local school system was in dire need of Khmer-speaking teachers, but potentially eligible teachers had lost their documentation in the Cambodian civil war. Local university representatives and members of the Cambodian American community worked together to develop an alternative teacher certification procedure so that immigrant teachers could teach in U.S. classrooms.

In the PNO intervention, workers did not incorporate community resident perspectives and resources into their intervention. Professionals predetermined the relevant problems and strategies in their grant proposal, which was expressly written to attract funding from a government organization that had a social agenda of its own. Despite the intentions of the program founders to design an empowerment intervention, clients gained no real access to resources. Strawn (1994) concluded, "the social organization of disempowerment was embedded in the macro-environment and filtered down to the interpersonal interactions between well-intentioned helpers and communities" (p. 172).

Proyecto Esfuerzo. Irma Serrano-García's (1984) description of Proyecto Esfuerzo also demonstrated how higher-level factors can sabotage empowerment interventions. Esfuerzo is a rural community of 1400 poor families in Puerto Rico. Residents' meager income derives mostly from welfare and other governmental programs. In 1980, a Community Mental Health Center in collaboration with University of Puerto Rico faculty and students launched Proyecto Esfuerzo to assist this impoverished community.

The project began with a familiarization stage during which personnel learned all they could about Esfuerzo as unobtrusively as possible (e.g., reading newspaper articles, visiting the community informally). The next stage consisted of a formal assessment of community needs, resources, and expectations. The most pressing community need was for relocation; residents believed that their land was in imminent danger of flooding. Other community problems included disastrous road conditions, erratic garbage collection, lack of telephone service, and a shortage of recreational activities. Resources included ideas about desirable activities and a willingness to work together to solve problems.

Community leaders and residents were then helped to organize into task forces to meet identified needs. Proyecto staff confirmed the seriousness of the threat posed by flooding, but decided not to address this long-standing and politically charged issue because other groups were spearheading relocation efforts. Instead task forces were formed to meet the social and recreational needs of the community and to share information gleaned from Proyecto interviews with the entire community. Residents were helped to develop the skills necessary to accomplish these tasks.

In assessing this intervention, Serrano-García noted some successes and some failures. The project succeeded in developing resident skills. Task force members increasingly took over group functions and expressed awareness of their learning. Community members also identified community resources and developed an internal sense of self-sufficiency. The project might even have succeeded in combating some components of colonialist ideology, such as a rigid value stance and an intolerance of dissidence. The larger social, economic, and political systems that kept residents in poverty and in danger of decimation by flooding remained unchallenged, however. Serrano-García concluded that the intervention created an *illusion* of empowerment. Residents felt more control over their lives but did not confront the colonial context that determined their lives and, in many ways, their thoughts.

Serrano-García became convinced that the project's small successes were possible only because the low-status residents were not recognized as a threat by people who controlled resources and because the project did not choose to deal with problems that led to direct confrontations with governmental institutions and other power brokers. Serrano-García reasoned that disenfranchised people are permitted to gain control only until they become threatening to dominant groups. Change efforts that hold the promise of redistributing societal power inspire counterforces that maintain the status quo.

Larger systems can limit empowerment efforts originating at lower levels, or they can support them. Serrano-García (1984) posited that Proyecto Esfuerzo might have grown into a powerful social change effort if there had been larger community or national organizations ready to build on the intervention's successes.

The examples of the Perinatal Outreach Program and Proyecto Esfuerzo demonstrate that interventions aimed at a particular level (individual, microsystem, or community) need to consider ever-higher levels of analysis in their quest for empowerment. Empowerment may be seen as a reiterative process. Individual empowerment and group empowerment are mutually enhancing and lead to increased engagement with civic life and concern for higher levels of influence (e.g., Saegert & Winkel, 1996). Empowerment efforts may be most complete when they connect proximal conditions and distal events in society and when actions are increasingly directed at less and less local conditions.

⌘ Empowerment and Community Psychology's Guiding Principles

Empowerment, as an orienting concept, has direct implications for each of community psychology's guiding principles (see Perkins & Zimmerman, 1995). We have already touched on how empowerment embodies several of these principles, but let's examine each more closely.

EMPOWERMENT AND CONTEXT

The preceding discussion of levels of analysis has already examined empowerment beyond the level of the individual, and so this section will be relatively brief. As described above, empowerment links individual well-being with larger social and political processes (see also Kroeker, 1995). A consideration of empowerment as a multilevel construct also highlights the need to view empowerment is a dynamic, context-dependent construct that varies across individuals (e.g., Keiffer, 1984) and across settings (e.g., Stewart & Weinstein, 1997).

Empowerment cannot be reduced to a single universal definition or set of rules (Zimmerman, 1995; 2000). Because the empowerment process is tied to context, its meaning varies across individuals,

settings, and cultures (Rappaport, 1987). Empowerment is indeed, as Edison Trickett (1994) proclaimed, "ecological in spirit" (p. 587). Precise definitions cannot be preordained by researchers, politicians, or any other outside force. Those of us dedicated to empowerment must take James Kelly's (1971) notion of an eco-identity (see Chapter Seven) to heart. Without "a grounding in local conditions, the concept runs the risk of becoming either a slogan lacking in substance or an imperialist activity once again done to people rather than with them" (Trickett, 1994, p. 591).

Consider, for example, the meaning of empowerment among the women dairy farmers described in the Community Intervention box (Shefner-Rogers et al., 1998). Researchers developed an empowerment scale that included such items as whether or not the woman made decisions about vaccinating milk animals or belonged to the dairy cooperative. Obviously community organizers working with youth in urban Detroit would need to devise a very different measure of empowerment that reflected the resources, barriers, and mechanisms for change relevant to that group.

EMPOWERMENT AND SOCIAL CHANGE

Some community psychologists have described Julian Rappaport's (1981, 1987) call for empowerment as a rallying cry for social change (Price, 1990; Zimmerman, 2000). Empowerment rests on the belief that people must work together to address the unequal distribution of and access to resources that is at the root of many problems in society. This conception of empowerment is not universal, however.

LIBERAL AND CONSERVATIVE PERSPECTIVES

In politics, the term empowerment enjoys bipartisan support. Members of both liberal and conservative parties advocate an empowerment agenda, although not the *same* agenda. More conservative individuals view empowerment as consistent with self-reliance, private voluntarism, and the reduction of big government. More liberal people, including many community psychologists concerned about righting inequities, watch with dismay as the rhetoric of empowerment is used to individualize responsibility for social problems. The theme of self-sufficiency seems empowering, but it is often used to relieve governmental institutions of their obligation to provide care and to justify the withdrawal of federal funds that previously supported empowerment initiatives (Silka & Tip, 1994; Strawn, 1994; Zimmerman, 2000). In his seminal address twenty years ago, Julian Rappaport (1981) anticipated this misuse of the term. Along with his hopes for empowerment as a unifying concept, he expressed his fear that a position of benign neglect would be cloaked as deep respect for individual freedoms. Empowerment would then be misconstrued as a rationale for doing nothing to change the status quo.

More recently Rappaport (1995) has suggested that community psychologists not be so quick to dismiss conservative viewpoints. Although he confessed his willingness to join other progressives in disapproving of the ideologies and actions of many groups claiming an interest in empowerment, he also admitted to finding the debate more useful than not. Ultimately, he advised, we must engage in dialogue not with only like-minded colleagues, but with all interested citizens. Conservative perspectives can push liberals past the borders of political correctness into more meaningful territory (see also Redding, 2001). Polarization of the two political camps only limits thinking. Liberals may resist attempts to relieve government of responsibility for promoting equality, arguing that disenfranchised groups require basic resources and technical assistance in order to level the playing field. There are, however, significant areas of overlap in the conservative and liberal meanings of the term on which to build. We might agree, for example, about the importance of mediating structures in driving empowerment efforts.

SOCIAL CHANGE AND COMMUNITY PSYCHOLOGISTS' HABITS OF THOUGHT

Despite the popularity of the term, widespread social transformation has not resulted from the plethora of empowerment initiatives implemented over the past decades. Community psychologists cannot simply blame conservative co-optation of the term for this state affairs. Our own habits of thoughts also interfere with social change agendas. Three shifts in perspective might increase the likelihood that empowerment-oriented interventions lead to social change.

The first, discussed above, is the need to attend to evermore remote levels of analysis. The second is a consideration of both the *process* and the *outcomes* of empowerment efforts (e.g., Perkins & Zimmerman, 1995; Swift & Levin, 1987). Influential definitions encourage a view of empowerment as a process (e.g., Cornell Empowerment Group, 1989; Rappaport 1984c), but Stephanie Riger (1993) questioned community psychology's willingness to equate empowerment with participation in the political process, as if changes in procedure automatically led to changes in the distribution of resources. Organizations can have quality circles (Klein et al., 2000) and schools can have policy councils (Gruber & Trickett, 1987), but these "decision-making bodies" may actually wield very little power. As Arthur Himmelman suggests (Himmelman, Johnson, Kaye, Salzman, & Wolff, 2001), token participation can actually reinforce the status quo. The true test of an empowerment effort is whether a real redistribution of valued resources actually occurs.

A third potentially useful shift in perspective is a recognition of the ways that marginalized groups, *not* people in power, control the social change process. Empowerment theory simultaneously sees disenfranchised groups as marginalized and lacking in social power, but also strong and capable agents of social transformation (see Riger, 2001). Some argue that ultimate control of the power relationship lies with the target group members. Paulo Freire (1970/1992) posited that the oppressor has neither the insight nor the motivation to create change, and so oppressed people must unite to transform unjust systems in ways that ultimately liberate the oppressed and oppressor alike.

Irma Serrano-García (1994) identified two ways in which target groups have the power to define the terms of power struggles. First, they can disrupt existing power relationships by altering the importance of the resource in question. They might, for example, obtain the resource elsewhere or perhaps find ways to generate it themselves. On Dudley Street, residents grow much of their own food, lessening their dependence on factory farms and large supermarket chains. Alternatively, target group members can redefine the importance of the resource. A community's consideration of the meaning of wealth may lead to the conclusion that collective wisdom of community residents and youth energy are important resources to nurture, thereby de-emphasizing traditional indicators of wealth, such as the average square footage of the homes or per capita income.

EMPOWERMENT AND DIVERSITY

The majority of work on empowerment with diverse groups has focused on one population at a time. Also important is a consideration of how empowerment can take shape in a multicultural system where different groups seek control over resources. Such expanded notions of empowerment might benefit from a cross-cultural analysis of the very concept of empowerment.

POPULATION-SPECIFIC EMPOWERMENT

In 1994 the *American Journal of Community Psychology* devoted a special issue to the empowerment of marginalized groups. Articles examined the implications of empowerment to people with disabilities, gay and lesbian people, Southeast Asians, Latinas and Latinos, and Black women. Each article identified relevant issues for the group in question. The article on people with disabilities discussed the barriers imposed by the environment (Fawcett, White, Balcazar, Suarez-Balcazar, Mathews, Paine, Seekins, & Smith, 1994). The article on lesbian and gay people highlighted the challenges of creating community for a group whose members are exceedingly diverse, invisible to each other, and have no intergenerational continuity (Garnets and D'Augelli, 1994; see also Kofkin & Schwartz, 1995). A different set of issues pertains to Southeast Asians, who face challenges arising from immigration, language barriers, and other factors (Silka & Tip, 1994).

Population-specific examinations of disenfranchised groups demonstrate how empowerment interfaces with a particular local culture. In addition, some general challenges exist. As one example, each marginalized group struggles with attempts from outsiders to "help" them adapt to society (see Silka & Tip, 1994). These efforts may be labeled empowering, but encouraging minority group members to conform to the dominant culture actually supports the status quo and reinforces their marginalization. The editors of the special issue also noted several empowerment strategies that cut across group boundaries (Serrano-García & Bond, 1994). Diverse groups all experienced the need to generate new or strengthen existing social networks in order to maximize resources. All groups sought to develop political participation through grassroots movements and attempted to strengthen group identity as a means of achieving broad social goals.

COEMPOWERMENT

A new set of concerns emerges when we go beyond population-specific analyses of empowerment and consider the difficulties inherent in honoring diversity in a multicultural society where various disenfranchised groups with different agendas seek to create change. Stephanie Riger (1993) framed the question as follows, "If the empowerment of the disenfranchised group is the primary value, then what is to hold together societies made up of different groups?" (p. 290). Let's look at some ways of tackling Riger's question.

First we must question conceptualizations of empowerment in which one group's gain is another's loss. If the empowerment of one person or group requires the oppression of another, then the more things change, the more they remain the same (Moss, 1991). A system of inequity is a system of inequity regardless of which particular group manages to climb its way to the "top." We need to think of empowerment as something other than a shift in the balance of power that enables a new group to gain power over others. Empowerment cannot be a zero-sum game. Julian Rappaport (1987) proposed that empowerment itself may be seen not as a scarce resource, but as an ideology that once adopted can expand.

Meg Bond and Chris Keys (1993) explored the possibility that different groups with different values and different priorities can be simultaneously empowered. They conducted a case study of a community board working to improve services for children with developmental disabilities. Members of this board included parents and nonparents of different socioeconomic levels. They coined the term **coempowerment** to refer to the goal of shared authority over agenda setting, discussion, and decision making. It overlaps with the notion of "collaborative empowerment," (Fawcett, Paine-Andrews, Francisco, Schultz, Richter, Lewis, Williams, Harris, Berkley, Fisher, & Lopez., 1995; Himmelman, 2001; see also van Uchelen's [2000] notion of "field control"). When coempowerment occurs, multiple groups with divergent perspectives jointly influence the direction of a setting. Although the influence of any particular group ebbs and flows, a sense of mutuality exists (Bond, 1999). Coempowerment exemplifies synergy: different groups connect and strengthen the total system in ways no one could alone (Bond & Keys, 1993).

When culturally different groups come together, they bring with them different motivations, perspectives, investments, class and cultural backgrounds, and approaches to collaboration. These differences often cause bickering, entrenchment in opposing camps, and a variety of other "power struggles" (Bond & Keys, 1993). Sometimes the coalition is co-opted by the strongest subgroup (Gruber & Trickett, 1987), and sometimes one or more subgroups leave the coalition. However, differences do not inevitably lead to alienation, apathy, insurmountable conflict, irreversible organizational upheaval, or the disintegration of a setting.

Bond and Keys identified several aspects of a system's culture that promote the coempowerment of subgroups. First, mutual empowerment increases if the system culture supports each group's meaningful inclusion. This means recognizing both the differences and similarities among group members. As described earlier, boundary-spanning people and structures also facilitate inter-group un-

derstanding. The community board Bond and Keys studied initially included parents who were of low socioeconomic status and nonparents who were middle class. When the setting expanded to include boundary-spanning people (i.e., parents from middle class backgrounds and nonparents from working class backgrounds), functioning of the board improved, in part because the boundary spanners could facilitate inter-group understanding. Finally, Bond and Keys recognized the importance of an organizational system that appreciated the interdependence of subgroups. This is reminiscent the findings of Muzafer Sherif and colleagues (1961) in their work with boys in Robber's Cave. The reduction of negative intergroup attitudes and interactions required contexts of mutual interdependence and collaboration towards a common goal. Shared visions can bring people together across differences.

The Dudley Street Neighborhood Initiative provides another example of coempowerment. On Dudley Street, neighborhood diversity is honored. The uniqueness of different cultures is celebrated in restaurants, theaters, and festivals. The need for diverse groups to work together is also appreciated. The DSNI board composition reflects the neighborhood's diversity, with designated seats for different groups. The board is able to function as a whole because the common vision of an urban village serves as a superordinate goal that unites the diverse membership.

Another example involves a small tribe of Indians who live just north of Phoenix on the Fort McDowell reservation (O'Sullivan, Tausig, & Lindsey, 1984). In 1961, the reservation became the focus of government attention as it lay near the confluence of the Salt and Verde Rivers—the site of a proposed dam. Most people believed that the dam would solve two pressing problems in the area. It would alleviate water shortages in this desert state and also reduce the threat of flooding in heavily populated areas. Plans for the dam enjoyed tremendous support from the business, agricultural, and political leaders of Arizona. The Yavapai Indians, who now faced the prospect of their third forced relocation, did not share in the enthusiasm.

The tribe seemed to have little power to resist. They were small in number, poor, and inexperienced in political maneuvering. The government offered the Yavapai monetary compensation for the land and income from the recreational facilities that the new reservoir would make possible. Business leaders characterized the dam as "the best thing that could happen to the Indians" (O'Sullivan et al., 1984, p. 79).

Plans proceeded slowly, and the Yavapai united in their opposition. A few others, including environmentalists, pro-Indian supporters, antigovernment advocates, and river recreationists joined the resistance. In 1977 they convinced President Carter to refuse funding for the dam project. In 1978 however, the first of three major floods hit the Phoenix area and the ban on the dam project was lifted. The Yavapai realized that through legal and political wrangling, they could tie up the project for the foreseeable future. In order to move beyond this impasse, a four-year study was launched to explore flood control options. The study was to include a highly visible public participation program. In addition, the governor of Arizona, Bruce Babbitt, appointed a Governor's Advisory Committee comprised of twenty-nine representatives from cities, organizations, and interest groups that had a stake in the outcome. Babbitt purposely put representatives of significant competing interests on this committee and charged them with making one consensual recommendation to him at the completion of the study. This provided an opportunity for coempowerment (or disaster!).

The Yavapai gradually convinced other stakeholders of the unfairness of the dam project. They launched media campaigns and made entreaties that were both logical and spiritual. Religious organizations were among the first to become convinced. Eventually, all major religious groups came out in opposition to relocation and held prayer services on behalf of the Indians. The Yavapai appealed to their opponents' consciences by stressing the impact of being torn from a sacred land to which they had historical, emotional, cultural, and spiritual ties. The commissioned study of the flood control options recognized the psychological impact of compulsory relocation. Researchers warned that if forced relocation occurred, the Yavapai would suffer from a lost sense of control and destroyed cultural identity, conditions that would seriously compromise their physical and psychological health.

On October 2, 1981, the Governor's Advisory Committee opposed the dam and recommended an alternative plan with a vote of 19 to 1 (one environmentalist cast a vote for "no action"). It seems that one reason this committee of diverse and conflicting parties was able to reach consensus was because the research study provided a forum for the public participation of all stakeholders. Thus, every viewpoint was heard. In addition, the information generated during the research study was available to all. A reciprocal process where all parties became aware of and responsive to the needs of others resulted in a decision in which everyone had a say, and with which everyone could live.

LEARNING FROM THE MARGINS

Coempowerment is only one innovative response to Riger's question of how we can hold together diverse groups of empowered people. There are others. Every group, because of its unique position, will have a slightly different view of empowerment. If empowerment scholars can draw out alternative visions of what is meant by empowerment, we will gain new insight and build more complete models.

As described earlier, feminist perspectives on power suggest a model of empowerment based on receptivity rather than agency (e.g., Rosenwasser, 1992b; 1992c). African American perspectives suggest that a place exists for spiritual perspectives; virtually every African American empowerment effort has had God at its center (Watts, 1997).

People with disabilities might have important lessons to share on how to think about *control* (Fine & Asch, 1988). Empowerment is often framed as an effort to gain control. People in modern societies seek to gain more and more control over life. Indeed, cloning and genetic engineering are two examples of our efforts to control life itself. People with disabilities remind us that we *cannot* control everything. As human beings with physical existences, we are sometimes in control and sometime not. As members of social groups, we are sometimes in control, and sometimes not. What *kind* of control is important to well-being? And what benefits accrue from relinquishing control? There are important paradoxes to uncover. I am reminded, for example, that one step in twelve-step programs is to recognize that we as people do not ultimately have control, which paradoxically allows us to assume more control.

EMPOWERMENT AND VALUES

Values enter into discussions of empowerment from several directions. This section examines three. First, values underlie the very construct of empowerment. Second values affect the actions of both the interventionist interested in empowerment and the disenfranchised groups with whom interventionist works. Finally, values may themselves be a resource relevant to empowerment efforts.

THE VALUES OF EMPOWERMENT

A few scholars have discussed the values underlying the construct of empowerment. Julian Rappaport (1981) highlighted empowerment's emphasis on citizen's rights as compared to prevention's focus on people's needs. Isaac Prilleltensky (1998) examined the value base of empowerment in relation to the values he identified as important to psychologists. He noted that empowerment challenges the status quo in its attention to *distributive justice,* but aligns with traditional psychological approaches in its valuing of *self-determination.* He argued that popular models of empowerment, which focus on obtaining resources for oneself and one's group, fail to disengage from *individualism* and so undermine the important values of *collaboration* and *caring compassion.*

Empowerment efforts that augment the mastery or control of one individual or group may actually work against a larger sense of community (Perkins, 1995; Speer, 2000). Stephanie Riger (1993) identified a primary task for community psychologists as articulating

the relationship between empowerment and community. Riger warned that a view of empowerment that emphasized individuation, mastery, and control overlooked the connectedness of human life. Empowerment research, theory, and practice can do a better job of balancing the existing attention to agency with an increased commitment to communion (Rappaport, 1995).

There exists a dialectical relationship between self and community in all societies. The question is to what degree each is emphasized. The strongly egalitarian !Kung society uses collaborative, community-based approaches to the distribution of both plentiful resources (e.g., building materials for their shelters) and scarce resources (e.g., water) (Katz, 1984). On the other hand, the strongly individualized society of the U.S. tends to adopt individualistic approaches to resource distribution no matter how plentiful the resource. Empowerment scholars can help balance the current focus in the U.S. on individuation by stressing the potential for empowerment to foster community.

THE VALUES OF EMPOWERMENT SEEKERS

Research and practice that promote empowerment (like all research and practice) are based in the interventionist's own values. These values may or may not conform to the values of the groups with which he or she works. In this section we will first examine the importance of a value match between interventionists and the targeted group, and then examine the implications of decisions to reveal or not reveal our values.

The Value Match. Several community psychologists have asked whether we really want to empower *all* disenfranchised groups (e.g., Price, 1990; Riger, 1993). Should we seek, for example, to empower neo-Nazis? Although many would have no problem responding to that question in the negative, not all value conflicts are as straightforward.

Value dilemmas revolve around not only who deserves to be empowered, but also what we want to empower people to do. A community psychologist may collaborate with a group deemed worthy of empowerment only to find that the group's empowerment agenda conflicts with her or his deeply held values. What should nonviolent interventionists who believe that children are a disempowered group do when efforts to honor the voices of powerless parents in school council meetings result in parental demands for the corporal punishment of children (Trickett, 1994)?

A more complete understanding of the local context can increase interventionists' sensitivity to different empowerment agendas. Still, community psychologists must grapple with the fact that empowerment does *not* mean helping people to do only what *we* think they should do.

The Veiling of Values. Because scientists enjoy a position of power in this society, the way in which our values affect our work requires careful consideration. The implications of expressing our values also merit attention.

Numerous community psychologists have argued for the importance of revealing our values whenever possible. In some instances, however, we may not have the freedom to do so. Irma Serrano-García's (1984) report on Proyecto Esfuerzo made clear that the project leaders operated from a particular value stance. They favored the independence of Puerto Rico from colonial rule. This belief put them in the minority; most Puerto Ricans favor either gaining statehood (Puerto Rico would become the fifty-first state of the United States) or remaining a commonwealth. When Proyecto Esfuerzo was launched, community members questioned the project staff about their political persuasions. The staff dodged these questions with reference to the nonpartisan position of their employer, the University of Puerto Rico. As employees of this purportedly apolitical organization, project staff did not have the freedom to express their pro-independence stance.

Serrano-García recognized the possibility that had the staff expressed their ideological views, the community would have rejected their involvement. Value differences may have created an insurmountable barrier. On the other hand, the staff's supposed neutrality hindered their consciousness-raising efforts by forcing the avoidance of pressing partisan issues. Had they not been shackled by university policy, project staff may well have decided to take the risk of unveiling their values. True, they may then have lost the opportunity to work with the disempowered community. They would not have ended up, however, in the morally compromised position of supporting the development of a community group that did not challenge and may even have supported a political ideology that the staff believed caused the community's problems in the first place.

VALUES AS A RESOURCE

Ten years after recounting her perceived failures with Proyecto Esfuerzo, Irma Serrano-García (1994) published a groundbreaking article on power. In this article she proposed that morality should be considered a resource. It can be an instrumental resource in that two parties may engage in conflict over whose vision of morality should prevail (that is, which value system is most valuable). It can also be an infraresource—a resource that facilitates access to instrumental resources.

The success of the Yavapai Indians in defeating the proposed dam stemmed, in large part, from their ability to use morality as an infraresource. When their plight became understood, people in power could not in good conscience build a dam that would force the Yavapai to leave their homeland for the third time. Nonviolent protesters in the civil rights movements also gained empowerment through appeals to morality. Perhaps moral power should be added to the list of power sources begun by French and Raven (1960). While legitimate power accrues only to people in positions of organizational or societal power, moral authority is conferred by a higher source.

You will remember that Serrano-García (1994) delineated different strategies disenfranchised people can use to disrupt power relationships. They can gain control of a resource, alter its importance by meeting their needs in other ways, or redefine the importance of the resource. Mahatma Gandhi, Martin Luther King, Jr., and other visionary leaders redefined the importance of *all* resources relative to morality. Their actions conveyed the conviction that morality was more important than job security, more important than food, more important than physical safety, and ultimately, more important than life itself. When disenfranchised people redefine the terms of power struggles and expose the moral emptiness of policies that enforce inequities, then "the power of morality will prevail over the morality of the powerful" (Serrano-García, 1994, p. 17).

EMPOWERMENT AND STRENGTHS

Empowerment directs attention toward health and competence. It promotes images of people as powerful, worthy, and capable. Individuals join forces to exercise their rights instead of passively waiting to have their needs fulfilled by others. In order for empowerment to occur, help providers need to relinquish their sense of omnipotence and omniscience and cease to defend professional territories and prerogatives (Katz, 1984).

Although empowerment efforts have a place for expertise (e.g., the building of *expert power*) there is no room for expert-helper models of helping.

Katz (1984) asserted that helpers must offer themselves and their knowledge under the same conditions as the people they seek to help. This includes being vulnerable to the same risks they face. Similarly, Serrano-García (1984) held that consciousness raising requires horizontal relationships between the change agent and participants. In the context of nonhierarchical relationships, genuine dialogue, respectful attention, and optimism about the possibility of change can lead to social transformation. As Ram Dass and Paul Gorman (1985) put it, "Our aim is to awaken together and see what follows, not to manipulate one another into this action or that" (p. 163).

For empowerment to occur, a change in roles must take place where client–expert relationships are replaced by relationships built on collaboration and co-participation. Lessons can be learned from a comparison of models of helping in mutual help groups as compared to professional helping relationships (Biklen, 1983). Mutual help groups:

1. Make professional information available to all and subject to questioning;
2. Value personal experience as a way of knowing;
3. Dispense with hierarchy and build a community where all members have equal status;
4. Operate via membership control;
5. Encourage active involvement of members;
6. Utilize problem definitions and solutions developed by the members;
7. Embrace a holistic orientation in which personal difficulties are seen as embedded in a developmental and social context;
8. Prefer flexibility in responding to individuals rather than bureaucratic routines.

In empowerment models, professionals develop, implement, and evaluate interventions in collaboration with community members. This requires the formation of an eco-identity—professionals must become members of the community in which they work, at least temporarily. We create opportunities for community members to learn our skills and so reduce their dependence on outsiders, thereby planning our own obsolescence.

⌘ The Promise of Community Psychology: Telling Stories

Julian Rappaport maintained his commitment to the concept of empowerment in the two decades that followed his seminal article. In his more recent writings, he has wedded the concept of empowerment to the notion of narrative.

Narratives can be understood as resources, and like most resources they are distributed unevenly throughout society. Stories about disenfranchised people are written by more powerful people, who present the others in a negative light (Rappaport, 1995). When people lack power, they are objects rather than subjects. They do not act in the world, rather their environments act upon them (Keiffer, 1984). One goal of empowerment is to establish the self as subject—to assist people who lack social, economic, and political power in becoming the authors of their own life stories. Thus, it is important to consider which stories are legitimated by whom and who has the right to tell whose story (Rappaport, 1995).

Supportive others can help disenfranchised and voiceless people become the authors of their own stories. When story-making happens in the context of community, the results can be profound. One of the functions of mutual help groups is that they provide a forum for people to reformulate and share personal stories. As people talk together about their experiences, they discover new ways to think about themselves (Rappaport, 1993). Sharing stories can also lead to social change. Ram Dass and Paul Gorman (1985) contended that "[t]he most effective political action often grows out of telling one another our stories" (p. 164). In the 1960s, stories shared by countless women gathered around kitchen tables and coffee tables gave shape and energy to a renewed women's movement. When people share stories, they gain insights about who they are, where they came from, what they believe, and perhaps most importantly, what they can become (Rappaport, 1995). This happens not only at the individual level, but the group level as well. Just as individuals have stories about their lives, so too do groups develop **community narratives**. Indeed, Rappaport (2000a) proposed that a community cannot be a community without shared stories. Similarly, David McMillan (1996) posited that a sense of community requires a shared *emotional connection* that results from shared stories about the community's history, traditions, and accomplishments.

Stories are not always spoken. Local arts projects of all types (theater, dance, music) provide a means for silenced groups to uncover, create, interpret, and control their narratives and therefore their identities (Thomas & Rappaport, 1996). Art also brings diverse people together. In outlining a change agenda to reverse the breakdown of community, Robert Putnam (2000) noted the importance of participation in cultural activities, from community theater to rap festivals. He encouraged activists to discover new ways of using art to build social capital.

The arts have always played an important role in empowerment efforts. As one of many examples, consider community mural making (Cockcroft, Weber, & Cockcroft, 1977/1998). Murals are community narratives in which disenfranchised people represent their history and their current lives on a heroic scale. Murals challenge existing stories written by others and present new interpretations of the community's reality. Neighborhood beautification comes second to meaning making, and so murals stir controversy. They involve community members who might never think to enter a museum in public discourse about art, identity, and politics. Every man, woman, and child can form an opinion about a mural that exists on the walls of their building, overlooking the streets on which they walk. No matter who actually painted it, the mural belongs to the community.

One role of the community psychologist is to find ways to give voice to stories that challenge dominant cultural narratives (Thomas & Rappaport, 1996). Some stories and narratives are terrifying, based in fear and oppression and shaped by the voices of others. Community psychologists can "use our tools (methods, critical observation and analysis, scholarship and social influence) to assist others in turning tales of terror into tales of joy" (Rappaport, 2000a, p. 7). As researchers and practitioners, we can aid empowerment efforts by creating settings where people participate in the discovery, creation, and enhancement of personal stories and community narratives (Rappaport, 1995).

This new role requires new approaches to intervention and research. Some innovative projects offer us direction. Charles Keiffer (1984) gathered information on the life courses of activists using what he called "dialogic retrospection." Researcher and activist engaged in a process of joint inquiry, and follow-up interviews were used to extend, correct, and clarify earlier conversations. Thus, the research participants validated and elaborated on the researcher's emerging interpretations of the activists' words. More recently, Lynne Bond and her colleagues (2000) established a group called "The Listening Partners Program," where rural mothers who felt unheard and powerless took turns telling their life stories to each other and found strength in their voices as a result. Autophotography might be a way for people to tell their stories without words (e.g., Ziller, 1990; Wang, 1999). In the process of developing new techniques for community psychology's research and practice, we have much to learn from other disciplines: anthropology, communications, the arts.

The payoff may be substantial. New research and intervention strategies will allow us to gain insights into the worlds of others that could never be gained through more traditional and constrained approaches. In addition, these strategies convey an important meta-message. Being listened to with respect is itself a transforming experience. (Rappaport, 1995).

Action Agenda

Power Animal Shield

Flor Fernandez is one of the women featured in *Visionary Voices: Women on Power* (Rosenwasser, 1992b). Fernandez is a psychologist, shaman, and psychic healer who works with abused women and children. In her work she has developed an activity drawn from ancient traditions. She asks people to draw or paint on shields their "power animals"; their personal symbols of empowerment. In Native American cultures, images used to decorate shields represents the spirit, the self, and one's journey through the lifetime. Fernandez recounted, "When you paint your symbols on the shield, you're actually using symbols that will remind you of your own personal power" (p. 126). In Native American traditions, the power animal connects the person to the earth and serves as a reminder that no one is alone in the universe; other kingdoms offer protection and support.

Think about your power animal. To what animal do you feel a special connection or affinity? What characteristics of that animal are attractive? Is it the graceful speed of a gazelle? The night vision of an owl? The good-natured cleverness of a fox? My power animal is a rhinoceros. I resonate to its solidity, its earth-boundedness, and I look to it for lessons about developing a tougher skin!

Make some sketches of your power animal (or several possible animals and see to which you most resonate). You may want to base your sketches on pictures from photography books or perhaps take a trip to the zoo or to an animal preserve to connect with that animal's essence. Your final drawing is not intended to be a realistic representation, however. It is *your* representation, and so it cannot be wrong. What colors do you associate with your animal? Is it a purple lion with a green mane? A red buffalo? When you think of your power animal, how is does it appear? Is it standing on a windblown cliff? Is it relaxing in the jungle sun? When you have a clear vision of your power animal, find or create a shield (a cardboard cutout would suffice) and draw or paint your power animal on it. Perhaps you will want to share your shields with classmates and tell each other the stories of your power animals.

Identification of Resources

Irma Serrano-García (1994) noted that most people interested in social change are unaware of the many resources available to them. She proposed that the ability to identify resources is a resource in and of itself.

Choose one of the empowerment efforts described in this chapter and consider the resources relevant to that effort. Think about the resources the group seeking power actually had, as well as the resources they sought (or could have/should have sought). For example, what resources were of interest to Dudley Street residents when the Neighborhood Initiative was formed? What resources did the residents of Dudley Street possess that enabled them to build their urban village? What resources were desired by the women dairy farmers in India, and on what resources did the community organizers build? You might consider resources at different levels.

Also consider the resources a community psychologist might bring to the empowerment initiative. For example, in Proyecto Esfuerzo, the intervention team brought to the community the results of the needs assessments, expertise on research methods, and access to information about governmental agencies (Serrano-García, 1994). The status and respect mental health professionals enjoy can also be a resource, providing a sort of power by proxy. Professionals can serve as advocates with inside knowledge about social institutions and an ability to speak the language of the powerful (e.g., Paradis, 2000). After brainstorming about resources, consider the strategies you might have adopted if you were a part of the intervention. Also consider the extent to which you believe the resources you identified are limited or expandable. How would the expandable versus limited nature of the resources affect the strategies you would attempt? After considering resources in the text examples, you might choose an intervention or social change effort in your community and conduct a similar analysis. Does this exercise suggest any next steps to create change in your community?

Shapes of Empowerment

Zimmerman (2000) suggested that measures of empowerment need to be developed in each setting of interest. Think about the settings that matter to you—your classroom, a religious fellowship, your neighborhood. What would empowerment look like in those settings? If you were developing a measure to assess empowerment, as Connie Shefner-Rogers and her colleagues (1998) did (see the Community Intervention box), what items would you include?

Key Terms

citizen participation

coempowerment

community narratives

empowered organizations

empowering organizations

infraresources

instrumental resources

mediating structures

nomological net

political efficacy

possible selves

psychological empowerment

resources

scarcity paradigm

synergy paradigm

tyranny of structurelessness

CHAPTER 14

The Dilemmas of Dissent and Political Response

We hold these Truths to be self-evident, that all Men are created equal, that they are endowed by their Creator with certain unalienable Rights, that among these are Life, Liberty, and the Pursuit of Happiness—That to secure these Rights, Governments are instituted among Men, deriving their just Powers from the Consent of the Governed, that whenever any Form of Government becomes destructive of these Ends, it is the Right of the People to alter or abolish it, and to institute a new Government, laying its Foundation on such Principles, and organizing its Powers in such Form, as to them shall seem most likely to effect their Safety and Happiness.

—DECLARATION OF INDEPENDENCE, 1776

KEY CONCEPTS

Acceptable Dissent	Human Dynamics	Right to Dissent
Civil Disobedience	Legalistic Position	Strategies of Dissent
De-escalation of Conflict	Neutralizing Disorder	Strategies of Response
Escalation of Conflict	Power Tactics	Upward Spiral of Violence

LEARNING OBJECTIVES

Studying this chapter will enable you to:

1. Define the parameters of the right to dissent under the U.S. Constitution.
2. Present contrasting views of acceptable dissent.
3. Describe the interaction of the strategies of dissent and response.
4. Identify the significant aspects of escalation and de-escalation.
5. Analyze the ways in which police, courts, and corrections become instruments of power in relation to dissent.
6. Describe the necessary components for effectively neutralizing disorder without increasing violent dissent.

Police-Community Relations and the Administration of Justice, Eighth Edition
by Ronald D. Hunter, Thomas Barker

C hange and resistance to change are part of every system. For change to occur, some amount of "deviance" takes place and the "normal way of things" is disturbed or—as perceived by some—threatened.

The rights guaranteed to individuals and groups by the First Amendment to the Constitution of the United States reflect a commitment to allowing dissent as a means of bringing about needed social, legal, and political change. However, powerful social and political forces everywhere have always been resistant to change, so dissent has often led to intense and even violent confrontation. In 2009, the entire world was watching as peaceful dissent was violently repressed in the Islamic Republic of Iran. The brutal actions of the ruling theocracy demonstrated that its rhetoric of democracy is a sham. Freedom is never free, someone pays for it.

Dissent may be active or passive, nonviolent or violent, individual or mass. In a democratic society, the major dilemma becomes how to avoid social disorder, while at the same time avoiding total social control.

To better understand the dilemmas of dissent and political response, we must first understand the concept of dissent. Toward that end, in this chapter we consider contrasting views of dissent and study current social conflicts as they relate to both the strategies of dissent and response and the consequences for all parties involved. We address the processes of escalation, de-escalation, and resolution of social conflicts, and the involvement of police, courts, and corrections in them.

DISSENT: CATALYST OF PROGRESS

Change versus Order

One of the problems in political history is the conflict between change and order. It is difficult to say that any specific historical time was in a "state of order" because the patterns of conflict and resolution that were current then have led to new conflicts. This process will continue to occur. Our present society is complex, technologically communicative, and composed of many groups of people who have different interests, lifestyles, and values. Our political reality is that we are essentially a society of groups rather than of persons. These groups are pressing for change at an accelerating rate because more and more individuals feel they cannot bring about change unless they represent, or are represented by, a power base (Cummings and Wise, 2005).

Why Seek Change?

Why are so many groups seeking change? The answer, perhaps, can be found by examining our culture. Our contemporary culture places great emphasis on achievement, but it also emphasizes dissatisfaction with one's present state. Thus, achievement and its companion value, individual self-determination, promote the right to protest and to have grievances addressed—indispensable elements of a "free society."

The Right to Dissent

The First Amendment protects the freedoms of speech, the press, the right of the people to assemble peacefully, and the right to petition the government for a redress of grievances (Figure 14.1). The amendment protects not only the *individual's* **right to dissent** but also the right of *groups* to dissent, assemble, petition, and demonstrate. The First Amendment is a principle—a symbolic commitment

FIGURE 14.1 **First Amendment to the U.S. Constitution.**

Congress shall make no law respecting an establishment of religion, or prohibiting the free exercise thereof; or abridging the freedom of speech, or of the press; or the right of the people peaceably to assemble, and to petition the Government for a redress of grievances.

by our government to permit dissent and debate on public issues. Dissent, in the words of the National Commission on the Causes and Prevention of Violence, is the "catalyst of progress."

Keeping Dissent Peaceful

The survival of our democratic system is dependent on accommodating dissent, solving disagreements, peacefully containing social conflicts, righting wrongs, and modifying the structure of the system as conditions change. Although these changes are necessary to keep the government alive, the organization of government itself is fundamentally resistant to change. This resistance by the government to peaceful change leads to violence, a problem that the National Commission on the Causes and Prevention of Violence found has occurred throughout the history of the United States. The commission's conclusions remain accurate:

1. America has always been a relatively violent nation. Considering the tumultuous historical forces that have shaped the United States, it would be astonishing were it otherwise.
2. Since rapid social change in America has produced different forms of violence with widely varying patterns of motivation, aggression, and victimization, violence in America has waxed and waned with the social tides. The decade just ending, for example, has been one of our most violent eras, although probably not the most violent.
3. Exclusive emphasis in a society on law enforcement rather than on a sensible balance of remedial action and enforcement tends to lead to a decaying cycle in which resistance grows and becomes ever more violent.
4. For remedial social change to be an effective moderator of violence, the changes must command a wide measure of support throughout the community. Official efforts to impose change that is resisted by a dominant majority frequently prompt counterviolence.

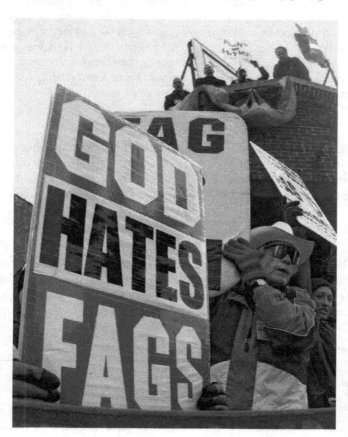

FIGURE 14.2 Religious extremists protesting against gay rights.

Tim Boyle, Getty Images Inc.–Liaison.

5. Finally, Americans have been, paradoxically, a turbulent people that have enjoyed a relatively stable republic. Our liberal and pluralistic system has historically both generated and accommodated itself to a high level of unrest, and our turmoil has reflected far more demonstration and protest than conspiracy and revolution (The National Commission on the Causes and Prevention of Violence, 1969, pp. 1–2).

Acceptable Dissent

Our current concern with militant and dissident groups involves the strategies they use to apply pressures in an attempt to bring about changes in society (see Figure 14.3). The men who wrote the Constitution did not define "**acceptable dissent** tactics" in the First Amendment. Therefore, the meaning of what is considered acceptable strategies of dissent constantly changes. For example, the acceptability of such protest strategies as civil disobedience, direct action, violent confrontation, sit-ins, boycotts, parades, and draft-card burnings varies greatly, depending on who is defining these actions. Such tactics may be acceptable to a protest leader or even a bystander, but not to a Supreme Court justice or a police officer. Even legal scholars concede that drawing constitutional lines on acceptable dissent procedures is a difficult task (Magleby et al., 2006). The U.S. flag desecrations of the 1960s, 1970s, and 1980s produced varied definitions of acceptable and unacceptable dissent practices, depending on the state where they happened, the law enforcement agency that arrested the offenders, the court that tried the offenders, and whether or not the convictions (and not all were convicted) were appealed (Welch, 1999). The U.S. Supreme Court declared in 1989 that desecrating the flag constitutes a form of political protest that is protected by the First Amendment. This set off a storm of protest and several attempts by the U.S. Congress to pass federal statutes to ban flag desecration (one passed and was declared unconstitutional by the Supreme Court) (Welch, 1999). The effort by Congress to pass a constitutional amendment against flag desecration still continues.

FIGURE 14.3   Birmingham, Alabama. American Nazi Party demonstration.
Courtesy of Birmingham Police Department.

A Legalistic Position

A MODEL DEFINITION A model definition of acceptable dissent was developed by former Supreme Court Justice Abe Fortas, who wrote the following:

> The First Amendment protects dissent if it is belief and not acts, if it is speech and does not create a clear and present danger of injury to others, if it is against a specific law or enforcement thereof by silent and reproachful presence, in a place where the dissenter has every right to be. Violation of a valid law is not justified by either conscience or a good cause. (1968, pp. 106–111)

SUPPORTIVE LEGALISTIC VIEWS A similar position was taken by Archibald Cox, special prosecutor during the Watergate scandal, who said that the Constitution guarantees a wide variety of public actions to express sentiment, dramatize a cause, and demonstrate aroused indignation, power, or solidarity. As Cox explained, "One may disregard with legal impunity the commands of civil authorities if what the authorities forbid is in truth only the exercise of a privilege guaranteed by the Constitution" (1971, p. 386). Such action does not involve a violation of law in the ultimate sense because the orders given by the authorities are not law at all. However, the Constitution does not give us the right to disobey *valid* laws. Conducting a sit-in demonstration in someone's office, for example, would plainly violate valid and constitutional laws. The Constitution does not give anyone the privilege to violate a law even if the protest demonstration is designed to test the law's constitutionality. Citizens cannot pick and choose which laws they will obey without destroying the whole concept of law. The privilege of freedom and the right to peaceful change are eroded by such lawbreaking, although some changes have occurred as a result of such tactics.

Most of the members of the Violence Commission took a similar position. They said that no matter how a person feels about the dissenters' cause, he must not violate valid laws. In their views, "respect for the judicial process is a small price to pay for the civilizing hand of law, which alone can give abiding meaning to constitutional freedom" (*Walker* v. *Birmingham*). The Violence Commission suggests that the best way to challenge the constitutionality of a law is by initiating legal action, and while the judicial test is in progress, all other dissenters should abide by the law (National Commission on the Causes and Prevention of Violence, 1969, pp. 90–91). Every time a court order is disobeyed and each time an injunction is violated, the effectiveness of our judicial system is eroded. Defiance of the law is the surest road to tyranny. Disobeying valid laws does not contribute to the emergence of a more humane society, but leads instead to the emergence of a totalitarian state.

THE LEGALISTIC POSITION: A SUMMARY Under this view, protesters are justified in disobeying the commands of civil authorities who try to forbid actions that exercise privileges guaranteed by the Constitution. Those who hold this view, however, insist that no one has the right to disobey valid laws. Three important corollaries of this position are as follows:

- Protest actions that break valid laws weaken the legal system, thus creating a threat to the privilege of freedom and the right to peaceful change, and compel the state to resort to its power.
- A distinction must be made between laws violated through protest actions (e.g., trespass and traffic laws) and laws violated because they are the object of dissent.
- The law and legal institutions are the only viable mechanisms for change in a democracy. Consequently, the best way to challenge the constitutionality of a law is through legal action; while the judicial test is in progress, all other dissenters should abide by the law.

CONTRASTING POSITIONS In contrast to the legalistic positions taken by Fortas, Cox, and the Violence Commission, others feel that (1) the traditional methods of dissent are insufficient or have fallen on deaf ears; (2) dissent is often focused on organizational policies or administrative decisions and not laws; and (3) the dissent issue is often not negotiable to those in the power structure. Thus, one cannot legally protest those procedures or institutional practices that the legal system assumes to be "correct." For example, few legal options are available to people who want to alter school curriculums or textbooks that devalue the role of minority groups in U.S. history. Conversely, a person can protest discriminatory employment practices through the law but not through the economic system itself.

A KEY ISSUE   Both the legalists and the advocates of dissent agree that creative disruptive tactics are legitimate, yet they also realize that many protest strategies pose a serious political problem: *how to avoid social disorder while at the same time avoiding total social control.*

A CLASSIC ARGUMENT   Howard Zinn, an advocate of civil disobedience, argued that government has abdicated its duty to meet the needs of the people in order to serve the needs of those in power (1968). To right the balance, therefore, he urged strategies of dissent that go far beyond what is legally acceptable. He also argued that the Constitution should be interpreted boldly and broadly in order to augment what he called "the natural rights of the citizen."

> Why should not the equal protection clause of the Fourteenth Amendment be applied to economics, as well as race, to require the state to give equal economic rights to its citizens: food, shelter, education, medical care? Why should not the Thirteenth Amendment barring involuntary servitude be extended to military conscription? Why should not the cruel and unusual punishment clause of the Eighth Amendment be applied in such a way as to bar all imprisonment except in the most stringent of cases, where confinement is necessary to prevent a clear and immediate danger to others? Why should not the Ninth Amendment, which says citizens have unnamed rights beyond those enumerated in the Constitution, be applied to a host of areas: rights to carry on whatever family arrangements (marriage, divorce, etc.) are desired, whatever sexual relationships are voluntarily entered into, whatever private activities one wants to carry on, so long as others are not harmed (even if they are irritated)? (Zinn, 1968, pp. 115–116)

Zinn suggested some guidelines for deciding when to disobey the law through protest activity:

1. **Civil disobedience**—the deliberate violation of the law for a vital social purpose—is not only justifiable, but necessary whenever a fundamental human right is at stake and the right cannot be secured through existing legal channels.
2. Government and laws are *instruments* to life, liberty, and happiness, not ends in themselves. Consequently, obeying "the rule of law" has *no* social value—and has *negative* social value if laws are bad ones.
3. Civil disobedience can involve violating laws that are not in themselves wrong in order to protest an important issue (e.g., illegally occupying a building, although normally wrong, is justified as part of a protest against, say, racism).
4. If a specific act of civil disobedience is morally justifiable, then jailing those who performed the act is *immoral* and should be opposed.
5. The tactics used in civil disobedience should be as nonviolent as possible, and the distinction between harm to property and harm to people should be a paramount consideration. However, the appropriate degree of force or disorder must be determined in light of the significance of the issue at stake.
6. The degree of disorder in civil disobedience should be measured not against some misleading degree of "peace" or "order" associated with the status quo, but against the real disorder or violence produced by the abuse that led to protest.
7. The state and the citizen have opposed interests. The state seeks power, influence, and wealth as ends in themselves and is in a favored position to obtain them, even if this means depriving individuals of the health, peace, creative activity, and love they seek. Each citizen, therefore, must learn to think and act on his or her own or in concert with fellow citizens against the state (Zinn, 1968, pp. 119–122).

ARENAS FOR DISSENT

The United States is a politically diverse nation. The numerous cultural influences, in conjunction with a wide variety of perspectives in regard to what the role of government and the extent of individual freedoms should be, frequently lead to bitter conflicts among competing political parties and interest groups. The major disagreements in the U.S. political system tend to occur between liberals and conservatives. Liberals seek to increase governmental (particularly federal) control over the modes of production and to promote social programs designed to help the poor. Conservatives argue for limited government and promotion of self-reliance by individuals. Both liberals and conservatives claim to cherish individual freedoms but tend to interpret them differently. Liberals argue that government must provide protections to ensure that the poor, minorities, and those living alternative lifestyles are treated fairly and equally. Conservatives argue that government intervention discriminates against the middle and upper classes, the white majority, and those who hold traditional American values (Magleby et al., 2006).

The nature of the liberal–conservative debate is not as easily defined as the preceding might cause one to believe. There is not one type of conservative, nor is there one type of liberal. Instead, liberalism ranges from socialists on the far left, who make American social policies similar to those found in "democratic socialist" nations such as Sweden (Basirico, Cashion, and Esheleman, 2005), to "neoliberals," who are skeptical of welfare programs and governmental bureaucracies (Magleby et al., 2006). Conservatives range from "ultraconservatives" on the far right who favor religious fundamentalism and strict enforcement of morality in addition to strongly opposing a "welfare state" to "neoconservatives" who support limited government involvement in solving social problems but fear that "excessive liberalism" threatens individual liberties and social stability.

A great many Americans occupy the middle of the political spectrum in that they consider themselves to be neither liberals nor conservatives. These citizens hold divergent views that cannot readily be classified by political scientists. Such persons might favor both capital punishment and abortion. They might vote for a Republican for one political office and a Democrat for another, and they would feel no obligation to abide by the wishes of a particular political party or interest group in making political decisions (Cummings and Wise, 2005).

Other Americans may have political ideologies that are far more extreme than those found within the liberal–conservative spectrum. Communists (and many remain despite the decline of Communism in the former Eastern bloc nations) feel that even the welfare capitalism found in the United States is evil and must be eliminated. Anarchists (a limited few) argue that all government is evil. Libertarians, who are considerably more moderate, criticize both liberals and conservatives as abusing the power of the government and infringing on individual liberties. Like conservatives, libertarians would sharply limit the size and power of the federal government. Like liberals, libertarians are very concerned with protecting individual freedoms.

Due to the nature of democracy in the United States, many compromises are made in order for the political system (and subsequently, the social and economic systems) to function. This compromise causes many (on the left, on the right, and in the middle) to feel that their views are being ignored by those in power. When this occurs, many Americans frequently utilize dissent in an effort to effect change. In U.S. society, dissent can be said to occur in at least five major areas: political, social, economic, religious, and environmental. Although these are not mutually exclusive, they often serve individually as primary targets for dissent.

Political Dissent

Political dissent is concerned primarily with effecting change in political policy. Power is sought in political decision making. Examples of nonviolent political dissent include the historic protests that were waged during the 1960s in opposition to the Vietnam War and in support of civil rights protection for minorities. More recent demonstrations in the United States have resulted from the efforts of opponents seeking to eliminate lawful abortions within the United States and from gay rights advocates seeking to eliminate laws and regulations that are considered discriminatory against homosexuals.

When advocates of political change resort to violence, it is frequently the activities of a single person or a small group of extremists within a predominantly peaceful organization. However, it may be calculated actions of an organization that is willing to use terrorism to bring attention to themselves or their cause (White, 2006). While most civilized peoples deplore terrorism, a person classified as a terrorist by one group may be considered a hero or freedom fighter by others (Fagin, 2006). For example, to most Americans (including opponents of abortion), the bombing of abortion clinics and/or the murder of doctors who perform abortions are acts of terrorism, but to some they are morally justified acts taken in defense of unborn children. However, those same persons would define terrorism quite differently if their churches were attacked by pro-abortion forces.

Social Dissent

Social dissent is concerned primarily with gaining social equality. Often, the conflict is over the counting and discounting of minority-group concerns in our society (Henslin, 2007). Social acceptance and rejection, changes in public opinion and social institutions, and having a "viable place" in the community are all social concerns. Social dissent in the United States was pioneered by Martin Luther King Jr., who utilized nonviolent protests as a means of drawing attention to inequitable treatment of African Americans (Greenberg and Page, 2005).

During the 1990s, the groups that most frequently utilized social dissent were gay rights advocates, feminists, and ethnic minorities. Many of these groups are also involved in political dissent, because changes in the law, a part of structuring social change, are a political prerogative.

Economic Dissent

Economic dissent is concerned primarily with effecting change in the economy and meeting material needs. Economic dissent addresses in general issues of unemployment; underemployment; poverty; and food, clothing, and shelter. Strikes and protests regarding unfair labor practices and demonstrations on behalf of the homeless may be considered economic dissent. One example was the Los Angeles Riot of 1992. Although the initial spark was the acquittal of the police officers accused in the videotaped beating of black motorist Rodney King, the real issues dealt with living conditions, unemployment, lack of opportunity, and what residents saw as social and economic oppression.

Religious Dissent

Religious dissent is concerned primarily with effecting change in the definition of religious freedoms or specific religious practices that may violate existing law. In this instance, conflict may be between opposing values or religious beliefs or between church and secular law. Much antiabortion dissent is couched in a religious context. Other examples include the ongoing debate over prayer in the schools, atheist–religious conflicts, Catholic–Protestant and Jewish–Gentile conflicts, and the refusal of religious groups such as the Amish and Mennonites to comply with compulsory school attendance laws. The attacks on doctors and abortion clinics by supporters of "Operation Rescue," the dramatic events that led to the 1993 deaths of approximately 90 people in the Branch Davidian compound near Waco, Texas, during an FBI assault, and the 1993 bombing of the World Trade Center by Muslim fundamentalists demonstrate the extremes that religious dissent in the United States can reach.

Freedom to believe is absolutely protected by the First Amendment to the U.S. Constitution, but freedom to act is not totally free from interference (Cummings and Wise, 2005). This is particularly true if those actions obstruct the rights of others, are seen as detrimental to the health and well-being of group members (especially juveniles), if the group or individual is found to be only incidentally religious, or when fraud or deception is involved (Lucksted and Martell, 1982).

Environmental Dissent

Environmental dissent is concerned primarily with effecting change in the surroundings or settings in which we live. Issues might include zoning changes, health hazards, and threats to wildlife. Recent environmental debates have ranged from preserving endangered species, halting the inappropriate disposal of chemical waste, eliminating pollution of air and water, guarding against radioactive or toxic risk to populations, and the harvesting of public forests. This dissent can range from community resistance to building chemical incinerators, to assaults on hunters or people wearing furs by animal rights extremists, to acts of sabotage and terrorism against perceived environmental offenders.

STRATEGIES OF DISSENT AND RESPONSE

Legalists and advocates of dissent differ in many critical respects, but they all recognize the need for "justice," "order," and "change" and agree that dissent must be analyzed in relation to crises in American institutions. This factor was also recognized by the National Commission on the Causes and Prevention of Violence. In a staff report, the commission suggests that mass protest is an outgrowth of social, economic, and political conditions and the violence that occurs in these protests arises from an interaction between protesters and the authorities.

Commission observations include the following:

- Political processes establish what "violence" is. Whoever has the power to disseminate and enforce their definitions blames the other party for the violence.
- Both the authorities and the protesters often exaggerate the violence committed against them in order to discredit the other party, gain sympathy from third parties, and deflect attention from their own violence.

FIGURE 14.4   Dissenting shipbuilders on strike in Newport News, Virginia.
Courtesy of Newport News Police Department.

- The interplay of protest and violence must be seen in light of the surrounding structure of power and authority and the conceptions held by the authorities of the nature of protest and the proper uses of official violence.
- Participants in mass protest today see their activity as political action aimed at the existing arrangements of power and authority that produced their grievances (Popenoe, 2000; Tischler, 2007).

The Labeling Process

In most issues of social conflict, a variety of groups and individuals with differing demands and differing strategies of dissent wish to be heard. These dissenters, however, generally have much less power than the political authorities or other parties whose actions, beliefs, policies, or laws the dissenters are protesting. Because dissenters usually have the least amount of power in a social conflict, the views of the more powerful authorities or organizations generally become the accepted ones.

The authorities, or those who have power (the "establishment"), generally label dissenters as "militants." This label may be applied to whole groups of dissenters or to individual spokespeople for a particular group of dissenters. No clear-cut definitions exist for the word "militant." This label has been used by the opponents of a movement to discredit everyone in the movement; it has also been used selectively by persons who partially agree with the objectives of the movement but who regard some of its demands as nonnegotiable. It is generally agreed that militants (1) approve of violence as a protest tactic, (2) are hostile toward their adversaries, and (3) do not accept the legitimacy of the structural system or its institutions.

Strategies of Dissent

Strategies of dissent differ with regard to three concerns: (1) the nature of the desired changes, (2) the means of achieving change (specifically, the degree of adherence to the rules of the system), and (3) attitudes toward the people who defend the system. Three strategies can be distinguished: strategies of order, disorder, and violence.

In the strategy of order, dissidents divide their attention between the changes to be accomplished and the accepted rules regarding legitimate ways of bringing about change; dissidents who use this strategy follow the rules.

In the strategy of disorder, dissidents have less interest in both the given rules and the powerful persons who stand in the way of change; they focus strongly on the changes needed.

In the strategy of violence, dissidents divide their attention between the changes needed and the powerful persons who stand in the way of change; dissidents who use this strategy attack their enemies.

Presumably, we can define any particular dissident group's strategy at any given time simply by analyzing its rhetoric and observing its deeds.

Strategies of Response

To understand the dynamics of dissent strategies, we must also understand the **strategies of response** utilized by political authorities or other parties who are the targets of dissident groups (Table 14.1). These can vary as widely as the strategies of protest groups and generally differ with respect to the same three concerns: the nature of desired changes, the means of achieving change, and attitudes toward the people who defend the system. The strategies of response are the response of law, of order, and of violence.

In the response of law, authorities do not respond at all or only respond in a protective manner as long as dissenters adopt legal strategies of protest (i.e., strategies of order). If the dissenters adopt illegal means of protest, however, the response of law strategy involves arresting dissenters and processing them in a legally acceptable manner. In this response, authorities follow proper legal procedures.

TABLE 14.1 Strategies of Dissent and Response

Dissent		Response	
Concerns		*Concerns*	
1. The nature of desired changes		1. The nature of desired changes	
2. The means of achieving change		2. The means of achieving change	
3. Attitudes toward people who defend system		3. Attitudes toward people who defend system	
Strategies	*Focus On*	*Strategies*	*Focus On*
1. Of order:	legitimate ways of bringing about change	1. Response of law:	no response or protective response
2. Of disorder:	changes needed; less concern with rules or powerful persons who stand in the way	2. Response of order:	arresting and processing dissenters in legal and acceptable manner
3. Of violence:	attacking enemies; change needed and powerful persons who stand in the way of change	3. Response of violence:	issue in conflict and people who are dissenting; attack enemies

Possible Interactional Outcomes

Changes in orientation and strategy

Violent action

Resolution of conflict

In the response of order, authorities make no response or only a protective one to legal protest (strategies of order). Illegal dissent, however, is met by attempting nonviolent bargaining over the social issue. The authorities place less emphasis on the demanded change than on maintaining order or preventing violence.

In the response of violence, authorities are concerned with the issue in conflict and focus on the people who are dissenting (regardless of what strategy of dissent they use). In other words, they attack their enemies.

Interaction between Strategies

When the strategies of dissent and response meet head-on, three outcomes are possible: changes in orientation and strategy, violent action, or resolution of the conflict.

CHANGES IN ORIENTATION AND STRATEGY   Those who adopt a given strategy of dissent usually expect it to have a specific effect on third parties or to elicit a specific strategy of response from the authorities. Thus, the civil disobedience of Martin Luther King was a strategy of order designed to draw attention to a particular issue and to educate the public about it; to a large extent, it succeeded. Problems arise, however, when dissidents and those in power find that their efforts are not producing the results they want. Their strategy may change toward greater use of violence.

VIOLENT ACTIONS   Some dissident groups seem committed to violence from the outset, engaging in guerrilla warfare and terrorist activities. Moreover, many law enforcement officials favor violent response to dissent; if they disagree with the dissenters on the issues, they are likely to consider acts of civil disobedience as simply another type of crime, and they often try to divert attention from the issues by defining the dissidents as terrorists, "crazies," or common criminals.

Guerrilla warfare, as a strategy of violence, exists throughout the world. Underground armies and terrorist organizations are particularly prevalent in underdeveloped nations that are ruled by dictatorship.

Terrorism and guerrilla insurgency have appeared in all segments of major U.S. cities. The use of terrorism as a tactic of dissent usually is directed at persons who exercise power and at the symbols of that power. The goal of this form of dissent is often terror and anarchy.

Some observers predict that the police officer on the street in the future will be required to deal with criminal violence arising from violent political dissent. The National Advisory Commission on Criminal Justice Standards and Goals (1976) and subsequent presidential commissions on terrorism have encouraged local police to increase their ability to deal with such activity.

A key element in violent dissent is that the dissenters seek to achieve their goals by whatever means necessary. Some domestic terrorist groups that are active or have been active in the United States in recent years include the Aryan Nation; the Black Liberation Army; the Christian Patriots Defense League; The Covenant, the Sword, and the Arm of the Lord (CSA); the Jewish Defense League; the Ku Klux Klan; Macheteros; Move; Neo-Nazis; the New World Liberation Front; Alpha 66; Omega 7; The Order; Posse Comitatus; Puerto Rican Armed Forces of the Revolution (FALN); the United Freedom Front; the Weather Underground; Fuqra; the Armenian Secret Army for the Liberation of Armenia (ASLA); Justice Commandos for Armenian Genocide (JCAG); the Croation National Liberation Forces; the Animal Liberation Front; and, arguably, Operation Rescue (Poland, 2005; Simonsen and Spindlove, 2007; White, 2006). In addition to these politically motivated groups, many individuals and criminal gangs engage in activities that could also be classified as terrorism. As if there were not enough of a harm potential from these "homegrown terrorists," the number of international terrorists operating in America is increasing. Due to the events of September 11, 2001, local and state law enforcement in the United States have had to assume responsibility for "Homeland Security" along with the federal agencies (Fagin, 2006; White, 2006).

RESOLUTION OF THE CONFLICT   This outcome, of course, would seem the most desirable, and it is often possible, although the struggle to reach it may be long. Those who adopt strategies or responses of violence, however, may not want any resolution other than the complete surrender or destruction of the other side.

The Role of Third Parties

Both dissidents and authorities plan tactics, publicity, and media communications to win over third parties. This is especially important when power differences are great between the conflicting parties, and the weaker party can obtain a compromise or achieve its goals only if strong third parties become its allies. In the civil rights movement in the South, the goal the protesters sought was inclusion in the political system; thus, these groups aimed their messages not only at the persons directly affected but also at third-party persons sympathetic to these goals and at those who believed in the legal inclusion of African Americans in the political system. As a result, media coverage and the violent response of political authorities to the civil rights movement had the consequences of affecting third-party intervention by the federal government, expanding the issues in conflict, and obtaining participants in the movement as well as allies.

The Role of the Media

Because media coverage is so necessary for reaching third parties, all parties try to influence the way conflict and the parties to it are portrayed in newspaper and magazine articles and on radio and television. Dissenters create events for media that will draw attention to the conflict and hopefully build bargaining power for them. Political authorities, on the other hand, attempt to control what the media present by exercising power through regulatory agencies and political pressure. They attempt to control sources of information by making government documents secret, infiltrating dissident groups with agents of the government, cutting off dissident groups from media visibility, and attacking the media for their "underdog" bias. When political authorities are pressed by dissent, freedom of the press comes under increasing fire.

ESCALATION AND DE-ESCALATION OF CONFLICT

Once conflict has started, each party tends to undergo changes that make the conflict more intense. Conflict, however, cannot escalate indefinitely. Sooner or later, forces or events that de-escalate conflict will influence the behavior of the parties involved.

Escalation Factors

INCREASE IN LOYALTY AND COMMITMENT   Feelings of loyalty and commitment to one's position increase if the other side responds with coercion, threats, or injuries. Increased commitment leads to and justifies further efforts toward the attainment of one's goals, creates anxiety, and heightens a sense that *now* is the time to act. For example, dissident or militant leaders state, "Seize the time!" "Freedom now!" "Peace now!" or other rhetoric emphasizing urgency:

> This is our last gasp as a sovereign people, and if we don't get these treaty rights recognized, then you might as well kill me because I have no reason for living. (Means, 1973)

He was not killed. And at this writing, more than 40 years later, Mr. Means has not given up on living.

> My hunger is for liberation of my people, my thirst is for the ending of oppression. I am a political prisoner, jailed for my beliefs that black people must be free. . . . Death can no longer alter our path to freedom. For our people death has been the only known exit from slavery and oppression. We must open others. Our will to live must no longer supersede our will to fight, for our fighting will determine if our race shall live. . . . Brothers and sisters, and all oppressed peoples, we must prepare ourselves both mentally and physically, for the major confrontation is yet to come. We must fight. (Brown, 1968)

Fortunately, the race war that Mr. Brown (who is now in prison for murdering an African American deputy sheriff) called for has not taken place. Despite frequent setbacks and the combined efforts of both white and black militants, race relations in the United States continue to progress.

PERSISTENCE IN A COURSE OF ACTION   Once conflict begins, it often escalates because leaders acting as representatives of an entire group usually persist on a course of action, even if no success is achieved. Mistakes are rarely admitted by either the dissenters or the responders. However, admission of mistakes does tend to occur when the group's constituency changes, when the futility of the strategy becomes apparent, or when escalation and reaction reach the point where survival of the group is threatened. Thus, the Black Panthers party retracted its focus on the police when party programs were seriously threatened by police actions. Party leaders recognized that other authorities are more important than the police and began to concentrate more deeply on other issues.

WITHDRAWAL OF MODERATE MEMBERSHIP   Another factor influencing the escalation of conflict is the withdrawal of members who are unwilling to participate in more intense conflict, leaving the group to those who are more eager to engage in hostile actions. With the withdrawal of moderates, dissident groups that have previously been viewed as peaceful activists (e.g., Operation Rescue) may begin to emerge as terrorist threats.

AN UPWARD SPIRAL OF VIOLENCE   Hostility and aggression from one side will very likely be answered in kind from the other side, so that an **upward spiral of violence** is created. Once the spiral begins, a relatively weak response from one side is unlikely to stop it; the other side will react with even more violence in order to defeat a seemingly "weakened enemy." If the police see a group of dissidents as a threat or as a source of violence and respond with violence, the dissident group tends to increase its violent activities. Once intensely engaged, even efforts by police to de-escalate the conflict may be interpreted as retreat and evidence of weakness. Therefore, such efforts will require careful planning and execution in order to avoid increasing the level of violence.

De-escalation Factors

Conflict cannot escalate indefinitely. The processes of de-escalation are embedded in those of escalation. Although participation in conflict behavior produces greater commitment to the group and willingness to escalate conflict, it also becomes increasingly costly if the attainment of the group's demands is not in sight.

SUPERIOR COERCIVE POWER   One side may use its superior coercive power to repress the opposition through harassment or by imprisoning its leaders. However, actions that are perceived as too extreme can lead to both heightened resistance on the part of the dissidents and increased sympathy from those who were neutral or somewhat opposed to dissent.

DIVIDE AND CONQUER   One side may split the conflict by being conciliatory in a divisive way (e.g., by granting the demands of some members of the opposition and thus removing their reasons for continuing the conflict). Placating the more moderate factions within the opposition may seriously weaken those who hold more extreme positions. The product is a deeply divided opposition that may force extremists to either capitulate or be rejected by their previous allies.

THIRD-PARTY INVOLVEMENT   One side may introduce issues that involve third parties who then either act as negotiators or increase one side's power to the point where the other side can no longer bear the cost of intense conflict. For example, during the Vietnam War, raising the POW issue brought new third parties into the peace movement. The intervention of third parties also can have a de-escalating impact on the authorities by increasing the political costs of continuing the practices being protested.

A REDEFINITION OF "REASONABLE"   The struggle may become so intense that leaders who formerly seemed militant now appear "reasonable"—an appearance that can only increase their bargaining power, if authorities have not repressed the entire movement.

Success Factors

In general, dissident groups are more likely to be successful if they have the following:

1. A specific goal or a broad goal (e.g., equality of job opportunity) that can realistically be achieved (e.g., by reserving a specific percentage of construction jobs for minority group applicants).
2. A specific, identifiable target (e.g., a particular political leader, landlord, or company).
3. Demands that realistically can be met. Some demands are defined as nonnegotiable by the conflict authority (e.g., state sovereignty, capitalism, or student control of school administration), and some demands are not grantable by the targets chosen (e.g., police and mayor).

OUTCOMES

Determinants of Outcomes

DIFFERENCES IN POWER   Power differences seem to be the major determinant in the outcome of social conflict. Extreme power differences almost invite domination and repression if the conflict has escalated to highly coercive strategies. In general, the greater the power difference, the more the outcome is likely to be withdrawal or domination of the dissidents (Eitzen and Zinn, 2007).

PERCEIVED PERMANENCE OF CONFLICT   The outcomes of different conflicts also vary according to the perceived permanence of the conflict. The Vietnam War has long since ended; mass rioting does not prevail over periods of weeks and months. Underlying social conflicts, however, such as the status of black, brown, and Native American citizens in our society seem to be continuing and painfully direct issues (Skolnick and Currie, 2007).

In a sense, the call for "black power" during the 1960s grew out of the perception that there would have to be many years of resistance and protest against white institutions and attitudes for African Americans to gain equality. In this view, to bargain from a position of strength, blacks first had to establish group solidarity. This same strategy is currently being utilized by advocates of gay rights, who are seeking to establish a group identity based on sexual preference.

Enhancing group solidarity to improve bargaining position is the objective of many other groups in our society with similar issues. Group solidarity is often defined in terms of self-defense, cultural autonomy, a sense of community, and community control.

The role of "militant" groups where conflict is perceived to be ongoing or permanent might include the following:

1. Correct the illusions of progress through critical, pessimistic attitudes.
2. Identify unresolved issues through confrontations.
3. Radicalize membership of the movement and increase polarization between the movement and its opposition.
4. Create an awareness of injustice among nonmovement third parties.

Schools and the police are among the primary targets of such movements; other targets involve issues such as housing, welfare, and social services.

PERCEIVED INSTRUMENTS OF POWER   In the midst of conflict, police, courts, and corrections administration and personnel are often seen as political instruments of power rather than as instruments of law.

The Police

In the drama of dissent, police frequently find themselves acting as substitutes for necessary political and social reform. Labor history demonstrates that the police served as the main bulwark against the labor movement. Picket lines were violently dispersed; meetings were disrupted; and organizers and activists were shot, beaten, and jailed. Police harassment of unions, such as the United Farm Workers, was common. Denial of strikers' legal rights; physical and verbal abuse; detaining organizers for long periods; encouraging workers to cross picket lines; and arresting strikers for trespass, unlawful assembly, secondary boycott, and illegal picketing were common practices. The police have also sought at times to prevent the political organization of Native Americans, Chicanos, and blacks by harassing and intimidating organization members and arresting leaders.

RESPONSES OF VIOLENCE   In some of our larger cities, tenant groups, students, war protesters, gays, browns, and blacks have drawn similar responses from the police. For example, some of the most highly publicized responses of violence occurred in Chicago at the 1968 Democratic

National Convention and in police confrontations with the Black Panther party. The shooting outbreaks between Panthers and police in San Francisco, Oakland, New Orleans, Detroit, Toledo, Philadelphia, New York, Houston, and Chicago were touched off by harassment (the Panther view) or minor offenses (the police view). These incidents involved the selling of a Panther newspaper on a Detroit street corner, the assault upon two police infiltrators in New Orleans, and the stockpiling of weapons in the other cities. The Black Panthers argued that police respond violently for a number of reasons:

- Many of them are "racists."
- Few minority persons serve on police forces.
- The police are isolated from the people they serve.
- Police are ill-trained for sensitive peacekeeping jobs.
- Police have a special view of dissent and dissenters.

This same theme was echoed in the Los Angeles Riot of 1992 and the Cincinnati Riots in 2000.

POLICE VIEW OF DISSENT   Many police officers (and administrators) view protest as unequivocally illegitimate. They tend to regard organized protest as the conspiratorial product of authoritarian agitators, Communists, rabble-rousers, spoiled kids, outsiders, or anarchists. This view does not distinguish dissent from subversion and lumps all dissent strategies into one category (Skolnick, 1969, p. 199). As a result, police may tend to be hostile to most strategies of dissent and make the reduction of dissent their goal. The dangers of such a position are many. The police may underestimate both the number of people involved and the emotionality of dissent. They may arrest leaders or speakers at mass rallies, thereby heightening the cycle of escalating violence. They may equate the law with their own situational use of power. As the police have become more comfortable with their role as protectors of individual rights rather than as strictly law enforcers, this view of protest has become less prevalent (Barker, Hunter, and Rush, 1994).

DISSENTERS AS DELIBERATE PROVOKERS OF VIOLENCE   Violent dissent and violent response are generally an interactional product of short-term situational escalation or a product of a history of unsuccessful dissent and/or response strategy. Some dissenters, however, purposely provoke hostility and violence in order to gain attention, increase membership, enlist third-party support, or simply show how "violent" the system is. Thus, the greater the resistance the groups encounter, the greater their motivation to continue their "just" struggle. Threats of punishment have little deterrent value on dissenters of this type, because they can use such threats to increase sympathy for their cause (Simonsen and Spindlove, 2007; White, 2006).

POWER AND THE RESPONSE OF ORDER   The response of order is more likely to occur if the power of the dissenting group approaches that of the powerful group. When a large number of people become involved in dissent and when their goals become specific and clear, police response of order is more frequent. If negotiation is on side issues that are not seen as critical by a majority of the dissenters, the strength of the dissent becomes diffused.

THE POLICE AND "DIRTY WORK"   The police frequently provide the most visible direct response to dissent. It is a response that the powerful and/or larger segments in society wish to see made, even though they themselves do not wish to be personally involved in the response. In such instances, the police find themselves doing the "dirty work" of larger political and social forces. As the police have become more representative of the communities they serve, many are beginning to resent that position (Barker, Hunter, and Rush, 1994). The accepted approach today is an attempt to balance the rights of protesters with the need to maintain law and order. Law enforcement officials are encouraged not to condemn the cause but, rather, to denounce the illegal acts and tactics of the protestors (King, 2000, p. 12).

Sometimes police seem to have been forced unwillingly into violent confrontations by the actions of legislative and judicial bodies over which they had no control. For example, city officials may decide to take steps to block what might have been a peaceful demonstration. The dissenters, with increased commitment, decide to demonstrate anyway. The police are caught in the middle.

POLITICAL SURVEILLANCE   The FBI, CIA, IRS, Army, Secret Service, Civil Service Commission, Department of Justice, and other government agencies sometimes, like the police, equate dissent with subversion. As a result, they maintain surveillance of the activities of dissidents. One major purpose of this surveillance is political control of dissent. Fortunately, the misuse of surveillance has led to congressional inquiries and the imposition of restrictions on those agencies with surveillance capabilities (Cummings and Wise, 2005).

Agents Provocateurs   To keep tabs on dissident groups, law enforcement agencies often have tried to infiltrate them with undercover agents, who may well commit provocative acts—or encourage others to commit them—to gain the dissenters' confidence and to obtain concrete evidence of illegal activity. The need for undercover agents is quite clear. Without them, terrorist acts would be extremely difficult to prevent. The 2006 arrests of terrorists in Canada who were planning on planting bombs and the arrests in Great Britain of a group of terrorists planning to blow up airliners flying to the United States were due to excellent intelligence gathering and the use of undercover operatives.

NATIONAL SECURITY   When the national security is believed to be at stake, political intelligence sweeps up dissenters of all styles. To protect the national security, all groups and individuals committed to social or political change, however peaceful, nonviolent, or legal, must be scrutinized because they may be "subversive." These intelligence activities are designed to demoralize, intimidate, and frighten citizens into not dissenting. The harassment, invasion of privacy, prosecution on drug charges, vandalism of offices and homes, blacklisting, and illegal searches by these intelligence services are chilling. When a covert force plays an important role in political decisions, the selection of candidates, the publication of false opinion polls, and the conducting of "smear" campaigns, then this nation's stated democratic political processes cease to exist. The First Amendment becomes meaningless when dissenting individuals are not allowed to exercise their rights. If there are great personal costs involved in the process of dissent, then there is no freedom. Driving political activity underground tends to escalate strategies to the more organized forms of violence, paramilitarism, terror, sabotage, assassination, guerrilla warfare, espionage, counterintelligence, and extreme political repression (Henslin, 2007; Simonsen and Spindlove, 2007).

NEW LIMITS ON POLITICAL SURVEILLANCE   To the concern of those who believe intelligence efforts are important, the trend in the recent past has been for legislatures, courts, and administrators to establish a tighter rein on police intelligence units. Some of the most restrictive guidelines have been placed on the FBI. After the guidelines went into effect in 1976, domestic security investigations by that agency fell dramatically. Most state guidelines are not as restrictive as those of the FBI. For those who believe that every "scrap of information" should be kept, such guidelines are a great handicap to police. For those who believe that intelligence gathering should be a highly selective activity and should exclude much political information, the new rules are a means of streamlining and professionalizing the intelligence process.

The Courts

The passage of laws that attempt to stifle dissent, such as riot conspiracy laws, mob action laws, and administrative laws, all make the court an arena for the politics of protest. Intelligence gathering, selective prosecution, and the response of violence tend to underwrite the perception that the courts are also political instruments of power.

The court process assumes that the activities defined as crimes are disapproved of by the community as a whole. In contemporary dissent situations, however, these conditions may not be met. As dissent increases and as a strategy of dissent gains acceptability, a majority of the citizens may not define the activity as criminal. Moreover, they may not accept the court's authority to decide the dispute. This presents a crisis for the courts and the legal system. The court becomes a political arena in which actors attempt to win third parties to their side (Skolnick, 1969, p. 243).

THE ISSUE OF IMPARTIALITY   It is difficult for the court to function as an impartial arbiter of conflict when the government itself is a party to the conflict. In the United States, lower courts have often set aside their independence and become instruments of political need, without regard for legality. In the civil turmoil of the 1960s and early 1970s, courts often took the following view:

1. Civil disorders were emergency situations that required extraordinary measures of control and resistance.
2. The courts must support the police and other public agencies acting to restore order.
3. Because of the emergency, defendants must be presumed guilty (until proven innocent).
4. High bail is required to prevent rioters from returning to the riot.
5. The niceties of due process cannot and should not be observed while an emergency lasts.
6. Due process should be restored as soon as the emergency passes (Skolnick, 1969, p. 237).

No recent period in history has provided such powerful examples of the courts as political arenas than the decade in which the government moved in several dramatic trials against well-known dissidents such as Dr. Benjamin Spock, the Chicago Seven, the Panther Twenty-One, and Angela Davis. The government sought conviction; the defendants sought acquittal. Both parties also had other, perhaps greater, concerns. The dissenters were willing to accept the legal penalties for their acts to raise the moral justice of their cause. The government's main purpose, particularly in the Spock trial, was probably to deter draft resistance and adult support of this resistance. However, the event was also used to discredit these dissenters symbolically, to blame dissent on Spock for his permissive child-rearing philosophy, and to rally patriotic third parties to the government's side. Actually, the Spock trial may have produced the opposite effect: It became a rallying point for the entire movement. Through the trial, citizens were informed about the issues of war.

ATTACKS ON THE COURTS   During their trials, dissidents of that period frequently tried not only to publicize their grievances, but also to attack the courts themselves, the criminal justice system, and, ultimately, the entire U.S. socioeconomic and political system.

Corrections: The Prison

THE REALITIES OF PRISON LIFE   Citizens want those whom they consider to be "deviants" to be "disposed of" safely, quickly, and invisibly. This invisibility creates a need for prisoners to escalate the strategy of dissent if they wish to obtain attention. Most prison dissent—in the form of hunger strikes, building takeovers, and hostage taking—is directed toward making third parties aware that "just" ideals are perverted both inside prison and out. Prisons are the breeding grounds of the strategy of violence and the marketplace of the response of total control.

Dissenters often claim that prisons, like the courts, are instruments of political oppression. Whether or not the claim is justified, punitive confinement is the essence of American penal institutions.

REACTIONS TO PRISON LIFE   Reactions to prison life may be docility, cooperativeness, and un-complaining conformity, or it may be rebellion in the name of liberty. Often prisoners feel that to be subject to the arbitrary exercise of power is to be a slave (Zimbardo, 1972, p. 8). Prison authorities may feel that prison dissent is caused by a small band of militants, the circulation of militant revolutionary literature, the influence of militant lawyers, and the strategies of dissent occurring outside the institution. They respond to threat by transferring inmates, placing them in solitary confinement, censoring mail and reading materials, and limiting contacts.

Systems for Solution

The Task Force on Disorders and Terrorism, whose report was released in late 1976, addressed setting standards and goals for the criminal justice system and for the nonofficial community in prevention, evaluation of threats, and management strategies for riots, urban disorders, prison disorders, and terrorism (National Advisory Commission on Criminal Justice Standards and Goals, 1976).

Currently, much emphasis is being placed on the use of negotiation, which stresses human dynamics, rather than "power" tactics, as an effective means of **neutralizing disorder**. However, as exemplified by the 1993 FBI assault on the Branch Davidian compound near Waco, Texas, authorities tend to revert to the use of force when negotiations fail. Whether or not that FBI response was correct will remain a matter of debate for many years.

AWARENESS   The best solution is prevention. If the police maintain close, ongoing contact with community members and help to keep channels for communication open, mutual trust will help to open legitimate peaceful options for dissent and deter the escalation of dissent to violent action. Close positive contact will also allow the police and community members to be aware of increasing tensions in a community, the factors involved in that tension, and ways to diffuse it.

Police officers also need to be self-aware. Their own assumptions and reactive behavior may increase the intensity of problems. Their level of hopefulness that what they do can make a difference influences the behavior of dissenters.

Agency administrators affect the officer's level of hopefulness and his or her ability to deal with fear and anxiety. They affect the officer's emotional and physical preparedness for situations of dissent. Support for the officers in the form of guidelines, education and training, planning, and coordination of function is a key element of success.

EDUCATION   Officers who understand human dynamics and mass behavior (e.g., that riots have a classic lull between 3:00 and 9:00 A.M.), the interaction of strategies of dissent and political response, the element of surprise, how to deal with their own fear and anxiety, and how to gain consistently reliable information are better prepared to respond to dissent in ways that prevent violence. In addition to gaining information as a resource, officers need to gain response skills. This may be accomplished through role play and should be provided over a period of time so that skills can be acquired, tested, and sharpened.

PLANNING AND PREPARATION   Planned, practiced tactical response can be successful. If police agencies are prepared, they can effectively use the wide range of options that they have and seize the initiative in a situation. Perhaps many different responses will be needed. If planning has been effective, the roles of each cooperating agency and jurisdiction are defined, and coordination of resources exists, disorder can be neutralized without extinguishing dissent or imposing excessive social control.

Cooperation and coordination among units in a single police agency (e.g., those trained in the various tactics of countersniper, assault, negotiation, and intelligence) are critical. Just as critical is cooperation of police with other agencies. A system response must be an organized one. Usually such response is from the "bottom up." The local agency is the key decision maker, and other agencies provide support. If this division of responsibility is not followed, procedures may be imposed from the "top down" (e.g., federal agencies making decisions for the local police).

Jealousies, conflicting philosophies, and poor planning can lead to immobility and disaster. Many of these problems can be avoided if police–community relations are conducted effectively with members of the justice community and clear guidelines for cooperation are developed. This includes not only other police agencies, but also courts and corrections.

HUMAN DYNAMICS VERSUS POWER TACTICS   Political response to dissent may shape the intensity of the dissent. Restraint on the part of the police will help to prevent violent confrontation. In contrast, heavy-handed harassment increases anger and invites violence.

Establishing dialogues with dissenting groups and applying an understanding of **human dynamics** are much more effective than **power tactics** in maintaining long-term peace, even if it is somewhat uneasy.

THE BATTLE OF SEATTLE

Background

The most serious incident involving the police and political dissent in the United States since the Age of Dissent (1965–1975), maybe in U.S. history, occurred in a city where it should not have happened: Seattle, Washington, a city known for its liberal lifestyle. It involved a police department well known for its community policing philosophy and style, and a department commanded by a well-respected police chief with a Ph.D.: Chief Norm Stamper. While with the San Diego Police Department, Chief Stamper introduced a community-oriented policing program, considered by many to be the first in the nation. His undergraduate senior thesis was titled "The Community as DMZ: Breaking Down the Police Paramilitary Bureaucracy." Stamper's doctoral dissertation described how civil service and paramilitary structures contribute to police losing touch with communities (Wilson, 1999). However, the city, the chief, and the police department became caught up in a situation they neither asked for nor created.

President Bill Clinton volunteered the city of Seattle as the site for a meeting of the World Trade Organization (WTO). Clinton wanted the WTO meetings to be held in the United States to spotlight the benefits America receives from international trade (Beveridge, 1999). This controversial organization was opposed by environmentalists, unions, and human rights groups around the globe. The WTO was well known as a "lightning rod for critics on the left and right, nationally and internationally, and had caused bitter diplomatic tensions" (Collier, 1999). The president himself had publicly criticized the actions of the WTO one month before the meeting:

> The WTO has been treated for too long like some private priesthood for experts where we know what's right and we pat you on the head and tell you to go along and play by the rules that we reach. (Collier, 1999)

It was known well in advance of the meeting that tens of thousands of protesters, some estimates said 50,000, would show up. The nature of the WTO allowed protesters to pick their cause from protecting clean air, sea turtles and dolphins, job exports and pest imports; curbing child labor; to eliminating beef hormones and genetically modified food (Postmand and Mapes, 1999). Protest organizers hoped for a "protest of the century" (Phillips, 1999). By the time the meeting ended, demonstrators had come from a Ralph Nader group, Greenpeace, the Sierra Club, Direct Action Network, the United Steel Workers of America, the Teamsters, the AFL–CIO, Students Against Sweatshops, an anarchist group calling themselves the Black Bloc, and numerous other self-proclaimed protest groups. The majority of the protesters were expected to be peaceful, but even they had forewarned the police that small radical fringes were planning violence (Collier, November 24, 1999). "Battle in Seattle" T-shirts had been on sale a week before the meeting (Postman and Mapes, 1999). Six thousand delegates from 135 countries were expected for the meeting.

Events

The morning of the first day, Tuesday, November 30, 1999, Teamsters Union President James Hoffa Jr. spoke at the organizing site and said, "We're basically putting a human face on the WTO. It has to consider human rights and workers' rights along with trade" (Beveridge, 1999). As he was speaking, 9,600 workers of the International Longshore and Warehouse Union began shutting down cargo movements up and down the West Coast in solidarity with the anti-WTO protests. Twenty thousand labor activists walked along a designated parade route from the organizing point to downtown. Their march was peaceful and uneventful.

Downtown the protests had turned ugly. Thousands of people, estimates range from 6,000 to 10,000, gathered in two locations and began to march toward the convention center where the meetings were to be held. They linked arms and prevented the delegates from entering the convention center. Some of the more radical demonstrators lay down in the streets, and some even chained themselves together. Beveridge (1999) says the police say they fired red pepper gas into these groups of chained demonstrators. The resulting clash between the demonstrators and the police and pepper spraying prevented the delegates from reaching the convention center. U.N. Secretary-General Kofi Annan and U.S. Secretary of State Madeline Albright were scheduled to talk at the opening ceremony; however, neither could reach the convention center. By the end of the day, police had fired their entire supply of pepper spray and tear gas at the demonstrators, forcing them to borrow from other agencies (*Seattle Times* staff and news services, 1999). The police had also used rubber bullets and batons to control the demonstrators. By the end of the day, protesters had defied the police, lit small fires, smashed windows, and scrawled graffiti; the opinion session of the WTO had been canceled; the mayor had declared a civil emergency and imposed a curfew; the governor had called up 200 unarmed National Guardsmen; and 300 Washington State Patrol troopers were on their way (Cook, 1999). The clashes between the police and demonstrators continued until the end of the meeting on Friday, December 3, 1999.

There is no question that the majority of the protesters in Seattle were nonviolent, but it appears also that they were gassed, pepper sprayed, shot with rubber bullets, and hit with batons along with a number of residents not engaged in the demonstrations. Residents were gassed and arbitrarily stopped, and some claim brutalized, when the downtown area was declared a protest-free zone, thereby driving the protesters into the Capitol Hill residential neighborhood. The minority demonstrators, such as the black-clad anarchists, the Black Bloc, who were more interested in violence and riot than political dissent, triggered the violent confrontations between the police and the demonstrators and the vandalism that occurred. There was also looting by criminal elements attracted, as they always are, to such chaotic situations.

Thankfully, no one was killed during the Battle of Seattle. However, a number of injuries occurred (to police and demonstrators), and almost 600 persons were arrested. Almost all arrested were charged with misdemeanors and out of jail in a week, released on their own recognizance (Rahner, 1999). Chief Norm Stamper resigned four days after the Battle of Seattle ended, acknowledging that his officers did not get all the support they needed and that he and the city had pursued a policy of negotiation, not confrontation, with the demonstrators (Wilson, 1999). The ranking officer in charge of the departments planning for the WTO meeting would retire in less than a year. Chief Stamper also confirmed that the trained anarchists were behind the violence. Stamper admitted that his department did not have enough staff, even with the help of the National Guard and the Washington State Patrol, to cope with the tens of thousands of protesters (Wilson, 1999). The cost to the city was more than $9 million. The city's reputation was damaged throughout the world, and numerous agencies—including the FBI—began investigations.

What Can Be Learned from the Battle of Seattle

The U.S. Constitution guarantees citizens freedom of speech and the right to assemble as long as they do so peacefully. The delegates to the WTO meeting also had constitutionally protected rights of free speech and assembly. In failing to get the WTO delegates through the protesters and into the opening ceremony on Tuesday, the badly outnumbered police gave the demonstrators the upper hand, caused the police to overreact and set in motion the events that followed (*Seattle Times* staff and news services, 1999). Mayor Schell said that a massive police presence at a peaceful demonstration, which he expected at the WTO conference, would create unruliness. Los Angeles Sheriff's Department Captain Richard Odenthal, a veteran of the Rodney King riots, says that he advised Seattle officials they needed to have an adequate perimeter around the conference site (*Seattle Times* staff and news service, 1999).

The situation spiraled out of control because of a lack of preparation, adequate staff, and coordination with other agencies. Jerome Skolnick in defense of the Seattle Police Department is quoted thus:

> The Seattle Police Department has a reputation as a very fine, community-oriented department, but because we haven't had that much recent experience with civil disorder, they may have underestimated the need for preparation, for intelligence, for manpower. Obviously, they were caught unprepared, and I think it's because everybody looked upon this as a very positive occasion, a chance to promote the city as an international trading place. (*Seattle Times* staff and news service, 1999)

The Seattle Fire Department even criticized the Seattle Police Department for its lack of preparation. "Several months before the WTO conference, the Seattle Fire Department, based on information it had received, was preparing for the worst. SFD told the police department to do the same and was ignored" (Henderson, 2000, p. 43). The Seattle Police Department also turned down offers for assistance from several law enforcement agencies before the WTO conference took place. This lack of coordination with other agencies, inadequate planning, and insufficient manpower had tragic results.

REALITY CHECK

Privacy versus Security?

On March 9, 2006, the PATRIOT Act was renewed by Congress and President Bush. Despite the efforts of Senate Democrats and libertarian-leaning Republicans who had sought to amend portions of the Act thought to undermine civil liberties, the Act was passed without revision.

The PATRIOT Act makes it easier for federal agents to gather and share information in terrorism investigations, install wiretaps, and conduct secret searches of households and businesses. Civil libertarians have voiced concerns about the PATRIOT Act since it was first proposed as part of the government's Homeland Security efforts after 9/11. These concerns have been highlighted by revelations that the Bush administration has authorized wiretaps and is monitoring e-mails of individuals thought to be communicating with terrorists.

The PATRIOT Act received approval without concessions to protect civil liberties. Despite the best efforts of the national media to create opposition among the American populace to the Bush administration "excesses," polls continue to show that Americans are willing to sacrifice some of their privacy in order to be safer from terrorism. The fear of civil libertarians (and of the authors) is that once personal freedoms are lost (or devalued) they will not only be difficult to regain, but will also serve as precedent for further losses. What do you think?

Conclusions

Change and resistance to change are part of every system. For change to occur, some amount of "deviance" takes place, and the "normal way of things" is disturbed. Dissent—acts designed to bring about needed social, legal, and political change—grows out of people's desire to shape their own destiny and to be more active in the processes and structures that shape their lives.

Political authority can, if it chooses, adapt and be responsive to change by encouraging solutions that will alleviate the conditions that have led to dissent. Political authority can also respond to dissent by trying to control it, either through persuasion, reward, compromise, or force. The latter alternative will induce some people to be docile, but may drive others to violent resistance.

If authority recognizes the issues raised by dissent, institutions may be transformed; if authority defines these issues as nonnegotiable and tries to control or stifle dissent, democratic political institutions will turn into prisons that are run without the consent of the governed.

When political dissent turns to demonstrations and protest in the community, the responsible officials must plan, prepare, and coordinate with all community agencies and outside agencies to meet the possible threat of violence and disorder.

Student Checklist

1. Define the parameters of the right to dissent under the U.S. Constitution.
2. Present contrasting views of acceptable dissent.
3. Describe the interaction of the strategies of dissent and response.
4. Identify the significant aspects of escalation and de-escalation.
5. Analyze the ways in which police, courts, and corrections become instruments of power in relation to dissent.
6. Describe the necessary components for effectively neutralizing disorder without increasing violent dissent.
7. Describe the events leading up to the Battle of Seattle. How could the city and the police department have been better prepared?

Topics for Discussion

1. Discuss the conflict between the right to dissent and the need to maintain order.
2. Discuss several positive ways of resolving social conflict.
3. In what ways is power a central issue in dissent and political response?

Bibliography

Barker, T., Hunter, R. D., and Rush, J. P. (1994). *Police Systems and Practices: An Introduction.* Upper Saddle River, NJ: Prentice Hall.

Basirico, L. A., Cashion, S. G., and Eshleman, J. R. (2005). *Introduction to Sociology,* 2nd ed. Redding, CA: Best Value Books.

Beveridge, D. (November 30, 1999). "Pepper gas fired on demonstrators against World Trade Organizations," *Seattle Times.*

Brown, R. (1968). March speech on "The Black Panther."

Collier, R. (November 24, 1999). "World-Trade Showdown: Wide-ranging WTO summit will spotlight division, dissent," *Seattle Times.*

Cook, R. (December 1, 1999). "City struggles to regain control of downtown streets after rampage," *Seattle Times.*

Cox, A. (1971). "Direct action, civil disobedience and the Constitution," in J. B. Grossman and M. H., Grossman (Eds.), *Law and Change in Modern America.* Pacific Palisades, CA: Goodyear.

Cummings, M. C., Jr., and Wise, D. (2005). *Democracy under Pressure: An Introduction to the American Political System,* 10th ed. Pacific Grove, CA: Thomson/Wadsworth.

Eitzen, D. S., and Zinn, M. B. (2007). *In Conflict and Order: Understanding Society,* 11th ed. Boston, MA: Pearson/Allyn and Bacon.

Fagin, J. A. (2006). *When Terrorism Strikes Home: Defending the United States.* Boston, MA: Pearson/Allyn and Bacon.

Fortas, A. (1968). *Concerning Dissent and Civil Disobedience.* New York: New American Library.

Greenberg, E. S., and Page, B. I. (2005). *The Struggle for Democracy,* 7th ed. New York: Pearson/Longman.

Henderson, J. (November 24, 2000). "Demonstrating success," *Police.*

Henslin, J. M. (2007). *Sociology: A Down-to-Earth Approach,* 8th ed. Boston, MA: Pearson/Allyn and Bacon.

King, T. R. (September 2000). "Managing protests on public land," *FBI Law Enforcement Bulletin,* pp. 10–13.

Lucksted, O. D., and Martell, D. F. (April 1982). "Cults: A conflict between religious liberty and involuntary servitude? Part I," *FBI Law Enforcement Bulletin,* pp. 16–20.

Magleby, D. B., O'Brien, D. M., Light, P. C., Burns, J. M., Peltason, J. W., and Cronin, T. E. (2006). *Government by the People,* 21st ed. Upper Saddle River, NJ: Pearson/Prentice Hall.

Means, R. (1973). "American Indian movement," *Chicago Express,* p. 1.

National Advisory Commission on Criminal Justice Standards and Goals. (1976). *Disorders and Terrorism: Report of the Task Force on Disorders and Terrorism.* Washington, D.C.: U.S. Government Printing Office.

National Commission on the Causes and Prevention of Violence. (1969). *To Establish Justice, To Insure Domestic Tranquility.* Washington, D.C.: U.S. Government Printing Office.

Phillips, K. (November 29, 1999). "Is the World Trade Organization a blessing or a curse? Con: More Power and Wealth for the Elite," *Seattle Times.*

Poland, J. M. (2005). *Understanding Terrorism: Groups, Strategies, and Responses*, 2nd ed. Upper Saddle River, NJ: Pearson/Prentice Hall.

Popenoe, D. (2000). *Sociology*, 11th ed. Upper Saddle River, NJ: Pearson/Prentice Hall.

Postmand, D., and Mapes, L. (December 6, 1999). "Why WTO united so many foes," *Seattle Times*.

Rahner, M. (December 6, 1999). "Most jailed WTO protestors are no longer behind bars," *Seattle Times*.

Seattle Times staff and news services. (December 6, 1999). "How did the police do? Everyone has an opinion," *Seattle Times*.

Simonsen, C. E., and Spindlove, J. R. (2007). *Terrorism Today: The Past, the Players, the Future*, 3rd ed. Upper Saddle River, NJ: Pearson/Prentice Hall.

Skolnick, J. (1969). *The Politics of Protest: Violent Aspects of Protest and Confrontation*, a staff report to the National Commission on the Causes and Prevention of Violence. Washington, D.C.: U.S. Government Printing Office.

Skolnick, J., and Currie, E. (2007). *Crisis in American Institutions*, 13th ed. Boston, MA: Pearson/Allyn and Bacon.

Tischler, H. L. (2007). *Introduction to Sociology*, 9th ed. Pacific Grove, CA: Thomson/Wadsworth.

Welch, M. (1999). "Social movements and political protests: Exploring flag desecrations in the 1960s, 1970s, and 1980s," *Social Pathology*, Vol. 5, No. 2, pp. 167–186.

White, J. R. (2006). *Terrorism and Homeland Security*, 5th ed. Pacific Grove, CA: Thomson/Wadsworth.

Wilson, K. A. C. (December 7, 1999). "Embattled police chief resigns," *Seattle Times*.

Zimbardo, P. G. (April 1972). "Pathology of imprisonment," *Society*, p. 8.

Zinn, H. (1968). *Disobedience and Democracy: Nine Fallacies on Law and Order*. New York: Random House.